DATE DUE

DEMCO 38-296

CHRONOLOGY OF EUROPEAN HISTORY

CHRONOLOGY OF EUROPEAN HISTORY
15,000 B.C. to 1997

Volume 3
1898 – 1997
Indexes

Edited by
JOHN POWELL

Editor, Great Events from History
FRANK N. MAGILL

Associate Editors

E. G. WELTIN   JOSÉ M. SÁNCHEZ
THOMAS P. NEILL   EDWARD P. KELEHER

Project Editor
WENDY SACKET

Salem Press, Inc.
Pasadena, California   Englewood Cliffs, N.J.

Editor in Chief: Dawn P. Dawson
Project Editor: Wendy Sacket
Acquisitions Editor: Mark Rehn
Research Supervisor: Jeffry Jensen
Photograph Editor: Karrie Hyatt
Production Editor: Joyce I. Buchea
Map Design and Layout: James Hutson

This edition includes: materials from *Great Events from History: Ancient and Medieval*, Frank N. Magill, editor, E. G. Weltin, associate editor, 1972; *Great Events from History: Modern European*, Frank N. Magill, editor, Thomas P. Neill and José M. Sánchez, associate editors, 1973; *Great Events from History: Worldwide Twentieth Century*, Frank N. Magill, editor, Edward P. Keleher, associate editor, 1980; and material new to this edition.

Library of Congress Cataloging-in-Publication Data

Chronology of European history, 15,000 B.C. to 1997 / edited by John Powell ; editor, Great events from history, Frank Magill ; associate editors, E. G. Weltin . . . [et al.] ; project editor, Wendy Sacket.

    p.   cm.

  "Combines updated entries from Magill's Great events from history : ancient and medieval series (1972) and Great events from history : modern European series (1973) with selected entries from Great events from history : worldwide twentieth century series (1980) and 266 completely new entries"—Vol. 1, Publisher's note.

  Includes bibliographical references and index.

  ISBN 0-89356-418-4 (set : alk. paper). — ISBN 0-89356-421-4 (v. 3)

  1. Europe—History—Chronology. I. Powell, John, 1954-   . II. Magill, Frank Northen, 1907-1997. III. Sacket, Wendy, 1962-   . IV. Great events from history. Ancient and medieval series. V. Great events from history. Modern European series. VI. Great events from history—worldwide twentieth century series.

D11.C57   1997

940'.02'02—dc21

97-33219
CIP

First Printing

CONTENTS

LIST OF MAPS

Volume I

Volume II

Volume III

CHRONOLOGY OF EUROPEAN HISTORY

1898-1899
THE FASHODA INCIDENT

The Fashoda incident on the Upper Nile brings England and France to the brink of war, changing the course of European domestic diplomacy.

DATE: July, 1898-March, 1899

LOCALE: Fashoda, a small village on the Upper Nile River

CATEGORIES: Diplomacy and international relations; Expansion and land acquisition; Wars, uprisings, and civil unrest

KEY FIGURES:

'Abd Allāh ibn Muhammad, member of the Ta'āishah tribe and successor to the Mahdī as leader of the dervishes in the Sudan in 1885

Robert Arthur Talbot Gascoyne-Cecil, marquis of Salisbury (1830-1903), British prime minister and foreign secretary, 1895-1902

Théophile Delcassé (1852-1923), French minister of foreign affairs, 1898-1905

General Horatio Herbert Kitchener (1850-1916), British conqueror of the Sudan

Captain Jean-Baptiste Marchand (1863-1934), leader of the French expedition to Fashoda

Sir Herbert Monson, British ambassador to Paris

SUMMARY OF EVENT. In the summer of 1897, Great Britain approached its zenith as an imperial power, and the British empire celebrated the Diamond Jubilee of Queen Victoria's accession to the throne. Nowhere was British influence more apparent than in Africa, the arena where the Great Powers struggled for colonies.

The most heated rivalry in Africa was between Great Britain and France over Egypt and the large, relatively isolated, desolate area known as the Sudan. Friction had been increasing since the mid-nineteenth century. British and French business interests had combined to construct the Suez Canal and a number of Egyptian railroads, but Ismail Pasha, the khedive of Egypt, had plunged his country into hopeless debt through reckless spending on private and public projects. To get out of debt, he had sold his Suez Canal company shares to the British government in 1875, thereby focusing British interest on the future of Egypt and the canal.

Resentment in Egypt over foreign control of its affairs led to violence which provoked a British naval bombardment of Alexandria and the appointment of a British consul general to supervise the activities of the new khedive, Tewfik, in order to protect British interests. Egypt had become a British protectorate, and by abstaining from these affairs France had been eased out of the picture. The French consoled themselves by searching for other areas in Africa to control.

After about 1895, Great Britain had visions of a continuous strip of British-held territory, "a thin red line," stretching from north to south across Africa, from Cairo to the Cape of Good Hope. To make this dream a reality, a gap had to be filled by annexing the area known as the Sudan, from the southern boundary of Egypt to northern Uganda. This area had fallen into the hands of the fanatical Mahdī and his dervish followers after the defeat and death of the British general Charles George "Chinese" Gordon at Khartoum in 1885. Since that time, Great Britain had not seen fit to challenge the climate, the terrain, and the wild dervishes who now followed the successor to the Mahdī, 'Abd Allāh ibn Muhammad, known as the khalifa, or caliph. British policy had been to maintain, at least temporarily, the status quo in the Sudan.

Gabriel Hanotaux, the French foreign minister from 1894 to 1898, was a militant expansionist. He was determined that the French would annex as much territory as possible even if it involved heated diplomacy with the European states. He challenged the British over long-standing trading rights in Tunisia, which had become a French protectorate in 1881. Hanotaux constantly put forth French claim of dominance in Morocco, although the British, Germans, and Spanish had considerable interests there. His policies were equally aggressive in Africa, south of the Sahara, and in Asia. Hanotaux's diplomacy was supported by an equally militant minister of colonies, Théophile Delcassé, and by a host of aggressive French colonialist organizations.

France envisioned a strip of French-held territory stretching from west to east across Africa from Senegal on the Atlantic coast to Somaliland on the Red Sea. Still chafing at the British takeover in Egypt, the French planned to control the water supply of Egypt by seizing the headwaters of the Nile River. After a brief period of diplomatic maneuvers and intrigues, which included providing arms to the Ethiopians enabling them to defeat Italian forces at the Battle of Adowa in 1896, the French launched the operation.

The British minister of war, Sir Edward Grey, announced in the House of Commons that any French move toward the Nile River "would be viewed as an unfriendly act," and Great Britain took immediate steps to meet such a threat. Sir Horatio Herbert Kitchener, then Sirdar of the Egyptian army, was provided with a strong Anglo-Egyptian force, and he began the reconquest of the Sudan by moving up the Nile River. At the same time a very small French force of Senegalese soldiers and French officers under Captain Jean-Baptiste Marchand began to move eastward from Brazzaville in the French Congo. Both sides were racing to a derelict fortress at Fashoda, a position of strategic importance for controlling the headwaters of the Nile.

After an epic journey, which included transporting all the parts of a steamboat, including the boiler, across the wilderness of Central Africa, Marchand arrived at Fashoda on July 10, 1898. Two months later, after defeating the dervishes, Kitchener arrived with five gunboats and a superior force. Marchand expected reinforcements to come from the Red Sea coast, but they did not materialize. The French had won the race, but they were outgunned.

Marchand and Kitchener, observing correct military etiquette, had a whisky and soda together and decided to fly their respective flags over different parts of the fortress while awaiting orders from their governments. The confrontation brought Great Britain and France to the brink of war. Public opinion, inflamed by irresponsible reporting in the press, demanded a decision by force of arms. Théophile Delcassé, who had recently been appointed French minister of foreign affairs, wisely realized that the French position at Fashoda was hopeless. Added to Kitchener's numerical superiority on the spot was Great Britain's overwhelming naval superiority in the Mediterranean; for France, a military confrontation in East Africa was not only undesirable but also potentially catastrophic. Even more significant, the French diplomatic machine was preparing for the inevitable confrontation with Germany. When the time came for a show of force, France wanted to be certain of being able to count on support from Great Britain. Under unrelenting pressure from the British government led by Lord Salisbury, who was prime minister and foreign secretary, the French gave ground and on November 3, 1898, ordered Marchand to withdraw.

Lord Salisbury, who had prepared for the clash at Fashoda since 1897, sincerely believed that any confrontation between France and Britain could only benefit imperial Germany. Since the 1870's, Salisbury had come to distrust the national and international goals of Germany, feeling that Germany, if not checked, could very well emerge as the dominant power on the Continent. In the long run, this would be a serious blow to British policies. Salisbury also understood that if he humiliated France the possibilities of ever achieving a Franco-British rapprochement would be almost nonexistent.

With that in mind, Salisbury, as early as 1897, envisioned making it clear to France that Britain would assist France in obtaining Morocco, if the question of the Nile and Sudan was resolved in Britain's favor. France could receive some minor compensations in the short run, but the Nile question, in the long run, would have to be negotiated with greater colonial questions in mind. French claims were not settled until the following March, when France was obliged to renounce all territory along the Nile River in return for worthless districts in the Sahara.

Marchand was hailed as a mighty hero upon his return to France, and Kitchener rose to the highest military post in Britain. Beyond mortal glories and reputation, however, was the salient fact that Britain and France would not go to war over Fashoda. What began as a dangerous confrontation on the Nile would end up being an important part of the process bringing England and France together, and six years later the two nations would sign the historic Entente Cordiale in London.

—*Jack H. Greising, updated by James J. Cooke*

ADDITIONAL READING:

Andrew, Christopher. *Théophile Delcassé and the Making of the Entente Cordiale*. New York: St. Martin's Press, 1968. This is the best, most detailed work on Delcassé, who was a militant expansionist and who, as foreign minister, had to deal with the Fashoda crisis and its aftermath.

Bates, Darrell. *The Fashoda Incident of 1898: Encounter on the Nile*. New York: Oxford University Press, 1984. Bates's work covers all the facts about the crisis.

Brown, Roger T. *Fashoda Reconsidered*. Baltimore: The Johns Hopkins University Press, 1969. Brown reevaluates Fashoda, and its impact on European expansionism and diplomacy.

Lewis, David L. *The Race to Fashoda*. New York: Weidenfeld & Nicolson, 1987. This book discusses the motivations of the great powers and the race to control the Upper Nile.

Sanderson, George N. *England, Europe, and the Upper Nile, 1882-1899*. Edinburgh: Edinburgh University Press, 1965. A classic historical overview, this work places Fashoda into a broader historical context.

SEE ALSO: 1830, France Conquers Algeria; 1854-1869, The Suez Canal Is Built; 1904, The Entente Cordiale.

1899
FIRST HAGUE PEACE CONFERENCE

The First Hague Peace Conference is held at the invitation of Czar Nicholas II, and twenty-six nations agree to establish a voluntary permanent court of arbitration.

DATE: May-July, 1899
LOCALE: The Hague, the Netherlands
CATEGORY: Diplomacy and international relations

KEY FIGURES:

Léon-Victor-Auguste Bourgeois (1851-1925), head of
the French delegation to the First and Second Hague
Peace Conferences

Captain Alfred Thayer Mahan (1840-1914), U.S.
advocate of sea power

Nicholas II (1868-1918), czar of Russia, 1894-1917

Sir Julian Pauncefote (1828-1902), British ambassador
to the United States

Andrew Dickson White (1832-1918), head of the
American delegation to the First Hague Peace
Conference and U.S. minister to Russia

William II (1859-1941), emperor of Germany, 1888-1918

SUMMARY OF EVENT. As announced by Count Mikhail
Nikolaevich Muravyov, the Russian foreign affairs minister, on August 24, 1898, Czar Nicholas II issued an "imperial rescript" inviting the powers with diplomatic representatives at the court of St. Petersburg to participate in an
international conference aimed at a "possible reduction of
excessive armaments which weigh upon all nations."

The czar's initiative was greeted with different responses. The growing number of pacifists and humanitarians hailed the move as evidence that the czar's promise of
peace and progress would be brought to fruition soon after
the arrival of the new century. They sincerely believed that
a utopian ideal was about to be realized despite the source
of the initiative and the signs of war which seemed to lurk
everywhere. The antiwar advocates had representatives on
the Continent, although they were particularly strong in
Great Britain and the United States. In those two countries, militarism was not deeply rooted, even though 1898
was the year of the Spanish-American War and the confrontation between Great Britain and France at Fashoda.
The hope was that the reduction of armaments would
make war less likely and that the products and profits of
the rapidly expanding Western industrial complex could
be brought to bear on world problems. Arbitration could
solve international grievances, as had actually happened
in the successful negotiations for damages resulting from
the depredations caused by the *Alabama* and other Con-
federate cruisers during the American Civil War. In 1889,
humanitarians were also able to point to the formation of
the Interparliamentary Union and the convening of the
first Pan-American Conference as examples of international problems being solved without resorting to war.

On the other side, contemporary political realists of
every stripe were suspicious of the czar's motives and
were alarmed over possible consequences. It was obvious
that the bellicose Emperor William II of Germany, who
was already committed to the continuance and expansion
of newfound German strength, would not, under any cir-

cumstances, agree to disarm an empire created by force of
arms. While on friendly terms with Russia, France was
shocked at not being consulted by its ally before the
proposal was made. The thought of maintaining the status
quo as established by the French defeat in the Franco-
Prussian War was totally unacceptable. Nevertheless, Germany and France, along with twenty-three other nations,
accepted the invitation. The reasons for acceptance varied,
but generally it was held that the czar should not be
offended, and it was unlikely that any enforceable action
could come out of such a conference. Furthermore, to
decline the invitation would have put a nation in a bad light
with Liberals, pacifists, humanitarians, Socialists, and
similar groups.

On close examination, Russian motives do not appear
to have been entirely altruistic. The naïve Nicholas II may
have been more idealistic than his ministers, but it was
clear by 1898 that Russia, already lagging behind the West
in economic and industrial development, was unable to
compete in the armaments race. The financial burden
alone was too great. Count Sergei Witte, Russian finance
minister from 1892 to 1903, decided that a ten-year international moratorium on armaments could bring the leading military states down to the Russian level.

On May 18, 1899, the First International Peace Conference convened at The Hague in the Netherlands. Among
those who attended the conference and who were genuinely interested in the cause of peace were Sir Julian
Pauncefote, who represented Great Britain and served as
British ambassador to the United States, and Andrew
Dickson White, who represented the United States and
served as the American minister to Russia. The voices
which were most influential in the long run belonged to
blunt military-naval experts and apostles of military
strength, such as Captain Alfred Thayer Mahan of the
United States, Admiral Sir John Arbuthnot Fisher of Great
Britain, and Colonel Schwarzhoff of Germany. Basing
their arguments on individual, sovereign responsibility,
their clamor for the necessity of preparedness carried the
day. Confronted by the irrefutable military realities of the
international situation, the goals of the conference were
not realized.

Yet the means for preventing armed conflict was approved unanimously by the twenty-six nations present and
participating in the conference. International commissions
of inquiry were authorized to appease, investigate, and
prevent conflict. More important, participants devised a
permanent court of arbitration that was authorized to hear
and judge disputes that were voluntarily brought to its
purview. Although it was not a permanent sitting court, it
drew from a pool of jurists who could arbitrate in any

given situation. The weakness of this approach was less in its structure than in the reluctance of nations to risk their influence and prestige. Perhaps Nicholas II put it best when he remarked that "Peace is more important than anything, if honor is not affected."

—*Jack H. Greising, updated by John Quinn Imholte*

ADDITIONAL READING:

Cooper, Sandi E. *Patriotic Pacifism: Waging War on War in Europe, 1815-1914*. New York: Oxford University Press, 1991. This work contains scattered references to both Hague Peace Conferences within a European context.

Davis, Calvin D. *The United States and the First Hague Conference*. Ithaca, N.Y.: Cornell University Press, 1962. Davis explores reasons for the successes of the first conference and, according to Davis, its more significant failures. Although limited progress was achieved, his overall judgment is that it was unsuccessful in its goals, and thus was a failure.

Hull, William I. *The Two Hague Conferences and Their Contributions to International Law*. Boston: Ginn, 1908. Reprint. New York: Garland, 1972. Hull presents a positive assessment of the peace movement's internationalist direction.

Marchand, C. Roland. *The American Peace Movement and Social Reform, 1898-1918*. Princeton, N.J.: Princeton University Press, 1972. Emphasizes in brief references the relationship of the conference and the American peace movement.

Ralston, Jackson H. *International Arbitration from Athens to Locarno*. Stanford, Calif.: Stanford University Press, 1929. Places the origin and outcome of the First Hague Peace Conference in its historical context.

Tuchman, Barbara. "The Steady Drummer: The Hague, 1899 and 1907." In *The Proud Tower: A Portrait of the World Before the War, 1890-1914*. New York: Macmillan, 1966. A popular account of the personalities and highlights of both Hague conferences.

SEE ALSO: 1889, Great Britain Strengthens the Royal Navy; 1906, Launching of the *Dreadnought*; 1907, Second Hague Peace Conference; 1915, International Congress of Women.

1899-1902
BOER WAR

The Boer War ends Afrikaner hopes for independence in southern Africa, establishes the basis for a unified nation under British control, and introduces deadly forms of modern warfare to Europeans.

DATE: October 11, 1899-May 31, 1902
LOCALE: South Africa
CATEGORIES: Expansion and land acquisition; Wars, uprisings, and civil unrest
KEY FIGURES:

Louis Botha (1862-1919), a Boer general and commander of the Transvaal Republican army who was also a representative at the peace conference in 1902

Joseph Chamberlain (1836-1914), colonial secretary of Great Britain, 1895-1903

Christiaan Rudolf De Wet (1854-1922), a leader of guerrilla raids who rose to become a Boer (Afrikaner) general

General Horatio Herbert Kitchener (1850-1916), chief of staff to Roberts until November, 1900, when he took over command himself

Paul Kruger (1825-1904), president of the South African Republic (Transvaal), 1883-1902

Sir Alfred Milner (1854-1925), governor of the Cape of Good Hope and high commissioner for South Africa, 1897-1901

Cecil John Rhodes (1853-1902), mine owner, head of the British South Africa Company, and prime minister of the Cape of Good Hope, 1890-1896

Field Marshal Frederick Sleigh Roberts (1832-1914), commander in chief of British forces in South Africa, 1899-1900

Marthinus Theunis Steyn (1857-1916), president of the Orange Free State, 1896-1902, and representative at the peace conference in 1902

SUMMARY OF EVENT. The Boer War was a conflict between the Afrikaner republics of the Transvaal and the Orange Free State against Great Britain. It pitted the Afrikaners or Boers, who were mostly of Dutch descent and mainly farmers, against the British empire.

The area around the Cape of Good Hope had been colonized by the Dutch in 1652. Because of British expansion into the area after 1806, the Boer settlers, who resented the British advance, migrated north into the interior during the Great Trek of 1836-1838, and founded several independent republics, including the South African Republic, in the Transvaal, in 1852, and the Orange Free State in 1854.

The discovery of diamonds at Kimberley in the Orange Free State in 1867, and of gold on the Witwatersrand in the Transvaal in 1886, brought a large influx of foreigners into the area and transformed the economies of these agricultural societies. Under the leadership of Paul Kruger, president of the Transvaal, these outsiders, or "Uitlanders," were denied easy access to citizenship and were taxed heavily in an attempt by the Boers to maintain political control and autonomy. The Boers feared that if the Uitlanders were allowed citizenship and representation, they would seize control of the government. The British viewed these measures as repressive and protested against them.

The Boers feared that they might lose their independence, and these fears seemed to be confirmed by the Jameson Raid of 1895, part of a plot designed by Cecil John Rhodes to stir up the Uitlanders to internal revolution. Rhodes was a major mine owner who was also head of the British South Africa Company (in control of lands that later became Zimbabwe and Zambia), and prime minister of the Cape Colony; his coconspirator was Dr. Leander Starr Jameson, administrator of Rhodesia (Zimbabwe). The plot failed, and because Rhodes had pursued his policy against the advice of Joseph Chamberlain, the British colonial secretary, he resigned as prime minister. Further restrictions on the Uitlanders in the Transvaal resulted. The abortive conspiracy led to a military alliance between the Transvaal and the Orange Free State in 1896; it also provoked worldwide sympathy for the Boers and a general denunciation of British policy.

The British were concerned about what they considered to be their legitimate commercial interests. Sir Alfred Milner, the British governor of the Cape Colony, began a long series of negotiations with Kruger in an effort to resolve the grievances of the Uitlanders. In 1898, Milner returned to London to consult with Chamberlain, but while he was absent, his subordinate damaged the British position by suggesting that these grievances of the Uitlanders were being exploited from ulterior motives. The suspicions of the Afrikaners deepened. In the spring of 1899, Milner warned Chamberlain that the situation was becoming worse. A conference was suggested by Chamberlain and supported by Marthinus Theunis Steyn, president of the Orange Free State, who acted as host for discussions at Bloemfontein in May, 1899, between Milner and Kruger. No agreement, however, was reached. In August, Kruger offered substantial concession to the Uitlanders, but the British had reached the point where they believed that British hegemony over South Africa was the only solution.

An exodus of Uitlander refugees from the Transvaal in September, 1899, was accompanied by a British military

From 1900 to 1902, Boer fighters staged numerous guerrilla raids against British troop convoys and military posts in the Transvaal region of South Africa. (Archive Photos)

buildup. This military menace was the subject of an ultimatum from Kruger on October 9, followed by a declaration of war on October 11. The Orange Free State honored the alliance of 1896 and joined the Transvaal.

The Boer War can be divided into three well-defined phases. The first, from October, 1899, to February, 1900, was marked by a strong and successful Boer offensive. Britain's Natal colony was invaded, and the Boers besieged British forces at Ladysmith, Mafeking, and Kimberley; Boer forces also crossed the Orange River that separated the Orange Free State and the Cape Colony. In the second phase, from February to September, 1900, British forces under the command of Field Marshal Frederick Sleigh Roberts occupied all the major towns and annexed the Transvaal. The third and most painful phase, from September, 1900, to May, 1902, was marked by guerrilla warfare by the Boers under the leadership of their generals, notably Louis Botha and Christiaan Rudolf De Wet. After Roberts was made an earl in November, 1900, he handed over command to his chief of staff, General Horatio Herbert Kitchener. Kitchener rounded up Boer women and children and placed them in concentration camps; epidemics broke out and there was an appalling death rate among prisoners until British officials compelled the military to improve living conditions in the camps. The British also built a system of blockhouses throughout the countryside; they then proceeded to run down the guerrilla bands by combing the country section by section.

The signing of the Treaty of Vereeniging on May 31, 1902, ended the most serious challenge to the British empire since Napoleon had been met. The British effort had been marked by the participation of troops from Australia, Canada, and other colonies. The Afrikaners lost their independence and became British subjects. Although the war ultimately established the foundation for the Union of South Africa, the bitterness engendered by the war continued to affect the political life of South Africa.

The cost of the war was high for Britain, with more than one hundred thousand total casualties. For the Boers, however, the loss of seven thousand dead out of a population of eighty-seven thousand was enormous. Meanwhile, as historian Thomas Pakenham observed, the "central tactical lesson of the war eluded the British," who tended to credit Boer marksmanship or the enemy's superior weapons with prolonging the conflict. Instead, the appearance of smokeless guns (witnessed firsthand by American soldiers in Cuba at roughly the same time), and the use of the machine gun, when combined with trenches, had raised the defense to a new preeminence—a status that became even more apparent during World War I.

—*Martin L. Dolan, updated by Larry Schweikart*

ADDITIONAL READING:

Bidwell, Shelford, and Dominick Graham. *Fire-Power: British Army Weapons and Theories of War, 1904-1945*. London: Allen & Unwin, 1982. Although beginning just after the Boer War, this book traces the effects on British military strategy, tactics, and weapons that derived from the "lessons" of South Africa.

Doughty, Robert A., et al. *Warfare in the Western World, Vol. 2: Military Operations Since 1821*. Lexington, Mass.: D. C. Heath, 1996. Contains a brief chapter on the war, relying extensively on Pakenham (below).

Holt, Edgar. *The Boer War*. London: G. P. Putnam's Sons, 1958. Before Pakenham's book, this was probably the best single-volume military treatment of the war, although one that ignored the racial elements of the Boer positions.

Le May, G. H. L. *British Supremacy in South Africa, 1899-1907*. Oxford: Oxford University Press, 1965. More a political history, this interpretation views the war as deriving from Sir Alfred Milner's attempt to unify South Africa.

Newton, A. P., E. A. Benians, and Eric A. Walker, eds. *The Cambridge History of the British Empire*. Vol. VIII: *South Africa, Rhodesia and the High Commission Territories*. New York: Macmillan, 1936. This edition remains the standard, detailed, and authoritative account of the Boer War, with individual chapters contributed by leading empire historians.

Pakenham, Thomas. *The Boer War*. New York: Random House, 1979. A thoroughly researched, comprehensive study of the conflict. Unmatched in detail and use of primary sources.

Walker, Eric A. *A History of Southern Africa*. Rev. ed. London: Longmans, Green, 1962. A standard survey, full of detail and accompanied by a sympathetic, descriptive narrative by an accomplished scholar in his field.

SEE ALSO: 1487-1488, Dias Rounds the Cape of Good Hope; 1652, Dutch Begin to Colonize Southern Africa; 1814, Britain Acquires the Cape Colony.

1900
FREUD PUBLISHES THE INTERPRETATION OF DREAMS

Freud publishes The Interpretation of Dreams, *employing dream analysis to introduce his influential theory that unconscious motives, molded from relationships in childhood, are basic to adult personality.*

DATE: 1900
LOCALE: Vienna, Austria

CATEGORIES: Cultural and intellectual history; Health and medicine

KEY FIGURES:

Josef Breuer (1842-1925), Austrian physician who worked with Freud on hysteria

Erik Erikson (1902-1994), psychoanalyst who modified Freud's ideas

Sigmund Freud (1856-1939), Austrian neurologist who founded psychoanalysis

SUMMARY OF EVENT. *The Interpretation of Dreams* is widely considered to be the greatest work of Sigmund Freud. This work is important because it introduced the core ideas of psychoanalysis, the still influential theory that hidden, unconscious feelings and motives determine both the symptoms of mental patients and the normal thoughts and deeds of everyday life.

Even before he began his study of dreams, Freud, an Austrian neurologist, had already proved himself a capable medical researcher and produced several significant papers on neurological conditions. About 1885, Freud was introduced to the study of hypnotism and in the 1890's he worked with Josef Breuer and developed a theory of hysteria. Breuer had called to the attention of Freud the case of a young girl who suffered from apparent paralysis and psychic confusion. He noticed that if the girl were allowed to give verbal expression to her fantasies, the symptoms tended to disappear. Breuer also observed that, whereas the girl could not account for her symptoms in a conscious state, under hypnosis she well understood the connection between her symptoms and past experiences. From this case, Breuer and Freud developed their theory: that hysteria is a condition which imitates a physical or neurological disorder but for which no physical or neurological causes can be discovered. According to the theory, hysteria springs from the repression of desired acts and can be cured only by a kind of catharsis in which unconscious desires are rendered conscious and meaningful.

These studies in hysteria contained one basic idea which Freud was later to develop in his theory of psychoanalysis: that a significant aspect of mental life was "unconscious." Inexpressible in words, the unconscious had indirect and sometimes perverse effects upon daily activity. In the 1890's, Freud began to appreciate the general significance of his discovery. He began to analyze his own dreams and unintentional behavior. The unconscious, he realized, could be revealed in many ways other than hypnosis and its significance was not limited to mental patients. *The Interpretation of Dreams* was significant in that it introduced psychoanalysis not only as a treatment for hysteria but also as a comprehensive theory of human motivation and development.

Sigmund Freud's The Interpretation of Dreams *introduced the core ideas of psychoanalysis as part of a comprehensive theory of human motivation and development.* (Archive Photos)

The Interpretation of Dreams is distinguished both by the methodology with which it intends to investigate dreams and by the meaning which it assigns to dreams. Freud argues that the meaning of a dream is not to be discovered by some hidden logic, but rather through a process of free association, by getting the dreamer to uncover its meaning. What is the nature of a dream? Basically, Freud sees it as a protector of sleep which both expresses and censors the unconscious desires which are allowed free play once conscious mental activity is suspended. Thus the manifest dream (the dream that is remembered in a conscious state) is not the same as the latent dream thought or desire, because this desire is often of such a nature (usually sexual) that it conflicts with the requirements of society and the moral code which the individual self-imposes. The manifest dream partly censors this unconscious desire and at the same time expresses it in symbolic form. The decoding of such symbolism is the entrance into the complexes which, if not understood and rationally dealt with, lead to mental disorder.

The Interpretation of Dreams was not Freud's final word; in his attempts to chart the mechanism of the unconscious, he constantly revised his theories. Nevertheless, it contained the basis of his subsequent work on the psychology of the individual and his attempts to apply the insights of psychoanalysis to cultural anthropology. Certainly it expressed that ambiguity which Freud discovered at the heart of human existence, the conflict inherent in what he describes as the pleasure principle, and it explains that spirit of pessimism which was so strong a characteristic of Freud's thought.

Several core themes of Freud's "dream book" became further elaborated in his later writings. The centrality of forbidden wishes modified and deflected by a "censor" remained one such continuing theme. "The censor" was in later work subdivided into the realistic controls of the conscious self, the "ego," and less rational, moralistic restraints and demands of an internalized parental image, the "superego." One core theme, the eroticized love for one's parent of the opposite sex and jealousy of one's same-sex parental rival, recurred in many dreams. This, later labeled the Oedipus complex, was considered by Freud as basic to adult sexual identity and to neurosis. The mechanism of displaced symbolization which disguises forbidden dream wishes was later elaborated into Freud's many "mechanisms of defense."

Not all of Freud's assumptions in 1900 have withstood the test of time. Freud's theory of motivation rested upon a hydraulic, tension-reducing analogy where such motives as sex and aggression would build up a sort of pressure that would demand some sort of release. The thrust of more recent psychology gives far more attention than did Freud to the joys of seeking out self-enhancing activities which often involve increased tension and excitement. Major twentieth century psychoanalysts such as Erik Erikson give more emphasis than did Freud to the social interactions between parent and child quite apart from the sexual overtones of such relationships. Freud's writings suffer in several ways from male biases characteristic of views of women prevalent in his time. Freud's account of little girls' family affections and jealousies was heavily flavored by an assumption of the biologically rooted inadequacy of females, an assumption that finds few defenders a century later. It has been charged that Freud too readily dismissed as fantasies reports by female patients of sexual abuse by trusted males.

Other ideas found in Freud's "dream book" retain the vitality of having endured a century of research. Freud's thesis that dreams are meaningful clues to motives important in waking life is still treated with respect by many students of personality and biopsychology. With the dis-

covery by twentieth century neuropsychologists that dreaming episodes in sleep are accompanied by such distinctive neurophysiological signs as rapid eye movements, it became possible to study the nature of dreams with an objectivity greater than was possible for Freud. It appears that dreams are the result of random firing by neurons deep within the brain stem. Such dream episodes occur several times a night, and most are immediately forgotten. Yet the few dreams that are remembered may be precisely those that have personal significance.

Fundamentals of Freud's thought survive in psychoanalysis and in scientific psychology. In 1993, some 8,197 members of the International Psychoanalytic Association practiced their healing art. More important, basic Freudian ideas have become a vital, often unrecognized, part of mainstream psychology. Relationships between the quality of childhood-caretaker attachments and adult styles of relating to others is a popular research topic in developmental psychology. The importance of implicit ("unconscious") adaptive styles, to cite another example, has become an important concern of cognitive psychology.

Post-Freudian art, literature, films, and television, no less than psychology, treat human emotions as subtle, complex, and often paradoxical, a view more consistent with Freud's portrayal of human nature than of prior nineteenth century conceptions of human rationality. Most of all, the study of the mind, which was the domain of magic, religion, and speculative philosophy in 1900, has forever become the province of science. Without the stimulus of Freud's ideas, human understanding of life itself would not be at all the same.

—*Paul T. Mason, updated by Thomas E. DeWolfe*

ADDITIONAL READING:

Erikson, Erik. *Childhood and Society*. New York: W. W. Norton, 1950. This work incorporates major post-Freudian developments in psychoanalysis, especially the importance of social factors in childhood.

Gay, Peter. *Freud: A Life for Our Time*. New York: W. W. Norton, 1988. This biography of Freud is comprehensive, thoroughly researched, balanced, and fair, taking into account the criticisms of Freud and also respecting his magnificent achievements.

Jones, Ernest. *The Life and Works of Sigmund Freud*. 3 vols. New York: Basic Books, 1957. An exhaustive work that benefits from the author's long personal association with Freud, but possibly suffers from the positive biases of an admiring disciple.

Masson, Jeffrey M. *The Assault on Truth: Freud's Suppression of the Seduction Theory*. New York: Farrar, Straus, & Giroux, 1984. This author calls into question

Freud's fairness toward women and argues that Freud dismissed as Oedipal fantasies some accounts of real seduction of children.

Neu, Jerome, ed. *The Cambridge Companion to Freud.* New York: Cambridge University Press, 1991. This contains evaluative essays on such classic Freudian concepts as the interpretation of dreams and on more general topics such as Freud's attitude toward women.

Nye, Robert D. *Three Psychologies: Perspectives from Freud, Skinner, and Rogers.* Pacific Grove, Calif.: Brooks-Cole, 1992. This short work contains a clear, succinct, and accurate overview of Freud and psychoanalysis for the introductory student.

Sulloway, Frank J. *Freud: Biologist of the Mind.* New York: Basic Books, 1979. This author seeks to dispel the myth of Freud as a "psychoanalytic hero" alone facing a hostile world.

1900
BRITISH LABOUR PARTY IS FORMED

The British Labour Party is formed, giving voice to the growing industrial working class and ultimately replacing the Liberal Party as one of the two major political parties in Great Britain.

DATE: February, 1900

LOCALE: Great Britain

CATEGORIES: Government and politics; Social reform

KEY FIGURES:

Keir Hardie (1856-1915), Scottish miner who was a leading member of the Independent Labour Party (ILP) and sat as a member of the 1892 Parliament

Arthur Henderson (1863-1935), trade union leader who became leader of the Labour Party

George Lansbury (1859-1940), Socialist member of the ILP who later joined the Labour Party

Ramsay MacDonald (1866-1937), founding member of the Labour Party who later would become prime minister

SUMMARY OF EVENT. Although the British Labour Party did not formally exist under that name until after the general election of January, 1906, the party had actually become a reality after a London conference in February, 1900, established a "Labour Representation Committee." The creation of a political organization based upon the working class was the result of a number of intertwined and complex historical developments. The most obvious of these are the reforms of 1867 and 1884, which gave the vote to male blue-collar workers and increased the electoral weight of the working class.

Yet this development alone fails to explain the birth of

a working-class political party in Great Britain in comparison with the United States or Germany, two countries that also granted the vote to male workers. Excluding the brief significance of the Socialist Party in the early twentieth century, the United States never developed an independent working-class political party, while an explicitly socialist party was to have representation in Germany by the 1870's. One must look at the specific historical developments which led to a party that was separate from both mainstream multiclass parties and the Marxist-defined groups predominant on the European continent.

Among the factors that contributed to the birth of the Labour Party was the virtually homogeneous nature of the British working class at the end of the nineteenth century. There was a genuine material basis for class solidarity among laborers as the living standards of unskilled workers rose closer to those of skilled workers, who perceived an erosion in their social position. The "divide and conquer" technique that proved so successful in some countries had less chance in Great Britain. Instead, unskilled workers—preoccupied with achieving some minimum living standards—were able to make common cause with many alienated skilled workers. Furthermore, the decreasing importance of religious and regional differences made social class a more ready touchstone of identity than in an ethnically and regionally divided nation such as the United States.

None of these considerations assured the formation of a new political party: There remained the possibility of absorption of working-class aspirations by one of the established political parties. The natural candidate for such a development was the Liberal Party, which claimed to share many of the same concerns as those voiced by Labour. The late nineteenth century had seen an alliance between union leaders, working-class voters, and the Liberal Party. Yet, when faced with ever increasing demands for a greater role within the party, the Liberal associations proved too intractable to accommodate themselves to the rising labor movement. Thus, in sharp contrast to American urban political machines, which were largely effective in containing labor discontent, working-class political aspirations in Britain would tend toward the establishment of a new party.

A number of labor leaders initially split from the Liberal Party when they were refused nomination as candidates for Parliament. In 1892, Scottish miner Keir Hardie was elected to Parliament as an Independent Labour representative after just such a Liberal refusal. The following year brought the formation of the Independent Labour Party (ILP), whose express goal was sending working-class men to Parliament, independent of either the Liberal or Conservative parties. This new socialist organization drew support heavily from unions representing unskilled workers, who feared that without parliamentary support they would witness the destruction of their limited gains during the next recession. While the party was blessed with a number of important leaders who would later make their mark on British politics, including Ramsay MacDonald and George Lansbury, the ILP—even taken together with other left-wing groups—was far too weak to mount a threat to the two established political parties.

It proved essential that a more broad-based labor organization such as the Trade Union Congress (TUC) join the campaign for a new political party. Although this development had seemed unlikely only a few decades earlier, by February of 1900, the Trade Union Congress voted to become the vehicle that would ultimately form the Labour Party. The trade unions relatively rapid conversion to the cause of independent political action was prompted by a series of employer assaults on trade union rights.

Worried about foreign competition, employers had established their own national federations, which conducted lockouts against unionized workers and vigorously opposed union demands. Seventy thousand Scottish miners were defeated in an industrial struggle in 1894, followed by the defeat of the Boot and Shoe Operatives in 1895. Even one of the oldest established trade unions, the Amalgamated Society of Engineers, saw itself defeated by a lockout in 1897-1898.

These industrial assaults on the working class were combined with consistent erosion of the trade unions' legal rights. By the late 1890's, the right to picket—essential if unions were to win strikes—was being threatened in the judicial system. In this context, the Trade Union Congress held in autumn of 1899 considered a resolution from an ILP member from the Amalgamated Society of Railroad Servants to call a special meeting of trade unions, cooperatives, and socialist organizations to design a plan to elect workers to Parliament. After an intense debate that saw leaders of the new unskilled workers pitted against the miners, whose concentration in certain electoral districts forced the Liberal Party to accept their candidates, the motion carried by a vote of 546,000 to 434,000.

The Labour Representation Committee (LRC) was duly established at a meeting in London on February 27, 1900. Present were 129 delegates, of whom 65 represented unions with 568,000 members—the remainder representing the various socialist societies with less than 25,000 members combined. A twelve-member committee was elected with seven trade unionists and five socialists.

Although it was in the minority, the ILP was able to elect Ramsay MacDonald secretary of the LRC. During the first year, the trade unions that joined were primarily made up of unskilled workers, although unions representing railroad, boot and shoe, and printing workers joined as well.

The first general election took place only six months later and the results were hardly encouraging. With neither time nor money in great supply, only two of the LRC-endorsed candidates were able to secure victory. There was also tension between the socialists, such as the ILP, and traditional Liberal Party supporters, such as Arthur Henderson. Such problems might have meant the end of the organization had it not been for a further assault on trade union rights that produced a new wave of affiliations. In July of 1901, the House of Lords rendered their famous Taff Vale judgment, which not only reaffirmed limitation on picketing but also proclaimed that unions had to pay for all the costs caused by strike action. Although the legal implications were complicated, trade union leaders soon concluded that they had been forced into a extremely difficult position.

As Labour leaders increasingly questioned the willingness of the existing parties to pass legislation that would reverse Taff Vale, they moved in support of the LRC with the hope of electing their own members to the House of Commons. Unwilling to place their faith in either of the two existing parties, unions began to affiliate with the LRC. Thus, the pre-Taff Vale membership of the LRC, which stood at 376,000, jumped to 469,000 in 1902 and 861,000 by 1903. By the time of the 1906 general election, the Labour Representation Committee was able to run a skillful campaign with fifty serious candidates, resulting in the election of twenty-nine to the House of Commons. When the 1906 Parliament convened, the LRC took the name "Labour Party."　　　　　　　　*—William A. Pelz*

ADDITIONAL READING:

Cliff, Tony, and Donny Gluckstein. *The Labour Party— A Marxist History*. London: Bookmarks, 1988. Written from a clearly far left viewpoint, this work provides a thought-provoking, if controversial, treatment of the Labour Party from its beginning.

Coates, David. *The Labour Party and the Struggle for Socialism*. Cambridge, England: Cambridge University Press, 1975. Although focused on the question of Labour's ability to advance the cause of socialism, this study addresses questions which have been inherent since 1900.

Hobsbawm, Eric. "Workers of the World." In *The Age of Empire, 1875-1914*. New York: Pantheon Books, 1987. Written by a renowned labor historian, this chapter allows the reader to situate the birth of the Labour Party within the context of global labor developments.

Pelling, Henry. *Origins of the Labour Party*. Oxford: Oxford University Press, 1965. A fine study that examines the many and varied currents which were to come together with the establishment of the Labour Party.

_____. *A Short History of the Labour Party*. London: Macmillan, 1972. Although somewhat dated and dry in parts, this work remains the best general introduction to the subject.

SEE ALSO: 1838-1848, Chartist Movement; 1864, The First International Is Formed; 1884, Fabian Society Is Founded; 1945, Labour Party Forms Majority Government.

1903-1906
POGROMS IN IMPERIAL RUSSIA

Pogroms in imperial Russia mark the outbreak of mob violence against Jewish communities as part of a rising wave of popular unrest in Russia that culminates in the Revolution of 1905.

DATE: 1903-1906

LOCALE: Russian cities in the Pale of Jewish Settlement, including Gomel, Kiev, Kishinev, Odessa, Zhitomir

CATEGORIES: Government and politics; Religion; Wars, uprisings, and civil unrest

KEY FIGURES:

Alexander II (1818-1881), czar of Russia, 1855-1881

Alexander III (1845-1894), czar of Russia, 1881-1894

Nicholas II (1868-1918), czar of Russia, 1894-1917

Vyacheslav Konstantinovich Plehve (1846-1904), minister of internal affairs

Konstantin Petrovich Pobedonostsev (1827-1907), chief procurator of the Holy Synod

Count Sergei Yulievich Witte (1849-1915), Russian minister of finance, later premier, 1905-1906

SUMMARY OF EVENT. The early years of the twentieth century were a time of mounting popular unrest in Russia. Rapid but uneven economic change was producing serious social tensions. The peasants, who still made up about 70 percent of Russia's population, had to cope with a series of disappointing harvests in the central agricultural region as well as high taxes imposed by Minister of Finance Sergei Witte to pay for his program of state-sponsored industrial development. Industrial workers, who often were unskilled or semiskilled peasants who sought factory work to supplement their agricultural earnings, faced harsh living and working conditions for low wages. A severe depression, which lasted from 1900 through the end of 1902, worsened their plight. These circumstances

gave rise to a growing number of strikes by industrial workers and peasant attacks on the estates of the landed nobility. A new round of mob assaults on Jewish communities in Russia took place against this backdrop of rising tension and confrontation.

The situation of the Jews in Russia was difficult even without the threat of physical attacks. With few exceptions, Russia's five million Jews (almost half of the world's total number of Jews) were prohibited by law from living in the historical heartland of the Russian empire. They were confined either to the portion of Poland that was under Russian control, or to a region which had become known as the "Pale of Jewish Settlement." Included in the Pale of Settlement were Lithuania, Belarus, Ukraine, Moldova (Bessarabia), and the provinces immediately north of the Black Sea. Even in these territories, the Jews were a distinct and unpopular minority, comprising only 13 percent of the population. Most of the Jews lived in cities and the larger towns; they earned their livelihoods as merchants, craftsmen, or in the developing industrial sector of the economy. Jews rarely owned land, and those who lived in the countryside were under pressure from the government during most of the nineteenth century to abandon occupations, such as tavern keeping and the operation of mills, which brought them into close contact with the non-Jewish peasants. The government relaxed some of these coercive measures during the reign of Czar Alexander II (1855-1881). Yet this relatively liberal interlude ended with the assassination of the czar in March, 1881. His successors, Alexander III and Nicholas II, revived and even strengthened the discriminatory policies against the Jews, which remained in force until the overthrow of the monarchy in 1917.

The assassination of Alexander II by revolutionary terrorists touched off the first massive wave of pogroms. Anti-Jewish riots had occasionally broken out in Russia in previous years; indeed, an 1871 disturbance which took place in the Black Sea port of Odessa was the first to become known as a "pogrom," a term derived from a Russian verb meaning "to smash" or "to destroy." What was new about the pogroms of 1881 was that they were not isolated eruptions of violence. An official report counted 259 pogroms in 1881; many of these had spread like ripples from cities and large towns to nearby villages. The ripple effect was related to difficult economic circumstances that were afflicting Russia at the time. The assassination of the czar took place during an industrial downturn which coincided with a series of poor harvests. Unemployed factory workers and hungry peasants seem to have been responsible for the spread of the pogroms as they wandered from place to place in a desperate search for new sources of income. Their frustrations fed upon the shock of the murder of the czar, the long-standing antagonism toward Jews by the non-Jewish majority in the Pale of Settlement, and a consciousness of official discrimination against Jews, which was distorted into a belief that the government approved of assaults on the Jews. The rapid spread of the pogroms took the government by surprise, so its attempts to contain them were not effective at first. By 1882, however, the new czar, Alexander III, despite his personal hatred of Jews, ordered his provincial officials to take stern measures to catch and punish those who attacked Jews and their property. Once the government's opposition to pogroms became clear, anti-Jewish outbreaks once again became isolated occurrences.

The second wave of pogroms began in Kishenev, the provincial capital of Moldova, on May 2 (April 19 by the Julian calendar then used in Russia), 1903. Two days of rioting, which began on Easter Sunday and the last day of Passover, left nearly fifty Jews dead and hundreds more injured, and inflicted enormous damage on Jewish-owned property. A second pogrom took place in Gomel, in Mogilev province, in September. This time the attackers encountered effective resistance from Jewish self-defense units, which limited the damage inflicted upon the Jewish community of Gomel. This time the government, in marked contrast with Alexander III's stern measures after the 1881 pogroms, responded in a weak and confused manner. On one hand, the Holy Synod, headed by Konstantin Petrovich Pobedonostsev, ordered all Russian Orthodox priests to preach against physical assaults on the Jews. Yet the government did not vigorously prosecute the perpetrators of the Kishinev and Gomel pogroms. Only a handful of the hundreds of pogromists were convicted, and almost all of those received lenient sentences.

The government prosecutors even suggested during the Gomel trial that pogroms were actually the fault of the Jews. These mixed signals reflected the government's anxiety over its inability to stem the rising incidence of peasant and worker unrest produced by poor harvests and the recent depression. Although Russian officials, such as Vyacheslav Konstantinovich Plehve, the notoriously anti-Semitic minister of internal affairs, did not, as was widely believed at the time, actually conspire in the organization of the pogroms, they were reluctant to impose severe penalties on the anti-Jewish rioters. They feared that such action would further anger the workers and peasants, thereby leading to additional violent outbreaks. They even regarded the pogroms as convenient diversions for popular discontent, which might otherwise be directed against government authorities.

The government's weak response to the Kishinev and Gomel pogroms did not succeed in calming restless workers and peasants. The outbreak of the Russo-Japanese War in February, 1904, heightened the political and economic strains in Russia. Popular unrest of all kinds escalated in the summer and fall of 1904, and exploded into revolution in the aftermath of the Bloody Sunday massacre of demonstrating workers in St. Petersburg on January 22, 1905. There were forty-three pogroms in 1904, and an average of about six a month for the first nine months of 1905. The announcement on October 30, 1905 (October 17 on the Julian calendar), of the October Manifesto, which granted limited constitutional reforms, ignited a massive eruption of violence, which included at least six hundred pogroms during the next two weeks. At least thirty-one hundred Jews died, and more than fifteen thousand were injured. The largest pogrom took place in Odessa, where about eight hundred Jews lost their lives and another five thousand suffered injuries.

Having broken the unity of the revolutionary opposition by issuing the October Manifesto, the government now moved vigorously to suppress popular disturbances of all kinds: strikes, peasant uprisings, and pogroms. Once again, pogroms became only isolated occurrences rather than part of a general wave of popular unrest. Yet the czarist regime had not succeeded in solving the underlying problems which had produced popular violence in the first place. The government still tacitly encouraged ethnic hostility by preserving, at the czar's insistence, the Pale of Settlement and other discriminatory laws directed against Jews. The social and economic strains of World War I and the Russian Revolution once again touched off a new series of pogroms, which began in 1917 and reached its height in 1919-1920 during the Russian Civil War.

—Richard D. King

ADDITIONAL READING:

Baron, Salo W. *The Russian Jew Under Tsars and Soviets.* 2d ed. New York: Macmillan, 1976. This survey by a leading specialist in Jewish history pays scant attention to the pogroms, but is a good introduction to the social, economic, and cultural aspects of Jewish history in Russia.

Judge, Edward H. *Easter in Kishenev: Anatomy of a Pogrom.* New York: New York University Press, 1992. This case study of the Kishenev pogrom of April, 1903, illuminates the causes of the anti-Jewish riots and graphically illustrates their brutality.

Klier, John D., and Shlomo Lambroza, eds. *Pogroms: Anti-Jewish Violence in Modern Russian History.* New York: Cambridge University Press, 1992. A collection of scholarly essays on the waves of pogroms of 1881-1884, 1903-1906, and 1919-1921.

Löwe, Heinz-Dietrich. *The Tsars and the Jews: Reform, Reaction, and Anti-Semitism in Imperial Russia, 1772-1917*. Chur, Switzerland: Harwood Academic Publishers, 1993. A revised version of a book originally published in German in 1978.

Rogger, Hans. *Jewish Policies and Right-Wing Politics in Imperial Russia*. Berkeley: University of California Press, 1986. Explores government policies toward Jews, especially the issue of government complicity in the pogroms.

Wistrich, Robert S. *Antisemitism: The Longest Hatred*. New York: Schocken Books, 1991. A lucid introduction to the history of anti-Semitism since ancient times, written as a companion volume to a three-part British television documentary.

SEE ALSO: 1290-1306, Jews Are Expelled from England, France, and Southern Italy; 1478, Establishment of the Spanish Inquisition; 1492, Expulsion of Jews from Spain; 1894-1906, The Dreyfus Affair; 1905, Bloody Sunday; 1905, The October Manifesto; 1919-1933, Racist Theories Aid Nazi Rise to Political Power.

1904-1905
RUSSO-JAPANESE WAR

The Russo-Japanese war breaks out as a result of the clashing imperial ambitions of Russia and Japan.

DATE: February 9, 1904-September 5, 1905
LOCALE: Manchuria, Korea, and the Yellow Sea
CATEGORIES: Expansion and land acquisition; Wars, uprisings, and civil unrest
KEY FIGURES:

Admiral Evgeny Ivanovich Alexieff, Russian viceroy of the Far East

General Tamemoto Kuroki, commander of main Japanese forces in Manchuria

General Aleksei Nikolayevich Kuropatkin (1848-1921), Russian minister of war, commander of Russian forces in the Far East

Mutsuhito (1852-1912), emperor of Japan, 1867-1912

Nicholas II (1868-1918), czar of Russia, 1894-1917

Theodore Roosevelt (1858-1919), twenty-sixth president of the United States, 1901-1909

Admiral Zinovi Petrovich Rozhdestvenski, commander of the Russian Baltic Fleet

Admiral Heihachirō Togō (1846-1934), commander of the Imperial Japanese Fleet

SUMMARY OF EVENT. By the end of the nineteenth century, the imperial ambitions of Russia and Japan focused on the same regions of the Far East: Korea, Manchuria, and the northeastern part of China. Japan was a relative newcomer as an imperialistic power, only emerging from its self-imposed isolation in the middle of the century. Although Japan modernized, its leaders still felt that they lacked respect from the Western powers and they were concerned with their nation's security. To Japanese leaders, Korea became a key to the national expansion. To expand its influence over that neighbor, Japan engaged Korea's more powerful neighbor, China, in war from 1894 to 1895.

Among the concessions Japan wrested from China with her victory was control over the Chinese area of Manchuria contiguous to Korea. This acquisition alarmed the Western imperialists; France, Russia, and Germany (the Triple Intervention) jointly protested this expansion, forcing Japan to relinquish territorial claims outside Korea. China's defeat in the war led the Western imperialists, including Russia, to seek additional concessions of their own from China. As the construction of the trans- Siberian railroad progressed, Russia wrested from China the right to build a railroad across northern Manchuria and also gained possession of two ports on the Liaotung Peninsula in southern Manchuria—Dairen (Ta-lien) and Port Arthur. Thus, Russia gained without conflict much of what the Triple Intervention had denied to the victorious Japanese.

One outcome of China's humiliation was the growth of antiforeign feeling, marked by the appearance of the secret society popularly called the Boxers. Their attacks on foreigners in the Boxer Rebellion resulted in a multinational military intervention in northern China. During the course of this uprising, Russian troops had fanned out over Manchuria. Only strong protests by other nations forced a phased, but often delayed, withdrawal of the Russian troops. In 1902, isolated Japan signed a treaty with Great Britain. Under its terms, each participant would remain a friendly neutral if the other became engaged in a war. If additional nations involved themselves in the conflict, the treaty required armed intervention by the other signatory. By this treaty, Japan would not have to face the threat of a new Triple Intervention alone.

In 1898, a Russian company secured from Korea the right to harvest timber along the Yalu River; the Russian royal family became financially involved in its operations, which a small Russian military force protected. These expansionist moves on the part of Russia alarmed Japan. Tensions reached such a peak that a series of negotiations between the two countries began in 1903. The negotiations were hampered by the activities of Admiral Evgeni Alexieff, Russia's Far Eastern viceroy who, because of racial prejudices, consistently underestimated the pride and strength of the Japanese.

During the 1904-1905 Russo-Japanese War, Russian soldiers clashed with Japanese troops near the city of Mukden in Manchuria. (Library of Congress)

When no progress was made after several months, the Japanese recalled their ambassador on February 6, 1904. Two days later, Admiral Heihachirō Togō attacked the Russian fleet at Port Arthur in Manchuria. Suffering some damage, the Russian fleet remained in or close to that port until late in the war. At the same time that Togō struck at Port Arthur, Japanese troops landed in Korea and quickly marched to the Yalu River against token Russian opposition. With the neutralization of the Russian Far Eastern fleet, Japan moved troops into Manchuria both to invest Port Arthur and to defeat the main Russian forces near Liaoyang under General Aleksei Kuropatkin. Because of the Japanese willingness to take casualties in attack and the weakness of the Russians in numbers and resolve, Japan won an unbroken series of victories. The major battles included those fought at Liaoyang and Mukden under General Tamemoto Kuroki, and the successful siege of Port Arthur. Sent to change the balance of naval power in Asia, the Russian Baltic fleet was totally destroyed by Admiral Togō in the Battle of Tsushima Strait, May 27-28, 1905.

The unbroken series of Russian defeats contributed to growing unrest at home and led Nicholas II to seek an end to the war. Although victorious at sea and on land, Japan was militarily and economically exhausted by the struggle. When President Theodore Roosevelt offered to help bring the war to an end, negotiators of the two belligerents met at Portsmouth, New Hampshire, where a peace treaty was signed on September 5, 1905. Under its terms, Japan took possession of the Russian concessions in southern Manchuria and the railroad leading north to Mukden, gained official recognition of their predominance over Korea, and were given the southern half of Sakhalin Island. The lack of a sizable indemnity led to some rioting in Japan.

The Russo-Japanese War has been overshadowed by World War I, which followed so closely on its heels. In actuality, the struggle of 1904-1905 may have been one of the most significant conflicts of the twentieth century. For the first time in modern history, a major European power was defeated by a non-European nation. This event raised the hopes of nationalists in Asia and Africa that the days of European colonialism were numbered. Defeat for Russia played a major role in bringing on an incomplete reformist revolution in 1905, which so eroded feelings for the czar that it was a factor leading to the revolutions of 1917 and the emergence of the Bolshevik state. Failure to achieve all of its aims in the peace treaty fed a growing militarism in Japan and the conviction that their legitimate goals were thwarted by the Americans. Japanese military planners became convinced that they could defeat a stronger power by destroying its main naval forces at the very outbreak of war.

—Hans Heilbronner, updated by Art Barbeau

ADDITIONAL READING:

Borton, Hugh. *Japan's Modern Century*. New York: Ronald Press, 1955. Includes a brief account of the war from the Japanese perspective.

Hare, James H., ed. *A Photographic Record of the Russo-Japanese War*. New York: Collier and Son, 1905. Probably the best of the many contemporary accounts of the war in presenting a photographic account of the conflict.

Malozemoff, Andrew. *Russian Far Eastern Policy, 1881-1904: With Special Emphasis on the Causes of the Russo-Japanese War*. Berkeley: University of California Press, 1958. While attempting a revision of traditional interpretations on the war and its results, the book has a definite anti-Japanese bias.

Martin, Christopher. *The Russo-Japanese War*. New York, Abelard-Schuman, 1967. Written in simple language, Martin's work recounts the events of the time in almost reportorial style. Unlike many earlier accounts, it places the war in its historical setting, giving proper emphasis to its Asian causes, rather than treating it as a minor intrigue of Russian internal politics. This work is where the interested reader should start.

The Russo-Japanese War. 2 vols. London: H. M. Stationery Office, 1906-1908. A history and analysis of the Russo-Japanese War by the British General Staff. As an unofficial ally of Japan, the British sent many observers to the scene.

White, John A. *The Diplomacy of the Russo-Japanese War*. Princeton, N.J.: Princeton University Press, 1964. A careful and scholarly account of the war that places the blame for the conflict on the Far Eastern aims of the two protagonists, each of which was threatened by the actions and desires of the other.

SEE ALSO: 1893, Franco-Russian Alliance; 1905, Bloody Sunday; 1905, The October Manifesto; 1906, First Meeting of the Duma; 1911, Assassination of Peter Stolypin.

1904
THE ENTENTE CORDIALE

The Entente Cordiale settles long-standing disputes between England and France and begins an era of improved relations that eventually make them allies in World War I.

DATE: April 8, 1904
LOCALE: London and Paris
CATEGORY: Diplomacy and international relations
KEY FIGURES:

Sir Thomas Barclay, British official active in international relations
Pierre Paul Cambon, French ambassador in London
Théophile Delcassé (1852-1923), French minister of foreign affairs, 1899-1906
Edward VII (1841-1910), king of Great Britain, 1901-1910
Émile-François Loubet (1838-1929), president of France, 1899-1906
Henry Charles Keith Petty-Fitzmaurice, marquis of Lansdowne (1845-1927), foreign secretary of Great Britain, 1900-1905

SUMMARY OF EVENT. Rapprochement between Great Britain and France, culminating in 1904 in the Entente Cordiale, was born of the realization in both countries at the beginning of the twentieth century that each had more to gain by seeking the other's friendship than by perpetuating hostile and dangerous imperialistic rivalry. Anglo-French conflict was possible at a number of places around the globe. In the Far East, tension was growing between Japan (an ally of Great Britain) and Russia (an ally of France). The outbreak of the Russo-Japanese War in 1904 made it important for London and Paris to repair their damaged relations to avoid becoming involved in war against each other. They had, in fact, already come into conflict in 1898 over the Fashoda crisis, the climax of the struggle for the Sudan, but France was not in a very strong position at the time. A similar situation arose in North Africa, where Great Britain desired a free hand in Egypt while France wanted the same in Morocco; French financial interests in Egypt had long bothered Great Britain, whose large share of Moroccan trade was a source of major discomfort to France. Other minor problems, including the traditional dispute over the Newfoundland fisheries, marred Anglo-French relations.

The British and French had been in dangerous competition in Africa for over two decades. The French had an added burden in that they had been humiliated in the Franco-Prussian War and by the Treaty of Frankfurt of 1871. One aspect of the new imperialism of the late nineteenth century for France was a psychological one. Territorial annexation helped assuage some French sensibilities, but it also focused national ire on Britain, which had become France's chief competitor in Africa. On both sides of the channel political rhetoric often became heated. In the wake of the Fashoda crisis, Théophile Delcassé, who became French foreign minister in the aftermath of the embarrassment on the Nile, wanted to proceed with caution in dealing with any new relationship with Britain.

Inside Europe, the relations of both countries with Germany provided better reasons for mutual friendship. Great Britain no longer desired splendid isolation, and made repeated attempts between 1898 and 1901 to enter into an alliance with Germany, but anti-British feeling in Germany generated by the Boer War of 1899-1902 not only frustrated these attempts but also had the effect of bringing Great Britain closer to France. There were many British politicians who distrusted Germany's intentions on the continent. Many, including Lord Salisbury, who was prime minister at the time of the Fashoda crisis, believed that Germany, if left unchecked under William II, would emerge as the undisputed power in Europe. William II was

seen as aggressive, militant, and often erratic, and his near-paranoid distrust of England and King Edward VII were well known. This was not a solid foundation on which to make a mutually beneficial alliance.

On the other side, France, always fearful of Germany, came to realize by 1904 that an *entente* with England might compensate for the disappointing alliance with Russia which had turned out to be a financial drain without visible returns on the diplomatic level. Both the British and the French governments appointed new officials to improve relations between their countries.

In France, Théophile Delcassé, the new minister of foreign affairs, tried to persuade the British to acquiesce in French dominance of Morocco; for this he was willing to back down from a confrontation with British forces at Fashoda in 1898. On March 21, 1899, he reached agreement with Great Britain demarcating the French and English spheres of influence between the Upper Nile and the Congo. A year later, Delcassé gave his blessing to the efforts of Sir Thomas Barclay, a British official, to arrange for the visit of British Chambers of Commerce to the great Paris Exposition. Barclay also arranged a return visit of

King Edward VII met with French leader Émile-François Loubet in 1903 as a prelude to the signing of the Entente Cordiale. (Library of Congress)

French Chambers of Commerce to England. On October 14, 1903, both states signed the Anglo-French Treaty of Arbitration, promising to submit most of their disputes to the Permanent Court of Arbitration at The Hague. Barclay was as influential in arranging this treaty as he was in organizing an exchange of visits to the two capitals by King Edward VII and President Émile-François Loubet in 1903. Edward VII's visit to Paris was a huge success, attracting large, friendly, and cheering crowds. The British king, who had always been popular in France, did much to warm relations between the two countries.

Expressions of warmth and friendship on both visits helped to smother anti-British feeling in France as a result of the Boer War. Also, Delcassé accompanied Loubet on his visit to London and used the occasion to begin serious negotiations with the marquis of Lansdowne, the new British foreign secretary, about settlement of outstanding differences between the two governments. This led to the signing of the Entente Cordiale on April 8, 1904, by Lansdowne and Pierre Paul Cambon, the French ambassador at London.

Although not a military pact, the Entente Cordiale reestablished good relations between Great Britain and France so that military cooperation was possible in the dark days of August, 1914. Among minor disputes settled by the Entente Cordiale were those concerning the Newfoundland fisheries, West African boundaries, Siam, Madagascar, and the New Hebrides Islands. Most important was the provision that France agree to allow Great Britain a free hand in Egypt in exchange for being allowed a free hand in Morocco. Under a secret convention of the Entente Cordiale, Great Britain agreed to an eventual partition of Morocco between Spain and France whereby the Spanish controlled the coastal area opposite Gibraltar while the French occupied the hinterland.

While it is correct to see the Entente Cordiale in the light of a warming of relations between France and Britain and a settling of long-standing colonial conflicts, the military effects were indeed important. The Entente gave an opportunity for the general staffs of France and Britain to visit each other and discuss military matters of mutual interest. While serious misunderstandings still existed between the two armies, certain common ground was found, and plans were slowly formulated for concerted action if war with Germany ever began. Despite obvious Russian weaknesses, made manifest by the Russo-Japanese War, it was clear that France was in a much better position militarily and diplomatically than she had been since the Franco-Prussian War.

To Delcassé, this agreement with Great Britain, like a similar one made with Italy in 1902, was designed primarily to gain French ascendancy in Morocco. To an insulted Germany, whose Moroccan interests Delcassé believed he could ignore, the Anglo-French agreement took on far greater significance, especially since France was already allied to Russia. For Germany, the balance maintained for ten years between the Triple Alliance and the Franco-Russian Dual Alliance of 1894 had now shifted in favor of the newly emerging Triple Entente. The German foreign office was particularly angered by the fact that Great Britain and France had sealed their rapprochement at the expense of German interests in Morocco. German attempts to defend these interests in 1905 and 1911 touched off two serious Moroccan crises, which in turn led to the strengthening of the Anglo-French accord. The combined effect was to divide Europe into two armed camps which were to move against each other in 1914.

—*Edward P. Keleher, updated by James J. Cooke*

ADDITIONAL READING:

Andrew, Christopher. *Théophile Delcassé and the Making of the Entente Cordiale*. New York: St. Martin's Press, 1968. Andrew's work remains the best, most detailed account of the making of the 1904 Entente.

Fay, Sidney B. *The Origins of the World War*. 2 vols. New York: Free Press, 1966. Fay's revisionist study remains a classic, detailed analysis of the background, signing and results of the Entente Cordial.

Grey, Sir Edward. *Twenty-Five Years, 1892-1916*. New York: Frederick A. Stokes, 1925. Having been involved with the great events from the Entente to the outbreak of World War I, Grey's memoirs provide a good insight to the period.

Hale, Oron J. *The Grand Illusion, 1900-1914*. New York: Harper & Row, 1971. Hale deals with social as well as diplomatic crosscurrents of the period.

Kennedy, Paul. *The Rise of Anglo-German Antagonism, 1860-1914*. London: Allen & Unwin, 1980. Kennedy's work has an extensive analysis of the factors leading up to the Entente Cordiale.

SEE ALSO: 1893, Franco-Russian Alliance; 1898-1899, The Fashoda Incident; 1899-1902, Boer War; 1907, The Triple Entente.

1905
EINSTEIN PUBLISHES HIS SPECIAL THEORY OF RELATIVITY

Einstein publishes his Special Theory of Relativity and demonstrates the inadequacy of Newtonian physics to explain key experimental results, thus inaugurating an era of revolutionary change in physical theory.

Although known for his famous theory of relativity, Albert Einstein was awarded the Nobel Prize in Physics in 1921 for his work on the photoelectric effect. (The Nobel Foundation)

DATE: 1905

LOCALE: Berne, Switzerland

CATEGORIES: Cultural and intellectual history; Science and technology

KEY FIGURES:

Albert Einstein (1879-1955), theoretical physicist

Albert Abraham Michelson (1852-1931), and

Edward Williams Morley (1838-1923), American physicists who performed an experiment to detect the absolute motion of the earth through the ether

Hendrik Antoon Lorentz (1853-1928), Dutch physicist who first proposed relativistic transformation of space and time measurements

SUMMARY OF EVENT. Albert Einstein, born at Ulm in Germany in 1989, showed early precocity in mathematics and the natural sciences. After receiving a doctoral degree, he held several unsuccessful teaching posts before becoming examiner of patents at the Swiss Patent Office in Berne. He devoted his spare time to theoretical subjects, and in 1905 he published four scientific papers, the most

famous bearing the rather technical title "Electrodynamics of Moving Bodies," in which he stated the basic principles of what has come to be known as the Special Theory of Relativity. This theory was an attempt to reconcile the theory of electromagnetic fields which had been developed in the nineteenth century with the classical physics of Galileo and Newton.

According to classical physics, the laws of mechanics are the same for all inertial systems moving uniformly in relation to one another. It is not therefore possible to determine by mechanical experiment the absolute motion of a system moving uniformly. In a train moving uniformly, for example, a ball tossed into the air by a seated passenger will act in the same manner, as observed by the passenger, as it would if the train and passenger were at rest. Contemporary physical theory did, however, offer one prospect for measuring the absolute motion of an object. To explain the wave properties of light, physicists postulated that light involved the vibrations of a "luminiferous ether," which filled all space but through which material objects passed with no resistance. In principle, this ether could serve as a reference point for determining absolute motion.

Toward the end of the nineteenth century, American physicists Albert Abraham Michelson and Edward Williams Morley, who were working in Cleveland, Ohio, made an ingenious attempt to measure the absolute motion of the earth with respect to the ether. They reasoned that if the earth was in motion with respect to the ether, then light beams would have slightly different velocities depending on whether the light was traveling in the same direction as, opposite to, or at right angles to the earth's motion through the ether, just as sound waves travel faster downwind than upwind from their source. Their most careful measurements, however, could detect no difference in the velocity of light whatever its direction.

The Dutch physicist Hendrik Antoon Lorentz proposed a solution to this puzzle. He argued that no difference could be detected between the velocity of light in a system in motion and a system at rest because a system in motion contracts in the direction of the motion. A light beam moving upstream is actually slowed down, but the change cannot be detected because the distance which it travels is shortened. Lorentz also postulated that the movement of time is slowed for a body in motion. Lorentz's results are summarized in the Lorentz transformation which relates position and time measurements made by observers in relative motion to each other. The Lorentz transformation agrees with the classical or Galilean (after Galileo) transformation at low velocities but predicts radically different behavior at velocities comparable to the speed of light, or

186,000 miles per second. For example, a yardstick moving at 85 percent of this speed, or 158,000 miles per second, would measure only half a yard in length. Yet Lorentz did not abandon the assumptions of classical physics entirely. Classical physics assumed that "absolute" space and absolute time did exist, and that a privileged observer in a system at rest could measure distances and time intervals "correctly." The Lorentz transformation enabled values of distance and time obtained from a system in uniform motion to be adjusted in order to find out these "correct" values.

Einstein carried the ideas of Lorentz one step further, but in so doing he transformed their meaning radically. Einstein took as fundamental postulates of his theory that there was no physical way to distinguish between frames of reference moving with respect to each other and that the speed of light would be measured to have the same value by all observers in uniform motion with respect to each other, thus eliminating the need for an ether. Moreover, because absolute motion or absolute rest cannot be determined, absolute space and absolute time are meaningless concepts. There is no privileged observer whose values are "absolutely" correct; there can only be "measured" distances and "measured" time intervals. An observer in a uniformly moving system attempting to measure distances and time intervals in another uniformly moving system will obtain results dependent upon the relative velocity of the two uniformly moving systems. Any observer may in fact decide, for purposes of convenience, that his own system (or any other system) is at rest without affecting the laws of nature.

Later in 1905, Einstein published a second paper using his new approach, entitled "Does the Inertia of a Body Depend on Its Energy Content?" in which he showed that the emission of energy by a body resulted in a change of mass according to the now famous equation $E = mc^2$. Within two years, Einstein would use this relationship to explain the release of energy by radioactive materials. In 1905, he also published two papers unrelated to relativity theory, one on Brownian motion and one on the photoelectric effect, for which he later received the Nobel Prize for Physics in 1921. In 1916, he extended his ideas by publishing the *General Theory of Relativity*, in which he enlarged his theory to describe the relationship between measurements in reference frames in nonuniform motion with respect to each other. This theory included the now famous "principle of equivalence," which states that an isolated observer would be unable to distinguish between a gravitational field and uniform acceleration, which in turn implies that light actually travels along a curved path in gravitational fields. Confirmation by astronomers of the bending of starlight by the sun during a solar eclipse was reported in newspapers around the world and brought immense fame to Einstein after World War I.

In the 1930's, Einstein began to spend time abroad as a visiting professor at various institutions, including Oxford University and the California Institute of Technology. By 1933, fearing that he would be the target of persecution by the National Socialists (Nazis) who had taken over the German government, he decided to emigrate to the United States. In 1939, he was called upon by other émigré physicists to write to President Franklin D. Roosevelt and draw his attention to the discovery of atomic fission, which made possible the construction of an atomic bomb in which a significant amount of the mass-energy of uranium atoms could be released. Following the defeat of Germany, Einstein became a spokesman for peace and international collaboration. Albert Einstein died in 1955 in Princeton, New Jersey.

—Paul T. Mason, updated by Donald R. Franceschetti

ADDITIONAL READING:

Clark, Ronald W. *Einstein: The Life and Times*. New York: Avon Books, 1971. Probably the most detailed biography of Einstein by a professional biographer. Provides much information on Einstein's role in world affairs.

Frank, Philipp. *Einstein: His Life and Times*. Translated by George Rosen. New York: Alfred A. Knopf, 1963. An excellent biography of Einstein by one of his contemporaries, a philosopher and scientist who knew him well.

Highfield, Roger, and Paul C. Carter. *The Private Lives of Albert Einstein*. New York: St. Martin's Press, 1993. Einstein's immense popularity led many to view him as an almost superhuman individual. This book provides carefully researched information on Einstein's everyday life and the personal relationships that may have influenced his work.

Hoffmann, Banesh. *Albert Einstein, Creator and Rebel*. New York: Viking, 1972. Written in collaboration with Helen Dukas, Einstein's former secretary, by one of Einstein's American mathematical collaborators, this book combines insight into Einstein's personality with very clear discussions of his scientific ideas.

Pais, Abraham. *Subtle Is the Lord: The Science and the Life of Albert Einstein*. Oxford: Oxford University Press, 1982. For the more ambitious reader, this biography reviews Einstein's scientific achievements in the context of his life and the political events that affected it.

Rhodes, Richard. *The Making of the Atomic Bomb*. New York: Simon & Schuster, 1986. Describes the physical discoveries leading up to the first nuclear weapons and Einstein's role in the decision to develop the atomic bomb.

Sugimoto, Kenji. *Albert Einstein: A Photographic Biography*. Translated by Barbara Harshav. New York: Schocken Books, 1989. Provides many valuable photographs of Einstein and other scientific notables of the period along with a detailed chronology of Einstein's life and bibliography of his publications.

SEE ALSO: 1687, Newton Formulates His Theory of Universal Gravitation; 1831, Faraday Converts Magnetic Force into Electricity.

1905
BLOODY SUNDAY

Bloody Sunday marks the violent suppression of a demonstration of unarmed workers in St. Petersburg, precipitating revolutionary unrest throughout Russia that forces Czar Nicholas II to grant limited constitutional reforms.

DATE: January 22, 1905

LOCALE: St. Petersburg, Russia

CATEGORIES: Government and politics; Wars, uprisings, and civil unrest

KEY FIGURES:

Father Georgi Appollonovich Gapon, Russian Orthodox priest

Nicholas II (1868-1918), czar of Russia, 1894-1917

Count Sergei Yulievich Witte (1849-1915), Russian finance minister

Sergei Vasilievich Zubatov, head of the Moscow security police

SUMMARY OF EVENT. The popular demonstration of Sunday, January 22, 1905 (January 9 by the Julian calendar used at the time in Russia), which ended in its bloody suppression, was not only a reaction against the deplorable conditions prevailing in Russia at the beginning of the twentieth century but also against the government's studied inability and reluctance to do anything about them. Foremost among those who opposed change and whose conservative policies created widespread discontent were Czar Nicholas II and a number of his close advisers, including Sergei Witte, the minister of finance. Nicholas II was determined to preserve his autocratic power against demands for representative government. Witte had implemented a program of rapid industrial growth, which he believed was imperative if Russia was to remain a great power. After the severe depression of 1900-1902, the opposition of these leaders to badly needed political and social reform encouraged acts of desperation. Between 1900 and 1905, unemployment increased in large centers of industry such as Moscow and St. Petersburg, and workers went on strike over low wages and long hours. Peasant unrest also increased dramatically during these years. Burdened by high taxes and a rapidly growing population, the peasants saw the seizure of the estates of the landed nobility as the answer to their problems.

This growing discontent received encouragement from illegal political parties that were seeking radical political and social change. An underground Union of Liberation organized demonstrations in the fall of 1904 protesting government incompetence in waging the Russo-Japanese War and demanding constitutional reforms and representative government. The Socialist Revolutionary Party supported the peasants' desire for land; it was also responsible for the assassination of numerous government officials. A Marxist party, the Social Democrats, hoped to transform the strike movement into a revolutionary upheaval that would overthrow the autocracy and capitalism.

Sergei Zubatov, a former revolutionary who had become head of Moscow's security police, believed that the workers were more interested in tangible improvements in their living and working conditions than in Marxist ideology or a political reform program. They would, he argued, support the czar rather than the Social Democrats if the government would support their economic demands against their employers. To further this goal, Zubatov founded the "Council of Workers of Mechanical Factories of the City of Moscow" in 1901. Similar "police unions" were set up in other industrial cities, including Odessa and St. Petersburg. Witte, however, opposed government support for striking workers as harmful to his vision of rapid industrial growth, and this "police socialism" soon collapsed. It soon reappeared in St. Petersburg under the leadership of a Russian Orthodox priest, Father Georgi Appollonovich Gapon.

Father Gapon's organization, the "Assembly of Russian Factory and Mill Workers of the City of St. Petersburg," also received government recognition as being nonpolitical in nature, which it was at first, but by 1904, when its membership had grown to eight thousand, many workers inclined to the more militant, revolutionary tactics of the Social Democrats and Socialist Revolutionaries. Many laborers became more and more disgusted with their working conditions. The dismissal of workers in January, 1905, by a large factory in the capital led to a strike that became general within a few days.

In a series of meetings of Gapon's organization held in January, 1905, it was agreed that he should lead a march of workers to the czar's Winter Palace in St. Petersburg and present Nicholas II with a petition that reaffirmed the loyalty of the petitioners to the czar, but called upon him to lift from their shoulders the yoke of oppression which his corrupt officials had placed upon them. The workers and the radical intellectuals who helped to draft the petition demanded better treatment from officials and factory owners, and an end to the war. The petitioners, moreover, called upon the czar to institute sweeping civil and political reforms, including freedom of speech, freedom of the press, and freedom of association; a broadened franchise for local elections; equality before the law; and above all, the creation of a representative assembly. These reform demands, given the nature of the country in which they were made, were truly revolutionary. Although Father

czar. Nicholas, however, decided to stay away from the city and left the handling of the crisis to his police and military officials. Having failed in an attempt to arrest Gapon, these officials stationed military forces on the large square in front of the Winter Palace and at key points along the anticipated routes of the march. Despite this show of force, which included some instances of shooting, the military patrols failed to prevent the crowds from pressing on toward Palace Square, and when the workers surged toward the Winter Palace and refused to disperse,

Russian workers staging a protest outside the Winter Palace in St. Petersburg were massacred by czarist troops on "Bloody Sunday." (Library of Congress)

Gapon was personally opposed to making political demands at that time, he agreed to include them in the petition rather than lose the trust of the workers. Consequently, the bitter cold Sunday morning of January 22, 1905, found him leading his followers to the czar's Winter Palace.

Clad in his priestly robes, Father Gapon personally led one of the several long columns of workers from the outskirts of St. Petersburg toward the center of the city and the Winter Palace. The march was intended as a peaceful demonstration, and some marchers were accompanied by their families while others bore icons and portraits of the

the troops, who remained loyal to the czar, fired on them. At least 130 workers were killed and hundreds more were injured.

The "Bloody Sunday" episode was a debacle for the czarist regime. Liberal agitation for constitutional reforms, the rising wave of workers' strikes and peasant uprisings, and public disgust with the lack of success in the war with Japan had already raised tensions in Russia to a high level. News of the massacre in St. Petersburg unleashed the first Russian revolution in the twentieth century. Father Gapon managed to escape from the capital and flee into exile, where he issued an open letter to the czar which denounced him for having refused to accept the petition. "Let all blood which has to be shed fall upon thee, hangman, and thy kindred." In this statement, Gapon expressed the real historical significance of Bloody Sunday, namely that the Russian people had now completely lost faith in the czar. Indeed, the Bloody Sunday massacre exposed to all Russians the intransigence and incompetence of Romanov autocracy. The government was only able to contain the revolutionary outbreaks when Nicholas II reluctantly agreed to conclude an unfavorable peace with Japan and grant constitutional reforms, including the establishment of a representative assembly, the Duma. The czar only grudgingly made these concessions, which by satisfying some of the revolutionary opposition enabled the government to begin the work of reestablishing order in Russia. Yet his manifest reluctance to relinquish even a portion of his enormous power did not bode well for the success of Russia's new constitutional government.

—*Edward P. Keleher, updated by Richard D. King*

ADDITIONAL READING:

Ascher, Abraham. *The Revolution of 1905*. 2 vols. Stanford, Calif.: Stanford University Press, 1988-1992. A fine history of the first Russian revolution of the twentieth century.

Lincoln, W. Bruce. *In War's Dark Shadow: The Russians Before the Great War*. New York: Dial Press, 1984. A noted scholar offers a highly readable portrait of Russia during the years 1891 to 1914.

Sablinsky, Walter. *The Road to Bloody Sunday: Father Gapon and the St. Petersburg Massacre of 1905*. Princeton, N.J.: Princeton University Press, 1976. A detailed history of the workers' organization founded by Father Gapon and of the tragic demonstration of January 22, 1905.

Schneiderman, Jeremiah. *Sergei Zubatov and Revolutionary Marxism: The Struggle for the Working Class in Tsarist Russia*. Ithaca, N.Y.: Cornell University Press, 1976. This work traces the rise and fall of the "police union" movement, which served as the inspiration for Father Gapon's organization in St. Petersburg.

Verner, Andrew M. *The Crisis of Russian Autocracy: Nicholas II and the 1905 Revolution*. Princeton, N.J.: Princeton University Press, 1990. An fine analysis of Nicholas II's personality as well as his role in Bloody Sunday and its aftermath.

Von Laue, Theodore H. *Why Lenin? Why Stalin? Why Gorbachev? The Rise and Fall of the Soviet System*. 3d ed. New York: HarperCollins, 1993. A classic interpretive essay that situates the events of 1905 in the larger context of modern Russian and Soviet history.

SEE ALSO: 1903-1906, Pogroms in Imperial Russia; 1904-1905, Russo-Japanese War; 1905, The October Manifesto; 1906, First Meeting of the Duma; 1911, Assassination of Peter Stolypin; 1917, October Revolution.

1905
NORWAY BECOMES INDEPENDENT

Norway becomes independent, dissolving its union with Sweden after an almost century-long effort of heated debate, ongoing compromise, and persistent political maneuvering.

DATE: October 26, 1905
LOCALE: Norway and Sweden
CATEGORY: Government and politics
KEY FIGURES:
Björnstjerne Björnson (1832-1910), leader of the Norwegian nationalistic literary revival
Erik Gustaf Boström, prime minister of Sweden in 1904
Haakon VII (formerly Prince Carl of Denmark; 1872-1957), king of Norway, 1905-1957
Peter Christian Hersleb Kjerschow Michelsen (1857-1925), leader of the Norwegian Radical Party and first premier of independent Norway, 1905-1907
Oscar II (1829-1907), king of Sweden, 1872-1907, and king of Norway, 1872-1905
Johan Svedrup (1816-1892), leader of the Norwegian Liberal Party, president of the Storting, 1871-1881, and prime minister of Sweden, 1884-1889

SUMMARY OF EVENT. Norway successfully dissolved its union with Sweden in 1905, and became completely independent for the first time since 1380. Norway had entered into dynastic union with Denmark in 1380, a union which lasted until 1814. After the Vienna Settlement ending the Napoleonic Wars, Finland was taken from Sweden and given to Russia. In return, Czar Alexander I promised to support Swedish annexation of Norway, which was accomplished by the Treaty of Kiel in 1814 between Sweden and Denmark. Norway, however, refused to become a pawn in the game of international politics. On May 17, 1814, a Norwegian constituent assembly adopted a liberal constitution providing for a unicameral parliament, the Storting. It also denied to the king both the right of absolute veto and the right to dissolve the Storting. The constituent assembly then proceeded to elect unanimously Prince Christian Frederick of Denmark as king of Norway.

This independent course of action prompted Sweden to invade Norway, which then had no choice but to submit to Swedish rule. Yet the Norwegians refused to abandon their independence altogether. On November 4, 1814, the Storting declared Norway to be "a free, independent, and indivisible kingdom, united with Sweden under one king." In 1815, Sweden accepted this declaration and, by implication, Norway's constitution by a special act of union called the *Riksakt*. It remained, in the wake of later unsuccessful attempts to revise it, an ill-defined agreement, something more than a merely personal bond but less than a complete union. Its vague character was particularly evident in the administration of foreign affairs for the two countries. The Swedish government conducted foreign affairs for both, but the consular service was a joint arrangement.

It became increasingly evident that Norway and Sweden were incompatible. Norway's population consisted primarily of fishermen and a free peasantry; in Sweden, by contrast, a landed aristocracy prevailed over a dependent peasantry. By the middle of the nineteenth century, Sweden was becoming highly industrialized; but Norway remained predominantly an agricultural and commercial state. During the second half of the nineteenth century, Norway increased its maritime commerce tenfold, leaving Sweden far behind in this area. Politically, the liberal structure of Norway's government was altogether different from the conservative and aristocratic bent of Sweden's government, over whose parliament the king exercised an absolute veto.

The steady growth of Norwegian nationalism after 1815 underscored these differences and contributed to the eventual dissolution of the union. The publication of national histories and collections of folk songs, together with Norwegian dictionaries and grammars, created the prologue for the great Norwegian literary revival of the last third of the nineteenth century, led by playwright Henrik Ibsen, among others, and especially by Björnstjerne Björnson, who aroused considerable antiunionist sentiment among the youth of Norway. Politically, the young nationalists were drawn to the Liberal Party, led by Johan Svedrup, which emerged after 1870 as the champion of Norwegian democracy and greater freedom for Norway within the union. By 1890, however, the most militant Norwegian nationalists had gone over to the Radical Party, which came to advocate dissolution of the union with Sweden.

Norway's growing disaffection with the union was reflected in a number of serious disputes after 1859 between the Storting and the Swedish crown. In each case, Norway successfully challenged key prerogatives of the monarch, King Oscar II, and thereby undermined the foundations of the union.

The Radicals, upon assuming control of the ministry and the Storting in 1891, proceeded to raise the issue which ultimately ended the union, the demand for a separate Norwegian consular service. As had been the case with previous issues debated with the Swedish crown, the Radicals believed that the question of a separate consular service was purely a Norwegian affair. In this view, the Radicals encountered the opposition of both the Swedish government and the Norwegian Conservative Party. In 1902, Sweden decided to accept the Radical demand for separated consular services. Chances for settlement of the question seemed to improve with the fall of the Radical government in 1903, but the advent of the uncompromising Erik Gustaf Boström as prime minister of Sweden in 1904 more than offset any advantage gained by the momentary decline of the Norwegian Radicals. During 1904, Boström insisted upon certain "dependency clauses" in any agreement with Norway, which would have effectively nullified the real independence of a separate Norwegian consular service relative to the foreign ministry of Sweden. On February 7, 1905, both governments finally announced that negotiations had formally closed. Boström had succeeded in uniting the people of Norway as never before against Sweden. In March, the Radicals returned to power under the leadership of Peter Christian Hersleb Kjerschow Michelsen.

Prime Minister Michelsen and the Radical-dominated Storting now moved to destroy the union. Rejecting new Swedish offers for negotiations on the consular issue, the Storting passed a bill in May, 1905, which called for the establishment of a separated Norwegian consular service. When the king vetoed the bill, the entire Norwegian ministry resigned. King Oscar II refused to accept the resignation and was reluctant or unable to form a new government in Norway. As a result, the Storting declared on June 7 that royal power had ceased to function. The Storting requested the ministry to remain in office and to exercise the authority of the Swedish king. In a plebiscite held on August 13, the voters approved the dissolution of the union by the overwhelming majority of 368,208 to 184. The Swedish parliament reluctantly accepted the separation on September 24. A month later, on October 26, 1905, the two states signed a formal treaty dissolving the union. Norway then bestowed the Norwegian crown on Prince Carl of Denmark, grandson of King Christian IX of Denmark. Carl ruled Norway until 1957 as King Haakon VII.

—Edward P. Keleher, updated by John Quinn Imholte

ADDITIONAL READING:

Derry, Thomas K. *A History of Modern Norway, 1814-1972*. New York: Oxford University Press, 1973. Includes social, economic, literary, and artistic developments as well as political history. Objective and well written. Norway is depicted as aspiring toward political democracy, social reform, economic growth, and cultural accomplishment.

Greve, Tim. *Haakon VII of Norway: The Man and the Monarch—Founder of a New Monarchy*. New York: Hippocrene Books, 1983. Life of the first modern Norwegian monarch. Chapters 2 through 4 are especially pertinent to the dissolution of Norway's union with Sweden.

Hayes, Carlton J. H. *Contemporary Europe Since 1870*. Rev. ed. New York: Macmillan, 1958. A brief, reliable account of Norway's move toward independence.

Larsen, Karen. *A History of Norway*. Princeton, N.J.: Princeton University Press, 1948. Written in a formal but not pedantic style, this survey of Norwegian history to World War II provides a straightforward recitation of the facts. Chapters 18 and 19 are especially for gaining an understanding of the dissolution of the union.

Lindgren, Raymond E. *Norway-Sweden: Union, Disunion and Scandinavian Integration*. Princeton, N.J.: Princeton University Press, 1959. Lindgren provides a fine presentation of reasons for the dissolution of the Swedish-Norwegian union, emphasizing the final phase of the union's history. His objective account includes nonpolitical events and ideas.

SEE ALSO: 1397, The Kalmar Union Is Formed; 1814-1815, Congress of Vienna; 1940, German Invasion of Norway.

1905
THE OCTOBER MANIFESTO

The October Manifesto outlines Nicholas II's grudging concessions to political reform in the wake of massive civil discontent and revolutionary activity in Russia.

DATE: October 30, 1905

LOCALE: St. Petersburg, Russia

CATEGORY: Laws, acts, and legal history

KEY FIGURES:

Alexander Dubrovin (1855-1918), leader of the "Union of the Russian People," a reactionary group which supported the czarist government

Alexander Ivanovich Guchkov (1862-1936), founder and leader of the Octobrist Party, established in 1905

Vladimir Ilich Lenin (Ulyanov; 1870-1924), leader of the antigovernment Bolshevik Party

Paul Miliukov (1859-1943), Russian historian and leader of the Constitutional Democrats

Nicholas II (1868-1918), czar of Russia, 1894-1917

Leon Trotsky (1879-1940), radical leader of the leftist Soviet of Workers' Deputies

Count Sergei Yulievich Witte (1849-1915), Russian prime minister, 1905-1906

SUMMARY OF EVENT. In January, 1905, the czar's troops had ruthlessly fired upon a peaceful procession of peti-

tioners in the capital city of St. Petersburg in what came to be known as "Bloody Sunday." This tragedy, combined with the disasters befalling Russia in the Russo-Japanese War of 1904-1905, sparked the Revolution of 1905. The revolution in Russia proved to be largely abortive, but out of it came one famous document: the promulgation by Czar Nicholas II of the October Manifesto. It marked, at least at face value, Russia's first departure from czarist autocracy in favor of a constitutional government with substantial limits on the monarch's authority. The October Manifesto also revealed Nicholas II's begrudging and belated concessions to the growing demands of the people for sweeping reforms.

Between January and October, 1905, there were strikes in the industrial centers, peasant revolts in the countryside, periods of national and ethnic unrest in the western border areas, and mutinies in the army and navy. In order to conciliate his people, Czar Nicholas proclaimed in August the establishment of the Duma, or Russian parliament, to advise the monarch concerning legislation. Although an elective body, it was chosen by a limited and indirect franchise, and its function was solely consultative. Announcement of its creation proved to be completely ineffective in quieting the general unrest and the antagonism of political organizations. In October, a widespread general strike paralyzed the entire country for about ten days, forcing Nicholas to decide on his options in the crisis. As he noted in a letter to his mother dated November of 1905, he had two choices: one was to use military force to impose ruthless control within the major cities and across the nation or to make concessions to the opposition.

On October 30 (October 17 by the Julian calendar still in effect at that time), the czar made his decision. He reluctantly agreed to issue an imperial manifesto promising a constitution that would include a stronger Duma and also place limits on the royal authority. This document was largely the work of Count Sergei Witte, his former finance minister and now prime minister.

The October Manifesto promised the institutions and procedures of a constitutional limited monarchy in Russia. The government promised to make significant concessions: to guarantee fundamental civil liberties (including freedom of speech, assembly, and conscience; freedom of the press; freedom from arbitrary arrest; and the right to form trade unions); to extend the franchise for elections to the Duma to those excluded under the previous decree made in August; to guarantee that no law would be enacted without the consent of the Duma; and to provide that the Duma should have the right to decide upon the legality of decisions of the czar's administrators. A second body, the State Council, was created later to serve as the upper house of the promised parliament.

The government hoped that publication of the October Manifesto would quell unrest, but in fact it ushered in fresh waves of disorder throughout the country. The enthusiasm of those supporting the manifesto was matched by elements of the population who demonstrated against the government for what they saw as high-sounding but meaningless promises. To many, the document was no more than a clever trick to divide the opposition. Indeed, the October Manifesto did accentuate the divisions which already existed in the ranks of the revolutionary movement, and helped the government to restore much of its autocratic authority by late 1905 and early 1906.

Broadly speaking, there were different responses to the October Manifesto by the Right, the Center, and the Left. On the extreme right, conservative advocates of the czar's absolute power urged Nicholas to make no concessions to the reformers and revolutionaries. Reactionaries in the service of the government and the Russian Orthodox Church organized the Union of the Russian People under the presidency of Dr. Alexander Dubrovin. Elements from this group, to which Czar Nicholas himself belonged, led gangs of toughs known as the Black Hundreds in demonstrations on behalf of the czar against supporters of the manifesto. During the week after its publication, the Black Hundreds launched a wave of violent riots known as "pogroms" against the traditional scapegoats, the Jews, many of whom suffered loss of life or property. Meanwhile, moderate rightists fully in accord with the principles of the October Manifesto created a new political party known as the Octobrists and hailed the concessions as the climax of a successful revolution. They now gave their support to the government. In the Center, another new party was established in the fall. The Constitutional Democrats also favored the manifesto, but led by the historian Paul Miliukov, they wanted to move forward rapidly on such matters as land reform plus more certain guarantees of parliamentary authority and meaningful civil rights.

The leftist parties rejected the manifesto outright as unsatisfactory, if not an outright deception, and they attempted to continue the revolution. In St. Petersburg, the Soviet, or Council, of Workers' Deputies, included members of the Social Revolutionary, Bolshevik, and Menshevik parties. It had been established several days before the manifesto's publication. Lenin, the Bolshevik leader, was not in Russia at the time but sent frequent messages demanding continued militancy and violence against the authorities. After the manifesto's appearance, the leaders of the Soviet, among them Leon Trotsky, made plans for new strikes they hoped would expand into an armed upris-

ing. Although encouraged by continuing peasant revolts and sporadic troop mutinies, the radicals had clearly begun by November to lose their hold over the workers. The program of strikes failed, and by mid-December the government made many arrests. In Moscow, the Soviet of Workers' Deputies attempted an armed uprising in December, but by the end of that month the government was able to muster sufficient loyal troops to put it down. Severe measures, including prison and several executions, were taken against the most militant of the government's opponents.

The Revolution of 1905 was over. The czarist monarchy had survived the crisis. The authority of Nicholas II was shaken, but he now began to restore his traditional autocratic rule at the expense of the promises he had made in the October Manifesto. Witte, reluctantly willing to consider some limits on the monarchy, resigned as prime minister in the spring of 1906. The new constitution, known as the Fundamental Laws, went into effect at the same time.

The Revolution of 1905 was a prologue to the Revolution of 1917. In one sense the Revolution of 1905 was not a revolution at all; the czar remained on his throne, the throne remained autocratic despite promises made in the October Manifesto, and most of the army remained loyal. In 1917, however, the czar fell, partly because massive numbers of troops went over to swell the ranks of the revolutionaries. In 1905, concessions to the contrary notwithstanding, the czarist autocracy prevailed over the demands of the moderates and the radicals; in 1917, czarism gave way to a moderate regime which was in turn overthrown by Bolshevik radicals. The two revolutions are nevertheless similar in some respects. Both began when Russia was severely weakened by military disasters in unsuccessful wars. Both the Russo-Japanese War and World War I underscored longstanding political, social, and economic grievances that could not be redressed within the framework of government then in existence. Both revolutions took place partly because mediocre leadership had cut itself off from reality and the growing discontent of the Russian people.

—Edward P. Keleher, updated by Taylor Stults

ADDITIONAL READING:

Ascher, Abraham. *The Revolution of 1905: Russia in Disarray*. Stanford, Calif.: Stanford University Press, 1988. This survey explores the factionalism among the regime's opponents as well as within the Russian government itself.

Ferro, Marc. *Nicholas II: The Last of the Tsars*. New York: Oxford University Press, 1991. Informative description of Nicholas from 1905 to 1906, with good quotes from his diary and family correspondence.

Harcave, Sidney. *First Blood: The Russian Revolution of 1905*. New York: Macmillan, 1964. This readable account of the tumultuous year provides solid coverage of a complex period.

Mehlinger, H. D., and J. M. Thompson. *Count Witte and the Tsarist Government in the 1905 Revolution*. Bloomington: Indiana University Press, 1972. Witte's role during a critical period in Russian history is examined closely.

Miliukov, Paul. *Political Memoirs, 1905-1917*. Ann Arbor: University of Michigan Press, 1967. Revealing recollections by the founder of the Constitutional Democratic Party who was at the center of these events.

Verner, A. M. *The Crisis of Russian Autocracy: Nicholas II and the 1905 Revolution*. Princeton, N.J.: Princeton University Press, 1990. Traces the response of the government in the face of growing opposition to autocracy.

Witte, Sergei. *The Memoirs of Count Witte*. Translated and edited by Abraham Yarmolinsky. New York: Howard Fertig, 1967. This is a reprint edition of self-serving but informative memoirs by one of the central decision-making leaders of the Russian government.

SEE ALSO: 1903-1906, Pogroms in Imperial Russia; 1904-1905, Russo-Japanese War; 1906, First Meeting of the Duma; 1911, Assassination of Peter Stolypin; 1917, October Revolution.

1906
FIRST MEETING OF THE DUMA

The first meeting of the Duma increases the political clout of radical liberals who lobby for full parliamentary government and unsuccessfully pressure Czar Nicholas II to abandon attempts to preserve his personal autocratic rule.

DATE: May 10-July 21, 1906

LOCALE: St. Petersburg, Russia

CATEGORIES: Government and politics; Organizations and institutions

KEY FIGURES:

Ivan Logginovich Goremykin (1839-1917), premier of Russia, May-July, 1906

Alexander Ivanovich Guchkov (1862-1936), leader of the Octobrists

Paul Miliukov (1859-1943), leader of the Constitutional Democrats, or Cadets

Nicholas II (1868-1918), czar of Russia, 1894-1917

Peter Arkadyevich Stolypin (1862-1911), premier of Russia, July, 1906-1911

Count Sergei Yulievich Witte (1849-1915), first constitutional premier of Russia, November, 1905-May, 1906

SUMMARY OF EVENT. The first duma, or Russian parliament, met in May of 1906 to consolidate the constitutional government that had ostensibly been created by Czar Nicholas II by means of the October Manifesto of 1905. The czar granted the manifesto in the hope that further violence, such as that which had occurred in the Revolution of 1905, would be avoided. Events, however, disappointed him. Less than two months after promulgating the October Manifesto, the czar was forced to suppress uprisings in St. Petersburg, Moscow, and elsewhere in Russia. The relative ease with which Nicholas handled the rebellions indicated that he still held supreme power in Russia and made him cautious about granting further concessions to the constitutionalists. Thus, as 1906 dawned, two ideologies competed for political supremacy in Russia. The ideologies pitted a revised constitutional monarchy against the continuation and invigoration of an absolute monarchy.

While enthusiastic but inexperienced and uncompromising politicians prepared for the elections to the first Duma, the czar and his supporters were moving to undermine and circumvent the power of the soon-to-be elected parliament. Drawn up by the czar's appointee, Count Sergei Witte, on the basis of guidelines announced in an imperial decree in August of 1905, the election laws provided for indirect elections of representatives, a large proportion of whom were assigned to the rural elements of the population. The government believed that these landowners and peasants would adhere to more conservative views than would townspeople and industrial workers. In another attempt to ensure that conservative ideas were upheld, the czar elevated the State Council to an upper legislative chamber with powers equal to those of the Duma. Half the members of the State Council were appointed directly by the czar, and the other half were elected by traditionally conservative groups such as the clergy, provincial *zemstvos* or assemblies, the nobility, and managers of businesses, the universities, and the Academy of Sciences.

Finally, in the week before the first meeting of the Duma, the government issued the "Fundamental Laws," which specified the powers—or, more accurately, the lack of powers—of the legislative body. Although Russia would now have an elected legislature, Nicholas II insisted on keeping the title of autocrat. The Fundamental Laws consequently proclaimed: "The All-Russian Emperor possesses Supreme and Autocratic power. To obey His authority not only from fear but also from conscience is ordered by God Himself." These laws stipulated that no bills could become law until they were passed by both houses and were signed by the czar. There was provision for the Duma to override the czar's veto of legislation. The czar's ministers were responsible to him alone and not to the Duma. Control of the budget was not to rest with the Duma alone; if the two houses approved different budget figures, the czar could accept either. If no budget passed the legislature, the government could continue to use the one adopted the previous year. The czar retained absolute control over foreign policy, appointments, censorship, the armed forces, the police, and the summoning and dismissal of the Duma. When the Duma was not in session,

were making preparations for elections to the first Duma, planned for March of 1906. The two leading political parties, both of which could be described as moderate, were the Constitutional Democratic Party, or Cadets, and the Union of October 17, or Octobrists. Founded late in 1905, these two parties competed vigorously with each other in the election campaigns. The Cadets, led by the distinguished Russian historian Paul Miliukov, championed the establishment of a parliamentary government under a constitutional monarchy, full participation of the Duma in framing a new constitution, and the expropriation of large estates, whose owners were to be compensated, in order to make more land available to the peasants. The

The first meeting of the Duma, or Russian parliament, represented a reluctant and ultimately unsuccessful step toward establishing a constitutional monarchy in Russia. (Library of Congress)

the czar could rule by decree, theoretically subject to review by the Duma when it reconvened.

Altogether, Witte's election laws, the expansion of the State Council into a conservatively-oriented upper house, and the Fundamental Laws had the collective result of seriously compromising the October Manifesto and the constitutional government which it had promised to establish. The czar's attitude did not bode well for the success of even limited representative government in Russia.

Meanwhile, the various political parties and factions that had emerged in the wake of the Revolution of 1905

program of the Octobrists, led by Alexander Ivanovich Guchkov, was generally more conservative and was critical of the land expropriation scheme of the Cadets. The Octobrists were willing to work within the constitutional framework established by the Fundamental Laws and Witte's election laws. With some exceptions, the radial Socialist Revolutionaries and the Social Democrats boycotted the elections. When the votes were counted, the Cadets had won 180 of the 520 seats, while the Octobrists secured only twelve mandates. In all, some forty political groups comprised the first Duma.

With a speech from the throne, Nicholas II formally convened the first meeting of the Duma on May 10, 1906, in the Winter Palace in St. Petersburg. From the outset, it was clear that the government had no intention of permitting the Duma to exercise any real authority. The government was especially disturbed by the fact that the conservative elements failed to elect a single deputy to the Duma, which the czar naïvely believed would be largely conservative in tone. Hence he was surprised when the Duma, shortly after its convocation, presented an "address to the throne" in which it demanded universal suffrage, direct elections, abolition of the upper chamber, parliamentary government, and extensive land reform based on the expropriation of large estates.

Witte resigned as premier and was succeeded by Ivan Logginovich Goremykin. On May 26, Goremykin delivered an address to the Duma in which he categorically rejected all these demands. Undaunted, the Duma persisted in its demands for extensive reforms during the two months it was allowed to remain in session. During this period, a vacillating Nicholas considered a proposal to bring Cadets into the government as a means of quelling opposition in the Duma. Yet the reluctance of Miliukov to accept such a compromise, combined with the reservations of the minister of the Interior, Peter Arkadyevich Stolypin, led Nicholas to dissolve the Duma on July 21. Stolypin, appointed on the same day to succeed Goremykin, pursued a reactionary course in the wake of the Duma's fall.

Some two hundred deputies, however, refused to accept the dissolution of the Duma. Crossing the border into the grand duchy of Finland, they gathered in the town of Viborg and there signed the so-called Viborg Manifesto, drawn up by Paul Miliukov. In this appeal, the deputies rejected the government's dissolution of the Duma as illegal. They further insisted, without any legal foundation for their claims, that the government could not collect taxes or draft conscripts for military service without the consent of the Duma. What it truly significant about this appeal is that it earned its supporters a three-month's term in prison. Such imprisonment marked them as criminals and made them ineligible to stand for reelection to any further Dumas, the second of which was to meet early in 1907. Deprived of some of its most competent political leaders, the cause of constitutionalism declined considerably in the years until the outbreak of the great Revolution of 1917.

When the second Duma turned out to be even more radical than the first, Stolypin quickly dissolved it and, in June of 1907, carried out a virtual coup d'etat against the Fundamental Laws. He had the czar use his emergency power to enact legislation when the Duma was not in session to issue a decree that redesigned the election system. Stolypin's alteration of the election laws in this fashion was a violation of the Fundamental Laws. By increasing the representation of the nobility, Stolypin succeeded in producing a conservative majority in subsequent Duma elections. Yet the unconstitutional method he used to effect this change further undermined the viability of constitutional government in czarist Russia.

—*Edward P. Keleher, updated by Richard D. King*

ADDITIONAL READING:

Ascher, Abraham. *The Revolution of 1905.* 2 vols. Stanford, Calif.: Stanford University Press, 1988-1992. A history of the upheavals of 1905, which challenged the autocratic rule of Nicholas II, and the restoration of order in 1906 and 1907.

Emmons, Terence. *The Formation of Political Parties and the First National Elections in Russia.* Cambridge, Mass.: Harvard University Press, 1983. A scholarly monograph that analyzes the workings of the liberal political parties and the election to the first Duma in 1906.

Healy, Ann Erickson. *The Russian Autocracy in Crisis, 1905-1907.* Hamden, Conn.: Archon Books, 1976. This study of the 1905 revolution contains a detailed account of the meetings of the first Duma.

Mehlinger, Howard D., and John M. Thompson. *Count Witte and the Tsarist Government in the 1905 Revolution.* Bloomington: Indiana University Press, 1972. Focuses on the months between the October Manifesto and Witte's resignation in April of 1906. Contains an informative discussion regarding the writing of the Fundamental Laws.

Rawson, Don C. *Russian Rightists and the Revolution of 1905.* New York: Cambridge University Press, 1995. Rawson's work studies right-wing groups that opposed liberal constitutionalism and radical social reform.

Riha, Thomas. *A Russian European: Paul Milliukov in Russian Politics.* Notre Dame, Ind.: University of Notre Dame Press, 1969. A political biography of the most prominent leader of the Constitutional Democratic Party, this work focuses on the period between 1905 and 1917.

Rogger, Hans. *Russia in the Age of Modernisation and Revolution, 1881-1917.* London: Longman, 1983. A history of Russia during the reigns of the last two czars, Alexander III and Nicholas II.

SEE ALSO: 1903-1906, Pogroms in Imperial Russia; 1904-1905, Russo-Japanese War; 1905, The October Manifesto; 1911, Assassination of Peter Stolypin; 1917, October Revolution.

1906
LAUNCHING OF THE DREADNOUGHT

The launching of the Dreadnought *ushers in a new era in naval technology and improves Britain's edge in the contest for naval superiority among the European powers.*

DATE: October 6, 1906

LOCALE: Portsmouth, England

CATEGORIES: Science and technology; Transportation; Wars, uprisings, and civil unrest

KEY FIGURES:

Vittorio Cuniberti (1854-1913), Italian naval designer

John A. Fisher (1841-1920), admiral in the Royal Navy

Alfred Thayer Mahan (1840-1914), U.S. naval theorist

William II (1859-1941), German emperor

SUMMARY OF EVENT. By the twentieth century, the battleship was firmly established as the dominant weapon of the world's navies. The battleship had evolved from the clumsy U.S. Civil War ironclads of the 1860's into a relatively large and heavily armed vessel. The development of naval technology had been generally consistent in those nations building warships, so battleships shared many characteristics. A typical battleship was armed with four main battery guns (generally of twelve-inch caliber) backed by a multitude of secondary guns in the six-to-eight-inch caliber range, protected by armor belts nine to twelve inches thick, and propelled by piston engines. Naval technology was about to take a huge leap forward, however, as circumstances around the world influenced naval architecture.

By 1900, three elements combined to create an atmosphere in which naval innovation could thrive. The most important of these was the growing international tensions between Germany and its European neighbors. Having unified only in 1870, Germany was a late participant in the imperialism of the late nineteenth century. Germany could only watch as France and Great Britain carved up Africa and Asia between them. Having emerged as a European industrial power, Germany believed it was being denied a leading role in world affairs because it lacked an overseas empire. Without foreign possessions, the German kaiser, William II, opted in 1897 to use naval power as a means to wield influence, with plans to double the size of the imperial navy in seven years. England, whose economy relied on sea communications, could not allow a threat to its century-old naval domination and prepared to answer Germany's challenge to a naval arms race.

The second element was navalism, a philosophy that equated naval power with national status. The prophet of navalism was a U.S. officer, Alfred T. Mahan, whose book

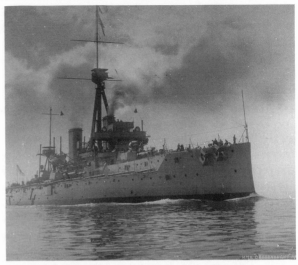

The HMS Dreadnought *represented a turning point in naval architecture, giving Britain an edge in the worldwide naval arms race.* (Library of Congress)

The Influence of Sea Power upon History (1890) provided naval officers and politicians around the world with justification to build large fleets. Mahan claimed that the most successful societies have been naval powers, and thus had the ability to control sea communications and commerce. To ensure control, navies needed battleships and colonies around the world as supply bases. Because Mahan justified the acquisition of empires and large navies, his theories were seized upon in Europe, the United States, and Japan to ensure large naval budgets.

Naval technology was the final element, as several innovations were perfected at the turn of the century, primarily fire control and propulsion. The largest problem facing naval gunnery in 1900 was range finding. Gunners had difficulty hitting targets that were constantly moving on a featureless ocean, obscured by smoke. Anticipated battle ranges were approximately four thousand yards, the effective range of a telescopic sight. Thus, battleships carried many secondary guns, as battles would take place well within their limited range, much less the longer range of the four main battery guns. New inventions, such as optical range finders and mechanical plotting boards (essentially mechanical computers), allowed accurate fire to beyond ten thousand yards, the range of the main batteries, by 1905. Propulsion also benefited from new innovation. Turbine engines, which had fewer moving parts and were thus more reliable than piston machinery, were first experimented with in 1897, and smaller warships began to be fitted with turbines by 1905.

With these three elements together, an atmosphere existed in which a technological leap was not only possible but probable. Only missing was an event that would shape how the next battleships would appear. That event took place on May 27, 1905, in the Strait of Tsushima, between Korea and Japan. Russian and Japanese competition for influence in Manchuria and Korea had led to war in February, 1904, and following the destruction of Russia's Asiatic Fleet, its Baltic Fleet was ordered to the Pacific. In May, 1905, the outmaneuvered Russian fleet was decisively defeated by the faster Japanese navy. Naval observers hurried to determine the lessons of the Battle of Tsushima and emerged with two conclusions: Accurate firepower at long range was absolutely vital, and the faster fleet had many tactical advantages. Coupled with international tension, navalism, and emerging technologies, the lessons of Tsushima formed the theoretical basis of the dreadnought-type battleship.

The first person to attempt to put theory into practice was Vittorio Cuniberti, a naval architect in the Italian navy. In 1903, Cuniberti published plans for a swift battleship armed with no less than twelve twelve-inch guns and no secondary armament. Influenced by the Battle of Tsushima, Cuniberti designed the ship on two premises. First, the large number of heavy guns, aimed by the new range finding devices, could destroy any current battleship before its secondary batteries could come into range. Second, Cuniberti's swift battleship could decide when and under what conditions battle would occur. The Italians, with their limited naval budget, rejected Cuniberti's design, but the project caught the attention of the driving force behind Great Britain's Royal Navy, Admiral Sir John Fisher.

Fisher was a man receptive to new ideas. Having risen through the ranks from cabin boy to commander of the Royal Navy, Fisher was not constrained by traditional methods of doing things. Cuniberti's design intrigued Fisher, for it seemed to fulfill two objectives: The new battleship would ensure Great Britain's technological dominance over the encroaching Germans, while increasing the Royal Navy's firepower. To refine Cuniberti's design, Fisher created a Committee on Designs in December, 1904, to produce a final blueprint for a ship to be named *Untakeable*. Besides Fisher, the committee consisted of naval designers, civilian scientists, gunnery officers, and representatives from naval intelligence to report on the latest German naval efforts.

Untakeable's design emerged from committee in May, 1905, and it reflected not only Cuniberti's theories but also particular British requirements. The ship had ten twelve-inch guns, which were sited to allow heavy fire in any direction. Fisher had insisted on maximum firepower ahead, presuming that in battle the Royal Navy would have to chase fleeing German ships. Hence, *Untakeable* had three twin turrets pivoting on the centerline, with two twin turrets on either side of the bridge, allowing six guns to fire ahead or astern, and eight guns to fire on the broadside. Prominent in *Untakeable*'s blueprint was a fire control tower, where officers could employ the new range-finding systems. The only other armament would be several small, rapid-fire guns to counter enemy torpedo boats; all other armament was dispensed with, causing some controversy among naval traditionalists.

Controversy also arose over the choice of propulsion systems. In order to give *Untakeable* a speed advantage over contemporaneous battleships (which traveled at about sixteen knots), the Committee on Designs wanted a top speed of twenty-one knots. Piston engines could not achieve this speed; the only way to attain the desired speed on a hull weighing eighteen thousand tons was to use the new turbine engines. Using such a new technology on such an important project caused great concern to the committee, but the advantages outnumbered the risks, and *Untakeable* received turbine engines.

As the ship was laid down at the Royal Navy Dockyard in Portsmouth, Fisher declared that the ship would be built in one year. Battleships typically required three years for construction, but Fisher had several reasons for wanting to hurry. First, a rapid construction time would generate public relations for the new ship. Second, completion would forestall opposition to the new design. Last, the sudden arrival of the new ship might deter the Germans.

The keel of the ship was laid on October 2, 1905, and the hull was ready for launching on February 10, 1906. Rather than using the name *Untakeable*, King Edward VII christened the ship *Dreadnought*, the eighth Royal Navy ship to bear the name. (The first had fought the Spanish Armada in 1688, while a later *Dreadnought* had served with Horatio Nelson at Trafalgar.) The ship then received its guns, engines, and other internal systems, leaving Portsmouth for sea trials on October 6, 1906, missing Fisher's deadline by only one day.

Dreadnought has remained a turning point in naval architecture. The ship gave its name to the battleship types that followed; any subsequent battleship armed with a single-caliber battery has been known as a dreadnought, while those battleships that came before 1905 have become pre-dreadnoughts. Dreadnoughts remained the focus of naval doctrine until the emergence of the aircraft carrier in World War II.

—*Steven J. Ramold*

ADDITIONAL READING:

Hodges, Peter. *The Big Gun: Battleship Main Armament, 1860-1945*. Annapolis, Md.: Naval Institute Press,

1981. Discusses battleship armament from the first iron-clads to the last dreadnought, with an emphasis on the adoption of single-caliber armament in 1906.

Massie, Robert K. *Dreadnought: Britain, Germany, and the Coming of the Great War.* New York: Random House, 1991. A voluminous study of the political and military impact of the Anglo-German naval arms race.

Padfield, Peter. *The Great Naval Race: The Anglo-German Naval Rivalry, 1900-1914.* New York: David McKay, 1974. The standard reference on this topic of naval history.

Roberts, John. *The Battleship "Dreadnought": Anatomy of the Ship.* Annapolis, Md.: Naval Institute Press, 1992. A highly technical study of the *Dreadnought*'s design, with many illustrations of internal systems.

Simkins, Peter J. *Battleship: The Development and Decline of the Dreadnought.* London: Imperial War Museum, 1979. A study of the dreadnought era, from its inception to its replacement by the aircraft carrier.

SEE ALSO: 1889, Great Britain Strengthens the Royal Navy; 1899, First Hague Peace Conference; 1904-1905, Russo-Japanese War; 1914, Germany Begins Extensive Submarine Warfare.

1907
SECOND HAGUE PEACE CONFERENCE

The Second Hague Peace Conference brings European nations together as part of a continuing attempt to regulate and contain wars through international agreement.

DATE: June-October, 1907

LOCALE: The Hague, the Netherlands

CATEGORY: Diplomacy and international relations

KEY FIGURES:

Sir Henry Campbell-Bannerman (1836-1908), British prime minister, 1905-1908

Joseph Hodges Choate (1832-1917), chief U.S. delegate to the Second Hague Peace Conference

Sir Edward Grey (1862-1933), British foreign secretary, 1905-1916

Aleksandr Petrovich Izvolski (1856-1919), Russian foreign affairs minister

Nicholas II (1868-1918), czar of Russia, 1894-1917

Theodore Roosevelt (1858-1919), twenty-sixth president of the United States, 1901-1909

Elihu Root (1845-1937), U.S. secretary of state, 1905-1909

William II (1859-1941), emperor of Germany, 1888-1918

SUMMARY OF EVENT. Between the adjournment of the International Peace Conference, or the First Hague Con-ference, on July 29, 1899, and the convening of the Second Hague Peace Conference in June, 1907, threats to peace had not diminished. Events indicated that the Great Powers had no intention of sacrificing sovereignty to achieve peaceful solutions to issues which they considered to be in their own national interests. Great Britain had involved itself in the Boer War, the Great Powers had joined to suppress the Boxer Rebellion in China, and sporadic fighting had occurred in the Philippines.

Significant though such events were, they were peripheral to the chain of events touched off by the decision of Germany in 1900 to begin a massive naval building program. This "Naval Law," if carried to its conclusion, would have effectively challenged British supremacy at sea within the following twenty years. The challenge inevitably led to abandonment of the British policy of "splendid isolation," as evidenced by the Hay-Pauncefote Treaty with the United States in 1901, an alliance with Japan in 1902, and the Entente Cordiale with France in 1904. Moreover, Arthur James Balfour, prime minister of Great Britain from 1902 to 1905, had taken steps to modernize British naval and military forces. All these acts had the effect of upsetting the precarious balance of power that existed in Europe and in the race for spheres of influence overseas.

In 1905, the first Moroccan crisis precipitated by William II, emperor of Germany, succeeded in convincing observers that an armed Germany was the ultimate threat to peace and would have to be dealt with eventually from a position of military strength. Also in 1905, Japan had stunned the world with unbelievably easy victories over Russia at Port Arthur and Mukden, together with the humiliation of the Russian Baltic Fleet in the Tsushima Strait. Against this gloomy background, the advocates of peace, disarmament, and arbitration, notably the Interparliamentary Union, began to agitate for a second International Peace Conference at The Hague to deal with the many unresolved questions of 1899. Theodore Roosevelt was approached as the obvious sponsor. Wishing to regain prestige lost in the Russo-Japanese War, however, Czar Nicholas II of Russia issued the invitations.

Once again, a group of sovereign states found themselves in the awkward position of attending a conference the aims of which were not consonant with their views of political or military realities. Possible exceptions were Great Britain, where the Liberal government of Sir Henry Campbell-Bannerman was in power, and the United States. Great Britain would have been happy to freeze the status quo, thus maintaining its naval superiority. Secretary of State Elihu Root believed that questions such as disarmament ought to be discussed even if nothing were decided, reasoning that some early failures were necessary to eventual success.

Russia and Germany let it be known from the outset that, while arbitration and rules of war were fit subjects for discussion, the limitation of armaments was not. Russia's position on disarmament in 1899 had been reversed by the lessons learned in the Russo-Japanese War. Germany remained consistent, firmly believing in its destiny based on military power.

The Second Hague Peace Conference opened on June 15, 1907. Forty-four nations were represented, in contrast to twenty-six in 1899. Four commissions were appointed to make recommendations concerning arbitration in international disputes, rules of land warfare, rules of war at sea, and maritime law. They proposed numerous conventions, many of which were adopted but promptly forgotten under the stress of modern warfare after 1914. In the case of war at sea, the basic British strategy of blockade was called into question, as was the submarine warfare already contemplated by Germany. Great Britain was determined to fight off attempts to curtail blockade and the free capture of ships, while the Germans were equally determined to use contact mines and submarines to break blockades.

The crucial issue of disarmament or an armament moratorium, though brought to the floor by Great Britain, was disposed of with a "serious study" type of resolution adopted without a vote in less than half an hour.

The problem of arbitration was centered on arguments about voluntary as opposed to compulsory arbitration. The latter principle was utterly rejected by the Germans. Although a Convention of Pacific Settlement of International Disputes was adopted, the compulsory principle was not contained in it. Once again, national sovereignty and self-interest defeated internationalism and pacifism. Finally, over the objections of the major European powers, the Americans successfully pushed through a resolution for the continuance of The Hague principle. A third conference was to be held in approximately eight years, the same lapse which separated the first two conferences. By 1915, however, World War I had made merely academic the problems which the conferences had been designed to solve.

—*Jack H. Greising, updated by John Quinn Imholte*

ADDITIONAL READING:

Choate, Joseph H. *The Two Hague Conferences.* Princeton, N.J.: Princeton University Press, 1913. Lectures by the chief delegate from the United States to the Second Hague Peace Conference.

Cooper, Sandi E. *Patriotic Pacifism: Waging War on*

War in Europe, 1815-1914. New York: Oxford University Press, 1991. Cooper's work contains scattered references to both Hague conferences within a European context.

Davis, Calvin D. *The United States and the Second Hague Peace Conference: American Diplomacy and International Organization, 1899-1914.* Durham, N.C.: Duke University Press, 1976. Davis includes various analyses of peacemaking through arbitration and internationalism. He also provides a thorough examination of why the movement for international organization failed.

Hull, William I. *The Two Hague Conferences and Their Contributions to International Law.* Boston: Ginn, 1908. Reprint. New York: Garland, 1972. This older study provides a positive assessment of the peace movement's internationalist direction.

Tate, Merze. "The Second Hague Conference." In *The United States and Armaments.* Cambridge, Mass.: Harvard University Press, 1948. A brief and straightforward account of the background and results of the conference.

Tuchman, Barbara. "The Steady Drummer: The Hague, 1899 and 1907." In *The Proud Tower: A Portrait of the World Before the War, 1890-1914.* New York: Macmillan, 1966. In this popular account of years leading up to World War I, Tuchman dedicates a lengthy chapter to the personalities and highlights of both Hague conferences.

SEE ALSO: 1882, The Triple Alliance; 1893, Franco-Russian Alliance; 1899, First Hague Peace Conference; 1899-1902, Boer War; 1904-1905, Russo-Japanese War; 1904, The Entente Cordiale; 1907, The Triple Entente; 1914, Outbreak of World War I; 1915, International Congress of Women.

1907
THE TRIPLE ENTENTE

The Triple Entente encourages Great Britain and Russia to set aside their differences and come together as allies with France to counter Germany and the Triple Alliance.

DATE: August 31, 1907
LOCALE: London, England, and St. Petersburg, Russia
CATEGORY: Diplomacy and international relations
KEY FIGURES:
Edward VII (1841-1910), king of Great Britain,
    1901-1910
Aleksandr Petrovich Izvolski (1856-1919), Russian
    foreign affairs minister, 1906-1910
Sir Edward Grey (1862-1933), British foreign secretary,
    1905-1916
Sir Charles Hardinge (1858-1944), permanent
    undersecretary at the British foreign office,
    1906-1910

Sir Arthur Nicolson, British ambassador to Russia, 1906-1910

SUMMARY OF EVENT. The mutual desire of Great Britain and Russia to settle their imperialistic rivalry in southern Asia can be traced to developments in international affairs of interest to both parties during 1904 and 1905: the rapprochement between Great Britain and France, the latter an ally of Russia; the deterioration of Anglo-German relations, underscored by the first Moroccan crisis and the growth of the German navy; and Germany's efforts to establish an alliance with Russia.

Great Britain's pursuit of an entente with Russia dates from April, 1904, when conversations took place between King Edward VII and Aleksandr Petrovich Izvolski, then Russia's envoy to Denmark. The British government had been an ally of Japan since 1902 and was concluding the Entente Cordiale with France. Although Russia had been at war with Japan since February, 1904, their agreement called for mutual aid only if one of the signatories was at war with two other powers. Consequently, Great Britain did not enter the conflict and was free to pursue its aim of rapprochement with Russia.

Among leading British officials who sought accord with Russia were Sir Edward Grey, the British foreign secretary since 1905, and Sir Charles Hardinge, the permanent undersecretary at the Foreign Office who had been ambassador to Russia from 1904 to 1906. Both these statesmen earnestly desired to settle Great Britain's outstanding differences with Russia in Persia and over India. They feared that continuing disagreement over these problems might cause Russia to accept the serious bids being made by Germany for a general alliance, especially since the signing of the Björkö Treaty in July, 1905, by William II, Emperor of Germany, and Nicholas II, czar of Russia, on each other's yachts had provided for mutual aid in case of attack by another European power. Germany had been prevented from extending the terms of the pact only by opposition from the Russian Foreign Office and the refusal of the French government to go along with such an agreement after the German emperor had precipitated the first Moroccan crisis. Grey and Hardinge were also aware of the expansion of the German navy, and in 1907 their attempts to reach agreement with Russia were aided by Sir Arthur Nicolson, who had succeeded Hardinge as British ambassador to the Russian court at St. Petersburg. Nicolson worked tirelessly to draft an agreement acceptable to the Russian government, which had been represented since May, 1906, by Izvolski as minister of foreign affairs.

Izvolski had for some years been a leading proponent in Russia of rapprochement with Great Britain. He be-

Sir Edward Grey, the British foreign secretary, was a key figure in negotiating the 1907 Anglo-Russian agreement that completed the network of treaties that became known as the Triple Entente. (Library of Congress)

lieved that an Anglo-Russian entente would accomplish at least four things for Russia, some of which complemented the thinking in London. First, in Izvolski's view, Russia could effect a genuine reconciliation with Japan, which in August, 1905, had renewed its alliance with Great Britain, thereby underscoring the Russian defeat in the Far East. Second, Izvolski believed that an Anglo-Russian entente would strengthen the Russian alliance with France and complement the Entente Cordiale of 1904. Third, it was as much in Russia's interest as Great Britain's to bring about settlement of major differences over Persia, India, and other sensitive areas in Asia. Finally, elimination of these sources of friction with Great Britain would in turn eliminate the need for an alliance with Germany, which would in any case be incompatible with the Franco-Russian alliance. Altogether, once its eastern and southern flanks were protected, Russia could once again assert itself in the Near East where, with the assistance of Great Britain and France, it could thwart Austrian ambitions in the Balkans, oppose those of Germany in Turkey, and eventually open the Dardanelles to Russian warships. Indeed, the question of these straits was uppermost in the mind of Izvolski when he agreed to negotiate an entente with Great Britain.

Negotiations began, in June, 1906, but dragged on until August, 1907, slowed by the air of mutual suspicion which prevailed between the two countries. Nicholas II, an autocratic czar, could not accept British Liberalism or the British Liberal press when it raised an outcry against Russian pogroms and the suspension of the Duma. The talks moved forward slowly. Izvolski pressed for the Dardanelles to be opened to Russian warships; from Grey he won the dubious and negative concession that in the future Great Britain would not oppose Russia on this issue. Grey, Hardinge, and Nicolson managed in turn to win more realistic concessions from Izvolski. First, he accepted London's demand for the partition of Persia into British and Russian spheres of influence, despite Russia's earlier insistence for domination over the whole of Persia in order to obtain access to the Persian Gulf. Second, the British government insisted that Russia should simultaneously negotiate a reconciliation with Japan, and on July 30, 1907, Russia signed a treaty with Japan under which both powers agreed to respect the status quo and the rights of each other in the Far East. A month later, Izvolski and Nicolson signed the convention which established the Anglo-Russian Entente.

The entente dealt exclusively with conflicting Anglo-Russian interests in the Middle East, specifically Afghanistan, Tibet, and Persia. By securing the Russian promise that each should respect the territorial integrity of Tibet (under Chinese sovereignty) and Afghanistan, Great Britain gained the assurance that these two viable buffer states would safeguard India from any future Russian advance. Even more important was the agreement of both parties to recognize the "independence" and "integrity" of Persia while proceeding to divide it into three spheres of influence. Russia received the northern zone, which was the largest but did not include the Persian Gulf, declared to be a neutral zone. The British received a desert wasteland in the south that contained roads leading to India. Nothing in the agreement bound the parties to mutual military obligations of the type that existed between France and Russia in the event of attack by an aggressor. Nevertheless, the Anglo-Russian agreement completed a network of treaties which bound together Great Britain, France, and Russia in what the press of these countries began to speak of as the "Triple Entente."

An entente in the sense of close cooperation and understanding on a wide range of issues it was certainly not. Great Britain's commitments to France and Russia were limited, and the agreement was confined geographically to Asia. Of somewhat questionable value to Great Britain, it did eliminate some of the causes of friction between the two countries. What happened between 1908 and 1914, against the background of recurring crises in Morocco and the Balkans, was gradual solidification of cooperation between Great Britain, France, and Russia in opposition to Germany and Austria-Hungary. The members of the Triple Entente began to coordinate their military and naval preparedness in anticipation of a clash with the Central Powers, preparations that served them well when they entered World War I as allies in 1914.

—Edward P. Keleher, updated by John Quinn Imholte

ADDITIONAL READING:

Gilbert, Felix. *The End of the European Era, 1890 to the Present.* New York: W. W. Norton, 1979. Both a broad and detailed account of the destruction of European centrality and its impact upon the twentieth century.

Jell, James. *The Origins of the First World War.* London: Longman, 1984. A general examination of the causes of World War I, emphasizing the international system, strategic planning and the arms race, domestic politics, international economics, and imperial rivalries.

Kennedy, Paul M. "The Coming of a Bipolar World and the Crisis of the 'Middle Powers': Part One, 1885-1918." In *The Rise and Fall of the Great Powers.* New York: Random House, 1987. Places the Triple Entente in its historical context. Concentrates upon the interaction of economics and strategy on the Great Powers.

Lee, Dwight E. *Europe's Crucial Years: The Diplomatic Background of World War I, 1902-1914.* Hanover, N.H.: Clark University Press, 1974. Suggests that each state acted in desperation to defend its own presumed interests.

Lieven, D. C. B. *Russia and the Origins of the First World War.* New York: St. Martin's Press, 1983. Argues that Russian foreign policy was the result of the czarist government's structure and the pressure of internal political factions. Result was the failure of its deterrence policy.

Massie, Robert K. "The Anglo-Russian Entente and the Bosnian Crisis." In *Dreadnought: Britain, Germany, and the Coming of the Great War.* New York: Random House, 1991. Describes the shift in British diplomacy from splendid isolation to the Triple Entente. Emphasizes prominent personalities and the importance of growing German naval power.

Schmitt, Bernadotte E. *Triple Alliance and Triple Entente.* New York: Howard Fertig, 1971. A detailed description of the background, substance, and results of the Triple Entente. An informative basic summary.

Steiner, Zara. *Britain and the Origins of the First World War*. New York: St. Martin's Press, 1977. A thorough analysis and investigation of the influence of external and diplomatic factors on one hand and domestic politics on the other in largely determining British foreign policy leading to war.

SEE ALSO: 1882, The Triple Alliance; 1893, Franco-Russian Alliance; 1898-1899, The Fashoda Incident; 1904-1905, Russo-Japanese War; 1904, The Entente Cordiale; 1914, Outbreak of World War I.

1908

AUSTRIA ANNEXES BOSNIA AND HERZEGOVINA

Austria annexes Bosnia and Herzegovina, creating an international crisis that lays the groundwork for the start of World War I.

DATE: October 7, 1908
LOCALE: The Balkans
CATEGORIES: Expansion and land acquisition; Government and politics
KEY FIGURES:

Count Alois Lexa von Aehrenthal (1854-1912), foreign minister of Austria-Hungary
Aleksandr Petrovich Izvolski (1856-1919), Russian foreign affairs minister
Alexander Obrenovic (1876-1903), ruler of Serbia, 1889-1903
Peter I (1844-1921), ruler of Serbia, 1903-1921

SUMMARY OF EVENT. Since the sixteenth century, the Balkan peninsula had been ruled by the Ottoman Empire. The Ottoman Turks had pushed their holdings westward into Europe until 1683, when their advance was stopped at the gates of Vienna by an army composed largely of Poles under their king, Jan Sobieski. Since that time, the Turkish hold had been gradually reduced, chiefly by the Habsburg rulers, who had successfully reclaimed Hungary in the eighteenth century.

In the nineteenth century, the Turkish hold on the Slavic inhabitants of the Balkans continued to weaken. Serbia had achieved de facto independence in 1829, and de jure independence in 1878. Increasingly, Russia had become a sponsor of the Slavic ethnic groups in the Balkans, particularly Serbia. Under the stimulus of the Pan-Slavic movement in Russia, the Serbs in Serbia began to dream of a great Slavic country in the Balkans with Serbia as its center. In 1876 Russia had gone to war with Turkey, largely to assist the Slavic ethnic groups in the Balkans to free themselves from Turkish control.

The Russian victories in the war with Turkey, and the revelation of Russian plans for the reorganization of the Balkan peninsula under her aegis, alarmed the other powers. Under the leadership of Bismarck, the chancellor of the German empire, an international congress met in Berlin in 1878 to revise the terms of the settlement the victorious Russians had planned to impose on the defeated Turks. While that settlement recognized the end of Turkish rule over large parts of the Balkans, it was concerned in preventing the extension of Russian control, particularly over the western Balkans. To prevent the expansion of Serbia, the Congress assigned the two principalities of Bosnia and Herzegovina to Austria to administer, although Turkish sovereignty was theoretically preserved.

The occupation of Bosnia and Herzegovina by the Austrians was generally beneficial to the inhabitants. The Austrians developed the Bosnia infrastructure and they provided administrators who replaced the rampant corruption of the older Turkish administration with relative honesty. The incorporation of the occupied principalities into the Austro-Hungarian economy provided increased economic opportunities for the Slavic inhabitants of the principalities.

Nevertheless, Austria's occupation of the principalities was resented by the Slavic inhabitants of the Balkans, particularly by neighboring Serbia. Serbia's army was no match for the Austro-Hungarian forces, and as long as the empire retained effective control of the two principalities the radical Serbians would have difficulty realizing their dream of a greater Serbia. Tensions were muted during the early years of the occupation, as the rulers of Serbia followed a policy of cooperating with the Austrians in return for economic advantages, notably an export market in Austria for Serbia's agricultural produce.

In 1903, however, the pro-Austrian king of Serbia, Alexander Obrenović, was assassinated by radical elements and his place taken by Peter I, of the hostile, anti-Austrian Karageorgevic dynasty. Under Peter I, Serbia veered away from the cooperative policy of his predecessor, and actively promoted anti-Austrian propaganda directed at arousing the Slavic sensibilities of the inhabitants of Bosnia and Herzegovina. In this new departure, the Serbians were encouraged by the Pan-Slavic movement in Russia. Austria felt threatened by this propaganda effort, fearing the loss not only of the occupied territories but also of other Slavic lands within the empire, such as Croatia and Slovenia, which the Serbs hoped to incorporate in a greater Serbia or Yugoslavia.

Alois Lexa von Aehrenthal, who had been appointed foreign minister of Austria-Hungary in 1906, believed that annexation of Bosnia and Herzegovina by the Dual Monarchy would frustrate Serbian machinations. In Russia, Aleksandr Petrovich Izvolski, the newly appointed minister of foreign affairs, sought to recoup Russian international standing following Russia's defeat by Japan in 1905 by a dramatic stroke in the European theater. Acting secretly, with the knowledge of Czar Nicholas II but not the ministers of the government, he informed Aehrenthal that Russia would be willing to support the annexation of Bosnia and Herzegovina by Austria-Hungary if in return the Dual Monarchy would sanction the opening of the Dardanelles to Russian warships. The straits had been closed to foreign warships since the straits convention of 1841. Aehrenthal reacted favorably to Izvolski's proposition, and the two statesmen then awaited the right moment to seal their bargain.

That moment came in the summer of 1908 with the outbreak of the Young Turk Revolution seeking to modernize the corrupt and ineffective government of the Ottoman Empire. While the Turks were preoccupied with civil war, the two foreign ministers, Aehrenthal and Izvolski, met in Buchlau in Moravia on September 15 and orally reiterated their earlier agreement to support Austria-Hungary's annexation of Bosnia and Herzegovina and the opening of the Dardanelles to Russian warships. Unfortunately, they drew up no written account of their decisions, nor did they set a date for the annexation. The result was that within three weeks a serious misunderstanding and a grave international crisis arose.

Izvolski left the conference with the impression that nothing would be done immediately (or so he later claimed). He set out to visit the European capitals in order to obtain the consent of the other Great Powers to the change in the status quo affecting the Dardanelles. Meanwhile, Aehrenthal was preparing for the annexation. He informed Bulgaria that the time was ripe for it to proclaim its independence from the Ottoman Empire, which it did on October 5. Two days later Aehrenthal announced to Europe that Austria-Hungary had annexed Bosnia and Herzegovina.

The storm of protest aroused by the annexation brought Austria to the brink of war with the other European nations. Serbia and Montenegro (then still an independent principality but closely allied with Serbia) were outraged over the move, viewing it as a deliberate effort to frustrate their dream of establishing a great South Slav state, a Yugoslavia. The Young Turks resented Austria's violation of Ottoman sovereignty. In Russia, where Pan-Slav sentiment was strong, Austria's annexation of Bosnia and Herzegovina and Izvolski's role in helping to make it possible were vociferously condemned. Peter Arkadyevich Stolypin, the Russian premier, ordered Izvolski to oppose

the annexation. He did so by denying any involvement and by calling on Great Britain and France to aid the Turks; but neither would come to the aid of Turkey. They were opposed in principle to the annexation as a violation of international agreements reached at the Congress of Berlin in 1878, but recognized the fact that Austria had been in control of Bosnia-Herzegovina for some thirty years, so that consequently the status quo in the Western Balkans would not really be changed much by the formal incorporation of these districts into the Dual Monarchy. Sir Edward Grey, the British foreign secretary, did reject Izvolski's plea for the opening of the Dardanelles to Russian warships.

The crisis lasted for almost six months. Serbia, with the reluctant support of Russia, drew near to war with Austria. Izvolski protracted the crisis by his insistence that the dispute be submitted to an international conference. Aehrenthal refused, and Great Britain and France, anxious to avoid war, declined any firm support to Russia. Finally, Germany backed Austria and Izvolski was forced to back down and accept the annexation, and on March 31, 1909, an isolated Serbia did likewise. Austria had previously compensated the Turks with a financial indemnity on February 26, 1909.

Peace was thus restored to the Balkans, but a precarious one. Relations between Austria and Serbia steadily deteriorated until they culminated in the assassination of the Austrian archduke Francis Ferdinand, heir to the Austrian throne, in July of 1914. The uneasy truce which Austria and Russia had maintained in the Balkans from 1878 to 1908 was now shattered beyond repair. In the long run, the Austrian annexation of Bosnia-Herzegovina raised more problems than it solved.

—Edward P. Keleher, updated by Nancy M. Gordon

ADDITIONAL READING:

Bridge, F. R. *From Sadowa to Sarajevo: The Foreign Policy of Austria-Hungary, 1866-1914*. London: Routledge & Kegan, 1972. Covers the Bosnian annexation within the context of Austro-Hungarian foreign policy.

Jelavich, Barbara. *History of the Balkans*. 2 vols. New York: Cambridge University Press, 1983. Jelavich gives a good, if brief, discussion of the administration of Bosnia-Herzegovina by Austria in volume 2.

_____. *Russia's Balkan Entanglements, 1806-1914*. New York: Cambridge University Press, 1991. Contains a detailed account of the negotiations between Aehrenthal and Izvolski.

Schmitt, Bernadotte E. *Annexation of Bosnia, 1908-09*. Reprint. New York: Howard Fertig, 1970. First published in 1937, this work provides an account of the diplomatic maneuvers associated with the annexation based on diplomatic documents published after World War I.

Sugar, Peter F. *The Industrialization of Bosnia-Hercegovina, 1878-1918*. Seattle: University of Washington Press, 1963. Gives the social and economic background to Austrian administration.

SEE ALSO: 1876, Bulgarian Massacres; 1878, Congress of Berlin; 1912-1913, Balkan Wars; 1914, Outbreak of World War I.

1909-1911
PARLIAMENT BILL

The Parliament Bill helps make Britain a democracy by regulating the relations between Lords and Commons by statute, allowing the House of Lords to delay legislation only for a short time.

DATE: April, 1909-August, 1911

LOCALE: Westminster, in the British Parliament

CATEGORIES: Government and politics; Laws, acts, and legal history

KEY FIGURES:

Herbert Henry Asquith (1852-1928), Liberal prime minister

Arthur Balfour (1848-1930), Conservative member of Parliament and leader of the Opposition, 1906-1911

Winston Leonard Spencer Churchill (1874-1965), Liberal member of Parliament and British home secretary, 1910-1911

George V (1865-1936), king of England, 1910-1936

David Lloyd George (1863-1945), Chancellor of the Exchequer, 1908-1915

Henry Charles Keith Petty-Fitzmaurice, marquis of Lansdowne (1845-1927), Conservative leader of the House of Lords

SUMMARY OF EVENT. The Parliament Act of 1911 was a major constitutional statute which limited the power of the House of Lords (the upper house) so that it could never again challenge the supremacy of the House of Commons (the lower house). It eliminated the theoretical equality of the upper and lower houses and allowed the democratic process to guide the nation from the House of Commons almost entirely unimpeded. Up until 1911, both Houses had to pass a bill before it became law. The only exception were money bills, which had to originate in the House of Commons and were not supposed to be rejected by the Lords. After the Parliament Act of 1911, the Lords had to accept all bills passed in three successive sessions of the House of Commons. This meant that the Lords' veto over bills passed in the Commons had been canceled and henceforth the upper house could only delay legislation

for approximately two years. After 1911, Britain's legislature was therefore functionally unicameral, or one-chambered, and much more effective in responding to the will of the electorate.

The drive for democracy in the late nineteenth and early twentieth centuries had made the House of Commons increasingly representative of the will of the majority of the British people at the same time that the House of Lords appeared increasingly anachronistic, that is, really belonging to another era long past.

Most of the Lords inherited their seats as leaders of wealthy landholding families. Some were leaders of families who had gained considerable riches recently and who had distributed some of their fortunes to help the campaigns of leading politicians. Whether they were the heads of newer or ancient noble families, members of the House of Lords tended to be strongly Conservative regardless of the inclination of the majority in the House of Commons. As long as the Conservative Party held a majority in the House of Commons cooperation between both houses could be maintained, but when the Liberal Party took over, either by itself or in alliance with the smaller Labour Party and Irish Nationalist Party, the two houses could easily become deadlocked.

Trouble that had been simmering between the Lords and Commons came to a head after the Liberals came to power with a large elected majority in the House of Commons in 1906. Several bills passed by the House of Commons on such important matters as education and voting qualifications were rejected by the House of Lords. While both the Liberal and Conservative parties were supposed to be fairly represented in the House of Lords, the number of Conservative Lords far outnumbered the number of Liberal Lords by the early twentieth century. That meant that the majority in the House of Lords followed the leadership of Arthur Balfour, the leader of the Conservatives in the House of Commons, even when he was in charge of a minority in opposition. Therefore, when he unsuccessfully opposed a measure in the Commons it was likely to be tossed out by the House of Lords. The situation gave rise to one of the most celebrated quips of the era: The House of Lords as the so-called "Watchdog of the Constitution" had become "Mr. Balfour's Poodle."

Resentment of the Lords focused dramatically after the House of Lords rejected of the so-called "People's Budget" of 1909 and thus violated the constitution as it was then interpreted. Money bills were regarded as the special responsibility of the House of Commons, and the Lords were supposed to accept them. The "People's Budget" passed in the House of Commons by 379 to 149, and was rejected by the Conservative majority in the Lords by an overwhelming 350 to 75. This budget had been brought forward in the Commons to help pay for old-age pensions and battleships called dreadnoughts. The budget imposed taxes on land and high incomes which were loathed by numerous Lords. The Chancellor of the Exchequer was David Lloyd George, a brilliant Welsh politician who bitterly resented the hereditary privilege embodied in the House of Lords. Yet no evidence has come to light that he designed the budget for the express purpose of bringing on a constitutional crisis with the House of Lords.

The justification for the Lords' rejection was included in an amendment fostered by its Conservative leader, Lord Lansdowne, which declared that the Lords could not vote for such a controversial measure until it had been "submitted to the judgement of the country." In other words, the Lords called for another election to be fought over the issue of the budget. Beyond this issue was the greater question of the relationship between Lords and Commons.

The atmosphere of this period was charged by a steady barrage of criticism against the House of Lords in the House of Commons by numerous Liberals, particularly David Lloyd George and Winston Churchill, who was himself the grandson and nephew of a duke.

Ridicule had the effect of goading many members of the upper house into outraged resistance. The election of 1910 left the Liberals only two seats ahead of the Conservatives and made them dependent upon the Irish nationalists and Labour members for a clear majority over the Conservatives. Nevertheless, the House of Lords passed the budget on the grounds that the election had confirmed the will of the electorate to have them do so. What they feared was legislation to alter the constitution and this came along promptly in the form of resolutions for a Parliament Bill to limit the powers of the House of Lords permanently. The resolutions were introduced by Prime Minister Herbert Asquith, and they passed resoundingly because the Irish nationalists knew that Home Rule would go through once the obstacle of the Lords was removed.

In essence, the resolutions which became the Parliament Bill of 1911 only allowed the Lords to delay legislation. Money bills, certified as such by the Speaker of the House, could only be held up one month and other bills could be delayed only for two years. If three successive sessions of the House of Commons passed a bill it would become law automatically, without the approval of the upper house. Another provision of this Parliament Bill was that general elections had to be held at least every five years instead of the seven years which had prevailed for centuries.

The death of Edward VII intervened before the issue could be fought out. Whenever a monarch dies new elections must be held, thus bringing on the second general election of 1910. The results were much the same. Liberals and Conservatives both had 272 seats and the a majority for the Parliament Bill was guaranteed by Irish Nationalist and Labour votes in the Commons.

Curiously, outside of Parliament the constitutional issue generated little interest compared to the inflamed passions of the legislature. The new king, George V, was persuaded to give assurances that he would support the Liberals' plan to swamp the Conservative majority in the Lords by creating new members. This prerogative right was the famous "safety-valve of the constitution," which was once applied in the early eighteenth century and used as a threat during the passage of the famous Reform Bill of 1832.

Faced with the prospect of inundation by newly minted Lords, many in the upper house were willing to accept defeat, but a number of die-hards, called "Ditchers" because they would resist to the last ditch, would not vote for the Parliament Bill when it came up to the Lords. Nevertheless, it passed by a vote of 131 to 114.

Ever since this constitutional milestone became law, the House of Lords has almost always cooperated with the House of Commons. Delay has only been invoked a few times.

—*Henry G. Weisser*

ADDITIONAL READING:

Allyn, Emily. *Lords Versus Commons: A Century of Conflict and Compromise, 1830-1930*. New York: Century, 1931. A University of Pennsylvania Ph.D. thesis that yields rich detail on all aspects of the topic.

Arnstein, Walter L. *Britain Yesterday and Today: 1830 to the Present*. 6th ed. Lexington, Mass.: D.C. Heath, 1992. This popular text treats the subject with great clarity, particularly for American readers.

Handcock, W. D., ed. *English Historical Documents, 1874-1914*. Vol. 12, part 2. Oxford: Oxford University Press, 1977. Key speeches by Asquith and Balfour are given prior to the complete statute itself.

Jenkins, Roy. *Mr. Balfour's Poodle: Peers Versus People*. New York: Chilmark Press, 1954. This very readable, detailed account is entirely devoted to describing the subject rather than arguing a thesis.

Lloyd, T. O. *Empire, Welfare State, Europe: English History 1906-1992*. 4th ed. New York: Oxford University Press, 1993. This text presents a detailed and solid account aimed at British readers.

SEE ALSO: 1838-1848, Chartist Movement; 1846, Repeal of the Corn Laws; 1867, Reform Act of 1867; 1912-1914, Irish Home Rule Bill.

1910

REPUBLIC OF PORTUGAL IS PROCLAIMED

The Republic of Portugal is proclaimed, beginning that nation's first, ill-fated experiment with democratic rule.

DATE: October 5, 1910

LOCALE: Lisbon, Portugal

CATEGORY: Government and politics

KEY FIGURES:

Manuel José de Arriaga (1842-1917), first constitutional president of the Republic of Portugal

Teófilo Braga (1843-1924), provisional president of the Republic of Portugal, 1910-1911

Carlos I (1863-1908), king of Portugal, 1889-1908

Afonso Augusto da Costa, minister of justice in 1910, who became leader of the Portuguese radical Democratic Party

Antonio Machado Dos Santos, leader of the *Carbonaria*, a secret Portuguese society of radical Republicans

Manuel II (1889-1932), king of Portugal, 1908-1910

Sidonio Bernardino Cardosa da Silva Pais, Portuguese Republican who led a coup in 1917 and became president of Portugal

SUMMARY OF EVENT. Since the late nineteenth century, successive governments in Portugal had been beset with difficulties. Basically, the problems were economic. Portugal had been unable to balance its budget since it had lost Brazil, and the legacy of civil war added to the national debt. Attempts to develop Portuguese Africa into an economic asset had contributed to loss of government prestige because British achievements in South Africa had forestalled success.

Within Portuguese society, much social reform was needed. The rise of a small socialist party pointed up the need for such reform. Government tenure was based on corruption, and all elections were decided in advance at Lisbon in imitation of the Spanish "cacique" system. A small republican movement protested against this corruption, but most of its anger was reserved for the clergy. The distinguishing characteristic of the movement, founded by Teófilo Braga, a scholarly, intellectual liberal, was a virulent anticlericalism.

Carlos I, who had become king of Portugal in 1889, could not cope with these problems, and his ministers could not solve them. By 1905, the clamor for reform led many observers to believe that the monarchy would soon be overthrown. In 1908, Carlos and his heir were assassinated. His second son ascended the throne as Manuel II, a young man with neither the training nor the inclination to rule Portugal. The Republicans increased their agitation

and, together with the *Carbonaria*, a secret society of radicals led by Antonio Machado Dos Santos, were mainly responsible for the overthrow of the government. These groups forced Manuel into exile and proclaimed the Republic of Portugal. Braga was named provisional president, and a constituent assembly was called to draft a republican constitution.

From the beginning, the Republic of Portugal was plagued by problems. The Portuguese Republican Party split into factions: a moderate group led by Machado and a radical group that separated and became the Democratic Party, led by Afonso Augusto da Costa, the minister of justice in the new regime. Political fighting between the Democrats and moderate Republicans occupied much time and energy that might have been devoted to constructive reform. With the support of his colleagues, Costa undertook a massive anticlerical campaign even before the *Cortes Gerais* (Portuguese parliament) drafted a constitution. The Church and the state were separated, clerical property was nationalized, the Jesuits were expelled, all monastic orders were dissolved, and complete state control of all education was decreed. After this first onrush of anticlerical activity, the moderate Republican decided to defend the Church and thereby caused tension to increase.

In 1911, a constitution was drafted and promulgated. Primarily a moderate document, it established a republican parliamentary system. Strikes by labor were permitted, and industrial turmoil increased as the proletariat demonstrated against the government's inaction regarding labor and social reform. The monarchists also began to agitate, and royalist plots caused great concern to the Republicans during the early years of the republic.

Manuel José de Arriaga was named president of the Republic after the constitution was promulgated, but he could do little to provide political peace. Costa's Democrats alternated in power with the moderate Republicans, but the main issue between the two parties concerned anticlericalism. Scant attention was given to fiscal problems or social reform. In 1916, the Portuguese government joined the Allies in declaring war on Germany and sent troops to the Western Front.

Historians have speculated as to the motivations for Portugal's sudden entry into the war. The most likely explanations that have been offered include fear of potential German annexation of the Portuguese African colonies of Angola and Mozambique; the traditional Portuguese alliance with Great Britain; and Portugal's desire to differentiate itself from its Iberian rival Spain, which was neutral in the war. Portugal was ill-prepared for war, and tension increased. In December of 1917, the army decided to intervene in politics. Major Sidonio Bernardino Car-

The assassination of King Carlos I in 1908 encouraged radical political factions in Portugal to agitate for the overthrow of the monarchy. (Library of Congress)

dosa da Silva Pais overthrew the government and established a dictatorship. This desperate act still did not solve Portugal's problems.

As admirable as the first Portuguese experiment in democracy was (and it should be remembered that in 1910 Portugal became only the third republic in Europe, following France and Switzerland), it possessed a fundamental flaw. The republican constitution was not accepted by the whole of the people; it represented one tendency in Portuguese society, the liberal, anticlerical current, but tended to exclude others, particularly the more conservative viewpoint that was stronger in Portugal's rural northern provinces. Rather than providing a neutral constitutional vehicle into which parties of both left and right could vie for elective power, the Republic was perceived as merely the constitutional vehicle for a moderately liberal, anticlerical viewpoint. Thus the coups of Sidonio Pais and later strongmen were seen less as violations of a democratic order than as partisan interventions against an already partisan system.

The Republic, though, was not a total failure. First of all, it permanently overthrew the long-established Bragança dynasty, and, even more, a tradition of Portuguese monarchy dating back eight centuries. Unlike in Spain, where the Bourbon dynasty was restored in name and later in fact, Portuguese monarchists never returned to power; Salazar's Fascism was a republican Fascism. Most important, the First Republic served as a crucial precedent for the time, after the overthrow of the military in 1974, when Portugal was finally ready to move to a full, stable multiparty democracy.

—*José M. Sánchez, updated by Nicholas Birns*

ADDITIONAL READING:

Bragança-Cunha, Vicente de. *Revolutionary Portugal: 1910-1936*. London: James Clarke, 1937. Outdated in analytical terms and prejudiced by its monarchist viewpoint, this source is still a useful source of facts and opinions.

Gallagher, Tom. *Portugal: A Twentieth-Century Interpretation*. Manchester, England: Manchester University Press, 1983. A razor-sharp account of twentieth century Portuguese politics; lively and spirited.

Livermore, H. W. *A New History of Portugal*. 2d ed. Cambridge, England: Cambridge University Press, 1976. The standard history of Portugal available in English, Livermore's work is a reliable, if unexciting, account.

Opello, Walter. *Portugal: From Monarchy to Pluralist Democracy*. Boulder, Colo.: Westview Press, 1991. Situates the Portugal's First Republic in the context of the political developments of the twentieth century.

Schwartzman, Kathleen. *The Social Origins of Democratic Collapse*. Lawrence: University Press of Kansas, 1989. This work takes a sociological look at unstable democracies, using republican Portugal as an example.

Wheeler, Douglas. *Republican Portugal: A Political History, 1910-1926*. Madison: University of Wisconsin Press, 1978. The most thorough survey devoted exclusively to the First Republic.

SEE ALSO: 1500-1530's, Portugal Begins to Colonize Brazil; 1505-1515, Portuguese Viceroys Establish Overseas Trade Empire; 1968, Caetano Becomes Premier of Portugal.

1911-1912
ITALY ANNEXES LIBYA
Italy annexes Libya in a belated assertion of colonial power status, but its seizure of the old Ottoman dependencies results in a failed imperialist experiment.

DATE: 1911-1912

LOCALE: Tripolitania, Cyrenaica, and Fezzan, Libya

CATEGORIES: Expansion and land acquisition; Wars, uprisings, and civil unrest

KEY FIGURES:

Count Alois Lexa von Aehrenthal (1854-1912), foreign minister of the Austro-Hungarian Empire

Mustafa Kemal Atatürk (1881-1938), Turkish officer and later founder of republican Turkey who, together with Enver Bey and Ali Fathi Bey, organized the resistance by Arab Sanusi tribesmen against the Italian forces in Libya

General Carlo Caneva (1845-1922), commander in chief of the Italian expeditionary force in Libya

Giovanni Giolitti (1842-1928), prime minister of Italy, 1892-1893, 1911-1914, and 1920-1921

Field Marshal Count Franz Conrad von Hötzendorf (1852-1925), chief of staff of the Austro-Hungarian Army, 1906-1911, 1912-1917

General Alberto Pollio (1852-1914), Italian chief of staff who planned the expedition to Libya

Victor Emmanuel III (1869-1947), king of Italy, 1900-1946, who acquiesced in the expedition to Libya

SUMMARY OF EVENT. Italy's annexation of the Ottoman dependency of Libya, comprising Tripolitania and Cyrenaica in North Africa, in the war of 1911-1912 represented the fulfillment of some thirty years of Italian imperial aspirations in Africa. In keeping with the traditions of those imperialist years, by 1902 Italy had secured the concurrence of Germany and Austria-Hungary, its partners in the Triple Alliance, as well as that of France and Great Britain for an eventual move into the southern Mediterranean. Approval from Russia, the most enthusiastic of all given its incentive to hasten the demise of the Ottoman Empire, was secured by 1909. Italy had put forward its fairly tenuous claims for living space for its impoverished and overcrowded peasants in its southern region and its economic interests in North Africa, which it had started to develop in the early twentieth century. More important, Italy's national ethos needed some balm to erase the memory of its embarrassing defeat in 1896 in its vain attempt to conquer Abyssinia (Ethiopia) in East Africa.

For the expansionist-minded leader of Italy's Liberal Party, Prime Minister Giovanni Giolitti, there were additional reasons for annexing Libya. First, there was always the possibility that France, having absorbed Morocco and Algeria to the west of Tripolitania, might decide to move farther east. At the same time, having suffered diplomatic humiliation in a second major international crisis in Morocco, Germany could also conceivably opt for its own compensation in Libya. Giolitti also considered that it would be easier to take the land from a decadent Ottoman Empire than to press Italian claims to parity with the Austrians in Albania, whose location on the Adriatic Sea Rome viewed as strategically crucial to its "Four Shores" policy. This policy anticipated the "Mare Nostrum" ("our sea") drive of Benito Mussolini in the 1920's and 1930's. Giolitti's other reasons had to do with internal Italian politics, especially winning the votes of the masses whom he was planning to enfranchise. Following an abrupt Italian ultimatum to the Turks on September 28, 1911, and with the concurrence of King Victor Emmanuel III while the Italian parliament was in recess, the government in Rome declared war the following day.

The Libyan War (also known as the Tripolitan War) was an ill-managed affair. Giolitti's transparent excuses that the small number of Italian settlers were being ill-treated or that Italian economic interests were being squeezed by the new government of Young Turks in Constantinople were not sustainable. In short order, Giolitti had Victor Emmanuel III issue a royal decree on November 5, 1911, placing Tripolitania and Cyrenaica "under the full and complete sovereignty of the kingdom of Italy." The Italian Parliament passed the corresponding enacting law on February 25, 1912.

While the Italian forces had little difficulty overwhelming the coastal Ottoman garrisons after their initial bombardment from the sea, there was spirited resistance by the Turks and Arabs in the interior. The Italian commander, General Carlo Caneva, and his chief of staff, General Alberto Pollio, made three serious miscalculations. First, they believed that the outnumbered Turks would quit after putting up a token fight. Second, the Italians had not anticipated that many native Arabs would side with their Turkish overlords, who had dispatched talented officers such as Mustafa Kemal (later known as Kemal Atatürk) to lead the insurrection by Sanusi warriors. Third, the Italians had expected to fight a conventional war. After the initial engagements, however, the conflict degenerated into guerrilla action. General Caneva and General Pollio were forced to increase the size of the Italian force from some twenty thousand to nearly one hundred thousand soldiers. Despite this change, the hostilities seemed to drag on, with neither side establishing conclusive victory. Accordingly, the Italians decided to launch a second front, capturing Rhodes and other Dodecanese islands in the Aegean Sea that were also Ottoman dependencies.

The peace talks that opened between the two belligerents in July, 1912, concluded with the signing of a peace treaty in Ouchy, a suburb of Lausanne, on October 18, 1912. The catalyst, however, was not the Italian feat of

As part of Italy's bid to annex Libya, Italian artillery units battled Turkish and Arab forces near Tripoli during the war of 1911-1912. (Library of Congress)

arms but rather the outbreak of the First Balkan War, in which the Greeks, Serbians, Montenegrans, and Bulgarians decided to settle their own scores with the Ottomans. The Treaty of Ouchy (also known as the Treaty of Lausanne) was an ambiguous document that left Italy in nominal control of Tripolitania and Cyrenaica but recognized some residual rights of the Ottomans, such as the supervision of Muslim religious affairs and the continuing acknowledgment of the Ottoman sultan as the Libyans' spiritual leader.

As for the other great powers, which had generally shown indifference or political guile in tacitly or actively acquiescing to Italy's conquest of Libya, most exhibited similar ambiguity in accepting the fait accompli even though some had gone through the motions of trying to mediate the conflict. Only Russia, which was the most to gain from a final solution of the "Eastern Question" and the further weakening of the Ottoman Empire, gave Italy unqualified endorsement. France had also supported Italy's action as part of its political maneuvering to annex Morocco, but its backing cooled in the wake of an incident in January, 1912, when the Italians boarded two French vessels suspected of aiding the Turkish war effort. Britain expressed concern over the further weakening and possible collapse of the Ottoman Empire and the consequent ascendancy of Russia in the Turkish Straits, which con-

trolled the passage from the Black Sea to the Mediterranean.

The strongest objection to Italy's conquest, however, came from its nominal partners in the Triple Alliance: Germany and Austria-Hungary. Many senior German officials mistrusted Italy as an ally, a policy that had been traditional since the days of Prussian Chancellor Otto von Bismarck. Austria-Hungary was the power most concerned with the consequences of Italy's aggressive stance. Austria's foreign minister, Count Alois Lexa von Aehrenthal, announced that his government would not permit the extension of Italian military operations against the Ottomans into the Balkans, where the Austro-Hungarian Empire was perceived to have vital interests. Because the chief of staff of the Imperial Army, Count Franz Conrad von Hötzendorf, wished to press Austrian opposition even further, Emperor Francis Joseph I was forced to relieve him of his command temporarily. Any relaxation of tensions which the European powers might have expected from the termination of hostilities between Italy and the Ottoman Empire in October, 1912, was entirely dissipated by the outbreak of the First Balkan War later that month.

In the meantime Italy could glory in the feeling that it had finally acquired great power status through its conquest of Libya. This conquest proved to be a Pyrrhic victory, however, for Libya was costly to maintain, impossible to subdue for some two decades, and unattractive to Italian migrants, who preferred opportunities in the Americas over the prospect of living in a desert wasteland people by mostly hostile natives.

The conquest of Libya altered the pattern of domestic Italian politics. The moderate parties that had controlled the centers of power were giving way to even more vocal nationalist groups. These groups pressed for Italy to pursue a more forceful imperialist course, and such demands colored much of Italian policy leading up to its second invasion of Abyssinia in 1935.

—*Edward P. Keleher, updated by Peter B. Heller*

ADDITIONAL READING:

Albertini, Luigi. *The Origins of the War of 1914*. Vol. 1. London: Oxford University Press, 1965. Explains how the Tripolitan War disrupted the unstable European balance of power and the shaky peace.

Askew, William C. *Europe and Italy's Acquisition of Libya, 1911-1912*. Durham, N.C.: Duke University Press, 1941. Stresses not only the diplomatic history leading to the Tripolitan War but also internal Italian politics and public opinion as contributing factors.

Barclay, Glen St. J. *The Rise and Fall of the New Roman Empire: Italy's Bid for World Power, 1890-1943*.

New York: St. Martin's Press, 1973. A diplomatic history that ridicules Italy's stated excuses for invading Libya in 1911.

Giolitti, Giovanni. *Memoirs of My Life*. Translated by Edward Storer. New York: Howard Fertig, 1973. First published in 1923, this memoir contains the recollections of the Italian statesman most instrumental in Italy's decision to conquer Libya.

Harris, Lillian C. *Libya: Qadhafi's Revolution and the Modern State*. Boulder, Colo.: Westview Press, 1986. A well-written account that stresses Italy's difficulties in absorbing its Libyan conquest.

Lowe, Cedric J., and F. Marzari. *Italian Foreign Policy, 1870-1940*. London: Routledge & Kegan Paul, 1975. The authors relate Italian policy regarding Ottoman Libya in 1911 to France's policy in North Africa and Austria's policy in the Balkans.

May, Arthur J. *The Hapsburg Monarchy, 1867-1914*. Cambridge, Mass.: Harvard University Press, 1960. May's work includes the Austrian perspective on the Tripolitan War and the Aehrenthal-von Hötzendorf squabble regarding Vienna's policy during the conflict.

SEE ALSO: 1853-1856, The Crimean War; 1861, Italy Is Proclaimed a Kingdom; 1882, The Triple Alliance; 1912-1913, Balkan Wars; 1935-1936, Italy Conquers Ethiopia.

1911
ASSASSINATION OF PETER STOLYPIN

The assassination of Peter Stolypin ends the possibility of a reconciliation between the czarist government and the elected Duma on the eve of World War I.

DATE: September 14, 1911
LOCALE: Kiev, Russia
CATEGORIES: Government and politics; Terrorism and political assassination
KEY FIGURES:
Alexandra (1872-1918), empress of Russia, 1894-1918
Dmitry Grigorievich Bogrov (died 1911), a police agent and revolutionary who assassinated Stolypin
Count Vladimir Nikolayevich Kokovtsev (1853-1943), Russian aristocrat who was with Stolypin in the theater when he was shot
Nicholas II (1868-1918), czar of Russia, 1894-1917
Grigory Rasputin (c. 1871-1916), monk, courtier, and confidante of Empress Alexandra
Peter Arkadyevich Stolypin (1862-1911), chairman of the Council of Ministers, 1906-1911

SUMMARY OF EVENT. The murder of Russia's premier in September, 1911, has long been a mystery. Peter Stolypin had numerous enemies both from the Right and Left. The assassin was well known to the police, both as a social revolutionary and police informer. *Agents provocateurs* were linked to numerous assassinations of political leaders, including a grand duke of the Romanov family. The mystery lies in the motive for this particular killing: Did the killer commit the act out of revolutionary zeal or did reactionary circles use him to eliminate a moderate voice in the government? How did Czar Nicholas figure in this story?

In the midst of revolution in Russia in 1905, the czar in his October Manifesto promised a nationally elected legislature, or Duma, which first met in April, 1906. In July, Stolypin was appointed chairman of the Council of Ministers. Concluding that absolutism was impossible to restore, his program called for further reforms but repression of revolutionaries; hence the source of his disfavor among reactionaries and radicals alike. Stolypin was called upon to deal with a Duma united in opposition to the government. In 1907, he suggested the electoral law that resulted in the Third Duma, with the conservative party (Octobrists) in a majority. Stolypin then introduced a land reform that freed peasants from the confinement of the village communes and opened up variations in peasant ownership. Although the immediate effects were harsh, the author reasoned that the benefits would take twenty years. Then, when terrorists bombed his own home, killing several people, and he was criticized for too quickly restoring the death penalty, opponents labeled the police hangings as "Stolypin's Neckties." Yet he also infuriated the ultrarightists by proposing an expansion of civil liberties and by dealing with the Duma as a legitimate instrument of state.

Early in 1911, Stolypin sponsored a measure to extend elected local assemblies to the western provinces. His measure was designed to strengthen the Russian peasant participation in government, one that pleased not only some liberal groups but also nationalists since Jewish merchants and Polish landowners would be underrepresented. Conservatives strongly resisted the proposal but Stolypin staked his career on this measure and threatened to resign if the czar did not support it. The Dowager Empress Maria Fedorovna wrote that if Stolypin held his ground, the czar would give in, but that Nicholas' pride would hide his inner agitation. She was correct; the czar invoked the emergency provision of the Fundamental Laws to override the vote of the Council of State, but he felt humiliated by pressure from his premier.

Meanwhile, reactionary elements at court undermined the chief minister, whispering that he was a traitor, willing to use the Duma to steal prerogatives assigned the czar by

God. Stolypin confided to associates that he was losing confidence in himself and even predicted that he would be killed by the ultraright factions. In addition to his house bombing, there were nine other attempts upon his life. Early in 1911, responding to appeals from numerous quarters, Stolypin forced the monk Rasputin to leave the capital. This move earned Stolypin the deep scorn of Empress Alexandra, who was certain that her son's life depended upon Rasputin's ability to cure his hemophilia. The consensus in government circles was that Stolypin soon would be replaced as head of state.

This would not be necessary. In September, Czar Nicholas II journeyed to Kiev to celebrate a new memorial to Alexander II, the czar who had freed the serfs fifty years earlier. He was accompanied by several ministers of state, including Stolypin and Count Vladimir N. Kokovtsev. There were the usual security precautions wherever the czar traveled, but none were extended to the premier, although he did have a bodyguard named Esaulov. At the parade through the streets of Kiev, one of the individuals in the crowd was Rasputin, who was heard saying that Stolypin soon would be dead.

On September 14, the party attended a performance of Rimsky-Korsakoff's opera *The Tale of Tsar Saltan* at the Kiev Municipal Theater. During the second intermission, a well-dressed man walked down the aisle to the first row of orchestra seats below the imperial box. Just a few feet away, Stolypin was standing and speaking to Kokovtsev, who was about to leave. The assassin, Dmitry Bogrov, shot the premier in the chest two times with a Browning revolver. The czar thought that something had dropped on the floor and stepped into the box to see Stolypin, facing him. He saw blood staining the white tunic of Stolypin, who crossed himself before falling into the chair. Bogrov, who was given a ticket to the theater by the police, allegedly to protect Stolypin, was captured in the direction of the only lightly guarded door, then seized by the police to protect him from mobs that were beating him mercilessly.

Stolypin was sent to a local hospital and lay in great pain for four days before he died. Kokovtsev was at his bedside throughout but Stolypin's wife refused to allow the czar to enter his room. Meanwhile, Bogrov, a lawyer and son of a Jewish merchant in Kiev, was kept incommunicado, and his trial and later execution on October 10 were handled with unusual dispatch. Although the Duma called for an investigation of the police in Kiev, the resulting report, highly critical of General P. G. Kurlov for negligence, was dismissed by Czar Nicholas who, rejoicing at the recovery of his son from a grave illness, was not in a mood, he said, to punish anyone. According to Duma member Alexander Kerensky, the prosecutor had told

Stolypin's son-in-law that the deed was carried out at Kurlov's instigation.

The suspension of the inquiry and failure to interrogate the prisoner left the public to speculate on the nature of the crime, its motive, and its backers. Was Bogrov acting on his own, using his police connections to commit a revolutionary crime? Richard Pipes argued that his deed was a desperate attempt to save his own life from terrorist comrades who had discovered his police connections and delivered an ultimatum to him in August. Or was he hired by reactionary forces who thought Stolypin too moderate? After the assassination of Stolypin, the State Duma was convened as scheduled on October 28, on the fortieth day after the government leader's tragic death, but members were told, not of Stolypin's death, but that of another Duma member from Minsk Province. Nevertheless, one deputy, the social democrat I. P. Pokrovskii, delivered a scathing attack upon the police and claimed that the Kiev Okhrana arranged the murder of the premier, just as other prominent persons were killed at the behest of the double agent, Yevno Azef, a few years before. In particular, he singled out General A. I. Spiridovich, commander of the Palace Okhrana, and Kurlov, as head of the Okhrana.

Stolypin was buried in the Pecherskii Monastery in Kiev. He was succeeded as premier by Kokovtsev who soon lost favor at court and was replaced by the aging and weak Ivan L. Goremykin. Neither could command the respect of court and Duma as the nation plunged into world war.

—*John D. Windhausen*

ADDITIONAL READING:

Ferro, Marc. *Nicholas II: The Last of the Tsars*. New York: Oxford University Press, 1993. The author accepts the conspiracy theory involving the security forces.

Kerensky, Alexander. *Russia and History's Turning Point*. New York: Duell, Sloan, and Pearce, 1965. These memoirs by the head of the provisional government in 1917 traced the public antagonism toward Stolypin to his restoration of capital punishment.

Lincoln, W. Bruce. *In War's Dark Shadow: The Russians Before the Great War*. New York: Simon & Schuster, 1983. This analysis took aim at the conservative reactionaries in the State Council and their hatred of the premier.

Massie, Robert K. *Nicholas and Alexandra*. New York: Atheneum, 1967. An attractive narrative that indicates Czar Nicholas' state of mind before, during, and after the murder.

Pares, Sir Bernard. *The Fall of the Russian Monarchy*. New York: Alfred A. Knopf, 1939. This Englishman had numerous interviews with many of the participants in the political drama of those years.

Pipes, Richard. *The Russian Revolution.* New York: Alfred A. Knopf, 1990. In this massive work, the author defends the police from the charge of instigating the murder.

Shulgin, V. V. *Memoirs of a Member of the Russian Duma, 1906-1917.* New York: Hippocrene, 1984. Includes the lengthy letter of Czar Nicholas to his mother about the assassination, and Pokrovskii's address that accused the Okhrana of responsibility.

SEE ALSO: 1904-1905, Russo-Japanese War; 1905, Bloody Sunday; 1905, The October Manifesto; 1906, First Meeting of the Duma; 1917, October Revolution.

1912-1914
IRISH HOME RULE BILL

The Irish Home Rule Bill marks the collision of Irish nationalism and British party politics, bringing about a constitutional crisis that nearly results in the enactment of a law that cannot be enforced.

DATE: April 11, 1912-September 15, 1914
LOCALE: London, and various parts of Ireland
CATEGORIES: Government and politics; Laws, acts, and legal history
KEY FIGURES:

Herbert Henry Asquith (1852-1928), Liberal prime minister, who advocated home rule for Ireland

Sir Edward Henry Carson (1854-1935), Ulster Unionist leader and member of Parliament, who opposed home rule for Ireland

Winston Leonard Spencer Churchill (1874-1965), first lord of the Admiralty and Liberal leader in the House of Commons, who supported home rule for Ireland

James Craig (1871-1940), Ulster Unionist leader and member of Parliament, who opposed home rule

Andrew Bonar Law (1858-1923), Unionist Party leader in the House of Commons, who opposed home rule for Ireland

David Lloyd George (1863-1945), Liberal politician and Chancellor of the Exchequer, who supported home rule

Eoin MacNeill, founder of the Nationalist Volunteers and leader of the Gaelic League

Patrick Pearse (1879-1916), leader of the Irish Republicans (Sinn Féin)

John Edward Redmond (1856-1918), leader of the Irish Nationalist Party, who advocated home rule for Ireland

Frederick Edwin Smith (1872-1930), Unionist Party member of Parliament and brilliant speaker, who opposed home rule

SUMMARY OF EVENT. The Act of Union of 1800 establishing the United Kingdom of Great Britain and Ireland had never been popular either in Catholic Ireland or in Protestant Ulster. When Catholic Irish Nationalists sought the restoration of the Irish Parliament, or home rule, during the nineteenth century, Ulster Protestants, fearing for their safety, turned to the Conservative Party for help. In the 1880's the matter became important in British politics when the Irish Nationalist Party delegates, led by Charles Stewart Parnell, used their eighty-five votes to keep the Liberal Party in power, in exchange for home rule. As a result, William Ewart Gladstone's Liberal government introduced the First Home Rule Bill in 1886, but it was defeated by thirty votes; and part of the Liberal Party, the Liberal Unionists, broke away to join with the Conservatives. Gladstone's Second Home Rule Bill passed the House of Commons by thirty-four votes in 1893, but it was overwhelmed in the House of Lords by a vote of 419 to 41.

In succeeding years Conservative-Unionist governments tried unsuccessfully to divert Irish attention from home rule by a series of economic reforms. John Redmond, a good Parliamentarian and an orator of repute, became leader of the united Irish Nationalist Party in the House of Commons in 1900; but since neither the Liberals nor the Conservatives needed Irish votes, no progress was made until 1910. In the campaign of that year, the Liberals supported home rule but lost so many seats that they needed the votes of the Irish Nationalists to form a cabinet and pass their legislative program. A new Home Rule Bill for Ireland was assured as a result of this political necessity. The obstacle to such a measure in the House of Lords had been removed with the passage of the Parliament Act of 1911 which had reduced the power of the upper chamber.

The Third Home Rule Bill was introduced into the House of Commons on April 11, 1912, by H. H. Asquith, the Liberal prime minister, and managed by Winston Churchill, who was then Liberal leader in the House of Commons and a strong proponent of home rule. The provisions proposed were similar to those of the earlier bills, which had proposed an Irish Parliament in Dublin while reserving for the British Parliament at Westminster control over foreign affairs, customs duties, and defense. The number of Irish members of Parliament at Westminster would be cut by half, to forty-two.

Redmond and the Irish Nationalists praised the bill and argued that it would strengthen the relationship between Great Britain and Ireland. Liberal leaders defended it as a rightful measure of self-determination and noted that home rule would relieve the British Parliament from being burdened by local Irish affairs. The Home Rule Bill met bitter opposition from the Unionists, including both the Conservative-Unionists and the Ulster Unionists. With the Conservative Party having lost three consecutive elections, newly elected Conservative Party leader Andrew Bonar Law seized upon Unionism as a means by which he could reunite a badly divided party. Edward Carson's goal was simpler: protection of the rights of Ulster, present-day Northern Ireland. This area was predominantly Protestant Scots-Irish and somewhat industrialized; it was bitterly opposed to joining the more rural Catholic South. The situation was complicated by the presence of a large Catholic minority in Ulster and a smaller but influential Protestant minority in the south of Ireland. Partition, however, was opposed by both sides. Irish Nationalists opposed it because they wanted Ireland to remain one nation, and the Ulster Protestants fought it because they did not wish to abandon the Protestants in the south. Ulster Unionists also argued that they were loyal Protestant Britons who were be being sacrificed to disloyal Catholic Irishmen for the sake of political expediency. They were convinced that the Catholic Irish would persecute them

As the leader of Sinn Féin, Patrick Pearse was committed to using military force to pressure the British parliament to pass the Irish Home Rule Bill. (Library of Congress)

religiously and economically.

The debate in the House of Commons was heated and disorderly, but the Liberal-Irish coalition had the votes and the Home Rule Bill passed the Commons on January 16, 1913. The House of Lords rejected it by a huge majority as expected, which meant that the bill would have to be passed again by the Commons at its next two sessions to overcome the Lords' veto. Nevertheless, it was almost certain to pass since the same Parliament would still be in session. Second passage was accomplished in the Commons on July 7, 1913; eight days later, the Lords again rejected the bill in uncompromising fashion.

It was clear that, if constitutional means were followed, there was no real obstacle to the Home Rule Bill becoming law in 1914. Thus Ulster Protestants and Conservative-Unionists were willing to use any means, even apparently unconstitutional ones, to stop home rule. At first, the Liberal government did not consider the threat of rebellion in Ulster to be real, and they believed that the situation would settle down if they avoided provocation. Carson was aware that there were hard-line Protestants who favored overt action against the bill, and he undertook measures which he hoped would control and direct Ulster Protestant emotions. A "covenant" was drawn up containing a total of 470,000 signatures, and the Ulster Unionists began to drill a militia, the "Ulster Volunteers." The Conservative-Unionist leaders, Bonar Law, F. E. Smith, and others, openly supported these measures in speeches throughout Great Britain. It was hoped that rhetoric and demonstrations could force the Liberal-Irish Nationalist coalition to the bargaining table.

Southern Irish Nationalists were much upset by Ulster's defiance and by the Liberal government's weakness in the face of Ulster threats. While Redmond continued to support Asquith and Parliament, other Irishmen became convinced of the need for stronger measures and for more than home rule. Groups such as the Irish Republicans and certain labor unions urged the South to imitate Ulster's tactics. In November 1913, the Nationalist Volunteers, led by their founder, Eoin MacNeill, and by Patrick Pearse, leader of Sinn Féin, began to drill in the South. In the face of such threats, Asquith backed down to some extent when the Home Rule Bill passed the Commons for the third and last time in March, 1914. He compromised by adding an Amending Bill, crafted by David Lloyd George, which provided a six-year exclusion clause for Ulster. Reluctantly, Redmond accepted it, but Nationalist groups objected. Neither Carson nor Bonar Law would, or could, accept the compromise.

Tragically, other events quickly outpaced the parliamentary leadership. In late March, the so-called "Mutiny at the Curragh" apparently left the government with the prospect of a Home Rule Act which it could not enforce. Under the leadership of James Craig, German rifles were smuggled to the Ulster Defense Force; weapons were now poised behind words. With the Nationalist Volunteers in the South growing in influence and restlessness, Redmond unwillingly took command of them in May to avoid a split with MacNeill and Pearse. In this atmosphere, the Home Rule Bill passed the Commons on May 25, and the Amending Bill passed on June 23. The House of Lords again amended the Bills far beyond what Asquith could accept. When Carson proclaimed the "Ulster Provisional Government" on July 12, Britain appeared poised on the brink of civil confrontation. King George V called a conference at Buckingham Palace on July 21; but the questions of permanent exclusion and the boundaries of Ulster could not be solved, and the conference broke up. The situation became even more tense when, on July 26, after some guns had been smuggled into town, British troops fired on an angry Irish crowd in Bachelors' Walk, Dublin, killing three and wounding many others.

Austria declared war on Serbia the next day, however, and Great Britain was plunged into World War I by August 4. There does appear to have been a collective sigh of relief when those events forced home rule to the back burner. Redmond, Carson, and Bonar Law all agreed to postpone the Amending Bill until the end of hostilities in Europe. Redmond, in a loudly applauded speech, stated that his Irish Nationalist Volunteers would aid Great Britain; the Ulster Defense Force volunteered en masse to serve in the British army. Finally, on September 15, the Home Rule Bill became law, but its operations were suspended for the duration of the war. Nevertheless, home rule was dead, and the Radical elements in Ireland soon split from Redmond. Eventually they were responsible for the Easter Rebellion of 1916, and civil war after 1918.

The passing of the Home Rule Bill had profound effects on both Great Britain and Ireland. The Conservative-Unionist preaching of revolution seriously threatened the entire Parliamentary system of government. Tragically, the danger of hyperbolic rhetoric is that there are always those who take such seriously and literally. Radical Irish groups, Protestant and Catholic, did so and broke with parliamentary tactics. The battle over the bill itself resulted in great domestic unrest throughout Ireland; and only the outbreak of World War I prevented an ominous constitutional crisis, and possibly even a bloody civil war, in Great Britain and Ireland. Ultimately, the failure to enforce home rule helped to sever the bonds between Great Britain and Ireland, preparing the way for the Irish Rebellion and eventual independence. Ulster opposition to home rule also resulted in the partition of Ireland which split off Northern Ireland from the rest of the island.

—James H. Steinel,
updated by William S. Brockington, Jr.

ADDITIONAL READING::

Bew, Paul. *Ideology and the Irish Question: Ulster Unionism and Irish Unionism, 1912-1916.* New York: Oxford University Press, 1995. Contends that conciliation was viable before the Easter Rising of 1916 brought Sinn Féin to dominance.

Blake, Robert. *The Unknown Prime Minister.* London: Eyre & Spottiswoode, 1955. A summary of Bonar Law's role in the Crisis which provides insight into the motivations of the Conservative-Unionist leadership.

Boyce, D. G. *The Irish Question and British Politics, 1868-1986.* Basingstoke, England: Macmillan Education, 1988. An overview of the use of the Irish Question by political parties during the period.

Dangerfield, George. *The Strange Death of Liberal England, 1910-1914.* New York: Capricorn Books, 1935. Brilliant exposition of the turmoil in Great Britain in the years just before World War I, but his conclusions bear careful scrutiny.

Hughes, Michael. *Ireland Divided: The Roots of the Modern Irish Problem.* New York: St. Martin's Press, 1994. Studies the nationalistic ideas and myths that provide the underpinning of the various Irish groups.

Jalland, Patricia. *The Liberals and Ireland: The Ulster Question in British Politics to 1914.* New York: St. Martin's Press, 1980. Provides an overview of the Irish Question as a political issue in Britain and its effect upon the Liberal Party.

Laffan, Michael. *The Partition of Ireland, 1911-1925.* Dundalk, Ireland: Dundalgan Press, 1983. A narrative of the issues and events from the introduction of home rule to partition.

Mansergh, Nicholas. *The Unsolved Question: The Anglo-Irish Settlement and Its Undoing, 1912-1972.* New Haven, Conn.: Yale University Press, 1991. Important for its analysis of the long-range impact of the failure of compromise.

Stewart, A. T. Q. *The Irish Question.* London: Edward Arnold, 1986. Although written by an Ulster Unionist historian, this brief account is quite balanced.

SEE ALSO: 1800, Act of Union Is Passed by Parliament; 1828-1829, Emancipation Acts of 1828 and 1829; 1845-1854, The Irish Famine and the Great Emigration; 1846, Repeal of the Corn Laws; 1909-1911, Parliament Bill; 1916, Easter Rebellion; 1932, Eamon de Valera Is Elected President of the Irish Dáil.

1912-1913
BALKAN WARS

The Balkan Wars reveal the weakening of the Austro-Hungarian Empire, the growth of Serbian power, and the infirmity of Russian policy—all of which contribute to the unsettled conditions leading to World War I.

DATE: October 18, 1912-August 10, 1913

LOCALE: The Balkans

CATEGORIES: Government and politics; Wars, uprisings, and civil unrest

KEY FIGURES:

Count Leopold von Berchtold (1863-1942), foreign minister of Austria-Hungary, 1912-1915

Ferdinand of Saxe-Coburg (1861-1948), prince and subsequently king of Bulgaria, 1887-1918

Sir Edward Grey (1862-1933), British foreign secretary, 1905-1916

Sergei Dmitrievich Sazonov (1861-1927), Russian foreign affairs minister, 1910-1916

SUMMARY OF EVENT. The Balkan Wars of 1912-1913 accelerated the already rapid disintegration of the Ottoman Empire, a process that had been going on since Austria had annexed the Turkish provinces of Bosnia and Herzegovina in 1908. Russia desired to forestall any further Austrian advance in the Balkans, especially against Serbia, and shore up the faltering Turks until Russia itself could become strong enough to move against them. Thus, from 1909 to 1913, Russia worked for the establishment of a Balkan League, based on separate agreements between Bulgaria on the one hand and Serbia, Greece, and Montenegro on the other, together with a Montenegrin-Serbian accord. The league finally came into existence in 1912, but the powers that comprised it were in no mood to act as mere caretakers on behalf of Russia. On the contrary, Austria's annexation of Bosnia and Herzegovina and Italy's annexation of Tripoli in 1912 more than encouraged the members of the Balkan League to drive the Turks out of Europe altogether and divide the territorial spoils between them.

The Ottoman Empire had more than demonstrated its inability to rule its subject nations adequately or carry out reforms on their behalf. Quarrels among the Great Powers and their failure to ensure that the Turks carry out the needed reforms in their subject territories led the Balkan states to conclude that the time was ripe for them to proceed with their own solution to the Balkan problems.

The effectiveness of Russian policy was reduced (as had happened before) because of the inability of the czarist government to control its own agents. Some Russian diplomats in the Balkans openly encouraged the Slavic

Montenegran forces were among the Balkan League allies who fought against the Turks in 1912 and 1913. (Library of Congress)

states to which they were accredited to drive the Turks out of Europe.

None of the Great Powers, particularly Austria and Russia, desired war, which, by dividing the Continent into two armed camps, might precipitate a conflict that could not be confined to the Balkans. Accordingly, on October 8, 1912, Count Leopold von Berchtold, the foreign minister of Austria-Hungary, and Sergei Dmitrievich Sazonov, the Russian minister of foreign affairs, issued a joint declaration on behalf of the European powers to the Balkan states, warning them not to make war on the Turks and stipulating that if they did so and won (an occurrence considered to be highly unlikely), they would not be permitted to annex any territory. Unfortunately, the warning came too late; on the same day that the declaration was issued, Montenegro, confident of support from other members of the Balkan League, boldly declared war on the Ottoman Empire.

War began in earnest on October 18, when Bulgaria, Serbia, and Greece entered the conflict. Six weeks later, on December 3, the shattered Turkish forces sued for an armistice. Meanwhile, Serbia's occupation of a stretch of the Adriatic Coast of northern Albania had precipitated a grave international crisis. Austria and Italy were unalterably opposed to the entrenchment of Serbia on the Adriatic coastline, where Serbia and Russia could challenge Habsburg and Italian naval supremacy. With some reluctance, Germany agreed to support Austria if Austria were attacked while defending its interests. Fearful that Austria might once again move against Serbian interests, as had happened in 1908, and desirous of maintaining the friendship of the surprisingly potent Balkan League to prevent such action, Sazonov made a pretense of supporting Serbian claims. Realizing, however, that Russia was not yet prepared for a major war, Sazonov obligingly staged a diplomatic retreat and worked for localizing the conflict at the London Peace Conference, which opened on December 16, 1912, under the chairmanship of Sir Edward Grey, the British foreign secretary.

The work of this conference was retarded by the complex Albanian question and the reopening of hostilities between members of the Balkan League and the Turks on January 30, 1913. Early in 1913, Austria and Italy were able to gain tentative international acceptance for the creation of an enlarged Albania, which would safely exclude Serbia from having an outlet into the Adriatic. Meanwhile, the Turks were again defeated, and the Treaty of London of May 30, 1913, brought the First Balkan War to a close. The unsatisfactory peace settlement, however, was imposed on disgruntled Serbs, their allies, and the Turks. None of the Balkan states was satisfied with the terms dictated to them in London. Because Serbia had been denied an outlet to the Adriatic, it now demanded compensation by insisting that Bulgaria cede a larger slice of Macedonian territory than had been assigned by the Treaty of London. Bulgaria indignantly refused and also rejected Greek claims to the Thessalonica area of Macedonia and Romania's claims to the Dobruja, an area adjacent to the mouth of the Danube River.

Surrounded by hostile powers, Ferdinand of Saxe-Coburg, who had been independent king of Bulgaria since 1908, decided to oust the Serbs and the Greeks from Macedonia. Bulgaria attacked on June 29, 1913, and consequently Serbia and Greece declared war on Bulgaria. They were soon joined by Montenegro and Romania, and eventually by the recent adversary of these protagonists, the Ottoman Empire. Bulgaria was badly mauled, and concluded peace in Bucharest on August 10 with the Balkan states and gave to those who demanded them the territories to which it had aspired. In a separate peace with Turkey signed at Constantinople on September 29, Bulgaria ceded to Turkey the greater part of Thrace, which it had gained in the First Balkan War, including the important city of Adrianople.

The Balkan Wars were over, but the peace of southeastern Europe was in ruins and that of the remainder of the Continent was in serious jeopardy. All the Balkan states increased their territories, but none was completely satisfied. The Treaty of Bucharest of August 10, 1913, which terminated the Second Balkan War, served to whet the appetite of Romania for more territory, and specifically for Austrian Transylvania, with its large Romanian population. So it was that Romania joined Serbia in coveting the crownlands of Austria-Hungary. Romanian sympathy for the Serbs, together with closer ties with the West, constituted a serious blow to the Triple Alliance during and after 1913.

The Second Balkan War proved to be a defeat for Austria. Serbia, Austria's archenemy in the Balkans, emerged from the second contest considerably strengthened at the expense of Bulgaria. Romania, however, mistrusted Austria-Hungary because it had given diplomatic support to Bulgaria during the recent war and because the Hungarians oppressed the Romanian population of Transylvania. —*Edward P. Keleher, updated by Carl Rollyson*

ADDITIONAL READING:

Kaplan, Robert D. *Balkan Ghosts: A Journey Through History*. New York: St. Martin's Press, 1993. Chapter 3 gives brief but deft descriptions of the Balkan Wars, especially from the perspective of the Turks, the Bulgarians, and other central European states.

May, Arthur J. *The Hapsburg Monarchy, 1867-1914*. Cambridge, Mass.: Harvard University Press, 1960. May's work provides a useful historical context for understanding Austria's role in the Balkan conflict.

Sked, Alan. *The Decline and Fall of the Habsburg Empire, 1815-1918*. New York: Dorset Press, 1991. See chapter 6, "The Road to Disaster" for a treatment of the Balkan Wars in the context of relationships between the Great Powers.

SEE ALSO: 1863-1913, Greece Is Unified Under the Glucksburg Dynasty; 1876, Bulgarian Massacres; 1878, Congress of Berlin; 1882, The Triple Alliance; 1908, Austria Annexes Bosnia and Herzegovina; 1914, Outbreak of World War I.

1914
OUTBREAK OF WORLD WAR I

The outbreak of World War I contributes to the collapse of the Russian, German, and Austrian empires, weakens Great Britain and France and their colonial empires, catapults the United States to a dominant position in world affairs, and sets the stage for an even more devastating world war.

DATE: June 28-August 4, 1914

LOCALE: Primarily Austria-Hungary, Germany, France, Russia, and Great Britain

Categories: Diplomacy and international relations; Government and politics; Wars, uprisings, and civil unrest

Key figures:

Count Leopold von Berchtold (1863-1942), foreign minister of Austria-Hungary

Theobald von Bethmann Hollweg (1856-1921), chancellor of the German empire

Sir Edward Grey (1862-1933), British foreign secretary

Aleksandr Petrovich Izvolski (1856-1919), Russian ambassador to France and former Russian foreign affairs minister

Nicholas II (1868-1918), czar of Russia, 1894-1917

Sergei Dmitrievich Sazonov (1861-1927), Russian foreign affairs minister, 1910-1916

William II (1859-1941), emperor of Germany, 1888-1918

Summary of event. The assassination of Archduke Francis Ferdinand, heir to the Austro-Hungarian throne, on June 28, 1914, set in motion a chain of events which resulted in a world war which profoundly affected the course of history. Virtually since its beginning, historians have attempted to explain how such a relatively minor event as the assassination could have had such devastating consequences. The war not only ravaged the economies of the major European states but also caused or made possible the triumph of communism in Russia, the rise of Nazism in Germany, and the international anarchy which led to World War II. Not least, World War I resulted in the deaths of between ten and twenty million people.

After the assassination of Francis Ferdinand, the chief of staff of the Austro-Hungarian army recommended that his emperor, Franz Joseph, mobilize his army on the border between Austria-Hungary and Serbia. The chief of staff argued along with civilian members of Franz Joseph's government that members of the Serbian government and armed forces had helped plan and carry out the assassination. He noted that individuals within the Serbian government, desirous of incorporating into their own territory that part of the Austrian empire which contained a large Serbian population, had good reason to wish the Austrian heir dead.

Austrian foreign minister Leopold von Berchtold feared that Russian troops might come to the aid of the Serbs in the event of war. Before agreeing to mobilize the Austrian army he first sent a letter of inquiry to the German government. The letter asked if their help would be forthcoming in the event of Russian intervention in a diplomatic or military struggle between Austria-Hungary and Serbia. German military and civil officials received the letter on July 5, 1914, and immediately assured the Austro-Hungarian envoy that they would support their

ally (Austria-Hungary had been partners with Germany and Italy since 1888 in a defensive treaty called the Triple Alliance).

The leaders of Austria-Hungary sent an ultimatum to the Serbian government on July 23. The ten-point ultimatum stipulated that (among other demands) Austro-Hungarian officials be allowed to conduct an investigation into the assassination in Serbia and try and punish any Serbs found guilty of involvement in Francis Ferdinand's death. The ultimatum gave the Serbs forty-eight hours to make a satisfactory reply or face a rupture of relations with the Austrians. When the contents of the ultimatum became known, leaders of other European governments became aware for the first time that a major crisis in international affairs had arisen. European leaders seemed incapable of halting the following sequence of events even though most of them wanted to avoid the catastrophe they saw looming ahead.

The Serbians ordered mobilization of their army on receipt of the Austrian ultimatum. Nicholas Pasic, Serbian prime minister, contacted members of the Russian and French governments (allied since 1892 in the Dual Alliance) in an effort to garner support. Pasic received assurances from Nicholas II of Russia that a secret agreement signed previously between Russian and Serbian officials would be honored. The agreement guaranteed Russian military assistance in any dispute between Serbia and Austria. The Serbs then sent a reply to the Austrian ultimatum on July 25.

The Serbians agreed to all Austrian demands except one. The Serbs declined to allow Austrian officials to participate in the internal Serbian investigation into any alleged plot to assassinate Ferdinand. Some historians say Pasic feared to permit Austrian participation in the inquiry because it would have revealed the complicity of the Serbian government. Other historians maintain that the Serbian rejection of the term resulted from the promise of Russian support.

The Austrians broke off diplomatic relations with the Serbs because of the unsatisfactory Serbian reply, and ordered the mobilization of their army on the Serbian border. Upon hearing of the Serb reply and the Austrian reaction, British foreign secretary Edward Grey sent an appeal to the governments of France, Germany, and Italy to convene an international conference the next day (July 26) to mediate a settlement of the crisis. Representatives of the German government declined the invitation, suggesting instead that the matter should be settled by direct negotiations between the Austrians and the Russians. Some German officials were privately urging Austrian officials to take immediate military action against the

Serbs to preempt any intervention by the Russians or the French. The French general staff began recalling its Moroccan garrisons to France, a move the German general staff considered provocative. The French ambassador to Russia, assured the Russian foreign minister, Sergei Sazonov, of French support for whatever action the Russian government decided to take.

On July 28, the Austrian government declared war on Serbia and the Austrian army began bombarding the Serbian city of Belgrade. The next day, the German ambassador to France warned the French foreign minister that French troop movements on the German border were about to cause a German declaration of "state of imminent danger of war"—the final step before mobilization of the German military. All European diplomats understood that the mobilization of the military forces of any of the major powers meant war.

The next day, the Russian czar signed two orders for the mobilization of Russian troops, one for partial mobilization (along the Austrian border only) the other for total mobilization along Russia's frontiers, including the border with Germany. Nicholas did not implement either order immediately. A few hours later, the German ambassador to Russia delivered a telegram from German chancellor Theobald von Bethmann Hollweg to Sazonov warning that the mobilization of Russian forces on the German border would mean war. To emphasize this point, German emperor William II sent a personal telegram to his cousin, Nicholas II, warning him of the danger of war and requesting that Russian steps toward mobilization be halted. Nicholas sent a reply assuring his cousin that Russia would not mobilize.

On July 30, Sazonov joined with the Russian minister of war and the chief of the Russian general staff in implementing Nicholas' previously signed order for full mobilization. The next day a representative of the French foreign ministry informed the Russian ambassador to France that the French government had decided to go to war against Germany. At about the same time, the German government issued a declaration of "imminent danger of war." Austrian officials simultaneously ordered mobilization of the Austrian army along its border with the Russian empire.

British government officials failed to make clear to any of the antagonists what action they might take in the event of war between the members of the Dual and Triple Alliance systems. A few members of the French government were aware of a secret agreement contained in the Anglo-French Entente of 1904, which guaranteed that the British fleet would protect French channel ports if France became involved in a war. The British government never made public this secret protocol, nor had the British parliament

The assassination of Archduke Francis Ferdinand (center) touched off the chain of events that involved all of the major powers of Europe in the outbreak of war in 1914. (National Archives)

ratified it. Nevertheless, Grey and other members of the British government talked privately throughout the crisis about British entry into the war on the side of the French.

On August 1, the French government mobilized its armed forces. The German government mobilized its own troops and declared war on Russia. German officials sent an ultimatum to the French to cease mobilization. When the French failed to comply, the Germans declared war on them the next day and delivered an ultimatum to the Belgians demanding that the German army be permitted to pass through their territory.

The Belgians rejected the German ultimatum on August 3, causing the Germans to declare war on the Belgians and invade their borders. The British government sent an ultimatum to the Germans, demanding that the German army withdraw from Belgium. When the ultimatum expired the next day, the British government declared war against the German empire. A war which eventually engulfed most of the world was under way.

—*Paul Madden*

ADDITIONAL READING:

Fay, Sidney B. *The Origins of the World War.* 2 vols. Rev. ed. New York: Macmillan, 1930. Argues persuasively that the actions of European governmental and military leaders, along with intellectuals and journalists, created a situation that by 1914 made a general war probable, if not inevitable.

Fischer, Fritz. *Germany's Aims in the First World War.* London: W. W. Norton, 1967. Blames the German government for the outbreak of the war.

Joll, James. *The Origins of the First World War.* London: Longman, 1984. A balanced synthesis of the enormous literature concerning the outbreak of war in 1914.

Lafore, Laurence. *The Long Fuse: An Interpretation of the Origins of World War I.* New York: J. B. Lippincott, 1971. A calm and balanced account of the origins of World War I which seeks to explain rather than to apportion blame.

Lee, Dwight E., ed. *The Outbreak of the First World War: Causes and Responsibilities.* Lexington, Mass.: D. C. Heath, 1975. Should be the starting place for anyone wishing to learn more about the outbreak of World War I.

SEE ALSO: 1882, The Triple Alliance; 1893, Franco-Russian Alliance; 1904, The Entente Cordiale; 1907, The Triple Entente; 1908, Austria Annexes Bosnia and Herzegovina; 1914, First Battle of the Marne; 1914, Spain Declares Neutrality in World War I.

1914
FIRST BATTLE OF THE MARNE

The First Battle of the Marne halts the German advance into Paris and changes the nature of World War I to one of position rather than movement.

DATE: September 5-9, 1914
LOCALE: The Marne River Valley, east of Paris, France
CATEGORY: Wars, uprisings, and civil unrest
KEY FIGURES:
General Karl von Bülow (1846-1921), commander of the German Second Army
General Ferdinand Foch (1851-1929), commander of the French Ninth Army
Louis-Félix-Marie-François Franchet d'Esperey (1856-1942), general commander of the French Fifth Army
Field Marshal Sir John Denton Pinkstone French (1852-1925), commander in chief of the British Expeditionary Force
General Joseph Simon Gallieni (1849-1916), military governor of Paris

General Joseph-Jacques-Césaire Joffre (1852-1931), commander in chief of the French armies
General Heinrich Rudolph Alexander von Kluck (1846-1934), commander of the German First Army
General Helmuth von Moltke (1848-1916), chief of staff of the German Army, 1906-1914
General Alfred von Schlieffen (1833-1913), chief of staff of the German Army, 1891-1906
William II (1859-1941), emperor of Germany, 1888-1918

SUMMARY OF EVENT. Before the outbreak of World War I, Germany's only battle plan to meet the contingency of war on two fronts against France and Russia was the 1905 Schlieffen Plan developed by General Alfred von Schlieffen, chief of staff of the Germany Army from 1891 to 1906. He knew that the vast size of Russia and its undeveloped railroad system meant that the mobilization and deployment of the Russian armies on the German frontier would take two months. France, on the other hand, being a compact country and possessing a dense network of railroads, could bring up all its troops against Germany in three weeks. Schlieffen's plan, accordingly, was to throw seven of the eight German armies against France initially. He proposed going around the strong fortifications on the border between France and Germany by marching two strong armies through Belgium in a westerly direction to the English Channel and then wheeling southward with the German First Army passing west of Paris and then turning back east to push the French against the German fortifications in the province of Lorraine. The French armies would be enveloped in a pocket southeast of Paris and they would be forced to surrender. Schlieffen's plan called for massing a strong force on the right flank and leaving the weaker left flank exposed to lure the French into an attack on the left flank while the main German force overran the French from behind their lines. "It would be like a revolving door," one military analyst explained, "if a man pressed heavily on one side, the other side would spring round and strike him in the back." Once the French were defeated, the German forces could then be sent to the Eastern Front to destroy the Russian armies, which in the meantime were expected to have advanced through east Prussia but no further than the Vistula River. Within about four months, the whole war should have been over.

General Helmuth von Moltke succeeded Schlieffen as chief of staff of the German army in 1906. Fearful that the French might invade German Alsace while the German army's right wing was still advancing, Moltke modified Schlieffen's plan by strengthening the German left flank with new divisions which were formed before 1913. Upon the outbreak of war in 1914, this variant of the original plan was put into effect. The German First and Second armies, consisting of thirty-two out of the seventy-eight German infantry divisions in the West, advanced through Belgium.

Meanwhile, the French launched a headlong offensive at the advancing Germans. Between August 20 and 24, 1914, a series of bloody collisions occurred along the Franco-Belgian frontier. Although the Germans were attacking, they were in fact more often thrown on the defensive, but their artillery and machine guns did repel the French attacks. On August 25, General Joseph-Jacques-

man field headquarters, Joffre remained in constant contact with his commanders in the field. Delayed communications between the German field commanders and Moltke's headquarters in Luxembourg would be a decisive factor in the Battle of the Marne.

The British Expeditionary Force under the command of Field Marshal Sir John French entered the fight on August 23. Three days later, Joffre ordered the formation of a new French Sixth Army in Paris, where it came under the orders of the capital's military governor, General Joseph Simon Gallieni. Joffre also created from elements

The victory of French and British forces over the German army at the First Battle of the Marne forced all combatants to engage in prolonged trench warfare along much of the western front. (Archive Photos)

Césaire Joffre, commander in chief of the French armies, was forced to order a general retreat of all the French armies. German troops followed the retreating French and British armies, who led them east of Paris and south toward the Marne River. There, the French would halt the retreat, turn around and fight the Germans in the First Battle of the Marne, September 6-9, 1914.

On August 4, the day after Germany declared war on France, General Joffre established his staff headquarters at Vitry-le-François on the Marne, where he would be within eighty to ninety miles of each of the five French army headquarters. Unlike Moltke, who never visited the Ger-

of other armies a French Ninth Army under the command of General Ferdinand Foch. Moltke was still intent on outflanking the French Fifth Army at the Franco-Belgian frontier, and on August 30, he abandoned that part of the Schlieffen plan which called for an advance to the west of Paris. Instead, he directed the German First Army to advance east of Paris as an echelon of the German Second Army and one day's march behind it. Nevertheless, the commander of the German First Army, General Heinrich Rudolph Alexander von Kluck, continued to push forward in line with the German Second Army on his left, commanded by General Karl von Bülow. Kluck did transfer one army corps from his left to his right as a flank guard against Paris, but this maneuver opened a small gap between himself and Bülow.

On September 3, Gallieni's reconnaissance reported that Kluck and Bülow's forces were slightly separated, and he suggested attacking Kluck's army. On September 4, Joffre ordered a general "about-face" of the Allied armies, and a general offensive against the Germans began on September 6. When Gallieni's troops made contact with Kluck's flanking corps, Kluck transferred more men from his left to his right in order to avoid being taken from the rear. This deployment widened the gap between himself and Bülow to some twenty miles, screened only partially by light infantry and cavalry. If the German right wing had had the extra troops that Moltke had sent to the German left flank upon mobilization, there might have been no gap and the Battle of the Marne might have developed differently. On September 6, however, the French Fifth Army, under the command of General Louis-Félix-Marie-François Franchet d'Esperey, and the British Expeditionary Force sent forward by Field Marshal French advanced slowly into the gap to threaten the flanks of both the German First and Second armies. General Foch's Ninth Army was instrumental in repelling German counterattacks for two days. Finally, on September 9, the Germans were driven back across the Marne and pushed sixty miles farther to positions across the Aisne River. Thus ended the First Battle of the Marne.

The German plan to overwhelm France rapidly and then crush Russia with the help of Austria-Hungary was frustrated by this Franco-British victory. The Germans now were faced with the stalemate of trench warfare on the Western Front. For more than three years the war wore on, with thousands of lives lost on both sides in futile efforts to break through the defensive positions marked by opposing trenches stretching from Switzerland to the North Sea.

During the First Battle of the Marne, none of the opposing generals proved to be a great leader. In the moment of crisis, Moltke lost his nerve, and German emperor William II consequently relieved him of his command on September 14. Joffre's victory, though aided by German mistakes, was largely a result of the brilliant execution of orders by his subordinates. The decision to turn and fight at the Marne halted the German invasion, saved France from defeat, and kept the Germans from imposing their hegemony on Europe.

—*Samuel K. Eddy, updated by Marguerite R. Plummer*

ADDITIONAL READING:

Asprey, Robert B. *The First Battle of the Marne.* New York: J. B. Lippincott, 1962. Analyzes military operations

and capabilities of commanders. Attributes Franco-British victory to an inspired will to win.

Gilbert, Martin. *The First World War: A Complete History.* New York: Henry Holt, 1994. Incisive analyses of causes and consequences, and detailed accounts of battles.

Isselin, Henri. *The Battle of the Marne.* Translated from the French by C. Connell. Garden City, N.Y.: Doubleday, 1966. Attributes Franco-British victory to German abandonment of Schlieffen Plan.

Liddell-Hart, B. H. *The Real War, 1914-1918.* Boston: Little, Brown, 1930. Reprint. *The History of the First World War.* London: Cassell, 1970. A concise narrative by an expert military historian.

Ritter, Gerhard. *The Schlieffen Plan: Critique of a Myth.* Translated from the German by Andrew and Eva Wilson. New York: Frederick A. Praeger, 1958. An exposition of the strategic thinking shared by Schlieffen and Moltke.

Tuchman, Barbara W. *The Guns of August.* New York: Macmillan, 1962. In-depth account of preparations of Germany, Russia, France, and Britain for World War I, including operations preceding the Battle of the Marne.

SEE ALSO: 1882, The Triple Alliance; 1893, Franco-Russian Alliance; 1904, The Entente Cordiale; 1907, The Triple Entente; 1914, Outbreak of World War I; 1914, Spain Declares Neutrality in World War I; 1916, Battle of Verdun.

1914
GERMANY BEGINS EXTENSIVE SUBMARINE WARFARE

Germany begins extensive submarine warfare as a strategy to cut off supplies to England before the United States or other neutral powers enter World War I.

DATE: September 22, 1914

LOCALE: The southern North Sea

CATEGORIES: Science and technology; Wars, uprisings, and civil unrest

KEY FIGURES:

Vice Admiral Prince Louis Alexander of Battenberg (later Louis Mountbatten; 1900-1979), first sea lord of the British Admiralty, 1912-October, 1914

Admiral Henry H. Campbell, commander of the British Seventh Cruiser Squadron

Lieutenant Otto Weddigen, captain of the German submarine *U 9*

SUMMARY OF EVENT. At the beginning of World War I, the first sea lord of the British admiralty, Vice Admiral Prince Louis Alexander of Battenberg, established patrols

In an attempt to blockade Britain into submission, German submarines conducted unrestricted warfare against all civilian shipping, including vessels belonging to the United States. (National Archives)

in the southern North Sea to protect the eastern entrance of the English Channel against raids by German destroyers and minelayers. The force assigned to this task included two flotillas of destroyers and a squadron of five old armored cruisers, but copies of the orders then given indicate that the risk of attack by German submarines was not taken seriously. On September 5, 1914, however, the British light cruiser HMS *Pathfinder* was sunk by the German submarine *U 21* off the Firth of Forth, and on September 13, the British submarine *E 9* destroyed the German light cruiser *Hela* off Heligoland. It should have been apparent that the submarine was making its appearance in war and would have to be regarded as a serious danger to surface ships, but nothing was done to alter the dispositions of the southern patrol.

On September 22, three ships of the British Seventh Cruiser Squadron, HMS *Aboukir*, *Cressy*, and *Hogue*, were patrolling west of the Dutch coast. The squadron commander, Admiral Henry H. Campbell, was on his flagship, which was refueling in port. When bad weather drove the escorting destroyers into port, the three cruisers were left without escort. In accordance with the admiral's orders, they were steaming on a straight course at less than ten knots.

Shortly after sunrise, they were sighted by Lieutenant Otto Weddigen, captain of the German submarine *U 9*. At 6:30 A.M., he hit the *Aboukir* with a single, skillfully directed torpedo. The cruiser quickly took on a dangerous list. The captain of the *Aboukir*, Captain John E. Drummond, believed that he had hit a mine, and being the senior officer present, he ordered the other two ships to close in on him. The *Hogue* neared the sinking ship, came to a stop, and launched her boats to rescue the crew of the *Aboukir*. *U 9* then took aim at the stationary *Hogue* and fired again at close range. Two torpedoes hit and mortally wounded the *Hogue*. Meanwhile, the *Aboukir* capsized and sank. Ten minutes later, the *Hogue* also foundered, and her survivors joined those from the *Aboukir* in the sea. Unwilling to abandon the struggling men, Captain R. W. Johnson, captain of the remaining ship *Cressy*, brought his vessel to a dead stop, thereby providing a helpless target. Weddigen did not miss the opportunity provided him. He reloaded his torpedo tubes and fired three missiles at the *Cressy*. Two torpedoes exploded against her, ripping out her side. The cruiser sank in fifteen minutes. In little more than an hour, Weddigen had accounted for three twelve-thousand-ton armored cruisers with his small 493-ton ship manned by twenty-nine men. British loss of life was extremely heavy; fourteen hundred men out of the twenty-two hundred in the crews of the three ships were either killed or drowned.

Shortly afterward, German submarines began to attack merchant vessels and proved themselves highly effective, although inhumane, destroyers of commerce. On October 20, 1914, *U 17* sank the British *Glitra*; it was the first of more than thirteen thousand merchant ships, thirty-six million tons in all, to be sunk by submarines of all navies in both world wars. In 1917, the Germans inaugurated a campaign of unrestricted submarine warfare. "Unrestricted" meant that the U-boats did not observe the rules of international law, which prescribed that warships must search merchantmen suspected of carrying contraband before sinking them, and that merchant ships must not be sunk at all if the crew could not first be put in a safe place. It was this offensive against civilian shipping, deemed brutish and cowardly by the standards of those days, that brought the United States into the war against Germany. Meanwhile, by unrestricted torpedo attacks and by mine-laying in the first four months of 1917, German submarines sank no less than 1,147 ships totaling 2,224,000 tons, forcing Great Britain to face the possibility of starvation and defeat. The British responded by collecting their merchant ships into convoys, where they could be directly protected by an escort of warships.

The risky strategy by Germany—that its U-boats could isolate and blockade Britain into submission before accidental sinkings of noncombatants brought neutrals such as the United States into war—failed. The sinking of the *Lusitania* on May 7, 1915, with more than one hundred Americans aboard, was met with sharp rebukes and general threats from Washington, D.C. Other sinkings, including those of the *Arabic* (August, 1915) and the *Sussex* six months later were followed by outrage in the United States and promises by Germany to end "unrestricted submarine warfare." When it became clear that Germany had no intention of ordering a change in tactics for the U-boats, the United States entered the war (April, 1917).

At first, a certain amount of disdain existed for submarines: It was not an "honorable" way to fight. Yet the nations of the world soon decided that the areas beneath the ocean surfaces were as much a part of the military map

as those above, and devised strategies accordingly. Admiralty staffs started to procure submarines and plan for their use. Likewise, those charged with defending against submarine attacks developed new strategies.

In World War II, the British and their allies used the convoy system from the beginning of hostilities. The Germans retaliated by grouping their U-boats into packs, and great actions between five or ten submarines and the convoy escorts were fought in the grim Battle of the Atlantic. In 1942 alone, German submarines sank 1,054 ships totaling 5,764,000 tons, seriously impeding the offensive capacity of the Allies. In the Mediterranean, British submarines dispatched a quarter of the entire Italian merchant marine, thus helping to cut off the Italo-German armies in Libya from their sources of food, fuel, and ammunition.

The antisubmarine warfare efforts in World War II featured new "combined arms" approaches to the submarine threats, utilizing aircraft, surface ships, and, by the 1950's, other submarines to track and kill submarines. By the 1960's and 1970's, attack submarines became a focal point of the antisubmarine warfare battle, especially against ballistic missile submarines.

—Samuel K. Eddy, updated by Larry Schweikart

ADDITIONAL READING:

Dalgleish, D. Douglas, and Larry Schweikart. *Trident*. Carbondale: Southern Illinois University Press, 1984. A case study of a ballistic missile submarine program, including detailed examinations of politics, technology, the struggles between the U.S. Navy and the contractor, and an entire chapter devoted to the (then) state-of-the-art antisubmarine warfare tactics and weapons.

Gray, Colin. *The Leverage of Sea Power*. New York: Free Press, 1992. Although far less specific to submarine warfare, Gray's book is the classic analysis of the effect of sea power upon land conflicts, and contains passages dealing with submarines. An excellent overview to more specialized books on undersea warfare.

Macintyre, Donald. *The Battle of the Atlantic*. London: B. T. Batsford, 1961. Another British review of antisubmarine warfare, this time in World War II, by a captain of British antisubmarine warfare units in World War II. Macintyre emphasizes not only the close cooperation between air and sea forces in fighting the U-boats, but also the coordination of military men and scientists, who provided the sophisticated electronic equipment that finally gave the Allies an edge.

Newbold, Henry. *Naval Operations*. Vol. 5. London: Longmans, Green, 1931. The last volume in a series concerned with the British response to U-boats, shows how unprepared the British were for the new type of warfare. Useful for discussions of antisubmarine warfare tactics in the Great War.

Terraine, John. *The U-Boat Wars, 1916-1945*. New York: G. P. Putnam's Sons, 1989. An exhaustive study of warfare and tactics in both world wars, laced with detail about individuals, flotillas, strategies, and technology. Highly recommended, and less overtly pro-British than the other books.

SEE ALSO: 1889, Great Britain Strengthens the Royal Navy; 1906, Launching of the *Dreadnought*; 1914, Outbreak of World War I; 1914, Spain Declares Neutrality in World War I; 1915, International Congress of Women; 1916, Battle of Verdun; 1916, Battle of Jutland.

1914

SPAIN DECLARES NEUTRALITY IN WORLD WAR I

Spain declares neutrality in World War I, bringing economic prosperity while heightening the nation's political polarization and instability.

DATE: October 30, 1914
LOCALE: Madrid, Spain
CATEGORY: Diplomacy and international relations
KEY FIGURES:

Alfonso XIII (1886-1941), king of Spain, 1886-1931
Francisco Cambó (1876-1947), leader of Catalonian Lliga
Eduardo Dato Iradier (1856-1923), Conservative premier of Spain, 1913-1915, 1917
Muley Ahmed El Raisuli (1868-1925), sharif of Djebala, Morocco
Alvaro de Figueroa y Torres, count of Romanones (1864-1950), Liberal premier of Spain, 1912-1913, 1916-1917, 1918
Alejandro Lerroux (1864-1949), Republican leader of Barcelona
Benito Márquez Martínez (1858-1923), Spanish colonel
SUMMARY OF EVENT. The outbreak of World War I exacerbated the fragmented, increasingly tumultuous quality of Spanish politics. In an unstable political environment, Alfonso XIII's control had brought continuity to foreign policy. Now the king's sympathies lay with the Franco-British Entente not the German-Austrian Central Powers because of the former's potential usefulness in developing Spain's Moroccan empire (compensation for her losses to the United States in 1898). The king's interest in Morocco also came from the loyalty of the *africanista* faction of Spain's army. On the other hand, most of Spain's conser-

vative classes, military personnel, and Eduardo Dato, premier in 1914, sympathized with Germany. They admired Germany for her military triumph over France in 1871, and they distrusted British and French liberalism. Besides, Britain and France had largely ignored Spain's interests in settling Moroccan crises in 1905 and 1911.

Spanish efforts to take effective control in Morocco had also been frustrated since 1909 by native resistance led by Sharif Muley Ahmed El Raisuli in the Rif region. Thus, at the outbreak of the European war, half of Spain's army was tied down in Morocco; the other half, underfunded, was not up to standards of modern warfare. From 1908, available money had gone into naval shipbuilding, but Spain's navy remained far behind those of the great powers in 1914.

Britain had not sought a Spanish alliance in the crucial months before the war's outbreak. Declaring neutrality on July 30, 1914, seemed the best course, and the Cortes (parliament) confirmed Premier Dato's decision an October 30.

Spaniards also believed that they might play a more influential role politically and economically as a neutral than as a combatant. During the early years of the war both Allies and Central Powers expended considerable effort propagandizing Spain. This effort escalated when Italy joined the Allies in 1915, after promises of postwar rewards. The Germans now promised Spain a free hand in Morocco and in revolutionary Portugal as well as possession of Tangier and Gibraltar. German agents encouraged Catalonian separatists in Barcelona, who also found encouragement in Allied propaganda favoring self-determination for subject peoples. The lively debate between Germanophiles and Francophiles (or *aliadofilos*) primarily reflected ongoing divisions between the Spanish Right and Left. Wartime prosperity also aggravated these divisions. Trade increased enormously as orders from belligerent nations poured in and investment funds from abroad increased. Spain's boom brought inflation, and wages lagged behind prices. Underclass persons not employed in industry suffered greatly, so prosperity encouraged already active socialism and anarchism. Wartime profiteers in Barcelona, Spain's industrial center, refused to pay taxes commensurate with the gains; instead, they rallied behind the *Lliga Regionalista* (Regional League), which stood for Catalonian autonomy. Increased taxes might have eased the lot of soldiers who also suffered from wartime inflation.

A crisis came on February 1, 1917, when Germany announced renewal of unrestricted submarine action against neutral shipping to Britain and France (even though German ships used Spanish ports). This declaration prompted the United States to enter the war in April, 1917. Spain's Francophile premier, the Count of Romanones, protested the declaration and was fiercely attacked by Madrid's pro-German press, which treated the protest as portending Spain's entry into the war. Romanones resigned in the midst of general domestic disorder and was succeeded by another Liberal premier, Manuel García Prieto, by Dato, and then by Conservative Antonio Maura. The policy of neutrality continued despite German submarine attacks on Spanish shipping. In late August, 1914, Dato and Romanones, both members of Maura's cabinet, supported a letter threatening the use of impounded German ships to replace sunken Spanish ships. Although this letter brought another fierce attack from Spanish Germanophiles, Germany agreed in the final month of World War I that six impounded ships might be so used for the duration.

In the meantime, wartime pressures had driven Spain to a general domestic breakdown in 1917. The king panicked, in part because of the collapse of Russia's monarchy in February after a revolt by soldiers and socialists. In June, Spain's junior officers formed "defense committees" (*juntas de defensa*) under Colonel Benito Márquez, calling for increased salaries and general army reform. In the course of that summer, defense committees were formed by civil servants, taxpayers, and others. Alejandro Lerroux, Barcelona's republican leader, offered to support the military junta with eight hundred men, but Márquez did not respond. In May, an assembly of parliamentarians, composed of republicans, reformists, and socialists, had convened in Barcelona and later in Madrid. The assembly demanded clarification of Spain's foreign policy and asserted the parliamentary right to control it. The assembly's larger goal was to reform the parliamentary system toward more effective democracy. Francisco Cambó, the *Lliga* leader, took the initiative in the Madrid meeting in October. After unsuccessfully inviting the military junta to join them, however, he left to join Maura's coalition cabinet, and the assembly collapsed. Earlier, Spanish laborers had formed an unprecedented alliance between the anarchist CNT (National Confederation of Labor) and the socialist UCT (General Confederation of Labor). In August, 1917, they declared a general strike. The government now gave in to the military junta in order to gain their assistance in suppressing the strike.

A total breakdown—even a revolution—had been averted, but at the cost of putting the army in control. The wartime experience of 1917-1918 set the scene for Spain during the next fifty years. The nation did emerge from World War I with increased diplomatic influence. Within the League of Nations, as a member of the Coun-

cil, Spain's continued neutrality made it a spokesperson for a coalition of small nations. Spain's military, secure in their power over domestic affairs, supported revolts and the dictatorships of General Miguel Primo de Rivera (1923-1930) and General Francisco Franco (1940-1975). Both military regimes remained committed to monarchy. Repressed by Primo and Franco, socialists, anarchists, and Catalonian extremists contributed to the failure of the liberal Second Republic (1930-1940) through their infighting and incoherent challenges to government authority. —*José M. Sánchez, updated by Paul Stewart*

ADDITIONAL READING:

Bledsoe, Gerie B. "Spanish Foreign Policy 1898-1936." In *Spain in the Twentieth Century World*, edited by James W. Cortada. Westport, Conn.: Greenwood Press, 1980. This succinct account puts the problem of Spanish neutrality in it diplomatic context.

Boyd, Carolyn P. *Pretorian Politics in Liberal Spain*. Chapel Hill: University of North Carolina Press, 1979. Emphasizing the period from 1898 to 1923 and the activities of the army, Boyd provides the most detailed treatment of the neutrality problem written in English.

Meaker, Gerald. *The Revolutionary Left in Spain 1914-1923*. Stanford, Calif.: Stanford University Press, 1974. Meaker presents a clear and objective account of the complex interaction of socialists, communists, and anarchists in a nation where regionalism and individualism often proved more important than political parties.

Payne, Stanley G. *Politics and the Military in Modern Spain*. Stanford, Calif.: Stanford University Press, 1967. Covering 1815 to 1965, Payne compensates for summary treatment (as compared to Boyd) by tracing Spain's problems from their roots to their logical conclusion in the dictatorship of Franco.

Pilapil, Vicente R. *Alfonso XIII*. New York: Twayne, 1969. This biography emphasizes the king's influence on foreign policy, including his manipulation of "pretorian politics," which is often lost in other treatments.

Rivas Cherif, Cipriano. *Portrait of an Unknown Man: Manuel Azaña and Modern Spain*. Edited and translated by Paul Stewart. Madison, N.J.: Fairleigh Dickinson University Press, 1995. A memoir from the vantage point of the moderate Left (a key element in divided Spain), this book gives a lively sense of what it was like to live through the turbulent wartime and postwar periods.

SEE ALSO: 1876, Spanish Constitution of 1876; 1882, The Triple Alliance; 1904, The Entente Cordiale; 1907, The Triple Entente; 1914, Outbreak of World War I; 1915, International Congress of Women; 1919, The League of Nations Is Established; 1919, Treaty of Versailles.

1915-1918
ARMENIAN GENOCIDE

The Armenian genocide results in the deportation and killing of between six hundred thousand and 1.5 million Armenians in the Ottoman Empire and marks the first state-organized genocide of an ethnic minority in the twentieth century.

DATE: 1915-1918

LOCALE: The Ottoman Empire

CATEGORIES: Race and ethnicity; Religion; Wars, uprisings, and civil unrest

KEY FIGURES:

Ahmed Cemal Pasha (1872-1922), Ottoman navy minister and governor of Syria

Enver Pasha (1881-1922), Ottoman minister of war

Ziya Gökalp (Mehmet Ziya; 1876-1924), Pan Turkism writer

Mehmed Kemal (1884-1919), inspector of deportations at Konya

Johannes Lepsius (1858-1926), German missionary and historian

Henry Morgenthau, Sr. (1856-1946), American ambassador in Constantinople, 1913-1916

Max Erwin von Scheubner-Richter (1884-1923), German vice consul in Erzerum and an early supporter of Adolf Hitler

Mehmed Talaat Pasha (1874-1921), Ottoman minister of the interior

SUMMARY OF EVENT. By the late nineteenth century, most of the historical territories of Armenia belonged to either the Ottoman Empire or the Russian empire. The Armenians represented an ethnic minority in both of these multicultural empires. In the predominantly Islamic Ottoman Empire, the Christian Armenians also constituted a religious minority. A majority of the Ottoman Armenians lived in eastern Anatolia, a region that bordered on the Russian Armenian provinces in the southern Caucasus area. In addition, Armenian businessmen and artisans were prominent in western Anatolia, particularly in Constantinople and Smyrna.

During the last quarter of the nineteenth century, both the Russians and the Turks discriminated against their Armenian populations. In the Russian empire, discrimination took the form of economic and cultural restrictions. Turkish persecution of the Armenians frequently resulted in massacres. Under the rule of Sultan Abdul Hamid II (1876-1909), thousands of Armenians were killed by Turkish mobs and Kurdish irregular forces in eastern Anatolia (1894-1896) and in Cilicia (1909) in southwestern Anatolia.

Armenian nationalist organizations directed their efforts primarily against the Turks rather than the Russians. Indeed, many Armenians considered the Turks inferior Asiatics. In turn, the Turkish population, according to Ernst Jäckh, a scholar and visitor to Cilicia in 1909, maintained that one Armenian "equals two devils."

Turkish attacks against Armenians resulted in the intervention of the great powers, including Russia. To prevent further foreign interventions and to establish a liberal constitution, "Young Turk" officers such as Enver Pasha, Talaat Pasha, and Cemal Pasha removed the sultan from power in 1909. Unfortunately for the Armenians, the Young Turks became intolerant Turkish nationalists. In a coup in 1913 in Constantinople, Enver, Talaat, and Cemal Pasha assumed power and took over the ministries of war, interior, and the navy. This reaction was based, in part, on an ideology of pan-Turkism and pan-Turanism advocated by Ziya Gökalp (Mehmed Ziya), one of the most influential writers and scholars on Turkish nationalism. His nationalism was based on the Turkish language, and he contemptuously identified Armenians with political and economic liberalism.

The conflict between the Young Turks and Russia over the Armenian question played a part in the decision of Constantinople to join Germany against Russia in World War I. In November of 1914, Enver Pasha launched an offensive against the Russians on the Caucasus front. Between December, 1914, and January, 1915, the Ottoman army suffered a devastating defeat at the battle of Sarikamis. At the same time, several Russian Armenian leaders urged support for the Russian army. These events produced the climate which enabled the Young Turk leaders to issue orders for the deportation of the entire Armenian population of eastern Anatolia in April of 1915. After the Russian victory, the Armenians could be accused of being security risks.

Even before the military disaster on the Caucasus front, the Armenians became targets for Turkish violence. Mahmud Kâmil, an associate of Ziya Gökalp and a fervent Turkish nationalist, was the commander in chief of the Turkish Third Army which had to face the brunt of the Russian offensive in 1915. Kâmil exaggerated incidents of Armenian resistance and sabotage in his reports to Constantinople. In private, however, he told the German vice-consul at Erzurum, Max Erwin von Scheubner-Richter, that after the war no Armenians would be left in Turkey.

The Ottoman government also organized "Special Organization" units which were recruited from prisons. German officials in Constantinople described these units as early as March of 1915 as "killer units." At least thirty thousand prisoners and brigands were recruited for the

"Special Organization." As early as December of 1914, foreign observers in Anatolia reported the plight of the Armenians in Ardahan, a Russian-Armenian city temporarily occupied by the Turks. At the same time, Armenians in the city of Van in eastern Anatolia reacted to Turkish atrocities by revolting and holding out until the Russians reoccupied Van in September, 1915.

Massive deportations and killings of Armenians were ordered after the military disaster in January 1915. On February 28, 1915, Talaat wrote to Jemal Bey of Adana stressing the need to "exterminate all Armenians." On April 15, 1915, an order was issued by Talaat, Enver, and Nazim Bey, the executive secretary of the ruling elite in Constantinople, which threatened punishment for anyone who attempted to protect Armenians from deportation.

On the night of April 24-25, 1915, hundreds of prominent Armenians were rounded up in Constantinople and killed. In addition, Armenian soldiers in the Ottoman armies were segregated in unarmed labor battalions and then murdered. Other males still living in the various villages of the Ottoman Empire were also killed. Women, children, and the elderly were deported to the deserts of Syria and Mesopotamia. On the way, the refugees were brutalized by Kurdish and Circassian bandits who raped and killed, often with the help of Special Organization or army units. In Syria, governor Cemal Pasha contributed to the misery of the survivors. These killings, together with malnutrition and diseases, resulted in the deaths of at least one million Armenians. When Russian soldiers occupied Armenian towns in eastern Anatolia in 1916, they found only empty communities.

Contemporary reports during World War I from Christian missionaries and German and American officials in the Ottoman Empire confirmed the testimonies of Armenian survivors. The German missionary Johannes Lepsius published reports about the genocide in Germany as early as 1916. The American ambassador in Constantinople, Henry Morgenthau, Sr., repeatedly reported the massacres to Washington. The historian Arnold Toynbee prepared a collection of documents for the British government which led to an official condemnation of the Turks in the British House of Lords.

During the war, the Allies had warned the Turkish leaders of the consequences of their actions against the Armenians. After the war, Turkish military courts condemned to death in absentia Enver, Talaat, Jemal, and Nazim, all of whom had already escaped to Germany. Armenians killed Talaat in Berlin in 1921, and Cemal Pasha in Tiflis in 1922. Enver died in a cavalry charge in 1922 in central Asia.

The attitude of the Turkish leaders after 1919 is well illustrated by reactions to the trial of Mehmed Kemal, governor of Yozgat and inspector of deportations at Konya. The testimony during the trial made it clear that Kemal enthusiastically supported the massacres although he claimed that he was only following the orders of his superiors. A Turkish military court found him guilty and hanged him on April 10, 1919. In October of 1922, however, the Turkish National Assembly in Ankara proclaimed Kemal a "National Martyr." The Armenian genocide was soon forgotten by the Allies who negotiated with the new Turkish leader, Kemal Atatürk. The treaty of Lausanne in 1923, unlike the original treaty of Sévres in 1919, returned the historic Armenian provinces to Turkey. Furthermore, because of the Russian revolution, Turkey regained control over Armenian territories in eastern Anatolia, which it had lost to the Russian empire in 1878. The Armenian genocide became the "forgotten holocaust" of the twentieth century. —*Johnpeter Horst Grill*

ADDITIONAL READING:

Boyajian, Dickran. *Armenia: The Case for a Forgotten Genocide*. Westwood, N.J.: Educational Book Crafters, 1972. A publication of primarily sources which document the origins and implementation of the Armenian genocide.

Dadrian, Vahakn. "The Role of the Special Organization in the Armenian Genocide During the First World War." In *Minorities in Wartime*, edited by Panikos Panayi. Providence, R.I.: Berg, 1993. This informative study examines the origins and activities of special units which were recruited from Ottoman prisons and used in actions against the Armenians.

Hovannisian, Richard G., ed. *The Armenian Genocide: History, Politics, Ethics*. New York: St. Martin's Press, 1992. This collection of fourteen essays by specialists examines various aspects of the Armenian genocide.

_____, ed. *The Armenian Genocide in Perspective*. New Brunswick, N.J.: Transaction Press-Rutgers University, 1986. These eleven multidisciplinary studies of the genocide incorporate findings from sociology, psychiatry, political science, literature, ethics, and history.

_____. *The Armenian Holocaust: A Bibliography Relating to the Deportations, Massacre, and Dispersion of the Armenian People, 1915-1923*. Cambridge, Mass.: Armenian Heritage Press, 1980. This book provides a convenient list of archival resources, collections of documents, and memoirs on the Armenian genocide.

Kloian, Richard D. ed. *The Armenian Genocide: News Accounts from the American Press, 1915-1922*. 3d ed. Berkeley, Calif.: AAC Books, 1985. These photocopies of major American journal and newspaper articles on this topic reveal how well informed the American press was.

Somakian, Manoug. *Empires in Conflict: Armenia and the Great Powers, 1912-1920*. London: Tauris Academic Studies, 1995. This work examines the Armenian question in the context of international relations before and after the genocide.

SEE ALSO: 1853-1856, The Crimean War; 1876, Bulgarian Massacres; 1903-1906, Pogroms in Imperial Russia; 1939-1945, Gypsies Are Exterminated in Nazi Death Camps; 1939-1945, Nazi Extermination of the Jews.

1915

INTERNATIONAL CONGRESS OF WOMEN

The International Congress of Women brings women peace activists together on the eve of the entry of the United States into World War I in an attempt to resolve the war and subsequent disputes through impartial, international mediation.

DATE: April 28 to May 1, 1915

LOCALE: The Hague, the Netherlands

CATEGORIES: Diplomacy and international relations; Social reform; Women's issues

KEY FIGURES:

Jane Addams (1860-1935), American humanitarian and Nobel Peace Prize recipient, 1931

Emily Balch, (1867-1961), American professor, activist, and Nobel Peace Prize recipient, 1946

Henry Ford (1863-1947), American automobile magnate, sponsor of the Ford Peace Ship

Alice Hamilton (1869-1970), expert on industrial medicine, reformer

Rosika Schwimmer (1877-1948), Hungarian pacifist and ambassador who later emigrated to the United States

SUMMARY OF EVENT. Women's opposition to World War I had roots in the Victorian perception of male-female roles, the "coming-of-age" of the first generation of women to have graduated college in large numbers, and the women's suffrage movement. In the Victorian view, motherhood, nurturing, and caring provided the core of a woman's being. Conversely, men were innately martial in spirit and might benefit (even if society did not), in terms of resoluteness and hardening of the manly spirit, from the crucible of war. In the late 1800's and early 1900's, women's caring nature would become sufficient cause to embrace issues beyond the confines of the home. This outreach to the larger society was facilitated by the fact that higher education of women was no longer viewed as a societal extravagance. Education and the maternal instinct combined in the espousal of a host of causes: including child labor, minimum wage, working conditions, pacifism, and women's suffrage. The leap from maternalism, to humanitarianism, to pacifism, to women's suffrage was neither long nor intricate. To ensure the welfare of the child implied activism to elevate society to a higher, more equitable plane. This elevation required an end to war and the full enfranchisement of women to enable the change. The correlation between pacifism and women's issues (feminism) was strong—but sometimes breakable, as World War I would prove.

The onset of World War I in 1914 was of grave concern to humanitarians such as Jane Addams, who, in her desire for a more equitable, less violent society than a free market could produce had hoped that society had progressed beyond the "need" for war. The fomentation of the peace movement in the United States would grow to include conservative groups such as the DAR and YWCA. In 1914, Hungarian feminist Rosika Schwimmer and English peace activist Emmeline Pethic-Lawrence toured the United States, advocating the mediation of the conflict by neutral nations. Together with Jane Addams, Schwimmer founded the Women's Peace Party (WPP) in January, 1915, as a cornerstone about which a better society might be built. The WPP drafted plans for an international conference of neutral interests which gained support from European organizations, such as the International Women's Suffrage Alliance (IWSA).

In February of 1915, Dutch physician Aletta Jacobs and a group of fellow IWSA members from Europe drafted a blanket invitation to an International Congress of Women at The Hague. Financing was forthcoming and Jane Addams, chair of the WPP, agreed to preside. The belligerent countries in World War I were almost uniformly opposed to the conference in neutral Netherlands. In fact, the *Noordam*, the ship carrying the American delegation to the conference was detained in England for four days before being allowed to proceed. Most of the British delegation was restrained from attending while the Germans sent five delegates and allowed five delegates from occupied Belgium to attend. The press in the United States, Britain, and France was hostile, labeling the group pro-Hun, while the American ambassador to Britain likened the *Noordam* to a cage of doves. In the face of imposing governmental barriers, fourteen hundred delegates attended the first session of the conference and twenty-four hundred attended the last. In all, twelve countries with delegates from 150 different organizations were represented.

The American delegation was an illustrious group of forty-seven including physicians (Dr. Alice Hamilton), journalists (Mary Heaton Vorse), social reformers (Elizabeth Gwendover Evans), union leaders (Annie Molloy), and political activists (Belle La Follette). A Canadian-born member of the *Noordam* group, Julia Grace Wales, had proposed a plan under which a group of neutral (non-political) experts would convene to mediate the war—after offering the disputants a menu of proposals which might end the conflict.

The actual meetings at The Hague were full of spirited discussion but constrained by a rigid system of rules of procedure, which galled Addams, more accustomed to the freer give-and-take of American democracy. The press continued to report in a biased manner. The German press accused its delegates of pro-Allied leanings; the British press regarded the conference as offering a pro-German agenda; and much of the nonaligned press reported the meetings as either underattended or terminated by dispute.

Nevertheless, the accomplishments of the conference were significant. The attendants somehow managed to avoid pointing the finger of blame on responsibility for the war or for use of some of the more heinous instruments (poison gas among others) in the war.

Instead, delegates focused on the purpose of the convention: establishment of a peace mechanism. The delegates engaged in considerable philosophical give-and-take with respect to immediate peace or peace with justice; the acceptability or inacceptability of some wars; and the unique role of women in the peace process. The landmark of the meetings, however, was agreement on a set of principles necessary for a lasting peace. Among the conditions agreed upon by the participants were: that conquests should not be recognized by nondisputants; that democracy should be the rule and foreign policy subject to the democratic process; that all governments should agree to submit international disagreements to mediation or arbitration; that nations which resort to arms in resolving disputes should be subject to economic sanctions; and that women deserve political equality with men. President Woodrow Wilson later complemented Addams on the peace proposals and reportedly used them as guidelines in establishing his Fourteen Points.

Additionally, the congress created the International Committee of Women for a Permanent Peace, which was intended to have a role in the postwar peace process. Rosika Schwimmer convinced the congress of the viability of her quixotic notion to physically present the leaders of belligerent and neutral countries with the findings and recommendations of the conference. To that end, Addams, Aletta Jacobs, and Alice Hamilton set off to visit political leaders from France, Austria-Hungary, Germany, Great Britain, Italy, and Belgium. Concurrently, Schwimmer, Emily Balch, and a second group journeyed to Russia and the Scandinavian nations to share the congress' recommendations.

Upon return from The Hague in the summer of 1915, having facilitated communications among belligerants and neutrals, the delegates realized there was little chance for government-sponsored mediation to succeed. There was a possibility, however, that private-sponsored mediation might fill the void. In a move that seemed more fancy than substance, delegate Rebuke Shelley arranged a meeting between American automobile magnate Henry Ford and Rosika Schwimmer, with the goal of obtaining financing for a private war-mediation effort. They made a colorful couple. Ford was self-educated, entrepreneurial, isolationist, and anti-Semitic in his preferences. Schwimmer was European, Jewish, educated, radical—practically the antithesis of Ford.

Surprisingly, Ford agreed to fund a new venture by the Women's International Committee to bring the instrument of independent mediation to all concerned parties. Previously, Ford had unsuccessfully tried to get President Wilson to accept the idea of a mediated peace. Undeterred, Henry Ford chartered the ocean liner *Oscar II*, quickly dubbed the Peace Ship, to transport the American delegation abroad. Sailing on December 4, 1915, the American contingent consisted of fifty-seven delegates from a spectrum of vocations, a clutch of animated reporters, and more than a few hangers-on wishing to benefit from an all expenses paid ocean vacation. The voyage did not proceed as smoothly as the congress at The Hague. Instead, bickering, political infighting, and mistrust were fueled by ever-skeptical reporters in search of a story. Upon reaching Europe, the delegates found their input unwelcome in what was regarded as a European affair. Wilson's call for military preparedness in the face of aggression had weakened the American peace movement. On December 21, Ford returned home, claiming illness. The Peace Ship had failed, yet it had succeeded in convening a conference of neutrals: the Neutral Conference for Continuous Mediation, conceived in Stockholm, funded by Ford, and convened in January, 1916. This six-nation group conducted studies, authored peace proposals, and was willing to put itself in the service of belligerents. German resumption of full-scale submarine warfare and Ford's withdrawal of funds, however, led to the conference's demise in the summer of 1916.

—*John A. Sondey*

ADDITIONAL READING:

Chatfield, Charles. *For Peace and Justice*. Knoxville: University of Tennessee Press, 1971. A well-documented, readable text that provides insight into the American pacifist movement from 1914 to World War II.

Elshtain, Jean Bethke, and Sheila Tobias, eds. *Women Militarism and War*. Savage, Md.: Rowan & Littlefield, 1990. A collection of essays in the politics and social theory of the feminist movement in its focus on war and pacifism.

Lundarini, Christine A. *The American Peace Movement in the Twentieth Century*. Santa Barbara, Calif.: ABC-Clio, 1994. A useful, instructive, alphabetically arranged compendium of historical factors in the American peace movement.

Randall, Mercedes. *Improper Bostonian*. New York: Twayne, 1964. An excellent biography of Emily Balch, professor, reformer, humanitarian, and pacifist.

Schneider, Carl J., and Dorothy Schneider. *Into the Breach*. A full and engaging record of American women in service during World War I, one that includes women at or against war.

SEE ALSO: 1882, First Birth Control Clinic Is Established in Amsterdam; 1899, First Hague Peace Conference; 1907, Second Hague Peace Conference; 1914, Germany Begins Extensive Submarine Warfare; 1919, The League of Nations Is Established.

1916
BATTLE OF VERDUN

The Battle of Verdun begins as part of a German plan to force surrender of France through excessive losses, but inflicts heavy costs on both sides.

DATE: February 21-summer, 1916
LOCALE: Verdun, France
CATEGORY: Wars, uprisings, and civil unrest
KEY FIGURES:

General Noël-Marie-Joseph-Édouard de Curières de Castelnau (1851-1944), chief of staff to General Joffre

General Erich Georg Anton Sebastian von Falkenhayn (1861-1936), chief of general staff of the German army, 1914-1916

General Joseph-Jacques-Césaire Joffre (1852-1931), commander in chief of the French armies

General Schmidt von Knobelsdorf, chief of staff to the crown prince

General Robert-Georges Nivelle (1856-1924), commander of the French Second Army

General Henri Philippe Pétain (1856-1951), commander of French forces at Verdun

William II (1859-1941), emperor of Germany, 1888-1918

William (Friedrich Wilhelm Viktor August Ernst; 1882-1951), crown prince of Germany and commander of the German Fifth Army

SUMMARY OF EVENT. When Allied and German forces reached a stalemate on the western front following the Battle of the Marne in 1914, they prepared different strategies. The French and the British tried to break through the German lines and repeatedly attacked German defenses along the hastily fortified northern portion of the front, but the German lines held despite bloody assaults at Ypres and elsewhere. In contrast, the Germans held to their defensive positions. They realized the great cost in troops spent on offensives in such a position war and chose to concentrate on an offensive in the East where they routed the Russian armies.

Sensing the effect that the loss of men was having on Allied forces, General Erich Georg Anton Sebastian von Falkenhayn, the chief of the General Staff of the German army, approached Emperor William II with a plan late in 1915. Falkenhayn suggested hurling an army against a fortified French position that the French could not surrender without a great loss of prestige. This hesitancy to lose such a position would force France to defend the position. In the process of defending such a position, Falkenhayn calculated that France would suffer such tremendous losses it would be forced to surrender. The plan was designed to inflict French casualties rather than to capture strategic positions. The emperor approved the plan, and the fortress town of Verdun was selected as the target.

Verdun, a small town ringed with fortresses, was in a salient and could be attacked on three sides. A fortified city, Verdun was 125 miles east of Paris and 40 miles from the German fortress of Metz. While the French valued Verdun as a defensive position, they did not believe a massive German attack on the city was likely. Indeed, shortly before the attack the French military command began moving supplies from Verdun to what were believed to be more threatened positions. Falkenhayn's plan called for the German army, led by Crown Prince William, to attack the ring of the fortress. German troops would then be supplied to the crown prince at a rate to ensure the attack kept pace, but not in sufficient numbers to enable a breakthrough by German forces. Neither the crown prince nor his chief of staff, General Schmidt von Knobelsdorf, was told anything about the design of the attack. Like their men, they believed that the assault was designed to achieve a military breakthrough. Falkenhayn was convinced that the plan would "bleed the French army white" and force them to negotiate with Germany. The German plan was code-named "Gericht," German for "a place of execution."

The German attack began with a massive artillery barrage on February 21, 1916. More than one million German shells pounded the French fortifications. A force of

WORLD WAR I: WESTERN FRONT, 1914-1917

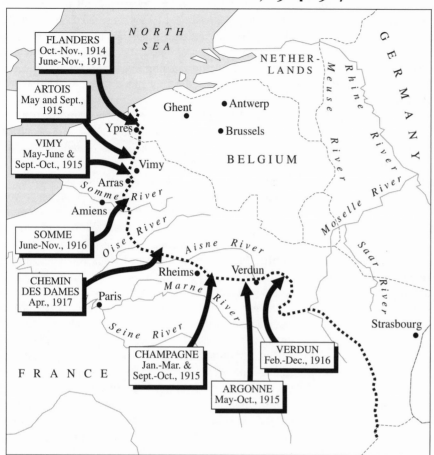

troops moved into the area to stop the German advance, supplies became jammed because German forces had managed to cut the southern and western rail links to the city. Transport was of utmost importance and the only access the French possessed were a narrow gauge railway and one small road. Pétain ordered the road rebuilt and organized a massive motorized supply column of more than three thousand trucks per day to supply French forces. The road became a critical supply route during the ten month battle and became known to the French as the "voie sacree" or "sacred path."

The crown prince and Knobelsdorf attempted to break through the French lines but were hampered by Falkenhayn's limitations on the number of troops as well as Pétain's organized defense. The Germans soon realized that their casualties began to equal and at times exceed those of the French. By mid-April, Pétain moved to the offensive, and Falkenhayn found that he had extended his troops into a danger-

140,000 German infantrymen attacked the French positions. The German troops made some early gains and captured a few of the key fortresses. German gas attacks on the first day of battle prompted the French to launch gas attacks on the advancing German forces. General Joseph-Jacques-Césaire Joffre, commander in chief of the French armies, and his chief of staff, General Noël-Marie-Joseph-Édouard de Curières de Castelnau, reacted as Falkenhayn had predicted. The French command concluded that Verdun was to be held at all costs and moved the French Second Army under General Henri Philippe Pétain to the defense of Verdun. A number of leaders in the French military believed that a German attack on Verdun would prove to be a strategic and military victory for the French. Before the battle, Joffre seemed to welcome the opportunity to confront the Germans at Verdun. He said "I ask only one thing, and this is that the Germans will attack me and if they do attack me, that it will be at Verdun."

Pétain immediately realized that the main problem was to keep Verdun supplied with troops and material. As

ous position. German prestige now demanded the capture of Verdun. In June, the Germans almost broke through the French lines, but French forces held firm. Complicating matters for the Germans was the British attack on the Somme which began in midsummer. German troops had to be pulled away from the Verdun sector to counter the Allied offensive. As the summer turned to fall, the fighting degenerated into vicious attacks and counterattacks amid the misery of trench warfare.

Pétain was elevated to commander of the entire central front and General Robert-Georges Nivelle was placed in command of the French Second Army. Like the Germans, the French now saw Verdun as a test of national will. Despite the fact that Verdun was never of great strategic importance to the French, political leaders now directed the military to hold the line at Verdun despite the tremendous loss of life. Aristide Briand, the French prime minister, told Joffre and his staff, "If you surrender at Verdun, you will be cowards, cowards. And you needn't wait till then to hand in your resignation. If you abandon Verdun, I sack you all on the spot." General Nivelle led a series of French counterattacks in the late summer and fall. By December, 1916, the exhausted German army gave up their positions and the Battle of Verdun was over.

The French had held the city, but the sacrifice was enormous. It was the longest and most costly battle of World War I. Militarily, the ten months of fighting were inconclusive. Both the Germans and the French failed to deliver a decisive strategic blow to end the battle. The French sustained five hundred thousand casualties and the Germans four hundred thousand. The battle also affected the futures of the commanders of both sides. Falkenhayn was dismissed and General Paul von Hindenberg succeeded him. Nivelle, covered with glory, attempted to repeat his performance at the Battle of the Aisne in 1917, which ended with disastrous results and a mutiny that almost broke the French army. Pétain gained the greatest prestige, eventually replacing Joffre as commander in chief of the French armies and later becoming the marshal of France. The psychological damage to the Germans was great, and for the French, Verdun became the outstanding symbol of French resistance and a factor in France's military defeat in 1940.

—*José M. Sánchez, updated by Lawrence I. Clark*

ADDITIONAL READING:

Gilbert, Martin. *The First World War: A Complete History*. New York: Henry Holt, 1994. A companion to his history of World War II, Gilbert provides thorough account of the diplomacy and battles of World War I.

Marshall, Samuel L. A. "Ordeal of Nations." In *World War I*. New York: American Heritage, 1985. Written by an American general, the chapter is a brief introduction to Verdun and other ill-fated battles designed by generals to deliver a decisive blow and bring the "Great War" to a close.

Winter, J. M. "1916-17—The Great Slaughter." In *The Experience of World War I*. New York: Oxford University Press, 1989. A valuable introduction to the Battle of Verdun that includes a chronology, photographs, and maps detailing the attacks and counterattacks.

SEE ALSO: 1914, Outbreak of World War I; 1914, First Battle of the Marne; 1916, Battle of Jutland; 1919, Treaty of Versailles.

1916
EASTER REBELLION

The Easter Rebellion against Britain fails, but it persuades the Irish people to seek freedom from British rule.

DATE: April 24-April 29, 1916
LOCALE: Dublin, Ireland
CATEGORIES: Government and politics; Wars, uprisings, and civil unrest
KEY FIGURES:
Augustine Birrell (1850-1933), chief secretary for Ireland
Sir Roger Casement (1864-1916), former British diplomat
Thomas Clarke (1857-1916), veteran from earlier rebellions
James Connolly (1868-1916), union official and military leader of 1916 rebellion
Ivor Churchill Guest, Baron Wimborne (1873-1939), lord-lieutenant of Ireland
General Sir John Maxwell (1859-1929), British commander who ended the rebellion
Patrick Pearse (1879-1916), chief spokesman for the rebellion

SUMMARY OF EVENT. On the Monday after Easter, 1916, several hundred Irishmen and Irishwomen began a rebellion against the British empire. The rising lasted until the following Saturday when, after considerable death and destruction, the survivors surrendered. The leaders were quickly executed, but within six years an independent Ireland came into existence; paradoxically from defeat came victory.

England's power and influence had hung over Ireland for hundreds of years, and throughout the nineteenth century many demanded greater independence for Ireland. Some were primarily peaceful and political—Daniel O'Connell and Charles Stewart Parnell—but some were violent, such as the Fenians of the 1860's. In 1910, with the British parliament deadlocked, the Liberal government promised the Irish delegates to introduce greater home rule in exchange for their support.

Opposition came mainly from Protestants in Ulster, fearing for their future in a largely Catholic Ireland. Forming a volunteer army, they were prepared to go to war against the British government in order to remain British. Their example inspired home rulers and Irish nationalists in the south to form their own volunteer movement to support home rule. When World War I began in August of 1914, Ireland was divided into two armed camps. Home rule became law, but its implementation was postponed until the war's end.

With the outbreak of war, many Irishmen, both Protestant and Catholic, joined the British army. Yet under the maxim that England's difficulty was Ireland's opportunity, a small group, connected to the old Fenian movement through the secret Irish Republican Brotherhood (IRB), infiltrated the remnant opposed to participating in a British war and began to plan a rising against Britain. The IRB's beliefs were exemplified in 1915 by Patrick Pearse, schoolteacher and poet who, at the Dublin funeral for an old Fenian, cried out that Ireland unfree could never be at peace.

The IRB leadership hoped to rely upon as many as ten thousand volunteers, and planned that weapons, even soldiers, would come from Germany, Britain's enemy. Sir Roger Casement, British diplomat turned Irish rebel, journeyed to Germany, but the German government promised only some weapons. Casement was captured on Good Friday before Easter after secretly returning to Ireland, and the German submarine carrying twenty thousand guns was scuttled when discovered by the British.

The uprising was planned for Easter Sunday, the resurrection of Ireland parallelling the resurrection of Christ. The head of the volunteers, Eoin MacNeill, was not part of the IRB, however, and when he heard of the proposed rebellion and that Casement had been captured, he can-

celed scheduled maneuvers. Yet the inner group decided to go ahead, a day late; thus about noon, on Monday, April 24, hundreds of rebels took to the streets of Dublin and quickly occupied several preselected sites, trusting that once the rising began others would join. As they marched forth that Monday, however, they could not have been overly optimistic. James Connolly, union leader with his own Citizens Army and only recently made privy to the IRB plans, commented that they were all going out to be slaughtered.

Among the several locations occupied by the small band of rebels—only about one thousand men and women took part—was the General Post Office (GPO), an imposing structure on Sackville Street, in the heart of Dublin. Shortly after noon, Patrick Pearse read the Proclamation of the Republic, beginning with the emotive words, "In the name of God and of the dead generations from which she receives her old tradition of nationhood, Ireland, through us, summons her children to her flag and strikes for her freedom." In addition to Pearse and Connolly, it was

Irish insurgents built strategic barricades on the streets of Dublin at the beginning of the Easter Rebellion. (Popperfoto/Archive Photos)

signed by Thomas Clarke, who had spent years in English jails, Joseph Plunkett, Sean MacDermott, Eamonn Ceannt, and Thomas MacDonagh. There were a few cheers from onlookers but mostly just curiosity, amusement, or even outright hostility: Irishmen were serving in the British army in Flanders and to many the rebel action was a cowardly stab in the back.

The British authorities were caught off balance. They had information about a rumored rebellion, but Casement was in jail, the German submarine was sunk, and MacNeill's cancellation of Easter Sunday's mobilization cast doubt upon any immediate threat. Monday was a holiday, and many of the British troops stationed in Dublin were out of the city. The chief secretary for Ireland, Augustine Birrell, who had doubted any threat, was away in London. Baron Wimborne, the lord-lieutenant and the king's representative in Ireland, wished for a stronger response to the rumors of rebellion, but before action could be taken, the rebels had occupied not only the GPO, but also the Four Courts along the River Liffey, St. Stephen's Green, and other positions, mostly on the south side of the city which could interdict any British support troops arriving by sea.

Lacking any creative strategy, the republicans merely occupied key places and waited, hoping for the best—a popular uprising by the populace of Dublin and throughout Ireland, a reversal of the German decision not to send troops, or a British collapse. All were unlikely, and none materialized. There were a few minor skirmishes elsewhere, but they had little effect. The Irish population did not rise up in support.

The British general staff preferred a cautionary approach, isolating the various rebel locations, wearing them down by attrition rather than frontal assaults against entrenched positions. Still, there were British casualties, most notably on Northumberland Road and Lower Mount Street where a small detachment of Irish rebels fired from nearby houses, decimating an inexperienced British force, causing about two hundred casualties. There were probing attacks by the British, but mainly they resorted to artillery against the rebel outposts.

Republican morale remained high, but superior force began to tell. At the GPO and Sackville Street, where the Republic's proclamation was first read, the destruction was the greatest. By Friday, British artillery had such an effect that the building was in danger of being engulfed by fire. Although Connolly had been shot twice on Thursday, most seriously in the ankle by a ricocheting bullet, the rebels had suffered relatively few casualties because of their defensive strategy. Pearse issued a statement on Friday morning, noting that "If we accomplish no more than we have accomplished, I am satisfied. I am satisfied that

we have saved Ireland's honour." Early on Saturday, concluding that the GPO must be abandoned, the rebels escaped into side streets to the north, but retreat was no longer possible, and at 12:45 P.M. a young nurse was sent out under a white flag to seek a truce. The British authorities would accept nothing less than unconditional surrender. At 3:45 P.M. on Saturday, April 29, Pearse signed the surrender document. Bypassed by the British, some of the rebel locations which had seen little fighting were reluctant to surrender, but did so.

Officially, 1,353 individuals were reported killed during the rising, with losses greater among the British soldiers than the rebels. Property damage was immense. None of the signers of the Proclamation had been killed, but the British commander, General Sir John Maxwell, established courts-martial to try the leaders for rebellion in time of war. On May 3, Pearse, Clarke, and MacDonagh were shot at Kilmainham Jail, and on the following day Plunkett, married in the jail chapel only a few hours earlier, and three others followed. More executions occurred, the last on May 12 with Connolly and MacDermott, a total of fifteen in all. Casement was hanged in August in Britain. As the executions dragged on, opinion changed in support of the rebels. Pearse, Connolly, and the others did not intend merely to make a blood sacrifice, but as martyrs they were more influential dead than alive. War broke out again in 1919, and in 1922 the Irish Free State came into being.

—Eugene Larson

ADDITIONAL READING:

Boyce, D. G., ed. *The Revolution in Ireland, 1879-1923*. London: Macmillan, 1988. A collection of articles with the Easter Uprising as a focus.

Caufield, Max. *The Easter Rebellion*. Reprint. Boulder, Colo.: Roberts Rinehart, 1995. First published in 1965, this is the most complete narrative.

Edwards, Ruth Dudley. *Patrick Pearse*. London: Victor Gollancz, 1977. A sympathetic but not uncritical analysis, subtitled "The Triumph of Failure."

Foster, R. F. *Modern Ireland, 1600-1972*. London: Penguin, 1988. Includes a scholarly and readable account of the rebellion by a leading scholar.

Lee, J. J. *Ireland, 1912-1985*. New York: Cambridge University Press, 1989. A valuable interpretative discussion of the causes and results of the rebellion.

SEE ALSO: 1800, Act of Union Is Passed by Parliament; 1828-1829, Emancipation Acts of 1828 and 1829; 1845-1854, Irish Famine and the Great Emigration; 1912-1914, Irish Home Rule Bill; 1932, Eamon de Valera Is Elected President of the Irish Dáil.

1916

BATTLE OF JUTLAND

The Battle of Jutland establishes the decisive superiority of the British Grand Fleet over its rival, the German High Seas Fleet, despite heavy British losses in ships and men.

DATE: May 31, 1916

LOCALE: The North Sea

CATEGORY: Wars, uprisings, and civil unrest

KEY FIGURES:

Vice Admiral Sir David Beatty (1871-1936), commander of the British Battle Cruiser Fleet

Vice Admiral Franz von Hipper, commander of German scouting forces

Admiral Sir John Rushworth Jellicoe (1859-1935), commander of the British Grand Fleet

Vice Admiral Reinhard Scheer (1863-1928), commander of the German High Seas Fleet

SUMMARY OF EVENT. Early in 1916, the German Naval Staff decided to undertake an offensive campaign against the British Grand Fleet in the North Sea. Vice Admiral Reinhard Scheer, commander of the German High Seas Fleet of twenty-three dreadnoughts, realized that he could conduct only limited operations against the British Grand Fleet of forty-two dreadnoughts under the command of Admiral Sir John Rushworth Jellicoe. So Scheer planned to lay minefields off the British naval bases and then lure the Grand Fleet out to sea. If German U-boats could take their toll of British battleships, Scheer imagined that he could offer battle on more equal terms.

At the same time, the British became more aggressive. They wanted to attack the Zeppelin bases in northern Germany and also support the Russian navy in the Baltic. They, too, hoped to lure the enemy fleet out to battle in the North Sea.

Minor sorties began in March, 1916. German battle cruisers bombarded a few British towns without inflicting or receiving much damage. The British bombarded selected targets in Germany with even less effect. At the end of May, Scheer took his fleet out to sea, with Vice Admiral Franz von Hipper scouting ahead with battle cruisers; fourteen U-boats were operating off British bases, and Scheer's strategy was to attack British shipping off the Norwegian coast in the hope that the British would take to sea in force. The plan was put into effect when the British intercepted a coded wireless signal which, they believed, indicated the prelude to a German advance. On the evening of May 30, the British Grand Fleet proceeded to sea from Scapa Flow, Invergordon, and Rosyth. They evaded Scheer's submarines and mines without difficulty, and the

Battle Cruiser Fleet under the command of Vice Admiral Sir David Beatty went ahead southeastward searching for the Germans.

On May 31, light cruisers of the British and German scouting forces came into chance contact, and at 2:18 P.M. they guided the heavy ships into action. At 3:48 P.M., the battle cruisers opened fire, and Hipper retired with his five ships toward the main German force under Scheer. Beatty pursued him with six cruisers supported by four fast battleships. A fierce and resolute action developed. Accurate German gunfire and weak British protection led to the destruction of two of Beatty's cruisers, which exploded with almost no survivors. Scheer arrived on the scene at 4:48 P.M. and, led by Hipper, chased Beatty northward. Jellicoe hurried southward with twenty-four battleships and joined forces with Beatty; together, they turned on the Germans. Between 6:30 P.M. and 6:45 P.M., the two battle fleets exchanged salvos briefly. The Germans blew up a third battle cruiser. The British built up a superior concentration of gunfire on Scheer's battleships, but he skillfully reversed course, laid down a smoke screen, and escaped serious damage, although one of Hipper's battle cruisers was so battered that it had to be sunk later. Once again Scheer returned to the attack but was forced to withdraw at 7:20 P.M. He covered his retreat with an attack by destroyers, from which Jellicoe, with great circumspection, turned away. The main bodies of the two fleets were now separated.

When darkness fell, Scheer firmly led his smaller, slower fleet homeward. By a remarkable combination of accurate gunfire and quick maneuvering, he succeeded during the night in cutting through the British destroyer flotillas to the rear of Jellicoe's battleships, and reached the safety of his mined home waters early the next morning. The battle was over. The British had lost fourteen ships, including three battle cruisers totaling 110,000 tons, and more than 6,200 men had been killed or taken prisoner. The Germans had lost eleven ships totaling 62,000 tons, including one battle cruiser and one battleship, and 2,500 men had been killed. Neither side had won a victory because the battle had done little to change the relative strengths of the two fleets.

The battle had thus fallen into five distinct segments. The first was the battle cruiser action during which Beatty pursued Scheer's force south. This was followed by Beatty's dash north after the encounter with Hipper's main battle fleet; the dual purpose was to protect the battle cruisers and simultaneously lure the High Seas Fleet within Jellicoe's range. The encounter between the two main battle fleets did indeed occur in two brief, destructive but essentially inconclusive actions. Once the two battle lines separated there remained only a confused series of night actions between the lighter ships, during which time Hipper's forces escaped to their home ports.

The statistics of the battle at first appeared to be in Germany's favor: for the loss of one modern battleship and one "pre-dreadnought" along with some smaller vessels, the High Seas Fleet had sunk three armored cruisers, eight destroyers, and three battleships. In strategic terms, however, Jutland was a British victory, even though its effects were long delayed. The Grand Fleet remained intact; upon his return to port, Jellicoe signaled the Admiralty that he could steam at four hours' notice. By contrast, Hipper's High Seas Fleet was so battered, morally as well as physically, that it hardly dared venture out for the remainder of the war.

After Jutland, Jellicoe abandoned his attacks on the German coast and instead sat back to await the reappearance of the Germans. In August, Scheer obliged, intending to bombard the British coast again. Once more his submarines lay in ambush. Forewarned again by the Germans' careless use of radio, the British came out to intercept. Scheer was then turned away from his objective by an erroneous report from a scouting zeppelin. He turned away from Jellicoe to pursue an isolated British squadron, which itself turned away from him. No contact was made, and both sides returned to their bases. The British had lost two light cruisers to German submarines, and the Germans suffered damage to one dreadnought. Scheer came out a third time in October, and that time the British Grand Fleet remained in port.

The German naval offensive of 1916 was essentially a failure. The German strategy had been to inflict unacceptable damage to the British fleet, thus severing that island nation's links to the outside world. The Germans relied upon a belief in the technical superiority of its ships over those of the British, especially in the vital area of armored protection, and also upon their willingness to risk their fleet in an all-out naval engagement. As Jutland and its aftermath demonstrated, German material superiority was real but not decisive, while the kaiser and his commanders clearly lacked the nerve to place again in harm's way the fleet which had cost them so dear and meant so much.

German hopes of sinking British dreadnoughts by mines or submarines were dashed, and the Germans themselves lost five capital ships to British mines and submarines. The reasons for the British successes were largely geographical. The shallow waters off the German coast were easy to mine, and German ships had to put to sea through the right angle formed by the German and Danish coasts. The exits from the British bases were broader, and the

British coastal waters were deeper, making them more difficult to mine effectively. The failure of Scheer's maritime guerrilla tactics led him to abandon his campaign in the North Sea. He did make a final bid for victory in November, 1918, but the German naval crews could not forget the Battle of Jutland. They refused to weigh anchor, and the final result of this mutinous outbreak and others was demonstrated on November 21, 1918, when Beatty received the surrender of the greater part of the German High Seas Fleet.

—*Samuel K. Eddy, updated by Michael Witkoski*

ADDITIONAL READING:

Costello, John. *Jutland, 1916*. New York: Holt, Rinehart and Winston, 1977. A very accessible and readable account of the engagement.

Halpern, Paul. *A Naval History of World War I*. Annapolis, Md.: Naval Institute Press, 1994. The chapter on the battle is clearly presented and incisive. Places the battle within the context of the larger struggle.

Hough, Richard. *The Great War at Sea: 1914-1918*. New York: Oxford University Press, 1983. Places the battle of Jutland and its aftermath within the larger confines of the Anglo-Germany naval rivalry as well as the war itself.

Keegan, John. *The Price of Admiralty: The Evolution of Naval Warfare*. New York: Viking, 1988. The chapter on Jutland is an outstanding example of military history at its finest.

Roskill, Stephen. *Admiral of the Fleet—Earl Beatty, the Last Naval Hero: An Intimate Biography*. New York: Atheneum, 1981. Presents a generally favorable yet fair picture of Beatty's pivotal role as commander of the British battle cruiser force at Jutland.

SEE ALSO: 1889, Great Britain Strengthens the Royal Navy; 1906, Launching of the *Dreadnought*; 1914, Germany Begins Extensive Submarine Warfare.

1917-1920
UKRAINIAN NATIONALISTS STRUGGLE FOR INDEPENDENCE

Ukrainian nationalists struggle for independence in the wake of the collapse of the czarist government and the October Revolution, but fail in their bid for autonomous statehood.

DATE: 1917-1920
LOCALE: Ukraine
CATEGORIES: Government and politics; Wars, uprisings, and civil unrest

KEY FIGURES:

Vladimir Alexandrovich Antonov-Ovseenko (1884-1934), revolutionary in Russia and Red Army officer who organized the Soviet army in the Ukraine

Anton Ivanovich Denikin (1872-1947), leader of the White armies in southern Russia during Russia's civil wars

Simon Vasilevich Petliura (1879-1926), French-backed Socialist leader of the Rada who was overthrown by the Reds in 1919

Józef Piłsudski (1867-1935), president of the new Poland that expanded into East Galicia, claimed by Ukraine

Khristian Georgievich Rakovsky (1873-1941), leader of the Bolshevik government in Kharkov

Pavel Petrovich Skoropadsky (1873-1945), Cossack hetman installed as president of Ukraine by the German occupiers in 1918

Volodimir Kirilovich Vinnichenko (1880-1951), co-leader of the Directory with Petliura

SUMMARY OF EVENT. Russia's new Time of Troubles, 1917-1921, involved foreign interventionist armies, civil wars among Russians, and wars of national liberation. One of the last was the Ukrainian bid for independence that began weeks after Bolsheviks seized St. Petersburg in November, 1917. The attempt to establish a separate Ukraine was made difficult by the Russian White forces that invaded the Ukraine under Anton Denikin from the Southeast in the name of imperial unity, by the occupying German armies which set up a puppet state under Hetman Pavel Skoropadsky, by the French armies in the Ukrainian port of Odessa, by the forces of newly independent Poland under Marshal Józef Piłsudski who seized the Western Ukrainian territories, and by the civil strife among Ukrainian parties.

An unrepresentative Ukrainian government called the Central Rada was set up in Kiev in March, 1917. Following the Bolshevik coup in St. Petersburg, the Rada desired a People's Republic within a Russian Federation. When the Rada allowed rebel Cossacks to cross its borders with impunity, Vladimir Lenin's government regarded that as a hostile act and responded with armed force that was resisted by the Ukrainians in the so-called Railway War. Russian forces moved into Kharkov using that Ukrainian city as a base from which to attack the White armies to the east and Ukrainians to the west. Disagreements within the Communist Party in Russia on how to deal with the Ukraine led to further confusion, but in December, the government of Lenin sent an ultimatum to Kiev to cease disarming Red Guard detachments and support the military campaign against the Whites. When the Ukrainian Congress of Soviets met in Kiev the delegates overwhelmingly supported the Rada and rejected the ultimatum. By the end of December, however, most Ukrainian towns, including Odessa, had fallen to the Red armies and only Kiev held out. Bolshevik agitators infiltrated the Rada forces led by Simon Petliura and on February 8, 1918, Bolshevik armies entered Kiev to reassert Russian control over the thirty-two million "Little Russians." In truth, Ukrainians were less than enthusiastic about independence since national feelings had not penetrated the peasant villages, and in the cities were large numbers of Great Russians and Jews. The Bolsheviks were not popular either, although they did manage to seize the moment to take more decisive actions.

The Germans, still fighting in World War I on the eastern front, sought to make a protectorate over the Ukraine. On February 12, 1918, the Central Powers (Germany and Austria-Hungary) signed a separate treaty of peace with the Ukrainian Rada in exile, sent an occupying army into the country, and were welcomed by some people anxious to restore order and prevent the Russian Bolsheviks from maintaining control. In March the Central Powers signed a treaty with Russia at Brest and compelled the Russians to withdraw from the Ukraine. Meanwhile, German armies continued to advance deep into Ukrainian and Russian lands, taking Kharkov on April 8, the Donbas region by April 29, and Sevastopol naval base on May day. The Rada, overthrown by Bolsheviks, restored by Germans, was soon (April 29) ousted by the Germans in favor of Hetman Pavel Skoropadsky who headed a puppet state supplying the Central Powers with much needed materials.

The Rada had been popular at least among the urban working classes but Skoropadsky's regime found less support. Consequently, when the armistice was signed ending World War I in November, 1918, the armies of the Central Powers evacuated the Ukraine and one month later the nationalists sent Skoropadsky packing to Germany; the Rada returned as the Directory under Simon Petliura and Volodimir Vinnichenko. Yet this nationalist government, calling itself the Ukrainian People's Government, was hampered by divisions in its ranks and fell prey to advancing Red armies from Russia. Although by the spring of 1919, the latter successfully removed the Directory leaders, by then much of the country had been overrun by the White armies of Denikin, who was also hostile to Ukrainian independence. After a year of fighting, Soviet armies had defeated the White forces and ensured that most of the Ukraine was again subservient to Russia. Vladimir Antonov-Ovseenko, the veteran revolutionary who arrested the provisional government in St. Petersburg in

The New York Times.

After the abdication of Czar Nicholas II in March of 1917, the province of Ukraine established an independent government known as the Central Rada in the city of Kiev. (Archive Photos)

November, 1917, organized the Ukrainian Soviet Army as the Bolsheviks established their own capital at Kharkov under G. L. Piatakov and Khristian Rakovsky. Their refusal to share power with other radical parties and their policy of requisitioning grain from the villagers ensured that support for the Bolsheviks would be minimal. Petliura mounted a counteroffensive in the West and briefly retook Kiev but monarchists and Whites (especially the Don Cossacks), took Kharkov from the Bolsheviks and arrived in Kiev to frustrate attempts at Ukrainian national unity, carrying out vicious pogroms against the Jewish communities. French armies in Odessa tried to protect that city against both Whites and Reds, rendering some support to Petliura. After the French withdrew, White forces took Odessa, and Ekaterinoslav, then crossed the Dnieper and chased Petliura westward where his troops were caught in the so-called triangle of death among hostile Polish, Russian, and White armies.

By June, 1919, the new Moscow government reversed itself by abandoning national armies in favor of centralized administrations, civil and military. Leon Trotsky told the Red armies that their duty was not to conquer, but liberate the Ukraine from German allies in the Rada. Meanwhile, Marshal Józef Piłsudski, the hero of Poland

reborn, invaded the western Ukraine and even captured Kiev by May, 1920. Making a deal with Petliura to take eastern Galicia from Ukraine, Piłsudski hoped that the forces of Petliura could be restored to power, but the nationalists of the Rada were no more popular than before and so were little help to the Poles. The resulting Russian-Polish war was a see-saw contest between the Polish leader and the armies of Marshal Mikhail Tukhashevsky who brought his Russian forces to the outskirts of Warsaw only to be pushed back again. The Treaty of Riga in March, 1921, left the west Ukraine in Polish control. Ukrainian resistance to Bolshevik rule ceased since there was too little support from the rank and file peasantry for a nationalist government and no national army of consequence remained. All leftist parties merged with the Reds, and Moscow controlled the Communist Party of the Ukraine.

In the end, the Russian government retained control of this large Slavic region. To many Russian historians, this episode was part of the historic struggle between North and South, the latter the traditional haven for rebels. To others, it was continued evidence of foreign interference in the internal life of the Russian land. Although Lenin had supported the principle of self-determination of all nations, he was surprised when some nationalities opted to take the Bolshevik slogan of The Declaration of Rights of Nations seriously and leave the new proletarian state. Lenin argued that such societies were unrepresentative of the working class; hence the justification to use force against those separatists. If Ukrainian nationalism was yet too weakly perceived in that region, the folklore emanating from the revolution helped to create a deeper feeling of nationhood in succeeding years.

—John D. Windhausen

ADDITIONAL READING:

Iroshnikov, M., D. Kovalenko, and V. Shishkin. *Genesis of the Soviet Federative State (1917-1921)*. Moscow: Progress, 1982. The authors provide a standard Soviet view of Ukrainian upheavals resulting from bourgeois class interests and leading to the triumph of Lenin's nationalist principles.

Lincoln, W. Bruce. *Red Victory: A History of the Russian Civil War*. New York: Simon & Schuster, 1989. As with other works by this master narrator, this book demonstrates that drama and scholarship are compatible. He agrees with Reshetar's conclusion below.

Mawdsley, Evan. *The Russian Civil War*. Boston: Allen & Unwin, 1987. A clear account of these troubles wherein the writer explains Russia's success by the favorable offer of some state independence coupled with centralization of the Soviet military and the party.

Pipes, Richard. *The Formation of the Soviet Union*. Rev. ed. New York: Atheneum, 1974. A classic account by the eminent Harvard historian who noted that divisions both in Kiev and in Moscow led to the tragic results.

Reshetar, John S., Jr. *The Ukrainian Revolution, 1917-20*. Princeton, N.J.: Princeton University Press, 1952. The author argues persuasively that the fundamental failure of Ukraine's bid for independence can be traced to the weak feelings of nationhood among the vast peasantry.

SEE ALSO: 1903-1906, Pogroms in Imperial Russia; 1917, October Revolution; 1917, Finland Gains Independence; 1918-1920, Baltic States Fight for Independence; 1918-1921, Russian Civil War.

1917

OCTOBER REVOLUTION

The October Revolution allows the Bolshevik Party to seize power from a weak coalition of liberals and moderate socialists and establish a Communist dictatorship.

DATE: November 6-7, 1917
LOCALE: Petrograd (formerly St. Petersburg), Russia

CATEGORY: Government and politics
KEY FIGURES:

Feliks Edmundovich Dzerzhinski (1877-1926), leading Bolshevik, head of the Cheka

Aleksandr Fyodorovich Kerensky (1881-1970), revolutionary leader, a Socialist revolutionary, successively minister of justice and minister of war in the provisional government, and premier, July-November 7, 1917

General Lavr Georgyevich Kornilov (1870-1918), supreme commander, July-September, 1917

Vladimir Ilich Lenin (Ulyanov; 1870-1924, leader of the Bolsheviks, head of the Soviet of People's Commissars

Prince Georgy Yevgenyevich Lvov (1861-1925), premier of the provisional government, March-July, 1917

Nicholas II (1868-1917), last czar of Russia, 1894-1917

Joseph Stalin (Iosif Vissarionovich Dzhugashvili; 1879-1953), leading Bolshevik, commissar for national minorities

Leon Trotsky (Leib Davydovich Bronstein; 1879-1940), leading Bolshevik, chairman of the Petrograd Soviet and commissar for foreign affairs

SUMMARY OF EVENT. The October Revolution of the Bolsheviks took place on November 6-7 (or October 24-25 by the Julian calendar), 1917. It was the second revolution to happen in Russia that year, and by it Vladimir Ilich Lenin, leader of the Bolsheviks, seized power from the provisional government, which had superseded the autocracy of the last Romanov czar of Russia, Nicholas II, in the February Revolution. The February Revolution had followed years of czarist misrule and the disastrous impact on Russia of World War I, during which stunning defeats had come to the Russian armies and deep privations had been inflicted upon the Russian people at home. In the second week of March, workers and soldiers in Petrograd (as St. Petersburg had been renamed during the war) had revolted and joined forces, thereby forcing the abdication of Nicholas II.

The provisional government which had then come into power was born out of negotiations between the previously elected assembly, or Duma, a moderate group dominated by the property-owning classes, and the recently established Petrograd Soviet, or council, of Workers' and Soldiers' Deputies, a relatively moderate socialist organization but clearly to the left of the Duma. It was agreed that the Duma was to form the provisional government, which would rule until a new constitution was written for Russia by a popularly elected Constituent Assembly, but the Petrograd Soviet (with the exception of Aleksandr Fyodorovich Kerensky) refused to participate because of the bourgeois nature of the Duma. The Petrograd Soviet regarded itself as the guardian of the working masses, who would in time transform the bourgeois revolution into a socialist one. The provisional government was composed mainly of Cadets (Constitutional Democrats) and Octobrists with Prince Georgy Yevgenyevich Lvov as premier and the lone Socialist, Kerensky, as minister of justice. There now existed two centers of authority, the liberal provisional government and the leftist Petrograd Soviet, but the real power was in the hands of the latter. The Petrograd Soviet quickly decreed that the soldiers of the Petrograd garrison should not obey orders which conflicted with the Soviet's commands. As news of the revolutionary events in Petrograd spread throughout the Russian empire, workers, soldiers, and peasants elected local soviets which proclaimed their loyalty to the Petrograd Soviet rather than the provisional government.

divided among them without delay, the provisional government answered that this matter could only be dealt with legally by the Constituent Assembly, elections for which were to be held later in the year. This answer did not satisfy the peasants, whose thirst for land was equaled only by their desire for peace. Yet the provisional government alienated the peasants still further by making it clear that they intended to prosecute the war vigorously in close cooperation with the Allies in order to secure a victorious

Violence erupted in the streets of Petrograd after Bolsheviks captured the Winter Palace and announced the fall of the provisional government in Russia. (Archive Photos/G. D. Hackett)

During the succeeding months, the absence of a strong central authority made it impossible for anything to be done about the terrible conditions facing Russia. The two most serious problems were the peasants' demands for land and Russia's future role in World War I. To the demand of the peasants that the great landed estates be

peace together with territorial annexations, namely, the Turkish Straits between the Mediterranean and the Black Sea. The insistence of the provisional government in pursuing these aims led, by May, to a serious clash with the Petrograd Soviet, which had approved continuing the war to defend Russian territory but had not approved fighting for the annexations. The crisis ended with a reorganization of the provisional government to include several members of the Petrograd Soviet as ministers. This "First Coalition," in which Kerensky became minister of war, represented the successful effort of the Petrograd Soviet not only to impose its views on the provisional government but also to attempt to close the ranks of the Center and moderate Left against the Bolsheviks.

The leader of this faction was Lenin, who had recently returned from exile in Switzerland with help from the German High Command. Lenin found the situation in Russia much to his liking; it encouraged him and his lieutenants, among them Leon Trotsky and Joseph Stalin, to begin plotting the takeover of the Petrograd Soviet and the overthrow of the provisional government. The German High Command was ultimately proved correct in its assumption that Lenin would in time undermine the pro-Allied provisional government. Lenin, a leading Russian Marxist revolutionary since 1895 and, after 1903, the head of the Bolshevik wing of the Russian Social Democratic Labor Party, had a program which was perfectly attuned to the unanswered grievances of the workers, peasants, and soldiers. He called for an immediate end to the war, immediate seizure of land by the peasants, control of industry by committees of workers, and the transfer of power from the provisional government to the Soviets ("All Power to the Soviets"), whose numbers were proliferating throughout Russia. Indeed, much of Lenin's success may be attributed to his ability to understand the feelings and desires of the masses and to act accordingly.

Kerensky, however, lacked this ability as was clearly demonstrated in June when he decided to launch an offensive against the Austro-German armies. A great victory at the front, or so he believed, would placate the discontented elements at home. Instead, the offensive was completely routed by July 7. In the wake of this disaster, the soldiers, sailors, and workers staged an uprising in Petrograd during July 16-18. A half-hearted attempt by the ill-prepared Bolsheviks to seize power was easily foiled by the government. Lenin fled into hiding in Finland; Trotsky was arrested together with several other leading Bolsheviks.

Kerensky now became premier in a second coalition of Liberals and moderate Socialists. The coup Kerensky had weathered from the Left was in September matched by one from the Right led by General Lavr Georgyevich Kornilov, recently appointed supreme commander of Russia's armies. Supported by conservative elements and property owners, this coup was directed against the Petrograd Soviet and probably against Kerensky as well. By September 14, the coup had collapsed, primarily because Kornilov's troops refused to obey him. Kornilov's movement also foundered because of the agitation carried on in his ranks by Bolshevik radicals, many of whom, including Trotsky, the government had released from prison to assist its cause. Kerensky won only a Pyrrhic victory, for his government was unable to contain the spread of popular unrest. Regular deliveries of food and other supplies were becoming harder to obtain, which drove increasingly desperate workers to take control of factories themselves.

After the failure of Kornilov's coup, the army began to disintegrate as entire units of peasant soldiers left the front to return to their villages. The arrival of armed deserters encouraged the impatient peasants to seize and divide up the privately owned estates. The provisional government almost completely lost control of the major cities, the army, and the countryside. Lenin and Trotsky now decided that the moment had come for them to seize power.

The Bolshevik Party had been growing progressively stronger since its defeat in the July coup. By August, its membership had grown to almost a quarter of a million, a tenfold increase since the start of the Russian Revolution in March. Significantly, the Bolsheviks secured a majority in both the Petrograd and Moscow Soviets during mid-September. Early in October, Trotsky was elected chairman of the Petrograd Soviet and later the head of the newly formed, Bolshevik-dominated Military Revolutionary Committee. Trotsky, as head of these organizations, had control of the Bolshevik militia, the Red Guard, and by the end of the month he managed to gain control of the Petrograd military garrison and contingents of sailors of the nearby Kronstadt naval base.

Lenin now emerged from hiding and on October 23, convinced the Central Committee of the Bolshevik Party that the moment had come to seize power. Finally, on the night of November 6, Bolshevik troops occupied key points in Petrograd and isolated the Winter Palace, headquarters of the Kerensky regime. The next morning, November 7, the Bolsheviks announced the fall of the provisional government. The Winter Palace, which held out until evening, was captured after a light skirmish in which a few lives were lost. Kerensky, who had left Petrograd in search of loyal troops to use against the Bolsheviks, managed to flee the country.

Lenin immediately began the consolidation of his power, a task he would not complete until the end of the Russian Civil War in 1921. In his efforts to assert authority outside the capital, he frequently encountered strong resistance from anti-Bolshevik elements. Moscow, for example, came under his control only after a week of fighting. Most of the Great Russian heartland, Siberia, and Central Asia, had come over, at least nominally, to the Bolshevik standard by the end of December, 1917. Years of bitter warfare lay ahead before these lands were brought under Bolshevik control. In Petrograd, meanwhile, Lenin issued two decrees in the meeting of the Bolshevik-dominated Second All-Russian Congress of Soviets of Workers', Soldiers', and Peasants' Deputies during November 8-9. One decree declared an end to the war (a manner of terminating the conflict which did not satisfy the Germans), and the other handed land over to the peasants.

Lenin also created the new government of the state, the Council of People's Commissars, a body made up entirely of Bolsheviks. Key figures in this cabinet were Lenin, the chairman; Stalin, commissar for national minorities; and Trotsky, commissar for foreign affairs. Lenin did allow the scheduled elections to the Constituent Assembly to take place within days of the Bolshevik takeover, but after permitting it one meeting in January, 1918, he decreed its dissolution. To combat opposition to the Bolshevik dictatorship, Lenin established the Cheka (from the Russian acronym for "Extraordinary Commission to Fight the Counterrevolution and Sabotage") in December, 1917. Headed by Feliks Dzerzhinski, this secret police force, which resembled the czarist internal security force that had been disbanded after the abdication of Nicholas II, was empowered to bypass normal legal procedures in investigating and punishing opponents of the new order. In other moves early in 1918, Lenin dissolved all ties between the church and the state, introduced the Gregorian in place of the Julian calendar, and decreed the nationalization of the land given to the peasants in November. Finally, in March, Lenin completed the first stage of his consolidation of power by concluding a formal peace with Germany at Brest-Litovsk, transferring the Russian capital back to Moscow, and adopting the name "Communist Party" to describe his movement.

The success of the Bolshevik movement was by no means completely assured in March, 1918; years of hard fighting and bloodshed lay ahead. The measure of success which the Bolsheviks had achieved by this time, however, was attributable to at least two factors. Negatively, they had succeeded not because they had the support of a majority of the people, but rather because the majority had never been in sympathy with the provisional government; most Russians considered the provisional government as aloof and unconcerned about their welfare as had been the czar. In the positive sense, it was much easier for people, whether Bolsheviks or not, to identify with the promises held out by Lenin for bread, peace, and land, promises he said would be fulfilled once he came to power. In the last analysis, the real measure of the Bolshevik success lay not in assuming power, but in consolidating that power against overwhelming odds during the years from 1918 to 1921. —*Edward P. Keleher, updated by Richard D. King*

ADDITIONAL READING:

Abraham, Richard. *Alexander Kerensky: The First Love of the Revolution*. New York: Columbia University Press, 1987. A sympathetic biography of a figure whom historians have often judged harshly.

Daniels, Robert V. *Red October: The Bolshevik Revo-lution of 1917*. New York: Charles Scribner's Sons, 1967. This book reconstructs the debates within the Bolshevik Party's Central Committee and the actual overthrow of the provisional government.

Katkov, George. *Russia, 1917—The Kornilov Affair: Kerensky and the Break-up of the Russian Army*. London: Longman, 1980. The author defends General Kornilov against charges that he plotted to overthrow the provisional government.

Lincoln, W. Bruce. *Passage Through Armageddon: The Russians in War and Revolution*. New York: Simon & Schuster, 1986. A lively history that shows the terrible impact of World War I and the revolution on the Russian empire and its peoples.

Pipes, Richard. *The Russian Revolution*. New York: Alfred A. Knopf, 1990. This massive history emphasizes the role of the radical intellectuals in shaping the course of the revolution.

Rabinowitch, Alexander. *The Bolsheviks Come to Power: The Revolution of 1917 in Petrograd*. New York: W. W. Norton, 1976. A detailed account of events in Petrograd from July to the Bolshevik seizure of power, this study stresses the radicalization of popular opinion.

Volkogonov, Dmitri. *Lenin: A New Biography*. Translated and edited by Harold Shukman. New York: Free Press, 1994. Written by a former Soviet general, this biography makes use of previously secret documents from the Soviet archives.

SEE ALSO: 1898, Social-Democratic Workers' Party Is Formed; 1905, The October Manifesto; 1917-1920, Ukrainian Nationalists Struggle for Independence; 1917, Finland Gains Independence; 1918-1920, Baltic States Fight for Independence; 1918-1921, Russian Civil War; 1918, Treaty of Brest-Litovsk.

1917-1920
FINLAND GAINS INDEPENDENCE

Finland gains independence from Russia on December 6, 1917, marking the emergence of a nation where one did not exist before.

DATE: December 6, 1917-1920

LOCALE: Finland

CATEGORIES: Government and politics; Wars, uprisings, and civil unrest

KEY FIGURES:

Alexander I (1777-1825), Russian czar at the time Sweden ceded Finland to Russia in 1809

Nikolai Ivanovich Bobrikov (1839-1904), Russian governor-general who was assassinated in the Finnish parliament building

Vladimir Ilich Lenin (Ulyanov; 1870-1924), leader of
the Russian Bolshevik Revolution

Carl Gustaf Mannerheim (1867-1951), Finnish military
leader who helped secure Finnish independence

Nicholas II (1868-1917), last of the Russian czars

Kaarlo Juho Ståhlberg (1864-1952), first president of
independent Finland

Joseph Stalin (Iosif Vissarionovich Dzhugashvili;
1879-1953), Russian communist and member of the
Revolutionary Council who recommended
recognizing Finnish independence

SUMMARY OF EVENT. World War I changed the map of
Europe as the once powerful Austro-Hungarian empire
fragmented, revolution swept the Russian czar from his
throne, and rising tides of nationalism created nations
from former imperial provinces. While the establishment
of some countries, such as Yugoslavia and Czechoslovakia, resulted from negotiations following the end of the
war, Finland declared its independence from Russia on
December 6, 1917, and established its borders well before
the victorious Allies determined the boundaries for the rest
of Europe with the 1919 Treaty of Versailles.

The most remote of the Scandinavian countries, Finland is bordered on the east by Russia, on the north by
Norway and Sweden, and to the west and south by the
Baltic Sea. Approximately one-third of the country lies
above the Arctic Circle. The climate is harsh with long
winters and short growing seasons. Not surprisingly, many
regions of Finland remained sparsely populated well into
the twentieth century. Scholars are not sure where the first
Finnish settlers originated, but speculate they came from
central Asia, as Finns speak a language unrelated to the
Germanic tongues, such as Swedish, spoken by their nearest neighbors. Finland's recorded history begins in the
thirteenth century, when, shortly after Swedish Christian
missionaries began proselytizing in Finland, the Swedish
king declared Finland a part of Sweden. The Swedish
church encouraged a sense of unity among the various
tribes in Finland, and gradually a sense of a common
national identity emerged. At the same time, Finland's
eastern border was the scene of almost constant warfare as
Russia and Sweden both attempted to expand into the
other's territory. The border shifted several times. Military
policies that often left Finnish troops to bear the brunt of
Russian attacks contributed to a growing Finnish disaffection for Sweden. Finally, as part of the Peace of Hamina,
Sweden lost Finland entirely in September of 1809. Torn
with internal dissension, the Swedes ceded Finland to
Russia and left the Finns to negotiate as best they could
with Czar Alexander I.

Alexander and his immediate successors allowed Finland to remain relatively autonomous. As a grand duchy,
Finland had its own civil service, staffed primarily by
Finns, and enjoyed privileges not granted to all Russians.
Finnish men, for example, were not subject to conscription into the Russian army, although many Finns did
choose to enter the military voluntarily. Swedish remained
the official written language of Finland for official purposes rather than Russian being imposed. At the time,
there was no written Finnish language. When, in the
1850's, a Finnish language movement developed and
Finnish language schools were founded, Alexander II issued a decree that, after allowing for a twenty-year transition period, placed Finnish on an equal footing with Swedish for use in public transactions. Finally, in 1863, the
Finnish parliament, or Lantdag, was reconstituted, and, in
1869, began to convene annually.

Under Czar Nicholas II, however, many of these liberal
policies were eliminated. In the 1890's the Russian government began a process of trying to make Finland more
Russian by imposing Russian postal and monetary systems on Finland, requiring the use of the Russian language, and removing freedoms Finns had enjoyed. By
1901, when a conscription law was passed requiring Finnish nationals to serve in the Russian army, a strong independence movement existed. Resistance to Russianiza-
tion intensified, until a Finnish student shot the Russian
governor-general, Nikolai Bobrikov, on a staircase in the
Finnish parliament building in 1904. Bobrikov walked
to his usual seat in the government chambers, brushing
off concern over his welfare, but died the next day. The
Russo-Japanese War provided a brief distraction, allowing
time for more reforms to take place in Finland, such as the
institution of universal suffrage that granted the right to
vote to all Finnish men and women, but by 1910 Russia
was again forcing closer ties. In 1914, Russia announced
an annexation program that would have eliminated Finland's status as an autonomous grand duchy.

World War I proved disastrous for Russia. Nicholas II,
a weak leader, was forced to abdicate in 1917, and Russia
withdrew from combat. Carl Gustaf Mannerheim, a Finn
who had made a career in the Russian army, returned to
Finland where he became a hero of the Finnish independence movement. The Finnish senate had officially
declared Finland an independent nation on December 6,
1917, but independence did not come easily. Like Russia,
Finland had many citizens who supported the Bolshevik
Revolution. Vladimir Lenin, leader of the Bolsheviks, had
spent August and September of 1917 in Finland, easily
evading attempts by Russian authorities to arrest him. The
Bolsheviks, or Reds, favored a communist form of government. Many other citizens, or Whites, remained loyal

monarchists. Four months of bloody fighting between the Whites and Reds followed the declaration of independence. Mannerheim assumed command of the Finnish White army in January, driving the Russians and Finnish Reds from Finland. By the summer of 1918, after concluding a decisive battle at Tampere, the Whites were left in clear control of the country.

Following the defeat of the Bolsheviks, Mannerheim was among the Finns who urged the establishment of a constitutional monarchy. Mannerheim was asked to serve as regent while plans for a monarchy went forward. German troops had fought with the Finns against the Russians in the war for independence and so the monarchists invited a minor German prince, Frederick Charles of Hessen, to become the first king of Finland. The offer was withdrawn following Germany's surrender in World War I and a republican form of government established instead. Mannerheim hoped to be elected president of the new republic, but his monarchist position alienated many Finns. Kaarlo Ståhlberg, a professor of law at the University of Helsinki who had drafted the republican constitution, became the first president of the new republic. Mannerheim retired from public life for a number of years, but later returned to again serve as commander in chief of the Finnish army and eventually, from 1944 to 1946, as president of Finland.

Finland adopted the constitution drafted by Ståhlberg on July 17, 1919, but was not recognized as an independent nation for almost another year. Finally, in 1920, Joseph Stalin, a member of the Revolutionary Council in the Soviet Union, urged the Soviets to acknowledge Finland's independence. The Soviet Union thus became the first nation to recognize Finland as a sovereign state. Following recognition of sovereignty, the Treaty of Tartu in 1920 resolved border disputes regarding the Karelia area in the east and access to the Arctic Ocean in the north.

—*Nancy Farm Mannikko*

ADDITIONAL READING:

Jutikkala, Eino. *A History of Finland*. Espoo, Finland: Weilin & Goos, 1984. A comprehensive history of Finland tracing the country's heritage from its origins to the 1980's.

Karvonen, Lauri. *From White to Blue-and-Black: Finnish Fascism in the Inter-War Era*. Helsinki, Finland: Finnish Society of Sciences and Letters, 1988. A discussion of Finnish politics following independence.

Kirby, D. G., ed. *Finland and Russia, 1808-1920: From Autonomy to Independence*. London: Macmillan, 1975. A thorough examination of conditions in the grand duchy of Finland and how the gradual loss of autonomy contributed to the nationalistic drive for independence from Russia.

Klinge, Matti. *Let Us Be Finns*. Helsinki, Finland: Otava Publishing, 1990. An interesting collection of essays on various aspects of Finnish history and culture.

Paasivirta, Juhani. *Finland and Europe: The Early Years of Independence, 1918-1939*. Helsinki, Finland: SHS, 1988. A social and cultural history that describes life in Finland in the inter-war period.

Singleton, Frederick Bernard. *A Short History of Finland*. New York: Cambridge University Press, 1989. A lively survey of the history of Finland that is easily accessible to the general reader.

Sjoderhjelm, Henning. *The Red Insurrection in Finland in 1918*. Westport, Conn.: Hyperion Press, 1977. The author presents an interesting discussion of the little-known civil war in Finland that erupted following Finland's declaration of independence from Russia.

Tillotson, H. M. *Finland at Peace and War, 1918-1993*. Wilby, Norwich, England: Michael Russell, 1993. A comprehensive history of Finland in the twentieth century.

Upton, Anthony F. *The Finnish Revolution, 1917-1918*. Minneapolis: University of Minnesota Press, 1980. Definitive English language history of the revolution. Extremely thorough, includes maps to help both clarify border issues and identify sites of military conflict.

SEE ALSO: 1904-1905, Russo-Japanese War; 1917-1920, Ukrainian Nationalists Struggle for Independence; 1918-1920, Baltic States Fight for Independence; 1918-1921, Russian Civil War; 1918, Treaty of Brest-Litovsk.

1918-1920
BALTIC STATES FIGHT FOR INDEPENDENCE

The Baltic states fight for independence and organize their own governments, allowing the three nations to consolidate a national political consciousness that later withstands a half century of Soviet rule.

DATE: 1918-1920

LOCALE: Lithuania, Latvia, and Estonia

CATEGORIES: Government and politics; Wars, uprisings, and civil unrest

KEY FIGURES:

Vladimir Ilich Lenin (Ulyanov; 1870-1924), chairman of the Council of People's Commissars of the Soviet Union

Konstantin Päts (1874-1956), prime minister of Estonia

Józef Piłsudski (1867-1935), chief of state of Poland

Antanas Smetona (1874-1944), president of Lithuania

Joseph Stalin (Iosif Vissarionovich Dzhugashvili; 1879-1953), commissar of nationalities of the Soviet Union

Karlis Ulmanis (1877-1942), prime minister of Latvia

SUMMARY OF EVENT. The emergence of the three Baltic states of Lithuania, Latvia, and Estonia at the end of World War I had an impact on the history of Eastern Europe throughout the twentieth century. An expression of the ideas of national self-determination, the creation of the states was made possible by the collapse of the two major East European empires, czarist Russia and the German Reich.

Before World War I, the territory that became the three states was a part of the Russian empire. The German offensive of 1915 basically occupied Lithuania and western Latvia. Eastern Latvia and Estonia therefore took part in the political revolutions sweeping Russia in 1917, from the collapse of the czarist order in March to the Bolshevik seizure of power, under the leadership of V. I. Lenin, in November. While new democratic ideas came to Estonia and Latvia in 1917, German authorities considered ways of incorporating Lithuania and western Latvia into the German empire. In February and March of 1918, German troops moved into eastern Latvia and Estonia. Thoughts of national independence for all three nations began to develop behind both the Russian and the German lines, but these became feasible only in the fall of 1918, after the collapse of the German war effort and the victory of the Allies in Western Europe. Even then, however, the new governments had to struggle to find their place in Eastern Europe.

The Estonians were the most advanced in organizing their own institutions. At the time of the collapse of the Russian czarist government in March of 1917, the Russians still occupied Estonia. In May of 1917, the Estonians elected their first local parliament, the Maapäev, and they also began to organize an Estonian military force. After the Bolshevik Revolution, Soviet authorities drove the Maapäev into the underground, but on February 24, 1918, when German forces occupied the region, the Maapäev's Committee of Elders declared Estonia's independence and formed a provisional government, headed by Konstantin Päts. The Germans suppressed Estonian institutions and arrested Päts. Only after the collapse of the German war effort in November could the Estonian government begin to build public institutions, and then it faced the challenge of the coming of the Red Army.

The Lithuanians, who had lived under German occupation since 1915, were able to organize a national council, the Taryba, only in September of 1917, and even then the Taryba, headed by Antanas Smetona, worked under the

supervision of the German military. In connection with the talks with Russia at Brest-Litovsk, the German authorities encouraged the Taryba to proclaim Lithuania's independence, but when the Lithuanians, on February 16, 1918, issued a declaration that made no mention of maintaining close future ties with Germany, the Germans refused to recognize it. The Lithuanians also were able to build public institutions only in the fall of 1918, after establishing a provisional government. In April of 1919, Smetona became president of Lithuania.

The Latvians were the last of the three to organize, establishing a council on November 18, 1918; the council immediately proclaimed the existence of a provisional government for the Republic of Latvia, headed by Karlis Ulmanis.

From the fall of 1918 to the fall of 1920, the Baltic area became a major battleground for the contending forces in the Russian Revolution. The Western Allies, fearing the expansion of the Bolshevik Revolution into central Europe, insisted that the Germans keep their forces in place in the territory of the former Russian empire. The troops, however, withdrew on their own initiative, and at a distance the Red Army followed their tracks into the Baltic.

The Communist leaders of Soviet Russia, after having seized power in November of 1917, proclaimed the right of all peoples to "national self-determination even to the point of separation and formation of an independent state." They did not, however, automatically recognize the right of the three Baltic peoples to separate from the empire; as Joseph Stalin, Soviet People's Commissar for Nationalities Affairs, explained, they insisted that they themselves would determine who could exercise the right of national self-determination. Although the Soviet government declared that it had no claim on the Baltic, the Bolsheviks organized their sympathizers from the region as local Communist Parties ready to follow the dictates of the leaders in Moscow. The parties then became the spearheads for the advance of the Soviet Red Army into the Baltic. The Soviet military also included troops from the Baltic, the most notable of these being the Latvian Rifles, known as the *strelnieki*, which were units organized in 1915 and 1916 as part of the Russian army.

To prepare the way for moving into the Baltic, Lenin and Stalin ordered the proclamation of Soviet Socialist Republics for Estonia, Latvia, and Lithuania. The Soviet troops succeeded in driving the provisional Latvian and Lithuanian governments out of their capitals, but the Soviet governments failed to win the support of the local peoples in any of the three territories. The men whom Moscow installed actually disapproved of establishing independent republics in the region, and on Moscow's orders they opposed extensive land reform, preferring to keep large estates intact for more efficient exploitation. The local populations supported their own national governments.

Outside aid helped the Baltic governments to withstand the Soviet attack. British ships provided equipment to Estonians and Latvians. Finnish volunteers arrived in Estonia to fight the Bolsheviks, and in both Latvia and Lithuania, German volunteers fought the Bolsheviks. The Bolsheviks had to withdraw and Moscow suppressed its puppet governments in the Baltic. The German volunteers, however, together with some Russian adventurers, posed new threats, and in Latvia pro-German forces briefly organized a countergovernment in the spring of 1919. In the summer, the Western Allies demanded that the German forces finally withdraw from the Baltic, and after battles with both Latvian and Lithuanian forces, the last German soldiers left the region in December, 1919.

The Lithuanians had a problem of a different sort in their relations with the new government of Poland, headed by Józef Piłsudski. Piłsudski wanted to extend the Polish frontier with the new Russia eastward as far as possible, and he dreamed of restoring the historic alliance of Poles and Lithuanians in a single state. The Lithuanians rejected his ideas, and in October of 1920, Polish forces seized the city of Vilnius (Wilno in Polish), which the Lithuanians claimed as their capital. The resulting tension between Poland and Lithuania constituted a major block to cooperation between the states of Eastern Europe between the world wars.

The Baltic governments won recognition of their independence in a series of peace treaties with Soviet Russia in 1920. In September of 1919, recognizing their failure in the Baltic, the Soviet leaders had agreed to enter into negotiations with the new governments, and in February of 1920, Estonia signed a peace treaty with Moscow. On July 12, 1920, the Lithuanians signed their peace treaty with the Russians, and the Latvians followed suit on August 11. The three republics became members of the League of Nations in 1921.

In the interwar period, all three Baltic governments consolidated the foundations of their independent existence. All three carried out extensive land reforms, which, in the case of the Estonians and Latvians, struck at the historic position of German landowners and in the case of the Lithuanians struck at Polish landowners. The cultural life of all three developed and grew, with the result that when the Soviet Union occupied and annexed the three republics in 1940, a half century of Soviet domination was unable to wipe away the memories and accomplishments of the period of independence. The Baltic peoples eventu-

ally played a major role in the collapse of the Soviet Union between 1990 and 1991.   —*Alfred Erich Senn*

ADDITIONAL READING:

Graham, Malbone. *The New Governments of Eastern Europe*. New York: Pitman, 1927. This study, although now outdated, offers a useful introduction to the events of 1917-1922 and appends important documents, including the constitutions of each state.

Plakans, Andrejs. *The Latvians: A Short History*. Stanford, Calif.: Hoover Institution Press, 1995. Written by an American historian of Latvian background, this is a very useful, balanced account of Latvian history, with about half of it devoted to the twentieth century.

Raun, Toivo. *Estonia and the Estonians*. 2d ed. Stanford, Calif.: Hoover Institution Press, 1991. Written by an American historian of Estonian heritage, this study concentrates on Estonian history in the twentieth century.

Royal Institute of International Affairs. *The Baltic States*. London: Oxford University Press, 1938. A reference work that is particularly useful for its account of the interwar economic history of the three republics.

Senn, Alfred Erich. *The Emergence of Modern Lithuania*. New York: Columbia University Press, 1959. A monograph on the creation of the Lithuanian state, 1918-1920.

SEE ALSO: 1917-1920, Ukrainian Nationalists Struggle for Independence; 1917, Finland Gains Independence; 1918-1921, Russian Civil War; 1918, Treaty of Brest-Litovsk.

1918-1921
RUSSIAN CIVIL WAR

The Russian Civil War marks the consolidation of Bolshevik power against an array of anti-Communist groups that are never able to unite politically or coordinate their military forces.

DATE: 1918-1921

LOCALE: The Soviet Union

CATEGORIES: Government and politics; Wars, uprisings, and civil unrest

KEY FIGURES:

Nikolai Vasilievich Chaikovski (1850-1926), Socialist Revolutionary Party leader of anti-Soviet movement in northern Russia

General Anton Ivanovich Denikin (1872-1947), commander of White forces in southern Russia

Admiral Aleksandr Vasilievich Kolchak (1874-1920), White commander in Siberia and White "Supreme Ruler," 1918-1920

General Lavr Georgyevich Kornilov (1870-1918),
  commander of White forces in southern Russia
Vladimir Ilich Lenin (Ulyanov; 1870-1924), Bolshevik
  leader and head of Communist Russia, 1917-1924
Nestor Makhno, Ukrainian anarchist peasant leader
Leon Trotsky (Leib Davydovich Bronstein; 1879-1940),
  Red Army commander and commissar of war after
  1918
General Pyotr Nikolayevich Wrangel (1878-1928),
  commander of White forces in southern Russia
General Nikolai Nikolaevich Yudënich (1862-1933),
  White commander in northwest Russia

SUMMARY OF EVENT. Any revolution that suddenly top-
ples a long-standing regime is likely to face continued
resistance from remnants of the "old order." Opposition
can be centered among embittered émigrés who flee to
distant havens of refuge, or opposition can take the form
of open counterrevolution. When Vladimir Ilich Lenin and
his Bolshevik followers staged their successful coup in
November, 1917 (October according to the Julian calendar in use in Russia at the time), the new Soviet government encountered both types of residual opposition. Many
anti-Bolshevik Russians, sensing the seriousness of Bolshevik aims, fled the country for Paris, New York, and
other Western cities, where they continued to oppose the
Bolshevik regime. By far the most serious threat to the
Bolshevik Revolution was a series of armed uprisings that
shook the edges of Soviet Russia between 1918 and 1921.
These uprisings, collectively grouped under the heading
"The Russian Civil War," for a time posed a serious threat
to the infant Soviet state. Lenin's eventual victory ensured
the triumph of the Communist experiment in Russia.

The White (anti-Bolshevik) movement included, at one
time or another, several politically incompatible groups:
patriotic socialists, liberals, and military officers who rejected Lenin's separate peace with Germany and his suppression of the Constituent Assembly; national minorities
seeking independence from Russia; reactionaries who
wished to revive the autocracy and restore all land seized
by the peasants to its former owners; and peasants who,
though fearing the return of the nobles whose lands they
had usurped, resented the forcible confiscation of grain by
armed Bolshevik detachments sent to collect food for the
cities. These disparate groups, moreover, were not concentrated in a single area, but widely scattered across the
vast Russian empire.

White forces in southern Russia centered in a Volunteer
Army augmented by Cossack forces. Led in succession by
Generals Lavr Kornilov, Anton Denikin, and Pyotr Wrangel between 1918 and 1920, the Volunteer Army attempted to maintain both an anti-Soviet and anti-German

campaign simultaneously. Politically, the campaign aimed
for restoration of an assembly form of government featur-
ing traditional political parties. The southern movement,
however, was hampered by a lack of cohesion in its daily
operations, which would lead to ultimate defeat.

Another important center of White activity proved to
be Siberia. Here fighting erupted in 1918 between Soviet
troops and the famous Czechoslovak Legion, which had
been recruited from captured Austro-Hungarian soldiers
to fight for the Allies against the Central Powers. The
legion was on its way through Siberia for eventual crossing into North America and from there to the western front
in Europe, when frictions with the Soviets erupted into
violence. The legion, comprising some thirty-five thousand troops, abandoned plans to leave Russia and effectively sealed off the Siberian east, creating a zone where
anti-Soviet movements might flourish. Ultimately, the Siberian White movement was led by Admiral Aleksandr
Kolchak.

Smaller White movements were based in seaports on
the White and Baltic Seas. Northern anti-Soviet movements, led by Nikolai V. Chaikovski, relied heavily on
British troops brought in as part of the Allied intervention.
So did the White forces in Estonia, where the White
movement was under the control of General Nikolai N.
Yudënich.

The first year of the civil war was characterized by
savage partisan warfare between small, mobile units. Unable to hold captured territory by leaving behind an army
of occupation, these units frequently resorted to terror to
pacify the population. By the fall of 1918, both Reds
(Soviets) and Whites had managed to form regular armies.
Although independent partisan units still operated and
both sides continued to use terror, the decisive engagements of 1919 and 1920 were fought by these better
organized armies along more clearly defined fronts.

At first, these White forces, peripheral though they
were, scored some impressive victories, and, indeed, for a
time in 1919 threatened the Soviet regime. In the south,
General Denikin scored key victories, notably his capture
of Kiev in September, 1919. By November, however, the
Red Army (Soviet) launched a resounding counteroffensive that drove the remnants of the Volunteer Army into the
Crimea, whence under Pyotr Wrangel they were later
evacuated in disarray. In Siberia, Admiral Kolchak began
an offensive against key sites near the Volga River. Kolchak rode a wave of military successes through March,
1919, but with the Volga threatened, the Red Army repelled his forces through the month of April. Attempts by
northern Whites based in Archangel to link up with Kolchak's troops failed, as did two attacks by Yudënich's

forces against Petrograd. By the winter of 1919-1920, impressive White campaigns ceased.

The anti-Soviet revolt was also joined by forces from Russia's minority nationalities, particularly in the Ukraine and the Caucasus, where fierce nationalist pride motivated many to use the civil war as a backdrop for national independence. The national minorities, however, were unwilling to cooperate with the White generals, who wanted to keep the Russian empire intact. Of great importance in the Ukrainian movement was the peasant leader Nestor Makhno, an avowed anarchist who was not aligned with either side. By 1920, the Soviets had crushed the Ukrainian independence movement and established control over most of the Caucasus.

Another aspect of the civil war had more diplomatic than military impact. This was the famous intervention of the Allied armed forces of Great Britain, France, the United States, and Japan in Russia in 1918. Japan, in landing its forces at Vladivostok, had definite territorial aims, a stance which did not characterize the other interventionist powers. British, French, and American troops were sent to Vladivostok, Odessa, and Archangel, but seldom played a direct combat role. Instead, these Western forces acted as suppliers of arms, aid, and advice to the White forces to help them fight both Germany and the Bolsheviks. By 1919, with the end of World War I, the Allied forces were withdrawn, as the rationale of restoring Russia to the Triple Entente no longer mattered.

By 1920, the Russian Civil War was nearing completion with Soviet victory. The Volunteer Army had been chased out of the Crimea, evacuated via Istanbul to the Kingdom of Serbs, Croats, and Slovenes (as Yugoslavia was then known), ending all southern resistance. In Siberia, the tired and demoralized Czechoslovak Legion, which had buttressed the eastern White forces, quit the field and handed Kolchak over to the Soviets, who promptly executed the admiral in February, 1920. With Allied forces gone, the civil uprising was over.

Several factors explain how the fledgling Soviet state won the civil war. The Soviet forces had the advantage of defending interior lines, while the Whites were fighting the offensive from the periphery of Russia. Transportation and communications had been difficult even before the destruction Russia had suffered because of World War I and the Bolshevik Revolution. It proved exceedingly difficult for the Whites to fight a united war, given their disparate locations and lack of political unity. Leon Trotsky, who was made commissar of war by the Lenin government in March, 1918, quickly abandoned many Bolshevik concepts of a people's army that had held sway since 1917. Discipline of a strict type was restored, as was

the practice of conscription. Trotsky recruited several thousand czarist officers who out of patriotism were willing to help the Bolsheviks defend Russia. The Red Army did not have to defend far-flung points such as those held by the Whites. The Bolsheviks controlled a larger population than the Whites, and most of the defense industries. The Red Army therefore enjoyed a decisive edge in manpower resources and armaments, and its rear was not threatened by rebellious national minorities. In addition, the Red Army, quite unlike the Whites, had a unified outlook and program which lifted its morale as the war continued. Finally, although the peasants frequently rebelled against Bolshevik grain requisitions, they feared a White victory and return of the nobility even more. Lenin's government, under a program of "War Communism," thus obtained the necessary sacrifices from the Soviet populace to secure victory.

—Edward A. Zivich, updated by Richard D. King

ADDITIONAL READING:

Fitzpatrick, Sheila. *The Russian Revolution.* 2d ed. New York: Oxford University Press, 1994. An interpretive essay of the years 1917-1938.

Kennan, George F. *Russia and the West Under Lenin and Stalin.* Boston: Little, Brown, 1961. Written by a distinguished scholar and diplomat, this book is a good starting point for studying the causes and consequences of Allied intervention in the Russian Civil War.

Lincoln, W. Bruce. *Red Victory: A History of the Russian Civil War.* New York: Simon & Schuster, 1989. A vivid narrative addressed to a general audience which captures the violence and brutality of the civil war.

Mawdsley, Evan. *The Russian Civil War.* Boston: Allen & Unwin, 1987. A balanced survey, particularly strong on military aspects of the civil war.

Pipes, Richard. *Russia Under the Bolshevik Regime.* New York: Alfred A. Knopf, 1994. This book addresses cultural and religious affairs, the non-Russian nationalities, and Soviet attempts to export the Bolshevik Revolution.

Swain, Geoffrey. *The Origins of the Russian Civil War.* London: Longman, 1996. Concentrating on events in 1918, this study emphasizes foreign intervention and the desires of the peasants, who were caught between the Reds and the Whites.

Volkogonov, Dmitri. *Lenin: A New Biography.* Translated and edited by Harold Shukman. New York: Free Press, 1994. Written by a former Soviet general who became highly critical of the Soviet system created by the October Revolution and the Russian Civil War.

SEE ALSO: 1905, The October Manifesto; 1917-1920,

Ukrainian Nationalists Struggle for Independence; 1917, Finland Gains Independence; 1918-1920, Baltic States Fight for Independence; 1918, Treaty of Brest-Litovsk; 1921-1928, Lenin's New Economic Policy.

1918
BRITISH WOMEN GAIN THE VOTE

British women gain the vote when Parliament passes a limited suffrage bill in the wake of a half century of increasingly militant women's rights efforts.

DATE: February 6, 1918
LOCALE: England
CATEGORIES: Government and politics; Social reform; Women's issues
KEY FIGURES:

Barbara Leigh Smith Bodichon (1827-1892), important early British suffrage organizer

Millicent Garrett Fawcett (1847-1929), British writer, leader, and political lobbyist for suffrage from 1869 until 1920

John Stuart Mill (1806-1873), British philosopher who presented first women's suffrage bill to Parliament

Christabel Pankhurst (1880-1958), militant suffrage leader and daughter of Emmeline Pankhurst

Emmeline Goulden Pankhurst (1858-1928), leader of militant, sometimes violent, suffrage protesters

Sylvia Pankhurst (1882-1960), militant suffrage activist and daughter of Emmeline Pankhurst

SUMMARY OF EVENT. Demands for women's suffrage arose as debate raged over the 1832 Reform Bill, which gave the vote to approximately one of every five British men, with eligibility established by a property qualification. In reaction, the House of Commons inserted the word "male" into voter qualifications for the first time. Female suffrage again briefly emerged among Chartist demands that began in 1838. The Chartists backed down from the issue for fear that insistence on female suffrage would handicap the effort to gain universal male suffrage. Nevertheless, the issue was debated in newspapers and journals of the 1830's and 1840's and resulted in formation of some women's political associations, many short-lived.

Interest was renewed in 1840, when female American delegates were excluded from the first World Anti-Slavery Convention in London. While no British women participated, Anne Knight, as a result of the ban, wrote a suffrage pamphlet and in 1847 joined with other Chartist women in Sheffield to form the first British suffrage group, the Female Political Association. Their 1852 petition to Parliament was rejected.

The movement was revitalized in 1865, as a result of

Parliamentary debate over further extension of the franchise. On March 18, 1867, Benjamin Disraeli introduced a bill that ultimately would add 938,000 male voters to an electorate of 1,057,000 in England and Wales. Barbara Bodichon, Emily Davies, and Elizabeth Garrett were among the leaders who collected 1,499 signatures on a petition to demand votes for women. John Stuart Mill, who had campaigned for election to Parliament on a platform that included women's rights, presented the petition on May 20, 1867. Thereafter, except in 1880, suffrage bills were introduced annually from 1870 to 1883 and were defeated, although women won other victories in areas such as property, child custody, and municipal voting rights. Women were not included in the 1884 Reform Bill that extended the franchise to male agricultural workers.

In the face of opposition and defeat, new women's political organizations were founded. A Ladies' Discussion Society was formed in Kensington, London, in 1865. Its members included Bodichon, Emily Davies, and Garrett. Lydia Becker, after hearing a suffrage paper by Bodichon in 1866, helped form the Manchester Women's Suffrage Committee in 1867. Other societies were formed in London, Edinburgh, and Bristol. The London National Society for Women (later, for Women's Suffrage) was founded in July, 1867, to coordinate policy and activities. Millicent Fawcett was a member of the executive board. Periodicals were established: the *English Woman's Journal* in 1858, to be succeeded by the *Englishwoman's Review* in 1865; the *Shield* in 1870; *Woman and Work* in 1874, and the *Woman's Gazette* in 1875. Lydia Becker edited the *Women's Suffrage Journal* from 1870 until her death in 1890. Outside London, organizations began to engage working women in a movement thus far primarily of interest to the middle classes. The Women's Trade Union League (WTUL), for example, began in 1874 as the Women's Protective and Provident League. While not a suffrage organization, its organizers came to believe that the vote was a necessary condition for the improvement of working conditions.

Organizations multiplied in part because the movement was often split by dissension. Feminists privately supported Josephine Baker's Ladies' National Association, founded in 1869, to oppose the Contagious Diseases Acts of 1864. These acts, which threatened all working-class women in garrison and seaport towns with forcible inspection for venereal disease, brought questions of sexuality into daily papers. Conservative feminists, such as Millicent Fawcett, feared that the association of suffrage with this scandalous subject would jeopardize suffrage. In 1888, the National Society for Women's Suffrage (NSWS) split over whether to admit women's mainstream social and political organizations. Dissidents formed the Central National Society for Women's Suffrage.

Formation of Keir Hardie's Independent Labour Party (ILP) in 1893, which would challenge and later replace the Liberal Party, marked the changing political climate at the century's end. By 1896, the Central Committee of the NSWS obtained 258,000 signatures on a petition to Parliament. In February, 1897, a woman's suffrage bill secured more than two hundred votes in the House of Commons and, for the first time, passed a second reading before being defeated. That year saw federation of suffrage societies through the National Union of Women's Suffrage Societies (NUWSS), led by Fawcett, with some seventeen member organizations; it held its first national convention in 1903. By 1914, it had 602 affiliated branches and societies. Fawcett and others spoke to crowds of tens of thousands in 1910, 1912, 1913, and 1914.

At the same time, some women grew impatient with traditional techniques. Emmeline Pankhurst at first worked with the ILP. In 1903, Pankhurst and her two oldest daughters, Christabel and Sylvia, organized the militant Women's Social and Political Union (WSPU). While traditional suffragists had lobbied Parliament and petitioned, the WSPU provoked headline-making confrontations. In 1905, Christabel and Annie Kenney, one of the few working class members, were arrested for disturbing crowds leaving a Liberal Party meeting. The first massive public demonstration took place in 1907. About three thousand women participated in a "Mud March" from Hyde Park to Exeter Hall. The *Daily Mail* coined the term "suffragette" to describe these women. Traditional suffragists, such as Fawcett, drew away after 1909 when WSPU tactics changed from rock-throwing to window-breaking and arson. Those arrested began hunger strikes in 1909.

Violence intensified in 1910, when Prime Minister Herbert Asquith offered, then abandoned, a Conciliation Bill that would have enfranchised propertied women. Asquith's manipulations assured political calm for the 1911 coronation of George V, but two weeks after Asquith destroyed the conciliation measure, suffrage activists smashed windows in eleven government offices. In 1912, they began stone-throwing in the fashionable West End and at the prime minister's headquarters at 10 Downing Street. As arrests increased and newspapers brought attention to the brutal force feeding of hunger strikers, Parliament passed the Prisoners (Temporary Discharge for Ill Health) Bill, called the "Cat and Mouse" act, which allowed hunger strikers to be released but rearrested when recovered. Between July and December, 1913, Emmeline

Pankhurst was arrested and discharged six times under this act. At the same time, the military discipline enforced by Emmeline and Christabel Pankhurst caused additional dissension. Sylvia and her sister Adele were among those expelled, as were male sympathizers. With the entry of England into World War I in August, 1914, political activity ceased. Fawcett dedicated NUWSS to war work; Emmeline and Christabel Pankhurst did the same. Unprecedented war casualties definitively changed the role of

Once suffrage was extended to British women in February of 1918, activists encouraged women to exercise their rights by participating in the British general elections of 1918. (Archive Photos)

women, who were drawn from domestic service and housework to relatively high paying jobs. The number of unionized women rose 160 percent to about 1,086,000. Public opinion changed in reaction to women's demonstrated abilities.

When the war ended in 1918, the electoral register had to be changed. Qualifications before the war included twelve months unbroken residence in one place. To enforce this would be to disenfranchise all military veterans. A Representation of the People Bill was introduced, and women could no longer be ignored. The bill granted suffrage to all men above the age of twenty-one and to unmarried or widowed women above the age of thirty who met certain property qualifications. It gave the vote to about six million of approximately eleven million British women. The WSPU disbanded. Fawcett's NUWSS, renamed the National Union of Societies for Equal Citizenship, continued to work for equal legal rights. The legislation, signed into law by George V on February 6, 1918, was followed, in July of 1928, by an act of Parliament extending the vote to all women above age twenty-one.

—*Betty Richardson*

ADDITIONAL READING:

Hamilton, Susan, ed. *"Criminals, Idiots, Women, and Minors": Victorian Writing by Women on Women*. Peterborough, Ontario, Canada: Broadview Press, 1995. Collects essays, not otherwise easily accessible, from writers ranging from suffragist Millicent Fawcett to antisuffrage writer Eliza Lynn Linton. Includes biographical notes.

Kent, Susan Kingsley. *Sex and Suffrage in Britain, 1860-1914*. Princeton, N.J.: Princeton University Press, 1987. Synthesizing a considerable body of scholarship, this scholarly but readable work shows relationship between suffrage and other issues such as marriage laws, prostitution, and medicine.

Liddington, Jill, and Jill Norris. *One Hand Tied Behind Us: The Rise of the Women's Suffrage Movement*. London: Virago, 1978. One of few to do so, this study focuses on the rise of the suffrage movement among working-class women in industrial towns.

Mackenzie, Midge. *Shoulder to Shoulder: A Documentary*. New York: Alfred A. Knopf, 1975. Compiled as a companion for a BBC-Warner Bros. television series, this excellently illustrated work is based on autobiographical fragments from militant suffrage activists.

Mitchell, David. *The Fighting Pankhursts: A Study in Tenacity*. New York: Macmillan, 1967. While Mitchell's work has been criticized by feminists for lack of understanding, this remains the best study of the militant suffrage leaders.

Rubinstein, David. *A Different World for Women: The Life of Millicent Garrett Fawcett*. London: Harvester Wheatsheaf, 1991. Reevaluates life of long-term suffrage leader in the light of postsuffrage scholarship.

Strachey, Ray. *"The Cause": A Short History of the Women's Movement in Great Britain*. London: G. Bell, 1928. Authoritative history by an NUWSS officer, but should be read together with later scholarship. Appendix includes Florence Nightingale's important essay, "Cassandra."

SEE ALSO: 1832, Reform Act of 1832; 1867, Reform Act of 1867; 1884, Franchise Act of 1884; 1900, British Labour Party Is Formed; 1909-1911, Parliament Bill; 1970, Parliament Passes the Equal Pay Act of 1970.

1918-1919
INFLUENZA EPIDEMIC STRIKES

The influenza epidemic strikes, unleashing a major medical plague not witnessed since the fourteenth century and spurring the discovery of its viral agent and a vaccine.

DATE: March, 1918-1919
LOCALE: Europe and worldwide
CATEGORIES: Health and medicine; Science and technology
KEY FIGURES:

Sir Christopher Howard Andrewes (1896-1988), British pathologist and member of the team which isolated influenza Virus A in 1933

Thomas Francis, Jr. (1900-1969), American epidemiologist who isolated influenza Virus B in 1940

Sir Patrick Playfair Laidlaw (1881-1940), British researcher who also helped identify influenza Virus A in 1933

Richard Friedrich Wilhelm Johannes Pfeiffer (1858-1945), German bacteriologist and immunologist who discovered *Haemophilus influenzae* (also known as Pfeiffer's bacillus) in 1892 and identified it as a cause of the disease

Richard Edwin Shope (1901-1966), American animal pathologist and virologist who, in the late 1920's, confirmed veterinarian J. S. Koen's theory formulated in 1918 that swine influenza could be transmitted to humans

Wilson Smith (1897-1965), British bacteriologist who helped identify influenza Virus A in humans in 1933 and cultivated it in chick embryos in 1935

Sir Charles Herbert Stuart-Harris (born 1909), British virologist and influenza researcher

SUMMARY OF EVENT. The influenza (or grippe) pandemic of 1918-1919 was deadlier than any war in history with its fatalities estimated at more than twenty but possibly as high as forty million throughout the world. All told, about a billion of the total world population of two billion at the time are thought to have been exposed to the virus. Too, this epidemic spread faster and more widely than any previous plague. A noted American epidemiologist, Edwin Oakes Jordan, eventually computed the estimated breakdown of mortality by continents as follows: North and Central America, about 1 million; Latin America,

In the United States and Europe, women volunteered as nurses to help care for victims of the widespread influenza epidemic that struck between 1918 and 1919. (Archive Photos)

about 300,000; Europe, about 2.2 million; Asia, about 15.8 million; Australia and Oceania, about 1 million; Africa, about 1.4 million. In the United States alone, some 550,000 died from influenza or its frequent pneumonic complications.

One peculiarity of the 1918 version of the flu was that it especially affected young adults between the ages of twenty and forty. Uncharacteristically, older citizens above sixty years, normally the most vulnerable, were now least so. Accordingly, it is on the basis of substantial increases in young adult deaths that pandemic pathways around the globe could be traced.

The world debut of influenza in 1918 is uncertain. The United States was hit as early as March of that year as were France, Japan, China, and others. This initial wave of the attack was fairly mild and attracted little notice. Indeed, in recent times influenza had appeared identifiably in 1627, 1729, 1788, 1830, 1847, 1872, and 1889-1892 but is known to have existed since the distant past, breaking out frequently but irregularly. In the early days, influenza epidemics had been attributed by astrologers to the influence (hence influenza) of the heavenly bodies. Only when

the second, much more lethal, wave broke out in August-September, 1918, did the world witness an unprecedented flu epidemic. The added virulence of this newer onslaught was subsequently explained as having been caused synergistically by a fairly mild hog flu virus acting in conjunction with an equally benign Pfeiffer bacillus. In combination, these two parasites produced a maverick killer that injured human lungs beyond their capacity to recover. During its peak in October-November, 1918, the influenza morbidity rate in the United States ranged from two hundred to four hundred per thousand population while the mortality rate was about fifty, compared to the normal thirteen from all causes. Even though the pandemic visited all continents, this new strain of an old affliction was dubbed the "Spanish flu," since uncensored news of its devastation was coming out of that neutral country, Spain, during the world conflict.

Wartime conditions—individuals in their prime crowded in cities, in military camps, on vessels, in hospitals, and elsewhere and moving about in unprecedented numbers—contributed to the rapid spread of the disease. On the western front in Europe, major offensives, first by the Germans and then by the Allies, were blunted in the summer and fall of 1918, partly because of the large number of troops victimized by the flu. The ailment recognized no regions, races, or categories other than age. The epidemic seems, however, to have found easy victims among peoples worn down by the deprivations of war and/or poverty, as in India. Even important World War I leaders were not spared, including President Woodrow Wilson (who nearly died of influenza in April of 1919), Premier Georges Clemenceau of France, and Prime Minister David Lloyd George of Great Britain.

At the time, the specific cause of this highly contagious respiratory infection was unknown. Its symptoms, since its identification as the "English sweat" in the sixteenth century, were, however, familiar: sudden fever, inflammation of the mucous membranes, coughing, a headache, acute perspiration, occasional nosebleed, muscular discomfort, prostration. Even though an attempt was made in 1951 to exhume the well-preserved bodies of Eskimo victims known to have died of influenza in the pandemic and buried in Alaska's permafrost, there was no trace of what was by then known conclusively to be the general cause of influenza: Any of three distinct types of viruses, A, B, and C. These minute organisms mutate rapidly and resurface in several strains, or subtypes. Type A was identified in 1933 by Dr. Wilson Smith, Sir Christopher Andrewes, and Sir Patrick Laidlaw as a filterable virus which was experimentally transmitted to animals and which the latter—not just hogs but also horses and birds among others—are suspected of harboring "underground" without causing outbreaks, except on occasion. One of these instances was in 1918-1919.

The countermeasures taken in that epidemic, most vigorously in cities such as San Francisco, were generally gauze masks, at times medicated, worn on the face, and even some makeshift attempts at vaccination. Nevertheless, such countermeasures did not seem to be effective. Indeed, it was not until the 1930's that virology had advanced sufficiently to pinpoint the basic agent which had killed more in a year than World War I had done in four. Without a miracle drug or appropriate vaccine, rest, warmth, fresh air, and good nursing care were about the best that the medical profession could prescribe in 1918-1919, since immediate priorities at that time necessarily had to focus on symptoms and disease control rather than prevention.

While individual survivors of the pandemic vividly recall how the event affected them, surprisingly, though cataclysmic, this plague seems to have had little impact on the collective psyche. Mention of the epidemic by historians and writers describing the period has been generally casual, brief, or nonexistent. Notable exceptions are authors Katherine Anne Porter, Thomas Wolfe, Mary McCarthy, and others, who, in different ways, were markedly affected by the event. There may be at least two reasons for such treatment. First, influenza is usually an uncomplicated illness and a minor inconvenience. Second, because it recurs frequently, the ailment is only too familiar. In short, it lacks the drama of other killers, such as tuberculosis.

There have been several influenza epidemics since that of 1918-1919 going by different names, including "swine flu," "Hong Kong flu," or "Asian flu." The reason is that most epidemics are caused by different strains of the Group A virus, and there are about a thousand of them. Samples of these are stored at the Influenza Center of the World Health Organization in London. Yet second-guessing the particular subtype that will hit in any particular flu season—essential to preparing an appropriate vaccination response in time—remained problematic even at the close of the twentieth century. The variation of the virus is still not fully understood, and the world may again witness the visitation of the "Spanish Lady."

—*Peter B. Heller*

ADDITIONAL READING:

Beveridge, W. I. B. Influenza, *The Last Great Plague: An Unfinished Story of Discovery*. New York: Prodist, 1977. The author, a British veterinarian, speculates on the possible animal origins of the 1918 epidemic.

Collier, Richard. *The Plague of the Spanish Lady: The Influenza Pandemic of 1918-1919*. New York: Atheneum, 1974. Based on the personal accounts of 1708 survivors of the epidemic and thus highly anecdotal but nevertheless informative. Illustrated and with a good bibliography.

Crosby, Alfred W., Jr. *America's Forgotten Pandemic: The Influenza of 1918*. New York: Cambridge University Press, 1989. This American medical writer puzzles over why the epidemic, despite its magnitude, was, generally speaking, neither traumatic nor memorable.

Jordan, Edwin O. *Epidemic Influenza: A Survey*. Chicago: American Medical Association, 1927. Though dated, still one of the most authoritative sources by an eminent American epidemiologist.

Kilbourne, Edwin D. *Influenza*. New York: Plenum, 1987. In chapter 1, "History of Influenza," this medical doctor considers technical aspects of the 1918 pandemic.

Osborn, June E., ed. *Influenza in America 1918-1976*. New York: Prodist, 1977. Includes an essay by Alfred W. Crosby, Jr., "The Pandemic of 1918," which provides an excellent synopsis.

Pettigrew, Eileen. *The Silent Enemy: Canada and the*

Deadly Flu of 1918. Saskatoon, Saskatchewan, Canada: Western Producer Prairie Books, 1983. An account of how the epidemic killed more Canadians than World War I. Includes illustrations and a good bibliography.

Pyle, Gerald F. *The Diffusion of Influenza: Patterns and Paradigms.* Totowa, N.J.: Rowman & Littlefield, 1986. Chapter 3, "Calamity and Discovery: The Early Twentieth Century," describes the epidemic of 1918 with considerable statistical information. Maps by the author-geographer graphically illustrate the spread of the plague.

SEE ALSO: 1882-1884, Koch Isolates Microorganisms That Cause Tuberculosis and Cholera; 1928, Fleming Discovers Penicillin.

1918
TREATY OF BREST-LITOVSK

The Treaty of Brest-Litovsk ends hostilities between Russia and Germany, giving Germany a break from a two-front war and the Soviet communist regime in Russia a chance to organize.

DATE: March 3, 1918

LOCALE: Brest-Litovsk, Russia (modern Belorus)

CATEGORIES: Diplomacy and international relations; Wars, uprisings, and civil unrest

KEY FIGURES:

Field Marshal Paul von Hindenberg (1847-1934),
 high-ranking leader of the German High Command

Major General Max Hoffmann (1869-1927),
 commander of German armies on the eastern front

Adolf Joffe, Bolshevik representative at the cease-fire negotiations

Baron Richard von Kühlmann (1873-1948), German foreign secretary

Vladimir Ilich Lenin (Ulyanov; 1870-1924), Bolshevik leader in Russia, 1917-1924

General Erich Friedrich Wilhelm Ludendorff
 (1865-1937), leader of the German High Command

Nicholas II (1868-1918), czar of Russia, 1894-1917

Leon Trotsky (Leib Davydovich Bronstein; 1879-1940),
 foreign commissar of the Bolshevik government and negotiator at the Brest-Litovsk conference

SUMMARY OF EVENT. Since 1914, Germany had been conducting a two-front war. The eastern front was the war between Germany and Russia. By 1917, Czar Nicholas II was in personal command of the army since all his officers had deserted him. There was growing unrest in Russia, with Vladimir Lenin leading the Bolshevik Party, in conjunction with the Menshevik Party, advocating overthrow of the Romanov dynasty and the establishment of a Marxist government in Russia. The agitation of Lenin and his

followers originated outside Russia since the leaders were in exile. The soldiers and people of Russia were tired of war and the Bolsheviks promised that if they were in power, they would end the war immediately.

Meanwhile, Germany was being stretched as far as it could be by trying to defend both fronts. General Hoffmann had eighty divisions under his command, but while all of this political maneuvering was occurring, the Soviet troops piled their weapons and began to consort with the idle German soldiers. During the confusion of the overthrow of the Russian czar and, later, the provisional government, Germany did not attack the idle troops for two reasons: By treating the enemy gently, the Germans were likely to receive a bid for peace from Petrograd and could conserve the German troops for the western front.

Germany, in an attempt to continue its war aims by signing a separate peace with one of the Entente powers, and end a war on at least one front, agreed to allow Lenin to return from exile in what became known as the infamous "sealed train," which carried Lenin and his party from Switzerland to Finland via Germany. Germany agreed to allow Lenin through their country in the hope that he would soon gain power and fulfill his promise of ending the war.

The Bolsheviks seized power in Petrograd on November 7-8, 1917, and gained control of much of European and Asiatic Russia by the following spring. Lenin published his Decree on Peace on November 8, proposing a three-month armistice and negotiations for a general settlement without annexations or indemnities.

On December 2, the Bolshevik Armistice Delegation passed through German lines to enter Brest-Litovsk. Heading the Russian delegation was Adolf Joffe, and for the Germans, General Hoffmann. At the peace table, the difference in power could be seen by the representatives of each government. Germany sent elegant diplomatic and grimly correct military staff officers to the table, while Russia sent unkempt, bearded peasants and workers of the soviets with only one military adviser. Lenin was trying to gain political clout by including representatives of each strata, except the aristocracy, at the talks, including a woman, Madame Anastasia Bizenko.

On December 15, Russia signed a separate cease-fire with the Central Powers at Brest-Litovsk, where peace negotiations began a week later. The Russians presented a six-point plan for peace without annexations or indemnities, which the Central Powers accepted with reservations on Christmas Day, on the condition that the Allies should do the same.

The Allied response to the negotiations in Brest-Litovsk was confused. The French were convinced that an "eastern barrier" of nations, declaring their independence from Imperial Russia, would counterbalance the power of Germany. The British, on the other hand, believed that drawing Austria into a separate peace with the Allies, with the assistance of America, would cause the downfall of the German coalition. For the most part, the Allies condemned the plan, with President Woodrow Wilson stating his Fourteen Points and Prime Minister David Lloyd George making a fiery speech to rouse the English nation.

From the German perspective, if the Allies could not be drawn into negotiations based on no annexations and the prewar status quo, a separate peace with Russia would allow the Germans to reach Paris and force the West to negotiate. The German leadership, however, was caught in a power struggle between the German High Command, in the guise of General Erich Ludendorff and Field Marshall Paul von Hindenberg, and Baron Richard von Kühlmann, the kaiser's adviser on foreign policy. Ludendorff believed that the Russians could be overwhelmed by a display of force by the German troops, allowing Germany to annex more land, and forced to sign the treaty on German terms. Kühlmann, the civilian adviser in charge of foreign policy, wanted to sign the treaty in order to release the troops to the western front.

On January 5, 1918, after the Allied response, the Central Powers declared the plan null and void, and imposed their own plan on Russia in the Treaty of Brest-Litovsk. Leon Trotsky, one of the leaders of the Bolshevik regime, personally headed the Russian delegation when negotiations began again on January 9. When the Central Powers signed a separate peace treaty with representatives of the Rada parliament of Ukraine one month later, Trotsky walked out of the conference, declaring unilaterally that hostilities were ended, but refusing to accept Germany's terms. This was Russia's famous slogan of "no war, no peace." This brought the internal conflict between Kühlmann and the German High Command to a head.

Kühlmann wished to accept the no war, no peace scenario and continue to fight against the Allies on the western front. He believed that continuing the assault into Russia would lead to the same results that Napoleon experienced and would stretch the German forces to the breaking point. Hindenberg and Ludendorff insisted upon an imposed peace, in the hope of uniting Germany and perhaps toppling the Bolshevik regime in Russia. Hindenberg and Ludendorff won the support of the kaiser and proceeded to call Trotsky's bluff by resuming the German advances into Russia on February 18, 1918.

German forces advanced almost at will. The Central Power's new terms required Russia to yield sovereignty over territory west of the line from the Gulf of Riga to Brest-Litovsk, including Poland, Courland, and Lithuania. In the south, Russia would evacuate the districts of Kars, Ardahan, and Batum to Turkish overrule. Russia would also give up all rights to the Ukraine and Finland.

On March 3, 1918, Lenin was forced to accept terms for Russia worse than those they had previously rejected in February in order to save the Bolshevik regime. Russia's loss in human life, territory, and prestige was horrendous. Russia lost more than 30 percent of its former lands and more than fifty-five million people by accepting these terms. Russia also lost nearly all of its iron-ore and coal resources. Lenin's justification was that this was breathing space until Russia could recover its strength. Although the "no war, no peace" cry was the beginning of the downfall of Trotsky, Lenin emerged from this treaty in a stronger political position.

The immediate consequences of the Treaty of Brest-Litovsk were the civil wars that broke out in Finland and Russia. These wars promoted Allied "intervention" into Russia and Finland in 1918 as part of an undeclared war between the Reds and the Whites (Bolshevik forces and Royalist-Provisional forces), with the Allies supporting the Whites.

While the Treaty of Brest-Litovsk was an unqualified disaster for all parties, the consequences of the negotiations lingered into the late twentieth century. Wilson's Fourteen Points became the basis of the American commitment to European affairs and the basis for the establishment of the League of Nations, the forerunner to the United Nations. Wilson also stated that nationality should be a factor in determining a nation's borders, with some references to the Balkans. These points became the basis of the Armistice that was signed with Germany at the end of World War I.

—Elizabeth L. Scully

ADDITIONAL READING:

Farrar, L. L. *Divide and Conquer: German Efforts to Conclude a Separate Peace, 1914-1918*. New York: Columbia University Press, 1978. Interesting German perspective detailing German efforts to shatter the Entente by concluding a separate peace with one of its members.

Marshall, S. L. A. *World War I*. Boston: Houghton Mifflin, 1992. Concise one-volume work that discusses the major events of World War I, with two excellent chapters on the consequences of the Brest-Litovsk Treaty.

Mayer, Arno J. *Political Origins of the New Diplomacy, 1917-1918*. New York: Howard Fertig, 1969. Investigates the war aims of the various nations involved based on military stalemate, the Russian Revolution, and the American intervention and the creation of the New Diplomacy in world politics.

Stevenson, David. *The First World War and International Politics*. Oxford, England: Oxford University Press, 1988. While probing the political dynamics of World War I, this work contains an excellent chapter on the Brest-Litovsk Treaty and its consequences.

Wheeler-Bennett, John W. *Brest-Litovsk: The Forgotten Peace, March, 1918*. London: Macmillan, 1963. Examines all aspects of the Brest-Litovsk negotiations and the long-term effects of the treaty.

SEE ALSO: 1914, Outbreak of World War I; 1917, October Revolution; 1918-1921, Russian Civil War; 1919, The League of Nations Is Established; 1919, Treaty of Versailles; 1919, Weimar Constitution.

1919-1933
RACIST THEORIES AID NAZI RISE TO POLITICAL POWER

Racist theories aid the Nazi rise to political power as the incorporation of several popular ideas concerning human racial types and human evolution into its political ideology contributes significantly to the party's political triumph in 1933.

DATE: 1919-1933
LOCALE: Germany
CATEGORIES: Government and politics; Race and ethnicity
KEY FIGURES:

Houston Stewart Chamberlain (1855-1927), son-in-law of composer Richard Wagner and British-born scholar who published a book emphasizing the importance of race in the development of human history, which greatly influenced Hitler's ideas on the subject

Sir Francis Galton (1822-1911), British scientist and founder of the eugenics movement, which heavily influenced Nazi racial ideas

Count Joseph Arthur de Gobineau (1816-1882), widely read French champion of "scientific" theories concerning the superiority of the German (Teutonic) race

Joseph Goebbels (1897-1945), master propagandist of the Nazi Party who simplified racist theories for mass consumption

Adolf Hitler (1889-1945), führer of the Nazi Party who incorporated racist theories into the Nazi political platform

Wilhelm Marr, one of the earliest German exponents of a racial interpretation of history

Alfred Rosenberg (1893-1946), leading theorist for the Nazi racial interpretation of history, editor of the Nazi newspaper *Völischer Beobachter*, and author of *The Myth of the Twentieth Century* (1930)

SUMMARY OF EVENT. In the German parliamentary elections of March, 1933, the *Nationelsozialistische Deutsche Arbeiterpartei* (National Socialist German Workers' Party, NSDAP, or Nazis for short) attracted slightly more than 44 percent of the total vote. The Nazi leader, or führer, Adolf Hitler, immediately formed a coalition government with another nationalist party, giving his movement a slim majority in the German Reichstag (parliament). Hitler then proceeded to establish a totalitarian dictatorship which attempted to make every aspect of German society conform to his own peculiar ideology.

Many historians have pointed out the importance of the racism of Hitler's program as a major element in the endorsement of his movement by many German voters at the polls in 1933. Once the Nazis were in power, racism formed a major component of their reorganization of German society. Hitler, his chief propagandist, Joseph Goebbels, and the self-proclaimed leading "theorist" of the NSDAP, Alfred Rosenberg, did not invent the racial theories and ideas they helped popularize before 1933 and tried to implement in subsequent years. They took them from a number of divergent and largely unrelated movements and ideas of the nineteenth and early twentieth centuries from all parts of Europe and blended them into a powerful political force in the turbulent years following World War I.

Some historians trace the origins of Nazi racial ideas to the anti-Semitism of the Christian churches in Europe during the Middle Ages. Many church leaders preached against acceptance of Jews in Christian communities, leading to the implementation of special laws which curtailed Jewish legal rights and sometimes led to outbreaks of violence against Jews. This religious anti-Semitism prepared the groundwork among the rural masses of Germany and Europe for the much more complex racism that emerged after the French Revolution of 1789.

The lifting during the revolutionary era of most of the legal and economic restrictions that Jews had suffered for centuries allowed many Jews to prosper in Europe. Some Jews amassed great fortunes during the spread of industrialization during the nineteenth century. Many Christians bitterly resented the success of people they considered aliens. Some European writers in the middle of the century began to refer to Jews as parasites, who accumulated wealth not through honest labor, but through duplicitous exploitation of Christians. This new economic anti-Semitism complemented and supported the older Christian anti-Semitism, which never disappeared.

During the final quarter of the nineteenth century and the first years of the twentieth century, writers in several European countries began calling for political action to eliminate the threat posed by "aliens," especially Jews, to native European civilization. Wilhelm Marr and Adolf Stoecker in Germany, Charles Maurras in France, and Karl Luger in Austria, attracted large popular followings by advocating political action to limit or eliminate Jewish influence in their countries.

Books by Adolf Hitler and Alfred Rosenberg fueled the spread of racist theories in Nazi Germany. (Library of Congress)

Marr's *Judentum und Deutschtum (Jewishness and Germanness,* 1876) argued persuasively that Jewish materialism corrupted the idealistic essence of the Germanic soul and would, if left unchallenged, eventually destroy German civilization. At least partly in response to Marr's contentions, Stoecker (once court chaplain to Emperor William II of Germany) formed the Christian Socialist Union, which had as its primary purpose the elimination of Jewish economic and political influence in Germany. During the Dreyfus affair in France during the 1890's, Maurras' newspaper *Action Français* gained a huge popular following by denouncing the pernicious influence on French society of "alien" and unpatriotic Jews. The people

of Vienna elected Luger as their mayor several times even though his political platform consisted of little more than denunciation of Jews and promises to limit their influence.

During this same era of European history, "scientific" theories of race emerged which seemed to lend credibility to this rapidly spreading religious, economic, and political anti-Semitism. Anthropologists and linguists produced works that suggested "Indo-European" or "Aryan" origins of many of the great civilizations of antiquity. Count Joseph Arthur de Gobineau produced a work entitled *Essay on the Inequality of Races* (1876), which used the terminology of Charles Darwin's theory of evolution. Gobineau ranked the races of the world according to their "evolution," concluding that the "Germanic" (Aryan/ Teutonic/Indo-European) race had evolved to the highest level, with the Australian aborigines at the bottom. According to Gobineau and others who elaborated on his thesis, only the Germanic race was capable of producing true civilization. Gobineau's imitators reserved a special place for the Jews, whom they characterized as parasites—destroyers of civilization which they themselves were incapable of creating. While these racist ideas were spreading, they became enmeshed with a new science founded by a first cousin of Darwin, which lent them a more sinister dimension.

Francis Galton, a cousin of Charles Darwin and scientist in his own right, published a book in 1883 which marked the beginning of a new science called eugenics. Galton and the huge international following which he attracted began to argue that the human race could and should be improved through encouraging mating between physically and intellectually superior persons and discouraging reproduction by persons with physically or mentally undesirable characteristics. In every European nation, the United States, and many other countries as well, prominent citizens (often led by prominent academicians) formed eugenics societies which brought pressure on politicians to implement Galton's ideas about racial hygiene. Many of the members of these eugenics societies also subscribed to the theories popularized by Gobineau, Maurras, Marr, and others. These racist ideas received further popular impetus from the works of Helena Blavatsky and Richard Wagner.

Blavatsky founded the Theosophical Society, which incorporated occult philosophies into a racial interpretation of history that attracted many pseudo-intellectuals during the generation before World War I. Wagner's immensely popular music drew on themes from Germanic mythology. Both Blavatsky and Wagner appealed to the irrational emotions of their audiences, which included many of the religious, economic, scientific, and political racists of European society.

European governments at least indirectly encouraged the wide dissemination of these racist ideas by deliberately attempting to inspire nationalist fervor in their citizens. Many European political leaders saw a blind and unquestioning loyalty to the "Fatherland" as necessary if citizens were to be convinced of the importance of imperialistic expansion and the high financial expenditures of military buildup justified. Some political leaders also felt that by inspiring a chauvinistic nationalism in their citizens through the educational system and the popular press they could divert the working class from the growing political appeal of socialism.

In Germany, all the racist ideas mentioned above merged during the late nineteenth and early twentieth centuries into something called the *Völkisch* movement. Popular writers and newspaper publishers such as Georg von Schoenerer, Arthur Moeller van den Bruck, and Houston Stewart Chamberlain, whose *Die Grundlagen des Neunzehnten Jahrhunderts* (1899; *The Foundations of the Nineteenth Century*, 1911) influenced Hitler, Rosenberg, and other Nazis, along with the influential publicist Friedrich Lienhard, spread *Völkisch* ideas to every area of Germany and throughout all segments of the German population. The *Völkisch* movement also disseminated *The Protocols of the Elders of Zion*, purportedly a Jewish plan for world domination, which fanned the flames of the spreading racist hysteria. Hitler's movement was only a small and (at first) insignificant part of the hyperracist *Völkisch* movement. He and his party propagandists used the groundwork laid by decades of *Völkisch* agitation to convince German voters to support the Nazi Party at the polls.

—*Paul Madden*

ADDITIONAL READING:

Field, Geoffrey C. *Evangelist of Race: The Germanic Vision of Houston Stewart Chamberlain*. New York: Columbia University Press, 1981. Critiques Chamberlain's racial theories and evaluates their influence on the evolution of European racism.

Hay, Malcolm. *Thy Brother's Blood: The Roots of Christian Anti-Semitism*. New York: Hart, 1975. Traces the origins and influence of Christian anti-Semitism. Argues that hatred of Jews preached by Christian ministers contributed heavily to Nazi racism and the Holocaust.

Katz, Jacob. *From Prejudice to Destruction: Anti-Semitism, 1700-1933*. Cambridge, Mass.: Harvard University Press, 1980. Shows the evolution of anti-Semitism from its Christian origins through the stages of economic, political, scientific, and occult racism before 1933.

Mosse, George Lachmann. *Toward the Final Solution: A History of European Racism*. Madison: University of Wisconsin Press, 1985. Considers European racism within the larger context of the industrial and scientific revolutions. Shows the influence of previous ideas of race on Nazi racist doctrine.

Weiss, Sheila Faith. *Race Hygiene and National Efficiency: The Eugenics of Wilhelm Schallmayer*. Berkeley: University of California Press, 1987. Examines the nature of the German eugenics movement and its influence on Nazi racial ideas. Shows the cross-fertilization between scientific racism and the *Völkisch* movement.

SEE ALSO: 1859, Darwin Publishes *On the Origin of Species*; 1894-1906, The Dreyfus Affair; 1903-1906, Pogroms in Imperial Russia; 1939-1945, Gypsies Are Exterminated in Nazi Death Camps; 1939-1945, Nazi Extermination of the Jews.

1919
ROSA LUXEMBURG IS ASSASSINATED

Rosa Luxemburg is assassinated, elevating her to the status of a martyr for socialism.

DATE: January 15, 1919

LOCALE: Berlin, Germany

CATEGORIES: Government and politics; Terrorism and political assassination

KEY FIGURES:

Friedrich Ebert (1871-1925), German chancellor when Luxemburg was murdered

Leo Jogiches (1867-1919), Luxemburg's associate and lover

Karl Liebknecht (1871-1919), lawyer, Reichstag member, and organizer of the Sparticists, who was also murdered January 15, 1919

Rosa Luxemburg (1870-1919), Marxist philosopher, orator, and Sparticist leader

Otto Runge, participant in the assassinations of Luxemburg and Liebknecht

Kurt Vogel, German lieutenant responsible for Luxemburg's death

SUMMARY OF EVENT. The murder of Rosa Luxemburg in January, 1919, can best be understood in the context of her life, career, and political philosophy. Born in Zamose, Poland, on March 5, 1870, of Jewish parentage, handicapped by a limp at an early age, she left her home in Warsaw for Zurich, Switzerland, in 1889, and enrolled at the University. In Zurich she met Leo Jogiches, who throughout her life would be her confidant, her collaborator, and intermittently her lover. Luxemburg graduated from the university in 1897 with a doctorate in law and political science; her thesis, *The Development of Industry in Poland*, was published in July, 1898, and an article,

"Step by Step," a study of the Polish middle class, appeared in an important German newspaper.

In April, 1898, in order to obtain German citizenship, Luxemburg married Gustav Lubeck. (they were divorced in 1903). The next month she left Zurich for Berlin, where she immediately became involved in the activities of the German Social Democratic Party. She was sent to Upper Silesia, a part of Poland annexed by Prussia, where she campaigned for Social Democratic candidates for the Reichstag. She wrote *Social Reform and Revolution*, appearing in six installments in September, 1898, one of her most important contributions to socialist thought. In contrast and in conflict with the arguments of Eduard Bernstein, who advocated a policy of peaceful social and political reform in Germany, she restated and refined Marxist doctrine, insisting on the need and inevitability of social revolution.

Luxemburg's speeches and writing, her organizing on behalf of the Social Democratic Party of the kingdoms of Poland and Lithuania, and her participation in international socialist conferences attracted the attention and reaction of both German and Russian authorities. In May,

A noted political activist and organizer, Rosa Luxemburg attracted attention for her public speeches advocating socialist revolution in Germany. (Archive Photos)

1903, addressing audiences in twelve cities, she spoke to fifteen hundred people in Bydgoszcz, five hundred the next day in Pila, and two thousand in Liechtenstein a few days later. Her speeches were usually two hours in length, followed by questions and answers and long meetings. A few months later in 1904, Luxemburg spent two months in prison for insulting Emperor William II of Germany. In 1906, along with Leo Jogiches, she was arrested by the czarist police and for a time incarcerated in the Warsaw Citadel.

Between her two prison terms, mass strikes had erupted in Germany, Poland, and Russia in 1905, and Czar Nicholas II was forced to permit the organization of the Duma, a representative assembly. Luxemburg spoke out against a policy of caution urged by the leadership of the General Commission of the German Trade Unions. At the Jena Party Congress in September, 1905, she argued that "we must remind ourselves that for us the final words of the *Communist Manifesto* are not merely fine phrases . . . but that we are in bloody earnest when we appeal to the masses [saying] the workers have nothing to lose but their chains—but a whole world to gain."

Luxemburg believed strongly in the importance and spontaneity of mass strikes ushering in the socialist revolution; for the German opposition to her ideas, she would become known as "Bloody Rosa." Despite another imprisonment in Berlin in 1907, and despite arguments in the factional struggles of the German and Russian socialist parties, Luxemburg persisted and persevered. She found time to write *The National Question and Autonomy*, published in 1908, condemning nationalistic movements in Poland, India, and Latin America as middle-class obsessions, unworthy of the support of Social Democrats.

"Social Democracy," she said, "is called to realize not the right of self-determination of nations [but] the self-determination of the working class." Increasingly, she was at odds with the leadership of the German Social Democratic Party, embittering her relations with Karl Kautsky, one of Germany's most prominent Marxists, and humiliating him in the party press. There were charges and countercharges between Luxemburg and other radicals, accusations that she betrayed the party; she was being politically isolated, finding difficulties in placing her articles in party journals and disseminating her viewpoints. Yet she was determined to remain within the party, discouraging efforts by her supporters to form a new political organization.

The beginning of the final rupture with the German Social Democratic Party came during World War I. In the Reichstag, the Social Democratic deputies, adopting the position that the German declaration of war against France and Russia was a defensive posture against czarist despotism, voted to endorse the government's appeal for war credits. Despite another conviction for pro- republican and anti-imperial sentiments, Luxemburg, along with Karl Liebknecht, denounced the policy of the Social Democratic majority. With Liebknecht, she formed the "International Group," soon to become known as the Sparticists, and published their own newspaper. Luxemburg wrote "The Crisis of Social Democracy," an analysis of the events that led to the European War and criticizing the mistakes of the Social Democratic Party "in the abdication of our will to struggle, of our courage, our fidelity to our convictions." Luxemburg herself did not lack a "will to struggle . . . courage . . . fidelity." She was in prison for a year from February, 1915, to February, 1916; later, she was placed in "protective custody" in July, 1916, where she remained until November, 1918. She was in prison during the March Revolution of 1917 in Russia, remained there during the Bolshevik Revolution in October, and was still incarcerated when there were mass strikes in Germany in March, 1918, as its leaders prepared to leave the war.

By the time of Luxemburg's release on November 9, 1918, the German emperor had abdicated his throne and gone into exile in neutral Holland, and Social Democratic deputies had joined the new government. On her return to Berlin, a republic had been proclaimed by the Social Democratic deputy, Phillip Scheiderman, and the Social Democratic deputy Fritz Ebert had become Reichschancellor.

Yet neither Karl Liebknecht nor Rosa Luxemburg were satisfied with the establishment of a republic. While Luxemburg was still in prison, the Sparticists had joined in an uneasy coalition with the Independent Social Democratic Party of Germany, the pacifist wing of the Social Democrats, after their expulsion from the party in 1917. In December, 1918, after a government attack on the People's Naval Division, which had mutinied in Kiel a year before, the Sparticists demanded that the Independent Social Democrats convene a party congress. The refusal of the Independent Social Democrats led to the establishment of the Communist Party of Germany.

On January 4, 1919, the Ebert government discharged Emil Eichhorn, the radical Berlin police chief. There was a protest demonstration; the Sparticists took control of the offices of the Social Democratic newspaper, and Liebknecht joined a Revolutionary Commission which declared the end of the Ebert government. Yet the Sparticists had acted too precipitously in fomenting an insurrection. The army supported the government, and Luxemburg and Liebknecht went into hiding, moving from place to

place as hunted fugitives with a price on their heads.

The end came on the evening of January 15, 1919. Luxemburg and Liebknecht were arrested by army troopers, taken to the Eden Hotel, the headquarters of the Guards Cavalry Rifle Division. There, they were informed that they would be transferred to the Moabit Prison. Liebknecht went first. As he left the hotel under army escort past jeering guests, an army rifleman, Otto Runge, hit Liebknecht with his rifle butt. Luxemburg then followed, also past whistling and spitting guests. Runge also hit her with his rifle, and blood poured from her nose and mouth. Dragged into a waiting car, Rosa Luxemburg was shot in the left temple by Lieutenant Kurt Vogel, her body then thrown from the Liechtenstein Bridge into the Landwehr Canal. At approximately the same time, Liebknecht was killed "while attempting to escape."

In May, 1919, by a military court-martial, Otto Runge and Kurt Vogel were sentenced to two years in prison. The escorts of Karl Liebknecht were acquitted of all charges. Two months earlier in March, 1919, Leo Jogiches, who revealed the identity of the perpetrators of the Luxemburg-Liebknecht murders, was taken into custody, severely beaten, and then shot "while attempting to escape."

—*David L. Sterling*

ADDITIONAL READING:

Abraham, Richard. *Rosa Luxemburg: A Life for the International*. Oxford: Berg Publishers, 1989. A concise analysis of Luxemburg's life and thought with an extensive and helpful bibliography and a guide to political parties and factions.

Ettinger, Elzbieta. *Rosa Luxemburg: A Life*. Boston: Beacon Press, 1986. This biography focuses on Luxemburg's personal life and her relations with Leo Jogiches and other men.

Geras, Norman. *The Legacy of Rosa Luxemburg*. London: NLB, 1976. Four essays on the political theories of Luxemburg including a study of her views on the mass strike.

Howard, Dick, ed. *Selected Political Writings of Rosa Luxemburg*. New York: The Monthly Review Press, 1971. A sampling of articles including *Social Reform or Revolution* and "The Crisis in German Social Democracy."

Netti, John Peter. *Rosa Luxemburg*. 2 vols. London: Oxford University Press, 1966. At 984 pages, this work is the most exhaustive and probably the best biography of Luxemburg.

SEE ALSO: 1848, Marx and Engels Publish the *Communist Manifesto*; 1864, The First International Is Formed; 1898, Social-Democratic Workers' Party Is Formed.

1919
THE LEAGUE OF NATIONS IS ESTABLISHED

The League of Nations is established, fulfilling Woodrow Wilson's dream of an international organization to prevent future wars.

DATE: June 28, 1919
LOCALE: Versailles, near Paris, France
CATEGORY: Diplomacy and international relations
KEY FIGURES:

Leon-Victor-Auguste Bourgeois (1851-1925), French statesman, chairman of the first meeting of the League of Nations

Lord Robert Cecil (Edgar Algernon Robert Gascoyne-Cecil; 1864-1958), assistant foreign secretary of Great Britain

Sir James Eric Drummond (1876-1951), first secretary-general of the League of Nations, 1919-1933

Edward Mandell House (known as "Colonel" House; 1858-1938), American diplomat, confidant of President Wilson

David Lloyd George (1863-1945), British prime minister, 1916-1922

Jan Christian Smuts (1870-1950, prime minister of the Union of South Africa, 1919-1924

Woodrow Wilson (1856-1924), twenty-eighth president of the United States, 1913-1921

SUMMARY OF EVENT. The idea of an international peace-keeping organization arose during World War I when leading statesmen decided that such a catastrophe should never again happen. For a hundred years before 1914, the absence of general war in Europe convinced most people that peace had become a tradition characteristic of modern industrialized society. None of the major European states, it was optimistically assumed, would condone a general conflict simply because they were too far advanced. In fact, the modern technological development of the European countries meant that when war came the ability to mobilize the whole nation would increase the destructive power of the conflict. When combined with the reverence attached to the idea of the sovereign national state, the potential existed for the kind of total war that erupted during the late summer of 1914. The interlocking system of secret alliances and rival interests which existed at that time guaranteed that the crisis that began at Sarajevo would result in a general European war.

As the war dragged on through four bloody years, many statesmen and leaders in Europe and America came to the conclusion that some kind of world forum should be established to prevent the repetition of the events that had plunged Europe into chaos. For President Woodrow Wilson, it seemed the special task of the United States to take the lead in establishing the mechanism that would forestall a future conflict.

In January of 1918, Wilson addressed Congress and proposed his Fourteen Points as the basis for world peace. Summarized, they were: open covenants of peace openly arrived at, freedom of navigation upon the seas, removal of all economic barriers and establishment of equal trade conditions among all nations, reduction of national armaments as consistent with internal security, impartial adjustment of colonial claims, friendly settlement of questions affecting Russia, evacuation and restoration of Belgium, restoration of invaded territory of France and return of Alsace-Lorraine, readjustment of frontiers of Italy, autonomy of Austro-Hungarian peoples, guarantees of free determination to Balkan States, sovereignty of Turkey with autonomous development of nationalities under Turkish rule and free passage through the Dardanelles, an independent Polish state with access to the sea, and formation of a permanent association of states to preserve peace. Both President Wilson and David Lloyd George, prime minister of Great Britain, emphasized the establishment of an association of nations to preserve peace. For Woodrow Wilson, this League of Nations would make the terrible sacrifice of World War I mean something permanent and lasting. By November, most of the belligerents had expressed their commitment to support the creation of the League of Nations. In the case of the defeated Germans, they had been compelled to agree to the Fourteen Points as the price for an armistice to stop the fighting.

The peace conference at Versailles convened on January 10, 1919. After one week of debate among leading statesmen, a plenary session of January 25, 1919, at the insistence of President Wilson, decided that the Covenant of the League of Nations should be incorporated into the peace treaty with Germany. The same resolution set up a committee of the associated governments "to work out the details of the constitution and functions of the League." In addition to its chairman, President Woodrow Wilson, this committee comprised staunch proponents of the League idea, including American diplomat Edward Mandell House, who represented the United States; Prime Minister Jan Christian Smuts of the Union of South Africa, who represented the British empire; Lord Robert Cecil, the British assistant foreign secretary, who represented Great Britain; and Leon-Victor-Auguste Bourgeois, the former premier of France, who represented France.

The committee began work on February 3 and labored until April on drafting a constitution for the League. It made use of plans submitted by President Wilson, Colonel House, and others, and it relied heavily on the pamphlet by Smuts entitled *The League of Nations: A Practical Suggestion*. This pamphlet was noteworthy for its lofty idealism and its clear definition of the three primary functions of the League of Nations: to safeguard the peace, to organize and regulate steadily expanding international business of all kinds, and to assist states needing help.

The basic vision of the League, however, remained that of Woodrow Wilson, and international acceptance of the concept rested on the confidence that the United States would play a leading part in the new world organization. On April 28, President Wilson presented the Covenant of the League of Nations to a plenary session of the peace conference. It was incorporated into the Treaty of Versailles which was signed on June 28, 1919. When that treaty officially became effective on January 10, 1920, the League of Nations also began to function. By that time, however, it was already evident that the United States was not going to be a member of the League; in March the Senate rejected the Treaty of Versailles for the second and last time.

The Covenant of the League of Nations (the first twenty-six articles of the Treaty of Versailles) defined the conditions of membership, the structure of the new body, the machinery for the creation of a Permanent Court of International Justice, the methods for the settlement of international disputes, and the mandate system. It also defined the role of the League of Nations in such important matters as disarmament, treaties negotiated between member states, and various humanitarian activities. The original or "charter" members of the League of Nations included those signing the Versailles treaty, and "invited" states which accepted the covenant without reservation within two months of the League's official inauguration. Under the covenant, other sovereign states could obtain membership by a two-thirds vote of the Assembly. After an advance notice of two years, a nation might withdraw from the League.

The Assembly, together with the Council and permanent Secretariat, composed the basic structure of the League. All member states were represented in the Assembly, which was empowered to deal with any matter pertaining to the affairs of the League or affecting the interests of world peace. The Council was composed of one delegate from each state entitled to representation, and according to the covenant these were to be five permanent and four nonpermanent seats. The Great Powers were to fill the five permanent seats, but as the United States refused to enter the League, the fifth seat remained vacant until occupied by Germany in 1926. By 1933, the Assembly had

President Woodrow Wilson envisioned the League of Nations as a means of preserving world peace through diplomatic settlement of international disputes. (Library of Congress)

increased the number of nonpermanent seats to ten.

The Council's sphere of competence was as broad as the Assembly's, but in practice it concentrated on such matters as the peaceful settlement of disputes and disarmament, aims to which the League was specifically committed. The permanent Secretariat, which formed the bureaucracy of the League, was composed of the secretary-general and his staff. Sir Eric Drummond, a British diplomat, was named in the Annex of the Covenant, as the first secretary-general, a post which he held until 1933; subsequent secretaries-general were appointed by the Council with the approval of the Assembly. Augmenting this basic structure of the League was the Permanent Court of International Justice, or World Court, established in 1921 by Article XIV of the covenant, and the International Labor Organization, provided for by the Treaty of Versailles.

These agencies of the League were designated by the covenant to fulfill basic functions, the most important of which was the peaceful settlement of international disputes. The covenant established several procedures for the settlement of such disputes, including arbitration or reference to one of the three bodies of the League: the World

Court, the Council, or the Assembly. To implement further the preservation of peace, the covenant required that all treaties conform to its principles and that all future treaties negotiated by member states be registered with the secretary-general. Another responsibility of the League was the supervision of former German and Turkish dependent territories assigned to various states under the mandate system. The covenant also dealt with the humanitarian activities of the League, which involved such matters as attempts to prevent disease, stop illegal traffic in drugs, and improve labor conditions. In its final article, the covenant provided machinery for its own amendment.

The lofty ideals expressed in the covenant were capable of realization only in so far as members of the League intended to carry them out. The League, located permanently in Geneva, Switzerland, was weakened from the outset by the nonparticipation of the United States and the absence of the Soviet Union. The American government rejected the League because of strong Republican opposition to President Wilson's foreign policy and the expansion of American involvement overseas; the Senate, indeed, refused to ratify the Treaty of Versailles because it included the Covenant of the League of Nations. The Soviet Union remained excluded from the League until 1934 because of its declared intention to promote worldwide revolution, a policy that was at odds with the ideals and substance of the covenant.

The most important work of the League after 1920 consisted in trying to secure both a program of disarmament and the pacific settlement of disputes involving the Great Powers. In these endeavors, the League proved to be a complete failure. Because of its inability to force Fascist Italy to abandon aggression against Ethiopia, the League virtually collapsed by 1936. In the wake of the Ethiopian crisis, Italy withdrew from the League, joining Japan and Nazi Germany who had withdrawn earlier. The League did have several unsung successes, notably its supervision of the financial rehabilitation of Austria between 1922 and 1926, but these were overshadowed by its inability to preserve the peace settlement and prevent the outbreak of what proved to be an even more disastrous world war.

Despite its failure to fulfill Wilson's dream, the League of Nations did serve as a testing ground for the problems of an international organization between the world wars. The United Nations which succeeded the League after 1945 sought in its organization to avoid the mistakes that had flawed its predecessor. The continued existence of the United Nations, despite its drawbacks, attests to the power of the Wilsonian ideal of a world organization to maintain peace, which first began in the aftermath of World War I.

—*Edward P. Keleher, updated by Lewis L. Gould*

ADDITIONAL READING:

Ambrosius, Lloyd E. *Woodrow Wilson and the American Diplomatic Tradition: The Treaty Fight in Perspective.* New York: Cambridge University Press, 1987. A thorough narrative of the development of the League concept in Woodrow Wilson's political thought and his efforts to create an international organization in 1919-1920.

Bailey, Thomas A. *Woodrow Wilson and the Lost Peace.* New York: Macmillan, 1944. An older, but still useful, account of how Woodrow Wilson put the League of Nations idea into the Treaty of Versailles.

Egerton, George W. *Great Britain and the Creation of the League of Nations: Strategy, Politics and International Organization, 1914-1919.* Chapel Hill: University of North Carolina Press, 1978. Important for an understanding of how the British and Americans cooperated and differed in framing the League of Nations during World War I.

Knock, Thomas. *To End All Wars: Woodrow Wilson and the Quest for a New World Order.* New York: Oxford University Press, 1992. Examines how Wilson's ideals for a League of Nations emerged from the American political environment and his own political thought.

Link, Arthur S. *Woodrow Wilson: Revolution, War, and Peace.* Arlington Heights, Ill.: Harlan Davidson, 1979. A good brief analysis of Wilson's thinking about the League of Nations by the foremost student of his life.

Zimmern, Alfred. *The League of Nations and the Rule of Law, 1918-1935.* London: Macmillan, 1936. A good survey of the constructive work of the League before its collapse as a result of the rise of the dictators during the 1930's.

SEE ALSO: 1899, First Hague Peace Conference; 1907, Second Hague Peace Conference; 1915, International Congress of Women; 1919, Treaty of Versailles; 1935-1936, Italy Conquers Ethiopia.

1919
TREATY OF VERSAILLES
The Treaty of Versailles ends World War I, but its provisions lay the foundation for another world conflict within a generation.
DATE: June 28, 1919
LOCALE: Versailles, near Paris
CATEGORIES: Diplomacy and international relations; Wars, uprisings, and civil unrest
KEY FIGURES:
Count Ulrich von Brockdorff-Rantzau (1869-1928), German foreign minister summoned to Versailles to receive the treaty on behalf of Germany

Georges Clemenceau (1841-1929), premier of France, 1917-1920, and president of the peace conference at Versailles

David Lloyd George (1863-1945), prime minister and chief representative of Great Britain at the peace conference at Versailles

Vittorio Emanuele Orlando (1860-1952), prime minister of Italy, 1917-1919, and head of the Italian delegation to the peace conference at Versailles

Woodrow Wilson (1856-1924), twenty-eighth president of the United States and his own representative at the peace conference at Versailles

SUMMARY OF EVENT. The Treaty of Versailles was the first and most important of the several peace treaties concluded at the Peace Conference of Paris in 1919. Not only did it formally assert the defeat of Germany in World War I, but as the basis of the peace settlement the Treaty of Versailles also represented the attempt of the victorious powers to regulate the new international order which had emerged in Europe as a result of the outcome of World War I. This new international order was the product of the most far-reaching political and social changes that had taken place in modern European history. Chief among these was the disappearance or imminent collapse of the Ottoman Empire, the Russian, Austrian, and German empires, and their ruling dynasties.

In Russia, Romanov rule collapsed in the Russian Revolution of 1917, followed after a brief interlude by the Bolshevik seizure of power in November and the breakup of the czarist presence in Eastern Europe. As the war drew to a close late in 1918, Austria-Hungary virtually disappeared from the map of Europe. Germany, meanwhile, faced the prospect of extensive territorial losses along its western and eastern frontiers to a victorious France and a revived Polish state, respectively. The collapse of Ottoman rule in Europe had actually preceded the war and had helped to set it off; after the war, the Turks lost control over non-Turkish peoples in the Near East. In the place of these empires, there emerged in Eastern Europe a series of new states stretching from Finland in the North to Yugoslavia in the South, all of which reflected the spirit of nationalism that the upheaval of World War I had promoted.

Situated between Germany and Russia, these states collectively constituted a large unstable power vacuum. Russia had been defeated by Germany early in 1918 and been forced to sign the harsh Treaty of Brest-Litovsk. Germany had in turn been defeated by the combined French, British, and American armies in November, 1918.

Both Russia and Germany were still potentially powerful and posed a threat to the smaller powers located between them. Russia, under Bolshevik rule, was bent on fomenting revolution among the proletariat throughout war-torn Europe, while Germany regarded the middle Danube Valley, now vacated by the Habsburgs, as an area in which to seek compensation for the expected territorial losses mentioned above. Hence, as the diplomats representing the victorious powers made their way to Paris in December of 1918, they sought ways to prevent Germany from once again posing a threat to the peace of Europe and to stave off the menace of Communism as represented by Bolshevik Russia.

The Peace Conference of Paris formally convened on January 18, 1919, amid the tumult and confusion of the immediate postwar period and with nations and diplomats from all over the world clamoring for attention. The presence of President Woodrow Wilson from the United States attested the emergence of a new power on the European scene. Major decisions at the conference were made initially by the Council of Ten, which comprised two representatives from each of the five great powers: France, Great Britain, the United States, Italy, and Japan. These sessions soon proved unwieldy, and the significant decisions fell to the leaders of the major powers. After March 24, the first ranking delegates of these states ceased to attend the sessions of the Council of Ten, which became known as the Council of Five, an agency of relatively secondary importance.

To expedite the completion of the German treaty, the four top western delegates called themselves the Council of Four: Georges Clemenceau, premier of France and president of the Peace Conference; David Lloyd George, the British prime minister; Woodrow Wilson, president of the United States; and Vittorio Emanuele Orlando, prime minister of Italy. During the three months when these statesmen were drafting the German treaty, all were agreed upon the necessity of providing safeguards that would ensure the perpetuation of peace as well as German defeat. Beyond this general aim, the Big Four found it difficult to agree upon which provisions should be incorporated into a treaty. Seeking to safeguard France against another German invasion, Clemenceau wanted to strip Germany of the Rhineland and the Saar, the former to be set up as a separate state and the latter to be annexed directly to France. In addition, he vigorously opposed German annexation (*Anschluss*) of the new state of Austria. Lloyd George rejected the French effort to establish a weak Germany; instead, he called for a restoration of the traditional European balance of power, but with guarantees to France against another German attack.

President Wilson's program, the famous Fourteen Points, was the best known of the Allies' war aims. Wilson, however, was prepared to sacrifice complete realization of

Georges Clemenceau (front left), Woodrow Wilson (center right), and David Lloyd George (far right) were among the world leaders who negotiated the terms of the Treaty of Versailles. (Archive Photos)

many of the principles embodied in the first thirteen points, including self-determination, in order to secure the fourteenth, the League of Nations. Aware of political problems in the United States with the Senate that had to approve whatever treaty he negotiated, Wilson was convinced that the League of Nations, if established, could in time deal with any shortcomings that might be incorporated into the treaty. Hence, he pressed for the inclusion of the Covenant of the League into the treaty itself. The Italian spokesman, Orlando, played a relatively minor role at the conference; he appeared, primarily, in what proved to be an unsuccessful attempt to secure territories in the Adriatic region which Great Britain and France had promised to Italy in the secret Treaty of London in 1915 as a means of bringing Italy into the war on their side. Despite

these and other areas of disagreement among the Big Four, they managed to complete their work on the Germany treaty by the end of April. The Allies then instructed the German provisional government to send a delegation to Paris to receive the terms.

After some delay caused by Germany's insistence that it ought to be allowed to "negotiate" and not merely "receive" the treaty, the Allies on May 7 formally presented the document to the German delegation headed by Count Ulrich von Brockdorff-Rantzau, the foreign minister of Germany. No negotiations took place; the Germans were merely given three weeks to submit their written observations on the harsh treaty. In their lengthy response of May 28, the Germans deplored among other matters those provisions in the treaty which forbade the German-speaking peoples of Austria and Czechoslovakia from uniting with Germany, and the German representatives denounced in strong terms the double standard which existed on the principle of self-determination. The Allies, in their reply of June 16 to the German observations, made only a few concessions and gave the German government seven days to accept the treaty without any further alterations. Germany did so on June 22. On June 28, 1919, the fifth anniversary of the assassination of Archduke Francis Ferdinand, the treaty was signed in the Hall of Mirrors of Versailles. Of the great powers which signed the Versailles Treaty, only the United States refused to ratify it when the Senate failed to give its approval in 1919 and 1920; not until August 25, 1921, was a separate peace concluded with Germany.

The Peace Conference of Paris formally came to a close on January 21, 1920, following the conclusion of the Treaty of St. Germain with Austria on September 10, 1919, and the Treaty of Neuilly with Bulgaria on November 27. Treaties with Hungary and Turkey remained to be signed after the conference had officially ended, but these two instruments may be regarded as part of the same peace settlement.

The Treaty of Versailles, in its major provisions, embraced the following areas: the Covenant of the League of Nations, territorial arrangements affecting Germany's frontiers and its former colonies, German disarmament, and reparations.

Throughout the opening months of 1919, President Wilson had insisted upon the incorporation of the Covenant of the League of Nations into the treaty as the best means of safeguarding the peace, and the covenant was incorporated into the treaty as the first twenty-six articles. In the section of the treaty dealing with territorial arrangements, Germany experienced substantial losses along its western and eastern frontiers. Its western boundary was reduced by the return of Alsace-Lorraine, taken after the Franco-Prussian War in 1871, to France, and by the cession of small territories to Belgium. Clemenceau, however, did not secure his demand for the creation of a Rhineland buffer state; instead the treaty set up the Rhineland as a perpetually demilitarized area to be occupied by an inter-Allied force for a period of fifteen years.

The Saar, in similar fashion, was surrendered to international control for the same length of time. At the end of this period, the people of the Saar could decide by plebiscite whether they wanted to join France or Germany. In the east, Germany was obliged to recognize a new, independent Polish state to which it had to cede substantial portions of Prussian territory in order to give the Poles an outlet to the sea. The German city of Danzig now became a free state under the protection of the League of Nations. Plebiscites were to be held for ethnically mixed German-Polish areas; some of these districts voted to remain with Germany, others voted to join with Poland; Germany was also strictly forbidden from annexing Austria. Outside Europe, Germany had to surrender all its colonies in Africa and Oceania, most of which were declared mandates or protectorates of the League of Nations and assigned to France, Great Britain, Japan, and other countries. These states were to be responsible to the League of Nations for the welfare of their mandates.

Germany was accorded equally demanding treatment in the areas of disarmament and reparations. The German military and naval forces were reduced substantially. The army was not to exceed one hundred thousand men, all of whom were to be volunteers, serving for long periods, in order to preclude the establishment of a large reserve. Germany's vaunted General Staff was disbanded. Limitations were placed on the production of war matériel. The German navy was reduced to a mere token force which could not include any submarines. The treaty also forbade Germany to maintain an air force.

In the section of the treaty dealing with reparations, the famous Article 231 or "war guilt" clause required Germany to acknowledge responsibility for starting the war and for all the damage caused by it. The Allies, after much haggling among themselves, finally agreed that Germany should pay only for actual damages, the Allied costs of war being excluded except in the case of Belgium. No definitive comprehensive sum was fixed in the treaty, but by May 1, 1921, Germany was to pay in case or kind the sum of five billion dollars. The Allies soon found that a Germany deprived of much of its former mineral-rich territory, could not begin to meet their reparation demands. The war guilt clause and the issue of reparations contributed to the bitterness with which Germans regarded the Treaty of Versailles and made them highly receptive to the criticisms of it leveled by Adolf Hitler and the Nazis during the 1930's.

The place of the Treaty of Versailles in history has always been controversial. Certainly the treaty was severe, reflecting the bitterness generated in the Allied camp by a long war which had taken millions of lives, left countless others ruined with wounds of the body or wounds of the spirit, and had completely devastated parts of several countries. Nevertheless, the treaty also represented a settlement that mirrored the military balance of power at the time and did more to draw reasonable national boundaries than any similar pact that had preceded it. Two major guarantors of the peace settlement, Great Britain and France, found their task difficult because of their frequently conflicting foreign policies. A greater difficulty for them rested in the fact that the United States and Russia never officially recognized the treaty and therefore played no role in upholding the peace settlement. The United States, whose leading statesmen had contributed so much to the Treaty of Versailles, afterward turned its back in isolation from direct intervention in European affairs during the 1920's and 1930's. Bolshevik Russia, which had not taken part in the drafting of the treaty that was at least implicitly directed against her, promoted the cause of worldwide revolution of the proletariat, a direct challenge to the stability and order that the framers of the Versailles Treaty pursued. Despite these handicaps, Great Britain and France, with the qualified support of Italy, did manage to uphold the Treaty of Versailles until 1935, when they began to give way in appeasement to the demands of Hitler's Germany for revision of the Treaty. The Allies, it is true, shirked their obligations in not standing up to Nazi Germany in the 1930's, but then Germany proved unwilling to honor the precepts of international law as it stood when Germany invaded the neutral state of Belgium in 1914. In historical perspective, the Treaty of Versailles was a better peace settlement than its critics claimed in the 1930's, but it also caused resentments that led the way to a second general war in Europe in 1939.

—*Edward P. Keleher, updated by Lewis L. Gould*

ADDITIONAL READING:

Ambrosius, Lloyd E. *Woodrow Wilson and the American Diplomatic Tradition: The Treaty Fight in Perspective*. New York: Cambridge University Press, 1987. A well informed and thoughtful analysis of Woodrow Wilson's role in shaping the Treaty of Versailles and the response to the pact in the United States Senate.

Floto, Inga. *Colonel House in Paris: A Study of American Policy at the Paris Peace Conference*. Princeton, N.J.: Princeton University Press, 1973. Looks at the role of Wilson's closest adviser and the impact of his contribution to the development of the peace treaty.

Knock, Thomas J. *To End All Wars: Woodrow Wilson and the Quest for a New World Order*. New York: Oxford University Press, 1992. Places the negotiations over the Treaty of Versailles in the context of Wilson's wartime diplomacy and the relations with other European nations.

Mayer, Arno J. *Politics and Diplomacy of Peacemaking: Containment and Counterrevolution at Versailles, 1918-1919*. New York: Alfred A. Knopf, 1967. A provocative study that emphasizes the impact of Bolshevik Russia on the deliberations in Paris. A very thorough treatment of key aspects of the Peace Conference.

Nordholt, Jan Willem Schulte. *Woodrow Wilson: A Life*

for World Peace. Berkeley: University of California Press, 1991. A Dutch scholar takes a critical look at Wilson's attitude toward the peace treaty and the League. Very useful for a European perspective on the events of 1919.

Tillman, Seth P. *Anglo-American Relations at the Paris Peace Conference of 1919*. Princeton, N.J.: Princeton University Press, 1961. Deals with the crucial problem of how the United States and Great Britain viewed the consequences of the war and the best way of maintaining peace in the future.

SEE ALSO: 1918, Treaty of Brest-Litovsk; 1919, The League of Nations Is Established; 1919, Weimar Constitution; 1933, Hitler Comes to Power in Germany; 1938, The *Anschluss*.

1919
WEIMAR CONSTITUTION

The Weimar Constitution gives the German people the opportunity to create their own form of government after the overthrow of the monarchy.

DATE: July 31, 1919
LOCALE: Weimar, Germany
CATEGORY: Government and politics
KEY FIGURES:

Friedrich Ebert (1871-1925), moderate Socialist who succeeded Prince Maximilian of Baden and who became first president of the Weimar Republic in 1919

Karl Liebknecht (1871-1919), left-wing Socialist who sought to establish a socialist council-style democracy

Rosa Luxemburg (1870-1919), left-wing Socialist who opposed the Weimar Republic as a betrayal of socialism

Prince Maximilian of Baden (Maximilian Alexander Friedrich Wilhelm; 1869-1929), former president of the Baden diet and heir to the Baden dukedom, chancellor of the German empire, October-November, 1918

Hugo Preuss (1860-1925), German jurist and politician, chief author of the Weimar Constitution

Philipp Scheidemann (1865-1939), moderate Socialist in Prince Maximilian of Baden's cabinet who became briefly in 1919 first prime minister of the Weimar Republic

William II, emperor of Germany, 1888-1918

SUMMARY OF EVENT. On November 9, 1918, after massive uprisings within all major cities and two days before the armistice ending World War I was signed, Germany was proclaimed a Socialist republic by revolutionary Karl Liebknecht. In immediate response, Philipp Scheidemann, a moderate Socialist, proclaimed a non-socialist republic to forestall these more radical designs. In this situation of often chaotic political struggle, exhausted by four years of warfare, the German empire that had been created in 1871 by Prince Otto von Bismarck came to an end. William II, the last emperor of Germany, fled to Holland, where he formally renounced his throne on November 28.

Prince Maximilian of Baden, the last chancellor of the German empire, turned over the government to the moderate Majority Socialists, led by Friedrich Ebert and Philipp Scheidemann. As the new chancellor, Ebert created a Directory of six men, three Majority Socialists and three radical Independent Socialists, to govern the country until a constituent assembly could be elected. Elections for the National Assembly took place on January 19, 1919, after radical workers had been suppressed and Liebknecht and Luxemburg murdered. With many radicals boycotting the voting, more than 80 percent of the population voted. The results indicated that most voters wanted Germany to be a republic; the parties committed to a republic won more than three quarters of the total vote.

The National Assembly met in Weimar on February 6, 1919, to ratify the peace treaty and thereafter to proceed to the drafting of a constitution. As early as November 15, 1918, Hugo Preuss, a professor of constitutional law and well known as a liberal jurist, had been appointed as secretary of the interior, and he presented his draft of the constitution to the National Assembly on February 24, 1919. After three days of general debate, the draft was referred to a constitutional committee which held about forty sessions from March to July examining each article of the constitution. Adopted on July 31, the constitution went into effect on August 11, 1919.

The constitution set up a liberal, democratic regime in Germany. Many ideas were borrowed from the constitutions of western Europe and the United States, but—in order to placate conservatives—much of the Bismarckian constitution was preserved. For example, the word "Reich" with all its imperial associations was retained to designate "the Republic" as distinguished from individual Lander, or states. As later events would prove, this compromise neither appeased the extreme right nor satisfied the radical Left.

The constitution created the office of *Reichsprasident* elected by the people for seven years with the possibility of reelection. The Majority Socialists opposed a strong presidency because they feared that the office might be used as a vehicle for the restoration of monarchy, as had happened in France with Napoleon III. At their insistence, presidential powers were weakened to the extent that the president had to have all his orders countersigned by the chancellor.

The German president, who stood somewhere between the strong American president and the weak French president, appointed the chancellor; he could dissolve the Reichstag and call for new elections. If he did not want to enact a law passed by the Reichstag, he could call for a referendum of the people on the matter.

A bicameral legislature was set up consisting of a Reichstag, representing the people, and a Reichsrat, representing the states. Members of the Reichstag were to be elected for four years by secret, direct, universal suffrage and according to proportional representation. As the expression of the will of the people and the sovereign legislative power, the Reichstag initiated and enacted laws, subject to a suspensive veto. The cabinet was made responsible to the Reichstag.

In the Reichsrat, each state was to have at least one member, but no state could control more than two-fifths of the membership. The Reichsrat could also initiate legislation and, if it disapproved of a bill passed by the Reichstag, it could return the measure to that body. The Reichstag, however, could override the veto by a two-thirds vote.

No part of the constitution caused more controversy than Article 48. This provision gave the president the right to suspend temporarily the fundamental rights guaranteed by the constitution in an emergency which threatened public safety and order. Because of the fear of social revolution in Germany after the war, this provision was considered necessary to prevent the young republic from being overthrown by revolutionaries. Designed to prevent the radical Left from taking power as they had in Russia, it was this article that later enabled Adolf Hitler to become dictator. The makers of the constitution made the mistake of thinking that, since the Reichstag could demand the termination of such measures, the actions of the president were ultimately controlled by the Reichstag.

Although Preuss's original draft had undergone considerable modification, his basic aim remained; he had seen the creation of a parliamentary, liberal, democratic government. As this new republic left untouched the traditional sources of power—the army, big business, and the courts—the high hopes of the Weimar Constitution were to remain unfulfilled. In little more than a decade, this liberal government would be overthrown and replaced with the Nazi dictatorship of Adolf Hitler.

—*Harry E. Wade, updated by William A. Pelz*

ADDITIONAL READING:

Eyck, Erich. *A History of the Weimar Republic.* Cambridge, Mass.: Harvard University Press, 1962. Critical of the voting system established by the constitution. Eyck chides the Social Democrats for being too theoretical, particularly in the case of extending the franchise.

Halperin, S. William. *Germany Tried Democracy*. New York: W. W. Norton, 1965. A work that many scholars believe to be the best political history in English of the Weimar Republic. In analyzing the Weimar Constitution, he points out that it furthered the trend toward administrative centralization which had begun before 1918.

Hunt, Richard N. *The Creation of the Weimar Republic: Stillborn Democracy?* Boston: D. C. Heath, 1969. Interpretations by leading historians regarding the nature of the Weimar Republic.

Mommsen, Hans. *From Weimar to Auschwitz*. Princeton, N.J.: Princeton University Press, 1991. A collection of essays which brilliantly explores various aspects of the Republic.

Peukert, Detlev J. *The Weimar Republic*. New York: Hill & Wang, 1989. Puts the Weimar Republic in a larger European context and examines the significance of anti-modern reactions.

Rosenberg, Arthur. *A History of the German Republic*. London: Methuen, 1936. Probably the best Marxist account of the Weimar Republic.

Snyder, Louis L. *The Weimar Republic*. New York: D. Van Nostrand, 1966. An analysis of the topic, together with pertinent documents.

SEE ALSO: 1919, Rosa Luxemburg Is Assassinated; 1919, Treaty of Versailles; 1933, Hitler Comes to Power in Germany.

1921-1928
LENIN'S NEW ECONOMIC POLICY

Lenin's New Economic Policy allows the leadership of the Soviet Union to experiment with a relaxation of the party's control over the economy while maintaining a monopoly on political power.

DATE: 1921-1928
LOCALE: The Soviet Union
CATEGORIES: Economics; Government and politics
KEY FIGURES:

Nikolai Ivanovich Bukharin (1888-1938), Bolshevik revolutionary schooled in economics in Austria who, although an early supporter of radical socialism, later became one of the leaders of the so-called moderates who supported the development of the New Economic Policy

Vladimir Ilich Lenin (Ulyanov; 1870-1924), leading Russian revolutionary and chairman of the Council of People's Commissars 1918-1924

Joseph Stalin (Iosif Vissarionovich Dzhugashvili; 1879-1953), general secretary of the Communist Party and preeminent leader of the Soviet Union from 1924 to 1953

Leon Trotsky (Leib Davydovich Bronstein; 1879-1940), leading associate of Lenin who organized labor battalions to rescue the economy of the Soviet Union in 1920

SUMMARY OF EVENT. When the Bolsheviks seized power in Russia in 1917, they were faced not only with the problem of ending the fighting against the Central Powers, but also with the difficulty of producing reforms within Russia consistent with the theories of Marxism. They were committed to abolishing the private ownership of property, nationalizing industry, and socializing state services. Vladimir Lenin, chairman of the Council of People's Commissars, found that the Russian economy could not sustain both a war against Germany and a fight against anti-Bolshevik groups while simultaneously implementing Marxist reforms.

Lenin therefore improvised a policy known as "War Communism," a plan to establish socialism in Russia and impose economic and political control over the Russian people. All industry was nationalized, but the government only had the power to supervise the nationalization of heavy industry. Trade was taken over by the state, but a black market in necessary items was allowed to flourish. Property owned by landlords was officially taken over, and officials decreed that peasants were required to turn over their entire harvests to government food cooperatives.

When the anti-Bolshevik forces were defeated and the Allies withdrew from Russia in 1921, War Communism no longer worked. Peasant resentment toward collectivization and bad weather contributed to the famines that killed an estimated five million Russians in 1920 and 1921. Food shortages and an increasingly authoritarian bureaucracy contributed to the peasants' alienation toward the Bolshevik regime. Sailors in the Kronstadt garrison revolted and were brutally crushed by fellow Soviet troops. Even before the revolt, Lenin was searching for a solution to Russia's economic problems. As the economy spiraled out of control, it became clear that the increasingly disgruntled populous had the potential to destabilize the Bolshevik government.

Between March and December, 1921, Lenin issued a series of decrees which established the New Economic Policy (NEP) in the Soviet Union. The first and most fundamental of these decrees ended the forced requisition of grain and other agricultural products from Soviet peasants, and substituted a new tax in kind. Small businesses were denationalized, and peasants were allowed to sell crops on the open market after state quotas were fulfilled. The party maintained control of large industries such as coal, oil, electricity, and heavy manufacturing. Even the cumbersome government bureaucracy which had attempted to run industry between 1918 and 1921 was broken up, and direction was turned over to government-related trusts. By the end of 1921, the process had gone so far that Lenin publicly admitted that War Communism had been a mistake and not, as many believed, a solution to the problem of a socialized economy. In 1922, the Bolshevik regime even experimented with allowing owners of small industrial firms to operate their former enterprises in state approved cooperatives.

Lenin rationalized the New Economic Policy, trying to bring it into line with the official doctrine that Russia was progressing toward a socialist society. He noted that the party kept control of heavy industry, banking, and foreign trade, which Marxists believed were the keys for developing a modern and efficient economy of abundance. Over the objections of some hard-line socialists, money was reintroduced in 1921. Lenin explained that the design of the party was to make the public sector of the economy more productive than the newly authorized private sector. Lenin's New Economic Policy was put forth as a kind of peaceful coexistence with capitalism in which the state controlled sector would demonstrate superior productivity. On the basis of the economic and social gains brought about by rational planning, the state sector was to gradually expand until it was once more in full control. In this period, the working population would have realized that the rewards were greater in state-run industries than in the private sector. Wide-ranging concessions to peasants were intended to neutralize peasant resistance to socialism until the position of the party was stronger, and the world Communist revolution would come to the assistance of the struggling Soviet regime.

In practice, however, the New Economic Policy was centered upon the precarious balance between the growth of the private and public sectors. As peasants entered the market with large quantities of agricultural products and competed for scarce industrial goods, inflation grew. It required three years of trial and error before the Soviet leadership learned to use fiscal policy, subsidies, wage and price controls, and foreign trade to stabilize the economy. From 1924 until 1927, NEP worked fairly well, food rationing ended and the Soviet Union reached an economic level roughly equal to 1913 levels. Yet maintenance of the New Economic Policy entailed a steady drift away from the goals of the Communist Party, possibly leading to almost complete economic independence for Soviet

Vladimir Lenin implemented his New Economic Policy to place the Communist Party in full control of the state sector of the Soviet economy. (Archive Photos)

peasants. Indeed, the tacit approval of a free market spawned so called "nepmen," entrepreneurs who had struck it rich through the ownership and management of small scale industrial enterprises. While the number of wealthy "nepmen" was small, their presence alienated the peasantry and embarrassed Communist Party officials. Fear that economic affluence would lead to political power in the majority peasant class compelled the Communist Party, after a series of fierce debates, to jettison NEP in favor of the First Five-Year Plan in 1928. Lenin, the architect of NEP, had died in 1924. Joseph Stalin, the general secretary of the Communist Party, began to replace free market mechanisms with a strict state controlled economy and political structure that remained largely intact until the collapse of the Soviet Union in 1991.

—George F. Putnam, updated by Lawrence I. Clark

ADDITIONAL READING:

Carr, E. H. *The Bolshevik Revolution, 1917-1923.* Vol. 2. Baltimore: Penguin Books, 1966. A treatment known for its admiration for Lenin, who is portrayed as always being abreast of developments in the Soviet Union and ready with correct "realistic" action.

Dziewanowski, M. K. "From War Communism to the New Economic Policy." In *A History of Soviet Russia*. Englewood Cliffs, N.J.: Prentice Hall, 1989. A basic historical introduction to the background, policies, and impact of NEP on Soviet economics, politics, and culture.

Nove, Alec. "NEP," "The Great Debate," and "The End of NEP." In *An Economic History of the U.S.S.R., 1917-1991*. New York: Penguin Books, 1992. A detailed economic history of the Soviet economy during the 1920's. Nove uses many primary sources in this useful account of the conditions that spawned the New Economic Policy and the mounting opposition to NEP after Lenin's death.

Pipes, Richard. "NEP: The False Thermidor." In *Russia Under the Bolshevik Regime*. New York: Alfred A. Knopf, 1994. A critic of the Soviet system, Pipes argues that NEP was a tactical retreat designed to save the Bolshevik government from the chaos of War Communism. Pipes also provides an account of the famine of the early 1920's and the effect of NEP on Soviet foreign policy of the period.

SEE ALSO: 1898, Social-Democratic Workers' Party Is Formed; 1917, October Revolution; 1918-1921, Russian Civil War; 1928-1933, Soviet Union Launches First Five-Year Plan.

1922
MUSSOLINI'S "MARCH ON ROME"

The "March on Rome" helps Benito Mussolini become the Fascist premier of Italy by threatening the application of force.

DATE: October 24-30, 1922
LOCALE: Rome, Italy
CATEGORIES: Government and politics; Wars, uprisings, and civil unrest
KEY FIGURES:
Italo Balbo (1896-1940),
Michele Bianchi,
Emilio De Bono (1866-1944), and
Cesare De Vecchi, Fascists who planned to lead the March on Rome
Luigi Facta (1861-1930), premier of Italy in 1922
Benito Amilcare Andrea Mussolini (1883-1945), leader of the Fascists in Italy
Victor Emmanuel III (1869-1947), king of Italy, 1900-1946

SUMMARY OF EVENT. Weary of the apparent chaos into which Italy had fallen following the end of World War I, an increasing number of Italians turned to the dynamic Fascist leader, Benito Mussolini, for a solution. Elements attracted to Fascism included: wealthy landowners and industrialists who were afraid that the recent Bolshevik Revolution in Russia might be repeated in Italy; ardent nationalists, frustrated by the government's failure to secure significant territorial concessions from the Allies following World War I; discharged servicemen who found it difficult to adjust to civilian life and who were repelled by Communist insults hurled against anyone who had served in the military; former Socialists who, like Mussolini, had shifted to the radical right during the war; and other groups, ranging from frightened bourgeoisie to a few members of the royal family of Italy.

Many of these elements strengthened their support of Mussolini after he modified his views. In 1919, Mussolini violently denounced all social classes and institutions. By late 1920, however, he had dropped his attacks against the landed proprietors, the industrialists, and the middle class, and thereafter attacked only the parliamentary system, the Socialists, the labor unions, and the cowardly politicians of all parties.

If many were attracted to Fascism because of the social strife, they overlooked the fact that most of the violence was caused by the very group they were supporting. From the beginning of the movement and especially after 1920, the Fascists terrorized much of Italy. Fascist squads invaded cities, intimidating, bludgeoning, and occasionally murdering known opponents. Forcing castor oil down the throats of opposition leaders was one popular technique. After removing government-appointed prefects from their offices, members of the Fascist squads took over the positions themselves; they burned down headquarters of the Socialists and local Chambers of Labor; they destroyed opposition newspapers; and they invaded and took command of local post offices, railway depots, and radio stations.

Mussolini was aided in his quest for power by a lack of resolve and foresight, caused by pettiness and factionalism, among his political rivals. After the Communists withdrew from the Socialist Party in September, 1921, the Socialists were still divided into factions. As a result, measures taken by the Socialists to combat Fascism were either too late or too mild to be effective. A general strike called at the end of July, 1922, failed miserably. The Socialist Party resisted uniting with the Christian Democrat Party until it was too late. Within other groups, veteran political leaders, such as Francesco Nitti, Giovanni Giolitti, and Antonio Salandra, were not able to cope with Mussolini because of personal rivalries and because they failed to comprehend Mussolini's driving force. Most of these men believed that a taste of political power would soften Mussolini's extreme views, that he would learn to function within the existing political structure.

Mussolini's actions from the time when he and thirty-five other Fascists were elected to the Chamber of Deputies in May, 1921, did little to discourage this opinion; up to this time, he had shown himself to be a cautious revolutionary. If he threatened, bullied, and terrorized, he also negotiated. In the late summer and early autumn of 1922, he negotiated with nearly all the prominent political figures from the center and the right.

On October 16, 1922, Mussolini and his cohorts—Italo Balbo, Michele Bianchi, Emilio De Bono, and Cesare De Vecchi—agreed in principle on the March on Rome. Bianchi was to be in charge of political matters, and the other three were to take charge of the military operations, leaving Mussolini free of responsibility. According to the plan, the Fascists were to seize control of certain key towns near Rome, after which Fascist columns would converge on Rome itself. By their use of force, they intended to place Mussolini at the head of a Fascist government. Mussolini issued a call for the march on October 24 at a Fascist assembly in Naples, and then went immediately to Milan to await developments. Despite his call, Mussolini was still unwilling to commit himself entirely to violent means for gaining power, and he continued to talk with other political figures in an effort to gain power legally.

As the time for the March on Rome grew near, the premier of Italy, Luigi Facta, at last decided that strong action was necessary to repel the threat. On the morning of October 28, the Italian cabinet prepared a declaration of martial law to take effect at noon. It committed the military to resist the attempted Fascist takeover of the government. The proclamation was distributed, but it could not be enforced legally until it had been signed by the king of Italy, Victor Emmanuel III. The king was torn by conflicting advice, and he hesitated, afraid for his own position and uncertain of the loyalty of the army. Finally, he refused to sign the declaration.

After Facta resigned, the king sent a telegram the next day to Mussolini and invited him to form a cabinet. It was in this way that Mussolini came to power, only through the threat of force and not by the use of it. Fascist columns eventually entered Rome, but only after Mussolini had been proclaimed premier of Italy. He arrived in Rome on October 30 in a railroad sleeping car instead of at the head of Fascist columns, and after he had been proclaimed premier of Italy. Wearing a black shirt, he presented himself to the king by announcing, "Majesty, I come from the battlefield—fortunately bloodless."

—*Harold A. Schofield, updated by John Quinn Imholte*

ADDITIONAL READING:

Carsten, Francis L. *The Rise of Fascism.* 2d ed. Berkeley: University of California Press, 1980. An intro-

Fascist military forces eventually entered Rome, but only after Benito Mussolini was invited to form a cabinet as the new premier of Italy. (National Archives)

duction to European Fascism. Argues that Fascism's rise had little to do with doctrine and was more the result of World War II. Includes neo-Fascism.

De Grand, Alexander J. *Italian Fascism: Its Origins and Development.* 2d. ed. Lincoln: University of Nebraska Press, 1989. An overview of Italian Fascism stressing its purposes and policies.

_____. "The March on Rome. " In *The Italian Nationalist Association and the Rise of Fascism in Italy.* Lincoln: University of Nebraska Press, 1978. A short, factual description of the March on Rome from April to August, 1922.

Hoyt, Edwin P. *Mussolini's Empire: The Rise and Fall of the Fascist Vision.* New York: John Wiley, 1994. The author suggests that Mussolini's flaws were political rather than moral. Psychological insights are emphasized.

Kirkpatrick, Ivone. *Mussolini: A Study in Power.* New York: Hawthorne Books, 1964. A British diplomat's detailed account of the man and his personality.

Lyttleton, Adrian. *The Seizure of Power: Fascism in Italy, 1919-1929.* New York: Charles Scribner's Sons,

1973. Stresses Fascism's changing relationship with the state. Examines origin and growth, as well as the contributions made by different social groups to its ideology and action.

Mack Smith, Denis. *Mussolini*. New York: Alfred A. Knopf, 1982. Deals with Mussolini's inconsistencies. Argues that Italian Fascism lacked a coherent ideology and was primarily a technique for seizing power.

SEE ALSO: 1911-1912, Italy Annexes Libya; 1919, The League of Nations Is Established; 1919, Treaty of Versailles; 1935-1936, Italy Conquers Ethiopia; 1943, Allied Invasion of Italy.

1926
BRITISH WORKERS LAUNCH GENERAL STRIKE

British workers launch a general strike conducted over nine days in support of striking miners and resulting in a dramatic and traumatic defeat for organized labor.

DATE: May 3-May 12, 1926

LOCALE: Great Britain

CATEGORIES: Business and labor; Government and politics; Social reform

KEY FIGURES:

Stanley Baldwin (1867-1947), British prime minister, 1924-1929

Sir Winston Leonard Spencer Churchill (1874-1965), Chancellor of the Exchequer and advocate of a militant government antistrike stand

Arthur J. Cook (1883-1931), general secretary of the Miners Union and an effective orator

William Joynson-Hicks (1865-1932), British home secretary who joined with Churchill in pushing Baldwin toward a hard stand

John Charles Walsham Reith (1889-1971), head of the British Broadcasting Corporation (BBC)

Herbert Samuel (1870-1963), head of the Royal Commission to investigate the coal industry and recommend reforms

Herbert Smith (1862-1938), president of the Miners Union

James H. Thomas (1874-1949), railway union leader

SUMMARY OF EVENT. The General Strike of May, 1926, was, in reality, a sympathy strike called for by the Trade Union Council (TUC) in support of British miners. For nine days, more than two million workers joined a million striking miners in an effort to exert pressure to prevent a salary rollback for miners. "Not a penny off the pay, not a minute off the day," became the slogan of the strikers.

In 1926, coal mining was England's largest industry, employing twice the workers of the textile industry, its nearest competitor. Since World War I, the mining industry had been heavily subsidized by government. By 1925, however, a rapid reversal in the demand for British coal was taking place because of a general increase in European coal production. In addition, Britain's return to the gold standard in 1925 made its coal uncompetitive and expensive, especially since the pound was set at the prewar level of 4.86, not the existing world rate of 4.40. Other British exports also slumped sharply, threatening increased unemployment.

The solution for Britain's economic woes, announced by the Conservative prime minister, Stanley Baldwin, on July 30, 1925, was a reduction in workers' wages to lessen the cost of British products. When Baldwin's solution was first applied to miners nine months later, union workers could not help but identify with the miners' dilemma, and use every possible means to blunt the instrument of salary cuts. Baldwin's speech was made the day before a mining strike was set to protest wage cuts. To prevent the strike, he extended government subsidies for nine months while a Royal Commission, headed by Sir Herbert Samuel, investigated changes in the mining industry.

On March 11, 1926, Samuel presented his massive three-hundred-page report on the mining industry. During the interim, the miners and the Trade Union Council were making coordinated strike plans, while the government worked on its own comprehensive plans to deal with a major strike. The Samuel Commission Report recommended many significant changes in the coal industry for the future, most of which were denounced by the mine owners. For the present, however, the sole recommendation was for an end to the coal subsidy with the inevitable rollback in wages.

During the seven weeks that followed the issuance of the Commission report, both the government and Trade Union Council leaders tried to narrow the gap between miners and mine owners before the existing agreement expired. These efforts proved fruitless, and on May 1, 1926, the mine owners locked the mine gates. Also on May 1, the Trade Union Council held a major conference, approved a sympathy strike in support of the miners to begin at midnight on May 3, and elected a general council to provide leadership during the strike. The Trade Union Council hoped that the threat of a national strike would force the government to intervene and moderate the intransigence of mine owners. The following day, negotiators from the Trade Union Council explored a number of stopgap measures with Baldwin, yet key members of his cabinet, such as Winston Churchill and William Joynson-

Hicks, wanted a showdown. Clearly, they would not have the Trade Union Council dictating policy to the government.

At midnight on May 3, Britain's brief and bloodless "class war" began. It would prove to be a remarkable event, involving more active participants than any other event during the interwar period.

The response to the strike was beyond the council's most optimistic projections. Although nearly two-thirds of the workforce was nonunion, large numbers joined the strike. Of the more than one million unemployed, only a small number succumbed to the temptation of becoming strikebreakers. Trains and trams came to a halt, docks were still, construction work ceased, steel mills closed, and power plant workers stayed away from work. Moreover, the strike was conducted with almost a holiday-like atmosphere. Although the army was called out to maintain order, no violent clashes occurred. While Churchill paraded armored cars through the streets and used them to accompany convoys, these armored vehicles were regarded more for pompous display than for use. As the days progressed, working-class support continued to grow,

peaking on May 12, the last day of the strike. In theory, the Trade Union Council had organized a tremendous show of solidarity, one which should have given it all the leverage needed to bring about a negotiated settlement. Nevertheless, the national strike was about to fail.

Members of the Trade Union Council had not foreseen that they were using a tactic more appropriate for an earlier part of the industrial age. The sympathy strike would catalyze upper- and middle-class solidarity against the strikers. Except for leftist intellectuals, there was little beyond working-class support for the action. Moreover, stoppage of railroad transportation was offset by road transportation, and the flow of supplies was only slowed by the strike. What the government lacked in the ability to attract working-class strikebreakers was more than offset by a tremendous outpouring of university students, former army officers, and upper- and middle-class volunteers who drove trucks, buses, and trollies. Volunteers drove an assortment of personal vehicles to bring white-collar workers to the office. Bicycling or walking became fashionable during the nine days of the strike.

The capacity to control communications was another

Women volunteers helped sort mail at London's General Post Office during the British General Strike of 1926. (Popperfoto/Archive Photos)

area the Trade Union Council failed to dominate. The newspapers were shut down, but this was the radio age and more than 2.5 million of the Crown's subjects owned crystal sets. In order to maintain future autonomy, John Reith, the head of the recently formed British Broadcasting Corporation (BBC), caved in to government pressures to accentuate all the negative aspects of the strike. During the strike, Churchill edited a mini-newspaper, *The British Gazette*, which stressed that a war was taking place with the stakes being either the overthrow of parliamentary government or its continuance. Human interest stories about strikers and police playing football together, or the fact that this was a national sympathy strike in support of miners, not a general strike to establish a Soviet-styled worker dictatorship, failed to appear in the paper.

Faced with the government taking a hard stand (including the threat of arrest for what was defined as an illegal action), and no end in sight to the situation that had been produced, the general council of the Trade Union Council called off the strike on May 12, although the strike was at its peak. Clearly essential services were not shut down and a position of leverage could not easily be obtained. The government held up possible implementation of the Samuel Commission proposal as an out to the strike, and the Trade Union Council's leadership rapidly acquiesced.

While other workers returned to work, the miners remained on strike for seven months. Eventually, they were starved into returning to work, those that were not part of the large number that had been blacklisted. For the miners, the fact that they had been betrayed remained permanently etched in their minds.

The General Strike was a bitter defeat for union solidarity. Over the short run, it led to a significant decline in union membership. As a means of achieving union goals, syndicalism faded away in England, and even strikes became a tactic of last resort. For the middle and upper classes, the fear of a working-class revolt diminished, as they had experienced the worst of it from British labor and it was not all that bad. Workers, too, experienced no real conflicts with the army or police, reducing fears of authoritarian repression by the establishment. Paranoia about class conflict faded after 1926, because of the low level of violence during the strike.

In 1927, Stanley Baldwin sponsored the Trade Union Act, which outlawed sympathy strikes designed to coerce the government. For the British labor movement, which eventually recovered from the General Strike, focus shifted to collective bargaining within the established system as a means of achieving worker objectives.

—*Irwin Halfond*

ADDITIONAL READING:

Boyce, Robert. *British Capitalism at the Crossroads 1919-1932*. New York: Cambridge University Press, 1988. This study provides an excellent background for economic policies leading up to and following the General Strike, along with a perceptive analysis of the strike.

Farmen, Christopher. *The General Strike, May 1926*. London: Hart-Davis, 1972. This study re-creates the complicated series of negotiations and colorful events taking place during the General Strike.

Florey, R. A. *The General Strike of 1926: The Economic, Political and Social Causes of That Class War*. New York: Riverrun Press, 1987. An in-depth analysis of the strike written from a working-class perspective.

Morris, Margaret. *The General Strike*. Harmondsworth, England: Penguin, 1976. A comprehensive treatment of the General Strike, its causes, main events, and significance, along with special studies by leading experts on aspects of the strike.

Ranshaw, Patrick. *Nine Days in May: The General Strike*. London: Methuen, 1975. A captivating picture book of the General Strike, and a good starting point for the topic, containing a clear synoptic summary.

Symons, Julian. *The General Strike: A Historical Portrait*. London: Cresset Press, 1957. A landmark study, written as narrative history and capturing the spirit of the strike.

SEE ALSO: 1884, Fabian Society Is Founded; 1900, British Labour Party Is Formed; 1945, Labour Party Forms Majority Government.

1928
FLEMING DISCOVERS PENICILLIN

Fleming discovers penicillin and revolutionizes modern medicine with the use of this powerful antibacterial agent.

DATE: 1928
LOCALE: London, England
CATEGORIES: Health and medicine; Science and technology
KEY FIGURES:
Ernst Boris Chain (1906-1979), German-English biochemist
Sir Alexander Fleming (1881-1955), British bacteriologist
Sir Howard Walter Florey (1898-1968), Australian pathologist
Harold Raistrick, English biochemist
Almroth Edward Wright (1861-1947), British bacteriologist

SUMMARY OF EVENT. The discovery of penicillin by Alexander Fleming in 1928 was the result of one of those happy accidents which, from time to time, turn scientific exploration in new directions. Fleming, who was born in 1881 and graduated from St. Mary's Hospital and the University of London Medical School in 1908, had extensive medical experience with the Royal Army Medical Corps during World War I when he dealt with bacterial infections of wounds. Afterward, while carrying out research at the University of London, Fleming discovered a natural substance in tears and mucous secretions that was capable of destroying bacteria—a substance he called a lysozyme.

Although seemingly the result of pure chance, Fleming's discovery occurred because of his recognition of the significance of a phenomenon that other scientists had often observed: the ability of chance contaminants to destroy bacteria growing in laboratory cultures. During the summer of 1928, Fleming was carrying out studies on various strains of staphylococcal bacteria, the organisms frequently associated with both boils and serious blood infections. Fleming was planning on writing a section on the subject for an upcoming medical encyclopedia and was consequently observing characteristics of bacterial colonies, including color and shape. From time to time, it was necessary to lift the lid from the culture plates in order to make the examinations.

The late summer weather was particularly hot, and the windows of the laboratory were often open, creating air currents. Consequently, during one such examination, mold spores fell on Fleming's culture dish. The dish sat for several weeks while Fleming was away; the mold spores germinated and around each mold colony was a zone in which the bacteria had died and disintegrated. No new growth developed in the culture. Fleming isolated the mold, and it was later identified by Charles Thom, an American mycologist, as *Penicillium notatum*, a mold related to one which grows on stale bread. Fleming regarded the mold as an agent which liberated an antibacterial chemical which he named penicillin.

Through further experimentation, Fleming was able to demonstrate that the mold affected some bacteria but not others. He also found that it was not poisonous to white blood cells, which would have made it useless as an antibacterial agent. Fleming tried it on a few patients with sinusitis, but with no miraculous results. He was unable to isolate or identify the chemical agent that destroyed bacteria, and it was noted that the agent lost its potency in a relatively short time. In spite of the fact that Fleming made his discovery known to the medical world in 1929, physicians showed remarkable disinterest in it as a medical

weapon. For the next few years, it was used primarily as a laboratory tool for the isolating of various strains of bacteria.

In part, this reflected Fleming's own expertise. Fleming was not a clinician; his interest was in the application of such antibacterial substances for solving other problems.

Sir Alexander Fleming's discovery of the antibacterial effect of mold spores was acknowledged when he was awarded the Nobel Prize in Physiology or Medicine in 1945. (The Nobel Foundation)

Fleming's research activity at the time was in the isolation and study of the bacillus thought to cause influenza, *Haemophilus influenzae*. Since this organism was not affected by penicillin, the antibiotic could be included in culture media used for its isolation, to the exclusion of other bacterial contaminants. It required the catalyst of world events to turn the application of such substance in another direction.

The coming of World War II changed the situation; the treatment of war wounds, with emphasis upon reducing the incidence of infections, became uppermost in the minds of many members of the medical profession. In 1939, a team of researchers from Oxford University, headed by Howard Walter Florey, began to study antibiotic agents.

Although Fleming recognized the potential application of antibacterial agents such as penicillin in the treatment of disease, he was never able to produce such chemicals in the quantity necessary for therapeutic application. Fleming also recognized the potential of artificial synthesis of the drug in overcoming such difficulties. Nevertheless, it remained for Florey to bring such dreams to fruition.

In collaboration with the German-born biochemist Ernst Chain, and working with the knowledge about penicillin which had earlier been gained by Harold Raistrick, an English biochemist, Florey and his group soon isolated a yellow powder which was penicillin. Florey demonstrated its potency on a variety of infections in mice and human beings, and he went to the United States in 1941 with his samples and his evidence. His purpose was to gain the support of American pharmaceutical manufacturers for the production of penicillin on a large scale.

This support was readily given, under the auspices of the Office of Scientific Research and Development; Dr. Vannevar Bush was appointed director by President Franklin Roosevelt. By 1945, American manufacturers were producing the drug at the rate of half a ton per month. It was first used on war casualties during the Tunis and Sicily campaigns of 1943, and the success of its application was truly astonishing.

Fleming discovered the properties of penicillin in 1928, but it did not become a commonly used medical agent until approximately fourteen years later. Fleming was not a chemist, Raistrick was not a bacteriologist, and the medical profession indicated no sense of urgency for the introduction of new antibacterial agents. Fleming knew the worth of the substance when he first discovered it, but circumstances, and the instability of the drug itself, militated against its development. Only the urgency of war brought penicillin into the center of medical research, and it was then recognized that Fleming was responsible for an entirely new direction in medical treatment. For his discovery, he, along with Florey and Chain, was awarded the 1945 Nobel Prize in Physiology or Medicine.

In its role as a wonder drug, penicillin found widespread application for only a period of some thirty to forty years. Bacteria, including the staphylococci, gradually developed resistance to its effects, a phenomenon initially observed by Fleming himself. Nevertheless, the isolation and application of penicillin opened the door to the widespread use of antibacterial agents in fighting disease.

—*Robert F. Erickson, updated by Richard Adler*

ADDITIONAL READING:

Epstein, Samuel, and Beryl Williams. *Miracles from Microbes*. New Brunswick, N.J.: Rutgers University Press, 1946. Presents the background history of the development of several antibiotics, including penicillin and streptomycin.

Ludovici, L. J. *Fleming: Discoverer of Penicillin*. London: Andrew Dakers, 1952. An older contemporary biography of Fleming, a man revered both by the author and the general public.

Macfarlane, Gwyn. *Alexander Fleming: The Man and the Myth*. Cambridge, Mass.: Harvard University Press, 1984. An authoritative biography on Fleming and his career. Macfarlane based the work on interviews as well as Fleming's own notes.

Marti-Ibanez, Felix. *Men, Molds and History*. New York: MD Publications, 1958. Essays on antibiotics written by a physician.

Reinfeld, Fred. *Miracle Drugs and the New Age of Medicine*. New York: Sterling, 1962. A brief work of interest because of its many photographs.

Rosenblum, Joseph. "Sir Alexander Fleming." In *The Nobel Prize Winners: Physiology or Medicine*, edited by Frank N. Magill. Pasadena, Calif.: Salem Press, 1991. Both a biographical sketch of Fleming and a discussion of his work, this profile includes a description of Fleming's talk before the Nobel committee. Includes a list of Fleming's major publications.

Ryan, Frank. *The Forgotten Plague: How the Battle Against Tuberculosis Was Won—and Lost*. Boston: Little, Brown, 1993. Written for nontechnical readers, a significant proportion of Ryan's book discusses the methodology behind the discovery and testing of many major antibiotics.

Sheehan, John C. *The Enchanted Ring: The Untold Story of Penicillin*. Cambridge, Mass.: MIT Press, 1982. A definitive history on the discovery, development, and marketing of penicillin. Although detailed in places, this account is accessible to nontechnical readers.

SEE ALSO: 1865, Lister Promotes Antiseptic Surgery; 1882-1884, Koch Isolates Microorganisms That Cause Tuberculosis and Cholera; 1951-1953, Model of DNA Molecular Structure Is Developed.

1928-1933
Soviet Union Launches First Five-Year Plan
The Soviet Union launches the First Five-Year Plan, creating a state-controlled economy based on the

forcible collectivization of agriculture and government investment in heavy industry.

DATE: 1928-1933

LOCALE: The Soviet Union

CATEGORIES: Economics; Government and politics

KEY FIGURES:

Nikolai Ivanovich Bukharin (1888-1938), Bolshevik leader, economist, and theorist who led the Right Opposition to the First Five-Year Plan

Lev Borisovich Kamenev (Rosenfeld; 1883-1936), Bolshevik leader, member of the Left Opposition

Aleksei Ivanovich Rykov (1881-1938), Bolshevik party and state leader, member of the Right Opposition

Joseph Stalin (Iosif Vissarionovich Dzhugashvili; 1879-1953), dictator of the Soviet Union, 1928-1953, and promulgator of the First Five-Year Plan

Mikhail Pavlovich Tomsky, Communist and trade union leader, member of the Right Opposition

Leon Trotsky (Leib Davydovich Bronstein; 1879-1940), major figure in the Bolshevik *coup d'état* and creator of the Red Army

Grigori Yevseyevich Zinovyev (Ovsel Gershon Aronov Radomyslsky; 1883-1936), Bolshevik leader, member of the Left Opposition

SUMMARY OF EVENT. The First Five-Year Plan, enunciated by Joseph Stalin in 1928, is the major turning point in the history of the Soviet Union. This plan set the stage for the "Great Change," a deep revolution that altered the personal lives of the entire population of Russia in a manner not even approached by the 1917 Revolution. It established the economic foundation for the social and political structure of the Soviet Union, which, with insignificant change, lasted until the communist government's collapse in 1991.

The implementation of the First Five-Year Plan came in the wake of Stalin's victory in the struggle for leadership of the Russian Communist Party after the death of Vladimir Ilich Lenin in January, 1924. Stalin formed an alliance with Grigori Zinovyev and Lev Kamenev against Leon Trotsky. Having defeated Trotsky, Stalin turned against Zinovyev and Kamenev, charging that their call for rapid industrial growth would endanger the economic recovery which the adoption of the New Economic Policy in 1921 had produced. Stalin now allied himself politically with Nikolai Bukharin, Aleksei Rykov, and Mikhail Tomsky against the "Left Opposition" of Zinovyev and Kamenev.

According to Bukharin, the Russian Civil War had shown that efforts by the state to control the production and sale of grain would be disastrous. He argued that private trade at prices set by the market should be tolerated

in order to supply the needs of Soviet Russia's urban population. When a grain shortage developed in 1927-1928, Stalin denounced Bukharin, Rykov, and Tomsky as a "Right Opposition" and had them removed from their posts. Stalin then embraced the Left Opposition's call for rapid industrialization. To solve the grain problem, he advocated the forcible collectivization of agriculture.

The First Five-Year Plan enunciated economic and social goals to be achieved by 1933. In its broadest terms, the plan called for immediate collectivization of the Russian peasantry and rapid strides toward massive industrialization. The instrument of collectivization was to be the *kolkhoz*, or collective farm, which was to be the home and working place of all Russian peasants. Massive industrialization was to take place through the disciplining of the Russian labor force and its employment in the building and operation of factories, mines, great dams, canals, and electric power stations. Industrialization was to be financed from the profits reaped from collectivized agriculture.

The imposition of the directives of the First Five-Year Plan brought about extreme difficulties in Russian agriculture and industry. Most of the peasants bitterly resisted general collectivization. All private holdings in a given area were to be turned over to a collective to be cultivated collectively, and the peasants were required to turn over their tools, draft animals, cows, sheep, pigs, and chickens. While there was nothing the peasants could do about land collectivization, they resisted collectivization of their other property by destroying tools and slaughtering livestock. The government responded with shootings, mass deportations, and an artificially induced famine that caused between five and ten million deaths. In addition, the slaughter of livestock during this period set Russian agriculture back so far that, by 1953, it had not reached prerevolutionary numbers of horses, cattle, sheep, and chickens. Long after 1953, production of meat, milk, and poultry in the Soviet Union remained inadequate to supply the country's growing population.

Other difficulties arose in the internal organization of the collective farms, and they were brought under control by the introduction of party bureaucrats, who ran them dictatorially at great cost to the country. Under such conditions, little progress was made toward achieving the agricultural goals of the First Five-Year Plan. Nevertheless, the efforts of the party did establish the *kolkhoz* as a relatively secure, functioning institution, so that substantial gains were made in agricultural productivity in the period of the Second Five-Year Plan.

The problem of rapid large-scale industrialization also proved immense. First, the government faced the challenge of securing a pool of laborers, most of whom had to be recruited from agricultural areas. Such labor lacked the discipline, steady work habits, and skills needed to operate modern machinery. In order to discipline an incompetent, ever-shifting, tardy, occasionally drunk, and often absent labor force, the "black book" was introduced. In this book, overseers kept a detailed record of each worker's misdemeanors, and workers were subjected to harsh penalties, including exile to Siberian labor battalions, if they did not conform. The question of material incentives also arose, for it soon became apparent that only piece-work rates encouraged higher productivity and only higher wages induced workers to take on supervisory duties.

The Soviet Union tried to create in a few years an industrial labor force as efficient and disciplined as those developed by Western countries during centuries of effort and experience. The problem was compounded by a severe shortage of housing in Russian industrial cities. Inadequate before the massive influx of new workers, housing was lamentably insufficient to provide accommodations for even more people. Indeed, for a family to have an apartment to itself in a Russian city remained a luxury. As was the case in agriculture, posited industrial goals could not be reached, though the basis was set during the First Five-Year Plan for substantial advances later.

At great cost in men and material the ruthless Stalin and the Communist Party faithfully dedicated themselves to the First Five-Year Plan. Although its material accomplishments were meager in comparison with the goals it had set, the party nevertheless set the stage for the stabilization of Russian society in the years to come.

—*George F. Putnam, updated by Richard D. King*

ADDITIONAL READING:

Davies, R. W. *The Socialist Offensive: The Collectivisation of Soviet Agriculture, 1929-1930*. Cambridge, Mass.: Harvard University Press, 1980. A detailed history of the establishment of the collective farm system from the perspective of the Soviet leadership.

Fitzpatrick, Sheila. *Stalin's Peasants: Resistance and Survival in the Russian Village After Collectivization*. New York: Oxford University Press, 1994. A pioneering work on collectivization from the point of view of the peasants based on previously secret Soviet archives.

Kuromiya, Hiroaki. *Stalin's Industrial Revolution: Politics and Workers, 1928-1932*. New York: Cambridge University Press, 1988. Studies the implementation of rapid industrialization during the First Five-Year Plan and analyzes support and resistance among industrial workers.

Lewin, Moshe. *Russian Peasants and Soviet Power: A Study of Collectivization*. Translated by Irene Nove with

the assistance of John Biggart. New York: W. W. Norton, 1968. Focuses on debates over economic policy within the Communist Party during the 1920's and the pivotal grain procurement crisis of 1928.

Scott, John. *Behind the Urals: An American Worker in Russia's City of Steel*. Enlarged edition prepared by Stephen Kotkin. Bloomington: Indiana University Press, 1989. These memoirs by an American who worked in Magnitogorsk, a steel-producing city founded during the First Five-Year Plan, vividly describe working and living conditions.

Tucker, Robert C. *Stalin in Power: The Revolution from Above, 1928-1941*. New York: W. W. Norton, 1990. Argues that Stalin forged a new autocracy modeled on Russia's Muscovite and czarist past to carry out his revolutionary policy of state-sponsored industrial development.

SEE ALSO: 1917, October Revolution; 1921-1928, Lenin's New Economic Policy; 1929, Trotsky Is Sent into Exile.

1929-1940
THE MAGINOT LINE IS BUILT

The Maginot line is built as a defense of France, but it fails because of the rigidity of its design and the mindset of those who command it.

DATE: 1929-1940

LOCALE: The border between France and Germany

CATEGORIES: Government and politics; Science and technology

KEY FIGURES:

Édouard Daladier (1884-1970), premier of France, 1933, 1934, and 1938-1940

General Charles-André-Marie-Joseph de Gaulle (1890-1970), French undersecretary of state for national defense, 1940, and leader of the Free French, 1940-1945

General Joseph-Jacques-Césaire Joffre (1852-1931), commander in chief of the French armies during World War I

André-Louis-René Maginot (1877-1932), French minister of war, 1922-1924 and 1929-1932

Paul Painlevé (1863-1933), French minister of war, 1925-1929

General Henri Philippe Pétain (1856-1951), commander in chief of the French armies after World War I, minister of war, 1934-1935

SUMMARY OF EVENT. The Maginot line was created in the aftermath of the carnage of World War I, but its designers failed to take into account the technical advances of 1918 which made it obsolete long before construction began.

Workers plowed the earth in preparation for the construction of the Maginot line along France's eastern border with Germany. (National Archives)

After November 11, 1918, France began to explore different means of defense against a possible resurgent Germany. Having lost more young men per capita than any other nation, the French were convinced that without an adequate system of security, the country would lose to Germany if war should break out again.

The French based their plan upon three aims. First, they sought a defensive alliance with Great Britain against Germany. England, however, perceived France as the strongest nation in Western Europe and therefore refused to commit to a Continental ally in the interest of a balance of power. Second, France concluded treaties with nations on Germany's eastern border including Poland, Czechoslovakia, Yugoslavia, Romania, and in 1934 the Soviet Union, in order to replace the security of the prewar Franco-Russian alliance. Finally, as a deterrent to Germany, the French signed a defensive alliance with Belgium and then began to construct a system of fortifications along their border with Germany which became known as the Maginot line.

The construction of the Maginot line had its genesis in

the experience of World War I. Following their defeat in 1871, the French sought as their national goal the reconquest of Alsace and Lorraine from Germany. The country's only strategy for success in 1914 depended on a sustained offensive. As Allied casualties mounted, both British and French trenches were designed to be as uncomfortable as possible to encourage troops to attack. By contrast, the Germans attempted to create both strong and relatively comfortable positions which could be easily held. After French mutinies in 1917, the French military commanders, Marshal Joseph-Jacques-Césaire Joffre and Marshal Henri Philippe Pétain, drew the conclusion that switching to a defensive posture would significantly reduce losses. They did, however, fail to take into consideration that new offensive techniques using tanks and mobile infantry overcame Germany's well-constructed defenses. Instead, the French concluded that a future war should find France maintaining a defensive position against an offensive Germany; only then would the odds be in France's favor.

After World War I, Joffre was appointed head of a special commission to plan the military defense of France. Both he and Pétain suggested that a system of fortifications be constructed along the Franco-German border. These fortresses would be so impenetrable that the Germans would face great losses if they attempted to attack France. The suggestions were taken up by the two men who served as ministers of war in the 1920's, Andre Maginot and Paul Painlevé.

A sergeant who was wounded in World War I and served as a member of the National Assembly, Maginot was primarily concerned with helping veterans to obtain benefits. After he oversaw the occupation of the Ruhr in 1923, however, Maginot became convinced that a fortified line was needed to protect France. During the last nine years of his life, he worked to convince the French legislature to vote funds for its construction using the double themes of jobs and patriotism. After Maginot's death, successive ministers of war continued his work and had the fortifications named in his honor in recognition of his interest and determination.

In 1930, the Chamber of Deputies approved the expenditure of 2,900 million francs over four years for frontier defenses, but the undertaking proved so immense that by 1940 the cost had doubled. Finished shortly before the start of World War II, the Maginot line was a continuous system of advance posts, casemates, and ourages, holding between two hundred and twelve hundred men, running from Switzerland to Belgium along the entire length of the Franco-German border. Vast underground bunkers, cannon that could be raised automatically, and the most modern equipment were installed. The government made the existence of the Maginot line, but not the details of its armaments, public in the hope of convincing the Germans that it would be folly to assault it.

By advertising its presence, a myth was established about the Maginot line. Most citizens of the republic believed that it ran the entire length of France's eastern border, passing Belgium to the English Channel. At the time of the fortification's construction, Belgium was a friendly nation with its own defenses on the German border. Pétain foresaw that in the event of war with Germany, French troops on the Maginot line would be able to hold the border while the bulk of the mobile French forces would move into Belgium to help that country hold its lines against the Germans. In 1914, the British had joined France to protect Belgium, and the French believed that this might be the only means to gain England's support in the future. The Maginot line's strength, it was believed, would invite such a German attack. When Belgium signed a pact with Germany in 1939, France's northern flank became exposed, but few foresaw the weakness that a static defense now posed.

In 1940, the Germans both outflanked the Maginot line and split the Allied forces by launching a mobile attack through the Ardennes Forest. Although many Germans marched through France as their fathers had done in 1914, dramatic penetrations were made by Panzer tank units. The success of such an attack had been envisioned as early as 1922 by Major-General J. F. C. Fuller and Captain Basil Liddell Hart of Great Britain and championed by Charles de Gaulle. Much to de Gaulle's frustration and the country's detriment, the General Staff failed to take his arguments seriously.

After the French garrisons surrendered on June 25, 1940, the Germans made an in-depth study of the Maginot line. Impressed by the small amount of damage wrought by their aerial bombardment, the army used both French construction techniques and many of the guns in the construction of the Atlantic Wall. The Germans converted much of the Maginot line to storage or factory space until the Allied liberation of Europe in June, 1944. At this stage, part of the fortifications at Faulquemont and Wittring were rearmed and successfully slowed the advance of General Patton's Third U.S. Army. Following the war, the French military began a reconstruction of the line which continued until 1964, when the fortifications were abandoned for defense and parts were opened to tourists and historians.

—*José M. Sánchez,*
updated by Edmund Dickenson Potter

ADDITIONAL READING:

Chapman, Guy. *Why France Fell: The Defeat of the French Army in 1940*. New York: Henry Holt, 1968. Chapman examines the fall of France by first studying the victory of 1918 and the mistakes which were made outside the political front involving the military.

De Gaulle, Charles. *War Memoirs, Vol. I: The Call to Honour, 1940-1942*. Translated by Jonathan Griffin. London: Collins, 1955. As the champion of mobile warfare in France before 1940, de Gaulle uses his autobiography to contradict the notion that the Maginot line and a policy of defense were created without protest.

Fuller, General J. F. C. *The Second World War, 1939-1945*. London: Eyre & Spottiswoode, 1948. As an early theorist on mobile warfare and the use of the tank, Fuller brings a unique perspective to the study of the war.

Hughes, Judith M. *To the Maginot Line: The Politics of French Military Preparation in the 1920's*. Cambridge, Mass.: Harvard University Press, 1971. Hughes addresses how the debate between peace and security created an atmosphere from which the Maginot line was born.

Joseph-Maginot, Marguerite. *Maginot: He Might Have Saved France*. Translated by Allan Updegraff. New York: Doubleday, 1941. This work provides not only a contemporary biography of Maginot, but also includes not so subtle recriminations for the fall of France shortly after it took place.

Kemp, Anthony. *The Maginot Line: Myth and Reality*. New York: Stein & Day, 1982. Kemp provides not only the history of the fortifications construction but also diagrams and photographs which illustrate the immense nature of the project. Further, he follows the history of the Maginot line through the German occupation into the Cold War when France and her neighbor became allies.

Rowe, Vivian. *The Great Wall of France*. New York: G. P. Putnam's Sons, 1961. While Rowe provides detailed accounts of the battles around the Maginot line, he suggests that it was the best defense for France at the time.

Weinberg, Gerald L. *A World at Arms: A Global History of World War II*. New York: Cambridge University Press, 1994. This comprehensive work addresses the world war chronologically rather than thematically.

SEE ALSO: 1919, The League of Nations Is Established; 1919, Treaty of Versailles; 1938, Munich Conference; 1940, Collapse of France; 1940, Evacuation of Dunkirk.

1929
TROTSKY IS SENT INTO EXILE

Trotsky is sent into exile, putting an end to significant opposition within the Russian Communist Party to Stalin's personal rule and his establishment of a totalitarian state.

DATE: January 19, 1929
LOCALE: Moscow, the Soviet Union
CATEGORY: Government and politics
KEY FIGURES:

Lev Borisovich Kamenev (Rosenfeld; 1883-1936), Bolshevik leader
Vladimir Ilich Lenin (Ulyanov; 1870-1924), leader of the Bolsheviks before and during the Russian Revolution of 1917, and creator and first leader of the Communist Party
Joseph Stalin (Iosif Vissarionovich Dzhugashvili; 1879-1953), dictator of the Soviet Union from 1928 to 1953, and creator of the Soviet totalitarian state
Leon Trotsky (Leib Davydovich Bronstein; 1879-1940), leading figure in the Russian Revolution of 1917 and the ensuing civil war and Stalin's main opponent in the power struggles of the 1920's
Grigori Yevseyevich Zinovyev (Ovsel Gershon Aronov

Radomyslsky; 1883-1936), Bolshevik leader involved in the struggle for power in the 1920's

SUMMARY OF EVENT. Both Leon Trotsky and Vladimir Ilyich Lenin played important parts in the Bolshevik seizure of power in Russia. Like Lenin, Trotsky may have been indispensable. No one agitated more effectively among the working classes to bring them to the side of the Bolsheviks and no one showed more skill and determination in organizing them into a military force capable of winning power in Petrograd in 1917. No one stood more steadfastly beside Lenin in the crucial days of October when several of the leading Bolsheviks opposed the leader's decision to try to seize power. In the summer and fall of 1917 the special talents which Trotsky possessed—energy, determination, ruthlessness, and flaming oratory—found a situation in which they could be most effective.

In the hard days of the civil war (1918-1921), Trotsky's abilities and courage once again served the Bolsheviks well. It was he who, as People's Commissar of War, organized and directed the Red Army. In less than one year by the force of his will and intelligence, he transformed an undisciplined group of youthful enthusiasts into an organized disciplined army. He also tirelessly and ruthlessly directed that army in its struggle to the death against White counterrevolution and foreign intervention. The Bolsheviks might not have survived the civil war, and the Red regime might have been merely a passing phenomenon in world history without Trotsky. Yet only ten short years later he became an outcast, exiled from his native land by the Communist Party he had done so much to defend and perpetuate. His victorious rival, Joseph Stalin, rewrote history to conceal Trotsky's important role in the Bolshevik seizure of power and victory in the civil war. Trotsky virtually became an "unperson" in the Soviet Union, remembered only for the false charge that he was a traitor to the revolution rather than one of its principal leaders.

After the death of Lenin in 1924, Trotsky lost the struggle for power in a personality clash with Joseph Stalin in which fateful aspects of Russian Communist policy were thrashed out. Should the party continue the semicapitalistic New Economic Policy (NEP) within Russia? Should it govern democratically or dictatorially? Should it stake all on the victory of world revolution, or should it try to consolidate "socialism" in Russia? These were the policy questions intertwined within the struggle for personal power. Between 1923 and 1925, Trotsky tried to turn the party away from NEP to a policy of collectivization of the peasants and massive industrialization. Stalin, with the help of important Bolsheviks, such as Lev Borisovich Kamenev and Grigori Yevseyevich Zinovyev),

As a leading figure with Lenin when the Bolsheviks came to power in Russia, Leon Trotsky was forced into exile when Joseph Stalin took control of the Party Congress in 1927. (Archive Photos)

and with overwhelming support among the mass of party members, brought about Trotsky's defeat on this issue in the Party Congresses of 1923 and 1924. Feeling against Trotsky ran so high that Kamenev and Zinovyev at a Central Committee meeting in January, 1925, demanded his expulsion from the party, but Stalin, still unsure of himself, rejected their proposal. Trotsky was merely forced to give up his post as People's Commissar of War.

By mid-1925, however, Kamenev and Zinovyev became alarmed at Stalin's demonstrated strength in the rank and file. They now saw him as a greater threat to their positions in the party than Trotsky, whom they, like many others, had suspected of a dictatorial tendency. Moreover they had come to believe that it was time to abandon the New Economic Policy. Accordingly, they joined forces with Trotsky as he once again called for a rapid beginning of collectivization and industrialization. They also fought for the restoration of democracy in the party, which Stalin as head of the Orgburo, which made party personnel decisions, and of the Secretariat, which controlled the party's records and conducted all correspondence between

Moscow and local party organizations, had transformed into a centrally directed, bureaucratic machine. They also fought for an active Communist role in international affairs against Stalin's doctrine of "Socialism in one country." At the Party Congress in December, 1925, Stalin and his supporters easily overcame this opposition group.

Defeated in the higher echelons of the party, Trotsky returned to the fray in 1926 and 1927, but in a different way. He now tried to reach the rank and file by speeches, articles, and pamphlets, and by the surreptitious organization of an opposition faction. Such overt oppositional activity had been banned by the Tenth Party Congress in March, 1921. Trotsky's violation of the rule against factions led in October, 1926, to Trotsky's expulsion from the Politburo, the leading policy-making organ of the party, the last bastion of his strength after his defeats in the Party Congresses of 1923-1925. His acts ran counter to the party's deep need and desire for unity, and eroded rather than increased his strength. His last attempt was made in October, 1927, on the anniversary of the revolution, by mounting public parades and demonstrations against Stalin and the party leadership. These pathetic efforts were easily crushed by Stalin's loyal followers, and in December, 1927, at the Fifteenth Party Congress, Trotsky, Kamenev, Zinovyev, and seventy-five of their most prominent followers were expelled from the party.

In a prophetic act, Stalin allowed the "guilty" to return to the womb of the party if they would publicly recant their errors. Kamenev, Zinovyev, and numerous others did so. Trotsky refused, and he was exiled, first to Alma Ata in Kazakhstan, and later out of the Soviet Union altogether. He lived on in exile, the center of forces opposing Stalin in world Communism, and the source of many polemical writings against the regime. Not content with the physical expulsion of Trotsky from the Soviet Union, Stalin sought to erase all memory of Trotsky's vital role in the Russian Revolution and Russian Civil War. Soviet history books were rewritten to misrepresent the roles of both Trotsky and Stalin. Trotsky was falsely accused of opposing Lenin in 1917 and secretly working for the defeat of Communism in the civil war, while Stalin was given credit for Trotsky's achievements. This falsification of history reached its height in Stalin's Great Purge of 1936-1938, when thousands of Stalin's former opponents, including Zinovyev and Kamenev, were imprisoned or executed on trumped-up charges of trying to sabotage the building of socialism in Russia in collaboration with Trotsky. The exiled Trotsky was hounded by Soviet agents until 1940, when Stalin silenced him with an assassin's ice pick in the brain. *—George F. Putnam, updated by Richard D. King*

ADDITIONAL READING:

Carr, E. H. *Socialism in One Country, 1924-1926.* 3 vols. New York: Macmillan, 1958-1964. A detailed investigation of the personal and policy struggles in the period following Lenin's death.

Deutscher, Isaac. *The Prophet Unarmed: Trotsky, 1921-1929.* New York: Oxford University Press, 1959. The second volume of a sympathetic three-volume biography, this book recounts the power struggles of the 1920's.

Fitzpatrick, Sheila. *The Russian Revolution.* 2d ed. New York: Oxford University Press, 1994. An introduction to the first two decades of Soviet history which effectively brings out Stalin's and Trotsky's different programs for building socialism.

Knei-Paz, Baruch. *The Social and Political Thought of Leon Trotsky.* Oxford: Clarendon Press, 1978. A comprehensive analysis of Trotsky's writings, with particular emphasis on Trotsky's interpretation of Stalinism.

Trotsky, Leon. *My Life: An Attempt at Autobiography.* Magnolia, Mass.: Peter Smith, 1930. Trotsky wrote this autobiography, which has been reissued several times, immediately after his exile from the Soviet Union in 1929.

Tucker, Robert C. *Stalin as Revolutionary, 1879-1929: A Study in History and Personality.* New York: W. W. Norton, 1973. This study of Stalin's rise to power offers a psychological interpretation of his rivalry with Trotsky.

Volkogonov, Dmitri. *Trotsky: The Eternal Revolutionary.* Translated and edited by Harold Shukman. New York: Free Press, 1996. Written by a retired Soviet general who has also published books on Lenin and Stalin, this is the first biography of Trotsky based on access to Soviet as well as Western archives.

SEE ALSO: 1917, October Revolution; 1918-1921, Russian Civil War; 1934-1939, Stalin Begins the Purge Trials.

1929

THE VATICAN TREATY

The Vatican Treaty initiates an end to the conflict, begun in 1870, between church and state in Italy.

DATE: February 11, 1929

LOCALE: Rome, Italy

CATEGORIES: Diplomacy and international relations; Religion

KEY FIGURES:

Domenico Barone, Italian diplomat

Cardinal Pietro Gasparri (1852-1934), papal secretary of state, 1914-1934

Benito Amilcare Andrea Mussolini (1883-1945), Fascist premier of Italy, 1922-1943

Francesco Pacelli, papal diplomat

Pius XI (Ambrogio Damiano Achille Ratti; 1857-1939), Roman Catholic pope, 1922-1939

Victor Emmanuel III (1869-1947), king of Italy, 1900-1946

SUMMARY OF EVENT. When the army of the new Italian state took the city of Rome from the papacy in 1870, Pope Pius IX retreated to the Vatican palace and proclaimed himself "Prisoner of the Vatican." Alleging that the Italian government had usurped lands which were the heritage of the Roman Catholic Church, he condemned the government and refused to have anything to do with it. The pope hoped that his condemnation would rally pro-papal forces to overthrow the Italian State and restore him to his temporal possessions. He furthermore prohibited Catholics, by threat of excommunication, from running or holding office in the national government or voting in state parliamentary elections, hoping that their abstention would also weaken the government.

Instead, the Italian government flourished, and in the absence of Catholic deputies, passed anticlerical legislation. Successive governments, however, respected papal possession of the Vatican palace and Saint Peter's basilica, and offered the papacy a Law of Guarantees, guaranteeing the pope residence at the Vatican and a large sum of money. The pope rejected this offer because acceptance would mean the Vatican would exist as charity of the state and imply that the pope serve under allegiance to the state.

After 1870, despite official unwillingness on both sides to solve the Roman Question, an expression referring to the politioreligious conflict between the papacy and the kingdom of Italy, a tacit understanding was worked out between the papacy and the state. Neither interfered in the other's affairs, but the underlying conflict between church and state still existed as a constant strain to the whole country in a time of political unrest throughout the world and the threat of communism at Italy's border. With the exception of extreme clericals, both sides wanted to effect a compromise settlement of the Roman Question, but it was a matter of prestige that neither side give in.

Early in the twentieth century, the papacy began to lift the ban on Catholic participation in national political life. In 1919, it was completely removed to allow the formation of the Catholic-oriented Popular Party led by Sicilian priest Don Luigi Sturzo. The Popular Party originated with the hope of propagating faith in the Church among the Italian people, for the pope knew that no answer to the Roman Question could be settled by treaty alone.

In 1922, Benito Mussolini, leader of the Fascist Party,

was named premier, and he set out to establish a dictatorship. In the process, Mussolini was anxious to reconcile with conservative groups and institutions to win them over to his side. He maintained the monarchy, assuring King Victor Emmanuel III that he had no intention of overthrowing the Italian Royal House. In order to gain support of both the papacy and the Catholics, he announced his desire to settle the Roman Question.

Mussolini's seizure of power coincided with the election of Pius XI as pope. Although Mussolini made public his desire to work with the papacy, Pope Pius XI cautiously proceeded to cooperate with Mussolini in an effort to ward off a mutual foe of the Vatican and Mussolini: communism.

In 1926, the two leaders made secret preliminary contacts for negotiation of the problem. The pope selected Francesco Pacelli, brother of the future Pope Pius XII, as his envoy, and Mussolini directed the Italian diplomat, Domenico Barone, to represent him in the talks. Early in 1929, agreement was reached, and the Vatican Treaty was officially signed on February 11, 1929, by Mussolini and the papal secretary of state, Cardinal Pietro Gasparri.

The Vatican Treaty, also known as the Lateran Accords, contained three separate sections: a treaty, a financial agreement, and a concordat. The first was an agreement between the Italian State and the Vatican State. By its terms, Italy recognized the Vatican as a separate and sovereign state with all the attributes of an independent nation. Italy furthermore recognized its usurpation of papal lands in 1870 by compensating the papacy for its loss of temporal possessions. A cash settlement of forty million dollars was paid to the pope along with another fifty-two million dollars of interest-bearing Italian government bonds. In return, the Vatican recognized the Italian government. The terms of the concordat between the Italian State and the Holy See, as representing the Catholic Church in Italy, were that the anticlerical laws were formally revoked. The Catholic religion was to be taught in all state schools, and Catholicism was proclaimed as the official religion of the state. The clergy were given a generally favorable position in civil law. In return, the Italian government obtained the privilege of nominating the higher clergy in Italy.

The announcement of the signing of the treaty immediately raised Mussolini's prestige both in Italy and throughout the Catholic world. Hailed for having solved one of the world's outstanding problems, Mussolini transformed his international image from that of a violent Blackshirt to a wise and compassionate statesman. Pius also reaped prestige for recognizing that the necessity for papal temporal possessions need not encompass large amounts of territory.

The Vatican Treaty was, however, the prelude to further disagreement between the pope and Mussolini. The concordat had specifically guaranteed Catholic lay organizations freedom to function in Italy. One of these societies, the Italian Catholic Action, soon became a refuge for anti-Fascist elements who used the organization to criticize the regime. Mussolini sent his Blackshirts to break up Catholic Action meetings, and the pope responded in 1931 by condemning Fascism in the encyclical *Non Abbiamo Bisogno*. After threats and counterthreats, the state and the papacy reached a tacit agreement: Catholic Action would no longer criticize the regime, and in return it would be allowed full freedom to operate outside this restriction. The pope thereafter maintained a discreet caution toward Mussolini, and when he died in 1939, Pius was considerably disenchanted with the Fascist regime.

Not all reactions to the signing of the treaty were positive. Anti-Laterans were as strongly opposed to the treaty as supporters highly exalted Pius and Mussolini. The issue of equality between the pope and the state was called into question by Americans and Europeans who viewed the treaty as an opportunistic maneuver by Mussolini and believed that the pope lost prestige for the Church by compromising with a political power whose beliefs were opposite humanity and religious devotion. Opponents of the Lateran agreements hated the implied surrender to Fascism that the treaty invoked rather than the settlement itself.

The Vatican Treaty was essentially respected by the various governments of the Italian State throughout the confusion of the war years: In 1948 it was officially incorporated into the constitution of the new Italian Republic and remained in force thereafter. With regard to peace and mutual understanding, however, the treaty barely survived its birth in 1929.

—*José M. Sánchez, updated by Diane Lise Hendrix*

ADDITIONAL READING:

DeGrand, Alexander J. "Cracks in the Facade: The Failure of Fascist Totalitarianism in Italy 1935-9." *European History Quarterly* 21, no. 4 (1991): 515-535. Describes weaknesses in Benito Mussolini's fascist reign which made it impossible for totalitarianism to survive.

Drake, Richard. "Julius Evola, Radical Fascism, and the Lateran Accords." *Catholic Historical Review* 74, no. 3 (1988): 403-419. A profile of anti-Lateran Julius Evola that critiques the Catholic Church and discusses the complexity of Fascism.

Knee, Stuart E. "The Strange Alliance: Mussolini, Pope Pius XI, and the Lateran Treaty." *Mediterranean Historical Review* 5, no. 2 (1990): 183-206. The Lateran

Accords sought to end antagonism between the Italian state and the papacy. Optimism following the agreement did not last long. Discussion of Fascist and papal motivations behind the Vatican Treaty.

O'Brien, Albert C. "Italian Youth in Conflict: Catholic Action and Fascist Italy, 1929-1931." *Catholic Historical Review* 68, no. 4 (1982): 624-635. Discusses the conflict and competition between the Catholic Church and Italian Fascists for control of Italian youth.

Rhodes, Anthony. *The Vatican in the Age of the Dictators, 1922-1945*. New York: Holt, Rinehart and Winston, 1973. An in-depth look at the motivations behind initiation of the Vatican Treaty and the consequences for church and state after signing the treaty.

SEE ALSO: 1861, Italy Is Proclaimed a Kingdom; 1922, Mussolini's "March on Rome"; 1943, Allied Invasion of Italy.

1931
SECOND SPANISH REPUBLIC IS PROCLAIMED

The Second Spanish Republic is proclaimed after the abdication of the king and the election of a constituent Cortes.

DATE: April 14, 1931
LOCALE: Madrid, Spain
CATEGORY: Government and politics
KEY FIGURES:

Niceto Alcalá Zamora y Torres (1877-1949), president of the Second Spanish Republic, 1931-1936
Alfonso XIII (1886-1941), king of Spain, 1886-1931
Manuel Azaña y Díaz (1880-1940), founder and leader of the Republican Action Party, prime minister of Spain, 1931-1933 and 1936-1939
Julián Besteiro, Socialist and speaker of the Cortes
José María Gil Robles y Quiñones (1898-1980), journalist and leader of the Confederación Española de Derechos Autónomos (CEDA), the moderate Catholic Party
Francisco Largo Caballero (1869-1946), leader of radical elements in the Socialist Party
Alejandro Lerroux García (1864-1949), leader of the Radical Party, and Spanish prime minister, 1933-1935
Miguel Maura y Gamazo, minister of the interior, 1931
Indalecio Prieto, leader of moderate elements in the Socialist Party
General José Sanjurjo, leader of attempted coup by the right wing

SUMMARY OF EVENT. By 1931, Alfonso XIII of Spain was a bankrupt monarch. In addition to his failure to provide Spain with the leadership necessary to solve its problems, he had approved the 1923 *coup d'état* of Miguel Primo de Rivera y Orbaneja, which had established a dictatorship. When the dictator resigned in 1930, Alfonso hoped to provide a transitional regime that would prepare the way for a return to constitutional government.

The reformist parties, however, had gained great strength since the mid-1920's. The Socialist Party, led by Indalecio Prieto and Francisco Largo Caballero, and the Republican Radical Party, led by Alejandro Lerroux García, joined newly established liberal parties and groups under Manuel Azaña y Díaz and Niceto Alcalá Zamora y Torres to demand the establishment of a reform republican government. When the king announced municipal elections in April, 1931, to test this republican sentiment, the results indicated that the Crown had lost. On April 14, 1931, the republican politicians proclaimed the Second Spanish Republic, and Alfonso went into exile.

In July, 1931, elections were held for a constituent Cortes, or parliament, and a liberal Republican-Socialist coalition was formed to govern Spain. The first cabinet reflected the overwhelming support of the electorate for Republican and Socialist deputies. Right-wing Republicans, the majority of whom were from the Radical Party of Alejandro Lerroux García, and left-wing Republicans under Manuel Azaña y Díaz held more than half of the seats in the Cortes, while Socialists, led by Largo Caballero and Indalecio Prieto, held an additional 115 seats. Alcalá Zamora was chosen as prime minister, but became the first president of the Republic later that year, after Azaña was selected to be prime minister of the governing coalition. Other members of the first government included Miguel Maura y Gamazo, minister of the interior; Alejandro Lerroux García, foreign minister; and Manuel Azaña y Díaz, minister of war.

The Cortes wrote a constitution incorporating many liberal reforms and providing regional autonomy for those provinces that desired it, thereby solving the Catalan problem. It provided for reform of the military and action against the Catholic Church, which had been one of the supporters of the old regime. The Catholic Church was disestablished, the clergy's salaries were abolished, the Jesuit order was dissolved, and provisions were made to prevent the clergy from teaching. This attack on the Church, however, precipitated a crisis that brought down the first cabinet. When Article 26 of the constitution went into effect, many excellent schools operated by Jesuits and Augustinians closed; there were no state schools immediately to take their place. This action angered both devout

Catholics and other members of the middle class whose children's schooling was disrupted.

Other reforms established machinery for wide and sweeping land reform, because solving Spain's agrarian problems was critical to the new government. These reforms did not do enough to satisfy many peasants, and incidents in several small villages led to riots and murder.

The government's actions began to polarize the country. Liberal reforms satisfied many moderates, but practicing Catholics were unhappy. Furthermore, extremist ele-

cals, then becoming more conservative under their leader Lerroux. Because the CEDA had unsavory monarchist connections, the Republican-Socialists in the newly elected Cortes rejected Gil Robles' bid for power. Instead, Lerroux became prime minister with CEDA backing.

CEDA-Radical ministries governed Spain from 1933 to 1935. As the CEDA's main concern was revision of the anticlerical legislation and the Radicals had no reform plans, little action was taken during these years. Most of the Republican-Socialist reform legislation was allowed

President Niceto Alcalá Zamora (center) assembled a coalition cabinet after the Second Spanish Republic was proclaimed in 1931. (National Archives)

ments opposed the Republican-Socialists. On the right, the monarchists schemed with the military to restore Alfonso. General José Sanjurjo led a coup against the Republic in 1932, but he and his followers were arrested. Anarchists of the Left called the reforms too moderate. They countered with strikes and industrial violence and tried to provoke the clergy by burning churches and monasteries.

In 1933, the Republican-Socialist coalition fell and the election was won by CEDA, the moderate Catholic party led by José María Gil Robles y Quiñones, and the Radi-

to lapse or was not implemented, causing the parties of the left to refer to the period as "The Two Black Years." The Anarchists protested and, along with certain Republicans and Socialists, revolted against the government in 1934. The revolt was put down, and many of the proletarian party leaders were imprisoned. Finally, in late 1935, Alcalá Zamora dissolved the Cortes and ordered new elections in order to break the parliamentary impasse.

In the elections of early 1936, the forces of the Left—Liberals and Socialists, with the tacit approval of the Anarchists—joined in a coalition known as the Popular

Front. They defeated the disunited Rightists and gained control of the Cortes. The Republican-Socialist reforms were once again implemented, but there was so much opposition from both extremes that public order was gravely compromised, thus provoking a military uprising by the right wing in July, 1936.

—*José M. Sánchez, updated by James A. Baer*

ADDITIONAL READING:

Brenan, Gerald. *The Spanish Labyrinth: An Account of the Social and Political Background of the Civil War.* Canto ed. New York: Cambridge University Press, 1990. Gives an excellent background to the civil war, and provides much information on the most important political forces in Spain.

Carr, Raymond. *Spain, 1808-1939.* Oxford: Clarendon Press, 1961. A comprehensive history of Spain with a chapter on the period of the Second Spanish Republic.

Crow, John A. *Spain, the Root and the Flower: An Interpretation of Spain and the Spanish People.* 3d ed. Berkeley: University of California Press, 1985. Offers a cultural history of Spain, with chapters 12 and 13 specifically on the background and events of the Second Spanish Republic.

Jackson, Gabriel. *The Spanish Republic and the Civil War, 1931-1939.* Princeton, N.J.: Princeton University Press, 1964. Political analysis sympathetic to the Second Republic and critical of "extremist" elements on both the left and the right.

Madariaga, Salvado de. *Spain: A Modern History.* New York: Frederick A. Praeger, 1958. A history of Spain and the events of the Second Republic from a minister of Education in the Republican government. Author states in Introduction that he does not treat Nationalist side evenly because he did not know these men and was sympathetic to those he knew in the Republican government.

Smith, Rhea Marsh. *Spain: A Modern History.* Ann Arbor: University of Michigan Press, 1965. While the book is a general history of Spain from prehistory to the twentieth century, its chapters on the dictatorship of Primo de Rivera and the Second Republic give a clear presentation of events.

Thomas, Hugh. *The Spanish Civil War.* New York: Harper & Row, 1961. A classic study of the background of the civil war and its major events from a political as well as military perspective. While the analysis is not especially original, the massive research is impressive.

SEE ALSO: 1868, Spanish Revolution of 1868; 1876, Spanish Constitution of 1876; 1914, Spain Declares Neutrality in World War I; 1936, Spanish Civil War Begins.

1932
EAMON DE VALERA IS ELECTED PRESIDENT OF THE IRISH DÁIL

Eamon de Valera is elected president of the Irish Dáil and, as president of the executive council, becomes in effect the prime minister of the Irish Free State after the Fianna Fáil establishes a majority in the Irish parliament.

DATE: March 9, 1932
LOCALE: Dublin, Ireland
CATEGORY: Government and politics
KEY FIGURES:
William T. Cosgrave (1880-1965), leader of Cumann na nGaedheal
Eamon de Valera (1882-1975), head of Fianna Fáil
Vivion de Valera (1911-1982), son of Eamon de Valera
Sean Lemass (1899-1969), Fianna Fáil official
James McNeil (1869-1938), governor-general of Ireland

SUMMARY OF EVENT. The elections of February, 1932, saw Eamon de Valera's Fianna Fáil become the majority party in the Dáil Éireann, the parliament of the Irish Free State. On March 9, de Valera, long a major figure in Irish life and lore, was chosen as president of the executive council of the Dáil, equivalent to the British prime minister, and came to command the state he had violently opposed at the time of its birth in 1922.

Irish history is full of irony and paradox, much of it tragic, and de Valera's career exhibits those qualities to the fullest. He had been at the center of the Irish consciousness since the failed Easter Monday Rising against Britain in 1916. A number of leaders were executed but de Valera was spared, possibly because of the perception that the earlier executions had created sympathy for the rebels, perhaps because de Valera had been born in the United States.

In 1919, war broke out between Britain and the Irish rebels, who were politically organized as Sinn Féin (ourselves alone) and militarily in the Irish Republican Army (IRA). De Valera, as head of Sinn Féin, and David Lloyd George, the British prime minister, agreed to a truce in the summer of 1921, but de Valera refused to participate in the subsequent negotiations, sending as head of the delegation his rival, Michael Collins. An "Irish Republic" was never a possibility, as de Valera undoubtedly knew, and Collins and his associates accepted dominion status within the British empire. Designated the "Irish Free State," the constitutional head would still be the British monarch, who lacked substantive power but was a symbol of the British connection, represented in Ireland by a governor-general. Supported by Collins but opposed by de Valera, the treaty was narrowly adopted. The result was a new civil war in Ireland, green against green, the Free State forces against Sinn Féin and the IRA, and before it ended with a Free State victory, Collins and numerous others on both sides were killed.

De Valera survived, but was imprisoned by the Free State and ignored by the military leaders of the IRA. During the years which followed, the Free State government, led by William Cosgrave, got the fledgling state underway. The shadow of history and Britain lay heavily over the new nation, and the partition of Ireland into the Free State and Northern Ireland generated controversy. Yet the greatest threat came not from Britain or Northern Ireland but from the losers in the treaty debate: de Valera's Sinn Féin and the IRA.

One of the most brilliant politicians in Irish history— he was an avowed student of Machiavelli's *The Prince*— de Valera combined idealistic nationalism with ruthless self-interest. He was never as hard-line as many republicans, being willing to settle for what he called "external

After severing ties with Sinn Féin and founding his own Fianna Fáil political organization, Eamon de Valera (right) secured a seat in the Irish Dáil and became president of its executive council in 1932. (Archive Photos/ Frederic Lewis, Inc.)

association" with Britain, but like everyone involved on both sides, symbols were important, and for de Valera the required oath to the British crown remained a seemingly insurmountable obstacle. De Valera decided to disengage himself from the IRA's violence and use the mechanisms of the hated Free State to gain power, but when many of his Sinn Féin colleagues refused to follow, de Valera resigned as president of the organization and founded Fianna Fáil (warriors of destiny) in May, 1926. In the 1927 elections, Fianna Fáil became the second largest party, with Sinn Féin reduced to a rump. To take one's seat in the Dáil, one had to sign his name as evidence of subscribing to the oath. In a gesture worthy of Machiavelli, de Valera signed his name but denied he was taking the oath and entered the Dáil in 1927.

Cosgrave's Cumann na nGaedheal, as the largest party in the multiparty Dáil, dominated the political arena throughout the 1920's. Like its British and American counterparts, the government's economic philosophy tended toward classic liberalism: the less government involvement the better. The coming of the Great Depression, however, made such attitudes less tenable. In addition, Cosgrave attempted to enlist the Catholic Church's support for his regime. The Irish church was, if anything, more conservative than the Vatican in political and social matters. The Free State outlawed divorce and established a censorship board to search out any obscenities, including any reference to birth control. Suspicious of socialism and adamantly against the IRA's violence, the bishops were a political prize worth having. De Valera also needed the Church, or at least its neutrality. Sincere in his own Catholicism, his Sinn Féin connections were a barrier to be overcome, but he and Fianna Fáil did so by complaining that Cosgrave had not taken a firm enough approach to entrenching the Catholic Church into Irish life. Also, as the established newspapers largely supported Cosgrave, in 1931 de Valera founded his own daily newspaper, the *Irish Press*, which became and remained de Valera's political mouthpiece: He owned it, he controlled it.

Cosgrave called an election for February 16, 1932, several months earlier than constitutionally required. Yet with the economy worsening, earlier elections seemed the lesser evil. Predictably, the government said little about economic policy, relying in its platform on being the party of religion, law and order, and accusing Fianna Fáil of being crypto-communists with ties to the IRA. De Valera committed himself to abolishing the oath, but stressed his economic programs which would increase welfare and reduce unemployment through public housing and other social programs. The Machiavellian de Valera's chief adviser, Sean Lemass, reassured the IRA of Fianna Fáil's friendship, Cosgrave's party was accused of being Masons and British unionists, and de Valera used every opportunity to identify himself with the Church.

The election results saw Fianna Fáil become the largest party in the Dáil with seventy-two seats, up fifteen from 1927. Cosgrave's party won only fifty-seven seats. Although lacking an absolute majority—Labour and other minor parties held the balance of power—it was understood that de Valera would head the new government. During the campaign he had assured the voters that in the event of a Fianna Fáil victory there would be no untoward measures taken against their political opponents. There were rumors that elements of the army would resort to a military coup in order to nullify Fianna Fáil's victory, but Cosgrave, committed to democracy, had consistently reduced the influence of the military throughout his long tenure.

On March 9, 1932, de Valera entered the Dáil, with Vivion, his son, at his side, armed with a revolver because of assassination rumors. Yet, there was no violence. Cosgrave did not even offer himself as a candidate, and thus de Valera, long a legend, as hero or villain, by a margin of eighty-one to sixty-eight was elected as president of the executive council and came to preside over the state he had disowned at its birth. Governor-General James McNeil, in a gesture of conciliation, took the initiative and went to the Dáil instead of requiring that de Valera come to the Vice-regal Lodge to confirm his election. McNeil was soon replaced, however, by a de Valera sycophant, much reducing the governor-general's position as a imperial symbol. De Valera also suspended land annuity payments due the British government, beginning an economic war which lasted until the eve of World War II. In power, de Valera was to prove no friend to the IRA, cracking down on its activities like Cosgrave before him. In 1937, a new constitution was promulgated, further weakening Free State ties with Britain, but it was not until 1947, ironically with de Valera briefly out of power, that the Irish Republic was established.

The election of 1932 was a crucial event in Irish history. It brought de Valera into office as head of the government, and through the peaceful transition of power between two groups which had been shooting at each other only a few years earlier, it proved to many that Irish democracy was a reality.

—Eugene Larson

ADDITIONAL READING:

Coogan, Tim Pat. *De Valera: Long Fellow, Long Shadow.* London: Random House, 1993. Often critical, this work is the most satisfactory biography of de Valera.

Edwards, Owen Dudley. *Eamon de Valera.* Cardiff:

University of Wales Press, 1987. This interpretative biography discusses de Valera's character and motives.

Foley, Conor. *Legion of the Rear Guard.* London: Pluto Press, 1992. A history of the IRA, which discusses its relationship with the 1932 election.

Lee, J. J. *Ireland, 1912-1985.* New York: Cambridge University Press, 1989. Comprehensive account of Irish politics and society in the twentieth century.

Longford, Earl of, and Thomas P. O'Neill. *Eamon de Valera.* London: Hutchinson, 1970. This authorized biography is a sympathetic portrayal of de Valera.

SEE ALSO: 1912-1914, Irish Home Rule Bill; 1916, Easter Rebellion; 1972, "Bloody Sunday" in Northern Ireland.

1933
HITLER COMES TO POWER IN GERMANY

Hitler comes to power in Germany and leads the Nazi Party, marking the end of German democracy in the 1930's and ushering in political changes that lead to World War II.

DATE: January 30, 1933
LOCALE: Berlin and the rest of Germany
CATEGORY: Government and politics
KEY FIGURES:

Paul Joseph Goebbels (1897-1945), Nazi leader of Berlin and later propaganda minister under Hitler
Hermann Göring (1893-1946), president of the Reichstag, 1932-1933, and minister in Hitler's cabinet
Paul von Hindenburg (Paul Ludwig Hans Anton von Beneckendorff und von Hindenburg; 1847-1934), president of the Weimar Republic, 1925-1934
Adolf Hitler (1889-1945), chancellor and führer of Germany, 1933-1945
Franz von Papen (1879-1969), German chancellor, 1932, and vice-chancellor under Hitler, 1933-1934
Ernst Röhm (1887-1934), chief of staff of the paramilitary *Sturm Abteilung* (Nazi stormtroopers or SA), also known as the Brown Shirts
Kurt von Schleicher (1882-1934), last German chancellor before Hitler, 1932-1933

SUMMARY OF EVENT. On the morning of January 30, 1933, Adolf Hitler took the oath of office from the venerable president of the Weimar Republic, Field Marshal Paul von Hindenburg. That evening thousands of torch-bearing Nazi Brown Shirts, or members of the paramilitary *Sturm Abteilung* (SA), marched through the Brandenburg Gate past the new chancellor, celebrating their victory over the forces of German democracy. The Third Reich, which would bring Hitler the fanatical allegiance of the majority of Germans and which would lead to the vast holocaust of World War II, had begun.

Hitler's movement, the National Socialist German Workers' Party (NSDAP), had begun with a handful of malcontents in Munich shortly after World War I. His ruthlessly brilliant leadership differentiated it from the many other racist-nationalist groups of the era. Hitler had first tried to grasp power in 1923 at the Beer Hall Putsch, but Weimar democracy had prevailed, and by the time of the 1928 elections, the Nazis appeared to be no more than an annoying inconsequential party of the lunatic fringe radical right. Their combination of nationalism, anti-Marxism, anti-Semitism, anti-big business "socialism," militaristic agitation, and raucous oratory had gained them less than 3 percent of the popular vote. Yet, in less than five years, Hitler was chancellor of Germany, placing such key men as Hermann Göring and Joseph Goebbels in charge of the mechanisms of the state. By the time of Hindenburg's death in August, 1934, Hitler had totalitarian control of the state.

Historians have noted a number of causes for the Nazi rise. Few will still argue that the German intellectual traditions which venerated the authority of the state, lauded the military virtues, and praised the greatness of the German people, made Hitler's victory inevitable. Nevertheless, this background provided traditions which Hitler could pervert and exploit. The depression, which hit Germany soon after the 1929 stock market crash in the United States, gave Hitler's movement its greatest boost. As business indicators fell and the unemployment lines grew, the Nazis scored impressive electoral gains. Curiously, however, it was not primarily the unemployed who gave their votes to Hitler; most of those were working-class people devoted to Marxism. If moderate, they voted Social Democrat, if radical, they voted Communist. While research supports the contention that the Nazi voters appear to have come largely from the ranks of the middle classes, including shopkeepers, managers, small farmers, white-collar workers, civil servants, and others of the *petite bourgeoisie*, some studies indicate that Hitler's support was even broader than this. For the most part, those who voted for Hitler's NSDAP feared the rhetoric of the Marxists and abandoned the traditional bourgeois parties in frustration.

Nationalistic appeals, based on denunciation of the Treaty of Versailles imposed on Germany after World War I, excited their support. Hitler, portrayed through careful and manipulative propaganda as a humble soldier from the ranks, a man of German "race" although of Austrian citizenship, appealed to their pride with his calls for a Greater Germany. The German people were not as lacking in democratic traditions as some commentators (including Hitler) would have one believe. Nevertheless, their feelings for the Weimar Constitution were pragmatic, and when unstable parliamentary coalitions proved unable to handle the economic crisis, they were quite prepared to try more authoritarian solutions.

The Nazis, with their vigor, toughness, and aggressive (if somewhat ill-defined) program, stood out in stark contrast to the modesty and fatigue which characterized the other middle-class parties. Hitler's leadership, amplified by the Goebbels propaganda machine, brought many solid German burghers to his side. It was the intrigues of reactionary politicians, rather than the votes of Germans, that put Hitler in power. The Nazis became the largest single power in the German multiparty system, but they never received an absolute majority in a free national election.

The year of the many elections, 1932, shows the dynamics of the Nazi rise. In March, Hitler ran for president against the aging Hindenburg. Hitler received 30.1 percent of the votes to Hindenburg's 49.6 percent, with the remaining votes going to the Communist candidate (13.2 percent), and two minor candidates. Clearly, Hitler had lost; but a second ballot was necessary since no one had received an absolute majority. In April, Hindenburg beat Hitler, receiving 53 percent of the vote as compared to Hitler's 36.8 percent. There followed several state legislative elections, the most significant being in Prussia. The Nazis emerged as the largest single party there, with 36.2 percent of the votes. In July, the National Parliament (the Reichstag) was elected. The Nazis won 37.3 percent of the votes; they and the Communists—the antidemocratic forces, respectively, of the radical Right and the radical Left—held a majority of Reichstag seats between them. A government based on even the broadest coalition of the middle parties was impossible, so in November the German people voted again. This time the Nazi vote totals fell, giving Hitler and his party only 33.1 percent. The Nazi campaign coffers were depleted, and the flood of Nazi votes seemed to have crested and receded. Hindenburg refused to give Hitler the dictatorial powers he demanded as his price for supporting a government with his votes in the Reichstag. Both Hitler and Goebbels became despondent.

The chancellorship had been held since midyear by a reactionary aristocrat once active in the Catholic Center Party, Franz von Papen. After the November elections, Papen found his position undermined not only by the Nazis but by General Kurt von Schleicher, army chief and an inveterate political manipulator. Hindenburg appointed

Schleicher to serve as chancellor in December, 1932. The clever general tried to split the Nazi Party and form a coalition of left-wing Nazis, right-wing Social Democrats, and conservatives, in order to keep Hitler from power. Schleicher's plan gathered little support, while Papen worked behind the scenes to unseat Schleicher and create a coalition of Nazis and Nationalists (German National People's Party) in which he would hold a key position. Papen assured Hindenburg and others on the traditional right that Hitler could be controlled by the conservatives in the cabinet. Indeed, only three Nazis, Hermann Göring, Wilhelm Frick, and Hitler himself, would be in the cabinet. Thus Hindenburg agreed to make the fatal appointment.

The first few months of Hitler's rule were crucial to his success, since during that period he accomplished a revolution *after* coming to power. Far from controlling Hitler, Papen and the other conservatives found themselves outmaneuvered by him at every turn. Hitler skillfully dismantled the constitutional guarantees he had sworn to uphold and went on to establish a totalitarian dictatorship in the years that followed. Upon Hindenburg's death in August of 1934, Hitler assumed his powers as president and exacted an oath of personal loyalty from the military.

The Nazi revolution after Hitler's rise to power can be seen as occurring in four phases. First, Hitler prevailed upon Hindenburg to call new elections for the Reichstag. Nazis now controlled the police, so Brown Shirt terrorism went unchecked while the opposition parties labored under severe handicaps. A few days before the election, a former Communist Dutch arsonist set fire to the Reichstag building. Quickly, the Nazis fabricated evidence of a Communist uprising and promulgated emergency decrees suspending civil rights. The decrees were never lifted. Even with all the power of the state behind them, the Nazis missed a majority, receiving 43.9 percent of the votes on March 5, 1933.

The second phase was the forcing through the Reichstag of the "Enabling Act," which was written to give Hitler dictatorial powers for a period of four years and required a two-thirds vote of the Reichstag for passage. The Communists had been forcibly excluded and many Social Democrats had been threatened and did not appear. Nevertheless, Hitler needed the votes of the big Catholic Center Party, so he combined honeyed words and threats to gain its support. When the vote came, only the Social Democratic Party voted "no." All of the other parties supported Hitler. Thus on March 23, 1933, his dictatorship gained its legal basis.

The third phase of the Nazi revolution was the policy of *Gleichschaltung* ("coordination"), which subordinated

every organization to the Nazi state. All other political parties dissolved more or less "voluntarily." The mass media and the arts were coordinated under Goebbels' leadership. Youth organizations, unions, professional societies, and even singing groups and garden clubs found it prudent either to amalgamate with the parallel Nazi organizations or simply to go out of business. Coordination was a process rather than a single action, so it overlapped the other phases in the Nazi takeover chronologically. Its results were uneven. Within the churches, for example, pockets of independence continued to exist, although the vast majority of both Protestants and Catholics formally accepted Nazi dominance. Anyone who actively and publicly opposed coordination faced the prospect of joining the thousands of dissidents in the concentration camps.

The fourth phase included two events in 1934 that placed the capstone on Hitler's control of the state. In late June, rumors of a putsch—an attempt to overthrow the government—by Ernst Röhm and certain other "radicals" among the SA provided an excuse for a bloody purge. Some 150 to 200 potential or real opponents of the regime were shot on Hitler's orders by the *Schutzstafel* (SS) under the direction of Heinrich Himmler. Not only Röhm, but a number of prominent conservatives including Schleicher, were killed. On August 2, 1934, the eighty-six-year-old Hindenburg finally died. Swiftly, Hitler assumed the powers of the deceased president and had the military swear a personal oath of loyalty to him as "führer" (leader). He then arranged for a plebiscite in which 89.9 percent of the valid votes cast supported him. Adolf Hitler, the ne'er-do-well Austrian painter, World War I lance corporal, convicted putschist, and fanatic leader of the NSDAP, was the unchallenged führer of Germany.

—George R. Mitchell, updated by Liesel Ashley Miller

ADDITIONAL READING:

Abel, Theodore. *Why Hitler Came into Power*. Cambridge, Mass.: Harvard University Press, 1986. Originally published in 1938, Abel's study remains an analytical cornerstone in the question of why Hitler was successful in becoming Germany's leader. This edition has a foreword by Thomas Childers.

Allen, William Sheridan. *The Nazi Seizure of Power: The Experience of a Single German Town, 1930-1935*. Chicago: Quadrangle Books, 1965. Allen's book shows the local impact of Nazism and how the grassroots organization and support of the party made possible Hitler's ultimate seizure of power.

Bullock, Alan. *Hitler: A Study in Tyranny*. New York: Harper & Row, 1962. Bullock's work remains one of the best, most thorough standard biographies of the führer;

this book shows how Hitler carried out his "revolution after power."

Childers, Thomas. *The Nazi Voter*. Chapel Hill: University of North Carolina Press, 1983. In this statistical analysis of German voting behavior, Childers contends that Hitler's supporters came not simply from an indistinguishable middle class, but from very diverse backgrounds.

Flood, Charles Bracelen. *Hitler: The Path to Power*. Boston: Houghton Mifflin, 1989. An insightful addition to accounts of Hitler and his rise to power, this work provides an exhaustive bibliography of both primary and secondary sources.

Hamilton, Richard F. *Who Voted for Hitler?* Princeton, N.J.: Princeton University Press, 1982. In this controversial book, Hamilton rejects the traditional centrist argument—that of the dominant lower-middle-class support for the NSDAP—and suggests alternative explanations for the Nazi rise to power.

Maier, Charles S., Stanley Hoffmann, and Andrew Gould, eds. *The Rise of the Nazi Regime: Historical Reassessments*. Boulder, Colo.: Westview Press, 1986. This collection of essays begins with an informative overview by Charles Maier, while subsequent contributors address the collapse of Weimar and the Nazi rise to power.

SEE ALSO: 1919, Weimar Constitution; 1919-1933, Racist Theories Aid Nazi Rise to Political Power; 1933, The Reichstag Fire; 1933, Enabling Act of 1933; 1934, The Great Blood Purge.

1933
THE REICHSTAG FIRE

The Reichstag fire prompts the president of Germany to grant the Nazis emergency powers to suppress a feared Communist revolution, resulting in the arrests of Hitler's political opponents.

DATE: February 27, 1933
LOCALE: Berlin, Germany
CATEGORY: Government and politics
KEY FIGURES:

Georgi Dimitrov, prominent Bulgarian Communist
Paul Joseph Goebbels (1893-1946), Nazi minister of propaganda and national enlightenment
Hermann Göring, Nazi president of the Reichstag, 1932
Paul von Hindenburg (Paul Ludwig Hans Anton von Beneckendorff und von Hindenburg; 1847-1934), president of the German Republic
Adolf Hitler (1889-1945), chancellor and führer of Germany, 1933-1945
Ernst Torgler, leader of Communist members of the German parliament

Marinus van der Lubbe, a former Dutch Communist convicted of treason for setting fire to the German parliament building

SUMMARY OF EVENT. On the night of February 27, 1933, arsonists set fire to the German parliament building (Reichstag). The spectacular blaze sent flames shooting up through the Debating chamber and illuminated the Berlin skyline. The tense political situation in Germany turned what would ordinarily have resulted only in newspaper headlines for a few days into the catalyst that resulted in Adolf Hitler gaining dictatorial power in Germany.

When the fire took place, Hitler was chancellor in a coalition government with the nationalists in the Reichstag which rested not on a parliamentary majority but on the authority granted to President Paul von Hindenburg under Article 48 of the Weimar Constitution. Parliamentary elections were only six days away and Hitler's National Socialist German Workers' Party (NSDAP or Nazis) needed to win a majority in the parliament. In the general elections held in November, 1932, the Nazis had lost almost two million votes and thirty-four seats in the Reichstag from the previous election, while the Communists gained three-quarters of a million votes and eleven seats.

A mysterious fire in a key public building during the height of a general election campaign was certain to arouse suspicion. Public tensions increased when Hitler and his two chief lieutenants, Joseph Goebbels (minister of propaganda) and Hermann Göring (president of the Reichstag and head of the secret police) blamed the fire on the Communists. Goebbels officially proclaimed the fire to be the work of the Communists, whom he alleged were thereby giving the signal for a Communist uprising.

The Nazis had been predicting such an uprising for several weeks. As early as January 31, Goebbels had written in his diary that the Nazi leaders had decided to wait for the Communist attempt at a revolution before making their own bid for power. Goebbels speculated that his party would gain power by crushing the Communist threat that so alarmed many Germans, including President Hindenburg. On February 24, only three days before the Reichstag fire, the secret police headed by Göring raided the Karl Liebknecht House, which had served as headquarters for the Communist Party in Berlin. The Communist Party had earlier abandoned the building, but the police found piles of pamphlets in the cellar. Göring issued an official communique stating that the police had found documents which proved that the Communists were planning a general uprising. Despite his promise to do so, Göring never released these documents for public scrutiny.

At the scene of the Reichstag fire the Berlin police captured twenty-four-year-old Dutch national Marinus van der Lubbe. Van der Lubbe, who had been a member of the Communist Party in Holland, admitted to the police that he had set fire to the building to encourage German workers to fight the Nazis. He insisted that he had acted entirely on his own, with no accomplices.

The Nazis leaders, however, refused to accept this explanation and began rounding up suspects on the actual night of the fire. Göring's police arrested and jailed between four and five thousand persons whose names appeared on a list prepared by the Nazis before the fire took place. Those arrested included Ernst Torgler, chairman of the Communist Reichstag delegation, and three Bulgarian Communists who happened to be in Berlin (Georgi Dimitrov, Simon Popov, and Vassili Taneu). The Nazis charged those four men along with van der Lubbe with responsibility for the fire.

The day after the fire, February 28, Hitler used the threat of a Communist uprising to persuade President Hindenburg to sign an emergency decree. The decree "for the protection of the people and the state" suspended individual and civil liberties guaranteed by the German constitution and authorized severe penalties for political crimes. The emergency decree enabled Hitler and Göring to restrict the efforts of their political opponents during the remainder of the election campaign. Members of the Nazi paramilitary *Sturm Abteilung* (SA or storm troopers) harassed members of rival political parties while the Nazis and their nationalist allies campaigned unhindered.

Despite the strenuous efforts made by the Nazis and the great advantage they gained by the emergency decree, the German voters did not give Hitler the parliamentary majority that he sought. In the elections held on March 5, the NSDAP received about five-and-a-half million more votes than in the previous election but they still had only 44 percent of the total vote. Together with the *Deutschnational Volkspartei* (DNVP or Nationalist Party), however, they had a slim majority of sixteen seats in the Reichstag. During the election campaign, the Nazis had cleverly postponed outlawing the Communist Party in order to split the working-class vote between the Social Democrats (another Marxist party) and the Communists. The Nazi leaders were not slow to realize that they would have a clear majority in the Reichstag without their Nationalist allies if they proscribed the Communist deputies. Thus the Reichstag fire and the emergency decree which followed played a crucial role in Hitler's rise to power.

The importance of the Reichstag fire for the Nazi electoral triumph led many contemporary observers and subsequent historians to suspect that the Nazis set fire to the building in order to frighten the voters with stories of an imminent Communist revolution. The Nazis did their utmost to allay such suspicions and prove that the Communists were responsible for the fire during the famous Reichstag fire trial held before the Supreme Court at Leipzig in the fall of 1933. While the German government was conducting the official trial at Leipzig, Jewish and Communist opponents of Nazism held their own "counter-trial" in London. The verdict of the London "countertrial" was that van der Lubbe could not have acted alone as he claimed, and that the Communist Party had no connection with the fire. The London mock jurists concluded that there were grave grounds for placing the guilt on the National Socialists.

The Leipzig court found van der Lubbe guilty and sentenced him to death. The German tribunal agreed with the London mock jurists on one point: Van der Lubbe could not have acted alone. Despite the fact that the German court acquitted Torgler and the three Bulgarian Communists for lack of evidence, it also charged that all the evidence pointed to the fact that the accomplices of van der Lubbe were to be found in the ranks of the Communist Party.　　　—*Harry E. Wade, updated by Paul Madden*

ADDITIONAL READING:

Fischer, Klaus P. *A History of Nazi Germany*. New York: Continuum, 1995. The most recent comprehensive account of the Nazi regime, based on research up to the time of its publication. Concludes that the Reichstag fire most likely resulted from the efforts of van der Lubbe and unnamed accomplices.

Gilfond, Henry. *The Reichstag Fire, February, 1933: Hitler Utilizes Arson to Extend His Dictatorship*. New York: Franklin Watts, 1973. An unconvincing argument that the Nazis deliberately burned the Reichstag building in order to stampede Hindenburg into granting Hitler the power to suppress the anticipated Communist revolution.

Leers, Johann von [Paulus van Obbergen, pseud.]. *The Oberfohren Memorandum*. London: German Information Bureau, 1933. An attempt by an official organ of the German government to refute the so-called Oberfohren memorandum. Ostensibly written by Ernst Oberfohren, a former leader of a German political party, and published in the *Manchester Guardian* on April 27, 1933, the memorandum accused the Nazis of setting the Reichstag fire.

Reed, Douglas. *The Burning of the Reichstag*. New York: Covici-Friede, 1934. Concludes that van der Lubbe was not guilty, or at least did not act alone.

Spielvogel, Jackson J. *Hitler and Nazi Germany: A History*. Englewood Cliffs, N.J.: Prentice-Hall, 1988. A widely used college text on the Nazi era which leaves open the question of responsibility for the Reichstag fire, but points out that Hitler gained much from the fire, while it cost the Communists dearly.

Tobias, Fritz. *The Reichstag Fire Trial*. Translated by Arnold J. Pomerantz. New York: G. P. Putnam's Sons, 1964. Argues that van der Lubbe was guilty of setting fire to the Reichstag building and did act alone. An introduction by famed British historian A. J. P. Taylor supports the author's position.

SEE ALSO: 1919-1933, Racist Theories Aid Nazi Rise to Political Power; 1933, Hitler Comes to Power in Germany; 1933, Enabling Act of 1933; 1934, The Great Blood Purge; 1938, The *Anschluss*.

1933

ENABLING ACT OF 1933

The Enabling Act of 1933 ultimately dooms the Weimar Republic by granting Hitler unprecedented powers and lending his totalitarian ends the illusion of legitimacy.

DATE: March 23, 1933

LOCALE: Kroll Opera House in Berlin, Germany

CATEGORY: Laws, acts, and legal history

KEY FIGURES:

Paul Joseph Goebbels (1897-1945), German minister of propaganda

Hermann Göring (1893-1946), chairman of the Reichstag, 1933

Paul von Hindenburg (Paul Ludwig Hans Anton von Beneckendorff und von Hindenburg; 1847-1934), president of Germany, 1925-1934

Adolf Hitler (1889-1945), chancellor and führer of Germany, 1933-1945

Monsignor Ludwig Kaas (1881-1952), leader of the Center Party

Franz von Papen (1879-1969), chancellor of Germany, 1932, and Hitler's vice chancellor, 1933

Otto Wels (1873-1939), leader of the Social Democratic Party

SUMMARY OF EVENT. Only two months after becoming chancellor, Adolf Hitler sought a legal foundation for dictatorship of Germany by proposing the Act for Ending the Distress of People and Nation—commonly known as the Enabling Act. In five short paragraphs, this bill transferred key legislative powers held by the Reichstag, or parliament, to Hitler's Nationalist Socialist (Nazi) party for a period of four years. Specifically, it would allow him and his cabinet to draft and pass laws without the Reichstag's consent; to propose amendments to the constitution and even to suspend it; to control the national budget; and to enter into foreign treaties. Although it contained reas-

suring phrases about not curtailing the power of either President Paul von Hindenburg or the parliament, the bill actually enabled Hitler to bypass all opposition. Since it modified the Weimar Constitution, however, Hitler needed a two-thirds majority in the Reichstag for enactment of the bill; more than two-thirds of the deputies had to be present, and at least two-thirds of those present had to vote for it so that it could pass into law.

The general elections of March 5, 1933, had given the National Socialists forty-four percent of the total vote and 288 out of the 647 seats in the Reichstag. After the elections Hitler turned his attention to the task of obtaining the two-thirds majority in the Reichstag that would make it possible for him to become dictator. First, he expelled the eighty-one Communist deputies. Those not arrested were threatened with arrest if they attempted to take their seats in the Reichstag. Second, Hitler persuaded the Center Party and the Nationalists to vote for the Enabling Act. The Center Party, under the leadership of Monsignor Ludwig Kaas, was pessimistic about blocking the bill and decided to support it in the hope of gaining Hitler's consideration for its own Catholic interests. Hesitant to trust Hitler's spoken pledge, however, the party demanded a written promise that he would abide by the president's power of veto. Kaas never received such an assurance from Hitler, but he accepted instead a letter from President Hindenburg, stating that he had been assured by Hitler that the Enabling Act would not be used without prior consultation with the president. Thus Kaas made the same error as his fellow Center Party member Franz von Papen, who had agitated for Hitler's instatement after his own dismissal from the chancellorship because he hoped to share and profit from Hitler's power.

To win the support of the Nationalists and the army, Hitler and his newly appointed minister of propaganda, Joseph Goebbels, staged a ceremony in the Garrison Church at Potsdam that was a master stroke of grand strategy. The ceremony was held on March 21 to mark the opening of the new Reichstag, two days before it was to consider the Enabling Act. Hitler and Goebbels selected Potsdam, the royal residence of the Hohenzollerns, and the Garrison Church, containing the grave of Frederick the Great, to marry symbolically the past glories of Prussia to the new Nazi regime. Even the date of the ceremony had significance, for on March 21, 1871, Otto von Bismarck as chancellor of the German empire had opened the first Reichstag. At noon, Hitler entered the church beside the fading, eighty-six-year-old Hindenburg, who endorsed the simple former corporal's new government to the crowd; Hitler's own speech emphasized the national renewal evident since he had taken office. The two men's handclasp

Seated behind Paul von Hindenburg (center), Adolf Hitler staged the ceremony at the Garrison Church at Potsdam that marked the opening of the new Reichstag on March 21, 1933. (Library of Congress)

at the climax of the ceremony convinced many that Hitler stood for a restoration of the old order in Germany.

The success of Hitler's policy was demonstrated when the Reichstag convened two days later in the Kroll Opera House in Berlin to vote on the Enabling Bill. The building was surrounded by belligerent SS and SA troops. Hitler opened the session with a speech noticeable for its restraint; he pointed out that the new powers would be used only to carry out measures vitally necessary, and that such occasions were unlikely to occur very often.

The only deputy to speak out against the bill was Otto Wels, leader of the Social Democrats. Amid the menacing jeers of swastika-waving storm troopers, Wels began a speech condemning the gangster mentality of the Nazis, but he was soon interrupted by Hitler. Infuriated by Wels's opposition, Hitler threw off all restraint. After savagely attacking the Social Democrats, he told them that he did not need their votes; Germany would be free, but not through them. Moreover, Hitler reminded Wels, the Nazis had merely observed legal niceties by seeking Reichstag

approval for something that they could and would readily have "taken in any case."

Despite this clue to Hitler's ruthlessness, when the vote was taken, the Enabling Bill passed by a huge majority: 441 votes for, 94 votes against. The opposition votes were cast by the Social Democrats. When Hermann Göring, president of the Reichstag and Hitler's trusted henchman, made the votes known, the Nazi deputies sprang to their feet and sang the *Horst Wessel* song while giving the Nazi salute. The Nazis had reason to be happy: Their leader had just freed himself from dependency on the Reichstag and the president. Hitler could now issues decrees without the president's approval, even if they modified the Weimar Constitution.

Technically, through a provision introduced by Hindenburg, the Enabling Act limited the appropriation of legislative powers to the particular cabinet in office on January 31, 1933. Hitler soon flouted this restriction. He also seized upon Hindenburg's death on August 1, 1934, as a pretext for fusing the presidency and chancellorship, again seeking a legal veneer by claiming that Hindenburg's will named him successor.

—*Harry E. Wade, updated by Margaret Bozenna Goscilo*

ADDITIONAL READING:

Bracher, Karl Dietrich. "The Technique of Nationalist Socialist Seizure of Power." In *The Path to Dictatorship, 1918-1933*, edited by Theodor Eschenburg et al. New York: Frederick A. Praeger, 1966. The author analyzes how the concept of "legal revolution" led to the middle-class parties' naïve trust in Hitler and their consequent passage of the Enabling Act.

Fischer, Klaus P. *Nazi Germany: A New History*. New York: Continuum, 1995. Fischer's masterful study stresses the Nazi cynicism and terrorism underlying both the Potsdam ceremony and the ratification of the Enabling Act.

Hoffmann, Peter. *The History of the German Resistance 1933-1945*. Translated by Richard Barry. Cambridge, Mass.: MIT Press, 1977. Hoffmann convincingly roots the lack of meaningful opposition to Hitler's pseudo-legal seizure of power in terrorism, ignorance and denial about Nazi values, and weak democracy.

Krausnick, Helmut. "Stages of 'Co-ordination.'" In *The Path to Dictatorship*, edited by Theodor Eschenburg et al. New York: Frederick A. Praeger, 1966. Krausnick views the Enabling Act as a decisive step in the "coordination" of German institutions to Hitler's will, second only to the February 28, 1933, decree suspending basic constitutional rights.

Shirer, William L. *The Rise and Fall of the Third Reich: A History of Nazi Germany*. New York: Simon & Schuster, 1960. Shirer's account of the Enabling Act emphasizes Hitler's manipulation of Prussian patriotism—and the Social Democrats' weakness—in bringing the nation "under the Nazi heel."

SEE ALSO: 1919, Weimar Constitution; 1919-1933, Racist Theories Aid Nazi Rise to Political Power; 1933, Hitler Comes to Power in Germany; 1933, The Reichstag Fire; 1934, The Great Blood Purge; 1938, The *Anschluss*.

1934-1939
STALIN BEGINS THE PURGE TRIALS

Stalin begins the purge trials, resulting in massive arrests and executions that create widespread fear in the Soviet Union and increase Stalin's dictatorial powers.

DATE: 1934-1939
LOCALE: The Soviet Union
CATEGORY: Government and politics

KEY FIGURES:

Nikolai Ivanovich Bukharin (1883-1938), former Politburo member and editor of *Pravda*; leader of the "Right Opposition"

Sergei Mironovich Kirov (Kostrikov; 1886-1934), member of the Central Committee of the Communist Party of the Soviet Union, 1922-1934; leader of the Leningrad Communist Party, 1928-1934

Joseph Stalin (Iosif Vissarionovich Dzhugashvili; 1879-1953), general secretary of the Communist Party and ruler of the Soviet Union, 1924-1953

Leon Trotsky (Lev Davidovich Bronstein; 1879-1940), former prominent member of the Communist Party's Politburo, and a political opponent of Stalin

Andrei Yanuaryevich Vyshinsky (1883-1954), Soviet state prosecutor, 1935-1939

Nikolai Ivanovich Yezhov (1895-c. 1939), head of the Peoples' Commissariat of Internal Affairs, 1936-1938

Grigori Yevseyevich Zinovyev (Ovsel Gershon Aronov Radomyslsky; 1883-1936), former Politburo member and chairman of the Communist International; leader of the "Left Opposition"

SUMMARY OF EVENT. By 1934, Joseph Stalin had been leader of the Soviet state for ten years. He had defeated his rivals in the effort to succeed Vladimir Ilich Lenin, the first Soviet leader, by a combination of political maneuvering and intrigue and by the skillful use of the Communist Party bureaucracy, which he had developed as general-secretary of the party's Central Committee. His position, however, was still far from secure. Stalin had achieved his preeminent place in Soviet politics largely by opposing the policies of his Politburo associates such as Leon Trotsky and Grigori Zinovyev. Nevertheless, once they were defeated by the later 1920's, he reversed his position and adopted many of the policies he had originally denounced. Furthermore, the failures of some of these policies during the First Five-Year Plan (begun in 1928 and terminated by 1933) was causing Stalin some difficulties in the highest circles of the Communist ruling elite, the Politburo, and the Central Committee.

Stalin's political problem was simple—how to get rid of the "Old Bolsheviks," Lenin's former associates, whose reputations could once again make them his rivals. He also wanted, at the same time, to eliminate possible new rivals from the group which he had created and developed in the 1920's but who were not sullied by the political conflicts of the previous decade. To accomplish this, Stalin introduced into revolutionary Russia a heightened form of political terror and gave a new meaning to the word "purge."

Within the higher circles of the party the most likely

source of opposition was the popular Sergei Kirov, whom Stalin himself had sponsored in his rise to prominence in the Central Committee, the Politburo, and as head of the Leningrad party organization. He was regarded as one of the most capable of the country's political leaders. On December 1, 1934, an obscure assailant (Leonid Nikolayev) fatally shot Kirov at the Communist Party headquarters in Leningrad. It appears possible, though not absolutely certain, that the assassination was part of a wider conspiracy; but the extent of the presumed conspiracy and the identities of the participants have been shrouded in some mystery. Many Western historians, buttressing their arguments with an apparent confirmation by Stalin's successor Nikita Khrushchev in 1956 as well as the availability of more evidence, believe that Stalin himself had a hand in bringing about the assassination to eliminate a potential rival.

At the time, however, Stalin used the occasion of Kirov's murder to declare that the investigation of the assassination had uncovered the existence of an enormous plot to overthrow his rule. This conspiracy was directed, Stalin alleged, by his archrival Leon Trotsky (then living abroad). The plot supposedly involved tens of thousands of Soviet political and military personnel, cooperating with the Fascist and capitalist foreign enemies of the Soviet state.

Kirov's actual assassin and his closest associates accused as accessories were sentenced to death within a few weeks. Shortly thereafter, the state prosecutor arrested two prominent leaders of the former Left Opposition, Grigori Zinovyev and Lev Kamenev, together with a number of their sympathizers, and charged them with maintaining a clandestine and illegal opposition group in Moscow. The prosecutor's office also charged them with providing ideological support for Kirov's assassins. Although charges of conspiracy against the state were not unprecedented in Soviet history, this was the first time that members of the Communist Party were so charged because of political opposition. The group was quickly tried in secret and sentenced to varying terms of imprisonment.

For a year and a half, there were apparently no more major repercussions from the Kirov assassination. Behind the scenes, however, Stalin was preparing his full-scale assault on the "Old Bolsheviks." His primary allies were concentrated in the Peoples' Commissariat of Internal Affairs, headed by Nikolai Yezhov, as well as Andrei Vyshinsky's State Prosecutor's office. In August, 1936, Zinovyev and Kamenev were tried with fourteen others, accused of conspiring against the Soviet government.

This so-called Trial of the Sixteen was the first of three major show trials in the purge era, which included count-

less scores of other secret and public processes. In January, 1937, seventeen left-wing defendants went on trial for conspiracy and the next year, in the spring of 1938, twenty-one right-wing opponents of Stalin, including Nikolai Bukharin, were tried on the same charges.

The bizarre nature of the show trials added an eerie, unreal atmosphere to the tragedy of the decimation of the ranks of the "Old Bolsheviks." With brazen illogicality, the prosecutors charged lifelong socialists with conspiring with their most implacable foes, including Nazi Germany, to overthrow the Soviet government. Easily refutable evidence, including impossible meetings and charges which could be proven false by examining public records and the foreign press, were introduced into court. Confounding matters, the accused almost invariably confessed to these unlikely crimes. Behind all stood the figure of Trotsky, who was accused of masterminding everything, but who was actually living in exile, his influence in the Soviet Union a faded memory.

All of the accused were found guilty, and most of these high government and party officials were executed. Trotsky himself was assassinated in Mexico in August, 1940, by a Soviet agent. As a result of the purges, almost all of

Through public trials held in the wake of the 1934 assassination of Sergei Kirov, Stalin consolidated his control of the Communist Party by eliminating Lenin's former associates and potential new rivals. (Library of Congress)

the old political leaders fell from power or disappeared. Fourteen of the eighteen members of the Soviet Council of Ministers, the highest Soviet government body including the nation's prime minister, were purged. Of 139 members of the 1934 Central Committee 98 were arrested, and 78 were executed. Furthermore, while in 1934 more than 80 percent of the high Communist officials were "longtime" party members (having joined before 1921), only 19 percent of the party elite in 1939 fell into that category. Near the end of the political purges, Stalin turned on the Soviet military, and throughout 1937 and 1938 continuous waves of arrests decimated well over half of the Red Army command. Three of the five army marshals of the Soviet Union were secretly tried and executed after being accused of being foreign agents. Of the total population, it is estimated that a minimum of seven million persons were arrested and perhaps a half million were executed. Release of more data during the 1990's revealed even greater numbers of victims and the massive scope of the purges across the Soviet Union.

The Stalinist purges have remained something of a mystery to the democratic West, whose citizens find this violent repression so alien to their own societies. Many have wondered why the defendants confessed to the absurd accusations. Were they drugged or beaten into submission? Did they believe that the absurdity of their confessions would prove their innocence before the world? Some, perhaps, were promised leniency or ignored the question of their own guilt or innocence in the hope of saving the reputation of the Party to which they had devoted their lives. Some individuals confessed, hoping their families would be spared from further retribution. Yet there is no doubt that excessive pressure, even torture, was used against the accused to elicit their "confessions" to be presented in the public and meaningless "show trials."

Many years later, especially in 1988 and 1990, a special commission of the Communist Party took the unusual step of declaring the innocence of many of the prominent persons of the charges of the 1930's that led to their deaths. The Communist Party also admitted that the Kirov murder was not part of a massive conspiracy and that grave injustices had been committed. This belated effort to provide a degree of posthumous justice came a half century too late to help the victims and their families.

The question remains whether the purges were an inevitable part of the Communist Revolution or a product of Russia's peculiar history. Similarities to events in the reigns of Ivan the Terrible, Peter the Great, and Alexander I would indicate the latter. The massive reach of the purges across Soviet society, however, reveals a far more pervasive dictatorship than existed under Stalin's predecessors. One conclusion is certain: By means of the purges Stalin was able to secure his position from the threats of potential political and military rivals and rise above all his comrades to become a demigod beyond reproach in the Soviet Union. At the same time, however, his ruthless leadership seriously weakened the nation politically, economically, socially, militarily, and psychologically.

—Frederick B. Chary, updated by Taylor Stults

ADDITIONAL READING:

Conquest, Robert. *The Great Terror: A Reassessment.* New York: Oxford University Press, 1990. An expanded and revised edition of Conquest's pioneering 1968 work on the subject.

_____. *Stalin and the Kirov Murder.* New York: Oxford University Press, 1989. This small book investigates Stalin's probable responsibility in causing Kirov's death.

_____. *Stalin: Breaker of Nations.* New York: Penguin, 1991. This psychological study emphasizes Stalin's paranoia and his desire to achieve massive power.

Levytsky, Boris. *The Stalinist Terror in the Thirties: Documentation from the Soviet Press.* Stanford, Calif.: Hoover Institution Press, 1974. Includes more than two hundred biographies of purge victims, plus the later Soviet rehabilitation campaign of some of those unjustly accused and punished.

_____. *The Uses of Terror: The Soviet Secret Police, 1917-1970.* New York: Coward, McCann & Geoghegan, 1972. Broad survey of the topic includes a description and assessment of the purges of the 1930's.

Radzinsky, Edvard. *Stalin: The First In-Depth Biography Based on Explosive Documents from Russia's Secret Archives.* New York: Doubleday, 1996. Provides more details on specific cases and Stalin's role during the purges, based on previously classified files.

Volkogonov, Dmitri. *Stalin: Triumph and Tragedy.* New York: Grove Weidenfeld, 1991. This substantial biography by a noted Russian historian provides a post-Communist perspective of Stalin.

SEE ALSO: 1928-1933, Soviet Union Launches First Five-Year Plan; 1929, Trotsky Is Sent into Exile; 1939, Nazi-Soviet Pact; 1953, Death of Stalin.

1934
STAVISKY RIOTS

The Stavisky Riots help polarize political life in the Third French Republic, weakening the centrist parties' capacity to resist the growth of Fascism at home and abroad.

DATE: February 6, 1934

LOCALE: France

CATEGORIES: Economics; Government and politics; Wars, uprisings, and civil unrest

KEY FIGURES:

Léon Blum (1872-1950), Socialist Party leader and statesman

Camille Chautemps (1885-1963), Radical Party leader and premier of France, November, 1933, to January 27, 1934

Jean Chiappe (1878-1940), prefect of Paris police, 1928-1934

Édouard Daladier (1884-1970), Radical Party leader and premier of France, January-October, 1933, and January 28-February 7, 1934

Léon Daudet (1867-1942), novelist, anti-Semitic writer and politician, editor of *L'Action française*

Charles Maurras (1868-1952), philosopher of integral nationalism and coeditor of *L'Action française*

Serge Alexandre Stavisky (1886-1934), petty criminal turned international swindler who occasioned a major political scandal in France

SUMMARY OF EVENT. The French governmental crisis of 1934 began in late 1933, when newspapers noted that Serge Alexandre Stavisky, an underworld character, had been accused of defrauding hundreds of investors in Bayonne's municipal bonds. Stavisky had been a police informer, a cabaret backer, a theater promoter, and a political-influence peddler. Called "King of the Crooks," he was actually a petty gangster. The legal protection which he had received from both judges and police was not uncommon in the Third Republic, where officials frequently protected men of Stavisky's caliber in return for information. He had also contributed heavily to election funds of the dominant Radical Party.

Further revelations of his protection by politicians of the dominant Radical Party created a scandal, trumpeted by its right-wing critics. Long active as a financial swindler, Stavisky had been indicted for fraud in 1927, but nineteen attempts to try him had mysteriously failed. He fled the warrant issued for his arrest in 1933, and was found shot to death in January, 1934. Many French people doubted the police reports of suicide and asked two questions: Who had protected Stavisky? Who had killed him? The political scandal forced the Radical premier, Camille Chautemps, to resign in January, 1934, for it had been revealed that he had indirectly supported Stavisky.

France's problems helped to turn the scandal into a crisis. The French normally suspected public officials of incompetence or dishonesty. The right-wing press normally ranted about conspiracies to destroy France. It took

the economic and political failures of the Republic to convert myths and half-truths into politically potent beliefs. Adolf Hitler's Germany was challenging French predominance in Europe, gained at a terrible price in World War I. The Great Depression overwhelmed the Third Republic's politicians. Foreign threats and economic insecurity created an atmosphere in which radical propagandists could use the Stavisky scandal as an excuse to challenge republicanism. France's woes made the rightist version of the Stavisky affair credible.

Numerous political organizations wanted to destroy the Third Republic and replace it with an authoritarian regime, either republican or monarchical. Foremost was Action Française, a rightist and monarchist movement, whose daily newspaper, *L'Action française*, had exposed the Stavisky affair. Action Française also possessed a violent youth movement, the Camelots du Roi. Other rightist organizations made Action Française seem moderate by comparison. There was the semifascist Croix de Feu, which only the openly Fascist Francistes exceeded in radicalism. Politically embittered veterans had formed leagues, some of which sought an "honest and authoritarian" regime. Rightists led the opposition in 1934, the Communists playing a minor role.

Right-wing papers inflamed the public's suspicions. Perhaps the police, who were embroiled in politics, had Stavisky killed to protect unknown politicians. Perhaps Germans, Jews, Communists, or all three groups, had planned the entire affair. These opinions, and the government's silence, caused riots in January, in which the Camelots du Roi and similar young toughs gleefully participated.

Édouard Daladier, a relatively unknown moderate Radical politician, finally promised to investigate the case and restore order. His initial moves, aimed at forming a coalition government, provided the pretext for the February 6 riots. Unable to gather sufficient support from the rightist deputies, who often supported Action Française, Daladier turned to the Left, appointing the Socialist, Eugène Frot, to be minister of the interior. In a further bid for support, he dismissed the head of the Paris police, Jean Chiappe, a tough Corsican with a reputation for meting out harsh treatment to leftist demonstrators. In contrast, he had treated rightist demonstrators delicately. Chiappe refused to accept his dismissal gracefully. *L'Action française* declared him a martyr to the "rotten" Republic.

Although right-wing leaders were willing to take the Stavisky and Chiappe affairs to the people, they did not foresee their followers' enthusiasm. On February 6, an unplanned demonstration began while the new government presented itself to the Chamber of Deputies. People had filled the vast Place de la Concorde by 6:30 P.M. The crowd unsuccessfully charged police stationed on the Pont de la Concorde, a bridge which led to the Palais Bourbon where the deputies met. The police, disgruntled at Chiappe's dismissal, offered only half-hearted resistance until they were angered by the mob, which used lead pipes, paving bricks, and even razors fixed on poles to cripple the horses of the mounted police. The struggle raged until midnight, with both sides suffering heavy losses. Thirteen rioters and one police officer were killed, hundreds others were injured.

The events of February 6 greatly influenced subsequent French politics. Daladier's resignation on February 7 was a clear victory for the rioters. The right-wing factions were impressed by the Republic's weakness. Fascists argued that a more systematic attack on the government could end the Republic. In the short run, Action Française, whose Camelots du Roi had supplied the most committed members of the mob, gathered support from those who blamed the Republic and its police for the rioting. In the long run the crisis damaged Action Française. Its Fascist competitors emphasized that inept Action Française leadership had caused the February riots to fall short of their professed goal of a new, authoritarian regime.

This "failure" was inherent in Action Française. Its leaders could neither comprehend nor exploit the revolutionary possibilities in France before, during, and after the 1934 crisis. They needed to be mindful of their aristocratic and bourgeois allies, who could not approve of any serious disruption of public order. Action Française's failure to seize the opportunity for a coup drove rightist youth into more activist organizations. After 1934, Action Française declined before more radical rightist movements. Their new popularity helped to undermine French unity at a time when it was sorely needed.

The Left, frightened by February 6, became less revolutionary. Although its massive antifascist demonstration on February 12 frightened some legislators, it was meant to show leftist loyalty to the Republic. Communist workers eventually forced their leadership to support the existing regime. Leftist fear of a Fascist coup helped create the Popular Front coalition of Radicals, Socialists, and Communists in 1936, led by the Socialist, Léon Blum, who had also supported the government during the riots. Workers, realizing that there could be worse states than a bourgeois republic, intensified their plans to defend themselves if the next crisis became a coup. Thus, the riots strengthened both Left and Right, and helped to shatter the coalition of centrist parties which had long stabilized the Republic.

Stavisky's death officially remained a suicide. New mystery was added when a judge who supposedly possessed papers relevant to the case died under strange circumstances. The police were again accused of political murder. Even the relatively limited corruption revealed by commissions investigating the Stavisky case discredited some Republican politicians and led to charges that others were hiding evidence. The Stavisky affair remained a symbolic cause and effect of France's political sickness in the 1930's.   —*Charles H. O'Brien*

ADDITIONAL READING:

Agulhon, Maurice. *The French Republic 1879-1992*. Oxford: Blackwell, 1993. The first half of this prize-winning book offers a vivid, lucid, and comprehensive survey of the history of the Third Republic.

Colton, Joel. *Léon Blum, Humanist in Politics*. New York: Alfred A. Knopf, 1966. This biography of the great Socialist Party leader of the 1930's includes a discussion of the Left's reaction to the 1934 crisis.

Lamour, Peter J. *The French Radical Party in the 1930's*. Stanford, Calif.: Stanford University Press, 1964. Offers an entire chapter analyzing the impact of the 1934 crisis on the Radical Party.

Soucy, Robert. *French Fascism: The Second Wave, 1933-1939*. New Haven, Conn.: Yale University Press, 1995. The author exposes the conservative, traditionalist essence of French Fascism.

Weber, Eugen. *Action Française: Royalism and Reaction in Twentieth Century France*. Stanford, Calif.: Stanford University Press, 1962. An exhaustive, well-written, and fair-minded study, based almost entirely on original sources.

_____. *The Hollow Years: France in the 1930's*. New York: W. W. Norton, 1994. A lively, masterfully detailed picture of the riots and their social context.

Werth, Alexander. *The Twilight of France, 1933-1940*. New York: Harper & Row, 1942. Places the 1934 crisis within the general framework of France's decline.

SEE ALSO: 1871-1875, Third French Republic Is Established; 1919, Treaty of Versailles; 1929-1940, The Maginot Line Is Built; 1940, Collapse of France.

1934
THE GREAT BLOOD PURGE

The Great Blood Purge eliminates the SA leadership and gains support for Hitler's radical restructuring of German society among German military leaders and industrialists.

DATE: June 30-July 2, 1934

LOCALE: Berlin, Munich, Wiessee, and other locations in Germany

CATEGORIES: Government and politics; Terrorism and political assassination

KEY FIGURES:

Werner von Blomburg, German minister of war

Hermann Göring (1893-1946), prime minister of Prussia and president of the German parliament

Reinhard Heydrich (1904-1942), Himmler's second in command and commander of the *Sicherdienst* (SD) or security service

Heinrich Himmler (1900-1945), commander of the *Schutzstaffel* (SS), Hitler's elite guard

Adolf Hitler (1889-1945), chancellor of Germany, 1933-1945

Ernst Röhm (1887-1934), chief of staff of the paramilitary *Sturm Abteilung* (SA), or storm troopers

SUMMARY OF EVENT. Between June 30 and July 2, 1933, members of the SS summarily executed several hundred Germans on direct orders from Chancellor Adolf Hitler. Hitler targeted especially the top leadership of the SA (also known as the Brown Shirts), including the SA chief of staff, his old friend Ernst Röhm. These murders (usually called by historians the Röhm Purge or the Night of the Long Knives) resulted from a series of intrigues among top leaders of the Nazi Party, members of the German general staff, and non-Nazi members of the German government. The origins of the purge dated back almost to the beginnings of Hitler's movement.

Röhm, a World War I hero and career army officer, joined the fledgling Nazi Party shortly after Hitler's own entry, in 1919. Röhm became an valuable liaison between Hitler and the German general staff during the years before Hitler's first attempt to seize political power in Germany in 1923. During the eleven months of Hitler's imprisonment after the putsch failed, Röhm, with Hitler's authorization, managed to reorganize the SA under another name and keep its members together despite a government ban on the Nazi Party and its affiliated organizations. In 1922, Hitler had authorized the formation of the SA as the paramilitary arm of the Nazi Party. Its members had protected party meetings and rallies from being broken up by similar organizations affiliated with rival political parties, particularly the Marxist parties. Members of the SA had also broken up the rallies of other parties in bloody confrontations on the streets of many German cities.

By the time the German government released Hitler from prison in December, 1924, Röhm had built the SA into an organization thirty thousand strong. Röhm wanted to maintain the SA as an autonomous organization under his own direct command. When Hitler insisted that the SA be subordinated to the party leadership rather than to

Röhm, Röhm resigned from the party and the SA. During the next five years, Röhm tried several jobs with little success. In 1928, he accepted a position as an instructor for the Bolivian army.

In 1930, Röhm's successor as chief of staff of the SA, Franz Pfeffer von Salomon, resigned his post after a dispute with Hitler. Röhm returned to Germany the next year to resume his command of the SA on Hitler's personal invitation. During the next two politically turbulent years, Röhm built the SA into a private army almost a million strong (the German army, by comparison, had slightly more than one hundred thousand officers and enlisted men). The members of the organization came largely from the ranks of the unemployed, were mostly young (under age twenty-five), and espoused radical solutions to Germany's social and economic problems. Röhm himself began to envision the SA as becoming a people's militia, which would absorb the regular army once the Nazis came to power.

During the period from 1931 to 1933, Hitler came under increasing criticism from conservative circles in German society because of Röhm's open homosexuality, and his appointment of other homosexuals to high posts in the SA. Röhm and his friends gained reputations as being corrupt and engaged in criminal activities as well as being morally dissolute. Despite this criticism, Hitler refused to replace Röhm. He argued that only Röhm could control the radicalism of the SA members and turn it to the advantage of the Nazi struggle for political power. After the parliamentary elections of March, 1933, however, Hitler's attitude toward his old comrade began to change.

The March elections gave the Nazis and their coalition partners a slight majority in the German parliament. The parliament immediately passed the Enabling Act, which gave Hitler dictatorial powers to solve the problems created by the Great Depression in Germany. Rank-and-file members of the SA became uncontrollable after Hitler's success. Many of them began to launch physical attacks against Germans they considered inimical to the creation of an egalitarian society. Wealthy and prominent Jews became favorite targets of SA violence. Members of the SA membership and leadership talked openly of an imminent "second revolution" during which they would replace the old institutions of Germany with new, socialist institutions.

As his men and officers became more impatient with Hitler's failure to elevate them to top positions in Germany and institute the "second revolution," Röhm began to criticize the Nazi Party leaders openly. He also began to criticize Hitler in private, although he remained loyal to his leader. SA violence, Röhm's homosexuality, and his criticism of members of the NSDAP's top hierarchy won him the enmity of several Nazi officials by early 1934. Hermann Göring, minister president of Prussia and the most powerful Nazi after Hitler, joined forces with Wilhelm Frick, minister of the interior. These two men began conspiring to oust Röhm from the leadership of the SA. Göring and Frick gained an important ally when Heinrich Himmler, commander of the SS, joined the anti-Röhm coalition. Despite the mounting criticism of Röhm, Hitler refused to dismiss the man who had been instrumental in the Nazi electoral successes of 1930-1933.

In April, 1934, Hitler met with leaders of the German General Staff. He needed the support of the army if his plans for a rejuvenated Germany were to succeed. The representatives of the General Staff demanded that in return for their support Hitler must initiate a massive expansion of the German armed forces and greatly diminish the size and power of the SA. The army leadership feared Röhm's plan to absorb the regular army into the SA might actually be realized.

On June 17, 1933, Hitler's vice chancellor, Franz von Papen (a member of the conservative establishment of Germany and never a Nazi Party member), delivered a speech at Marburg critical of Röhm and the SA leadership. Hitler interpreted Papen's speech as the official position of the conservatives in Germany. President Paul von Hindenburg of Germany confirmed the conservative determination to be rid of Röhm in a meeting with Hitler on June 21. Hindenburg and Minister of War Werner von Blomberg warned that unless Hitler dismissed Röhm and curbed the SA, they were prepared to declare martial law. Even in the face of mounting pressure from his own party leadership and the conservative circles whose support he needed, Hitler continued to vacillate about replacing Röhm. In reaction to the growing criticism of Röhm and the SA, Hitler ordered the entire membership of the SA to go on leave effective July 1. He also scheduled a meeting with Röhm for 11:00 A.M. on June 30.

Göring finally pushed Hitler into taking action. Göring and Himmler met with Hitler shortly after 1:00 A.M. on June 30 and gave him details of a supposed plot by Röhm and his SA officers to arrest Hitler and take control of the government. Accepting the accusations without investigation, Hitler ordered Himmler's SS to arrest and execute the SA officers supposedly involved in the plot. Hitler personally led a detachment of SS troops in the predawn hours to arrest Ernst Röhm. Over the next three days, SS troops executed many SA officers, including Röhm, in several German cities.

Röhm and his SA leaders were not the only victims of the purge. As early as June 24, Göring and his co-conspirators began drawing up lists of Germans to be eliminated. Included on the list were their own personal enemies and people they felt were dangerous to Nazi aspirations. Hitler added other names to the list on July 1 and 2. Included among the non-SA victims of the purge were individuals who had opposed Hitler during the preceding years. Murdered along with the SA leadership were Kurt von Schleicher (Hitler's immediate predecessor as German chancellor) and his wife, and Gregor Strasser, one-time challenger to Hitler for leadership of the NSDAP.

Hitler announced to the German parliament on July 13 that the SS executed seventy-seven people during the purge, all of whom were involved in a plot to overthrow his government. The parliament immediately passed a law legalizing everything Hitler had done to protect Germany. President Hindenburg sent him a congratulatory message. The purge won for Hitler the support of the army, and eliminated the primary target of domestic criticism of the Nazi party. Historians of the period put the death toll much higher; estimates range from 150 to more than 1000. Although Hitler consolidated his position in Germany, the brutality and lawlessness of the purges revealed the true face of Nazism for the first time. —*Paul Madden*

ADDITIONAL READING:

Bornstein, Joseph. *The Politics of Murder*. Toronto, Canada: George J. McLeod, 1950. Surveys political murders in the twentieth century, including the Röhm purge.

Gallo, Max. *The Night of the Long Knives*. Translated by Lily Emmet. Toronto, Canada: Harper & Row, 1972. The most complete account of the Röhm purge in English.

Smelser, Ronald, and Rainer Zitelmann, eds. *The Nazi Elite*. Translated by Mary Fischer. New York: New York University Press, 1989. Biographical sketches of twenty-two leading Nazis, including Ernst Röhm. Concise account of Röhm's life and the events of the purge.

Spielvogel, Jackson J. *Hitler and Nazi Germany: A History*. Englewood Cliffs, N.J.: Prentice-Hall, 1988. Intended as an introductory college text, Spielvogel's book contains a brief account of the Röhm purge based on the most recent scholarship on the subject.

Tolstoy, Nikolai. *Night of the Long Knives*. New York: Ballantine, 1972. Concise account of the purge, accessible to most readers. Replete with a number of rare photographs.

SEE ALSO: 1919, Weimar Constitution; 1919-1933, Racist Theories Aid Nazi Rise to Political Power; 1933, Hitler Comes to Power in Germany; 1933, The Reichstag Fire; 1933, Enabling Act of 1933; 1938, The *Anschluss*.

1935-1936
ITALY CONQUERS ETHIOPIA

Italy conquers Ethiopia through overwhelming military force, revealing the ineffectiveness of the League of Nations and encouraging Mussolini's exaggerated estimate of his nation's military power.

DATE: October 2, 1935-May 9, 1936

LOCALE: Ethiopia and Geneva

CATEGORIES: Expansion and land acquisition; Government and politics; Wars, uprisings, and civil unrest

KEY FIGURES:

Pietro Badoglio (1871-1956), commander of Italian forces in Ethiopia, 1935-1936

Haile Selassie I (Tafari Makonnen; 1892-1975), emperor of Ethiopia, 1930-1936 and 1941-1974

Sir Samuel John Gurney Hoare (1880-1959), British foreign secretary, 1935

Pierre Laval (1883-1945), French foreign affairs minister, 1931-1932, and later premier of France, 1931-1932 and 1935-1936

Benito Amilcare Andrea Mussolini (1883-1945), Fascist premier of Italy, 1922-1943

SUMMARY OF EVENT. Since expansion seemed to be inherent in Fascism, it is not surprising that Benito Mussolini, Fascist dictator of Italy after 1922, eventually looked toward Ethiopia. Since the opening of the Suez Canal in 1869, this East African land had become increasingly significant, especially to any nation wishing to pursue an active Mediterranean policy. Ethiopia adjoined two already existing Italian colonies: Eritrea and Italian Somaliland. It was the last large piece of Africa that still remained outside the sphere of European domination. It held more potential value than the trackless deserts Italy already possessed in Africa. Finally, Mussolini's interest can also be regarded as a continuation of Italian policy, since active Italian interest in that area began in the 1880's.

Early in his regime, Mussolini was too busy with European affairs to pay much attention to developing an African policy. His one overture came in 1928, when he signed a Treaty of Friendship with Ethiopia. In 1934, however, Mussolini switched the focus of his foreign policy for two main reasons. First, while the 1928 Treaty of Friendship had granted economic concessions to Italy, Haile Selassie I, the emperor of Ethiopia since 1930, was afraid of the aggressive Italians and did not live up to his agreements. Second, European developments forced Mussolini's hand. Adolf Hitler became chancellor of Germany in 1933; the following year, Germany began to rearm. Since Italian and German aims clashed in Austria, Mussolini realized he must move quickly if he wished to acquire Ethiopia; he had to act before the German military was strong enough to take advantage of the Italian army's absence from Europe. The time was also opportune because British and French attention was focused on the German problem and might allow Italy's conquest of Ethiopia in order to retain Italy's friendship and hold a united front against Nazi Germany.

The actual crisis began in December, 1934, when a royal Ethiopian force attempted to drive an Italian expedition from an encampment at Walwal, an oasis clearly within Ethiopian territory. The Italians used the attack as proof of Ethiopian perfidy and began to strengthen their forces in their East African colonies. Frightened, Haile Selassie appealed to the League of Nations, which, in turn, caused alarm in Great Britain and France. If the matter were brought before the League of Nations and the Western powers ignored the obviously just and valid grievances of the Ethiopians, Italian friendship would be retained, but in all likelihood, such an act would destroy the League as a viable institution. Support for Ethiopia would preserve the League, but would incur Italian wrath and consequently threaten the recently created united front against Germany.

The Ethiopians, therefore, were persuaded to discuss the Walwal incident with Italy according to the terms established for arbitration between the two nations by their 1928 treaty. Mussolini, who now realized the need for time to build up his army in Africa, agreed to the suggestion and then used delaying tactics to prevent meaningful discussion. The British and French, meanwhile, alternately used mild threats and promises of support to persuade Mussolini to modify his demands.

After a summer of frustration, Ethiopia finally managed to bring the affair before the Council of the League of Nations on September 4. The session began with a ringing denunciation of Ethiopia by the Italian delegate, who attempted to prove that Ethiopia was an untrustworthy neighbor and unfit for membership in the League. The charge convinced no one and the League began to investigate the matter. The Italians accused the British of leading League opposition, and a speech given by Sir Samuel John Gurney Hoare, the British foreign secretary, reinforced their suspicions. Many Italians were panicked by Hoare's strong speech, realizing that the Ethiopian venture was doomed if Great Britain, in control of the Suez Canal and with its strong fleet, opposed Italy. In reality, Hoare's speech was stronger than he meant it to be. He had no intention of overtly opposing the Italians.

Despite the uncertainty of what Great Britain's role would be, Mussolini decided to move ahead. His army was positioned, and on October 3, 1935, it moved into Ethiopia. With this act, the League branded Italy the aggressor and voted to impose economic sanctions on that nation. Unfortunately, with the continued uncertainty of British policy and the unwillingness of France to anger Italy, no military sanctions were considered, and the economic sanctions were incomplete. Oil and other vital raw materials continued to enter Italian ports.

The Ethiopian army was utterly unprepared to resist a modern European force. In the spring of 1936, Ethiopian resistance collapsed, and on May 5, Pietro Badoglio, commander of Italian forces in Ethiopia, entered Addis Ababa, the capital. Four days later, the nation was proclaimed a part the new Italian empire.

The tragic result of the conquest of Ethiopia ultimately was an unrealistic and unjustifiably positive estimate of Italian military might by Mussolini. By 1943, however, optimistic foolhardiness turned to disastrous defeat when Italy surrendered to the Allies.

—*Harold A. Schofield, updated by John Quinn Imholte*

ADDITIONAL READING:

Baer, George W. *The Coming of the Italian-Ethiopian War.* Cambridge, Mass.: Harvard University Press, 1967. Examines Italy's preparation for invasion and Ethiopia's for defense. Presents a study of the political, diplomatic, and military decisions that were made and their implications. Also deals with relevance of the war within a European context.

_____. *Test Case: Italy, Ethiopia and the League of Nations.* Stanford, Calif.: Hoover Institution Press, 1976. Baer describes the policy of appeasement pursued by the League of Nations, combining limited sanctions and conciliation toward Italy. The outcome was a triple win for Mussolini in Africa, against the League, and at home.

Del Boca, Angelo. *The Ethiopian War, 1935-1941.* Chicago: University of Chicago Press, 1965. A straightforward account of the war and of the short-lived Italian rule in Ethiopia. Del Boca strongly supports Haile Selassie's efforts to maintain Ethiopian independence.

Macartney, M. H. H., and P. Cremona. *Italy's Foreign and Colonial Policy, 1914-1937.* London: Oxford University Press, 1938. The Ethiopian conquest allowed Italy to sever its traditional relationship with Great Britain and establish closer relations with Hitler's Germany. Even so, the authors argue that Mussolini's foreign policy was consistent with his predecessors.

Marcus, Harold G. *A History of Ethiopia.* Berkeley: University of California Press, 1994. A survey of Ethiopian history from pre-historic times to the present. Marcus' account is supportive of Haile Selassie and his efforts to modernize Ethiopia and to maintain its independence.

Mockler, Anthony. *Haile Selassie's War: The Italian-Ethiopian Campaign, 1935-1941.* New York: Random House, 1984. Includes detailed factual information about Ethiopia. A lengthy "tale of blood and war" which the author hopes is objective and accurate. Covers not only the Italian invasion but also the British invasion in 1941.

SEE ALSO: 1854-1869, The Suez Canal Is Built; 1861, Italy Is Proclaimed a Kingdom; 1919, The League of Nations Is Established; 1922, Mussolini's "March on Rome"; 1943, Allied Invasion of Italy.

1936
SPANISH CIVIL WAR BEGINS

The Spanish Civil War begins as a military uprising against the Spanish Republic and results in a three-year civil conflict that brings Franco and the Fascist Falange to power.

DATE: July 17, 1936

LOCALE: Military garrisons throughout Spain and Morocco

CATEGORIES: Government and politics; Wars, uprisings, and civil unrest

KEY FIGURES:

Manuel Azaña y Díaz (1880-1940), president of the Spanish Republic, 1936-1939

José Calvo Sotelo, Monarchist parliamentary leader

Santiago Casares Quiroga, prime minister of the Spanish Republic at the outbreak of the Spanish Civil War

General Francisco Franco (Francisco Paulino Hermengildo Teódulo Franco y Bahamonde; 1892-1975), leader of the uprising and later *caudillo* of Spain, 1939-1975

Adolf Hitler (1889-1945), chancellor and führer of Germany, 1933-1945

Francisco Largo Caballero (1869-1946), leader of the Socialist Party, prime minister of the Spanish Republic, 1936-1937

Benito Amilcare Andrea Mussolini (1883-1945), Fascist dictator of Italy

José Antonio Primo de Rivera (1903-1936), leader of the Falange, or Spanish Fascist Party

General José Sanjurjo, one of the plotters of the military uprising

Joseph Stalin (Iosif Vissarionovich Dzhugashvili; 1879-1953), chairman of the Soviet Council of Commissars and ruler of the Soviet Union, 1924-1953

SUMMARY OF EVENT. In the spring of 1936, Spain was on the verge of chaos. Five years of Republican government had heightened the tensions of the previous hundred years. A liberal, reform government had been defeated by conservatives in 1933, who began to reverse changes that had benefited workers and supporters of federalism. The elections of February brought the Popular Front government to power, but its varied composition of Liberals and Socialists, with tacit support from the Anarchists, meant that it could not act effectively to curb public and civil disorder caused by the Anarchists and the right-wing Falange. The Anarchists, impatient with Republican reforms and desiring a revolution immediately, had begun uprisings and takeovers of land after the election. There were many strikes, and economic chaos threatened. The Falange, the Fascist Party organized and led by José Antonio Primo de Rivera, son of the former dictator of Spain, responded

with violence to the Anarchists' actions to show the Republican government's inability to cope with the problem. There were assassinations and gun fights in the streets. In addition, military and right-wing groups were organizing to oppose the newly elected government. Finally, the election victory of the Popular Front polarized both left-wing and right-wing extremes, and the country seemed to be moving inexorably toward violence. Even so, the government of Prime Minister Santiago Casares Quiroga refused to believe reports of military plots, while President Manuel Azaña frantically sought a political solution that would not require arming workers against the military.

José Calvo Sotelo, a Monarchist deputy in the Cortes, José Antonio Primo de Rivera, and General José Sanjurjo formed a conspiracy to overthrow the government and

DIVISION OF SPAIN, 1936

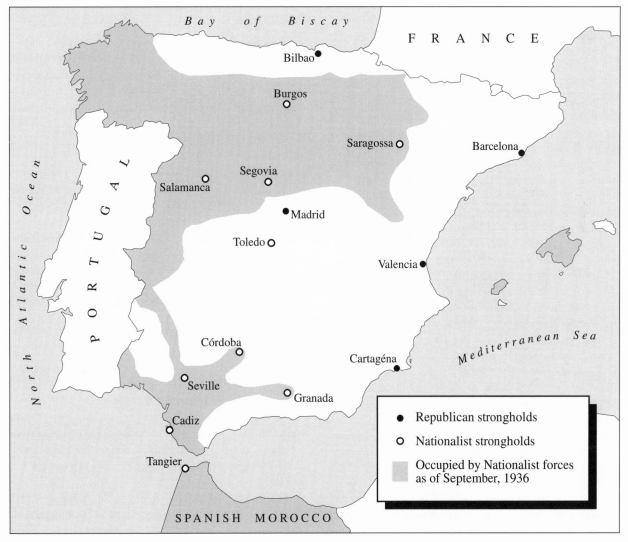

- ● Republican strongholds
- ○ Nationalist strongholds
- ▨ Occupied by Nationalist forces as of September, 1936

restore order to Spain. Although they did not commit themselves to a specific form of government, they were able to get the support of the monarchist leaders, who hoped for the restoration of Alfonso XIII, and the Falangists, who wanted to establish a Fascist state. Throughout the spring of 1936, they made plans for an uprising that summer.

In the Cortes, the government could not answer the complaints of its critics, where Calvo Sotelo regularly complained of the civil disorder. President Azaña did little except wait for the situation to improve, for he feared the leftist extremists. Francisco Largo Caballero, leader of the Socialist Party and one of the mainstays of the Republic, staged a march of ten thousand workers on the First of May in Madrid to demand a workers' government. There was talk about a leftist revolution to prevent a rightist coup and to implement long-desired radical reforms.

On July 13, 1936, Calvo Sotelo was arrested and murdered in revenge for a Falangist assassination of a Liberal policeman. So great was the shock at this deed that the military conspirators decided to take advantage of the public mood and advanced the date of their planned uprising. On July 17, military garrisons of the Canary Islands, Morocco, and throughout Spain pronounced against the Republican government and began taking over control of the local governments. Despite the uprisings, Azaña and the government refused to distribute arms to proletarian organizations and the trade unions. Nevertheless, workers seized arms and resisted the military. In Madrid and Barcelona armed workers were responsible for the failure of the insurrection, which had triumphed in about half of Spain. The conflict then settled into a prolonged civil war.

The conspirators, called the Nationalists, had the support of the rightist elements—the Church, the landed classes, and many moderates—but more important, they were able to get military aid and material from the Italian Fascist dictator, Benito Mussolini, and from Adolf Hitler, the German chancellor and führer. Mussolini wanted influence in Spanish affairs, and Hitler wanted to keep Mussolini embroiled in war so as to draw him away from the Western powers. By October, 1936, General Francisco Franco had emerged as the leader of the Nationalists, and in that month he proclaimed himself *caudillo*, or military leader, of Spain.

On the Republican, or Loyalist, side chaos prevailed. The military uprising allowed the Anarchists to implement a proletarian revolution in several areas of Spain. Workers seized factories and elected committees to oversee operations, while owners were murdered or fled. Azaña and Caballero, who had become prime minister, were powerless to stop Anarchist workers whose activities, while

fulfilling the hopes of many workers, antagonized many moderates who came to support the Nationalists. The Republicans' only source of outside aid was Soviet Russia, whose leader Joseph Stalin sent supplies and military advisers. In this manner, the Spanish Communist Party, a relatively small and powerless group before the uprising, became powerful, having control of the distribution of Russian aid. The democratic Western powers stood aside from the conflict, hoping that it would not spread into a general European war.

Throughout 1936 and 1937, the Nationalists slowly encircled the Republicans, whose army was largely undisciplined. By 1939, the superior military force of the Nationalists had prevailed, and in April, General Franco seized Madrid, the last Republican stronghold, and the war was over.

—José M. Sánchez, updated by James A. Baer

ADDITIONAL READING:

Bolloten, Burnett. *The Spanish Civil War: Revolution and Counterrevolution*. Chapel Hill: University of North Carolina Press, 1991. A massive study of the outbreak of the Civil War and the revolution that occurred, with much detail regarding the role of the Communist Party in undermining that revolution and the efforts of the Spanish Republic to operate outside of Stalin's control.

Hills, George. *The Battle for Madrid*. New York: St. Martin's Press, 1976. Provides a detailed history of both the political and the military battle for Madrid during the Spanish Civil War. Good maps and photographs, and thoughtful analysis of events.

Payne, Stanley G. *The Spanish Revolution*. New York: W. W. Norton, 1970. A thorough, although biased toward the liberal republic, account of events in Spain from the early twentieth century through the Civil War, focusing on the revolutionary changes occurring in the Republican Zone.

Preston, Paul. *The Spanish Civil War, 1936-1939*. Chicago: Dorsey Press, 1986. A short interpretive work, in which the author makes clear his belief that the military uprising under Franco ended a Republican government that was doing the best it could for Spain.

Thomas, Hugh. *The Spanish Civil War*. New York: Harper & Row, 1961. A classic study of the civil war from a political as well as military perspective. While the analysis is not especially original, the massive research is impressive.

SEE ALSO: 1914, Spain Declares Neutrality in World War I; 1931, Second Spanish Republic Is Proclaimed; 1937, Raids on Guernica; 1975, Death of Franco.

1936
EDWARD VIII ABDICATES THE BRITISH THRONE

Edward VIII abdicates the British throne in the wake of the public scandal surrounding his romantic involvement with an American divorcée.

DATE: December 10, 1936

LOCALE: Great Britain

CATEGORY: Government and politics

KEY FIGURES:

Stanley Baldwin (1867-1947), Conservative prime minister of Great Britain, 1935-1937

Sir Winston Leonard Spencer Churchill (1874-1965), British statesman and author

George Geoffrey Dawson (1874-1944), English journalist and editor of the London *Times*, 1923-1941

Edward VIII (1894-1972), king of Great Britain, January 20, 1936-December 11, 1936

William Cosmo Gordon Lang (1864-1945), archbishop of Canterbury, 1928-1942

Wallis Warfield Simpson (1896-1986), the twice-divorced American woman whom Edward VIII wished to marry

SUMMARY OF EVENT. Edward VIII was unconventional but popular both as Prince of Wales and as king; popular, perhaps, because he seemed modern and unconventional. His father, George V, had endowed the British monarchy with a comfortable image of middle-class propriety. His eldest son had a less clear sense of the duties and responsibilities of the monarch. Edward wanted to attune the monarchy to the times and to the people, and he was suspicious of what seemed to him the unimaginative and insensitive leadership of tired old men that characterized British politics in the 1930's. Because of his intimate relationships with married women and his pro-German sympathies, the Prince of Wales was regarded in many circles with distaste and even suspicion. A constitutional crisis drove him from the throne before he had reigned one year.

The king, who at age forty-one was still a bachelor, fell in love with Wallis Warfield Simpson, an American and a commoner. Not only was Mrs. Simpson married to Ernest Simpson, a London stockbroker, but she had a former husband from whom she had been divorced many years before. The intimate friendship of the king and Mrs. Simpson soon became a matter of gossip in London society and of comment in the American press. The British press, with its traditional respect for the royal family's privacy, treated Mrs. Simpson as if she did not exist. Stanley Baldwin, the Conservative prime minister, chose to bide his time and

wait for the king to make a mistake or come to his senses.

In October of 1936, Mrs. Simpson sought and was awarded a divorce from her husband. This decree freed her to marry again after six months. At this point, the king told Baldwin that he intended to marry Mrs. Simpson. Baldwin and the entire cabinet opposed the marriage. They believed that having the king marry a twice-divorced woman would violate the principles of the Church of England, of which the king was Supreme Governor, regarding divorce and remarriage. The archbishop of Canterbury, Cosmo Gordon Lang, strongly upheld the church's view. Divorce still barred a man from public life in Britain, and it would be an intolerable affront if the king were to marry Mrs. Simpson. The cabinet correctly assumed that public opinion, in Great Britain and in the even more conservative countries of the Commonwealth, would display a similar outrage at what the king wanted to do. The king, the monarchy, and the government would be drawn into the storm of political controversy. There would likely be permanent political damage to the monarchy and all that it represented for the unity of the British people and the solidarity of the Commonwealth.

The king was legally free to marry any woman he wished, but he was constitutionally obliged to accept the advice of the cabinet. If he did not, the cabinet would be justified in resigning, as it now threatened to do. The question of the king's marriage became a constitutional crisis. Baldwin endeavored to convince the king to renounce Mrs. Simpson; otherwise it was his duty to abdicate. For Edward VIII, who apparently had little sense of the duties of the royal family, the choice was simple. He decided to marry the woman he loved.

Meanwhile, the British public knew nothing, because the secret was so well guarded. Then, suddenly, on December 3, the press broke its self-imposed silence. The nation was shocked and disbelieving. There was some popular support for the king and numerous demonstrations were held. Yet Baldwin and the cabinet had been right; most of the British people disapproved and public sentiment in the Commonwealth against the king also ran high. Most of the British press was against the monarch. Winston Churchill's attempts to stir up support in the House of Commons failed dismally.

The king notified Baldwin on December 5 of his decision to abdicate. Certain conventions had to be honored, and Parliament was not informed until December 10. On December 11, a Declaration of Abdication Bill was introduced in Parliament, passed both houses, and received royal assent. Edward was now a private citizen. The new king, the former Duke of York, succeeded as George VI. That evening Edward broadcast a touching farewell mes-

Constitutional provisions obliged King Edward VIII to accept the advice of the British cabinet regarding his decision to marry Wallis Warfield Simpson. (Library of Congress)

sage to the people of Great Britain and the Commonwealth. He said that he could not continue his life without the help of "the woman I love." Immediately afterward he went into self-imposed exile in France, where he married Mrs. Simpson the following June.

Although Edward was created duke of Windsor, his wife was not accorded the title of royal highness. The British royal family, bitter at how Edward had behaved during the abdication crisis and convinced that Mrs. Simpson was responsible, refused to receive her or acknowledge her as duchess of Windsor. There was some softening of their attitude, however, before the duke of Windsor's death in 1972.

Edward VIII's abdication became one of the most controversial episodes in the history of the British monarchy. Modern scholarship now contends that Edward VIII mishandled his personal and public affairs throughout the period that led up to the abdication. His later expressions of pro-German sentiment in the 1930's and 1940's have also hurt his historical reputation. So far as the monarchy was concerned, the crisis fortunately proved no more than a minor tremor. Because of the excellent performance of

George VI as king, the abdication controversy passed quickly, and was almost as quickly forgotten.

—James M. Haas, updated by Lewis L. Gould

ADDITIONAL READING:

Bloch, Michael, ed. *Wallis and Edward: Letters, 1931-1937: The Intimate Correspondence of the Duke and Duchess of Windsor.* New York: Summit Books, 1986. A valuable primary source for understanding how King Edward VIII and the woman he loved viewed the constitutional crisis that had changed their lives.

Bradford, Sarah. *The Reluctant King: The Life & Reign of George VI, 1985-1952.* New York: St. Martin's Press, 1989. Looks at the abdication crisis from the point of view of Edward VIII's brother and successor, and is critical of the performance of the future duke of Windsor.

Donaldson, Frances. *Edward VIII: A Biography of the Duke of Windsor.* New York: J. B. Lippincott, 1974. The first thorough and critical biography of the duke of Windsor which began the reappraisal of his life and the implications of the abdication and its background.

Windsor, Duchess of. *The Heart Has Its Reasons: The Memoirs of the Duchess of Windsor.* New York: David McKay, 1956. The duchess of Windsor offers her account of the abdication crisis, which reveals how little she understood the British monarchy and the political system of the country.

Windsor, Duke of. *A King's Story: The Memoirs of H.R.H. the Duke of Windsor.* New York: G. P. Putnam's Sons, 1951. The ghostwritten memoirs of the king illustrate the strengths and weaknesses of his personality and approach to his royal responsibilities.

Ziegler, Philip. *King Edward VIII: A Biography.* New York: Alfred A. Knopf, 1991. The best modern biography of the king, with a thorough and balanced treatment of the abdication crisis and its aftermath.

1937
RAIDS ON GUERNICA

Raids on Guernica make civilians the target of military assaults in the Spanish Civil War, placing Franco in complicity with Hitler's agenda for world domination.

DATE: April 26, 1937
LOCALE: Guernica, Spain
CATEGORY: Wars, uprisings, and civil unrest
KEY FIGURES:
General Francisco Franco (1892-1975), dictator of Spain, 1939-1975
Adolf Hitler (1889-1945), chancellor and führer of Germany, 1933-1945

Benito Amilcare Andrea Mussolini (1883-1945), Fascist premier, 1922-1943

SUMMARY OF EVENT. Probably the most notorious event linked with war to precede Hitler's "Final Solution," the bombing of a completely civilian target in the Basque area of Spain—the town of Guernica—revealed to the world the tactics of Spain's General Francisco Franco and his ability to enlist the aid of Fascist dictators Benito Mussolini and Adolf Hitler.

By April, 1937, the civil war in Spain between Republicans and Nationalist troops fighting under Franco had been raging for some months. Many Republicans fled to France to live and carry out raids across the border. Ill-equipped, they depended on the hospitality of and news carried by peasants in the Basque region of Spain, including Guernica.

The Republican forces had also received much-needed assistance from the American volunteer fighters of the Abraham Lincoln Brigade, although it was to fail in its objectives and was ultimately disbanded without having contributed in a palpable way to the war. Nevertheless, writers and authors began to take notice of this war, most notably Ernest Hemingway in *For Whom the Bell Tolls* and several short stories. These works would be precursors to reactions to the bombing of Guernica, which created the largest artistic protest since the introduction of mustard gas in World War I.

Further studies have shed light on the genesis of the bombing raid on Guernica. One actor in this drama who has often been ignored is Italian dictator Benito Mussolini. Apparently, Mussolini had been in constant contact with Franco about the "Basque problem." With intelligence assistance from Franco's troops, Mussolini had singled out the town of Guernica as one that would send a message to the provinces. Having chosen Guernica as a likely target, Mussolini met on several occasions with Hitler. Hitler's role in the bombing went far beyond his action in dispatching the German bombers that attacked Guernica. All three dictators knew that Guernica constituted a civilian target. Only with Mussolini's discussion with Hitler was the bombing of Guernica finalized as part of Hitler's plans to "impress" the world with the extent of Germany's military might. Hitler's easy agreement to bomb civilians in another country served to prefigure future German actions during World War II.

The attack on Guernica surprised many contemporary observers because Germany had largely left Spain alone to its own struggles in its civil war. Although Franco and Hitler shared similar right-wing philosophies, they were not on particularly friendly terms with each other. Mussolini and Hitler had developed far more amicable rela-

tions, however, and that is why Mussolini's actions as a go-between were so important to carrying out the bombing raid on Guernica.

Early on the morning of April 26, 1937, while it was still dark, the people of Guernica were awakened to the unfamiliar sound of waves of high-flying German bombers. No fighter planes accompanied these bombers because no resistance was expected. The bombers soon released their payloads of solid and shrapnel bombs over the town. When they landed, the solid bombs obliterated entire buildings and started fires throughout the town. The shrapnel bombs split apart upon impact, spraying fragmented pieces across a wide area.

As more people were roused from sleep or interrupted in their chores by German planes and the sound of falling bombs, they rushed into the streets, where most were cut down by pieces of shrapnel bombs. Unsure of what was happening, many people who lived on nearby farms made the mistake of running to Guernica in a vain attempt to rescue relatives and friends. Some survivors later spoke of climbing into their root cellars until they could hear nothing overhead; a few managed to escape into the countryside and found shelter in areas less devastated by the bombing. Reports about how long the bombing lasted differ, but some scholars have estimated that the attack itself may have lasted little more than an hour. A tremendous payload of bombs were dropped in that time, destroying people, houses, churches, and a hospital.

Other Basque villages tried to assist the survivors of Guernica, sharing the few medical supplies that they had, and additional assistance came from France. The destruction was so complete that at the conclusion of World War II, some eight years later, the town of Guernica had not been rebuilt.

Despite this attempt to halt their efforts, the Republicans continued to conduct even more raids from across the French border against Nationalist targets. Although most Basque residents stopped taking up arms against Franco, they provided secret assistance to the rebels. Although Franco had proved that he could call upon Germany's powerful military resources with the intercession of the Italian government, Guernica was not truly a triumph for the leadership of Spain, Italy, or Germany.

The bombing of civilians spoke volumes about Franco's character and encouraged a growing distrust of Hitler and his motives—a conviction that was reinforced during the years leading up to the outbreak of World War II. Artists from throughout the world responded to the horror of the bombing. Pablo Picasso created his powerful and enduring antiwar painting entitled *Guernica*, and Paul Éluard was inspired to write his famous poem "La

Liberté," which was later dropped in bundles across war-torn France by the RAF in 1940. The 1984 book *Cries from a Wounded Madrid: Poetry of the Spanish Civil War* estimates that some twenty thousand poems were written by five thousand poets in response to the Spanish Civil War, and many of these poems were written about Guernica.   —*John Jacob*

ADDITIONAL READING:

Friends of Spain. *The Spanish War: Foreign Wings over the Basque Country.* London: Author, 1937. Sympathizers of the Spanish Civil War react specifically to the bombing of Guernica.

MacDonald, Nancy. *Homage to the Spanish Exiles: Voices from the Spanish Civil War.* New York: Human Sciences Press, 1987. This volume discusses the value of the Basque rebels and those exiled to France.

North American Committee to Aid Spanish Democracy. *The Crime of Guernica.* New York: The Committee, 1937. This volume represents one of the first published reactions of North Americans (particularly U.S. citizens) to the bombing.

Oppler, Ellen C. *Picasso's Guernica: Illustrations, Introductory Essay, Documents, Poetry, Criticism, Analysis.* New York: W. W. Norton, 1988. This volume represents a scholarly discussion of the political motives behind Guernica and the artistic impulse it unleashed.

Perez, Janet, and Wendell Aycock, eds. *The Spanish Civil War in Literature.* Lubbock: Texas Tech University Press, 1990. An important ancillary text discussing literary reactions to the Spanish Civil War, including the bombing of Guernica.

Thomas, Gordon. *The Day Guernica Died.* London: Hodder & Stoughton, 1975. A blow-by-blow account of the atrocities at Guernica.

Thomas, Gordon, and Max Morgan Witts. *Guernica, the Crucible of World War II.* New York: Stein & Day, 1975. Thomas and Witts discuss how Guernica prefigured further atrocities and military campaigns during World War II and the relationship between Franco, Mussolini, and Hitler.

SEE ALSO: 1933, Hitler Comes to Power in Germany; 1936, Spanish Civil War Begins; 1975, Death of Franco.

1938

THE ANSCHLUSS

The Anschluss *marks the absorption of Austria by Nazi Germany, underscoring Hitler's aggressive designs and the tacit acceptance of his aggression by other European powers.*

DATE: February 12-April 10, 1938
LOCALE: Vienna, Austria; Berchtesgaden and Berlin, Germany
CATEGORIES: Expansion and land acquisition; Government and politics
KEY FIGURES:
Englebert Dollfuss (1892-1934), chancellor of Austria, 1932-1934
Hermann Göring (1893-1946), German field marshal, 1938-1945
Adolf Hitler (1889-1945), chancellor and führer of Germany, 1933-1945
Benito Amilcare Andrea Mussolini (1883-1945), Fascist dictator of Italy, 1922-1943
Kurt von Schuschnigg (1897-1977), chancellor of Austria, 1934-1938
Arthur Seyss-Inquart (1892-1946), Austrian security minister in 1938

SUMMARY OF EVENT. With the disintegration of Austria-Hungary in 1918, most of the German-speaking areas of the Habsburg domains were organized into a Federal Republic of Austria. From the start, this truncated state was handicapped by a lack of a national consciousness strong enough to infuse an organic unity. The Habsburg state had been based on the principle of dynastic nationalism, and when the Habsburgs were deposed, no other approach to nationalism seemed adequate to sustain an independent Austria. Most Austrians began to favor *Anschluss,* or union with Germany, even though such union was prohibited by both the Treaty of Versailles and the Treaty of St. Germain.

Agitation for the *Anschluss* continued in Austria and Germany throughout the 1920's and led to negotiations for a customs union, which was, however, abandoned in 1931 as a result of the opposition of France, Italy, and the Little Entente states of Czechoslovakia, Yugoslavia, and Romania.

When Adolf Hitler became chancellor of Germany early in 1933, most Austrians turned away from the *Anschluss* because union with Germany then meant union under Nazism. On the other hand, the Austrian Nazi Party hoped that with support from the new government in Germany its aim of seizing control in Austria would be aided.

In the *Putsch* of July 25, 1934, Austrian Nazis seized several members of the Austrian government, assassinated Chancellor Englebert Dollfuss, and captured the Vienna radio station. Yet the *Putsch* aborted when the rest of the Austrian government and the army effectively opposed the insurgents, and when Benito Mussolini, the Italian Fascist dictator, moved four divisions to the Austrian frontier. Hitler quickly decided against providing assistance to the rebels and pursued a strictly evolutionary approach to the *Anschluss.*

Financial problems and political division in France after 1934 impeded French intervention in central Europe, and the outbreak of the Italo-Ethiopian War brought an Italo-German rapprochement. These factors forced the Austrian government, under Chancellor Kurt von Schuschnigg, to seek accommodation with Hitler. In the Austro-German Agreement of July, 1936, Schuschnigg won from Hitler a promise to respect Austrian independence, but he had to admit two crypto-Nazis into his government and pledge that Austria's foreign policy would always correspond to the fact that Austria considered itself to be a German state.

By 1938, Hitler believed that he was strong enough diplomatically and militarily to apply new pressures on Schuschnigg; in February, he called him to a meeting at Berchtesgaden. Hitler demanded vast new concessions, including the appointment of Arthur Seyss-Inquart and two other Austrian Nazis to key ministerial posts. Schuschnigg consented, but when he returned to Vienna he sought to limit the German gains by announcing a plebiscite on the subject of Austrian independence. Field Marshal Hermann Göring ordered Seyss-Inquart to demand Schuschnigg's resignation, which was tendered on March 11. The plebiscite, scheduled to take place in only two more days, was postponed. About midnight on March 11, President Wilhelm Miklas of Austria acknowledged that the German-backed Austrian Nazis had seized control of the cities and government, and consented to Seyss-Inquart's appointment as chancellor.

Although the Austrian Nazis had now achieved their ultimate goal, Berlin could not resist pushing for the formal absorption of Austria into the Third Reich. Göring instructed Seyss-Inquart to request the German army to occupy Austria in order "to restore order." On the morning of March 12, Hitler ordered the occupation half an hour before Seyss-Inquart's telegram even arrived in Berlin. German troops entered Vienna and other cities to cheering crowds. A subsequent Nazi-controlled plebiscite on April 10 recorded a vote of 99.73 percent in favor of the *Anschluss.* Although the plebiscite was rigged, a substantial number of Austrians supported the *Anschluss.*

—*William Harrigan, updated by Steve D. Boilard*

ADDITIONAL READING:

Brook-Shepherd, Gordon. *Anschluss: The Rape of Austria.* Westport, Conn.: Greenwood Press, 1976. A highly readable, engaging account of events leading up to the *Anschluss.*

Gardiner, Muriel. *Code Name "Mary": Memoirs of an American Woman in the Austrian Underground.* New Haven, Conn.: Yale University Press, 1983. An autobiographical account with first-hand observations of Austria in the 1930's. Chapter 3 describes the *Anschluss.*

Parkinson, F., ed. *Conquering the Past: Austrian Nazism Yesterday and Today.* Detroit: Wayne State University Press, 1989. A collection of nineteen essays on various aspects of Austrian Nazism. Most relate to the *Anschluss* at least indirectly; several focus on the *Anschluss* in detail.

Pauley, Bruce F. *Hitler and the Forgotten Nazis: A History of Austrian National Socialism.* Chapel Hill: University of North Carolina Press, 1981. Political events in pre-World War II Austria, with a focus on the Austrian Nazi Party. The *Anschluss* is detailed in chapter 12.

Suval, Stanley. *The Anschluss Question in the Weimar Era: A Study of Nationalism in Germany and Austria, 1918-1932.* Baltimore: The Johns Hopkins University Press, 1974. Although this book does not detail the actual absorption of Austria by Germany, it does examine how the issue of *Anschluss* occupied the Germans and Austrians after the demise of the Austro-Hungarian empire in 1918.

Wright, William E., ed. *Austria, 1938-1988: Anschluss and Fifty Years.* Riverside, Calif.: Ariadne Press, 1995. A collection of essays focusing on various aspects of the *Anschluss.* Includes bibliography.

SEE ALSO: 1919, Treaty of Versailles; 1933, Hitler Comes to Power in Germany; 1933, Enabling Act of 1933; 1938, Munich Conference; 1939, Nazi-Soviet Pact.

1938
MUNICH CONFERENCE

The Munich Conference formalizes the capitulation of Prime Minister Neville Chamberlain and his French ally to Hitler's demands for the Sudetenland but fails to slake Hitler's thirst for power.

DATE: September 29-30, 1938

LOCALE: Munich, Germany

CATEGORIES: Diplomacy and international relations; Expansion and land acquisition

KEY FIGURES:

Edvard Beneš (1884-1948), president of Czechoslovakia, 1935-1938

Georges Bonnet (1889-1973), French foreign affairs minister, 1938-1939

Arthur Neville Chamberlain (1869-1940), British prime minister, 1937-1940

Édouard Daladier (1884-1970), premier of France, 1938-1940

Emil Hácha (1872-1945), president of Czechoslovakia, 1938-1939

Adolf Hitler (1889-1945), chancellor and führer of Germany, 1933-1945

Benito Amilcare Andrea Mussolini (1883-1945), Fascist premier of Italy, 1922-1943

Walter Runciman (1870-1949), head of the British mission to Czechoslovakia

SUMMARY OF EVENT. As soon as Germany had annexed Austria in March of 1938, Adolf Hitler, chancellor and führer of Germany, accelerated his political operations against the democracy of Czechoslovakia. Although Czechoslovakia was stronger and more populous than Austria, it was also more divided internally as a result of the decision of the Paris Peace Conference in 1919 to draw its frontiers along economic and strategic rather than ethnic lines. Included in the new Czech state was the Sudetenland, a mountainous border area in western Czechoslovakia that was historically Austrian, linguistically German, and inhabited by more than three million

Neville Chamberlain's decision to concede the transfer of the Sudetenland to Germany ultimately did little to appease Hitler's military goals in Europe. (Archive Photos)

people who were opposed to Czech domination. The region was strongly pro-Nazi. The *Anschluss* greatly intensified Pan-German sentiment in the Sudetenland and correspondingly increased the power of the Sudeten German Party. Outwardly, the party worked for Sudeten autonomy within the Czech state, but during the summer months of 1938, Sudeten negotiators continually rejected proposals for settlements put forth by the Czech government in Prague. Secretly, the Sudeten German Party took orders from Hitler, who unknown to the rest of the world, sought to dismember and ultimately destroy Czechoslovakia. As early as April, 1938, Hitler discussed with his cabinet plans to provide additional *Lebensraum* (living space) for the German people. This undisclosed plan, known to insiders as Operation Green, was the blueprint for the invasion of Czechoslovakia.

Since 1924, Czechoslovakia had been allied with France, an alliance which provided also for Soviet support, contingent upon prior French support. By 1938, France had decided that it could not maintain its East European alliances without the support of Great Britain. In the last analysis, support of Czechoslovakia against German aims depended upon Great Britain. Neville Chamberlain, the British prime minister, was convinced that there were injustices in the treaties of 1919 which had to be removed if peace were to be preserved. He mistakenly believed that Hitler shared his abhorrence of war, and that Hitler's objectives in Czechoslovakia were limited; he therefore favored a policy of appeasement. Instead of standing firmly behind Edvard Beneš, president of Czechoslovakia, and his government in their efforts to resist German pressure, Chamberlain continually urged Beneš to make maximum concessions. In August he sent Walter Runciman, the English politician and millionaire shipbuilder, as an "impartial mediator" to investigate Czech-Sudeten differences at first hand. Runciman had no prior experience in such matters, and his pro-German sympathies were soon detected. The fact that Hitler was instructing the Sudeten leaders to keep on increasing their demands to impossible limits remained hidden.

In September, when it became evident that Hitler was preparing an armed attack on Czechoslovakia and that the Czechs intended to resist, Chamberlain made three visits to Germany in the space of fourteen days. On September 15, at Hitler's mountain retreat near Berchtesgaden, he conceded the right of self-determination to the Sudetens and promised to win acceptance of this point from the French and Czech governments. After this initial meeting, Chamberlain believed he had averted a general war, telling his sister "I have no doubt whatever . . . that my visit alone prevented an invasion." He met Hitler again on September 22 at Bad Godesburg, a small town on the Rhine River, only to find that this concession was no longer enough. Hitler now demanded immediate Czech evacuation of the Sudetenland and German military occupation before the holding of any plebiscite. Even Chamberlain balked at such bullying; the outbreak of a general war seemed imminent, and on September 24 the Czechs mobilized in preparation for war, refusing to give in to Hitler. Chamberlain made a final effort to prevent hostilities, however, by proposing a four-power conference which he asked Benito Mussolini, the Fascist dictator of Italy, to urge upon Hitler. On September 29, Chamberlain, Hitler, Mussolini, and the French premier, Édouard Daladier, met at Munich, at what became known as the Munich Conference. Together, without representatives of Czechoslovakia or its Soviet ally, they reached agreement on the Sudeten question. Relieved at the outcome of the Munich Conference, Chamberlain declared the settlement a "peace with honor." Abandoned by its allies, Czechoslovakia had no alternative but to relinquish the region to Hitler.

The Munich agreement provided for the speedy but peaceful transfer of the Sudetenland to Germany and for an international guarantee of the reduced Czech state once the territorial demands of the Poles and Hungarians had been fulfilled. Chamberlain did prevent, at least temporarily, Hitler's military advance on the Czechs. He also secured Hitler's signature to an Anglo-German consultative pact, which he naïvely hoped would prevent the Nazi leader from acting unilaterally in the future. Yet he paid an enormous price. Soon the connotations of "sell-out" and "peace at any price" would become attached to the terms "appeasement" and "Munich."

Czechoslovakia made its settlement with Poland, but difficulties with Hungary brought German and Italian intervention to determine the new Czech-Hungarian frontier. The British and French did not seem disturbed by the fact that they were not consulted, and they did not press strongly for the promised guarantee of the remainder of the Czech state.

Hitler worked through the Slovak and Ruthenian nationalist groups to complete the destruction of the Czech state. Finally, in March of 1939, after brutally browbeating the new Czech president, Emil Hácha, in Berlin, Hitler forced the surrender of Bohemia and Moravia, established Slovakia as a German satellite, and assigned Ruthenia to Hungary. Thus, after months of negotiations and concessions to appease Hitler, Nazi armies finally occupied the remainder of Czechoslovakia, which had been Hitler's plan from the outset. These flagrant violations of the Munich agreement belatedly awakened Chamberlain to the fact that Hitler was seeking not merely the self-

determination of German-speaking people, but the domination of all Europe.

As historian David Clay Large pointed out in *Between Two Fires: Europe's Path in the 1930's* (1990), the Munich agreement has remained a source of debate. Although it is "one of the most widely condemned acts of diplomacy in modern history," defenders of the pact insist that even the slightest chance for peace warranted the agreement with Germany. Moreover, Chamberlain's efforts allowed the western powers a vital year to improve their armaments, strengthen military weaknesses, plan their strategies, and prepare their countries psychologically for another war. Opponents of the agreement contend the Germans actually improved their military position relative to the West in that same vital year, and that the agreement predisposed the Soviet Union toward an accommodation with Germany. Whatever the case, clearly Hitler never intended peace, but war.

—*William Harrigan, updated by Liesel Ashley Miller*

ADDITIONAL READING:

Adams, R. J. Q. *British Appeasement and the Origins of World War II*. Lexington, Mass.: D. C. Heath, 1994. Highlights Britain's role in appeasement and the origins of World War II. Sections on "Variety of Opinion" and "The Search for Lessons" are especially noteworthy.

Baumont, Maurice. *The Origins of the Second World War*. Translated by Simone de Couvreur Ferguson. London: Yale University Press, 1978. A concise yet thorough review of events leading up to and including the Munich Conference. Baumont looks also at the Soviet response to the pact.

Eubank, Keith. *The Origins of World War II*. 2d ed. Arlington Heights, Ill.: Harlan Davidson, 1990. A chapter on "The Road to War, 1938" focuses on Czechoslovakia, negotiations between Hitler and Chamberlain, and the agreement between Germany, Britain, France, and Italy.

Jensen, Kenneth M., and David Hendrickson, eds. *The Meaning of Munich Fifty Years Later*. Washington, D.C.: The United States Institute of Peace, 1990. A collection of essays useful for general study as well as detailed reviews. Important for advanced reading and a variety of analyses.

Large, David Clay. *Between Two Fires: Europe's Path in the 1930's*. New York: W. W. Norton, 1990. Chapter 8, "Peace for Our Time," provides an insightful, detailed narrative of the process of appeasement, meetings between Hitler and Chamberlain, and the Munich Conference.

Taylor, Telford. *Munich: The Price of Peace*. Garden City, N.Y.: Doubleday, 1979. A lengthy and exhaustive study of every facet of the Munich Agreement, replete with details of the events leading to, during, and following the fateful conference.

Watt, Donald Cameron. *How War Came: The Immediate Origins of the Second World War, 1938-1939.* New York: Pantheon Books, 1989. Examines the final two years of peace and discusses the roles of appeasement and the Munich Conference in the onset of general war.

SEE ALSO: 1919, Treaty of Versailles; 1929-1940, The Maginot Line Is Built; 1933, Hitler Comes to Power in Germany; 1939, Nazi-Soviet Pact; 1939, Germany Invades Poland.

1939-1945
GYPSIES ARE EXTERMINATED IN NAZI DEATH CAMPS

Gypsies are exterminated in Nazi death camps after being transported from areas of Europe occupied by the German armed forces to the camps in an effort to "purify" the Aryan race.

DATE: 1939-1945

LOCALE: German-occupied Europe, especially modern Poland

CATEGORIES: Government and politics; Race and ethnicity

KEY FIGURES:

Eugen Fischer, professor of anthropology and leading advocate of eugenic racial policies

Reinhard Heydrich (1904-1942), commander of the *Sicherheitdienst* (SD), or secret service, and commander of the concentration camp system until his death in 1943

Heinrich Himmler (1900-1945), commander of the *Schutzstaffel* (SS) and overseer of the efforts to exterminate all persons deemed "asocial" or "alien"

Adolf Hitler (1889-1945), chancellor and führer of Germany, 1933-1945

Robert Ritter, anthropologist and leading German expert on the "Gypsy Problem"

Ernst Zindel, senior councilor and bureaucratic coordinator of government policies concerning the Gypsies

SUMMARY OF EVENT. On May 16, 1940, German police rounded up almost three thousand Gypsies living in western and northwestern Germany and put them on trains bound for German-occupied Poland. The deportations initiated a more radical phase of the attempt by the German government to solve what they called the "Gypsy Problem." The solution to the "problem" resulted in tens of thousands of Gypsy deaths over the next five years. Al-

though the total number of Gypsies who died during what Gypsies call the *Porajmos* (the Gypsy holocaust) remains unknown, some estimates range as high as half a million. Four distinct but related factors in European history contributed to this massive destruction of human lives: The lifestyle of the Gypsies and their reputation in European folklore, the eugenics movement, the euthanasia movement, and the Nazi seizure of power in Germany.

According to ethnologists, ancestors of the modern Gypsies began emigrating from northwestern India around A.D. 1000. They developed a nomadic lifestyle, never staying in one area for long. They retained their own distinct language. They earned money by fortune-telling, entertaining audiences with their unique music and dancing, and by theft and chicanery. Arriving in Europe sometime during the fourteenth century, they were often viewed as criminals and pests. Many European monarchs decreed laws limiting their mobility and contact with their own settled populations. By the twentieth century, many Europeans viewed the Gypsies as nomadic criminals who were a danger to the public welfare. Even the European scientific community began to denounce the Gypsies in the late nineteenth century with the advent of the science of eugenics.

Sir Francis Galton, a first cousin to Charles Darwin, founded the science of eugenics in the 1870's. In several influential books, Galton argued that governments should encourage the genetically well-endowed members of their countries to reproduce in order to improve the human race. He also maintained that persons with congenital diseases and deformities should not be allowed to pass on their flawed genes to future generations. A number of scientists and laypeople around the world took up Galton's cause and began to push their lawmakers to implement eugenics laws. Eugenics societies emerged in most of the European nations and in the United States which began to demand that their governments adopt laws for the mandatory sterilization of people they identified as genetically deficient.

Some, if not all, of these eugenics societies adopted distinctly racist agendas, identifying blacks, Jews, Gypsies, and other "people of color" as being genetically inferior to the "white" races. In Germany, Eugen Fischer and Ernst Ruedin emerged as the most outspoken advocates of eugenics. Both were professors and both warned of an impending "biological crisis" which could irreparably damage the German race. Adolf Hitler, führer of the Nazi Party, read one of Fischer's books while imprisoned after his failed attempt to overthrow the German government in 1923. Hitler was so impressed by Fischer's arguments that he incorporated many of them into his own semiautobiographical book *Mein Kampf* (1925-1927).

When Hitler became chancellor of Germany in 1933, the eugenicists realized they had a powerful ally in the highest position of the German government. Although many of the leading eugenicists never joined the Nazi Party, they worked closely with Nazis in the German government to develop a sound racial policy for the German people. The Nazis created a number of government agencies such as the Reich Office for Research on Race Hygiene and Population Biology to identify and solve the racial problems of Germany. They also established university chairs of Racial Hygiene in many of the most prestigious institutions of higher learning to study the racial problem.

By 1935, the racial experts proposed that allegedly undesirable elements (homosexuals, carriers of hereditary diseases, the terminally insane, and others) be excluded from German society through incarceration. The eugenicists also proposed that "alien" minorities in Germany (particularly the Jews and the Gypsies) be excluded as well, and forbidden to intermarry with Germans. The German parliament responded by passing the infamous Nuremberg laws that deprived Jews and Gypsies of German citizenship and provided stiff penalties for sexual relations between Germans and non-Germans. The government also established bureaus to deal with the several racially undesirable elements in Germany. To deal with the Gypsies, the government established the *Zentralstelle zur Bekaempfung des Ziguenerunwesen* (the ZBZ, Central Office to Combat the Gypsy Pest).

One career bureaucrat of the ZBZ, Senior Council Ernst Zindel, recommended in 1935 that the Gypsies be identified and placed on reservations under close supervision. Accordingly, Reinhard Heydrich, head of the SD and the ZBZ, commissioned a young scientist named Robert Ritter to study and identify all Gypsies living in Germany. Ritter performed a number of tests on more than twenty thousand German Gypsies over the next ten years, including blood types, cranial and skeletal measurements, and eye, hair, and skin pigmentation. As Ritter's work progressed, Heydrich adopted ever more restrictive legislation concerning the Gypsies.

In 1935, Heydrich ordered that all municipal governments establish Gypsy camps. By law, nomadic Gypsies could stay only in these camps. After 1937, Gypsies could leave these camps only during the day. Also in 1937, Heydrich adopted a regulation which permitted "preventive arrest" of anyone his police deemed likely to commit a crime. The police in German cities often used this law to arrest Gypsies and send them to concentration camps. In 1938, Heydrich ordered that all Gypsies must register with the local police whenever they entered a

new district. In January of 1940, Ritter issued a report to Heydrich recommending that all pure and "mixed blood" Gypsies be sent to work camps and completely isolated from German society. The May, 1940, deportations represented Heydrich's first step in implementing Ritter's recommendation. The mass deportation of Gypsies from all over occupied Europe did not begin until November of 1941, when members of the German government had apparently decided on a more radical solution to the Gypsy problem.

The so-called Final Solution to the racial problems as defined by the Nazis owed much to a movement in the German medical profession related to but distinct from the eugenics movement. Beginning shortly after World War I, some German doctors advocated the medical termination of "lives unworthy to be lived." These doctors, including many eugenicists, argued that the terminally ill, the hopelessly insane, and persons incapable of thought, be granted mercy deaths—euthanasia. A number of doctors began to practice euthanasia illegally and without authorization. After the outbreak of World War II, Hitler personally authorized the implementation of euthanasia under the strict surveillance of competent doctors. Between 1939 and 1945, German doctors killed many thousands of their own citizens without the consent of the patients or their relatives. Some estimates put the number of "mercy deaths" as high as seventy thousand. A special group of German medical personnel called T-4 usually carried out the actual killing of patients.

The T-4 group worked out several methods for killing large numbers of people at one time, including the use of carbon monoxide gas. Sometime in 1940 or 1941 (the exact date is uncertain because no written order exists), Hitler apparently made the decision to apply the methods of mass euthanasia to solve the Jewish and Gypsy problems. Heydrich and Himmler entrusted the deportation of Jews and Gypsies living in the German occupied territories to Adolf Eichmann. In 1942, Eichmann began the mass transport of Jews and Gypsies to concentration camps and ghettos in Poland, where the T-4 group had set up mass extermination centers in January, 1942. In camps such as Auschwitz, Chelmno, Sobibor, Belzec, Majdanek, and Treblinka, SS personnel began the systematic murder of millions of Jews, Gypsies, Slavs, and other racially undesirable or asocial persons. According to some Polish sources, the SS also began to murder Gypsies wherever they found them in the occupied territories without bothering to ship them to the camps in Poland. According to witnesses, at least twenty thousand Gypsies perished in Auschwitz alone, many dying from malnutrition or typhus.

By the time the death camps halted operations in late

1944, tens of thousands of Gypsies had died from various causes directly related to their incarceration. One historian puts the Gypsy death toll at five hundred thousand. The Gypsies died because some scientists deemed them unworthy to live based on their supposed racial characteristics. *—Paul Madden*

ADDITIONAL READING:

Crowe, David M. *A History of the Gypsies of Eastern Europe and Russia*. New York: St. Martin's Press, 1994. Surveys the Gypsy communities of all the Eastern European and Russian areas during the Holocaust.

Editors of Time-Life Books. *The Apparatus of Death*. Alexandria, Va.: Time-Life Books, 1991. A brief account of the Gypsy holocaust, along with a number of rare photographs of the deportation of Gypsies from occupied Europe and the death camps.

Friedlander, Henry. *The Origins of Nazi Genocide: From Euthanasia to the Final Solution*. Chapel Hill: University of North Carolina Press, 1995. Incorporates accounts of Nazi policies toward the Gypsies throughout the book.

Mueller-Hill, Benno. *Murderous Science: Elimination by Scientific Selection of Jews, Gypsies, and Others, Germany 1933-1945*. New York: Oxford University Press, 1988. Shows the complicity of the non-Nazi German scientific community in the "final solution."

SEE ALSO: 1919-1933, Racist Theories Aid Nazi Rise to Political Power; 1919, Treaty of Versailles; 1933, Hitler Comes to Power in Germany; 1939, Nazi-Soviet Pact; 1939, Germany Invades Poland.

1939-1945
NAZI EXTERMINATION OF THE JEWS

Nazi extermination of the Jews is begun in an effort to achieve Hitler's goal of eradicating the Jewish race, resulting in the deaths of six million Jews from Germany and from areas of Europe occupied by the German armed forces.

DATE: 1939-1945

LOCALE: Europe

CATEGORIES: Government and politics; Race and ethnicity; Religion

KEY FIGURES:

Adolf Eichmann (1906-1962), head of the Austrian Central Immigration Office and chief of the German deportation system during World War II

Reinhard Heydrich (1904-1942), Himmler's second in command and commander of the *Sicherdienst* (SD) or security service

Heinrich Himmler (1900-1945), commander of the *Schutzstaffel* (SS), Hitler's elite guard, and chief of the German Gestapo

Adolf Hitler (1889-1945), chancellor and führer of Germany, 1933-1945

Josef Mengele (1922-1979), chief physician of Auschwitz who was known as the "Angel of Death"

SUMMARY OF EVENT. The Nazi extermination of European Jews during World War II was the outgrowth of Adolf Hitler's violent persecution of Germany's Jews through tactics that began with his ascent to power in 1933. Deprived of their political rights, occupations, and property, the Jews in Germany suffered physical violence, mental anguish, exile, and death at the hands of the Nazis. On January 30, 1939, Hitler predicted that the coming world war would bring "the annihilation of the Jewish race throughout Europe." World War II began seven months later on September 1, when Hitler's armed forces invaded Poland. Simultaneously, the Nazis initiated policies and programs they hoped would bring about the extermination of the Jews.

At the time of the Nazi invasion of Poland, Reinhard Heydrich was placed in charge of German actions affecting the Jews in Poland, who comprised about two million of the Polish population in 1939. They had, during medieval and early modern times, been driven to Poland because of persecution and expulsion from Western Europe. Moreover, Polish borders as redrawn after World War I included many Jews. Heydrich first began to deal with them in his September 21, 1939, directive. This order was issued to the heads of the *Einsatzgruppen*, or mobile killing squads. First, Jewish property was to be "Aryanized" or expropriated. Second, Jews were to be forced into ghettos in the large cities. Over each ghetto, Jews were required to establish a Council of Elders, or *Judenrat*, which was to administer the ghetto in conformity with Nazi orders. Heydrich's directive was regarded as the preliminary step to the Final Solution, which eventually accomplished the near-destruction of European Jewry.

If ghettoization was one of Hitler's policies toward the Jews in 1939, another was murder, even at that early date. The *Einsatzgruppen* that accompanied the German armies in Poland and elsewhere were given orders to massacre Polish civilians, especially the Jews. Eventually, members of the *Einsatzgruppen* operated throughout Eastern Europe and, with the assistance of some two hundred thousand collaborators, tortured and murdered about one and a half million Jews by the end of World War II. Two difficulties arose, however, with the *Einsatzgruppen*. First, as diligent as they were in murdering Jews, they could not possibly accomplish the destruction of all of Europe's

Jews. In only two days at Babi Yar in Russia, thirty-five thousand Jews had been shot, but there was a Russian Jewish population of four to five million people. Second, there was some concern about the ability of members of this Nazi elite to retain their sanity as they went about their duties. "The unlimited brutalization and moral depravity," wrote German General Johannes Blaskowitz, "will spread like an epidemic through the most valuable German human material" and "brutal men will soon reign supreme."

MAP OF THE DEATH CAMPS IN NAZI-OCCUPIED TERRITORIES

Source: Yitzhak Arad, ed., *The Pictorial History of the Holocaust* (New York: Macmillan, 1990).

In order to help solve these two problems, a more efficient means of murder was devised that was expected to have a less brutalizing effect on the Nazi murderers. Ghettoization had concentrated the Jews into a rather small area, including the central Polish cities of Radom, Lvov, Lodz, Lublin, Warsaw, and Cracow, which were then sealed. Jews from throughout Europe, including Germany, were deported to the Polish ghettos. Concentrated in the worst parts of cities and required to subsist on a few calories per day, many Jews fell ill or starved. Since starvation was too slow, the Nazis prepared other means of extermination. In the meantime, however, the Jews were exploited as a natural resource.

The largest form of exploitation involved using Jews as forced laborers for large-scale projects of various sorts. Soon, the Jews were literally being worked to death constructing concentration and labor camps. Once the labor camps were in operation, major German industrial corporations, such as Krupp and I. G. Farben, continued the brutal process of killing Jewish laborers with overwork. At the I. G. Farben synthetic rubber works at Auschwitz, it was estimated that the life expectancy of workers was three to four months. The ghettos were also centers of labor where Jews were required to produce a variety of manufactured goods for the Nazis. Although the Jews were, by their labor, contributing significantly to the German war effort, Hitler's implacable objective remained the destruction of their race, regardless of the impact on the German economy or the war.

By the winter of 1942, rumors of the Nazi determination to destroy all Jews began to circulate. Actually, that decision had already been made and was being carried out. Since the mass shooting of the *Einsatzgruppen* had certain drawbacks, as had the program of starvation, German technical skill solved the problem by devising an orderly technology of murder. Facilities for mass extermination by gas were constructed at six camps: Auschwitz, Treblinka, Sobibor, Majdanek, Belzec, and Chelmno. At the same time, the Nazi bureaucracy was now skillfully organized to undertake mass murder and process the corpses as efficiently as possible. Top Nazi officials coordinated the entire procedure at the Wannsee Conference held near Berlin on January 20, 1942. As a result of the decisions made at that conference, Jews from all over Europe began to be transported by rail to the extermination camps.

To illustrate the efficiency of the camps, in two months of the summer of 1942, three hundred thousand Jews from the ghetto of Warsaw were gassed at Treblinka, and the *Judenrat* of the Warsaw ghetto was forced to furnish six thousand Jews per day for transportation to Treblinka. Throughout German-occupied Europe, Jews were sent to

In the wake of decisions made at the Wannsee Conference in January of 1942, Jews from all over Nazi-dominated Europe began to be transported by rail to extermination camps in Poland and Germany. (Leo Baeck Institute/Archive Photos)

Polish and German extermination camps until one and three-quarter million had been exterminated at Auschwitz, one and a half million had died at Maidanek, and hundreds of thousands had been killed elsewhere by 1944.

About fifty thousand people were engaged in carrying out the extermination process. Two types of gas were used: carbon monoxide and hydrogen cyanide (Zyklon B), which was considered to be much quicker than carbon monoxide. The procedure was much the same in the various death camps. Jews would arrive jammed into railroad boxcars. Forced out of the cars, they were sent to barber shops where their heads were shaved and the hair carefully retained for various manufacturing purposes. Then they would be required to surrender all their clothing, valuables, spectacles, and everything else they possessed—even artificial limbs. Those Jews not spared for forced labor were then marched to large open areas in front of gas chambers, where they were forced to wait, often for hours, until smaller groups were "processed." These smaller groups were marched into the gas chambers, which were filled so full that there was no room even to fall down. The doors were sealed, and while the remainder waited, the

gas was turned on for about half an hour. When all inside were dead, doors at the opposite end from the entrances were opened and the corpses removed. Gold fillings and valuable dental bridges were salvaged, and the bodies were cremated while the next group entered the chamber. By 1944, this process had become so efficient that tens of thousands of Jews were being slaughtered daily. Auschwitz held the record: In July of 1944, thirty-four thousand people were killed there in a single day.

In addition to efforts at extermination, the Nazis also undertook medical experiments on the Jews. Regarding Jews as potential research animals, the Germans were ready to test literally any drug or attempt any type of experiment on them, as Dr. Josef Mengele demonstrated with his experiments on twins, eye color, and genetics. All segments of the German scientific community took part in the experiments, for reasons that were frequently obscene and sadistic as well as scientific. Almost all of the experiments involved torture, and resulted in the deformity or death of the victims. In short, such "research" was little more than one aspect of the extermination process, since Mengele himself performed the daily selection at Auschwitz. By the end of World War II, the combined activities of the *Einsatzgruppen*, the medical experimenters, and the extermination camps had brought death to approximately six million Jews.

Hitler's program of extermination was not limited to the Jews. The SS also attempted to exterminate all intellectuals, priests, deformed persons, Gypsies, homosexuals, and other "undesirables," bringing the total number exterminated to between ten and twelve million.

Hitler failed to decimate the Jewish race or even to eliminate Jews from Europe. In many countries, brave individuals stepped forward to give Jews food and lodging, often claiming them for their own relatives. Raoul Wallenberg saved many Jews from certain death in his role as a foreign diplomat.

Hitler underestimated the human nature of many of those Germans in his employ, not to mention people in Poland, Lithuania, and France who did not believe in mass extermination. Hitler's plan was highly mechanistic, relying on an unfeeling, cold bureaucracy. Much discussion has been fostered regarding why six million or more people allowed themselves to be systematically slaughtered, but the more that the record is analyzed and the more that survivors of the Holocaust come forward, the world has learned that such slaughter was hardly automatic.

Many died because they were physically ill with typhus, cholera, and especially dysentery. Many had lost their faith in God and therefore in the world. Nevertheless, Jewish resistance, as some critics have described it, was not unknown. The Warsaw ghetto uprising drew thousands of German soldiers away from the front, and minor events within the camps distracted the soldiers each day. The Jews were not directly involved in their own destruction. They fought back when and as they could, including a number of American Jews whom scholars have discovered were caught behind German lines.

To "choose life" under the conditions of the concentration camp had to have been one of the hardest choices that one could make. Nobel Prize-winner Elie Wiesel did so, but it was an internal pact—one that he has written about in most of his books, most notably *Night* and *The Accident*. Those who chose to continue living had to confront tremendous guilt; among the men and women who survived the camps, it was not uncommon for them to commit suicide decades later, as Italian author Primo Levi did. Some Jews felt the biblical need to "bear witness" so such mass destruction of human life could never happen again and so that those responsible could be brought to justice.

—*Saul Lerner, updated by John Jacob*

ADDITIONAL READING:

Des Pres, Terrence. *The Survivor: An Anatomy of Life in the Death Camps.* New York: Oxford University Press, 1976. Des Pres is best at describing how camp survivors had to live one day at a time and how they had no past, history, or future. Any other way was suicidal.

Druks, Herbert. *Jewish Resistance During the Holocaust.* New York: Irvington, 1983. A recitation of events that prove Jewish resistance.

Friedlander, Henry. *The Origins of Nazi Genocide: From Euthanasia to the Final Solution.* Chapel Hill: University of North Carolina Press, 1995. The book makes clear the Nazi intentions and stresses each step along the way to the "final solution."

Hilberg, Raul. *Perpetrators, Victims, Bystanders: The Jewish Catastrophe, 1933-1945.* New York: HarperCollins, 1992. Hilberg explains early German interest in eradication of the Jews and discusses the various roles taken by individuals whose actions fit his chosen categories.

Langer, Lawrence L. *Admitting the Holocaust: Collected Essays.* New York: Oxford University Press, 1996. In a misguided revisionism, some critics at the end of the twentieth century argued that the Holocaust did not happen. Langer's book attacks those theories and forces the German people to admit their complicity in the acts.

Levi, Primo. *"Survival in Auschwitz" and "The Reawakening": Two Memoirs.* New York: Summit Books, 1986. These are two of the most visceral commentaries on camp life by a survivor who later killed himself.

Marcus, Michael R., ed. *The Nazi Holocaust: Historical Articles on the Destruction of European Jews.* 9 vols. Westport, Conn.: Meckler, 1989. This nine-volume work is the definitive study of the Nazi execution of European Jews, collected over decades of writing.

SEE ALSO: 1919-1933, Racist Theories Aid Nazi Rise to Political Power; 1919, Treaty of Versailles; 1933, Hitler Comes to Power in Germany; 1939, Nazi-Soviet Pact; 1939, Germany Invades Poland; 1940, Collapse of France.

1939
NAZI-SOVIET PACT

The Nazi-Soviet pact frees Hitler from the immediate possibility of a two-front war, allowing him to attack Poland and trigger the beginning of World War II hostilities.

DATE: August 23-24, 1939
LOCALE: Moscow, the Soviet Union
CATEGORY: Diplomacy and international relations

KEY FIGURES:

Arthur Neville Chamberlain (1869-1940), British prime minister, 1937-1940

Édouard Daladier (1884-1970), premier of France, 1938-1940

Adolf Hitler (1889-1945), chancellor and führer of Germany, 1933-1945

Maksim Maksimovich Litvinov (Meir Walach; 1876-1951), Soviet commissar for foreign affairs, 1930-1939

Vyacheslav Mikhailovich Molotov (Skryabin; 1890-1986), Soviet commissar for foreign affairs, 1939-1949

Joachim von Ribbentrop (1893-1946), German foreign minister, 1938-1945

Joseph Stalin (Iosif Vissarionovich Dzhugashvili; 1879-1953), dictator of the Soviet Union, 1929-1953

SUMMARY OF EVENT. The signing of the Treaty of Nonaggression between Nazi Germany and Communist Russia in August, 1939, surprised most European observers, who believed that a rapprochement between the diametrically opposed dictatorships was impossible. Relations between the Soviet Union and Germany had declined substantially since 1933, when the National Socialist regime under Adolf Hitler had assumed power in Germany. Before 1933, Hitler had frequently denounced Bolshevism; in his political autobiography, *Mein Kampf* (1925-1927), he had stressed the need for Germany to acquire living space (*Lebensraum*) in Eastern Europe at the expense of the Soviet Union. Hitler's genuine interest in Eastern Europe was demonstrated in January, 1934, when he signed a nonaggression treaty with Poland, a traditional enemy of Russia.

Viewing this pact as a potential threat to Russia's security, Soviet leader Joseph Stalin was suspicious, and he concluded that sooner or later Hitler would start a war somewhere in Europe. Beginning with a successful bid for membership in the League of Nations in September, 1934, Stalin and his foreign minister Maksim Litvinov, became the leading champions of "collective security," the concert of European governments against Hitler, and the "Popular Front," the cooperative effort of European moderate leftists and Communist Parties against Fascism. During the Abyssinian crisis, the Soviet Union made a staunch defense of the covenant only to find this an irritant rather than an aid in warming up to the West. When the Popular Front coalition in republican Spain came under assault from German and French support to France's forces, the Soviets provided critical military supplies while the Western forces avoided participating in the Spanish Civil War.

The activities of the world revolutionary Communist International, or *Comintern*, supported and sustained by Moscow, were now sharply curtailed. In May, 1935, the Soviet government took major steps to encircle Germany by concluding pacts of mutual assistance with France and Czechoslovakia; the agreement with the latter, however, was to bind the Soviet Union only if France made the first move in rendering aid to the Czechs in the event of a German attack. Hitler used these treaties as an excuse to occupy the Rhineland in 1936, and in the fall of that year, he countered them by signing an agreement with Italy and the Anti-Comintern Pact with Japan, which was directed against the Soviet Union.

Meanwhile, the Stalinist purge trials and the execution of numerous army officers did nothing to strengthen Western confidence in the Soviet Union as a viable military ally against Hitler. This attitude toward the Soviet military posture contributed by 1937-1938 to the genesis of the appeasement policy in the French and British governments, led respectively at that time by Édouard Daladier and Neville Chamberlain. The fruit of this policy was Hitler's bloodless conquest of Austria and Czechoslovakia during 1938 and 1939. The Soviets were prepared to come to Czechoslovakia's defense in 1938, but Western appeasement doomed such a move. As a result, Stalin was driven to accept a policy of "Fortress Russia" in 1939. In response, the collective security coalition collapsed, and Stalin now set about to reexamine all available options in the conduct of his foreign affairs.

Stalin's subsequent exercise of one of these options, namely the conclusion of a nonaggression pact with Germany, was the result of the last prewar crisis involving Nazi demands on Poland. Shortly after the Nazi occupation of Prague in mid-March, 1939, the German foreign minister, Joachim von Ribbentrop, submitted a series of demands to Poland that were categorically refused. Although he was furious, Hitler could not undertake an immediate solution of the Polish question for a number of reasons. First, in the light of Anglo-French promises of late March and early April, 1939, to aid the Poles if attacked by Germany, Hitler appeared to suspect that, in contrast to 1938, the Western powers might fight if he embarked on another venture, this time against Poland. Second, Hitler was as uncertain as the Western powers were about the role that the Soviet Union might play in the event of a German attack on Poland. If the Soviet Union joined the Western powers in an alliance, Hitler would be caught in a two-front war. If he could engage the Soviets in a pact of nonaggression, however, Hitler might be able to force Great Britain and France to back down as in the past. If this pattern were not repeated, he would at least be in a better position to dispose of a military thrust from the

West. Hitler also delayed aggression because he had to draft extensive military plans that would provide the operational details for both the invasion of Poland and the defense of the Reich from an attack by the Western powers.

On April 3, Hitler ordered his military commanders to

country if Hitler invaded Poland. Since the Soviet leader was still uncommitted regarding the Polish question, however, the diplomacy surrounding it assumed the character of a contest between the Western powers and the German Reich for the prize of Russia's favor. From mid-April to mid-August, 1939, the British and French government

Soviet foreign minister V. M. Molotov signs the nonaggression pact, while Joachim von Ribbentrop and Joseph Stalin observe from behind. (National Archives)

draw up such plans; those for the Polish campaign, known by its code name "Operation White," were to be ready by September 1, 1939, the scheduled date of their implementation. Parallel with these military preparations, Hitler was beginning to giver serious consideration to rapprochement with the Soviet Union by the end of April.

Stalin, too, was anxious to prevent the isolation of his

attempted in a most clumsy and careless fashion to negotiate a common defense against Hitler's designs on Poland. Actually, neither Chamberlain nor Daladier relished the idea of negotiating with the hated Bolsheviks. Consequently, they carried on talks with the Soviet Union at a slow pace through second-rank officials. When they finally dispatched a joint Anglo-French military mission to

Moscow in the critical days of August, it traveled by boat rather than by airplane.

Apart from these problems, a Soviet-Western pact foundered almost immediately on traditional Russo-Polish animosity. Russian leaders insisted that a Soviet-Polish military agreement would have to be arranged before the Soviet Union would conclude any pact with Great Britain and France. Poland, however, adamantly rejected any such agreement with the Soviet Union. The prospects for accord between the West and the Soviet Union were not promising.

Often overlooked are the British and German talks, which reveal that Neville Chamberlain preferred further appeasement of Hitler to a grand alliance with the Soviet Union. Chamberlain's proposals to the Third Reich were quite generous. They included an enormous loan to Germany and settlement of colonial problems as well as the Polish crisis on terms favorable to Hitler. Still more, the British offered Germany an Anglo-German condominium over Europe—all of this in exchange for a mere promise from Hitler that he would not invade Poland. Yet Hitler, for the moment, preferred the destruction of Poland in a short, local war to another Munich agreement.

The Anglo-French-Russian negotiations, carried on with considerable publicity, were closely watched by the German Foreign Office. By the end of April, Berlin had decided to explore the possibilities of a Russo-German rapprochement to which the Soviet ambassador had alluded earlier in the month. In his speech of April 28 before the Reichstag, Hitler formally renounced Germany's nonaggression pact with Poland. Surprisingly, his address was devoid of his usual invective against Bolshevism and the Soviet Union.

Initially, Stalin pursued a cautious policy designed to avoid Soviet isolation in an increasingly dangerous international environment. By early 1939, however, increasing Soviet economic and military strength gave him sufficient confidence to take the diplomatic offensive. Stalin believed that Germany was far weaker than the Western powers and, thus, more likely to grant his demands. In response to Germany's apparent interest in better relations, the Soviet Union announced on May 3 the dismissal of Litvinov, a pro-Western Jew with a British wife, as Soviet commissar for foreign affairs. He was replaced by Vyacheslav Molotov, a determined negotiator who was Stalin's oldest and closest associate. Although the two dictatorships negotiated in an atmosphere of deep distrust, the Russo-German talks made steady progress in contrast to the negotiations between the Soviet Union and the other Western powers. Finally, at the end of July, Molotov indicated, through his negotiators, a willingness on the part of

the Soviet Union to enter into a commercial treaty with Germany, to be followed later by a political agreement.

By this time, however, Germany was desperate for a political pact, as the planned date for the invasion of Poland was only a month away. The Soviet-German trade talks were more than a mere preliminary to the pact. Because economically strapped Germany needed Soviet-supplied raw materials, Soviet negotiators extracted German agreement to deliver Germany's most up-to-date weapons and vast quantities of strategic goods. Now the arch appeaser, Stalin gained additional time to build up the Red Army by buying off Hitler with fresh trade deals. The signing of a commercial agreement on August 19 only served to intensify the impatience of Hitler and Ribbentrop for an immediate political arrangement with the Soviet Union. Stalin apparently wanted to be sure that Germany would become embroiled in war with the West over Poland. He was fearful that Great Britain might back down on her support to Poland, thus containing Hitler's aggression in Eastern Europe to the Soviet frontier. Therefore, in trying to attain an essential goal of Soviet foreign policy, namely the escape from isolation, Stalin had to take the risk that he might actually deepen his country's isolation. When he decided that Great Britain would fight, when his mistrust of the West outweighed his suspicion of the Nazis, and when he became convinced that there were real advantages to be gained from a bargain with Hitler, then and only then did Stalin approve the signing of the nonaggression pact so desperately sought by his German counterparts.

Once Stalin decided to go ahead, Ribbentrop was received in Moscow on August 23. The treaty as signed by Ribbentrop and Molotov early on August 24 contained a mutual promise of neutrality and nonaggression. A "Secret Additional Protocol" attached to the treaty divided Eastern Europe into German and Soviet spheres of interest. Poland was to be partitioned between the two powers; Germany was allowed influence over Lithuania, while the Soviet Union was given a free hand in Estonia, Latvia, and Finland, and it declared its "interest" in Romania's Bessarabia.

The Nazi-Soviet Pact of August, 1939, had various results. The immediate effect was to precipitate World War II. Assured of Russian neutrality, Hitler launched his invasion of Poland as originally planned on September 1; the British and French declared war on Germany two days later when Hitler failed to respond to their demand for immediate withdrawal from Poland. Meanwhile, Stalin gained at least temporary immunity from German attack, and he proceeded to build up Soviet armed forces. The sphere of interest granted to Stalin in Eastern Europe appeared to provide him with a strong forward defensive zone against possible German attack. Russia attacked Finland on November 30, 1939, after the Finns refused to grant territorial and naval base concessions. Led by Carl Gustaf Mannerheim, the Finns resisted astonishingly, annihilating five Soviet divisions. Yet a new Soviet offensive in February, 1940, succeeded. Stalin then dictated peace terms more severe than the original Soviet demands. He later absorbed the Baltic states, including Lithuania, which Hitler conceded to him in a readjustment of their pact. Simultaneously in the Far East, the Nazi-Soviet Pact enabled Stalin to relieve the pressure which Japan had been exerting on the Soviet Union's Asian frontier since the outbreak of an undeclared Russo-Japanese war in 1938. Nominally an ally of Nazi Germany, Japan terminated the conflict in April, 1939, and signed a mutual agreement on September 15, 1939.

Intermediately, however, the alliance nearly proved disastrous for Stalin. Hitler got the better of the pact because he was able to conquer most of Europe and turn on the Soviet Union at a time of his choosing. Stalin assumed that he was dealing with Hitler from a position of unassailable strength. Thus, he was able to secure the favorable revision of the secret protocol of the Soviet-Nazi pact on several occasions and, in late 1940, was preparing to do so again. Stalin thought that Hitler could not do without his political and economic support in Germany's continuing war with Great Britain and that this dependence would increase with time. Refusing to believe mounting evidence that Hitler was preparing to attack, Stalin was genuinely shocked by Operation Barbarossa. For Hitler, Stalin's misplaced trust in him almost spelled a German victory over Russia in 1941-1942. Viewed in wider perspective, however, the Nazi-Soviet Pact added considerably to Hitler's overconfident attitude toward Russia. The ultimate failure of Hitler's military campaign against Russia and his loss of the war brought about an extension of Soviet influence into central Europe that existed into the 1990's.

The ramifications of the Nazi-Soviet Pact are tantalizing. How would the course of World War II have changed if Hitler had maintained the pact against Britain before the United States launched its all-out intervention? Britain might have surrendered. Even after Barbarossa began, the possibility of a Nazi-Soviet truce on the eastern front would have stiffened considerably German resistance against Allied forces. A negotiated armistice to World War II could have occurred in Europe because British intelligence learned that Heinrich Himmler made overtures to an interested Stalin about a Russian front truce.

—*Edward P. Keleher, updated by Douglas W. Richmond*

ADDITIONAL READING:

Bullock, Alan. *Hitler: A Study in Tyranny.* 2d rev. ed. New York: Harper & Row, 1962. A detailed account, from the German vantage point, of how the development of the Polish crisis led to the Nazi-Soviet accord in August, 1939.

Carr, E. H. *German-Soviet Relations Between the Two Wars, 1919-1939.* Baltimore: The Johns Hopkins University Press, 1951. Contains a discussion of the 1939 Nazi-Soviet Pact.

Churchill, Winston S. *The Second World War.* Vol. I: *The Gathering Storm.* Boston: Houghton Mifflin, 1948. Chapters 20 and 21 trace the course of the Polish crisis and the rapprochement between Germany and Russia.

Haslam, Jonathan. *The Soviet Union and the Struggle for Collective Security in Europe, 1933-39.* New York: St. Martin's Press, 1984. Haslam defends the sincerity of Soviet attempts to ensure collective security.

Read, Anthony, and David Fisher. *The Deadly Embrace: Hitler, Stalin, and the Nazi-Soviet Pact, 1939-1941.* New York: W. W. Norton, 1988. A skillful correlation of concurrent sets of secret negotiations that outline the British and German talks.

Rossi, Angelo. *The Russo-German Alliance, August 1939-June 1941.* Translated by John and Micheline Cullen. Boston: Beacon Press, 1951. This study deals with the uneasy relations between Nazi Germany and Soviet Russia after the negotiation of their nonaggression pact in August, 1939.

Ulam, Adam B. *Expansion and Coexistence: The History of Soviet Foreign Policy, 1917-67.* New York: Frederick A. Praeger, 1968. Ulam's study offers a controversial evaluation of the diplomatic background of the Nazi-Soviet Pact from the Russian vantage point.

SEE ALSO: 1938, The *Anschluss*; 1938, Munich Conference; 1939, Germany Invades Poland; 1939-1940, Russo-Finnish War.

1939
GERMANY INVADES POLAND

Germany invades Poland, initiating the first hostile fighting in World War II and launching the policies that result in the Holocaust.

DATE: September 1, 1939

LOCALE: The German-Polish frontiers

CATEGORIES: Expansion and land acquisition; Government and politics; Wars, uprisings, and civil unrest

KEY FIGURES:

Józef Beck (1894-1944), Polish foreign minister, 1932-1939

Georges-Étienne Bonnet (1889-1973), French foreign affairs minister, 1938-1939

Arthur Neville Chamberlain (1869-1940), British prime minister, 1937-1940

Galeazzo Ciano, conte di Cortellazzo (1903-1944), Italian foreign minister, 1936-1943, and son-in-law of Benito Mussolini

Édouard Daladier (1884-1970), premier of France, 1938-1940

Adolf Hitler (1889-1945), chancellor and führer of Germany, 1933-1945

Maksim Maksimovich Litvinov (Meir Walach; 1876-1951), Soviet commissar for foreign affairs, 1930-1939

Vyacheslav Mikhailovich Molotov (Skryabin; 1890-1986), Soviet commissar for foreign affairs, 1939-1949

Benito Amilcare Andrea Mussolini (1883-1945), Fascist premier of Italy, 1922-1943

Joachim von Ribbentrop (1893-1946), German foreign minister, 1938-1945

Joseph Stalin (Iosif Vissarionovich Dzhugashvili; 1879-1953), dictator of the Soviet Union, 1929-1953

Edward Frederick Lindley Wood, earl of Halifax (1881-1959), British foreign secretary, 1938-1940

SUMMARY OF EVENT. On March 15, 1939, after the Nazis had staged a bogus crisis, German troops marched into Czechoslovakia and occupied Prague, thus completing the annexation of the Czech state which Adolf Hitler had planned in 1938. Hitler and his henchmen then turned their attention to Poland. On March 21, Joachim von Ribbentrop, foreign minister of Germany, summoned Józef Beck, the foreign minister of Poland, to Berlin and gave him a list of German demands. Danzig, a free city administered under the supervision of the League of Nations, in which Poland had certain economic rights, was to revert to German control; Germany would receive an extraterritorial road and railway across the Polish Corridor, a strip of Polish territory separating East Prussia from the remainder of the German Reich; and Poland would agree to associate itself with Germany in an anti-Russian policy. Colonel Beck rejected these demands. In the meantime, alarmed by the seizure of Prague, Great Britain and France guaranteed Poland's independence and territorial integrity. On March 31, Prime Minister Neville Chamberlain announced that if Germany invaded Poland, Great Britain and France would give Poland all the support in their power. London and Paris could not, however, give effective direct assistance to Warsaw because Poland was separated from them geographically by Germany. Poland's best help could come only from the Soviet Union, and in the weeks following the Anglo-French guarantee, Moscow became the center of European diplomacy.

Soviet dictator Josef Stalin was worried about Hitler's rising power, especially because the Red Army was undergoing reorganization in the wake of the executions of so many of its high officers in 1937. Stalin decided to explore the feelings of both the Allies and the Nazis. On April 16, Maksim Maksimovich Litvinov, the Soviet commissar for foreign affairs, who was believed to be friendly toward the West, approached the Allies with an offer to conclude a Mutual Assistance Pact. The next day, the Soviet ambassador in Berlin inquired of the Reich foreign ministry whether Russo-German relations might be improved. The Germans made some noncommittal answers at once. The Allies made no answer at all until, after a delay of three weeks, Chamberlain and his Conservative cabinet, with their inveterate suspicion of Russian motives, virtually rejected Litvinov's advances. Meanwhile, Litvinov had been replaced by the iron-willed opportunist, Vyacheslav Mikhailovich Molotov.

Hitler now scored a success in another quarter. On May 22, he made the "Pact of Steel" with Italy, in which the two powers pledged themselves to fight as allies in the event one of them went to war. Benito Mussolini, the Fascist dictator of Italy, was anxious for gain and, over the protest of his son-in-law and foreign minister, Galeazzo Ciano, committed his country to war on Hitler's terms. This alliance strengthened Hitler's position, and on May 23, he told his generals that war with Poland was now inevitable. Hoping to prevent the Soviet Union from helping Poland, the Nazis opened serious talks with the Russians on May 30.

During the next two months, the situation did not develop rapidly. The Russian and German negotiators hesitated to commit their countries to a clearly defined pact. By now, the West had also sent delegates to Moscow, but they also acted slowly, unable to carry the strongly anti-communist and anti-Russian Colonel Beck with them. Because most of their country had been occupied by Russia for more than a century prior to 1918, the Poles were understandably reluctant to readmit the Red Army in 1939. On the other side, Stalin distrusted the West. With the events in Munich still in mind, he doubted their determination to resist Hitler and suspected them of wishing to embroil him in war with Germany. In August, it became apparent that Stalin had chosen Hitler, because Hitler could give more and ask for less than Chamberlain or French premier Édouard Daladier. In the early hours of

German armored tank units had little difficulty breaching Poland's border defenses, supported by heavy air attacks launched by the German Luftwaffe. (Archive Photos)

August 24, the Russo-German nonaggression pact was signed; a secret protocol spelled out the share of Poland that each power would take.

Poland's situation was now critical. On August 23, believing that his pact with Stalin would convince Chamberlain and Daladier that helping Poland would be futile, Hitler ordered his attack to begin at dawn on August 26. The British, however, were determined to honor their guarantee, and they signed a formal treaty with Poland on August 25. The same day, facing the prospect of war with less than ten fully equipped divisions, Mussolini informed Hitler that he would remain neutral in the event of a conflict. At this point, Hitler paused; in the evening, he ordered the invasion, then only twelve hours away, to be postponed.

Hitler now attempted to separate the Poles from their allies. Daladier and Chamberlain stood firm, however, and when it became apparent that his efforts to shake them had failed, Hitler unleashed his army and air force on Poland. On September 1, at 4:45 A.M., six armored divisions (*panzers*) rolled forward, while the pilots of the German Luftwaffe struck at the Polish airfields. A new kind of

lightning warfare of tanks and mobile artillery, closely supported by aircraft, was launched with devastating success. The Luftwaffe smashed the Polish railway system, with the result that Polish attempts to mobilize effectively failed. Air strikes against Polish troops attempting to defend Warsaw were so successful that Polish forces collapsed completely in that area. Heavy air attacks also occurred against military targets inside Warsaw once the Germans realized that their armor could not operate effectively in the narrow streets. Considerable collateral damage and casualties among the civilian populace also resulted from air attacks. Having hoped that, with good luck and bad weather, Poland could resist for six months, the West watched the Polish army become torn to pieces within two weeks.

The Poles were in an impossible strategic situation; the entire country was a flat plain. The only defensible feature was the Bug River. It lay so far to the east, however, that a defense along it would have forced the Poles to surrender all their economic assets and political centers. Nevertheless, by placing most of their troops in the Polish corridor and between Warsaw and the industrial city of Ladz, the rest of the Polish army was stretched dangerously thin. German armored forces quickly broke through Poland's border defenses and penetrated deep into the interior. On September 17, the Russians hastily invaded Poland from the east to secure their portion of the spoils; by October 2, 1939, all organized Polish resistance had ceased.

On September 3, the British and French government fulfilled their commitment to Poland by declaring war. Nevertheless, they were unable to do anything to avert Poland's fate. World War II had now begun.

The process by which the *Wehrmacht* analyzed its performance after the Polish invasion explains why the German army did so well on World War II battlefields. By early October, the high command obtained reports from units down to the regimental level. The army then established a rigorous training program throughout to correct mistakes. Thereafter the army trained for sixteen hours a day and six to seven days a week. When the *Wehrmacht* streamed west in May, 1940, few armies in the twentieth century had been as well trained or disciplined.

From the beginning, the invaders embarked on Hitler's racial and ideological crusade. Atrocities fell immediately upon Jews as well as Poles. Hitler ordered that Poland's ruling and intellectual elites be liquidated. Stalin's secret police also wiped out large numbers of army officers and the Polish intelligentsia. An even deadlier fate devastated the Jews. There were 3.25 million Jews in Poland in 1939; less than 10 percent survived to 1945. The largest number were exterminated in various death camps, of which Treblinka, Sobibor, Belsen, and Auschwitz have become the symbols of the Holocaust. The Jewish partisan movement began in the summer of 1942 as a result of the German action to liquidate the ghettos by transporting the Jews to the death camps. The nightmare lasted only a few years, but wounds of the German invasion lingered long after the fighting ended.

—*Samuel K. Eddy, updated by Douglas W. Richmond*

ADDITIONAL READING:

Bullock, Alan. *Hitler: A Study in Tyranny.* Rev. ed. New York: Harper & Row, 1964. This definitive biography tells the story of Hitler's career, which culminated in the outbreak of World War II.

Colvin, Ian. *Vansittart in Office.* London: Victor Gollancz, 1965. Fills in details of British diplomatic activity behind the Chamberlain administration.

Garliński, Jozef. *Poland in the Second World War.* New York: Hippocrene Books, 1985. Concludes that despite the mistakes it committed, the Polish government could not have avoided confrontation with Germany and the Soviet Union.

Gross, Jan. *Polish Society Under German Occupation: The General Government, 1939-1944.* Princeton, N.J.: Princeton University Press, 1979. The longest and most severe occupation by Germany of any European country receives detailed consideration here.

Krakowski, Shmuel. *The War of the Damned: Jewish Armed Resistance in Poland, 1942-1944.* New York: Holmes & Meier, 1984. Krakowski describes the conflict in Poland between Hitler's forces and the Jews, who were determined to resist the Third Reich even at the cost of their lives.

Namier, Lewis B. *Europe in Decay: A Study of Disintegration, 1936-1940.* London: Macmillan, 1949. Reprint. Gloucester, Mass.: Peter Smith, 1963. Namier's book is a series of well-written, analytical reviews of the memoirs of some of the principal leaders who participated in the diplomatic prelude to the war—a series of pictures of demoralized and debased European ministers of state.

Reynaud, Paul. *In the Thick of the Fight.* Translated by J. D. Lambert. New York: Simon & Schuster, 1955. A personal memoir by the French statesman and cabinet minister.

Taylor, A. J. P. *The Origins of the Second World War.* London: Hamish Hamilton, 1961. An interpretation of the events leading up to the invasion of Poland that blames Britain and France for causing the war.

Toynbee, Arnold, and Veronica M. Toynbee, eds. *Survey of International Affairs, 1939-1946. The Eve of War, 1939.* London: Oxford University Press, 1959. A detailed study, country by country, of the events of the summer of 1939, written by experts.

SEE ALSO: 1938, The *Anschluss*; 1938, Munich Conference; 1939, Nazi-Soviet Pact; 1940, Collapse of France; 1940-1941, Battle of Britain.

1939-1940
RUSSO-FINNISH WAR

The Russo-Finnish War begins after the Soviet Union annexes some Finnish territory, but staunch fighting by Finnish soldiers allows Finland to retain its independence.

DATE: November 30, 1939-February 13, 1940
LOCALE: Finland and the Soviet Union
CATEGORIES: Expansion and land acquisition; Government and politics; Wars, uprisings, and civil unrest
KEY FIGURES:
Carl Gustaf Mannerheim (1867-1951), Finnish
    president and commander in chief of the Finnish army
Kirill Meretskov, planner of the Russian invasion of

Finland and overall commander of Russian forces on the Finnish front until 1940

Vyacheslav Mikhailovich Molotov (Skryabin; 1890-1986), Russian foreign minister before and during the Russo-Finnish War

Joseph Stalin (Iosif Vissarionovich Dzhugashvili; 1879-1953), dictator of the Soviet Union, 1928-1953

Kliment Yefremovich Voroshilov (1881-1969), Russian overall commander on Finnish front, January-March, 1940

of 295,000 men with virtually no aircraft or tanks. This invasion resulted from a number of factors in the tumultuous history of the two nations.

The czars of Russia and the kings of Sweden long battled for domination of the area that later became Finland. Peter I of Russia (1689-1725) incorporated most of Finland into his empire at the conclusion of the Great Northern War in 1721. During the Napoleonic wars, Alexander I of Russia (1801-1825) declared Finland to be a grand duchy with himself as its grand duke. Although

In the aftermath of the invasion of Poland, the Soviet government launched an invasion of Finnish territory, setting off a bitter winter war that killed thousands of troops before the Finns negotiated an armistice in February of 1940. (Popperfoto/Archive Photos)

SUMMARY OF EVENT. On November 30, 1939, the armed forces of the Soviet Union launched an invasion of Finnish territory. While the Soviet air force bombed Finnish cities, Soviet troops advanced into Finland on two fronts. Some units advanced eastward on a front bordered by the White Sea on the north and Lake Ladoga on the south, while a larger Soviet force advanced northward into the Karelian Isthmus between Lake Ladoga and the Gulf of Bothnia. The Soviets deployed 470,000 troops, supported by 2,200 tanks and more than 2,000 aircraft against a Finnish force

many Finns were unhappy with Russian rule, no opportunity presented itself to them to break away until the Russian Revolution of 1905.

With Czar Nicholas II (1894-1917), the last Russian czar, distracted by revolt in his far-flung dominions, Finnish students led a revolt against the Russian ruler. Two revolutionary military forces, the Red Guard and the Nationalists, led armed assaults on Russian military garrisons. When the revolutionaries fell out among themselves over political issues, Nicholas managed to regain control of the grand duchy by granting its people nearly complete autonomy and the world's first parliament elected by universal suffrage.

When the great Russian Revolution of 1917 came, many Finns opted for complete independence. Taking advantage of Russian preoccupation with civil war between the Communists and White (royalist and non-Communist) forces and the concurrent foreign intervention in Russia, Finnish nationalists declared Finland's independence on July 18, 1917, and suppressed the Finnish Bolsheviks. The Red Army of the Soviet Union attempted to suppress the Finnish government, but was defeated by German troops and a Finnish army commanded by Carl Gustaf Mannerheim in May, 1918. Finnish and Soviet representatives confirmed Finland's independence and settled the borders between their countries in the Treaty of Dorpat in 1922. Relations between the Finnish and Soviet governments remained stable and friendly until the beginnings of German rearmament and territorial expansion in the mid-1930's.

German dictator Adolf Hitler made it plain in his book *Mein Kampf* (1925-1927) that he planned to destroy communism and acquire living space for Germany's excess population in the Ukraine. Soviet dictator Joseph Stalin realized that Hitler could accomplish his ambitions only through a successful war against the Soviet Union. Stalin became increasingly anxious to strengthen Soviet defenses as Hitler became more aggressive in throwing off the territorial and military terms of the Treaty of Versailles. In planning the defense of their nation, Soviet leaders decided that they must garrison troops and ships in areas belonging to Finland. In 1937, Soviet emissaries proposed a military alliance between the two countries. The Finns turned down the Russian proposals because they wanted to remain neutral in the event of a new European war, which seemed likely.

By 1939, the Soviet proposals for an alliance turned into demands for military bases for their troops on Finnish territory. The Finnish government resisted these demands, thinking that the rivalry between Germany and the Soviet Union would guarantee their own continued neutrality. The Nazi-Soviet nonaggression pact of August, 1939, shattered the Finnish hope that they could continue to walk a tightrope between the two great-power antagonists. Secret protocols of the pact divided Europe into German and Soviet spheres of influence. The Soviet sphere included Finland and the small Baltic republics of Estonia, Latvia, and Lithuania, as well as eastern Poland.

When the German army invaded Poland and defeated its armed forces in September of 1939, the Soviets occupied the eastern part of the country. The German invasion brought Great Britain and France into the war, which quickly escalated into a global conflict. While the European countries confronted each other, Stalin occupied and annexed the Baltic republics during October and November, 1939. On October 5, Stalin summoned Finnish emissaries to Moscow. The Finnish government sent the emissaries, but at the same time ordered the mobilization of the Finnish army. The Soviet foreign minister Vyacheslav Molotov demanded of the emissaries that their government allow Soviet troops to establish bases on Finnish territory. As the Finnish representatives continued to resist Soviet demands, Stalin ordered a massive military buildup on the Russo-Finnish border. He also ordered general Kirill Meretskov to plan an invasion of Finland.

When Molotov reported to Stalin that the Finns would never accept the Soviet demands, the dictator ordered an invasion of Finland. On November 26, the Soviet government claimed Finnish troops had shelled the border village of Mainila. Using this supposed aggression as an excuse, the Soviet government broke off relations with the Finns on November 29 and invaded Finland the next day. Concurrently, Soviet bombers launched attacks against Finnish cities including Helsinki.

Gustaf Mannerheim, president of Finland and the hero of the Finnish war of independence in 1918, assumed command of the Finnish army. A career soldier who had risen to the rank of general in the imperial Russian army during World War I, Mannerheim was an able commander who well understood the rigors of a winter war. Mannerheim and the Finnish General Staff had long planned for the possibility of a Soviet invasion of their country. Their plan called for the small Finnish army to hold the Russians at bay in the Karelian Isthmus while reserves could be called to active service. Both in the isthmus and on a front north of Lake Ladoga the Finns fought the Red Army to a standstill in November and December.

During the fighting, the Finnish government tried to secure military aid from abroad. The Germans held fast to their nonaggression pact with the Soviet Union. The French and the British seemed willing to send military aid if the Finns would grant them bases for their armed forces on Finnish territory. U.S. president Franklin Roosevelt publicly denounced Soviet actions, but was not inclined to send military aid. The Finns were no more willing to have French and British bases on their soil than they were to have Soviet bases, so the appeal of Finnish representatives did not succeed.

The Soviet troops at the front proved to be poorly led and ill-equipped for war in conditions where the temperature often reached forty degrees below zero and lower. Their offensive halted, the Red Army found itself constantly harassed by the Finns and without supplies. Thousands were killed in the fighting and thousands more froze or starved to death. Even while his troops were dying, Stalin was planning a new offensive.

In December, the Soviet dictator replaced most of the generals on the Finnish front. General Kliment Voroshilov became the commander of Soviet forces and launched a new offensive against the Finns in February of 1940 with overwhelming force.

The Finnish army gave up a considerable amount of territory but managed to fight the Russians to a standstill once again. By this time Mannerheim had given up on aid from the French or British, and he advised the Finnish government to make peace on any terms short of unconditional surrender.

The Finns negotiated an armistice on February 13, 1940. The Finns had lost 22,425 men killed, 43,557 wounded, and 1,434 missing in action. The Russians had lost 53,500 killed, 176,000 wounded, and 16,000 missing in action. Civilian casualties are unknown, but hundreds of Finnish civilians died in the Russian bombings, which intensified during January and February, 1940.

The terms of the Treaty of Moscow, signed several months later to officially end the war, forced the Finns to give up more than thirty-five thousand square kilometers of their territory. The Finns also agreed to the establishment of Russian military bases on their territory and signed a mutual assistance pact with the Soviets. Harsh as these terms were, the Finns kept their independence and did not suffer the fate of the Baltic republics, which were annexed outright into the Soviet Union. Through the sacrifice of their soldiers in the face of overwhelming odds, the Finns managed to keep their freedom.

—Paul Madden

ADDITIONAL READING:

Engle, Eloise, and Lauri Paananen. *The Winter War: The Soviet Attack on Finland, 1939-1940*. Harrisburg, Pa.: Stackpole Books, 1973. Written for a popular audience, concentrates primarily on the soldiers and battles on the front lines.

Jakobson, Max. *Finland Survived: An Account of the Finnish-Soviet Winter War, 1939-1940*. Helsinki, Finland: Otava, 1961. Pro-Finnish account of origins and course of the war suitable for general readers. Written by a Finn, the language is sometimes confusing and the book reveals some obvious biases.

Tillotson, H. M. *Finland at Peace and War, 1918-1993*. Wilby Hall, England: Michael Russell, 1993. Heavily weighted toward military history, contains an account of Finnish history which puts the 1939-1940 war into a broader perspective of Finnish history.

Trotter, William R. *A Frozen Hell: The Russo-Finnish Winter War of 1939-1940*. Chapel Hill, N.C.: Algonquin Books, 1991. Surveys the origins, course, and results of the war in language accessible to most readers.

Upton, Anthony F. *Finland, 1939-1940*. Newark: University of Delaware Press, 1974. A concise overview of the origins of the war, the battles of the war, and the war's results. Recommended for high school audiences and above.

SEE ALSO: 1917, Finland Gains Independence; 1939, Nazi-Soviet Pact.

1940
GERMAN INVASION OF NORWAY

The German invasion of Norway begins with a successful surprise attack by land, sea, and air and challenges the traditional dominance of British sea power in Europe.

DATE: April 9, 1940

LOCALE: Norway

CATEGORIES: Expansion and land acquisition; Government and politics; Wars, uprisings, and civil unrest

KEY FIGURES:

Sir Winston Leonard Spencer Churchill (1874-1965), first lord of the British Admiralty

General Nikolaus von Falkenhorst (1885-1968), commander of German infantry, later general govern of Norway, 1940-1944

Haakon VII (1872-1957), king of Norway, 1905-1957

Carl Joachim Hambro (1885-1964), president of the Norwegian Storting

Adolf Hitler (1889-1945), chancellor and führer of Germany, 1933-1945

Vidkun Abraham Lauritz Jonsson Quisling (1887-1945), Norwegian politician and traitor

General Otto Ruge, Norwegian army commander

SUMMARY OF EVENT. Soon after the outbreak of World War II, Grand Admiral Erich Raeder, commander in chief of the German navy, drew Adolf Hitler's attention to the importance of Norway's coast for Germany's submarines, surface raiders, and blockade runners. He emphasized that an Allied capture of the ice-free port of Narvik in northern Norway would prevent Germany from importing vital Swedish iron ore. The führer did not show much interest in Scandinavia until he received reports that Britain was in fact considering a descent on Norway, spurred on by Winston Churchill, the first lord of the Admiralty. The Russo-Finnish War, which began on November 30, 1939, also prompted Allied agitation for sending troops to Finland via Narvik and northern Sweden.

On December 10, 1939, Vidkun Quisling, a Norwegian nationalist with Nazi sympathies, came to Berlin to propose to Hitler a Norwegian *coup d'état* to forestall the British, and Hitler appointed a staff to study ways of intervening. When Churchill, on February 16, 1940, sent the destroyer *Cossack* into Norwegian territorial waters to rescue British prisoners from the supply ship *Altmark*, Hitler accelerated preparations for a German invasion, code-named "Weserubung." A British cabinet decision on March 12 for landing troops at Narvik was reversed that same day by the end of the Russo-Finnish War, but Hitler decided not to risk further delay. Britain started mining Norway's shipping channels on April 8, but by then German invasion forces were on their way—most of the navy, twelve hundred aircraft, and the vanguard of six reinforced army divisions under the capable command of General Nikolaus von Falkenhorst—moving toward an April 9 surprise dawn attack on Denmark and Norway.

Thus, the Norwegian cabinet, after discussing British minelaying into the evening of April 8, had to reconvene in the early hours of April 9 to face reports of an approaching German threat. Norwegian mobilization orders were delayed and muddled. The army, short on rifles, artillery, ammunition, and without tanks, was also between drafts, with almost no men in barracks. Norway's planes were obsolete, and most of the navy's ships were museum pieces. Soldiers and civilians alike were surprised and confused, and the unexpected German dawn attack quickly seized most of its objectives—seaports and air fields at Narvik, Trondheim, Bergen, Stavanger, and Kristiansand.

The most important opposition occurred at the narrows of the Oslofjord, where the fortress at Oskarsborg sank a German heavy cruiser (*Blucher*), damaged a pocket battleship (*Lutzow*), and delayed the invasion flotilla more than twelve hours. This enabled King Haakon VII, the cabinet, and the Storting (parliament) to escape the German plan for their capture, taking a special train north at 7:23 A.M., followed by commandeered trucks carrying the nation's gold reserves. Six German airborne companies seized Fornebu airport on the morning of April 9 and occupied Oslo that afternoon, followed the next day by reinforcements from Falkenhorst's main army. The seizure of Oslo had the effect of isolating Norwegian troops in Ostfold, southern Norway, and Telemark from the Norwegian forces retreating northward.

On the evening of April 9, Storting president Carl Joachim Hambro persuaded that assembly to grant full emergency powers to the king and cabinet for the duration of the war. Ongoing attempts to capture the king or persuade him to name Nazi puppet Quisling prime minister failed, as did an air raid intended to kill the Norwegian leaders. By evening on April 9, however, the Germans held all the main ports and airfields, and by April 10 strong squadrons of fighters and bombers were already operating from them. The new commander in chief of Norway's army, Otto Ruge, retreating northward, relied chiefly on help from Britain, where Prime Minister Neville Chamberlain assured him, "we are coming as soon as possible, and in great strength."

Indeed, on the morning of April 9, the British Home Fleet under Admiral Sir Charles Forbes was in a position to sail into Bergen after the Germans with a far superior naval force. Strong German air attacks on his fleet that afternoon, however, persuaded Forbes to abandon his planned attack. A British cabinet project for a naval attack on Trondheim was also canceled because of the threat of German air power. Instead, from April 14-17, Britain landed an Allied expedition in the region of Narvik and sent smaller contingents to the west coast ports of Andalsnes and Namsos in the hope of converging on Trondheim and linking up with Norwegians in the Gudbrandsdal. The Allied soldiers arrived too late, however, and were too few in number. Without armored vehicles, field artillery, or effective aircraft, the British were no match for the well-equipped and fast-moving Germans. Defeated in the Gudbrandsdal and Trondheim areas, the Allies on May 28 drove the isolated German garrison out of the port of Narvik, but by then defeat in France forced the Allies to abandon Norway. The Allied evacuation of June 5-8 carried the Norwegian king and political leaders to England as a government-in-exile, while General Ruge remained behind to surrender his troops on June 10.

In the Norway campaign, the Germans had and employed superior forces, took the offensive and achieved surprise. The Luftwaffe outmatched British naval power in ways that seemed to threaten the security of Britain itself. The Norway invasion also marked the first major combined operation of the three service branches, demonstrating the necessity for cooperation between air, land, and sea forces in future campaigns. Allied weaponry and methods were exposed in Norway as outmoded, and their intelligence system ineffective.

The German capture of Norway had wartime consequences for both sides. Germany gained secure access to Sweden's iron ore, Trondheim became an important German submarine base, and other air and naval bases in the far north were used for attacks on Allied ship convoys to Russia between 1941 and 1945.

Britain, although beaten in the struggle for Norway,

avoided significant losses, while inflicting enough damage on the German navy to reduce its importance during the 1940 Battle of Britain. Another significant benefit for Great Britain was the fall of Chamberlain's ineffectual administration, and its replacement by the national coalition government headed by Churchill.

The Norwegian population of less than three million could not be a major factor in the war, but their large merchant marine helped the Allies, and their example of continuing underground resistance was a moral asset and also tied down three hundred thousand German occupation troops until 1945. At the end of the war, King Haakon VII and the government returned to Oslo, Falkenhorst and Raeder went on trial as war criminals, and Vidkun Quisling was convicted of treason and shot.

—Samuel K. Eddy, updated by K. Fred Gillum

ADDITIONAL READING:

British army, navy, and air force operations in Norway have been well covered by the official service histories. Norwegian army and navy operations have also been detailed in multivolume histories which have not been translated and are nearly unobtainable in the United States. The same is true of General Otto Ruge's *Krigens dagbok* (1946-1947). The best German account of overall operations is by Walther Hubatsch, *Die deutsche Besetzung von Danemark und Norwegen 1940*. This 1952 work has not been translated, but is increasingly employed in English language histories. The widest scope has been achieved, as noted below, by François Kersaudy, a French historian with a working command of the English, German, and Norwegian languages.

Churchill, Winston S. *The Second World War*. Vol I: *The Gathering Storm*. London: Cassell, 1948. An indispensable account of the author's role.

Derry, T. K. *The Campaign in Norway*. London: Her Majesty's Stationery Office, 1952. The official history of British army operations.

Gray, Edwyn. *Hitler's Battleships*. London: Leo Cooper, 1992. Includes an account of German landing operations taken largely from Hubatsch (above).

Kaufmann, J. E., and H. W. Kaufmann. *Hitler's Blitzkrieg Campaigns*. Conshohocken, Pa.: Combined Books, 1993. Chapter 4 includes material from Hubatsch and Derry (above).

Kersaudy, François. *Norway 1940*. New York: St. Martin's Press, 1991. Brief, balanced, broadly researched account that is also well translated. Includes the clearest account of Norwegian operations so far available in English.

Moulton, J. L. *The Norwegian Campaign of 1940*.

London: Eyre and Spottiswode, 1966. Analytical critique of the British campaign, with a few references to German and Norwegian sources.

Ruge, Friedrich. *Der Seekrieg*. Annapolis: U.S. Naval Institute, 1957. Chapter 5 gives a decidedly German perspective on the campaign.

SEE ALSO: 1939, Nazi-Soviet Pact; 1939, Germany Invades Poland; 1940, Collapse of France; 1940, Evacuation of Dunkirk; 1940-1941, Battle of Britain.

1940
COLLAPSE OF FRANCE

The collapse of France occurs after German forces breach the Maginot line and overwhelm the combined French and British military forces, eliminating France as a serious opponent to Germany for the remainder of World War II.

DATE: May 10-June 22, 1940

LOCALE: France

CATEGORIES: Expansion and land acquisition; Wars, uprisings, and civil unrest

KEY FIGURES:

Sir Winston Leonard Spencer Churchill (1874-1965), British prime minister, 1940-1945

Gustave-Maurice Gamelin (1872-1958), inspector general of French army and vice president of Higher Council of War, 1935-1940

Adolf Hitler (1889-1945), chancellor and führer of Germany, 1933-1945

Fritz Erich von Manstein (von Lewinksi; 1887-1973), Gerd von Rundstedt's chief of staff

Benito Amilcare Andrea Mussolini (1883-1945), Fascist premier of Italy, 1922-1943

General Henri Philippe Pétain (1856-1951), premier of Vichy France

Paul Reynaud (1878-1966), premier of France, March-June, 1940

General Karl Rudolf Gerd von Rundstedt (1875-1953), German commander in France

Maxime Weygand (1867-1965), French general and successor to Gamelin in 1940

SUMMARY OF EVENT. When World War II broke out in September, 1939, France was weak and demoralized. Unable to face a resurgent Germany alone and unaided, French leaders had followed the British in appeasing the aggressions of Adolf Hitler, chancellor and führer of Germany. France's domestic political problems had worsened during the interwar years, and there was a feeling of disillusionment with the politicians of the Third French Republic. Finally, France's military establishment, ostensibly strong, was actually weak both in planning and practice. Hidden behind the daunting series of fortifications known as the Maginot line, the French army waited for the Germans to attack and did not go to the aid of Poland when the Germans invaded it. From September, 1939, to May, 1940, the border between France and Germany was characterized by inactivity, for the French were reluctant to move out of their defenses. What mobile forces the French had were concentrated on the Belgian border, prepared to go to that country's aid should the Germans invade.

Residents began a frantic evacuation of Paris as German armies approached the city in June of 1940. (Archive Photos/ Potter Collection)

Meanwhile, following his successes in the east, Hitler made plans to invade France. In the winter of 1939-1940, he appointed General Karl Rudolf Gerd von Rundstedt as commander of Army Group A, and approved a modified Schlieffen Plan which would call for the Germans to sweep through Belgium and attack northern France. The French expected such an attack and moved their mobile forces north along the Belgian border. Rundstedt's chief of staff, General Fritz Erich von Manstein, a strong proponent of the utility of the armored division, proposed instead that the German armies concentrate on a push through the Ardennes forest, outflanking both the Maginot

line and the French mobile forces. The French considered the Ardennes impassable to armor, and the area was lightly defended. Hitler approved of Manstein's plan, and following his Blitzkrieg invasion of Norway and Denmark in April, 1940, he prepared to attack France.

The British and French were totally unprepared militarily and psychologically for the German assault. During the 1930's, France had focused on the building of the Maginot line. Military preparedness lagged behind that of Germany which, after 1936, had concentrated on building mobile, armored forces along with new aircraft such as the Stuka divebomber. The lessons of the successful, rapid German campaign in Poland in September, 1939, were also lost on the French high command. The senior French leadership was basically very old. For example, General Maurice Gamelin, overall commander of Allied forces in France, was sixty-eight years old in 1940. Very few senior French generals grasped the fact that new battlefield technology had changed the face of combat since 1918. The French and British General Staffs made few substantive inspections of the front and remained dangerously ignorant of the poor state of training of the armies or of the low state of morale of the troops.

On May 10, 1940, the German armies invaded Belgium, and Army Group A struck through the Ardennes, achieving an immediate breakthrough. The French cabinet, led by Premier Paul Reynaud, removed General Gamelin from command because he had committed all his armored forces to the fighting in Belgium and held none in reserve. General Maxime Weygand was appointed to replace Gamelin. To bolster the French cabinet and increase its prestige, Reynaud took over the Ministry of War himself and recalled Marshal Philippe Pétain, the aged hero of World War I, to act as his deputy.

Weygand could not contain the German forces, and they swept close to Paris, encircling and trapping the French troops against the back of the Maginot line. Reynaud appealed to Great Britain for additional aid, particularly fighter planes, but Winston Churchill, the British prime minister, refused the request because he foresaw that he would need them to protect England.

Reynaud's cabinet was in a state of indecision and confusion over the obvious deteriorating military and political situation. Word reached Paris that the roads from northern and eastern France were jammed with hundreds of thousands of fleeing, terrified refugees. German tanks were moving with no significant opposition from the defeated and demoralized Allied armies. There were obvious signs of panic in Paris, where the train stations were overwhelmed with citizens and government officials who were trying to evacuate the city before the Germans arrived. To spare the historic city and its population, Paris was declared to be an open city.

On June 11, the French cabinet withdrew to Tours as the German armies approached Paris. Churchill implored the French not to surrender but to retreat to North Africa and carry on the fight from there. Although Reynaud agreed, the French military saw no reason to carry on the fight, especially after Benito Mussolini, the Fascist dictator of Italy, declared war and sent Italian troops into southern France.

On June 16, in the face of almost certain defeat, Reynaud resigned his cabinet positions, and since the majority of the government wanted to conclude an armistice with Germany, Pétain was named premier with full powers. He appealed to Hitler, and on June 22, 1940, the French surrendered to Germany.

When it became clear that France was no longer able or willing to fight, Brigadier General Charles de Gaulle, serving as an undersecretary of state for war, fled to England. On June 18, 1940, de Gaulle broadcast from London his first appeal for France to continue the struggle against Nazi Germany. In June of 1940, however, few Frenchmen had the will to resist any further.

According to the terms of the surrender, France was divided into two parts; northern France was to be under German occupation, and southern France was to be nominally independent. The French fleet was to be interned in its home ports and was not to be used for the duration of the war. Pétain formed a government at the small southern town of Vichy, and in July formally abolished the constitution of the Third French Republic and established himself as virtual dictator. It was France's most inglorious moment and Germany's greatest, for Hitler had captured in one month what the German armies of 1914 had failed to take in four years of fighting.

—*José M. Sánchez, updated by James J. Cooke*

ADDITIONAL READING:

Corum, James S. *The Roots of Blitzkrieg: Hans von Seeckt and German Military Reform.* Lawrence: University of Kansas Press, 1992. This is a fine study of the rebuilding of the German army which eventually defeated France and Britain in 1940.

Doughty, Robert A. *The Breaking Point: Sedan and the Fall of France.* Hamden, Conn.: Archon Books, 1992. This is an analysis of the German breakthrough at Sedan, a battle which destroyed Allied defensive plans.

_____. *The Seeds of Disaster: The Development of French Army Doctrine, 1919-1939.* Hamden, Conn.: Archon Books, 1985. The author discusses the decisions and the doctrine which brought France to the disaster of 1940.

Horne, Alistair. *To Lose a Battle: France, 1940.* Boston: Little, Brown, 1969. Horne's classic work remains an excellent, detailed account of the French military disaster in 1940.

Weygand, Maxime. *Recalled to Service.* London: William Hinemann, 1952. These memoirs by a key player shed much light on the lost battles of 1940.

SEE ALSO: 1929-1940, The Maginot Line Is Built; 1938, Munich Conference; 1939, Nazi-Soviet Pact; 1940, Evacuation of Dunkirk; 1940-1944, The French Resistance; 1940-1941, Battle of Britain; 1944, Allied Invasion of France.

1940
EVACUATION OF DUNKIRK

The evacuation of Dunkirk transports members of the British Expeditionary Force and French troops across the English Channel, ensuring that the British army will continue in the war and a Free French armed force will be created.

DATE: May 26-June 4, 1940

LOCALE: Dunkirk and its beaches in northeastern France

CATEGORY: Wars, uprisings, and civil unrest

KEY FIGURES:

Admiral Jean Abrial, commander of French naval forces at Dunkirk

Sir Winston Leonard Spencer Churchill (1874-1965), British prime minister, 1941-1945

Robert Anthony Eden (1897-1977), British secretary of war, 1940

Hermann Göring (1893-1946), commander of the German Luftwaffe

Adolf Hitler (1889-1945), chancellor and führer of Germany, 1933-1945

Admiral Sir Bertram H. Ramsay, British flag officer at Dover

General Karl Rudolf Gerd von Rundstedt (1875-1953), German commander in France

General John Standish Surtees Prendergast Vereker, Lord Gort (1886-1946), commander in chief of the British Expeditionary Force

SUMMARY OF EVENT. When the Germans invaded Poland in 1939, the British sent an expeditionary force to France. By May of 1940, it had risen to a strength of ten infantry divisions. In the meantime, Adolf Hitler, chancellor and führer of Germany, had issued orders for a general offensive, planned by General Erich von Manstein, against France, Belgium, and Holland. At dawn on May 10, the German army and air force struck. In accordance with Allied plans, two French armies and nine divisions of the

Despite heroic evacuation efforts at Dunkirk, many British soldiers who are wounded are taken prisoner by victorious German forces. (National Archives)

British Expeditionary Force advanced into Belgium, to confront the German attack there.

On May 13, six German divisions broke through the French defenses farther south along the Meuse River, and struck northwestward toward the English Channel. On May 20, German forces reached the English Channel coast at the mouth of the Somme near Abbeyville, trapping the Allied forces in Belgium and northern France.

The progress of the Germans toward the coast had seriously alarmed General Lord Gort, the commander in chief of the British Expeditionary Force, and as early as May 19, he informed the British government that he was considering withdrawing his nine divisions to the English Channel for possible evacuation. The British Admiralty, the War Office, and Admiral Ramsay, the flag officer commanding Dover, began to improvise plans for such an evacuation under the code name "Dynamo."

A successful evacuation did not appear promising, as German forces moved northeastward along the coast. Boulogne and Calais were quickly surrounded, and a German force moved toward Dunkirk, the last port through which an Allied evacuation could take place. Yet on May 24, Rundstedt ordered the German armor to halt, less than fifteen miles from Dunkirk. This decision be-

came one of the most controversial of the entire war. After the war, German generals singled out Hitler as responsible for the failure to finish off the Allied forces. In fact, a number of senior generals shared the blame.

The halt, however, allowed the British and French to establish a defense line around Dunkirk and provided them time to put Operation Dynamo into motion. Hermann Göring, the German Luftwaffe commander, told Hitler that if the Allies left Dunkirk by sea, the German air force could stop them by bombing alone. Evacuation of the British began during the night of May 26. The French continued to consider defending Dunkirk as a fortress; it was not until May 28 that they decided to withdraw their troops and issued orders to Admiral Jean Abrial, in command of their forces at Dunkirk, to cooperate with the British. The Royal Navy recruited hundreds of small civilian pleasure craft to ferry troops from the beaches to the larger naval ships waiting offshore. The Luftwaffe's attempt to stop the evacuation proved much more difficult than Göring had imagined. German fighters, still operating from bases in western Germany, were farther from Dunkirk than British fighters operating from England. Although the British could not gain control of the air over Dunkirk, the British did hamper the German air attacks, destroying 240 German aircraft, while losing 177 planes.

On May 26, Hitler rescinded the halt order, but problems in the German command structure slowed the German advance, and it was not until May 30 that they even realized that the British were evacuating their troops. In the early morning hours of June 4, the last British ship left Dunkirk. The evacuation was over, a feat of heroism and great organizational skill on the part of the Royal Navy and Ramsay. Altogether, the British, with some French assistance, rescued 338,000 men, 224,000 of them British, many more than anticipated. Yet the cost was heavy. The British used 760 ships, of which 228, mostly small craft, were sunk by air attack, and the French had about 300, of which 60 were lost.

The evacuation of the British Expeditionary Force from Dunkirk ensured that the British army could continue in the war. Although the British had been forced to leave behind all their heavy equipment, tanks, artillery, and transport, their trained men were rescued, and they formed the nucleus of the British army of the future.

—Samuel K. Eddy, updated by Donald L. Layton

ADDITIONAL READING:

Carse, Robert. *Dunkirk, 1940: A History*. Englewood Cliffs, N.J.: Prentice Hall, 1970. This book recaptures the horror, shock, and excitement which surrounded the withdrawal, but it is not a detailed analysis of the event.

Collier, Richard. *The Sands of Dunkirk*. New York: E. P. Dutton, 1961. An attempt to reconstruct the fighting at Dunkirk, this book's greatest strengths are its full tables of units and ships.

Divine, A. D. *Dunkirk*. New York: E. P. Dutton, 1948. This is a dated but good account of the evacuation based on the logs of small boat masters and Admiralty reports.

Gelb, Norman. *Dunkirk: The Complete Story of the First Step in the Defeat of Hitler*. New York: William Morrow, 1989. An anecdotal reprise of the Dunkirk story based mostly on the standard secondary sources.

Harman, Nicholas. *Dunkirk, the Necessary Myth*. London: Hodder & Stoughton, 1989. A revisionist account of the evacuation, emphasizing British manipulation of the press at home.

Lord, Walter. *The Miracle of Dunkirk*. New York: Viking, 1982. This is the best and most up-to-date account of the Dunkirk evacuation. Lord's interpretations of major issues are soundly based on recent scholarship.

SEE ALSO: 1938, Munich Conference; 1939, Nazi-Soviet Pact; 1940, Collapse of France; 1940-1944, The French Resistance; 1940-1941, Battle of Britain; 1944, Allied Invasion of France.

1940-1944
THE FRENCH RESISTANCE

The French Resistance brings French citizens together in a spontaneous patriotic movement to fight the German occupation during World War II.

DATE: June, 1940-August, 1944

LOCALE: France

CATEGORIES: Organizations and institutions; Wars, uprisings, and civil unrest

KEY FIGURES:

General Charles-André-Marie-Joseph de Gaulle (1890-1970), leader of the Free French in Great Britain from 1940-1942, who eventually joined forces with the French Resistance on the mainland in 1944

Jean Moulin (1899-1943), delegate chosen by de Gaulle to head the Resistance in France and president of the National Resistance Council in 1943, until his capture and death at the hands of the Gestapo

General Henri Philippe Pétain (1856-1951), premier of Vichy France, 1940-1944

SUMMARY OF EVENT. When France declared war on Germany in 1939, it remembered the atrocities of World War I and hoped that an actual war would not break out. In May of 1940, however, the Germans entered and conquered northern France. On June 14, Paris surrendered. On June 17, Henri Philippe Pétain, the eighty-four-year-old general who had served France during World War I and to whom the defeated French looked as a savior, announced over the radio from Vichy France, that he was seeking an armistice with the Germans. The next day, Charles de Gaulle spoke on a BBC radio broadcast from London, telling the French that "the flame of French resistance must not die," and ten days later, Churchill recognized de Gaulle as the leader of the Free French movement in Great Britain. Few back in France, however, paid much attention. The armistice became official on June 25, 1940.

Yet there were many French citizens who could tolerate neither the fall of France nor the armistice. These men and women, known as the First Resisters, began to meet spontaneously with one another in opposition to the Vichy government and the German occupation. This small group, largely autonomous and unconnected to the Free French movement led by de Gaulle, formed the nucleus of what was to become the French Resistance. At first, they scarcely knew what to do.

After the armistice, France was divided into two zones: the North, which was occupied by the Germans, and the free South, where the Vichy government ruled. As the premier of the Vichy government, Pétain quickly made drastic changes in the government. Although promising that the government was to be run by the French, Pétain abolished the Third French Republic, called for a new constitution, and began a series of reforms known as the National Revolution. A new motto, "Work, Family, Country," replaced the traditional one of "Liberty, Equality, and Fraternity." By November of 1940, the Vichy government abolished all free elections, dissolved the trade unions, established a secret police, and banished Jews from government jobs and the professions. Even worse, on October 30, 1940, Pétain used the word " collaborate" with the Germans at the same time as he was filmed shaking hands with Hitler. This behavior shocked and galvanized many of the resisters to action.

Among these early resisters was Jean Moulin, who had been arrested and tortured when the Germans entered the town of Chartres in 1940. Rather than sign a paper stating that the French were responsible for the atrocities committed by the Germans, Moulin cut his own throat. He was then hospitalized and, after his recovery, managed to get to London. De Gaulle sent Moulin back to France in 1942 to head and unify the Resistance movement there. For the next year until his death, he was a ubiquitous figure throughout France. Known as "Max," which was only one of a dozen aliases, he appeared, speaking hoarsely and wearing a scarf around his injured throat.

By 1942, the Vichy government had lost much of its

credibility with the French citizens. In November, the Germans moved South, so that now all of France became occupied territory. In addition, Vichy lost its foothold in North Africa. In 1942, the Germans asked France to send workers to Germany voluntarily. Out of the 350,000 requested, only 50,000 signed up. By 1943, this voluntary service became obligatory forced labor. In response, new groups of individuals joined the Resistance movement. Their name derived from *maquis*, the term for the dense brush of the Corsican hill country, where those traditionally in trouble could seek refuge. Now, those who refused to go to Germany became known as the maquis or outlaw branch of the Resistance. They found refuge with local sympathetic French citizens. Indeed, later on some of the maquis lived up to their name of outlaw and committed violent acts against the French citizenry.

By May of 1943, de Gaulle, who had from 1941 insisted on his right to speak for France, became from his station in North Africa, the titular leader of the Resistance. He commissioned Moulin to establish and lead the National Resistance Council in France. In June of 1943, his whereabouts betrayed, Moulin was arrested in Lyon by Klaus Barbie and the Gestapo. He was tortured and then put to death. The identity of the one who betrayed him has never been determined.

Moulin's death notwithstanding, the Resistance movement continued to grow largely in response to the sustained repression by the Vichy government. With the establishment of the Milice in 1943, an outgrowth of the French secret police started earlier by Vichy, and the obligatory service in Germany, the ranks of the Resistance swelled to more than two hundred thousand. Resistance members undertook a multitude of tasks. First, the Resistance needed to make information available to their fellow French and to the Allies and so published numerous clandestine newspapers. By 1944, the resistance press was publishing two million papers a month. Second, through the services of doctors and other professionals, the Resistance produced the false papers which made discovery of its membership difficult. Next, resisters engaged in sabotage, destroying factories turning out weapons for the war effort and shutting down power stations which fed such factories. Last, they tried to assist in the escape of Jews and to ambush German patrols.

This activity escalated when the Allies landed in Normandy on June 6, 1944, and began to push the Germans back toward central Europe. At this point, the Resistance blew up bridges, cut electrical cables and telephone wires, blocked tunnels, delayed railway movements, and removed signposts and milestones so as to confuse the Germans. In addition, they used several delaying tactics to slow the German march. In some instances, the Resistance would place explosives amid piles of stones along the roads; soon the Germans became suspicious of any pile of stones. The resisters also buried boxes of explosives in holes in the road underneath clumps of cattle dung. The explosion was sufficient to dismantle a tank. The Resistance then encouraged French children to spread the dung in the roads without the explosives. When the Germans saw the dung, they spent at least twenty minutes investigating it for the explosive. They thus lost valuable time in their retreat across France.

The Allies pushed the Germans back toward Paris. While the Allied troops had no intention of entering the city initially, on August 19, 1944, when Resistance fighters rose up against the Germans in Paris, the Allies decided to intervene. On August 25, 1944, the Allies declared victory and de Gaulle, flanked by members of the Resistance, walked through the Arc du Triomphe in the heart of the city. Although de Gaulle would not have been there without the efforts of these resisters, he gave them little recognition.

As the Resistance had traveled behind the Allies forcing the Germans back across France, they had spontaneously eliminated ten thousand Vichy officials. After the liberation of Paris, the French courts assumed the task of administering justice to those suspected of collaborating with the Germans. Fifty thousand of those placed on trial lost their civil rights, another forty thousand were sent to prison, and between seven and eight hundred were executed. Pétain was one of those who was tried and sentenced to death in 1945. The government commuted his sentence to life imprisonment, and he died in prison off the coast of Brittany in 1951.

The French Resistance kept few written records during its existence, for these would have jeopardized the membership. Because their language was one of the few things left to them under the German occupation, some resisters wrote poetry. As values of the Resistance were felt rather than learned, these few used the language of emotion—poetry—to memorialize their actions. This poetry and subsequent memoirs remain as the major legacy of the French Resistance.

—Jennifer Eastman

ADDITIONAL READING:

Aubrac, Lucie. *Outwitting the Gestapo*. Lincoln: University of Nebraska Press, 1993. Written by the wife of the noted resister, Raymond Aubrac, the book details nine months of the couple's activity in the movement. An excellent introduction.

Camus, Albert. *The Plague*. New York: Modern Library, 1948. A fictionalized account purporting in part to concern the French resistance against the German occupation.

De Vomecourt, Phillipe. *An Army of Amateurs*. Garden City, N.Y.: Doubleday, 1961. Detailed and lively memoir from a resister present at the beginning of the movement in 1940 until the Paris liberation in 1944.

Ehrlich, Blake. *Resistance, France 1940-1945*. Boston: Little, Brown, 1965. The most comprehensive, factual account of the activities of the French Resistance.

Frenay, Henri. *The Night Will End*. New York: McGraw-Hill, 1976. Eyewitness account of early participant in the movement. Frenay is critical of de Gaulle and Moulin, although he worked for both of them.

Kedward, Roderick, and Roger Austin, eds. *Vichy France and the Resistance Culture and Ideology*. Kent, England: Croom Helm, 1985. Interesting collection of essays by British and Irish scholars emphasizing the ambiguities of the times.

SEE ALSO: 1940, Collapse of France; 1940, Evacuation of Dunkirk; 1940-1941, Battle of Britain; 1944, Allied Invasion of France.

1940-1941
BATTLE OF BRITAIN

The Battle of Britain results in a successful deflection of German air assaults, forcing Hitler to postpone the invasion of Britain and turn toward the Soviet Union instead.

DATE: Late summer, 1940-1941
LOCALE: England and the English Channel
CATEGORY: Wars, uprisings, and civil unrest
KEY FIGURES:

Sir Alan Francis Brooke (1883-1963), general officer and commander in chief of the Southern Command
Sir Winston Leonard Spencer Churchill (1874-1965), British prime minister, 1940-1945 and 1951-1955
Sir Hugh Dowding (1882-1970), commander in chief of the Fighter Command with the Royal Air Force
Hermann Göring (1893-1946), commander in chief of the German Luftwaffe
Albert Kesselring (1885-1960), commander of the Luftwaffe Air Group II
Keith R. Park (1892-1975), commander of the Num-ber 11 Group in the Fighter Command with the Royal Air Force
Erich Raeder (1876-1960), commander in chief of the German navy
Hugh Sperrle (1885-1953), commander of the Luftwaffe Air Group III

SUMMARY OF EVENT. With the German conquests of the Low Countries and France completed by June of 1940,

Britain stood alone to confront Adolf Hitler's forces. Winston Churchill spoke to his countrymen: "Hitler knows he will have to break us on this Island or lose the War." British military leaders assumed that a German invasion of Britain from across the English Channel was likely to begin in the near future.

While the British Royal Navy did control the seas immediately around Britain, its forces were strained by the need to protect the Atlantic supply routes used by American supply ships against German U-boat attacks. Some fifty-five army divisions could be mustered to defend the island, and many of those divisions were only at half strength. Prospects of defending against a German ground attack were further complicated by the fact that British forces fleeing Dunkirk earlier in June were forced to abandon most of their supplies while retreating from German forces.

An army general observed at the time that the defense of Britain would fall primarily on the Royal Air Force (RAF), particularly on the Fighter Command planes. Since 1936, Sir Hugh Dowding, head of the Fighter Command, had tried to convince the cabinet and the Air Council that, in the next war, Britain would be on the offensive. For that reason, priority in aircraft planning and production should be given to a buildup of fighter plane strength, not bombers as the Air Council wanted. Dowding also stressed the need for improved detection and early warning of enemy aircraft. Over much opposition and after much delay, Dowding's warnings persuaded the Air Council to alter its contingency plans. In 1939, the Air Council ordered stepped-up production of more fighters, as well as the construction of an early warning system.

British designers developed two types of improved fighter planes: the Hurricanes and the Spitfires. Both flew at maximum speeds of three hundred miles per hour (fast for the time), had heavy armor, constant speed propellers, self-sealing fuel tanks, and eight machine guns. The innovative design of these planes had a major impact on the course of Britain's air battle with the German Luftwaffe.

During 1937, British physicists had worked on aircraft detection by means of radio wave signals, and what would later be known as radar was quickly developed. Work began on building a linked system of radar stations, ground observation units, and Fighter Command sector control bases which would enable the Fighter Command to anticipate and intercept enemy bombers. Hundreds of barrage balloons and antiaircraft artillery added to the British defensive shield.

Since the German invasion of France, Hitler had sought to persuade the British to negotiate a settlement and end the fighting between their nations. His peace overtures were rejected out of hand by Churchill. Although he believed the mission "technically unfeasible," Hitler approved Operation Sea Lion, the military plan for the German invasion of England. The invasion was tentatively set to begin on September 21, some two months later. Ninety thousand German troops would make up the initial assault force, building to ten divisions within two weeks. Preparations for Operation Sea Lion went forward rapidly. More than twelve hundred boats and barges were assembled at French ports across the Channel from England. Troops were trained in landing procedures, and bases were built

trated front in Kent and Sussex. Admiral Raeder insisted that his ships could not assure protection of the assault forces over the broad front, while the generals feared that the narrow front would enable the British to place their full force in one locality and so more effectively contest the invasion. Raeder finally won his point, and the narrow front plan was adopted; but the delay had further shortened the time margin for implementation. Logistic revisions had to be made with dangerous haste to get Operation Sea Lion under way before autumn storms closed the Channel.

The Tower Bridge stands in stark relief against a background of smoke in the wake of the first mass air raid on London in September of 1940. (National Archives)

for the aircraft which were to provide air cover during the landing. A central element in the plan was to neutralize Britain's Air Force before German troops crossed the English Channel.

Serious disagreements then arose between the German naval and army high commands as to whether the landings should be made along a broad front in southern and eastern England as the army wanted, or on a more concen-

Across the Channel, British ground and air defense preparations were also proceeding. Under General Alan Brooke, the Home Guard was increased to five hundred thousand men; mobile field guns, antitank weapons, and small arms were provided in ever larger amounts; more than two million bomb shelters were built and distributed; and plans to resist German landings from the sea, or by parachutes from the air were developed.

It was increasingly apparent to both sides that control of the air over southern England would be the critical factor in determining the success or failure of Operation Sea Lion. Göring had no doubt that his Luftwaffe could gain that control. Indeed, he believed that his bombers would so pulverize British defenses within a month's time that they would have to surrender and a cross-Channel invasion would be unnecessary. Göring had cause for optimism. With more than thirteen hundred bombers and twelve hundred fighter planes, the Luftwaffe in Western Europe greatly overmatched the Royal Air Force. The Luftwaffe squadrons were organized into three air groups (Luftflotten); of these, the latest was the Luftflotte Two (Kesselring) and Luftflotte Three (Sperrle) stationed in France and the Netherlands. They would spearhead the German air offensive.

To confront the German air power, Dowding's Fighter Command had only about 700 front line fighter aircraft, with another 350 in reserve. And those were, of necessity, deployed all over the island. Even the heaviest concentration of fighter planes—those in Park's Number 11 Group in the southeast—would probably be outnumbered by as much as ten to one by the attacking German planes. Dowding's most serious shortage, however, was men to fly the planes. There were only a few more than fourteen hundred fully trained fighter pilots and almost no reserves available to replace them if they were disabled or killed.

The Battle of Britain for air supremacy cannot be said to have taken place on any one specific day. Rather, the fighting consisted of a number of bomber attacks and fighter plane encounters, increasing in size and intensity from July to September, 1940. During July and into early August, the Luftwaffe carried out intermittent strikes, mostly on British shipping in the Channel and on the port of Dover. Some 150 civilians were killed and twenty ships were sunk in these strikes, but dozens of Luftwaffe planes were downed by RAF fighters and antiaircraft fire. On August 1, Hitler ordered the Luftwaffe to destroy the Royal Air Force and establish air superiority. "The German air force is to overcome the British air force with all means at its disposal, and as soon as possible," Hitler ordered.

The next phase of the German air offensive was directed at the radar stations and airfields in the southeastern counties of England. British losses of men and machine were heavy, and the prospects of clearing the area for the Sea Lion landings were enhanced. The airfields were quickly repaired, radar stations were rebuilt, and the Fighter Command was able to complete most of its operations by mid-August. As a result of the energetic efforts of Lord Beaverbrook, the minister of aircraft production,

Britain more than made up its losses in fighter aircraft. The pilot shortage was partly rectified through increased graduation from training schools, the retraining of bomber pilots, and shifting pilots from other branches of the military.

Meanwhile, Göring had been planning Operation Eagle, a massive saturation bombing of Britain's southern ports and airfields. Operation Eagle had to be postponed several times in early August because of bad weather. Then on August 13, designated "eagle day" by the German Command, British radar stations picked up signals of very large formations of approaching aircraft: Operation Eagle had begun. The German attackers came in several waves, and Park's fighters rose to meet them. Some of the German bombers penetrated British defenses and did further damage, but the Hurricanes and Spitfires shot down forty-seven of the enemy planes at the cost of thirteen British craft.

Bad flying weather returned, causing a two-day suspension of the operation. By August 15, favorable weather prompted Göring to order a renewal of the bombings. He declared that the objective was to obliterate the Royal Air Force planes and facilities. On that day, and into August 16, four successive waves came across the Channel and across the North Sea from bases in Norway. Luftflotte Two and Luftflotte Three bombers eluded Park's fighters and the antiaircraft guns in sufficient numbers to destroy four aircraft factories and five airfields around London. The bombers from Norway had been sent with insufficient fighter escort and they were brought down in large numbers. In those two days, the Luftwaffe had seventy-six planes shot down, the worst damage in a short period the German air force would ever suffer.

In all, between August 8 and August 26, the British fighters destroyed 602 German aircraft—mostly bombers, especially the Stuka dive bombers, which proved very vulnerable to British defenses. In that same period, 259 British fighters were shot down during these daylight raids. Under intense bombardment, Britain refused to yield to German air power. Churchill praised the efforts of the Royal Air Force and the British military in his famous speech to the House of Commons on August 20, 1940. "Never in the field of human conflict has so much been owed by so many to so few," Churchill observed.

Yet, despite the growing German losses, the Luftwaffe attacks intensified. Göring was convinced that, weather permitting, Britain could be brought to its knees in approximately two weeks. During the last week of August and the first week of September, 1940, there were more than thirty major attacks averaging more than one thousand planes per raid. Most of the bombs were directed at the airfields and sector stations of Number 11 Group. Vice Marshal Park admitted that the damage was extensive and that the fighting efficiency of his command was being seriously impaired. Dowding saw the mounting loss of fighter pilots as critical: In those two weeks, 103 RAF pilots were killed or missing. By September 6, the Fighter Command (and therefore all of Britain) appeared on the verge of defeat. Across the Channel, Operation Sea Lion preparations were stepped up with the news of the Luftwaffe successes.

Then, in early September, Göring made a serious tactical error. He ordered the Luftwaffe to shift its attacks from RAF facilities toward massive attacks on London and other population centers. Göring had received intelligence reports that the Fighter Command had been neutralized and no longer had sufficient strength to defend against German bombers. Those reports were wrong, as the events of the following week would illustrate. If Göring had pursued his objective of destroying the Fighter Command, Germany may have won the Battle of Britain.

On September 7, the British government sent out the code signal "Cromwell," signifying that the expected invasion was now at hand. On that same day, nearly two hundred German bombers hit East London, killing more than three hundred civilians and inflicting extensive damage to houses, docks, and warehouses. That night, another 250 bombers, guided by the light of the extensive fires, did more damage to the British capital. Park sent up his fighters to intercept. In the air battles that ensued, another thirty-eight German planes were shot down, as were twenty-eight British aircraft. Most important, Park had demonstrated that the Fighter Command was still functioning and lethal. London was again bombed on September 9, but with less effect than on September 7 because only about half of the attacking planes were able to penetrate and attack their targets. As the attacks continued, nearly one thousand civilians a week were dying in raids on London. Churchill, fearing any show of weakness, ordered the Royal Navy and the RAF Bomber Command to attack French port facilities that could be used by Germany in a cross-Channel invasion. It was increasingly obvious that the Germans did not yet control the Channel or the air space over England. Faced with that knowledge, Hitler postponed Operation Sea Lion to the spring of 1940.

What proved to be Göring's last effort to clear the way for the invasion came on September 15, 1940. He threw everything he had into the day's fighting. One hundred twenty-three bombers with five fighter escorts each went out from the continental bases. Park's squadrons, reinforced by planes from other British Air Groups, went to meet the Luftwaffe. The air battle began about noon and lasted until late in the evening. When the day ended, sixty German planes had been destroyed, with British losses of only twenty-six aircraft. September 15, 1940, would later be identified by many as the day the RAF won the Battle of Britain. "We still keep this day, and I hope we will always keep it," Harold Macmillan would write, "in commemoration of our victory."

Two days later, realizing that the Luftwaffe could not gain air supremacy and that is was now too late for favorable weather, Hitler ordered the indefinite postponement of Operation Sea Lion. His interest turned eastward instead, and German plans for the invasion of Russia (Operation Barbarossa) began. Britain would still have to endure repeated pounding by German bombers in the later so-called Blitz of 1940-1941, but in the summer of 1940, the "gallant few" of the RAF Command had saved Britain from invasion. Adding up the final cost, more than forty thousand British civilians were killed. In addition, more than forty-six thousand were injured and more than one million homes were destroyed. Six to seven hundred British military aircraft had been destroyed between July and September of 1940, as against some fourteen hundred German aircraft of all types.

—James W. Pringle, updated by Lawrence I. Clark

ADDITIONAL READING:

Bickers, Richard Townsend, ed. *The Battle of Britain: The Greatest Battle in the History of Air Warfare*. New York: Prentice Hall Press, 1990. A detailed examination of the Battle of Britain written by a former RAF pilot and British military historian. Contains photographs, detailed information on military aircraft, day-to-day analysis of the air battles, index, and chapter on "RAF Heroes" killed during the Battle of Britain.

Franks, Norman. *Battle of Britain*. New York: Gallery Books, 1990. A useful general introduction to Battle of Britain written by a British aviation writer. Includes photographs, appendix, and index.

Gilbert, Martin. "France's Agony, Britain's Resolve" and "The Battle for Britain." In *The Second World War: A Complete History*. New York: Henry Holt, 1989. In this widely acclaimed book, the official biographer of Winston Churchill provides a valuable history of German strategy and the defiance of the British people.

Hough, Richards, and Denis Richards. *The Battle of Britain: The Greatest Air Battle of World War II*. New York: W. W. Norton, 1989. Richards, the coauthor of the official history of the Royal Air Force, and Hough, a former RAF pilot, draw heavily on official sources in this detailed military history. Includes photographs, illustrations, maps, detailed appendix, index, and day-to-day chronology of the fighting.

SEE ALSO: 1938, Munich Conference; 1939, Nazi-Soviet Pact; 1939, Germany Invades Poland; 1940, Collapse of France; 1940, Evacuation of Dunkirk; 1941, Atlantic Charter Is Signed; 1942, Battle of El Alamein.

1941
ATLANTIC CHARTER IS SIGNED

The Atlantic Charter is signed, creating guidelines that have a more profound impact on the evolution of the postwar global order than its framers may have originally intended.

DATE: August, 1941-postwar years
LOCALE: Europe
CATEGORIES: Diplomacy and international relations; Government and politics
KEY FIGURES:
Sir Winston Leonard Spencer Churchill (1874-1965), British prime minister, 1940-1945 and 1951-1955
Franklin Delano Roosevelt (1882-1945), thirty-second president of the United States, 1933-1945

SUMMARY OF EVENT. President Franklin D. Roosevelt and Prime Minister Winston Churchill secretly met August 7-12, 1941, along the quiet coast of Placentia Bay harbor in Newfoundland. By summit's end, the Atlantic Charter was approved by both leaders. Although it was never signed by either party and was redrafted numerous times, the final text was telegraphed to London and Washington. The Charter established common principles shared by both countries' national policies and their ambitions for a more secure global future.

The text contained in its body eight principles. First, both countries sought no aggrandizement, territorial or other. Second, they desired to see no territorial changes that did not accord with the freely expressed wishes of the people concerned. Third, they respected the right of all peoples to choose the form of government under which they will live; and they wished to see sovereign rights and self-government restored to those who had been forcibly deprived of them. Fourth, they endeavored, with due respect for their existent obligations, to provide all states, great or small, victor or vanquished, with equal access to the trade and to the raw materials of the world which were needed for their economic prosperity. Fifth, they desired to bring about the fullest collaboration between all nations in the economic field, with the object of securing for all improved labor standards, economic advancement, and social security. Sixth, after the destruction of the Nazi tyranny, they hoped to see a peace established which would afford to all nations the means of dwelling in safety within their own boundaries, and which would afford assurance that all people in all the lands may live out their lives in freedom from fear and want. Seventh, such a peace would enable all people to traverse the high seas and oceans without hindrance. Finally, they believed that all nations of the world, for realistic as well as spiritual reasons, must abandon the use of force. Since no future peace can be maintained if land, sea, or air armaments continue to be employed by nations which threaten, or may threaten, aggression outside their frontiers, they believed, pending the establishment of a wider and permanent system of general security, that the disarmament of such nations is essential. They would likewise aid and encourage all other practicable measures which would lighten for peace-loving peoples the crushing burden of armaments.

Following the victory of the Allied forces over the Nazi threat, subsequent problems with regard to each of the eight points became great. Surviving identification with the immediate crisis of Nazi dominance of the European continent in 1941, and later global conflict from 1941 through 1945, the Charter evolved into strongly worded principles instead of limited national policies. The new global order and embryonic United Nations charter took its creative and spiritual guidance from the Atlantic Charter's earlier preestablished points. In practical application, the fundamental policies and basic principles and ideas of the Charter became universal. Large, small, and newly emergent nations in the decades that followed sought to put into effect if not apply its tenets to their diverse national policies. That is where the trouble began.

Postwar European and later Third World development placed the United States, Britain, and their Western allies in a defensive posture. Determined to break out of the limitations of containment imposed upon them by the United States and the alliance, the Soviet government countered such restraints with consistent policies to influence in its favor the process of "self-determination." The Soviets employed subtler tactics than the Nazis. These policies were referred to as "subversive" by the Allied powers. Several European capitals, including Paris, Athens, and Rome, emerged as the battleground for the minds of the populace. Left-wing organizations were swayed by Soviet resources and, in turn, sought to sway the body politics of their societies through their domestic elections.

American policy, as a result, took a more urgent turn. To the principle of self-determination, a Cold War corollary was added by U.S. policymakers. War-devastated Europe needed a massive infusion of capital in order to rebuild. The Marshall Plan was created to fill that void.

European recovery was regarded by American policymakers as crucial to future prosperity in the United States. Thirteen billion dollars was distributed to seventeen west European nations, with the largest amounts going to Britain, France, and Germany. The effect was immediate. Living standards throughout the region were raised. The power of the Communists in France and Italy began to wane, with the ensuing crackdown on left-wing organizations in their respective government ministries and throughout much of their societies by government forces. With a revived Europe and stronger West Germany, the Soviets interpreted the impact of the Marshall Plan as representative of a calculated offensive that sought to subvert their country's security interests.

By the late 1940's and throughout the 1950's and 1960's, most of the former colonies of Britain, France, the Netherlands, and Belgium gained independence. In this new political environment of increased sovereignty, the Soviets found more room in which to maneuver. Not only did the issue of self-determination maintain its urgency, but other important issues—including development and modernization, colonialism and anticolonialism, and foreign aid to poor and developing societies—also concerned the superpowers and the newly emergent states. This better explains why events such as the war in Indochina, the 1956 Suez crisis, Soviet penetration of the Middle East, and Palestinian self-determination were dominant issues addressed by both superpowers.

President Franklin D. Roosevelt and Prime Minister Winston Churchill's secret rendezvous in August, 1941, bore unexpected fruit many decades later. To many postwar participants, a more stable and secure global order seemed to be on the horizon. —*Talaat E. Shehata*

ADDITIONAL READING:

Fish, M. Steven. "After Stalin's Death: The Anglo-American Debate over a New Cold War." *Diplomatic History* 10 (Fall, 1986): 343-353. Describes debate in which Winston Churchill took part, and provides a clearer focus on American and British policies during the postwar years, in comparison with their earlier Atlantic Charter agreement in August, 1941.

Herring, George C., and Richard H. Immerman. "Eisenhower, Dulles, and Dienbienphu." *Journal of American History* 71 (September, 1984): 356-357. Provides important insights into how American policy began to change, with its increased global responsibilities after the early Cold War years of the Truman administration.

Mee, Charles L., Jr. *The Marshall Plan: The Launching of the Pax Americana.* New York: Simon & Schuster, 1984. A backdrop on growing American hegemony in

Europe during the postwar era, and how that would color American and Western European perceptions of the aspirations of Third World nations in a bipolar world.

Paterson, Thomas G. *On Every Front: The Making of the Cold War.* New York: W. W. Norton, 1979. Paterson's introductory work provides valuable explanations of the environment in which the concept of self-determination developed and survived.

Smith, T. *The Pattern of Imperialism: The United States, Great Britain and the Late-Industrializing World Since 1815.* Cambridge, England: Cambridge University Press, 1981. A relevant chronological guide to the gradual process of Western global dominance.

SEE ALSO: 1938, Munich Conference; 1939, Nazi-Soviet Pact; 1943, The Casablanca Conference; 1945, The Yalta Conference; 1945, The United Nations Is Founded; 1947, Marshall Plan Is Announced.

1942-1943
STAND AT STALINGRAD

The stand at Stalingrad marks one of the most significant turning points in World War II when Soviet forces successfully defeat the German Sixth Army after a hard-fought campaign lasting five months.

DATE: August 24, 1942-January 31, 1943
LOCALE: Stalingrad, the Soviet Union
CATEGORY: Wars, uprisings, and civil unrest
KEY FIGURES:

General Vasili Chuikov (1900-1982), Russian commander of the Sixty-second Army, responsible for the immediate defense of Stalingrad

Field Marshal Hermann Göring (1893-1946), commander of the German Luftwaffe

Adolf Hitler (1889-1945), chancellor and führer of Germany, 1933-1945

Field Marshal Fritz Erich von Manstein (von Lewinski; 1887-1973), commander of the German army group on the Don front

Field Marshal Friedrich Paulus (1890-1957), commander of the German Sixth Army at Stalingrad

General Konstantin Rokossovski (1896-1968), Russian commander at the Don front

General Andrei Yeremenko (1892-1970), Russian commander at the southeast front, including Stalingrad

General Georgy Kostantinovich Zhukov (1896-1974), Soviet deputy commander in chief

SUMMARY OF EVENT. When Germany invaded the Soviet Union in June of 1941, Adolf Hitler was determined to conquer that nation and force a surrender within six

Women, children, and elderly residents were among the refugees who were trapped during the lengthy siege of Stalingrad in 1942-1943. (Archive Photos)

months. German armies using Blitzkrieg ("lightning war") tactics were victorious in the south, with the capture of Kiev, and their soldiers reached the outskirts of Leningrad in the north. Hitler's goal of a rapid and total victory was not realized, however, because of delays in beginning the invasion, bad weather, logistical problems, Soviet resistance, and the German strategic plan calling for a broad frontal attack instead of a decisive single thrust to Moscow. German forces were halted before Moscow in December, 1941, and Joseph Stalin ordered a successful counteroffensive that forced a partial German withdrawal in that sector. Hitler ordered the German troops to stand fast, however, and they dug in for the winter. By the spring of 1942, when major military operations resumed, the Germans were still deep within the Soviet Union and Hitler could plan a renewed assault aimed at forcing Russia to surrender.

Hitler increasingly took personal command of the German troops on the eastern front, issuing orders to his commanders and interfering with military operations. His plans for 1942 had two primary objectives: the capture of Leningrad in the north, and a drive upon the Donets industrial basin in the Ukraine and the Caucasus oil fields in southern Russia. By midsummer, the Germans still had been unable to capture Leningrad. To the south, the Germans drove the Russians back and were advancing toward the vital oil fields. Hitler now turned his attention upon the city of Stalingrad, to protect his left flank from Soviet counterattack.

Stalingrad, an industrial city, was situated on the Volga River. If the city could be captured, vital river traffic, especially oil being shipped to Moscow, could be stopped. Furthermore, an attack would draw in the Russian army to battle the German forces with the expectation of further German victories. Hitler believed that Russian reserves were small and the defeat of these Soviet troops would topple Stalin's regime. To achieve his goal, he ordered General Friedrich Paulus and the German Sixth Army to capture Stalingrad and seize the left bank of the Volga in order to halt river traffic.

Troops of the Sixth Army reached the Stalingrad area by late August. As foreseen, the Russians rallied to the defense of the city. During the extended fighting, lasting several months, the city was reduced to rubble. This made the German task even more difficult, for pockets of resistance within the city continued to plague the Germans even after the main portion of the town was taken. Fighting continued into November.

Meanwhile General Georgy Zhukov, in charge of overall Soviet forces, planned a counteroffensive to relieve Stalingrad and break the German advance toward the Caucasus region. Because Paulus' Sixth Army was overextended and German troops were forced to cover a long flank, Zhukov formed two armies, commanded by General Andrei Yeremenko and General Konstantin Rokossovski. Their assignment was to encircle the Germans. On November 19, 1942, these two armies began an enveloping maneuver to trap Paulus in Stalingrad. By November 24, Paulus and 250,000 men were encircled in the Stalingrad "pocket."

The Germans had a reasonable chance to break out from the Stalingrad area until approximately mid-December. Despite pleas from his generals, Hitler ordered Paulus to stand fast and hold the ground already captured. The German führer also ordered Field Marshal Erich von Manstein, commander of Germany Army Group Don, to advance toward Stalingrad to lift the siege and supply Paulus. Hermann Göring, commander of the Luftwaffe, the German air force, assured Hitler that he could supply Paulus by air.

When it became apparent that the Luftwaffe would not be able to carry out its task, partly because of logistical problems and severe weather conditions, Manstein asked Hitler to order Paulus to break out of the city and join his relief force; otherwise, Manstein said he would not be able to relieve Paulus. Hitler refused Manstein's request, for the possession of Stalingrad had become a point of prestige. Manstein's forces fought their way to within thirty miles of Stalingrad, but could get no farther, especially after Zhukov launched an offensive against his supply lines.

By early January, 1943, Paulus had lost any chance of breaking out of the encirclement. His troops were tired, cold, hungry, and lacked adequate ammunition. Relentless Soviet attacks, plus growing casualties and freezing weather, wore down the Germans in the "pocket." Hitler still ordered Paulus not to surrender but to fight to the last man if necessary. He even promoted Paulus to the rank of Field Marshal, on the theory that no German officer of such high rank had surrendered. Yet Paulus' men could not resist further, and on January 31, 1943, the Sixth Army capitulated to the Russians. All fighting ended by February 2. Approximately one hundred thousand Germans became prisoners when the battle ended.

Casualties on both sides in the Stalingrad campaign likely will never be known with precision. Estimates suggest that as many as two hundred thousand Germans had died by the final capitulation. Germany and its allies (Hungarians, Italians, and Romanians) may have suffered as many as one million total casualties in the overall campaign. Soviet military casualties are estimated at a minimum of 750,000 killed, wounded, and missing. Civilian losses are in addition. These numbers scarcely begin to convey the full horror of the battle for the participants.

The massive German defeat at Stalingrad marked the turn of the tide on the eastern front, for they never again won a major battle in that region. Powerful and numerically superior Soviet forces now undertook a series of offensive campaigns to liberate their nation from Nazi control. They continued to push the Germans back for the next two years, until the Russians captured Berlin in April, 1945, and World War II came to an end in early May.

—José M. Sánchez, updated by Taylor Stults

ADDITIONAL READING:

Carell, Paul. *Hitler Moves East, 1941-1943*. Translated by Ewald Osers. Boston: Little, Brown, 1965. Comprehensive coverage of military campaigns on the eastern front.

Chuikov, Vasily I. *The Battle for Stalingrad*. New York: Holt, Rinehart & Winston, 1964. Memoirs by the Russian commander of the Sixty-second Army at Stalingrad.

Craig, William. *Enemy at the Gates: The Battle for Stalingrad*. New York: E. P. Dutton, 1973. Includes events leading to the Stalingrad campaign, plus many details of the battle itself.

Goerlitz, Walter. *Paulus and Stalingrad*. New York: Citadel Press, 1964. Uneven but useful biography of the German commander of the Sixth Army.

Richardson, William, and Seymour Freiden, eds. *The Fatal Decisions*. Translated by Constantine FitzGibbon. London: Michael Joseph, 1956. Includes a useful analysis of the Stalingrad campaign, by the former chief of the German army General Staff.

Tarrant, V. E. *Stalingrad: Anatomy of an Agony*. New York: Hippocrene Books, 1992. Clearly written account based on German and Russian sources.

Ziemke, Earl F., and M. E. Bauer. *Moscow to Stalingrad: Decision in the East*. New York: Military Heritage Press, 1988. Covers the 1941 German invasion to the end of the Stalingrad campaign in early 1943.

SEE ALSO: 1939, Nazi-Soviet Pact; 1939, Germany Invades Poland; 1945, The Yalta Conference.

1942
BATTLE OF EL ALAMEIN

The Battle of El Alamein pits British forces in the Middle East against the German Afrika Corps and results in a British victory.

DATE: October 23-November 3, 1942
LOCALE: El Alamein, Egypt
CATEGORY: Wars, uprisings, and civil unrest
KEY FIGURES:

Sir Harold Rupert Leofric George Alexander (1891-1969), commander in chief of British forces in the Middle East, 1942-1943

Sir Claude John Eyre Auchinleck (1884-1981), commander in chief of British forces in the Middle East, 1941-1942

Sir Alan Francis Brooke (1883-1963), chief of the British General Staff, 1941-1946

Sir Winston Leonard Spencer Churchill (1874-1965), prime minister of Great Britain, 1940-1945

Rodolfo Graziani, marchese di Neghelli (1882-1955), Italian commander in Libya, 1940-1941

Adolf Hitler (1889-1945), chancellor and führer of Germany, 1933-1945

Bernard Law Montgomery (1887-1976), commander of the British Eighth Army, 1942

Erich Raeder (1876-1960), admiral and commander in chief of the German navy

Erwin Johannes Eugen Rommel (1891-1944), commander of the German Afrika Korps, 1941-1943

Sir Archibald Percival Wavell (1883-1950), commander in chief of British forces in the Middle East, 1938-1941

SUMMARY OF EVENT. Declaration of war on the Allies by Italy in June, 1940, gave the British the opportunity of striking at Italy's possessions in North Africa. Fighting alone against Germany and Italy, the British were in no position to mount an offensive on the European continent, and it was essential for them to hold the "Imperial Lifeline" of Gibraltar, Malta, and Suez. Victory in North Africa would not only help to maintain British control in the Mediterranean but would also weaken the enemy. Accordingly, Winston Churchill, the British prime minister, and General Sir Alan Brooke, chief of the Imperial General Staff, ordered General Sir Archibald Wavell, commander of Middle East Forces, to begin operations against the Italian army in North Africa.

Throughout 1940 and 1941, Wavell's small but highly trained forces inflicted defeat after defeat on the Italian troops under the command of Marshal Rodolfo Graziani, and drove them out of Libya and Ethiopia. Hundreds of thousands of Italians surrendered to the British. The cam-

paign was an outstanding success as far as it went.

Adolph Hitler, chancellor and führer of Germany, began to be perturbed over his ally's losses. Grand Admiral Erich Raeder, though officially commander of the German navy, was probably the best strategist among Hitler's military advisers, and he advised Hitler to send large forces to North Africa to sever the "Imperial Lifeline," capture Suez, and gain the oil riches of the Middle East. Toward the end of 1940, however, Hitler had committed himself to the invasion of Russia, and he would agree to sending only a small force to North Africa, appointing General Erwin Rommel as commander.

Rommel, who became known as the "Desert Fox," arrived in Africa at a propitious moment. Wavell had been forced to send many of his troops to the defense of Greece, and the British forces were weak when Rommel began an offensive in April, 1941. The British were pushed back eastward toward Cairo. As a countermeasure, Churchill and Brooke appointed General Sir Claude Auchinleck as commander of British forces in the Middle East. It was not a good choice, and when Auchinleck, never a forceful soldier, found himself in a poor defensive position, he gave more ground to Rommel, who captured the key town of Tobruk in June, 1942. The British fell back to a fine defensive position at El Alamein, sixty-five miles from Alexandria and the Nile Delta. Anchored on the sea and running to the Qattara Depression in the south, the thirty-mile front could not be flanked.

In desperation, Churchill and Brooke replaced Auchinleck with General Sir Harold Alexander. To command the main British force, they appointed General Bernard Montgomery as commander of the British Eighth Army. Montgomery immediately realized the military situation and planned an offensive that would turn back the Axis forces.

When Rommel tried to resume the offensive in September, Montgomery forced him to a standstill at the Battle of Alam el Halfa. Meanwhile British troops and supplies, particularly tanks, were arriving in great numbers, while the Germans were overextended and suffering a severe scarcity of fuel. Because of the "Ultra Secret," coded German radio traffic reached British commanders as quickly as it reached Rommel. Knowing when shipments of fuel were scheduled, the British were able to destroy the vast majority of such transports before the ships could reach their destination. By mid-October, the British had numerical superiority in men, tanks, air power and artillery.

On October 23, 1942, Montgomery struck. At this crucial moment, Rommel was on sick leave in Germany. He hurried back to take command of the Axis forces, but the British were able to force a break in his lines and, in a tank battle that lasted a week, Rommel's forces were defeated. Rommel had ordered a systematic general withdrawal to positions nearer his source of supplies. Hitler personally insisted that the position at El Alamein be held at all costs. When Rommel finally ordered the retreat on November 3, the situation was desperate; much of the German armor and nonmotorized infantry units were lost. Montgomery had achieved the first major defeat of a German army in World War II.

The Battle of El Alamein has been hailed by the British as a major turning point in the war. German military historians generally agree with this assessment. To the British, it was their last great single victory over the Axis. The final day of the battle coincided with the Anglo-American invasion of northwest Africa. These two events, coupled with the German defeat at Stalingrad two months later, put the Germans on the defensive for the remainder of the war. El Alamein also highlighted the importance of winning the battle of supply in modern warfare.   —*Art Barbeau*

ADDITIONAL READING:

Bryant, Arthur. *The Turn of the Tide: A History of the War Years Based on the Diaries of Field Marshal Lord Alanbrooke*. Garden City, N.Y.: Doubleday, 1957.

Churchill, Winston S. *The Second World War*. Vol. 4: *The Hinge of Fate*. Boston: Houghton Mifflin, 1950.

Montgomery of Alamein, Field Marshal. *Memoirs*. Cleveland: World Publishing Company, 1958.

Rommel, Field Marshal Erwin. *The Rommel Papers*. Edited by Captain B. H. Liddle Hart. Translated by Paul Findlay. New York: Harcourt, Brace, and World, 1953.

The above are pertinent memoirs of the leading figures in the Battle of El Alamein.

Carver, General Michael. *El Alamein*. New York: Macmillan, 1962. A thorough, reasoned, and objective account of the battle, placing the opposing leaders in perspective. Carver is sympathetic to Rommel's problems, particularly his lack of material support, but he blames Rommel for originally overextending his chosen position

General Bernard Montgomery watches his British tanks advance on the North African front in November of 1942. (National Archives)

at El Alamein. In the end, Carver says: "The victory was won by the determination, realism, and professional skill of Montgomery; the greatly superior material at his disposal . . . and his superiority in numbers of men."

Freiden, Seymour, and William Richardson, eds. *The Fatal Decisions*. New York: Berkeley Publishing Corporation, 1956. Freiden and Richardson present reports on six major battles of World War II, each written by one of the German commanders present at the battle. Lieutenant-General Fritz Bayerlein, who was chief of staff of the Afrika Korps and then held the same position on Rommel's staff, presents his account of the battle of El Alamein.

Jacobsen, H. A., and J. Rohwer, eds. *Decisive Battles of World War II: The German View*. Translated by Edward Fitzgerald. New York: G. P. Putnam's Sons, 1965. A history of World War II written by German military historians who present the German view of the war. Because some of the contributors had formerly been highly placed military men, they are able to give readers the benefit of their hindsight as well as their research.

Lucas, James. *War in the Desert*. New York: Beaufort Books, 1982. One of the best accounts of El Alamein, putting the final battle in its proper perspective. Lucas' own service in the desert provides insights lacking in many other accounts. Lucas is among the few writers to give the "Ultra Secret" its proper place in the victory, and the crucial role of air power is better illustrated by Lucas than in many other accounts.

Moorehead, Alan. *The March to Tunis: The North African War, 1940-1943*. New York: Harper & Row, 1967. A reportorial history of the entire African campaign.

Philips, C. E. Lucas. *Alamein*. Boston: Little, Brown, 1962. A popular writer, Philips concentrates on narrative, making Montgomery a hero, while Rommel is less than a villain.

Young, Desmond. *Rommel: The Desert Fox*. New York: Harper & Row, 1951. Flattering biography of the German commander at the Battle of El Alamein.

SEE ALSO: 1898-1899, The Fashoda Incident; 1911-1912, Italy Annexes Libya; 1935-1936, Italy Conquers Ethiopia; 1940-1941, Battle of Britain; 1942, Stand at Stalingrad; 1943, The Casablanca Conference.

1943
THE CASABLANCA CONFERENCE

The Casablanca Conference allows British and American diplomats to establish policies and draw up a blueprint for the Allied conduct of World War II in Europe and the Pacific.

DATE: January 14-24, 1943
LOCALE: Casablanca, Morocco
CATEGORY: Diplomacy and international relations
KEY FIGURES:
Sir Harold Rupert Leofric George Alexander (1891-1969), British commander in chief of Middle East Forces
Sir Alan Francis Brooke (1883-1963), chief of the British General Staff, 1941-1946
Sir Winston Leonard Spencer Churchill (1874-1965), prime minister of Great Britain, 1940-1945
Charles-Andre-Joseph-Marie de Gaulle (1890-1970), French general and head of the French Committee of National Liberation
Dwight David Eisenhower (1890-1969), American general and supreme Allied commander in North Africa and the western Mediterranean
Henri Honoré Giraud (1879-1949), French commander in North Africa
Harry Lloyd Hopkins (1890-1946), special assistant to Roosevelt
Ernest Joseph King (1878-1956), American admiral and chief of U.S. naval operations, 1942-1945
George Catlett Marshall (1880-1959), American general and chief of staff of the U.S. Army
Franklin Delano Roosevelt (1882-1945), thirty-second president of the United States, 1933-1945
Joseph Stalin (Iosif Vissarionovich Dzhugashvili; 1879-1953), premier of the Soviet Union, 1924-1953

SUMMARY OF EVENT. Late in 1942, after the defeat of the Axis forces at the Battle of El Alamein and after the Anglo-American invasion of northwest Africa, President Franklin D. Roosevelt suggested a meeting of the Allied leaders to plan further wartime strategy. Prime Minister Winston Churchill of Great Britain accepted, but Soviet dictator Joseph Stalin declined because the Battle of Stalingrad had just begun and he could not leave his country. The recently liberated town of Casablanca in Morocco was selected for the conference, which opened on January 14, 1943.

Roosevelt was accompanied by his chief civilian adviser, Harry Hopkins, and by his two military advisers, General George C. Marshall, chief of staff of the U.S. Army, and Admiral Ernest King, chief of U.S. naval operations. Churchill arrived with his military and naval advisers, notably General Sir Alan Brooke, chief of the British General Staff. The Allied leaders had no difficulty in agreeing upon a number of military matters, such as continuation of the bombing of Germany and the priority given to naval resources to transport supplies across the Atlantic. Nor did they oppose each other on the French problem. With the liberation of French Africa, the Allies had to find a leader for the French. Instead of turning to General Charles de Gaulle, leader of the Free French forces, whom both Churchill and Roosevelt distrusted, they selected General Henri Giraud as supreme French commander for North Africa. Considerably angered by this selection, de Gaulle refused to have anything to do with Giraud or his government. At Casablanca, Roosevelt and Churchill invited de Gaulle to make peace with Giraud and named him commander with Giraud; a temporary reconciliation was reluctantly achieved.

The problem that revealed disagreement was the planning of future strategy. The British wanted a continuation of the war in the Mediterranean until a large number of troops could be concentrated for a cross-Channel invasion of France. Churchill hoped that Italy could be invaded and forced to surrender, which in turn would bring Turkey in on the Allied side and perhaps permit an invasion of the Balkans. In this way, Germany could be attacked through the "soft-underbelly of Europe." Maximum gains could be exploited with a minimum risk without committing insufficient troops to a difficult struggle in France. The Americans, particularly Marshall and King, opposed this plan. They viewed Mediterranean action as merely diversionary and said that the only way Germany could be brought to defeat was through a massive cross-Channel invasion.

King was particularly opposed to the British idea and threatened to divert landing-craft production to the war against Japan in the Pacific, which he believed should have the priority anyway. He was overruled, however, by Roosevelt on the basis of a 1940 agreement among the American chiefs of staff that in a two-front war, the European conflict should take priority. Roosevelt agreed to a limited continuation of the Mediterranean war, and General Dwight D. Eisenhower was appointed supreme commander of the Allied forces in the Mediterranean. His deputy was the British commander, General Sir Harold Alexander. Eisenhower and Alexander were told to plan an invasion of Sicily that would take place when the Axis powers were driven out of North Africa. In the meantime, planning of the cross-Channel invasion proceeded.

Twelve decisions emerged from the conference. Three were rather unimportant, but nine became significant to the overall planning and implementation process of the Allied powers during the war. They included strengthening the attacks on U-boats in the North Atlantic; stepping up the strategic bombing of Germany; providing material support for Russia; going on a limited offensive in the Pacific, specifically attacking Rabaul; opening up the Burma Road and supporting China; increasing air activities in China-Burma; stabilizing North Africa and invad-

ing Sicily; agreeing to plan for opening up the western front; and adopting a policy for the unconditional surrender of Germany, Italy, and Japan.

The most controversial decision made at Casablanca appeared to be impromptu. Roosevelt, who remembered the mistakes made by Woodrow Wilson during World War I, wanted to send a clear message that the forms of government in the Axis countries were unacceptable, and their defeat and removal were significant as an objective of the Allies. He would frequently reiterate this position throughout the war. Thus, at a press conference held on the final day at Casablanca, Roosevelt announced that the "elimination of German, Japanese, and Italian war power means the unconditional surrender by Germany, Italy, and Japan. He went on to say that he did not mean the destruction of the people of those countries but rather "the destruction of the philosophies which are based on conquest and the subjugation of other people." Reportedly taken aback by this statement, Churchill nevertheless indicated his agreement.

Critics came to contend that the statement of unconditional surrender hurt the Allied cause more than it helped, for it indicated to the Axis people that nothing less than total defeat would be accepted and therefore prolonged the war and reduced the chances of resistance groups within those countries overthrowing the regimes in order to obtain reasonable concessions from the Allies. Furthermore, such critics have maintained, Roosevelt's statement established an idealistic goal that could be achieved only with great human suffering and which was not in accord with the realities of the conflict.

Other scholars have disagreed, pointing out that the policy did not undercut resistance groups in Germany, who were not strong enough to succeed. Some historians have argued that the policy was unimportant to the Germans until late in the war, when it did provide some propaganda value. Ultimately, it allowed the Allies to defeat the Axis powers "according to an accepted formula," and although it did not allay Allied suspicions of one another, it obviously lessened them to some extent.

—José M. Sánchez,
updated by Robert Franklin Maddox

ADDITIONAL READING:

Armstrong, Anne. *Unconditional Surrender: The Impact of the Casablanca Conference on World War II.* New Brunswick, N.J.: Rutgers University Press, 1961. The author analyzes the impact of the unconditional surrender policy on the conduct of the war and on the Germans.

Churchill, Winston S. *The Second World War.* Vol. 4: *The Hinge of Fate.* Boston: Houghton Mifflin, 1950. This volume includes Churchill's memoirs of the Casablanca Conference.

Feis, Herbert. *Churchill, Roosevelt, Stalin*. Princeton, N.J.: Princeton University Press, 1957. Written by a distinguished diplomatic historian, this solid work analyzes the major events at the Casablanca Conference.

Kimball, Warren F. *The Juggler: Franklin Roosevelt as Wartime Statesman*. Princeton, N.J.: Princeton University Press, 1991. Kimball places emphasis on Roosevelt's personal diplomacy and sees Casablanca and unconditional surrender as a commitment of Russia to the Allied effort and a sense that the Anglo-Americans would run the show after the war.

Sherwood, Robert E. *Roosevelt and Hopkins*. New York: Harper & Row, 1948. This work gives a thorough treatment of the Roosevelt polices from the perspective of a close adviser.

Smith, Gaddis. *American Diplomacy During the Second World War*. New York: Harper & Row, 1985. This work does not regard the statement of unconditional surrender as being particularly important.

Wilt, Alan F. "The Significance of the Casablanca Decisions, January, 1943." *The Journal of Military History* 55 (October, 1991): 517-529. The author concludes that this meeting provided a realistic agenda for the Anglo-American conduct of the war.

SEE ALSO: 1942, Stand at Stalingrad; 1942, Battle of El Alamein; 1943, Allied Invasion of Italy; 1944, Allied Invasion of France.

1943
ALLIED INVASION OF ITALY

The Allied invasion of Italy is initially planned as a temporary substitute for the cross-Channel invasion of France, but becomes an unexpectedly costly effort surrounded by controversy and mixed results.

DATE: September 3 and 9, 1943
LOCALE: Reggio, Taranto, and Salerno, Italy
CATEGORY: Wars, uprisings, and civil unrest
KEY FIGURES:
Pietro Badoglio (1871-1956), premier of Italy, 1943-1944
Sir Winston Leonard Spencer Churchill (1874-1965), British prime minister, 1940-1945
General Mark Wayne Clark (1896-1984), U.S. Army commander in North Africa and Italy
General Dwight Eisenhower (1890-1969), supreme Allied commander in the western Mediterranean
Adolf Hitler (1889-1945), chancellor and führer of Germany, 1933-1945

Field Marshal Albert Kesselring (1885-1960), German commander on Mediterranean and Italian fronts
General George Catlett Marshall (1880-1959), chief of staff of the U.S. Army
General Bernard Law Montgomery (1887-1976), commander of the British Eighth Army
Benito Amilcare Andrea Mussolini (1883-1945), Fascist premier of Italy, 1922-1943
Franklin Delano Roosevelt (1882-1945), thirty-second president of the United States, 1933-1945
Victor Emmanuel III (1869-1947), king of Italy, 1900-1946

SUMMARY OF EVENT. After the American and British leaders had agreed at the Casablanca Conference upon an invasion of Sicily after the Axis powers were defeated in North Africa, Prime Minister Winston Churchill of Great Britain came to Washington, D.C., in May, 1943, to confer with President Franklin D. Roosevelt. Noting the rapidity with which the Axis forces had been driven out of North Africa, Churchill proposed that the Allies invade Italy at the earliest possible moment to take advantage of Italian war-weariness and perhaps force an Italian surrender.

Roosevelt and General George C. Marshall, chief of staff of the U.S. Army, were opposed to the idea of committing large numbers of troops to an invasion of Italy, which they considered a merely diversionary effort. Instead, they proposed that the troops be sent to England to prepare for a cross-Channel invasion of France. Nevertheless, they gave in to Churchill's urgings and agreed to a limited invasion of Italy, but specified that troops from the Mediterranean were to be transported to England on schedule no matter what occurred in Italy. General Dwight D. Eisenhower, supreme Allied commander in the Mediterranean, was ordered to command the operation.

Sicily was invaded in July, 1943. Within a month, Italian and German forces on the island were defeated. Success led the Allies to believe that a minimal use of force could be employed to invade the Italian mainland and quickly defeat the German and Italian defenders.

Events in Italy confirmed their hopes, but also raised problems. On July 24-25, Benito Mussolini, the Fascist dictator of Italy, met with the Fascist Grand Council to discuss the problem of Italian defeatism. The Italian people were clearly tired of the war and a recent bombing of Rome had raised the clamor for peace. The council recommended that Mussolini be dismissed. When Mussolini appealed to King Victor Emmanuel III, the monarch dismissed and arrested him. Marshal Pietro Badoglio was appointed premier of Italy. The Fascist dictatorship was overthrown.

Although the king and Badoglio wanted to surrender

Italy to the Allies, they had to take account of the German plans. Adolf Hitler, chancellor and führer of Germany, had no intention of allowing the Allies to capture Italy by the simple act of a surrender by the king. Hitler ordered the German commander in Italy, Field Marshal Albert Kesselring to look into the situation. Kesselring recommended that large numbers of German troops be brought into Italy to fight the Allies if Italy should surrender or if the Allies should invade. Hitler ordered the troops sent to Kesselring. Badoglio, aware that German troops were concen-

took place on September 9, when the American Fifth Army, commanded by General Mark Wayne Clark, landed at Salerno, south of Naples.

The fighting immediately bogged down. The Germans had moved enough troops into Italy to contain the Allies, and the rugged terrain of southern Italy further slowed the Allied advance. No additional troops could be sent to Italy, nor could the transfer of troops to England for D-day preparation be stopped. It was not until June, 1944, that the Allies were able to capture Rome; when Germany

In 1944, Allied troops marched through the bombed out ruins of the city of Cassino in central Italy. (Archive Photos)

trating in Italy, wanted to surrender, but to avoid German occupation of Italy in its entirety, he was unwilling to sign the surrender instrument until the Allies landed an invasion force. He contacted the Allies and indicated his willingness to surrender, but only on the condition that the Allies invade when the surrender took effect. The Allies, having recently issued a statement that nothing less than unconditional surrender would be accepted, had to scrutinize Badoglio's plea to decide whether and when it could be accepted.

Over a month of secret negotiations took place. In the meantime, German troops poured into Italy, taking up defensive positions. The document was finally signed on September 3, 1943, and on the same day, elements of the British Eighth Army, commanded by General Bernard Law Montgomery, landed at Reggio. The largest invasion

surrendered in May, 1945, the Allied armies were still fighting in northern Italy in what was probably the most difficult campaign of the entire war.

—José M. Sánchez, updated by John Quinn Imholte

ADDITIONAL READING:

Deakin, Frederick. *The Brutal Friendship*. New York: Harper & Row, 1962. A discussion of Italian war-weariness leading directly to Mussolini's removal. The author argues that protracted negotiations over the Italian surrender to the Allies enabled the German defenders to build up their defensive strength.

Graham, Dominick, and Shelford Bidwell. *Tug of War: The Battle for Italy, 1943-1945*. New York: St. Martin's Press, 1986. For both general and more serious readers. Not a blow-by-blow account, but rather a lucid history of a complicated campaign. Special attention is given to General Mark Clark.

Howard, Michael. *The Mediterranean Strategy in the Second World War*. London: Greenhill Books, 1968. Three brief, first-rate lectures delivered in 1966 by the British historian, Michael Howard. Emphasis is on the less than coherent Mediterranean strategy and its effect on American strategic planning.

Jackson, W. G. F. *The Battle for Italy*. New York: Harper & Row, 1967. The author was a British participant in the planning for the invasion. An objective and well-documented presentation of the arguments for and against decisions that were made. At the very least, the Italian campaign was a valuable rehearsal for the upcoming invasion of France.

Lamb, Richard. *The War in Italy, 1943-1945: A Brutal Story*. New York: St. Martin's Press, 1993. Lamb served as a British officer in the Italian campaign. His book is a blunt and thoughtful account of the immediate results of the campaign.

Lorelli, John A. *To Foreign Shores: U.S. Amphibious Operations in World War II*. Annapolis, Md.: Naval Institute Press, 1995. Description of the planning and execution of "Avalanche," the invasion at Salerno. Through use of the index, the book is a good source for gaining a brief account of the American amphibious offensive.

SEE ALSO: 1942, Battle of El Alamein; 1943, The Casablanca Conference; 1944, Allied Invasion of France; 1944-1945, Battle of the Bulge; 1945, The Yalta Conference.

1944
ALLIED INVASION OF FRANCE

The Allied invasion of France is one of the most complicated military exercises in history and, along with the invasion of southern France, provides Allied forces with beachheads from which German forces can be attacked.

DATE: June 6, 1944, and August 10, 1944

LOCALE: France's Normandy and Mediterranean beaches

CATEGORY: Wars, uprisings, and civil unrest

KEY FIGURES:

Sir Winston Leonard Spencer Churchill (1874-1965), British prime minister, 1940-1945

General Dwight David Eisenhower (1890-1969), supreme commander of the Allied Expeditionary Force

Adolf Hitler (1889-1945), chancellor and führer of Germany, 1933-1945

General George Catlett Marshall (1880-1959), chief of staff of the U.S. Army

General Bernard Law Montgomery (1887-1976), commander of the Allied armies in northern France

Field Marshal Erwin Johannes Eugen Rommel (1891-1944), German commander of Army Group B and inspector of coastal defenses

Franklin Delano Roosevelt (1882-1945), thirty-second president of the United States, 1933-1945

Field Marshal Karl Rudolf Gerd von Rundstedt (1875-1953), German commander in chief of the western front

SUMMARY OF EVENT. After the German victory over France in 1940, one of the main objectives of the Allied powers was to invade France and inflict defeat upon Germany. Indeed, when the United States entered the European conflict in 1941, American generals proposed an immediate Anglo-American invasion of France as the first and most important step in defeating Germany. This proposal for an immediate invasion did not match British plans; Winston Churchill, was afraid that an invasion with the limited resources then available would fail. He proposed instead that an attack upon German and Italian troops in the Mediterranean would offer greater advantages with fewer troops.

Franklin D. Roosevelt, together with General George C. Marshall, continued to press for an invasion of France. So also did Joseph Stalin, the Soviet dictator, who wanted a second front to take German pressure off the battlefields in Russia. Although adequate troops were available, landing craft were insufficient for such a large operation because they were divided between the Pacific and European theaters. It was not until 1944 that the Allies had sufficient craft to support an invasion of France.

In 1943, planning for two invasions of France, named Operations Hammer (later named Overlord) and Anvil (later named Dragoon) began. As the time for invasion came closer, however, the Allies abandoned the Hammer and Anvil plan for strategic and practical reasons. First, Winston Churchill wanted Allied forces to move east out of Italy and opposed drawing down the Italian occupying forces to invade southern France. Second, resources were simply inadequate to launch two invasions simultaneously. For these reasons, invasion planners decided to concentrate on the Normandy invasion. Operation Dragoon was postponed until after Operation Overlord had been completed.

Planning for Operation Overlord required Anglo-American troops to be moved from the Mediterranean, where an invasion of Italy had already taken place, to a staging area in southern England. The invasion was scheduled to take place in May or June of 1944. General Dwight D. Eisenhower and British general Bernard Law Montgomery, the hero of El Alamein, were appointed to command the Twenty-first Army Group, the main Allied land force. The beaches of Normandy were selected for the primary invasion. Eisenhower knew that the invasion would have to be successful on the first day; with the scarcity of landing craft, a beachhead had to be established in order to land enough men to achieve numerical superiority over the German defenders. Thus, everything depended on the outcome of the first day's operations.

On the Continent, Adolf Hitler was aware that the Allies were planning an invasion and had ordered his armies to construct coastal defenses in northern France. In 1944, he appointed Field Marshal Erwin Rommel as commander of Army Group B, the main German army in northern France. He also made Rommel inspector of coastal defenses. Because Hitler retained personal command of the entire defense operation, there was much overlapping of responsibility, producing poor defense planning.

Field Marshal von Rundstedt contended that the Allies would be able to land anywhere along the coast, and therefore the best defense would be to hold armor in reserve and send it to the battlefield after the Allies landed. The Allies anticipated this strategy, and in the spring of 1944, they bombed communication and transportation lines along the entire coastal area to prevent the armor from moving fast enough to prevent the establishment of a beachhead. Given the air situation, Rommel believed that the best chance of defense lay in making a guess where the Allies would land and building up coastal defenses in that area. Like Eisenhower, Rommel knew that all would be decided on the first day. Rommel chose the Pas de Calais area for his strong defense.

The Allies waited patiently for the proper combination of tides and weather. Then, on June 6, 1944, Operation Overlord began. It was one of the largest combined air, sea, and land operations in history. After a day of bitter fighting, the Allies established a beachhead at Normandy. Both Rommel and Hitler believed that the Normandy invasion was a feint for a larger invasion at Calais and kept troops away form Normandy. Von Rundstedt was unable to move his armor in time to stem the Allied troops.

During the preliminary planning for the invasion of Europe, the Allies planned landings in the south of France as part of a strategy that would force German forces in France to defend their conquests on two fronts at once. The first Allied bombing attacks began in April, 1944, and intensified throughout the summer until the actual invasion on August 10. German planners assumed that the Allies would attempt to invade by landing on the broad beaches between Nice and Cannes and, partly because of orders given by Field Marshal Erwin Rommel during a May inspection, built extensive and elaborate defensive structures in the area.

The Riviera defenses were never tested. Ten divisions of the American Seventh Army, led by General Alexander M. Patch, Jr., and the French First Army, led by General de Lattre de Tassigny, landed on the beaches east of Toulon. The first landing on the mainland took place at Cap-Nègre, and the islands of Levant and Port-Cros were secured. These successes were followed by landings farther to the east on the beaches of Cavalaire, Pampelonne, Saint-Raphael, Cap de Dramont, and Anthéor.

After the successful invasion French units moved west toward Toulon and Marseilles, and American units moved east. Cannes and Antibes fell on August 25, and Nice and Lyon were liberated on August 28. The Allies then proceeded north through the Rhône valley. Lyons fell on September 3; on September 10, a forward unit of Free French fighters met units from Leclerc's second armored division at Sombernon, a town slightly west of Dijon. The northern and southern invasion forces were finally linked.

—José M. Sánchez, updated by C. James Haug

ADDITIONAL READING:

Azema, Jean-Pierre. *From Munich to the Liberation: 1938-1944.* Translated by Janet Lloyd. New York: Cambridge University Press, 1984. Written by a leading French leftist historian of the Third Republic and Vichy, this work examines the role of the Resistance and the Free French in liberating France.

Clarke, Jeffrey J., and Robert R. Smith. *Riviera to the Rhine.* Washington, D.C.: Center of Military History, U.S. Army, 1993. An illustrated, commemorative work that extols the virtues of the U.S. Army.

Jacobsen, H. A., and J. Rohwer, eds. *Decisive Battles of World War II: The German View.* Translated by Edward Fitzgerald. New York: G. P. Putnam's Sons, 1965. Outlines the German failings that led to Allied success. The work attributes the Allied success to a superior chain of command.

Wilmot, Chester. *The Struggle for Europe.* New York: Harper & Row, 1952. In this study written from an Anglophile perspective, Wilmot is critical of Eisenhower and American soldiers in general.

Wilt, Alan F. *The French Riviera Campaign of August, 1944.* Carbondale: Southern Illinois University Press, 1981. A workmanlike and detailed discussion of the Allied invasion of southern France.

SEE ALSO: 1943, The Casablanca Conference; 1943, Allied Invasion of Italy; 1944-1945, Battle of the Bulge.

WORLD WAR II: THE FIGHT FOR EUROPE

1939

Sept. 1	German forces invade Poland. *See* **1939 Germany Invades Poland.**
Sept. 3	Great Britain declares war on Germany.
Sept. 17	Soviet troops invade Poland, crossing its eastern border.
Nov. 30	Soviet forces launch an unprovoked air attack on Helsinki, marking the beginning of its war against Finland. *See* **1939-1940 Russo-Finnish War.**

1940

Apr. 9	Germany invades Norway. *See* **1940 German Invasion of Norway.**
May 10	Germany invades Luxembourg, the Netherlands, and Belgium.
May 11	British prime minister Neville Chamberlain is succeeded by Winston Churchill.
May 28-June 11	EVACUATION OF DUNKIRK: Nearly 350,000 French and British troops leave France. *See* **1940 Evacuation of Dunkirk.**

WORLD WAR II: THE EUROPEAN THEATER, 1943-1944

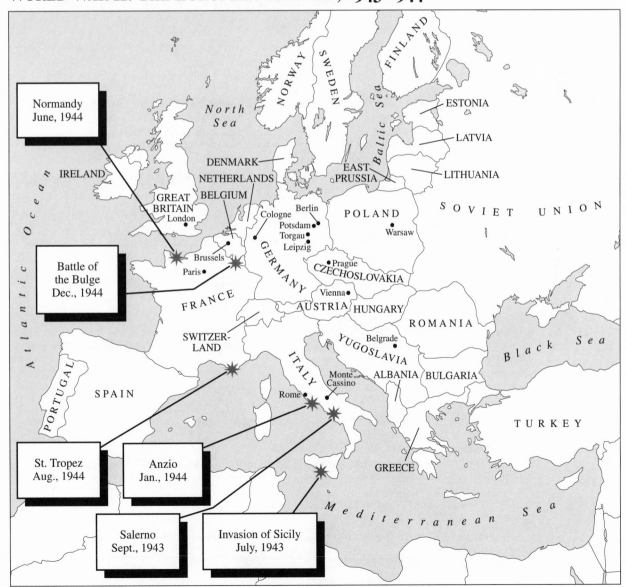

1940 *continued*

June 5	BATTLE OF FRANCE: Germans invade France across the Somme River and the Aisne-Oise canal. *See* **1940 Collapse of France.**
June 10	Italy declares war on France and Great Britain. Italian forces enter southern France.
June 14	German forces enter Paris.
Aug. 8-Oct. 31	BATTLE OF BRITAIN: Germany bombs Great Britain in preparation for a land invasion as part of Operation Sea Lion; despite great losses on both sides, British air squadrons repulse German air power and avoid German occupation. *See* **1940-1941 Battle of Britain.**
Oct. 8	Germany occupies Romania.
Oct. 28	Italy invades Greece.

1941

Feb.-May	Germany mounts a naval campaign against Allies and neutral powers in the Atlantic Ocean, using submarines as well as battleships.
Mar. 11	Despite dwindling finances, Great Britain is able to secure war matériel from the United States under the terms of the Lend-Lease Act.
Mar. 24	German general Erwin Rommel begins a North African campaign forcing the British to retreat to Egypt.
Apr. 17	Yugoslavia falls to the Germans.
Apr. 23	Greece falls to the Germans.
June 18	French general Charles de Gaulle pledges continued French resistance against coming Vichy dictatorship. *See* **1940-1944 The French Resistance.**
June 22	France under Henri Philippe Pétain signs a German-French armistice; a similar armistice with Italy is signed two days later. Pétain is installed at Vichy as French dictator on July 10.
June 22	Germany invades the Soviet Union; occupies Ukraine, then Leningrad, then Sevastopol, reaching Moscow by November.
Sept. 24	Fifteen nations have endorsed the anti-Axis Atlantic Charter, drawn up by Roosevelt and Churchill during secret talks conducted aboard U.S. and British ships in August. *See* **1941 Atlantic Charter Is Signed.**
Nov. 1	United States extends lend-lease credit to the Soviet Union.
Dec. 11	Germany and Italy declare war on the United States, and the United States responds with its own declaration.

1942

Jan. 20	Russians begin German counteroffensive.
May 30	Allies begin their thousand-bomber air raids on Germany.
Sept. 13	Germans enter Stalingrad. *See* **1942-1943 Stand at Stalingrad.**
Nov. 4	BATTLE OF EL ALAMEIN: British victory forces a German retreat from Egypt. U.S. and British amphibious forces land in North Africa at Casablanca, Oran, and Algiers on Nov. 8, leading to an armistice with the Vichy leader in North Africa (Nov. 11). British go on to take Bardia, Tobruk, and Bengasi by Nov. 20. *See* **1942 Battle of El Alamein.**

1943

Jan. 14-24	Roosevelt, Churchill, and their chief advisers meet in the newly liberated Moroccan city of Casablanca to draw up a blueprint for the Allied conduct of World War II in Europe and the Pacific. *See* **1943 The Casablanca Conference.**
Feb. 2	Germans surrender at Stalingrad.
Feb. 14-16	Rostov and Kharkov fall to the Russians.
Mar. 9	Rzhev falls to the Russians.
Apr. 7	U.S. and British lines meet in North Africa.
May 13	Axis surrenders in North Africa.
July 10-Aug. 17	Allied forces invade and occupy Sicily in Operation Husky.
July 25	Italian dictator Benito Mussolini resigns, replaced by Pietro Badoglio as head of the Italian government. Badoglio dissolves the Fascist Party on July 28.
Aug. 4	Russians take Orel and Belgorod.
Sept. 3	British forces invade Italy. *See* **1943 Allied Invasion of Italy.**
Sept. 8	Italy surrenders unconditionally.
Sept. 9	U.S. amphibious forces land at Salerno, launching Operation Avalanche against German-occupied Italy.
Sept. 25	Russians take Smolensk.
Oct. 9	Yugoslavians under Marshal Tito (Josip Broz) begin their campaign against Axis powers.
Dec. 25	Allied invasion of Italy reaches the Sangro River.

1944

Jan. 3	Russians enter Poland.
Jan. 11-May	Allied air raids of the Continent from Great Britain begin to soften Normandy for a ground-force invasion.
Jan. 16	Respected for his role in the North African campaign, U.S. general Dwight D. Eisenhower arrives in England as Supreme Commander of the Allied Expeditionary Forces.
Jan. 22	Allied amphibious forces land at Anzio beachhead and begin an assault on Germans in central Italy.
Jan. 29	Russians evacuate German troops from the Moscow-Leningrad region.
Apr. 10	Russians take Odessa.
May 9	Russians take Sevastopol.
May 18	Monte Cassino falls to Allied forces in Italy.
June 4	Rome is liberated by Allied forces.
June 6	OPERATION OVERLORD: Crossing the English Channel, massive Allied amphibious forces invade Normandy along the coast between the Orne River and the Cotentin Peninsula. With an initial force of more than 150,000 troops, 4,000 invasion craft, 600 warships, and 11,000 airplanes, the invasion is the largest amphibious campaign in history. *See* **1944 Allied Invasion of France.**
June 14	Germans launch V-1 pilotless aircraft to bomb England.
June 23	Russians begin a counteroffensive south of Leningrad.
June 27	U.S. forces capture Cherbourg.
July 9	Caen falls to the British.
July 20	An attempt to assassinate German chancellor Adolf Hitler fails.
July 25	U.S. forces break German lines at St. Lô, launching the Allied thrust into Brittany, ending the Normandy invasion, and initiating the campaign to secure the interior of France.
Aug. 12	The Italian city of Florence falls to the British.
Aug. 15	In Operation Dragoon, U.S. forces invade southern France and begin to move up the Rhone River Valley.
Aug. 25	Allied forces liberate Paris.
Sept. 4	Brussels and Antwerp are liberated from German control.
Sept. 7	Germans launch V-2 rockets toward London.
Sept. 8	Bulgaria surrenders to the Allies.
Sept. 11	Liberation of Luxembourg.
Sept. 12	Battle for Germany begins when U.S. forces enter Germany near Trier and Eupen.
Sept. 22	Russians take Tallinn in Estonia.
Oct. 2	Polish forces surrender to Germany. In Germany, U.S. forces begin the battle for Aachen.
Oct. 20	Russians and Yugoslavs take Belgrade.
Dec. 16-28	BATTLE OF THE BULGE: Along an eight-mile front in the Ardennes region of Belgium, the Germans launch a surprise attack, advancing nearly to the Meuse River, where they are stopped by the Allies. *See* **1944-1945 Battle of the Bulge.**
Dec. 29	Russians enter Budapest.

1945

Jan. 17-19	Warsaw and Lodz fall to the Russians.
Feb. 4-11	Roosevelt, Churchill, Stalin, and their diplomatic advisers meet at Yalta in the Soviet Crimea to discuss postwar occupation of conquered nations and other political problems arising out of the approaching defeat of Germany. *See* **1945 The Yalta Conference.**
Feb. 8	British forces launch offensive in the Netherlands.
Feb. 22	U.S. forces cross the Saar River and reach the Ruhr Valley the next day.
Mar. 7	Fall of Cologne and Düsseldorf.
Mar. 23	U.S. forces cross the Rhine River and reach the Elbe River by Apr. 11.
Apr. 21	Fall of Nuremberg and Bologna.
Apr. 25	U.S. forces, coming from the west, and Russian forces, from the east, meet in Germany at Torgau.
Apr. 28	U.S. forces invade the Po River Valley in Italy. Italian partisans assassinate Mussolini.
May 2	Fall of Berlin. German forces in Italy surrender.
May 4	German forces in Denmark and the Netherlands surrender.
May 7	Germany surrenders unconditionally. The next day is declared V-E ("victory in Europe") day.
Jul. 17-Aug. 2	Stalin and Churchill are joined by two new political leaders—U.S. president Harry Truman and British Labour Party leader Clement Atlee—at a diplomatic conference held in Potsdam, Germany. The conference serves as a follow-up to agreements made at Yalta and as a vehicle to deal with important postwar issues, particularly the military occupation of Germany. *See* **1945 The Potsdam Conference.**

1944-1945

BATTLE OF THE BULGE

The Battle of the Bulge marks Germany's last desperate attempt to stave off defeat on the western front in World War II by attempting to break through the Allied lines in Belgium.

DATE: December 16, 1944-January 28, 1945

LOCALE: The Ardennes, Belgium

CATEGORY: Wars, uprisings, and civil unrest

KEY FIGURES:

Omar Nelson Bradley (1893-1981), American general and commander of the Allied Twelfth Army Group

Sepp Dietrich, German commander of the Sixth Panzer Army

Dwight David Eisenhower (1890-1969), American general and supreme commander of the Allied Expeditionary Force

Adolf Hitler (1889-1945), chancellor and führer of Germany, 1933-1945

Courtney Hicks Hodges (1887-1966), American general in command of the U.S. First Army

Hasso von Manteuffel, German commander of the Fifth *Panzer* Army

Bernard Law Montgomery (1887-1976), British general and commander of the Allied Twenty-First Army Group

George Smith Patton (1885-1945), American general in command of the U.S. Third Army

Karl Rudolf Gerd von Rundstedt (1875-1953), German commander on the western front

SUMMARY OF EVENT. In September, 1944, Adolf Hitler, the chancellor and führer of Germany, realized that the German armies were being pushed back on all fronts. In the east, the Russian army stood poised before Warsaw and threatened the Balkans, having regained all the ground lost in the German offensive of 1941. In northern Italy, the Germans were hard pressed to hold their defensive position, the Gothic Line. Allied bombers raided German cities daily, and the German Luftwaffe, or air force, had few operational defensive planes left. The German navy was confined to its ports, and only a few submarines could be adequately fueled to go on voyages of destruction. In the West, there was the greatest threat of all—an Allied army that had swept from Normandy to Belgium and stood poised to invade Germany.

At a conference with his generals in September, 1944, Hitler unveiled his plans for a massive counteroffensive against the Anglo-American army. Following Carl von Clausewitz's maxim that the best defense is a good offense, he proposed to scour Germany for all men capable of fighting and throw all his reserves into battle against the British and the Americans. To those who questioned this strategy and warned that the Russians presented a more immediate threat to Germany, Hitler answered that he did not have the force to counter Russia immediately. The Allied forces were weaker, he pointed out, for the Allies did not have as many men as did the Russians, and their supply lines were long and tenuous. Since June they had been supplying their army from the Normandy ports, and the capture of Antwerp in September did not solve their supply problem, for the port was blocked by debris and the Germans still controlled the estuary of the Scheldt River.

Therefore, Hitler planned a strike aimed at splitting the Allied army. The attack would be launched in the lightly defended area of the Ardennes Forest in Belgium and pushed forward until Antwerp was captured. This coup would deal the Allies such a blow that their leaders would quickly negotiate an armistice. Then, the German armies could be turned eastward to defeat the Russians. In addition to his army thrust, Hitler intended to use V-1 and V-2 rockets to bombard both London and Antwerp, and in the coming offensive, air cover would be provided by his new jet airplanes, which could travel much faster than any Allied airplane.

The German forces were gathered with great secrecy, and when, on December 16, 1944, the weather forecast indicated that Allied air superiority would be nullified because of poor visibility, the German forces struck. The Allies were caught completely off guard and the Germans scored a decisive breakthrough.

Field-Marshal Gerd von Rundstedt commanded the operation, and two German armies—the Sixth Panzer Army, commanded by General Sepp Dietrich, and the Fifth Panzer Army, under General Hasso von Manteuffel—formed the arms of a pincer movement aimed at Antwerp. The U.S. First Army under General Courtney Hicks Hodges was defending the Ardennes and was the hardest hit. General Dwight D. Eisenhower, supreme commander of the Allied Expeditionary Force, decided upon a defensive tactic. He divided command of the Allied forces around the "bulge" created by the German thrust: the northern armies were to be commanded by General Bernard Law Montgomery, British commander of the Twenty-First Army Group, and the southern armies by General Omar N. Bradley, American commander of the Twelfth Army Group. They were ordered to allow their defensive line to give, but not to split. In the meantime, defensive reserves would be brought in to help drive back the Germans. General George S. Patton's Third Army would swing in from the south to relieve the defenders of the bulge.

The main fighting soon centered around the town of Bastogne. American defenders of the town were besieged by Manteuffel's army, but a fortunate break in the weather allowed Eisenhower to airdrop supplies to the defenders. By late December, the Germans had to give up their siege of the town, and they began a tactical withdrawal. Throughout January, 1945, Dietrich's and Manteuffel's armies were pushed back, although Hitler continued to pour his last remaining reserves into the bulge. By January 28, 1945, the German armies were in full retreat and the Allies had recovered the areas they had previously lost.

While the resistance at Bastogne was heroic, the relief effort in the south by General George S. Patton was instantaneous. He swung the U.S. Third Army to counterattack, advising Eisenhower that even if the Germans pushed through the areas he temporarily evacuated they could not maintain the offensive.

Air power also proved decisive once again. When the weather lifted on December 23, more than five thousand Allied planes pounded German positions, isolating Nazi forces. Patton's relief of Bastogne on December 26 marked, in the words of the authors of *Warfare in the Western World*, "his finest hour. " Responding to the improvement in weather, Patton decorated his chaplain for a "particularly bloodthirsty prayer. " The Battle of the Bulge had cost the Germans one hundred thousand men and gained the Reich nothing.

This last major German offensive of the war confirmed the demise of the German army and made total defeat merely a matter of months. Hitler had no reserves left to counter either the Allied forces or the Russians; nevertheless, he resolved to defend Germany to the very end, and it was not until late April, 1945, that Hitler gave up and committed suicide. By that time, Allied forces had reached the Elbe River and the Russians were entering Berlin. The Germans surrendered on May 7, 1945.

—*José M. Sánchez, updated by Larry Schweikart*

ADDITIONAL READING:

Bradley, Omar N. *A Soldier's Story*. New York: Holt, Rinehart and Winston, 1951. Bradley's memoir provides interesting counterpoints to Eisenhower's book.

Doughty, Robert, et al. *Warfare in the Western World*. 2 vols. Lexington, Mass.: D. C. Heath, 1996. A comprehensive set that includes detailed discussions of World War II by a team of distinguished historians.

Eisenhower, Dwight D. *Crusade in Europe*. New York: Doubleday, 1948. An assessment of the war from the American commander in chief of European forces.

Jacobsen, H. A., and J. Rohwer, eds. *Decisive Battles of World War II: The German View*. Translated by Edward

Fitzgerald. New York: G. P. Putnam's Sons, 1965. Another work from the German viewpoint, emphasizing the perspective of Manteuffel. The Germans misread the Allied slowdown in the fall of 1944, interpreting it as a broad collapse instead of a minor supply problem.

Adopting defensive tactics, Eisenhower divided the Allied troops under his command to meet the thrust of the advancing German armies at the Battle of the Bulge in the Ardennes region of Belgium. (Archive Photos)

Leckie, Robert. *The Wars of America*. Rev. ed. New York: Harper & Row, 1981. A history of American involvement in conflicts with extensive discussions of the major battles of World War II.

Luttichau, Charles V. P. von. "The German Counteroffensive in the Ardennes." In *Command Decisions*, edited by Rent Roberts Greenfield. Washington, D.C.: U.S. Government Printing Office, 1960. A thorough treatment of the Ardennes offensive from the German perspective, based on German war documents. Luttichau argues that the assassination attempt on Hitler convinced him that divine powers protected him, and gave him the inspiration to order the offensive.

SEE ALSO: 1943, The Casablanca Conference; 1943, Allied Invasion of Italy; 1944, Allied Invasion of France; 1945, The Yalta Conference.

1945
THE YALTA CONFERENCE

The Yalta Conference between British, American, and Soviet representatives provides a controversial blueprint for how major issues will be dealt with in the postwar world, and its problems presage the coming of the Cold War.

DATE: February 4-11, 1945
LOCALE: Yalta, in the Russian Crimea
CATEGORY: Diplomacy and international relations
KEY FIGURES:

Sir Winston Leonard Spencer Churchill (1874-1965), British prime minister, 1940-1945 and 1951-1955

Robert Anthony Eden (1897-1977), British foreign secretary, 1940-1945

Harry Lloyd Hopkins (1890-1946), special assistant to Roosevelt

Vyacheslav Mikhailovich Molotov (Skryabin; 1890-1986), Soviet commissar of foreign affairs

Franklin Delano Roosevelt (1882-1945), thirty-second president of the United States, 1933-1945

Joseph Stalin (Iosif Vissarionovich Dzhugashvili; 1879-1953), premier of the Soviet Union, 1924-1953

Edward Reilly Stettinius, Jr. (1900-1949), U.S. secretary of state, 1944-1945

SUMMARY OF EVENT. Early in 1945, as Russian armies were advancing on Germany through Eastern Europe and American and British armies were entering western Germany, the leaders of the Allied nations met at Yalta, in the Russian Crimea, to consider the political problems arising out of the approaching defeat of Germany, to plan an occupation policy for the conquered nations, and to discuss the problems of the United Nations, Eastern Europe, and the Far East.

At the conference, the United States was represented by President Franklin D. Roosevelt; his closest adviser was Harry Hopkins, and they were accompanied by Edward Stettinius, Jr., the U.S. secretary of state. The British were represented by Prime Minister Winston Churchill and Anthony Eden, the British foreign secretary. As host country, the Soviet Union was represented by Joseph Stalin, the Soviet premier, and Vyacheslav Molotov, the Soviet commissar of foreign affairs. The three Allied leaders had met together once before, at Teheran in 1943, but had postponed many of their decisions to be discussed later or to be worked out by their foreign ministers for

presentation at Yalta. Generally, the atmosphere at Yalta was cordial. Churchill and Stalin, however, were suspicious of each other's motives, and Roosevelt, who died two months later, was in failing health.

Many of the decisions made at Yalta were ratifications of earlier accords worked out by the foreign ministers; some agreements were reached only after much bargaining. For purposes of convenience, the main issues and agreements can be grouped in the following categories: the United Nations, Poland and Eastern Europe, Germany, and the Far East.

The United Nations had been proposed as far back as 1941. In 1944, the foreign ministers had established the organizational structure. The Russians had insisted upon a Security Council veto on all matters, even procedural ones, and had demanded sixteen seats in the General Assembly on the basis that each of the Soviet Republics was autonomous. These demands were intended to offset the Pan American and British Commonwealth blocks that would likely emerge in the future organization. Viewing the establishment of the United Nations along American lines as a prime objective, Roosevelt believed that it "was the only device that could keep the United States from slipping back into isolationism" after the war. Thus, when Stalin agreed to drop his demands for an unlimited veto in the Security Council, Roosevelt agreed to the Soviet Union's request for membership in the General Assembly for the Soviet Ukrainian and Byelorussian republics. After all, members of the British Commonwealth had six votes in the Assembly. Thus, Stalin agreed to drop his demands and to send Molotov to the founding meeting of the United Nations to be held in San Francisco in April, 1945.

Poland presented two problems: frontiers and government. When Poland had been conquered by the Germans and the Russians in 1939, a Polish government-in-exile had been established in London. After the Soviet Union joined the Allies in 1941 and began liberating Poland from Nazi rule in 1944, Stalin had formed the Polish Committee of National Liberation, essentially a Communist government-in-exile, which was known as the Lüblin government.

Stalin wanted the Communist government to be recognized as the legitimate government by the Allies. Furthermore, he wanted the Curzon Line—the ethnic boundary—to be the frontier between the Soviet Union and Poland, with Poland's western frontier moved farther west into Germany. Stalin stood in a strong position, since the Russian army was moving through Poland, and he possessed the argument that he needed a Polish security buffer between Germany and the Soviet Union.

The discussions, which were primarily between Churchill and Stalin, centered around the type of government and the Polish boundaries. Stalin won the concession that the eastern boundary basically follow the Curzon Line and that Poland would receive substantial territories in the north and west, with the final boundary to be decided at the peace conference at war's end. He did, however, agree that the Polish provisional government be reorganized on a broader "democratic" basis to include democratic lead-

were to be preponderant in Greece; the Russians, in Romania and Bulgaria; and each country was to have equal shares in Hungary and Yugoslavia. This agreement was not discussed at Yalta, nor was there discussion on the future of Czechoslovakia, Finland, or the Baltic states, all of which later came under Russian influence or control.

The future of Germany was the most divisive problem taken up at Yalta. Most of the decisions were based on

Winston Churchill, Franklin Roosevelt, and Joseph Stalin met in Yalta in the Soviet Crimea to discuss tentative plans for postwar policy. (AP/Wide World Photos)

ers from within Poland and from abroad. Moreover, he agreed the elections for this united Polish government would occur "as soon as possible."

As for the other countries of newly liberated Eastern Europe, the Allies agreed to support and help all interim governments until free elections could be held. Specific problems in the Balkans had already been settled by Stalin and Churchill at a meeting held in Moscow in October, 1944, when they agreed that spheres of temporary influence would be established. The Americans and the British

recommendations made by the foreign ministers, who had been discussing this problem since 1943. Stalin favored a partition of Germany in order to keep it under control, and Churchill toyed with the idea of a dismembered Germany. Since Roosevelt was vague, they decided to refer the matter to the ministers of foreign affairs. Ironically, the Soviets would abandon this position by late March. The Allies did approve a temporary military occupation policy; Germany was to be divided into four zones of military occupation, with France (whose section would be carved out of the Anglo-American part) being included as an occupying power, and joint-occupation policy was to be defined by a four-power Allied control commission in Berlin. Berlin itself was to be divided and occupied by all four powers, and the Allies agreed that common occupation policies were to be imposed, by mutual agreement, on the whole of Germany.

As for German reparations and the German economy, Stalin favored a plan proposed earlier by U.S. secretary of the Treasury Henry Morgenthau, Jr. Morgenthau's plan favored complete deindustrialization of Germany; all of Germany's industry was to be given to the Allies as reparations, and Germany would be allowed to maintain only an agrarian economy. At Yalta, neither Churchill nor Roosevelt favored this plan, nor could they agree with Stalin on the exact amount of reparations to demand from Germany. Roosevelt did agree in principle, however, to a ten-billion-dollar figure for reparations in favor of the Soviet Union as a "basis for discussion." The only agreement made was the appointment of a reparations commission to study the problem and to make recommendations.

Apart from military occupation, there was no agreement whether Germany should be dismembered, kept intact, or given new frontiers, other than that Poland would be given compensation in Germany and that East Prussia would be divided between the Soviet Union and Poland. The Allies agreed to appoint another commission to make recommendations on these questions.

The question of the Far East loomed as a major priority with Roosevelt and to some degree with Churchill. Even though the British prime minister did not participate in these discussions, he did sign off on the resultant understanding. At the time of Yalta, the Japanese seemed a long way from surrender. The atomic bomb had not been tested, and Allied forces in the Pacific were a long way from closing in on the homeland of Japan. Likewise, Japanese armed forces had proved to be able fighters who were not inclined to surrender easily. Thus, Roosevelt wanted to pin down Stalin on a Russian entry into the war against Japan in order to save hundreds of thousands of American lives. Earlier at Teheran, he and Stalin had reached substantial agreement concerning the Far East, and at Yalta, by secret accords, the agreement was formalized. Thus, the Soviet Union would declare war on Japan within three months after the surrender of Germany. In return, the Soviets would be given control over certain areas in the Far East, including the Kurile Islands and the southern portion of Sakhalin Island, concessions in Manchuria (granted without the knowledge or agreement of the Chinese leaders), and the internationalization of the port of Dairen and a lease on Port Arthur, both on China's Liaodong Peninsula.

Most of the agreements made at Yalta were considered to be temporary in nature. Nevertheless, when World War II ended and the Cold War began, these temporary agreements quickly became permanent.

—*José M. Sánchez, updated by Robert Franklin Maddox*

ADDITIONAL READING:

Buhite, Russell D. *Decisions at Yalta: An Appraisal of Summit Diplomacy*. Wilmington, Del.: Scholarly Resources, 1986. The author concludes that Roosevelt pursued a policy of détente with cooperation with the Soviets as his main goal.

Churchill, Winston S. *The Second World War*. Vol. 6: *Triumph and Tragedy*. Boston: Houghton Mifflin, 1953. This memoir deals with the events of the conference from the British perspective.

Feis, Herbert. *Churchill, Roosevelt, Stalin*. Princeton, N.J.: Princeton University Press, 1957. This volume evaluates each decision and concludes that it was a victory for the West in that it limited Russian aims.

Freidel, Frank. *Franklin D. Roosevelt: A Rendezvous with Destiny*. Boston: Little, Brown, 1990. Written after four decades of research, this definitive political biography deals with the major issues surrounding Yalta.

Laloy, Jean. *Yalta: Yesterday, Today, Tomorrow*. New York: Harper & Row, 1988. Written by a French historian, this work places Yalta's impact in the perspective of the European community.

Sherwood, Robert E. *Roosevelt and Hopkins*. New York: Harper & Row, 1948. This revealing work is written from the perspective of the key Roosevelt adviser.

Snell, John L., ed. *The Meaning of Yalta*. Baton Rouge: Louisiana State University Press, 1956. This group of essays by noted historians treats the various issues that dominated the Yalta Conference.

SEE ALSO: 1941, Atlantic Charter Is Signed; 1943, The Casablanca Conference; 1945, The United Nations Is Formed; 1945, The Potsdam Conference.

1945
THE UNITED NATIONS IS FORMED

The United Nations is formed in the aftermath of World War II in an attempt to create a new world government of peace-loving nations through international cooperation based on the sovereign equality of its members.

DATE: April 26-June 26, 1945
LOCALE: San Francisco, California
CATEGORIES: Diplomacy and international relations; Organizations and institutions

KEY FIGURES:

Sir Winston Leonard Spencer Churchill (1874-1965),
   British prime minister, 1940-1945 and 1951-1955
Cordell Hull (1871-1955), U.S. secretary of state,
   1933-1944
Franklin Delano Roosevelt (1882-1945), thirty-second
   president of the United States, 1933-1945
Joseph Stalin (Iosif Vissarionovich Dzhugashvili; 1879-
   1953), premier of the Soviet Union, 1924-1953
Edward Reilly Stettinius, Jr. (1900-1949), U.S. secretary
   of state, 1944-1945

SUMMARY OF EVENT. The United Nations, a worldwide
organization of nation-states, was founded at the Conference on International Organization held April 26-June 26,
1945, in San Francisco, California. The organization was
intended to maintain international peace and security, especially by encouraging friendly relations among states,
based on the principle that all nations have equal rights
and are entitled to self-determination. The United Nations
was expected to promote international cooperation in
solving social, economic, cultural, and humanitarian problems and to encourage respect for human rights and fundamental freedoms. It was also intended to serve as an
agency through which member states can act to achieve
these goals. Member nations are pledged to fulfill the
obligations they have assumed, to settle international disputes by peaceful means, to refrain from the threat or the
use of force except in self-defense, to assist the United
Nations in actions ordered under the charter and to refrain
from assisting any country against which such United
Nations action is being taken, and to act in accord with the
charter's principles.

The roots of the United Nations began within the
League of Nations, which was formed in Geneva, Switzerland, after the conclusion of World War I. The League of
Nations represented one of the first attempts to foster
international cooperation for peacekeeping. Yet the League
of Nations grew progressively weaker in influence, failed
to prevent the outbreak of World War II, and was formally
dissolved in 1946. During World War II, organizational
steps were taken by the major Allied powers (United
States, Great Britain, Soviet Union, France, China) to pave
the way for the United Nations based on their struggles
with the Axis powers (Germany, Italy, Japan).

Secretary of State Cordell Hull initiated America's preparatory work for the United Nations soon after World
War II began in Europe. When health problems forced his
resignation months before the beginning of the San Francisco conference, Hull was succeeded by Edward R. Stettinius, Jr., who had been undersecretary of state since
1933.

The first significant action toward the foundation of the
United Nations took place in August, 1941, when President Franklin D. Roosevelt and Prime Minister Winston
Churchill met on a warship off the coast of Newfoundland
in the mid-Atlantic to discuss principles for international
conduct after the war. Aware of President Woodrow Wilson's failure to obtain approval from Congress to enter the
United States into the League of Nations, Roosevelt was
initially reluctant to join any postwar international political organization. The League of Nations idea was the last
of Wilson's Fourteen Points for ending the war with Germany. On August 14, 1941, however, the Atlantic Charter
was signed by Roosevelt and Churchill with the commitment that the establishment of a "wider and permanent
system of general security" designed to "bring about the
fullest collaboration between all nations in the economic
field" in the form of a new world organization would begin
after peace was restored. The title of "United Nations"
first formally appeared when the Declaration of the United
Nations was signed by representatives of twenty-six Allied nations who pledged to continue fighting against the
Axis powers on January 1, 1942, in Washington, D.C.
Churchill originally proposed to call the organization
"The Grand Alliance" but Roosevelt persuaded him and
others to call it the United Nations.

More formational steps toward this new world organization were taken at the "Moscow Pact" conference in the
Soviet Union on October 30, 1943, where representatives
of the Union of Soviet Socialist Republics (Vyacheslav
Mikhailovich Molotov), Great Britain (Anthony Eden),
the United States (Hull), and China signed a declaration
which recognized the need to establish "at the earliest
practicable date a general international organization,
based on the principle of the sovereign equality of all
peace-loving states and open to membership by all such
states, large and small, for the maintenance of international peace and security." Meeting in Teheran, Iran, a
month later, Roosevelt, Churchill, and Soviet premier
Joseph Stalin reaffirmed "the supreme responsibility resting upon us and all the United Nations to make a peace
which will . . . banish the scourge and terror of war."
Representatives of the four powers then met at the Dumbarton Oaks Estate near Washington, D.C., from August
21 to October 7, 1944, to attempt to draft a series of
proposals for the United Nations. Agreed upon was a draft
charter that specified the purposes, structure, and methods
of operation of the United Nations, but further negotiations were needed to specify the method of voting for the
Security Council, which was to have the major responsibility for peace and security. The much-contended issue
regarding voting strength of the major powers in the Gen-

eral Assembly and Security Council was later settled, February 4-11, 1945, at the Yalta Conference of the big five powers (United States, Great Britain, Soviet Union, China, France), when Roosevelt, Churchill, and Stalin met for the last of their wartime conferences, and at the San Francisco Conference itself. After considerable negotiation and compromise, Stalin finally accepted the Anglo-American position that limited great-power prerogatives on procedural matters, but retained the right of veto on substantive issues.

At the Yalta Conference, the Allied leaders called for the first United Nations Conference on International Organization to be held April 26-June 26, 1945, in San Francisco, California, which would include delegates from the fifty founding nations (who were later joined by Poland). During this two-month period at the first international conference not dominated by Europe, a charter based on the draft developed at Dumbarton Oaks and consisting of 111 articles was completed. The charter included six principal organs (General Assembly, Security Council, Economic and Social Council, Trusteeship Council, International Court of Justice, and Secretariat), and was approved on June 25, signed the next day, and became effective on October 24, 1945, after ratification by a majority of its members. The General Assembly was to be, as U.S. senator Arthur Vandenberg later called it, "the town meeting of the world." The bonds of the wartime alliance against common enemies unquestionably hastened agreement on several key issues, with October 24 being commemorated as United Nations Day. On December 10, 1945, the U.S. Congress invited the United Nations to establish its permanent headquarters in the United States. The United Nations accepted and moved to a temporary location in Lake Success, New York, in August, 1946. Later that year, a site was purchased bordering the East River in Manhattan and the United Nations complex, which included the General Assembly Hall, the Secretariat Building, the Conference Building, and the Dag Hammarskjold Library, was completed in mid-1952. Even as the United Nations was being formed under U.S. leadership, problems were already being born within the foundation of its great-power agreement with the development of the Cold War between the Soviet Union and the Western alliance. —*Daniel G. Graetzer*

ADDITIONAL READING:

Feis, Herbert. *Churchill, Roosevelt, and Stalin*. Princeton, N.J.: Princeton University Press, 1967. An important documentary on the relationships between the three men who dominated the political climate surrounding the formation of the United Nations.

Goodspeed, Stephen. *The Nature and Function of International Organizations*. 2d ed. New York: Oxford University Press, 1967. A well-written textbook on the nature and functioning of the United Nations and other international organizations.

Min-chuan, Ku. *A Comprehensive Handbook of the United Nations: A Documentary Presentation in Two Volumes*. New York: Monarch Press, 1979. Compiled and edited by Min-chuan, this handbook highlights the formation of the United Nations and documents the successes and failures that occurred during the design and implementation of its charter.

Parsons, Anthony. "Birth, Death, and Rebirth: League of Nations to the United Nations." *Modern History Review* 2, no. 3 (1991): 2-4. Examines the origins and structure of the League of Nations and the United Nations, comparing the differences and similarities of their major functions.

Russell, Ruth B. *A History of the United Nations Charter: The Role of the United States, 1940-1945*. Washington, D.C.: The Brookings Institute, 1958. This exhaustive work utilized many State Department documents and represents research by a large staff originally under the direction of Dr. Leo Pasvolsky, whose advice guided many American representatives at the San Francisco conference.

SEE ALSO: 1919, The League of Nations Is Established; 1941, Atlantic Charter Is Signed; 1943, The Casablanca Conference; 1945, The Potsdam Conference; 1967, United Nations Declaration on Equality for Women; 1972, United Nations Environmental Conference.

1945
THE POTSDAM CONFERENCE

The Potsdam Conference serves as a follow-up to agreements made at Yalta and as a vehicle to deal with important postwar issues.

DATE: July 17-August 2, 1945
LOCALE: Potsdam, Germany
CATEGORY: Diplomacy and international relations
KEY FIGURES:

Clement Richard Attlee (1883-1967), British prime minister, 1945-1951

Ernest Bevin (1884-1951), British foreign secretary, 1945-1951

James Francis Byrnes (1879-1972), U.S. secretary of state, 1945-1947

Sir Winston Leonard Spencer Churchill (1874-1965), British prime minister, 1940-1945

General Charles-André-Marie-Joseph de Gaulle (1890-1970), president of France, 1944-1946

Robert Anthony Eden (1897-1977), British foreign
secretary, 1940-1945

Harry Lloyd Hopkins (1890-1946), special assistant to
Roosevelt

Vyacheslav Mikhailovich Molotov (Skryabin; 1890-
1986), Soviet commissar for foreign affairs

Joseph Stalin (Iosif Vissarionovich Dzhugashvili; 1879-
1953), premier of the Soviet Union, 1924-1953

Harry S Truman (1884-1972), thirty-third president of
the United States, 1945-1953

SUMMARY OF EVENT. At the close of the Yalta Conference
in February of 1945, the leaders of the United States, Great
Britain, and the Soviet Union had agreed that they would
meet again to settle European problems resulting from the
defeat of Germany. These problems concerned peace treaties with the former Axis nations and satellites. For the
Western Allies, the problems dealt with the Soviet Union's
violation of the agreement to allow the establishment of
free governments in Eastern Europe.

When Germany surrendered in May, 1945, the Allied
leaders began preparations for another conference. Prime
Minister Winston Churchill was particularly anxious that
the meeting be held as soon as possible, not only to
forestall further Soviet gains in Europe but also because of
the possibility that upcoming British elections to be held
in July might vote him out of office before he could
participate in these important foreign policy decisions.
Harry Truman, who had taken office as president of the
United States in April after the death of Franklin D.
Roosevelt, wanted to delay the meeting long enough to
familiarize himself with the problems. Soviet premier
Joseph Stalin had no apparent preference regarding the
scheduling of the meeting. It was finally agreed that the
conference would open on July 17 and be held in Potsdam,
Germany.

Two other problems had to be solved. One involved the
provisional president of France, Charles de Gaulle. France
had been allotted an occupational zone in Germany, but
past relations between the Allies and de Gaulle had been
so trying that no one wanted him at the Potsdam Conference and he was not invited. The other problem concerned
the occupation armies in Germany. During the course of
the war, both Western Allied troops and Soviet troops had
occupied German areas not included in their respective
occupational zones. In particular, there were no American
troops in Berlin, and the American military commanders
wanted soldiers there to protect the president on his trip to
Potsdam. The Soviet Union refused to allow troops into
Berlin until Western soldiers left the Russian zone. Despite Churchill's misgivings, Truman ordered a retreat,
and the British and Americans were allowed into Berlin.

*In need of time to familiarize himself with agreements made
by Franklin Roosevelt, President Harry Truman (center) asked
for a delay before convening the Potsdam Conference.* (National Archives)

The Potsdam Conference began on July 17, 1945, and
lasted for two weeks. In the middle of the conference,
British election returns proclaimed the defeat of Churchill
and the triumph of the Labour Party. Churchill was replaced as prime minister by Labour Party leader Clement
Atlee. Since Atlee had attended the conference earlier,
there was no change in British policy. The agenda listed
peace treaties, Eastern Europe, and Germany.

Recalling the hasty decisions and mistakes made at the
Paris Peace Conference of 1919, Truman proposed that the
Council of Foreign Ministers meet at leisure to draft peace
treaties for the defeated Axis nations. This proposal was
accepted by all; within two years, the foreign ministers
produced acceptable treaties.

Eastern Europe, however, was another matter. Stalin
wanted Western diplomatic recognition for the pro-
Communist governments there, but Truman and Churchill
refused. As for Poland, the Allies had agreed at Yalta that
free elections be held "as soon as possible"; since Yalta,
the Communist-controlled Warsaw government had taken
over Poland and had made no plans for free elections.
Furthermore, members of the anti-Communist Polish
government-in-exile had been arrested when they had

returned from London to Poland after the German surrender. Truman had sent his special assistant, Harry Hopkins, to Moscow in May to inquire into this matter. Hopkins had arranged a compromise between the London and Warsaw Poles on a coalition government, despite the fact that the Communists held fourteen out of twenty-one cabinet seats, and the Polish government had agreed to hold free elections. At Potsdam, this agreement was ratified with the stipulation that the Allied press be admitted and allowed to report on the elections. The Polish interim government was granted Western diplomatic recognition.

As for the Polish-German frontier, when Soviet troops had liberated Poland, they had turned over all German lands east of the Oder-Western Neisse River line to the Poles. The southern half of East Prussia had been turned over to the Poles. Stalin proposed that the Allies recognize these boundaries as permanent frontiers. Truman and Churchill accepted them only as temporary frontiers pending a final peace treaty with Germany.

The German problem was the central issue at Potsdam. The main dispute was between the Soviet desire for a weak Germany and harsh reparations and the Western Allied aim of a restored and pacified Germany to act as a buffer against Soviet expansion. So intense was this dispute that the leaders could agree only on noncontroversial issues. Thus, the Allies agreed on the abolition of Nazi institutions and the prohibition of arms manufacturing, although they agreed that Germany was to be treated as a single economic unit and the Control Council in Berlin was to make unanimous decisions for Germany as a whole. Within each zone, however, each military commander was to have sovereign authority. Local self-government was to be encouraged, and the German economy was to be geared toward peaceful pursuits.

On the question of reparations, the conference members agreed that each power could take what it wanted from its own zone, but the Soviets wanted industrial equipment from the Ruhr complex (located in the British zone) in order to compensate for the meager resources in their zone. The Soviets finally agreed to accept a percentage of the Ruhr industrial machinery in return for food products that they were to ship from their zone to the zones of the Western Allies. These Western zones needed food supplies because they had become heavily crowded with refugees who had fled the Russian zone in the last days of the war. All other reparations were renounced.

In other matters, the Potsdam Conference members agreed on an occupational zone arrangement for Austria similar to that in Germany. They condemned Spain for having supported the Axis powers during the war and forbade Spain's entry into the United Nations. Finally, they agreed upon the orderly and human transfer to Germany of nine million displaced German civilians living in areas outside Germany.

In a final gesture, the Potsdam Declaration was issued to the Japanese government, calling upon it to surrender unconditionally or face total destruction. On August 2, a statement of the agreements, known as the Potsdam Protocol, was signed, and the participants went home.

The issue of atomic weapons has loomed as a major backdrop to this conference, causing much historical debate. Some scholars argue that the United States helped bring on the Cold War by taking a tough stance with the Soviets as a result of the atomic bomb. Some have even argued that the exact date of the nuclear arms race can be traced to Truman's conversation with Stalin on July 24, 1945, in which he revealed that the United States had a weapon of "unusual destructive force." Others point out that the United States no longer needed Soviet intervention in the Pacific war after they had successfully tested the bomb. Many conservative historians see Potsdam as part of an overall sellout to the Communists. Nevertheless, given the military strength and strategic location of Soviet troops, the agreements reached at Potsdam generally have been accepted as being quite realistic. Finally, the leaders negotiated compromise in a number of areas, with all sides gaining certain major strategic concessions, and they established a mechanism to deal with the details of the peace treaties in the postwar period.

—*José M. Sánchez, updated by Robert Franklin Maddox*

ADDITIONAL READING:

Alperovitz, Gar. *Atomic Diplomacy: Hiroshima and Potsdam*. New York: Simon & Schuster, 1965. This revisionist historian blames American bellicosity at Potsdam on the fact that Truman knew about the successful explosion of the atomic bomb. Thus, the United States helped bring on the Cold War.

Feis, Herbert. *Between War and Peace: The Potsdam Conference*. Princeton, N.J.: Princeton University Press, 1960. The author maintains that compromise was necessary since the Russian army stood in a strong European position, which placed them in control of Eastern Europe in 1945, and since the war against Japan was still in progress.

Ferrell, Robert H. *Harry S. Truman: A Life*. Columbia: University of Missouri Press, 1994. Written by a premier Truman scholar, this work argues that no Western figure could allow the status quo to be defined by the presence of Soviet troops in the eastern part of Europe.

Maddox, Robert James. *From War to Cold War: The Education of Harry S. Truman*. Boulder, Colo.: Westview

Press, 1988. Maddox analyzes the Potsdam Conference in the overall context of Truman's coming to grips with the problems of the ending of the war and the subsequent unraveling of the coalition.

Mee, Charles L., Jr. *Meeting at Potsdam.* New York: M. Evans, 1975. This volume argues that the victorious leaders acted in a Machiavellian fashion to achieve their goals, and that the origins of the Cold War and nuclear arms race can be found in this conference.

Robertson, David. *Sly and Able: A Political Biography of James F. Byrnes.* New York: W. W. Norton, 1994. Critical of revisionists, the author concludes that Byrnes's primary motivation for use of the atomic bomb was to end the war with Japan and not to impress the Russians.

Woods, Randall, and Howard Jones. *Dawning of the Cold War: The United States' Quest for Order.* Athens: University of Georgia Press, 1991. This work, which is based on a synthesis of scholarship, concludes that the potential impact the atomic bomb would have on Russia was "not decisive" in Truman's decision.

SEE ALSO: 1941, Atlantic Charter Is Signed; 1943, The Casablanca Conference; 1945, The Yalta Conference; 1945, The United Nations Is Formed; 1945, Labour Party Forms Majority Government; 1945-1946, Nuremberg Trials; 1946, Churchill's "Iron Curtain" Speech.

1945
LABOUR PARTY FORMS MAJORITY GOVERNMENT

The Labour Party forms a majority government, introducing a planned economy, nationalizing several industries, and creating the modern welfare state.

DATE: July 26, 1945
LOCALE: Great Britain
CATEGORIES: Economics; Government and politics; Social reform
KEY FIGURES:

Clement Richard Attlee (1883-1967), Labour prime minister, 1945-1951
Aneurin Bevan (1897-1960), minister of health, 1945-1951, and minister of labour and national service, 1951
Ernest Bevin (1881-1951), British foreign secretary, 1945-1951
Sir Winston Leonard Spencer Churchill (1874-1965), Conservative prime minister of the National Coalition cabinet, 1940-1945
George VI (1895-1952), king of the United Kingdom of Great Britain and Northern Ireland, 1936-1952

SUMMARY OF EVENT. The victory of the Labour Party in the parliamentary elections of July, 1945, marked the end of the National Coalition government which had held office in Great Britain since 1931. This government, comprising Conservatives, Liberals, and a few Labourites, represented the effort of its members to find solutions to the grave financial problems which had been brought on by the Great Depression of 1929. In reality, the National Coalition government was only a facade for the rule of the Conservative Party, which in its own right commanded an absolute majority in Parliament as constituted in the elections of 1931 and 1935.

The Conservative leader Stanley Baldwin headed the coalition as prime minister from 1935 to 1937. Following his resignation, King George VI called upon Neville Chamberlain, also a Conservative, to lead the nation. Chamberlain's policy of appeasing Nazi Germany in the late 1930's led to his resignation in 1940, when Adolf Hitler, chancellor and führer of Germany, ordered German troops to overrun Western Europe. King George thereupon asked Winston Churchill, the spokesman for those Conservatives who had condemned appeasement, to form a government. Churchill reorganized the cabinet extensively, bringing in both Labourites and Conservatives, who, like himself, had opposed Chamberlain's conciliatory policy toward Germany. A tough, aggressive leader, Churchill played a major role in the Allied victory over Germany in May, 1945. As Parliament had by then prolonged its session for ten years, Churchill agreed shortly after the German surrender to hold a general election. The king dissolved Parliament on June 15.

In order to prepare the way for the general election scheduled for July 5, the coalition cabinet resigned and Churchill appointed an exclusively Conservative cabinet. The election campaign was primarily a contest between the Conservative and Labour parties. Both parties presented themselves to the electorate as being best qualified to solve Great Britain's desperate postwar economic problems, which included the necessity of funding a staggering debt of more than three billion pounds and of replacing personal property, shipping, and industry destroyed during the war. The Labour Party proposed a comprehensive economic plan which called for, among other things, the nationalization of many industries and the establishment of extensive controls over those in private hands. The Conservatives, while recognizing the need to continue certain economic controls, denounced the Labour program of nationalization as a major infringement upon the private enterprise system. Both parties promised an extension of social services and full employment. During the campaign it was obvious that Labour had superior party organization, and Churchill made an appalling gaff, implying that Labour's sweeping economic changes would bring in a "gestapo" state, a clearly unfair charge against a party with an admirable war record. In addition, many voters still blamed the Conservatives for their alleged mean-spirited social policies during the Great Depression and for their bungling policy of appeasement prior to the war. The election gave the Labour Party a substantial majority with 393 seats as opposed to the 213 seats retained by the Conservatives. Attlee replaced Churchill as prime minister on July 27, 1945, one day after the vote was officially tabulated. By virtue of his victory, Attlee became Great Britain's chief representative at the Potsdam Conference, which was then meeting to decide the fate of postwar Germany.

The Labour Party remained in power from 1945 through most of 1951, during which period it attempted, with the aid of loans from the United States, to deal with Great Britain's economic and social problems by implementing its socialistic program. Attlee, unimposing in appearance and totally lacking charisma, nevertheless turned out to be a first-rate leader and put together a formidable cabinet team. In October, 1945, he secured from the House of Commons an extension of the government's wartime emergency powers for five years. During this period, the government nationalized the Bank of England, overseas cable and wireless services, civil aviation, coal mines, railroads, road haulage (trucking), canals and docks, gas and electricity companies, and the iron and steel industries. Owners of these industries were generously compensated. It was estimated that roughly 20 percent of the nation's economy was now in state hands. Labour subjected industry left in private hands to extensive controls, primarily to establish a healthy balance of trade between exports and imports. Strict government regulations also maintained rationing in the buying of food, clothing, and fuel. In agriculture, the Attlee government established price supports for milk, livestock, eggs, and potatoes, and set detailed standards of efficient production which farmers had to follow.

Yet it was Labour's domestic program for which it is chiefly remembered. It constructed the modern welfare state, or in the parlance of that time, offered security "from the womb to the tomb." In 1946, Parliament passed the National Insurance Act. Funded by contributions from employers, employees, and the state, this act dispensed funds for unemployment benefits, old age pensions, and grants to mothers having children. Yet the National Health Service, which began operation in 1948, was by far the government's most popular program. Pushed by Aneurin Bevan, minister of health, this act provided to everyone

After his Labour Party wins a majority in Parliament, Prime Minister Clement Attlee (right) is invited by King George VI to form a new government. (National Archives)

free medical services and supplies, hospital care, and nursing aid. Bevan was also responsible for directing the government-sponsored housing program, which built approximately one million units during Labour's term of office. In conjunction with the expansion of social services, Attlee attempted to bring about a modest redistribution of Great Britain's wealth by changing the tax laws whereby the heaviest burden fell upon the wealthy. Because of the resistance to these and other reform measures in the House of Lords, the Attlee government pushed an act through Parliament which restricted the powers of the House of Lords to delay legislation.

Foreign policy during this period was directed by Ernest Bevin, a former trade union leader who was appointed secretary of state for foreign affairs. The country played a positive role in creating the United Nations. Consistent with its socialist principles, the Labour government granted independence to India (1947), Pakistan (1947), Ceylon (1948), Burma (1948), and in something of a diplomatic debacle, Britain voluntarily surrendered its mandate for Palestine in 1948, which immediately led to fighting between Jews and Arabs in that area. During the early stages of the Cold War, Britain remained a staunch ally of the United States, joining the North Atlantic Treaty Organization in 1949, and offering military support during the Korean War. Much to America's displeasure, however, Britain recognized the Communist regime of China in 1950. Significantly, Britain spurned any negotiations dealing with the creation of a European political and economic union, preferring instead to maintain close ties with the Commonwealth and the United States.

With the expiration of its term in February, 1950, the Labour government stood for reelection. The Labour Party ran on a platform that called for the consolidation of the gains which it had made since the end of the war. The Conservatives promised to supply more housing and to end further nationalization and excessive controls. In addition, they attempted to assure the electorate that, contrary to statements from the Labour camp, they would not bring back unemployment and reduce the social services. Many people who had supported the Labour Party in 1945 now cast their votes for the Conservatives who captured 297 seats. The Labour Party, however, retained control with 315 seats. During the following months, the Labour Party barely managed to maintain this slender majority. A split in the ranks of Labour between right and left wingers during the middle of 1951 finally induced Attlee to call another election in October. This time the Conservatives won a slim majority of seats and once again Churchill returned to 10 Downing Street. The Conservatives were to remain in power for the next thirteen years.

The Labour government of 1945-1951 is regarded as one of the most important in modern British history. Correctly or incorrectly, it is credited with creating the modern welfare state, demonstrating the virtues of rational economic planning, and attempting to build a society embodying the virtues of social justice and economic security. Significantly, the Conservative Party after it returned to office accepted almost all of the welfare state and much of the nationalization program. This consensus was to last until the 1980's when it was vigorously challenged by Margaret Thatcher's Conservative government.

—Edward P. Keleher, updated by David C. Lukowitz

ADDITIONAL READING:

Bullock, Alan. *Ernest Bevin: Foreign Secretary, 1945-1951*. New York: W. W. Norton, 1983. A flattering account of Bevin's days at the Foreign Office by a respected Oxford historian.

Burridge, Trevor. *Clement Attlee: A Political Biography*. London: Jonathan Cape, 1985. A detailed, heavily documented study of Attlee's political career. Includes photographs and a lengthy bibliography.

Cairncross, Alec. *Years of Recovery: British Economic Policy, 1945-51*. New York: Methuen, 1985. An expert analysis of Britain's economy with special emphasis upon the financial crises of this period. For the advanced student.

McCullum, R. B., and A. Readman. *The British General Election of 1945*. Oxford: Oxford University Press, 1947. A good analysis of the election which brought the Labour Party to power.

Morgan, Kenneth O. *Labour in Power, 1945-1951*. Oxford: Clarendon Press, 1984. This lengthy, detailed account is arguably the finest study on the topic. Written by a distinguished Oxford historian.

Pearce, Robert. *Attlee's Labour Governments, 1945-1951*. New York: Routledge, 1994. A brief readable introduction to the topic designed specifically for students. Excellent bibliographical essay.

SEE ALSO: 1900, British Labour Party Is Formed; 1945, The Potsdam Conference; 1949, North Atlantic Treaty.

1945-1946
NUREMBERG TRIALS

The Nuremberg Trials establish an international tribunal for the punishment of defeated German military commanders and civilian representatives as war criminals.

DATE: November 20, 1945-August 31, 1946

LOCALE: Nuremberg, Germany

CATEGORIES: Government and politics; Laws, acts, and legal history

KEY FIGURES:

Karl Dönitz (1891-1980), commander of the German navy, 1943-1945, and Hitler's designated successor as führer and chancellor, April-May, 1945

Hermann Göring (1893-1946), former commander of the German Luftwaffe

Walther Richard Rudolf Hess (1894-1987), Hitler's deputy, 1934-1941

Albert Speer (1905-1981), German minister of armaments, 1942-1945

SUMMARY OF EVENT. As early as 1942, the Allies in the war against Nazi Germany had learned from various sources that the Germans in occupied territories were committing countless atrocities against Jews, prisoners of war, and the civilian population. The Germans after World War I never carried out the provision in the Versailles Treaty (articles 227-230) which required them to bring war criminals to trial. The atrocities reported during World War II seemed to be of an even greater magnitude, and the Allies determined early in the war that German war criminals had to be brought to justice. On October 7, 1942, the United States and Great Britain took the lead in establishing the War Crimes Commission, which started to collect evidence and drew up a list of German war criminals. During the Moscow Conference of Foreign Ministers on November 1, 1943, the Soviet Union joined the Western Allies in a declaration on war crimes, promulgated over the names of Churchill, Roosevelt, and Stalin.

Following the defeat of Nazi Germany in May of 1945,

the United States, Soviet Union, Britain, and France made more detailed plans at the London Conference of Foreign Ministers. This conference provided for the two legal instruments under which these trials were to be held: The London Agreement of August 8, 1945, and the Control Council Law No. 10, promulgated by the Allied Control Council in Berlin on December 20, 1945. A list was drafted containing twenty-four Nazi leaders and six Nazi organizations which were to be brought to trial soon. The city of Nuremberg, site of the annual Nazi Party rally, was chosen as the location for the International Military Tribunal (IMT), as it was reasoned that the Nazis should be brought to justice at the place of their greatest triumphs and face their crimes where they had originated.

The list of the accused included Hermann Göring, leader of the Luftwaffe; Rudolf Hess, former deputy of the führer; Joachim von Ribbentrop, foreign minister; Ernst Kaltenbrunner, head of the *Sicherheitsdienst* (security police force, known as the SD) of the *Schutzstaffel* (protective rank, known as the SS), standing in for Heinrich Himmler and Reinhard Heydrich, both dead; Baldur von Schirach, leader of the Nazi youth organization; Arthur Seyss-Inquart, German high commissioner in the occupied Netherlands; Hans Frank, governor general of occupied Poland; Fritz Saukel, commissioner general of forced labor in occupied territories; Alfred Rosenberg, minister for the conquered eastern territories; Albert Speer, minister of armaments; Wilhelm Frick, minister of the interior; Robert Ley, head of the German Labor Front; Hans Fritzsche, a high official of the ministry of propaganda, standing in for Goebbels; Julius Streicher, editor of the racial and anti-Semitic publication *Der Stürmer*; Hjalmar Schacht, financial wizard, minister of economics and president of the Reichsbank until 1938; Walter Funk, minister of economics and head of the Reichsbank from 1938 to 1945; Grand Admiral Karl Dönitz, commander of the navy and Hitler's designated successor; Admiral Erich Raeder, commander of the German navy; Field Marshal Wilhelm Keitel, chief of the German General Staff; General Alfred Jodl, chief of staff to Keitel; Constantine von Neurath, German foreign minister from 1932 to 1938; Franz von Papen, German vice chancellor, 1932-1934, and German ambassador to Turkey, 1939-1944; and Gustav Krupp von Bohlen und Halbach, retired industrialist of armaments.

Martin Bormann, Hitler's secretary and last deputy, was also indicted, but his whereabouts were unknown. Excluded from the list were Adolf Hitler; Joseph Goebbels, minister of propaganda; and Heinrich Himmler, head of the SS and the Gestapo; all of whom had committed suicide.

The six organizations named as defendants were the Reich cabinet, the leadership corps of the Nazi Party, the SS, the SD, the Gestapo, the paramilitary *Sturm Abteilung* (storm troopers, known as the SA), and the General Staff and High Command of the German army. The indictments, promulgated by the Allies in their final form on October 6, 1945, were made up of four counts: crimes against peace; war crimes; crimes against humanity; and participation in a conspiracy to commit crimes against peace, war crimes, and crimes against humanity.

The International Military Tribunal consisted of four members and four alternates, two judges from each of the four Allied powers. Its charter stipulated that neither the prosecution nor the defense could challenge the competence of the tribunal, and that persons could be held accountable for actions carried out while following orders of a superior.

The Nuremberg Trials convened on November 20, 1945, with the reading of the long indictment against the German war criminals. Only twenty-one of the twenty-four Nazis were seated in the dock. Martin Bormann was never apprehended but tried in absentia, Gustav Krupp was excused because of failing health, and Robert Ley had committed suicide while in prison. The trials lasted over nine months, during which the prosecution made use of numerous eyewitnesses and captured German documents describing details of the crimes perpetrated by the Nazis. No effective defense could be devised against the overwhelming evidence.

The trials finished on August 31, 1946. The tribunal handed down its judgments on October 1. Papen, Schacht, and Fritzsche were acquitted. The others accused were found guilty under one or more of the four counts of the indictment: Hess, Funk, and Raeder were sentenced to life imprisonment; Dönitz, Speer, Schirach, and Neurath were sentenced to lesser terms, and the remainder were sentenced to death by hanging. The capital sentences were carried out on the night of October 15-16. Göring managed to escape the gallows by swallowing poison that had been smuggled into his cell. The tribunal also handed down verdicts of guilty on the leadership corps of the Nazi Party, on the SS and the SD, and on the Gestapo. After the first Nuremberg trial, twelve more trials were held under the Control Council Law No. 10. In these trials, 185 persons were indicted. These trials resulted in the hanging of thirty-five doctors, concentration camp guards, and SS leaders; in the remaining cases, 120 defendants received prison sentences and 35 were acquitted.

The Nuremberg Trials have remained a subject of controversy. Those who oppose the trials claim that the trials themselves were illegal, that the military tribunal had no jurisdiction and was not a legal court of law, that there was no world state from which the tribunal's authority could emanate, and that the tribunal's proceedings constituted *ex post facto* prosecutions of the victors on the vanquished. Others questioned the trials because Stalin's Soviet Union was prosecuting and judging Nazi crimes that were not much different from the ones it had committed. Critics also believed that the Allied bombing of Dresden on February 13, 1945, should be tried as a war crime under the criteria of Nuremberg.

Those who have upheld the legality of the trials have advanced the view that the crimes committed by the Nazis violated every standard of human behavior; while there is not international law code against the slaughter and torture of millions of people, such acts are so odious that they need no prohibition by formal statute. The Nuremberg Trials proved to be precedent-setting in the development of international law. In November of 1945, the United Nations General Assembly adopted Resolution 95 (I) which endorsed "the principles of International Law rec-

ognized by the Charter of the Nuremberg Tribunal and the judgment of the Tribunal." Under this provision, the U.N. Security Council established an international war crimes tribunal in 1992 and 1993 to try war crimes committed in the former Yugoslavia.

—Edward P. Keleher, updated by Herbert Luft

Additional reading:

Kelley, Douglas M. *Twenty-two Cells at Nuremberg*. New York: Greenberg, 1947. This classic is by an American psychiatrist who spoke almost daily with the defendants and analyzed them in prison.

Maser, Werner. *Nuremberg: A Nation on Trial*. Translated by Richard Barry. New York: Charles Scribner's Sons, 1979. An account of the trials written by a German historian; though critical of many procedures, Maser is in general agreement with the outcome.

Nazi Conspiracy and Aggression. 8 vols. and 2 supplementary vols. Washington, D.C.: Office of United States Chief of Counsel for Prosecution of Axis Criminality,

Military troops stand guard over the war criminals seated in the defendants' dock at the Nuremberg Trials. In the lower row (left to right) are Hermann Göring, Rudolf Hess, and Joachim von Ribbentrop; Karl Dönitz and Erich Raeder are seated behind Hess and Ribbentrop. (AP/Wide World Photos)

1946-1948. An official collection of documentary evidence based on captured German documents.

Persico, Joseph E. *Nuremberg: Infamy on Trial*. New York: Viking, 1994. A well-written narrative of the trials.

Taylor, Telford. *The Anatomy of the Nuremberg Trials: A Personal Memoir*. New York: Alfred A. Knopf, 1992. A well-documented memoir by the U.S. chief prosecutor at Nuremberg. Described as the ablest American legal mind at the trials, Taylor provides background information and analysis from the perspective of almost fifty years of hindsight.

SEE ALSO: 1939-1945, Gypsies Are Exterminated in Nazi Death Camps; 1939-1945, Nazi Extermination of the Jews; 1940-1944, The French Resistance; 1945, The United Nations Is Formed.

1946
CHURCHILL'S "IRON CURTAIN" SPEECH

Churchill's "Iron Curtain" speech sounds an alarm about Soviet encroachments in Eastern Europe and the Middle East, reflecting a simultaneous change in U.S. foreign policy regarding relations with the Soviet Union.

DATE: March 5, 1946

LOCALE: Fulton, Missouri

CATEGORY: Diplomacy and international relations

KEY FIGURES:

James Francis Byrnes (1879-1972), U.S. secretary of state, 1945-1947

Sir Winston Leonard Spencer Churchill (1874-1965), former prime minister of Great Britain, 1940-1945

Harry S Truman (1884-1972), thirty-third president of the United States, 1945-1953

SUMMARY OF EVENT. When Winston Churchill delivered his historic "Iron Curtain" speech, he uttered a phrase which may be considered the first rhetorical shot of the Cold War. The Soviet Union's postwar posture was exposed, and the once-great ally of the West was portrayed as the arch-aggressor. The dramatic character of the speech is intensified when one recalls that the United States, fresh from victory, was sighing with profound relief; war-torn Western Europe was on the brink of total economic collapse; and Great Britain had recently rejected its great wartime prime minister, preferring instead Clement Attlee's Labour Party with its bold democratic socialistic schemes.

The phrase "Iron Curtain" was first used by Joseph Goebbels, Adolf Hitler's propaganda minister, but Churchill initially used it in a dispatch sent to President Harry

Truman on May 12, 1945, exactly one month after President Franklin Roosevelt's death. With the German defeat imminent, Churchill tried to persuade Truman to disregard the occupation zones arranged at the Quebec Conference in August of 1943, and to continue to hold firmly the Anglo-American positions in Yugoslavia, Austria, Czechoslovakia, Germany north to Lübeck, and into Denmark.

Churchill concluded his message by advising Truman not to move his armies until the three chiefs of state had met and the Western Allies had reached agreement about their Eastern partner's occupation policy. Although Great Britain's primary enemy, Germany, was virtually defeated, the United States was still fighting Japan in the Pacific. Truman was suspicious of the Soviet Union, but he was advised to hope for a settlement by exercising restraint. If he had pursued a hard line, the Soviet Union might have responded with an equally tough line and shut the West out of Berlin and Vienna. Since the atomic bomb had not been tested, Truman's advisers stressed the need for cooperation with the Russians so they would keep the promises they had made at Yalta to enter the Pacific war and to work toward the establishment of a world organization (the United Nations). Thus, the first "Iron Curtain" message, a top-level wartime dispatch, was rejected in Washington, D.C. When Churchill used his "Iron Curtain" phrase publicly a year later, the context had greatly changed.

In the winter of 1946, Churchill was visiting Washington, D.C., and was invited to deliver the John Findley Green Foundation Lecture at Westminster College in Fulton, Missouri. Since Truman assured Churchill that he would preside at the lecture, the occasion assumed an official character. American foreign policy still reflected confidence in the United Nations, faith in the cooperation of the Soviet Union, and a belief in the idea that power politics was an obsolete diplomatic procedure. Although traditional American isolationism supported this policy of restraint and hope, the State Department was actually experiencing the severe limitations of the policy, particularly in Poland and Iran. Secretary of State James F. Byrnes's agreement with the content of Churchill's preparatory notes seems to indicate that the Truman administration was groping for new directions in foreign policy. The transition of U.S. foreign policy toward the Soviet Union actually began in mid-February of 1946, as it moved from a position of accommodation to a position of firmness. Beginning in late 1945, The New York Times had buttressed this change by stepping up its anti-Soviet stance.

Churchill's speech, entitled "The Sinews of Peace," was delivered on March 5, 1946, to an audience of forty thousand people. He opened with an urgent reminder to the American people that victory in war had left them at the pinnacle of power where they must be sensitive to the demands of peace. He urged all nations to cooperate with the United Nations and to add to its effectiveness by establishing an "International Armed Force." Churchill argued that the secrets of atomic weaponry, still restricted to the United States, Canada, and Great Britain, must remain safely guarded in their hands until "the essential brotherhood of men is truly embodied and expressed in a world organization."

Speaking again in general terms, he warned the American people that, while they must be vigilant to any threat of war, they should beware of another "world marauder"—tyranny—and join with all liberty-loving people, particularly their British cousins, in proclaiming "in fearless tones the great principles of freedom and the rights of man. As a complement to the United Nations, Churchill specifically called for a "fraternal association of English-speaking peoples," which would include a permanent defense agreement whereby British and American military forces would pursue a mutual security policy. A strong Anglo-American pact was needed to stabilize the foundations of peace.

Before the rising action of this dramatic speech reached its "Iron Curtain" climax, Churchill eased into his attack upon the Soviet Union's bellicose behavior by stating his admiration for the Russian people and his wartime comrade, Joseph Stalin. As if he were talking directly to the Kremlin, Churchill acknowledged their right to be secure on their western frontiers against the possibility of German aggression and assured them of the Anglo-American resolve to establish lasting friendship with the Soviet Union in spite of "the many differences and rebuffs." He noted, however, that it was his duty "not to misstate the facts . . . about the present position in Europe." Churchill then uttered his famous warning:

> From Stettin in the Baltic to Trieste in the Adriatic, an iron curtain has descended across the Continent. Behind that line lie all the capitals of the ancient states of Central and Eastern Europe. Warsaw, Berlin, Prague, Vienna, Budapest, Belgrade, Bucharest, and Sophia . . . lie in what I must call the Soviet sphere and all are subject in one form or another, not only to Soviet influence but to a very high and increasing measure of control from Moscow.

Churchill was convinced that while the Soviet Union did not want war, it did aim at the indefinite expansion of its power and doctrine. Because Churchill contended that the Soviet Union admired strength and scoffed at military weakness, his response to the descent of the "Iron Curtain" was to propose the establishment of Western military

and moral unity. The first step toward such unity was to cement an Anglo-American defense pact. As a sign of solidarity, on the day of Churchill's speech, Byrnes sent three strong messages to the Soviet Union, questioning their actions in Eastern Europe, China, and Iran.

In an America seeking postwar tranquillity, the Soviet Union's military occupation of Eastern Europe did not clearly reveal its political design. Confidence in the United Nations bolstered American hopes for a cooperative policy with the Soviet Union. In general, Churchill's speech was considered shocking in its bold references to Russian bellicosity. Although Churchill recalled that Truman and Byrnes indicated their approval of his remarks immediately following the speech, Eleanor Roosevelt, Henry Wallace (former vice president under Franklin Roosevelt and Truman's secretary of commerce), and *The New York Herald Tribune* openly disagreed with the tone and content of Churchill's Fulton address. Eight days after the speech, *Pravda* published a bitter condemnation of the speech, expressing Stalin's indignation that Churchill's remarks were sowing discord among the Allied governments. When Prime Minister Clement Attlee of Great Britain was asked to comment on the speech, he diplomatically retreated with a "no comment" response to Churchill's warnings.

Churchill delivered his "Iron Curtain" address at Westminster College in Fulton, Missouri, in 1946. (Winston Churchill Memorial and Library in the United States)

The Truman administration greeted Churchill's plea with ambivalence. Although privately respecting the former prime minister's vision, both Truman and Byrnes publicly responded to the Russian rejoinder and the rift in public opinion by dissociating American policy from Churchill's belligerence toward the Soviet Union. Iran, Manchuria, and the Balkans were points of conflict in U.S.-Soviet relations, but the Truman administration continued to pursue a cooperative policy. During the transition from "cooperation" to "containment," public opinion appeared to be capricious in the extreme. The public opinion polls indicated a shift from an anti-"Iron Curtain" stance to agreement with it in a matter of a few weeks.

Despite Truman's public stance, on February 12, 1946, Secretary of State James Byrnes initiated the reorientation of policy by taking firmer actions in Eastern Europe. He refused to recognize a Soviet inspired accommodation in Bulgaria, and he took the position that the Soviet-inspired Romanian government was not in compliance with earlier Allied agreements. Moreover, he formally complained of harassment of U.S. officials in Albania, and he threatened to withhold U.S. recognition of their government. Likewise, he charged the Russians with holding up economic recovery in Hungary, and he complained vigorously about noncompliance with the Potsdam Declaration in Eastern Europe.

As part of this reorientation, Byrnes went to Miami for a February 17 meeting with Churchill, where the former prime minister's upcoming speech was discussed. On February 22, Byrnes initiated a change in policy toward Iran, which encouraged that government to resist Soviet pressure, a move which thrust the United States into confrontation with the Soviet Union in the eastern Mediterranean and Middle East. In a speech delivered on February 28 in New York, Byrnes announced a new policy of "patience and firmness" toward the Soviet Union. He even called for universal military training in the United States. Finally, he appointed Bernard Baruch to the United Nations Atomic Energy Commission to preserve the atomic monopoly for the United States. A columnist for *The New York Post* wrote on March 1, "A stiffening American attitude towards Russia is in prospect. . . . evidence will soon be forthcoming." Prior to the Churchill speech, President Truman read it with approval.

The rhetoric for a foreign policy change had been clearly enunciated in Churchill's dramatic "Iron Curtain" speech. By 1947, Churchill's Fulton utterances had worked their way into diplomatic realities when certain Cold War facts became clearly visible. The Soviet Union was exerting greater political pressure in Central and Eastern Europe, was uncooperative in the joint occupation of Berlin, was threatening to secure bases in Turkey, and was interfering in a guerrilla war in Greece. When Great Britain announced its withdrawal from Greece, President Truman responded in March, 1947, with his Truman Doctrine, promising military and economic aid to Greece and Turkey. The development of the Marshall Plan in 1948 and the North Atlantic Treaty Organization (NATO) in 1949 further cemented the American commitment to European stability. By that time, the phrase "iron curtain" was a common term in the diplomatic rhetoric of the day.

—*Christopher J. Kauffman,*
updated by Robert Franklin Maddox

ADDITIONAL READING:

Churchill, Winston S. *Memoirs of the Second World War.* Boston: Houghton Mifflin, 1959. This volume is an abridgment of the six volumes of *The Second World War.* In this work, Churchill recalls events surrounding his famous speech.

Ferrell, Robert H. *Harry S. Truman: A Life.* Columbia: University of Missouri Press, 1994. Ferrell concludes that Churchill's speech "embarrassed" the president, who backed away from it.

Halle, Louis J. *The Cold War as History.* London: Chatto & Windus, 1967. Halle views the Fulton speech as a lesson in the foreign policy education of the American people.

Harburt, Fraser J. *The Iron Curtain: Churchill, America, and the Origins of the Cold War.* New York: Oxford University Press, 1986. This work focuses attention on the role of Winston Churchill as "the most active protagonist of a joint Anglo-American political front against the Soviet Union" during and after World War II.

Robertson, David. *Sly and Able: A Political Biography of James F. Byrnes.* New York: W. W. Norton, 1994. This work places the "iron curtain" speech and Byrnes's role in context.

Taylor, A. J. P., ed. *Churchill Revised: A Critical Assessment.* New York: Dial Press, 1969. This collection of essays from four historians and one psychiatrist attempts to bring into focus one of the major figures of the period.

Truman, Harry S. *Memoirs of Harry S. Truman.* Vol. 2: *The Years of Trial and Hope.* New York: Doubleday, 1956. Truman's account of his administration provides an interesting contrast to Churchill's vision.

SEE ALSO: 1945, The Yalta Conference; 1945, The Potsdam Conference; 1947, Marshall Plan Is Announced; 1948-1949, Berlin Airlift; 1949, North Atlantic Treaty.

1947
Marshall Plan Is Announced

The Marshall Plan is announced to assist in the economic rebuilding of Europe; it forms the keystone of U.S. foreign policy concerning the containment of communism.

Date: March 12, 1947

Locale: Washington, D.C.

Categories: Diplomacy and international relations; Economics

Key figures:

Ernest Bevin (1881-1951), British foreign secretary, 1945-1951

Georges Bidault (1899-1983), French foreign minister, 1944-1947

George F. Kennan (born 1904), director of the policy planning staff of the U.S. State Department

George Catlett Marshall (1880-1959), U.S. secretary of state, 1947-1949

Vyacheslav Mikhailovich Molotov (Skryabin; 1890-1986), Soviet commissar for foreign affairs

Harry S Truman (1884-1972), thirty-third president of the United States, 1945-1953

Summary of event. World War II devastated the economies of all the countries in Europe. Even with American aid, Western European nations struggled for two years to reconstruct productivity at prewar levels. In addition, the war had greatly affected the world economic structure. While manufacturing, transportation, and agriculture were far below prewar levels, raw materials from Germany and Eastern Europe and food imports from Asia were unavailable. Thus, Russia's expansion into Eastern Europe and the collapse of the European colonial empire had widespread economic ramifications. The general need for fuel, food, and machinery was acute.

By 1947, recovery was at its lowest. Low productivity, inflation, and a dollar shortage had continuously plagued Western Europe. A dislocated labor force, underfed and ill trained, was attached to a war-battered industrial complex, slow to adapt to peacetime needs and badly in need of raw materials and capital investment. Postwar inflation, brought on by scarcity and its attendant price-wage spiral, and the crying need for social welfare spending created a diseased circulatory system in the economic body politic.

The dollar shortage was related to Western Europe's dependency on American goods and its inability to produce sufficient exports to balance its gold and dollar payments. Without dollars, Western Europe could not invest in the capital goods necessary to increase production, curtail inflation, and redress the balance of trade.

Social unrest and political instability accompanied economic depression. Observers could foresee another rise of totalitarianism in Western Europe. The rapid growth of the French and Italian Communist Parties and a revival of Russian militancy substantiated such fears.

Europe's importance to the United States became very clear in the emerging bipolar world. It ranked second only to the United States in its potential power in industry, productivity, skilled manpower, scientists, and engineers. If these assets had come under the control of the Soviet Union, the military balance would swing sharply in its favor and American security would had been endangered.

Secretary of State George C. Marshall believed that the United States should take the initiative in leading Europe to a long-range plan for revival. He presented the principles of his plan in a Harvard commencement address on June 5, 1947. He focused on Europe's low yield productivity, the need for raw materials, fuel, and modern machinery, and the lack of capital and dollar resources. Marshall warned Americans that a European depression would mean political instability and a threat to peace, and would have adverse effects upon the American economy.

He ended his address with a firm commitment by the United States to underwrite a plan for recovery, one which would be drawn up by representatives of all willing European states. While he invited all governments to participate in the plan, he warned that any government, political party, or groups "which seek to perpetuate human misery in order to profit therefrom politically or otherwise will encounter the opposition of the United States." The transformation of the idea into the Marshall Plan was dependent upon European response.

The United States had never intended the Soviet Union to receive this aid, unless it was willing to open up Eastern Europe. By attaching conditions to the Marshall Plan, the United States hoped to maneuver the Soviet Union into rejecting what seemed to be a generous offer of assistance. The principal planners in Europe would be Great Britain and France, who responded swiftly and decisively. They were instructed to meet with the Russians to formulate a response to the American offer. British foreign secretary Ernest Bevin joined French foreign minister Georges Bidault, and they met with Vyacheslav M. Molotov, the Soviet commissar for foreign affairs, on June 23, 1947. The offer included the required American conditions of private American investment in Eastern Europe, mutual exchange of economic intelligence, and a common, coordinated program for the Continent as a whole. The two Western powers proposed the establishment of a coordinating committee to arrange and evaluate the work of the various committees investigating the resources and needs

Secretary of State George C. Marshall (right) presented the bare outlines of his recovery plan for Europe in a commencement address at Harvard in 1947. (National Archives)

ously undermined. The Soviet Union attacked the Marshall idea as an expression of American imperialism.

A sixteen-member conference opened in Paris on July 22, called the Committee of European Economic Cooperation (CEEC), consisting of delegates from Austria, Belgium, Denmark, France, Greece, Iceland, Ireland, Italy, Luxembourg, the Netherlands, Norway, Portugal, Sweden, Switzerland, Turkey, and the United Kingdom. On September 23, the conference issued a report which outlined a four-year plan for recovery for the sixteen nations and West Germany.

In general, the participating nations pledged to coordinate self-help and mutual aid projects to increase agricultural and industrial productivity, thereby maximizing exports and minimizing imports while reducing their balance of payments deficit. Stabilization of the various currencies was dependent on the amount of foreign assistance. The most significant section of the report was the proposal

of participating nations and to devise a general plan for recovery. Molotov rejected the proposal on the grounds that such a committee would necessarily intervene in the internal affairs of sovereign states. As a substitute, Molotov's plan called for the participating states to indicate their needs after the United States had specified the amount of aid it was willing to grant. Such a proposal was a complete reversal of Marshall's idea for European cooperation, which Bevin and Bidault persistently pursued. Consequently, Molotov rejected the American offer, and the Soviets were forced to take the blame for the worsening Cold War.

On July 3, the day after Molotov left the meeting, Bevin and Bidault invited twenty-two other European nations to a Paris meeting. Because of Russian dominance, Czechoslovakia was the only Eastern European state to accept the invitation, and Poland had also expressed an interest in the offer. Under pressure from Molotov, however, they would reject it. Without such solidarity, Soviet authority in Eastern Europe would have been seri-

to establish a European recovery organization insuring continuous economic cooperation in resources, productivity, transportation, trade, and labor supply. Plans for mutual interests, disregarding national boundaries, included the construction of a series of power plants to exploit natural resources in Germany, the Alps, and Italy. The CEEC Report projected that more than fifty-seven billion dollars in non-European imports of food, fuel, machinery, iron, and steel would be required if the participating nations were to increase productivity and eventually reduce their balance of payments deficit during the four-year recovery period.

Throughout the summer and fall of 1947, the Truman administration investigated the ramifications of the Marshall Plan with the aim of outlining an aid program acceptable to Congress. On April 3, 1948, however, the Marshall Plan became law in the form of the Foreign Assistance Act of 1948. This act created a new administrative agency, the Economic Cooperation Administration (ECA), which was commissioned to engage in bilateral agreements with the participating countries and coordinate the first year's appropriation, which was not to exceed $4.3 billion, plus another $1 billion for assistance on a loan basis.

The ECA worked closely with the sixteen-nation committee which in March, 1948, became the Organization for European Economic Cooperation (OEEC). At the urging of the United States, the economic aid was funneled into European development through the OEEC. The ECA's aim was to encourage freer trade and rational planning throughout the Continent and lead to an open world market. At American insistence, the smaller nations in OEEC were protected by a rule requiring unanimous consent to any OEEC decision. The OEEC pledged to cooperate in planning production, reducing economic barriers, and establishing a multilateral system of payments. To translate the pledges into reality, OEEC created an administrative council, executive committee, various technical committees, and an executive secretariat. Through these bodies the American and European organizations processed $8.6 billion in aid in three years. The United Kingdom received $2.2 billion, France $1.7 billion, Germany $1.7 billion, Italy $9.18 million, Greece $3.53 million, the Netherlands $6.18 million, and others $1.6 billion.

By 1950, Western European productivity had increased by 45 percent compared to 1947, while exports during the same period increased by 91 percent. Net agricultural production for 1950-1951 exceeded the prewar average level. The economic crisis and the emergence of the Cold War forced the United States and Western Europe to move into a new phase in the development of a viable Atlantic community.

—*Christopher J. Kauffman, updated by Bill T. Manikas*

ADDITIONAL READING:

Brower, Daniel R. *The World in the Twentieth Century: The Age of Global War and Revolution.* Upper Saddle River, N.J.: Prentice Hall, 1996. Brower's work emphasizes the increasing interaction among states and peoples on a global scale.

Paterson, Thomas G., et al. *American Foreign Policy: A History Since 1900.* Lexington, Mass.: D. C. Heath, 1991. This broad survey of American foreign policy provides a comparative treatment of ideology, economics, and strategy and the importance of personalities and domestic politics.

Paxton, Robert O. *Europe in the Twentieth Century.* New York: Harcourt Brace Jovanovich, 1975. Surveying the history of the twentieth century, Paxton illustrates how Europe rapidly lost its dominant status as a result of war, revolution, and economic crisis.

Spanier, John. *American Foreign Policy Since World War II.* Washington, D.C: Congressional Quarterly, 1992. The author strongly emphasizes the international system in explaining the origins and conduct of the Cold War.

Vadney, T. E. *The World Since 1945.* 2nd ed. New York: Penguin Books, 1992. Vadney provides a detailed account of the events of the post-World War II period.

SEE ALSO: 1945, The United Nations Is Formed; 1946, Churchill's "Iron Curtain" Speech; 1948-1949, Berlin Airlift; 1949, North Atlantic Treaty; 1949, Creation of Two German Republics; 1950-1963, Italy's Postwar Economic Boom; 1957, Common Market Is Formed.

1948-1949
BERLIN AIRLIFT

The Berlin Airlift allows the United States and Britain to provide relief to West Berlin in the face of Soviet attempts to cut off West Berlin from the zones of Germany administered by the Western Allies.

DATE: June 24, 1948-May, 1949
LOCALE: Berlin, Germany
CATEGORY: Diplomacy and international relations
KEY FIGURES:
General Lucius DuBignon Clay (1897-1978), U.S. military governor in Germany and commander of U.S. forces in Europe
George Catlett Marshall (1880-1959), U.S. secretary of state, 1947-1949
Ernst Reuter (1889-1953), lord mayor of West Berlin, 1948-1953
Joseph Stalin (Iosif Vissarionovich Dzhugashvili; 1879-1953), marshal of the Soviet Union and general secretary of the Central Committee of the Communist Party, 1922-1953
Harry S Truman (1884-1972), thirty-third president of the United States, 1945-1953

SUMMARY OF EVENT. The most important and dramatic European confrontation of the United States and the Soviet Union in the formative period of the Cold War was the blockade of Berlin and the airlift that subsequently resulted. The Soviet challenge to the West's rights of access to Berlin seems to have been designed not only to expel the Western powers from the former German capital but also to prevent the creation of a workable West German government. Yet President Harry Truman, Secretary of State George C. Marshall, General Lucius D. Clay, and the British recognized that the continued Western presence in Berlin was a test of the determination of the Western powers regarding the German question, and they made it clear that the West was not going to submit to Stalin's demands.

The problem of Berlin arose from the wartime agreements among the Allies for postwar administration of Germany. Zones of occupation were agreed upon for Germany itself. Although Berlin was deep within the Soviet zone, the powers also arranged sectors in Berlin. American, British, and French authorities dutifully assumed their responsibilities in the ruined capital, seeking every opportunity to cooperate with the Soviet authorities in the Allied Control Council (for all of Germany) and the Kommandatura (for Berlin itself). Soviet obstructionism, however, convinced American leaders that the Soviet Union sought to dominate all of Berlin and eventually Germany as a whole.

In early 1948, the British and the Americans developed plans to merge their two zones in western Germany economically, and they encouraged the French to cooperate. The Soviet Union protested these actions bitterly and responded by exerting more economic pressure on the western sectors of Berlin. In March, the London Conference recommended that West Germany be united to form a federal state, and that it take part in the Marshall Plan of economic recovery. In response, the Soviet Union withdrew its representatives for the Allied Control Council in Berlin, and on April 1 it began the "small Berlin Blockade" by restricting land access to Berlin and deliveries of food and fuel.

American leaders realized that should the Soviets cordon off Berlin entirely, the situation of the city's inhabitants and the token Western garrisons would be desperate. There was no written agreement guaranteeing free access to Berlin by surface transportation, but merely oral understandings. There was a specific agreement on air corridors between Berlin and West Germany, but few believed that the needs of the 2.25 million people in the western sectors could be met by air transport alone.

Aware of the West's dilemma, the Soviets pushed forward with plans to isolate the city. Apparently their goal was to discourage the economic and political unification of West Germany, and eventually to take control of Berlin, by demonstrating that the Western powers were unwilling or unable to protect their rights. The Western powers nevertheless went ahead with economic and currency reform in their zones of Germany and Berlin, introducing the deutsche mark to replace the worthlessly inflated old currency beginning on June 20, 1948. The full-scale Soviet blockade of West Berlin followed on June 24.

General Clay organized an immediate but modest airlift to keep the Western garrisons in Berlin supplied. Battered old C-47 "Gooney birds," veterans of the Normandy Invasion and the "Asian Hump" airlift, took the first eighty tons of medicine and food to Berlin. Clay went to Washington to consult with President Truman. Clay favored forcing the issue with the Soviet Union by sending an armed transport convoy along the main highway from West Germany into the city. Secretary of State Marshall favored an expanded airlift instead, coupled with a direct but informal approach to Stalin. Truman decided on the airlift rather than the armed convoy, and he told the U.S. ambassador in Moscow to contact Stalin.

An airlift to ferry all necessary supplies for more than two million people was a most difficult undertaking. Moreover, the logistical triumph would have proved fruitless if it had not been for the dogged determination of the people of West Berlin. Berliners knew Soviet troops could take over the city in a few hours. The Western Allies had only some sixty-five hundred combat troops in Berlin to face more than three hundred thousand troops in the Soviet zone. Yet the Berliners refused to give into fear, hunger, or discouragement. Ernst Reuter, a Social Democrat and staunch opponent of Communist rule, was elected lord mayor of West Berlin in December. During the blockade many non-Communist professors abandoned the Humboldt University in the Soviet sector and, with American aid, established the Free University of Berlin. Reuter's leadership and the Free University became rallying points for the West Berliners, strengthening their resolve.

The airlift proved more and more successful, with tons of coal and food staples, and enough luxuries such as fish, coffee, and children's candies arriving each day to buoy popular spirits. Politically, the blockade and the airlift brought unwelcome results for the Soviet Union. Rather than forcing a humiliating retreat on the Western powers, it showed them to be solid allies of the Berliners, willing to pay any price to save the people from either Soviet domination or war. West Germany continued on its way to becoming a unified state and eventually an ally of the North Atlantic Treaty Organization rather than merely a conquered enemy. Truman, who was facing a difficult election campaign at home, emerged as a hero, willing to face up to Communist threats without actually going to war. He not only ordered the full power of U.S. transport aircraft into the airlift, but he moved B-29 bombers, capable of carrying atomic weapons, to British bases within range of Moscow. Soviet attempts to intimidate the American and British fliers on airlift duty by holding "air maneuvers" along the approaches to the West Berlin airfields were brushed aside, and radar-aided deliveries continued to increase even in the bad winter weather.

At the same time, behind the scenes diplomatic efforts by Truman tried to bring an end to the crisis. Already in August of 1948, the U.S. ambassador in Moscow spoke directly to Stalin. At times Stalin appeared reasonable.

"After all," the Soviet leader commented, "we are still allies." At other times Stalin seemed elusive and belligerent, and Truman commented privately in September that he feared that the United States and the Soviet Union were slipping toward war.

By February of 1949, it had become clear that the Western powers could sustain the airlift indefinitely and that the blockade was driving the Germans into the arms of the West. Stalin hinted to a Western newsman that he was willing to give up his objections to the use of the West German deutsche mark in West Berlin and eventually drop the blockade. Soviet and American diplomats soon began meeting secretly at the United Nations in New York.

In early May, the secret talks at the United Nations were nearing successful completion. Simultaneously, the West German parliamentary council was moving toward approval of the constitutional document that would establish the Federal Republic of Germany. On May 10, 1949, the Soviets published the orders for lifting their restrictions, and the Berlin blockade was over. The airlift had lasted a total of 321 days, from June 24, 1948, until May 12, 1949, and brought into Berlin 1,592,787 tons of supplies. The achievements of the airlift were not without cost. It was a heavy burden for the American and British taxpayers, some $200 million, and the Berliners had to make do with very short rations. Moreover, accidental deaths did occur. Twenty-four planes crashed, and seventy-six persons lost their lives.

Although additional Berlin crises would occur, including the building of the Berlin Wall in 1961, the Berlin blockade and the airlift response had been a clear turning point in the history of postwar Europe. Hostilities had been avoided, yet the Soviet Union was forced to back down, and West Germany and West Berlin were clearly linked to the United States and Western Europe for the remainder of the Cold War.

—*Paul A. Whelan, updated by Gordon R. Mork*

ADDITIONAL READING:

Clay, Lucius D. *Decision in Germany*. Garden City, N.Y.: Doubleday, 1950. The American commander in Germany recounts his personal experiences.

Davidson, Walter Phillips. *The Berlin Blockade: A Study in Cold War Politics*. Princeton, N.J.: Princeton University Press, 1958. A well-documented account, originally a Rand Corporation study, emphasizes the brilliant improvisations of the airlift and the political significance, as seen from the perspective of the 1950's.

Ferrell, Robert H. *George C. Marshall*. New York: Cooper Square, 1966. An exhaustive treatment of Marshall's tenure at the State Department, though because of its early publication the author had to rely on memoirs and other published information for most of his information.

Grathwol, Robert P., and Donita M. Moorhus. *American Forces in Berlin, 1945-1994: Cold War Outpost*. Washington, D.C.: Department of Defense, 1994. Partly a commemorative volume, partly a documentary history, this well-illustrated book adds significant details on the American achievements in Berlin.

Shlaim, Avi. *The United States and the Berlin Blockade, 1948-1949: A Study in Crisis Decision-Making*. Berkeley: University of California Press, 1983. A scholarly analysis of U.S. decision making, step by step, during the crises of the blockade and airlift.

Tusa, Ann, and John Tusa. *The Berlin Airlift*. New York: Atheneum, 1988. A well-documented narrative account of the blockade and the airlift by two British authors, within the context of Cold War diplomacy.

SEE ALSO: 1946, Churchill's "Iron Curtain" Speech; 1949, North Atlantic Treaty; 1949, Creation of Two German Republics; 1955, Warsaw Pact Is Signed.

American C-47 cargo planes carried medicine and food staples as part of the Berlin Airlift. (Smithsonian Institution)

1949
NORTH ATLANTIC TREATY

The North Atlantic Treaty creates a defense alliance among twelve democratic nations for assistance in the event of Soviet attack.

DATE: April 4, 1949

LOCALE: Washington, D.C.

CATEGORIES: Diplomacy and international relations; Organizations and institutions

KEY FIGURES:

Dean Acheson (1893-1971), U.S. secretary of state, 1949-1953

Ernest Bevin (1884-1951), British foreign secretary, 1945-1951

Dwight David Eisenhower (1890-1969), U.S. commander of NATO forces, 1951-1952

Robert A. Lovett (1895-1986), U.S. undersecretary of state, 1947-1949

George Catlett Marshall (1880-1959), U.S. secretary of state, 1947-1949

Robert Schuman (1886-1963), French foreign affairs minister, 1948-1952

Harry S Truman (1884-1972), thirty-third president of the United States, 1945-1953

Arthur Vandenberg, Jr. (1884-1951), U.S. senator from Michigan

SUMMARY OF EVENT. Cold War diplomacy originated in the aftermath of World War II, when relations between the two world superpowers—the United States and the Soviet Union—shifted from wartime cooperation to postwar competition. The United States had planned to rely upon the United Nations as the major instrument for an orderly peaceful Europe, but the United Nations also became a forum of Cold War confrontation. When Soviet foreign policy became increasingly militant in occupied Germany as well as increasing its hold on Eastern Europe, however, traditional American isolationism changed to a policy of active interventionism under the label of "containment" of Soviet expansion.

The Truman Doctrine of March, 1947, was the first official step in containing the expansion of the Soviet orbit. It pledged military and economic assistance to Greece and Turkey, as well as to all nations threatened by totalitarianism. The proposal for the European Recovery Program (ERP), better known as the Marshall Plan in honor of its author, was enunciated a few months after the Truman Doctrine. This ambitious assistance project was America's response to Europe's economic instability, and all states in that continent were eligible to apply for funds.

The Kremlin initially participated in early negotiations but later rejected the Marshall Plan, forbidding its satellites to participate in what it considered to be American imperialism. Marshall Plan assistance therefore did not reach the Communist nations of Central and Eastern Europe. The Soviet Union also established the Cominform (Communist Information Bureau) as a means of tightening its control over the Communist parties of Europe. The adoption and implementation of the Truman Doctrine and the Marshall Plan illustrate America's commitment to assist democratic Europe in defending itself against communist militancy.

Mutual distrust between the United States and the Soviet Union became more evident in the unfolding events of 1947-1948. While Washington and Moscow exchanged accusations and threats, Western Europe, caught in the throes of economic stagnation, saw itself caught in the cross fire. As cooperation between the former Allies continued to break down, it became evident to Great Britain, France, and other countries that some form of military security was imperative if democracy was to maintain itself against the potential Soviet challenge. France and Great Britain signed the Treaty of Dunkirk in March of 1947, creating a defense alliance against an attack from Soviet-occupied central Europe. Although pleased with this agreement, France and Great Britain believed an expanded and stronger defense association was needed.

Growing distrust of the Soviet Union, combined with the Greek and Turkish crises of 1946-1947, the Communist coup in Czechoslovakia in February of 1948, and the beginning of the Berlin blockade in the late spring of 1948, impelled the United States to support a military partnership with Western Europe, leading to the establishment of the North Atlantic Treaty Organization (NATO) in 1949. American forces already were deployed in Europe, primarily as occupation forces in its zone of defeated Germany. Prior to NATO, the United States had never undertaken a peacetime military alliance with any state; this fact indicates the revolutionary character of NATO in American foreign policy and helps to explain the relatively long birth process of the alliance.

George F. Kennan, the chief of the policy planning staff of the State Department and author of the theory of containment, dates the conception of the NATO idea as January 13, 1948, the date of a letter from British foreign secretary Ernest Bevin to Secretary of State George Marshall. Bevin inquired about the State Department's view of a British proposal to initiate discussions on common defense problems, and Marshall's reply supported this proposal. On March 17, shortly after democratic Czechoslovakia had fallen to a communist *coup d'état*, the United Kingdom, France, Belgium, the Netherlands, and Luxembourg signed the Brussels Pact. Although this pact was an attempt to provide for an economic and cultural community, it created a union which was primarily an expanded military alliance. As European economic stability rested upon American support, so European military security was obviously dependent upon American assistance. The United States, however, was not a signatory to the treaty.

When Washington eventually responded to an invitation from the Brussels Pact members, it did so through a Senate resolution. Undersecretary of State Robert A. Lovett and Senator Arthur Vandenberg, a Republican who led bipartisan support for the Marshall Plan, were responsible for the Vandenberg Resolution which gained overwhelming Senate approval on June 11, 1948. This opened the way for more serious consultation with the governments of democratic European nations, as well as Canada, to develop a broader and more inclusive military association.

These negotiations led to the formal signing of the NATO treaty in Washington on April 4, 1949. This collective defense treaty pledged to support the purposes and principles of the United Nations, established under the provision in article 51 of the U.N. Charter for a regional mutual defense agreement. Article 5 of the NATO agreement states the central purpose of the treaty: "The Parties agree that an armed attack against one or more of them in Europe or North America shall be considered an attack against them all." The treaty envisioned American military aid to the Allies, a permanent organization, and joint military commands. Eventually the NATO structure included a North Atlantic Council, a secretary-general, an international staff, chiefs of staff of NATO members forming the Military Committee, and supplementary regional planning staffs.

Twelve nations signed the treaty: Belgium, Canada, Denmark, France, Iceland, Italy, Luxembourg, the Netherlands, Norway, Portugal, Great Britain, and the United States. The inclusion of Italy indicates the alliance was not geographically limited to the northern Atlantic Ocean region, despite its name, and this was further illustrated by the entrance of Greece and Turkey in 1952. For ideological and political reasons Franco's Spain and Tito's Yugoslavia were excluded from the treaty. Germany was still under four-power Allied occupation and this fact, plus concern about the effects of German rearmament, precluded West Germany's participation as a treaty signatory. After the return of full sovereignty in the new West German state, however, the Bonn government became a NATO member in 1955. Spain joined as NATO's sixteenth member in 1981.

NATO strategy was primarily based upon the nuclear deterrent of the United States. The Americans also sup-

plied the preponderance of naval and air power while the European nations were responsible for maintaining the bulk of the ground forces. The Soviet Union had approximately 175 divisions along its western frontiers in 1949, but the NATO nations combined had a mere fourteen, two of which were American. This thin protective shield could do little more than temporarily slow a Red Army attack, but such an assault would presumably lead to American nuclear retaliation.

With the Soviet Union's explosion of its own nuclear bomb late in 1949 and the outbreak of the Korean War in 1950, America's European allies demanded an increase in U.S. ground forces to guarantee that it would come to the aid of its allies in the event of a Soviet attack. Thus, by 1951 a substantial NATO defense force had been established. With an American as supreme commander and a large American contingent, NATO military forces indicated the depth of American commitment to the defense of Western Europe.

—José M. Sánchez, updated by C. James Haug

ADDITIONAL READING:

Acheson, Dean. *Present at the Creation: My Years in the State Department*. New York: W. W. Norton, 1969. Acheson's memoirs of his years as secretary of state under Truman.

Feis, Herbert. *From Trust to Terror: The Onset of the Cold War, 1945-1950*. New York: W. W. Norton, 1970. A detailed account of the issues during the early period of the Cold War.

Isaacson, Walter. *The Wise Men: Six Friends and the World They Made: Acheson, Bohlen, Harriman, Kennan, Lovett, McCloy*. New York: Simon & Schuster, 1986. Profiles of major foreign policy specialists and their influence.

Kaplan, Lawrence S. *NATO and the United States: The Enduring Alliance*. New York: Twayne, 1988. Surveys America's relationship with its NATO partners, including NATO's creation.

Sherwen, Nicholas, ed. *NATO's Anxious Birth: The Prophetic Vision of the 1940's*. New York: St. Martin's Press, 1985. Topical essays cover the formative period of the alliance.

Truman, Harry. *Memoirs: Years of Trial and Hope, 1946-1952*. Garden City, N.Y.: Doubleday, 1956. The president's personal account of the Cold War period and the negotiations leading to the Western alliance.

Vandenberg, Arthur H., Jr., ed. *The Private Papers of Senator Vandenberg*. Boston: Houghton Mifflin, 1952. Observations of a prominent supporter of Western defense.

SEE ALSO: 1945, The United Nations Is Founded; 1947, Marshall Plan Is Announced; 1955, Warsaw Pact Is Signed; 1966-1995, France Withdraws from NATO's Military Structure.

1949
CREATION OF TWO GERMAN REPUBLICS

The creation of two German republics powerfully symbolizes the division of Cold War-era Europe into two hostile blocs.

DATE: May 23 and October 7, 1949
LOCALE: Bonn and Berlin, Germany
CATEGORY: Government and politics
KEY FIGURES:

Konrad Adenauer (1876-1967), chancellor of the Federal Republic of Germany (FRG) and chairman of the Christian Democratic Union, 1949-1963

James Francis Byrnes (1879-1972), U.S. secretary of state, 1945-1947

Lucius DuBignon Clay (1897-1978), U.S. Army general and military governor of the American occupation zone, 1947-1949

Theodor Heuss (1884-1963), president of the Federal Republic of Germany and chairman of the Free Democratic Party, 1949-1959

Walter Ulbricht (1893-1973), head of the ruling Socialist Unity Party of East Germany

SUMMARY OF EVENT. Set in motion by passage of the Basic Law on May 23, 1949, the formal establishment of the Federal Republic of Germany (FRG) and the German Democratic Republic (GDR) occurred on September 21 and October 7, 1949, respectively. The creation of these two separate German states was the ultimate consequence of the Cold War between the United States and the Soviet Union that evolved soon after the defeat of Nazi Germany. The division of Germany came to symbolize the division of the world into Eastern and Western blocs and represented one of the most serious threats to world peace.

At the close of World War II, the Allied Powers had concerned themselves only in a limited way with the future of Germany. In effect, they had decided to divide the prewar territory of the German Reich into eight separate parts. The most important were the four zones of occupation. The capital city of Berlin was given separate special status, placed under four-power control and divided into four occupation sectors. East Prussia was divided, the northern half given to the Soviet Union and the southern half placed under Polish administration, along with all the territory east of a line formed by the Oder and the western Neisse rivers. In addition, the Saar region was given special status and placed under French control. Regarding the control machinery for the occupation zones, it was stipulated that each Allied commander in chief would function as military governor in his respective occupation zone. Matters of common concern to all of occupied Germany were to be dealt with by an Allied Control Council. These arrangements were intended to be temporary, pending more detailed and permanent agreements for the uniform political and economic administration of Germany. Such agreements, however, would not materialize for thirty-five years.

At the Potsdam Conference in the summer of 1945, the victorious Allies reiterated their intentions for defeated Germany. These included complete disarmament and demilitarization; the eradication of all vestiges of Nazism and the restructuring of German political life along democratic lines; the destruction of the industrial cartels and monopolies; and the extraction of reparations. At this time, major differences regarding the future of Germany between the United States and Great Britain on one side and the Soviet Union on the other were already apparent. Disagreement over the issue of reparations was the major reason for the failure to reach a permanent agreement on all of occupied Germany.

The United States and Great Britain were becoming apprehensive about Soviet power extending deep into central Europe, and they envisioned a revived Germany serving as a barrier to the expansion of communism. Conversely, the Soviet Union was unwilling to relinquish its claim to participate in the determination of policies regarding the western zones and to face the prospect of having the resources of that area turned against it. In the end, it was agreed that each occupying power could draw reparations from its own zone and the Soviet Union, in view of the greater industrial wealth in the western zones, would receive from these zones an additional 25 percent of the industrial equipment considered unessential for the German peace economy. The provisions were highly ambiguous and the subject of considerable polemics between the occupying powers. A major item of contention was whether the Soviet Union's share of reparations should be derived from the removal of plants existing at the end of the war or from current production. The United States refused to allow payments from current production.

The functioning of the Allied Control Council came to an end when the Soviet commandant walked out of the Control Council on March 20, 1948, and the Soviet military administration began to impose a blockade on Berlin shortly thereafter. As the hostilities and suspicions between the powers mounted, the Soviets used their control over the military and civilian traffic between the western sectors and Berlin to retaliate for what they considered hostile acts. In this case, it was the introduction into West Berlin of the German mark, the new currency of the western zones. On July 24, the Soviets halted all rail and road traffic with the West. The Berlin blockade was the most serious crisis of the evolving Cold War. The United States responded by supplying the daily needs of the western sectors through the most massive airlift in history, for a period of eleven months. The consequence was the definite split of Berlin. The sobering crisis also had the effect of ending the stubborn French opposition to the creation of a West German government. Moreover, the path was clear for twelve nations to respond to the United States initiatives and to negotiate the North Atlantic Pact, signed on April 4, 1949.

The United States and Great Britain had already agreed to an economic fusion of their zones as early as December, 1946. The area, known as Bizonia, was to become self-sustaining in three years and thus reduce occupation costs. With the assistance of selected German leaders, an administrative machinery was established in Frankfurt. By 1947, an Economic Council was in existence, the members of which were selected by the popular branches of the newly established provincial legislatures within Bizonia. This body could adopt and promulgate ordinances, with the approval of an Anglo-American Bipartite Board. Soon an executive committee and a German high court were added to the Economic Council. Thus, the organs of a central German government were gradually emerging for the American and British zones. The growing split between the Soviet Union and the three western Allies ultimately induced France to join in the establishment of a central German government for all three western zones.

The United States had been on public record since September, 1946, when Secretary of State James F. Byrnes declared that the United States would grant the German people the right to manage their own affairs, as soon as they were able to do so in a democratic manner. This matter was more deliberately taken up at the meeting of the Council of Ministers in London, in February, 1948. In addition to the three western Allies, Belgium, the Netherlands, and Luxembourg were participating in the deliberations. At this time, basic agreement on the fusion of the three western zones was achieved. As the four-power control apparatus had come to a complete standstill in mid-1948, the western Allies proceeded with specific trizonal arrangements. The heads of the various German provincial governments were empowered by the military governors to convene a constituent assembly for the pur-

Signs in Berlin warned passersby of the boundary dividing West Berlin from the sector of the city controlled by the Communist-dominated German Democratic Republic. (National Archives)

pose of drafting a democratic, federal constitution. The German assembly, apprehensive about finalizing the division of Germany and desirous to give the formal arrangements a kind of provisional status, called itself "Parliamentary Council" and the new constitution came to be referred to as "Basic Law." The composition of the Parliamentary Council reflected the proportionate strength of the political parties. Konrad Adenauer, the chairman of the Christian Democratic Union (CDU), was elected the presiding officer.

On May 23, 1949, the Basic Law was formally adopted. The Allies approved it with some reservations and negotiated for the arrangements paving the way for civilian control. Residual occupation powers were exercised by a new Allied High Commission. Following the first postwar elections, the new Parliament convened in Bonn for its inaugural session on September 7, 1949. A federal convention elected Theodor Heuss, the chairman of the Free Democratic Party (FDP), as federal president. Heuss then nominated Konrad Adenauer for federal chancellor. Adenauer was elected by the Parliament with a one-vote margin and formed a coalition government. Thus, all the basic arrangements being attended to, the Federal Republic of Germany was officially launched in a formal ceremony on September 21, 1949.

The Soviet Union strongly and bitterly protested the establishment of the West German state. In its zone, however, fundamental societal changes had begun to be implemented, with the objective of eliminating all aspects of capitalism and creating a socialist society. The Soviet military administration had for some time permitted the formation of German central organs. These were controlled by the Communist-dominated Socialist Unity Party (SED), under the effective leadership of Walter Ulbricht. The Soviet Union was, therefore, able to follow suit quickly in the formal division of Germany. It authorized the drafting of a constitution for an East German state. On October 7, 1949, a so-called German People's Council convened in Berlin and voted unanimously to transform itself into the provisional People's Chamber of the German Democratic Republic and adopted the new constitution, thereby formally launching the GDR.

—*Manfred Grote, updated by Steve D. Boilard*

ADDITIONAL READING:

Adenauer, Konrad. *Memoirs, 1945-53.* Translated by Beate Ruhm von Oppen. Chicago: Henry Regnery, 1966. West Germany's first Chancellor describes the first years after the defeat of Hitler. The establishment of the FRG is treated in chapter 12.

Clay, Lucius D. *Decision in Germany.* Garden City, N.Y.: Doubleday, 1950. A detailed, firsthand account of the occupation of defeated Germany by the Allies, and the subsequent partition and division of the country. Clay was the military governor of the American occupation zone.

Committee on Foreign Relations, United States Senate. *Documents on Germany, 1944-1970.* Washington, D.C.: U.S. Government Printing Office, 1971. Includes text of numerous official documents relating to the division of Germany.

Sowden, J. K. "Division 1949-55." In *The German Question, 1945-1973: Continuity in Change.* New York: St. Martin's Press, 1975. Chapter 4 of Sowden's work presents an account of the procedural details surrounding the creation of the FRG and GDR.

Turner, Henry Ashby, Jr. "The Birth of Two New Governments." In *Germany from Partition to Reunification.* New Haven, Conn.: Yale University Press, 1992. Chapter 2 of Turner's work gives a brief account of the formal creation of the two German states.

SEE ALSO: 1948-1949, Berlin Airlift; 1949, North Atlantic Treaty; 1955, Warsaw Pact Is Signed; 1961, Building of the Berlin Wall; 1973, East and West Germany Establish Diplomatic Relations; 1989, The Berlin Wall Falls; 1990, German Reunification..

1950-1963
ITALY'S POSTWAR ECONOMIC BOOM

Italy's postwar economic boom transforms it from a relatively backward agricultural society into one of the most advanced industrial nations in the world.

DATE: 1950-1963

LOCALE: Italy

CATEGORIES: Economics; Government and politics

KEY FIGURES:

Alcide De Gasperi (1881-1954), Italian prime minister, 1945-1953

Luigi Einaudi (1874-1961), minister of the budget, 1947-1948, president of Italy, 1948-1955

Amintore Fanfani (born 1908), Italian prime minister, 1954, 1960-1963

Enrico Mattei (1906-1962), director of the National Hydrocarbons Agency, 1953-1962

SUMMARY OF EVENT. Italy's rapid rise to economic prominence represents one of the most significant historical developments of the European postwar era. Prior to World War II, Italy was, in many respects, still an economically underdeveloped country. Although pockets of modern industry existed in the northwest, almost half of the population was still engaged in agriculture, and most manufacturing was labor intensive and small scale. The war, with its widespread destruction and massive economic dislocations, only served to compound these problems. By 1945, Italian industrial production stood at only 25 percent of its 1938 level, and per capita income was actually lower than in 1861.

Nevertheless, during the following two decades, Italy would experience a spectacular economic revival. Propelled by a unique combination of national and international forces, it would rebuild its shattered industry, update its antiquated technology, and become a major exporter on a global scale. By 1965, it would rank among the world's seven largest industrial powers, and its people would enjoy a level of affluence comparable to the most advanced societies of the West.

At the center of Italy's postwar economic recovery lay the extraordinary growth of Italian industry. Between 1950 and 1963, Italian industrial production increased by 8.1 percent per annum, faster than any country in the world except West Germany and Japan. During the same period, gross domestic product more than doubled, unemployment dropped from two million to five hundred thousand, and exports increased by an annual average rate of more than 14 percent. By 1963, the economy's ability to create new jobs was three times higher than in 1950, capital investment, saving, and productivity were all at record levels, and the country's total net capital stock had increased by more than 100 percent.

While virtually all sectors of Italian industry participated in this general economic expansion, some grew faster than others. Among those recording the greatest gains were the chemical industry (235 percent between 1953 and 1962), petroleum and coal products (203 percent), automobiles (201 percent), and food production (68 percent). In 1951, Italy produced 18,500 refrigerators; by 1967, it was producing 3.2 million, more than any other country in Europe. At the same time, Italy also became Europe's largest producer of washing machines and dishwashers, and the production of Italian plastics increased twenty-fold. By the mid-1960's, Italian cars, scooters, home appliances, and clothing had become staples throughout much of Western Europe, and companies such as Fiat, Olivetti, and Zanussi became household names. Overall, during the thirteen years after 1950, Italian exports tripled. Western journalists began to speak buoyantly of an Italian "economic miracle," and, for millions of Italians living in northern and central Italy in particular, the poverty and privations of the immediate postwar period were clearly things of the past.

The reasons for Italy's rapid postwar economic recovery are both complex and varied. Among them, one of the most important, particularly for the early years, was American aid. Between 1945 and 1948, the United States supplied Italy with more than $2 billion in economic assistance. This was followed by an additional $1.5 billion under the Marshall Plan from 1949 to 1953. The money—which was granted in the form of food, fuel, machinery, technical assistance, and loans—did a great deal to help restart the Italian economy, and thus provided the foundation upon which much of subsequent expansion was based.

Once started, however, Italian economic growth proved to be self-sustaining. The main reason for this was Italy's astonishing ability to export its products abroad. Low price and excellence in design made Italian manufactured goods highly desirable on the international market. Competitive prices, in turn, were a function of the artificially low exchange rate which had been established for the lira against the dollar, inexpensive energy costs, and suppressed wages.

Of the three, it was wages which were clearly the most important. The Italian economic "miracle" was made possible, to a large extent, by the human resources of the south. Between 1951 and 1970, almost four million people

left southern Italy, most of them impoverished peasants seeking jobs in northern Italian cities. In an age of high unemployment and weak unions, they supplied the cheap labor necessary for Italian products to remain competitive on the open market, and thus gave Italian entrepreneurs the edge that they needed to compete abroad. This factor became especially important after 1957, when Italy joined with five other countries to found the European Economic Community (EEC), or "Common Market." Membership in the Common Market allowed Italian companies to export their products to EEC countries without tariffs, and thus produced six years of unprecedented economic boom. Between 1958 and 1961 alone, Italy's gross domestic product increased by more than 30 percent in real terms, the highest rate of growth in Italian history, and almost 50 percent greater than that of the EEC as a whole.

Finally, among the factors which helped to produce Italy's postwar economic revival, special emphasis must be given to the role played by the state. Between 1948 and 1962, Italy was governed by a long series of Center-Right Coalitions led by the politically-moderate Christian Democratic Party. The party's founder, Alcide De Gasperi, who was prime minister from 1945 to 1953, was a determined advocate of European integration and strongly pro-business. In 1947, he chose as his minister of the budget, Luigi Einaudi, an economic liberal who was a firm believer in a market economy and a vociferous exponent of free trade. Together, they enacted a series of measures which freed Italian companies from wartime restrictions, stabilized the currency, reduced the budget deficit, and, more generally, created a fiscal and regulatory atmosphere in which Italian business could thrive.

In addition, De Gasperi and his successors, most notably Amintore Fanfani, used a number of government holding companies and agencies, many of which dated from the Fascist era, to stimulate the economy directly. Among the most important were the Institute for Industrial Reconstruction, which provided funds for the development of industry, the National Hydrocarbons Agency, which helped supply low cost energy, and the gigantic Fund for the South, which was created in 1950 to facilitate the development of southern Italy.

By 1970, more than 350 Italian firms were either partially or wholly state owned or state controlled, including Alitalia (the national airline), Alfa Romeo (automobiles), and Finsider (the steel giant). Overall, these firms employed more than four hundred thousand people, and many, such as the state-owned petroleum company directed by Enrico Mattei, were brilliantly administered and contributed enormously to Italy's economic success. Thus, by the late 1960's, Italy had developed its own unique form of "mixed economy" in which a capital-intensive and state-controlled public sector and an export-oriented private sector existed side by side.

Italy's postwar economic "miracle" was not without its problems. First, Italian industrialization, despite its impressive achievements, was geographically limited, confining itself almost exclusively to a small triangle in the northwest enclosed by Turin, Genoa, and Milan. As such, it failed to bridge the historic gap in wealth, education, and productivity which existed between the country's northern and southern regions. By 1971, per capita income in the north was double that of the rest of the peninsula, and the south had fallen further behind. Second, the Italian working class—whose labor was crucial to the process of modernization—never received its fair share of the wealth produced by Italy's burgeoning economy. Between 1953 and 1960, for example, while industrial production rose by 89 percent, and labor productivity increased by 62 percent, real wages in industry actually experienced a slight decline. As a result, many Italian workers carried within them deep-seated feelings of resentment and alienation, and their anger would explode in a renewed wave of labor unrest in 1969.

Nevertheless, despite these shortcomings, between 1950 and 1963, Italy had undergone a remarkable transformation. By the late 1960's, the average Italian lived longer, ate better, and was healthier than at any other time in Italian history. Millions experienced new levels of affluence and personal liberty, and many millions more confronted the challenges of urban life for the first time. Italy, in short, had become an industrial society, and the values and aspirations of its people had come to reflect those of the modern world. —*John Santore*

ADDITIONAL READING:

Clark, Martin. *Modern Italy, 1871-1982*. New York: Longman, 1984. Chapter 17 of this work is succinct and scholarly and provides an excellent place to begin the study of the postwar Italian economy.

Clough, Shepard B. *The Economic History of Modern Italy*. New York: Columbia University Press, 1964. A comprehensive overview of Italian economic development since unification, with special emphasis on the period after 1945.

Ginsborg, Paul. *A History of Contemporary Italy: Society and Politics, 1943-1988*. New York: Penguin Books, 1990. Written by a noted expert on postwar Italy, this book offers a number of brilliant insights into the social consequences of Italy's economic transformation.

Hine, David. *Governing Italy: The Politics of Bargained Pluralism*. Oxford: Clarendon Press, 1993. A penetrating study of Italy's postwar political system, with an unusually concise discussion of Italian economic development since 1945.

Scimone, Giuseppe. "The Italian 'Miracle.'" In *Economic 'Miracles.'* Introduction by J. Enoch Powell. London: Andre Deutsch, for The Institute of Economic Affairs, 1964. A compact account emphasizing the role played by industry.

SEE ALSO: 1947, Marshall Plan Is Announced; 1957, Common Market Is Formed; 1961, Organization for Economic Cooperation and Development Forms; 1987, European Community Adopts the Single Europe Act.

1950

EUROPEAN CONVENTION ON HUMAN RIGHTS IS SIGNED

The European Convention on Human Rights is signed to implement the policies established in the Genocide Convention treaty.

DATE: November 4, 1950

LOCALE: Rome, Italy

CATEGORY: Diplomacy and international relations

KEY FIGURE:

René Cassin (1887-1976), French judge on the European Court of Human Rights and winner of the Nobel Peace Prize in 1968

Fernand Dehousse (born 1906), Belgian university professor, politician, and member of the Council of Europe

Raphael Lemkin (1901-1959), European jurist who coined the term "genocide"

Broc Arvid Sture Petren (1908-1976), Swedish lawyer, adviser to the Swedish delegation at the United Nations, and member of the European Commission of Human Rights

Pierre-Henri Teitgen (born 1908), French statesman and lawyer who was a member of the Council of Europe

Sir Humphrey Waldock (1904-1981), British delegate who became first elected president of the European Commission of Human Rights

SUMMARY OF EVENT. Because of the appalling Jewish Holocaust during World War II, the United Nations General Assembly passed a resolution during the first meeting, December 11, 1946, condemning genocide. The term "genocide" was coined for the occasion by the jurist Raphael Lemkin. Genocide refers to the systematic destruction by a government of a racial, religious, or ethnic group. The basic right underlying the condemnation of genocide is the right to life. Two basic treaties or conventions resulted from the 1946 resolution: the 1948 Universal Declaration of Human Rights, and the 1951 Genocide Convention.

Development of the Universal Declaration and Genocide Convention, therefore, is designed to apply to the whole world, the first part of a human rights pattern in which the European Convention participates. The second part of that pattern involved the implementation of the Genocide Convention. The 1953 European Convention on Human Rights was first signed November 4, 1950, in Rome. This convention, or treaty agreement, went into effect in 1953. The full title is "European Convention for the Protection of Human Rights and Fundamental Freedoms." The treaty created the European Court of Human Rights. The convention also guarantees to the citizens of its member-states the right to appeal for redress for human rights violations. Granting that right of an individual to bring a petition for redress against a state caused many states to hesitate in agreement.

The Genocide Convention itself left major responsibility for enforcement up to the individual states. The Council of Europe and the Organization of American States are the two most significant groups of states to undertake enforcement of the Genocide Convention. The Council of Europe is responsible for the European Convention on Human Rights.

The European Convention operates through two sections of the European Council: the Commission of Human Rights, and the European Court of Human Rights. The Commission and the Court have influenced the national legislation and administrative practices of states found in violation. One net effect of the impetus is to offer some measure of unity to Europe. Some of these rights involve prisoner's rights, freedom from censorship and undue discipline and the right to remain silent in order to avoid self-incrimination.

Prisoner's rights have flowed out of the European Convention, rights such as access to legal advice, freedom from censorship and undue discipline. The original European Convention document included the right to remain silent in order to avoid self-incrimination. The original document regarded the death penalty as an exception to the right to life. That notwithstanding, the signatories of the convention have been gradually eliminating the death penalty and affording the right to remain silent.

The 1950 European Court of Human Rights is a political creature of the Council of Europe. The European Court of Human Rights eschewed a literal reading of treaty provisions and relied upon the purpose of the treaty for interpretation. This meant that the court served as a fulcrum for evolving community standards of human rights.

The Court developed a custom of offering preliminary rulings for national courts, thereby guiding the development of law.

Historically, individuals have been the main source of complaints before the European Court of Human Rights. Those individuals have been able to obtain reparation and damages from the Court. Member states may add further punitive damages to the damages awarded by the Court. While twenty states had ratified the European Convention in 1985, only sixteen accepted the right of individual petition.

The third part of the developing human rights pattern extends the effects of the original intention or purpose of the treaty into the details of law and custom. Effective enforcement of the European Convention permits authoritative breach of domestic jurisdiction which, otherwise, ensures that states have exclusive legal competence within their borders over their citizens. In 1984, the European Court of Human Rights exercised such jurisdiction from over a dozen European states. At that time approximately fifty decisions had been rendered by the European Court. Areas affected included: public school languages, state security methods, and local moral standards.

The fourth part of the human rights pattern both extends and receives the influence of the European Convention, back and forth, outside of Europe. Two agreements outlawing the death penalty were prepared for the European Convention: the 1976 Civil and Political Rights Covenant and the 1978 American Convention on Human Rights. By 1993, twenty countries had ratified those agreements. A total of thirty-six countries worldwide ascribed to the abolishment of the death penalty. Outside of the realm of formal treaties, international custom is developing an unwritten code severely limiting the application of the death penalty.

In 1978, the European Court of Human Rights defined inhuman and degrading treatment and torture for the first time. Inhuman and degrading treatment included wall standing, hooding, subjection to noise, deprivation of sleep, and deprivation of food and drink. Torture constituted a deliberate form of cruel, inhuman, or degrading treatment or punishment motivated by cruel disposition as well as by a desire to collect information.

The main effect of the European Convention on Human Rights has been informal and along friendly lines. The Council of Europe has been known to denounce nonmember states. The Parliamentary Assembly of the European Council, for one example, denounced the persecution of the Bahā'īs in Iran.

Among themselves, procedures in the European Convention do exist for a more adversarial approach to violations. Complaints are first registered with the European Council Commission of Human Rights. If the Commission of Human Rights develops an unresolved bill of particulars, the dispute is transmitted to the Committee of Ministers of the Council of Europe and to the states concerned.

Whether the alleged violations are to appear before the Court of Human Rights is a separate issue. The Commission can ordain that the judgment of the ministers be implemented. The Committee of Ministers does not prescribe how its judgment is to be implemented. Implementation is left up to the states involved. Should the committee be dissatisfied with how its judgment is implemented, its members may issue a report to that effect. Issuing such reports is the only sanction provided in the European Convention on Human Rights. The right to refer a case to the European Court of Human Rights is limited to the Commission on Human Rights, the states concerned, or a state party whose citizen has alleged to have been a victim. The Court may decide that remedial action is required, but it is left up to the individual states involved to implement that remedial action. The court is never specific about what remedial action to take. The Committee of Ministers has the task of supervising the execution of the Court decisions.

The European Court of Human Rights only has jurisdiction over those states which agree to such jurisdiction. That jurisdiction can either be general or specific toward a particular case. In 1985, eighteen states accepted that jurisdiction. Should the Committee of Ministers want to go beyond issuing a report, the Committee may suspend or expel an offending state from membership in the Council of Europe.

The fifth part of the human rights pattern is more theoretical. Welfare rights flow from the basic right to life. The welfare state is a beneficiary of the European Convention. The growth of the welfare state arose from an unarticulated expansion of political rights to social rights.

The European Convention had an important impact on human rights in Europe. Although international law generally regulated relations between states, the granting of the right of individual petition to the European Commission established an important precedent upholding the rights of private citizens against those of the state. The European Commission and Court of Human Rights were also granted power to examine and judge the activities of states that adhere to the convention. This arrangement stands in contrast with the United Nations charter, which prohibits the United Nations from intervening in the domestic affairs of any state. In addition, some European nations have applied the provisions of the treaty directly to their domestic law, allowing rights guaranteed by the convention to be invoked by litigants and to be held to prevail over any national laws and administrative decisions that contradict the convention. Finally, the European Convention also served as a precedent for conventions on human rights adopted by the Organization of American States and by human rights conventions held in Africa and Southeast Asia.
                                                    —*Raymond J. Jirran*

ADDITIONAL READING:

Fawcett, J. E. S. *The Application of the European Convention on Human Rights.* Reprint. Oxford: Clarendon Press, 1987. First published in 1969, Fawcett's book provides a thorough examination of the convention section by section and article by article.

Hufton, Olwen, ed. *Historical Change and Human Rights: The Oxford Amnesty Lectures: 1994.* New York: Basic Books, 1995. This contemporary source provides a useful exposition on the topic of human rights.

Jacobs, Francis G. *The European Convention on Human Rights.* 3d ed. Oxford: Clarendon Press, 1995. In its third edition, this volume provides a well-written general survey of background and history of the convention.

Kauffman, Natalie Hevener. *Human Rights Treaties and the Senate: A History of Opposition.* Chapel Hill: University of North Carolina Press, 1990. Relationship of the U.S. to the principles in the European Convention.

SEE ALSO: 1945, The United Nations Is Founded; 1945-1946, Nuremberg Trials; 1967, United Nations Declaration on Equality for Women; 1972, United Nations Environmental Conference.

1951-1953
MODEL OF DNA MOLECULAR STRUCTURE IS DEVELOPED

The model of DNA molecular structure is developed, solving the mystery of how genetic information is transmitted from generation to generation.

DATE: October, 1951-1953
LOCALE: England
CATEGORY: Science and technology
KEY FIGURES:

Oswald T. Avery (1877-1955), the British physician who identified DNA as the genetic molecule

Erwin Chargaff (born 1905), the Austrian-born chemist who discovered the nucleotide ratios in DNA

Francis H. C. Crick (born 1916), a British physicist who became interested in biology and became a biochemist

Rosalind Franklin (1921-1958), a British physicist and colleague of Wilkins who obtained X-ray photographs key to the solution of DNA's structure

Linus Pauling (1901-1994), American scientist who pioneered the use of models in molecular structure determination

James D. Watson (born 1928), an American geneticist who persuaded Crick to collaborate on the structure of DNA

Maurice H. F. Wilkins (born 1916), the British physicist who shared the Nobel Prize with Watson and Crick

SUMMARY OF EVENT. In 1866, Gregor Johann Mendel published the first scientific evidence describing the process of heredity. He demonstrated that physical characteristics are transmitted from one generation to the next and that inheritable traits are controlled by the combination of separate units of heredity. His work was ignored until 1909, when the Dutch biologist Willhelm Johannsen termed these units of heredity genes. While the chemical constitution of these genes was unknown, biologists believed that either proteins or nucleic acids must be involved in hereditary processes. Initial analyses of the nucleic acid DNA showed that it contained only four types of subunits called nucleotides each made up of a phosphate, the sugar deoxyribose and one of four bases: cytosine, thymine, adenine, or guanine. Individual nucleotides differ only in the identity of the base. Since DNA appeared to be a simple molecule, it seemed unlikely that it was responsible for the extraordinary capabilities of a gene, and many researchers felt that proteins, which are combinations of twenty different amino acids, were more appropriate candidates for transmitting genetic information.

In 1928, Fred Griffith discovered that nonpathogenic cells could be transformed into pathogenic cells, and, in the early 1940's, Oswald T. Avery determined that DNA was the essential molecule of this transformation process. What now remained was for someone to decipher how the DNA orchestrated such processes. Although James D. Watson and Francis Crick carried out no laboratory experiments, they utilized the experimental results of others to assemble the pieces of the puzzle into a complete picture.

In 1950, Erwin Chargaff's studies into the chemical composition of DNA molecules produced two pieces of the puzzle: first, the relative amounts of the four nucleotides differ considerably depending on species; and second, the amount of adenine always equals the amount of thymine while guanine equals cytosine in a sample of DNA. Although certain that these nucleotide relationships had structural significance, Chargaff's purely chemical approach could not solve the problem.

Linus Pauling's work also influenced Watson and Crick. Pauling was considered the expert on determining three-dimensional shapes of molecules using models, constructed of cardboard, wood, and metal. Such models can be manipulated by the scientist until a reasonable molecular structure is obtained. Pauling had combined experimental information about structural features with a model to deduce the alpha-helix structure of proteins, work for which he won a Nobel Prize in 1954. Pauling's work showed Watson and Crick that exact and careful model construction can detect the constraints that must be satisfied in the final structural solution.

Maurice Wilkins, a physicist at London's King's College, and his assistant Rosalind Franklin provided X-ray photographs which turned out to be of great importance. Although she did not recognize it, Franklin's photographs showed that DNA consists of two chains running in opposite directions arranged in a helical structure.

Watson, the geneticist, and Crick, the physicist, undertook the construction of a model of the structure of DNA in October, 1951. Before long, Lawrence Bragg, the head of the Cavendish Laboratory where Watson and Crick worked, ordered them to stop work on the DNA problem. This was a politically based request, since the department head did not wish to interfere with the work going on at King's College. Although they ceased active work on the project, Watson and Crick continued to discuss the subject. In the spring of 1952, John Griffith, a mathematician and Fred Griffith's nephew, performed calculations indicating that adenine should be attracted to thymine while cytosine should be attracted to guanine in DNA molecules. This information coupled with Chargaff's nucleotide ratios lead to the idea that these bases must pair in some complementary way.

In the fall of 1952, Pauling decided to enter the race to solve the structure of DNA. By early 1953, Bragg, again motivated by politics, permitted Watson and Crick to resume their investigation since neither Pauling nor Wilkins and Franklin seemed close to a solution. At this time, Wilkins allowed Crick to see some of Franklin's X-ray pictures. These pictures provided the final piece necessary to complete the puzzle: DNA consisted of a double helix with its chains running in opposite directions. On February 28, Watson constructed cardboard cutouts of the shapes of the four nucleotide bases and found that the complementary base pairs superimposed perfectly. These bases were attached to the phosphate-sugar chain to form a DNA strand. When two chains were placed side-by-side with the bases pointing inward, the two chains could be held together by attachments between the complementary bases. The joining of the two chains was analogous to the joining together of the two halves of a clothing zipper. The

James Watson (left) and Francis Crick (right) display a three-dimensional model of the complex double-helix structure of DNA. (Archive Photos)

unveiling of the structure for peer review occurred on March 7, 1953, and on April 25, 1953, Watson and Crick's article "Molecular Structure of Nucleic Acids: A Structure For Deoxyribose Nucleic Acid" was published in the journal *Nature*.

The structural determination of DNA led Watson and Crick to quickly infer a possible copying mechanism called replication for the genetic material from DNA's specific base pairing. A second paper appeared in the May 30, 1953, issue of *Nature* discussing the significance of the structure in the transmission of genetic information. Experiments conducted in other laboratories validated the Watson-Crick model.

In 1962, the Nobel Prize was awarded to Watson, Crick, and Wilkins. Since the X-ray photographs which provided crucial data were actually Rosalind Franklin's work, her role in solving the structure of DNA has become a point of historical debate. It appears that Wilkins divulged Franklin's work without her knowledge. Two technical reasons may have prohibited Franklin from sharing in the Nobel Prize—it was customary to avoid awarding prizes posthumously (there had been only one exception)

and no more than three individuals could share one prize. Rosalind Franklin died of cancer in 1958.

The era of molecular biology was opened by Watson and Crick's discovery of the DNA double helix. They were responsible for developing the central dogma of molecular biology which states that the expression of genetic information is encoded in the DNA molecule. The DNA molecule serves as a template for replication, the reproduction of itself to be passed on from generation to generation, as well as a template for the dissemination to other parts of the cell of the recipes for the production of proteins.

By the mid-1960's, the central dogma had been proven, and researchers had learned to read the "words" of the genetic code stored in the DNA molecule. Thus, the biological question of how molecules pass on genetic information had been solved. There is no life science discipline, either pure or applied, which has not been transformed by the development of molecular biology. In agriculture, molecular biology allows improvement of plant characteristics through genetic engineering. Genetic fingerprinting allows us to scientifically identify criminals. Molecular medicine identifies the genetic abnormalities causing diseases such as cystic fibrosis and Huntington's disease. Knowledge of the structure of DNA has opened the door to the study of the entire human genome— identification of the location of all the important human genes within the DNA.   —*Arlene R. Courtney*

ADDITIONAL READING:

Crick, Francis. *What Mad Pursuit: A Personal View of Scientific Discovery*. New York: Basic Books, 1988. An autobiography allowing the reader to view the discovery of the structure of DNA through the scientist's eyes. The book concentrates on the science of the discovery.

Davis, Joel. *Mapping The Code: The Human Genome Project and the Choices of Modern Science*. New York: John Wiley & Sons, 1990. The story of the Human Genome Project—how it developed, the personages involved, and ethical and moral questions.

Hoagland, Mahlon. *Discovery: The Search For DNA's Secrets*. Boston: Houghton Mifflin, 1981. A layman's guide to the development of molecular biology beginning with Mendel and his peas.

Watson, James D. *The Double Helix: A Personal Account of the Discovery of the Structure of DNA*. New York: Atheneum, 1968. An account of the events which led to the solution of the structure of DNA focusing on the people involved in the discovery.

SEE ALSO: 1859, Darwin Publishes *On the Origin of Species*; 1882-1884, Koch Isolates Microorganisms That Cause Tuberculosis and Cholera; 1905, Einstein Publishes His Special Theory of Relativity; 1928, Fleming Discovers Penicillin.

1952
LONDON SMOG KILLS THOUSANDS

In December of 1952, a London smog kills thousands, bringing about the enactment of a law in 1956 virtually eliminating serious smoke pollution in England.

DATE: December 5-8, 1952

LOCALE: London, England

CATEGORIES: Environment; Laws, acts, and legal history

KEY FIGURES:

Sir Hugh Beaver (1890-1967), chairman of British committee on air pollution

Gerald Nabarro (1913-1973), British proponent of a clean air law

SUMMARY OF EVENT. The fog which engulfed Greater London in early December of 1952 was not London's first, or perhaps not even its most deadly, but its importance was immense as, unlike earlier fogs, it triggered enough public

concern to force remedial action. The fog caused passage of the Clean Air Act of 1956, Britain's major antismoke act, an act which was startlingly successful and which assured that the fog of 1952 would be remembered as one of the last significant air-pollution disasters in British history.

London, built on both banks of the tidal River Thames, forty miles from the ocean, was inevitably subject to fog. Early in its history naturally forming fog, or suspended water particles, entrapped additional particles arising from fuel burned for heat. Virtually all the dwelling units in London in 1952 were heated by soft (bituminous) coal, burned in open fireplaces. Each fireplace produced substantial smoke and soot. Millions of fireplaces burning soft coal produced over a thousand tons of soot every day, and when the fog rolled in from the ocean and the marshes of the Thames, that fog entrapped the soot. The result was "smog," a term coined in 1905. Smog soiled and decayed the buildings of London, seriously limited visibility, and settled into the lungs of Londoners, amplifying respiratory problems of the old and ill and sometimes bringing a slow and gasping death.

The same sequence of events has occurred many times. As early as the fourteenth century, efforts had been made to limit the burning of soft coal in London, but these efforts had never worked, and the problem grew worse as London's population increased. Serious attacks of fog blanketed London in the nineteenth century, fogs which constituted the "London Particulars" which create literary atmosphere in some of Charles Dickens' novels and shroud the activities of criminals pursued by Arthur Conan Doyle's fictitious Sherlock Holmes. The nineteenth century Parliament enacted legislation to reduce smoke pollution, but the acts were largely ineffective, in part because of a countervailing pressure to avoid inflicting hardship on industry, and in part because none of the acts applied to domestic heating arrangements which, all the experts agreed, created the greater part of the problem. So fogs continued as a persistent, sometimes deadly, but oddly loved part of the London winter scene. In 1898, reformers who realized fogs were serious threats to health, rather than merely mysterious and romantic interludes, founded the Coal Smoke Abatement Society, which, as the National Smoke Abatement Society, continued on into the twentieth century campaigning against air pollution.

The fog of December 5-8, 1952, settled on the metropolis as had hundreds of earlier winter fogs. No special alarms were raised. No feeling of panic gripped the eight million inhabitants of Greater London. Those who died, most of them elderly, did not attract much attention beyond that of their immediate families. It was not realized, during the four days of the fog, how many were dying. Funeral directors noticed an extraordinary demand for their services, but it was only later, when the ordinary statistics of applications for sickness benefits and of deaths were routinely collected and tabulated, that the fog's impact was recognized. It was discovered that in December of 1952, twenty-five thousand more people had filed claims for sickness benefits than in the previous December. The statisticians were struck by the vast number of excess deaths, deaths beyond those which experience indicated could be expected in a normal December. The fog, it was revealed, had killed, slowly and insidiously, about four thousand people, people who had died, one by one, in hospitals and houses scattered throughout the metropolis. It was not until late December, when the newspapers began to pick up the story, that the existence and magnitude of the disaster began to be recognized, and it was a statistical summary compiled by the National Smoke Abatement Society and distributed to every member of Parliament in the spring of 1953 that finally caught public attention and led to action designed to ensure that a similar disaster would never happen again.

The government, a complacent administration led by the octogenarian Winston Churchill, was initially slow to respond. It was only back-bench pressure in the House of Commons that forced the government to take a minimal step, appointment of a committee to study and report. This was a traditional way of avoiding, or at least postponing, action. The result was the Beaver Committee on Smoke Pollution, headed by industrialist Sir Hugh Beaver. The resultant Beaver Report of 1954 acknowledged the seriousness of the problem revealed by the smog of 1952 and outlined practical steps which could be followed to avoid similar problems in the future. Nevertheless, the government hesitated to suggest any new legislation. Parliamentarians stepped into the breach. In December of 1954, Gerald Nabarro, a west-of-England Conservative, habitually dressed in country tweeds and sporting an immense handlebar mustache, introduced a private member's bill for smoke control, based on the Beaver Report's recommendations. Private member's bills, defined as bills not sponsored by the government and therefore allotted little parliamentary time, rarely pass, but they may be used to prod a government into action, which was actually the consequence of Nabarro's effort.

The resultant Clean Air Act of 1956, introduced by the government as a condition of withdrawal of Nabarro's bill, was a practical act, eschewing impossible utopias to focus on what could actually be done. The act used the concept of smokeless areas, areas in which smoke was prohibited, initially minute in number, to be augmented year by year

Many London residents took to wearing surgical-style masks to avoid inhaling the polluted air that blanketed the city in early December of 1952. (Popperfoto/Archive Photos)

until eventually the whole country was covered. In areas declared smokeless, both commercial and private structures would have to be equipped with smoke-free heating devices: furnaces so designed as to avoid production of smoke by burning smokeless fuels, such as coke and other products made by removing the sooty particles of coal, or by using natural gas or electricity. The act also appropriated funds to aid in converting premises to domestic smokeless heating technologies. For each conversion, the central government would pay 40 percent of the cost, and the local authority 30 percent, leaving the home owner responsible for only the remaining 30 percent. Smokeless areas were to be carefully selected, including, for example, only those areas where modern factories were being built or where British Rail was already phasing out steam locomotives, and the spread of smokeless areas was not to be allowed to outrun the expected increasing capacity for manufacture of smokeless fuels and apparatus.

The Clean Air Act of 1956 proved extraordinarily effective, much more so than even its most optimistic supporters had predicted. Not only did industry and the public react favorably to smokeless areas, but soon a desire for greater convenience and heightened living standards led to conversions even before they were required by the law. That is, many people whose houses were not yet in smokeless areas converted to smokeless fuel anyway, even without governmental financial assistance, when they discovered that electric heat, for example, was simply easier and more effective than the old coal-burning fireplace. Consumption of soft coal steadily declined, the hours of sunshine reported by the London meteorological officials steadily increased, and the severity of fogs diminished. Although about 750 people died in the fog of December, 1957, the fog of January, 1963, proved to be the last which produced significant mortality. The disaster of 1952 had triggered legislative action so effective that within a dozen years an ancient scourge had virtually disappeared. —*John Ranlett*

ADDITIONAL READING:

Brimblecombe, Peter. *The Big Smoke: A History of Air Pollution in London Since Medieval Times.* London: Methuen, 1987. Uneven account that is stronger on technology than on legislation, this work supplies an odd blend of minute detail and vague generalization.

Morgan, Kenneth O. *The People's Peace: British History, 1945-1990.* Oxford: Oxford University Press, 1990. A detailed discussion of the political and social history of Britain in the period surrounding the smog of 1952.

Sanderson, J. B. "The National Smoke Abatement Society and the Clean Air Act (1956)." *Political Studies* 9 (October, 1961): 236-253. Evaluates the role played by the National Smoke Abatement Society in passage of the Clean Air Act of 1956.

Scarrow, Howard A. "The Impact of British Domestic Air Pollution Legislation." *British Journal of Political Science* 2 (July, 1972): 261-282. A detailed analysis of the effect of the Clean Air Act of 1956.

Wise, William. *Killer Smog: The World's Worst Air Pollution Disaster.* Chicago: Rand McNally, 1968. A popular journalistic account, often lacking in precision.

SEE ALSO: 1969, Pesticide Poisons the Rhine River; 1972, United Nations Environmental Conference; 1986, Chernobyl Nuclear Disaster.

1953
DEATH OF STALIN

The death of Stalin ends several decades of dictatorial rule and terminates the initial stages of a new wave of purges in the Soviet Union.

DATE: March 5, 1953
LOCALE: Moscow, the Soviet Union
CATEGORY: Government and politics
KEY FIGURES:

Lavrenti Pavlovich Beria (1899-1953), chief of the secret police under Stalin, 1938-1953

Nikita Sergeyevich Khrushchev (1894-1971), first secretary of the Communist Party, 1953-1964

Georgi Maksimilianovich Malenkov (1902-1988), deputy premier of the Soviet Union, 1946-1953, premier, 1953-1955

Vyacheslav Mikhailovich Molotov (Skryabin; 1890-1986), Soviet foreign minister in 1953

Joseph Stalin (Iosif Vissarionovich Dzhugashvili; 1879-1953), Soviet dictator, 1924-1953

SUMMARY OF EVENT. On March 4, 1953, Radio Moscow announced that on March 1, Joseph Stalin had suffered a stroke, which had led to partial paralysis with heart and breathing difficulties. On the morning of March 6, it reported that Stalin had died on the evening of March 5. He was seventy-three years old at the time of his death.

The news aroused consternation throughout the country that Stalin had ruled for more than a quarter of a century. Following Lenin's death in January, 1924, Stalin had become the most powerful figure in the party and governed the nation until his own death nearly three decades later.

He had led his people victoriously through World War II, which brought death and destruction to the Soviet Union on an unprecedented scale as a result of the Nazi invasion, and he seemed to be the indispensable center about which all Soviet life revolved. Despite the terror, bloodshed, and suffering associated with his policies, Stalin provided the security of the familiar in Soviet citizens from the poorest collective farmers to the top leaders of the Communist Party. It was logical that his associates feared the possible disruptive consequences in the aftermath of his death and the removal of his dominating and guiding hand.

In the last years of his life, Stalin had been preparing to plunge his people once again into the suffering and killing which had characterized his rule. Suspicious of everyone and growing more paranoid in his final years, the old dictator appeared to be setting the stage for a repeat performance. The death penalty, abolished in 1947, was restored to deal with "spies and traitors." The so-called Leningrad Affair of 1949 led to further demotions and even execution of significant party leaders. The Soviet press, by the early 1950's, published numerous criticisms and even denunciations of individuals and groups.

Events surrounding the Nineteenth Party Congress of

October, 1952, provided ominous signs of the purge spreading throughout the highest echelons of the party and extending to other areas of society to produce another destructive wave of terror. Technically, the actions of the Congress did not on the surface look unduly serious. A new leadership committee, the Presidium, replaced the ruling Politburo, substantially increasing its membership as compared to its predecessor. Significant changes modified the Secretariat as the Communist Party's central bureaucratic and organizational structure. Rumors began to spread that even the most important of Stalin's associates during the previous fifteen years were among those likely to be demoted, ousted from power in the government or the Communist Party, or possibly arrested.

Moreover, a major part of Stalin's scheme was the conscious use of political anti-Semitism, a clear threat to the Jewish population of the Soviet Union. The dossier which Stalin prepared against his intended victims included numerous indictments of prominent Jews in the party and the government bureaucracy. Anti-Semitic language and the prevalence of Jews among the alleged "criminals" seemed to indicate that Stalin planned to capitalize upon existing anti-Semitism in Russia to get public support for at least the beginning of his purge. Allegations of Jews recruited by the American Central Intelligence Agency (CIA) to work for "American-Zionist imperialism" inside the Soviet Union became more frequent. The executions of several Jews in 1952, after allegations of collaboration with Russia's enemies, further added to the atmosphere of suspicion and fear.

Most frightening of all was the announcement in January, 1953, of the discovery of a "Doctors' Plot" which charged that nine prominent doctors, six of whom were Jews, had been guilty of trying to kill, by improper medical treatment, leaders of the Communist Party and the armed forces. The list of alleged murdered victims included Andrei Zhdanov, the party leader of Leningrad and widely believed to have been Stalin's choice as his eventual heir, who died in 1948. The secret police and investigative agencies came under special attack for their apparent laxity in discovering these opponents.

It became clear that Stalin was piecing together allegations involving assassination plots, economic crimes, sabotage, and collaboration with foreign enemies in which prominent party figures and many lesser officials would be swept up and punished.

Only his death saved Russia from the bloodshed that would have followed the implementation of his plans. On March 4, Soviet authorities announced that Stalin suffered a major stroke on the night of March 1-2. A brain hemorrhage caused major paralysis of his right side, plus loss of speech and consciousness. The medical team provided what care they could, even using leeches to reduce the blood pressure of their patient. He died at 9:50 P.M. on March 5.

In announcing Stalin's death and in their speeches in succeeding weeks, Communist Party leaders, fearing civil disorder upon the death of the much feared leader, appealed to the people in the name of "collective leadership" to remain calm. They took steps to tighten control over the party and other political and economic organs by placing themselves in key positions. The powerful party leaders carefully avoided any suggestion that any individual would rule the party as Stalin had done. Malenkov became Soviet premier, while Khrushchev assumed the responsibility as head of the party.

Stalin's successors began almost immediately to reduce the most hated features of the Stalinist system, including the secret police apparatus and the terror by which it had infected Russian life. The "Doctors' Plot" was admitted to have been fabricated, and those physicians still in prison were released. By the end of the year, it was announced that Beria had been ousted as head of the secret police, expelled from the party, and executed. Articles in the party newspaper *Pravda* assured the people that their rights under the Soviet constitution would be respected and that more consumer goods would be made available. So the Communist Party, under the concept of "collective leadership," rode out of the days of uncertainly, fear, and turmoil surrounding Stalin's death, and a new era in Russian history began.

—George F. Putnam, updated by Taylor Stults

ADDITIONAL READING:

Bortoli, Georges. *The Death of Stalin*. New York: Frederick A. Praeger, 1975. The title is misleading, as this account traces events from 1952 through Stalin's death and effectively juxtaposes general social conditions with the activities of the Communist Party leadership.

Conquest, Robert. *Stalin: Breaker of Nations*. New York: Penguin, 1991. This psychological study emphasizes Stalin's paranoia and his desire to achieve massive power.

Hyde, H. Montgomery. *Stalin: The History of a Dictator*. New York: Farrar, Straus & Giroux, 1972. A critical assessment of Stalin, but a solid biography.

Radzinsky, Edvard. *Stalin: The First In-Depth Biography Based on Explosive Documents from Russia's Secret Archives*. New York: Doubleday, 1996. A Russian historian provides more information based on previously inaccessible files.

Salisbury, Harrison E. *Moscow Journal: The End of*

Stalin. Chicago: University of Chicago Press, 1961. Engaging and detailed account of conditions in the Soviet Union in the late Stalin era, including Stalin's demise, by a *New York Times* correspondent living in Moscow.

Ulam, Adam B. *Stalin: The Man and His Era*. Boston: Beacon Press, 1989. Expanded edition of an earlier biography of Stalin by a highly regarded Soviet scholar at Harvard University.

Volkogonov, Dmitri. *Stalin: Triumph and Tragedy*. New York: Grove Weidenfeld, 1991. Substantial biography by a noted Russian historian provides a post-Communist perspective of Stalin.

SEE ALSO: 1928-1933, Soviet Union Launches First Five-Year Plan; 1929, Trotsky Is Sent into Exile; 1934-1939, Stalin Begins the Purge Trials; 1946, Churchill's "Iron Curtain" Speech.

1955
WARSAW PACT IS SIGNED

The Warsaw Pact is signed in response to the arming of West Germany, consolidating Soviet power in eastern and central Europe.

DATE: May 14, 1955

LOCALE: Warsaw, Poland

CATEGORIES: Diplomacy and international relations; Wars, uprisings, and civil unrest

KEY FIGURES:

Nikolai Aleksandrovich Bulganin (1895-1975), chairman of the Council of Ministers (premier) of the Soviet Union, 1955-1958

Marshal Ivan Stepanovich Konev (1897-1973), commander in chief of Warsaw Pact armed forces

Nikita Sergeyevich Khrushchev (1894-1971), first secretary of the Communist Party of the Soviet Union, 1953-1964, and premier of the Soviet Union, 1958-1964

Vyacheslav Mikhailovich Molotov (Skryabin; 1890-1986), Soviet foreign minister, 1953-1956

SUMMARY OF EVENT. The Warsaw Pact, formally known as the Treaty of Friendship, Cooperation, and Mutual Assistance Between the People's Republic of Albania, the People's Republic of Bulgaria, the Hungarian People's Republic, the German Democratic Republic, the Polish People's Republic, the Rumanian People's Republic, the Union of Soviet Socialist Republics, and the Czechoslovak Republic, was signed on May 14, 1955. To a large extent, this multilateral alliance must be seen as an outgrowth of Soviet concerns over the rearming of the Federal Republic of Germany (West Germany). The Soviet Union formally protested the Western arrangements providing for the creation of West German armed forces and the entry of West Germany into the North Atlantic Treaty Organization (NATO). The Soviets served notice in November, 1954, that the remilitarization of West Germany would lead to new security measures in Eastern Europe. The actual signing of the Warsaw Pact was preceded by the Moscow Conference of the future members in November-December, 1954. At this time, V. M. Molotov, the Soviet foreign minister, presented a rather blunt statement regarding the revival of German militarism and the need for "special vigilance" and "practical measures."

Molotov's militant anti-Western stance was not entirely maintained by the subsequent Warsaw Conference. The new Soviet leaders, Nikita Khrushchev and Nikolai Bulganin, had only recently asserted themselves in a power struggle with Georgii Malenkov, who led a faction in the Soviet Politburo associated with the commitment to détente. The Khrushchev-Bulganin leadership, however, was similarly inclined to adopt a somewhat softer foreign policy posture than the one advocated by Molotov. Molotov saw the pact as an instrument of military preparedness and socialist consolidation, whereas Khrushchev viewed it as a Cold War political device. Thus, the language and terms of the Warsaw Pact reflected the new Soviet priorities in international affairs.

It is certainly appropriate to view the Warsaw Pact as the Soviet counterpart to NATO. Indeed, the Warsaw Pact's role as a military alliance opposing NATO continued to increase over the years. The Soviet Union maintained sizable combat-equipped forces in a forward deployment in the Warsaw Pact area, supported by tactical air and missile elements and reinforceable from the Soviet Union. Nevertheless, concern over the developments in NATO was not the sole reason for the Warsaw Pact. The period following Stalin's death in 1953 had seen considerable diversity and agitation for increased independence on the part of the Eastern European satellite states, a phenomenon known as polycentrism. The changing political environment in Eastern Europe required new approaches and methods in the continuing efforts to sustain Soviet control over the area. The creation of a formal treaty organization, together with invigoration of the Council for Mutual Economic Assistance (COMECON), established under Soviet auspices in 1949, appeared to be an excellent response to Soviet needs.

The eleven articles of the Warsaw Pact provided for consultation on all issues of common interest, the peaceful settlement of conflicts, and joint defense. The military convention was the most important part of the treaty; it allowed for the disposition of troops under the joint command for purposes of mutual defense. Soviet marshal I. S.

Konev was appointed commander in chief, and the ministers of defense of the other member states became his deputies. Each of these deputy commanders was put in charge of the troops contributed by his own state. The headquarters, with a permanent staff of the joint armed forces and certain auxiliary bodies, were located in Moscow. For purposes of policy coordination, a political consultative committee was established.

Subsequent military integration efforts by the Soviet Union included the standardization of equipment and the development of a common infrastructure. Moreover, considerable effort was made to indoctrinate officers and men in loyalty to the "socialist camp." Key positions in the satellite armies were awarded, as a matter of course, to Soviet-trained officers. The German Democratic Republic was initially excluded from participation in the joint command; it was given equal status at the first meeting of the political consultative committee held in Prague in January, 1956. As a deliberate counter to the developments in NATO, the East German National People's Army was created and integrated into the joint command.

In retrospect, it is important to note that at the time of its inception, the Warsaw Pact was primarily designed to strengthen the Soviet position at the Geneva Summit Conference, held in July, 1955. The Soviet government envisioned a European collective security treaty, which, when achieved, would provide for the simultaneous termination of NATO, the supplementary Paris agreements, and the Warsaw Pact. As an alternative to this maximum goal, the Soviets proposed a nonaggression treaty between the members of each alliance. No steps were taken, however, on either proposal at that time.

In its initial stages, then, the Warsaw Pact served the Soviet Union essentially as a Cold War political device. Indeed, during the first years of the treaty's existence, the Soviet Union was not very intent on developing its potential as an integrated military alliance. The existing bilateral agreements with individual European states were sufficient with regard to the deployment of Soviet troops to counter American influence in Europe. Certain features of the pact, however, such as its "legitimizing" the presence of Soviet troops on Eastern European soil, gradually appreciated in value for the Soviet Union. The latter came to regard the Warsaw Pact as a highly useful instrument in East-West relations and in furthering its hegemonal interests in Eastern Europe. The pact could be effectively used as a coordinating mechanism for foreign policy and the achievement of a uniform external posture. More important, it facilitated the achievement of general conformity to Moscow's policy line for the area itself. Moscow was able to promote what it called "fraternal bloc solidarity,"

and any member straying too far from the line could be subjected to disciplinary action behind the collective facade of the Warsaw Pact.

Riots and massive public demonstrations flared up in Poland and Hungary in the fall of 1956. The respective regimes attempted to respond to some of the demands and expectations, defying directives to the contrary from Moscow. Clearly, Soviet control over political developments in Eastern Europe was slipping. In October of 1956, the Soviets decided to intervene directly in Poland and Hungary. In the case of Poland, a Soviet delegation went to Warsaw and, backed by alerted Soviet troops stationed in the vicinity, was able to bring matters back under control. In the case of Hungary, the great popular uprising ultimately led to the massive use of Soviet military force to crush the rebellion and to reestablish a regime subservient to Moscow. The Soviet use of armed might was justified under the Warsaw Pact terms, although these terms refer only to aiding a members state threatened by aggression and do not state what to do in case of civil war. The Soviet action was presented as a response to "the sacred duty" to protect the "achievements of socialism." Reviewing the events in Hungary, there was no consultation within the context of the Warsaw Pact. The political consultative committee did not meet at all during this time of crisis.

The provisions of the treaty were reinterpreted to allow for "legitimate" intervention in the affairs of member states, including the use of force, under the doctrine of "proletarian internationalism." Such disciplinary and policing functions became a significant part of Soviet policy and practice over the years. The most extreme instances were the interventions in Hungary in 1956 and in Czechoslovakia in 1968. The resort to military force to bring these countries to heel did not truly depend on the Warsaw Pact. It was, however, politically and ideologically most expedient to give these operations a multilateral appearance.

—Manfred Grote, updated by Carl Rollyson

ADDITIONAL READING:

Brzezinski, Zbigniew. *The New Eastern Europe: The Khrushchev Era and After*. New York: Praeger, 1961. Early and highly acclaimed systematic study of the relations among Communist states, containing useful information on the Warsaw Pact.

Clawson, Robert W., and Lawrence S. Kaplan, eds. *The Warsaw Pact: Political Purpose & Military Means*. Wilmington, Del.: Scholarly Resources, 1982. Chapters on the principal political relationships within the Warsaw Pact, on NATO and the Warsaw Pact, the pact's military strength and weaponry, and its doctrines and capabilities.

Epstein, Joshua M. *Conventional Force Reductions: A*

Dynamic Assessment. Washington, D.C.: The Brookings Institution, 1990. See index for entries on the Warsaw Pact's combat power, its overall military significance, and its relationship to NATO. See also the section in chapter 5, "Soviet Perceptions."

Holloway, David, and Jane M. O. Sharp. *The Warsaw Pact: Alliance in Transition?* Ithaca, N.Y.: Cornell University Press, 1984. Chapters on the Warsaw Pact's history, defense capability, Soviet crisis management, foreign policy goals, the later policy of security through détente, and the Warsaw Pact in the context of the world system.

Kelleher, Catherine McArdle. *The Future of European Security: An Interim Assessment*. Washington, D.C.: The Brookings Institution, 1995. Chapters 3 and 4 discuss the politics of European security and the relationship between Eastern and Western Europe. An excellent study of how the Cold War alliance system broke down, with extensive notes and bibliography.

Remington, Robin Alison. *The Warsaw Pact: Case Studies in Communist Conflict Resolution*. Cambridge, Mass.: MIT Press, 1971. Still among the best studies of the resolution of various conflicts between the Soviet Union and other member states. A detailed study of the origins of the Warsaw Pact and its relationship to the struggle for power in the Soviet Union.

SEE ALSO: 1946, Churchill's "Iron Curtain" Speech; 1949, North Atlantic Treaty; 1949, Creation of Two German Republics; 1953, Death of Stalin; 1956, Hungarian Revolution; 1968, Soviet Union Invades Czechoslovakia.

1956
HUNGARIAN REVOLUTION

The Hungarian Revolution against a repressive Communist government is brutally suppressed by the Soviet Union.

DATE: October-November, 1956
LOCALE: Hungary
CATEGORIES: Government and politics; Social reform
KEY FIGURES:
Erno Gerö (1898-1980), Rákosi's henchman and successor as first secretary of the Hungarian Communist Party
János Kádár (1912-1989), prime minister of Hungary, 1956-1958 and 1961-1968
Nikita Sergeyevich Khrushchev (1894-1971), premier of the Soviet Union, 1958-1964
Colonel Pal Maléter, Hungarian army officer
Imre Nagy (1896-1958), popular reformist Communist, premier of Hungary, 1953-1955, and head of the Hungarian revolutionary regime

Mátyás Rákosi (1892-1971), Stalinist first secretary of the Hungarian Communist Party, 1949-1953, and prime minister of Hungary, 1952-1953
Tito (Josip Broz; 1892-1980), president of the republic of Yugoslavia, 1953-1980

SUMMARY OF EVENT. In 1953, Stalin's successor, Georgi Malenkov, forced Hungarian leader Mátyás Rákosi to make an uneasy coalition with reformist Hungarian Communists led by Imre Nagy. After July 4, 1953, when Nagy entered the government, Hungarians enjoyed the policies that he called his "new course." The dreaded secret police had its power curtailed, and political prisoners were released. Peasants were allowed to dissolve their collective farms. Economic planners who had formerly emphasized heavy industry now foresaw increased production of badly needed consumer goods. The fact that almost all Hungarians applauded the "new course" placed Nagy among the Communist world's most popular leaders. He faced an unceasing struggle, however, with Rákosi, whose Stalinists retained control of the party and bureaucracy. Events within Hungary and the replacement of Malenkov by Nikita Khrushchev in Russia caused the Hungarian party leadership to eject Nagy from the party in April, 1955.

The restored Rákosi regime found itself in an awkward position. Moscow supported Rákosi primarily because it needed strong leadership in the satellite states while the power struggle continued within Russia. With Khrushchev initiating his own anti-Stalinist program, Rákosi could not rule as he had previously. The contradiction between the government's Stalinist political heritage and increasing Russian pressure for de-Stalinization made the Hungarian regime ineffective. When Khrushchev denounced Stalin's purges at the Twentieth Party Congress in February, 1956, Hungarians noted that Rákosi was also guilty of Stalinist political murder. During the spring and summer of 1956, Hungarian intellectuals, many of whom were Communists, attacked Rákosi in journals and literary circles. Dissident Communists rallied around Nagy and urged a return to the "new course." Between June 30 and July 21, Rákosi challenged Nagy's supporters and lost. He was promptly removed by Moscow. Unfortunately for Russo-Hungarian relations, his successor was not Nagy, but Erno Gerö, whom Hungarians considered to be only a slightly less despicable Stalinist than Rákosi.

Gerö mixed repressive and conciliatory policies, but he could not stifle demands for liberalization. At a ceremony reburying the rehabilitated Communist leader, Lazlo Rajk, whom Rákosi had executed, three hundred thousand people heard party leaders make formal apologies for past deeds. On October 14, the party readmitted Nagy. In order to gain support, Gerö left for Yugoslavia to seek the blessing of Marshal Tito, the Communist world's first and most respected anti-Stalinist.

The Hungarian revolution began with meetings held during Gerö's absence. When Gerö returned to Hungary late on October 23, enormous crowds filled the streets. By midnight, the crowds were fighting police and some Russian units. The government adopted Machiavellian tactics. Nagy was appointed to head a new cabinet, but a false communiqué was released stating that he had requested Russian intervention. Disillusioned by Nagy's apparent treachery and reinforced by some Hungarian soldiers, the rebels continued the struggle despite Nagy's appeals for order. Nagy, who had to operate under close observation by the police, was gambling that he could stop the uprising with his persuasive abilities, a certain amount of force, and his somewhat diminished reputation. Simultaneously, he had to act as a loyal Communist lest the Russians remove him and initiate a bloody repression aimed at restoring Gerö or, even worse, Rákosi.

By October 28, Nagy had succeeded in arranging a cease-fire agreement with the rebel leader, Colonel Pal Maléter. Nagy promised to grant amnesty to all rebels, abolish the secret police, and convince the Russians to leave Hungary. Russian leaders Mikhail Suslov and Anastas Mikoyan had arrived from Moscow to start negotiations. The public again rallied around Nagy. Despite later Russian claims that Nagy desired to restore capitalism, the Hungarian revolution at this stage represented the victory of nationalist Hungarian Communists over both Russian and Hungarian Stalinists. Maléter, who became minister of defense on October 31, envisioned a "free, independent, and socialist" Hungary. He indicated that he would use force against anyone desiring to restore the capitalist social and economic structure.

Meanwhile, the Russians watched the Hungarian experiment with intense interest. At some point, probably about November 1, they decided that it could not continue. Historians can only surmise some of the reasons for this decision. Conservative groups in the Kremlin, undoubtedly appalled at the revolt and at the congratulations that reached Nagy from Poland and Yugoslavia, began a campaign against him. They could cite the presence of one definitely anti-Communist rebel leader, Josef Dudas, although Nagy disavowed him, and they could quote the gloating of those Western commentators to whom the revolution seemed only the first step in destroying Com-

Violent clashes between Hungarian rebels and police units persuaded the Soviet Union that military intervention was necessary to prevent Hungary from abandoning the Warsaw Pact alliance. (Archive Photos)

munism. Nagy had legitimized the old political parties, including small Fascist groups in two counties. Some rebel bands continued to attack police, mistakenly killing even those loyal to, or appointed by, Nagy. On October 31, Nagy told Mikoyan that Hungary intended to quit the Communist Warsaw Pact alliance. On the same day, the joint Anglo-French-Israeli attack on Egypt distracted world attention from Hungary, split the Western powers, and provided Russian interventionists with the argument that it was a propitious moment to crush Nagy.

On November 1, Russian troops reentered Hungary, and János Kádár formed a puppet government. Hungarian armed resistance, although ferocious, was hopeless, and appeals to the outside world to recognize and protect Hungarian neutrality failed. On November 3, Maléter and his staff were arrested while they were negotiating at Russian headquarters. Nagy fled to the Yugoslavian embassy in Budapest. By November 14, Kádár had established himself as a Russian puppet ruler with the help of Russian troops and secret police. The Hungarian revolution had ended.

Nagy was perfidiously abducted after the Hungarian government had granted him release from the Yugoslavian embassy under guarantee of safe conduct. He and Maléter were shot in 1958. Josof Revai, an associate of Rákosi, died in 1959, and Gabor Peter, the chief of Rákosi's secret police, began work as a tailor's apprentice. Rákosi, who never returned from Moscow, died there in 1963. About two hundred thousand Hungarians fled to the West. Kádár, the traitor of 1956, felt sufficiently secure by 1960 to begin reforms that began to liberalize Hungarian life, although to a lesser extent than Nagy's "new course."

The Hungarian revolution was the crucial test of national Communism. Hungary's traditional Russophobia and resentment of Rákosi's vicious suppression made Hungary an especially difficult country in which to lift the controls. According to some scholars, Nagy's "new course" might have surmounted even these obstacles if it had been permitted to develop unimpeded after 1953. The Russians' major error was allowing Rákosi to return in 1955. Diplomat and historian Zbigniew Brzezinski stated that this mistake contributed much to Hungarian ferocity toward, and distrust of, the Russians in 1956. In this sense, the experiment of 1956 was hampered from its very inception.

The Hungarian revolution had major implications for subsequent developments within the Communist bloc. It convinced Russia that there were limits beyond which national Communism was unallowable without relinquishing control of the satellites.

—*Wayne D. Santoni, updated by Carl Rollyson*

ADDITIONAL READING:

Aczel, Tamas, ed. *Ten Years After*. New York: Holt, Rinehart and Winston, 1966. Analyzes the Hungarian Revolution and its aftermath by means of essays by various authors, mainly Hungarian.

Barany, Zoltan D. *Eastern Europe, 1945-1990*. New York: St. Martin's Press, 1993. See chapter 3 for a detailed analysis of the political background of the Hungarian Revolution, the role of the Hungarian army, and the repercussions of the revolution, especially its relationship to other revolts in Eastern Europe.

Borsody, Stephen, ed. *The Hungarians: A Divided Nation*. New Haven, Conn.: Yale Center for International and Area Studies, 1988. See chapter 5, "The Soviet Union and the Hungarian Question." Extensive chronology, bibliography, and notes.

Brzezinski, Zbigniew K. *The Soviet Bloc: Unity and Conflict*. New York: Praeger, 1961. Places the Hungarian Revolution with the context of the history of the Communist world and argues that the events of 1956 marked the end of an era in the history of the Communist Eastern bloc.

Felkay, Andrew. *Hungary and the USSR, 1956-1988*. New York: Greenwood Press, 1989. Chapters on the history of relations between Hungary and the Soviet Union, the early development of János Kádár as a Communist, the power struggle in the 1950's between national and Stalinist Communists, and Kádár's consolidation of power.

Sugar, Peter F., Peter Hanak, and Tibor Frank. *A History of Hungary*. Bloomington: Indiana University Press, 1990. See chapters 20 and 21 on the development of post-World War II Hungary, the Hungarian Revolution, and its aftermath. Detailed bibliography.

SEE ALSO: 1946, Churchill's "Iron Curtain" Speech; 1955, Warsaw Pact Is Signed; 1968-1989, Brezhnev Doctrine; 1968, Soviet Union Invades Czechoslovakia; 1989, Hungary Adopts a Multiparty System.

1957
COMMON MARKET IS FORMED

The Common Market is formed, providing the basis for resolving long-standing trade and political differences among the European nations and paving the way for a more sophisticated united Europe.

DATE: March 25, 1957
LOCALE: Rome, Italy
CATEGORIES: Economics; Government and politics
KEY FIGURES:
Konrad Adenauer (1876-1967), chancellor of West Germany, 1949-1963

Alcide De Gasperi (1881-1954), prime minister of Italy, 1945-1953

Jean Monnet (1888-1979), director of France's National Planning Council, 1945-1947, and later president of the European Coal and Steel Community, 1952-1955

Helmut Michael Kohl (born 1930), chancellor of West Germany, 1982-1990, and later chancellor of unified Germany beginning in 1990

François Mitterrand (1916-1996), president of France, 1981-1995

Robert Schuman (1886-1963), foreign minister of France, 1948-1952

Paul-Henri Spaak (1899-1972), premier of Belgium, 1947-1950; secretary-general of NATO, 1957-1961

Margaret Thatcher (born 1925), prime minister of Great Britain, 1979-1990

SUMMARY OF EVENT. The Common Market, officially called the European Economic Community, had its origins in the dark days immediately after World War II. At that time, Europe was both weak and destitute, and the various nations were in a position to discuss their mutual problems. As they looked about they saw that their former glory and power had been captured by the United States and the Soviet Union. Men such as Konrad Adenauer of Germany, Alcide de Gasperi of Italy, and Jean Monnet of France thought in terms of a strong, unified Europe.

Faced with mutual economic problems, Europe was forced to work as a unit. The United States provided an outright gift in the form of the Marshall Plan. The Organization of European Economic Cooperation was established with fifteen nations participating in 1948 to act as an agency to oversee the Plan's funds. Later, the Netherlands, Belgium, and Luxembourg created Benelux and abolished all frontier duties. In 1951, under the able direction of Robert Schuman, the European Coal and Steel Community (ECSC) was formed; its purpose was to abolish trade barriers, to coordinate industry, restrict trusts, and control the production of arms. A further step toward a unified Europe was the ill-fated European Defense Community which died in the summer of 1954 in the French Assembly. The result of these actions was an economically healthy and prosperous Europe, which produced a desire for closer economic cooperation.

As a result, the foreign ministers of the ECSC nations met in Messina, Italy, in 1955 and discussed further moves. The British walked out of this meeting, thinking that it was of no importance. The Messina talks continued under the direction of Paul Henri Spaak of Belgium in a secluded chateau outside of Brussels. In May, 1956, the Spaak Committee erected the foundations of the Common Market.

The Suez Crisis and the Hungarian revolt highlighted Europe's lack of direction and weakness. Consequently, the foreign ministers of Belgium, France, Germany, Italy, Luxembourg, and the Netherlands met and signed the Treaty of Rome on March 25, 1957, which created the Common Market. At the same time, they also created the European Atomic Energy Community (Euratom) which unified the development of nuclear power as a source of future power.

The treaty contains 248 articles which constitute a framework of progressive partnership and gradual economic integration. The treaty regards economic union as the first step in "an even closer union among European peoples." Thus the ideals of Adenauer, Gasperi, and Schuman were at last coming to fruition in the most ambitious attempt that had been undertaken, up to that time, for economic and, through it, political unification of Europe.

Gradual elimination of national custom barriers within twelve to fifteen years was a treaty objective. This customs union or free trade area would encompass 160 million people and from it would evolve an integrated mass market. Social and tax legislation would be harmonized and eventually common agriculture and transportation policies would emerge.

Institutions were created to implement the treaty. The Council of Ministers consists of ministers of member states who decide major issues by unanimity. The European Commission, an executive body whose decisions are subject to council veto, consists of nine members. The Assembly consists of 132 delegates, appointed by their respective parliaments according to population, whose task is to review council and commission proposals. Seven judges comprise the Court of Justice, which hears cases of violations of the Treaty. The headquarters of the Common Market is in Brussels, Belgium.

The Common Market went into effect in January, 1958, and by the end of 1961 the results were beginning to be seen and felt by member nations. Tariffs had been cut by 40 percent on industrial goods and 30 percent on agricultural products. Twelve former African territories were given provisional association status. The Common Market provided them with tariff advantages, development funds, and protection for their own infant industries. As the decade of the 1970's began, Europe was experiencing vigorous economic growth as a result of the Common Market. In October, 1970, the Werner Report called for full economic and monetary unity by the close of the decade.

The question of membership came up in 1961 for Great Britain, which had not taken earlier negotiations seriously. After two years of study, President Charles de Gaulle of France vetoed British admission. He did not consider

Great Britain a part of the European continent and feared its economic ties with the United States. After the death of de Gaulle in 1970, France took a new position. In May, 1971, Prime Minister Edward Heath of Great Britain and President Georges Pompidou of France met in Paris and concluded their talks on an optimistic note, thus setting the tenor of future negotiations between Great Britain and the Common Market. Finally, on January 1, 1973, not only Great Britain but also Ireland and Denmark formally joined their European neighbors and became participating members of the Common Market.

Other nations were admitted over time: Greece in 1981, and Spain and Portugal in 1986. After the collapse of the Communist systems dominated by the Soviet Union, many former Soviet-bloc countries also considered joining. The reunification of Germany in 1990 brought the former East Germany into the European Economic Community (EEC), by which name the organization was called after the 1980's.

The addition of Britain caused a number of problems, not the least of which was the concessions the mainland European nations had to give Britain in agricultural tariffs and prices. Moreover, the difficulty of conducting transactions with many currencies of different values made trade less efficient. In 1979, the EEC approved the European Monetary System (EMS), which regulated currency exchange rates by keeping the fluctuations within a "grid" of rates. No nation, therefore, could unilaterally raise the value of its currency or devalue it without simultaneous movement in other currencies.

In 1987, the EEC governments negotiated the Single European Act, which was the first major revision of the treaties. That act greatly expanded the role of the European Parliament and provided greater assistance to new members from the south, ensured some foreign policy cooperation, and laid the groundwork for the economic and monetary union (Emu). Following the reunification of Germany, the community members decided to press for a political union similar to the economic union, with the crucial meetings taking place at Maastricht, the Netherlands, in December, 1991. During that time, resistance to the delegation of national sovereignty by individual nations to the collective European parliament caused debates to rage in various countries, particularly England, where Prime Minister Margaret Thatcher—an otherwise exceptionally popular leader and the longest serving British prime minister in the twentieth century—was forced out of office. Primarily through the efforts of Helmut Kohl, chancellor of the newly unified Germany, and François Mitterrand, president of France, the negotiations retained their momentum.

The Maastricht meetings produced the European Union, which gave the European parliament new powers over some international agreements and broad new powers over monetary policy. Signed in March, 1992, the Maastricht Treaty wound its way through a difficult ratification process, and in some cases the vote in favor of the treaty was extremely close. Britain proved the most recalcitrant, but France and Denmark also resisted some of the provisions. The advantages of the Union attracted other nations, however, including Austria, Finland, Norway, Sweden, Hungary, and Poland, all of which applied for membership.

Other nations, including the Czech Republic, Slovakia, Bulgaria, and Romania had gained "privileged associated status" in 1995, making them the equal of Poland and Hungary, while Norway, upon further review, decided against joining the Union. Union officials wanted to move slowly in accepting new members out of a concern that too numerous and diverse a membership might make the institutions unwieldy or inefficient.

—*Russell M. Magnaghi, updated by Larry Schweikart*

ADDITIONAL READING:

Bloed, Arie, and Ramses A. Wessel, eds. *The Changing Functions of the Western European Union (WEU)*. Dordrecht, the Netherlands: Martinus Nijhoff, 1994. An excellent collection of the documents of the European Union, with a brief introduction and history.

Broad, Roger, and Robert Jarret. *Community Europe: A Short Guide to the Common Market*. London: Oswald Wolff, 1967. This volume deals with the societal and communal aspects of the market and less with the economic. Although this account provides an adequate history of events, its predictions are dated. Good bibliography.

Deniau, Jean François. *The Common Market*. Translated by Graham Heath. New York: Frederick A. Praeger, 1960. A brief and critical analysis of the Common Market that emphasizes the decisions to place economic issues ahead of political differences. Although dated, the book nevertheless reflects the views and predictions of some of those who observed the market in its growing period.

Finder, John. *European Community: The Building of a Nation*. 2d ed. New York: Oxford University Press. 1995. An excellent summary of the history of the EU, as well as a detailed look at each of the component parts of the treaties. A required reference for students.

Thatcher, Margaret. *The Downing Street Years*. New York: HarperCollins, 1993. An "inside" look at one European leader's struggle with maintaining sovereignty while moving toward community. Thatcher includes excerpts from some of her speeches on the issues of the Maastricht Treaty.

Western European Union: History. Structure. Prospects. Brussels: WEU Press and Information Service, 1994. The official publicity guide to the Union and its activities.

SEE ALSO: 1947, Marshall Plan Is Announced; 1949, North Atlantic Treaty; 1950-1963, Italy's Postwar Economic Boom; 1961, Organization for Economic Cooperation and Development Forms; 1987, European Community Adopts the Single Europe Act; 1993, Maastricht Treaty Is Ratified.

1957

SOVIET UNION LAUNCHES SPUTNIK

The Soviet Union launches Sputnik, the first artificial Earth satellite, dramatically altering the science and technology programs of the West.

DATE: October 4, 1957

LOCALE: Baikonur Cosmodrome in the Soviet Union

CATEGORIES: Exploration and discovery; Science and technology

KEY FIGURES:

Dwight David Eisenhower (1890-1969), thirty-fourth president of the United States, 1953-1961

Valentin P. Glushko, Soviet rocket-engine designer

Lyndon Baines Johnson (1908-1973), majority party leader in the United States Senate at the time of Sputnik's launch

Nikita Sergeyevich Khrushchev (1894-1971), premier of the Soviet Union, 1958-1964

Sergei Korolev (1906-1966), referred to as the chief designer of Soviet space programs, 1957-1966

SUMMARY OF EVENT. Sputnik 1 was the first in a relatively long list of early space flight achievements made by the Soviet Union in the years 1957 through 1965, the period in which the Soviets were heralded, correctly or incorrectly (depending upon one's point of view), as world leaders in the area of space technology. It is commonly believed that orbiting an artificial satellite by the Soviets caught the Western world totally by surprise. This is certainly not the case. As part of their contributions to the International Geophysical Year (IGY), both the Soviet Union and the United States publicly acknowledged a commitment to the development and launch of a satellite before IGY ended in 1958. In the United States, there had been programs advanced by agencies in the Department of Defense. Some of these programs were championed by the group of German rocket scientists (led by Wernher von Braun) that had emigrated to the United States near the end of World War II in Europe under Project Paperclip, to modify existing boosters under development as weapons-delivery systems to place a scientific satellite into orbit. None of these programs received tremendous support by the Eisenhower administration. In particular, Eisenhower was deeply concerned that large science and technology programs could seriously impact growth of the federal budget, and did not want a satellite program, which he did not view with high priority, to interfere with development of intercontinental ballistic missiles (ICBMs). To prevent multiplicity of effort by each branch of the armed services, the Eisenhower administration placed the American satellite program in the hands of scientists external to the Department of Defense, yet required a new, supposedly civilian, booster called Vanguard (to be developed by the U.S. Navy) to launch the satellite. The U.S. Army already had a booster (called Redstone) capable of being modified to become a satellite-delivery system, but its Project Orbiter was refused permission to attempt launching such a payload.

One other concern of the Eisenhower administration was the potential claim against the right of over-flight by a foreign nation. The Eisenhower administration was more interested in developing reconnaissance satellites to collect intelligence information, particularly about the Soviet Union. High-altitude flights by aircraft such as the U-2 were rapidly becoming quite risky and provided relatively limited data. When Sputnik entered space, passing over vast areas of the Free World, the issue of international sovereignty against over-flight became moot. The Soviets could not object to over-flight by American satellites, if their own payloads passed over the United States and NATO allies.

In the Soviet Union, development of heavy-lift launch vehicles proceeded with higher priority than similar programs in the United States, largely because the Soviet Union had a greater need for such missiles as nuclear weapons delivery systems. Soviet nuclear weapons were too large and heavy for available long-range bombers to carry. The edge in aviation enjoyed by the American Department of Defense combined with greater sophistication in nuclear weapons placed strategic defense initially with squadrons of B-52 bombers. Development of the MX-774 missile, later redefined as the Atlas ICBM, received a much lower priority. The purported "missile gap" became a central theme in the 1960 presidential race between Richard M. Nixon and John F. Kennedy, Jr.

Sputnik 1 was launched from the Baikonur Cosmodrome on October 4, 1957, atop an SL-3 booster. This booster was known in the West as the SS-6 Sapwood, capable of half-a-million kilograms of thrust at liftoff. (Baikonur was the name Soviets referred to as their launching site. In actuality it was located at Tyuratam.)

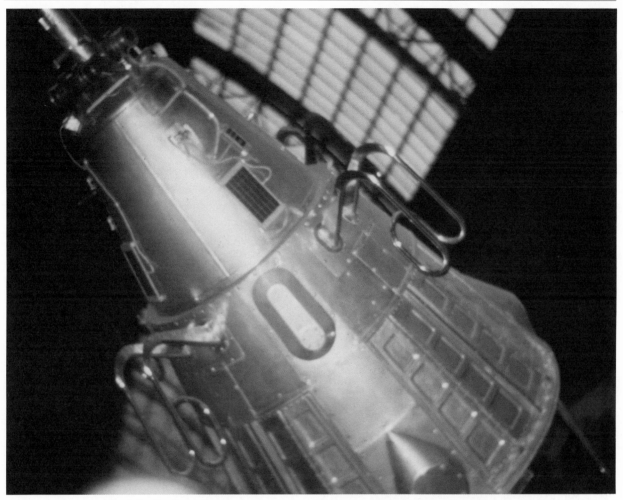

After its historic launch in October of 1957, Sputnik 1 was visible in the night skies around the world. (Archive Photos)

Khrushchev approved launching this satellite one day after the first successful full-range test-flight of the SL-3 booster on August 3, 1957. Originally, Sputnik was to be orbited on or near the birthday of Konstantin Tsiolkovsky, hailed throughout the Soviet Union as the father of cosmonautics. Delays in launch preparations precluded that.

Sputnik 1, referred to in Russian as *Iskustvennyi Sputnik Zemli* (fellow traveler of Earth), entered an orbit inclined 65.1 degrees with Earth's equator. Sputnik's orbit ranged from a low point (perigee) of 228 kilometers to a high point (apogee) of 947 kilometers. The satellite completed one revolution around the earth every 96.2 minutes. Its onboard power supply lasted until October 22, and the satellite itself reentered the atmosphere, burning up after ninety-four days in space.

The satellite was equipped only with a temperature sensor, a pair of battery-powered radio transmitters, a circulating fan, and four external folding antennae. The antennae, each nearly a meter long, unfurled once Sputnik separated from its booster. The transmitters operated at 20.005 and 40.002 megahertz (million cycles per second), providing signals of 0.3 seconds duration separated by 0.3-second breaks. The fan circulated nitrogen gas used to pressurize the satellite's interior.

Sputnik's characteristic beeping signal was transmitted at a frequency especially chosen to be significantly lower than the frequency used by American tracking systems, but accessible to amateur HAM radio operators throughout the world. Not only was Sputnik heard, heralding the dawn of the space age, but it also provided dazzling proof of its celestial voyage, appearing as a steady, brilliant light passing from horizon to horizon in a matter of minutes, illuminated by sunlight as it flew over a region of the earth shortly after local sunset. Sputnik watchers were both amazed and frightened by the satellite's appearance in the night sky.

One of the most infamous descriptions of Sputnik's flight came from Senator Lyndon B. Johnson, who exclaimed that he for one did not wish to go to sleep under a communist moon. If the Soviets were capable of putting a satellite into orbit, then perhaps they also were able to send hydrogen bombs raining down from the sky. Cold War politics were fueled significantly by the orbiting of Sputnik, and Sputnik was perceived by many as the technological equivalent of the surprise attack by the Japanese upon Pearl Harbor. This hysteria was unanticipated by Khrushchev. He quickly took advantage of the situation, however, using space flight as a means to purport technological superiority of the Soviet Union over the United States, and, by inference, superiority of communism over democratic rule. This manipulation of Soviet space programs resulted in a series of spectacular stunts (in the period 1957 to early 1965) that ultimately fell short of Khrushchev's boasts and doomed the Soviet space program to failure in the moon race.

Sputnik 1 provided relatively little scientific data. By observing Sputnik's rising time with optical and radio means, estimates of electron density in the ionosphere were made. By monitoring the decay of Sputnik's orbit, estimates of drag forces were inferred.

The first Sputnik was quickly followed by another satellite launch. Sputnik 2, launched from Tyuratam on November 3, carried a dog named Laika. The size of the payload, 7.8 metric tons, was startling to Western observers. This feat was achieved by keeping the booster's upper stage attached to the satellite. Nevertheless, Sputnik 2 further spread hysteria throughout the Western world. Desperation increased after the United States Vanguard 1 blew up after rising but a few feet off its launch pad on December 6, 1957. The Soviets referred to Vanguard as a "Flopnik" or "Kaputnik." Eventually the American satellite Explorer 1 achieved orbit, launched from Cape Canaveral, Florida, on January 31, 1958, by a Jupiter-C variant of the Redstone intermediate-range ballistic missile.   —*David G. Fisher*

ADDITIONAL READING:

Braun, Wernher von, and Frederick I. Ordway III. *History of Rocketry and Space Travel*. New York: Thomas Y. Crowell, 1977. A detailed historical review of rocketry and astronautics with an international basis.

Divine, Robert A. *The Sputnik Challenge*. New York: Oxford University Press, 1993. Detailed presentation of Eisenhower's response to Sputnik.

McDougall, Walter A. *The Heavens and the Earth: A Political History of the Space Age*. New York: Basic Books, 1985. Winner of the 1986 Pulitzer Prize for history, McDougall gives an excellent presentation of political and technological developments that brought about the space race. Particularly strong in its presentation of satellite program decisions made during the Eisenhower presidency.

Reeves, Robert. "The Sputnik Program." In *Magill's Survey of Science: Space Exploration Series*. Vol. 5. Pasadena, Calif.: Salem Press, 1989. Places Sputnik's launch in context with the remainder of the Sputnik series, and the reaction in the United States which eventually led to the creation of NASA.

Stoiko, Michael. *Soviet Rocketry: The First Decade of Achievement*. London: David & Charles, 1970. A thorough presentation of the development of Soviet rocketry from Tsiolkovsky's theoretical dreams to the reality of Vostok, Voshkod, and early Soyuz manned space flights. Description of pre-Sputnik development is particularly good.

SEE ALSO: 1949, North Atlantic Treaty; 1955, Warsaw Pact Is Signed; 1961, Soviet Union Puts a Human in Space; 1963, Limited Nuclear Test Ban Treaty Is Signed; 1973, European Space Agency Is Formed.

1958
RACE RIOTS ERUPT IN LONDON

Race riots erupt in London, revealing racial tensions that have been simmering in English cities and establishing race as a significant political issue for the future.

DATE: September 9, 1958

LOCALE: London, England

CATEGORIES: Government and politics; Race and ethnicity

KEY FIGURES:

Richard Austen "Rab" Butler (1902-1982), British home secretary, 1957-1962

Harold Macmillan (1894-1986), British prime minister, 1957-1963

Sir Oswald Ernald Mosley (1896-1980), the leader of English Fascism in the 1930's, who returned from exile to run for office after the 1958 riots

SUMMARY OF EVENT. After World War II, British Commonwealth citizens began to immigrate to the British Isles, and because they held British passports, no restriction on their entry was legally possible. Most decided to move for economic reasons, believing that their employment opportunities would be significantly improved in what they had been taught for generations was the home country. Many of these citizens were nonwhite, the largest numbers being from the West Indies, India, and Pakistan.

The immigrants, particularly the West Indians, were sincerely shocked to find that they were not welcomed. In the 1950's, the numbers of nonwhites grew rapidly but were never large by American standards. In 1951, there were approximately 15,000 West Indians in England and Wales out of a total nonwhite population of 74,500. The latter figure had more than quadrupled to 336,600 by 1961 and the proportion of West Indians in the nonwhite population to about half. In the same period, the total population had grown from 43,759,000 to 46,106,000. Clearly nonwhites were not demographically significant, but they were concentrated in particular districts of major cities, especially London.

The initial discontent about immigration revolved around the perception of competition for jobs and the drain on the British welfare system, and although some of unhappiness was certainly racial, prejudice does not seem to have been enormous. An opinion poll of 1956 indicated that only 10 percent of white Englishmen would object to nonwhite neighbors and only 1 percent felt that nonwhites should be kept out of the country. This did not mean, however, that there was no discontent. In 1954, the colonial secretary called immigration a "problem"; in 1956, a Home Office undersecretary said it was a "headache." Although the terms were guarded, both of these remarks were clearly in the context of nonwhite immigration. The government leaders, however, were not inclined to think there was any cause for entry restrictions or other controls. Studies in 1955 and 1958 indicated that the immigrants took menial jobs that white Englishmen usually did not want, and despite higher than average unemployment—8 percent of newcomers compared to an overall national rate of 2 percent—they were not a significant drain on the British welfare system. Thus, the trouble of late summer, 1958, was largely unexpected.

The first disturbances occurred in the city of Nottingham's Chase district in July and August. The result was that eight whites, including a policeman, were hospitalized. Since fighting among white gangs, called Teddy Boys, followed, the authorities dismissed the racial elements and blamed drink and youth. About the same time, a gang of about fifteen Teddy Boys raided a black-owned café in the Shepherd's Bush district of London. The attackers were gone before the police arrived, and no one was ever charged with the crime. The attack was repeated by a larger group in about two weeks, and this time six youths aged eighteen to twenty-three were arrested, convicted of causing malicious damage, and fined.

The authorities hoped that the trouble was no more than isolated incidents. In late August, however, there was fighting in Nottingham and several London districts.

Blacks reported numerous incidents of white drivers, often reputedly older men, trying to run them down. Graffiti such as "Keep Britain White" began to appear. On August 23, there were several attacks on blacks and their homes, and nine youths were arrested for driving around Shepherd's Bush and surrounding districts with clubs and a knife for, as they put it, "nigger hunting." They attacked a number of black individuals and couples on the streets. Five of their victims were hospitalized, three seriously hurt, and the youths ultimately were sentenced to four years imprisonment each. Londoners, however, seem to have continued to believe that there was no serious racial problem and little was done to alleviate the situation.

There was a serious problem, despite the sanguine attitude of the metropolis. On Saturday, August 30, there was much wider violence centered in Bromley Road near Notting Dale, the most overcrowded district in London. Although it was not a particular center of nonwhite residence, several black-owned homes were attacked and one burned. Fighting spread and for several days there were disturbances in much of west London. Black Londoners tended to avoid trouble, but there was some retaliation to

Concerned about public safety, British police officers maintained a high profile to discourage rioting and attacks against black Londoners that broke out in August of 1958. (Archive Photos)

Chronology of

white attacks. Teddy Boys used this as provocation for more trouble.

On August 31, a crowd estimated by some at seven hundred called for killing blacks, and rioting resulted in several injuries and damage to two police cars. The climax came on the first two days of September with widespread fighting, Teddy Boy attacks against blacks, and trouble with the police who were trying to control the situation. For several weeks, there were sporadic outbreaks of violence, especially in the Notting Hill, Notting Dale, and Paddington districts, but this tapered off until peace was generally restored by late September.

Opinion polls after the rioting showed that the English were most likely to blame whites or both whites and blacks for the riots. Perhaps more tellingly, however, some 30 percent of whites now expressed an unwillingness to have black neighbors. Rab Butler, the British home secretary, was initially concerned about the possibility of violence spreading as it had in the United States in similar situations. He soon calmed, and he decided the proper course was to refer such problems as housing to local authorities, who were, in fact, reluctant to act. He also spoke of the need to restrict immigration, especially from the Caribbean, but talks with governments in that area went nowhere. Since the economic situation in the British Isles remained better than in most of the Commonwealth states, the flow of immigrants continued, peaking in 1961. The racist party called the National Front became more active, and Fascist expatriate Oswald Mosley returned to England to run for office in the 1959 general election. Although Mosley never regained his prewar prominence, Enoch Powell would gain notable support as leader of the National Front over the next decade. Controlled by the Labour Party for the first time since the riots, Parliament passed the Race Relations Act, Britain's first legislation to govern racial interaction, in 1965. Although it banned overt public acts of racism, the legislation did not address such problems in housing and employment. It was a grudging attempt, but it was at least the beginning of an effort to resolve the questions of race that had so clearly emerged in 1958.   —*Fred R. van Hartesveldt*

ADDITIONAL READING:

Glass, Ruth, assisted by Harold Pollins. *London's Newcomers: The West Indian Migrants.* Cambridge, Mass.: Harvard University Press, 1961. Glass provides a detailed account of the events during the riots along with some insightful comments about the problems of the immigrants.

Katznelson, Ira. *Black Men, White Cities: Race, Politics, and Migration in the United States 1900-30, and*

Britain, 1948-68. London: Oxford University Press, 1973. The comparison of the situations in the United States and Britain helps set the situation of 1958 into context. This book also provides information concerning the political responses to the growth of nonwhite population.

Morgan, Kenneth O. *The People's Peace: British History, 1945-1989.* New York: Oxford University Press, 1990. Written by one of the best and most prolific of modern British historians, this volume is an excellent analysis of postwar British society and provides the background necessary for an understanding of the racial situation in the late 1950's.

Schaefer, Richard T. *The Extent and Content of Racial Prejudice in Great Britain.* San Francisco: R. and E. Research Associates, 1976. This volume provides the results of a number of public opinion polls concerning racial attitudes.

Van Hartesveldt, Fred R. "Race and Political Parties in Britain, 1954-1965." *Phylon* 44 (June, 1983): 126-133. This article provides background to the situation and an analysis of the reaction of the Conservative and Labour Parties to the emerging issue of race in British politics.

SEE ALSO: 1945, Labour Party Forms Majority Government; 1972, "Bloody Sunday" in Northern Ireland; 1973, West Germany Restricts Immigration of Foreign Workers; 1992, Protests and Violence Against Foreigners in Germany.

1961
SOVIET UNION PUTS A HUMAN IN SPACE

The Soviet Union puts a human in space, launching a new era of exploration and demonstrating that humans can survive the rigors of spaceflight.

DATE: April 12, 1961

LOCALE: Baikonur, the Soviet Union

CATEGORIES: Exploration and discovery; Science and technology

KEY FIGURES:

Yuri Alekseyevich Gagarin (1934-1968), the first Soviet cosmonaut

John Fitzgerald Kennedy (1917-1963), thirty-fifth president of the United States, 1961-1963

Nikita Sergeyevich Khrushchev (1894-1971), premier of the Soviet Union, 1958-1964

SUMMARY OF EVENT. The space age was inaugurated with the launching of Sputnik 1 on October 4, 1957, yet astronautics originated in the late nineteenth century. Konstantine E. Ziolkovsky, the "founding father" of Russian space science, predicted in 1898 that a space rocket could be constructed using liquid fuel and liquid oxygen capable of thrusting humans into space. It has been reported that Vladimir Lenin was a firm believer in astronautics, prophesying a time when a Soviet citizen would make the space odyssey.

After World War II, German scientists in both the United States and the Soviet Union perfected the German V-2 war rockets. Russia constructed rockets capable of launching large payloads, while the United States concentrated on smaller, efficient, and more agile rocket-missiles. Sputnik 1 dramatically demonstrated the immediate success of the development of larger rockets. From 1957 to 1961, Russian spaceships were the first to carry live animals, to reach the vicinity of the moon and orbit the sun, to photograph the far side of the moon, and to return live animals from space. While the United States was also scoring significant progress in space science, Russia clearly monopolized the drama of space exploration.

In March of 1961, Soviet premier Nikita Khrushchev announced that the Soviet Union would soon place a human being in space. A few weeks later on April 12, Yuri A. Gagarin became that first human in space. Until that day, history recorded only imaginative flights toward the stars. With Gagarin's flight, science and the Cold War arms race had converged to change dream into reality.

The spaceship Vostok 1 weighed 10,395 pounds and orbited the earth in 89 minutes at a top speed of 17,000 miles per hour—three times faster than the previous manned-flight record. Gagarin's journey was weightlessly smooth. He reported being able to write a note in addition to drinking and eating. The Vostok 1 spacecraft was controlled by radio signals from the ground, but Gagarin maintained radio communication with flight controllers, reported his visual observations of the earth, and relayed information about onboard experiments, demonstrating the ability of humans to function in space.

Although rapid reentry into the earth's atmosphere marred the space capsule, Gagarin landed safely at Smelovaka, near Saratov on the Volga River. Secrecy surrounded the technical details of the flight. Although the Russian press reported that Gagarin landed in his capsule, disclosures made more than twenty-five years later indicated that he parachuted to Earth from a height of about twenty thousand feet. The reason for this misinformation may have been that the Fédération Aeronautique Internationale, which certifies all international aviation records, requires pilots to land with their aircraft. Gagarin's landing site was later marked by a titanium obelisk measuring 130 feet (40 meters) in height commemorating the flight.

Shortly after the launching, Radio Moscow announced

Soviet cosmonaut Yuri A. Gagarin became the first human to be launched into space, flying aboard the spaceship Vostok 1 in April of 1961. (Archive Photos)

to the world that "the world's first manned spacecraft . . . has been launched into orbit around the earth," and crowds began to gather in Moscow's Red Square and around the country to follow the progress of the flight. During the flight, Russian factories and businesses were closed to allow everyone the opportunity to listen to radio broadcasts about the flight. The Soviet propaganda office was prepared for the historic event, and a commemorative stamp rolled off the presses on the same day that Gagarin reached space. Two days later, jubilant Muscovites heralded their latest hero as a triumphant Gagarin stood with Khrushchev atop the Lenin-Stalin mausoleum to view a four-hour parade honoring the first human in space. Later that evening, President Leonid Brezhnev presented the first cosmonaut with the nation's highest award, the title of Hero of the Soviet Union.

President John F. Kennedy's immediate response was to congratulate the Soviet Union on a victory that would be beneficial to all nations. While Kennedy encouraged international cooperation in space exploration, it was not long before he announced that the United States would place a human being on the moon by 1970. Having campaigned for office on a promise to close the missile gap, Kennedy was now confronting the American people with a promise to close the spaceship gap.

The Vostok launch system was veiled in secrecy until 1967. Until then, the United States knew only that the Soviet-made rockets had a greater total thrust than those used at Cape Kennedy. When the Vostok launch vehicle was displayed at the Paris Air Show in 1967, American space scientists were surprised to discover that the vehicle was not equipped with enormous engines, but instead was an amalgamation of small engines. The Sputnik launch vehicle, a converted intercontinental ballistic missile (ICBM), had been a one-and-a-half-stage rocket with four booster engines and one additional half-stage engine which provided the final thrust into space. Used between 1961 and 1965, the Vostok series included the addition of another full upper stage, allowing it to place the huge manned spaceships into orbit.

Gagarin's flight was followed by the seventeen-orbit journey of Major Gherman S. Titov, who had been Gagarin's back-up, on August 6-7, 1961. Vostok 2 remained in orbit for twenty-five hours, allowing Titov to record the effects of a full day of weightlessness in space on the human capacity to work. During 1961, the United States did not attempt an orbital flight. Between the flights of Vostok 1 and Vostok 2, the United States launched the Project Mercury capsule *Freedom 7* on May 5, 1961. Alan B. Shepard rode the capsule 115 miles into space before returning to Earth. Shortly after this first U.S. space flight, President Kennedy requested a new congressional appropriation for space and defense-related programs amounting to $1.8 billion. To take a leading role in space, the United States would need to spend approximately $7-$9 billion between 1962 and 1967. Gagarin's flight greatly intensified the space race that climaxed with the dramatic moon landing of America's Apollo 11 in 1969.

The Soviet Union dominated the first decade of the space age. Between 1961 and 1967, they launched the first group of manned spacecraft, placed the first woman in space, launched the first multipassenger spacecraft, and executed the first spacewalk. In the area of space exploration, Soviet-built spacecraft were the first to make a successful landing on another planet (Venus), to make a soft landing on the Moon and send back photographs, to orbit as the first functioning satellite of the moon, and to carry out automated rendezvous and docking. By 1967, it was apparent that the space race between the Soviet Union and the United States was close, since American-built vehicles were scoring firsts in communications and weather satel-

lites and in nonautomated rendezvous and docking.

The relationship between Cold War weaponry and space technology is clearly evident in the ICBM spaceship development. The prestige gained from Gagarin's historic flight was also a valuable Cold War weapon for the Soviet Union. Sputnik 1 and Vostok 1 served as visible projections of increasing Soviet power. From Khrushchev's point of view, a Soviet space victory was a dramatic response to those who criticized his country's backwardness. Since the United States and the Soviet Union were both struggling for world prestige, the Kremlin eagerly exploited Gagarin's journey as an illustration of Soviet progress not only as the leader in astronautics but also as a representative of the most dynamic political system—Marxist Communism. The immediate gain in prestige, however, was bought at a high price. While both superpowers were spending an equivalent sum of money on space exploration, the gross national product of the Soviet Union was approximately one half that of the United States. The long-range consequences of Soviet space victory and its attendant propaganda campaign were far more costly to the economic health of the Soviet Union than the short-term gains they produced.

As the Cold War began to thaw with the advent of détente, Russian leader Leonid Brezhnev and U.S. president Richard Nixon agreed, in 1972, to a joint mission linking spacecraft from the two nations. In July of 1975, the Apollo-Soyuz Test Project was launched. Three astronauts from the Apollo program maneuvered their vehicle to dock with a Soyuz spacecraft, which contained two Soviet cosmonauts, thus exchanging the first international handshake in space.

Following the American success in reaching the Moon, the Soviet space program concentrated on developing a series of space stations orbiting the earth. Soviet success in this area prompted an invitation from the United States and its international partners to develop an international space station, to be operated jointly by the United States, Canada, a consortium of European nations, Russia, and Japan. Officials from the Russian Republic and the United States also discussed the possibility of a joint human mission to Mars in the twenty-first century.

—Christopher J. Kauffman,
updated by George J. Flynn

ADDITIONAL READING:

Bloomfield, Lincoln P., ed. *Outer Space: Prospects for Man and Society.* Rev. ed. New York: Frederick A. Praeger, 1968. A collection of essays by nine experts on the political, scientific, economic, and diplomatic aspects of space exploration.

Bond, Peter. *Heroes in Space: From Gagarin to Challenger*. New York: Basil Blackwell, 1987. Focuses on the cosmonauts and astronauts and their achievements, with an opening chapter describing Yuri Gagarin's life and his spaceflight.

Hart, Douglas. *The Encyclopedia of Soviet Spacecraft*. New York: Bison Books, 1987. Provides the technical details on the rockets, spacecraft, technological achievements and scientific experiments of the Soviet Union's space program,

Riabchikov, Evgeny. *Russians in Space*. Translated by Guy Daniels. Garden City, N.Y.: Doubleday, 1971. An in-depth account of the early Soviet space program, including chapters on the flights of Gagarin and Titov, by a Russian journalist with access to the participants.

Shelton, William R. *Soviet Space Exploration: The First Decade*. New York: Washington Square Press, 1968. One of the foremost writers on Soviet space achievements describes the first human flight and includes a brief biography of Yuri Gagarin.

SEE ALSO: 1949, North Atlantic Treaty; 1955, Warsaw Pact Is Signed; 1957, Soviet Union Launches Sputnik; 1963, Limited Nuclear Test Ban Treaty Is Signed; 1973, European Space Agency Is Formed.

1961
AMNESTY INTERNATIONAL IS FOUNDED

Amnesty International is founded, giving a collective voice to those concerned about human rights violations around the world and helping to free thousands of political prisoners.

DATE: May 28, 1961
LOCALE: London, England
CATEGORIES: Organizations and institutions; Social reform
KEY FIGURES:
David Astor (born 1912), editor of the London *Observer*
Eric Baker, prominent British Quaker
Peter Benenson (born 1921), London lawyer and visionary
Louis Blom-Cooper (born 1926), London lawyer
Diana Redhouse, professional designer in London
SUMMARY OF EVENT. The story of Amnesty International begins with one man: a Catholic lawyer of Jewish descent named Peter Benenson, who lived in London. During the 1950's, Benenson had dedicated himself to human rights causes in different countries, defending people (often at his own expense) accused of crimes because of their religious or political beliefs. He wrote articles and made radio addresses about human rights violations, trying to make more people aware of wrongdoings committed by governments around the world. His work was not influenced by politics, but by an overriding belief in human rights. Therefore, he spoke out against abuses wherever he found them, whether the oppressive government was socialist or communist or democratic, whether it was considered friend or foe.

In the late 1950's he formed an organization of British lawyers who used their collective voices to campaign for human rights. This group took the name Justice, and chose to work specifically to see that the 1948 United Nations Universal Declaration on Human Rights was observed.

In November of 1960, Peter Benenson was reading the newspaper as he traveled in the subway to his London office. He saw a brief article about two students in Portugal who had been arrested in a restaurant and sentenced to seven years in prison. Their crime: raising their glasses in a toast to freedom. Benenson's initial reaction was that he ought to register a protest, and he made plans to appear in person at the Portuguese Embassy in London. He quickly saw, however, that the protest of one man would not make enough of an impression to bring about the prisoners' release. Neither would the protests of a group of London lawyers. In an instant a vision came to him—an international network of people who would bombard the Portuguese government with letters and telegrams. Perhaps the pressure of worldwide public opinion would be enough to impress a dictator.

As he thought more about his plan, Benenson began to see that he might be able to reach more than just one government, and help more than these two unfortunate victims. Gradually he developed an idea for a massive one-year campaign, to dramatically increase public awareness of political and religious persecution, and to work for the freedom of at least some political prisoners. He chose 1961 as the starting date for his program, in commemoration of the one hundredth anniversary of the beginning of the process of freeing slaves in the United States, and also the hundredth anniversary of the freedom of Russian serfs.

A campaign of the magnitude Benenson envisioned would require the efforts of many people, and he turned first to two other well-known men to help him. Eric Baker was a prominent Quaker, and Louis Blom-Cooper was another lawyer who had provided the defense for several high-profile human rights cases himself. With the influence and contacts of these three men, and the help and support of the members of Justice, "Appeal for Amnesty

1961" would reach an international audience.

The goals of the campaign were formalized in writing before the first public call for support. "Appeal for Amnesty 1961" would work impartially for the release of those imprisoned for their opinions, seek a fair and public trial for such people, enlarge the right of asylum and help find work for political refugees, and urge the formation of an international machinery to guarantee freedom of opinion. Benenson's law office would be used as a center for gathering and disseminating information about political prisoners.

On May 28, 1961, with the full cooperation of editor David Astor, Peter Benenson published a full-page appeal in one of London's most influential Sunday newspapers, the liberal *Observer*. Other major newspapers in France, the United States, Denmark, India, South Africa, and other nations carried similar articles the next day. Benenson's piece, titled "The Forgotten Prisoners," described the situations of eight "prisoners of conscience" in Angola, Czechoslovakia, Greece, Hungary, Romania, South Africa, Spain, and the United States, and explained Benenson's theory that massive public outcry could influence governments. The prisoners described had been chosen to appeal to a wide range of concerned people. Among the eight were two white men—in the United States and South Africa—jailed by other whites because of their work for the rights of black people in their own country; a poet and doctor; a philosopher; a Roman Catholic Cardinal and an archbishop. The appeal was carefully timed to appear on May 28, observed in England as a religious holiday, Trinity Sunday. Amnesty's operations were secular, but echoed the idea of "three": volunteers would work in groups of three, each group writing letters in support of three prisoners, one from a communist country, one from a Western country, and one from a developing nation in the "Third World." Volunteers would not become involved in cases in their own countries. This system was intended to guarantee that all efforts on behalf of prisoners would be strictly impartial.

The appeal was effective, and reaction was immediate. Hundreds of letters, phone calls, and cash contributions were received, and newspapers published editorials supporting the new organization. People who had information about other prisoners of conscience shared what they knew, adding thousands of names to the lists Amnesty had already compiled. Schools, churches, and business and civic clubs volunteered to work together on behalf of the prisoners.

A network was formed. A group would take a few names of prisoners and write letters to their governments, demanding again and again that the prisoners be released.

Volunteers would also try to contact the prisoners' families, send financial support if possible, and attempt to get at least one letter to each prisoner, so that they would know the world was aware of their situations. Within weeks, branches of Amnesty had formed in seven other countries. In the first year, Amnesty took up the cases of 210 prisoners. With the ever-increasing awareness of the need for this work, and an increasing supply of volunteers to do it, Amnesty founders decided that the campaign must not stop after a year, but continue as long as there was a need. The name of the organization became Amnesty International.

Each of the branches took its system of organization from the central London branch and also adopted its emblem. Designed by London artist Diana Redhouse during the first days after the appeal, the emblem shows a lit candle encircled by barbed wire. The idea was from Benenson, who remembered the ancient saying "It is better to light one candle than to curse the darkness."

From this simple start, great things were accomplished. On October 10, 1977, Amnesty International was awarded the Nobel Peace Prize, in recognition of its work "to protect the value of human life." By 1993, the organization had more than one million members in 150 countries, and had investigated more than forty thousand cases. Many thousands of former political prisoners owe their freedom to the direct or indirect intervention of Amnesty International.

—*Cynthia A. Bily*

ADDITIONAL READING:

Amnesty International Photo File, 1961-1981. London: Amnesty International Publications, 1981. Twenty-one full-page black-and-white photos of important moments in the organization's first twenty years, including a reproduction of Peter Benenson's newspaper article, "The Forgotten Prisoners."

Desmond, Cosmos. *Persecution East and West: Human Rights, Political Prisoners and Amnesty*. Harmondsworth, England: Penguin, 1983. Written by a former director of the British section of Amnesty International, this book represents a rethinking of how Amnesty can and should achieve its goals.

Larsen, Egon. *A Flame in Barbed Wire: The Story of Amnesty International*. New York: W. W. Norton, 1979. A chronological account of Amnesty International's work and evolving philosophy, from its founding through its winning the Nobel Prize for Peace in 1977.

Power, Jonathan. *Against Oblivion: Amnesty International's Fight for Human Rights*. Glasgow, Scotland: Fontana Paperbacks, 1981. A thorough history of the first two decades of Amnesty International, and a detailed look at the human rights issues facing nine countries around the world at the start of the 1980's.

_____. *Amnesty International: The Human Rights Story*. New York: McGraw-Hill, 1981. Commemorating the twentieth anniversary of Amnesty's founding, this book offers an insightful history with detailed explanations of four "special efforts" and several targeted countries. Includes over one hundred photographs and maps.

Staunton, Marie, Sally Fenn, and Amnesty International U.S.A. *The Amnesty International Handbook*. Claremont, Calif.: Hunter House, 1991. A handbook for those who wish to become involved in Amnesty's efforts, this book includes a brief history of the group's founding and accomplishments over its first thirty years, and descriptions of ten major issues of interest to the organization.

SEE ALSO: 1945, The United Nations Is Founded; 1945-1946, Nuremberg Trials; 1950, European Convention on Human Rights Is Signed; 1963-1970, Soviet Jews Demand Cultural and Religious Rights; 1976, IRA Hunger Striker Dies in an English Prison.

1961
BUILDING OF THE BERLIN WALL

The building of the Berlin Wall precipitates an international crisis between East Germany and the West.

DATE: August 13, 1961
LOCALE: Berlin, East Germany
CATEGORY: Government and politics
KEY FIGURES:

Konrad Adenauer (1876-1967), chancellor of the Federal Republic of Germany (West Germany), 1949-1963

Willy Brandt (Herbert Ernst Karl Frahm; 1913-1992), mayor of West Berlin, 1957-1966

Dwight David Eisenhower (1890-1969), thirty-fourth president of the United States, 1953-1961

John Fitzgerald Kennedy (1917-1963), thirty-fifth president of the United States, 1961-1963

Nikita Sergeyevich Khrushchev (1894-1971), premier of the Soviet Union, 1958-1964

Walter Ulbricht (1893-1973), chairman of the State Council, German Democratic Republic (East Germany), 1960-1973

SUMMARY OF EVENT. From the time the military occupation zones had been agreed upon at the Yalta Conference (February, 1944) and Potsdam Conference (July-August, 1945), the status of Berlin had been a bone of contention between the victorious powers of the Soviet Union, the United States, France, and Britain.

At these conferences, as well as at the London meeting of the Allied foreign ministers in 1944, it was agreed that Germany and its capital Berlin was to be divided into four occupational zones. The city of Berlin although inside the Soviet zone became a separate unit. Access to the city from the Western zones was guaranteed by the Soviets, but only the air corridors were especially mentioned in writing. According to the agreements, Berlin was to be jointly administered by an Allied Control Council, whose decisions had to be unanimous.

The Soviets, soon after occupying Central Germany, started to convert their zone into a communist satellite, thus boycotting the joint administration of defeated Germany. The Western powers responded by encouraging the foundation of the Federal Republic of Germany along the lines of democracy and free enterprise. In 1948, the Soviets walked out of the Allied Control Council, and the joint administration of Germany and Berlin came to an end. The Soviets claimed that Berlin had now lost its four-power status and tried to incorporate the city into their sphere of influence. In trying to get the Western powers to withdraw from Berlin, the Soviets blockaded all land access to the city for eleven months (March, 1948-May, 1949). During this time the western part of the city's population of 2.5 million was entirely supplied by Allied airplanes in a logistical masterpiece: the Berlin Airlift.

After the Soviets lifted the blockade, the eastern and western sectors of the city were ruled separately, by tacit agreement. The Western Allies allowed the newly founded West German government (August, 1949), under the leadership of Chancellor Konrad Adenauer, to extend its political and economic system to West Berlin, while the Soviets established Communism in East Berlin by founding the Communist German Democratic Republic (GDR) in October of 1949, under Walter Ulbricht. Although incorporated into the respective systems, Berlin retained a special status as an occupied city, with the final authority in each of the zones resting with the occupational powers.

In the 1950's, the Soviets tried to incorporate Berlin into East Germany, mainly on the grounds that actual four-power rule had ended when the Allied Control Commission ceased functioning in 1948, but also on the contention that the Potsdam agreement had been nullified by the creation of the West German government. The problem was not crucial in the early 1950's, although there were sporadic East German interruptions of the transit routes through the GDR in an attempt to hamper Western access to the city.

On June 17, 1953, the unpopularity of the Soviet occupation and the communist regime in East Germany became evident when workers in East Berlin demonstrated and rioted after the government increased production quotas. The uprising was beaten down by riot police and Soviet tanks. Following these uprisings, the East Germans closed the border between East and West Germany with barbed wire and armed watchtowers. Berlin remained the only opening in the Iron Curtain.

Between 1954 and the building of the wall in 1961, about three million East Germans escaped to the West via Berlin by leaving the Soviet zone and entering a Western sector of the city. This was as easy as crossing the street or taking a subway ride and disembarking at a Western zone station.

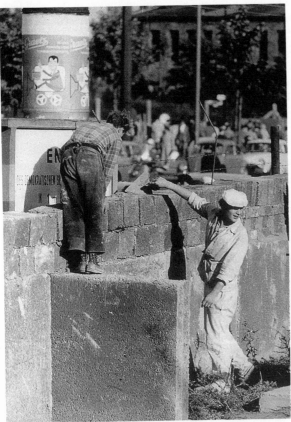

In 1961, East German workers labored to construct a cement block wall between West Berlin and the Soviet-controlled eastern sector of Berlin. (Archive Photos)

Following the death of the Soviet dictator Joseph Stalin, Nikita Khrushchev won the power struggle for succession. Some of his domestic economic reforms aroused opposition from old line Stalinists. He placated these domestic opponents by taking a harder line on foreign policy. On November 10, 1958, he delivered an ultimatum stating that if the German problem was not solved by mutual agreement within six months, he would turn over control of the city and its approaches to the East Germans. He softened his demands somewhat by proposing on November 27, 1958, that Berlin become a "free city." Both declarations were rejected by the Western powers. The Berlin problem was being discussed, however, at a series of summit meetings between Khrushchev and President Dwight D. Eisenhower. In September of 1959, Khrushchev visited the United States and met with Eisenhower. They agreed on the Camp David Formula: a statement of mutual willingness to solve the Berlin problem but without any time limit. Further negotiations on Berlin were scheduled at the Paris Summit of 1960; however, Khrushchev embarrassed President Eisenhower at Paris with the announcement that the Soviets had shot down an American U-2 spy plane over Russia. This incident led to an immediate cancellation of the conference.

By 1961, the crisis in Berlin had become acute. Large numbers of refugees from East Germany and Communist Europe were using the open interzonal borders of Berlin as an escape route to the West. In 1960, more than 230,000 Germans left East Germany, three-fourths of them below the age of forty-five. Ulbricht was losing many of his skilled workers and most productive people.

When John F. Kennedy, the new U.S. president, was inaugurated in January of 1961, Khrushchev seized the opportunity to settle the Berlin problem. The Bay of Pigs fiasco in Cuba and the deteriorating American influence in Laos convinced Khrushchev that Kennedy was inexperienced and weak and could be made to yield on Berlin. He invited Kennedy to a summit in Vienna in June, 1961, where he renewed his demands for a settlement. The constant Soviet ultimatums and threats regarding Berlin caused an increase in the flood of refugees. The German boulevard press, especially the *Bild Zeitung*, heated up the hysteria by publishing the number of refugees in big headlines each day on the front page. The rest of the Western media joined in publicizing the hemorrhaging of East Germany. Despite the efforts of the East German police to restrict citizens' access to Berlin and by aggressively patrolling the borders of the Soviet sector, by June of 1961, the rate of refugees had risen to more than twenty thousand per month. On August 12, 1961, twenty-four hundred individuals left East Berlin on that day alone.

On August 13, at 2:00 A.M. on a Sunday night, the East German troops and police closed the checkpoints between East and West and sealed off the entire Soviet sector with barbed wire, which was replaced on August 15 by a crude cement block wall running thirty miles through the middle of the city. The West was completely taken by surprise. The small garrison of Western troops in Berlin moved tanks to the demarcation line, but they did not intervene in the sealing off of the eastern third of the city nor interfere with the construction of the wall. Khrushchev then announced that he was turning over control of the city and its access routes to the East Germans. Kennedy mobilized reservists in the United States and sent a token force of fifteen hundred troops through East Germany, to enlarge the American garrison in Berlin and to demonstrate Western rights. Despite the urging of West Berlin's mayor Willy Brandt, no action was taken by the Western Allies to tear down the wall. Soviet and East German authorities led the Kennedy administration to believe that the wall was only a temporary measure to control the refugee problem. By the time it became apparent to the West that the wall was intended to be permanent, it could have only torn it down at the risk of nuclear war.

In the following weeks, the United States demonstrated its rights by sending diplomats and troop patrols into East Berlin without submitting to East German border controls. High-profile politicians were dispatched to Berlin, including Vice President Lyndon Johnson and Lucius D. Clay, the former U.S. high commissioner during the Berlin Airlift. President Kennedy personally visited the divided city, inspected the wall and gave his famous speech to reassure the population of West Berlin of continued American support. Two points were made, namely that the United States, Great Britain, and France still had rights in the city under the Potsdam agreement, and that the Soviets, despite their claims of turning over control of Berlin to East Germany, were still the controlling power in East Germany and East Berlin.

Although West Berliners were now denied the right to visit East Berlin, the crises soon abated. The flow of refugees was stopped and East Germany began a period of consolidation and economic growth. The West accepted the Berlin Wall as an alternative to bringing this international crisis to the brink of war.

—*José M. Sánchez, updated by Herbert Luft*

ADDITIONAL READING:

Attwood, William. *The Twilight Struggle.* New York: Harper & Row, 1987. This work provides anecdotal information on the Cold War.

Beschloss, Michael R. *The Crisis Years: Kennedy and Khrushchev, 1960-1963.* New York: HarperCollins, 1991. Details of the encounters between the American president and the Soviet leader.

Gelb, Norman. *The Berlin Wall.* London: Michael Joseph, 1986. The building of the Berlin Wall embedded in a discussion of the Cold War.

Rees, David. *The Age of Containment: The Cold War, 1945-1965.* New York: St. Martin's Press, 1967. An excellent older study that places the Berlin problem in the perspective of the Cold War.

Turner, Henry Ashby. *Two Germanies Since 1945.* New Haven, Conn.: Yale University Press, 1987. Compares the two German states since the end of World War II and discusses in detail the crises surrounding Berlin.

SEE ALSO: 1945, The Yalta Conference; 1945, The Potsdam Conference; 1948-1949, Berlin Airlift; 1949, North Atlantic Treaty; 1949, Creation of Two German Republics; 1955, Warsaw Pact Is Signed; 1989, The Berlin Wall Falls.

1961
ORGANIZATION FOR ECONOMIC COOPERATION AND DEVELOPMENT FORMS

The Organization for Economic Cooperation and Development forms to further trade and economic growth in all nations, rich and poor.

DATE: September 30, 1961

LOCALE: Paris, France

CATEGORIES: Economics; Government and politics; Organizations and institutions

KEY FIGURES:

George Catlett Marshall (1880-1959), U.S. secretary of state, 1947-1949, and founder of Marshall Plan for European recovery from World War II

Jean Monnet (1888-1979), father of concept of a United States of Europe

Robert Schuman (1886-1963), French founder of European Coal and Steel Community (ECSC)

SUMMARY OF EVENT. The beginnings of what was to become the OECD lie in the Organization for European Economic Cooperation (OEEC), established in 1948 to screen requests from European nations for Marshall Plan aid. The European Recovery Plan (ERP), more commonly known as the Marshall Plan, was a bill passed by the U.S. Congress in 1948 that authorized U.S. aid for the reconstruction of war-devastated Europe. Both Secretary of State George C. Marshall and Congress were mindful of the fact that the Cold War with the Soviet Union was intensifying, and that the Iron Curtain separating command and free economies was moving toward Western Europe. In 1948, Czechoslovakia's free government (a requester of Marshall Plan aid) was toppled in a communist takeover. Moreover, the city of Berlin in East Germany was sealed off by Soviet troops and was reliant on an airlift of Western food and supplies for survival. Even France seemed in danger of a communist takeover. Congress saw that only an economically resurgent and politically stable Europe could withstand communist expansionism.

In authorizing the massive aid program, however, Congress was careful to extract formal commitments from the sixteen recipient nations in the OEEC. The commitments were concentrated in four major areas, and the ramifications of those resolutions were later quite evident in the subsequent European Union. The sixteen beneficiary countries were obligated (by Congress) to increase the economic growth rate, implement the necessary policies for economic and political stability, expand international trade, and establish a greater degree of cooperation with other (European) beneficiaries.

The Marshall Plan proved a resounding success. In all, nearly $13 billion in American aid was parceled out among OEEC nations. Not coincidentally, most of the aid was spent on purchases of capital equipment and technology from the United States. By the mid-1950's, virtually all European economies were fully reconstructed and the political situation, vis-à-vis Russian expansionism in Europe, had stabilized somewhat.

By the late 1950's, the tasks of the OEEC had essentially been completed. The cooperative effort to rebuild in the aftermath of World War II was a success. Global economics, however, were changing. Currency convertibility and reduction of trade barriers fostered both growth and interdependencies between economies. The threat from the Soviet Union had taken on a new dimension—economic and technological competition with the West. In view of new challenges and economic alliances, the role and the continued existence of the OEEC were reconsidered. In a series of meetings commencing in 1959, Western leaders of the twenty OEEC member or associate member nations convened and reconvened to rethink and eventually transform the organization. In January of 1960, the Special Economic Committee formed of OEEC members and associates proposed that a group of four, "the Four Wise Men," be selected to conduct a formal study of the focus of a new, reconstituted Pan-Atlantic organization and the best means for attaining these aims. The goals of the this new "Atlantic Alliance" would be consistent with mutually held beliefs in enhanced economic growth rates for less developed nations and in expanding trade so that economic welfare is enhanced on a global level.

The report of the "Wise Men" was published on April 6, 1960. Entitled "A Remodelled Economic Organization," the report recommended a list of defined and redefined goals for the new organization, outlined its membership, proposed provisions for adding new mem-

bers, and suggested the selection of a new organizational name. The name selected was "Organization for Economic Cooperation and Development." It was proposed that the name OECD would suggest both the interdependence and need for cooperation among member nations and emphasize that enhanced global welfare was contingent, as well, on the growth of the least developed nations. A final recommendation involved the appointment of a preparatory committee, which would guide the institution through its transitional phase as well as detail the reconstitution of the OEEC as the OECD. The work of the preparatory committee was completed by November of 1960, and approved at a ministerial meeting in Paris on December 13, 1960. Despite this progress, spadework on the reorganization continued into 1961. By September 30, 1961, ratifications from seventeen of the twenty original member nations were received, enabling official acknowledgement of the new organization as the OECD.

The twenty charter members of the OECD included Austria, Belgium, Canada, Denmark, France, Germany, Greece, Iceland, Ireland, Italy, Luxembourg, the Netherlands, Norway, Portugal, Spain, Sweden, Switzerland, Turkey, the United Kingdom, and the United States. During the next fifteen years, Japan, Finland, Australia, and New Zealand were admitted to "the Rich Man's Club," as the OECD came to be known. In 1995, however, Mexico became the first less developed nation and Latin American country to join the OECD.

As itemized in its charter, the goals of the OECD were general and quite diverse in nature. The lack of a definite focus may have been intentional by the founders of the OECD. By its structure, the OECD spanned an ocean as well as a full spectrum of thought as to what its purpose should be. Some of its founders regarded cementing the North American-European alliance as paramount. Others regarded the founding of an economic union between Europe and America as most important. Another group focused on the economics of lower trade barriers and higher growth rates, while maintaining a nationalist, anti-union stance. The participating nations may have regarded a tightly specified agenda for action as a catalyst for conflicting legislative debates at the national level and chose instead to position the OECD as a forum where ideas might be aired, studies commissioned, and controversy minimized.

Nevertheless, consistent with the general intent to expand growth and development, a number of explicit goals were specified for the emergent OECD. The broad functions of the OECD were enumerated as economic policy coordination, aid to lesser developed nations, trade, and a microeconomic focus on technology, agriculture, and labor productivity within member nations. The coordination of economic policy is facilitated by OECD annual reviews of member-nation economic performance. The reviews are shared with OECD partners before being published. Coordination of economic policy between members is achieved through meetings of the Economic Policy Committee. Emphasis is placed on currency stability and balance of payment problems.

The OECD acts to further the welfare of developing economies through the activities of its Development Assistance Committee (DAC). Unlike the International Monetary Fund (IMF) or World Bank, DAC does not make loans or grants to less developed countries. Rather, DAC seeks to promote foreign aid by member nations and to measure and compare the effectiveness of aid programs among member nations. The OECD addresses the issue of trade and balance of payments difficulties through its trade committee, which acts to air issues raised by trade officials in member nations. Additionally, through its committees and member-nation studies, the OECD gathers, compares, and disseminates data regarding agricultural production, technological change, productivity, energy, and relative efficiencies in resource allocation.

The OECD evolved from OEEC in 1961 as a vehicle for furthering economic coordination among developed economies. Its role is vaguely defined by its charter. With the passage of time and growth in membership, the composition of the OECD increasingly resembles that of parallel institutions, such as the IMF, the European Union, and NATO. The unique functions it may have once performed are now also performed by the parallel institutions. The OECD's role in coordinating economic policies between members has been partially usurped by the IMF. Many of its country studies can be performed by private research firms.

Nevertheless, the OECD is more than another research firm. Much of its activity goes toward gathering data and making comparisons among nations which becomes input into national and supranational policy. The OECD's study of microeconomic issues such as wage, taxes, and social service reforms is thorough and much valued by end-users. The OECD involves national officials in its research, which allows for more thorough and comprehensive studies and makes the end product more valuable. Therefore, a strategy of pruning OECD activities in line with current informational needs is a superior argument to demanding its abolition.   *—John A. Sondey*

ADDITIONAL READING:

Bromberger, Merry, and Serge Bromberger. *Jean Monnet and the United States of Europe*. New York: Coward-McCann, 1969. Excellent account of Monnet's role in a United States of Europe.

Cerami, Charles A. *Alliance Born of Danger*. New York: Harcourt, Brace & World, 1963. Easy to read and informative detailing of the building and maintenance of the Atlantic Alliance.

The Organization for Economic Cooperation and Development. Paris: OECD Publications, 1963. An official delineation of the origin, organization, and functions of the OECD. Complete organizational appendix.

"Rich Man's Club." *Economist*, April 16, 1994, 17-18. Provides insight into whether expenditures on OECD bureaucracy can be justified by its product.

Wexler, Imanuel. *The Marshall Plan Revisited*. Westport, Conn.: Greenwood Press, 1983. A second look at the Marshall Plan and European recovery from the perspective of economic rather than political planning.

SEE ALSO: 1947, Marshall Plan Is Announced; 1949, North Atlantic Treaty; 1950-1963, Italy's Postwar Economic Boom; 1957, Common Market Is Formed; 1987, European Community Adopts the Single Europe Act; 1993, Maastricht Treaty Is Ratified.

1963-1970
SOVIET JEWS DEMAND CULTURAL AND RELIGIOUS RIGHTS

Soviet Jews demand cultural and religious rights, protesting the anti-Semitic policy of the Soviet Union in the wake of Israel's victory in the Six Day War.

DATE: 1963-1970

LOCALE: Soviet Union

CATEGORIES: Cultural and intellectual history; Government and politics; Religion

KEY FIGURES:

Leonid Ilich Brezhnev (1906-1982), general secretary of the Communist Party in the Soviet Union, 1964-1982

Nikita Sergeyevich Khrushchev (1894-1971), general secretary of the Communist Party in the Soviet Union, 1953-1964, who implemented moderate reforms and was responsible for "de-Stalinization"

Aleksei Nikolayevich Kosygin (1904-1980), premier of the Soviet Union under Brezhnev, 1964-1980

SUMMARY OF EVENT. The history of Soviet Jewry has been that of frustration, denial, bigotry, hostility, and fear. Regardless of the varied methodologies employed by the regime in the Soviet Union, official anti-Semitism was consistent in perpetrating acts of national, racial, and religious discrimination upon the Jews in the name of national unity. Operating under the guise of anti-Zionism, modern anti-Semitism, in its ramifications of cultural suppression, forced assimilation, and denial of equality with other Russian citizens, failed to achieve its goal of integrating Jews into socialist society. The new variety of anti-Semitism—forced assimilation—made of the Jews nonpersons. While Jews were systematically denied the means to exercise their rights as a separate nationality as guaranteed by the Soviet constitution, they were also denied the full privileges of Soviet citizenship.

Article 74 of the Criminal Code of the Russian Soviet Federated Socialist Republic (RSFSR) prohibited "any direct or indirect limitation of rights or the establishment of direct or indirect privileges" based on race or nationality. While classified as a separate nationality, they were denied the rights of one.

The Jews of the Soviet Union suffered from being categorized in two of the groups perceived by the Soviets as potentially inimical to national security—a religious and a racial minority. By clinging to religious customs and beliefs as well as ethnic customs, language and, in some instances, loyalty to a Zionist homeland, the Jews have been stigmatized by the government as collaborators with Western intellectuals and governments and as such have frequently been subjected to detention and internment and restrictions on freedom of movement.

Comprising a nationality, a majority of whose world membership resided outside the Soviet Union, the Jewish people thus represented an alien heritage and, as such, were subject to substantial suspicion. As part of the policy of forced assimilation, the Jews were not to be allowed to act in unison, to establish cultural, social, religious, or national groups. Contact with Israel or world Jewish organizations, with the culture, language, literature, or religion of the Jewish people of other nations was not permitted, as it would only encourage a greater reawakening of their Jewish identity.

The practice of the Jewish religion in the Soviet Union was forbidden. Hebrew, the language of Judaism and thus essential to participation in the religious services, was proscribed in the Soviet Union. Similarly, the authorities prohibited the publication of the Hebrew Bible.

The Israeli victory over Egypt, Syria, and Jordan in the 1967 Six Day War became the catalyst in the Jewish-Soviet conflict. What had before only been a whisper suddenly erupted in a shout as thousands of Soviet Jews awakened to a resurgence of pride in their unique culture and young homeland. As the fever of Zionism and the desire to emigrate to Israel grew, the Kremlin, fearing not only worldwide condemnation but also Soviet national minorities' clamor for independence, launched a severe propaganda campaign against "international Zionism" as an external threat against national security.

As the propaganda attacks on Jews increased, popular anti-Semitism in the Soviet Union also increased. The denial of rights to the Jews was a major cause of the Jewish desire to emigrate. Cultural, religious, and political suppression and inequality concerning the Soviet Jews led to a slowly mounting tide of Zionist activity by the oppressed as well as increased numbers of requests for exit visas for emigration to Israel. That emigration had become a problem for the Kremlin was evidenced by the aggressive press campaign perpetrated by Khrushchev's successor, Aleksei Kosygin. Departure for Israel was branded an unpatriotic act since loyalty to the native socialist fatherland took precedence over notions of a spiritual homeland.

Individual or group petitions were the first noticeable demonstrations of the consciousness among the Jews. The novelty of these petitions was not in the criticism of government policies of repression and harassment or in the pleas for exit visas to Israel, but in the willingness of the authors to defiantly sign names, addresses, ages, and places of employment. Alarming to the authorities was the volume of such documents as well as the background of the signers. Most were between twenty and forty years of age with a high educational level and employed in scientific and humanities areas—skills and fields important to the Soviet Union.

Finding negligible response from the government to individual or group petitions, the Jews inaugurated the program of "internationalization of protest" based on the premise that the Kremlin was sensitive to world opinion and pressure. In the period from February, 1968, to October, 1970, world leaders received more than 220 such appeals from Soviet Jews.

Adopting as their standard the Universal Declaration of Human Rights and the International Convention on the Elimination of Racial Discrimination rather than the Soviet constitution, the Jews thus appealed to the international conscience. The significance of their strategy lay in the fact that the Soviet Union had ratified the International Convention and had consistently complied with the Universal Declaration, both of which bound the cooperating powers to acknowledge that "everyone has the right to leave the country, including his own."

Aware of the approaching Twenty-fourth Party Congress and the vast number of foreign party delegates who would be in attendance, the Jews circulated a petition to all regions of the Soviet Union. The result was a total of more than four thousand signatures on a document addressed to the United Nations and all the major Western powers, complaining of imposed assimilation and the liquidation of the cultural and religious institutions of the

Jews. A "police-gendarme terror" attacked those who applied for exit visas. It concluded with a plea to the United Nations and the Western governments for intervention on the right of Jews to emigrate.

On the anniversary of the Universal Declaration of Human Rights, 123 Jews from Moscow and Minsk attached their names to a petition addressed to the secretary-general of the United Nations. The authors of the petition appealed to the United Nations to establish a commission to evaluate the Soviet violation of the Declaration.

The Soviet reply to this petition was delivered by the Russian representative to the United Nations. Referring to the petition as "a typical slanderous letter," he accused the Soviet Jews of bringing up an issue that "was concocted by the Zionists for anti-Soviet purposes."

The authority of the Kremlin was confronted as never before when 156 Jews from eight various cities throughout the country staged a combined sit-in and hunger strike in the Supreme Soviet reception room. This action was indicative of the degree of frustration, desperation, and boldness which had been engendered among the Jews in 1970. A document addressed to the Presidium seeking the release of those arrested in connection with a hijacking plot and requesting permission to emigrate to Israel was also presented to the Secretariat of the Supreme Soviet.

Thus, by 1970, it had become apparent that state-sponsored anti-Semitism or anti-Zionism, which had been intended to instill fear and submissiveness in the Soviet Jews, had backfired. A new national pride, a sense of personal dignity, and a hunger for contact with the new Jewish homeland manifested themselves in audacity as the oppressed openly protested against the government's anti-Semitism. As the Kremlin countered with increased ethnic and racial propaganda as well as further cultural and individual discrimination, it became futile to deny the existence of a degree of interdependence and interaction between Zionism and anti-Semitism. Decades of repression of Soviet Jews only led to an awakening of Zionist sentiments. It was not until the advent of *glasnost* and *perestroika* in the mid-1980's under Mikhail Gorbachev, however, that the Soviet government moved toward allowing unrestricted Jewish emigration and greater religious freedom within the Soviet Union.   *—LaRae Larkin*

ADDITIONAL READING:

Baradat, Leon P. *Soviet Political Society.* 2d ed. Englewood Cliffs, N.J.: Prentice-Hall, 1989. Covers a broad scope of Soviet political life, including religion and dissident movements.

Brumberg, Abraham, ed. *In Quest of Justice—Protest and Dissent in the Soviet Union Today.* New York: Praeger, 1970. A detailed analysis of dissent in the Soviet Union from the death of Stalin to the early Brezhnev years.

Cohen, Richard, ed. *Let My People Go!* New York: Popular Library, 1971. An extremely readable and emotional account of the efforts of Soviet Jews to emigrate.

Korey, William. *The Soviet Cage: Anti-Semitism in Russia.* New York: Viking Press, 1973. Describes the official policy of anti-Semitism in the Soviet Union, particularly during the regimes of Khrushchev and Brezhnev.

Reddaway, Peter, ed. *Uncensored Russia: Protest and Dissent in the Soviet Union.* New York: American Heritage Press, 1972. Uses case studies and trial documents in research on the dissent movement.

Rubenstein, Joshua. *Soviet Dissidents: Their Struggle for Human Rights.* 2d ed. Boston: Beacon Press, 1985. Focuses on events and personalities of the democratic movement in Moscow.

SEE ALSO: 1950, European Convention on Human Rights Is Signed; 1961, Amnesty International Is Founded; 1966-1991, Soviet Intellectuals Express Disagreement with Party Policy; 1972, Munich Olympic Massacre; 1975, Helsinki Agreement.

1963
LIMITED NUCLEAR TEST BAN TREATY IS SIGNED

The Limited Nuclear Test Ban Treaty is signed by the United States, Great Britain, and the Soviet Union as part of the first significant step toward controlling nuclear weapons.

DATE: August 5, 1963

LOCALE: Moscow, the Soviet Union

CATEGORIES: Diplomacy and international relations; Science and technology

KEY FIGURES:

Leonid Ilich Brezhnev (1906-1982), general secretary of the Communist Party of the Soviet Union, 1964-1982

Sir Alexander Frederick Douglas-Home (1903-1995), British foreign secretary, 1960-1963

Andrei Andreyevich Gromyko (1909-1989), Soviet foreign affairs minister, 1957-1985

John Fitzgerald Kennedy (1917-1963), thirty-fifth president of the United States, 1961-1963

Nikita Sergeyevich Khrushchev (1894-1971), first secretary of the Communist Party of the Soviet Union, 1953-1964, and premier of the Soviet Union, 1958-1964

Harold Macmillan (1894-1986), British prime minister, 1957-1963

Richard Milhous Nixon (1913-1994), thirty-seventh
   president of the United States, 1969-1974

Dean Rusk (1909-1994), U.S. secretary of state,
   1961-1969

SUMMARY OF EVENT. On August 5, 1963, the United
States, the Soviet Union, and Great Britain signed the
Treaty Banning Nuclear Weapons Tests in the Atmosphere, in Outer Space and Under Water. Following ratification by the parties the treaty entered into force on October 10, 1963. This treaty was the first significant arms
control agreement to be reached by the nuclear powers.

Underground nuclear tests were not covered by this
treaty because the three states could not agree on a method
of detection and verification of underground explosions.
The problem with underground explosions was that they
could not be distinguished from earthquakes without some
form of on-site inspection, and the United States and the
Soviet Union both occupied territories that were prone to
frequent earthquakes. This problem did not apply to explosions in the atmosphere, under water, or in outer space
which could be detected and identified by "national means
of detection" without the need for on-site inspection.

The limited test ban treaty was the culmination of years
of efforts to control nuclear weapons which began with
negotiations in the United Nations Atomic Energy Agency
to prohibit the production and use of atomic weapons.
That effort was abandoned in the late 1940's as negotiations broke down in complete deadlock. The United States
introduced a plan—the Baruch Plan, named after its draf-
ter—designed to bring under international control everything connected with the development of atomic energy.
An International Atomic Development Authority would
supervise the development of atomic energy to guarantee
that it be used for peaceful purposes only. The Soviet
Union proposed a prior commitment by the nuclear powers to destroy nuclear weapons before a system of control
was established. The issue of which was to come first,
disarmament or control, became an enduring point of
difference between Moscow and Washington.

Efforts to prohibit nuclear weapons were supplanted by
the more modest goal of banning the testing of nuclear
weapons. In November of 1952, the United States detonated it first hydrogen bomb, followed in August, 1953, by
a Soviet explosion of a hydrogen device. Throughout the
1950's both countries engaged in extensive nuclear weapons testing. These tests caused worldwide alarm because
of the fear of radioactive fallout and the prospects of ever
more powerful weapons being tested. An American ther-
monuclear test at Bikini Atoll in March of 1954 created a
worldwide reaction because of its size—fifteen mega-
tons—and the fact that radioactive fallout accidentally

contaminated the crew of a Japanese fishing vessel. Soviet
tests also produced fallout, inducing the United Nations
General Assembly to call for an end to nuclear testing.

During the eight years in which a ban on nuclear
weapons testing was on the agenda of East-West negotiations, a cardinal issue in dispute was whether on-site
inspections were necessary and, if so, how many would be
required to guarantee observance of a complete test ban.
The United States insisted upon on-site inspections while
the Soviet Union balked at the idea as unwarranted interference in its internal affairs. Unable to bridge their differences the two nuclear powers agreed to suspend testing
while they negotiated a solution. On November 3, 1958, a
voluntary moratorium on testing went into effect. It lasted
until September of 1961, when the Soviet Union violated
the moratorium with a fifty-eight-megaton atmospheric
test, the largest ever made. One factor in the decision of
Nikita Khrushchev to break the moratorium was the deto-
nation of an atomic bomb by France on February 13, 1960,
making France the world's fourth nuclear power. The
resumption of nuclear tests by both sides added to the
tension in their relations.

The adversarial relations between the United States
and the Soviet Union reached a peak with the Cuban
Missile Crisis in October, 1962. That confrontation
brought the two superpowers to the brink of nuclear war
and led to profound reassessment on both sides of their
relations and of the dangers of a nuclear holocaust. Following the resolution of the Cuban Missile Crisis, both
Kennedy and Khrushchev made a determined effort to
find some form of an accommodation on the nuclear issue.
In December of 1962, the Soviet leader offered a concession of two or three on-site inspections and the Americans
came down to seven. By the summer of 1963, both leaders
were prepared to halt nuclear testing again while a new
intensive effort was made to reach agreement. In July, an
American delegation led by Averell Harriman, a British
delegation led by Lord Hailsham, and a Soviet delegation
led by Andrei Gromyko met in Moscow to hammer out a
test ban treaty. Unable to resolve the inspection problem,
they agreed on a limited test ban treaty.

While the treaty permitted underground testing, it did
not permit an explosion which vented radioactive debris
outside the borders of the state conducting the test. The
treaty was of unlimited duration and open to accession by
all states. The vast majority of states in the world have
adhered to this treaty, including France and China, the
fourth and fifth nuclear powers, respectively.

The Limited Nuclear Test Ban Treaty ended the problem of contamination of the atmosphere, but it did not
satisfy the demands of those who wanted a complete test

ban in order to stop the proliferation of nuclear weapons or to slow down the development of new nuclear military technologies or to end completely the nuclear arms race. Efforts to eliminate all nuclear testing continued and achieved a partial success when President Richard Nixon and General-Secretary Leonid Brezhnev signed the Threshold Test Ban Treaty in Moscow on July 3, 1974. This treaty prohibited underground nuclear tests with a yield of more than 150 kilotons. The two test ban treaties were part of a diplomatic effort between the superpowers to improve their relationship. When the Cold War ended in 1990, the prospects improved greatly for a complete ban on nuclear weapons tests. In 1991, the superpowers signed the START I treaty, which brought the first reductions in strategic nuclear weapons, and, in 1993, the START II treaty committing the United States and Russia (the successor state to the Soviet Union) to even further reductions. In 1994, the United Nations General Assembly called for the adoption of a Comprehensive Nuclear Test Ban Treaty as a "priority" objective. That goal was assigned to the Conference on Disarmament, a thirty-eight-member body created by the United Nations. China and France continued their own underground nuclear tests through 1995, but with the completion of those tests both states joined Great Britain, the United States and Russia in a pledge to work for a Comprehensive Test Ban Treaty.

—*Joseph L. Nogee*

ADDITIONAL READING:

Blacker, Coit D., and Gloria Duffy, eds. *International Arms Control: Issues and Agreements.* Stanford, Calif.: Stanford University Press, 1984. This is a balanced analysis of arms control negotiations and includes the texts of the major arms control agreements.

Bundy, McGeorge. *Danger and Survival: Choices About the Bomb in the First Fifty Years.* New York: Random House, 1988. Bundy, who died in 1996, was both a scholar and policymaker. This a comprehensive and authoritative history which explains the many factors that determined American atomic energy policy.

Carnesale, Albert, and Richard N. Haass, eds. *Superpower Arms Control: Setting the Record Straight.* Cambridge, Mass.: Ballinger Publishing, 1987. These essays examine eight arms control agreements including the limited test ban treaty to test ten hypotheses regarding popular beliefs about arms control. They find that many popular conceptions about arms control are untrue.

Mandelbaum, Michael, ed. *The Other Side of the Table: The Soviet Approach to Arms Control.* New York: Council on Foreign Relations Press, 1990. Five authors examine the politics of Soviet policy on several different arms control issues including the nuclear test ban treaty, SALT I, and the intermediate-range nuclear forces agreement.

United States Arms Control and Disarmament Agency. *Arms Control and Disarmament Agreements: Texts and Histories of Negotiations.* Washington, D.C.: U.S. Government Printing Office, 1982. This government publication contains the complete texts of the nuclear test ban treaties and a brief history of the negotiations.

SEE ALSO: 1949, North Atlantic Treaty; 1955, Warsaw Pact Is Signed; 1957, Soviet Union Launches Sputnik; 1979, SALT II Is Signed; 1985, Sinking of the *Rainbow Warrior*; 1987, Intermediate-Range Nuclear Forces Treaty.

1963
GREEK AND TURKISH CYPRIOTS CLASH OVER POLITICAL RIGHTS

DATE: December 21, 1963
LOCALE: Cyprus
CATEGORIES: Government and politics; Race and ethnicity
KEY FIGURES:

George Grivas (1898-1974), Cypriot and an officer in the Greek army, leader of anti-British forces in Cyprus, rightist supporter of union of Cyprus with Greece

Fazil Kutchuk (born 1906), leader of Turkish Cypriots, first vice president of Cyprus, 1960-1973

Makarios III (Michael Mouskos; 1913-1977), archbishop of Cyprus and president of the Republic of Cyprus, 1960-1977

SUMMARY OF EVENT. Situated in the eastern Mediterranean, the island of Cyprus has had its fortunes tied to a larger power since ancient times. Greeks have inhabited Cyprus since the time of Homer and they gradually developed their own traditions. With the spread of Christianity, the Orthodox Church was established on the island. An autocephalos church, it retains the right to elect an archbishop as its own religious leader.

In 1571, the Ottoman Turks conquered Cyprus and Turkish immigrants from Anatolia began to settle there. Their communities were scattered among those of the Greeks but the two peoples remained apart socially. By the twentieth century, the Greeks made up 80 percent of the six hundred thousand inhabitants, while the Turks numbered less than 20 percent of the population.

The Ottoman sultan agreed in 1878 to allow British administration of the island, a mutually beneficial ar-

Despite years of talks between Greek and Turkish Cypriot leaders before and after Cyprus achieved independence in 1960, neither side was satisfied with the tenuous balance of power established under the country's constitution. (Archive Photos)

rangement. During World War I, when the Ottoman Empire fought on the side of Germany, Britain annexed Cyprus. Cyprus became a Crown Colony in 1925.

Relations between the two peoples began to change, however, when the Greek War of Independence (1821-1829) led to the establishment of a sovereign Greek state. Greek leaders took up the cause of fellow nationals still under what they considered foreign Ottoman rule. Their goal was the liberation of unredeemed lands and their union (*enosis*) with the Greek motherland.

By the late nineteenth century, under British administration, which allowed the two communities control of their respective educational institutions, nationalist ideology became pervasive among both Greek and Turkish Cypriots. The Cypriot Orthodox Church, with the archbishop as ethnarch, or national community leader, supported aspirations for *enosis* with Greece. The Turkish side adamantly opposed any action by the British that might bring them under Greek authority.

In 1931, agitation for *enosis* led to a serious incident in the capital of Cyprus, Nicosia. Greek Cypriots, unhappy

with British demands for more taxation, burned the Government House. Troops restored order, the leading agitators were exiled, the constitution was suspended, and Britain ruled by decree.

Political activity revived during World War II. A leftist trade union movement, the Reform Party of the Working People (AKEL), was formed to protest economic grievances and to speak for the Cypriots' national interests. Although interest in *enosis* abated during the war, it emerged at the end of World War II as Greek Cypriots expected to be rewarded with union with Greece for supporting the war effort. Greek Cypriot nationalists contested British plans for moderate political reforms, including a consultative assembly, and gained the upper hand over communist-led AKEL, which had called for self-government. Turkish Cypriots responded by seeking the sympathetic attention of Turkey.

In January of 1950, the Orthodox Church organized a plebiscite among Greek Cypriots regarding *enosis*. They voted overwhelmingly (96 percent) in favor. Michael Mouskos, who promoted the plebiscite, was elected archbishop of Cyprus as Makarios III later that year. As ethnarch, he was firmly committed to lead his people in their quest for *enosis*.

Politically astute, Makarios worked to consolidate the position of the *enosist* nationalists against AKEL, sought support from Greece, and looked to the United Nations to apply pressure on the British by involving other countries in determining the fate of Cyprus.

More forceful action was being planned by Colonel George Grivas, a Cypriot who had organized a rightist resistance organization in Greece during World War II. Grivas visited Cyprus in 1951 and met Makarios. While both believed in *enosis*, Makarios was reluctant to agree to large-scale and long-term guerrilla warfare that Grivas was planning against the British.

The struggle commenced in the spring of 1955. Grivas' group, the National Organization of Cypriot Fighters (EOKA) carried out attacks and distributed leaflets in Cyprus. Many in Cyprus were concerned over the consequences of a revolt. Harold Macmillan, British foreign secretary, convened a conference at which Greece and Turkey were represented but not Cypriots. The British offered only limited self-government, which was rejected by Greece and Turkey, and sent Field Marshall Sir John Harding as governor to restore order.

Talks between Harding and Makarios eventually broke down, and in March of 1956, the archbishop was exiled to the Seychelles. EOKA-initiated violence mounted against the British as well as Greek and Turkish Cypriots. Makarios was released the following spring but was not allowed to return to Cyprus. In November of 1957, Harding was replaced as governor by Sir Hugh Foot. He attempted more conciliatory policies and Britain tried to involve Greece and Turkey in a "partnership" to administer the island. Both states rejected the proposal and violence in Cyprus continued.

By the fall of 1958, all the interested parties recognized that a settlement through compromise was necessary. Archbishop Makarios was willing to put off *enosis* and accept independence. Greece was in political turmoil, unable to obtain a solution of the Cyprus problem through the United Nations, and fearful that Britain might sanction *taksim* or partition of the island. Prime Minister Konstantinos Karamanlis was, therefore, amenable to compromise. The Turkish Cypriots, who opposed rule by Greece and favored partition, found independence acceptable. Anxious about the situation in the Middle East, the United States encouraged talks.

Prime Minister Karamanlis and his Turkish counterpart, Adnan Menderes, met in Zurich in February, 1959. They worked out an agreement for an independent Cyprus. At a meeting in London later in the month, Britain, Greece, and Turkey presented the agreement to Archbishop Makarios, leader of the Greek Cypriots, and Dr. Fazil Kutchuk, representing the Turkish Cypriots. Britain promised independence in return for sovereign control of military bases on Cyprus. The island's independence was guaranteed by Britain, Greece, and Turkey, each having the right of unilateral intervention. The latter two states had the right to station a small contingent of troops on the island.

Cyprus became independent in August of 1960. Yet the constitutional arrangements were cumbersome and potentially troublesome. Power was shared between the executive, parliament, and the civil administration. Each ethnic community was represented in the civil service, though the Turks got disproportionately more positions than their number warranted. The president was to be a Greek and the vice president a Turk. Both had veto power in internal and foreign affairs. Accordingly, the archbishop was elected president, and Kutchuk, vice president. Grivas, a staunch *enosist*, was opposed to the agreements.

Constitutional order broke down as each community looked to its own interests. Ethnic separation developed in the large towns. Recognizing that the constitution needed changing, Archbishop Makarios submitted thirteen proposals to rectify the problems to Kutchuk. They included ending the veto power of the president and vice president, modifying the proportional representation of Greeks and Turks in public service to more closely reflect the actual population, and ending the requirement of separate majorities for enacting certain laws. Turkey and then Kutchuk rejected the proposals.

On December 21, 1963, an incident in Nicosia led to fighting between the two communities. The violence brought Turkey and Greece near to war and there were rumors of an impending invasion of Cyprus by Turkey. The United States and Britain were alarmed at the prospect of two NATO allies in conflict. A United Nations peacekeeping force was dispatched in March of 1964.

Tensions on the island remained high as members of the two communities separated into enclaves. Secretary of State Dean Acheson floated a plan in the summer of 1964 to unite Cyprus with Greece in return for establishing a large Turkish military base on the island to protect the Turkish community. Prime Minister George Papandreou of Greece rejected the plan, while Colonel Grivas returned to Cyprus to promote Greek national interests and serve as a counterbalance to the archbishop.

In the mid-1960's, the two communities strengthened their military forces and periodically a communal crisis broke out. Intercommunal talks began in 1968 between Glafkos Clerides, representing the Greek Cypriots, and Rauf Denktash, speaking for the Turkish Cypriots, in the wake of another crisis that ended with the departure of Grivas and a large Greek force from the island.

Greece was now under the control of a military regime. Tension between the military in Athens and Archbishop Makarios mounted as the junta secretly sent Grivas back to Cyprus to start up a new organization, EOKA-B. On July 15, 1974, the Cyprus National Guard, supported by Greek army forces on the island and approved by the Athens junta, launched a coup against Archbishop Makarios. The archbishop was able to escape. A few days later, Turkish forces invaded and occupied 40 percent of the island. Hostilities ended quickly, but Cyprus was divided by force into two ethnic communities.

—Gerasimos Augustinos

ADDITIONAL READING:

Crawshaw, Nancy. *The Cyprus Revolt*. London: Allen & Unwin, 1978. Account focusing on the struggles from the 1950's to independence.

Maynes, Stanley. *Makarios: A Biography*. New York: St. Martin's Press, 1981. Sympathetic account based on numerous interviews.

Panteli, Stavros. *A New History of Cyprus*. London: East-West Publications, 1984. Well-researched study with emphasis on the British era.

SEE ALSO: 1821-1827, Greeks Fight for Independence; 1967, Greek Coup Leads to a Military Dictatorship; 1981, Greek Socialists Win Parliamentary Majority.

1964

KHRUSHCHEV FALLS FROM POWER

Khrushchev falls from power, marking the first peaceful removal of a Soviet leader and establishing a new sense of normalcy in Soviet politics.

DATE: October 13-14, 1964
LOCALE: The Soviet Union
CATEGORY: Government and politics
KEY FIGURES:

Leonid Ilich Brezhnev (1906-1982), a member of the Politburo and, after the removal of Khrushchev, first secretary of the Communist Party of the Soviet Union, 1964-1982

Nikita Sergeyevich Khrushchev (1894-1971), first secretary of the Communist Party of the Soviet Union, 1953-1964, and premier of the Soviet Union, 1958-1964

Aleksei Nikolayevich Kosygin (1904-1980), a member of the Politburo and, after the removal of Khrushchev, the premier of the Soviet Union, 1964-1980

Nikolai Podgorny (1903-1983), a member of the Politburo and later its chairman, 1965-1977

Mikhail Andreyevich Suslov (1902-1982), a member of the Politburo and an opponent of Khrushchev's policies

Alexander Shelepin (born 1918), a trade union leader and a leader of the movement to remove Khrushchev

Vladimir Semichastny (born 1924), head of the KGB and a leader of the movement to remove Khrushchev

SUMMARY OF EVENT. On March 5, 1953, long-time Soviet leader Joseph Stalin died after an apparent cerebral hemorrhage. Stalin, who became general secretary of the Communist Party of the Soviet Union in 1922, had assumed power within the Politburo after V. I. Lenin died in 1924. A struggle for power continued in the 1920's and 1930's. In his drive to consolidate control, Stalin conducted extensive purges of the Communist Party and the citizenry in the 1930's. In 1941, he assumed the title of chairman of the Council of Ministers, or premier, becoming head of the government as well as the party. In his final years, although unchallenged as a leader, Stalin conducted several purges, ascertaining that potential successors would be subservient.

In the aftermath of Stalin's death, there was a power struggle among the members of the Politburo, or Presidium. The leadership was reluctant to allow one man to head the party and government as Stalin had done. Georgi Malenkov served as premier from 1953 to 1955, and Nikita Khrushchev served as first secretary of the Communist Party from 1953 to 1964. Although Malenkov was removed as premier in 1955, he remained a member of the Politburo. Nikolai Bulganin succeeded Malenkov as premier in 1955 and served until 1957, but the power struggle continued, as Malenkov and Vyacheslav M. Molotov, among others, opposed Khrushchev's policies and growing power. In June of 1957, the Politburo voted to remove Khrushchev, who appealed the vote to the Central Committee of the Communist Party and emerged victorious. His rivals were labeled the anti-Party group, dismissed from the party, and given other assignments or retired. In early 1958, Khrushchev was named premier of the Soviet government as well as head of the party. Nevertheless, the memory of Stalin's absolute dictatorship and ruthless methods was too vivid and too deep to allow Khrushchev to become more than "first among equals" within the Politburo, the highest decision-making body in the country.

Khrushchev faced opposition within the Soviet leadership elite in his remaining years in power. He initiated new policies, reorganized the party, and reshuffled the leadership but rarely without opposition. On the domestic front, Khrushchev reversed the Soviet Union's traditional economic priorities by spending more on consumer goods production and less on heavy industry and defense. Khrushchev initiated decentralization of governmental control over economic planning and decision making by creating 107 economic regions, each operated by a regional economic council supervised by the Communist Party. In 1962, the regional party organizations were subdivided into agricultural and industrial sectors, further decentralizing power.

Khrushchev launched the first of several campaigns for de-Stalinization in 1956, criticizing Stalin's crimes against the party, but not challenging Stalin's policies of economic development. He denounced terror but was not always consistent in exposing past evils. Khrushchev was instrumental in rehabilitating many of Stalin's victims, and in the publication of Alexander Solzhenitsyn's novella about the Stalinist prison camps, *One Day in the Life of Ivan Denisovich* (1962). In the early 1960's, Khrushchev conducted another de-Stalinization campaign, removing Stalin's name and statues from many streets, towns, and institutions. Stalingrad became Volgograd, and Stalin was removed from the mausoleum he shared with Lenin, the founder of the Soviet state.

A literary and intellectual "thaw" during the Khrushchev era relaxed somewhat the severe censorship of the Stalin era in literature and films. Although Khrushchev permitted publication of some books critical of the system, Boris Pasternak's internationally acclaimed novel *Doctor Zhivago* was not published in the Soviet Union.

Khrushchev's foreign policy was innovative yet inconsistent. His redefinition of the policy of "peaceful coexistence" involved better relations with the West and the Third World. He advocated a policy of rapprochement and reduced tension between communist and capitalist states, emphasizing peaceful economic competition instead of the confrontations of the Cold War. The emphasis on economic competition with the West reflected de-emphasis of the military competition and a reduction of defense spending in the Soviet Union. Improved Soviet relations with the Third World were seen as part of global competition with the West for the loyalty of neutral nations. Khrushchev liberalized Stalin's rigid policies toward Eastern Europe but also formed the Warsaw Pact to legitimize continuing Soviet military presence there. At the Twentieth Party Congress in 1956, Khrushchev declared that there were "many roads to socialism." Several states of Eastern Europe, foremost among them Hungary, tested the limits of Soviet intentions during the next few months. The Hungarian Revolution of October, 1956, challenged Soviet and Warsaw Pact influence and was forcefully suppressed.

Khrushchev's policies and reforms had the air of spontaneous improvisations. His policies were usually bold but not well organized—a series of ad hoc measures to rectify pressing problems rather than methodical, carefully articulated solutions. To most observers, it seemed Khrushchev was pursuing his goals by a series of zigzags, and critics complained that his goals were seldom achieved. Khrushchev's critics comprised a sizable segment of the Communist Party leadership, since his innovative policies had run roughshod over many vested interests. Military leaders and those involved in heavy industry looked askance at the greater emphasis on consumer goods; the central planners and ministries were dubious about the decentralization of economic policy making; the party leaders were disturbed about the reorganization of the party organs and frequent shuffling of positions. Some party leaders believed de-Stalinization had been too rapid and disruptive. Although Khrushchev and his colleagues distanced themselves from Stalin, those leaders, including Khrushchev, who emerged into prominence during the 1930's and 1940's, participated in the Stalinist era policies. Some also believed that de-Stalinization was at times used as a rationale for settling current political differences.

Khrushchev's years in power were characterized by numerous policy failures from the perspective of the other Soviet leaders. Liberalization in Eastern Europe resulted in the Hungarian Revolution, whose suppression was costly to the international prestige of the Soviet Union. The Sino-Soviet split began in the initial days of de-Stalinization and escalated throughout the Khrushchev

years. Khrushchev's failure to consult the Chinese about policy and ideological changes, the cutback of aid to China, the growing hostility between Khrushchev and Mao Zedong, and the public exchange of insults between the two communist parties were, rightly or wrongly, blamed on Khrushchev by his colleagues.

Khrushchev's policies toward the West were sometimes less than successful. The U-2 incident and subsequent collapse of the Paris Summit Conference in 1960, his failure to resolve the issue of a divided Berlin, and the placement of nuclear missiles in Cuba resulting in Khrushchev's seeming capitulation in the Cuban Missile Crisis led the Soviet leadership to question his policies toward the West.

Khrushchev's domestic policies fared little better. Some of his agricultural policies, including the Virgin Lands campaign, achieved mixed results. A poor harvest in 1963 led to grain purchases from the West in 1964, and some leaders attributed the crop failure to Khrushchev's interference and inconsistencies in agricultural policy. Although economic specialists were exploring systematic economic reform, policies associated with Khrushchev often emerged as public campaigns, rather than as full-

Nikita Khrushchev pursued innovative policies and reforms that upset many high-ranking Soviet officials, leading to his ouster in 1964. (AP/Wide World Photos)

fledged plans. A notable example was his 1964 campaign to improve production and use of synthetic materials, known as "Big Chemistry."

Criticism and opposition to Khrushchev within the Presidium mounted. Mikhail Suslov often disagreed with Khrushchev, especially with Khrushchev's program to build the "material-technical bases of communism" in twenty years, but apparently was not a key player in the plot to remove him. Insiders have suggested the key plotters included Leonid Brezhnev and Nikolai Podgorny from the Presidium; Alexander Shelepin, head of the trade unions and a Presidium member; and Vladimir Semichastny, head of the KGB. Brezhnev, a cautious man, was Khrushchev's chosen heir but wanted power sooner rather than later. Publicly Brezhnev praised Khrushchev but privately plotted against him. In the late summer of 1964, Khrushchev vacationed in the south and then went on his fall agricultural tour. Meanwhile in Moscow, a group of top leaders planned his removal. Deputy Premier Aleksei Kosygin and Party Secretary Suslov were probably informed of plans late in the process. Khrushchev was warned of the plot, but had difficulty believing it.

On October 12, 1964, the Presidium voted to remove Khrushchev. They summoned him to a meeting in Moscow on October 13 and informed him of their decision. The Central Committee was hastily convened on October 14 and officially dismissed Khrushchev as first secretary. Suslov led the discussions at these sessions. In the subsequent negotiations, Khrushchev agreed to resign from all positions and retire. Brezhnev became first secretary of the Communist Party and Kosygin chairman of the Council of Ministers.

In the aftermath of the announcement, Pravda, the party's official organ, on October 17, 1964, indicated that the leaders sought a return to collective leadership and an end to "harebrained scheming, immature conclusions and hasty decisions and actions divorced from reality." Khrushchev was the first Soviet political leader to be removed without violence and struggle, and therefore his passing from the political scene was remarkable. His successors Brezhnev and Kosygin initially worked well together, but their partnership later became strained. The economic reorganization of the Khrushchev era was reversed, and major economic reforms were introduced in 1965. On balance, the Soviet economy was no more successful under Kosygin's more measured approach to change than under Khrushchev. Soviet foreign policy was more smoothly executed under Kosygin and Brezhnev, but there were still inconsistencies. Although there was a partial retreat from de-Stalinization and the literary thaw, the Brezhnev era continued many of the Khrushchev initiatives.

In retirement, Khrushchev lived in the Moscow region, occasionally coming into the city. After his initial shock, Khrushchev worked on his memoirs and read extensively. He died in 1971, and was buried in Novodevichy Cemetery in Moscow.

—*Paul Ashin, updated by Norma Corigliano Noonan*

ADDITIONAL READING:

Conquest, Robert. *Power and Policy in the USSR: The Struggle for Stalin's Succession, 1945-1960*. New York: Harper & Row, 1967. An overview of the power maneuvers among the Soviet elite in the postwar era.

Khrushchev, Nikita. *Khrushchev Remembers*. 2 vols. Translated and edited by Strobe Talbott. Boston: Little, Brown, 1970-1974. Khrushchev's memoirs give his interpretation of his twelve-year rule.

Khrushchev, Sergei. *Khrushchev on Khrushchev: An Inside Account of the Man and His Era*. Boston: Little, Brown, 1990. An insider's view of the Soviet elite, Khrushchev's last year in power, and his political defeat.

Medvedev, Roy. *Khrushchev: A Biography*. Garden City, N.Y.: Anchor Books, 1984. A Soviet historian's view of Khrushchev from his early years, to his work in the Ukraine, to his years in power and afterward.

Richter, James G. *Khrushchev's Double Bind: International Pressures and Domestic Coalition Politics*. Baltimore: The Johns Hopkins University Press, 1994. An issue-oriented approach that examines both internal and international pressures faced by the Khrushchev administration.

Tatu, Michel. *Power in the Kremlin: From Khrushchev to Kosygin*. New York: Viking Press, 1969. An encyclopedic treatment of the period, 1960-1969, with a focus on the decline of Khrushchev.

SEE ALSO: 1953, Death of Stalin; 1955, Warsaw Pact Is Signed; 1956, Hungarian Revolution; 1957, Soviet Union Launches Sputnik; 1968-1989, Brezhnev Doctrine; 1974, Solzhenitsyn Is Expelled from the Soviet Union; 1985, Gorbachev Is Elected General Secretary of the Communist Party; 1991, Soviet Union Dissolves into Loosely Allied Republics.

1966-1991
SOVIET INTELLECTUALS EXPRESS DISAGREEMENT WITH PARTY POLICY

Soviet intellectuals express disagreement with party policy to achieve creative freedom, but they face powerful government pressures to make them conform to communist expectations.

DATE: 1966-1991

LOCALE: The Soviet Union

CATEGORIES: Cultural and intellectual history; Government and politics; Social reform

KEY FIGURES:

Leonid Ilich Brezhnev (1906-1982), general secretary of the Communist Party, 1964-1982

Mikhail Sergeyevich Gorbachev (born 1931), general secretary of the Communist Party, 1985-1991

Andrei D. Sakharov (1921-1989), scientist and human rights activist

Aleksandr Solzhenitsyn (born 1918), Russian novelist and human rights activist

Yevgeny Yevtushenko (born 1933), Russian poet

SUMMARY OF EVENT. Seven decades of communist rule in the Soviet Union between 1917 and 1991 attempted to modernize a traditional and largely illiterate society. The new government assigned specific tasks to each social class in the creation of a communist society. Intellectuals, especially writers, were expected to explain and promote the promised utopia. Yet the communist dictatorship imposed numerous controls and limitations on its population, and intellectuals suffered under Lenin, Stalin, and their successors.

The authorities developed the "Socialist Realism" theory in the 1930's to direct the intellectuals' creative efforts. Many Soviet writers worked within these limitations, including several (as Mikhail Sholokhov) who received international acclaim. Other intellectuals, however, chafed under the excessive ideological rigidity that interfered with their creative talents. An undercurrent of unrest and frustration existed among these individuals, bringing them periodically into confrontation with the authorities who responded with various measures to punish these "freethinkers."

A famous example of the regime's control over intellectuals can be seen in the Nikita Khrushchev period (1953-1964) when Boris Pasternak was selected to receive the Nobel Prize in Literature in 1958 for his novel *Doctor Zhivago* (1957). Widespread and scathing official criticism of his work caused Pasternak to renounce this internationally prestigious award. Such a practice of permitting only limited intellectual independence continued under Leonid Brezhnev, who succeeded Khrushchev in 1964 as Communist Party head.

The Brezhnev era quickly developed a reputation among intellectuals for toughness. Arrests of several writers by the mid-1960's, followed by public trials and lengthy sentences in forced labor camps, clearly revealed the new regime's determination to suppress intellectual independence that might stray too far from Socialist Real-

Boris Pasternak's refusal to accept the 1958 Nobel Prize in Literature to avoid further official criticism reflected the stifling atmosphere which Soviet intellectuals were forced to endure. (AP/Wide World Photos)

ism or other approved behavior. Another indication of placing intellectual life under state control was the appointment of a member of the party's powerful Politburo to be the nation's minister of culture.

The Union of Soviet Writers served as the primary official professional association that authors were expected both to join and follow its designated guidance. (Similar organizations monitored other cultural fields such as theater, film, media, and so forth.) As pressure and harassment of intellectuals grew by the mid-1960's, however, several brave individuals protested these destructive limitations on intellectual freedom.

Aleksandr Solzhenitsyn became the most famous example, as seen in his 1967 "manifesto" sent to the Union of Soviet Writers protesting its ideological criticism of his novels that could not be published in the Soviet Union. (Several, such as *Cancer Ward* and *First Circle*, were smuggled to the West and published there, which made Soviet authorities even more outraged at his independent behavior.) He was ousted from the writers' group in 1969 and prohibited from any further literary activity in the Soviet Union. Nevertheless, he was awarded the Nobel

Prize in Literature in 1970. After confiscating a manuscript copy of his exposé of communist dictatorship, later published in the West as *The Gulag Archipelago*, the government arrested Solzhenitsyn in 1974 and forcibly deported him from the country. His citizenship also was revoked.

Punishments of the sort meted out to Solzhenitsyn illustrate the various methods the government used against its opponents: lack of publication opportunities; withdrawal of subsidies or other government support; arrest and imprisonment; or deportation and loss of citizenship, to name a few. Nonetheless, all these techniques had the similar objective of controlling intellectuals who sought the right to freely develop their own work in such subjects as science and technology, politics and economics, philosophy and religion, ethnic issues, literature, and numerous other fields. Many noted figures, including the ballet dancer Mikhail Baryshnikov in 1974 and the poet Joseph Brodsky in 1972, abandoned the Soviet Union for the West in their search for a more hospitable artistic environment.

To surreptitiously circumvent official restrictions and harassment, many intellectuals utilized *samizdat* to share their views. They prepared "underground" manuscripts, usually in typed carbon copies, to be passed only between the most trustworthy. The state energetically opposed this illegal technique. Those preparing or even possessing *samizdat* materials, if caught, usually faced a minimum three-year prison term.

Others, like Solzhenitsyn, confronted the authorities directly by written and verbal criticisms. Andrei Sakharov, a noted physicist who began his human rights activity by the later 1960's, also became famous for this approach. He wrote a significant assessment of the Soviet Union, published in the West in 1968 under the title *Progress, Coexistence and Intellectual Freedom*. This important statement made him a prominent leader of the intellectual community. His dedicated public support for human-rights reform in his country drew world attention to the former physicist, now stripped of his numerous honors and former reputation.

Following Solzhenitsyn's deportation, and with the Nobel Peace Prize being conferred on Sakharov in 1975, the physicist's reputation grew. The authorities intensified efforts to stem Sakharov's controversial writing and speaking, and vilified him in the Soviet press and public opinion as a virtual traitor to his country. Finally, in early 1980, Soviet authorities banned Sakharov to internal exile in the city of Gorky. Located many miles east of Moscow, Gorky was a "closed city" forbidden to foreigners, and this substantially reduced his influence.

New leadership finally emerged in the Soviet Union in the mid-1980's, as Mikhail Gorbachev became the Communist Party head in 1985. His policies included limited changes in economic, political, social, and intellectual life. Identified by terms as *perestroika* (restructuring) and *glasnost* (openness), the Gorbachev period permitted more freedom of expression on diverse and controversial subjects. Especially noteworthy was Gorbachev's personal decision to permit Sakharov and his wife Elena Bonner to return to Moscow in December, 1986, to resume their human-rights efforts in the capital.

Additional examples illustrate the improved atmosphere for intellectuals by the later 1980's. The old shibboleths of communist ideology that determined the study and interpretation of history and politics gradually began to disappear. Writers and other cultural leaders took advantage of the relaxed environment. Anatoly Rybakov published *Children of the Arbat*, a Stalin-era novel written two decades earlier but never published. *Repentance*, a famous allegorical film of life under a dictatorship, finally was released in 1988 and shown to large audiences.

The celebration in 1988 of the millennial anniversary of Christianity in Russia provided opportunities for more active religious activity. The emergence of a reformed parliamentary system in 1989 permitted more public discussion of issues, and in early 1990 the parliamentary body eliminated the constitutional provision confirming the Communist Party as the sole political party in the Soviet Union. New political groups began to form, gradually evolving into actual parties. The press covered more topics, and journalists presented a variety of views in their stories.

Yet the efforts of a society moving hesitatingly toward reform had many unforeseen consequences. The reform movement lost an important voice when Sakharov died in late 1989, greatly mourned by many Russians. Expanded public discussion and spirited criticism, compounded by massive economic and ethnic problems in the various regions of the country, brought the country to domestic crisis by 1990. The Soviet Union as a nation finally disintegrated into fifteen separate states, breaking up by the end of 1991.

Yevgeny Yevtushenko, a leading poet of this era, described the potential dangers of change in a 1989 poem. Titled "Half Measures," he noted that moving halfway toward reform was not a satisfactory answer any more than trying to keep half of the old system. Gorbachev's reform commitment and achievements were partial and inconclusive, and they failed. Yevtushenko over many years has consistently called on his fellow citizens, both intellectuals and others, to work for the renewal of Russia, free of government oppression and also avoiding the historical tendency of the population to adopt a subordinate and passive position in the face of authority.

—*Taylor Stults*

ADDITIONAL READING:

Bonner, Elena. *Alone Together: My Years with Sakharov*. New York: Alfred A. Knopf, 1986. Memoirs of Sakharov's wife, a leading opponent of the communist regime and a human rights activist in her own right.

Cerf, Christopher, and Marina Albee, eds. *Small Fires: Letters from the Soviet People to Ogonyok Magazine, 1987-1990*. New York: Simon & Schuster, 1990. Selection of commentary and letters, including material by Andrei Sakharov, submitted to a reformist publication.

Sakharov, Andrei. *Memoirs*. New York: Alfred A. Knopf, 1990. Memoirs by the noted Russian human rights activist show the state's attempts to thwart his efforts.

_____. *Moscow and Beyond: 1986-1989*. New York: Alfred A. Knopf, 1991. Sequel to his memoirs, covering the period of liberalization during the Gorbachev era.

Scammel, Michael. *Solzhenitsyn: A Biography*. New York: W. W. Norton, 1984. Lengthy biography of the famous Russian author and dissident.

Tolkes, Rudolf L., ed. *Dissent in the USSR: Politics, Ideology and People*. Baltimore: The Johns Hopkins University Press, 1975. Essays describe the views, concerns, and problems of Soviet intellectuals.

Yevtushenko, Yevgeny. *Fatal Half Measures: The Culture of Democracy in the Soviet Union*. Boston: Little, Brown, 1991. Collected writings of a prominent poet who interpreted political and social issues facing his nation.

SEE ALSO: 1929, Trotsky Is Sent into Exile; 1934-1939, Stalin Begins the Purge Trials; 1953, Death of Stalin; 1963-1970, Soviet Jews Demand Cultural and Religious Rights; 1974, Solzhenitsyn Is Expelled from the Soviet Union; 1975, Helsinki Agreement; 1985, Gorbachev Is Elected General Secretary of the Communist Party.

1966-1995
FRANCE WITHDRAWS FROM NATO'S MILITARY STRUCTURE

France withdraws from NATO's military structure, initially leaving the Atlantic Alliance more vulnerable defensively, but eventually returns, under completely different circumstances, some three decades later.
DATE: February-March, 1966; December, 1995
LOCALE: Paris, France
CATEGORY: Diplomacy and international relations

KEY FIGURES:
Jacques René Chirac (born 1932), president of France beginning in 1995
Hervé Marie Joseph de Charette de la Contrie (born 1938), foreign minister of France under Chirac
General Charles-André-Marie-Joseph de Gaulle (1890-1970), head of the Free French Forces, 1940-1945; prime minister of France, 1958; and president of France, 1959-1969
Lyndon Baines Johnson (1908-1973), thirty-sixth president of the United States, 1963-1969
Maurice Couve de Murville (born 1907), foreign minister of France, 1958-1968, and later prime minister of France, 1968-1969
Georges Pompidou (1911-1974), prime minister of France, 1962-1968, and later president of France, 1969-1974
Dean Rusk (1909-1994), U.S. secretary of state, 1961-1969

SUMMARY OF EVENT. In a televised press conference on September 9, 1965, President Charles de Gaulle of France startled his Western allies with a threat to pull his country out of the North Atlantic Treaty Organization (NATO) (NATO) by 1969 at the latest, when its twenty-year term expired, because of his wish to "end the subordination which is described as integration." Suddenly, the essentially political and defensive Atlantic Alliance, which for a generation had stood as Western Europe's seemingly indispensable bulwark against possible Soviet aggression, was in jeopardy of collapsing from within. De Gaulle's pronouncement reflected his long-held fear that France was losing its independence in foreign policy by participating in NATO's combined military command dominated by the United States. In the weeks following this press conference, while campaigning for his reelection as president, de Gaulle raised a new and more concrete objection to NATO. Through the organization, he warned, France might be unwillingly drawn into the growing American involvement in Vietnam to which de Gaulle objected strenuously.

Since joining NATO, France had concluded its own Algerian War and had become a nuclear power with its own strike force. At the same time, the Soviet Union's status as a formidable nuclear power may have convinced France that the destructive consequences of a possible nuclear conflict would give the United States pause before coming to the assistance of its NATO allies.

Accordingly, de Gaulle resolved to leave NATO's integrated military structure forthwith. Within two months of his reelection in December of 1965, he made his decision public. At a further press conference on February 21, 1966, the French president reiterated his fear that the

Vietnam War might become a general conflagration in which Europe might become involved through NATO even when it did not wish to be. To avoid such a possibility, he would withdraw all French units from NATO command and allow no NATO forces in his country unless under direct French control. And indeed, on March 7, 1966, France formally notified the Atlantic Alliance of its decision, spelling out the details later that month. In a letter of March 9 to President Lyndon B. Johnson, de Gaulle explained: "France intends to restore within her territory the full exercise of her sovereignty—currently modified by the permanent presence of Allied military forces or by the use made of her air space—to end her participation in the integrated command and no longer to place her forces at the disposal of NATO."

By July 1, 1966, all French troops in Germany were to be removed from NATO command. By July 23, all French officers would be withdrawn from the NATO War College. Finally, by April 1, 1967, all foreign bases and troops (twenty-six thousand Americans and Canadians) were to leave French soil. NATO headquarters, known as Supreme Headquarters Allied Powers Europe (SHAPE), were also to be moved from Paris by then. For all that, France would remain a member of the Atlantic Alliance.

De Gaulle's unilateral action and short notice for withdrawal in 1966—the major agenda topic at the Atlantic Council's ministerial meeting on June 7 and 8—shocked and angered France's NATO allies. Yet his decision to abandon the organization's military structure had been clearly foreshadowed. France and its allies had clashed on various issues since the signing of the North Atlantic Treaty on April 4, 1949. In the early 1950's, the French had opposed the addition of German forces to NATO and a plan to combine all Western European forces in a single organization, the European Defense Community (EDC).

France never really challenged the fundamental purpose and structure of NATO, however, until Charles de Gaulle returned to power in 1958. By that time, the introduction of intercontinental ballistic missiles (ICBMs) was putting into question Western Europe's role as America's first line of defense against the Soviet Union and thus raising doubts about Washington's determination to stand by Europe in a crisis.

These doubts were exploited by General de Gaulle in his efforts to undercut American dominance in NATO military planning. In September of 1958, while he was still France's prime minister, de Gaulle called for a three-power directorate consisting of France, Great Britain, and the United States to formulate NATO military strategy, including nuclear strategy. Yet the United States refused to share authority over its atomic arsenal. This refusal must

have catalyzed the French leader's idea to build his independent nuclear capability and correspondingly to withdraw from NATO's nuclear umbrella.

Thus, in 1962, President de Gaulle withdrew the French Mediterranean fleet from NATO command. In 1963, France removed its Atlantic fleet from NATO command. In September of 1964, French units did not participate in NATO's naval maneuvers and in May, 1965, France boycotted NATO land maneuvers as well. Thus, over a period of years, de Gaulle had set the stage for France's complete military withdrawal from NATO.

In addition to his grievance against American dominance in the multilateral organization, de Gaulle also read the political evolution as justifying his move. Following the Soviet setback in the Cuban Missile Crisis of October, 1962, he believed that the Communist bloc posed a lesser potential threat to Western Europe. De Gaulle began to envision an independent Europe, led by France, playing an important role in world affairs similar to that of the United States and the Soviet Union. Feeling blunted by Washington in his wish to establish parity with the United States in NATO, de Gaulle abandoned his efforts to expand French influence there and engaged in reducing its participation in the organization and in pursuing a new foreign policy.

France's allies protested the lack of consultation and the apparent violation of the North Atlantic Treaty requiring two years' notice before the withdrawal of a member's forces. Yet the West Germans were the first to accept France's new position. Facing the imminent withdrawal of French forces from Germany, which would have left a strategic gap in its defenses, the government in Bonn agreed to have French troops remain in West Germany outside the NATO framework. In France itself, domestic opposition to the withdrawal was overcome in April, 1966, when Prime Minister Georges Pompidou and Foreign Minister Maurice Couve de Murville successfully defended the decision before the National Assembly, where the motion to censure the government failed by a large margin. For good or ill, the earlier united Western military front had unraveled.

Many years later, on December 5, 1995, climaxing France's increasing involvement with NATO in connection with the latter's peacekeeping efforts in Bosnia, the new French foreign minister, Hervé de Charette, announced his country's reintegration into NATO's Military Committee, War College, and other defense bodies. De Charette characterized the French decision as reflecting its willingness to join the "new," not the "old," NATO to "participate actively in the renewal of the alliance."

—Michael S. Smith, updated by Peter B. Heller

ADDITIONAL READING:

Flynn, Gregory. *French NATO Policy: The Next Five Years*. Santa Monica, Calif.: Rand Corporation, 1990. An update of an earlier study by Carl H. Amme, Jr., on the impact of the French withdrawal from NATO's military structure. Flynn's five-year projection about France's continued nonreintegration into the organization has turned out to be incorrect.

Harrison, Michael M. *The Reluctant Ally: France and Atlantic Security*. Baltimore: The Johns Hopkins University Press, 1981. A scholarly but readable work, based heavily on French sources with an authoritative bibliography. Harrison analyzes the effects of France's moves on NATO and its defense strategy.

Kelleher, Catherine M. *The Future of European Security: An Interim Assessment*. Washington, D.C.: The Brookings Institution, 1995. This work traces the increasing involvement of France in the former Yugoslavia through NATO's Military Committee, heralding its formal reintegration into NATO's military structure.

Millon, Charles. "France and the Renewal of the Atlantic Alliance." *NATO Review* 44 (May, 1996): 13-16. Considers the implications of France's decision of December 5, 1995, to resume its earlier military participation in NATO.

Rose, François de. *European Security and France*. Translated by Richard Nice. Urbana: University of Illinois Press, 1984. Written from the French perspective, this work cogently explains de Gaulle's decision to withdraw from NATO's integrated military structure in 1966.

Sherwood, Elizabeth D. *Allies in Crisis: Meeting Global Challenges to Western Security*. New Haven, Conn.: Yale University Press, 1990. Sherwood discusses the context in which France's withdrawal from NATO's integrated military structure occurred. The endnotes to the chapters contain excellent bibliographic references.

SEE ALSO: 1947, Marshall Plan Is Announced; 1949, North Atlantic Treaty; 1969, De Gaulle Steps Down; 1991, Coalition Defeats Iraq in Gulf War; 1991-1992, Civil War Rages in Yugoslavia.

1967

GREEK COUP LEADS TO A MILITARY DICTATORSHIP

A Greek coup leads to a military dictatorship when a group of right-wing military officers take over the government and inaugurate seven years of military control of the country.

DATE: April 21, 1967
LOCALE: Athens, Greece
CATEGORIES: Government and politics; Wars, uprisings, and civil unrest
KEY FIGURES:

Constantine II (born 1940), king of Greece, crowned in 1964, left Greece 1967, deposed in 1973

Konstantinos Karamanlis (born 1907), prime minister of Greece, 1955-1963 and 1974-1980

George Papandreou (1888-1968), prime minister of Greece, 1944 and 1963-1965

Andreas Papandreou (1919-1996), member of Greek parliament, 1964-1968 and 1974-1981, later prime minister, 1981-1989 and 1993-1996

George Papadopoulos (born 1919), army colonel on staff of Greek intelligence agency who later led a coup and served as prime minister, 1967-1973, regent, 1972-1973, and president of the Greek republic, 1973, before being imprisoned for life

Stylianos Pattakos (born 1912), army brigadier who served as Greek minister of interior, 1967-1973, and deputy prime minister, 1971-1973, before being imprisoned for life

SUMMARY OF EVENT. After World War II, Greece suffered a traumatic civil war between a leftist, communist-led movement and anti-communist government forces that ended with the defeat of the former in the fall of 1949. Elections held in 1952 led to a parliamentary majority for the rightists. In 1955, Konstantinos Karamanlis became their leader. He formed the National Radical Union (ERE) Party and remained in power until 1963.

Although the Communist Party was declared illegal, the Left was represented in parliament through the United Democratic Left (EDA). It gained support as resentment mounted in the country over British control of Cyprus, with its majority Greek population, and as demands for *enosis*, or union of the island with Greece, increased. A number of small parties made up the political center and center-left, particularly the Liberals led by George Papandreou. Their inability to unite allowed Karamanlis and ERE to remain in control of the government.

In the fall of 1961, concerned in part over mounting opposition to the storing of nuclear weapons on American bases in Greece, Karamanlis called for an early election. Papandreou had now formed the Centre Union Party and in alliance with another centrist party came in second in the election. Although Karamanlis and the ERE won, there were complaints of election fraud by the opposition culminating in Papandreou's demand for new elections.

In May of 1963, Gregory Lambrakis, a leftist parliamentary deputy, was assassinated. After an investigation, accusations flew that extremist right-wing elements were responsible. Karamanlis resigned the next month in a dispute with the monarchy over its close ties to the military and overt involvement in political affairs. Elections held in November gave Papandreou a small victory. Refusing to form a coalition government, he sought new elections, which were held in February, 1964. The Centre Union gained an absolute majority in the popular vote and in parliament. Karamanlis left the country for self-imposed exile in Paris.

Papandreou's victory at the polls seemed propitious for stable political development. Yet events soon proved otherwise. In foreign affairs, there was concern with Cyprus because of deteriorating relations between the Greek and Turkish ethnic communities and the increasingly independent political line that Archbishop Makarios, the country's president, was taking. Domestically, the Right was apprehensive at Papandreou's efforts to improve relations with the communist countries, his release of individuals imprisoned for acts committed during the civil war, and the more liberal economic and social policies of his son, Andreas, who was in the government. In the military, a leftist conspiratorial group was uncovered and Andreas linked to it by his enemies, while on the Right, ultranationalists, such as Colonel George Papadopoulos, were also active.

As prime minister, Papandreou sought greater supervision over the military and KYP, the Greek intelligence agency. Yet he clashed with the young king, Constantine II, who had come to the throne in 1964 determined to maintain his prerogatives. In July of 1965, Papandreou resigned and a political crisis ensued. Papandreou demanded new elections, which were to be held in May, 1967.

On the morning of April 21, 1967, citizens in the capital, Athens, awoke to the sound of tanks rumbling through the streets and the proclamation of martial law. A conspiratorial group led by Colonel Papadopoulos seized control in an almost bloodless *coup d'état*. The leaders of the junta abolished the political parties, suspended civil rights guaranteed in the constitution, and arrested people they considered leftist sympathizers, exiling them to detention camps. They claimed to have saved the country from a communist-inspired conspiracy, which was patently untrue.

A civilian government was quickly formed, but real power was in the hands of the junta, which consisted of a triumvirate that included Papadopoulos, Colonel Nicholas Makarezos, and Brigadier Stylianos Pattakos. Although the pretext for the coup was a purported communist threat, the colonels were really motivated by the fear that Papandreou would win the election and then proceed to purge the military of extremist right-wing officers such as themselves. Moreover, there was disaffection among the conspirators at what they perceived as their poor status in the military. Many of them were from the lower middle class and they resented those above them in social status and military rank.

In December, 1967, the king attempted a countercoup. Hoping to rally civilians and the military loyal to him, Constantine called for support, but most people did not even hear his appeal. Unwilling to countenance the use of force, the king instead left the country.

The junta reacted by doing away with the civilian government. A general was named regent and Papadopoulos became the prime minister. He subsequently took on other ministries such as defense and foreign affairs. A number of officers were retired and many in the civil service and education were terminated. To minimize any opposition, the junta used the security and military police to full effect. Reports of torture circulated in the country adding to the intimidation.

The military regime settled in and tried to boost its legitimacy. In September, 1968, it organized a referendum for a new constitution which heightened the military's role as guarantor of the country's integrity. The junta attempted to associate itself with the nation's past by concocting the slogan a "Greece of Helleno-Christians" and plastered the countryside with simplistic posters proclaiming a "revolution of the 21st of April."

There was a populist tone and a cathartic vein in the regime's rhetoric. The junta attacked moral decadence (miniskirts and long hair associated with Western influences) among the youth and promised to do away with parties and politics as they had existed in the past. Although Europe and the United States might be experiencing great political and social ferment, the colonels touted their country as a haven of stability and calm.

The junta also promoted economic development, which they hoped would satisfy consumer demand and gain public support for the regime. It supported public works projects that benefited small contractors, extended favorable terms for investment in tourism, especially hotels, and offered tax breaks to shipowners if they based their businesses in Greece. The regime counted on remittances from Greeks working abroad and in the merchant marine, and the growing tourist industry, while borrowing to meet fiscal needs. Although they claimed to be aiding the masses, the junta's unevenly targeted economic policies, combined with continued intervention in the labor and agricultural sectors, produced both inequitable and gradually diminishing economic results.

An attempted mutiny within the navy in May, 1973,

prompted Papadopoulos to declare that the king was behind it and to depose him in June. He then proclaimed a republic and held a referendum in July, 1973, with himself as the only candidate for president, promising elections for parliament the following year. He won more than 75 percent of the vote, though many voted no.

University students challenged the junta's facade of legitimacy in November, 1973, when they occupied buildings at the Polytechnic University in Athens. On November 17, Papadopoulos used the army's tanks to brutally repress the students at the Polytechnic. Although he restored order, he was himself overthrown about a week later and replaced as president by a senior military officer. Power, however, was in the hands of the man behind the scene, Brigadier Dimitrios Ioannidis, commander of the military police. He, along with some others, felt that Papadopoulos had deviated from the regime's goals.

Although more authoritarian and ruthless than Papadopoulos, Ioannidis was inept and ineffectual in handling the country's affairs. Relations with Turkey worsened in the spring of 1974 when the two countries confronted each other over territorial rights in the Aegean. Matters were no better between the junta and Archbishop Makarios. Ioannidis disliked the archbishop's independent ways, and the military in Athens surreptitiously supported anti-Makarios terrorist activities on Cyprus in the name of *enosis*. On July 15, 1974, opponents of the archbishop attempted a coup and were joined by Greek army forces stationed on Cyprus. Turkey then unilaterally intervened and occupied much of the island. The military regime attempted to mobilize the armed forces, but senior officers refused to retaliate against Turkey. The commander of army forces in northern Greece demanded a return to civilian government and the junta dissolved. Karamanlis returned to lead Greece on July 24, 1974. Elections for a new government were held, civilian supporters of the junta were ousted from their posts, and the leaders of the military regime were tried in the courts.

—*Gerasimos Augustinos*

ADDITIONAL READING:

Clogg, Richard, and George Yannopoulos, eds. *Greece Under Military Rule*. New York: Basic Books, 1972. Essays covering various aspects of affairs in Greece written during the junta period.

Woodhouse, C. M. *The Rise and Fall of the Greek Colonels*. New York: Franklin Watts, 1985. A detailed political account of the junta years.

SEE ALSO: 1963, Greek and Turkish Cypriots Clash over Political Rights; 1981, Greek Socialists Win Parliamentary Majority.

1967
UNITED NATIONS ISSUES A DECLARATION ON EQUALITY FOR WOMEN

The United Nations issues a declaration on equality for women, bringing to fruition earlier United Nations efforts to promote the equality of men and women and providing the basis for numerous subsequent actions to achieve this end.

DATE: November 7, 1967
LOCALE: New York, New York
CATEGORIES: Laws, acts, and legal history; Women's issues
KEY FIGURES:
Margaret K. Bruce, chief of the U.N. Section on the Status of Women, which had primary responsibility for implementing programs to advance women's rights
Annie R. Jiagge, chair of the Commission on the Status of Women
Helvi Sipila (born 1915), chair of the Committee on the Status of Women (1967) and secretary-general of the International Women's Year Conference held in Mexico City

SUMMARY OF EVENT. Adopted unanimously by the U.N. General Assembly on November 7, 1967, the Declaration on Elimination of Discrimination against Women sought to eliminate the extensive worldwide exploitation of women. From its inception in 1945, the United Nations had worked to raise the status of women. Its charter emphasized the "equal rights of men and women." Recognizing that member nations had not granted women the same political rights as men and that women faced many other limitations and liabilities, the United Nations in 1946 established the Commission on the Status of Women as a part of its Economic and Social Council. Its mandate was to recommend to the council ways to promote "women's rights in the political, economic, civil, social and educational fields" and to implement equal rights for men and women. The United Nations adopted a Universal Declaration of Human Rights in 1948 to further explain the civil, economic, social, and cultural rights to which individuals of both sexes are entitled.

Between 1951 and 1962, six conventions meeting under the auspices of the United Nations passed recommendations pertaining to the rights of women. In 1951, an International Labor Organization (ILO) convention urged countries to pay men and women equal wages for doing work of equal value. The next year, the U.N. Convention on the Political Rights of Women declared that women

In the wake of its 1967 Declaration on Elimination of Discrimination against Women, the United Nations adopted a proposal at the 1975 Mexico City conference to establish the U.N. Decade for Women. (Archive Photos)

should have the same rights as men to vote, hold public office, and participate in all civil activities. The Convention on the Nationality of Married Women, meeting in 1957, declared that the nationality of women should not be affected by their marriage to or divorce from aliens. Nations that signed the ILO Discrimination (Employment and Occupation) Convention of 1958 pledged to allow women full access to vocational training and to all occupations and not to discriminate against them in the terms and conditions of their employment. The declaration of a 1960 UNESCO convention on discrimination in education bound ratifying nations to provide women with the same opportunities as men to attend schools and universities and to study whatever subjects they chose. Recommendations adopted by United Nations conventions in 1962 and 1965 stipulated that only those marriages that involved the full and free consent of both parties were legally binding,

that minimum ages be established for marriage, that nations create uniform standards for marriages, and that men and women have equal access to divorce.

Because women continued to be discriminated against in a variety of ways, the U.N. General Assembly on December 5, 1963, asked the Commission on the Status of Women to prepare a declaration delineating the rights of women and suggesting ways to end this exploitation. First meeting in 1965, commission members argued that this declaration was needed to promote the principles ratified in previous conventions, encourage more nations to ratify these statements, and help educate women about the rights they already had. They proposed to devise a document that recognized the different, but equally important, and complementary roles men and women played in society. The commission aimed to proclaim the aspirations of women throughout the world, enunciate principles that would be

valid for future generations, and provide a solid foundation for programs designed to eradicate deeply rooted
local and national attitudes and customs thwarting the
advancement of women.

The commission created a committee of delegates representing different countries and cultures to draft the declaration. After lengthy discussion, including critical analysis of proposals submitted by member nations, United
Nations specialized agencies, and key nongovernmental
organizations, the commission presented a proposed declaration to the General Assembly in 1966. The Assembly
then asked the commission to revise this draft to take into
account further recommendations made by various member states. The commission ratified a revised text in
March, 1967, which was approved by the General Assembly's Third (Social, Humanitarian and Cultural) Committee in October and then unanimously adopted by the Assembly itself on November 7, 1967.

The resulting declaration asserts that all discrimination
against women is "fundamentally unjust" and "an offence
against human dignity." Despite the commitment to "fundamental human rights" expressed in the U.N. Charter and
the Universal Declaration of Human Rights and the substantial progress women had made, the declaration argued, they continued to be the victims of "considerable
discrimination." Because this situation was "incompatible
with human dignity," undermined the welfare of the family and society, prevented the equal participation of
women with men in political, social, economic, and cultural life, and thwarted their personal development as well
as the advancement of their countries, the world, and the
cause of peace, it must be changed. The declaration called
for the elimination of "all existing laws, customs, regulations and practices" that discriminated against women.
Reaffirming earlier declarations, it pledged to ensure
women the right to vote in all elections and public refer-
enda, hold all public offices, and exercise all civic functions. It also argued that women should have the same
rights as men to "acquire, change or retain their nationality," to "acquire, administer, enjoy, dispose of and inherit
property," and to choose a spouse. The declaration insisted
further that women had a right to "enter into marriage only
with their free and full consent" and had equal rights with
men pertaining to marriage and parenting. It bound all
signers to ensure that all girls and women have the same
opportunities as men to study at "educational institutions
of all types," take the same curricula and the same examinations, receive scholarships, and participate in continuing education programs. The declaration asserted that
women should enjoy equal rights with men to work,
choose vocations, and receive remuneration and work-
related benefits. Moreover, nations adopting the declaration agreed to take measures to "prevent their dismissal in
the event of marriage or maternity and to provide paid
maternity leave, with the guarantee of returning to former
employment." Its final article exhorted governments, nongovernmental organizations, and individuals to do everything they could to implement the declaration's principles.

After its adoption, the Declaration on Elimination of
Discrimination against Women became an impetus for
action to improve the status of women. Insisting that the
document would be a "mere piece of paper" unless it was
"known, understood and discussed in cities, towns and
villages all over the world," its authors strove to use both
written and audio-visual means to reach audiences everywhere. The United Nations issued pamphlets containing
the text of the declaration, background material, and commentary. The Commission on the Status of Women urged
member governments to revise their laws to accord
women all the rights specified in the declaration and to
furnish information describing how they were doing so.

Several subsequent actions built upon the foundation
laid by the declaration. During the International Women's
Year (1975) the United Nations redoubled its efforts to
promote sexual equality, expand the opportunities of
women to contribute to national and international development, and ensure that women realized all the rights
specified in the 1967 declaration. A declaration adopted at
the World Conference held in Mexico City in July, 1975,
explained why additional measures were needed to further
women's rights and linked their advancement with economic and political objectives. The next year the Commission on the Status of Women adopted a Programme for the
United Nations Decade for Women: Equality, Development and Peace (1976-1985). Its principal goals were to
formulate and implement national and international standards for ending discrimination against women and to
increase their participation in politics, economic development, and peacekeeping efforts. An important aspect of
the United Nations Decade for Women was the adoption
in 1979 of the Convention on the Elimination of All Forms
of Discrimination against Women. Nations signing this
convention (which numbered 130 by 1993) pledged to
implement the principles delineated in the 1967 declaration and take all necessary steps to end all forms and
manifestations of discrimination against women. Another
statement inspired in part by the 1967 declaration was the
Declaration on the Elimination of Violence against
Women. Adopted by the Commission on the Status of
Women in 1993, it defined violence against women as
including all physical, sexual, and psychological abuse as
well as sexual harassment and intimidation. The 1967

declaration also helped inspire studies of the status of women in many individual nations and the publication of numerous books on women's rights. —*Gary Scott Smith*

ADDITIONAL READING:

Bruce, Margaret K. "An Account of United Nations Action to Advance the Status of Women." *The Annals of the American Academy of Political and Social Science* 375 (January, 1967): 163-174. An analysis of the work of the Commission on the Status of Women and UNESCO to further women's rights.

"The Expanding Social Agenda." In *Yearbook of the United Nations—Special Edition: U.N. Fiftieth Anniversary, 1945-1995*. The Hague: Martinus Nijhoff Publishers, 1995. A discussion of the impact of the declaration on subsequent U.N. conventions and actions.

Jiagge, Annie R. "An Introduction to the Declaration on Elimination of Discrimination Against Women." *United Nations Monthly Chronicle* 5 (March, 1968): 55-61. A concise summary of the events leading of the adoption of the declaration by a leading participant.

SEE ALSO: 1882, First Birth Control Clinic Is Established in Amsterdam; 1915, International Congress of Women; 1918, British Women Gain the Vote; 1950, European Convention on Human Rights Is Signed; 1970, Parliament Passes the Equal Pay Act of 1970.

1968-1989
BREZHNEV DOCTRINE

The Brezhnev Doctrine justifies military intervention to keep Soviet satellites in line and maintains centralized control over the Soviet empire.

DATE: 1968-1989
LOCALE: The Soviet Union and Eastern Europe
CATEGORY: Diplomacy and international relations
KEY FIGURES:

Leonid Ilich Brezhnev (1906-1982), secretary general of the Communist Party of the Soviet Union, 1964-1982, and creator of the Brezhnev Doctrine

Alexander Dubček (1921-1992), first secretary of the Czechoslovakian Communist Party, January, 1968-April, 1969

Mikhail Sergeyevich Gorbachev (born 1931), Soviet leader, 1985-1991, who was responsible for the collapse of the Brezhnev Doctrine

Aleksei Nikolayevich Kosygin (1904-1980), Russian premier, 1964-1980

Ivan G. Paulovsky, general-commander of the Warsaw Pact units that invaded Czechoslovakia in 1968

Mikhail Andreyevich Suslov (1902-1982), Russian politician and senior member of the Politburo, 1952-1982, who was responsible for helping to formulate the Brezhnev Doctrine

Ludvik Svoboda (1895-1979), Communist hard-liner and president of Czechoslovakia, 1968-1975

SUMMARY OF EVENT. The Brezhnev Doctrine was a Soviet foreign policy directed toward keeping the East European satellite countries in line. It was used to justify Soviet military intervention to restore Soviet Communist authority over the satellites and to strengthen the Soviet's grip over them. The Brezhnev Doctrine was also used as the ideological basis of Soviet empire.

The origins of the Brezhnev Doctrine were articulated by Vladimir Lenin and Joseph Stalin in the 1920's. This included the principle of a strong, centralized authority to direct policies and a firm, conscientious discipline in creating a socialist society. Although Lenin and Stalin applied these principles domestically to the republics that made up the Union of Soviet Socialist Republics (USSR), Leonid Brezhnev used these same principles in his foreign policy toward the Eastern European countries that looked to the Soviet Union for guidance. These countries were known as the Eastern bloc, or the Soviet satellites, or the Warsaw Pact and consisted at various times of Yugoslavia, Poland, Czechoslovakia, East Germany, Romania, Bulgaria, and Hungary.

With the overthrow of Nikita Khrushchev in 1964, the Soviet Communist Party began a return to the hard-line orthodox policies of Lenin and Stalin. These policies affected all aspects of life for the Soviet Union as well as its satellites. Any deviation from these policies was considered tantamount to treason and brought swift action on the part of the Soviet Union.

In the mid-1960's, Alexander Dubček and a party of liberals began to gain power in Czechoslovakia. Dubček became the first secretary of the Czechoslovak Communist Party in 1968. As leader, he immediately began to radically modify several aspects of communism in Czechoslovakia, enacting a domestic policy of reform and liberalization, to create, in his words, "Communism with a human face."

The Soviet Union would not countenance any other or new models of Soviet socialism other than its own. The fear and concern was that the entire Communist bloc may have followed, especially in the Soviet Union itself, and would have broken the monopoly of power upon which the leadership depended. The Soviet leadership of that time, consisting of Aleksei Kosygin as the Soviet premier and Leonid Brezhnev as secretary general, would not tolerate any domestic political policies among its allies that were more liberal than those practiced in the Soviet

Union. This perceived threat to the power structure of the Soviet Union had to be eradicated. Control must be maintained by the Soviet Union at all costs. This return to the orthodox Stalinist principle of control from a single center was difficult for Dubček to accept.

Dubček's refusal to change his policies led to an invasion of Czechoslovakia by Warsaw Pact units, mainly Soviet, in the spring of 1968. After capitulation, Dubček was allowed to retain his position in the Communist Party as a figurehead until 1969, when he was stripped of his powers. Dubček was replaced by a Communist hard-liner, Ludvik Svoboda.

The invasion, which ended the period known as "The Prague Spring," was the first instance of the use of Soviet military intervention to keep satellite countries in line. To justify Soviet military intervention in Czechoslovakia, Brezhnev formulated the theory of "qualified sovereignty of socialist countries" and the obligation of the Soviet Union to intervene where "socialism is imperiled." Any deviation from the Soviet path meant that Communism was imperiled. It established the principle of Soviet hegemony over the East European empire, creating its own sphere of totalitarian influence. This theory became known as the Brezhnev Doctrine and was practiced by the Soviet Union until 1989.

In reality, the Brezhnev Doctrine was a combination of theories melded into an ideological basis for the Soviet imperial system. The doctrine acknowledged that socialist countries and their Communist Parties have the freedom to determine the means of advancement for their respective countries. This qualified sovereignty is severely limited by the second aspect of the Brezhnev Doctrine. This aspect stated that decisions should not harm socialism in the Soviet Union or any other socialist country. Each Communist Party is responsible not only to its own people, but also to all the socialist countries in the entire communist movement. If this was true, then any deviation from the Soviet Union's policies would be a betrayal of socialism. This policy allowed the Soviet Union to dominate the republics and dictate policy.

The Brezhnev Doctrine was not a comprehensive foreign policy, but an attempt to form a single anti-imperialist front and to dictate the return of the Communist Party to an orthodox foreign policy line. Control from the center, meaning Moscow, was emphasized. The Brezhnev Doctrine, however, needed to be rationalized and legitimized in order to be used again.

The Brezhnev Doctrine was formalized in the constitution of 1977. Foreign policy issues were a distinct and notable addition to the constitution. This completed the continuity of Brezhnev's policies in 1968, by linking for-eign policy with military preparedness, and establishing the right of military intervention as reasonable and legal. Relations with other socialist countries should be based on "socialist internationalism" and "comradely mutual aid." These same ideological premises were used to justify Soviet intervention into Czechoslovakia in 1968.

The Brezhnev Doctrine was enforced diligently until 1980. With a new perspective toward conciliation with the West, and the dying off of the old order that had served under Stalin, the Eastern European bloc countries began to slowly develop individually. With a new generation in the power structure, new forms of public debate opened and a general loosening up of restrictions occurred. The first signs of collapse of the Brezhnev Doctrine occurred in Poland in 1980 with the growth of the Solidarity movement and the collapse of Communist Party control. With mob activity, national strikes, and the disintegration of authority, the leadership in Poland was in a precarious position. Deviation from Soviet policies was rampant in Poland. Yet the Soviet Union made no move to intervene in Poland.

As the 1980's continued, each of the Soviet satellite

Leonid Brezhnev justified Soviet military intervention in Czechoslovakia by claiming that the Soviet Union had an obligation to intervene where socialism was imperiled. (AP/Wide World Photos)

countries experienced political turmoil. With the death of three Russian leaders in the space of twenty-eight months, the Soviet Union was in disarray. The Soviet Union had difficulty in containing domestic situations, much less foreign entanglements. Mikhail Gorbachev, the Soviet leader, believed in allowing each communist country to find its own path and a policy of public examination of all acts of the Soviet government, past and present. Fittingly, the most significant surrender of the Brezhnev Doctrine occurred in Czechoslovakia. Gorbachev announced to the ideologist of the Czechoslovak Party, Jon Fojtik, in November, 1989, that the Soviet Union was about to repudiate the 1968 invasion of Czechoslovakia. Simultaneously, Soviet military officers hinted to their Czechoslovakian counterparts that they might block any attempt from Czechoslovakian hard-liner Miloś Jakeś to suppress dissent. Under pressure from national strikes, and without support of the Soviet Union, Czechoslovakian Communists released their monopoly on power in December, 1989. This surrender of power became known as the Velvet Revolution and was seen as a symbol of a successful political change.

In 1990, the Warsaw Pact, with Gorbachev as its leader, formally announced to the world that the 1968 invasion of Czechoslovakia had been an illegal error. This announcement was the official termination of the Brezhnev Doctrine and the abandonment of the Soviet quest for empire. —*Elizabeth L. Scully*

ADDITIONAL READING:

Chafetz, Glenn R. *Gorbachev, Reform and the Brezhnev Doctrine: Soviet Policy Toward Eastern Europe, 1985-1990.* Westport, Conn.: Praeger, 1993. Excellent study of all aspects of the collapse of the Brezhnev Doctrine from the Soviet perspective.

Dornberg, John. *Brezhnev: The Masks of Power.* New York: Basic Books, 1974. Biography of Leonid Brezhnev, explaining his philosophical and political development.

Jones, Robert A. *The Soviet Concept of "Limited Sovereignty" from Lenin to Gorbachev: The Brezhnev Doctrine.* Basingstoke, England: Macmillan, 1990. Examines the philosophical origins of the Brezhnev Doctrine, actual implementation, and the eventual dissolution.

Kanet, Roger E., ed. *Soviet Foreign Policy in the 1980's.* New York: Praeger, 1982. Good introduction to several aspects of Soviet foreign policy with two sections related to the Brezhnev Doctrine.

Moore, John Norton. *International Law and the Brezhnev Doctrine.* London: University Press of America, 1987. Explores the ramifications of the Brezhnev Doctrine in the arena of international law.

Murphy, Paul J. *Brezhnev: Soviet Politician.* Jefferson, N.C.: McFarland, 1981. Informative look at the rise of power of Leonid Brezhnev and vivid political struggle of Soviet politics.

SEE ALSO: 1955, Warsaw Pact Is Signed; 1956, Hungarian Revolution; 1964, Khrushchev Falls from Power; 1968, Soviet Union Invades Czechoslovakia; 1980, Solidarity Is Founded in Poland; 1989, Hungary Adopts a Multiparty System; 1989, The Berlin Wall Falls; 1989, Velvet Revolution in Czechoslovakia.

1968
FRENCH WORKERS ENGAGE IN A NATIONAL STRIKE

French workers engage in a national strike, paralyzing much of the country's economy but eventually resulting in substantial wage and benefit gains.

DATE: May-June, 1968

LOCALE: France

CATEGORIES: Business and labor; Government and politics; Social reform

KEY FIGURES:

Daniel Cohn-Bendit (born 1945), radical student leader

Charles-André-Marie-Joseph de Gaulle (1890-1970), president of France, 1958-1969

Georges Pompidou (1911-1974), prime minister of France, 1962-1968

Georges Séguy (born 1927), general-secretary of the Confédération Générale du Travail, 1967-1982

SUMMARY OF EVENT. During the months of May and June, 1968, France experienced a social upheaval so profound that it almost toppled the regime of president Charles de Gaulle. What became known as "the May Revolt" began with serious student disturbances at the University of Paris. France's university student population had exploded from 170,000 to more than 500,000 in the preceding decade, but government funding and physical expansion failed to keep pace. Students had legitimate grievances concerning overcrowded classes, poor facilities, too few professors, arrogant academic bureaucrats, outdated curriculums, and questionable job prospects. By May 3, student unrest at the bleak suburban Nanterre campus spilled over into the Sorbonne, the symbolic center of the huge University of Paris, located in the Latin Quarter on the Left Bank of the city. The university rector called in police to expel the demonstrators, and soon the entire Latin Quarter was in an uproar.

On May 6, there were pitched battles on the streets between students and the much hated riot police, the CRS.

The final toll was some six hundred injured, more than four hundred arrested, and perhaps two hundred vehicles destroyed. Even worse was the "Night of the Barricades" on May 10-11, which resulted in more than fifteen hundred injured, almost five hundred arrests, and substantial property damage. Initially, the students had wanted reform of the university system, but their demands quickly escalated to the point of calling for a revolution to topple the Gaullist regime and create a utopian society. Student leaders, such as Daniel Cohn-Bendit, denounced both capitalism and communism for embracing a hierarchical society, characterized by mindless consumerism, rampant materialism, and an obsessive quest for economic growth and technological efficiency regardless of what it did to the human spirit. Yet these radicals, an uneasy coalition of Maoists, Trotskyites, anarchists, and nihilists, had considerably more difficulty agreeing on the precise nature of their new society.

After the events of May 10-11, this potentially revolutionary situation entered a new and dangerous phase. Previously, students had dominated the action, but now the working classes entered the fray. Industrial workers believed they had not shared in the very prosperity they had helped to create, while middle-class professionals resented the hierarchical structure of the workplace and the failure to see their worth properly compensated. The major trade unions called for a general strike on May 13, which resulted in a massive demonstration of almost one million marchers.

Then a tidal wave of strikes engulfed France. On May 14, workers at Sud-Aviation in the city of Nantes engaged in a sit-down strike. Over the next week, some thirty-five thousand workers struck at the huge Renault auto factory in Billancourt, near Paris, and soon Peugeot and Citroen workers followed suit. Miners went out on strike, as did huge numbers of railway workers. Shipyards were shut down, vital ports were closed, and public service employees in gas, electricity, and the post office ceased working or occupied their premises. In Marseilles, France's second largest city, some two hundred thousand were on strike. White collar workers and middle-class professionals showed equal militancy, the most serious a strike at ORTF, the state-owned radio and television corporation. Even famous film directors and professional soccer players joined. High school teachers emulated university professors in striking. By May 22, it was estimated that perhaps nine million workers were on strike.

In most cases, these strikes started spontaneously on the local level and frequently caught the national union leadership off guard. For the most part workers were concerned about local economic issues, not national po-

The French trade union strikes of 1968 were initially sparked by student protests that broke out at the Sorbonne in Paris. (Archive Photos)

litical ones, such as overthrowing governments. In addition to wages and benefits, employees expressed concern over such qualitative issues as hierarchy, regimentation, and dehumanization in the workplace. France had three major national trade union organizations, but the largest by far was the Communist-dominated Confédération Générale du Travail (CGT), having two million members and led by Georges Séguy.

From the beginning, the French Communist Party had castigated the student revolutionaries as adventurers and spoiled children of the petite-bourgeoisie. Party ideology dictated that authentic revolutions could only be led by the working classes, not students, and that the vanguard of the working classes, the Communist Party, alone could determine whether a genuine revolutionary situation existed. Therefore, the party tried to prevent fraternization between workers and students, fearing the latter might infect the former with utopian schemes and revolutionary fervor, reducing Communist control over unionists and perhaps leading the working classes to a slaughter. Only one major trade union, the Force Ouvrière, closely allied with democratic socialists and possessing a membership of six hundred thousand, showed pronounced sympathy for the student cause.

Georges Séguy and the CGT, however, did wish to use this crisis to extract economic concessions for the striking workers. From May 25 to May 27, the CGT participated in the "Grenelle talks," a joint meeting of representatives from the government, employer groups, and the major trade unions, designed to hammer out an agreement to end the strikes. Prime Minister Georges Pompidou, who hoped to avoid any dramatic confrontation with either the students or the strikers, played a conciliatory role. The final settlement included increasing the minimum wage by a third, a 10 percent raise in regular wages, larger family allowances, a reduction of the work week, and partial payment for wages lost during the strike. When this attractive package was presented to local unions, however, it was decisively rejected as insufficient. At this stage, it seemed the Gaullist government was in deadly peril. Students controlled the streets of Paris, militant unions had paralyzed the French economy, and the government appeared weak, indecisive, almost pathetically resigned to events. At a huge rally held at Charlety stadium in Paris, radical speakers called for replacing the Gaullist regime with a government representing the forces of the Left.

It was at this juncture that President de Gaulle recovered the initiative. After receiving assurances that he could count on the loyalty of the French army in a crisis, he dissolved the National Assembly on May 30 and called for new parliamentary elections in late June, warning the public that France faced a terrible danger from totalitarian communism. That same day, there was a massive rally of more than five hundred thousand Gaullist supporters on the Champs-Élysées. In the following days, the strikes came to an end, partly because many workers were rather pleased by the Grenelle accord, and partly because the government cleverly negotiated further wage and benefit packages with any remaining disaffected workers. Students continued to demonstrate and riot, but Parisians were beginning to resent the constant turmoil and senseless destruction associated with student unrest. The Communist Party, anxious to do well in the elections, tried to appear as a party of law and order dedicated to the parliamentary system, and therefore discouraged any illegal activity in their own ranks as well as in the CGT.

The Gaullists won the June parliamentary elections decisively, dramatically increasing their representation in the National Assembly to 296 deputies, and with their political allies, the Independent Republicans, actually controlled 360 seats out of a total of 485. Left-wing parties suffered heavy losses, including the Communist Party, which elected only thirty-four deputies compared to seventy-three in the previous election.

The results of the May Revolt were mixed. French industrial workers secured substantial economic benefits, especially those allied with powerful trade unions, but the professional managerial classes fared less well.

Students did see some modest reform of the university system, although not nearly as much as hoped. The Gaullist regime emerged triumphant, and Georges Pompidou's conciliatory stance during the crisis helped play a role in his being elected president of France the following year. The Communists suffered a temporary electoral setback, but regained most of the lost ground in the 1973 parliamentary elections. More serious for the party was that idealistic and radical youth blamed the Communists for having betrayed the cause of revolution by its alleged conservative and cowardly stance. Finally, the events of May solidified the reputation of France in general and Paris in particular as places where the revolutionary tradition was as strong as ever.   —*David C. Lukowitz*

ADDITIONAL READING:

Brown, Bernard. *Protest in Paris: Anatomy of a Revolt.* Morristown, N.J.: General Learning Press, 1974. Arguably the most lucid, thoughtful, and impartial analysis of the meaning of the May Revolt.

Caute, David. *The Year of the Barricades: A Journey Through 1968.* New York: Harper & Row, 1988. Entertaining and lively, this book places the May Revolt in an international context. See chapters 11 and 12 for events in France.

Johnson, Richard. *The French Communist Party Versus the Students: Revolutionary Politics in May-June, 1968.* New Haven, Conn.: Yale University Press, 1972. Analyzes the reasons behind the French Communist Party's antipathy toward radical left-wing students.

Ross, George. *Workers and Communists in France.* Berkeley: University of California Press, 1982. Chapter 7 contains a scholarly account of the CGT's role in the great strike of 1968. For the advanced student.

Touraine, Alain. *The May Movement: Revolt and Reform, May, 1968.* Translated by Leonard Mayhew. New York: Random House, 1971. A French sociologist, Touraine argues that students and workers were questioning the modern world dominated by scientific elites, mindless consumerism, and dehumanizing assembly lines.

SEE ALSO: 1966-1995, France Withdraws from NATO's Military Structure; 1969, De Gaulle Steps Down; 1981, Mitterrand Is Elected to the French Presidency; 1995, Chirac Takes Office as President of France.

1968
SOVIET UNION INVADES CZECHOSLOVAKIA

The Soviet Union invades Czechoslovakia, using Warsaw Pact forces to demonstrate its belief that any liberalization of the Communist dictatorships in Eastern Europe threatens Soviet interests.

DATE: August 20-21, 1968

LOCALE: Czechoslovakia

CATEGORIES: Government and politics; Wars, uprisings, and civil unrest

KEY FIGURES:

Leonid Ilich Brezhnev (1906-1982), general secretary of the Soviet Communist Party, 1964-1982

Oldrich Černik, chairman of the Council of Ministers (premier) of Czechoslovakia

Alexander Dubček (1921-1992), first secretary of the Czechoslovak Communist Party, January, 1968-April, 1969

Gustav Husák, deputy premier of Czechoslovakia, and first secretary of the Czechoslovak Communist Party

Aleksei Kosygin (1904-1980), prime minister of the Soviet Union

Antonín Novotný (1904-1975), president of Czechoslovakia, 1957-1968, and first secretary of the Czechoslovak Communist Party, 1953-1968

Ludvík Svoboda (1895-1979), president of Czechoslovakia

Walter Ulbricht (1893-1973), chairman of the state council of the German Democratic Republic, 1960-1973

SUMMARY OF EVENT. The Soviet-led invasion of Czechoslovakia in August, 1968, was the third major disaster to befall that hapless country within a generation. Thirty years earlier, in 1938, Nazi Germany began the piecemeal annexation of the Czechoslovak Republic. Restored to independence after World War II, Czechoslovakia fell victim to a communist coup in 1948, which transformed the country into a full-fledged satellite of the Soviet Union. For the next twenty years, the Czechoslovak Communist Party exercised, with the blessing of Moscow, a dictatorial authority characterized by terror, purges, and the repression of basic liberties. A leading figure in this brutal regime was Antonín Novotný, first secretary of the Czechoslovak Communist Party and president of the Republic. Particularly hostile to the Novotný regime were Czech writers and intellectuals. In late June, 1967, the writers, on the occasion of their fourth congress, unleashed a vigorous attack upon the repressive policies of the regime. This event marked the first step toward the liberalization of Czech life and government that flowered during 1968. Novotný's position steadily deteriorated. Unrest spread rapidly among students. On October 31, 1967, a serious clash took place in Prague between police and students who were critical of the regime. Moderate Communists, meanwhile, had begun to blame Novotný for the bad state of the Czech economy. By the end of the year, the ranks of the Czech Communist Party were seriously split between the old-guard Novotný faction and the moderates who sought to introduce political as well as economic reforms. Finally, on January 5, 1968, the moderates succeeded in ousting Novotný from his position as first secretary. He was succeeded by a Slovak Communist, Alexander Dubček. The "Prague Spring" had begun.

Dubček and his supporters soon inaugurated a series of sweeping reforms designed to liberalize Czech life and politics. Almost immediately, the government released the press, radio, and television from twenty years of rigorous censorship. Groups and organizations such as the Sokol and Boy Scouts, which had been suppressed following the communist coup in 1948, now reemerged. Within a few months, the new regime had bloodlessly purged itself of Communist hardliners, including Novotný, who was forced to resign from the presidency in March. Elected as new president was the highly respected Ludvík Svoboda. Shortly thereafter, Oldrich Černik, another liberal, became chairman of the Council of Ministers and organized a government of moderates. Early in April, the Central Committee of the Czechoslovak Communist Party adopted the so-called Action Program, which established the guidelines for the "New Model of Socialist Democracy." This program guaranteed the basic freedoms of speech, press, assembly, organization, and religious worship while assuring all people the free choice of work, fair trial, personal property rights, and the right of free movement inside and outside the country. In addition, the New Model called for the creation of an independent judiciary and promised to "give reality to the constitutional status of the National Assembly as the highest organ of state power." The Council of Ministers was to assume its rightful place as the highest executive organ of the state rather than leave major decisions to the Communist Party apparatus. These innovations were eventually to be incorporated into a new constitution.

Despite Dubček's frequent pronouncements that these reforms would neither compromise the continuation of Communist one-party rule nor Czechoslovakia's participation in the Warsaw Pact, criticism of his policies began to mount in various capitals of the Soviet bloc. As early as May 9, Soviet troop movements were reported near Czechoslovakia's frontiers. Later in the month, Aleksei

Residents of Prague kept a wary eye on the Soviet troops who invaded Czechoslovakia to bring an end to the Prague Spring of 1968. (Archive Photos)

Kosygin, the Soviet prime minister, abruptly terminated a surprise visit to Prague, having failed in his efforts to check the tide of Czech liberalism. The Czechs, undaunted by these developments, continued their program of reform, despite the press campaign launched against them in Russia, Poland, East Germany, Hungary, and Bulgaria. Exasperated at the attitude of the Czechs, the leaders of these countries met in Warsaw on May 15, where they drafted a virtual ultimatum to the Dubček government, demanding that it put an end to the liberalization program. The Czechs responded to this demand by meeting in early August, first with the Soviet leaders in private talks, and subsequently with these same leaders and their allies in a larger session to arrange what appeared to be a tentative compromise. An uneasy calm was momentarily restored in the Soviet bloc.

On August 10, however, the reformers issued a draft of proposed new party statutes which would be debated at a special Congress of the Czechoslovak Communist Party in September, 1968. The proposed statutes went far beyond the Action Program. The reformers now were proposing

fundamental changes which they believed would ensure that the party would not be able to violate the civil liberties promised in the Action Program. The proposed new statutes called for all party elections to be conducted by secret ballot, for the separation of party and state offices, for term limits on the holding of any party or state office, and for the transfer of decisions on the disciplining of party members from the central party organs to the local organizations. Even though the proposed statutes did not call for an end to one-party rule by the Czechoslovak Communist Party, they would have greatly weakened the power of the central organs and have made party officers responsible to the rank-and-file members for their policies and conduct.

The publication of the proposed party statutes undid the tentative compromise which had been reached a few days before. On August 12, Dubček held an important meeting in Karlsbad, Czechoslovakia, with Walter Ulbricht, chairman of the East German Democratic Republic, who without success demanded an end to the reforms. A frustrated Ulbricht now strongly urged Soviet leaders openly to intervene in Czech affairs. This appeal seems to have been a key element in the Kremlin's decision to invade Czechoslovakia on August 20-21.

There were several reasons why the Soviet Union decided to use military force against Czechoslovakia. Most Communist leaders feared that unless the Czech liberalization program was immediately and ruthlessly quashed, it might encourage moderates elsewhere in the Soviet bloc to attempt similar experiments, thus threatening the stability of several autocratic communist regimes. The Soviet leadership felt that a liberal Czechoslovakia would not only be a danger ideologically but also militarily.

Czechoslovakia, strategically located in the geographic heart of the Soviet bloc, shared common frontiers with West Germany and the four communist states of East Germany, Poland, Hungary, and the Soviet Union. The Russians feared that Czechoslovakia might one day provide the North Atlantic Treaty Organization alliance with a corridor leading directly to the Soviet frontier, a corridor that would separate East Germany and Poland from the other Warsaw Pact states to the south. Economically, Moscow believed that a free Czechoslovakia would in time establish closer trade relations with the West to the detriment of those with the Soviet Union. Not all Russian leaders, Kosygin among them, agreed that the use of armed force was the best or most prudent way discipline the Czechs. The militants, however, led by Leonid Brezhnev, general secretary of the Soviet Communist Party, prevailed.

On August 20-21, some two hundred thousand troops of the Soviet Union, East Germany, Poland, Bulgaria, and Hungary invaded Czechoslovakia from all directions. Romania refused to participate. Before he was arrested on August 21 and taken to Moscow under armed guard, Dubček ordered the Czech army and people not to resist. There were, however, numerous sporadic clashes between Czech citizens and Russian troops, especially in Prague. Brezhnev justified the invasion by stating that the interests of international socialism took precedence over the rights of state sovereignty. The "Brezhnev Doctrine" represented Soviet Communism at its ideological best and Russian nationalism at its traditional worst.

The invasion of Czechoslovakia had significant repercussions both in that country and throughout the world. On August 26, Dubček, Svoboda, and Černik were obliged to sign the Moscow Agreement under which they promised to curtail liberalization, allow Soviet forces to remain in Czechoslovakia, and to reestablish the leading position of the Communist Party in the state. In the year that followed, the Czech government, under constant pressure from Moscow, steadily retreated from the Dubček program. Dubček himself stepped down as first secretary

of the Communist Party in April, 1969, his place being taken by Gustav Husák, a Slovak Communist usually styled as a "realist" because of his willingness to cooperate with Soviet Russia. In reaction to the nationwide "Day of Shame" that was staged on the first anniversary of the invasion, Husák declared a state of emergency and had the federal assembly draft a drastic decree "for the defense of public order." He vigorously employed this measure during the late summer and early fall of 1969 by carrying out mass arrests and clearing the ranks of the Czech Communist Party of all remaining reformers. By the end of the year, Husák had "normalized" the situation in Czechoslovakia to the satisfaction of the Soviet government. Dubček's plans for the creation of "socialism with a human face" were dead, at least for the moment.

On the international front, the Soviet-led invasion created an air of intense indignation rather than an immediate threat to peace. Nevertheless, it dispelled the notion that the Soviet government was mellowing, a thesis which had been gathering support since the late 1950's. The 1968 invasion proved, as had suppression of the German revolt of 1953 and the Hungarian uprising of 1956, that Soviet leadership would take any steps to maintain the integrity of its vast empire, even at the risk of losing claim to the moral leadership of the world Communist movement. Soviet control of Eastern Europe came to an end only in 1989, when a new Soviet leader, Mikhail Gorbachev, attempted to implement policies similar to those favored by the Czechoslovak reformers of 1968. The removal of Russian support for one-party Communist dictatorship made it possible for reformers in Czechoslovakia, and throughout Eastern Europe to carry through democratic reforms even more radical than the ones which the Soviet invasion of Czechoslovakia had thwarted.

—*Edward P. Keleher, updated by Richard D. King*

ADDITIONAL READING:

Crampton, R. J. *Eastern Europe in the Twentieth Century.* New York: Routledge, 1994. This general survey of Eastern European history since World War I contains an extensive bibliography of works published in English.

Dawisha, Karen. *The Kremlin and the Prague Spring.* Berkeley: University of California Press, 1984. Based on declassified American intelligence sources, this study examines the way in which Soviet leaders responded to the unfolding crisis in Czechoslovakia.

Dubček, Alexander. *Hope Dies Last: The Autobiography of Alexander Dubcek.* Edited and translated by Jiri Hochman. New York: Kodansha International, 1993. The posthumously published memoirs of the leader of the Prague Spring, written in collaboration with a former

Czech journalist who emigrated to the United States after the Warsaw Pact invasion.

Golan, Galia. *The Czechoslovak Reform Movement: Communism in Crisis, 1962-1968*. Cambridge, England: Cambridge University Press, 1971. Concentrates on the economic and political background to the emergence of the reform movement within the Czechoslovak Communist Party.

Kusin, Vladimir V. *The Intellectual Origins of the Prague Spring: The Development of Reformist Ideas in Czechoslovakia*. Cambridge, England: Cambridge University Press, 1971. This analysis of the reform movement emphasizes its moderation and the willingness of the reformers to effect change by working within existing institutions.

Renner, Hans. *A History of Czechoslovakia Since 1945*. New York: Routledge, 1989. This narrative history of Czechoslovakia since World War II was published in the year that Communist rule was overthrown.

Skilling, H. Gordon. *Czechoslovakia's Interrupted Revolution*. Princeton, N.J.: Princeton University Press, 1976. In this massive scholarly study, Skilling argues, in contrast to Kusin and Golan, that the Prague Spring was a revolutionary movement that presented a radical challenge to existing institutions.

SEE ALSO: 1955, Warsaw Pact Is Signed; 1956, Hungarian Revolution; 1968-1989, Brezhnev Doctrine; 1985, Gorbachev Is Elected General Secretary of the Communist Party; 1989, Velvet Revolution in Czechoslovakia; 1993, Czechoslovakia Splits into Two Republics.

1968
CAETANO BECOMES PREMIER OF PORTUGAL

Caetano becomes premier of Portugal after being appointed by President Américo Tomás to succeed António de Oliveira Salazar's forty-year conservative regime.

DATE: September 27, 1968
LOCALE: Portugal
CATEGORY: Government and politics
KEY FIGURES:
Marcelo José de Neves Alves Caetano (1906-1980), Portuguese premier (prime minister), 1968-1974
António de Oliveira Salazar (1899-1970), Portuguese dictator, 1932-1968
Mário Alberto Nobre Lopes Soares (born 1924), Portuguese prime minister, 1976-1978 and 1983-1985, and later president, 1986-1995

Américo Deus Rodrigues Tomás (1894-1987), Portuguese president, 1958-1974

SUMMARY OF EVENT. Marcelo José de Neves Alves Caetano was born in Lisbon on August 17, 1906, into a middle-class family. He attended law school at the University of Lisbon. While there he became involved with the right-wing group, the Integralists, whose ultraconservative views were based on the monarchy and the theories of the French writer Charles Maurras. Caetano obtained his law degree in 1927, and became a legal consultant to the finance ministry and a protégé of Finance Minister António de Oliveira Salazar.

In 1933, Caetano became an assistant professor of social science and administrative law at the University of Lisbon School of Law. Caetano helped write the 1933 constitution for Salazar's fascist new state. Salazar's Portugal consisted of balancing power within the country among the military, landowners, business and commerce, colonial interests, and the Catholic Church. No criticism or discussion was allowed outside this intimate circle of Salazar supporters. All political parties were banned, and Salazar's leadership consisted of a small, informal ruling political and commercial elite. The philosophical tenets of the Salazarist regime were authoritarian government, patriotic unity, Christian morality, and the work ethic. The regime also indulged in ideological fascist-like rallies and youth movements. The government assumed greater control over politics, business, and labor. It also authorized the establishment of a police force known as PIDE (International Police in Defense of the State). PIDE, which resembled the Gestapo, had the power to arrest and imprison, without formal charges, anyone who was accused of having committed a crime "against the safety of the state."

For more than twenty years, Caetano held a variety of appointments under Salazar's dictatorship: In 1936, Caetano was elected to the Council of the Colonial Empire; in 1940, he headed Portugal's state-organized youth movement; in 1941, he was a special envoy to Brazil. Caetano was appointed minister for overseas territories from 1944 to 1947; in 1947, he became president of the National Union, the party that controlled Portugal's political life. From 1950 to 1955, he was president of the Corporate Chamber, an appointed parliamentary body of the nation's economic, cultural, administrative, and religious associations. As an ex-officio member of the council of state, Caetano and his advisory body rendered opinions to the supreme court and to the national president. From 1953 to 1958, Caetano was vice president of the Overseas Council, and in 1955, he became minister of state of the presidency (deputy premier).

As Caetano became more moderate in his conservative,

right-wing views, he decided to leave government service. He became rector (president) of the University of Lisbon in 1959. Three years later, he resigned in protest of police arrests of student demonstrators; afterward he wrote an article in defense of the police action. For the next six years, Caetano taught at the university, practiced law, and served on the board of various companies. Caetano was a teacher, jurist, and scholar of international reputation who had helped draft the 1933 Portuguese constitution. He was also the editor of a law journal, *O Direito* (the law) and author of several books on political science and law. He wrote the first complete treatise on administrative law in Portugal.

When Salazar fell ill on September 16, 1968, with no hope for recovery, President Américo Deus Rodrigues Tomás met with the Council of State to choose a successor. After convincing ultra right-wing conservatives that he would continue Salazar's policies (especially in the colonies), Caetano became premier of Portugal on September 27, 1968. For the most part, the Portuguese seemed content with the choice of Caetano to succeed the dying dictator; the right wing was convinced that Caetano would follow Salazar's policies, while the left wing saw him as the only liberal hope who had any possibility of being chosen by the ruling regime.

In his short acceptance speech Caetano spoke of "evolution within continuity." In other words, he wanted changes to keep up with reform expectations, but not so fast as to antagonize Salazar's conservative supporters. Thus, he promised to continue Salazar's policies (retaining the African colonies, fighting communism, and repressing dissent at home). In his speech, however, he also recognized the need for government reform and advocated an expansionist economic policy. Portugal's new leader, Marcelo Caetano, renamed Salazar's new state as the social state. As if to reassure conservatives, Caetano reappointed Salazar's ministers to their former posts. Caetano's modest reforms began in his fifth year of office. He eased police repression and censorship laws, but, while he allowed freedom of expression in newspapers, he would not allow criticism of Salazar. Politically exiled citizens were allowed to return to Portugal. The outspoken bishop of Porto, along with Alvaro Cunhal (of the Portuguese Communist Party), and Mário Soares, a socialist lawyer (who had been exiled on the island of São Tomé) among others were allowed to return to continental Portugal.

Little by little, Marcelo Caetano replaced Salazar's ministers with his own appointees, particularly younger and more progressive economists, and began moderate government reforms. Although his policies toward the Portuguese African territories remained unchanged,

Caetano called for increased autonomy in the colonies during his 1969 visit. Voting laws were liberalized, giving women equal voting rights and allowing all literate Portuguese adults, without criminal records, the right to vote. In October of 1969, the first "free" elections in forty years were allowed, however, opposition groups were not allowed to form parties. Although newspapers could report on opposition groups, candidates were not allowed to use radio, television, or public rallies to further their causes. As a result of restrictions, all pro-government candidates were reelected. One month after the election, Marcelo Caetano abolished the dreaded secret police, PIDE, established by Salazar in 1945. During Caetano's tenure, the Portuguese capital of Lisbon became the headquarters for North Atlantic Treaty Organization's (NATO) Iberian Atlantic Command (IBERLANT), the Treaty of Friendship and Nonaggression. Caetano continued Portugal's agreement with the United States to maintain a military base, Lajes, on the island of Terceira of the Azores archipelago. Although he inherited Salazar's post of prime minister, Caetano faced the ultraconservative authority of President Tomás, who was emerging as increasingly more powerful. With Salazar's death in 1970, President Tomás was given more freedom to exercise constitutional power to its fullest. Tomás went so far as to threaten Caetano with a military coup if he continued liberalized economic changes.

Like Salazar, Caetano was a conservative Roman Catholic who continued Portugal's concordatas (agreements) with the Vatican and discouraged divorce and birth control, and provided state assistance for Catholic education in public schools. Unlike Salazar, however, Caetano appeared to have a more global vision and visited other Western European nations, the African colonies, and other countries to bring higher recognition for Portugal (one of the least affluent European states) abroad. Caetano was decorated by the governments of Portugal, Spain, Belgium, and Brazil. In an effort to appear more open to the people, Caetano inaugurated televised fireside chats. This apparent openness to public opinion rendered him more popular than Salazar. Although Caetano brought about some reforms, his government lacked a democratic vision and achieved modest economic growth. Increased consumption without adequate production led to a rise of 15 percent inflation. The gap between the rich and the poor continued to widen, as well as the slow development in literacy and educational reform. The military junta of General António de Spinola ousted Caetano's government and took command of the Portuguese Republic on April 25, 1974. The bloodless revolution led to the establishment of democracy in Portugal. Mário Soares (of the Socialist Party) would serve as the prime minister of

Portugal from 1976 to 1978 and 1983 to 1985 and as president from 1986 to 1995. Marcelo Caetano was exiled to Brazil where he died, in Rio de Janeiro, on October 26, 1980. —*Maria A. Pacino*

ADDITIONAL READING:

Figueiredo, Antonio de. *Portugal: Fifty Years of Dictatorship.* New York: Holmes & Meier, 1975. Provides a comprehensive perspective on the Portuguese regimes of Salazar and Marcelo Caetano.

Gallagher, Tom. *Portugal: A Twentieth-Century Interpretation.* Manchester, England: Manchester University Press, 1983. Presents a historical interpretation of Portuguese government, including the Salazar and Caetano years, and subsequent democratic changes, after the 1974 "revolution."

Jenkins, L. "New Style of Tyranny." *Nation* 209 (November 13, 1969): 532-534. The article implied that Caetano's regime is a perpetuation of Salazar's tyrannical policies with Marcelo Caetano as another dictator.

Soares, Mário. "Stagnant Dictatorship: The Legacy of Salazar." *Nation* 214 (April 17, 1972): 491-492. Soares, who served as Portugal's prime minister (1976-1978 and 1983-1985) and as president (1986-1995), criticizes the government of Caetano and his apparent continuation of Salazar's dictatorial policies.

Solsten, Eric, ed. *Portugal: A Country Study.* 2d ed. Lanham, Md.: Bernan Press, 1994. Complete and informative handbook whose chapters include history, society and environment, sthe economy, government and politics, and national security. Includes statistical tables, bibliography, and glossary.

SEE ALSO: 1910, Republic of Portugal Is Proclaimed; 1974, Portugal Grants Independence to Its African Colonies.

1969
DE GAULLE STEPS DOWN

De Gaulle steps down from the French presidency, easing France's struggle for a place among the world's great nations and marking the emergence of domestic concerns as the predominant theme in French national politics.

DATE: April 28, 1969
LOCALE: Paris, France
CATEGORY: Government and politics
KEY FIGURES:

Daniel Cohn-Bendit (born 1945), student with leftist leanings at Nanterre, a branch of the University of Paris

Charles-André-Marie-Joseph de Gaulle (1890-1970), president of the French Republic, 1958-1969

Roger Frey, minister of state under de Gaulle

Valéry Giscard d'Estaing (born 1926), former finance minister

Pierre Messmer, defense minister under de Gaulle

François Mitterrand (1916-1996), leader of a splinter group of French Socialists

Guy Mollet (1905-1975), head of the French Socialist Party

François-Xavier Ortoli, finance minister under de Gaulle

Alain Poher, president of the French Senate

Georges Pompidou (1911-1974), premier of France, 1962-1968, president of France, 1969

SUMMARY OF EVENT. On April 28, 1969, President Charles de Gaulle of France picked up the telephone in his home in Colombey-les-Deux-Eglises and dictated a brief farewell statement to the Elysée Palace in Paris: "I am ceasing to exercise my functions as President of the Republic. This decision takes effect today at noon." The call signaled the end of de Gaulle's eleven-year reign as president of the French Republic. This period witnessed the birth of the Fifth French Republic, the end of the Algerian Crisis, and the exit of France from the North Atlantic Treaty Organization's defense structure. It saw the end of the Algerian crisis, the development of a French nuclear arsenal and striking force, and a French drive for leadership of the "Third World" in Africa and Asia. The French people reacted with optimistic anticipation of new leadership with its greater attention to pressing social and economic problems at home. Nostalgia and a sense of loss tempered their reflections upon de Gaulle and the end of a great era in French history.

De Gaulle's downfall began eleven months before his official resignation. On March 22, 1968, a student demonstration against the Vietnam War, led by Daniel Cohn-Bendit, erupted at the Nanterre branch of the University of Paris; five Nanterre students were jailed. Nanterre's Rector closed the Nanterre branch of the University after consulting the French ministry of education. Incensed by the rector's arbitrary action, Nanterre's faculty joined the fray on the side of the students.

Cohn-Bendit, who was known as "Danny the Red," was ordered to appear before the disciplinary council at the Sorbonne in Paris. He made the three-hour walk from Nanterre to his hearing in Paris at the head of a student procession. At the Sorbonne campus in Paris, the procession was met by a group of hard-core anticommunist war veterans. The rector of the Sorbonne called on the police to keep order. There were 596 arrests.

French labor unions joined the protest by staging one-day general strikes throughout industrial France. After six weeks of chaos, the one-day protest strikes had burgeoned into a national strike of the national workforce. Airports, railroads, and bus lines were shut down; utilities were cut off; mail delivery ceased. Restaurants and hotels closed for lack of business. By early 1969, France had approached a state of anarchy.

At the height of the unrest, President de Gaulle called for a national referendum. He vowed to resign "without delay" if his bid for a personal power mandate was defeated. The fifty-three percent "no" vote registered by the French electorate on April 27, 1969, was the immediate cause of de Gaulle's retirement.

In the long-term view, de Gaulle and the French people had drawn apart on many issues. The president had concerned himself more with the French military, France's foreign policy, and the pursuit of "greatness" abroad, than with domestic problems. By 1969, the high cost of making France a power on the international scene went far beyond the country's economic military resources, and the French electorate was weary of the austerity in domestic spending it dictated.

France had moved into the age of mass consumerism, pop culture, discotheques, and travel abroad. French interest in reorganization of business and farming along American lines, involving computers and computer management, required lower taxes and tax incentives to produce money for these activities. De Gaulle neither understood these needs nor addressed them in budgetary matters. To the French people who voted "no" on April 27, his lack of foresight made him seem out of step with the times. De Gaulle's domineering style and omnipresent personality had become an embarrassment to many and a frequent irritant to French sensibilities.

The president's cabinet members joined in the massive effort to achieve an affirmative vote for de Gaulle. Pierre Messmer, de Gaulle's defense minister, informed voters that the government planned to reduce compulsory military service from sixteen to twelve months. Finance Minister François Xavier Ortoli promised that no new taxes would be levied in the year ahead. Minister of State Roger Frey drew a frightening picture of France without de Gaulle. Even Georges Pompidou, the former premier who had been dismissed by de Gaulle after his successful management of the campaign for a "yes" vote in the 1968 referendum, campaigned vigorously in support of the president's proposals. In opposition to de Gaulle, Valéry Giscard d'Estaing, the former minister of finance, and Alain Poher, president of the French senate, stumped France in defense of "the separation of powers." Socialist Party chief Guy Mollet and the Socialist maverick

François Mitterrand supported their efforts.

A new emphasis on domestic problems followed de Gaulle's exit from power. France's archaic road system, which had only one-fifth of the turnpike miles of West Germany, now received greater funding. The new budget allowed for a preliminary attack on France's outmoded and inefficient telephone system. As de Gaulle's successor, Pompidou no longer denied French workers higher wages because of "prestige" projects abroad. He rescued the French educational system, far too rigid and woefully overcrowded, from Gaullist inattention. The French began to feel a shift in governmental policy.

In the wake of a French national strike that paralyzed the country, President Charles de Gaulle called for a national referendum to determine whether he should retain his political mandate to rule. (AP/Wide World Photos)

In foreign affairs, where de Gaulle had registered his greatest successes, Pompidou moved less boldly. Nevertheless, unmistakable shifts in policy direction were visible. De Gaulle's pro-Arab stance in the Middle East relaxed. This shift eased tension in the Western bloc and possibly paved the way for more cordial Franco-Israeli relations. France's adamant insistence on British exclusion from the Common Market appeared certain to dissolve under Pompidou. British inclusion in the Common Market meant a unified Western Europe, strong enough to be independent of both the United States and Soviet Union. Pompidou moved quickly after his election to extend the *rapprochement* that de Gaulle had begun with the United States. Two important programs of the Gaullist Period, however, stayed in place. French forces remained outside NATO, and the French government continued to enhance its nuclear power facilities and weaponry.

—*Barry L. Knight, updated by Barbara C. Stanley*

ADDITIONAL READING:

Cook, Don. *Charles de Gaulle: A Biography*. New York: G. P. Putnam's Sons, 1983. As Paris Bureau Chief, Don Cook covered the European political arena for the *Los Angeles Times*. He produced this de Gaulle biography from an American viewpoint.

Furniss, Edgar S., Jr. *France, Troubled Ally: De Gaulle's Heritage and Prospects*. New York: Harper & Row, 1960. Produced by the Council on Foreign Relations, this volume reviews the key episodes of French foreign policy since World War II, centering on the prime influence of French domestic demands on the policy-making process and the continuity of policy as the Fourth French Republic gave way to the Fifth.

Hoffmann, Stanley, et al. *In Search of France: The Economy, Society, and the Political System in the Twentieth Century*. Cambridge, Mass.: Harvard University Press, 1963. Six knowledgeable students of French history, social structure, politics, and economy focus on the changed and changing French situation; a well-integrated and informative discussion of postwar France that concludes with a reassessment of the national character.

Lacouture, Jean. *De Gaulle: The Ruler, 1945-1970*. Translated from the French by Alan Sheridan. New York: W. W. Norton, 1991. Lacouture's extensively annotated and indexed second volume of his biography of de Gaulle covers the creation of France's Fourth Republic to de Gaulle's death in 1970.

Macridis, Roy C., and Bernard E. Brown. *The De Gaulle Republic: Quest for Unity*. Homewood, Ill.: The Dorsey Press, 1960. This analysis of de Gaulle's Fifth Republic outlines and submits to careful critical scrutiny the origins, institutions, and prospects of the new constitution and leadership.

Pickles, Dorothy. *The Fifth French Republic: Institutions and Politics*. New York: Frederick A. Praeger, 1960. This book analyzes the nature and purposes of the Constitution of the Fifth Republic adopted on October 4, 1958. The author employs her understanding of French politics to estimate how its purposes were achieved after a brief period of implementation.

Williams, Charles. *The Last Great Frenchman: A Life of General De Gaulle*. New York: John Wiley & Sons, 1993. The author, Lord Williams of Elvel and deputy leader of the opposition in the British House of Lords in 1993, has put together this fine analysis of Charles de Gaulle, the private man and the public figure.

SEE ALSO: 1940-1944, The French Resistance; 1966-1995, France Withdraws from NATO's Military Structure; 1968, French Workers Engage in a National Strike; 1981, Mitterrand Is Elected to the French Presidency; 1995, Chirac Takes Office as President of France.

1969
PESTICIDE POISONS THE RHINE RIVER

Pesticide poisons the Rhine River, killing thousands of tons of fish and bringing awareness of water pollution to Europe.

DATE: June 18, 1969
LOCALE: The Rhine River near Bingen, West Germany
CATEGORIES: Environment; Government and politics
KEY FIGURES:

J. A. Bakker, Dutch minister of transport and waterways, who announced that the Dutch government would hold West Germany responsible for damages resulting from the spill of the insecticide endosulfan

Diether Deneke, agricultural minister of North Rhine-Westphalia in West Germany and official spokesperson for the West German government during the crisis

Hans-Erich Klotter, chemical director for the Rhineland-Palatinate government, who helped lead the investigation into the spill

SUMMARY OF EVENT. The Rhine is Europe's best known and most economically important river, stretching 865 miles (1,392 kilometers) from Lake Constance in the Swiss Alps to the North Sea, on the way forming an eastern border of France and passing through Germany and the Netherlands. As an international waterway open to all, thousands of barges navigate the Rhine every year, and this region of Germany is heavily industrialized. One fifth of the world's chemical industries have factories located along the Rhine. In the late nineteenth century, heavy industry began to build on the Rhine and used the river as dumping grounds, thus earning it the opprobrious label of being "the sewer of Europe" by the middle of the twentieth century. Scientific measurements carried out in the late 1960's showed that the Rhine dumped 15.6 million cubic yards (11.9 million cubic meters) of industrial waste and sewage into the North Sea each year, an amount equal to one-fifth of its total discharge. Salmon and other prized game fish were plentiful at the turn of the century; by mid-century they were all extinct. Between 1940 and 1960, the Rhine saw the amount of chloride in its water increase by 20 percent, ammonia by 7,000 percent, and phosphorus by 300 percent. Thirty-three million bacteria could be found in one cubic inch (two million in one cubic centimeter) of water in the Netherlands. Thousands of foreign substances were found in the water, most of them toxic.

water pollution in Europe's rivers, yet, again, the council was not able to pass any laws against industrial or illegal polluters.

In Germany, laws were in place by 1913 that forced industries to pay to discharge wastewater, hence making it economically feasible for companies to reuse water at every opportunity. Many manufacturers did this as a matter of course for decades. Despite the widespread reuse of

Because the pesticide spill could not be traced to an exact source, local governments along the Rhine River were forced to pay for the removal of dead fish that clogged the river. (Archive Photos)

As early as the 1940's, the Netherlands saw a need for international cooperation concerning control of the Rhine's pollution. In 1950, the International Commission for Protection of the Rhine from Pollution met for the first time. Delegates from the Netherlands, West Germany, Switzerland, France, and Luxembourg (which does not border the Rhine but which is in its floodplain) drew up a plan to monitor the Rhine and to make suggestions to their respective governments. The commission was not composed of state leaders and hence had no authority to enforce any pollution laws. In 1968, eighteen member nations of the Council of Europe met at the United Nations headquarters in Geneva to draw up Europe's first water charter, hoping to stir up public interest in the problem of

water in West Germany, contamination of the Rhine was still a major problem that was exacerbated by West Germany's policy of letting the five states bordering the Rhine enforce water pollution laws. In 1959, the federal government attempted to secure authority over pollution laws, but the states seized control again in 1962.

According to many political experts, the states are more susceptible of being lenient to polluters because significant industries can threaten to leave if taxed and create an economic loss to the state. Also, while the law ensured that polluters who were caught would pay to clean up their spills into the Rhine, it could not ensure that anyone would do so in those cases in which the perpetrator could not be found. No system of federal monies was in place to pay for cleaning up the Rhine under these circumstances. Because of all these factors, no significant cleanup of the Rhine had taken place by 1969.

On June 18, 1969, huge numbers of dead fish in the Rhine were noted by authorities near St. Goar, a small agrarian village in the West German state of North Rhine-Westphalia, located roughly two hundred miles from the Rhine delta at the North Sea. German police reacted by warning farmers to keep cattle away from the river and by warning swimmers along its length to avoid the contaminated water. As the unknown chemical causing the fish kill floated downstream, Germany notified the Netherlands. The Dutch, who obtained more than 60 percent of their drinking water from the Rhine, responded by closing off the source and resorting to reservoir water. German authorities began an investigation as to what was causing the fish kill. Some thought it could be nerve gas stored in drums that the Nazis had dumped into the Rhine some twenty-five years before the incident. The drums could have corroded over the years and released the gas. It was deemed, however, that, since the region around St. Goar was not home to any major industries, the fish kill most likely was caused from a chemical that either fell off or was deliberately tossed from a barge that day. Dutch scientists also investigated the matter, searching the chemical-laden waters of the Rhine for the culprit, finally determining that it was endosulfan, an insecticide manufactured by three large chemical companies in West Germany.

Endosulfan is widely used as an agricultural insecticide on many food and nonfood crops. It is also used in home gardens and in Africa to combat the tsetse fly. The World Health Organization lists it as moderately hazardous, claiming that it does not accumulate in tissue nor harm mammals. It is, however, extremely toxic to fish. In the hope of finding the barge that had dumped the insecticide, German authorities investigated the twenty-two barges that had passed the area near St. Goar between noon and two o'clock on the afternoon of the June 18. On June 27, they had narrowed the search to two barges that had passed by at noon, yet no missing canisters were reported. On July 4, they investigated a report that two years ago Dutch ships carrying endosulfan from Germany had claimed that some canisters were missing. Further investigation led to the discovery that the canisters had not been lost en route to the Netherlands, but only after they had reached their destination, invalidating the possibility that they had fallen overboard. German authorities then agreed that the spill must have been caused by the corrosion of canisters of liquid endosulfan that had been dumped years ago. Despite further investigation, no exact source for the

endosulfan was ever found. Since the spill could not be blamed on any particular company or individual, no one could be forced to pay for the damage to the fishing industry or for the cost of cleaning the river.

Within a week after the spill, the pesticide had reached the North Sea, continuing to kill millions of fish along the way. Thousands of tons of fish had to be removed from the river and incinerated. By the time the endosulfan reached the ocean, the immediate danger was over, but experts estimated that it would take four years for the fish to come back. On August 29, 1969, officials of the North Rhine-Westphalia region announced that they would buy $21,250 worth of live fish from Hamburg and place them in Rhine tributaries in the hope of replenishing the Rhine's natural supply.

Negotiations between West Germany and the Netherlands were begun immediately following the incident. The countries agreed to improve surveillance of the Rhine by building more monitoring stations. The Dutch built a barge that would float near the German border and monitor the condition of the water. Germany responded by outlawing all pesticide dumping and by contracting to build five thousand new sewer treatment plants during the 1970's. Companies in Germany pledged 6 percent of their new construction budgets to go toward pollution reduction facilities. By 1980, the Rhine could boast of being the cleanest river in Europe. The crisis was heard the world over and brought many countries' attention to the problem of water pollution.

—*Rose Secrest*

ADDITIONAL READING:

International Programme on Chemical Safety. *Endosulfan Health and Safety Guide*. Geneva: World Health Organization, 1988. In clear language, discusses the physical and chemical properties of endosulfan, as well as its intended use, legal restrictions, safety precautions and toxicity levels.

Johnson, Ralph W., and Gardner M. Brown, Jr. "Water Quality Management in the Netherlands" and "Water Quality Management in West Germany." In *Cleaning Up Europe's Waters: Economics, Management, and Policies*. New York: Praeger, 1976. Covers water conditions and the history of increasing water pollution for each country, and efforts each country has made to control water pollution.

"The Longest Sewer." *Newsweek* 74 (July 7, 1969): 30. Brief article that neatly sums up the disaster from its initial discovery to the pinpointing of the culprit endosulfan.

Pearce, Fred. "Greenprint for Rescuing the Rhine." *New Scientist* 138 (June 26, 1993): 25-29. A wide-ranging article that provides background on the efforts to clean the Rhine over the last several decades.

"The Rancid Rhine." *Time* 94 (July 4, 1969): 26. Brief article that covers industrial pollution of the Rhine, the spill itself, political tensions between the Netherlands and Germany, and possible rectification of the problem.

SEE ALSO: 1972, United Nations Environmental Conference; 1986, Chernobyl Nuclear Disaster.

1970
PARLIAMENT PASSES THE EQUAL PAY ACT OF 1970

Parliament passes the Equal Pay Act of 1970, establishing a legal basis and remedies for women to receive equal pay and benefits for work that is similar, or of equal value, to work performed by men in Britain.

DATE: May 29, 1970

LOCALE: Great Britain

CATEGORIES: Economics; Laws, acts, and legal history; Women's issues

SUMMARY OF EVENT. Prior to the passage of the Equal Pay Act of 1970, the labor force in Great Britain was characterized by differential salary structures for women workers compared to male workers. In addition, the labor force was segmented, on the basis of gender, in that women worked in a secondary labor market, which had its unique qualities, while their male counterparts were over-represented in jobs that constituted the primary sector of the civilian labor force. Women workers generally were employed in occupations that were female-intensive or jobs defined as feminine. In 1971, women comprised 36.5 percent of the labor force; yet, they were employed in occupations in which 70 percent or more of the workers were females. There were a handful of occupations in which more than 71 percent of the employees were women. These occupations that had an overrepresentation of women were typists, shorthand writers, secretaries, maids, counter-workers, nurses, machine sewers, domestic workers and housekeepers.

Typically, the occupations in which women were employed reflected the functions that women performed in the home or as helpmates to men. Accordingly, these jobs, like the homemaker functions to which they are related, were not highly valued. Therefore, women were usually consigned to low-paying, dead-end jobs or short-career ladder occupations throughout Great Britain. Alternatively, men workers were employed in higher paying occupations, including professional and managerial positions. Further, because women's work was culturally devalued, even when women performed basically the same job as men the job titles were different, with men

being assigned titles that were more highly valued, thereby justifying a higher salary structure and benefits. For example, women were cooks and men chefs; women were secretaries and men personal assistants; and women were shop assistants while men were salesmen. Therefore, women were subjected to pay differentials that were often a result of negative stereotypes regarding women's abilities and occupational and professional interests. Clearly, the Equal Pay Act of 1970 was necessary to improve the pay differential of women workers compared to men workers performing similar jobs and working in occupations that were of equal value according to job evaluations.

The Equal Pay Act of 1970 was passed on May 29, 1970, and implemented in 1975. It was designed to prevent the most blatant forms of pay discrimination in Great Britain. Essentially, this law prohibited unequal pay for the same work or similar work. In addition, this legislation forbade unequal pay for work that was rated as equivalent by employers based on an evaluation scheme that was purported to be gender neutral. In effect, the Equal Pay Act of 1970 made it illegal for women to be paid less for the same work, or work rated to be of equal value to that which was performed by men.

The act also provided remedies for comparable work that was devalued regarding salaries and benefits for women workers. Further, the Equal Pay Act contained a stipulation that required pay structures and collective agreements that contained provisions that applied exclusively to men or women to be referred to the Central Arbitration Committee for the purpose of amending this overt form of gender discrimination. Consequently, the Equal Pay Act of 1970 served as the impetus for gender neutral or unisex grading or evaluation schemes. In order for the jobs to be rated as "like" work or similar work they must be determined to be of equal value relative to the demands placed on a worker in terms of decision making, skill, effort, and so forth.

The fact that the Equal Pay Act is a statute that is geared toward addressing gender discrimination in pay means that when employees file claims they must compare their pay to that of a worker of the opposite sex. Therefore, women can only claim equal pay with men and men can only claim equal pay with women. Moreover, the filing of claims must occur within the same firm. In other words, a claim cannot be filed between a man and a woman who are employed in different firms, even if they are employed in the same industry or occupation. While the Equal Pay Act is primarily a legal measure that makes it unlawful to pay women workers less than their male counterparts, the legislation encompasses all of the terms of the contractual agreement, excluding provisions for death or retirement benefits. Therefore, a claim filed under the Equal Pay Act does not have to be a simple wage claim but can be an attempt to equalize other conditions of employment. Other benefits for which equal value claims can seek remedies include sick pay benefits, bonuses, subsidized mortgages and other nonwage contractual terms of the claimant's employment.

According to the Equal Pay Act the claimant, rather than the employer or the tribunal, is permitted to choose the comparator, or the individual who is allegedly paid at a higher rate because of gender discrimination. Claimants are also allowed to identify multiple comparisons or in the case of female complainants, a woman may compare her case to many men who are more highly paid, as opposed to only one man.

While the Equal Pay Act was able to diminish the existence of pay inequality based on gender it could not eliminate gender discrimination regarding pay for men and women workers. Clearly, there are many factors that contribute to pay inequality between men and women workers that this legislation as well as its subsequent amendments could not resolve. Specifically, factors such as discrimination in education in which female students are perceived as better suited for female-intensive, lower-paying occupations, culturally prescribed socialization of females into acceptable women's roles within and outside of the labor market, the familial division of labor that requires women to assume more responsibility for caregiving and tasks of domesticity, discrimination in preemployment training, and so forth.

Another obvious deficiency in the Equal Pay Act of 1970 is that it could not provide remedies for innumerable women who were currently working in occupations over-represented by women workers, and for whom there were no male comparators. Finally, although the Equal Pay Act permitted individual claims it did not make provisions for class action claims. Thus, an individual may not litigate on behalf of similarly situated workers.

Subsequent to the implementation of the Equal Pay Act of 1970 the earnings gap between men and women workers was reduced by 15 percent. Clearly, the Equal Pay Act contributed to this occurrence. Further, applications that were processed after the passage of the Equal Pay Act decreased from 1,742 in 1976 to 39 in 1982.

Perhaps the Equal Pay Act would have been more effective in decreasing the earnings gap between men and women workers if it had not been for the level of resistance that was presented by employers. According to the Equal Pay Act of 1970, if the Industrial Tribunal concludes that a claim has merit, and the claimant is being paid a lesser salary for a job of equal value, the burden of proof is on the employer to show that the variation in pay is the result of a material factor that is not based on gender. For example, employers may cite tenure or length of service, differential work experience, or disparate educational preparation. Yet the Equal Pay Act not only makes the employer responsible for justifying the pay differential but also makes gender discrimination unlawful whether it is intentional or unintentional on the part of the employer.

Unquestionably, the Equal Pay Act of 1970 had a definite effect on reducing the differential salary structure based on gender. Equally important, this act served as a precursor to, and impetus for, amendments as well as related legislation, such as the Sex Discrimination Act of 1975. Generally, the effectiveness of the Equal Pay Act of 1970, as well as other legislation designed to improve the social and economic opportunities for women workers, has been contingent upon the extent to which they have been able to make gender discrimination unprofitable for employers.

—*K. Sue Jewell*

ADDITIONAL READING:

Hastings, Sue. "Equal Value in the Local Authority Sector in Great Britain." In *Equal Value/Comparable Worth in the UK and the USA*, edited by Peggy Kahn and Elizabeth Meehan. New York: St. Martin's Press, 1992. Hastings discusses the impact of the Equal Pay Act of 1970 on manual and non-manual workers in Great Britain.

Middleton, Chris. "Gender Divisions and Wage Labour in English History." In *Gender Segregation at Work*, edited by Sylvia Walby. Milton Keynes, England: Open University Press, 1988. The author of this article provides a discussion of the origins of wage labour, in an effort to refute theorists that contend that wage labor is a function of capitalism.

Rubenstein, Michael. *Equal Pay for Work of Equal Value: The New Regulations and Their Implications*. London: Macmillan, 1984. This work contains an examination of the Equal Pay Act of 1970, the implementation of this act, its impact on employers, and an analysis of its interpretation by the courts.

Wilborn, Steven L. *A Secretary and a Cook: Challenging Women's Wages in the Courts of the United States and Great Britain*. Ithaca, N.Y.: ILR Press, 1989. Wilborn discusses issues related to comparable worth by examining two major legal cases—those of Helen Castrilli and Julie Hayward.

SEE ALSO: 1918, British Women Gain the Vote; 1967, United Nations Declaration on Equality for Women.

1972
"BLOODY SUNDAY" IN NORTHERN IRELAND

"Bloody Sunday" in Northern Ireland occurs when a peaceful demonstration leads to a violent confrontation with British troops.

DATE: January 30, 1972

LOCALE: Londonderry, Northern Ireland

CATEGORIES: Government and politics; Wars, uprisings, and civil unrest

KEY FIGURES:

William Craig (born 1924), leader of the Vanguard Unionist Party in Northern Ireland

Bernadette Devlin (born 1947), a student leader, 1967-1969, and later a member of Parliament, 1969-1974

Brian Faulkner (1921-1977), prime minister of Northern Ireland, 1970-1972

Edward Heath (born 1916), prime minister of Great Britain, 1970-1974

Reginald Maulding, British home secretary

The Reverend Ian Paisley (born 1926), leader of the Democratic Unionist Party in Northern Ireland

William Whitelaw (born 1918), secretary of state for Northern Ireland following the dissolution of the Northern Ireland Parliament, 1972-1973

SUMMARY OF EVENT. On January 30, 1972, a protest rally organized by the Northern Ireland Civil Rights Association (NICRA) in Londonderry, Northern Ireland, to demand an end to the internment without trial of suspected terrorists resulted in a clash with British troops. Thirteen of the protesters, all Catholics, died, and more were wounded. The event, which quickly became known as "Bloody Sunday," led to claims that the British had fired without provocation, a charge rejected by the official British investigation called the Widgery Report, although it was confirmed by various eyewitnesses.

Shocking as the deaths were to the Irish and British people, they were only part of a long, complex, and continuing struggle in Northern Ireland. This struggle may be said to have begun anew with the civil rights movement of 1967-1968, but it lay deep in the history of the "damnable question" of Anglo-Irish relations over many generations.

Northern Ireland came into existence on December 6, 1921, as a result of the Anglo-Irish Treaty, a pragmatic compromise negotiated by Prime Minister David Lloyd George in the wake of the Easter Rising of 1916, the electoral victory of the Sinn Féin over the Parliamentary Party in the elections of 1918, and the establishment by the Sinn Féin of an independent Irish Parliament in 1919. The

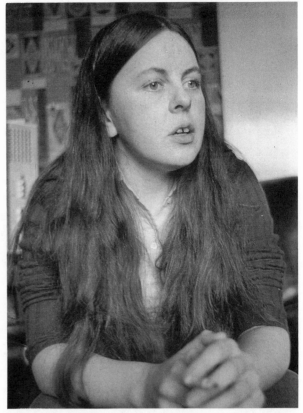

A vocal critic of British rule in Northern Ireland, Bernadette Devlin was a member of Parliament who was scheduled to address marchers in Londonderry on "Bloody Sunday." (AP/Wide World Photos)

political division of Ireland corresponded neither to historical reality (the old Province of Ulster) nor to religious differences, but rather represented the maximum area over which those elements favorable to Britain held political control. The six northern counties of Ireland were granted limited local autonomy under the North Ireland Parliament meeting in Stormont.

By the middle of the twentieth century, the area contained within the borders of Northern Ireland held a Protestant population of about one million and a Catholic population of about half a million. The religious division was accentuated by an economic division, for while two distinct "classes" could not be said to exist in the society, there was a clear tendency for Protestants to be wealthier and more politically powerful, and for Catholics to be poorer and politically weak. Most Protestants wished to continue the union with the United Kingdom of Great Britain and Ireland and were thus known as "unionists" or "loyalists," while many Catholics, who hoped to incorporate Northern Ireland into the Republic of Ireland, were referred to as "nationalists.

The chain of events leading to the confrontation of 1972 began with the emergence of a civil rights movement. Irish activists took as their model the civil rights marches in the American South and endorsed the nonviolent tactics of Mohandas K. Gandhi and the Reverend Martin Luther King, Jr. During the late 1960's, Bernadette Devlin, a leader of the Student People's Democracy group, became one of the most vocal critics of British rule in Northern Ireland. In 1968, the Northern Ireland Civil

though now illegal armed force favoring union of all Ireland, split into "official" and "provisional" factions over the question of tactics in January, 1970. The "officials" supported the nonviolent methods of NICRA and provided marshals and other assistance during the marches. The "provisionals" advocated more violent means. They ultimately took the initiative from all other groups with an argument that appealed to the Catholics, who formed the bulk of the ostensibly nonsectarian civil

A peaceful protest rally in Londonderry was interrupted when British paratroopers and rowdy elements of the crowd clashed, resulting in thirteen deaths on "Bloody Sunday." (Archive Photos)

Rights Association, espousing a nonsectarian unity of disadvantaged Protestants and Catholics, organized a series of marches, the first of which took place at Dungannon without incident. Then, in October of 1969, the first violent clash between marchers, police, and militant Protestant groups occurred in Londonderry. Confrontations became increasingly frequent in late 1968 and into 1969. In August, 1969, British troops assumed riot duty for the first time.

The Irish Republican Army (IRA), the traditional

rights movement. The "provisionals" argued that only violent resistance could protect the Catholic minority from the Protestant-leaning "B-Specials" police militia, and, as they later began to take form, from the various Protestant paramilitary groups.

Faced with escalating violence, the Northern Ireland Parliament introduced the internment without trial of suspected terrorists in August, 1971. This measure, permitted under the Special Powers Act of 1922, was declared necessary by Brian Faulkner, the prime minister of Northern

Ireland, to bring the increasingly militant IRA under control. The internments elicited negative responses from both foreign and domestic critics, and soon observers alleged that the internees were being kept under brutal conditions. Those charges provided the immediate occasion for the demonstration of January 30, 1972.

Although all demonstrations had been banned by the government of Northern Ireland, at mid-afternoon on January 30, six thousand demonstrators marched from Bishop's Fields, their point of assembly, toward the Bogside district of Londonderry (commonly known as Derry to most Catholics and nationalists). To avoid an impending confrontation, the march was diverted from its original course toward the Guildhall and redirected toward an alternate rally site at Free Derry Corner. One of the highlights of the rally was to have been a speech by Bernadette Devlin, who had held a seat in Parliament since 1969. At about 3:30 P.M., however, a group of Derry youths broke away from the main column and confronted the army barricades that had been erected to contain the march. British paratroopers were pelted with stones and bottles, and they responded with tear gars and fire hoses. The paratroopers then crossed the barricades, intending to arrest demonstrators. Encountering resistance and fearing attack, the paratroopers began firing their weapons into the crowd. In the next twenty minutes, thirteen young and unarmed men were dead and perhaps as many as eighteen other people were injured. The paratroopers later justified their actions by claiming that they had been fired upon but evidence in support was controversial.

The thirteen deaths on Bloody Sunday brought shock and rage to the nationalist Irish community, many of whom saw the British cast in a role that they had played so often in Irish history—a repressive force against the Irish people. The Irish ambassador was withdrawn from London, and the British Embassy in Dublin was fire-bombed. The continuing conflict and the differing interpretations between the two sides was dramatized on the following day, Monday, January 31, when Reginald Maulding, the British home secretary, announced in the House of Commons that an investigation would take place, but his remarks also seemed to defend the paratroopers' actions. In response, Bernadette Devlin physically assaulted Maulding, accusing him of being a "murdering hypocrite."

On March 24, 1972, Prime Minister Edward Heath of Great Britain announced plans for a solution of the problems of Northern Ireland, including the resignation of Prime Minister Faulkner and the effective dissolution of the Stormont government. William Whitelaw was appointed secretary of state for Northern Ireland. Fifty years after the partition of Ireland and the establishment of Northern Ireland with its own home-rule parliament, the British had again assumed direct rule over a part of the island. The dissolution was approved by the Catholic community, which had little love for the Protestant-dominated Stormont, but it was ill-received by such Protestant leaders as William Craig of the Vanguard Unionist Party, who desired independence for Northern Ireland. Led by their spokesman, the Reverend Ian Paisley, another group of Protestants received the news of direct rule by England with moderate satisfaction, seeing it as a step toward full union with Britain and protection against "popery." Direct British rule, however, proved not to be the panacea for a peaceful resolution of "the troubles" of Northern Ireland, as that fractured society continued on its path of increasing violence.

—*James W. Pringle, updated by Eugene Larson*

ADDITIONAL READING:

Bardon, Jonathan. *A History of Ulster*. Belfast: Blackstaff Press, 1992. This is a well-written one-volume history of Ulster that includes a sensitive discussion of the events in Northern Ireland during the late 1980's and early 1990's.

Bell, J. Bowyer. *The Irish Troubles*. New York: St. Martin's Press, 1993. This analysis of Northern Ireland from 1967 to 1992 includes a brilliant account of "Bloody Sunday."

Devlin, Bernadette. *The Price of My Soul*. New York: Alfred A. Knopf, 1969. Although published before the events of "Bloody Sunday," this work remains a valuable source regarding the nationalist and Catholic position in Northern Ireland.

Hamill, Desmond. *Pig in the Middle*. London: Methuen, 1985. A discussion of the difficult position of the British army in the Northern Ireland, including a commentary on "Bloody Sunday."

McClean, Raymond. *The Road to Bloody Sunday*. Dublin: Ward River Press, 1983. An eyewitness account by a medical doctor who tried to treat the wounded and dying during the firing on "Bloody Sunday."

McCluskey, Conn. *Up Off Their Knees*. Galway: Conn McCluskey and Associates, 1989. This excellent work is written by an early and active participant in the civil rights movement in Northern Ireland.

SEE ALSO: 1916, Easter Rebellion; 1932, Eamon de Valera Is Elected President of the Irish Dáil; 1974, IRA Terrorists Bomb Parliament Building; 1976, IRA Hunger Striker Dies in an English Prison; 1985, Anglo-Irish Agreement Is Signed; 1993, Ulster Peace Accord.

1972

UNITED NATIONS ENVIRONMENTAL CONFERENCE

The United Nations Environmental Conference marks the beginning of the United Nations Environment Programme (UNEP) to address global environmental problems.

DATE: June 5-16, 1972

LOCALE: Stockholm, Sweden

CATEGORIES: Environment; Government and politics; Social reform

KEY FIGURES:

René Jules Dubos (1901-1982), a world-renowned environmentalist and bacteriologist whose report, *Only One Earth*, set the agenda for the conference

Maurice F. Strong, Canadian businessman who served as secretary-general of the Stockholm Conference

Barbara Mary Ward (1914-1981), a British environmentalist and economist who assisted Dubos in writing *Only One Earth*

SUMMARY OF EVENT. The United Nations Conference on the Human Environment, held at Stockholm in 1972, is commonly thought of as the event where international debate on the environment began, but it was in reality the culmination of a considerable process of discussion. It was also a presentation of rather different points of view. The industrialized world came to discuss international solutions to pollution problems which resulted from the growth of industrial activity. Their emphasis was on regulation and pollution control. They were also concerned with nature conservation, and especially with threats to particular species (such as whales) and habitats (such as rain forests). The developing countries expressed little interest in these problems as compared with "the pollution of poverty" and the inefficiency of resource use caused by underdevelopment.

This divergence became a serious issue in the months leading up to the Stockholm Conference, and at one point seemed to endanger it. An important meeting that began to bridge the gap in perception was held at Founex, Switzerland, in June, 1971. The report produced at this meeting clearly defined many of the issues that were to confront governments from both developed and developing countries. It became clear at this meeting that "development" and "environment" were linked.

The extent of activity within the United Nations system was familiar to the governmental delegations at Stockholm, many whom were also members of a number of other nonaffiliated institutions who were playing an active part in evaluating and responding to emerging environ-mental concerns. There were three main concentrations behind the Stockholm agenda. First, there was a recognition that the developing nations faced massive environmental problems, especially linked to poverty, that needed to be overcome through economic development, while developed countries had problems because their development had followed the wrong course. Second, there was a growing scientific understanding of the interrelatedness of natural systems which indicated that action was required by all countries if success was to be achieved. Third, a growing public concern had arisen concerning the cumulative impacts of human activities on the global environment. This had been stimulated by disasters such as the 1967 wreck of the *Torrey Canyon* (the world's first super-tanker accident) and reports of damage to wildlife through persistent contamination by industrial chemicals and other substances.

The U.N. organizations were hardly in a position to respond coherently to the Stockholm agenda. Those agencies with programs directly relevant to the environment, presented points of view which naturally reflected close links to their own mandates. Stockholm came before the time when all applicable natural sciences were grouped as environmental science. The holistic, or systems, approach was still something left to academics for debate. Moreover, the knowledge of social scientists was hardly ever presented in the debate. Economic questions were discussed largely in relation to development and natural resource depletion. Government organization was also sectoral (and there, hardly any departments of the environment). The overall approach was compartmentalized, and the diplomatic community did not consider the environment as a central concern at all.

The Stockholm Conference was the culmination of a two year preparatory process, and the beginning of a new and intensified program. In the preparatory process, International working groups drew up plans, later endorsed by the conference and implemented by the United Nations Environment Programme (UNEP), for the Global Environmental Monitoring System (GEMS), an International Register for Potentially Toxic Chemicals (IRPTC), and an International Referral System for Sources of Environmental Information (INFOTERRA). Concern over marine pollution led to the negotiation of the Convention on the Prevention of Pollution of the Sea by the Dumping of Wastes and Other Matter, finalized in London in October, 1972. Parallel conventions raised issues concerning wetland conservation (Ramsar), the control of trade in endangered species (CITES; held in Washington, D.C.), and world heritage sites (Paris).

The Stockholm Conference decided on a system of

environmental coordination for the United Nations that took the participating nations a full fifteen years to adopt themselves. Although the resolutions were not systematically organized, and few were global or regional in scope, they did cover a wide variety of issues. The need for global information, provided by EarthWatch, led toward global standard setting. The establishment of the UNEP with its voluntary fund, was a major advance, and a spur both to the development of the U.N. system and to the adoption of a more integrated approach by governments. The limiting factor to the success of the Stockholm Conference lies in the slow implementation of a similar intersectoral approaches at the national level by the participants.

The Stockholm Conference was successful because it created a tremendous public interest in the environment and provided directives for international and national action. It began a process that linked the environment with economic development. The Stockholm Declaration on the Human Environment and the Declaration of Principles constituted a solid foundation for future work, and the Stockholm Action Plan was embodied in the United Nations Environment Programme.

The impact of the Stockholm Conference on the Western European countries was largely carried through the supranational mechanism of the European Economic Community (EEC) and later of the European Union (EU). The EEC had no official environmental policy until 1972. The event which triggered this action was the participation of each of the member states at the Stockholm Conference.

The original Treaty of Rome (which created the European Economic Community) makes no mention of the environment and this continued until it was amended by the Single European Act in 1987. Nevertheless, the Heads of State and their respective governments decided in October of 1972 that the EEC should develop an environmental policy, and since 1973, this has been subsequently presented in Five Action Programmes (1973-1976, 1977-1981, 1982-1986, 1987-1992, 1992-2000).

These plans contain the environmental policy intentions of the European Commission and the European Council of Ministers. To varying degrees, and typically after a considerable period of time, these have been translated into a series of council decisions (regulations, directives, recommendations, and nonbinding opinions). After a further interval and to varying degrees, given compliance problems, these have been translated into member-state laws to achieve formal compliance, followed later by practical compliance (implementation on the ground). The interval between statement of intention and practical compliance can be substantial (in excess of ten years in some cases) and the content with its associated costs and bene-

fits may be greatly transformed in the process.

The first plan of 1973 charted a new path in EEC policy making. As such, it was a long and comprehensive document. It started with a general statement of the objectives and principles of the EEC's environmental policy and then went on to delineate the proposed actions. The commission proposed to reduce pollution and nuisances; to improve the natural and urban environments; to deal with environmental problems caused by the depletion of certain natural resources; and to promote awareness of environmental problems and education. These principles have largely been incorporated in subsequent legislation. Member states have also subsequently created their own departments of the environment and worked closely to harmonize their policies.   —*Kevin B. Vichcales*

ADDITIONAL READING:

"Action to Save Our Environment." *UN Chronicle* 25 (June, 1988): 42-43. This article is part of a cover story on U.N. efforts to protect the environment. It covers the activities of UNEP and assesses prospects for the future.

Bassow, Whitman. "The World Environment Center." *Environment* 28 (November, 1986): 3-4. This article provides an overview of the history, accomplishments, and plans of the World Environment Center (WEC), established in 1974 with help from the United Nations Environment Programme.

Bequette, France. "UNESCO: Helping to Save the Earth." *The Unesco Courier* 46 (November, 1993): 25-29. The author provides an update on UNESCO. As part of its ongoing environmental initiative in collaboration with the UNEP, the organization continues to employ a wide range of methods to improve awareness of environmental issues. Several UNESCO environmental programs are described. Sidebars present environmental news briefs from various countries and a suggested reading list.

Dubos, René, and Barbara Ward Jackson. *Only One Earth: The Care and Maintenance of a Small Planet.* New York: W. W. Norton, 1972. The contents of this book inspired many of the initiatives and recommendations that came out of the Stockholm Conference. Provides a useful context for understanding environmental concerns of the period.

Haas, Peter M. "United Nations Environment Programme." *Environment* 36 (September, 1994): 43-45. The author contends that the focus of the United Nations Environment Programme (UNEP) has become unclear. Created by the General Assembly of the United Nations in 1972, UNEP was designed to coordinate the environment-related activities of other U.N. agencies and to spur them to integrate environmental considerations into their activities. UNEP's success at coordinating efforts with other U.N. agencies has been spotty, and its mission in the aftermath of the 1992 U.N. Conference on Environment and Development in Rio de Janeiro will likely be redesigned.

Tolba, Mostafa K., and Osama A. El-Kholy, eds. *The World Environment 1972-1992: Two Decades of Challenge.* New York: Chapman and Hall, 1992. This work examines the twenty years since the Stockholm Conference to see how the world has changed, and to what extent the world community has responded to these changes since that time.

United Nations. *The Results from Stockholm.* Berlin: Erich Schmidt Verlag, 1973. This work is a complete report of the actions of the United Nations Conference on the Human Environment held in Stockholm. It also contains the reports of the experts to the Second International Parliamentary Conference on the Environment, demonstrating their reactions as observers to the discussions held at the conference.

SEE ALSO: 1945, The United Nations Is Founded; 1969, Pesticide Poisons the Rhine River; 1985, Sinking of the *Rainbow Warrior*; 1986, Chernobyl Nuclear Disaster.

1972
MUNICH OLYMPIC MASSACRE

The Munich Olympic massacre draws international attention to the Palestinian cause in the wake of the killing of eleven Israeli athletes by the terrorist group, Black September.

DATE: September 5, 1972
LOCALE: Munich, West Germany
CATEGORIES: Government and politics; Race and ethnicity; Terrorism and political assassination
KEY FIGURES:

Avery Brundage (1887-1975), elder statesmen of modern Olympic competition and chairman of the International Olympic Committee

Abu Daoud (born 1937), founder of Black September who was involved in planning the Munich operation

Golda Meir (1898-1978), Israeli prime minister during the Munich Olympics

Colonel Muammar al-Qaddafi (born 1942), Libyan leader who provided funding and supplies for the Munich operation

Ali Hassan Salameh (1940-1979), founder of Black September and mastermind behind the Munich massacre

SUMMARY OF EVENT. The Twentieth Summer Olympiad opened on August 26, 1972, in Munich, West Germany.

Heralded as the first computerized modern games, more than 8,500 athletes representing 121 countries came to participate. The $650 million Olympic Village and other facilities had been built on a site used in World War II to dump refuse from Allied bombings. The German Olympic Committee hoped to erase not only the memories of the war, but the Nazi arrogance associated with the elaborate and racially motivated 1936 Berlin Olympics. Spirits ran high during the Opening Ceremony, and as competition began, outside tensions including the Vietnam War were put aside. Highlights included the performances of American swimmer Mark Spitz, who won an unprecedented seven gold medals, and Russian gymnast Olga Korbut, who tumbled into the hearts of the world.

On the eleventh day of competition, the excitement of these games would come to a sudden halt. At 4:30 A.M. on September 5, eight men scaled the fence surrounding the Olympic Village. Dressed as athletes, the men quickly moved undetected to Connolly Street Building 31, which housed the teams from Hong Kong, Uruguay, and Israel. Armed with machine guns and grenades, the terrorist team reached the door of Israeli wrestling coach Moshe Weinberg at approximately 5:00 A.M. Shouting a warning to others, Weinberg held off the perpetrators long enough for six Israeli athletes to escape before he was fatally shot. Weightlifter Joseph Romano was also fatally shot as the terrorists rounded up and roped together the remaining nine Israeli team members. News of possible gunfire reached authorities, and within an hour, Munich and Olympic officials began negotiations with the Black September terrorists.

Black September, the assassination faction of the al-Fatah wing of the Palestine Liberation Organization (PLO), took its name from the September, 1970, incident when Palestinian guerrillas were expelled from Jordan for terrorist activities. Substantially funded by Libya's Muammar al-Qaddafi, Black September operated in the Middle East and Europe to attract attention to the Palestinian cause. The ultimate goal of the group was to disband Israel and return the area to the Palestinians. One founder, Ali Hassan Salameh, drew additional support from neo-Nazi groups and used the anti-Semitic connections to create an elaborate European terrorist branch. Salameh and Abu Daoud, another founder, initiated the plans to take the Israeli team hostage in early 1972.

The terrorists communicated their demands through a Munich policewoman and Walter Troger, the mayor of the Olympic Village. The main demand was the release of 236 fellow guerrillas held in Israel, including Kozo Okamoto, the surviving terrorist from the Lod Airport massacre in March, 1972. Additional demands included free passage

Eight of the Israeli hostages slain in the Munich Olympic massacre received a state funeral in Tel Aviv. (Popperfoto/Archive Photos)

to Cairo, Egypt. While the German foreign ministry tried to find an Arab leader who would act as mediator, Munich chief of police Manfred Schreiber and Interior Minister Hans-Dietrich Genscher of West Germany offered to pay unlimited ransom or to exchange themselves for the hostages. Prime Minister Golda Meir of Israel officially refused to negotiate but encouraged the use of force in dealing with the terrorists. Adding to the tension was the minute-by-minute live coverage by the media sent to cover the Olympic games. Some five hundred million people worldwide saw the maneuvering by the Munich police and other officials before coverage was halted to keep information from the terrorists.

The official International Olympic Committee (IOC) response was spearheaded by chairman Avery Brundage. Wanting to maintain Olympic autonomy while protecting the athletes, the IOC suspended the games beginning at 4:00 P.M. Marking the first temporary suspension in modern Olympic history, the IOC resented the use of the competition in an attempt to evoke political change.

A break in the negotiation finally came around 9:00 P.M., when the terrorists agreed to leave the Olympic Village and be flown to a nearby airbase where a Boeing 707 awaited. German helicopters picked up the nine Israeli hostages and the eight terrorists at 10:00 P.M. and flew to Furstenfeldbrück NATO airbase fifteen miles away. The world breathed a sigh of relief as international media reported the hostages had been freed. Behind the scenes, the German government and Munich police, with IOC and Israeli approval, had planned to place police sharpshooters at the airbase to remove the terrorist threat. As the terrorists went to inspect the jet, sharpshooters opened fire and killed three. The remaining terrorists shot out the flood lights, threw grenades toward the helicopters holding the hostages, and an hour-long gunfight ensued.

The entire hostage taking and massacre lasted twenty-three hours. In the aftermath, seventeen men were dead, including Munich police officer Anton Fliegenbauer, five terrorists, and all the Israeli hostages—twenty-six-year-old David Berger and twenty-eight-year-old Zeev Friedman, both of whom were weightlifters; eighteen-year-old Mark Slavin and twenty-eight-year-old Eliezer Halfin, both wrestlers; fifty-three-year-old shooting coach Kehat Schorr; forty-five-year-old fencing coach Andre Spitzer;

forty-one-year-old wrestling referee Yosef Gutfreund; fifty-one-year-old weightlifting coach Yacov Springer; and thirty-two-year-old track coach Amitzur Shapira. The remaining Israeli delegation returned home with their fallen comrades on September 7. Weinberg, Romano, and eight of the slain hostages received a state funeral in Tel Aviv. The body of David Berger, an émigré from the United States, was returned to his family.

The Olympic and world community faced the horrifying news with solemn reserve. Flags around the world flew at half mast and international outrage called for answers. The IOC scheduled a memorial service on September 6 in the main stadium where the athletes had last come together for the Opening Ceremonies. Some eighty thousand people came to mourn the tragedy and share the loss. After a thirty-four-hour suspension, the IOC decided to resume the games and not allow the Olympic tradition fall victim to terrorism. The Closing Ceremony also included a moment of silent prayer in honor of the Israeli athletes.

Three Black September members—Ibrahim Badran, age twenty; Mahmud el-Safadi, twenty-one; and Samer Mohammad Abdullah, twenty-two—were captured and charged with murder and kidnapping. The three admitted to participating in the raid but not to using their weapons. The five dead terrorists were flown to Tripoli where they received a martyr's funeral headed by Qaddafi. The Libyan leader also gave $5 million to Fatah in recognition of their efforts for the Palestinian plight. The three accused terrorists were released by West Germany on October 29, after two Palestinian guerrillas hijacked a Lufthansa 727, holding its passengers and crew hostage and demanding the release of the three surviving Munich terrorists. The three terrorists returned to Libya and received a hero's welcome. The seemingly quick release of the terrorists by the West German government heightened efforts by the Israeli government to seek revenge. The Wrath of God, an Israeli secret service group, actively sought out and assassinated Black September members into the late 1980's. Their efforts followed other Israeli retaliatory actions, including attacks on Palestinian commando bases in Syria and Lebanon.

The Munich police force faced stark criticism for the failed rescue attempt. Despite an official report clearing them, Schreiber and his sharpshooting team would continue to confront scrutiny for decades to come. The West German government made a $1 million settlement with the athletes' families in 1973, although allegations over blame in the hostage deaths continued into the mid-1990's.

Both local and international security, especially in air-

ports, heightened as Arabs around the world found their comings and goings monitored. The PLO initially denied involvement and blamed the media for anti-Palestinian propaganda. The Munich massacre did bring increased attention to the Palestinian cause as it ushered in a new image of terrorism. Subsequent terrorist activities would follow the pattern of sudden, small scale operations that draw the attention of the international media. The Munich massacre would come to represent a major turning point in the scope of terrorism.

—Jennifer Davis

ADDITIONAL READING:

Doctorow, E. L. "After the Nightmare." *Sports Illustrated* 44 (June 28, 1976): 72-82. An emotional look at the personal losses and aftermath of the massacre, this article traces a number of the murdered athletes' families on the eve of the 1976 Olympics.

McForan, Desmond. *The World Held Hostage: The War Waged by International Terrorism.* New York: St. Martin's Press, 1986. This book is a well-respected study of the problems of and responses to international terrorism.

Rubenstein, Richard E. *Alchemists of Revolution: Terrorism in the Modern World.* New York: Basic Books, 1987. While examining the various definitions of terrorist activities, this books questions the role of nationalism and political connections used to achieve political ends.

Sterling, Claire. *The Terror Network: The Secret War of International Terrorism.* New York: Holt, Rinehart and Winston, 1981. An extensive look at the terrorist connections within Europe and the Middle East, this book gives particular attention to the leaders of various organizations.

Thackrah, John Richard. *Encyclopedia of Terrorism and Political Violence.* New York: Routledge & Kegan Paul, 1987. Designed to place terrorist groups and activities into historical context, this book includes concise entries that are extensively cross-referenced for further study.

SEE ALSO: 776 B.C., Olympic Games; 1974, IRA Terrorists Bomb Parliament Building; 1978, Aldo Moro Is Kidnapped and Murdered by Italian Terrorists.

1973
EAST AND WEST GERMANY ESTABLISH DIPLOMATIC RELATIONS

East and West Germany establish diplomatic relations in a watershed of the détente era, one symbolizing the acceptance of the post-World War II European order by the two blocs.

DATE: June 21, 1973

LOCALE: Bonn, West Germany, and East Berlin, East Germany

CATEGORY: Diplomacy and international relations

KEY FIGURES:

Egon Bahr (born 1922), state secretary in the West German Federal Chancery and principal negotiator for the West German government in Berlin, 1969-1972

Willy Brandt (Herbert Ernst Karl Frahm; 1913-1992), chancellor of the Federal Republic of Germany (West Germany), 1969-1974, and chairman of the Social Democratic Party (SPD)

Michael Kohl (born 1929), state secretary to the East German Council of Ministers and plenipotentiary for the East German government in Bonn

Willi Stoph (born 1914), chairman of the Council of Ministers of the German Democratic Republic (East Germany)

SUMMARY OF EVENT. The Treaty on the Basis of Relations Between the Federal Republic of Germany and the German Democratic Republic, the so-called Basic Treaty, entered into force on June 21, 1973. It was the instrument through which the two German states formally recognized each other as sovereign entities. The termination of the strict nonrecognition policy pursued by the American-allied Federal Republic of Germany (FRG) opened the door for the worldwide de jure recognition of the socialist German Democratic Republic (GDR). The establishment by the German states of mere "permanent representations" in each other's capitals, instead of full diplomatic embassies, was a concession to the West German position on the state of the German nation. This position insisted on the continued existence of two German states within one German nation. Accordingly, the relationship between the two German states would have to be of a special nature, for the two entities could not deal with each other as if they were foreign states.

The Basic Treaty was a significant milestone in Chancellor Willy Brandt's innovative *Ostpolitik* (literally "East politic," or Eastern policy), aiming toward normalization of affairs with the East and the softening of the harsh impact of the division of Germany. The new Eastern policy represented a complete turn-about from the earlier West German posture, expressed by the so-called Hallstein Doctrine. This doctrine pursued as its principal objective the prevention of diplomatic recognition of the GDR by the non-Communist world. The West German government's earlier position maintained that Germany continued to exist in its 1937 borders. It also claimed that the German state, continuing as a subject before interna-

tional law, was recognized in reorganized form in 1949 as the Federal Republic of Germany. This legal standpoint, according to which the FRG represented the whole of the German nation, assumed that the borders of the former German Reich of 1937 maintained full validity in the legal sense, in spite of the fact that the constitution of the FRG could not be extended over the same area. A further deduction was that the FRG should pursue a foreign policy that would enable the other parts of Germany to enter into the realm of the Basic Law of the FRG. Thus, reunification of Germany within the 1937 borders was among the expressed goals of the West German government.

The new West German flexibility began to emerge with the "Grand Coalition" government in November, 1966, formed by the two largest West German political parties: the Christian Democrats and the Social Democrats (SPD). As a junior party in the coalition, the SPD was able to play a significant role in outlining a common denominator for the new West German policy thrust toward achieving normalized relations with Eastern Europe. The foremost goal would continue to be the construction of a satisfactory solution to the German problem, but the approach would be changed. Later, the parliamentary elections of 1969 enabled the SPD to form the government, in coalition with the small Free Democratic Party (FDP), and to determine the basic guidelines of public policy.

The new government, led by Willy Brandt, fully conceded the reality of the two German states and abandoned the earlier legal claims. The new foundation regarding the German national question was: "Two states within one nation." Although it did not totally eliminate the core of the earlier posture, this new formulation buried the West German government's claim of superiority over the East German regime.

West Germany's new position, making both states equal, was consistent with an earlier East German position respecting the German question. The East German Socialist Unity Party of Germany (SED) had often expressed its commitment to the reestablishment of national unity. When Brandt began his new *Ostpolitik* initiatives, however, the GDR changed its position. Where before it had spoken of itself as a socialist state of German nation, reference was now made to a "socialist German nation-state." The new East German posture was designed to make possible a sharper ideological demarcation, to protect against possible undermining influences resulting from increased contacts with the West. With the Soviet Union's course set on détente, the East German regime had little choice but to respond to the West German policy initiatives, lest it face the prospect of isolation within the Communist camp.

Toward the end of 1969, the GDR expressed readiness for talks with the FRG, no longer insisting on its earlier precondition of formal diplomatic recognition. These developments led to the historic meeting between Brandt and Willi Stroph, chairman of the Council of Ministers of the GDR, in Erfurt on March 19, 1970. The subsequent negotiations between the two German states were very difficult and often intractable. Simultaneously, the West German government conducted talks with other Warsaw Pact states. Treaties with the Soviet Union and Poland were concluded, entailing the acceptance of the existing frontiers in central Europe, particularly the Oder-Neisse Line, thereby formally conceding the loss of the former German eastern territories. In return, the Eastern Bloc was expected to accept certain realities as well, such as West Berlin being a de facto part of the FRG.

To some extent, Bonn's concerns regarding the security of West Berlin were accommodated by the Four Power Agreement on Berlin signed on September 3, 1971. Essentially, this agreement reaffirmed West Berlin's special status. In addition, it made possible the achievement of practical improvements involving civilian traffic between West Germany and West Berlin, the facilitation and simplification of border clearance, and the general expansion of freedom of movement for West Berliners, all to be settled through specific arrangements between the governments of the GDR and the FRG or the Senate of West Berlin.

On November 8, 1972, Egon Bahr and Michael Kohl, the two principal negotiators in the West German-East German talks, initialed the Basic Treaty. The document provided for relations based on sovereign equality, peaceful settlement of disputes, respect for the signatories' territorial integrity, mutual support of arms control and disarmament, resolution of all problems of a practical and humanitarian nature, and the establishment of permanent missions in the respective capitals. A number of issues, varying in importance and scope, were treated in supplementary protocols. These included the resolution of problems relating to the border line, the creation of additional border crossings, the easing of travel restrictions for West Germans, the reuniting of families, the improvement of traffic in noncommercial goods, the working conditions for journalists, and the simultaneous application for membership in the United Nations.

The question regarding the continuing existence of the German nation was not settled by the Basic Treaty; it merely made it possible for both sides to maintain their differing legal positions. For West Germany, it was imperative to uphold the concept of one German nation, to insist that the relationship between the two German states

was of a special nature. There was no formal reference anywhere in the document to diplomatic relations. The substantial trade between the two states was to continue to be conducted on the basis of existing agreements. These agreements considered it to be intra-German, rather than foreign, trade. The GDR quietly accepted this arrangement because it provided substantial economic benefits. Nevertheless, the Basic Treaty entailed the mutual recognition of the signatories as sovereign states, irrespective of the specific terminology. The subsequent wave of de jure diplomatic recognitions of the GDR by Western and Third World countries and the existence of two German ambassadors in the capitals of the world legitimized and finalized the partition of Germany. In that sense, the German problem appeared to have been solved. A tolerable coexistence, rather than hostile confrontation, was given precedence. In short, the normalization of affairs and the attendant easing of the daily lives of the people of West Germany and East Germany was made possible.

The normalization of relations between the two Germanies was symbolic of the stabilization of relations between the two military-ideological blocs in Europe. Yet normalization also facilitated the increased exposure of East Germany to Western visitors and media. Toward the end of the following decade, East Germans' dissatisfaction with their living conditions would contribute to the overthrow of their Communist government and the subsequent absorption of the GDR by the FRG.

—Manfred Grote, updated by Steve D. Boilard

ADDITIONAL READING:

Birnbaum, Karl E. *East and West Germany: A Modus Vivendi*. Lexington, Mass.: D. C. Heath, 1973. A concise review of the so-called détente treaties of 1970-1972, including texts of the treaties.

Brandt, Willy. *People and Politics: The Years 1960-1975*. Translated by J. Maxwell Brownjohn. Boston: Little, Brown, 1978. The author of the New Ostpolitik describes the era of détente. A highly readable, personal account.

Hanrieder, Wolfram F. "A New Ostpolitik for the 1970s and 1980s." In *Germany, America, Europe: Forty Years of German Foreign Policy*. New Haven, Conn.: Yale University Press, 1989. Chapter 7 in Hanrieder's work provides penetrating analysis of the German problem in the late détente period. The entire book offers valuable historical background and contemporary evaluation of intra-German relations.

Hess, Frederick W., ed. *German Unity: Documentation and Commentaries on the Basic Treaty*. East Europe Monographs series, #4. Kansas City, Mo.: Park College

Governmental Research Bureau, 1974. Includes text of the Basic Treaty and analysis by scholars.

McAdams, A. James. *Germany Divided: From the Wall to Reunification*. Princeton, N.J.: Princeton University Press, 1993. Examines intra-German relations from the 1960's until reunification in 1990. Heavy emphasis on the events leading up to and surrounding the Basic Treaty. Includes extensive bibliography.

Whetten, Lawrence L. *Germany's Ostpolitik: Relations Between the Federal Republic and the Warsaw Pact Countries*. London: Oxford University Press for the Royal Institute of International Affairs, 1971. Although published before the signing of the Basic Treaty, this volume presents a valuable analysis of the logic behind Bonn's *Ostpolitik*.

SEE ALSO: 1949, Creation of Two German Republics; 1955, Warsaw Pact Is Signed; 1989, The Berlin Wall Falls; 1990, German Reunification.

1973
EUROPEAN SPACE AGENCY IS FORMED

The European Space Agency is formed, becoming a model of international cooperation by uniting many European countries to reach common scientific and commercial goals in space technology.

DATE: July 31, 1973

LOCALE: Brussels, Belgium

CATEGORIES: Government and politics; Science and technology

KEY FIGURES:

Edoardo Amaldi (1908-1989), cofounder of the European Space Research Organization

Pierre Auger (born 1899), cofounder of the European Space Research Organization

Charles-André-Marie-Joseph de Gaulle (1890-1970), president of France, 1958-1969

Roy Gibson (born 1924), director general of the European Space Agency, 1975-1981

Harold Macmillan (1894-1986), British prime minister, 1957-1963

Ulf Merbold (born 1941), West German astronaut aboard Spacelab

SUMMARY OF EVENT. At the dawn of the space age in 1957, the United States and the Soviet Union began to develop space programs, and the larger countries of Europe, such as France and Great Britain, followed suit. While the two superpowers could focus on orbiting satellites, large rocket launcher facilities, placing human beings into orbit, and the race to the moon, Europe had to satisfy itself with the launching of small sounding rockets into the upper atmosphere to study such phenomena as the aurora borealis.

As early as 1960, some Europeans working in the field of space science saw the need for space agencies of various European countries to work together in order to sponsor larger projects. Scientists Edoardo Amaldi of Italy and Pierre Auger of France witnessed the success of Conseil Europeen Pour La Recherche Nucleaire (CERN), an organization of European countries dedicated to nuclear research. Because of the pooled monies and efforts from the governments and scientists of many European countries, CERN was able to build many powerful particle accelerators. Amaldi and Auger thought it might be possible to have such an organization for space research, too.

On June 14, 1963, the European Space Research Organization (ESRO) was formed. Belgium, France, Italy, the Netherlands, Spain, Sweden, Switzerland, the United Kingdom, and West Germany were the initial members, followed later by Denmark. Norway and Austria agreed to be nonparticipating associate members. ESRO had a rocket engineering center in the Netherlands, a computer center in West Germany, and a research laboratory in Italy. Dedicated to space science research, ESRO had no plans to place human beings into space, and whenever they needed launcher facilities to place large satellites into space, they did so with the help of the United States. From 1964 until its demise in 1972, ESRO sent seven satellites into orbit around Earth and sent up a total of 183 small sounding rockets into the upper atmosphere. In the realm of atmospheric studies, ESRO was a success.

ESRO was not the only European space cooperative of the 1960's. Many European countries, in particular France, sought to go beyond small scale space science studies. On January 30, 1961, President Charles de Gaulle of France met with Prime Minister Harold Macmillan of Great Britain to discuss the possibility of the two countries working together to build a rocket launcher. No longer would Europe have to rely on the United States for such facilities. In February of 1964, the European Launcher Development Organization (ELDO) was formed. Australia, Belgium, France, Italy, the Netherlands, the United Kingdom, and West Germany signed the agreement, with Switzerland and Denmark as nonparticipating associate members. Australia would provide Woomera Range as a launching site. Belgium, Italy, and the Netherlands would develop the test satellites, guidance systems, and communications. Britain would be responsible for the first stage of the launcher, France for the second stage, and West Germany for the third stage. There were eleven ELDO launches in all. Ten Europa I rockets were launched from the Woomera Range, and one Europa II rocket was sent from Kourou in French Guinea on November 5, 1971, but none of the launches successfully put a satellite into orbit.

As early as the late 1960's many European representatives of both ESRO and ELDO were dissatisfied. Some claimed that ESRO stressed space science and small projects over rocket launcher development and larger projects. Many scientists and politicians chafed over having to rely on the United States for launchers. Others looked to ELDO's string of failures and pointed out that ELDO had no effective central authority nor enough money to do what it had originally planned. As the money allocated to ESRO was to run out in the early 1970's, some representatives of smaller countries expressed their dissatisfaction with programs that required all member countries to fully participate in all approved projects, whether or not they would receive direct benefits from these projects.

In June of 1967, a European Space Committee (ESC) met in Rome, Italy, to study the problems associated with ESRO and ELDO. In November of 1968, in Bad Godesberg, West Germany, a second ESC met and decided that the best solution would be to fuse ESRO and ELDO into one organization to be called the European Space Agency (ESA). A plan was developed that addressed Europe's need for the production of a successful rocket launcher and the subsequent launching of scientific and telecommunications satellites. Delegates of the ESC were chosen to iron out any difficulties and come up with specific programs that would reach the stated goals. At a meeting held in Brussels, Belgium, in December of 1972, a revised plan was submitted. Special projects included a plan whereby France would develop their launcher Ariane to replace Europa. West Germany would cooperate with American scientists from the National Aeronautics and Space Administration (NASA) to build Spacelab, a unit dedicated to scientific experiments that would be sent into space by NASA's space shuttle. The United Kingdom would develop a maritime communications satellite. The United Kingdom was also the source for ESA's first director general, Roy Gibson, who was formerly director general of ESRO.

The most significant aspect of the structure of ESA was its flexibility. Participating countries were required to contribute to ESA according to the size of their gross national products. This mandatory program would cover the general budget of ESA, its technological research, fellowships, and science program. Member countries of ESA could then select optional programs in which they were willing to participate, and separate agreements among participants would determine the amount each would pay and what benefits each would accrue.

The formation of the ESA was made official on July 31,

1973, in Brussels, Belgium. Austria, Belgium, Denmark, France, Ireland, Italy, the Netherlands, Norway, Spain, Sweden, Switzerland, the United Kingdom, and West Germany became the charter members of ESA, with Finland and Canada as associate members.

With the formation of ESA, Europe became the third largest space power in the world after the United States and the Soviet Union. While its budget is usually about one-tenth that of NASA, ESA's projects have been noteworthy successes. ESA assisted NASA with the Hubble Space Telescope by building the Faint Object Camera, and they also assisted NASA with the International Solar Polar Mission by building the Ulysses spacecraft. ESA's Giotto spacecraft was sent up to study Halley's Comet in 1986. Ariane, the rocket launcher developed by France, had the largest payload capability of any launcher of its time and it was the most utilized series of launchers for commercial satellites during the 1980's and the 1990's. The most publicized European success story began on September 24, 1973, in Washington, D.C., when West Germany signed an agreement with NASA to develop Spacelab for the United States space shuttle program. On November 28, 1983, Spacelab went into orbit with Europe's first astronaut, West Germany's Ulf Merbold, on board. During the ten-day flight, more than seventy scientific experiments were carried out by a seven-member crew. With these scientific and economic successes, Europe demonstrated to the world the benefits of international cooperation.

—Rose Secrest

ADDITIONAL READING:

Arnold, H. J. P., ed. "Space for All: The End of the Superpower Monopoly." In *Man in Space: An Illustrated History of Space Flight*. New York: Smithmark, 1993. Provides crucial information on the political situation that shaped the formation of the ESA. Illustrated with plenty of color photographs.

Bonnet, Roger M., and Vittorio Manno. "The Birth of ESA" and "Governing Principles." In *International Cooperation in Space: The Example of the European Space Agency*. Cambridge, Mass.: Harvard University Press, 1994. While the entire book gives a clear picture of how ESA operates, these two chapters are good introductory material that explains ESA's origins and structure.

"Europe in Space: The Emergence of ESA." *Sky and Telescope* 49 (May, 1975): 284-302. Summarizes the history of ESRO and ELDO and the founding of ESA. Also details ESA's major projects of the 1970's and 1980's.

Gibson, Roy. "National and Regional Space Activities: A Brief Survey." In *Space*. New York: Oxford University Press, 1992. From the former director general of ESA comes a book that discusses its predecessors ESRO and ELDO and its current setup.

Gibson, Roy, and Werner J. Kleen. "Europe's 'NASA' Gets off the Ground." *IEEE Spectrum* 13 (February, 1976): 66-70. Technical and detailed account of ESA's facilities and staff, as well as a listing of ESA's major projects of the 1970's and 1980's.

Zabusky, Stacia E. "The European Space Agency and the Structure of Cooperation." *In Launching Europe: An Ethnography of European Cooperation in Space Science.* Princeton, N.J.: Princeton University Press, 1995. An anthropological text on human cooperation, yet surprisingly helpful in showing how ESA is organized and what ESA's goals are.

SEE ALSO: 1957, Common Market Is Formed; 1957, Soviet Union Launches Sputnik; 1961, Soviet Union Puts a Human in Space; 1961, Organization for Economic Cooperation and Development Forms; 1963, Limited Nuclear Test Ban Treaty Is Signed.

1973
WEST GERMANY RESTRICTS IMMIGRATION OF FOREIGN WORKERS

West Germany restricts immigration of foreign workers, marking a change in the nation's postwar policies toward its foreign-born population.

DATE: November 23, 1973
LOCALE: West Germany
CATEGORIES: Business and labor; Government and politics; Immigration
KEY FIGURES:

Walter Arendt (born 1925), West German minister of labor and social welfare, 1969-1976
Willy Brandt (Herbert Ernst Karl Frahm; 1913-1992), chancellor of West Germany, 1969-1974
Josef Stingl (born 1919), director of the German Labor Exchange, 1968-1984

SUMMARY OF EVENT. The ban on labor immigration by the West German government, with the exception of the countries of the European Economic Community (EEC), was one of two closely related 1973 events that represented milestones in that government's immigration policy. The earlier event was the initiation of the "Action Program on the Employment of Foreigners" in June, 1973. This program was a response to the growing unemployment and lack of social integration of the foreign population. It included closer government scrutiny of foreign workers' housing, higher recruitment fees, and penalties for employers of illegal immigrants; measures that were designed to discourage foreign recruitment. This was part of a new policy of encouraging the voluntary return of the foreign born to their homelands, and promoting the integration of those who stayed. Since comprehensive forced repatriation was deemed unacceptable, the goal was to contain the "integration problem" by curtailing further foreign population growth. With that goal in mind, on November 23, 1973, the government announced a complete stop to all labor immigration from non-EEC nations.

In order to fully appreciate the significance of this event, it is necessary to understand the reasons for foreign labor recruitment and immigration policy objectives in West Germany after World War II. During this period, the age structure in West Germany was shaped in part by the low fertility rate during the war and the increase of that rate from 1945 to 1964. After that, the birthrate for the indigenous West German population dropped until the growth rate for that population became negative, which has been the case since 1972. The large labor-force age losses and small birth cohorts during the war combined with the postwar economic recovery and reconstruction of the military resulted in "overemployment," or, more jobs than workers, as early as 1955. The options for addressing this labor shortage were either to increase female labor force participation or to actively recruit foreign workers. The government, with the support of the labor unions, opted for the latter approach, because the former was predicted to be socially and economically disruptive.

Labor recruitment agreements were signed with Italy in 1955, and Spain and Greece in 1960. The building of the Berlin Wall in 1961 exacerbated the labor shortages, and additional agreements were signed with Turkey in 1961, Morocco in 1963, Portugal in 1964, Tunisia in 1965, and Yugoslavia in 1968. Foreign labor immigration was coordinated by West German government recruitment offices, and control was exerted through visas, and work and residence permits. The recruitment offices in foreign countries selected workers on the basis of their qualifications, health, and work record, issued them work and residence permits, and arranged transportation to West Germany. Employers were charged a recruitment fee.

The influx of "guest workers" was great until 1973 because this program was attractive to foreign workers and West Germans alike. The robust West German economy with its promise of jobs, and the generous structure of social welfare attracted immigrants. Foreign workers were legally entitled to publicly funded benefits, including child allowances, rent subsidies, and unemployment benefits. On the other hand, West Germany benefitted because of "overemployment," and what was seen as the enhancement of upward mobility of the indigenous population.

Several authors have asserted that immigrant laborers were predominantly recruited for the least skilled and most physically demanding jobs, making it possible for West German youths to attain more formal education. It was also claimed that the rebuilding of the West German army was similarly facilitated. Thus, foreign worker recruitment was seen as being desirable by West Germany until the large postwar birth cohorts created increases in unemployment rates. The response was the 1973 recruitment stop.

One must consider the history and nature of West German immigration policy in order to assess the importance of this measure. West Germany's lack of a comprehensive clearly stated immigration policy was a longstanding tradition by the post-World War II era. Foreign citizens had never been officially recognized as "immigrants" or "minorities," but only as "guest workers" or "foreigners." The government's position was that West Germany "was not a country of immigration." Therefore, the laws relating to labor recruitment and refugees constituted the country's immigration policy. The fundamental legislation that underlay all such laws during the height of worker recruitment was the Aliens Act of 1965. This act restated the principle that any foreigner's residence in West Germany would only be permitted as long as it was economically and politically beneficial to the host country. The position of the Aliens Act was that all foreigners in West Germany would eventually return home voluntarily, but it clearly stated that among the rights not extended to foreigners were the freedoms of movement, choice of occupation, place of work, place of education, and protection from extradition.

This position was reiterated in worker recruitment agreements that originally specified that work and residence permits would be issued for one year and renewed for one additional year, creating a system of forced rotation for foreign workers. As long as the demand for foreign labor continued, new guest workers could be recruited. By the mid-1960's, however, the principle of forced rotation after two years had been abandoned, and in 1971 a law was enacted allowing foreigners who had worked in West Germany for five years to obtain five-year extensions on their work permits. The need for the social and political integration of a large and growing foreign population was not anticipated by the West German government. By the early 1970's, it was apparent that foreign workers had become an indispensable part of the West German economy. They were doing jobs that West Germans would no longer do, and, by facilitating the upward mobility of the indigenous population, had secured a permanent niche at the low end of the paid labor force. By 1973, the need for more than just a guest worker policy was obvious.

The recruitment stop of 1973 became the foundation of West German immigration policy by accentuating the need for an expansion of policy objectives regarding the foreign-born population and for the development of more comprehensive legislation. This event, and the Action Program of 1973, which addressed deficiencies in foreigners' social services—housing, preschool education, and education in general—had the effect of increasing both the size and the unemployment rate of that population. The recruitment stop provided that a foreigner who had worked for three years in West Germany could obtain residence permits for his spouse and children under twenty-one if he or she could provide suitable housing. Children under sixteen required no residence permit. As a result, family reunification among foreigners increased dramatically in West Germany. Since work permits were not guaranteed for family reunification immigrants, the number of foreign employees did decrease as hoped, but the size of the immigrant population dropped very little, and began to increase by 1976, partly because of foreigners' relatively high birth rates.

Because of these circumstances, the government was moved to officially recognize a need to consider not only foreign workers' economic benefits to West Germany, but also these people's social needs. In 1975, the federal government initiated a program of immigrant employment, and produced the "Guidelines for an Immigration Policy." Both insisted that, although West Germany still was not an immigration country, there was a need to forge a policy that created a balance between the social and economic interests of West Germany and humanitarian concerns regarding immigrants' social needs. The suggested solution was to decrease the foreign population as much as possible without forced rotation, and promote the "temporary integration" of those remaining. These seemingly contradictory objectives resulted from the following factors: There was a demonstrated need for guest workers, who were complimenting, not competing with the indigenous labor force; humanitarian concerns over institutional discrimination affecting second and third generation immigrants' educational and career opportunities; projected future labor shortages, that could not be filled by uneducated and unskilled laborers, as the small post-1970 West German birth cohorts came of labor force age; and the possibility of future social, political, and economic instability that might result from the perpetuation of a permanent foreign-born underclass. The 1973 foreign worker recruitment stop continues to be a pivotal event in the ongoing debates over and changes in Germany's immigration policies.

—*Jack Carter*

ADDITIONAL READING:

Buechler, Hans Christian, and Judith-Maria Buechler, eds. *Migrants in Europe: The Role of Family, Labor, and Politics.* New York: Greenwood Press, 1987. Chapters examine the development of German labor migration policies from the perspective of two important countries of origin.

Collinson, Sarah. *Europe and International Migration.* London: Printer Publishers, 1993. This work provides an introduction to contemporary European labor and family immigration- and minorities-related issues.

Fassmann, Heinz, and Rainer Münz, eds. *European Migration in the Late Twentieth Century: Historical Patterns, Actual Trends, and Social Implications.* Laxenburg, Austria: Edgar Elgar, 1994. Included are chapters on the complexities of German immigration policy and on former sources of immigrant workers, such as Poland and Yugoslavia.

King, Russell, ed. *Mass Migrations in Europe: The Legacy and the Future.* London: Belhaven Press, 1993. Chapters examine worker recruitment's effect on German demographics, and contemporary and future German immigration.

Soysal, Yasemin Nuhoglu. *Limits of Citizenship: Migrants and Postnational Membership in Europe.* Chicago: University of Chicago Press, 1994. This work delves into the importance of European international organizations, such as the EEC.

SEE ALSO: 1949, Creation of Two German Republics; 1957, Common Market Is Formed; 1987, European Community Adopts the Single Europe Act; 1990, German Reunification; 1992, Protests and Violence Against Immigrants in Germany.

1974
PORTUGAL GRANTS INDEPENDENCE TO ITS AFRICAN COLONIES

Portugal grants independence to its African colonies, freeing itself from an economically disastrous series of wars and signaling the dissolution of one of the few remaining colonial empires.

DATE: 1974
LOCALE: Portugal
CATEGORY: Diplomacy and international relations
KEY FIGURES:

Amilcar Cabral (1926-1973), secretary general of the African Party for the Independence of Guinea and the Cape Verde Islands
Marcello José Das Neves Alves Caetano (1906-1980), dictator of Portugal, 1968-1974

Francisco da Costa Gomes (born 1914), president of Portugal, 1974-1976
António de Spínola (born 1910), president of Portugal, 1974

SUMMARY OF EVENT. At the middle of the twentieth century, the small European country of Portugal still retained nine colonies in various parts of the world: some small settlements in India, the port of Macau opposite Hong Kong on the Chinese coast, parts of the island of Timor in the East Indies, and the African territories of the Cape Verde Islands, Guinea, Ajudá, São Tomé and Príncipe, Angola, and Mozambique. These colonies had been in its possession for centuries, but change was in the air.

India invaded Goa and the other Portuguese settlements on the subcontinent in 1961, and annexed them quickly and with little bloodshed. The tiny enclave of Ajudá was seized by Dahomey the same year. More seriously, organized internal revolt had broken out as early as 1961 in Angola, in 1963 in Guinea, and in 1964 in Mozambique.

Although a minor European power, Portugal had long prided itself on its possession of an overseas colonial empire. Thus the loss of Ajudá and the settlements in India damaged the self-image of the nation and of its armed forces. The remaining African colonies, particularly Angola, were of far greater economic importance, and had attracted significant numbers of Portuguese settlers. The uprisings in these territories were countered at first by local troops, but their scale and vehemence soon forced Portugal to send large expeditionary forces to Africa, initiating a chain of events ruinous to the African territories and to Portugal itself. The result was that long after other European powers such as Great Britain and France had begun peaceful if reluctant programs of decolonization, Portugal found itself fighting lengthy, savage, and costly wars on a number of fronts. By 1974, nearly two hundred thousand Portuguese troops were involved.

Under dictator António de Oliveira Salazar and his successor Marcello José Das Neves Alves Caetano, retention of the colonies had been an article of faith. The first prominent Portuguese figure to question this policy was Senior Army General António de Spínola. A veteran of the fighting in Angola and Guinea, Spínola had witnessed the failure of Portugal's efforts, and had been reprimanded by Caetano for expressing a desire for a political solution to the conflict. He was also reported to have met secretly with Amilcar Cabral, secretary general of the African Party for the Independence of Guinea and the Cape Verde Islands (PAIGC) and a major architect of African resistance.

Spínola returned to Portugal in 1973 as chief of staff of

the armed forces, and proceeded to publish *Portugal and the Future* on February 22, 1974. It called publicly for liberalization of his country's government and for a political solution to its continuing wars. The book's publication led to Spínola's dismissal by Caetano on March 14, as well as the dismissal of Spínola's superior, General Francisco de Costa Gomes. Many of the junior army officers who had served under Spínola in Guinea went on to participate in a virtually bloodless coup on April 25, 1974, that ended Portugal's dictatorship.

Although Spínola was named the new government's provisional president, he and his colleagues held divergent opinions about Portugal's empire. Spínola himself hoped for a referendum in the colonies that would allow them to choose a loose union with Portugal. Spínola's fellow officers favored turning over control to the colonies' independence movements and an immediate withdrawal of troops. These differences led to Spínola's resignation on September 30, and his replacement by Costa Gomes, under whom Portugal's decolonization then took place.

As it turned out, public opinion in the colonies overwhelmingly favored immediate independence. Guinea was already largely controlled by an indigenous government, represented by PAIGC. Portugal recognized the country's independence (as Guinea-Bissau) on September 9, 1974, and withdrew its troops quickly and effortlessly.

The situation was more complicated in Angola, where the insurgents were splintered into a number of groups. At first, Spínola encouraged the formation of a government that would favor union with Portugal, a plan that fell through when Spínola himself left office. Portugal had negotiated a cease-fire with one of the groups, the Union for the Total Independence of Angola (UNITA), on June 17, 1974. Cease-fires with the National Front for the Liberation of Angola and the Popular Movement for the Liberation of Angola followed on October 14 and 21, respectively. Portugal managed to negotiate an official cease-fire with the Front for the Liberation of Mozambique on September 7, 1974. The resulting agreement called for significant cooperation between the two governments, both before and after a projected independence date of June 25, 1975, but rioting by Portuguese settlers threatened the fragile agreement. Subsequently as many as a thousand Europeans a week began fleeing the country.

The process of decolonization begun so hurriedly in 1974 was concluded, sometimes under almost equally adverse conditions, the following year. The situation in Angola was particularly chaotic. An agreement was reached January 15, setting up a transitional government in that country involving Portugal and the three major independence movements and leading to elections and total independence on November 11. Long before that date, however, Angola had slid into nearly total anarchy as various factions battled for supremacy. Portugal proceeded with a complete withdrawal of troops and declared Angola independent as of the agreed-upon date without transferring power to any of the competing parties.

Mozambique achieved independence on June 25 as scheduled, but in this case with a Portuguese official present to hand over power to the African majority. The Cape Verde Islands became independent July 5, after which it was anticipated that they would join in a union with Guinea-Bissau. Freedom followed for the island territory of São Tomé and Príncipe on July 12. None of the islands had been touched by the fighting on the mainland, and São Tomé and Príncipe in particular seemed inclined to pursue close ties with Portugal.

The Portuguese sections of the East Indian island of Timor declared their independence on November 28, 1975, but were invaded within days by Indonesian forces. This forced annexation, which resulted in continued bloodshed in the years ahead, was not recognized by Portugal. On the other hand, Portuguese authorities offered to return the enclave of Macau to China, but the latter declined. The two countries did, however, agree that Macau would become part of China by the end of the century.

Portugal's revolution and its subsequent abandonment of its empire lifted the weight of years of oppression and senseless combat. The colonial wars—the longest fought by any European power in the latter half of the twentieth century—had drained the national economy while provoking cynicism and suspicion among the country's population. Despite much initial euphoria, however, Portugal failed to prosper in the immediate post-revolutionary period. It was only during the mid-1980's that such problems as the flow of refugees from the former colonies were brought under control.

In most of the former colonies themselves conditions were far worse. Angola and Mozambique were both in ruins. Fighting among various liberation groups continued in the former country, and the loss of two hundred thousand Portuguese—many of them administrators and skilled workers—had crippled the latter. The Cape Verde Islands (which never attained union with Guinea) were debilitated by drought in the 1970's, as were São Tomé and Príncipe in the 1980's, and both territories found themselves dependent upon the steadily dwindling economic bases left by the Portuguese. In all the African territories Marxist-dominated governments pursued authoritarian political and social programs that generally exacerbated the countries' problems. *—Grove Koger*

ADDITIONAL READING:

Birmingham, David. "The Dictatorship and the African Empire." In *A Concise History of Portugal*. New York: Cambridge University Press, 1993. A succinct history of Portugal and its empire from the late 1920's to the revolution of 1974. A subsequent chapter examines the aftermath of the revolution.

Gallagher, Tom. *Portugal: A Twentieth-Century Interpretation*. Manchester, England: Manchester University Press, 1983. A political analysis concentrating on events since the proclamation of the first Portuguese Republic in 1910. Several of the latter chapters treat the colonial wars in Africa.

Grayson, George W. "Portugal and the Future." *Current History* 68 (March, 1975): 109-113. Good background on the 1974 revolution and its implications for the empire, and an early evaluation of António de Spínola's rise and fall.

Henriksen, Thomas H. "End of an Empire: Portugal's Collapse in Africa." *Current History* 68 (May, 1975): 211-215. A brief examination of latter-day resistance to Portuguese rule in Africa. Particularly good on the complicated situations in Angola and Mozambique.

Hunt, Christ. *Portuguese Revolution, 1974-76*. New York: Facts On File, 1976. A day-by-day account of the revolution, but with many references to events involving the colonies.

Wheeler, Douglas L. *Historical Dictionary of Portugal*. Metuchen, N.J.: Scarecrow Press, 1993. An A-Z arrangement of brief articles about Portugal, the empire, and the leading figures involved in their history. Concludes with a lengthy bibliography.

SEE ALSO: 1910, Republic of Portugal Is Proclaimed; 1968, Caetano Becomes Premier of Portugal.

1974

SOLZHENITSYN IS EXPELLED FROM THE SOVIET UNION

Solzhenitsyn is expelled from the Soviet Union, resulting in a crushing blow to the dissident movement within the Soviet Union.

DATE: February 13, 1974

LOCALE: The Soviet Union; Frankfurt, West Germany; Zurich, Switzerland; and Cavendish, Vermont

CATEGORIES: Cultural and intellectual history; Government and politics

KEY FIGURES:

Heinrich Böll (1917-1985), West German writer and friend of Solzhenitsyn

Mikhail P. Malyrov, deputy prosecutor general of the Soviet Union

Aleksandr Solzhenitsyn (born 1918), Soviet writer

Natalia Svetlova, Solzhenitsyn's second wife

Elizaveta Voronyanskaya, Solzhenitsyn's former secretary

SUMMARY OF EVENT. On February 12, 1974, Soviet writer Aleksandr Solzhenitsyn was arrested for the second time in his life. His first arrest had been in 1945, and had been followed by imprisonment in the Soviet camp (Gulag) system. The second arrest was followed by exile from his native country, the first famous Soviet citizen to be expelled from his country since Leon Trotsky in 1929.

Solzhenitsyn had created a sensation when his *One Day in the Life of Ivan Denisovich* was published in 1962 in the Soviet literary magazine, *Novy mir*. This novel portrays in grim detail life in a Stalinist concentration camp—a life to which Solzhenitsyn himself had been unjustly condemned—and is a damning indictment of the Stalinist past. Beginning in 1964, under Leonid Brezhnev, the Soviet Union began a period of limited "re-Stalinization." For Solzhenitsyn this meant that none of his subsequent novels were to be published in the Soviet Union, although they did circulate clandestinely, through *samizdat* or self-publication.

For some time before Solzhenitsyn's arrest, rumors had circulated within the Soviet Union that he had written a large work about the Soviet concentration camp system. In late 1973, the Soviet secret police (Komitet Gosudarstvennoi Bezopasnosti, or KGB) brought in for interrogation a Leningrad woman, Elizaveta Voronyanskaya, who had once worked as a secretary for Solzhenitsyn. After five days and five nights of nonstop interrogation and torture, she finally told KGB agents where she had hidden a manuscript of *The Gulag Archipelago*, an exposé of the Soviet camp system. The work also exposed the inherent illegitimacy of the regime and every Soviet leader, including Vladimir Ilich Lenin. The regime could not tolerate this. Shortly after her release, Voronyanskaya was found dead of an apparent suicide, although Solzhenitsyn believed that the KGB had killed her.

On January 14, 1974, *Pravda* published an 1,800-word commentary, "The Path of a Traitor," by I. Solovyov, a pseudonymous author. This article set in greatest detail yet, the case against Solzhenitsyn. He was accused of being a counterrevolutionary, an internal émigré, and a defector to the camp of the enemies of peace, democracy, and socialism by attempting to disrupt détente. The article also asserted that Solzhenitsyn had been a renegade from the beginning, was anti-patriotic, anti-Russian, and pro-German (the equivalent of being a Nazi). He was further

Although he was expecting to face lengthy imprisonment on charges of treason as a result of his writings, Aleksandr Solzhenitsyn was deprived of his Soviet citizenship and deported to the West in February of 1974. (Archive Photos)

characterized as a rich speculator, who owned three cars and a dacha (country cottage) and had earned a small fortune from his "anti-Soviet lampoons." Other Soviet publications followed *Pravda*'s lead, and in a radio broadcast, an old adversary, Sergei Mikhilov, stated that no one would hold Solzhenitsyn back if he should find a place in another society. Mikhilov said he doubted that Solzhenitsyn would go voluntarily. Solzhenitsyn and his second wife, Natalia Svetlova, were threatened, but things eventually quieted down and Solzhenitsyn believed that the authorities were unlikely to do anything in the near future.

On February 11, 1974, Solzhenitsyn left the dacha of Kornei Chukovsky at Peredelkino, where he did his writing, for Moscow. The next day, two men from the prosecutor's office knocked on his apartment door in Moscow. When Solzhenitsyn opened the door, they burst inside, followed by six others who had been waiting around the corner of the landing. Their leader gave Solzhenitsyn a document to sign and informed him that he must accom-

pany them to the prosecutor's office immediately. Ironically, Solzhenitsyn had described just such a procedure in the opening pages of *The Gulag Archipelago*. Before he left the apartment, Solzhenitsyn put on a threadbare cap and a sheepskin overcoat that he had preserved from his previous imprisonment and that he had been saving for such an eventuality.

At Lefortovo prison, where he was taken, Solzhenitsyn was stripped and searched and forced to hand over his watch and other belongings. Soon after his arrival, Solzhenitsyn was summoned from his cell by Colonel Komarov, the prison commandant, and led into the office of Mikhail P. Malyrov, the deputy prosecutor general of the Soviet Union. Malyrov informed Solzhenitsyn that he was being charged under Article 64 of the penal code, with treason—a charge that carried a penalty ranging from ten years in prison to the death penalty. Solzhenitsyn told Malyrov that he would take no part in the investigation or subsequent trial.

The next day, February 13, Solzhenitsyn was given a suit and new shoes, a fresh white shirt, a tie, an overcoat and a cap. In Malyrov's office he was informed that he was being deported and deprived of his Soviet citizenship. A limousine drove him to Sheremetovo Airport, where he was placed in the forward cabin of a waiting Aeroflot jet. Accompanying him were seven secret agents and one doctor, all in civilian clothes. The plane was a regularly scheduled flight to Frankfurt-am-Main in West Germany (although Solzhenitsyn did not know that). The flight had been held back for three hours and other passengers had been told that the delay was the result of fog.

Solzhenitsyn's parting words to his countrymen dated to the day he was arrested and were published a few days later by Western newspapers under the title, "Live not by Lies." It called upon Soviet citizens to assert their spiritual liberation simply by refusing to participate in the system's official lies. It was to be the first piece to be printed in the Soviet press while Solzhenitsyn was in the West in 1989.

The flight arrived in Frankfurt at 4:00 P.M. local time (6:00 P.M. Moscow time). One of the secret service men handed Solzhenitsyn a gift from the KGB, five hundred German marks. As Solzhenitsyn stepped from the plane, he was greeted by Peter Dingens, a German official, who greeted him on behalf of the German foreign ministry. Solzhenitsyn was then driven to the country home of his old friend, Heinrich Böll, in the hamlet of Langenbrouck, west of Bonn.

Natalia Svetlova and the children were in complete ignorance of what was happening to Solzhenitsyn until he finally called them from Böll's house. On March 29, a little more than six weeks after Solzhenitsyn's expulsion, his family was allowed to leave Moscow, preceded by 1,400 pounds of baggage, including part of Solzhenitsyn's archive and library.

By the time his family was able to leave the Soviet Union, Solzhenitsyn was living in Zurich, Switzerland, having rejected both West Germany and Norway as possible locations for his exile. He eventuality tired of the publicity and attention he attracted in Switzerland. After a tour of the United States, he decided to move with his family to a secluded area of Vermont, near the town of Cavendish. He and his family remained there until after the fall of the Soviet Union. Solzhenitsyn's return to Russia in May of 1994 fulfilled his prophecy that he would one day return to his homeland, but it was quite a different country from the one he had left.

From the government's point of view, the exile of Solzhenitsyn was the right strategy. To have put Solzhenitsyn on trial and in jail would have created worldwide reaction, disrupted relations with the West, and put an end to détente. Expulsion allowed the regime to rid itself of its most bitter opponent, while avoiding charges of cruelty and oppression.

To Solzhenitsyn, exile abroad was the equivalent of execution by shooting. It was also a crushing blow to his hopes of continuing his fight against oppression within the Soviet Union. His exile was also a serious blow to the dwindling band of Soviet dissidents. —*Donald L. Layton*

ADDITIONAL READING:

Dunlop, John, Richard Haugh, and Michael Nicholson, eds. *Solzhenitsyn in Exile: Critical Essays and Documentary Materials.* Stanford, Calif.: Hoover Institute/Stanford University Press, 1985. This collection contains an important memoir by Lidia Chukovskaia, a dissident novelist and friend of Solzhenitsyn.

Erickson, Edward E., Jr. *Solzhenitsyn and the Modern World.* Washington, D.C.: Regnery Gateway, 1993. A scholarly reassessment of Solzhenitsyn's ideas and their relevance for the modern world.

Rzhevsky, Leonid. *Solzhenitsyn: Creator and Heroic Deed.* Translated from Russian by Sonja Miller. University: University of Alabama Press, 1978. A study of Solzhenitsyn's literary works by a Russian critic living in the United States.

Scammel, Michael. *Solzhenitsyn: A Biography.* New York: W. W. Norton, 1984. This biography puts heavy emphasis on the nature of the society in which Solzhenitsyn lived and its impact upon him.

Solzhenitsyn, Aleksandr I. *The Oak and the Calf.* Translated from Russian by Harry Willets. New York: Harper & Row, 1975. These memoirs take their title from

a Russian proverb in which a tender calf, oblivious to the odds against him, keeps butting his head against a massive oak tree trying to knock it down.

SEE ALSO: 1966-1991, Soviet Intellectuals Express Disagreement with Party Policy; 1975, Helsinki Agreement; 1985, Gorbachev Is Elected General Secretary of the Communist Party; 1991, Soviet Union Dissolves into Loosely Allied Republics.

1974
IRA TERRORISTS BOMB PARLIAMENT BUILDING

IRA terrorists bomb the Parliament building, attacking the symbol of English parliamentary law and government in its terrorist campaign to force British withdrawal from Northern Ireland.

DATE: June 17, 1974
LOCALE: London, England
CATEGORIES: Government and politics; Terrorism and political assassination
KEY FIGURES:
Daniel O'Connell (1775-1847), founder of the Repeal Association
Charles Stewart Parnell (1846-1891), Irish nationalist leader and member of Parliament, 1875-1891
John Edward Redmond (1856-1918), Irish nationalist leader and member of Parliament, 1881 and 1891-1918
Theobald Wolfe Tone (1763-1798), founder of the Society of United Irishmen
Lord Harold James Wilson (1916-1995), British prime minister, 1964-1970 and 1974-1976
SUMMARY OF EVENT. The genesis of England's claim to Ireland lies in an agreement between King Henry II and Pope Adrian IV in the twelfth century, when the pope granted the king lordship of Ireland. Norman invasions followed and for several hundred years the English maintained and enforced their intermittently challenged power.

During the eighteenth and nineteenth centuries, a number of Irish nationalist movements emerged. In radically different ways, two Catholic barristers—Theobald Wolfe Tone and Daniel O'Connell—greatly influenced the development of Irish nationalism. In 1791, Wolfe Tone formed the Society of the United Irishmen, whose armed actions in 1798 became the ideal for many later Irish nationalists. The United Irishmen's color, green, was adopted as the national color. Daniel O'Connell, the leader of the emancipation movement, supported constitutional rather than revolutionary action.

On January 1, 1801, the Act of Union between Great Britain and Ireland was enacted, thereby ending the five-hundred-year-old Irish Parliament. It moved the political power from Ireland to Westminster (the Houses of Parliament), and established the United Kingdom. In 1830, O'Connell began campaigning for the repeal of the Act of Union, and he founded the Repeal Association in 1840. For a while, the Young Ireland movement supported O'Connell, but the Young Irelanders left the Repeal Association in 1845 and openly advocated rebellion, a "holy war to sweep this island clear of the English name and nation." The British politicians used the increased sectarian unrest to justify their refusal to support the repeal. O'Connell's constitutional approach, however, served as a model for the Irish Home Rule Party of Charles Stewart Parnell in the late nineteenth century, and of John Redmond in the early twentieth century.

The English Liberal Party's third Home Rule Bill passed in 1914, and was signed into law on August 4, 1914. Since the United Kingdom had declared war on Germany six weeks prior to the act's passage, it was

Onlookers view the smoky aftermath of a bomb that exploded near Westminster Hall and the Houses of Parliament in London. (Archive Photos)

decided the act would not be implemented until the war was concluded.

Meanwhile, in 1905, Sinn Féin (a Gaelic phrase meaning "ourselves alone"), a more extreme Irish nationalist movement was formed. Their initial support for home rule was dropped in 1917 in favor of securing "international recognition of Ireland as an independent Irish republic." Sinn Féin members won seats in the 1918 General Election. In 1919, they established Sinn Féin's constituent Assembly, the Dáil Éireann (parliament of Ireland), by whose order the Irish Republican Army (IRA) officially came into existence. The first IRA campaign against the British administration lasted from 1919 to 1921.

The combined political and military campaign by Irish nationalists prompted Britain to reconsider its view of Ireland as a single unit. In 1920, the British legislature passed the Government of Ireland Act dividing Ireland into two separate states, the Republic of Ireland (Eire), containing twenty-six of Ireland's thirty-two counties, and Northern Ireland, containing the remaining six counties. A bloody civil war broke out in Eire in 1922 involving "savage atrocities on both sides" until its end in 1923.

The Ulster parliament in Northern Ireland held considerable local powers even though they were circumscribed by the British government. In 1922, in order to contain sectarian conflict and civil disorder, the Special Powers Act was passed and renewed annually until 1933, when it was made permanent. It encompassed a wide range of regulations including curfews, searches without a warrant, legal forcible entry, and the banning of organizations such as the IRA. The Protestant paramilitary organizations were not outlawed until the 1960's.

The IRA's drive to oust the British from Northern Ireland increased between 1955 and 1962, in the so-called Border Campaign. The Protestant Unionist Party won the 1965 election and the Nationalist Party became, for the first time, the official opposition. Antagonism, acted out in civil disobedience and violence increased throughout the 1960's. An illegal march from Belfast to Londonderry in October, 1968, erupted into rioting. The following summer, serious rioting resumed in Londonderry. For the first time since 1922, Westminster became directly involved in Northern Ireland when it sent the British Army to intervene. As terrorist violence between Catholics and Protestants increased, the Provisional IRA, a breakaway faction of the IRA, was formed.

In August of 1971, the British government introduced internment, the holding without trial of people suspected of terrorist violence. When Harold Wilson's government ended it four years later in December of 1975, 2,158 people had been interned. The techniques used by the

British on some of those detained led the Irish government to enter a petition against Britain in the European Commission on Human Rights. (In 1978, Britain was exonerated of the charge of torture, but was found guilty of degrading and inhuman treatment.) In 1972, the British government assumed direct rule of Northern Ireland, and Westminster's Northern Ireland Act replaced the Special Powers Act of 1933.

On January 1, 1974, a new power-sharing executive body of Protestants and Catholics took office in Northern Ireland. This followed twenty-one months of British rule during which the death rate from killings had fallen and the number of explosions had decreased. Yet the arrival of the year 1974 was accompanied by an event familiar to the people of Northern Ireland. Outside a Roman Catholic dance hall in Glenary, a bomb believed to have been planted by Protestant extremists exploded, injuring five people. On January 2, the government of the Irish Republic announced that anyone seeking refuge in the Irish Republic while accused of murder in Northern Ireland would be brought to trial in Irish courts. For the first time in four years, the IRA singled out an individual by name for execution by imposing a "death sentence" on Francis Pym, the secretary of state for Northern Ireland, on January 3. The following day the Unionist Party, the largest Protestant party in Northern Ireland, defeated a proposal that would have allowed Northern Ireland to enter the Council of Ireland.

Throughout the first half of 1974, bombings and terrorist attacks were reported almost daily in Belfast and London. In February, on the eve of the British General Election, the Provisional wing of the IRA took responsibility for major bomb attacks in Belfast. Election results showed hard-line Protestants had won eleven of the twelve seats in the British House of Commons. March brought renewed violence in London, Manchester, and Birmingham. By May, the terrorism had spread to Dublin, where three car bombs killed twenty-three people and critically injured eighty others. On May 19, Britain declared a state of emergency. When an Irish prisoner serving a jail sentence in England died in June, following a two-month hunger strike, the IRA threatened reprisals.

On June 16, one of the world's most famous paintings, Adoration of the Magi by Peter Paul Rubens, was defaced by IRA members in King's College Chapel, Cambridge. The next day at 8:28 A.M., a twenty-pound bomb exploded, injuring eleven people and causing considerable damage to Westminster Hall adjoining the Houses of Parliament. Built in the eleventh century by King William Rufus and improved three centuries later by Richard II, the Hall was part of the original Royal Palace of Westminster and was used for special occasions only. It had survived a fire in 1834 and bombing attacks during World War II. Two thousand people visited the Hall daily. Six minutes before the explosion, a man telephoned the Press Association. Using the IRA code word that identified his call as genuine, he warned of the event. Neither the House of Lords nor the House of Commons were damaged, but for several hours smoke shrouded Big Ben as firemen fought the blaze fed by an ignited gas main. Security at the Houses of Parliament and surrounding the British royal family was immediately strengthened. Since August of 1969, the campaign of violence had resulted in 1,040 deaths. There were fears that the IRA would increase their violent attacks. The IRA's Provisional wing warned that until Britain declared its intention of withdrawing from the province the attacks would continue.   *—Susan E. Hamilton*

ADDITIONAL READING:

Conner, Ulick, ed. *Irish Liberation*. New York: Grove Press, 1975. An anthology of major writings dealing with the theme of Irish liberation including contemporary reports, essays, and stories.

Finnegan, Richard B. *Ireland: The Challenge of Conflict and Change*. Boulder, Colo.: Westview Press, 1983. An introduction to Ireland's history, society, economy, government, and politics, and a thoughtful examination of changes during the 1960's and 1970's.

Ranelagh, John O'Beirne. *A Short History of Ireland*. New York: Cambridge University Press, 1994. A highly readable concise history covering pre-Norman to 1993, that presents a clear and objective account of the conflict in Northern Ireland, and contains an excellent bibliography.

Wright, Joanne. *Terrorist Propaganda, the Red Army Faction, and the Provisional IRA, 1968-86*. New York: St. Martin's Press, 1990. This complex examination of terrorist violence presents the ideology and propaganda of the Provisional IRA.

SEE ALSO: 1916, Easter Rebellion; 1932, Eamon de Valera Is Elected President of the Irish Dáil; 1972, "Bloody Sunday" in Northern Ireland; 1976, IRA Hunger Striker Dies in an English Prison; 1985, Anglo-Irish Agreement Is Signed; 1993, Ulster Peace Accord.

1975
HELSINKI AGREEMENT

The Helsinki Agreement provides for increased security and economic cooperation between the two military blocs in Europe, while at the same time providing mechanisms for challenging human rights abuses in the Soviet bloc.

DATE: August 1, 1975
LOCALE: Helsinki, Finland
CATEGORY: Diplomacy and international relations
KEY FIGURES:
Leonid Ilich Brezhnev (1906-1982), first secretary of the
    Communist Party of the Soviet Union, 1964-1982
Gerald Rudolph Ford (born 1913), thirty-eighth
    president of the United States, 1974-1977
Valéry Giscard d'Estaing (born 1926), president of
    France, 1974-1981
Henry Alfred Kissinger (born 1923), U.S. secretary of
    state, 1973-1977
Helmut Schmidt (born 1918), chancellor of the Federal
    Republic of Germany, 1974-1982
SUMMARY OF EVENT. The Conference on Security and
Cooperation in Europe (CSCE), held in Helsinki, invites
comparison with the Congress of Vienna in 1815. Unlike
the latter, the "Congress" of Helsinki never danced, but it
was a similarly momentous diplomatic undertaking and
may be considered the beginning of a new era. The gathering of such ranking world statesmen as Gerald Ford,
Henry Kissinger, Leonid Brezhnev, Valéry Giscard
d'Estaing, Helmut Schmidt, and the many others representing the thirty-five participating states during the final
ceremonies, gave fleeting form to a vision of Europe free
of confrontations and divisions. The CSCE formally
opened at the foreign ministers level on July 3, 1973, in
Helsinki and concluded there on August 1, 1975, when the
national leaders of the United States, Canada, the Soviet
Union, and thirty-two European countries (including the
ministates) signed the Final Act. The actual working phase
of the CSCE was held in Geneva, Switzerland, from September, 1973, to July, 1975. The Final Act, the so-called
Helsinki Agreement, must be regarded as a political statement of intent, rather than a legally binding treaty.

The Soviet Union had first proposed such a conference
as early as 1954, but at that time the United States and its
allies were not receptive to the idea. The subject was again
broached in July, 1966, by the Bucharest Declaration of
the Warsaw Pact members. Although the relaxation of
tensions between East and West in the 1960's made the
prospect for such a conference less remote, the Soviet-led
invasion of Czechoslovakia in 1968 foreclosed serious
Western consideration of the proposal at that time. Moscow continued to pursue the matter. The need to convene
an all-European conference on security and cooperation
was a dominant theme in Soviet statements concerning
European affairs. The keen Soviet interest in the CSCE
was, obviously, based on the fact that such a conference
could serve the Soviet Union most beneficially in several
different ways. One of these was the possible furtherance

of the longstanding objective of driving a wedge between
the United States and Western Europe. While campaigning for the CSCE, the Soviets depicted the United States
as the main obstacle to peace and security in Europe.
American opposition to the conference unless certain conditions were met was decried as evidence of the incom-
patibility of basic American and European interests.

Eventually the Warsaw Pact states accepted the conditions imposed by the United States and Canada in the
conference; an agreement on Berlin providing for improved conditions; and the holding of talks for the mutual
reduction of armed forces. Thus, multilateral preparatory
talks began in November, 1972, and established sufficient
common ground to justify the convocation of the CSCE.
As to the actual holding of the conference, Moscow was
most eager to secure multilateral recognition of the prevailing conditions in Central and Eastern Europe. On the
basis of such a consolidated position, the Soviet leaders
then intended to pursue more economic and technological
cooperation with the major Western nations and to enter-
tain considerations on mutual force reductions in Central
Europe. The United States and Western Europe saw an
opportunity in Moscow's strong interest in the CSCE to
facilitate progress in the human rights area; concessions
by the East on human rights issues were to be the quid pro
quo for the formal acknowledgment by the West of prevailing circumstances.

The Helsinki Agreement consists of a declaration of
principles guiding the relations between the signatories
and three main sections, referred to by the term "basket."
Basket One contains so-called confidence-building measures, security, and disarmament. Outlined in this section
are ways and means by which military confidence can be
strengthened and tension reduced, thereby diminishing
the danger of war between the signatories. Basket Two
contains a variety of measures which are expected to
enhance economic, scientific, technical, and environmental cooperation. Such areas as commercial exchanges,
industrial cooperation, and the promotion of tourism are
referred to. Basket Three includes cooperation in humanitarian and other fields. In this section are to be found
statements advocating the freer movement of people,
ideas, and information; family reunification and visits;
binational marriages; travel; access to printed, broadcast,
and filmed information; improved working conditions for
journalists; and increased cultural and educational exchanges.

The Western emphasis regarding the Helsinki Agreement was on improvement, not on the freezing of the
status quo. The United States, in particular, pressed the
Soviet Union and other East European states to follow

through on implementing the provisions of the Final Act. Basket Three drew the most public attention in the United States, which engaged in an intensified campaign for human rights during the presidency of Jimmy Carter.

The Helsinki Agreement came under strong criticism immediately after the signing. The principal argument of the opponents was that Moscow made rich gains, while the West obtained only meager ones at best. It was charged that, by agreeing to the inviolability of the existing frontiers, the stamp of legitimacy was put on the Soviet annexations of territory, including the former Baltic states of Estonia, Latvia, and Lithuania. Along with exiled Soviet writer Aleksandr Solzhenitsyn, opponents warned that any concessions to the Soviet Union would only help consolidate the oppressive regime; they saw the Soviet Union deceitfully using détente to lull the West into complacency.

Although the Soviet bloc may well have bought some time with the trade opportunities and security guarantees provided by the Helsinki Accords, Basket Three turned out to be the sleeper clause that helped facilitate the ultimate demise of the Communist regimes. The several follow-up meetings to the CSCE examined the progress (or lack thereof) in terms of human rights, and provided an international forum for Soviet and other East European dissidents to point to abuses by their regimes. Basket Three provided moral support and institutional power to human rights movements in the Soviet bloc, and helped to galvanize a set of international expectations which Soviet leader Mikhail Gorbachev sought to address in the late 1980's. In trying to meet those expectations, Gorbachev presided over the ultimate demise of the eastern bloc.

—Manfred Grote, updated by Steve D. Boilard

ADDITIONAL READING:

Bleed, A., and P. Van Dijk, eds. *Essays on Human Rights in the Helsinki Process.* Dordrecht, the Netherlands: Martinus Nijhoff, 1985. A collection of essays examining the follow-up meeting to the Helsinki Conference at Madrid between 1980 and 1983. Most essays assess the value of and prospects for Basket Three provisions.

Maresca, John J. *To Helsinki: The Conference on Security and Cooperation in Europe, 1973-1975.* Durham, N.C.: Duke University Press, 1985. An in-depth analysis of the Helsinki Conference and the agreement that ultimately emerged from it. Includes text of the agreements.

Novak, Michael. *Taking Glasnost Seriously: Toward an Open Soviet Union.* Washington, D.C.: American Enterprise Institute for Public Policy Research, 1988. An assessment of the Soviet Union's willingness to meet the spirit of the Helsinki Accords as part of Gorbachev's reform program. The book is a collection of speeches the author gave at the Helsinki Review Conference on Human Contacts in 1986. The author generally supports the value of the Helsinki process, although they are frequently critical of the Soviet Union.

Redefining the CSCE: Challenges and Opportunities in the New Europe. New York: Institute for East-West Studies, 1992. An assessment of the Helsinki Process at it entered its second phase ("Helsinki II") after the end of the Cold War. Since the collapse of communism in Europe, the CSCE has become a more permanent institution (called the Organization for Security and Cooperation in Europe) and is characterized by greater cooperation between East and West.

Russell, Harold S. "The Helsinki Declaration: Brobdingnag or Lilliput?" *American Journal of International Law* 70 (April, 1976): 242-272. A principal U.S. negotiator at Helsinki offers an insider's assessment of the Final Act's legal provisions.

SEE ALSO: 1955, Warsaw Pact Is Signed; 1961, Amnesty International Is Founded; 1963, Limited Nuclear Test Ban Treaty Is Signed; 1968, Soviet Union Invades Czechoslovakia; 1979, SALT II Is Signed; 1987, Intermediate-Range Nuclear Forces Treaty.

1975
DEATH OF FRANCO

The death of Franco ends authoritarian dictatorship in Spain and elevates King Juan Carlos as head of state.

DATE: November 20, 1975
LOCALE: Spain
CATEGORY: Government and politics
KEY FIGURES:
Francisco Franco (1892-1975), fascist dictator of Spain, 1936-1975
Juan Carlos (born 1938), king of Spain beginning in 1975

SUMMARY OF EVENT. From his victory over the Second Republic on April 1, 1939, until his death on November 20, 1975, Francisco Franco ruled as the undisputed leader of Spain. Immediately after the Spanish Civil War, Franco imposed a stifling repression on Spanish society. He enjoyed refereeing disputes between the fascist Falange movement, the army, and the Roman Catholic Church. Such quarrels only increased his power, encouraging many to believe that Franco was indispensable.

Franco wielded more power than any Spanish king. Franco ruled as chief of the Falange Española, prime minister, chief of state, and commander in chief of the armed forces. As such, his position was almost unassailable.

The physical and ideological exhaustion of Spain from its bloody civil war also contributed to the longevity of Franco's rule. With the beginning of World War II in September, 1939, the people of Spain feared renewed conflict. Marxist leaders either became swallowed up in Moscow or sulked in exile in Latin America or western Europe. Catalonia and the Basque provinces suffered severe repression; no self-government was permitted and local dances and dialects were prohibited. Such regional deterioration made Franco the first Spanish ruler to have absolute control over the entire country. Shortages of food supplies produced general suffering that continued until the 1950's. To avenge the death of so many of his followers during the Spanish Civil War, Franco executed tens of thousands of Republicans and imprisoned many more.

With the end of World War II, the Roman Catholic Church recovered its dominant position in Spanish society. The Church chose the minister of education, civil marriages were decreed null, and the Church again received state subsidies and land that had earlier been seized by Republican authorities. Even the Falange was ordered to bow to clerical objections concerning publication. The Church also received permission to impose a suffocating campaign against any behavior (dancing) or form of personal attire (bare legs, dresses, bathing suits) deemed to be indecent, suggestive, or immoral.

The army remained the foundation of the regime until Franco's death. The army supported Franco partially because he was one of their most illustrious figures, having been the youngest general in Europe during the 1920's. Like Franco, the army was conservative and not rigidly fascist in its political leanings. Army officers held important positions in the national administration, police, and local government for decades.

The aristocracy had minimal influence with Franco, but hundreds of dukes, marquises, counts, and viscounts continued to enjoy their established privilege. The number of landowners may have shrunk during the civil war, but the amount of land they owned increased. Towns and villages were often answerable to the local landowners. Franco frequently allowed landowners to use concentration camp prisoners as day laborers for a fee of a peseta per person.

The monarchists also worked behind the scenes to restore the royal family. The Carlists aided the monarchists' efforts greatly, because the Carlists rightly considered themselves and the Moors as the shock troops of the nationalist forces. Franco disliked Don Juan, the pretender to the Spanish throne, but decided to restore the monarchy in 1947. Franco had good relations with Prince Juan Carlos and approved his 1961 engagement to Princess Sofia,

eldest daughter of King Paul and Queen Frederika of Greece. The Spanish dynasty provided the regime with a traditional continuity that was favored by nearly everyone. Problems arose because Franco had deliberately left open the question of when and how the transition of power would take place. Nevertheless, Prince Juan Carlos began to stand at Franco's elbow on important occasions.

By the 1960's, Franco began to age noticeably. Nearly seventy years old, he was suffering from Parkinson's disease, a paralytic illness caused by the progressive degeneration of nerve cells at the base of the brain. Hastening his physical demise was a hunting accident that Franco suffered on Christmas Eve, 1961. His shotgun exploded in his left hand, seriously injuring it. This incident made Franco's followers realize that he was indeed mortal. Although the injury caused him considerable pain, Franco broadcast his traditional end-of-the-year message. By 1968, Franco began to withdraw completely into leisure pursuits and family activities to the growing exclusion of official duties. On January 15, 1969, Franco finally informed Juan Carlos that he would be officially designated as the political heir.

Franco's final years were agonizing. In the summer of 1974, Franco had to be hospitalized because he suffered phlebitis in his right leg. Shortly afterward, Franco suffered a major relapse, probably from watching a television program concerning his career. The next day, Prince Juan Carlos took over as head of state. Nevertheless, the stubborn Franco resumed his duties on September 9, 1974, despite the necessity of participating in an intensive program of physiotherapy to help him recover his mobility. Constant bouts with depression also hindered Franco's determination to rule. He appeared in public for the last time on October 1, 1975. Although he was barely able to raise his hand to salute his cheering supporters from the balcony of the Royal Palace in Madrid, Franco was determined to eradicate all vestiges of Marxist ideology in Spain.

On October 15, Franco suffered a heart attack, and Juan Carlos once again assumed the duties of head of state. Meanwhile, Franco agonized with respiratory and intestinal complications that began to set in. Soon, his transfer to the hospital became permanent and he underwent major intestinal surgery in November to stop massive internal hemorrhaging. Franco finally died in the early hours of the morning of November 20, 1975. The Spanish minister for Information and Tourism later announced that at 5:25 A.M. that morning, the *generalísimo* had died as the result of a cardiac arrest, leading to toxic shock caused by peritonitis. Shortly after the announcement, Prime Minister Carlos Arias Navarro read Franco's last message. He had written this testimony in October and had entrusted it to his daughter Carmen. In it, Franco sought forgiveness from his enemies and expressed gratitude for his supporters. His other request was that all people of Spain pledge their support to the monarchy. An atmosphere of disbelief seemed to descend upon the country in the wake of Franco's death. Newspapers could not keep up with demand for copies of the ultimate events of Franco's life. Thirty days of official mourning were declared, during which academic activities, cinemas, theaters, and sporting events ceased. Radio stations broadcast a steady stream of appropriately solemn music, interspersed with news bulletins.

On November 22, Juan Carlos was installed as official head of state during his appearance before the Spanish parliament. After a short speech, Juan Carlos became the new king of Spain. Franco's state funeral took place the next day. For nearly fourteen hours, members of the public lined up to walk past Franco's casket as he lay in state, attired in his uniform of Captain-General. Several mourners raised their arms in a Falangist salute, but most knelt in prayer. Overwhelmed with emotion while viewing Franco's body, one young man fell dead at the site. After the mass, a unit of Franco's personal guard carried his coffin to an open military vehicle, which served as a hearse.

Franco's legacy is complex. Always a traditionalist, he accepted aid from Benito Mussolini and Adolf Hitler at the beginning of the Spanish Civil War, but he disliked fascism. Franco's foremost concern was the defeat of Marxists and liberals and the preservation of the Church and the monarchy. For these reasons, he had no serious desire to pursue a career in politics and no interest in leading a political party. Above all, Franco was a representative of the Spanish army and its greatest twentieth century leader. He trusted the armed forces more than anything else. An ambitious man, Franco nevertheless maintained a certain detachment from the pursuit of power that belied his interest in keeping rival factions fighting among themselves while he settled all disputes. An astute judge of character and a master of the art of exploiting others to enhance his own needs, Franco once confided to Juan Carlos that he never trusted anyone. Despite constant repression and censorship, Spain changed greatly in the 1960's and 1970's.

The speed with which Franco's policies dissolved after his death would undoubtedly have shocked him. He intended to see little alteration of his policies. The decision to restore the monarchy, however, proved to be the best of all Franco's decisions. Once in power, Juan Carlos proved to be astute as well as independent of Franco's old political

At the conclusion of Franco's state funeral, King Juan Carlos gave a military salute to show his respect for the late general. (Archive Photos)

cronies. Within fourteen months of Franco's death, the Spanish parliament passed a law of political reform with the king's clear approval. This statute opened up the political system by legalizing political parties and the holding of a general election based on universal suffrage. The 1977 election was the first democratic election to be held in Spain since 1936. A popular referendum held on December 6, 1978, approved a new constitution, drawn up earlier by a seven-member committee. The new charter wisely granted considerable autonomy to regions such as Catalonia and the Basque provinces.

Perhaps the last gasp of Francoist tendencies took place on February 23, 1981, when a group of extreme rightist Civil Guards and army officers attempted a *coup d'état*. Firing submachine guns inside the legislature, the officers took the entire Chamber of Deputies hostage in the center of Madrid. The king, however, intervened decisively. Wearing his uniform as commander in chief of the armed forces, Juan Carlos condemned the revolt and dispatched forces to crush it. Few supported the rebels, and the revolt lasted less than two days. A sense of relief swept over the country, secure in the knowledge that a democratic Spain would not be turned aside and that its relations with other European and world nations would not be altered.

By the 1990's, few signs of Franco's institutions existed, and no statues of the dictator were erected since his death. Streets and squares named to honor Franco and his wartime collaborators have reverted to their pre-1936 designations. As Spain has become more tightly integrated with the rest of Europe, the possibility of a Francoist revival has become ever more remote.

—*Douglas W. Richmond*

ADDITIONAL READING:

Carr, Raymond. *Modern Spain, 1875-1980.* New York: Oxford University Press, 1980.

———. *Spain, 1808-1975.* New York: Oxford University Press, 1982. These two works by a noted scholar of modern Spanish history provide important background material for understanding post-Franco Spain.

Ellwood, Sheelaugh. *Franco.* New York: Longman, 1994. A well-written contemporary biography of the Spanish leader.

Hooper, John. *The Spaniards.* Harmondsworth, England: Penguin, 1987. A useful overview of Spanish life and culture that is accessible to general readers.

Payne, Stanley G. *The Franco Regime, 1936-1975.* Stanford, Calif.: Stanford University Press, 1987. This scholarly work is essential for placing Franco and the Falange within the context of Spanish politics.

Preston, Paul. *Franco.* New York: HarperCollins, 1993. Serves as a useful companion to the biography by Ellwood, cited above.

SEE ALSO: 1936, Spanish Civil War Begins; 1937, Raids on Guernica.

1976
CONCORDE FLIES PASSENGERS AT SUPERSONIC SPEEDS

The Concorde flies passengers at supersonic speeds, proving the technological viability of supersonic passenger flight despite high initial costs.

DATE: January 21, 1976
LOCALE: London, England, and Paris, France
CATEGORIES: Science and technology; Transportation
KEY FIGURES:

Julian Amery (born 1919), the British minister of aviation, 1962-1964

Geoffroy De Cource (born 1912), the French minister of aviation, 1962

Charles-André-Joseph-Marie de Gaulle (1890-1970), president of France, 1958-1969, and chief political supporter of the Concorde

Sir George Edwards, chairman of British Aircraft Corporation (later British Aerospace)

Harold Macmillan (1894-1986), British prime minister, 1957-1963

Lucien Servanty, director of aviation at Sud-Aviation (later Aérospatiale)

William Strang, chief engineer at Bristol-Siddeley (later Rolls-Royce)

Brian Trubshaw, first British test pilot to fly the Concorde

André Turcat, first French test pilot to fly the Concorde

Henri Ziegler, president of Aérospatiale

SUMMARY OF EVENT. On January 21, 1976, the Concorde became the first Supersonic Transport (SST) to fly in commercial service. It had been under development since 1962, when the French and British governments signed an agreement to build an aircraft that could transport passengers at more than twice the speed of sound. The aircraft is exceptionally graceful. It is 202 feet long with long, slightly curved delta wings and no tail. The nose section is hinged which allows it to be parallel with the plane's body while in flight, but be angled down to enhance pilot visibility during take-off and landing. Concorde is powered by four Bristol-Siddeley (Rolls-Royce) Olympus turbojets enclosed in two underwing nacelles. It is capable of carrying up to 130 passengers at a cruising speed of twice the speed of sound (Mach 2 or 1,350 miles per hour.) It has a range of four thousand miles and cruises at between fifty thousand and sixty thousand feet, much higher than ordinary jet passenger planes.

Britain and France had different motives in building the aircraft. Both nations wanted to use the project to enhance their national aircraft industries and give them tools to compete with American manufacturers that controlled 80 percent of the civil aviation market. Both nations wanted to preserve jobs in their aerospace industries and enhance national prestige. The British had an additional reason for initiating the project. France, under the leadership of President Charles de Gaulle, had been blocking British entry into the Common Market because de Gaulle was suspicious of Britain's "special relationship" with the United States. Prime Minister Harold Macmillan of Great Britain wanted to use the project to establish Britain's European credentials. By cooperating on the Concorde, the British hoped to show the French that they could be reliable European partners.

Confidence in technology was high in the 1960's, and many assumed that supersonic flight was a logical next step for the world's aircraft manufacturers. The United States had begun research in the area in 1961, and President John F. Kennedy had committed the country to developing a SST in 1963. The Soviet Union began work on its SST in 1962. None of these projects was backed by the airline industry; it had been financially devastated in

the parties to break the agreement. The first prototype (known as 001), piloted by test-pilot André Turcot, a popular French hero, flew on March 2, 1969, from its home airport in Toulouse. The British prototype, piloted by Brian Trubshaw, chief of flight operations for British Aircraft Corporation, flew on April 9. The two airplanes

The development of the supersonic Concorde jet represented a cooperative economic venture supported by the French and British governments. (Archive Photos)

1958 when the Boeing 707 and the McDonnell-Douglas DC-8 arrived on the market, forcing them to replace their propeller-driven DC-7s and Super Constellations long before the costs of these aircraft had been recouped. Although many of the leading airlines placed options for purchases of the Concorde, they remained skeptical about its commercial viability.

The Anglo-French Supersonic Aircraft Agreement was signed on November 29, 1962. The agreement was unusual because it was solemnized as a formal international treaty, and because it contained no escape clause allowing

made an impressive public debut when they flew together at the Paris air show in June, 1969.

By this time, the Concorde had evolved into a major industrial project in both France and Britain. The main contractors were BAC and Rolls-Royce in Britain and Aérospatiale and the Société Nationale d'Etude et de Construction de Moteurs d'Aviation (SNECMA) in France. They, in turn, had subcontracts with many smaller suppliers of components and services. At its peak, the Concorde project employed some fifty thousand men in France and Britain.

Throughout the period of development and production cost estimates for the Concorde multiplied. Originally, the partner nations had estimated that around 160 million pounds sterling would be needed to develop and test the airplane over an eight year period. These estimates were hopelessly optimistic. The technical problems involved in building a Mach 2 airplane had proved to be much more formidable than anticipated. Capacity, noise, and pollution requirements changed, and inflation took its toll. By the end of 1975, the British and the French had spent a little more than a billion pounds in thirteen years on an airplane that had yet to transport a single paying passenger.

Besides the financial burden placed on the British and French governments, Concorde faced many other challenges during its development that probably would have killed it if the initial agreement had not been so ironclad. Concorde provided a highly visible target for those who thought that the advanced technology it represented was of little social value, and that the vast sums invested in it could be put to better use. The most powerful argument used by Concorde's opponents was the plane's potential harm to the environment. Since the Concorde flew much higher than conventional jets, it deposited its exhaust into the stratosphere. Some critics thought that the carbon dioxide and nitrogen oxides would deplete the ozone layer and contribute to the greenhouse effect. Others thought that the sonic booms it produced would cause physical damage to structures below and create intolerable conditions for all living beneath Concorde's flight paths. The most serious argument used by Concorde's opponents involved airport noise. The plane's immensely powerful engines created very high noise levels of about 118 decibels on take-off, and critics thought that such noise would make life miserable for those living near airports.

These arguments were powerful, especially when coupled with the great expense involved in producing a supersonic transport. Although such arguments killed the completion of the American SST project in May, 1971, Concorde's supporters worked tirelessly to refute these arguments, and the project stayed alive.

Concorde's most serious problem, however, was financial. Originally, the British and French thought that there might be a market for nearly two hundred Concordes produced in various configurations. Initially, sixteen airlines had placed options for seventy-four Concordes. Yet the key to Concorde's commercial viability rested in the hands of the large American airlines, Pan American (Pan Am) and Trans World Airlines (TWA). If Pan Am followed through on its options, Concorde's developers assumed, other airlines would have to follow to remain competitive. Unfortunately, the argument also worked in reverse, and

when Pan Am announced that it was canceling its options for the purchase of Concordes on January 30, 1973, the other airlines followed suit. The national carriers, Air France and British Airways, alone operated the sixteen Concordes ultimately produced.

The decisions to drop the Concorde options involved several factors. First, the world's airlines were in great financial difficulty. They had made massive purchases of wide-body Boeing 747's and were suffering from overcapacity. Fuel costs had risen dramatically in the wake of the energy crisis that had begun with the 1973 Arab-Israeli war. The environmental movement had become more powerful, especially in the United States, and environmentalists protested the Concorde by demonstrating around airports and by trying to persuade U.S. officials to deny it landing rights.

In spite of its financial and commercial difficulties, the Concorde was a remarkable technological and political achievement. The plane cut the trans-Atlantic voyage to around three-and-one-half hours and placed every major city on earth within twelve hours of all other urban centers. Its supersonic flights connected London and Paris to cities around the globe, including New York, Washington, D.C., Melbourne, and Singapore. It set new passenger aircraft speed records, including a 213-minute crossing from Washington to London. Britain's cooperation with France helped establish its European credentials, and Britain eventually became a full member of the Economic Community. The viability of cooperative high-technology ventures was tested, and the Concorde project was a major step in developing the European Airbus aircraft.

—*C. James Haug*

ADDITIONAL READING:

Bilstein, Roger. *Flight in America: From the Wright Brothers to the Astronauts.* Rev. ed. Baltimore: The Johns Hopkins University Press, 1994. Written by one of the most prominent historians of the space program, this book provides a balanced survey of the history of flight.

Costello, John, and Terry Hughes. *The Concorde Conspiracy.* New York: Charles Scribner's Sons, 1976. This work is an easy-to-read survey of the Concorde program which examines the motives of both its proponents and opponents.

Gardner, Charles. *Concorde: The Questions Answered.* London: British Aircraft Corporation, 1975. Although this is a short work written to defend the Concorde against its enemies, it provides many useful details in a concise format.

Gidwitz, Betsy. *The Politics of International Air Transport.* Lexington, Mass.: Lexington Books, 1980. This book is a survey of the relationship between national governments, their national carriers, and the American airline industry.

Knight, Geoffrey. *Concorde: The Inside Story*. London: Weidenfeld & Nicolson, 1976. An account of the development of the Concorde that focuses on the personalities involved.

SEE ALSO: 1957, Common Market Is Formed; 1961, Soviet Union Puts a Human in Space; 1973, European Space Agency Is Formed; 1993, Maastricht Treaty Is Ratified; 1994, Channel Tunnel Is Officially Opened.

1976
IRA HUNGER STRIKER DIES IN AN ENGLISH PRISON

An IRA hunger striker dies in an English prison, provoking reprisals from the Irish Republican Army.

DATE: February 12, 1976

LOCALE: Yorkshire, England

CATEGORIES: Government and politics; Wars, uprisings, and civil unrest

KEY FIGURES:

Liam Cosgrave (born 1920), prime minister of the Republic of Ireland

Seamus Loughran, organizer for Sinn Féin

Terence MacSwiney (1879-1920), mayor of Cork

Francis Stagg (1942-1976), member of the Irish Republican Army

Lord Harold James Wilson (1916-1995), prime minister of Britain, 1964-1970 and 1974-1976

SUMMARY OF EVENT. Francis Stagg began his hunger strike on December 13, 1975, knowing he had the support of fellow members of the Irish Republican Army (IRA), who were fighting to end the partition of Ireland. He also had the example of men such as Terence MacSwiney, the mayor of Cork, who during the Irish civil war in 1920 undertook a lengthy hunger strike to demonstrate against his arrest by the British government. MacSwiney died in Brixton Prison in England on the seventy-fourth day of his protest. Also, Stagg had earlier observed the gains in 1972 of IRA prison hunger strikers in Northern Ireland, when they successfully secured a "special category status" from the British government. Designated as political prisoners they could enjoy privileges such as wearing civilian clothes, access to education and recreation facilities, and the freedom to mix among themselves within their prison area. Furthermore, prisoners who had lost the remission of their sentences because of prison protests could have it reinstated.

To purposefully die from self-imposed starvation requires unlimited psychological commitment while coping with the erosion of physical stamina, the gradual loss of functions such as sight and hearing, and the mental confusion that results from nutritional deficiency. At about the forty-second day, visual competence becomes severely impaired because of muscle degeneration. For a while, an individual experiences rapid blinking of the eyes, accompanied by periods of dizziness and vomiting. Progressively the body withers away. For many IRA hunger strikers, withdrawing from the slow suicide meant not only personal failure but also dishonor among their paramilitary comrades.

Aware of its propaganda value and hoping to soften the possible impact of Stagg's immanent death, the British government placed two full-page advertisements in *The Irish News*, the Roman Catholic community's Belfast newspaper. The headlines read "Frank Stagg—The Facts." In these advertisements they sought to explain why Francis Stagg should remain in a British jail; that although he had been born in County Mayo in the Irish Republic and had married a woman from there, he moved to England in 1959, and since then had lived in the town of Coventry, England. Moreover, his sentence in Britain was for crimes carried out in Britain. Beneath the advertisement in capital letters was stated "Connections with Northern Ireland: None."

Francis Stagg was sentenced on November 1, 1973, for conspiracy to commit arson and criminal damage. He demanded a transfer from a prison in Yorkshire, England, to one in Northern Ireland, where he could complete his sentence with "special category status." When the English authorities rejected his demand, he started refusing food. His demise, closely followed by the British press, was inevitable. He died on the sixty-first day of his hunger strike at the age of thirty-four.

Fears of terrorist reprisals immediately surfaced in London and in Northern Ireland. Seamus Loughran, the Northern Ireland organizer for Provisional Sinn Féin, the political arm of the IRA provisionals, announced "Francis Stagg's death will not go unavenged. There is a debt of honor which must be paid." In the twenty-four-hour period following his death, 104 incidents of violence were reported, including the fatal shooting of a Protestant policeman in a village near Londonderry. On February 13, rioting erupted in the Roman Catholic areas of Belfast. Mobs of youths hurled bombs from behind barricades of hijacked cars. Three people were killed. In London's West End during the peak rush hour, an attache case containing twenty pounds of explosive was found at the entrance to the Oxford Circus subway station. The bomb was removed and defused. Violence continued to erupt in Northern Ireland and London. During the week following Stagg's death eleven people were killed, and there was extensive property damage. Two bombs exploded in the center of Belfast, destroying a market and a department store. On February 21, there were two explosions in London. The first, occurring in the basement of Selfridge's, a department store on Oxford Street, injured five people. The second, a car bomb, exploded six hours later not far from the Marble Arch intersection of Park Lane and Hyde Park. There, no one was reported injured.

Before being flown to Dublin, Michael Gaughan's coffin was paraded through London followed by an eight-man IRA honor guard. (Archive Photos)

Stagg's brother and sister requested a quiet funeral, but IRA officials, describing Stagg as a martyr, announced on February 14 their own plans to hold an IRA funeral honoring him with full military honors. Stagg had asked to be buried beside Michael Thomas Gaughan. In 1974, Gaughan had died in an English prison following a sixty-five-day hunger strike. He was serving a seven-year sentence for bank robbery, that he said was undertaken to raise funds for the IRA. Before being flown to Dublin Gaughan's body was paraded through London streets fol-

lowed by an eight-man honor guard wearing IRA paramilitary garb. Francis Stagg was buried on February 21, at Ballina, a remote village in Western Ireland, without the full military honors he had requested and which his comrades had promised. The grave for Francis Stagg was dug by police detectives some distance from that of Michael Gaughan.

On February 22, a memorial mass was said in the village of Hollymont in County Mayo. Demonstrators arrived in buses from all over Ireland and gathered in the center of the village. Led by a squadron of girls in dark glasses and uniformed youths, they marched the two miles to the cemetery. Prevented by police from approaching the grave, they assembled in other parts of the cemetery. The Provisional IRA fired a volley of shots. More than seven thousand sympathizers threw stones at the one thousand policemen and six hundred soldiers who had been brought to the area.

On February 29, memorial masses were held in Toronto, Canada, and several American cities, including Boston and New York. More than three thousand people marched through midtown Manhattan to a rally held at the United Nations.

Harold Wilson, the British prime minister, and Liam Cosgrave, the prime minister of the Republic of Ireland, arranged to meet in London on March 5 in order to assess subsequent moves in the Northern Ireland situation. Efforts to draft a new coalition for Northern Ireland allowing Roman Catholic participation in the government failed. The British announced their plans to govern the province of Northern Ireland indefinitely. This pleased neither the Protestant majority in Ulster nor the IRA. The former viewed the action as a denial of their desire to exclude Catholic politicians from power, while the IRA viewed the statement as an affirmation of Great Britain's intention of continued presence in Northern Ireland.

Throughout 1974, the violence did not subside. Civilians, soldiers, and police, both in Northern Ireland and England, were injured and killed. More bombs exploded in London's subway system prompting Scotland Yard to assign one thousand police for special duty there. In Belfast, the bombings were attributed both to the IRA and the Protestant extremists. In the wake of the continuing violence two Belfast women, Betty Williams and Mairead Corrigan, developed a series of small, silent marches and vigils to protest the violence. The Women's Peace Movement brought together twelve thousand supporters in October. They marched through the streets of Belfast urging an end to the sectarian violence and were harassed by IRA youths. Sixteen people were injured.

In November, after two bombs in Birmingham killed twenty-one people and injured more than 150, the government passed the Northern Ireland (Temporary Provisions) Act making the IRA illegal. It granted the home secretary powers to exclude from Britain (but not Northern Ireland) persons suspected of terrorist involvement. That month, fifteen thousand people attended a rally in Trafalgar Square urging an end to the violence in Northern Ireland. By years end, however, the death toll was the highest in any year except 1972. In Ulster, 296 people were killed and 1,342 were left injured from the violence.

The British government, having concluded "that the introduction of special category status was a serious mistake," ended it on March 1, 1976.   —*Susan E. Hamilton*

ADDITIONAL READING:

Bartlett, Jonathan, ed. *Northern Ireland.* New York: H. W. Wilson, 1983. This collection of essays includes five that deal with the hunger strikers and prison conditions in Northern Ireland.

Finnegan, Richard B. *Ireland: The Challenge of Conflict and Change.* Boulder, Colo.: Westview Press, 1983. An introduction to Ireland's history, society, economy, government, and politics, with a thoughtful examination of changes during the 1960's and 1970's.

Ranelagh, John O'Beirne. *A Short History of Ireland.* New York: Cambridge University Press, 1994. This edition presents an extremely detailed history of Ireland up to 1993.

Wright, Joanne. *Terrorist Propaganda, the Red Army Faction and the Provisional IRA, 1968-86.* New York: St. Martin's Press, 1990. This complex examination of terrorist violence presents the ideology and propaganda of the Provisional IRA. It briefly touches on the hunger strike as a propaganda tactic.

SEE ALSO: 1916, Easter Rebellion; 1972, "Bloody Sunday" in Northern Ireland; 1974, IRA Terrorists Bomb Parliament Building; 1985, Anglo-Irish Agreement Is Signed; 1993, Ulster Peace Accord.

1978

ALDO MORO IS KIDNAPPED AND MURDERED BY ITALIAN TERRORISTS

Aldo Moro is kidnapped and murdered by Italian terrorists, initiating the gradual disintegration of the Red Brigades, a left-wing terrorist group in Italy in the 1970's.

DATE: March 16-May 9, 1978
LOCALE: Rome, Italy
CATEGORIES: Government and politics; Terrorism and political assassination

KEY FIGURES:

Germano Maccari, a former Red Brigades member found guilty in 1996 of the 1978 shooting of Aldo Moro

Aldo Moro (1916-1978), prime minister of Italy, 1963-1968 and 1974-1976; foreign minister 1968-1974

SUMMARY OF EVENT. On March 16, 1978, former Italian prime minister Aldo Moro and his five-man security team, traveling in two cars, were en route to the Parliament Building in Rome, Italy, on a routine workday. At Moro's request, the small caravan had made an apparently unscheduled stop at a church on Via Fani in a well-to-do residential neighborhood. Moments later, the lead car suddenly halted in an unsuccessful effort to avoid hitting the car ahead. Behind the lead car, Moro's car stopped also. As gunshots sounded, bullets from unknown assailants struck bodyguards in both cars. All five men died as they attempted to protect Moro from the flying bullets. Bystanders observed a badly bruised and shaken Aldo Moro as he was quickly loaded into another car, never to be seen alive again. Fifty-five days later, on May 9, 1978, Moro's bullet-riddled body was discovered in the trunk of a Renault parked on Via Caetani in Rome.

Born on September 23, 1916, into a well-educated, well-to-do family in Maglie, Lecce, Italy, Aldo Moro experienced a sheltered childhood and grew to be a rather handsome young man, with a studious and religious bent. After moving to Bari, Italy, with his family in 1934, Moro attended the University of Bari. While at the university, he served as leader of the Italian Catholic University Federation from 1939 to 1942.

Aldo Moro lived at a time when Italy was zealously Fascist. The divergence between Catholicism and Fascism provoked serious thought on the part of the devoutly Catholic Moro. His aversion to Communism, however, bothered him more. He settled on an anti-Communist position that aligned him with the Italian dictator Mussolini's Fascists against Communist control. Moro made his peace with the differences between Fascist thought and Catholic tenets, and for a few years felt that the two systems of thought could coexist. Moro preferred this uneasy alliance to Communism. He maintained this political position until the collapse of Benito Mussolini's regime in 1943, when, finally convinced that Fascism was decadent, he urged Catholics to step forward and help rebuild the faltering Italian government. From that time, Moro assumed an active roll in politics, first on the local level and then in the upper tiers of government.

After graduation from the University of Bari in 1942, Moro taught law there as an untenured professor. He wrote for Catholic publications and edited *Studium*, a periodical

A terrorist group known as the Red Brigades claimed responsibility for kidnapping former Italian prime minister Aldo Moro in 1978. (Archive Photos)

of progressive Catholic thought, thus establishing his reputation as a Catholic intellectual long before he became a power in the political arena. From his editorial position at the helm of *Studium*, Moro called Italians to positions of moderation; he exhorted them to exhibit kindness and charity. His widely published political stance began to catch the attention of politicians on the national level, especially that of members of the Christian Democratic Party.

In 1959, the forty-three-year-old Aldo Moro became the Christian Democrats' party secretary. From his party platform, Moro preached Italy's need for a liaison between Socialists and Christian Democrats. Moro remained actively associated with the Christian Democratic Party, becoming its president again in 1976. As party president, having moderated his political views, Moro concentrated on an "opening to the left," in order to include the Communist Party in the Christian Democratic government's official parliamentary majority. As a lawyer, educator, author, and politician, Moro became known as the "Great Compromiser" because of his efforts to unify Italy.

A Marxist-Leninist rebel group called Brigate Rosse, or Red Brigades, emerged at the forefront of the renegade communist element among the Italian people and became a force in Italian politics. Originating in the late 1960's as part of the university ferment in northern Italy and the militant strikes of young factory workers, the Red Brigades aimed to destroy the democratic political base of the Italian government, ostensibly to eliminate the corruption of capitalism. This purpose set them squarely in opposition to the Christian Democratic Party, headed by Prime Minister Aldo Moro. At the pinnacle of his intellectual and political prowess and at the height of his popularity with the Italian people, Moro worked ceaselessly to hammer out a compromise position that would allow all legitimate political forces, including Communism, a fair share in Italy's government.

On March 16, 1978, members of the Red Brigades captured Aldo Moro. This terrorist act was intended to cause the collapse of the Christian Democratic Party, but this expected collapse did not occur.

Immediately upon claiming responsibility for the kidnapping, spokesmen for the Red Brigades demanded a ransom for the safe return of Aldo Moro—they offered to exchange Moro for thirteen imprisoned terrorists. The offer was dismissed by the Italian government, which had recently settled on a hard-line policy called *fermezza* (firmness): no negotiations with terrorists. From his place of incarceration in the "People's Prison," later learned to be on Via Montalcini in Rome, Moro wrote letters to then Prime Minister Giulio Andreotti and to other officials, encouraging negotiations and prisoner exchange. His letters, probably dictated by members of the Red Brigades, described the political calamity that would be caused by the Christian Democrats' failure to rescue him. Most investigators agree that Moro's written pleas, dramatically departing from his long-held views, were produced under torture and possibly the influence of drugs. For reasons never made clear, the Red Brigades ceased communications after fifty-five days and "executed" their captive.

Four trials and two parliamentary investigations have proved Aldo Moro's murderer, or murderers, to be members of the Red Brigades. The motivation of the crime was the terrorists' desire to set off a Marxist-Leninist revolution, which they hoped would trigger the collapse of the Christian Democrat Italian government.

Five years later, in 1983, three Brigades guerrillas, proved to have participated in Moro's incarceration and murder, were tried and sentenced to life imprisonment. A fourth suspect, also a Red Brigades member, was not apprehended until 1993. This suspect, Germano Maccari, was convicted of actually killing Moro. The trial court rejected Maccari's defense that, although he was present at the execution, another guerrilla had fired the gun that killed Moro. According to Italian legal custom, Maccari was released from jail in late 1996 pending his appeal.

Despite the conviction of several terrorists, many questions about the motives of Italy's government officials and the integrity of their efforts to find Moro alive remained unanswered. The possibility of conspiracy remained unresolved. A large portion of the Italian populace, headed by Aldo Moro's wife and children, believed that the Italian government was guilty of Aldo Moro's murder because it refused to meet ransom demands. Appeals from high-ranking Catholic intellectuals, who argued that life is sacred and should not be sacrificed to reasons of state, failed to sway the Italian government's position of no negotiation with terrorists. On the international level, Kurt Waldheim, then secretary-general of the United Nations, pleaded personally with the Red Brigades to release the former Italian prime minister. Waldheim's appeal was widely criticized because it seemed to raise the terrorist group to the status of a recognized power.

On the other hand, part of the populace felt that Italian democracy, defective as it might have been, was worth defending, even at the cost of the life of its former head of state. Members of other major political groups argued that if negotiations were entered into, and prisoner exchanges made, Italy's law enforcement and police agencies could no longer operate effectively.

In the last decade of the twentieth century, Moro's kidnapping and murder remained unresolved in Italy's turbulent and unwieldy legal system.   *—Barbara C. Stanley*

ADDITIONAL READING:

Drake, Richard. *The Aldo Moro Murder Case.* Cambridge, Mass.: Harvard University Press, 1996. Written by a well-regarded specialist in Italian politics, this book probably contains the greatest amount of specific information published on the murder of Aldo Moro through the end of 1995.

_____. *The Revolutionary Mystique and Terrorism in Contemporary Italy.* Bloomington: Indiana University Press, 1989. Pages 46-54 contain a short, concise description of the turmoil of Italian politics during the period in which Moro was kidnapped and murdered.

Katz, Robert. *Days of Wrath—The Ordeal of Aldo Moro: The Kidnapping, the Execution, the Aftermath.* Garden City, N.Y.: Doubleday, 1980. Excerpts from this American author's book were cited by an attorney who cross-examined Giulio Andreotti, a former prime minister and a key witness in the trial that attempted to sort out the truths in the Moro slaying.

Wagner-Pacifici, Robin Erica. *The Moro Morality Play: Terrorism as Social Drama.* Chicago: University of Chicago Press, 1986. One of several books dealing with the conspiracy theory. Deals with the influence of the Catholic Church on the trial of Aldo Moro's suspected murderers.

_____. "Negotiation in the Aldo Moro Affair: The Suppressed Alternative in a Case of Symbolic Politics." *Politics and Society* 12, no. 4 (1983): 487-517. This article provides background for the position taken by the Italian government as to negotiations in terrorist situations.

SEE ALSO: 1950-1963, Italy's Postwar Economic Boom; 1972, Munich Olympic Massacre; 1974, IRA Terrorists Bomb Parliament Building; 1986, Olof Palme Is Assassinated.

1979
MARGARET THATCHER BECOMES BRITAIN'S FIRST WOMAN PRIME MINISTER

When Margaret Thatcher takes office as Britain's first woman prime minister, she ushers in a tempestuous era of change, particularly in regard to international relations and domestic economic policy.

DATE: May 4, 1979
LOCALE: Great Britain
CATEGORY: Government and politics
KEY FIGURES:

Michael Heseltine (born 1933), British minister of environment, 1979-1983, minister of defense, 1983-1986

Sir Geoffrey Howe (born 1926), Chancellor of the Exchequer, 1979- 1983, British foreign secretary, 1983-1989

Sir Keith Joseph (born 1918), British minister of industry, 1979-1981, minister of education, 1981-1986

Margaret Thatcher (born 1925), British prime minister, 1979-1990

SUMMARY OF EVENT. Margaret Thatcher was the first woman prime minister in British history and also the first scientist to hold that office. She was the only person in the twentieth century to win three consecutive elections, and her eleven uninterrupted years in office was a feat that had not been accomplished since 1827. She also was the only prime minister to have an "ism " attached to her name.

Margaret Hilda Roberts was born in Grantham, Lincolnshire, on October 13, 1925. Her father, a grocer and town alderman, was a dominate influence in her development, along with Methodism. From both she absorbed such virtues as thrift, hard work, personal responsibility, and individual initiative. She attended Oxford University from 1943 to 1947, where she studied chemistry, and then worked as a research chemist. In 1951, she married Dennis Thatcher, a successful businessman, and after studying law she was admitted to the bar in 1954.

Thatcher was first elected to Parliament as a Conservative in the general election of 1959. When the Conservative Party won the 1970 election, she served as minister of education, and after the party lost office in 1974, she maintained a high profile as an Opposition spokesperson. Equally important she joined a group of energetic reform-minded Conservatives which opposed the consensus politics that dominated Britain during the 1960's and 1970's, whereby both major parties supported a mixed economy, the welfare state, and a powerful trade union presence in government. By the late 1970's, Britain was bedeviled by inefficient state enterprises, high inflation, punitive taxes, and constant strikes. Thatcher and other radicals, such as Sir Keith Joseph, who had a decided influence upon her economic theories, called for a program embracing sharp cuts in state expenditures, lowering taxes, tightening the money supply, unloading inefficient state enterprises,

After serving as the leader of the Opposition since 1975, Margaret Thatcher became Britain's first woman prime minister when the Conservative Party won a majority of seats in the general election of 1979. (Archive Photos)

curbing trade union excesses, and scaling back the welfare state. The underlying philosophy was freedom: Roll back the power of the state and give people control over their lives. This peculiar blend of philosophy, specific economic programs, and moral homilies was subsequently dubbed "Thatcherism."

In 1975, Thatcher challenged Ted Heath for the party's leadership and won. After gaining valuable experience as leader of the Opposition, she easily led the Conservatives to victory in the general election of 1979, thanks mainly to the Labour Party, which was divided, demoralized, and poorly led by James Callaghan, who was blamed for the crippling strikes of the preceding winter. She also convincingly won the elections of 1983 and 1987, although it is significant that the Conservative Party never won more than 44 percent of the vote, the majority of votes divided among three opposition parties.

Once in office, Thatcher proved a decisive leader. She dismissed dissenting or ineffective ministers with alacrity, and in the House of Commons proved a skilled debater. The government reduced the maximum income tax rate to 40 percent and the basic rate to 25 percent, among the lowest in Europe. Inefficient, aging smokestack industries were allowed to die off, while the more productive state companies were privatized, such as Jaguar, British Gas, British Telecom, and British Airways. The general public eagerly bought shares in these companies, tripling the number of shareholders and enabling Thatcher to claim that Britain had become a "share holding democracy." Legislation enabled people to buy their council houses, formerly rented from local governmental authorities, and approximately 1.6 million units were purchased under this popular program. The Education Reform Act of 1988 established a national curriculum to upgrade educational standards and established the principle of greater parental authority in choosing schools. No less than four significant pieces of legislation were passed during the 1980's designed to democratize trade unions, reduce the number of strikes, and eliminate violence and property damage on the picket lines. In March, 1984, the coal miners went on strike, one of the bitterest in modern British industrial history, but the Thatcher government stood firm and won a complete victory.

On the international scene, Thatcher demonstrated equal decisiveness and resolve. She secured a substantial reduction in British payments to the European Economic Community (EEC), and in the process made it clear to the EEC bureaucracy, which she regarded as undemocratic, wasteful, and working toward a socialist unitary government, that it would have no easy time securing Britain's consent to further integration. Her government convinced the white minority regime of Rhodesia, a former British colony, to transfer power to the black majority, and in April, 1980, the newly renamed country of Zimbabwe became independent. A major crisis confronted Thatcher in April, 1982, when Argentina, governed by a brutal military junta, seized the Falkland Islands, a British possession in the South Atlantic. Thatcher responded defiantly and ordered a naval task force to retake Britain's possessions, which it successfully did. In December, 1984, Britain signed a treaty which formalized the orderly transfer of Hong Kong, then a British possession, to China in 1997. In November, 1985, she negotiated the Anglo-Irish Agreement with the Republic of Ireland, which gave the latter an unprecedented consultative role in Northern Ireland affairs in the hope that this might expedite an end to the bitter conflict there.

A key element in Thatcher's foreign policy was anti-Communism, for which the Soviet Union labeled her "the Iron Lady." She formed a close alliance with the United States, made easy by the warm friendship that existed between her and President Ronald Reagan. She permitted American cruise missiles to be stationed on British soil, allowed American bombers based in Britain to bomb Libya for supporting terrorism, and played a constructive role in facilitating discussions between Reagan and the new Soviet leader, Mikhail Gorbachev, in order to end the arms race and reduce tensions.

It was Thatcher's policy toward further European integration that provoked her downfall. Her determined opposition to a federal European Union and her vigorous assertions of British sovereignty was seen as obstructive, if not eccentric. Influential pro-Europeans within the Conservative Party, such as Sir Geoffrey Howe, openly criticized her stance. Added to Thatcher's woes was the new poll tax, which proved to be immensely unpopular with the public. In November, 1992, Michael Heseltine, a pro-European, challenged her for the party leadership. A majority of Conservative members of Parliament voted for Thatcher, but she failed to win by the necessary numerical margin, and she was persuaded to step down rather than risk facing a possible humiliating defeat in the next ballot. The party subsequently chose John Major as leader, and on November 28, 1990, Margaret Thatcher officially resigned from office. On June 30, 1992, she entered the House of Lords as Baroness Thatcher of Kesteven.

By the mid-1990's, there was still no consensus regarding her record. Admirers emphasize the privatization of state industries, trade union reforms, initiating a national debate on Britain's declining educational standards, and the dramatic increase in share holding and home ownership, all of which were highly popular. They claim that

Britain emerged with enhanced international stature as a result of Thatcher's forceful opposition to tyranny, terrorism, and aggression, and because of the country's constructive role in attempting to resolve a number of issues in Africa, the Far East, and Northern Ireland. Equally significant, she legitimized capitalist activity, fostered an entrepreneurial spirit, and encouraged Britons to assume personal responsibility for their lives. Perhaps her greatest compliment is that the Labour Party repeatedly stated that if elected, it had no intention of undoing many of her popular reforms.

Thatcher's critics point out that much of Britain's industrial base was allowed to disappear, and that even the successful privatization program was accomplished at the expense of increased unemployment. Statistics also show that she failed to cut state expenditures, the overall tax burden did not decline noticeably, the welfare state continued to grow, and the gap widened between the rich and the poor. Most distressing, she exhibited a shocking indifference to the needs of Britain's alienated youth and growing nonwhite population. Perhaps the only area of agreement between admirers and detractors is that she dominated the political agenda of the 1980's and as a result British society was dramatically changed.   —*David C. Lukowitz*

ADDITIONAL READING:

Butler, David, and Dennis Kavanagh. *The British General Election of 1979*. London: Macmillan, 1980. The definitive account of the election that brought Thatcher to power.

Kavanagh, Dennis, and Anthony Seldon, eds. *The Thatcher Effect*. Oxford: Clarendon Press, 1989. A collection of articles by twenty-five authors with impressive credentials which assess how much change actually occurred during the Thatcher years.

Mikdadi, Faysal. *Margaret Thatcher: A Bibliography*. Westport, Conn.: Greenwood Press, 1993. This valuable book contains an excellent biographical sketch of Thatcher, a lengthy chronological list of important events in her life, and a fine bibliography.

Smith, Geoffrey. *Reagan and Thatcher*. London: Bodley Head, 1990. Based upon interviews with many of the key historical actors, this book explains the basis of their warm friendship and close cooperation.

Thatcher, Margaret. *The Downing Street Years*. New York: HarperCollins, 1993. A lengthy and detailed memoir of her years as prime minister. Those interested in her earlier years should read Thatcher's 1995 memoir *The Path to Power*, also published by HarperCollins.

Young, Hugo. *One of Us: A Biography of Margaret Thatcher*. London: Macmillan, 1991. A useful, if somewhat critical, account of Thatcher's life, written by a respected British journalist.

SEE ALSO: 1974, IRA Terrorists Bomb Parliament Building; 1982, Great Britain Recovers the Falkland Islands; 1984, Britain Signs Agreement to Leave Hong Kong in 1997; 1985, Anglo-Irish Agreement Is Signed.

1979
SALT II IS SIGNED

SALT II is signed, establishing limits on the size and technology of the nuclear arsenals of the Soviet Union and the United States thus limiting the nuclear arms race and creating a more stable deterrence.

DATE: June 18, 1979

LOCALE: Vienna, Austria

CATEGORIES: Diplomacy and international relations; Science and technology

KEY FIGURES:

Leonid Ilich Brezhnev (1906-1982), secretary of the Communist Party and the most powerful political leader of the Soviet Union from 1957-1982

James Earl "Jimmy" Carter, Jr. (born 1924), thirty-ninth president of the United States, 1977-1981

Gerald Rudolph Ford (born 1913), thirty-eighth president of the United States, 1974-1977

Andrei Andreyevich Gromyko (1909-1989), Soviet foreign affairs minister, 1957-1985

Henry "Scoop" Jackson (1912-1983), Democratic senator from the state of Washington

Henry Alfred Kissinger (born 1923), national security adviser, 1969-1975, and U.S. secretary of state, 1973-1977

Aleksei Nikolayevich Kosygin (1904-1980), Soviet premier, 1964-1980

Richard Milhous Nixon (1913-1994), thirty-seventh president of the United States, 1969-1974

Cyrus Roberts Vance (born 1917), U.S. secretary of state, 1977-1980

SUMMARY OF EVENT. To facilitate the passage of an international treaty to limit the spread of nuclear weapons (Nuclear Non-Proliferation Treaty, 1968), the United States and the Soviet Union pledged to begin a process of mutually agreed upon disarmament. Consequently, the two nations began the Strategic Arms Limitations Talks (SALT) in 1969. From the beginning, however, it was clear that the goal was not disarmament but rather to create a state of stable deterrence and reduce expenditures on new weapons systems. Both the United States and the Soviet Union had adopted a strategy of nuclear deterrence, a policy that attempts to reduce the likelihood of nuclear war by threat-

ening the other side with unacceptable levels of destruction. Deterrence, however, is undermined if one side gains a significant advantage in numbers of weapons or new technologies which would allow it to destroy its adversary in such a way that a counterattack becomes impossible. The purposes of SALT were thus to create a nuclear balance between the two superpowers and to limit the development of new technologies. Despite mutual suspicion, a treaty (SALT I), was completed in 1972. The treaty included a limited freeze on the construction of new long range missiles, but failed to take into account a new technology which permitted the placement of multiple independent reentry vehicles (MIRV; war heads) on each missile. The new technology thus defeated the purpose of the SALT I treaty of stabilizing the nuclear arsenals. In fact, this new technology allowed the Soviet Union to increase the number of its nuclear war heads from twenty-three hundred in 1972 to five thousand in 1979. The United States similarly increased its arsenal from 1,710 war heads to more than 8,000. As a response, both sides agreed to resume the Strategic Arms Limitations Talks (SALT II). SALT II thus began in 1972 and struggled episodically through the administrations of three American presidents before a treaty was finally signed in Vienna in June, 1979.

The talks which were initiated by the Nixon administration and by the Kosygin-Brezhnev politburo were begun under conditions of suspicion and animosity. Commitment to the talks further eroded as Richard Nixon became absorbed in the Watergate scandal and finally had to resign the presidency. Gerald Ford, who then assumed the presidency, entered the talks with some reluctance. He faced a great deal of opposition from members of his own political party (Republican) as well as opposition from a group of "hawkish" senators under the vocal leadership of Senator Henry Jackson. Nevertheless, by 1974 two agreements were signed, one of which further limited deployment of ABM (antiballistic missile) systems in accord with the SALT I treaty. The other was the Threshold Test Ban Treaty, which restricted the size of explosions of underground nuclear tests. A meeting between President Ford and Leonid Brezhnev in Vladivostok in 1974 also set limits on strategic launchers (missiles armed with warheads) at 2,400 for each side and on MIRV weapons at 1,320 for each side. These were to serve as guidelines for the remainder of the negotiations. Henry Kissinger was to be a central negotiator during both the Nixon and Ford administrations, while Andrei Gromyko would serve as his counterpart on the Soviet side.

Faced with a campaign for reelection, the Ford administration backed away from the talks, taking a tough stand to show the administration's opposition to the Soviet

Union. The election of 1976, however, was won by Jimmy Carter, who entered office with a strong commitment to arms control. He was severely limited, however, by ongoing Republican opposition to the SALT talks, continued opposition from Henry Jackson, and by the formation in 1976 of the Committee on the Present Danger. The Committee was a private lobbying group which attempted to convince the public and Congress that any concessions in the area of nuclear weapons would leave the United States at a distinct disadvantage in its relationships with the Soviet Union. Lacking popular support, the Carter administration was limited in its ability to negotiate with the Soviet Union. Nevertheless, by 1979, an agreement was reached in Geneva which was then signed in Vienna. Cyrus Vance was a principal negotiator, a role that continued to be filled by Andrei Gromyko on the Soviet side. The final treaty was lengthy and complex.

The final SALT II treaty included three major provisions. First, it agreed to equal limits on strategic launchers at 2,250. This limit required the Soviet Union to destroy 250 of its launchers while allowing the United States to add to its arsenal. The treaty set limits on MIRVs, limiting the number of warheads per missile to that of the current technological capability. Second, it placed a short term moratorium on the development of new weapons systems as a way of slowing the arms race. This limited the testing and deployment of new weapons systems, but did exclude testing of cruise missiles where the United States had a distinct advantage. Likewise, it excluded air launched cruise missiles, another area where the United States had superiority. Third, it included a Statement of Principles which pledged the two sides to actual arms reduction as the focus of what were intended to be the SALT III talks. The treaty also included provisions for verification of compliance with the treaty. Neither side was permitted to interfere in intelligence gathering related to weapons deployment and development as related to the treaty guidelines. While this agreement was viewed by other countries as a positive first step toward a safer world, the agreement continued to meet opposition by the public and the Senate in the United States. Presented with the treaty, the Senate initially refused to ratify it. Following the Soviet invasion of Afghanistan in 1979 to quell a violent revolution, suspicion of the Soviet Union and its motives further increased and all possibility of ratification was lost.

Carter lost to Ronald Reagan in the 1980 presidential election. Reagan had been a strong vocal opponent of the treaty and of arms negotiations with the Soviet Union. Following his election, the treaty was withdrawn from consideration by the Senate and the entire SALT process was discontinued. Nevertheless, while the Reagan administration did not recognize the validity of the treaty, it continued to abide by the provisions of it, as did the Soviet Union. While the treaty's provisions were very limited and did nothing to facilitate actual disarmament, the treaty did have the effect of slowing the arms race. In addition, the talks presented an ongoing forum for conversation between the two superpowers. Despite a period of mutual antagonism lasting until the mid-1980's, the SALT process created the conditions which would allow Mikhail Gorbachev to begin new disarmament initiatives in the 1980's.   —*Charles L. Kammer III*

ADDITIONAL READING:

Cimbala, Stephen J., ed. *Strategic Arms Control After SALT*. Wilmington, Del.: SR Books, 1989. A discussion of arms control negotiations in the wake of the SALT agreements.

Geyer, Alan. *The Idea of Disarmament: Rethinking the Unthinkable*. Elgin, Ill.: Brethren Press, 1985. Includes a critical discussion of SALT II in the context of the history of nuclear arms control policy.

Morris, Charles R. *Iron Destinies, Lost Opportunities: The Arms Race Between the USA and USSR*. New York: Harper & Row, 1988. Places a discussion of SALT within the broader context of American and Soviet relationships.

Panofsky, W. K. H. *Arms Control and SALT II*. Seattle: University of Washington Press, 1979. A very specific discussion of the issues confronting the SALT II negotiators.

Smith, Gerald. *Doubletalk: The Story of SALT I*. Garden City, N.Y.: Doubleday, 1980. Includes an analysis of SALT II as a follow up to SALT I by one of the chief negotiators of SALT I.

Talbott, Strobe. *Endgame: The Inside Story of SALT II*. New York: Harper & Row, 1979. A very detailed account of the SALT II negotiations.

SEE ALSO: 1963, Limited Nuclear Test Ban Treaty Is Signed; 1975, Helsinki Agreement; 1979, Soviet Union Invades Afghanistan; 1987, Intermediate-Range Nuclear Forces Treaty.

1979
SOVIET UNION INVADES AFGHANISTAN
The Soviet Union invades Afghanistan, resulting in more than a decade of internal guerrilla resistance, international negative public opinion, an estimated loss of thirteen thousand Russian lives, and an estimated cost of twelve billion dollars by the end of 1983.
DATE: December 25, 1979
LOCALE: Afghanistan

CATEGORIES: Government and politics; Wars, uprisings, and civil unrest

KEY FIGURES:

Hafizullah Amin (1929-1979), president of Afghanistan, 1979

Leonid Ilich Brezhnev (1906-1982), first secretary of the Communist Party of the Soviet Union, 1964-1982

Sardar Mohammad Daud (1908-1978), president of Afghanistan, 1973-1978

Babrak Karmal (born 1929), president of Afghanistan, 1979-1986

Nur Mohammad Taraki (1917-1979), president of Afghanistan, 1978-1979

SUMMARY OF EVENT. Afghanistan, an underdeveloped, impoverished, and tribal-oriented country with a history of political instability and factional infighting, would not seem to present an inviting invasion prospect for a superpower such as the Soviet Union in the 1970's. Yet, the Soviet government, and its czarist Russian predecessors, had developed an interest in Afghanistan for doctrinaire and global political reasons harking back to the "Great Game" of diplomacy and intrigue between colonial Russia and Great Britain, in which Afghanistan served as a buffer state separating the expansionist pretensions of the Russian empire in Central Asia from the British empire's interests in India and South Asia. With the cessation of British interests in the area and changes in Russia after the revolution of 1917, Afghanistan pursued its own path to nationhood under Islam and a native monarchy, subject to a number of changes in rulership and frequent recourse to economic aid from foreign countries, most notably Germany before World War II and the United States and the Soviet Union in the postwar era.

A significant change in political orientation came in April, 1978, with the Saur revolution, a quasi-military coup instigated by members of the People's Democratic Party of Afghanistan (PDPA), founded in 1965, and Soviet-trained military officers. This revolution, which did not have wide popular support, was inspired by Marxist-Leninist political views, and was intended to be followed by wide-ranging and radical reforms of the political and social milieu. These reforms not only failed to win acceptance among the overwhelmingly peasant population, but were actively opposed by Islamic leaders and feudal landowners.

Soon after its formation, the PDPA had split into two rival groups, the *khalqis* and the *parchamis*, who differed not only in their doctrinal and class associations, but also in their willingness to involve the Soviet Union in internal Afghan affairs. Each faction put out a newspaper under its own name which expressed the political philosophy of that group. The *khalqis* were primarily members of the rural based Pushtun ethnic community and favored a homegrown type of socialism. The *parchamis* were primarily urbanites, better educated, and non-Pushtun, and advocated cooperating with the Soviet Union in their revolutionary endeavors. The leaders of the religious elite, meanwhile, were influenced by their coreligionists in Egypt, Pakistan, and Iran, and organized their own Islamist movement in Kabul. A seizure of the government and proclamation of a republic in 1973 by Sardar Mohammad Daud, followed by repressive measures against political opponents and a leaning of foreign relations away from the Soviet Union and toward Iran and other Islamic states, caused Afghanistan's relations with the Soviet Union to become strained, and served to effect a rapprochement between the two Marxist factions of the PDPA in 1977.

The 1978 Saur coup was instigated by the assassination of a prominent Marxist leader and mass arrests of PDPA leaders. PDPA military officers led a demonstration in Kabul on April 27, seized the presidential palace, and assassinated Daud. Nur Mohammad Taraki, a *parcham* leader, emerged as the new president, with deputy prime ministers Amin and Karmal. Renewed infighting between the factions soon developed, however, and Amin engineered the ouster of Karmal and assumed the position of secretary-general of the party. The prospective reforms, such as massive reallocation of land, educational opportunity for women, and social changes, while laudable in themselves, took no account of the traditional Afghan culture and caused widespread disruption among the peasant population.

Although there is some evidence that the Soviet Union was implicated in the 1978 coup, there is no doubt that it watched with growing alarm the outcome of that event. Amin became the de facto power in Afghanistan and, when he learned of Soviet attempts to effect a reconciliation between the figurehead leader Taraki and the ousted leader Karmal, he and his henchmen executed Taraki in October, 1979. At this point, it became virtually certain that the Soviet Union would invade Afghanistan, since Amin was a leader with whom they could not cooperate. They were concerned about his inability to effect reform, his divisive leadership of the Marxist PDPA, and his growing assumption of dictatorial powers. Brezhnev was also personally incensed about Amin's disregard for his attempt to reconcile Taraki and Karmal, and the resultant murder of Taraki.

Amin was also ineffective in combating the mujahideen resistance. Thousands of refugees were fleeing Afghanistan for neighboring states, particularly Pakistan

Afghan resistance fighters waged an arduous guerrilla war against Soviet troops who invaded Afghanistan in December of 1979. (U.S. Department of Defense)

and Iran, and some were there regrouping to join the resistance. The Soviet Union believed that a brief intervention to oust Amin would prevent the mujahideen from taking power and would save the Marxist revolution. This would protect the geopolitical interest of the Soviet Union and contribute to the international cause of communism, while ridding them of a troublesome ally. Although Amin learned of the intentions of the Soviet Union for removing him from power, he had insufficient time to make a counterplan before Russian troops were flown in to carry out his execution and install Babrak Karmal as president in late December, 1979.

This action of the Soviets came as a shock to international public opinion, particularly in the United States. Security in the region had recently been severely upset by the fall of the Shah of Iran and the Iranian revolution. Détente between the United States and the Soviet Union at this point was strained, although the Soviet Union had planned that this intervention would be a swift one, as had

occurred in 1956 in Hungary and again in 1968 in Czechoslovakia. The claim was made that the Soviet Union had been "invited" to intervene by the legitimate government in Afghanistan to prop up a shaky Marxist government, which was in accord with the Brezhnev Doctrine of intervening militarily to defend Marxist regimes under attack.

What the Soviet Union failed to realize was the intransigence and staying power of the Afghan resistance movement. It also committed the signal error of sending in troops from the republics of Soviet Central Asia, who found themselves under orders to attack their ethnic cousins rather than the imperialists and capitalists Soviet propaganda had made them expect. Although there was massive international support for the resistance, particularly as the war progressed, most of the action on the ground was fought by native insurgents. The heavily armored troop movements of the Soviet Union were at a disadvantage under conditions of guerrilla warfare in a mountainous country where the surrounding population was uniformly hostile. To this was added morale problems as the Russian soldiers realized the unpopular nature of the war and faced lack of support, or even awareness, from their native country.

Nor was Babrak Karmal able to form a government acceptable to even a small percentage of the Afghan people, particularly in the light of the complete domination of his government by Soviet advisors. The *parcham* regime of Karmal was responsible for alienating many of the *khalqi* factionists, some of whom defected to the mujahideen, as did many of the regular Afghan troops. Massive starvation threatened, millions of Afghan citizens became refugees, and the Soviet Union was forced to import wheat in order to feed the starving population.

Reaction in the United Nations was to deplore the Soviet action and call for the withdrawal of foreign troops from Afghanistan. President Jimmy Carter of the United States stopped grain and technology exports, reduced the fishing fleet catch, delayed the opening of a Soviet consulate in New York, postponed negotiating a new cultural agreement, boycotted the 1980 Moscow Summer Olympics, withdrew the SALT II treaty from active consideration, and announced the Carter Doctrine whereby any attempt to gain control of the Persian Gulf region would be regarded as an assault on U.S. vital interests.

—*Gloria Fulton*

ADDITIONAL READING:

Collins, Joseph J. *The Soviet Invasion of Afghanistan: A Study in the Use of Force in Soviet Foreign Policy.* Lexington, Mass.: Lexington Books, 1986. Traces the background of Soviet-Afghan relations and the main political events in Afghanistan and the Soviet Union that precipitated the invasion.

Cordovez, Diego, and Selig S. Harrison. *Out of Afghanistan: The Inside Story of the Soviet Withdrawal.* New York: Oxford University Press, 1995. An account of the background, invasion, and peacemaking efforts by the principal U.N. peace negotiator and a foreign correspondent.

Girardet, Edward. *Afghanistan: The Soviet War.* New York: St. Martin's Press, 1985. A journalist's account of the invasion, including Soviet strategy, the resistance, political imperatives, refugees, and foreign aid.

Newell, Nancy Peabody, and Richard S. Newell. *The Struggle for Afghanistan.* Ithaca, N.Y.: Cornell University Press, 1981. A study of the internal conditions in Afghanistan and how they were changed by the invasion.

Rais, Rasul Bakhsh. *War Without Winners: Afghanistan's Uncertain Transition After the Cold War.* New York: Oxford University Press, 1994. A scholarly analysis of the Afghan tragedy from the Afghan perspective.

SEE ALSO: 1968-1989, Brezhnev Doctrine; 1975, Helsinki Agreement; 1979, SALT II Is Signed; 1985, Gorbachev Is Elected General Secretary of the Communist Party; 1991, Soviet Union Dissolves into Loosely Allied Republics; 1994, Russian Troops Invade Chechnya.

1980
DEATH OF TITO

The death of Tito leaves a power gap in his union of Serbs, Croats, and Muslims that ultimately results in Yugoslavia's dissolution in war.

DATE: May 4, 1980

LOCALE: Yugoslavia

CATEGORY: Government and politics

KEY FIGURES:

Sir Winston Leonard Spencer Churchill (1874-1965), British prime minister, 1940-1945 and 1951-1955

Draža Mihailović (1893-1946), leader of the Serbian Chetniks

Joseph Stalin (Iosif Vissarionovich Dzhugashvili; 1879-1953), Soviet leader, 1928-1953

Tito (Josip Broz; 1892-1980), general secretary of the Yugoslav Communist Party and Yugoslavian dictator, 1945-1980

SUMMARY OF EVENT. When Tito died in 1980, he left behind a unified but precarious Yugoslav state. He had been the undisputed leader of Yugoslavia since the end of World War II. Although a committed Communist, he broke with Stalin in 1948, rejecting Stalin's charges that he had been disloyal. Tito emphasized that his country could pursue an independent course and remain Communist. He later allied himself with President Gamal Abdel Nasser of Egypt and Prime Minister Jawaharlal Nehru of India in the nonaligned movement, a group of nations attempting to pursue common policies that put them between the rival Cold War powers, the United States and the Soviet Union.

Tito was a master at manipulating power blocs—both outside and within his own country. He had fought with distinction on the Communist side in the Russian Civil War (1918-1920), and he became Stalin's agent in Yugoslavia. Although he had condemned World War II as an imperialist war, he reversed his position when Germany invaded the Soviet Union and Yugoslavia. During World War II, he organized the Partisans, an underground organization of Yugoslavs fighting to remove the Germans and Italians from Yugoslavia. In 1943, he gained the support of Winston Churchill, who had been championing the cause of Draža Mihailović, leader of the Serb Chetniks, and a fervent anti-Communist. Churchill became convinced that

Mihailović was not fighting as hard as Tito and that he may even have been collaborating with the enemy. Churchill's switch to Tito is still a fiercely debated issue among historians, many of whom believe Tito's agents fed Churchill false information.

During the war, the Partisans and Chetniks fought each other, realizing that one group or the other would dominate the country when the Germans and Italians were defeated. Tito gained a reputation for drawing Communists and non-Communists to his cause, and American and British officers serving with his forces were impressed at his efforts to unify Serbs, Croats, and Muslims.

After the war, Tito quickly consolidated his power—executing Mihailović and purging some of his own followers whom he suspected of disloyalty. He continued his close relationship with Churchill and the Western powers, aware that they acted as a buffer against the Soviet Union, which dominated the countries of Eastern Europe. When Stalin expelled Tito from the Communist movement in 1948 and threatened to invade Yugoslavia, he was deterred by Tito's army, which would have inflicted considerable casualties and, more important, by the possibility that the Western powers would come to Tito's aid.

Tito dominated Yugoslavia's warring factions. The Serbs had taken the lead in post-World War I Yugoslavia, and other groups—particularly the Croats—resented Serb hegemony. Tito did not resolve tensions between the Roman Catholic Croats and the Orthodox Catholic Serbs; instead, he suppressed them. He stifled political and religious dissent of all kinds. He established a command economy, in which all economic decisions were made by the central government, so that farmers, for example, were given production quotas. Yet he did not collectivize agriculture—as in the Soviet Union with its huge government-owned farms. As a result, Tito's form of Communism was regarded in the West as less authoritarian and more worthy of support when compared to Soviet tyranny.

Besides his jailing and even murder of political opponents, Tito relied on his own charismatic personality. He dressed the part of war hero on a white horse with a chest full of medals. He downplayed his own ethnic origins (he was the son of a Croat village blacksmith) and made sure that no group had an undue influence in any branch of government. His powerful support from the Western powers, including economic and military aid, made it difficult for anyone within the country to oppose his policies.

Tito's overwhelming presence gave Yugoslavia a veneer of unity and economic health it never really possessed. His relaxation of central planning in the 1970's, for example, was not a sign of his liberalism or of the country's strength but rather a desperate effort to deal with

The death of Yugoslavian dictator Tito contributed to an escalation of tensions and ethnic rivalries among the various provinces and groups that composed the Yugoslav state. (Archive Photos)

failures in economic development. Similarly, he had achieved no workable model of a unified Yugoslav state. In 1971, realizing that he had not built the institutions that would ensure his nation's survival, he established a twenty-two member collective presidency, composed of the presidents of the six republics and representatives from their respective assemblies, elected for five-year terms. Tito was then chosen chairman of this unwieldy federation. He projected a sort of round-robin government, which after his death would be headed, in rotation, by the presidents of the republics. In the absence of a single strong leader, each republic would have its share of power.

Yet Tito's loosening of the central power proved problematic. Franjo Tudjman (later elected president of an independent Croatia) challenged Tito's concept of a unified Yugoslav state. Although dissenters such as Tudjman were punished, the idea of a single Yugoslav state was undermined as Tito's policies were shown to be ineffective and the economy weakened. Tito tried to reimpose censorship on intellectual life, but his death only showed how futile it had been to deny the tensions he could check but not eradicate.

Tito's death left the major issues of World War II unresolved and a country without the institutions or the political culture to deal peacefully with those issues. For example, Tito had not addressed the grievances of Serbs, whose leader had been executed after the war and whose king he had deposed. There were large Serb minorities in Croatia and Bosnia which felt threatened once politicians such as Tudjman were free to foment their ideas of independence. Who would protect Serb minority rights when Croatia was independent? The Croatian Ustachi (a Fascist organization) had slaughtered thousands of Serbs during World War II. When the new Croatian government adopted some of the Utaschi's symbols, Serbs feared another bloodbath. On the other hand, Croats, who had bridled under Serb dominance before the war, feared the resumption of calls for a "greater Serbia, which to Croats meant a loss of some of their lands where Serbs lived and wished to be united with the Serbian republic. Other minorities, such as the Muslims, were caught between the warring claims of Serbs and Croats.

For more than forty years—since the end of World War II—Tito had silenced all talk of national political rights. According to Communist ideology, ethnic rivalries could not be permitted or even acknowledged because the goal of the Communist state was to produce a culture free of racial, ethnic, or other group loyalties. Consequently, with no rational discussion of underlying problems, the debate about what happened in Yugoslavia remained frozen in the attitudes of World War II. To many Serbs, the Croat slaughter of their people during the war seemed like yesterday. To Croats, the Yugoslav state, and especially the army, became nothing more than a bastion of Serb tyranny.

Marshal Tito's death did not make the breakup of Yugoslavia inevitable, but it did contribute to a climate of intolerance and ignorance that his political program did nothing to ameliorate. The demise of Communism in the Soviet Union and elsewhere in Eastern Europe meant that Yugoslav leaders, devoid of any credible ideology, resorted to policies that played on people's memories of World War II and awakened their worst fears about inclusion in a nation-state in which they would find themselves once again despised and perhaps exterminated minorities.

—*Carl Rollyson*

ADDITIONAL READING:

Beloff, Nora. *Tito's Flawed Legacy: Yugoslavia and the West Since 1939.* Boulder, Colo: Westview Press, 1985. One of the key studies of postwar Yugoslavia, criticizing Churchill's support of Tito, Tito's rupture with Moscow, and his failure to encourage brotherhood or unity among Serbs, Croats, and Muslims.

Dedijer, Vladimir. *Tito.* New York: Simon & Schuster, 1952. The official biography still worth consulting for its authoritative detail.

Djilas, Milovan. *Tito: The Story from Inside.* New York: Harcourt Brace Jovanovich, 1980. An impressive and critical view by one of Tito's closest confidants turned dissident.

Stankovic, Slobodan. *The End of the Tito Era: Yugoslavia's Dilemmas.* Stanford, Calif.: Hoover Institution Press, 1981. Chapters on Yugoslavia's army, economic condition, the struggle to succeed Tito, and Soviet-Yugoslav relations.

West, Richard. *Tito and the Rise and Fall of Yugoslavia.* New York: Carroll & Graf, 1995. Detailed study of Tito's triumph in World War II, his consolidation of power, his quarrel with Stalin, and a reassessment of his final years leading to the disintegration of Yugoslavia and to war.

Wilson, Sir Duncan. *Tito's Yugoslavia.* New York: Cambridge University Press, 1979. Yugoslavia's history after World War I, its role in World War II, its early years as a Soviet satellite, the break with Stalin, the evolution of an independent Communist state, and economic development.

SEE ALSO: 1912-1913, Balkan Wars; 1918-1921, Russian Civil War; 1991-1992, Civil War Rages in Yugoslavia.

1980
SOLIDARITY IS FOUNDED IN POLAND

Solidarity is founded in Poland, bringing the grievances of Polish workers to the forefront of the nation's political consciousness and resulting in the eventual overthrow of its oppressive Communist regime.

DATE: September, 1980
LOCALE: Gdansk, Poland
CATEGORIES: Business and labor; Government and politics; Organizations and institutions
KEY FIGURES:

Edward Gierek (born 1913), leader of the Polish Communist Party, 1970-1980

Jozef Glemp (born 1929), primate of the Polish Roman Catholic Church during the rise of Solidarity

Wojciech Jaruzelski (born 1923), Polish general who declared martial law in 1981 and served as head of the Polish Communist Party, 1981-1989

Anna Walentynowicz, worker at the Lenin Shipyards in Gdansk whose unfair firing led to the revolt which led to the rise of Solidarity

Lech Wałęsa (born 1943), shipyard worker who became the leader of the Solidarity movement and later the first president of the newly independent Poland, 1990-1995

SUMMARY OF EVENT. The roots of the Polish trade union Solidarity extend deep into the soil of Polish history, ideology, and politics. In order to understand how Solidarity could and did successfully operate while under the rigid structures of the Soviet Union, it is important to understand Poland's unique relationship not only with Russia but also with its other neighbors, notably Germany and Austria. The Roman Catholic Church in Poland played a significant role, serving as a source of both spiritual nourishment and of political and social strength. Under the auspices of the trade union movement, the people of Poland mounted a vigorous nonviolent campaign against a Soviet-controlled military regime that had crushed similar protest movements in neighboring nations, most notably in Czechoslovakia.

The Poles have been a most independent people, as is demonstrated by their history. Their territory has been conquered but their spirit always remained free. No matter how long the occupation, Poles have always come back to prominence. They have been the only nation in Eastern Europe that consistently challenged and won when it came up against the Soviet Union. Part of this independence is their geographical situation as a major buffer between the Soviet Union and the West. Part of it is the result of their political and cultural preeminence since the Middle Ages. The city of Danzig was a "free city" during the Middle Ages, meaning a city almost like a state in itself. The same city of Danzig when it changed hands after World War II became a part of postwar Poland as the city of Gdansk, the birthplace of Solidarity.

Poland was partitioned several times during its history. Partition came at times from the East (Russia) and sometimes from the West (Austria and Germany). Sometimes partition came for religious reasons. The Russians, who adhered to Orthodox Christianity, disliked Roman Catholic Poland. Prussia, and later on Germany, which engulfed it, was largely Protestant. Poland was always very unified culturally. For the most part, the Poles spoke one language and primarily belonged to one set of historical and cultural forebears. These affinities were important in making Poland one of the few Eastern and Central European nations that retained an identity despite changes of boundaries and displacement of population. When Poland was occupied by Soviet troops, these troops controlled the geography, but they never gained control of the Polish people. While official government policy supported atheism, the cultural reality was a strong and vibrant Polish Roman Catholic

Polish shipyard worker Lech Wałęsa was honored for his leadership of the Solidarity trade union when he received the Nobel Peace Prize in 1983. (The Nobel Foundation)

Church. This vitality existed because the church not only was a place for spiritual support but it also acted as a social and cultural repository of things Polish when the Polish state did not exist. Thus the church helped Poland to survive as a nation and is seen as a nationalist phenomenon as well as a spiritual center. Although Soviet military might did indeed rule in Poland, the Polish attitude of "self-limitation" allowed Poles to work within the Soviet sphere. The goal was to make this sphere more and more Polish. This fluid and flexible relationship kept the Poles alive if not fully free.

The Solidarity movement was born when seventeen thousand workers at the Lenin shipyard in Gdansk launched a strike on August 15, 1980. Soon, other workers in Gdansk and Warsaw joined the strike. On August 23, Party leader Edward Gierek agreed to negotiate directly with the strike committee of the Gdansk shipyard where the strike began. As a result of the negotiations, the Polish government conceded certain rights to the strikers, including permission to form an independent trade union. By September, the independent trade unions joined to form a single organization calling itself Solidarnosc, the Polish word for "solidarity." The newly formed organization elected Lech Wałęsa to serve as its president. The legalization of Solidarity gave rise to more demonstrations in Poland for additional concessions, particularly in the political arena. These demonstrations led the Polish government to declare martial law in 1981, to outlaw Solidarity, and to arrest the union's leaders.

The trade union Solidarity was itself a mirror of the Polish people's response to outside opposition. Solidarity became so deeply rooted in the Polish people's lives that no repressive measures could erase either the idea of the labor union or the labor union itself. Solidarity's main thrust was not to eliminate socialism but to make socialism more relevant to the basically working-class nation which is Poland. What was revolutionary about this activity was that it was Solidarity that brought this renewed interest in socialism. It was to be a home-grown effort—one controlled by the Polish people rather than by the Polish Communist Party or by the Soviet Union. While Solidarity was working for Polish interests, it was doing so within the framework of socialism. Solidarity did not directly challenge the political authority of the Soviet-controlled Polish government, and it refused to surrender its trade union independence for a Soviet-style labor reality.

The 1980 Gdansk shipyard worker strike which led to the rise of Solidarity began with limited objectives, and expanded as situations allowed. As events developed, Solidarity responded to them, thus allowing the movement to move as it needed to, and not become entangled in processes which were not to the workers' advantages.

When Solidarity was given legal status, this status was won on its own ground and was thus not compromised by giving away its independence as a prerequisite for survival. Solidarity could legitimately claim that its action was not political but economic. It could claim that the change it wanted to bring about had to do with the workplace, not politics. It could do all of this and still secure its independent status. This independent status eventually led to real political clout, allowing Solidarity to become part of the foundation upon which political democracy arose in Poland.

Solidarity was an example of nonviolent revolution in its best form. Solidarity was a mix of piety and politics, a mix of working-class socialism and trade union democracy. Its members used nonviolent methods to change the system rather than abolish that system. The pragmatics of the situation (and the pragmatics of Polish history) suggested that any absolute procedure would fail. Solidarity is yet another example that ultimate political success is not always on the side of those with the most firepower but on the side that exhibits the most awareness of its surroundings. Solidarity indicates that those closest to the situation can win if they are willing to bide their time. The story of Solidarity is ultimately a kind of a guerrilla movement within Poland. History shows that guerrillas often have more advantage in the end than they seem to have in the beginning.

—*Paul Barton-Kriese*

ADDITIONAL READING:

Ash, Timothy Garton. *The Polish Revolution: Solidarity*. New York: Charles Scribner's Sons, 1984. An excellent journalistic report of the rise of the Solidarity movement to prominence in Poland. Ash covers the entire movement from the Lenin dockyards to Solidarity's underground days. An excellent chronology of events.

Barton-Kriese, Paul. *Nonviolent Revolution*. Nairobi, Kenya: Shirikon, 1995. One of the best analytical accounts of the political culture of Poland on the eve of Solidarity's nonviolent revolt. Solidarity participants rate this work as an accurate account of the broader issues involved in this event.

Blondi, Lawrence, et al., eds. *Poland's Solidarity Movement*. Chicago: Loyola University Press, 1984. An incisive account that provides a broad overview of the economic, political, and social components of the movement.

Kemp-Welch, Andrew. *The Birth of Solidarity: The Gdansk Negotiations, 1980*. New York: St. Martin's Press, 1980. An indispensable compendium of the most important documents of the era including the entire texts of the Gdansk Agreements. Kemp-Welch paints in much of what was said but did not appear in the final versions.

Steven, Stewart. *The Poles*. New York: Macmillan, 1982. A brief, easily read history of the Polish nation. It details the tapestry upon which the Solidarity movement moves.

Zielonka, Jan. "Strengths and Weaknesses of Nonviolent Action: The Polish Case." *Orbis* 30 (Spring, 1986): 91-110. The philosophical framework for the concept of "self-limiting" revolution, the major Solidarity theory.

SEE ALSO: 1955, Warsaw Pact Is Signed; 1968-1989, Brezhnev Doctrine; 1983, Martial Law in Poland Ends.

1981

MITTERRAND IS ELECTED TO THE FRENCH PRESIDENCY

Mitterrand is elected to the French presidency, bringing to power a president from the political Left for the first time since the Fifth Republic was established twenty-three years earlier.

DATE: May 10, 1981
LOCALE: France
CATEGORY: Government and politics
KEY FIGURES:

Raymond Barre (born 1924), prime minister of France, 1976-1981

Jacques René Chirac (born 1932), Gaullist leader who gave lukewarm support to Giscard d'Estaing

Jacques Delors (born 1925), moderate Socialist economist

Valéry Giscard d'Estaing (born 1922), president of France, 1974-1981

George Marchais (born 1920), general-secretary of the French Communist Party, 1972-1994

Pierre Mauroy (born 1928), first prime minister under Mitterrand, 1981-1984

François Mitterrand (1916-1996), Socialist president of France, 1981-1995

Michel Rocard (born 1930), moderate Socialist and rival to Mitterrand

SUMMARY OF EVENT. In 1981, many people believed that François Mitterrand's electoral victory was a watershed event that would inaugurate a long period of political dominance by the parties of the Left. Following the euphoria of his first year in power, however, severe economic difficulties forced the government to the political center. Although Mitterrand remained president for two full terms, his Socialist Party and other left-wing parties experienced electoral decline, and he left office in 1995 without accomplishing the structural changes which he had advocated.

By 1981, Mitterrand was a veteran politician with a most impressive record. One of the leaders of the Resistance in World War II, he was an influential member of eleven cabinets during the Fourth Republic (1946-1958). In the election of 1965, he gained great stature when he forced President Charles de Gaulle to submit to a second ballot. Elected first secretary of the new Socialist Party (PS) in 1971, Mitterrand skillfully mediated differences between the party's left-wing and its moderate reformist factions. His strategy was to seek a Union of the Left which included the French Communist Party (PCF), and in 1972 the PS and PCF agreed to a Common Program which envisioned nationalizing many private businesses and increasing social programs. In the presidential election of 1974, Mitterrand was narrowly defeated by the candidate of the Right, Valéry Giscard d'Estaing, with a vote of 49.1 percent to 50.9 percent.

During his seven-year term of office, Giscard's policies were moderately right of center. As explained in his book of 1976, *French Democracy*, Giscard wanted to promote a "liberal" capitalism with fewer class differences and more emphasis on social justice. He was able to reduce the voting age to eighteen, and he tried, but failed, to convince the parliament to pass a capital gains tax and a less restrictive abortion law. Giscard made a costly political blunder in 1980, when he became the first Western leader to meet with Leonid Brezhnev after the Soviet invasion of Afghanistan. Many people disliked Giscard's aloof, monarchial style of leadership.

There was widespread dissatisfaction with the economy during Giscard's presidency. In the two decades before the 1973 oil crisis, the French had become accustomed to an uninterrupted growth in the standard of living, and the new international challenges made it impossible to satisfy public expectations. After 1976, Prime Minister Raymond Barre pursued a deflationary policy which emphasized the free market and a restriction of the money supply. The austerity of the Barre plan was painful and only partially a success. While purchasing power increased by 24 percent during Giscard's presidency, by 1980 inflation had grown to almost 14 percent while unemployment stood at 7.5 percent.

Prior to the election of 1981, coalitions of both the Left and the Right were increasingly fragile. There was a growing split between Giscard's organization, the Union for French Democracy (UDF), and Chirac's followers, the Rally for the Republic (RPR). Likewise, in 1977 the Socialists and the Communists could not agree on the terms of their Common Program, and the PS-PCF alliance came to an end.

As specified in the French constitution, the presidential election of 1981 took place in two stages, with the first ballot scheduled for April 26 and the second ballot slated for May 10. The campaign officially opened on April 9, when the Constitutional Council announced ten candidates for the first round. The four major candidates were Giscard, Mitterrand, Chirac, and Marchais. Giscard defended his policies of the last seven years, and called for moderate reforms, including an expansion of youth training programs and a lowering of the retirement age. Chirac endorsed a program of reducing governmental spending and limiting regulations on business. Mitterrand advocated a watered-down version of the Common Program, including nationalization of ten unspecified industries, creation of new jobs in the public sector, a workweek of thirty-five hours, and an increase in the minimum wage and family allowances. Marchais wanted to go further than the Socialist agenda, and emphasized increased taxes on profits and capital. On April 26, Giscard and Mitterrand received the largest number of votes, with 28.3 percent and 25.8 percent respectively. This meant that the two

A skillful mediator who strove to unify the French Socialist Party, François Mitterrand won a 1981 run-off election against the incumbent president Valéry Giscard d'Estaing. (Archive Photos)

would face each other in the run-off election two weeks later.

In a television debate of May 5, neither candidate was considered to have gained a decisive advantage, but there was agreement that Mitterrand improved over his performance of four years earlier. In order to win, Giscard badly needed the support of the RPR, but Chirac only gave him a lukewarm endorsement, saying that everyone should vote "according to his conscience." The Left appeared to be more united than the Right, and Communist leaders instructed their followers to vote for the socialist candidate. Mitterrand announced that if elected he would dissolve the National Assembly and hold elections to gain a majority of the Left, but he refused to say whether he would include Communists as members of his cabinet.

In the vote of May 10, Mitterrand prevailed with 43.15 percent to 40.22 percent. In response, Mitterrand's supporters held jubilant celebrations that were compared with the liberation of Paris after World War II. Most informed

observed were surprised with the outcome, which represented the first substantial change of power in the history of the Fifth Republic.

Within two days, French stocks lost an average of 20 percent, but moderate socialists, especially economist Jacques Delors, assured investors that nationalizations would be based on fair compensation. The stock market rebounded on May 13. Installed as president on May 21, Mitterrand evoked socialist traditions but used a conciliatory tone aimed at calming fears of the center-Right. Taking office, his first major action was to announce that his prime minister would be Pierre Mauroy, a centrist leader of the SP, and the new cabinet included moderates such as Delors and Mitterrand's major rival, Michel Rocard. Mitterrand quickly scheduled elections for a new National Assembly to take place on June 14 and 21. In these elections, the Socialist Party won an absolute majority, and with this unprecedented triumph by the Left, Mitterrand predicted a "break with capitalism." During Mitterrand's "state of grace," he and Mauroy got the Assembly to pass an economic program based upon his campaign platform, including nationalizations, an increase in spending on social programs, and one hundred thousand public-sector jobs. By June of 1982, however, a combination of deficits and inflation forced Mitterrand to reverse course and begin a program of austerity. Thereafter, his policies became increasingly moderate, and in the presidential election of 1988 he ran on a platform of modernization, national union, and compromise.

By the end of Mitterrand's second term in 1995, most of the radical reforms of 1981-1982 had been reversed, and it appeared doubtful that there would be a repeat of such experiments in the foreseeable future. Although France had not become a socialist country, Mitterrand and the socialists did demonstrate that they could be responsible in managing a capitalist economy. Ironically, Mitterrand's most enduring legacy probably was his purging of the revolutionary ideology from the PS, so that it conformed to the model of reformist Social Democratic parties elsewhere in Europe. —*Thomas T. Lewis*

ADDITIONAL READING:

Friend, Julius. *Seven Years in France: François Mitterrand and the Unintended Revolution, 1981-1988.* Boulder, Colo.: Westview Press, 1989. A readable summary of Mitterrand's early policies and why he was forced to change direction.

McCarthy, Patrick, ed. *The French Socialists in Power, 1981-1986.* Excellent collection of articles, with chapter 1 devoted to the election of 1981.

Machin, Howard, and Vincent Wright. "Why Mitterrand Won: The French Presidential Elections of April-May, 1981." *West European Politics* 5 (January, 1982): 5-35. A detailed analysis of the election, with much voting data.

Northcutt, Wayne. *Mitterrand: A Political Biography*. New York: Holmes & Meier, 1992. Well-written account of Mitterrand's life and career, with excellent discussion of how he came to power.

Ryan, W. Francis. "France Under Giscard." *Current History* 80 (September, 1981): 201-205, 228-229. Useful summary of the policies of Valéry Giscard d'Estaing before 1981.

Singer, David. *Is Socialism Doomed? The Meaning of Mitterrand*. New York: Oxford University Press, 1988. A stimulating thesis about the impractical postulates of socialism.

SEE ALSO: 1969, De Gaulle Steps Down; 1983, Klaus Barbie Faces Nazi War Crimes Charges; 1985, Sinking of the *Rainbow Warrior*; 1995, Chirac Takes Office as President of France.

1981
GREEK SOCIALISTS WIN PARLIAMENTARY MAJORITY

Greek socialists win a parliamentary majority under the leadership of Andreas Papandreou, who forms the first socialist government in the country's history.

DATE: October 18, 1981
LOCALE: Greece
CATEGORY: Government and politics
KEY FIGURES:

Konstantinos Karamanlis (born 1907), prime minister of Greece, 1955-1963 and 1974-1980, and later president of the Greek Republic, 1980-1985 and 1990-1995

Konstantinos Mitsotakis (born 1918), member of Centre Union Party, later joined New Democracy and served as prime minister, 1990-1993

Andreas Papandreou (1919-1996), U.S.-educated economist, who served in the Greek parliament 1964 and 1974-1981 before serving as prime minister, 1981-1989 and 1993-1996

SUMMARY OF EVENT. The years of military rule in Greece (1967-1974) left a lasting legacy of revulsion against authoritarian rule and the determination to create a stable democracy. Called from self-imposed exile, Konstantinos Karamanlis returned to Athens where he had to deal immediately with a dangerous confrontation between Greece and Turkey over Cyprus and then with popular clamor for

the punishment of the junta leaders and their supporters and the depoliticization of the military.

Democratic government was reestablished but the people's joy was diminished by the national humiliation over Turkey's intervention in Cyprus. In the aftermath of that crisis, it was a political leader from the past, Karamanlis, who led the way to democratic politics, but it was a figure from the future, Andreas Papandreou, who took most advantage of it.

Under the leadership of American-born politician Andreas Papandreou, the Panhellenic Socialist Movement won a majority in the Greek parliamentary elections held in 1981. (Archive Photos)

Karamanlis would not countenance military action against Turkey over Cyprus. Some 40 percent of the island remained occupied by Turkish troops, and the Greek and Turkish Cypriot communities separated physically resulting in a major refugee problem. Greece withdrew from the NATO military wing in protest.

Before dealing with the military and other problems, Karamanlis called for elections quickly. Held in November, 1974, for parliament, and followed by a referendum on the monarchy in December, they were a milestone in several respects. The communists, illegal since before World War II, were able to participate. Voters rejected the return of the monarchy and Greece became a republic. Andreas Papandreou competed for votes leading the recently established Panhellenic Socialist Movement (PASOK).

Papandreou brought together center-leftist elements from his father's Centre Union Party, including members of youth organizations, and more radical leftists who had been members of his resistance organization against the junta. Ideologically, Papandreou called for a socialist "third way," neither capitalist nor communist. PASOK demanded national independence free of outside intervention, sovereignty based on the people, and the creation of democratic institutions emphasizing local self-rule. Specifically this meant an anti-NATO stance, demanding that American bases in Greece close, wariness of close ties to the European Economic Community (EEC), which Greece was to join as a full member, bitter criticism of the monarchy and the junta, and a pro-Third World position in foreign affairs.

In the 1974 election, PASOK came in third following the Centre Union Party. Overwhelming victory (54 percent of the vote and 219 of 300 parliamentary seats) went to Karamanlis and his New Democracy Party. A continuation of the National Radical Union Party of the 1950's, New Democracy was the mainstay of the moderate conservatives. Offering what most Greeks wanted at the time, stability and democracy, Karamanlis represented dignity for Greece, commitment to Western alliances and institutions, and a middle road in politics, allowing communists a voice while settling the monarchy issue. In 1975, Karamanlis pushed for a new constitution that strengthened presidential authority against that of parliament. Konstantinos Tsatsos, a New Democracy supporter, was elected president.

Because of pressing foreign issues, early parliamentary elections were held in November, 1977. New Democracy maintained control of parliament, though its percentage of the popular vote fell. More significantly, the share of the center vote dropped dramatically, while PASOK's percentage of the popular vote nearly doubled. With the second highest number of members in parliament, it was now the main opposition party.

Papandreou's rhetoric had proved popular at the polls, but governmental power still eluded him. Some in the party advocated ideological purity and preparing for the long run. Others counseled moderating the discourse and appealing to as broad a segment of the electorate as possible. Papandreou opted for the latter course, promoting PASOK as a noncommunist alternative for those who had been shut out of politics in the past.

Papandreou called for *allagi* (change), promising

widespread social reform. Party stalwarts built a solid grassroots organization, while their leader projected an alluring charisma, with speeches redolent of populism. This combination of factors produced a left-of-center party with mass appeal.

Such formidable competition from the left impelled political change on the right. In 1979, Karamanlis convened a party congress of New Democracy at which ideology was given a more liberal cast and the party's leadership was democratically elected by the parliamentary membership. Soon after, Karamanlis turned his eyes to the presidency, as Tsatsos stepped down. He was elected by parliament in 1980.

The following year, two historic events occurred. Greece became the tenth member of the European Community. In October, 1981, PASOK won the elections to become the first socialist government in Greek history. As a candidate, Papandreou spoke of the need for dramatic change in domestic and foreign affairs, but he was not about to remake society.

Although PASOK had promised much in the campaign, reality dictated otherwise. The double economic problem of inflation and stagnation that afflicted Greece in the late 1970's, led the PASOK government to adopt new fiscal policies while trying to keep its campaign promises. To combat stagnation, automatic cost-of-living increases stimulated consumer demand, but at the cost of further inflation. To assert Greece's national independence, PASOK technocrats argued for incentives to enterprises that embraced new technologies while increasing efficiency. Yet the government also stepped in to aid "problematic" industries, like the shipyards, that were foundering. Papandreou successfully demanded a redistribution of EEC funds to less developed member states such as Greece.

In a shrewd and long overdue move, on the civil front the government sought to heal the political breach resulting from the bitter civil war of the late 1940's by acknowledging the efforts of the leftist resistance movement during World War II and allowing political exiles of that era to return.

In 1985, Papandreou sought a mandate for a second term from the voters to carry out social reforms. Yet the election was held amid rancor between PASOK and New Democracy. Earlier that year the wily and autocratic Papandreou refused to support Karamanlis in his bid for a second term as president. He put forward his own candidate and proposed changes in the constitution that would limit the president's powers. Konstantinos Mitsotakis, now party leader of New Democracy, bitterly opposed Papandreou and painted the ideological differences between the two parties in stark contrasts. With a timely increase in public expenditures for new civil service jobs and financial aid to various segments of the populace, however, PASOK won as mundane concerns came first over ideological positions among the electorate.

The sweetness of political victory was diluted when PASOK had to take the harsh medicine of implementing an economic austerity program to curb public deficits and increase revenues. Protest strikes by public employees followed. In 1987, Papandreou tried to deal with criticism that the party and government were too closely linked and the party had lost its ideological momentum. Problems, both personal and political, mounted for Papandreou in 1988. He became seriously ill with heart problems while deciding to divorce his wife and marry a woman half his age. Financial scandal blew up and he was indicted in 1989.

As parliamentary commissions investigated the growing scandal, two elections in 1989 proved inconclusive, and it was not until April of 1990 that New Democracy formed a working majority. Mitsotakis became prime minister and embarked on an austerity program and the privatization of public enterprises as befitting a party committed to free enterprise. Karamanlis was again elected president and counseled Mitsotakis to exercise restraint as the new measures were hurting some more than others.

Papandreou overcame the indictment and was acquitted in 1992, the year when almost all in parliament approved the Maastricht Treaty of European Union integration. Defections from New Democracy in 1993 forced Mitsotakis to call elections that fall. Papandreou's star shone again and PASOK won a comfortable majority in parliament. Though in delicate health, Papandreou garnered support by criticizing the austerity program, promising to halt privatization, and projecting PASOK as a caring social democratic party.

Both major parties were committed to the economic convergence program for Greece to meet the requirements for integration in the European Union. Papandreou was, therefore, forced to follow austerity measures and some privatization. The Papandreou era ended, however, in January of 1996, when ill health forced him to resign as prime minister, though remaining as party leader.

Papandreou's legacy was mixed. An authoritarian figure who dominated his party's affairs, he used populist appeals to exploit fears in society. This resulted in disenchantment with politics by the electorate, limited social and economic progress, and few foreign relations successes. Disaffection with the role of the state in civil society remained. On the positive side, there were gains in women's property and legal rights, PASOK helped over-

come the deep political divisions between the left and the right, and a large segment of the petite bourgeoisie felt empowered.　　　　　*—Gerasimos Augustinos*

ADDITIONAL READING:

Clogg, Richard, ed. *Greece 1981-89: The Populist Decade*. New York: St. Martin's Press, 1993. Essays primarily on domestic politics and foreign affairs.

Spourdalakis, Michalis. *The Rise of the Greek Socialist Party*. London: Routledge, 1988. A penetrating study that places the development of PASOK in historical context.

Vryonis, Speros, Jr. *Greece on the Road to Democracy: From the Junta to PASOK, 1974-1986*. New Rochelle, N.Y.: Caratzas, 1991. Conference papers covering various aspects of Greek developments assessing changes since 1974.

SEE ALSO: 1963, Greek and Turkish Cypriots Clash over Political Rights; 1967, Greek Coup Leads to a Military Dictatorship; 1993, Maastricht Treaty Is Ratified.

1981
CONSTRUCTION OF SIBERIAN GAS PIPELINE BEGINS

The construction of the Siberian gas pipeline begins as part of an effort to increase Soviet natural gas supplies to Western Europe, but it leads to American sanctions and consequent stress in the Western alliance.

DATE: November 20, 1981

LOCALE: The Soviet Union from northwestern Siberia to Western Europe

CATEGORIES: Economics; Government and politics; Science and technology; Transportation

KEY FIGURES:

William Emerson Brock (born 1930), U.S. trade representative, 1981-1985

William J. Casey (1913-1987), director of the U.S. Central Intelligence Agency (CIA), 1981-1987

François Mitterrand (1916-1996), Socialist president of France, 1981-1995

Ronald Wilson Reagan (born 1911), fortieth president of the United States, 1981-1989

Boris E. Shcherbina (born 1919), Soviet minister for oil and gas construction, 1973-1984

George P. Shultz (born 1920), U.S. secretary of state, 1982-1989

Margaret Thatcher (born 1925), British prime minister, 1979-1990

Caspar W. Weinberger (born 1917), U.S. secretary of defense, 1981-1987

SUMMARY OF EVENT. This major undertaking—a natural gas pipeline from the Urengoi field in northwestern Siberia to Western Europe via Uzhgorod in the Ukraine— initiated on November 20, 1981, was noteworthy on several accounts. Because of its size and technical aspects the Urengoi-Uzhgorod line, nearly three thousand miles long, was to run through several time zones. Originating north of the Arctic Circle, its course, running south of the Northern Lights gas pipeline whose capacity was also being increased for the same purpose, was scheduled to be routed through nearly 100 miles of permafrost, 450 miles of swamp, and more than 1,200 miles of forest lands. Taking a more southerly route, the new line was to cross some 340 miles of mountain ranges in the Urals and the Carpathians. Among the numerous rivers to be spanned by the gas line were the Ob, the Volga, the Kama, the Dnieper, and the Dniester with total underwater crossings of about 125 miles. Highways and railroad lines were to be traversed 417 times.

The pipeline also called for the building of forty-one compressor stations in order to move the "blue fuel" at 75 atmospheres in each of the two pipelines. This was in preference to the even higher pressure of one hundred times normal atmosphere initially contemplated in a single pipeline at less cost. Simultaneously, major construction was also scheduled at the Urengoi oil field some three hundred miles southeast of the Yamal Peninsula in the Tycumen region. While the Soviet Union was the world's leading producer of natural gas, that country had never tackled a project of this magnitude before. Leaks and fires along the way were a constant possibility given the high pressure in the pipes and the inflammable nature of gas.

Yet, in short order, the project's political dimensions were to overshadow its engineering difficulties. For the plan had called for massive Western technology transfer to the Soviet Union to help it realize the line from which the West expected to benefit as an alternative energy source. The Middle East crises and "oil shocks" of 1973, 1979, and 1980 that had threatened Western energy supplies were in the background. Furthermore, the Soviets' record-high oil production itself was expected to decline soon, and natural gas was seen as an adequate substitute. Accordingly, a number of Western European countries and Japan were to make credits available to Moscow for its use in purchasing their huge earth-moving equipment, pipe-laying tractors, compressors, pumps, 25-megawatt turbines, and especially large-diameter 4.66-foot pipes (some 6 million tons of them). West Germany, France, Italy, Austria, and others were already receiving or contemplating to have access to this enlarged supply of Soviet natural gas through the existing grid.

Now, as the plan was taking shape, the new administration of President Ronald Reagan, in office since January of 1981, became concerned about several aspects of the project. Heading the list was the possible Western European overreliance on the Soviet Union as a major supplier of its energy. Such clout, according to Washington, could make these European states subject to Moscow's political or other leverage. Furthermore, the Reagan administration considered that the project would strengthen the Soviet economy by the contemplated Western hard currency credits to be extended to it, enabling the Communist state to divert a larger amount for its military preparedness. There was also fear that following closer ties between these Western European countries and President Reagan's "evil empire," the Europeans would be less likely to follow American leadership in the Cold War confrontation between the two power blocs, East and West. Questions were also being raised about the Soviets' technical ability to pull off such a huge undertaking expected to cost between $10 and $15 billion.

It so happened that a significant portion of the equipment for the project sought by the Russians was being produced by the affiliates of U.S. multinational corporations in Western Europe or by Western European firms using American-licensed designs. Accordingly, the sanctions issued by President Reagan on December 29, 1981, and extended on August 21, 1982, were premised on Washington's belief that the U.S. government could bar such items from reaching the Soviets until such time as they changed their policies. To wit, Washington was blaming Moscow primarily for the earlier imposition of martial law in Poland, the outlawing of its Solidarity union movement, and other repressive measures elsewhere.

Shortly after the sanctions were announced, however, there was a chorus of European protests against the ban. Opposition to the American sanctions was voiced on the grounds that U.S. national law could not be extended extraterritorially so far as to infringe on the sovereign decision-making rights of America's partners. Also, trying to deny the Soviets the ability to build their pipeline in this way was doomed to failure, given the capacity and willingness of other countries such as Japan to supply comparable equipment, not to mention the rapidly increasing capability of the Soviet Union itself to turn out the hardware. Also, that for the Western Europeans, especially a few of their hard-pressed firms, to forego such earnings as the sales of equipment could generate would be intolerable. Finally, that the United States had not come up with a viable alternative plan ensuring the Europeans' steady access to energy sources in future years.

Thus, several European leaders—predictably François

Mitterrand, the Socialist president of France, but even Ronald Reagan's personal and ideological ally, Prime Minister Margaret Thatcher of Great Britain—ordered the affected firms in their respective countries to ignore the American sanctions. In fact, the Western Europeans and the Japanese were already shipping hardware for the project.

In the meantime, the disagreements in the Atlantic alliance were being echoed within the Reagan administration itself. Thus, National Security Council adviser William P. Clark, Secretary of Defense Caspar Weinberger, CIA director William Casey, and others were arguing for coming down hard on the European violators of the embargo to reassert American leadership and President Reagan's credibility. Contrariwise, Secretary of State George Shultz and U.S. Trade Representative William Brock were cautioning against a showdown with the Western Europeans, one that could badly shake the North Atlantic Treaty Organization (NATO) of which they were members.

Possibly for these and other reasons, such as American multinationals complaining about their losing business following a month of intensive but little publicized negotiations between the parties in the controversy, on November 13, 1982, President Reagan announced his administration's decision to lift the sanctions on the sales of gas technology to the Soviets. He explained that an agreement had been reached on an alternative package of regulations applying to the export of strategic hardware to the Communist bloc. His decision came none too soon, since companies in several Western European countries were being blacklisted by the U.S. government for attempting to adhere to the terms of their suppliers' contracts.

While defying independent Western confirmation and despite a few mishaps such as fires during construction, the Soviets announced that the Urengoi gas pipeline had become operational in early 1984. Yet how much of the 32 billion cubic meters of gas planned to flow yearly through the pipeline was effectively delivered remained unreported.   —*Peter B. Heller*

ADDITIONAL READING:

"Energy Projects and Plans: Gas Piplines Move West from Urengoi." *The Current Digest of the Soviet Press* 34 (March 17, 1982): 3-4. Provides impressive numerical data and a map evidencing the scope of the pipeline.

Greer, Boyce I., and Jeremy L. Russell. "European Reliance on Soviet Gas Exports: The Yamburg-Urengoi Natural Gas Project." *The Energy Journal* 3 (July, 1982): 15-37. A thorough background of the undertaking, arguing the geographic and economic logic of not obstructing Soviet gas exports to Western Europe.

Griffin, Joseph P. and Michael R. Calabrese. "Coping with Extraterritoriality Disputes." *Journal of World Trade* 22 (June, 1988): 5-26. Two lawyers discuss the problematic application of American law in other sovereign states with reference to the Soviet pipeline to Western Europe.

Jentleson, Bruce W. *Pipeline Politics: The Complex Political Economy of East-West Energy Trade*. Ithaca, N.Y.: Cornell University Press, 1986. The chapter on the Reagan administration's sanctions focuses on the consequent near-split in the Western alliance.

Katzman, Julie E. "The Euro-Siberian Gas Pipeline Row: A Study in Community Development." *Millennium* 17 (Spring, 1988): 25-41. A good account of the disagreements following the Reagan administration's sanctions and consequent tension in U.S.-European relations.

Petroleum Economist. *Gas in the Former Soviet Union and Europe*. Energy Map Series 27. London: The Petroleum Economist and Ruhrgas, 1994. One of the best maps available of the gas pipeline grid, with relevant data statistics.

SEE ALSO: 1949, North Atlantic Treaty; 1972, United Nations Environmental Conference; 1986, Chernobyl Nuclear Disaster.

1982
GREAT BRITAIN RECOVERS THE FALKLAND ISLANDS

Great Britain recovers the Falkland Islands by dispatching a task force to wage a short, but hard-fought war in the wake of Argentina's unexpected seizure of the islands.

DATE: June 14, 1982
LOCALE: The Falkland Islands in the south Atlantic
CATEGORIES: Government and politics; Wars, uprisings, and civil unrest
KEY FIGURES:
Leopoldo Galtieri (born 1926), Argentine general who headed the military government that invaded the Falklands
Alexander Haig (born 1924), U.S. secretary of state during the presidency of Ronald Reagan
Margaret Thatcher (born 1925), British prime minister, 1979-1991
Julian Thompson (born 1934), commander of key units of British ground forces during the Falklands campaign
John Woodward (born 1932), British admiral who commanded the task force sent to recover the Falklands

SUMMARY OF EVENT. In the early morning hours of April 2, 1982, Argentine armed forces staged an amphibious invasion of the lightly defended Falkland Islands and within a few hours took control of Port Stanley (the capital) and the main airport. This unexpected aggression stunned British government officials. The two nations had been arguing about British possession of the Falkland Islands (the Argentines used the term Malvinas) since the 1830's. This long and complicated dispute proved difficult to resolve because both nations refused to compromise on their conflicting claims. The British pointed to nearly 150 years of continuous occupation by their settlers, but the Argentines argued that the British occupation of 1833 was illegal in the first place and, therefore, their claims were invalid. This dispute seemed to be largely a matter of pride for both nations since the Falklands had only limited economic value with much of the income of the approximately eighteen hundred inhabitants derived from increasingly marginal sheep ranching. The cold, windswept climate, dominated by the nearby Antarctic, gave the islands an inhospitable environment.

Margaret Thatcher's government was caught by surprise. While the Argentines had recently shown signs of impatience in the discussions regarding the Falklands, the dispute about these south Atlantic islands remained a fairly low priority for the British just as it had been since its beginnings in the 1830's. Thatcher and her cabinet emphatically expressed their outrage against the invasion and, by the end of the day (April 2), decided to organize a task force to reestablish British control of the islands. The build-up of forces on both sides brought a third party into the conflict. The administration of President Ronald Reagan, represented by Secretary of State Alexander Haig, attempted to mediate this dispute involving two allies of the United States. Haig used "shuttle diplomacy" between Buenos Aires and London in hopes of formulating an agreement that would bring both sides back to diplomacy and away from war. Haig faced great difficulty in part because of the intransigence of both sides on crucial issues. The Argentine government wanted Britain to surrender sovereignty, whereas the British government was determined to protect the self-determination of the islands' residents, who clearly wanted to remain British. Haig could not find a middle ground on which to revive negotiations.

After Haig's mediation efforts failed, Argentina and Great Britain intensified their preparations for combat. The British task force was a formidable presence as it made its way southward. Admiral John Woodward assumed command of an assemblage of ships that included two aircraft carriers, five state-of-the-art nuclear submarines, more than fifty additional warships and naval support vessels plus approximately forty-five civilian ships that the British government pressed into duty. The British military force included ten thousand men, many of whom were experienced in cold climate operations. The British air arm, limited because of the absence of a secure air base on the mainland within striking distance of the Falklands, consisted of 38 modern Harrier jets (capable of vertical take-offs) and 140 helicopters. The level of British training and technical expertise was quite high, reflecting their participation in the forces of the North Atlantic Treaty Organization (NATO).

Argentina's armed forces were impressive in certain areas, but did not equal the overall strength of the British forces. The Argentine navy consisted largely of World War II era ships that were no match for the modern surface vessels and submarines of the British Royal Navy. Argentina's army had some well-trained units, but President Galtieri did not send them to the Falklands. Most of the ten thousand soldiers stationed in Port Stanley and its environs were intended to serve in a pacification role and not in actual combat. Galtieri and his advisers had clearly underestimated British determination to retake the Falklands. The component of the Argentine armed forces that most concerned the British was air power. Argentina possessed an array of up-to-date jet aircraft and also the fully modern French-made Super Etendard fighter bombers capable of firing Exocet missiles. Such missiles had a great destructive potential when launched from distances of up to thirty to forty miles from their targets. The Super Etendard-Exocet combination posed a definite threat to the task force. In addition, Argentine fighter pilots in general were highly motivated and well trained in the tactics of attacking surface ships with conventional bombs.

Major combat began when the British nuclear submarine *Conqueror* sank the Argentine cruiser *General Belgrano* on May 2. The *Belgrano* was a partially modernized World War II warship that, from the British point of view, seemed to be involved in a large maneuver by the Argentine navy and therefore constituted a threat to the British task force. The heavy loss of life (368 Argentine sailors perished) shocked both sides and brought criticism even from British allies. The British fleet experienced another shock on May 4, when two Argentine Super Etendards launched their Exocet missiles, one of which hit and demolished the British destroyer *Sheffield*, killing twenty-one British personnel and wounding more than forty others. Admiral Woodward quickly realized that the task force, and therefore the entire mission, were threatened by Argentine air power.

The focal point of the fighting became East Falkland

Island. The Argentine army had established its defenses around Port Stanley on the eastern side of that island. The British decided to land their troops on the opposite side of the island, where the Falkland Sound offered shelter from rough seas. The surrounding land mass also provided protection from Exocet missiles. British soldiers poured ashore on May 21, led by Brigadier Julian Thompson. They encountered light resistance from the small Argentine units stationed on the western side of the island. Thompson's units quickly established a beachhead, only to watch with dismay as Argentine aircraft delivered more

between the rival armies ensued, with the Argentines suffering heavy casualties. Isolated, low on ammunition, and without hope of reinforcements, the Argentine forces surrendered on June 14, 1982.

The British victory brought a wave of patriotic celebrations to the home islands and buttressed the government of Prime Minister Margaret Thatcher. These celebrations somewhat obscured the difficulties involved in the mission, the narrow margin of survival against Argentine air attacks, and the uncertain value of the Falklands to the British nation. As a response to territorial aggression, the

British troops established a beachhead on East Falkland Island in May of 1982. (AP/Wide World Photos)

deadly blows to the British navy. The threat came not from Exocet missiles but from conventional five-hundred-pound bombs delivered primarily by American-made Skyhawk jets flown by Argentine pilots. In three days, the Argentines sank three frigates and inflicted severe damage on a destroyer. British Harriers responded with Sidewinder missiles, which took a heavy toll on Argentine aircraft. By May 23, the Argentines had lost most of their better aircraft and experienced pilots. As the Argentine air threat diminished, Thompson's forces completed the difficult march across the interior of the island, where the cold, damp climate and soggy soil were formidable enemies. British units soon concentrated around the Argentine troops dug in at Port Stanley. Brief but heavy fire fights

British action enjoyed widespread popular support at home and in the United States, but there were significant costs. Approximately one thousand lives were lost, including 255 British servicemen. The British government spent 780 million pounds (approximately 1.1 billion dollars) on the campaign and another billion or more pounds (more than 1.5 billion dollars) to reestablish their normal military operations after the war and to extend their defenses in the vicinity of the Falklands.   —*John A. Britton*

ADDITIONAL READING:

Ethell, Jeffrey, and Alfred Price. *Air War in the South Atlantic.* New York: Jove Books, 1986. Detailed account of the air combat based on official documents, press accounts, and interviews with both British and Argentine veterans.

Freedman, Lawrence. *Britain and the Falklands War*. London: Basil Blackwell, 1988. Conveniently brief, factual discussions of the historical origins, diplomacy, fighting, and consequences of the war, including an assessment of British public opinion.

Freedman, Lawrence, and Virginia Gamba-Stonehouse. *The Falklands Conflict of 1982*. Princeton, N.J.: Princeton University Press, 1991. A thorough, balanced examination of the causes and conduct of the war drawn from British and Argentine sources.

Gavshan, Arthur, and Desmond Rice. *The Sinking of the Belgrano*. London: Secker & Warburg, 1984. The focus of this critical, thought-provoking study is on the sinking of the Argentine cruiser, but the authors also consider the organization of the task force and the diplomacy of the war.

Hastings, Max, and Simon Jenkins. *The Battle for the Falklands*. London: Michael Joseph, 1983. An early journalistic account of the fighting that retains the strengths of a fast-paced narrative of key events.

SEE ALSO: 1949, North Atlantic Treaty; 1979, Margaret Thatcher Becomes Britain's First Woman Prime Minister.

1983
KLAUS BARBIE FACES NAZI WAR CRIMES CHARGES

Klaus Barbie faces Nazi war crimes charges and is prosecuted by the French government, affirming the legacy of the Nuremberg trials and the importance of collective memory about the Holocaust.

DATE: February 24, 1983

LOCALE: Lyons, France

CATEGORIES: Government and politics; Race and ethnicity; Wars, uprisings, and civil unrest

KEY FIGURES:

Klaus Barbie (alias Klaus Altmann, 1914-1991), Nazi chief of intelligence in Lyons, 1942-1944

Beate Klarsfeld (born 1939) and *Serge Klarsfeld* (born 1935), German-French team of Nazi-hunters who tracked Barbie down

François Mitterrand (1916-1996), premier of France during the Barbie trial

Jean Moulin (1899-1943), Lyonnais Resistance leader tortured to death by Barbie

Pierre Truche (born 1932), public prosecutor in Lyons

Jacques Vergès (born 1925), Barbie's defense lawyer

SUMMARY OF EVENT. On January 29, 1983, more than a decade after the Nazi hunters Beate and Serge Klarsfeld first located him in La Paz, Bolivia, a business man named Klaus Altmann was arrested on suspicion of being the war criminal Klaus Barbie. Between November, 1942, and August, 1944, Barbie, a second lieutenant in the SS (*Schutzstaffel* or protective rank), had headed the Section Four unit of the Gestapo-SD (*Sicherheitsdienst* or security police) forces in Lyons, then a city of seven hundred thousand residents. As an intelligence officer investigating "political crimes," Barbie had pursued the Nazi agenda with a ruthlessness that earned him the nickname "Butcher of Lyons." Unable to track Barbie down after his return to Germany in 1944, France twice tried him for war crimes in absentia; both times—1952 and 1954—the court sentenced him to death for his role in at least four thousand murders and eight thousand deportations to the concentration camps. By the time the Klarsfelds discovered him in La Paz in 1972, Barbie already faced no danger from these distant judgments. Not only had the statute of limitations lapsed on his war crimes after twenty years but also capital punishment had been abolished in France in the 1960's under François Mitterrand's government—ironically enough by Justice Minister Robert Badinter, whose father was among the Jews deported to Auschwitz on Barbie's orders.

Nevertheless, France had made special provision for keeping the case against such former Nazis open: On December 26, 1964, it had incorporated into its legal code the exact concept of "crimes against humanity" established at the Nuremberg Trials in 1945. Finding the standard term "war crimes" unequal to the magnitude of Nazi atrocities, the International Military Tribunal at Nuremberg formulated the new category to cover the perpetration of heinous acts against civilians as a matter of state policy. The tribunal thereby criminalized genocide and anti-Semitic, racial and ethnic persecution in a war context. Although the Nuremberg precedent had passed into international law in 1950 under the auspices of the United Nations, France was the first country to use it for domestic legislation. In so doing, the French court responsible for defining and interpreting law—the Cour de Cassation—reaffirmed that crimes against humanity transcend the passage of time, calling them *imprescriptible*. In January of 1983, Klaus Barbie, alias Altmann, was fully liable to French prosecution for war atrocities and then to life imprisonment if found guilty.

Despite years of pressure from the Klarsfelds and from the French government, Bolivia chose to cooperate with France's quest for justice only after the 1982 election of a democratic president, Hernan Siles Zuazo. President Zuazo followed up Barbie's arrest, supposedly for non-payment of a debt, with an unprecedented, irregular step. In February of 1983, given the continuing lack of an extradition treaty between the two countries, Zuazo's government simply "expelled" Klaus Altmann for his 1951 entry into Bolivia with false identity papers, putting him on a plane with the promise of exile in Paraguay but actually delivering him to Cayenne, the capital of French Guiana—and thus into French custody. In return, Bolivia received wheat, armaments, and financial aid from Mitterrand.

After a brief symbolic stay at Fort Montluc prison in Lyons, where he had tortured Resistance hero Jean Moulin and many others to death, Klaus Barbie was incarcerated in St. Joseph Prison. On February 24, 1983, he faced eight charges of crimes against humanity, which included the killing of hostages, the torture and execution of civilians, and the deportation of prisoners to the concentration camps; he could not be retried for his brutalities against members of the Resistance.

Although scheduled for 1984, the trial itself did not begin until May 11, 1987. In the intervening four years, the Examining Magistrate's massive investigation into the grounds for indictment yielded ten thousand pages of affidavits and documents. The painstaking, international inquiry allowed the French both to accumulate strong evidence for the "leftover" crimes with which Barbie could be charged and to avoid implications of a kangaroo court set up to avenge Barbie's notorious murder of Moulin. Eventually, the indictment was distilled into three specific charges: raiding the Jewish welfare office (UGIF) on February 6, 1943, and deporting 56 of the captured refugees to Auschwitz; seizing 44 children and 7 personnel at a children's shelter at Izieu, a neighboring farm village, on April 6, 1944 and deporting most of them to Auschwitz; designating 629 prisoners from Fort Montluc for deportation to Auschwitz or Ravensbrück on August 11, 1944.

Then, in December of 1986, the Cour de Cassation refined its interpretation of "crimes against humanity." In adapting the term to include systematic persecution of those opposed to a state ideology, the court put new instances of Barbie's barbarity toward the Resistance within the scope of the indictment. Consequently, the final case against Barbie consisted of five charges, and these charges in turn involved no fewer than 341 separate counts of crimes against humanity. Alongside the state's charges, there were depositions from thirty-nine lawyers filing civil suits against him on behalf of individual survivors, Jewish groups and Resistance groups. One of these lawyers seeking moral satisfaction and a token one-franc compensation was Serge Klarsfeld.

Ironically, Barbie's defense lawyer, Jacques Vergès,

used the charge of crimes against humanity to counterattack the prosecution, led by Pierre Truche, and the French nation. Born to French-Vietnamese parents during colonial rule and later active in the Algerian national movement, the left-wing Vergès impugned the government's right to charge Barbie with the same kind of atrocities that France itself had been guilty of in the Algerian war for independence in the 1950's.

Another irony was that even at this trial Barbie did not truly face his accusers. After the third day, he refused to appear at proceedings that he deemed illegal because of his "kidnapped" status. The presiding judge, André Cerdini, required his presence just three more times, for witnesses' identification and then for the reading of the verdict and sentencing. Found guilty on all counts by the nine-person jury and sentenced on July 4, 1987, Barbie responded to the outcome by disclaiming responsibility for deportations and then insisting on the distinction that the Cour de Cassation had blurred: "I fought a harsh combat against the Resistance, which I respect, but it was war, and now the war is over."

One of the most immediate impacts of the Barbie trial was its challenge to France's sense of national identity. Prosecuting Barbie two years before the bicentennial of the French Revolution afforded the French people a dramatic history lesson in patriotism. At the same time, however, the defense's emphasis on betrayal and collaboration during the occupation and on colonialist atrocities in Algeria forced France to confront the two darkest shadows in its own twentieth century past. More immediately, the trial constituted a landmark opposition to the nation's increasing tolerance for the reactionary, racist politics of Jean-Marie Le Pen, whose crusade to send nonwhite immigrants back to North Africa harmonized with his dismissal of the gas chambers as a mere detail of World War II. Indeed, the trial both flushed out and defied the resurgent racism, anti-Semitism, and Holocaust denial or negationism afflicting France and the rest of Europe in the 1980's. Finally, the charges against Barbie forced the United States to reexamine its use of him as an anti-Communist informant for the Counter Intelligence Corps from April, 1945, to March, 1951. After the publication on April 17, 1983, of the *Ryan Report*, a full-scale inquiry authorized by the Justice Department, America officially apologized to France for flouting international law and delaying justice.   —*Margaret Bozenna Goscilo*

ADDITIONAL READING:

Dabringhaus, Erhard. *Klaus Barbie: The Shocking Story of How the U.S. Used This Nazi War Criminal as an Intelligence Agent*. Washington, D.C.: Acropolis Books,

1984. Written by Barbie's Control Officer in the Counter Intelligence Corps, this book documents America's role in "rehabilitating" Barbie and facilitating his escape to Bolivia through the "rat-line."

Finkielkraut, Alain. *Remembering in Vain: The Klaus Barbie Trial and Crimes Against Humanity*. Translated by Roxanne Lapidus with Sima Godfrey. New York: Columbia University Press, 1992. A leading French intellectual ponders the trial's philosophical ramifications, particularly the defense's strategy of attacking French inhumanity in Algeria.

Morgan, Ted. *An Uncertain Hour: The French, the Germans, the Jews, the Klaus Barbie Trial, and the City of Lyon, 1940-1945*. New York: William Morrow, 1990. This account by the Lyons-born reporter who covered the trial for *The New York Times Magazine* vividly details the occupied city's everyday life, its resistance and collaboration, and its role in the Final Solution.

Rosenbaum, Alan S. *Prosecuting Nazi War Criminals*. Boulder, Colo.: Westview Press, 1993. An American professor urges the moral imperative of prosecuting Nazis, given the unique evil of the Holocaust.

SEE ALSO: 1940-1944, The French Resistance; 1945-1946, Nuremberg Trials; 1986, Election of Kurt Waldheim as President of Austria Stirs Controversy.

1983
GREEN PARTY WINS SEATS IN WEST GERMAN PARLIAMENT

The Green Party wins seats in the West German parliament, marking the first time since the 1950's that a new party wins seats in the West German legislature to compete with the three established parties.

DATE: March 6, 1983
LOCALE: West Germany
CATEGORIES: Government and politics; Social reform
KEY FIGURES:

Rudolf Bahro (born 1935), Green fundamentalist from East Germany

Gert Bastian (1923-1992), former West German army officer and associate of Petra Kelly

Marieluise Beck-Oberdorf (born 1953), one of the three leader of the Greens in the *Bundestag* in 1983

Jutta Ditfurth (born 1951), Green fundamentalist from Frankfurt

Josef (Joschka) Fischer (born 1937), first Green minister in a state government in Hesse

Petra Kelly (1947-1992), moderate Green fundamentalist and national leader

Otto Schily (born 1933), a Green political realist leader who left the party in 1989

SUMMARY OF EVENT. The election of twenty-seven members of the Green Party (and one member from the Alternative List in Berlin) to the German lower house (*Bundestag*) on March 6, 1983, marked the first time since the 1950's that a new party entered the West German national parliament. Since 1961, only three parties, Social Democrats, Christian Democrats, and Free Democrats, were represented in the West German parliament. The election of the Greens represented a political triumph for extraparliamentary mass protest movements, which had opposed the policies of the three West German parties since the late 1960's.

The first major extraparliamentary protest movement which attempted to create a mass movement originated in the student protests in the 1960's. Students used sit-ins and demonstrations to protest state authority, consumerism, and American policies in both Vietnam and West Germany. Many student activists found a new home in the 1970's in citizens' initiative movements which emerged spontaneously on the local and regional level seeking to protect the environment. The nonviolent protest tactics employed by these predominantly middle-class activists won the approval of millions of West Germans who were concerned with polluted rivers and forests.

By the mid-1970's, the most important single issue which galvanized the citizens' initiatives was the use of nuclear energy. Because of the oil crisis, the coalition government of Socialists and Free Democrats decided in 1973 to expand the nuclear power program. The antinuclear movement also attracted a number of left-wing groups, including communists. Typical was Rudolf Bahro, an East German Marxist who emigrated to West Germany in 1979. In 1983, he presented a plan in which he attacked industrial society and capitalistic growth and demanded radical anti-industrial solutions to environmental and social problems.

Beginning in 1977, environmentalists turned to politics in an effort to influence state and national governments and to block the construction of nuclear reactors. In 1979, the Greens of the northern city-state of Bremen became the first environmentalists to win parliamentary representation in a German state. In the same year, the Greens organized nationally to compete in elections to the European parliament in Brussels. They won 3.2 percent of the West German vote. Petra Kelly, an American-educated German activist, became one of the best-known national leaders of the Greens. Although she was an employee of the European Commission in Brussels (1971-1982), she still considered parliamentary government only a platform from which to espouse the Green philosophy.

In January of 1980, a national Green Party was organized in West Germany in order to compete at all levels of politics. Even though the Greens did not win any seats in the national election in 1980, during the following two years the Greens won seats in six out of eleven West German states. On March 6, 1983, they captured 5.6 percent of the national vote and entered the *Bundestag*.

Although environmental issues were still important to voters in 1983, even more crucial for the success of the Greens was the issue of American nuclear missiles in West Germany. In 1979, Socialist chancellor Helmut Schmidt asked the North Atlantic Treaty Organization (NATO) to place additional American nuclear missiles in Germany to counteract new Soviet weapons. Opposition to the deployment of these American missiles attracted the support of Gert Bastian, a commander of a West German armored division, who argued that there was no major Soviet threat to West Germany. He joined forces with Kelly and became active in the Green movement until 1984.

The typical West German voter who supported the Green Party in 1983 was a young, well-educated member of the new middle class primarily from Protestant urban centers. A large percentage of Green voters were former socialist supporters. Many Green representatives in the *Bundestag* were also well-educated professionals or civil servants.

Green leaders did not agree on many ideological issues and tactics. The more conservative environmentalists such as Herbert Gruhl had left the Green Party in 1980 in protest to the Greens' left-wing social programs. In truth, party leaders and delegates represented a variety of special interests, ranging from homosexuals and feminists to advocates of the rights of immigrants.

The most divisive issue was between "realist" Greens who accepted parliament and were willing to form alliances with the Socialists, and the "fundamentalist" Greens who wanted to use the legislature only as a platform for propaganda. Realists were more prominent in the *Bundestag*, while fundamentalist obtained leading positions in the party's executive bodies. Fundamentalists like Bahro and Jutta Ditfurth, a journalist and a Frankfurt city counselor, rejected political alliances with the Social Democrats and demanded a "qualitative change in society." Kelly was afraid that close association with the Social Democrats would destroy the independent identity of the Greens.

In contrast to the fundamentalists, realists such as Otto Schily and Joschka Fischer were willing to use parliament to introduce constructive environmental policies. Schily, a lawyer, had defended German terrorists, and Fischer had participated in student street battles in 1968. Schily, Kelly, and Marieluise Beck-Oberdorf were the party's official leaders in the *Bundestag* in 1983. Frustrated with the Greens' divisiveness, Schily joined the Social Democratic Party in 1989. Fischer became the first Green minister at the state level when he joined a coalition government in Hesse in October 1985.

In spite of the bitter differences within the Greens, the movement has been successful in inducing the government and the other parties to support environmental policies. After 1983, West Germany adopted one of the most stringent environmental programs in Europe. The collapse of communism and massive American withdrawal from Europe has resolved the dispute over American nuclear missiles.

The Greens have become a part of the established political scene. They are represented in a majority of German state legislatures, and, with the exception of the national election of 1990, the West German party continued its presence in the *Bundestag*. The Greens in the former East German states have not fared as well. Since German unification in 1990, a new leftist party, the Party of Democratic Socialism, the successor to the Communist Party of East Germany, has entered the *Bundestag*. The Greens have faced the problem of whether to collaborate with the former communists or to continue to form coalitions only with the socialists.

Many of the original Green leaders who were active in 1983 no longer play a major role in the party. Fundamentalists, such as Bahro and Ditfurth, either left the party or abandoned politics. Bastian shot his lover Kelly in October of 1992, and then committed suicide. Schily joined the Social Democratic Party in 1989, while Fischer, another realist, has remained the most prominent national leader. He was joined by Antje Vollmer, a former moderate fundamentalist, in an effort to reform the Green Party and make it more disciplined and effective. Whether realists or fundamentalists, however, the Greens have not been able to convince the German public to abandon capitalism or industrialism in order to return to a idyllic rural world.

—*Johnpeter Horst Grill*

ADDITIONAL READING:

Burns, Rob, and Wilfried van der Will. *Protest and Democracy in West Germany: Extra-Parliamentary Opposition and the Democratic Agenda.* New York: St. Martin's Press, 1988. The authors review the extraparliamentary protest movements which gave birth to the Greens.

Hülsberg, Werner. *The German Greens: A Social and Political Profile.* New York: Verso, 1988. This survey was written by a left-wing journalist who sympathizes with the ecosocialists, one wing of the Greens.

Kolinsky, Eva, ed. *The Greens in West Germany: Organization and Policy Making*. Oxford: Berg, 1989. Ten articles by specialists examine various aspects of the Green Party.

Müller-Rommel, Ferdinand, ed. *New Politics in Western Europe; The Rise and Success of Green Parties and Alternative Lists*. Boulder, Colo.: Westview Press, 1989. The thirteen essays in this comparative study examine the Greens in twelve European countries and in the European parliament.

Papadakis, Elim. *The Green Movement in West Germany*. New York: St. Martin's Press, 1984. This is a thorough survey of extraparliamentary protest movements which led to the Green Party's election success in 1983.

Rosolowsky, Diane. *West Germany's Foreign Policy: The Impact of the Social Democrats and the Greens*. Westport, Conn.: Greenwood Press, 1987. This work argues that the Greens' "ideological neutralism" primarily represents a challenge to the Social Democrats.

Scharf, Thomas. *The German Greens: Challenging the Consensus*. Oxford: Berg, 1994. The author suggests the Greens in some German states have become a part of the established parliamentary system.

SEE ALSO: 1949, Creation of Two German Republics; 1972, United Nations Environmental Conference; 1986, Chernobyl Nuclear Disaster; 1990, German Reunification.

1983
MARTIAL LAW IN POLAND ENDS

Martial law in Poland ends, marking the communist government's failure to govern without appealing to democratic elements—chiefly the banned trade union Solidarity.

DATE: July 21, 1983
LOCALE: Poland
CATEGORY: Government and politics
KEY FIGURES:
Wojciech Jaruzelski (born 1923), Poland's last
    Communist leader
Lech Wałęsa (born 1943), leader of the Solidarity trade
    union

SUMMARY OF EVENT. The ending of martial law signaled the final failure of communist governments in postwar Poland. General Wojciech Jaruzelski, prime minister and first secretary of the Polish Communist Party, decreed martial law in December of 1981, responding to the overwhelming popularity of Solidarity, a broad-based union with more than ten million members—nearly a third of the

country's population. In August of 1980, Solidarity staged strikes in the Gdansk shipyards, protesting government policies that prohibited free speech and democratic activities. The union called for higher wages, lower prices, and an end to censorship.

Poles had rebelled against their communist governments on other occasions—most notably in 1956—but earlier regimes had treated protestors brutally and reneged on promised reforms, relying on the fact that no cohesive dissident movement challenged their authority. Poland had enjoyed a brief period of improving economic conditions in the 1970's until the Arab oil embargo severely damaging its industrial development. In addition, Edward Gierek, first secretary of the Communist Party and the country's leader, had borrowed heavily from the West to finance his economic plans, and most of his efforts to modernize the Polish economy failed disastrously. Consequently, what little confidence Poles had in their government's ability to improve the standard of living vanished.

Solidarity was an unprecedented alliance of workers and intellectuals—indeed virtually a whole nation combining together to protest an unrepresentative and dictatorial government. Solidarity's leader, Lech Wałęsa, a shipyard electrician, symbolized the new spirit of social and political activism, which was so universal that the communist government could not simply resort to violence in order to break the strike. On the contrary, the government capitulated on many of the strikers' key demands. The Polish Communist Party removed Edward Gierek as leader and replace him with a reform-minded successor, Stanislaw Kania. Yet the instability in the Polish leadership and the strength of Solidarity led to Kania's replacement in 1981 by General Wojciech Jaruzelski, a highly respected military man who seemed less like the Communist Party professionals and who Poles regarded with cautious optimism.

Solidarity's endurance was sorely tested as the government stalled on fulfilling its promises and even began to repudiate agreements with the union. Solidarity continued to agitate for social, political, and economic reform, but it did so warily, well aware that its activities could provoke a Soviet invasion. In Hungary in 1956 and in Czechoslovakia in 1968, Soviet troops had overthrown communist governments which seemed to bow to the pressure of their citizens for reformed, democratic government. Poland itself had barely escape a Soviet intervention in 1956.

Finally the tensions between Solidarity and the government were resolved in General Jaruzelski's imposition of martial law. Unlike the previous government crackdowns in Poland, there was little violence—although many key Solidarity leaders, including Lech Wałęsa, were imprisoned. Instead, Jaruzelski cut Solidarity's lines of communication, so that the union could not communicate with the outside world and had difficulty meeting and planning for further action. Jaruzelski then ruled the country in a South-American style "junta"—a word in popular use in Poland to describe his seizure of power.

Martial law was shocking not only because it deprived people of the few democratic rights they had been allowed but because the Polish army had been used as a domestic force to suppress the opposition. Poles had been used to making a distinction between the Communist Party and the army, viewing the army as a patriotic institution, elements of which might even resist a Soviet invasion.

At first, martial law seemed a triumph for the communist government. There were no more strikes, and on the surface it seemed as though the government would be able to return to a centralized, command economy, in which the workers would have no say. Yet Poles did not join or cooperate with the government created unions, and gradually it became clear that the government could not function without the lifting of martial law. Jaruzelski continued the ban against Solidarity, but he conceded his defeat by agreeing to round table negotiations with the union in 1989, when it was once again legalized.

The ending of martial law not only doomed the communist's exclusive hold on power, it showed that a popular movement in a communist country could effectively change the terms of political debate and action. Solidarity's example, a union of all classes, made the communist claim to establishing a classless society ridiculous. In retrospect, it is clear that many communists could no longer pay even lip service to their Marxist program. Independent intellectuals such as Adam Michnik, a dissident and founding member of Solidarity, became role models and allies of intellectuals and union organizers in other Eastern European Soviet satellites such as Czechoslovakia and Hungary. Solidarity's persistent and nonviolent course proved immensely influential and earned worldwide sympathy and support.

The ending of martial law led to protracted and frustrating bargaining between the government and Solidarity. Still leery of Soviet intervention, Solidarity leader Lech Wałęsa haggled with Jaruzelski, the very man who had imprisoned him. Solidarity's strategy was called that of a "self-limiting revolution"; that is, it aspired to gradually change the country's form of government without directly confronting communist hegemony. To some extent, of course, the term was contradictory. How can a revolution be self-limiting? Yet the point was to forestall Soviet aggression and to give the Polish government and Solidarity time to work out an understanding.

In spite of Jaruzelski's resort to martial law, Solidarity relied on him to act in good faith, while still pressuring him to make political and economic reforms. Jaruzelski, it was said, had imposed martial as his own way of controlling Solidarity before the Soviets acted. Poles were divided as to his true motivations—whether his dictatorial approach had really prevented a Soviet attack or was just a rationalization for keeping the communists in power.

Even before 1989, when Solidarity reemerged in public as a legal union—both Jaruzelski's and Solidarity's positions became less precarious. In 1985, Gorbachev's assumption of power in the Soviet Union, represented the beginnings of a reform movement that relaxed tensions throughout the Eastern bloc. Polish reformers then worried about Gorbachev's ability to rule over the hard-line faction of the Soviet Communist Party. By the late 1980's, it was clear that not only did Gorbachev relinquish the idea of an invasion of Poland, but he was willing to relax and eventually abandon any direct Soviet role in Eastern Europe.

In 1989, Jaruzelski capitulated to Solidarity's demand for free parliamentary elections—in return for which Solidarity supported his election as president of Poland, supposing that the general was still needed to maintain stability and to ease the transition to a noncommunist government. Jaruzelski served until 1990, when he stepped down in favor of his former arch-opponent, Lech Wałęsa.

Although the ending of martial law brought only limited freedoms to Poles, it began the process of democratization and acknowledged that Polish leaders could not remain in power without the consent of the governed. Jaruzelski gradually accepted this democratic principle as he gave way to Solidarity's demands and eventually relinquished his office. Whether martial law itself was necessary to preempt a Soviet attack cannot be definitively answered. Soviet archives might answer this question, although there is some evidence that suggests the Soviet government itself was divided on what action to pursue. In other words, Poland's crisis and the imposition of martial reflected a larger crisis in the communist world and in communist leaders determination to stay in power.

—*Carl Rollyson*

ADDITIONAL READING:

Ascherson, Neal. *The Struggles for Poland.* New York: Random House, 1987. See especially the chapters on Gierek and the period leading to Solidarity (1970-1980), and a final chapter on Solidarity, martial law, and the future (1980-1986). Bibliography.

Ash, Timothy Garton. *The Polish Revolution: Solidarity.* New York: Charles Scribner's Sons, 1983. Explains why Poland erupted in political dissent in 1980, with a chronology, notes, and bibliography.

The Book of Lech Walesa. New York: Simon & Schuster, 1982. Essays on Wałęsa and Solidarity, with notes on contributors and a chronology of modern Poland.

Brandys, Kazimierz. *A Warsaw Diary 1978-1981.* New York: Random House, 1983. An important document about Poland in the years leading up to Solidarity. The diary ends on December 13, 1982, the day martial law is declared.

Cynkin, Thomas M. *Soviet and American Signalling in the Polish Crisis.* New York: St. Martin's Press, 1988. How the West responded to Solidarity and tried to manage the crisis and its relationship with the Soviet Union.

Lineberry, William, ed. *Poland.* New York: H. W. Wilson, 1984. Essays on communist government in Poland and martial law. Includes a useful bibliography.

Rachwald, Arthur R. *In Search of Poland: The Superpowers' Response to Solidarity, 1980-1989.* Stanford, Calif.: Hoover Institution Press, 1990. Chapters on Solidarity, the Soviet threat, martial law, and the banning of the union.

SEE ALSO: 1956, Hungarian Revolution; 1968, Soviet Union Invades Czechoslovakia; 1980, Solidarity Is Founded in Poland; 1989, The Berlin Wall Falls; 1989, Velvet Revolution in Czechoslovakia.

1984
BRITAIN SIGNS AGREEMENT TO LEAVE HONG KONG IN 1997

Britain signs an agreement to leave Hong Kong in 1997, marking one of the final steps away from its colonial heritage while bringing into question the continuing free market status of Hong Kong.

DATE: September 26, 1984

LOCALE: London, England, and Hong Kong

CATEGORIES: Diplomacy and international relations; Economics

KEY FIGURES:

Deng Xiaoping (1904-1997), leader of the People's Republic of China from 1978 until he resigned his last Central Committee position in 1989

Sir Geoffrey Howe (born 1926), British foreign secretary, 1983-1989

Margaret Thatcher (born 1925), British prime minister, 1979-1990

Zhao Ziyang (born 1919), premier of the People's Republic of China, 1980-1987

SUMMARY OF EVENT. British possession of Hong Kong Island was first obtained by the Treaty of Nanking (1842)

that settled the first Opium War. Although the sale of Indian opium in China was part of that agreement, the Chinese continued to resist, and after a second war, 1858-1860, China was forced to cede the southern Kowloon Peninsula by the Treaty of Peking (1860). The colony was completed in 1898, when China had to accept a ninety-nine-year lease of an additional 365 square miles, called the New Territories. Although initial expectations in London were that Hong Kong would be of little significance in the empire, the colony developed into an entrepôt for trade with China. It became an extremely valuable possession.

Until the Communist Revolution of 1949, the British position seemed quite secure. From early in its history, the People's Republic of China took the position that the treaties creating Hong Kong were "unequal" and therefore invalid. This attitude was not, however, translated into any active policy, and Hong Kong, enjoying free port status, low taxes, and a liberal capitalist economy was eventually the source of 30 to 35 percent of the foreign exchange of mainland China. The mainland also profited by selling the colony water, food, and cotton cloth. Chinese-owned banks and shops thrived as well. Hong Kong's place in the international economy is suggested by the fact that it was second only to Japan in U.S. investments in Asia. Disturbances in China such as the Cultural Revolution of 1966-1967, despite sometimes causing unrest in Hong Kong, emphasized the colony's importance as a source of hard currency and continued the push, begun by the 1949 revolution, of refugees to the labor-strapped city. Hong Kong's population grew from 2.4 million in 1951 to 5.5 million in 1984.

Normalization of Sino-British relations in 1972 resulted in more trade and an increased Chinese economic presence in Hong Kong. Travel between the mainland and the colony was even encouraged. The political confusion after the death of Mao Zedong in 1976 had little effect on Hong Kong, but afterward the authorities on both sides did begin to put effective restrictions on the movement of mainland Chinese to the colony. As far as the status of the city was concerned, however, Beijing would say no more than that the matter should be negotiated "when the time was ripe." A Chinese protest was lodged, however, when the United Nations listed Hong Kong as a colonial territory which should eventually be independent. The People's Republic of China insisted that Hong Kong was an occupied part of China.

By the early 1980's, the people in Hong Kong were increasingly concerned about the future. The 1997 expiration of the British lease put property mortgages made in 1982 and later in some doubt. (Although technically only

In addition to establishing political control of Hong Kong, the People's Republic of China wanted to take charge of the island's thriving economy, reflected in the bustling activity of Hong Kong Harbor. (AP/Wide World Photos)

the New Territories were leased, the rest of the colony is not viable without them.) The value of stocks, land, and the Hong Kong dollar fell sharply, despite reassurances from Beijing. In September, 1982, Prime Minister Margaret Thatcher conferred with Premier Zhao Ziyang about the colony. The Chinese position was clear: sovereignty and administration must pass to China but the economic arrangements might be negotiated. Thatcher insisted that Britain retain administrative control. This deadlock lasted a year during which Hong Kong suffered increasing economic problems.

The next summer, Thatcher yielded. Britain would concede Chinese sovereignty as soon as an arrangement ensuring Hong Kong's prosperity was settled. In July, formal talks, that would continue for fourteen months, began. On August 15, 1983, the government of mainland China increased the pressure by announcing that it would take control of Hong Kong on July 1, 1997, regardless of the outcome of the negotiations. For several weeks the value of the Hong Kong dollar fell sharply, leftists in the city asserted popular support for the People's Republic of

China, and Beijing accused Britain of encouraging the economic problems to stall the talks. In September, London took steps to support the dollar, and calm was restored. Progress was slow but steady, but the Chinese began to insist that an agreement be reached by October 1, 1984, the thirty-fifth anniversary of the founding of the People's Republic of China. The British took no official notice but made the extra effort necessary to meet this deadline. The final agreement was initialed on September 26, 1984.

The resulting Joint Declaration (and several addenda detailing and clarifying aspects of post-1997 government, land lease arrangements, and nationality) laid out the situation of Hong Kong after the shift of authority in 1997. The city would constitute a special administrative region of the People's Republic of China with "a high degree of [domestic] autonomy," and its government was to be made up of local people, except for the chief executive who would be appointed in Beijing. The existing economic system was not to be disturbed for fifty years after the People's Republic of China takes over, and Hong Kong could continue to participate in international trade organizations and agreements. Military forces of mainland China would not intervene in Hong Kong's domestic affairs but would be stationed in the city. Rights and freedoms were assured, and China pledged to prepare a Basic Law incorporating the points made in the Joint Declaration.

The Joint Declaration was greeted in Hong Kong with a mixture of relief and suspicion that it was too good to be true. It was certainly possible that the People's Republic of China might renege on parts or all of it, and the promise of governmental and economic systems that vary from the constitutional provisions guiding the rest of the country appeared to be of dubious legality. Few in the city were comfortable with the prospect of the presence of the People's Liberation Army. By the mid-1990's, there were some significant indications that Beijing actually intended to honor the agreement. The economy of mainland China certainly needed the foreign exchange to be gotten from Hong Kong's commerce, and special economic zones were created in coastal areas. The acquisition of Hong Kong appeared to fit neatly into this economic policy. Success with the Hong Kong arrangement was expected to provide a model for the eventual reabsorption of Taiwan by the People's Republic of China. Although the Hong Kong arrangement might fail to live up to the highly publicized promises given concerning it, it suggested to the Taiwanese that their suspicions of the communist regime on the mainland were well founded. Risks remained even in 1997, but the people of Hong Kong seemed to accept prospects for the future with cautious optimism.

—*Fred R. van Hartesveldt*

ADDITIONAL READING:

Bonavia, David. *Hong Kong 1997: The Final Settlement*. Hong Kong: South China Morning Post, 1985. Bonavia is clearly sympathetic with the people of Hong Kong, but he has not allowed feelings to cloud his assessment of reality. Building on a solid historical framework, first he sets the situation of Hong Kong in perspective, but the narrative moves rapidly to the post-World War II era.

Cheng, Joseph Y. S., ed. *Hong Kong: In Search of a Future*. New York: Oxford University Press, 1984. A collection of documents and the results of polls concerning the transfer of sovereignty of Hong Kong. Also contains press accounts.

Ching, Frank. *Hong Kong and China: For Better or Worse*. New York: Foreign Policy Association, 1985. Chin provides a meticulous account of the Sino-British negotiations that led to the Joint Declaration. An important aspect of the process was the economic and public response in Hong Kong, and Chin shows unusual skill at weaving the technical diplomatic arrangements and that response into one piece.

Chiu, Hungdah, Y. C. Jao, and Yuan-il Wu, eds. *The Future of Hong Kong: Toward 1997 and Beyond*. New York: Quorum Books, 1987. A collection of essays and relevant documents. Although scholarly in tone, the volume is accessible to the serious reader.

Domes, Jurgen, and Yu-ming Shaw, eds. *Hong Kong: A Chinese and International Concern*. Boulder, Colo.: Westview Press, 1988. A collection of essays concerning the history and future prospects of Hong Kong.

Geddes, Philip. *In the Mouth of the Dragon: Hong Kong—Past, Present and Future*. London: Century Publishing, 1982. The result of a television documentary, this book is easy reading and provides useful background. It is too old to include data concerning more than the beginning of the negotiation over sovereignty.

Kelly, Ian. *Hong Kong: A Political-Geographic Analysis*. Honolulu: University of Hawaii Press, 1986. An interesting account based on the political geographer's concept of "landscapes." Contains much information about the political-geographic elements affecting Hong Kong's situation. The methodological discussion may frustrate general readers.

Morris, Jan. *Hong Kong*. New York: Random House, 1988. A marvelous mix of travelogue, history, and comment on the current situation.

SEE ALSO: 1945, The United Nations Is Founded; 1979, Margaret Thatcher Becomes Britain's First Woman Prime Minister.

1985
GORBACHEV IS ELECTED GENERAL SECRETARY OF THE COMMUNIST PARTY

Gorbachev is elected general secretary of the Communist Party, raising hopes of positive changes in the Soviet Union, despite the opposition of many senior bureaucrats to his candidacy and leadership.

DATE: March 11, 1985
LOCALE: Moscow, the Soviet Union
CATEGORY: Government and politics
KEY FIGURES:

Yuri Andropov (1914-1984), general secretary of the Communist Party of the Soviet Union, 1982-1984
Leonid Ilich Brezhnev (1906-1982), general secretary of the Communist Party of the Soviet Union, 1964-1982
Konstantin Chernenko (1911-1985), general secretary of the Communist Party of the Soviet Union, 1984-1985

Mikhail Sergeyevich Gorbachev (born 1931), general
　secretary of the Communist Party of the Soviet
　Union, 1985-1991

Victor Grishin (1914-1992), first secretary of the
　Moscow Communist Party, 1967-1985

Andrei Andreyevich Gromyko (1909-1989), foreign
　minister of the Soviet Union, 1957-1985

Grigory Romanov (born 1923), first secretary of the
　Leningrad Communist Party, 1970-1983

SUMMARY OF EVENT. Since the Bolshevik Revolution of
November, 1917, the history of the Soviet Union has
largely depended on the personality, authority, and vision
of its communist leaders. The achievements and failures
of the Soviet Union reflect the influence of Vladimir
Lenin, Joseph Stalin, and their successors. The office of
general secretary of the Communist Party represented the
highest party leadership position as well as the guiding
force to the nation at large. In addition, the Party bureaucracy also played a role in shaping domestic and foreign
policies. The most powerful decision-making body in the
Communist Party was the Politburo, composed of the
highest officials of the party and the Soviet government.
Although small in size, usually between twelve and sixteen members, the Politburo's authority was far-reaching.
The general secretary always was selected from its midst.
Consequently, power struggles periodically existed within
the Politburo as individuals maneuvered to maintain their
positions or increase their authority.

As a result of the deaths of three major national leaders
in the early 1980's, a new era for the nation began with the
selection of Mikhail Gorbachev as general secretary of the
Soviet Communist Party in March, 1985. Gorbachev succeeded Leonid Brezhnev, Yuri Andropov, and Konstantin
Chernenko as general secretary. Brezhnev, the long-time
leader of the nation, died in November, 1982. His later
years were characterized by ill health and lack of strong
leadership. His successor, Yuri Andropov, was best known
as head of the nation's secret police from 1967 to 1982
under Brezhnev. Yet Andropov's skills and possible
achievements as general secretary were cut short by a
debilitating illness leading to his own death in February,
1984. Chernenko, the next selection as general secretary,
was the oldest of the three. At age seventy-two, he already
was ill and died a year later, on March 11, 1985.

These rapid transitions caused by illness and death
created confusion within the Communist Party and uncertainty in the nation, and made it impossible to deal effectively with the nation's political needs, economic problems, and foreign policy objectives. Various candidates
vied to become the new general secretary in 1985, and
Gorbachev at the relatively young age of fifty-four suc-

ceeded in winning over his rivals within the Politburo.

Full knowledge of the details behind his victory only
gradually became known in later years, since the Politburo
maintained a high level of secrecy about its inner workings
during the Soviet period. Gorbachev's name had been put
forth after Andropov's death, but his opponents successfully blocked his candidacy in favor of age and experience. Gorbachev had to overcome his comparative youth
and lack of seniority.

He did this by determination, a good party record,
ability, and patience. Son of a rural farm family in southern Russia, he joined the Communist Party in 1952 near
the end of the Stalin era. After earning a degree in law at
the University of Moscow in 1955, Gorbachev became
active in party work in his home province of Stavropol. He
was selected in 1970, at age thirty-nine, to be the head of
the Communist Party for the province. His reputation for
honesty and efficiency, plus good farm management policies and successful harvest results in his province, brought
this able communist administrator to the attention of top
party leaders in Moscow. They brought him to Moscow in
1978 to join the Communist Party Secretariat, given the
responsibility for providing the party's direction over all
Soviet agriculture.

Even the failing Brezhnev saw promise in this young
administrator from a remote southern province, and Gorbachev was added to the Politburo in 1979. Under Andropov from 1983 to 1984, Gorbachev oversaw party personnel policies. Under Chernenko from 1984 to 1985 he was
given responsibility for Communist Party ideology. This
latter position was widely interpreted as the second highest position in the Communist Party after the general
secretary. During Chernenko's short term, part of which
was spent in the hospital, Gorbachev chaired meetings of
the Politburo and assumed other duties that showed his
growing authority, stature, confidence, and experience.
Considering Chernenko's poor health, his closest associates could predict he would soon die or have to resign.
Hence the maneuvering for the succession already was
underway before Chernenko's death.

During this period, the West first became aware of
Gorbachev, particularly during an official visit he made to
Great Britain in December, 1984. Prime Minister Margaret Thatcher was impressed with the articulate Soviet
leader and spoke favorably of his abilities. When Chernenko died a few months later, the time was ripe for
Gorbachev to make his move to be Chernenko's successor.

One initial indication of Gorbachev's strength was his
selection to be chairman of the funeral committee planning the ceremonies for Chernenko's state funeral. Prior
experience suggested this might indicate the likely succes-

sion, since Andropov had this responsibility after Brezhnev's death in 1982. Chernenko was given a similar assignment after Andropov's demise in 1984.

Gorbachev had just turned fifty-four on March 2, 1985, and was a good deal younger than other possible candidates for general secretary. He was the youngest member of the Politburo. Victor Grishin, the long-time head of the Communist Party's Moscow organization and Gorbachev's most serious rival, was seventy years old. Another potential contender, sixty-one-year-old Grigory Romanov, was closer to Gorbachev's age but had longer service on the Politburo as well as a substantial power base from his long service as Party head in Leningrad. In 1985, Romanov's position in the Communist Party's Secretariat was a powerful one. Gorbachev's victory in the Politburo was not assured.

A power struggle at the highest level, the third in four years, thus played itself out in early March. Whoever emerged as the final winner would receive the quick endorsement of the Central Committee of the Communist Party, a body of more than three hundred members who had the designated function under party rules to formally elect and confirm the new general secretary.

The Politburo member who apparently swung sufficient support to Gorbachev's side was Andrei Gromyko, Soviet foreign minister since 1957 and a senior Politburo member. Gromyko pressed for Gorbachev's selection immediately upon news of Chernenko's death. A consensus for this decision was reached the same day, and news of Gorbachev's appointment appeared in the Soviet media almost immediately. At least one newspaper announced Gorbachev's appointment on page one while giving the news of Chernenko's death on page three.

Gorbachev's victory as general secretary was only the beginning of a dramatic era in Soviet and communist history. During his years in office from 1985 to 1991, Gorbachev undertook a series of policies and reforms that improved the Soviet economy, provided some movement toward partial democracy, and created a more open cultural atmosphere. These important steps are known as *perestroika* and *glasnost*. In foreign policy, an era of improved relations with the United States helped bring the Cold War toward an end. Gorbachev was awarded the Nobel Peace Prize in 1990. Yet, under his leadership, the Soviet Union fragmented internally and the country disappeared as a nation state in 1991. He ultimately failed to achieve the objectives he sought.   —*Taylor Stults*

ADDITIONAL READING:

Butson, Thomas G. *Gorbachev: A Biography*. Briarcliff Manor, N.Y.: Stein & Day, 1985. Gorbachev's life

from early years to his election as general secretary in 1985.

Doder, Dusko, and Louise Branson. *Gorbachev: Heretic in the Kremlin*. New York: Viking, 1990. Excellent biography, including earlier years plus his leadership as general secretary.

Kaiser, Robert G. *Why Gorbachev Happened: His Triumphs and His Failure*. New York: Simon & Schuster, 1991. Solid biography, with emphasis on how Gorbachev rose to power and was able to continue in the face of opposition and domestic crises.

Medvedev, Zhores A. *Gorbachev*. New York: W. W. Norton, 1986. Careful interpretive account by a former Soviet dissident now living in Great Britain. Sharp analysis with predictions of successes and failures.

Morrison, Donald, ed. *Mikhail S. Gorbachev: An Intimate Biography*. New York: Time, 1988. Informative biography from his childhood to 1987. Emphasis on personality and leadership. Good account for the general reader.

Murarka, Dev. *Gorbachev: The Limits of Power*. London: Hutchinson, 1988. Fresh and independent assessment of Gorbachev's policies and objectives, by an informed observer.

Schmidt-Haüer, Christian. *Gorbachev: The Path to Power*. Topsfield, Mass: Salem House, 1986. Readable account of Gorbachev's life, comparing him to earlier reformers such as Peter the Great.

SEE ALSO: 1968-1989, Brezhnev Doctrine; 1979, Soviet Union Invades Afghanistan; 1986, Chernobyl Nuclear Disaster; 1986, Riots in Kazakhstan; 1987, Intermediate-Range Nuclear Forces Treaty; 1988, Ethnic Riots Erupt in Armenia; 1989, The Berlin Wall Falls; 1991, Soviet Attack on Baltic Separatists; 1991, Soviet Union Dissolves into Loosely Allied Republics.

1985
SINKING OF THE RAINBOW WARRIOR

The sinking of the Rainbow Warrior *by French secret agents draws international attention to Greenpeace and its antinuclear message.*

DATE: July 10, 1985

LOCALE: Auckland, New Zealand

CATEGORIES: Environment; Government and politics; Organizations and institutions; Social reform

KEY FIGURES:

Christine Cabon (born 1951), French secret agent who infiltrated the Auckland Greenpeace office

Charles Hernu (1923-1990), French minister of defense forced to resign over the *Rainbow Warrior* affair

David McTaggart (born 1932), Greenpeace chief executive officer who demanded international investigation into incident

Alain Mafart, French agent imprisoned for bombing

Fernando Pereira (1950-1985), Greenpeace photographer killed in the sinking of the *Rainbow Warrior*

Dominique Prieur, French agent imprisoned for bombing

Bernard Tricot, wrote official French report clearing agents of any wrongdoing

to return in 1973. That protest ended when the French navy attacked McTaggart and another crew member. The government denied the assault but faced embarrassment when photographs revealed the coverup. Because of intense public outcry, the French moved nuclear testing underground in 1974. Greenpeace would again protest testing at Moruroa in 1981 and 1982.

In February of 1978, Greenpeace bought the fishing research trawler, *Sir William Hardy*, from the British ministry of agriculture for thirty-two thousand pounds. Once refurbished and renamed *Rainbow Warrior*, the ship

Publicity from the sinking of the original Rainbow Warrior *allowed Greenpeace to purchase a new ship and redouble its efforts against nuclear testing, particularly in the South Pacific.* (Reuters/RTV/Archive Photos)

SUMMARY OF EVENT. The environmental group, Greenpeace, had been founded in 1969 to protest against nuclear testing. In 1972, the group took on the French and forged a longstanding combatant relationship when future chief executive officer David McTaggart sailed the *Vega* into atmospheric test zones in the South Pacific near the Moruroa atoll. Failing to stop the test, McTaggart vowed

served on campaigns to protect whales and seals and protests against toxic and nuclear dumping. A symbol of the increasing power and scope of Greenpeace, the *Rainbow Warrior* drew crowds around the world.

On March 15, 1985, the flagship embarked on what would become its last voyage. Greenpeace assigned board member, Steve Sawyer, to lead a two-pronged expedition into the South Pacific. The first stage would be "Operation Exodus" to relocate the entire population of radiation-contaminated Rongelap atoll to a safer location. Health problems caused by atmospheric testing conducted by the United States in the 1940's and 1950's prompted Senator Jeton Anjain from the Marshall Islands parliament to ask Greenpeace for help. During a two-week period in May of 1985, the *Rainbow Warrior* made four trips moving 304 people and their possessions to Mejato, some ten hours away.

The second stage of the expedition had been announced in February of 1985, when Greenpeace learned of French plans to test a neutron bomb near Moruroa. The *Rainbow Warrior* was to be the lead ship in an international protest that would include several Polynesians from Tahiti. This Tahitian connection gave this protest an increased political element as the French colonies in the South Pacific were struggling for independence. As news of this reached the upper levels of the French government, a plan was set in motion to stop Greenpeace and the *Rainbow Warrior*.

In March of 1985, the French defense minister, Charles Hernu, ordered the secret service organization, General Directorate for External Security (DGSE), to gather information about the protest. DGSE leader Admiral Pierre Lacoste sent agent Christine Cabon to infiltrate the Greenpeace office in Auckland, New Zealand, where the *Rainbow Warrior* would dock before leaving for Moruroa. Posing as ecologist "Frédérique Bonlieu," Cabon arrived on April 24 and quickly relayed details about the operation as well as information on the Tahitian involvement. During her month-long stay, she also gathered prices on diving equipment, boats, and hotels for friends who were supposedly coming on vacation.

Based on Cabon's information, plans were made, under the direction of Lieutenant Colonel Louis-Pierre Dillais, to sabotage the protest. One DGSE group made their way to Auckland abroad the yacht, *Ouvéa*. Posing as tourists, four underwater combat school trained agents—Roland Verge, Gerald Andries, Jean-Michael Bartelo, and Dr. Xavier Maniguet—smuggled in diving gear, explosives, and an inflatable Zodiac raft. Another set of agents, Major Alain Mafart and Captain Dominique Prieur, arrived via the Auckland airport posing as a Swiss honeymoon couple, "Alain and Sophie Turenge." Dillais also arrived by air.

The *Rainbow Warrior* reached Marsden Wharf in the Auckland Harbor on Sunday, July 7. Volunteers and crew began cleaning and painting the ship in preparation for the journey to Moruroa. On July 10, sometime between 8:00 and 9:00 P.M. during a birthday party for Steve Sawyer,

agent Jean-Michael Bartelo crossed the harbor by Zodiac raft, donned scuba-diving gear, swam to the ship, and planted two bombs on its hull. Bartelo then went down the coast to an awaiting rental van. At 11:38 P.M., the first bomb went off, blowing a three-foot hole in the hull. Captain Peter Willcox gave the order to abandon ship as water quickly filled the lower decks. Portuguese photographer, Fernando Pereira, rushed to get his cameras when a second bomb detonated at 11:40 P.M. Rendered unconscious, Pereira drowned as the boat sank within four minutes. He was the first Greenpeace volunteer to die during a protest.

Acts of terrorism were unheard of in New Zealand and officials scrambled to gather information. On July 11, Superintendent Allan Galbraith took charge of the investigation that would ultimately collect more than four hundred statements and one thousand exhibits. Interviews quickly lead to the investigation to the rental van. On July 12, Mafart and Prieur were stopped and questioned when they attempted to return the rental van. The couple's falsified papers and suspicious activities pointed to a possible French government connection.

Despite adamant denials, the media hounded the French government over what became known as "Underwatergate." When a French magazine reported on August 8 that secret agents had been involved, the government agreed to open a formal impartial investigation. Under the direction of a former Gaullist counselor, Bernard Tricot, the formal report cleared French agents of any wrongdoing. Released on August 26, Tricot's report stated that the agents were merely collecting information. President François Mitterrand publicly denied any French involvement in the explosion on September 16. A day later, the French newspaper *Le Monde* reported Admiral Lacoste and Minister Henru knew of and probably ordered the attack. Within forty-eight hours, Lacoste was dismissed and Hernu resigned. Allegations that Mitterrand also knew brought calls for his resignation. Finally, on Sunday, September 22, Prime Minister Laurent Fabius admitted on television that secret agents had indeed bombed the *Rainbow Warrior* and the truth had been hidden from Tricot during the investigation.

Of the eight known agents involved in the attack, only Mafart and Prieur were formally charged. Their anticipated trial began on November 4. Greenpeace and the world media were surprised when the pair pleaded guilty to manslaughter and willful damage in a thirty-four-minute hearing. The pair each received ten-year sentences. Subsequent United Nations-led negotiations between France and New Zealand resulted in the release of the agents to the French military in July of 1986 for a three-year term on the Hao atoll. In exchange, France paid seven million dollars in compensation to New Zealand, made a formal apology and paid damages to Pereira's family. (Mafart returned to France in December of 1987, and Prieur in May of 1988, under the pretense of medical necessity.) In October of 1987, an independent panel of judges ordered France to pay $8.16 million in damages to Greenpeace marking the first governmental compensation to a private organization for military actions.

As for the *Rainbow Warrior*, the ship was damaged beyond repair. Crews removed the salvageable machinery and adapted the hull to serve as an artificial reef. On December 13, 1987, the *Rainbow Warrior* was placed along the coast of New Zealand. Gathering strength with the cry, "You Can't Sink a Rainbow," money and memberships poured in to Greenpeace. The planned protest in 1985 was carried out under the leadership of the *Vega*. Despite a larger international protest, the French testing went off on October 24. Buoyed to continue the protest he started, McTaggart maintained a strong stance against French nuclear testing. Greenpeace launched a new campaign, Nuclear Free Seas, in July of 1987, and used the increased support to purchase a new *Rainbow Warrior* dedicated on the fourth anniversary of the attack. The growing protest against nuclear testing that resulted in the sinking of the *Rainbow Warrior* would finally see its realization when the United States, Russia, and France agreed to halt testing in 1992.   —*Jennifer Davis*

ADDITIONAL READING:

Brown, Michael, and John May. *The Greenpeace Story*. New York: Dorling Kindersley, 1991. Written to commemorate the organization's twentieth anniversary, the text and numerous photographs provide an extensive look at the scope of Greenpeace.

Brown, Paul. *Greenpeace*. London: Exley Publication, 1993. Part of a series on organizations that help the world, this book gives a chronological look at the development of Greenpeace.

Dyson, John. *Sink the Rainbow!* London: Victor Gollancz, 1986. Written from perspective of a native New Zealander, the book gives insight into the local attitudes about French nuclear testing and the sinking of the boat.

Hunter, Robert. *Warriors of the Rainbow: A Chronicle of the Greenpeace Movement*. New York: Holt, Rinehart and Winston, 1979. This book, from a Greenpeace founder, covers the early years of organization including the basis of the French tensions.

Morgan, Robin, and Brian Whitaker, et al. *Rainbow Warrior: The French Attempt to Sink Greenpeace*. London: Hutchinson, 1986. Written by a team of reporters

from *The Sunday Times Insight*, this book provides historical information on the agencies involved and the tensions between France and Greenpeace.

SEE ALSO: 1966-1995, France Withdraws from NATO's Military Structure; 1972, United Nations Environmental Conference; 1986, Chernobyl Nuclear Disaster.

1985
ANGLO-IRISH AGREEMENT IS SIGNED

An Anglo-Irish agreement is signed in an attempt to meliorate the endemic problems of Northern Ireland.

DATE: November 15, 1985
LOCALE: Hillsborough, Northern Ireland
CATEGORY: Diplomacy and international relations
KEY FIGURES:

Garret FitzGerald (born 1926), *taoiseach* (prime minster) of the Republic of Ireland, 1981-1982 and 1982-1987, and head of Fine Gael party

Charles Haughey (born 1925), leader of Ireland's Fianna Fáil party

John Hume (born 1937), head of Northern Ireland's Social Democratic and Labour Party

James Molyneaux, leader of Northern Ireland's Official Unionist Party

Reverend Ian Paisley (born 1926), leader of Northern Ireland's Democratic Unionist Party

Margaret Thatcher (born 1925), prime minister of the United Kingdom of Great Britain and Northern Ireland, 1979-1989, and leader of the Conservative Party

SUMMARY OF EVENT. The Anglo-Irish Agreement, signed at Hillsborough, Northern Ireland, on November 15, 1985, was the most serious political attempt between the early 1970's and the truce of 1994 to settle the long, often violent dispute in Northern Ireland. In the 1960's another round of "the troubles" began with the "civil rights" movement, inspired in part by recent events in America, which motivated the largely have-not Catholic community to demand equality with the majority Protestant community who had wielded economic, political, and social power since Ireland was partitioned in 1921. Inevitably tied to the demand for equality was the issue of the ultimate future of Northern Ireland: Would it remain a part of the United Kingdom, or would it join the Irish Republic which had sovereignty over the rest of the island? Those who demanded the first were the unionists or loyalists; the latter were referred to as the nationalists. The former were overwhelmingly protestant, the latter largely Catholic.

Peaceful demonstrations led to confrontation and by the early 1970's violence had returned to the streets of

Northern Ireland, most infamously in the Bloody Sunday episode in Londonderry in January, 1972. The local police, largely protestant, were unable to keep order, and British troops were sent in but the violence continued. The Irish Republican Army, particularly the Provisional faction, or Provos, along with Sinn Féin, the IRA's political wing, moribund during the 1960's, were resurrected, demanding that the British leave and the north be incorporated into a "socialist" Irish Republic. The unionists/loyalists also spawned their own paramilitary groups. In a generation more than three thousand persons died.

The Protestant-dominated home-rule parliament was abolished in 1972, and a political solution was attempted in 1973-1974 through the establishment of a power-sharing government, representing both communities. This cooperation died almost at birth: The IRA instituted a new bombing campaign and the unionist majority, also opposed, resorted to a general strike in May of 1974 that brought the political agreement crashing down. The later 1970's and early 1980's were years of violence. For the British government, the primary concern was security, which meant more troops rather than the search for political solutions. The IRA's campaign of militancy spread to Britain itself, most notably in the bombing of Brighton's Grand Hotel during the Conservative Party Conference in October, 1984. The main target was Prime Minister Margaret Thatcher, who survived, but several others were killed. The focus on security had not succeeded.

Garret FitzGerald was the Taoiseach, or prime minister, of the Irish Republic. His Fine Gael party was traditionally less sympathetic to the IRA and its militaristic dreams of unity than was the other major party, Fianna Fáil, under the leadership of Charles Haughey. With FitzGerald's support, the New Ireland Forum met frequently in Dublin in 1983 and 1984. Because of its ties to the IRA, Sinn Féin was excluded, but in the absence of unionists, the forum, representing only the nationalist community, particularly the north's Social Democratic and Labour Party, headed by John Hume, was destined to come to nothing. Its vision was of a future unified Ireland, based not necessarily on a unitary state, but one constructed as a federation or confederation or encompassing a system of joint authority with Great Britain, at least temporarily. Thatcher dismissed out of hand the forum's proposals as compromising British sovereignty in Northern Ireland.

Discussions had already begun, however, between the two governments. Politics was not the least of the concerns: Both Thatcher and FitzGerald needed to appear to be doing something about the problems of Northern Ireland. Both sides also understood the continued threat of increased violence, not only in Northern Ireland but also in mainland Britain and even in the Irish Republic. In addition, the failure of the military solution led to the hope that peaceful discussions might prove to be a viable alternative to continued terrorism and violence. Unlike some of his more traditional Irish colleagues, FitzGerald was firmly convinced that a unified Ireland could only come into existence through majority consent in the north.

Thatcher's conservatism was instinctively sympathetic to the unionist demand to remain part of the United Kingdom, but reliance upon the military had not succeeded. In addition, the obstreperous nature of the unionists, notably Reverend Ian Paisley and James Molyneaux, the leaders of the two major unionist parties, saw Thatcher turn away from Northern Irish politicians. To what degree this was a matter of emotional reaction rather than considered policy is difficult to determine, but in the months leading up to the signing of the Anglo-Irish Agreement, Thatcher's government provided the unionist leaders in Northern Ireland with almost no information regarding the negotiations, in retrospect perhaps a fatal flaw.

The Anglo-Irish Agreement (AIA), signed on November 15, 1985, at Hillsborough, Northern Ireland, ostensibly satisfied the two sovereign governments but not necessarily all of the communities or traditions in Northern Ireland. Article One recognized that there could be no change in sovereignty until a majority in the north desired it, long a principal of British governments, but perhaps implicit was the belief that someday Northern Ireland would become part of the Republic. Article Two and Three established an Intergovernmental Conference to meet regularly regarding such matters as cross-border security, human rights, and elections. The agreement recognized that the Republic had the right to "put forward views and make proposals" regarding Northern Ireland, in effect becoming something of the advocate of nationalist and Catholic interests in the north. Article Four envisioned some sort of power-sharing or political devolution for the province, but ultimate control would continue to rest in the British Parliament with input from the Intergovernmental Conference.

The agreement was met with almost universal praise—except within Northern Ireland. The unionist majority, left out of the deliberations, were outraged, feeling that the assumption of the agreement's signatories was that someday, somehow, the north was to be joined to the Republic. On the other hand, in spite of FitzGerald's hopes, it did not bring peace. The IRA saw the agreement as a disaster because it stated that no change of sovereign status would come until a majority desired it, something the IRA could not admit. Ironically, both the IRA-Sinn Féin and the unionists/loyalists believed that the agreement was a sell-out, over their heads, by politicians and governments who should have been the advocates and defenders of the their positions. Politics does make for strange bedfellows.

The British parliament quickly approved the agreement, 473 to 47, with opposition from only the unionist representatives, a handful of Conservatives, and, ironically, several left-wing Labour supporters who wanted a unified Ireland immediately. The Dáil, Ireland's parliament, voted in favor, eighty-eight to seventy-five. Yet little that was positive resulted. The IRA increased its militancy, and the unionists, claiming that the Anglo-Irish Agreement was an example of "parliamentary despotism" imposed on the people of Northern Ireland without their consent, also rejected the agreement. On Saturday, November 23, 1985, more than two hundred thousand people reportedly gathered in front of the Belfast City Hall in protest, with Paisley, noted for his inflammatory oratory, crying "Never! Never! Never!" Fifteen unionist members of parliament resigned, forcing new elections. Seventy-eight percent of voters chose candidates opposed to the Hillsborough agreement, including unionists and supporters of Sinn Féin. Protests at the local council level, already begun, continued, strikes and boycotts were organized, and, fittingly in Northern Ireland, some resorted to prayer. Many unionist politicians urged that the agreement be suspended. It was not, but unionist defiance and IRA militancy ensured that the Anglo-Irish Agreement would ultimately become more a brief symbol and hope than lasting substance in the settling of the troubles in Northern Ireland.

—*Eugene Larson*

ADDITIONAL READING:

Aughey, Arthur. *Under Siege*. New York: St. Martin's Press, 1989. The author presents the unionist position in this highly critical analysis of the Angle-Irish Agreement.

Bell, J. Bowyer. *The Irish Troubles*. New York: St. Martin's Press, 1993. Subtitled "A Generation of Violence, 1967-1992," this is a comprehensive, exhaustive, and brilliant narrative by a noted scholar.

Kenny, Anthony. *The Road to Hillsborough*. New York: Pergamon Press, 1986. This account, written shortly after the signing of the Anglo-Irish Agreement, is a valuable summary by an English academic.

Keogh, Dermot, and Michael H. Haltzel. *Northern Ireland and the Politics of Reconciliation*. New York: Cambridge University Press, 1993. In this collection, Garret FitzGerald defends the Anglo-Irish Agreement. FitzGerald's autobiography, *All in a Life* (1991), is also worth considering.

Thatcher, Margaret. *The Downing Street Years*. New York: HarperCollins, 1993. Thatcher's autobiography suggests that her interest in the Anglo-Irish Agreement was more reactive than a concerted search for a solution to the problems of Northern Ireland.

SEE ALSO: 1972, "Bloody Sunday" in Northern Ireland; 1974, IRA Terrorists Bomb Parliament Building; 1976, IRA Hunger Striker Dies in an English Prison; 1993, Ulster Peace Accord.

1986
OLOF PALME IS ASSASSINATED

Olof Palme is assassinated, depriving the world of a great statesman dedicated to international peace and the nonproliferation of nuclear weapons.

DATE: February 28, 1986
LOCALE: Stockholm, Sweden
CATEGORIES: Government and politics; Terrorism and political assassination
KEY FIGURES:
Ebbe Carlsson (1948-1992), Swedish journalist and publisher
Ingvar Carlsson (born 1934), prime minister of Sweden, 1988-1991
Lisbeth Beck-Friis Palme, wife of Olof Palme
Olof Palme (1927-1986), prime minister of Sweden, 1969-1976 and 1982-1986

SUMMARY OF EVENT. On the evening of February 28, 1986, Prime Minister Olof Palme and his wife, Lisbeth Beck-Friis Palme, left a movie theater on Tunnelgaten (Tunnel Street) in Stockholm, and began walking home to their apartment in the Old Town. About fifteen minutes later, as they turned onto Sveavagen, a major city thoroughfare, from a few yards behind, a man fired two shots at Palme, hitting his chest and abdomen, and grazing Palme's wife. The man fled, reportedly in a car. A young female nurse passing by, not knowing who she was helping, attempted to assist the fallen prime minister. A taxi driver who had observed the incident phoned the police. Palme was taken to Sabbatsberg Hospital, where he was pronounced dead on arrival. The completed autopsy revealed that he died instantly from the gun shot wound in his chest. He was fifty-nine years old.

At the site of the shooting, the police questioned a number of people. Two witnesses reported they saw the gunman escaping through the downtown streets. Cars leaving the city were inspected at check points and patrols were set up at airports, ferry stations, and all other border crossings. The Associated Press announced that the police were looking for a dark haired man, thirty-five to forty years old, wearing a long, dark overcoat. This was the first assassination of a major Swedish official since King Gustav III was shot in 1972. No European head of government had been assassinated since 1973, when Prime Minister Luis Carrero Blanco of Spain was killed in a car bombing, apparently carried out by Basque terrorists.

Olof Palme was born on January 30, 1927, the youngest of three children of Baltic aristocrats. He graduated in 1948 from Kenyon College in Ohio. He had a "formidable intelligence," spoke fluent English, French, German, Spanish, and some Russian as well as the Scandinavian tongues. His career in politics began in 1956, the same year he married Lisbeth Beck-Freiis, a lawyer. Together, they had three children. His first cabinet position was minister of communications. In 1969, Palme was elected chairman of the Social Democratic Party. From 1969 until 1976, he served as prime minister of Sweden. The defeat of the Social Democratic Party in 1976 ended forty-four years of socialist rule. Six years later, when the party overwhelmingly won the election, Palme was reelected as prime minister, and he was reelected again in September of 1985.

Throughout the 1970's and 1980's, Palme was a dominant figure in Swedish politics. His work for active international cooperation reflected Sweden's strong policy of neutrality. At the time of his death, he was the special representative of the U.N. Secretary-General for the conflict between Iran and Iraq. Among Western leaders, Olof Palme held political views that were farthest to the Left. He opposed American involvement in the Vietnam War, supported nuclear disarmament, and wanted a nuclear-free Europe. He did not hold himself aloof from the general populace but was seen often on the streets of Stockholm, chatting with constituents. He said of himself once, "I was born in the upper class, but I belong to the labor movement."

The reaction to the news of Palme's death was immediate and heartfelt. People assembled around the metal barricades in front of the art supplies shop where the assassination had occurred. They brought bouquets of flowers to the police who carried them to the spot where Palme had died. Gradually a mound of flowers arose at the site. The Swedish radio suspended their regular programming and played somber classical music. Long lines of people waited to sign books of mourning. Condolences and tributes arrived from Asia, South Africa, Latin America, East Germany, Yugoslavia, Australia, Africa, the Middle East, and the Soviet Union. World leaders described the Swedish prime minister as a great statesman, a very peace loving man, and his loss to the world as "tragic." U.S. president Ronald Reagan expressed his shock and sorrow, and praised Palme as a "man who made compas-

sion the hallmark of Swedish policy." U.N. Secretary-General Javier Perez de Cuellar said, "There are few statesmen who have had such influence in international affairs and social change." The governments of Portugal, Nicaragua, Argentina, and India ordered periods of mourning. Palme's assassination in 1986 shocked the Swedish people as profoundly as the 1963 assassination of President John F. Kennedy had shocked the American public.

As officials and diplomats held a memorial service in Washington, D.C., sixty thousand people marched in a torchlight procession in Göteborg, Sweden, to a meeting where Palme was eulogized. *New York Times* journalist Anthony Lewis wrote, "When the political leader of a small country engages the imagination and the respect of leaders around the world, he must have special qualities of character. His persuasiveness comes not from power but from himself."

On March 16, a secular funeral for Palme held in Stockholm City Hall was attended by dignitaries from 125 nations, including thirteen presidents and nineteen prime ministers. Security at the event was the tightest Stockholm had ever known. Throughout the two-hour ceremony, as eulogies were given by several heads of state, Palme's body lay in a white coffin covered with a mass of red roses. One million Swedes watched the funeral procession as it moved from the City Hall to the Adolf Frederik Church for the Christian burial. The coffin was carried on a hand-drawn catafalque. When the procession reached the church, Swedish television, in respect for the family's wishes for privacy, ended its coverage of the event.

In the years prior to his assassination, Palme was accompanied at times by security guards, but on the night he died he had dismissed them earlier in the day. Following the assassination, Deputy Prime Minister Ingvar Carlsson, who served as acting prime minister, said his attitude toward personal security was the same as that of Olof Palme; he expected to walk the streets of Stockholm without guards. Unanimously elected prime minister in 1988, Ingvar Carlsson was often seen strolling through Stockholm, taking an ordinary train to a campaign rally, and casually mingling with the general public.

Despite investigations from leads provided to the police, an offer of five hundred thousand Swedish kroner (about eighty-six thousand U.S. dollars) for information that would help solve the murder, and advertisements placed in major newspapers around the world, the case remained unsolved a year after the assassination. Criticized for incompetence, the Swedish police chief resigned and national officials took over the investigation. In December of 1988, the Stockholm district court arraigned

Carl Gustaf Christer Patterson, a forty-two-year-old Swede with a criminal record that included manslaughter and drug abuse who had previously been questioned in connection with the case in 1986. Patterson was charged with the shooting. Throughout the trial held the following spring, Patterson maintained his innocence. Palme's widow told the court she was certain that Patterson was the man she had seen just after the shooting. The six lay judges on the panel of judges were convinced of Patterson's guilt, while the two professional judges voted for his acquittal. Patterson was convicted and sentenced to life imprisonment. Three months later, an appeals court overturned Patterson's conviction, saying the evidence was inadequate, and ordered him freed immediately.

Palme's widow accused the police and the press of sabotaging the inquiry into her husband's assassination and the subsequent trial. Ebbe Carlsson, a journalist and publisher who was a former confidant of Olof Palme, also believed the police investigations were inadequate. Until his death in 1992, and with endorsement from Swedish law officials, Ebbe Carlsson undertook a secret enquiry, the focus of which was Kurdish immigrants and refugees. Over the years a number of conspiracy theories surfaced.

In February of 1996, on the tenth anniversary of Olof Palme's death, the financial reward remained unclaimed and the crime remained unsolved. The crime scene was indistinguishable from other street corners except for the intersecting street sign, which had been renamed Olof Palme Street.

—*Susan E. Hamilton*

ADDITIONAL READING:

Canova, Timothy A. "The Swedish Model Betrayed." *Challenge* 17 (May-June 1994). This article, written by an attorney, discusses in detail Sweden's economic difficulties since 1986 and how Olof Palme might have dealt with them.

Fact Sheets on Sweden. This regularly updated series of comprehensive fact sheets, published by the Swedish Institute, provides a reliable general reference source for political, economical, historical, social, and cultural aspects of Sweden.

Mosay, Chris. *Cruel Awakening: Sweden and the Killing of Olof Palme*. New York: St. Martin's Press, 1991. An examination of Swedish society and politics by a British journalist living in Sweden who uses the unsolved assassination as his starting point.

SEE ALSO: 1978, Aldo Moro Is Kidnapped and Murdered by Italian Terrorists; 1991, Sweden Applies for Membership in the European Community.

1986
CHERNOBYL NUCLEAR DISASTER

The Chernobyl nuclear disaster spreads radioactive material over much of Europe, killing several hundred people, contaminating crops and animals, and undermining public confidence in the nuclear industry.

DATE: April 26, 1986
LOCALE: Chernobyl, Ukraine, the Soviet Union
CATEGORIES: Environment; Government and politics; Science and technology
KEY FIGURES:

Aleksandr Akimov, crew supervisor on duty at the Chernobyl nuclear plant when the accident began

Nikolai Fomin, chief engineer of the Chernobyl nuclear plant

Vitali Skiyerov, power minister of the Ukraine

Leonid Telyatnikof, fire chief of the Chernobyl nuclear plant

SUMMARY OF EVENT. In late April of 1986, reactor 4 at the Chernobyl nuclear plant was scheduled for shutdown for annual maintenance. The operators planned to test how long the plant's turbines, which generate electricity from the steam produced from the heat given off in nuclear decay, could produce electric power after the steam was shut off. Electricity from these turbines was required to operate the plant's safety systems until emergency diesel generators could take over.

The test began at 1:00 A.M. on April 25, but shortly after the operators reduced power they were asked to restore the reactor to full power to supply electricity needed in the Kiev area. They did this, but neglected to turn a critical emergency cooling system back on. At 11:10 P.M. on April 25, they again began shutting down the reactor, but this time they made a series of errors that resulted in the cooling water level dropping below its emergency level. Since the emergency cooling system had been shut down, it did not respond to the low water level.

At 1:23 A.M. on April 26, 1986, there were sounds of escaping steam followed by a fireball over the roof of the turbine hall at reactor 4 of the Chernobyl nuclear plant. The remaining water in the reactor core, where the uranium fuel decays generating heat, had expanded rapidly, producing an explosion that destroyed the core and part of the building and released radioactive material into the environment. Burning lumps of graphite and reactor fuel were dispersed around the site, starting fires that carried more radioactive material into the air. A study by the Lawrence Livermore Laboratory estimated that the Chernobyl accident released more long-lived radioactive material into the soil, air, and water than was released by all the nuclear weapons tests ever conducted.

About two hundred plant workers and firefighters were hospitalized with symptoms of radiation poisoning within thirty-six hours after the explosion. On the evening of April 26, everyone within ten kilometers of the plant was evacuated, except for crews still trying to contain the radiation release. The evacuation zone was extended to thirty kilometers on May 2, and more than one hundred thousand people were eventually moved from the danger area. The distribution of radioactive fallout outside the immediate vicinity of the Chernobyl site was spotty, with high concentrations in the areas where it was raining when the cloud of radioactive particles passed overhead. Outside the Soviet Union, Poland was the most seriously affected. Both Poland and Hungary restricted grazing by cattle, but local shortages of hay caused some farmers to ignore the rules. In Austria, nearly all of the strawberry crop was discarded because of radioactive contamination. Some areas of Sweden experienced the most extreme fallout outside the Eastern bloc. Rain near Gavle, about 150 miles north of Stockholm, resulted in such severe contamination that one thousand square kilometers of grass had to be harvested and burned, and many thousands of gallons of milk were contaminated.

In Lapland, meat from fifty thousand reindeer had to be discarded. Because the Lapps depend on the reindeer for food, the Swedish government had to arrange for the importation of reindeer meat. In 1987, the government raised the permissible level of radioactivity in reindeer meat to allow the Lapps to again consume local meat.

The British National Radiological Protection Board (NRPB) estimated that over the next fifty years about one thousand people in Western Europe would die of cancers induced by the Chernobyl radiation. Since thirty million people would die of cancer not related to Chernobyl during the same period, the NRPB concluded the effect would be undetectable. In the Soviet Union, where the fallout was more concentrated press accounts in 1989 indicated that about 250 persons who worked at the Chernobyl plant or assisted in the clean-up had died as a result of radiation exposure. In 1992, Ukrainian officials estimated that the Chernobyl accident would eventually be responsible for between six thousand and eight thousand deaths.

In 1985, nuclear reactors produced more than 18 percent of all the electricity generated in the world, and four nations generated more than 40 percent of their electricity using nuclear power: France, with 65 percent of its electricity being generated by nuclear plants, Belgium, with 60 percent, Taiwan, with 53 percent, and Sweden with 42 percent. Yet public confidence in nuclear power was shaken by the Chernobyl accident, and by the much less

serious accident at Three Mile Island in Pennsylvania in 1979.

The Soviet Union's commitment to nuclear power remained firm. Soviet authorities reacted quickly on May 20, 1986, to prevent a group of dissidents from collecting signatures outside Moscow's Vachtangova Theater on an antinuclear petition which they planned to present

Engineers and scientists worked to clean up and contain the damage to plant facilities that resulted from the nuclear explosion at Chernobyl in the Soviet Ukraine. (Reuters/Soviet Life/Archive Photos)

to Kremlin leaders. In May of 1986, the chairman of the Soviet State Committee on the Utilization of Atomic Energy said "the path of nuclear power development and the growth of nuclear power in the USSR are to remain unchanged." The two undamaged reactors at Chernobyl were returned to electricity production as soon the site cleanup progressed far enough to permit it.

In Poland, which was directly in the path of the Chernobyl fallout, three hundred residents signed a petition to halt construction of the country's first nuclear plant at Zarnowiec. In Hungary, Bulgaria, and Czechoslovakia, the governments took the position that there was no viable alternative to nuclear power plants. Of the Eastern European nations, only Yugoslavia altered its nuclear policy in the immediate aftermath of Chernobyl. On May 25, 1986, the government announced it would not build a new nuclear plant in the country's wheat growing region. In a 1980 referendum, the voters in Sweden endorsed a plan to build no additional nuclear power plants and to decommission the twelve existing nuclear power plants no later than 2010. The Chernobyl accident solidified support to move up that deadline, and, in May of 1986, the Swedish government announced that it would look into advancing the deadline.

Demonstrations in Germany protesting a proposed nuclear waste reprocessing plant near Wackersdorf, in Bavaria, had attracted about seven thousand protesters in December of 1985 and January of 1986. In the aftermath of the Chernobyl accident, twenty thousand protesters gathered at Wackersdorf in a two-day demonstration that turned violent and resulted in about four hundred injuries. More than fifteen thousand demonstrators stopped traffic in Munich in a protest on May 4-5, 1986, and six thousand demonstrators had to be dispersed by police using tear gas at the site of a planned nuclear waste dump in Gorbelen. Yet these protests produced no change in the plans of Chancellor Helmut Kohl's government to increase Germany's reliance on nuclear energy.

In 1985, the United States operated ninety-three nuclear power plants, more than any other nation in the world. Public concern about the hazards of nuclear power plants increased in the United States in the aftermath of the Three Mile Island accident, in 1979, and the Chernobyl accident focused public opinion on this issue. A poll conducted in May of 1986 and published in *The Washington Post* found that 78 percent of the people surveyed opposed construction of nuclear power plants and 40 percent of those surveyed wanted to phase out existing plants.

The Long Island Lighting Company (LILCO) planned to begin operation of a new nuclear plant at Shoreham, New York, in mid-1986, but approval of its operating license had been delayed because of concern over the lack of evacuation routes from the eastern tip of Long Island. LILCO struggled to save its $5.5 billion plant, but opponents battled to keep the plant from opening. Eventually the State of New York intervened, proposing a plan to close the Shoreham facility permanently. On June 12, 1992, the Nuclear Regulatory Commission approved a plan to decommission the Shoreham plant, which was radioactive because it had been operated for thirty hours in 1985 in a test.

The protests were not universal. France, which gener-ated 65 percent of its power by nuclear plants, saw only small protests. Only five thousand people demonstrated in Paris on May 24, 1986, and the French government announced plans to construct additional nuclear power plants. In Japan, which had few domestic sources of energy, the Advisory Committee for Energy announced plans to more than double production of electricity by nuclear plants by the year 2030.　　*—George J. Flynn*

ADDITIONAL READING:

Chernousenko, V. M. *Chernobyl: Insight from the Inside*. New York: Springer-Verlag, 1991. A well-illustrated account of the Chernobyl nuclear accident and the clean-up work by a scientist who served on the government commission that investigated the accident.

Gould, Peter. *Fire in the Rain: The Democratic Consequences of Chernobyl*. Baltimore: The Johns Hopkins University Press, 1990. An in-depth account of the consequences of Chernobyl, including the distribution of radioactive fallout throughout the world, the public reaction, and the government response.

Hawkes, Nigel, et al. *Chernobyl: The End of the Nuclear Dream*. New York: Vintage Books, 1986. A detailed account of the Chernobyl accident and its aftermath prepared by correspondents for the *London Observer* immediately following the accident.

Medvedev, Zhores A. *The Legacy of Chernobyl*. New York: W. W. Norton, 1990. Includes a detailed description of how the Chernobyl accident occurred, then focuses on the environmental and health impacts within the Soviet Union.

Park, Chris C. *Chernobyl: The Long Shadow*. London: Routledge Press, 1989. A detailed account of the environmental aspects of the Chernobyl accident, and an assessment of the public reaction around the world and its impact on the nuclear industry.

SEE ALSO: 1952, London Smog Kills Thousands; 1963, Limited Nuclear Test Ban Treaty Is Signed; 1969, Pesticide Poisons the Rhine River; 1987, Intermediate-Range Nuclear Forces Treaty.

1986

ELECTION OF KURT WALDHEIM AS PRESIDENT OF AUSTRIA STIRS CONTROVERSY

The election of Kurt Waldheim as president of Austria stirs controversy because his election victory, achieved despite his falsified autobiography, typifies Austria's eagerness to gloss over its Nazi past.

DATE: June 8, 1986
LOCALE: Vienna, Austria
CATEGORIES: Diplomacy and international relations;
Government and politics
KEY FIGURES:
Hubertus Czernin, Austrian journalist at *Profil* magazine
Michael Graff, general secretary of Austrian People's
Party
Robert Herzstein, American historian hired by World
Jewish Congress
Georg Tidl, Austrian historian and Socialist Party
member
Kurt Waldheim (born 1918), secretary-general of the
United Nations, 1972-1982, and president of Austria,
1986-1992
Simon Wiesenthal (born 1908), Austrian-based
Nazi-hunter

SUMMARY OF EVENT. On June 8, 1986, Kurt Waldheim, former secretary-general of the United Nations, became president of Austria amid continuing controversy about his wartime activities under the Nazis. Rumors about Waldheim's past had started circulating in Vienna in September of 1985, after his nomination to the presidency by the conservative People's Party. Nor were such rumors entirely new. They had surfaced previously during Waldheim's two terms as secretary-general, the office he was elected to on December 22, 1972, after losing the race for the Austrian presidency in 1971. On the very day he secured his U.N. position, Waldheim faced the first public questions about his past. Interviewed by an Israeli journalist who had heard rumors about his Nazi years from a member of the Austrian delegation—in which Waldheim had been ambassador between 1958 and 1962—Waldheim claimed an anti-Nazi patriot's past.

Speculation about Waldheim's past focused on his public account of his career in the last four years of World War II. Waldheim never denied serving as a lieutenant in Hitler's army or fighting on the Russian front. Yet he claimed that after a grenade wound to his right thigh on December 14, 1941, he was discharged and spent the rest of the war earning his master's degree in law at the University of Vienna. He also denied any links to the Nazi Party, stressing his family's resistance to the *Anschluss*.

Several years before Waldheim perpetuated this version of events in his 1985 memoir, *In the Eye of the Storm*, rumors about his past cropped up in print. In 1980, *The New Republic* ran articles by Shirley Hazzard and by its editor and publisher, Martin Peretz, accusing Waldheim of Nazi allegiances. Spurred by these articles and by his voters, Congressman Stephen J. Solarz wrote to both Kurt Waldheim and the Central Intelligence Agency (CIA) in

November of 1980, asking for information on Waldheim's activities under Hitler's regime. In December, the Legislative Counsel of the CIA cleared Waldheim, and he himself wrote to Solarz, insisting that he would hardly have been elected U.N. secretary-general by several governments if his past did not stand up to scrutiny. Then, as later in 1986, Waldheim dismissed the allegations as slander and threatened the press with legal action—which he never took. The difference was that in 1986, rediscovered documentation forced him into a less credible self-defense.

The intensified speculation during Waldheim's presidential campaign came about through Georg Tidl, an Austrian historian investigating General Alexander Loehr, whom the Yugoslavs had hanged in 1947 for war crimes. Tidl inadvertently discovered that Lieutenant Kurt Waldheim had served from 1942 through 1945 as a military intelligence officer in the Army Group E staff commanded by Loehr in the Balkans. Michael Graff, the general secretary of the People's Party, rejected this information and made the first countercharge of an international conspiracy against Waldheim's candidacy.

Several months later, on February 21, 1986, Waldheim inexplicably gave Hubertus Czernin, a young journalist at the independent-minded magazine *Profil*, permission to check his service records in the National Archives. There, Czernin found a review of Waldheim's career under the Nazis, conducted in 1945 by the Austrian government to clear Waldheim for the foreign service. That same evening, armed with evidence both of Waldheim's presence in the Balkans and of his membership in three Nazi organizations—the National Socialist Student Federation, the *Sturm Abteilung* (SA or Storm Troopers), and the SA Cavalry Troop—Czernin could not budge Waldheim from his doctored autobiography. In their next interview on February 24, however, Waldheim admitted his Balkan posting and further aroused the reporter's suspicions by his evasiveness. On March 3, nine weeks before the election, *Profil* published a detailed exposé of Czernin's findings; the following day, *The New York Times* took up the story, and the World Jewish Congress (WJC) held a press conference about Waldheim's prevarications. On March 22, the WJC revealed that the U.N. Central Registry of War Criminals and Security Suspects (CROWCASS) held a file on Waldheim based on the Yugoslav War Crimes Commission's request for his extradition in 1947.

In the following weeks, more data about Waldheim's hidden past emerged from research by journalists from various countries, by Eli Rosenbaum, a former Justice Department war crimes prosecutor and the WJC's counsel, and by Robert Herzstein, an independent historian hired by the WJC. As an Army Group E *ordonnanzoffizier* (staff officer) charged with writing reports on prisoner interrogations and antipartisan operations, Waldheim would inevitably have known about—if not necessarily participated in—the Nazi atrocities in the Balkans. Prominent among these was the Kozara offensive, in which the Germans killed more than four thousand rebels, took reprisal against civilians, and deported more than sixty thousand peasants to concentration camps. Documents also placed Waldheim in Arsakli, Greece, around the time of massive deportations of Greek Jews from nearby Salonika to the death camps—between March 15 and August 7, 1943. Thus, far from having been discharged in 1941, Waldheim was associated with two notorious Nazi brutalities in southern Europe. Waldheim, whose campaign slogan had been "An Austrian the world trusts," responded to international suspicion with an abundance of conflicting rebuttals. He first called all rumors a "monstrous lie" designed by his political opponents. On March 25, he insisted on Austrian television that there had been no massacre—only normal warfare—in the Kozara mountains. On April 13, he apologized on *CBS News* and *60 Minutes* for concealing his Balkan history; in a June 16 French radio interview after his presidential victory, he claimed that he had hidden his past because it was uninteresting: "I was a young man. . . . War is war."

Instead of turning Austria against Waldheim, the publicity about his lies led his party and some media to denounce the WJC and introduced a pronounced anti-Semitic element into his campaign. This reaction was consistent with Austria's record for accepting more former Nazis into positions of power than any other European nation. Simon Wiesenthal, the renowned Nazi hunter, added to the controversy by dismissing the WJC's condemnation of Waldheim's hypocrisy because he himself had never found evidence for the man's involvement in war crimes. Wiesenthal became less vocal about supporting Waldheim, however, when the latter claimed unlikely ignorance of the Salonika deportations.

On May 4, 1986, in the first election race, Waldheim missed the majority infinitesimally with a 49.3 percent vote. In the June 8 runoff between him and the Socialist candidate, Kurt Steyrer, a landslide win made Waldheim the ninth Austrian head of state since 1918. Yet ultimately, his victory proved a Pyrrhic one. Other Western European governments gave him the cold shoulder, so that his first official visit abroad did not come until June 25, 1987, when he traveled to the Vatican to meet Pope John Paul II. Soon afterward, only the Islamic governments welcomed Waldheim's visits.

Meanwhile, on April 27, 1987, the U.S. Attorney General put Waldheim's name on the Watch List of undesirable aliens denied entry into the United States; by 1990, the decision remained unchanged despite three voluminous defense folders submitted to the Justice Department by Waldheim's lawyers. In Austria, on February 8, 1988, a commission of historians established at Simon Wiesenthal's suggestion concurred that although not personally

Shown here casting his vote in the presidential elections, Kurt Waldheim faced intense public scrutiny in the wake of charges that he had been less than candid about his links to Nazi activities during World War II. (Reuters/Rick Wilking/Archive Photos)

involved in atrocities, Waldheim had been in "consultative proximity" to war crimes. The very next day, Wiesenthal called upon Waldheim to resign as an untrustworthy official.

Although Waldheim remained impervious to such demands and even gained ground through an official meeting in Salzburg with the German and the Czech presidents in 1990, his deceit about his past barred him from the respect and influence enjoyed by previous Austrian presidents. On June 21, 1991, on nationwide television, the seventy-two-year-old Waldheim announced that he would not seek reelection in 1992.

—*Margaret Bozenna Goscilo*

ADDITIONAL READING:

Cohen, Bernard, and Luc Rosenzweig. *Waldheim.* Translated by Josephine Bacon. New York: Adama Books, 1987. The authors offer a detailed investigation into Waldheim's military life and an indictment of Austria's amnesia about Nazi past.

Hazzard, Shirley. *Countenance of Truth: The United Nations and the Waldheim Case.* New York: Viking Press, 1989. A journalist who questioned Waldheim's past back in the 1980's condemns the United Nations' tolerance of his Nazi background and of his mediocrity and racism as its secretary-general.

Mitten, Richard. *The Politics of Antisemitic Prejudice: The Waldheim Phenomenon in Austria.* Boulder, Colo.: Westview Press, 1992. A historian who researched the Thames Television-Home Box Office production of *Kurt Waldheim: A Commission of Inquiry*, Mitten surveys Austrian anti-Semitism and meticulously examines errors and misrepresentations in the numerous Waldheim investigations.

Rosenbaum, Eli M. *Betrayal: The Untold Story of the Kurt Waldheim Investigation and Cover-Up.* New York: St. Martin's Press, 1993. A fascinating account, detailed and thriller-paced, of the inquiry Rosenbaum conducted into Waldheim's past at the request of the World Jewish Congress.

Wiesenthal, Simon. "The Waldheim Case." In *Justice Not Vengeance.* Translated by Ewald Osers. New York: Grove Weidenfeld, 1989. The Nazi-hunter establishes Waldheim's unworthiness for the Austrian presidency while criticizing the WJC's proceedings against him as reckless and self-serving.

SEE ALSO: 1945, The United Nations Is Founded; 1945-1946, Nuremberg Trials; 1983, Klaus Barbie Faces Nazi War Crimes Charges.

1986
RIOTS IN KAZAKHSTAN

Riots in Kazakhstan stimulate Kazakh nationalism while increasing the uneasiness of the republic's many non-Kazakh residents.

DATE: December 16-17, 1986
LOCALE: Alma-Ata, Kazakh Soviet Socialist Republic
CATEGORIES: Government and politics; Race and ethnicity; Wars, uprisings, and civil unrest
KEY FIGURES:
Mikhail Sergeyevich Gorbachev (born 1931), general secretary of the Soviet Communist Party and later president of the Soviet Union, 1985-1991
Gennadii V. Kolbin (born 1927), first secretary of the Communist Party of the Kazakh Soviet Socialist Republic, December, 1986-1989
Dinmukhamed Kunayev (born 1912), first secretary of the Communist Party of the Kazakh Soviet Socialist Republic, 1956-1962, 1964-1989, and member of the Politburo
Nursultan Nazarbaev, first secretary of the Communist Party of the Kazakh Soviet Socialist Republic, 1988-1991, and later president of the Republic of Kazakhstan, 1991-

SUMMARY OF EVENT. The Kazakhs are a central Asian people of Turkic origin. Living in the border area between Russia and China, they were nomads organized into family and clan groups. Traditionally, the largest social organizations among them were the three hordes, each occupying a traditional geographical area.

Russian contact with the Kazakhs began because of Kazakh control of the caravan routes connecting Imperial Russia to Central Asia and beyond. Russian penetration into this area began in the eighteenth century and was completed, not without military conquest, by about the middle of the nineteenth century. During the Russian civil war, Kazakhs enjoyed a brief period of autonomy, but this essentially ended by 1924.

The Kazakh Soviet Socialist Republic was separated from other central Asian areas by the end of the 1920's. During the purges of the 1930's, and with forced migrations of other Soviet nationals to Kazakhstan during World War II, the non-Kazakh population increased. During this same period, the shrinking of pasture lands and internal purges led to a serious reduction of the Kazakh population. An additional wave of European immigrants entered the area during the "virgin lands" movement in the 1950's when Nikita Khrushchev hoped that expansion of agriculture to new lands would solve Soviet food shortages.

The Kazakh Soviet Socialist Republic was the second

largest of the Soviet republics (next to the Russian SSR), stretching from the Caspian and Aral Seas to Siberia and to the border of the People's Republic of China. Because of the migration of outsiders, it was the only ethnic republic in which the titular group was a minority within the republic. Not until the end of the 1980's, when a Slavic outmigration combined with a higher Kazakh birth rate, did Kazakhs become the largest group within the state.

Ethnic tensions in the Kazakh region were heightened by several incidents of the post-Stalin era. Industrial development and mining in the north increased the urbanization of non-Kazakhs in that section. Also, Slavic farmers began to enter during the "virgin lands" period under Khrushchev. The northern area near Semipalatinsk was the center of Soviet nuclear testing. All of these activities resulted in serious environmental degradation and exacerbated problems for the land-hungry Kazakh nomads of the south whose living standards declined below those of the Europeans.

During the era of Leonid Brezhnev, who had himself held high office in the Kazakh SSR, the tradition developed that the regional first secretary of the Communist Party in an ethnic republic would come from the largest ethnic group; Dinmukhamed Kunayev led the Party in the Kazakh SSR and later became the first political leader of Soviet Central Asia elevated to the Politburo. Under his regime, Kazakhs advanced in the power elite controlling government and cultural positions. Kazakh youths had increased chances of rising because of favorable university admissions. The Kunayev regime, like many others, was also thoroughly corrupt.

When Mikhail Gorbachev took control of the Soviet Union, his policies were aimed at improving the efficiency of the economy. This included attacks on corruption within the system. As a result, Kunayev was dismissed as first secretary of the Party in the Kazakh SSR and replaced by Gennadii Kolbin, an ethnic Russian.

Young Kazakhs, including university students, immediately began a demonstration in Brezhnev Square in Alma-Ata. Rumors preceded the dismissal and it appears the initial demonstration was well planned. When authorities put pressure on the remaining demonstrators to disperse, rioting broke out. Estimates of the numbers involved range upward from ten thousand. Rioting lasted for two days. In its course, vehicles were overturned and set on fire; some shops were looted and torched. Some Russians were attacked, and there was fighting between rioters and security forces.

The Soviets officially admitted that two deaths occurred during the rioting and that there were a number of other casualties. Unofficial reports of the deaths were considerably higher, ranging from sixty to more than two hundred. More than seventeen hundred injuries occurred. Estimates of arrests range from more than one thousand to about eighty-five hundred; two temporary prison camps were cleared of inmates to hold those detained. At least one participant was sentenced to death, though the sentence was commuted.

Despite forcible suppression of the riots, ethnic tensions in the Kazakh SSR continued at least until the appointment of Nursultan Nazarbaev as regional first secretary of the Communist Party in 1989. Though he worked to ease ethnic tensions, problems with some minorities continued, and Russian uneasiness did not abate completely, especially following the creation of the Republic of Kazakhstan.

The rioting in Kazakhstan was the first major rift in Soviet ethnic relations following the death of Stalin. Despite more than a half century of stressing the multiethnic nature of the Soviet Union, ethnic tensions continued. The riots in Alma-Ata were followed in the next few years by ruptures of Russian relations with the Baltic States, with Ukraine, Georgia, Byelorussia, Armenia, Azerbaijan, and the Central Asian states. Even within Russia and those other states, nationalism has created an increasingly obvious number of ethnic problems.

Ten years after the Alma-Ata riots, there were still no complete accounts of the causes, extent, or results of that violence. At the time of the riots, there were no American or European reporters in the Kazakh SSR. Western news media paid little attention to the rioting.

The Moscow-appointed investigation commission conducted its investigation and made its report. Only a brief summary of that report has ever been made public. Even the independence of Kazakhstan shed little additional light. Some Kazakh leaders who played a role in ending the violence, and condemning it, changed their expressions on the event.

The Alma-Ata riots made clear the limitations of Gorbachev in approaching the question of nationalities, and his weakness in believing that his attacks on corruption and inefficiency were of primary importance to most Soviet citizens. Many observers were convinced that his outlook was Russian rather than Soviet. Beyond their significance in marking the decline of Gorbachev's political power, the riots in Alma-Ata initiated a chain of events that ultimately resulted in the collapse of the Soviet Union.

—*Art Barbeau*

ADDITIONAL READING:

Diuk, Nadia, and Adrian Karatnycky. *New Nations Rising: The Fall of the Soviets and the Challenge of Inde-*

pendence. New York: John Wiley & Sons, 1993. The few paragraphs dealing with the Alma-Ata riots are among the most complete in Western accounts. Their discussion of the cause, course, and results of the violence would seem to be reliable. Diuk and Karatnycky put the implications of the December, 1986, events in proper perspective for the Soviet Union as a whole.

Nahaylo, Bohdan, and Victor Swoboda. *Soviet Disunion: A History of the Nationalities Problem in the USSR*. New York: Free Press, 1989. Although the Alma-Ata riots play a minuscule role in this work, the few pages devoted to those events are among the most complete in a Western language. The riots are reveal the failure of Moscow politicians to assess the question of ethnicity in the Soviet Union.

Olcott, Martha Brill. *The Kazakhs*. Stanford, Calif.: Hoover Institution Press, 1987. Written before the events described, it is the best account of Kazakh history in a Western language.

_____. "Kazakhstan: A Republic of Minorities." In *Nations and Politics: The Soviet Successor States*, edited by Ian Bremmer and Ray Taras. New York: Cambridge University Press, 1993. Although giving little attention to the 1986 riots, Olcott's account places those events in the context of the subsequent history and independence of Kazakhstan, noting that the uprising stimulated both Kazakh nationalism and unease among Russian citizens of the new state.

Svanberg, Ingvar. "Kazakhs." In *The Nationalities Question in the Soviet Union*, edited by Ian Smith. New York: Longman, 1990.

_____. "Kazakhstan and the Kazakhs." In *The Nationalities Question in the Post-Soviet Union*, edited by Ian Smith. London: Longman, 1995. Both of Svanberg's accounts provide excellent descriptions of the position of Kazakhs and Kazakhstan in the last days of the Soviet Union and the first days of the independence of Kazakhstan. He makes some assessment of the extent of the rioting, and puts the rise of Kazakh nationalism in proper perspective.

Wimbush, S. Enders. "The Alma-Ata Riots," *Encounter* 69, no. 1 (1988): 62-68. Wimbush's account has both the advantages and the disadvantages of immediacy and suffers somewhat from his anti-Soviet and anti-Gorbachev biases. Still, ten years after the event, there is no better Western account. The director of the Society for Central Asian Studies at Oxford, Wimbush relied heavily on wire service and newspaper accounts. He places the riot securely in its central Asian and Islamic context, noting the impact of the war in Afghanistan in exacerbating tensions in Muslim central Asia.

SEE ALSO: 1979, Soviet Union Invades Afghanistan; 1988, Ethnic Riots Erupt in Armenia; 1991, Soviet Union Dissolves into Loosely Allied Republics; 1994, Russian Troops Invade Chechnya.

1987
EUROPEAN COMMUNITY ADOPTS THE SINGLE EUROPE ACT
The European Community adopts the Single Europe Act at the Luxembourg summit meeting of European leaders, establishing a single European market as a precursor for full European integration.

DATE: July, 1987

LOCALE: Luxembourg

CATEGORIES: Economics; Government and politics; Organizations and institutions

KEY FIGURES:

Konrad Adenauer (1887-1967), first chancellor of the Federal Republic of Germany, who presided over post-World War II reconstruction

Jacques Delors (born 1925), French statesman appointed president of the new European Commission in 1985 who was instrumental in passage of Single Europe Act and moving Europe toward full political and economic integration

Jean Monnet (1888-1979), the founding father of a European Union (EU)

Robert Schuman (1886-1963), French statesman and founder of the European Coal and Steel Community (ECSC)

SUMMARY OF EVENT. The concept of a unified Europe dates from the union under Christianity of medieval times. Many notable personages of that period, such as Thomas Aquinas, regarded themselves as Europeans, and moved freely between nations. William Penn (founder of the Pennsylvania colony) suggested the viability of a European Parliament in the 1700's. The major impetus toward European union, however, came during the reconstruction of Europe in the aftermath of World War II. Jean Monnet, who had assisted the Allies in a united effort against Nazi Germany, became a strong advocate of European postwar union. With Robert Schuman of France and Konrad Adenauer of Germany, Monnet engineered the European Coal and Steel Community (ECSC) in 1952 to coordinate resource allocation and production between nations (Belgium, the Netherlands, Luxembourg, West Germany, Italy, and France). In 1957, the same six nations signed the Treaty of Rome which brought a greater cross-section of economic activity under international coordination of the

European Economic Community (EEC). A decade later in 1967, three European agencies, the European Atomic Energy Community, ECSC, and EEC were merged. These agencies retained the acronym EEC, but were known as the European Community.

Since 1957, progress toward a true European union has been positive, but uneven—as if each step toward union required a digestive period by member nations. The Single Europe Act of 1985 was another step toward total union. It set in place a single European market and justifies a single European currency under a European Monetary Union. While the Maastricht Treaty of 1993 paved the way for the European Monetary Union, progress toward a single European currency (the Euro) was slow. In March, 1996, the fifteen European Union nations convened an intergovernmental conference to rework the union's institutional guidelines to allow for expansion, further integration, and revisions of the Maastricht Treaty.

The Single Europe Act of 1985 explicitly targeted six critical areas of economic concern. First, with a target date of December 31, 1992, member countries should take all necessary steps to ensure that a free, internal market exists for labor, capital, and other inputs in the production process within the European Union. This enhanced resource mobility, however, will not inhibit member nations' ability to reduce illegal immigration, or traffic in drugs or stolen properties. In all, 279 different directives would be brought to bear in creating a market free of internal barriers to trade and commerce by 1992. Second, layers of regulation on small and middle-sized business should be cut to stimulate productivity, jobs growth, and profitability. Third, while the preamble to the Single Europe Act refers to monetary union as a state to be ultimately arrived at, progress toward it can be gradual, without a time deadline. (The deadline that existed for a single market was 1992.) Fourth, inequalities of income distribution among more and less affluent areas of Europe should be reduced through prudent use of structural, regional, and social funds. Special attention should be paid to lesser developed areas. Therefore, impoverished areas of northern and southern England would benefit from increased European Union assistance as would poorer countries in southern Europe. Jacques Delors was instrumental in a doubling of structural assistance funds over the 1988 level.

Fifth, the European Parliament was given increased powers. In certain cases, Parliament could amend European Union legislation after a second consideration. The "two-reading" process became law. In this procedure, Parliament studies a law submitted by the European Commission, which is then submitted to the European Council for determination of a "common position." The Council returns the proposed law, with their findings, to the Parliament for a second reading, after which Parliament can amend or reject the bill. The law, affixed with Parliament's changes or rejection, is returned to the Commission who, in turn, can amend Parliament's findings before returning it to the Council for a final hearing. Certainly passing legislation within the European Union is a complex, lengthy affair; compounded by the fragmented powers of all the union's governing bodies.

Sixth, the Single Europe Act provided the process for coordination of foreign policy—as opposed to trade policy—among member nations. Controversial, in that it attempts to substitute a supranational for a national approach to foreign affairs, the provision is viewed as another step toward full integration of the European Union.

The Single Europe Act was intended to effect a much greater degree of economic integration among the union's members by 1992. The economic effects of Single Europe Act can be categorized under the headings of lower trade barriers, specialization to comparative advantage, increased scale economies, lower production costs, and geographic concentration.

In creating a single European market, four categories of trade barriers were to be eliminated gradually. First, differential taxes and subsidies on agricultural trade and less favorable taxation on nondomestic firms would be eliminated. Second, quantitative barriers would be ended, including quotas and a set maximum market share for nondomestic producers of services (for example, airlines). Common non-tariff barriers against nonmembers had to be agreed upon by the union's members. Third, restricted access of other member countries to entry into many service industries (finance, banking, professions) would cease. Finally, the "border costs" involved with trade, including delays, certifications, quality checks, and border personnel, would all be substantially lowered under a single European market.

Jacob Viner proposed that any effective customs union would be both "trade creating" and "trade diverting": "creating" in the sense that the volume of intraunion trade will expand; "diverting" in the sense that the flow of extraunion trade will contract. Early studies indicated that welfare gains from a single European market would be relatively small. Moreover, within the European Union, production to comparative advantage (efficient resource use) will be only slightly enhanced because of similar resource endowments in high-volume trading relationships.

With the advent of a single European market, competition would be enhanced as barriers to entry fell, as the market power of domestic firms declined because of foreign entry, and as supply costs of foreign firms declined as the result of smaller transborder costs. As foreign markets become more contestable for foreign firms, entry may increase (in the short run) or decrease (in the long run) the number of firms in an industry. Conceivably, stronger firms may buy rivals or expand capacity. If higher levels of output are consistent with lower per unit costs, scale economies exist. Lower costs can be reflected in lower consumer prices (and higher consumer surplus) while maintaining profit margins. Some evidence indicates that plant size in similar industry is larger in the United States relative to the point of minimum efficient scale than in Europe (minimum efficient scale measures minimum plant size necessary to realize lowest average costs). Therefore, potential economies of size exist for European producers.

Generally, firms have some degree of excess capacity or slack. Increased competition from foreign firms may increase domestic firm efforts to lower costs, and possibly price, to sustain market share. Also, there are indications that economic integration provides stimulus for geographic concentration, so that different industries, in proximity and in need of each other's product, can reduce some costs of operations.

By the mid-1990's, it was by no means clear that each of the 279 facilitating mechanisms for the Single Europe Act would unambiguously enhance welfare or efficiency in the European Union. The single European market was expected to improve resource allocation and heighten competition in European markets. The issue of complete integration, however, continued to be the subject of intense debate—with Germany advancing the concept while Britain and the Scandinavian nations favored a more flexible (and less comprehensive) union.   —*John A. Sondey*

ADDITIONAL READING:

Flam, Harry. "Product Markets and 1992: Full Integration, Large Gains." *Journal of Economic Perspectives* 6 (Fall, 1992): 7-30. Solid, nontechnical article which examines the economic effects of Single Europe Act, with specific attention to resource and productive efficiencies.

Holland, Martin. *European Integration.* London: Pinter Publishers, 1994. A detailed, textually complex account of the road to European Union. Informative, relevant appendices.

Hurwitz, Leon, and Christian Lequesne, eds. *The State of the European Community.* Boulder, Colo.: Lynne Rienner, 1991. A series of essays which provides a detailed snapshot of the European political, social, and economic situation as it moves toward full integration.

Owen, Richard, and Michael Dynes. *The Single European Market.* London: Times Books, 1993. A strong, readable compendium of the political, economic, and social ramifications of Single Europe Act.

SEE ALSO: 1957, Common Market Is Formed; 1961, Organization for Economic Cooperation and Development Forms; 1991, Sweden Applies for Membership in the European Community; 1993, Maastricht Treaty Is Ratified.

1987
INTERMEDIATE-RANGE NUCLEAR FORCES TREATY

The Intermediate-Range Nuclear Forces Treaty reduces the threshold of the dangers of a nuclear war on the Continent when the Soviet Union and the United States agree to eliminate existing intermediate range nuclear missiles deployed in Europe.

DATE: December 8, 1987
LOCALE: Washington, D.C.
CATEGORIES: Diplomacy and international relations; Science and technology
KEY FIGURES:
Yuri Andropov (1914-1984), general secretary of the Communist Party of the Soviet Union, 1982-1984
Mikhail Sergeyevich Gorbachev (born 1931), general secretary of the Communist Party of the Soviet Union, 1985-1991
Andrei Andreyevich Gromyko (1909-1989), Soviet foreign affairs minister, 1957-1985
Ronald Wilson Reagan (born 1911), fortieth president of the United States, 1981-1989
Eduard Shevardnadze (born 1928), Soviet foreign affairs minister, 1985-1990
George P. Shultz (born 1920), U.S. secretary of state, 1982-1989

SUMMARY OF EVENT. Decades of suspicion, misunderstanding, and confrontation during the Cold War years after 1945 greatly reduced the opportunity for the United States and the Soviet Union to find common ground and achieve breakthroughs in the complicated realm of nuclear arms control. The Intermediate Nuclear Forces (INF) agreement signed in December, 1987, represented a significant step, lessening the danger of potential nuclear war between the two major superpowers and the opposing alliances facing each other in Europe, the North Atlantic Treaty Organization (NATO) and the Warsaw Pact.

Efforts to successfully negotiate arms control agreements in the years before 1987 had been difficult but not

Mikhail Gorbachev and Ronald Reagan signed the Intermediate Range Nuclear Forces Treaty in 1987, the first such agreement to set in motion the total elimination of an entire category of nuclear weapons held by the Soviet Union and the United States. (Reuters/Dennis Paquin/Archive Photos)

impossible. The Strategic Arms Limitation Treaties (SALT) of 1972 and 1979, setting upper limits on the numbers of some types of nuclear weapons and their delivery systems, showed that bilateral agreements could be achieved. The 1987 Intermediate Range Nuclear Force (INF) treaty was the first agreement between the two superpowers to develop procedures for the total elimination of one entire category of nuclear weapons held by each nation.

The decade prior to the INF treaty had been characterized by an intensification of the Cold War and a rapidly expanding nuclear arms race. Despite the 1972 SALT agreement, both sides during the 1970's energetically developed their modern and potentially very destructive multiple-warhead nuclear weapons. These included improved long-range strategic weapons able to reach between the United States and the Soviet Union, as well as the shorter range missiles deployed in Europe. The maximum range of these intermediate range rockets (some with

multiple warheads) was approximately thirty-four hundred miles, still far enough to reach a massive target area throughout the continent. Population centers located in the arc of a probable war zone would bear the brunt of nuclear destruction, even if these intermediate range missiles were used on a limited scale.

The serious problem became evident when the Soviet Union began in 1977 to deploy its new intermediate range missile systems, known as SS-20's. These missiles, which had three nuclear warheads on each rocket, were aimed at western Europe. American efforts during the next several years failed to convince Moscow to remove or reduce these destabilizing weapons. As a consequence, beginning in 1983, the United States reciprocated by deploying comparable intermediate range nuclear weapons aimed at Soviet targets. These were the Pershing II missiles and the smaller but equally deadly "cruise missiles." This confrontational atmosphere created more tensions by the early 1980's, despite occasional bilateral meetings to discuss possible avenues to reduce the dangers of nuclear war.

Arms talks on the INF issue completely broke down in 1983, when the Soviet Union withdrew from further discussions with the Americans. It was during this period that President Ronald Reagan characterized the Soviet Union as the "evil empire," and the Soviet leadership under Leonid Brezhnev and his successor Yuri Andropov adopted a similar confrontational foreign policy toward the West.

Widespread public demonstrations and numerous petitions in Western Europe during these years urged the United States to remove all nuclear weapons that could jeopardize their safety and lives. Yet European public opinion was divided between those who opposed and those who supported the presence of these weapons in their midst. Many Europeans still sought tangible American protection and support in the event of Soviet aggression. The NATO governments in Europe consistently supported deployment of the American intermediate missile systems, to provide a balance of power or equilibrium that hopefully would deter the Soviet side from miscalculating and starting a war with conventional weapons that might "go nuclear."

This tense and dangerous atmosphere changed with the emergence of a new Soviet leader, after Mikhail Gorbachev became the general secretary of the Communist Party in 1985. Both sides, now approximately balanced in the comparative strength of their intermediate weapons systems deployed in Europe, returned to the negotiating table that year to resume the interrupted talks. Military and diplomatic delegations discussed the many complex technical issues that had to be resolved in reaching a satisfactory settlement.

Gradually the two governments made sufficient compromises related to this one category of nuclear weapon to meet the strategic objectives of both states. In 1986, negotiators for the two countries finally agreed that all intermediate nuclear missiles should be removed from the European region. This settlement would still protect the vital national interests of each superpower and their allies in Europe, while at the same time reducing the potential for conflict in Europe. Also, Gorbachev and Reagan personally began a series of high-level summit meetings in 1985 and 1986 that helped lead to the final result.

These discussions and negotiations eventually culminated in a successful agreement. The December 7-10, 1987, meeting in Washington, D.C., was the occasion for the official signing of the INF treaty on December 8. Gorbachev flew to the United States to sign the treaty on behalf of the Soviet Union. The importance of this agreement for arms control, and the presence of the leaders of the two world's superpowers, made this Washington summit a major media event.

The text of the INF treaty totaled 169 single-spaced typed pages, containing seventeen articles and three annexes. Composed of four topical sections, it detailed the removal and destruction of approximately 2,600 missiles (1,752 Soviet and 859 American missiles), plus the elimination or destruction of all rocket launchers, spare parts, test and training equipment, and other supplies or facilities needed for missile maintenance and possible use. These treaty obligations, requiring the physical removal and destruction of these materials, were to be fulfilled within a three-year period.

An extensive and detailed verification plan to monitor compliance with the INF treaty provided for mutual inspections of missile bases and facilities under U.S. and Soviet control. Observers were allowed to visit assembly and deployment sites, giving access to several of the most secret and sensitive locations in both countries. Once the treaty became effective in June of 1988, both sides were entitled to make short-notice inspections of designated facilities for a thirteen year period to see that no violations would occur. Mutual trust was the goal, and the verification provisions made it unlikely either side could cheat on their treaty obligations. President Reagan often repeated the Russian phrase *doveryai no proveryai* ("trust but verify") as the appropriate approach.

The United States Senate formally ratified the INF treaty by a 93-5 vote on May 27, 1988. This agreement was a significant step toward improved relations between the two superpowers. Other outstanding disputes and issues affecting Soviet-American relations still remained to be resolved, including disagreements over the "antiballistic missile" (ABM) systems in the arsenals of both nations, development of the American "Strategic Defense Initiative" (commonly called "Star Wars"), and Soviet policy in Africa and Latin America. Massive numbers of other nuclear weapons still existed, for the INF treaty only dealt with a small portion (approximately 5 percent) of nuclear delivery systems. Nevertheless, it promised a safer future.

The improved atmosphere emerging from the INF negotiations provided momentum for further negotiations on other arms control issues, such as decreasing the number of long-range strategic missiles. This important objective was achieved in the Strategic Arms Reduction Treaty (START) signed by the two governments in 1991. Reductions in conventional (non-nuclear) armaments also were initiated, after NATO and the Warsaw Pact signed the 1990 "Conventional Forces in Europe" (CFE) agreement. By the time the Soviet Union collapsed internally in late 1991, the potential dangers of a nuclear war had been substantially reduced. Within this context, the INF agreement represents an important turning point in the Cold War.   *—Taylor Stults*

ADDITIONAL READING:

Gorbachev, Mikhail. *At the Summit: Speeches and Interviews, February 1987-July 1988*. New York: Richardson, Steirman & Black. 1988. Full text of important Gorbachev foreign policy pronouncements.

Haslam, Jonathan. *The Soviet Union and the Politics of Nuclear Weapons in Europe, 1969-87*. Ithaca, N.Y.: Cornell University Press. 1990. Provides the Soviet perspective on the subject.

Oberdorfer, Don. *The Turn: From the Cold War to a New Era: The United States and the Soviet Union, 1983-1990*. New York: Poseidon Press, 1991. Comprehensive account of problems and changes in U.S.-Soviet relations.

Reagan, Ronald. *An American Life*. New York: Simon & Schuster, 1990. In his autobiography, Reagan gives his own account of the road to the INF agreement.

Shultz, George P. *Turmoil and Triumph: My Years as Secretary of State*. New York: Charles Scribner's Sons, 1993. Shultz's memoirs cover the period from 1982 to 1989 and include the INF issue.

SEE ALSO: 1949, North Atlantic Treaty; 1955, Warsaw Pact Is Signed; 1963, Limited Nuclear Test Ban Treaty Is Signed; 1975, Helsinki Agreement; 1979, SALT II Is Signed; 1991, Soviet Union Dissolves into Loosely Allied Republics.

1988
ETHNIC RIOTS ERUPT IN ARMENIA

Ethnic riots erupt in Armenia, touching off more ethnic turbulence in the wake of Gorbachev's policies of "openness" and "restructuring" and leading to the eventual dismantling of the multinational Soviet Communist empire.

DATE: February, 1988

LOCALE: Armenian Soviet Socialist Republic

CATEGORIES: Government and politics; Race and ethnicity

KEY FIGURES:

Suren G. Arutyunyan (born 1938), first secretary of the Central Committee of the Armenian Communist Party, May, 1988-April, 1990, and first deputy chairman, Council of Ministers, Armenian Soviet Socialist Republic, January, 1986-May, 1988

Kyamran M. Bagirov (born 1933), first secretary of the Politburo of the Central Committee of the Azerbaijani Communist Party, December, 1982-May, 1988, and member of the Central Committee of the Communist Party of the Soviet Union, 1986-1991

Karen S. Demirchyan (born 1932), first secretary of the Central Committee of the Armenian Communist Party, 1974-May, 1988

Mikhail Sergeyevich Gorbachev (born 1931), general secretary of the Central Committee of the Communist Party of the Soviet Union, March, 1985-December, 1991, and president of the Soviet Union, March, 1990-December, 1991

Boris S. Kevorkov (born 1932), ethnic-Armenian first secretary of the Nagorno-Karabakh Autonomous Oblast (Region) Communist Party, 1973- February, 1988

Vazgen M. Manukyan (born 1946), mathematician and early ideologue of the Karabakh Committee (1988), prime minister of the Armenian SSR, 1990-1991, and defense minister of the independent Republic of Armenia, 1991-1993

Henrik Pogosyan, ethnic-Armenian first secretary of the Nagorno-Karabakh Communist Party, February, 1988-1991

Andrei D. Sakharov (1921-1989), Russian nuclear physicist and Nobel Prize-winning human rights activist, who supported the Armenian national cause in 1988

Levon A. Ter-Petrosyan (born 1945), philologist and long-time Armenian dissident, head of the Karabakh Committee, 1988, and its successor Armenian National Movement, 1989-1991, chairman of the Armenian Supreme Soviet, 1990, and president of the independent Republic of Armenia, 1991-1996

SUMMARY OF EVENT. In order to end what he called the "period of stagnation" under his predecessors, Mikhail S. Gorbachev, general secretary of the Communist Party of the Soviet Union and later its head of state, introduced his policies of *glasnost* (openness) and *perestroika* (restructuring). In allowing greater freedom, he also inadvertently released the pent-up ethnic tensions in the multinational empire. Nationalist movements in several non-Russian republics of the Soviet Union believed that they would find the central party and government authorities in Moscow more tolerant of their political aspirations than during the earlier repressive Soviet era.

Following the restlessness in the Soviet Baltic republics, a series of events broke out in the Azerbaijani-ruled Nagorno-Karabakh Autonomous Oblast (an enclave with a predominantly ethnic-Armenian majority), in Armenia proper, and in Azerbaijan that were to lead to serious disturbances, violence, and undeclared warfare. Eventually, to the establishment of *de facto* Armenian military control over Nagorno-Karabakh, also called Mountainous Karabakh or simply Karabakh, as the Communist regime and the Soviet Union unraveled and Armenia and Azerbaijan became independent in 1991.

In the Caucasus, this chain of events started when, on February 20, 1988, the regional Karabakh Supreme Soviet (parliament) called for Nagorno-Karabakh to be reunified with Christian Armenia, from which it had been detached in 1923 and placed under Shiite Muslim Azerbaijani rule. Within days, there were supportive mass rallies in Erevan, the Armenian capital. On June 15, the Armenian Supreme Soviet in turn voted for the transfer of Karabakh to Armenia, only to be rebuffed two days later by the Azerbaijani Supreme Soviet. In the meantime, serious intercommunal violence had broken out on February 27 in the Azeri industrial city of Sumgait when dozens of ethnic-Armenians were tortured, raped, and killed.

When Gorbachev and the central party authorities in Moscow were confronted with the matter on July 18, they adopted a formal ruling rejecting any change in the constitutional status of Karabakh, despite Gorbachev's earlier assurances to Armenian representatives that a "just solution" would be found. Indeed, a Karabakh Committee of eleven Armenian intellectuals headed by Levon Ter-Petrosyan became the unofficial spokesmen for the reunification movement in Erevan. In the face of the opposition, the movement became more radical, with newer members demanding reunification with Karabakh, independence from the Soviet Union, and democracy in public affairs.

The unrest continued, however, for there was even more that underlay the Armenian nationalist cause in 1988. Erevan also complained of the alleged official stifling of their language and culture among the 75 percent ethnic-Armenian majority in the Karabakh autonomous region. At the same time, Armenia's deliberate industrialization and urbanization by the Soviet authorities over the previous decades had caused severe ecological problems and concern over the presence of a nuclear power plant near Erevan following the catastrophic accident in Chernobyl in the Soviet Ukraine in 1986. The region's citizenry also resented the entrenched and privileged Communist elite. Indeed, it was this state of political and bureaucratic behavior and Gorbachev's reformist agenda which now spurred various Armenian demands for change.

For all that, it was the status of the Karabakh autonomous enclave, at its closest point six miles from the Armenian border and with 127,000 ethnic-Armenians out of its total population of 160,000, which remained the crucible

of the Armenian nationalist cause. Neither Gorbachev's personal visit and appeal for calm nor Moscow's later sending troops to Azerbaijan to protect ethnic Armenians nor Azerbaijani opposition could make the issue abate. Mass rallies in Erevan continued, and on November 7, during the commemoration of the Communist Revolution of 1917, about one million Armenians out of the capital's total 1.2 million jeered both central Communist Party officials and government leaders. On November 22, there were further massacres of Armenians in Azerbaijan and the start of a massive two-way exodus involving several hundred thousand ethnic inhabitants from both countries regaining their homelands. From December 10 to 14, all eleven members of the Karabakh Committee were arrested and exiled to Moscow until their release on May 31, 1989.

Azerbaijan established an economic and communications blockade of Armenia in September, 1989. An undeclared war began between Armenian and Karabakh ethnic-Armenian forces on one side and the Azerbaijani army on the other. The Armenians managed to impose military control over the Azeri-ruled autonomous region and a direct link across the narrow Lachin corridor separating Karabakh from Armenia.

Eventually, ceasefire talks among the authorities of Erevan, Baku, and Stepanakert (Karabakh) bore fruit through multinational intermediation. Although independent Armenia's President Levon Ter-Petrosyan moved toward compromise, however, there was no definitive political settlement by the end of his first term in 1996. More than Karabakh's future status was involved, since its very borders were challenged by Armenians as having been arbitrarily drawn following their brief independence before the establishment of Communist rule in the 1920's.

The traumatic earthquake of December 7, 1988, in the Leninakan region of northern Armenia killed more than three percent of the country's total population, victimizing some hundred thousand residents. This event was not only physical drama but also a political catalyst. The lack of an effective response by Moscow in rescue aid enhanced the alienation of Armenians, formerly among the most loyal members of the Soviet community. Mikhail Gorbachev's criticism of the Karabakh Committee on December 10, 1998, for "seizing the initiative" in conjunction with foreign assistance sources did not bode well for the solution of the various problems distilled in Armenia's ethnic crucible.

—Peter B. Heller

ADDITIONAL READING:

Chorbajian, Levon, et al. *The Caucasian Knot: The History and Geopolitics of Nagorno-Karabakh.* London:

Zed Books, 1994. An Armenian-American sociologist and others present a thorough profile of the autonomous Azerbaijani enclave with emphasis on its ethnic problems. Includes a valuable appendix of documents and maps.

Curtis, Glenn E., ed. *Armenia, Azerbaijan, and Georgia: Country Studies*. Washington, D.C.: Library of Congress, 1995. This volume in the Area Handbook Series contains a thorough background with an extensive appendix, bibliography, and varied illustrations.

Hunter, Shireen T. *The Transcaucasus in Transition: Nation-Building and Conflict*. Washington, D.C.: Center for Strategic and International Studies, 1994. An authoritative account by an area specialist. The selected bibliography is also top-flight.

Libaridian, Gerard J., ed. *Armenia at the Crossroads: Democracy and Nationhood in the Post-Soviet Era*. Watertown, Conn.: Blue Crane Books, 1991. The historian-editor and later Armenian government official reproduces essays, interviews, and speeches which he considers to be milestones on the way to Armenia's independence. A sequel to the editor's *The Karabagh File: Documents and Facts, 1918-1988*, published in 1988.

Rost, Yuri. *Armenia Tragedy*. Translated by Elizabeth Roberts. New York: St. Martin's Press, 1990. A Soviet photojournalist covers both the interethnic conflict and the earthquake in Armenia in 1988. The accompanying halftones are dramatic.

Suny, Ronald G. *Looking Toward Ararat: Armenia in Modern History*. Bloomington: Indiana University Press, 1993. This professor of Armenian history at the University of Michigan provides one of the most thorough treatments of the nationalist-ethnic question. Includes an authoritative bibliography and endnotes.

Verluise, Pierre. *Armenia in Crisis: The 1988 Earthquake*. Translated by Levon Chorbajian. Detroit, Mich.: Wayne State University Press, 1995. A French writer's excellent account of both the political and physical earthquakes of that year, with an appendix and illustrations.

SEE ALSO: 1979, Soviet Union Invades Afghanistan; 1986, Riots in Kazakhstan; 1991, Soviet Union Dissolves into Loosely Allied Republics; 1994, Russian Troops Invade Chechnya.

1989
HUNGARY ADOPTS A MULTIPARTY SYSTEM

Hungary adopts a multiparty system, becoming the first Eastern bloc country to establish constitutional guarantees for free elections with competitive political parties.

DATE: January-October, 1989
LOCALE: Hungary, especially Budapest
CATEGORY: Government and politics
KEY FIGURES:
Mikhail Sergeyevich Gorbachev (born 1931), reformist leader of the Soviet Union, 1985-1991
Károly Grósz (1930-1996), Hungarian moderate who briefly served as Communist Party leader, May, 1988-October, 1989
János Kádár (1912-1989), secretary of Hungary's Communist Party, 1956-1988
Imre Nagy (1896-1958), reformist Communist who was rehabilitated in June, 1989
Miklós Németh (born 1948), last prime minister of the Communist regime in Hungary, November, 1988-May, 1990
Rezsö Nyers (born 1923), reformer and first president of the Hungarian Socialist Party, 1989-1990
Imre Pozsgay (born 1933), preeminent leader of reformist Communists in Hungary

SUMMARY OF EVENT. Years before the Eastern European revolutions of 1989-1990, Hungary's Communist regime, more than any other in the region, initiated a gradual process of political and economic liberalization. After the overthrow of Imre Nagy in 1956, there continued to be advocates of Nagy's liberalism within the communist party—named the Hungarian Social Workers Party (HSWP). In 1968, János Kádár's regime introduced a New Economic Mechanism (NEM), producing considerable economic decentralization and reliance on market forces. For a few years, Hungarians were able to see real improvements in their standards of living, described as "Goulash communism" or "communism with a capitalistic facelift." A conservative reversal in the 1970's was an economic failure, leading to extreme discontent with both Kádár and the HSWP. In the HSWP Congress of 1980, reformers managed to pass an endorsement of the legitimate role of small private enterprises, referred to as the "second economy."

The 1980 Congress also endorsed an expansion of political democracy. By this time, voters in some elections had a choice among party-approved candidates, and in 1983 the National Assembly mandated multiple candidates in almost all elections, a process called "socialist pluralism." When Mikhail Gorbachev came to power in the Soviet Union in 1985, his policies of *glasnost* (openness) and *perestroika* (restructuring) gave great encouragement to the reformist wing of the HSWP, which was led by the trio of Imre Pozsgay, Rezsö Nyers, and Miklós Németh. In 1987, Pozsgay issued a report, "Turning Point and Reform," which called for Hungary's integration into the world economy, protection of individual rights, limits on the role of the party, and an independent judiciary.

In May, 1988, party liberals successfully unseated Kádár as general secretary, and replaced him with Károly Grósz, a pragmatist known to favor limited reform. Of perhaps greater significance, Pozsgay, Nyers, and Németh were added to the ruling politburo of the party, where they were able to help guide the party's agenda. In July, Grósz announced that the party would soon introduce a law of associations permitting opposition groups to organize. Almost immediately, dozens of small opposition groups appeared, including the highly respected Democratic Forum.

The most immediate question was whether the Soviet Union, with sixty thousand troops stationed in Hungary, would allow such a radical change to occur. Until this time the Soviets had been ready to use force to prevent multiparty pluralism in Eastern Europe, as they made clear in 1956, 1968, and 1981. Gorbachev, however, was giving hints that he did not wish to intervene in the internal affairs of other countries, and then on December 7, he delivered a speech to the United Nations in which he appeared to repudiate the Brezhnev Doctrine, the basis for intervention since 1968.

Taking the speech as a green light, the Hungarian National Assembly on January 11, 1989, voted 357-6 to allow the formation of independent organizations (not yet full political parties), and on the same day the Parliament voted 364-7 to allow almost unrestricted rights for peaceful assembly. Justice Minister Kalman Kulscar publicly declared that the two laws represented "the transformation of an authoritarian political system into a pluralistic one." A few days later in a related development, Poland's Communist Party announced the legalization of the Solidarity labor union, to be followed by round-table talks aimed at the sharing of power. It appeared clear that the Soviets were not going to use military force in either Poland or Hungary.

The HSWP's Central Committee began to work seriously on a draft for fundamental changes in the Hungarian Constitution, and committee members soon disagreed about whether or not to eliminate the key phrase recognizing the party as "the leading power of society." Grósz and those committed to communist ideals wanted to keep the phrase, while reformers wanted its elimination, a change that would logically lead to multiparty elections. The Hungarian government on March 8 released a proposed compromise which did not mention the leading role of the party but did acknowledge Hungary's "socialist system." In addition, the party offered to follow Poland's recent example of holding serious round-table negotiations with opposition groups.

In April, the Central Committee approved of guidelines encouraging more private ownership of newspapers, television stations, and other media. In May, Hungary became the first Soviet-bloc country to open its borders to Western Europe, a move causing a major crisis in East Germany. A week later, Prime Minister Németh replaced six cabinet members with younger men whom he described as "fighters for political and economic reform." After the party's historical commission, chaired by Pozsgay, presented a very favorable interpretation of Nagy's policies, the government gave its full support for a memorial burial service for Nagy and four of his aids. On June 16, a quarter of a million people solemnly gathered as speakers eulogized Nagy and his associates for nine hours. Ironically, Kádár died three weeks later, the same day that the Supreme Court reversed Nagy's conviction for treason.

As numerous politicians announced they were leaving the HSWP, the Central Committee formed a new four-member ruling presidium which included Nyers, Pozsgay, and Németh. Round-table discussions with the opposition began on June 13, and Pozsgay said in a public debate that the HSWP leadership had accepted the principle of free elections with rival parties. In fact, three opposition candidates were elected to the National Assembly in special elections on August 5, something that had not occurred since 1947. Round-table participants announced agreements about several constitutional amendments and about a framework for holding multiparty elections the next year. On October 6-9, a special party congress voted in favor of these agreements, and it also voted to install Nyers as the new party leader, to endorse democratic socialism in place of Marxism-Leninism, and to change the party's name to the Hungarian Socialist Party (HSP).

On October 17-20, the National Assembly approved of ninety-four constitutional amendments, including abolition of the party's monopoly on political power and a guarantee that "political parties may be freely established and may freely function." Other key amendments codified civil liberties and human rights, and established a separation of powers among executive, legislative, and judicial branches. With these amendments, Hungary became the first Warsaw-Pact country unambiguously to discard Communist rule and to institute a Western model of pluralistic democracy. In a referendum of November 26, Hungarian voters overwhelmingly rejected a Communist-backed proposal for the direct election of the presidency, thus assuring that the next president would come from an opposition party. After another Communist defeat in the parliamentary elections of March-April, 1990, Democratic Forum organized a non-Communist coalition to take over the reigns of power. *—Thomas T. Lewis*

ADDITIONAL READING:

Ash, Timothy Garton. *The Magic Lantern: The Revolution of '89 Witnessed in Warsaw, Budapest, Berlin and Prague*. New York: Vintage Books, 1993. Chapter 3 gives an interesting description based on personal observations.

Berend, Ivan. *The Hungarian Economic Reforms, 1953-1988*. New York: Cambridge University Press, 1990. An eminent Hungarian economist's analysis of the gradual changes that prepared the country for peaceful transformation in 1989.

Brown, James F. *Surge to Freedom: The End of Communist Rule in Eastern Europe*. Durham, N.C.: Duke University Press, 1991. Readable accounts of the experiences of each country, with chapter 4 devoted to Hungary.

East, Roger. *Revolutions in Eastern Europe*. London: Pinter Publishing, 1992. Pages 87 through 106 provide a factual guide to the personalities and events of Hungary's negotiated revolution.

Stokes, Gale. *The Walls Came Tumbling Down: The Collapse of Communism in Eastern Europe*. New York: Oxford University Press, 1993. Highly recommended as the most interesting and balanced treatment of the political transformations of Hungary and other countries.

Swain, Geoffrey, and Nigel Swain. *Eastern Europe Since 1945*. New York: St. Martin's Press, 1993. Readable summary of the rise and fall of Communist systems in the entire region.

Volgyes, Ivan. "Hungary: Dancing in the Shackles of the Past." *History Today* 88 (November, 1989): 381-384, 399-400. A useful summary of the background and early achievements of the 1989 revolution.

SEE ALSO: 1956, Hungarian Revolution; 1968-1989, Brezhnev Doctrine; 1968, Soviet Union Invades Czechoslovakia; 1985, Gorbachev Is Elected General Secretary of the Communist Party; 1989, The Berlin Wall Falls; 1989, Velvet Revolution in Czechoslovakia; 1989, Ceausescu Is Overthrown in Romania; 1991, Soviet Union Dissolves into Loosely Allied Republics.

1989
THE BERLIN WALL FALLS

The Berlin Wall falls, beginning the process of reunifying East and West Germany.

DATE: November 9, 1989
LOCALE: Berlin, East Germany
CATEGORY: Government and politics
KEY FIGURES:

Willy Brandt (Herbert Ernst Karl Frahm; 1913-1992), chancellor of the Federal Republic of Germany

(FRG), 1969-1974, and former mayor of West Berlin, 1957-1969

Hans-Dietrich Genscher (born 1927), foreign minister of the Federal Republic of Germany, 1974-1992

Erich Honecker (born 1912), president of the German Democratic Republic (GDR), 1976-1989, chairman of the State Council of the GDR, 1973-1989, and secretary of the (Communist) Socialist Unity Party of Germany (SED), 1971-1989

Egon Krenz (born 1937), president of the GDR and secretary of the SED, October-December, 1989

Mikhail Sergeyevich Gorbachev (born 1931), president of the Soviet Union and general secretary of the Communist Party, 1985-1991

Guenter Schabowski, member of the Politburo of the (Communist) Socialist Unity Party's Central Committee of the German Democratic Republic

SUMMARY OF EVENT. Berlin, the capital of Germany, deep inside the Russian occupation zone, had been divided into four occupational sectors after the defeat of Nazi Germany in 1945. Since the Russian blockade of Berlin in 1948-1949, the eastern sector was under Communist domination, while the western sectors were under the protection of the United States, Britain, and France.

On August 13, 1961, the East German government under the patronage of the Soviet Union erected a wall through the center of Berlin to separate Communist East Berlin from the three western sectors of the city. In building the wall, the Communists intended to stop the mass exodus of East Germans (three million had fled via the open sectors since 1949) and to close the only hole in the tightly sealed Iron Curtain.

The thirty-mile-long barrier, originally an irregular, hastily constructed wall of cement blocks and barbed wire, eventually was replaced by ten-foot-high concrete prefabricated panels. This replacement wall gave a somewhat better appearance to the border but also provided West Berliners with ready-made surfaces for anti-Communist slogans and other graffiti. On certain prominent sites such as the Brandenburg Gate or the former Potsdamer Platz, visitor platforms allowed a look across the wall to witness how the East German regime kept its population imprisoned with trip wire and barbed wire, dogs on clothesline-leashes, watchtowers, and floodlights. All official state visitors to the Federal Republic of Germany were brought to see the Berlin Wall, and it became a public relations nightmare for the German Democratic Republic and the Communist east bloc.

After the wall was erected, West Berliners were barred from visiting relatives and friends in East Berlin. The situation of the beleaguered city improved when Willy

Brandt, former mayor of West Berlin, became West German chancellor in 1969 and initiated a policy of rapprochement with the East, known as *Ostpolitik*. As the result of Brandt's efforts to relax tension between East and West, the Quadripartite Agreement was signed in September of 1971, in which the United States, the Soviet Union, France, and Britain regulated access to West Berlin and outlined visa provisions for West Berliners. East Berliners continued to be trapped in the East by their government's refusal to issue visas to the West.

People made frequent attempts to flee over the Berlin Wall to West Germany. Many of these (sometimes ingenious) attempts were frustrated and quiet a number of refugees were apprehended. From 1961 to 1989, Communist border guards fatally shot seventy-nine people while trying to escape across the Wall.

When Mikhail Gorbachev emerged as leader of the Soviet Union in 1985, he introduced reforms under the policies of *perestroika* (restructuring) and *glasnost* (transparency or openness). These reforms transferred power from the Communist Party to democratically elected leaders. While the Soviet Union was undergoing fundamental reforms, East Germany remained staunchly Communist under Erich Honecker, its party and government leader. Encouraged by the reforms in Russia, East Germans practiced defiance of their Communist rulers by voting their disapproval of the party's candidates in the statewide municipal elections held in May of 1989. As usual, a vote of 98.85 percent approval of state candidates was announced. Heartened by the changes in Russia, East Germans openly protested the "election fraud."

On June 5, 1989, the official Communist Party newspaper of East Germany, *Neues Deutschland*, defended the massacre of Chinese dissidents in Beijing's Tiananmen Square on the previous day by calling the incident "the answer to counterrevolutionary revolt by an extremist minority." Finely atuned to Communist diction, many East Germans took this to mean that their government would not tolerate any demonstrations for democratization and would likely shoot at anyone who might attempt such demonstrations. Many East Germans revealed their lost hopes for reforms by "voting with their feet." During the vacation period in August of 1989, they visited neighboring Communist states where they were allowed to travel. There, they applied for West German passports at the Federal Republic's embassies in Hungary, Czechoslovakia, and Poland. (Instead of recognizing separate East German citizenship, the West German constitution only recognized All-German citizenship.) By mid-August of 1989, the international press was reporting on the growing number of East Germans with West German passports who found themselves trapped in Hungary, Czechoslovakia, and Poland. Their new passports did not contain the necessary visas to leave for the West. By September, many of these East Germans were running out of food and money and descended upon the West German embassies, which swiftly became hopelessly overcrowded. Others camped out in public parks. On September 11, Hungary canceled its bilateral travel treaty with East Germany and allowed sixty-five hundred refugees to leave for West Germany. On October 1, West Germany's foreign minister, Hans-Dietrich Genscher, succeeded in negotiating permission for sixty-two hundred refugees to leave Warsaw and Prague. This permission was granted on the East German condition that such refugees would be transported to the West on sealed railroad trains via East Germany, so they could be officially extradited as undesirable citizens. As these transports crossed the East German border, rioting broke out as other East Germans tried to climb aboard. The refugee drama was magnified by the world's media, especially television.

In East Germany, demonstrations were held with banners demanding "freedom to travel rather than mass

East and West German crews cooperate in pulling down a section of the Berlin Wall in November of 1989. (Robert McClenaghan)

flight." The East German police who monitored these demonstrations did not intervene. Their passiveness encouraged others to express their opposition to the regime openly. In Leipzig on September 4, a mere twelve hundred had demonstrated. By October 16, however, their ranks had swelled to 120,000 protesters.

On the eve of the GDR's fortieth anniversary on October 5, the East German regime was at a loss as what to do, as the number and size of demonstrations grew weekly and the refugee problem continued. The founding of the state was to be commemorated with all the pomp known to Communist celebrations and attended by the Soviet president, Mikhail Gorbachev. The hard-liners in the SED argued for a Chinese-type disposal of demonstrators; others warned that the loyalty of the security forces and the army could not be counted on. Getting through the anniversary without too much disruption and embarrassment and with encouragement from Gorbachev to inaugurate reforms, the SED finally replaced the aging and obstinate Honecker with the younger Egon Krenz. On October 18, Krenz assumed Honecker's duties and promised reforms. Krenz immediately started talks with the grassroots Democratic Forums that had sprung up all over the country. These attempts at making concessions became the familiar story of too little, too late. The people in their peaceful revolution sensed the vulnerability of the SED and its government and pressed even further.

A fatigued and terrified Communist leadership hurried from one emergency meeting to the other, trying to devise strategies that would stop the unraveling of their regime. At the end of a long day of Politburo deliberation on November 9, at 7:00 P.M., the members of the committee held an international televised press conference in East Berlin. The last question of the session was by a young American journalist asking in broken German what the Politburo's deliberations had been with reference to the refugee problem. Guenter Schabowski, member of the committee, shuffled through a mountain of papers looking for a declaration he claimed had been released to the press (it had not). Reading from this declaration, he announced that East Germans would henceforth be allowed to travel and migrate freely. Word of this statement spread throughout East Berlin like wildfire. Immediately, some East Berliners headed for the few checkpoints at the Wall to put the new policy to the test. The demands of passage caught the border officials by complete surprise. In panic, they telephoned the Communist Party leadership to confirm the policy and to ask what the new travel procedures were, adding that they did not have enough forces to contain the growing and angry crowd. They received word to let the people pass without formalities. When news of the free passage at the Berlin Wall reached others via Western radio and television, several hundred thousand East Berliners crossed into West Berlin that night and an unprecedented fiesta of celebration and fraternization commenced. The festivity lasted until dawn, when most Easterners returned home.

The events of the night of November 9 spelled the end of the Communist regime in East Germany and marked the beginning of German reunification. The very next day, East German authorities started to break down the Berlin Wall, which served no more useful purpose. They were aided by Berliners from both sides of the wall with hammer and chisel.   —*Herbert Luft*

ADDITIONAL READING:

Attwood, William. *The Twilight Struggle*. New York: Harper & Row, 1984. Provides anecdotal information on the Cold War.

Bernstein, Jerry. *The Wall Came Tumbling Down*. New York: Outlet, 1990. A prime narrative of the events leading to the end of the Wall.

Borneman, John. *After the Wall: East Meets West in the New Berlin*. New York: Basic Books, 1991. Impact of the Unification on East Berliners with personal accounts.

Gedmin, Jeffrey. *The Hidden Hand: Gorbachev and the Collapse of East Germany*. Washington, D.C.: American Enterprise Institute, 1991. Details the Russian role in the demise of East Germany.

McElroy, Amy. *The Saddled Cow: East Germany, Life and Legacy*. London: Faber & Faber, 1992. McElroy attended the press conference held on November 9.

SEE ALSO: 1948-1949, Berlin Airlift; 1949, Creation of Two German Republics; 1961, Building of the Berlin Wall; 1973, East and West Germany Establish Diplomatic Relations; 1985, Gorbachev Is Elected General Secretary of the Communist Party; 1990, German Reunification.

1989
VELVET REVOLUTION IN CZECHOSLOVAKIA

Czechoslovakia's Velvet Revolution marks the end of the Marxist-Leninist system and the beginning of a pluralistic democracy and a free-market economy.

DATE: November 17-December 29, 1989
LOCALE: Czechoslovakia
CATEGORIES: Government and politics; Social reform
KEY FIGURES:
Ladislav Adamec (born 1926), pragmatic prime minister of Czechoslovakia, 1988-1989

Marián Calfa (born 1946), interim prime minister of the first cabinet without a Communist majority, December, 1989

Alexander Dubček (1921-1990), reform leader of 1968 and the symbol of democracy in 1989

Mikhail Sergeyevich Gorbachev (born 1931), reformist leader of the Soviet Union, 1985-1991

Václav Havel (born 1936), non-Communist president of Czechoslovakia, 1989-1992, and later president of the Czech Republic, 1993

Gustáv Husák (1913-1991), hard-line President of Czechoslovakia, 1975-1989

Miloš Jakeš (born 1922), general secretary of the Communist Party, 1987-1989

Václav Klaus (born 1941), Civic Forum leader, who was appointed finance minister on December 10, 1989

Vasil Mohorita (born 1952), moderate Communist, who was appointed general secretary on December 21, 1989

Karel Urbanak (born 1941), general secretary of the Communist Party, November 24-December 21, 1989

SUMMARY OF EVENT. In its "gentle revolution," Czechoslovakia became the second Soviet bloc country, after Poland, to establish a non-Communist government. Although Czechoslovakia before 1989 had not undergone any of the political and economic liberalization that took place in Poland and Hungary, the country appeared to dismantle its communist system more thoroughly than any other former satellite of the Soviet Union. Based on their democratic foundations and mass support, Czechs and Slovaks appeared ready and able to construct and maintain a viable industrial economy as well as a stable constitutional democracy (whether or not the Czechs and Slovaks remained united).

Before World War II, Czechoslovakia was the Eastern European country that had been most successful in achieving economic and political modernization, and after 1918 it had been governed democratically for twenty years. Since becoming a Marxist-Leninist state in the "Prague coup" of 1948, however, Czechoslovakia generally adhered to the Stalinist model until Alexander Dubček promoted the "Prague Spring" of 1968. Following Soviet intervention, the new government under Gustáv Husák established one of the most authoritarian, repressive systems within the Warsaw Pact. Then, with the Helsinki Final Act of 1975, playwright Václav Havel and other liberal dissidents created an organization, Charter 77, to monitor respect for human rights, but the organization's leaders were often harassed and sometimes imprisoned.

When Mikhail Gorbachev began his reforms in the Soviet Union, the Czechoslovakian leaders tried a few of the reforms of economic "restructuring," but they distrusted and rejected the entire concept of political "openness." President Gustáv Husák and Miloš Jakeš, who replaced Husák as head of the Communist Party in 1987, permitted almost no deviation from "hard-line" Marxist-Leninist orthodoxy, but moderates such as Prime Minister Ladislav Adamec were willing to consider limited reforms. With the public, there was widespread dissatisfaction with the political regime, as well as growing awareness of economic stagnation and ecological degradation. In 1987, a new liberal group, Democratic Initiative, added to the many voices calling for political and economic change.

Early in 1989, there were indications that the year would be eventful. On January 15, two-thousand demonstrators assembled in Prague to honor the memory of Jan Palach, who had committed suicide in 1969 to protest the Soviet-led invasion. Riot police responded with tear gas and truncheons, driving the protesters out of Wenceslas Square. Demonstrations continued for six days and resulted in the arrest of eight hundred people, including Havel and nineteen other leaders of Charter 77. Czechoslovakia's Roman Catholic primate, Cardinal Frantisek Tomasek, issued a public letter criticizing the "crude violence" of the regime. On February 21, Havel was convicted and sentenced to nine months in jail for his attempt to place flowers at the St. Wenceslas statue, and the next day seven dissidents received similar sentences. Foreign governments everywhere protested, and even the French Communist Party called the convictions "inadmissible." The government released Havel and others on May 17, but the dissidents vowed to continue their activism.

Criticisms of the regime got louder, and on June 29, Charter 77 presented a petition of two-thousand citizens who supported a seven-point program of economic reform and religious freedom. On August 21, about three thousand protesters gathered in Prague at the twenty-first Anniversary of the 1968 invasion; they sang the national anthem, shouted anti-Communist slogans, and chanted the names of Dubček and Havel. Security police broke up the rally and made about 370 arrests.

The events called the Velvet Revolution began with a student march on November 17. In a rally to remember Jan Opletal, a student killed by the Nazis, twenty-thousand demonstrators began to shout antigovernment slogans, and riot police tried to prevent demonstrators from entering Wenceslas Square, with thirteen hospitalized and more than a hundred arrests. There was a false rumor that one student had been killed. On November 19, about two hundred thousand people gathered to protest violence against the students, and that day Havel and other dissi-

Young activists display the national flag and chant slogans in support of the 1989 "Velvet Revolution." (Reuters/Petar Kujundzic/Archive Photos)

dents formed a new organization, Civic Forum, modeled after the New Forum of East Germany. Fearing uncontrolled violence, Premier Adamic met with Havel and other representatives of Civic Forum, and agreed to future discussions about limited reform.

On November 24, Dubček returned to Prague for the first time since 1969, and before 250,000 cheering demonstrators, he declared: "Long live socialism with a human face." That same day there was an emergency meeting of the Central Committee of the Communist Party, at which time Jakeš, Husák, and eleven other conservatives were forced to resign from the Presidium. The new secretary general, Karol Urbanek, was considered to be flexible. Civic Forum demanded additional concessions, and on November 25, the Central Committee removed more hard-liners from the leadership. That same day, Gorbachev wrote an article in *Pravda* which implicitly endorsed the prodemocracy movement in Czechoslovakia.

By November 26, antigovernment demonstrations swelled to almost five hundred thousand people. On November 27, an estimated 60 percent of Czechoslovak workers participated in a two-hour general strike, with huge rallies in all of the major cities of the country. Faced

with the threat of longer strikes, Premier Adamec agreed to meet Havel for formal power-sharing talks. On November 28, Adamec effectively capitulated; among other concessions, he promised to change the constitution to abolish the "leading role" of the party and promised to put together a coalition cabinet with non-Communist members within a week.

As huge crowds continued to demand even more changes, Adamec resigned on December 7. Three days later Husák resigned as president, and a new interim prime minister, Marián Calfa, formed a new cabinet composed of a majority of non-Communists, including liberal economist Václav Klaus as finance minister. On December 21, a Communist congress apologized for "unjustified reprisals" against dissidents; it also installed the moderate Ladislaw Adamec as party chairman and suspended or expelled hard-liners of the old regime, including Vasil Bilak and Husák. On December 29, the National Assembly unanimously elected Havel as the Czechoslovak President, and elected Dubček as the chairman of the Assembly.

The euphoric "Velvet Revolution" was remarkable in achieving a rapid end to the Communist system. On June 8, 1990, the country would hold its first free multiparty election since 1946, and the Communist Party would adopt to the new situation by participating in the election and finishing second. Leaders of the new government would strongly disagree concerning how rapidly to move to a free market system, and the country faced other challenges such as environmental degradation and ethnic conflicts between Czechs and Slovaks. Despite the magnitude of the problems, nevertheless, only a tiny percentage of the population disagreed with the general direction of the revolution.   —*Thomas T. Lewis*

ADDITIONAL READING:

Ash, Timothy Garton. *The Magic Lantern: The Revolutions of '89 in Warsaw, Budapest, Berlin, and Prague.* New York: Random House, 1990. Pages 78-131 present a dramatic account of the events in Czechoslovakia.

Danac, Ivo, ed. *Eastern Europe in Revolution*. Ithaca, N.Y.: Cornell University Press. Stimulating articles by recognized scholars, including Tony Judt's perceptive analysis of the Velvet Revolution.

Dubček, Alexander. *Hope Dies Last: The Autobiography of Alexander Dubček*. Translated by Jiri Hochman. New York: Kodansha International, 1993. Fascinating account of Dubček's career and developing ideas, including his role in the events of 1989.

East, Roger. *Revolutions of Eastern Europe*. London: Pinter Publishers, 1992. Pages 38-61 provide a factual guide to the personalities and events of the Velvet Revolution.

Kriseova, Eda. *Václav Havel: The Authorized Biography.* New York: St. Martin's Press, 1993. A scholarly study of the life and career of the dominant figure of the revolution.

Stokes, Gale. *The Walls Came Tumbling Down: The Collapse of Communism in Eastern Europe.* New York: Oxford University Press, 1993. A most readable analysis, with pages 148-157 presenting an excellent summary of Czechoslovakia in 1989.

Wheaton, Bernard, and Zdenek Kavan. *The Velvet Revolution: Czechoslovakia, 1988-1991.* Boulder, Colo.: Westview Press, 1992. Detailed narrative of how and why the revolution occurred, with an appendix of useful documents and tables.

SEE ALSO: 1956, Hungarian Revolution; 1968-1989, Brezhnev Doctrine; 1968, Soviet Union Invades Czechoslovakia; 1985, Gorbachev Is Elected General Secretary of the Communist Party; 1989, Hungary Adopts a Multiparty System; 1989, The Berlin Wall Falls; 1989, Ceausescu Is Overthrown in Romania; 1991, Soviet Union Dissolves into Loosely Allied Republics; 1993, Czechoslovakia Splits into Two Republics.

1989
CEAUSESCU IS OVERTHROWN IN ROMANIA

Ceausescu is overthrown in Romania as part of a violent climax to the dissolution of the Soviet empire and the collapse of Communism in Europe.

DATE: December 25, 1989
LOCALE: Romania
CATEGORY: Government and politics
KEY FIGURES:
Ana Blandiana (born 1942), dissident Romanian poet
Elena Ceausescu (1918-1989), wife of Nicolae Ceausescu
Nicolae Ceausescu (1918-1989), president of Romania
Doina Cornea (born 1928), dissident university lecturer in Cluj
Ion Iliescu (born 1930), leader of Romania's National Salvation Front
General Vasile Milea (died 1989), Romanian minister of defense
Petre Roman (born 1946), National Salvation Front prime minister
Lazslo Tokes (born 1952), pastor of Timisoara church

SUMMARY OF EVENT. Before Nicolae Ceausescu's overthrow, Romania appeared quiescent, accepting the last unreformed, Stalinist ruling party in Soviet-dominated Europe. Actually Romania was ready to explode. On two previous occasions, popular discontent had turned violent, threatening the regime. In August, 1977, thirty thousand miners in the Jiu Valley went on strike and allegedly held important officials hostage until their demands had been negotiated. Again on November 15, 1987, protesting pay cuts and fearful about deprivations the coming winter, workers marched on the Brasov city center demanding food and destroying the local party headquarters before the army restored order and killed three protesters.

Although Romanian dissidents usually failed to attract the attention of the non-Communist world, they nevertheless existed. By the time of the revolution, Ana Blandiana was well known for her poignantly critical, anti-Communist poetry. Doina Cornea, a lecturer at Cluj University living under house arrest since 1982, continued to publicize human rights violations.

External events also pressured Ceausescu. In the Soviet world, Gorbachev's reforms spread quickly; by December of 1989, Romania alone among the Soviet allies had not begun a retreat from Communism, retaining many features of an earlier Stalinism.

A pervasive secret police, the Securitate, had informers throughout the society reporting on any anti-Communist thought or action. Romania's human rights record was subject to constant international criticism. Particularly egregious were the harsh, invasive laws encouraging large families, outlawing birth control, and forbidding abortions. A decision by Ceausescu in 1980 to retire Romania's international debt halted consumer imports and produced a drive for exports that left Romanians without enough food or energy for their homes. Standards of living in Romania and Albania were the lowest in all of Europe. A misconceived systematization policy called for some eleven thousand villages to be razed and their inhabitants consolidated in agro-industrial complexes, allegedly increasing agricultural land by 4.5 percent but destroying the peasant village life fundamental to Romanian culture. An urban variant of systematization destroyed the old center of Bucharest and displaced forty thousand people, making space for a gigantic, impractical Palace of the People and a Boulevard of the Victory of Socialism.

In the late 1980's, Laszlo Tokes, a Hungarian-Romanian pastor in Timisoara, criticized the systematization policy, to which he gave wide publicity, including taped broadcasts on Hungarian radio. A transfer was arranged to a small, remote village, but Tokes refused to go. On December 15, 1989, the authorities determined to remove him by force. His congregation defiantly linked arms to prevent his leaving, thus beginning the Romanian revolution.

The next day, the protesters were joined by Romanians and other nationalities in the multiethnic city. Although Tokes and his family were forcibly removed that night, the protest continued, increasing in size, soon moving to the city center, smashing the local party headquarters and adding to their demands democracy and free elections. At a meeting held on December 17, Ceausescu ordered the army and Securitate to fire on the demonstrators if necessary. That afternoon, the Securitate and probably the army opened fire, killing some and dispersing the demonstration. On December 18, confident the situation was under control, Ceausescu began a state visit to Iran.

A general strike broke out in Timisoara on December 19, and the demonstrations spread to Cluj, Oradea, and other provincial localities. On December 20, demonstrations resumed in earnest in Timisoara, and that evening more than one hundred thousand people gathered in the city center. Ordered again to open fire, the army and some Securitate units refused and returned to their barracks. A Timisoara Action Committee of the Romanian Democratic Front was announced and issued a manifesto of grievances and demands.

Ceausescu returned to Bucharest the afternoon of December 20, and that evening he made a radio broadcast blaming the disturbance on hooligans working with foreign imperialists and thanking the army and Securitate for doing their duty. The following day, thousands of workers were ordered into Bucharest's Square of the Republic, where they joined students and others in front of the Communist Party's Central Committee headquarters to hear an address by Ceausescu. Shortly after beginning, the speech was interrupted by catcalls and commotions at the back of the crowd. When Ceausescu hesitated in confusion and disbelief, his wife, Elena Ceausescu, dragged him back inside; but not before all Romania had seen live on national television its confused and flustered president.

Attempts to break up the demonstration after the aborted speech only succeeded in moving the demonstrators to the university where they kept up their confrontation with the army and the Securitate, which continued shooting that night, inflicting many casualties.

Confusion thereafter prevailed in the Central Committee building. Ceausescu's fury focused on the defense minister, General Vasile Milea, who reportedly refused Ceausescu's order to resume firing into the demonstrators. For this disobedience Milea was apparently summarily executed the morning of December 22, costing Ceausescu whatever army support he may still have enjoyed; none believed the government that Milea had committed suicide. With the army now fraternizing with demonstrators who threatened to storm the Central Committee building, the Ceausescus took off in a helicopter from the roof that noon.

Immediately thereafter, the Central Committee building as well as the television and radio studios across town were occupied by demonstrators. That afternoon Ion Iliescu, a former Communist youth leader who had been forced off the Central Committee in 1984, announced the formation of a National Salvation Front composed largely of such Communists as himself and Petre Roman, the future prime minister, with representatives of the Securitate and the army, together with some dissidents including Blandiana and Cornea. That evening a manifesto announced the Front now held governmental authority in Romania and outlined a program of free elections, protection of human and minority rights and far-reaching economic reforms.

Meanwhile, the Ceausescus had abandoned the helicopter and commandeered an automobile. They were soon captured and taken to a military installation in Tirgoviste. On December 25, they were tried and found guilty of genocide, a reference to the highly exaggerated figure of sixty-three thousand dead in the revolution, and of seeking to flee the country with vast sums in foreign banks. An edited video of the irregular judicial proceeding, resembling the mock trials the Communists themselves conducted in the past, was shown on Romanian television on December 26, as were pictures of the bullet-ridden Ceausescu. Intermittent firing had been continuing on the streets of Bucharest and elsewhere, allegedly by die-hard members of the Securitate; but incontrovertible evidence of Ceausescu's death and threats to execute gunmen not surrendering by December 27 brought an end to the violence.

Many disturbing questions, however, remained. How is it possible to account for the speed with which a group of Communists formed a government and issued a manifesto on December 22? Was it a popular revolution as the Timisoara events indicated or a coup d'etat as the immediate appearance of the National Salvation Front suggested? What exactly were the roles of the army and the Securitate, when and why had they gone over to the new government? Why were preposterous death figures cited at Ceausescu's trial, when the government admitted in June, 1990, that at the time of his flight only 144 persons had died? Who killed the 889 others the government reported killed after Ceausescu's flight when the new government was already in place? These and other such questions lingered unanswered long after the revolution and handicapped the National Salvation Front in its quest for international acceptance and approval.

—Ernest H. Latham, Jr.

ADDITIONAL READING:

Codrescu, Andrei. *The Hole in the Flag: A Romanian Exile's Story of Return and Revolution.* New York: William Morrow, 1991. Witty, insightful comments on Romanian events by a famous poet who returned to his native land in December, 1989.

Corley, Felix, and John Eibner. *In the Eye of the Romanian Storm: The Heroic Story of Pastor Laszlo Tokes.* Old Tappan, N.J.: Fleming H. Revell, 1990. A biography of Pastor Tokes with detailed narrative of Timisoara events through the December demonstrations.

Murphy, Dervla. *Transylvania and Beyond: A Travel Memoir.* Woodstock, N.Y.: The Overlook Press, 1992. Less travelogue than the perspicacious observations of a woman traveling alone in post-revolutionary Romania and early 1991.

Pilon, Juliana Geran. *The Bloody Flag: Post-Communist Nationalism in Eastern Europe, Spotlight on Romania.* New Brunswick, N.J.: Transaction Publishers, 1992. Emphasizing Romania, a Romanian-American political scientist examines the new nationalism that replaced Communism in eastern Europe.

Rady, Martyn. *Romania in Turmoil: A Contemporary History.* London: I. B. Tauris, 1992. Scholarly account of the Romanian revolution by a British historian in control of the available sources.

Ratesh, Nestor. *Romania: The Entangled Revolution.* Westport, Conn.: Praeger, 1992. A veteran chief of Radio Free Europe critically examines the Romanian revolution, highlighting many questions, inconsistencies and contradictions.

Sweeney, John. *The Life and Evil Times of Nicolae Ceausescu.* London: Hutchinson, 1991. A London journalist who covered Romanian events for the *Observer* took leave to write this well-researched, literate account.

SEE ALSO: 1985, Gorbachev Is Elected General Secretary of the Communist Party; 1989, The Berlin Wall Falls; 1989, Velvet Revolution in Czechoslovakia.

1990
ALBANIA OPENS DOORS TO FOREIGN NATIONALS

Albania opens its doors to foreign nationals, resulting in a mass exodus of Albanians and an influx of Albanian exiles and foreigners.

DATE: 1990
LOCALE: Albania
CATEGORIES: Government and politics; Immigration
KEY FIGURES:
Ramiz Alia (born 1925), leader of Albanian Communist Party and President of Albania, 1985-1992
Sali Berisha (born 1945), first non-Communist president of Albania, who succeeded Ramiz Alia in 1992
Enver Hoxha (1908-1985), leader of Albanian Communist Party, 1941-1985, and dictator from the end of World War II to 1985

SUMMARY OF EVENT. Led by Enver Hoxha, the Albanian Communist Party, later named the Albanian Party of Labor, established a tightly controlled, Stalinist regime following World War II. Hoxha's regime systematically isolated Albanians from external influences, excluding all foreigners excepting, successively Yugoslav, Russian, and Chinese advisers and technical experts. Albanians, excepting those sent abroad for training in professional fields and members of diplomatic or trade missions were strictly prohibited from leaving the country. Frontier guards literally shot down foreigners wandering into Albania and arrested or killed Albanians attempting to flee the country. After the Soviet invasion of Czechoslovakia, Hoxha's government began cautiously dealing with selected Western countries and Albania's neighbors. In 1973, Hoxha, following a heart attack, began planning for preservation of his system. In 1976, a new, very restrictive constitution, designed to ensure continuation of his policy after his death, was enacted. On July 7, 1977, an article entitled "The Theory and Practice of Revolution," published in *Zeri i Populit*, the official newspaper, attacked Chinese policy without mentioning China and marked the breaking point in Chinese-Albanian relationships. A rail link with Yugoslavia (completed on July 6, 1986), ferry service to Italy, and road crossings into Greece and Yugoslavia were established for trade and limited tourism. Albanians traveling outside the country were still limited to those traveling on state business or for advanced study. These people, however, were required to sign a statement prohibiting establishment of close personal relationships with foreigners. The U.S. State Department *Country Reports on Human Rights for 1985* cites punishment by ten years in prison or death for unauthorized flight from the country or defection on authorized trips abroad.

In April of 1985, Ramiz Alia became Communist Party First Secretary two days after Hoxha's death and continued slowly relaxing repressive and isolationist policies. In a public speech delivered in November of 1987, he stated, "We do not intend to stand aloof from the world, to live in isolation. We do not hesitate to cooperate with others, nor do we fear their power and wealth. On the contrary, we seek this cooperation."

By 1986, Albanians generally were obtaining news and other information about the outside world from Italian, Greek, and Yugoslav television broadcasts. Radio broadcasts, conversations with the few tourists entering the country, and the stories of Albanian truck drivers traveling to various European cities brought additional information from abroad. Albanians also began participating in professional, cultural, and scientific meetings, and athletic events in Europe.

Between 1985 and 1989, Albania opened trade relationships with France, Germany, Italy, Greece, and other countries. Albania sent exhibits to 180 trade fairs in thirty countries. By 1988-1989, Alitalia and Swissair had joined Olympic (Greek), Interflug (East German), Malev (Hungarian), Tarom (Romanian), and Jay (Yugoslavian) airlines in serving Albania. Foreign travel restrictions were reduced, and growing numbers of Albanians were allowed to visit relatives in foreign countries—mainly Greece, Yugoslavia, and a few Western European countries.

The first Albanian-American postwar tourists were admitted in 1985. This easing of restrictions was followed by increasing requests for visas. ALBTOURIST, the Albanian government tourist agency, announced early in 1988 that tourists wishing to visit Albania could arrange itineraries through agents in twenty countries for groups of ten to twenty for two week periods. This began expan-

sion of the tourist industry. Prior to the late 1980's, American citizens (with the exception of Americans of Albanian ancestry), Russians, South Africans, and South Koreans were excluded. Between 1987 and 1989, the total number of tourists admitted increased from 7,000 to 14,435 annually. These tourists reported lesser fear on the part of Albanians to interact with foreigners.

Between 1985 and 1989, however, many escapes or attempted escapes from Albania were reported. Some escapees paid money to the government; others crashed through border barriers in trucks, hid in shipping containers, swam to Corfu, or escaped by other dramatic means. A few foreign citizens of Albanian descent began to be admitted to visit relatives under extremely restrictive terms. In the summer of 1988, three Albanian American clergymen—Orthodox, Muslim, and Catholic—were admitted for short family visits. Also, Edwin Jacques and his wife, who had been associated with the Protestant mission school in Korcha in the 1930's, were permitted to visit in 1986. Mother Teresa, an Albanian from the Kossovo, after being excluded in 1960, was allowed to visit in 1990.

In January of 1990, the Plenary Session of the party's Central Committee approved moderate reforms, including allowing multicandidate parliamentary elections. Demonstrations and agitation, however, continued. On March 20, 1990, an automatic direct dialing system for inter-city and international service, financed by the United Nations Development Fund, was inaugurated linking Albanian to 54 foreign nations. Telephones were few and calls were monitored, but isolation was decreased. In April, 1990, Alia announced that reestablishment of diplomatic relations with the United States and the Soviet Union was under negotiation. This was followed by congressional visits and by William Post, a representative of the Commonwealth Gas Company, who came to discuss cooperation in modernizing the Albanian petroleum business.

In May and June, 1990, the official *New Albania* magazine announced reforms, including reducing the crime of flight from the country from treason to illegal border crossing and assuring a general right to passports and visas for foreign travel. This announcement came just three days before an invited visit of U.N. secretary general Javier Perez de Cuellar, who was investigating human rights violations. Following Perez de Cuellar's visit, several Albanians sought refuge in the Greek and Turkish embassies, precipitating official countermeasures, but, eventually, the government allowed the embassies to fly them out of the country.

Following a peaceful, but illegal, demonstration of about ten thousand people protesting governmental failure to implement announced reforms, including the pledge to grant passports, thousands sought asylum in the Italian, Polish, French, Greek, Czechoslovak, Hungarian, and Turkish embassies. Embassy gates and walls were broken down, security forces fired on the crowds, and laid siege to the embassies. After the European Economic Community expressed concern, the United Nations negotiated departure for these people. About 4,500 were taken to Durres for evacuation by ship, mostly to Italy. Others were flown out. At the same time other individuals and groups fled by sea or through the border barriers. Alia's government responded by cordoning off the embassies and revamping the cabinet, but disturbances and flight continued. During the last two weeks of December, 1990, 4,740 Albanians entered Greece according to the Greek government. A returning American newsman reported that "More than 500 people have been killed this year [1990] trying to flee to Greece or Yugoslavia."

On February 9, 1991, about twenty thousand people clashed with the police after hearing rumors of ships leaving the country. Early in March, Yugoslav news agencies reported five hundred refugees had just crossed their border from northern Albania. On March 5, five vessels carrying nine hundred refugees reached Italy, and the southern Adriatic was crowded with small boats and rafts bearing refugees. On March 7, about eight thousand refugees aboard two ships arrived in Italy from Durres. Reportedly an additional thirty thousand gathered in Durres awaiting transport, along with four thousand at Vlora. The Italian government, unable to handle the influx, interned Albanians in sports stadia, deported several shiploads, seized thirteen ships in port to prevent their returning to Albania, and set up a naval blockade to intercept refugee ships. Ultimately, the Italian government granted the equivalent of $85 million in aid and advanced $50 million in credit to Albanian commercial enterprises, all to stem the exodus.

On February 26, 1991, Albania established official relations with the Soviet Union; on March 15, 1991, relations with the United States were officially reopened. In response to continued unrest, multiparty elections were held March 31, 1991, under the watchful eyes of foreign observers. The Communists, however, won a two-thirds majority and attempts to leave the country followed immediately. On April 10, the Albanian Party of Labor presented a draft of a new constitution which was quickly approved by the new assembly. Continued disturbances and strikes, however, forced the government to call new elections for May, 1992. Disturbances continued, but Albania was admitted to the Conference on Security and Cooperation in Europe. James Baker, the U.S. secretary of state, visited Tirana in June of 1991, bringing encourage-

ment and six million dollars in aid.

On August 7, 1991, rumors that Durres port had reopened, brought thousands of hopeful refugees who, at a cost of twelve casualties, stormed boats and ferries in the harbor. Three ships and two fishing boats were boarded and forced to sail for Bari. Here, the Italians interned the refugees and deported them by August 12. After further demonstrations and riots, hundreds again headed for Durres because of rumors that boats were available. Police blocked the highway. An estimated two hundred thousand citizens were said to have fled the country during 1991.

Continued protests forced Albania's second free election on March 22, 1992. The Democratic Party, headed by heart surgeon Sali Berisha, decisively defeated the Albanian Socialists (formerly Albanian Party of Labor) on a platform calling for a complete break with the Communist political and economic system, including opening the country to foreign entrepreneurs and integration of Albania into the European political and economic structure. On April 4, Ramiz Alia resigned as president, and Sali Berisha was elected to succeed him.   —*Ralph L. Langenheim, Jr.*

ADDITIONAL READING:

Biberaj, Elez. *Albania: A Socialist Maverick*. Boulder, Colo.: Westview Press, 1990. Albanian politics, economic policies, and foreign policy under the Communist regime.

_____."Albania's Road to Democracy. *Current History* 92 (November, 1993): 381-385. Analyzes Albanian affairs subsequent to the fall of the Communist government in 1992.

Fonseca, Isabel. "Last to Leave, Turn Out the Lights." *The Nation* 255 (October, 5, 1993): 356-360. Anecdotal account of entrance and exit problems of 1990-1992.

Halliday, Jon. *The Artful Albanian Memoirs of Enver Hoxha*. London: Chatto & Windus, 1986. A critical partial translation of Hoxha's six-volume memoirs.

Jacques, Edwin C. *The Albanians: An Ethnic History from Prehistoric Times to the Present*. Jefferson, N.C.: McFarland, 1995. Concentrates on post-World War II events. Emphasizes religious issues.

SEE ALSO: 1989, The Berlin Wall Falls; 1989, Velvet Revolution in Czechoslovakia; 1991-1992, Civil War Rages in Yugoslavia.

1990

GERMAN REUNIFICATION

German reunification increases the nation's political weight in European affairs and clearly symbolizes the surmounting of the "Iron Curtain" that had divided Europe since 1945.

DATE: October 3, 1990

LOCALE: East Germany and West Germany

CATEGORY: Government and politics

KEY FIGURES:

James A. Baker III (born 1930), U.S. secretary of state, 1989-1993

Roland Dumas (born 1922), French foreign minister

Hans-Dietrich Genscher (born 1927), West German foreign minister

Sir Douglas Hurd (born 1930), British foreign secretary

Lothar de Maiziére (born 1940), prime minister of the German Democratic Republic

Helmut Michael Kohl (born 1930), chancellor of the Federal Republic of Germany, 1982-1990, and later chancellor of unified Germany beginning in 1990

Eduard Shevardnadze (born 1928), Soviet foreign affairs minister, 1985-1990

SUMMARY OF EVENT. The defeat of Nazi Germany in 1945 brought to the surface a recurrent "German question," which asked how the powerful German nation might be prevented from dominating European politics. Both of the world wars were in large part a consequence of German aggression. The rise of Hitler in the 1930's seemed to demonstrate the inadequacy of the presumed solution to the German question after World War I: to impose harsh restrictions and reparations policies.

Nevertheless, at the time of Nazi Germany's defeat, the Allies had developed no consensus as to how the reemergent German question should be resolved. Instead, the countries that defeated Germany—the United States, the United Kingdom, and the Soviet Union—made the "temporary" decision to administer Germany through occupation zones. In the meantime, a final settlement was to be negotiated. Three western zones were assigned to the United Kingdom, the United States, and France (which had fought against and was defeated by Germany at the beginning of the war). Eastern Germany was assigned to the Soviet Union. Within the East German borders, the historic capital of Berlin itself was split into four sectors, analogous to the four German zones.

The conclusion of World War II ushered in the Cold War, and the Western Allies found themselves increasingly at odds with the Soviets over Germany's status (among other things). In 1949, the three Western powers combined their three zones, creating the Federal Republic of Germany (FRG). The Soviet Union responded within a few weeks by creating the German Democratic Republic (GDR) from their zone. In 1955 both German states were incorporated into rival military alliances: the FRG into the North Atlantic Treaty Organization (NATO), and the GDR into the Warsaw Treaty Organization (WTO). The German

question thus was addressed by the division of Germany for over three decades.

In the late 1980's, popular unrest in the GDR reopened the German question. Prompted by democratic revolutions in other East European countries and encouraged by the Soviet leadership's newfound tolerance of political reform, the East German people began to press their demands for the resignation of their Communist government. The matter of reforming official ideology and introducing democracy were more sensitive for the GDR than other East European countries, because East Germany's very existence as a separate state was justified by its official ideology and maintained by nondemocratic means. Were it not for these, the East German people might as well be citizens of an expanded FRG.

At the same time as they were pressing for political reforms, the people of the GDR insisted upon the right to visit (or emigrate to) the FRG. For years East Germans had been enticed by the freedom and prosperity of the West, and encouraged by the West German government's promise of citizenship to any ethnic German who came to the FRG. Indeed, the Berlin Wall itself had been erected in 1961 by the East German government to stem the flow of its citizens into West Germany. In 1989, East Germans now insisted that their embattled government's good faith could be proven only by permitting freedom of movement. The regime had been responding with a frenzied dismissing and reshuffling of its leaders, and a confused, halting series of limited reforms. Finally, on the night of November 9-10, the government relented and allowed free movement between East and West Berlin. The Berlin Wall was opened.

Perhaps the East German government believed that by allowing greater freedom, its citizens would now be content to stay. Yet the flow of emigrants out of the GDR increased, as did the popular demands for further democratic reforms. At the same time, West German chancellor Helmut Kohl proposed a plan that would begin to move the two Germanys toward reunification. Although the plan was modest, it put the issue of German reunification squarely on the agenda. With increasing urgency the new East German prime minister, Hans Modrow, began implementing various reforms that would have been unthinkable only months earlier. As a member of the unpopular Socialist Unity Party (SED) that had maintained a monopoly on political power throughout the GDR's existence, his authority was waning. The ever-bolder populace demanded a new political system, and increasingly that came to mean reunification with Germany. By February of 1990, various opposition groups had been drawn into the East German government, and Modrow accepted the principle of German reunification.

The countries that had defeated Nazi Germany were keenly interested in how any reunification of Germany would be constructed. Legally, the Quadripartite powers (the United States, the Soviet Union, the United Kingdom, and France) reserved the right to approve any "final settlement" of German unification. Once again, the German question was a source of controversy. The French were especially anxious about a renewal of German power, as were the Poles (who had no formal right to approve unification). The Soviets, were dogmatically opposed to the simple absorption of the GDR by the FRG; this would fundamentally shift the European balance of power to the West. Moscow therefore argued that any unification of Germany should ensure German neutrality and military limits. The Americans were most committed to German unification within NATO.

These questions were debated within a framework dubbed "Two-plus-Four," whereby the two German states would negotiate the details of how unification might be achieved, while the four Allied powers would work out the larger security issues. While the talks were going on, East Germany finally held its first truly free elections. On March 18, 1990, the East Germans overwhelmingly elected to their parliament members of their newly-established Christian Democratic Union, which was unabashedly tied to the West German party of the same name. The East German elections in effect united the two Germanys under one political party. The new East German government proclaimed its intent "to achieve the unity of Germany swiftly and responsibly. . . . "

Now that the "two" of the Two-plus-Four were essentially agreed upon German reunification, all eyes turned to the "four." Negotiations now largely turned to the method, rather than the fact, of reunification. Two broad options were available: The simpler method was provided by

Huge crowds attended ceremonies in front of the historic Bundestag building celebrating the reunification of Germany in October of 1990. (Reuters/Sven Creutzman/Archive Photos)

Article 23 of the West German constitution, which provided for the incorporation of new regional states (*Länder*) into the FRG. The alternative would require a formal peace treaty with Germany, and the establishment of a new state. The simpler option was selected. In addition, procedures were established for merging the two economic systems. All that remained was the unified Germany's military status. The Soviets stubbornly opposed German unification within NATO, offering instead a range of alternatives including enforced neutrality and simultaneous membership in both NATO and the WTO. Ultimately the Soviet Union relented and permitted reunited Germany to freely choose its own alliances. It was understood it would choose NATO. As a concession to the Soviets, the other Quadripartite powers agreed to keep NATO troops out of the eastern part of Germany until the Soviets had withdrawn their troops.

A formal relinquishing of Allied legal claims on Germany was accomplished in a treaty signed by the Quadripartite powers and the two German states on September 12, 1990. On October 3, Germany formally reunified. On December 2, the entire country participated in the first all-German elections since 1932, and established Helmut Kohl's coalition government as the freely elected government of all Germany.   —*Steve D. Boilard*

ADDITIONAL READING:

Ash, Timothy Garton. *In Europe's Name: Germany and the Divided Continent*. New York: Vintage Books, 1993. A sweeping, engaging narrative that explores Germany's place in Europe, with special attention to the German question and Germany's unification. Includes some 270 pages of notes, tables, and appendices.

Kommers, Donald P. "The Basic Law and Reunification." In *The Federal Republic of Germany at Forty-Five: Union Without Unity*, edited by Peter H. Merkl. New York: New York University Press, 1995. A fairly brief summary of how the FRG's constitution facilitated unification, and how unification can be expected to affect Germany's constitution.

Neckermann, Peter. *The Unification of Germany, or the Anatomy of a Peaceful Revolution*. New York: Columbia University Press, 1991. A straightforward and brief account (113 pages, including notes) of the unification of Germany.

Stares, Paul B., ed. *The New Germany and the New Europe*. Washington, D.C.: The Brookings Institution, 1992. One of the first books to thoroughly assess the political, economic, and security implications of the unified German state. As such, it uniquely conveys the hope and anxiety that surrounded German unification.

Szabo, Stephen F. *The Diplomacy of German Unification*. New York: St. Martin's Press, 1992. A thorough, well-documented account of the negotiations and agreements that led up to German unification. A definitive work.

SEE ALSO: 1949, Creation of Two German Republics; 1961, Building of the Berlin Wall; 1973, East and West Germany Establish Diplomatic Relations; 1992, Protests and Violence Against Immigrants in Germany; 1993, Maastricht Treaty Is Ratified.

1991
SWEDEN APPLIES FOR MEMBERSHIP IN THE EUROPEAN COMMUNITY

Sweden applies for membership in the European Community in the wake of German reunification, overcoming its traditional view that membership is incompatible with its traditional policy of neutrality.

DATE: 1991

LOCALE: Sweden

CATEGORIES: Diplomacy and international relations; Economics; Government and politics

KEY FIGURES:

Carl Bildt (born 1949), prime minister of Sweden and leader of the Conservative Party, 1991-1994, and vigorous advocate of Sweden's membership in the EC

Ingvar Carlsson (born 1934), prime minister of Sweden and member of the Social Democratic party, 1986-1991 and 1994-1995

Tage Erlander (1901-1985), prime minister of Sweden and member of the Social Democratic Party, 1946-1969

Olof Palme (1927-1986), prime minister of Sweden and member of the Social Democratic Party, 1969-1976 and 1982-1986

Östen Undén (1886-1974), Swedish foreign minister, 1924-1926 and 1945-1962, who was architect of modern Swedish policy of neutrality

SUMMARY OF EVENT. The road to Sweden's application for membership in the European Community has been long. Sweden formed its attitude toward Europe and the world immediately following World War II, under the leadership of Foreign Minister Östen Undén. Guarding his country's traditional neutrality, which had served it well during two world wars, Undén set Sweden upon a course of well-armed nonalignment between the two hostile superpowers, NATO and the Soviet bloc. He also advocated free trade, a policy in the best interest of Sweden's export-oriented economy. Finally, while eager to see Sweden play an active role in the United Nations, Undén would not countenance any surrender of sovereignty to a supranational entity. His view of Europe, the dominant one in the country's political elite, envisaged Sweden in a Europe of sovereign states trading freely with one another.

At odds with this Swedish view of Europe was the gathering of nations that eventually became the European Community (later, the European Union). From its inception in 1951 as the European Coal and Steel Community, the institution was supranational in certain key economic and political matters. These issues were defined fundamentally in the Treaty of Rome, 1957, which joined France, the German Federal Republic, Italy, Belgium, the Netherlands, and Luxembourg in the European Economic Community (EEC). It called for the elimination of barriers to trade within the community and a common tariff policy toward the outside.

In 1960, several European nations outside the community, who shared Sweden's point of view on free trade and national sovereignty, formed the European Free Trade Area (EFTA). They included besides Sweden, the United Kingdom, Norway, Denmark, Switzerland, and Portugal, and later Iceland and Finland. In contrast to the European Economic Community, EFTA always had a loose, temporary character.

Throughout the 1960's a minority, chiefly among the Conservatives and Liberals, argued for Swedish membership, since the country traded much more with the EEC than with EFTA. The prevailing point of view, put forward by the governing Social Democratic Party and shared by the agrarian Center Party, was that Swedish neutrality ruled out joining the EEC, which appeared to overlap NATO too much. Moreover, Sweden appeared economically strong enough to need nothing more than friendly trade agreements with the EEC. It was also widely felt that membership in the EEC would threaten Swedish "identity." The EEC seemed too Catholic, capitalist, and conservative.

The question of Sweden's membership grew more urgent in the early 1970's, as EFTA virtually disintegrated. In 1973, after two earlier failed attempts, the United Kingdom entered the European Community (EC since 1970), together with Denmark and the Irish Republic. The Social Democratic prime minister, Olof Palme, inclined toward a Swedish application for full membership but bowed to opposition from within the party. In 1972, Palme's government negotiated a free trade agreement between Sweden and the EC, covering mainly industrial products.

During the 1970's, as Sweden's trade with the EC grew ever more significant, the country also was reminded that its policy of armed neutrality had certain limitations. Military expenses had to be cut during the recession that weakened Sweden's economy in the mid-1970's. At the same time, the Brezhnev regime in the Soviet Union heated up the Cold War. It became clear that Swedish national security increasingly depended on indirect support from NATO.

With the death of Soviet premier Leonid Brezhnev in 1982, and the thaw in the Cold War that followed, the basic assumptions of Sweden's foreign policy changed. In 1985, Mikhail Gorbachev came to power and initiated reforms in 1987, such as *glasnost* and *perestroika*, that promised the end of dictatorship in the Soviet Union. In 1989, the Berlin Wall came down, the Cold War ended, and Sweden could rethink the Undén doctrine of neutrality.

Simultaneously, the EC became a more attractive option for Sweden. By the mid-1980's, it had expanded to include Greece, Spain, and Portugal. Austria, a nonaligned country like Sweden, applied for membership in the EC in 1989.

In 1984, virtual free trade in industrial products having been achieved, the EC and EFTA reached an agreement in Luxembourg to expand cooperation in a common European Economic Area (EEA). In 1987, realizing that Europe was being restructured in accord with EC plans and that Swedish industry was being tempted to move to EC countries, the Swedish government declared its wish to join the EC single market. In 1990, as EEA negotiations began in Brussels, Sweden announced its goal of securing EC membership.

During that year, the question of membership became a major domestic issue, pressed by Carl Bildt on behalf of an alliance of Conservatives and Liberals. Influenced by a strong showing of popular support for membership— about 60 percent for, 20 percent against, and 20 percent undecided—the Social Democratic government led by Ingvar Carlsson laid the matter before the Riksdag. On December 2, 1990, the Riksdag voted overwhelmingly to apply under the condition of preserving Sweden's neutrality. Opposition came only from Communists and Environmentalists.

In the following months, the Riksdag's foreign affairs committee examined specific conditions for the application. Of particular concern was whether the EC might eventually impose a compulsory defense obligation on its members and, if so, whether Sweden could comply. The committee took the view that in the short run, such an obstacle was unlikely. If such an obligation arose, Sweden's membership in the EC would allow it to shape such future policy. On July 1, 1991, Prime Minister Carlsson submitted Sweden's application, without qualifications, to the EC in Brussels.

The swift changes in world affairs had swept the country's leaders into the application too fast for the Swedish public to examine what membership might mean to the country's special interests. A genuine national consensus in favor of membership had not yet formed. Popular support for membership peaked at 60 percent in October, 1991, shortly after the general election that brought Carl Bildt to power at the head of a coalition of middle-class parties. Thereafter, the EC's opponents exploited fears of its possible negative impact. The Bildt government's austerity program, linked in the public's mind with the need to adapt Sweden to the structures of the EC, drew popular resentment to the application. The EC became identified with Sweden's problems rather than with its opportunities. It also appeared to jeopardize Swedish identity, raising fears that foreigners would overrun the country and faceless bureaucrats in Brussels would govern it.

During December, 1991, at Maastricht in the Netherlands, the EC's members agreed to prepare themselves by 1999 for a common monetary system and other far-reaching measures of unification. In November of 1993, the European Community became known as the European Union. Negotiations with Sweden had begun in February, 1993; in March of the following year, an agreement was reached. Much of the work on this agreement had already been done when the EEA treaty was signed in 1992. Sweden's membership was approved, pending results of a national referendum. Prime Minister Bildt signed the accession treaty for Sweden at a European Union summit meeting held in the summer of 1994.

In the debate leading up to the referendum, public opinion remained evenly divided. Finally, it shifted in favor of the treaty, influenced by what seemed favorable to Sweden's long-term interest and appeared inevitable. On November 13, 1994, 52.3 percent voted in favor of membership in the European Union, 46.8 percent voted against, and 0.9 percent turned in blank ballots. The turnout was high: 83.3 percent of eligible voters. The Riksdag ratified the results on December 15, 1994. Sweden became a full European Union member January 1, 1995.

—*Charles H. O'Brien*

ADDITIONAL READING:

Hill, Richard, and David Haworth. *The New Comers: Austria, Finland and Sweden.* Brussels, Belgium: Europublications, 1995. This popular survey offers useful insights into those national characteristics that impeded the entry of Sweden as well as Finland and Austria into the European Union.

Huldt, Bo. "Sweden and European Community-Building, 1945-92." In *Neutral States and the European Commu-*nity, edited by Sheila Harden. New York: Macmillan, 1994. This well-balanced, detailed historical analysis discusses the forces pulling Sweden away from its traditional stance of neutrality toward full membership in the European Union.

Milward, Alan S., ed. *The Frontier of National Sovereignty, 1945-1992.* New York: Routledge, 1993. A collective work by Milward and four other expert contributors, this book argues that interrelated economic, social, and political changes in the postwar period have motivated Sweden and other Western European states to integrate.

Pedersen, Thomas. *European Union and the EFTA Countries: Enlargement and Integration.* London: Pinter, 1994. An authority on this topic, the author presents a succinct study of Sweden's reasons for abandoning EFTA on pages 85-94.

Scott, Franklin. *Sweden, the Nation's History.* 2d ed. Carbondale: Southern Illinois University Press, 1988. The standard English-language survey of Swedish history, this work offers a sound understanding of the growth of a national identity, marked by democratic social cohesion at home and neutrality in foreign affairs.

SEE ALSO: 1957, Common Market Is Formed; 1961, Organization for Economic Cooperation and Development Forms; 1986, Olof Palme Is Assassinated; 1987, European Community Adopts the Single Europe Act; 1993, Maastricht Treaty Is Ratified.

1991
SOVIET ATTACK ON BALTIC SEPARATISTS

The Soviet attack on Baltic separatists results in failure and foreshadows the subsequent collapse of the Soviet empire.

DATE: January 13, 1991
LOCALE: Lithuania and Latvia
CATEGORIES: Government and politics; Wars, uprisings, and civil unrest
KEY FIGURES:

Mikhail Sergeyevich Gorbachev (born 1931), president of the Soviet Union, and first secretary of the Soviet Communist Party, 1985-1991

Vladimir Kriuchkov (born 1924), head of the KGB

Vytautas Landsbergis (born 1932), chairman of the Lithuanian Supreme Council

Kazimiera Prunskiene (born 1943), prime minister of Lithuania

Oleg Shenin (born 1937), second secretary of the Soviet Communist Party

Boris Yeltsin (born 1931), president of the Russian Federation of the Soviet Union beginning in 1991

SUMMARY OF EVENT. After Mikhail Gorbachev came to power in the Soviet Union, he embarked on a program of reform, known as *perestroika*, that began to liberalize Soviet society. The reforms, however, released unexpected feelings and forces that he considered a threat to the stability of the Soviet state. Gorbachev had originally envisioned the decentralization of the Soviet government, but when local governments, driven by national movements, demanded more authority, he balked. His concern for holding the Soviet empire together prevailed over thoughts of political decentralization, and the Baltic became a prime battlefield for this struggle.

Taking advantage of Gorbachev's policy of *glasnost* (openness), which permitted discussion of previously forbidden topics, Lithuanians, Latvians, and Estonians insisted on examining and denouncing the Soviet Union's forcible annexation of their states in 1940. When the Lithuanian parliament, on March 11, 1990, declared the restoration of the independent Lithuanian state, Gorbachev objected and imposed an economic blockade on the region. Under the leadership of Vytautas Landsbergis, the chairman of the Lithuanian parliament, the Lithuanians refused to yield. In July of 1990, Gorbachev lifted the blockade, but the situation remained unresolved.

The Lithuanians were divided in their attitude toward Moscow. The Lithuanian Left, under the leadership of Prime Minister Kazimiera Prunskiene, tried to negotiate with Gorbachev. The Lithuanian Right, headed by Landsbergis, saw no purpose in dealing with Gorbachev and banked on the eventual success of his newly emerging rival, Boris Yeltsin, who in turn was building his base not in the Soviet administration but in the Russian republic, one of the constituent republics of the Soviet Union. Gorbachev himself headed toward confrontation; in the fall of 1990, Oleg Shenin, the second secretary of the Soviet Communist Party, worked with Vladimir Kriuchkov, head of the Soviet KGB, to plan the overthrow of Landsbergis and the elected government in Lithuania.

In January of 1991, Soviet troops moved into the Baltic in force, ostensibly to seek military deserters. Latvia appeared to be the first target; on January 2, Soviet forces seized the Press House in Riga, where the major Latvian newspapers were published. On January 7-8, the Soviet forces turned to Lithuania, which was experiencing a political crisis because of the government's decision to raise food prices. Prunskiene, the person in government most willing to negotiate with Gorbachev, resigned, and while Lithuania formed a new government, the Soviet authorities moved.

The original Soviet plan would seem to have aimed at inciting the minorities in the Baltic—Russians in Latvia and Russians and Poles in Lithuania—against the government, thereby opening the way for Moscow to play the peacemaker in an ethnic conflict. In Vilnius this plan failed when Lithuanians came out in great numbers to stand as an unarmed guard in front of the parliament building and a massive pro-Moscow demonstration on January 9 shied away from a forceful confrontation.

On January 10, Gorbachev accused the Lithuanians of planning the reestablishment of the "bourgeois order" and threatened action. On January 11, the Soviet military acted, first seizing the Lithuanian Press House. On the night of January 11-12, Vilnius was besieged: Soviet authorities closed down the airport, stopped trains from passing through the city, and closed the highway to the frontier. In the early morning of January 13, spearheaded by the special forces group Alfa, Soviet forces seized the television facilities in Vilnius. Fourteen people died in the violence. A group calling itself the Committee for the Salvation of Lithuania announced that it had taken power.

In the early morning of January 13, thousands of Lithuanians hurried to the parliament building, expecting the troops to attack, but the Soviets held off. A great number of foreign reporters had by now descended on Vilnius, and their reports, sent out through modern communications technology that the Soviet authorities could not control, aroused a storm of protest in Moscow and in the West.

The Lithuanian government, led by Landsbergis, remained in place, and although the Soviet armed forces could control the streets of Vilnius, they clearly functioned as an occupation army in hostile territory. A truce settled on Vilnius in the evening of January 13, and the Soviet special forces left the city in the next few days. A week later, on January 20, a shootout in Riga resulted in four deaths. An uneasy standoff ensued in both Lithuania and Latvia, marked by random violence perpetrated by the Soviet special forces. This situation continued until the August Putsch in Moscow.

By seizing the buildings in Vilnius and in Riga, Soviet forces had won a battle and lost the war. The members of the Committee for the Salvation of Lithuania insisted on remaining anonymous, and by the end of January Soviet authorities, embarrassed at having put troops at the service of an anonymous group, argued that the committee had never really existed. Gorbachev eventually recognized that the actions of the Soviet troops had been "unconstitutional," but he denied any responsibility on his own part and refused to restore any of the seized buildings. He blamed the Lithuanians for the violence.

The violence in Vilnius compromised Gorbachev's

program of *perestroika* and undermined his position as president of the Soviet Union. He had spoken of establishing a political system "ruled by law," and, in 1990, he had supervised the amendment of the Soviet constitution that eliminated the power of the Communist Party to dictate state policy. Yet in preparing the action in Vilnius, Shenin, in the name of the party, had worked with sympathizers in Lithuania to direct the military's use of force against unarmed Lithuanian civilians. Critics denounced Gorbachev's promises of reform as empty.

Boris Yeltsin, on the other hand, used the events in the Baltic to his own advantage. Just a few hours after the attack on the television tower, he traveled to Tallinn, Estonia, to proclaim his support for the rights of the Baltic peoples. The news of his declaration greatly bolstered the spirit of resistance in Vilnius, and he enjoyed considerable support among all who criticized the action of the Soviet troops.

The January events, as the Lithuanians call them, took place in the shadow of the beginning of the Gulf War, and they presented a painful dilemma for the United States. The U.S. government considered Gorbachev the pivotal figure for the process of reform in the Soviet Union, and it also valued Gorbachev's support in the campaign against Iraq. The United States, however, had never recognized the Soviet annexation of the Baltic republics, and it had to be mindful of the potential of Lithuanian American voters. Convinced that the question of working with Gorbachev was the major concern, the administration therefore moved cautiously, urging Gorbachev to refrain from violence. President George Bush pointedly delayed a scheduled summit meeting, but at the end of July of 1991, he traveled to Moscow to meet with the Soviet leader.

The events of January in Vilnius and Riga presaged the events of August in Moscow. As in Vilnius and Riga, opponents of the Moscow Putsch gathered to defend the parliamentary building with their bodies. In contrast to Vilnius, the Alfa forces, many of whom had participated in the Vilnius events, refused to attack the Russian parliament, believing that they had been misled and reviled for obeying just such orders in Lithuania. When the putsch failed, Soviet rule in the Baltic collapsed. The troops withdrew from the buildings they held in Vilnius; even the KGB gave up its building in the center of Vilnius. In September of 1991, Lithuania and Latvia, together with Estonia, won general international recognition as independent states.   —*Alfred Erich Senn*

ADDITIONAL READING:

Beschloss, Michael, and Strobe Talbott. *At the Highest Levels*. Boston: Little, Brown, 1993. An account of the direct relations between the leaders of the United States and the Soviet Union.

Lieven, Anatol. *The Baltic Revolution*. New Haven, Conn.: Yale University Press, 1993. A British journalist who worked in the Baltic offers a sharp analysis of events and personalities in 1990-1991.

Matlock, Jack F. *Autopsy on an Empire*. New York: Random House, 1995. The American ambassador to the Soviet Union, 1987-1991, analyzes the policies of Mikhail Gorbachev and the Soviet Union's collapse.

Plakans, Andrejs. *The Latvians: A Short History*. Stanford, Calif.: Hoover Institution Press, 1995. The last two chapters of this work by an American historian recount and analyze the events in Latvia from 1988 to 1991.

Senn, Alfred Erich. *Gorbachev's Failure in Lithuania*. New York: St. Martin's Press, 1995. A study of Gorbachev's policies by an American historian who was in Vilnius during the events described in this article.

SEE ALSO: 1918-1920, Baltic States Fight for Independence; 1985, Gorbachev Is Elected General Secretary of the Communist Party; 1991, Soviet Union Dissolves into Loosely Allied Republics.

1991
COALITION DEFEATS IRAQ IN GULF WAR

A coalition defeats Iraq in the Gulf War, uniting the forces of several European nations and the United States to drive Iraq from Kuwait.

DATE: January 17-February 28, 1991
LOCALE: Saudi Arabia, Kuwait, and Iraq
CATEGORIES: Government and politics; Wars, uprisings, and civil unrest
KEY FIGURES:

George Herbert Walker Bush (born 1924), forty-first president of the United States, 1989-1992
Saddam Hussein (born 1937), president of Iraq
John Major (born 1943), British prime minister, 1990-1997
François Mitterrand (1916-1996), French president, 1981-1995
Colin Luther Powell (born 1937), American general and chairman of the Joint Chiefs of Staff, 1989-1993
H. Norman Schwartzkopf (born 1934), American general and commander of allied forces during the Persian Gulf War

SUMMARY OF EVENT. At dawn on August 2, 1990, Iraqi armed forces, lead by the elite and heavily armed Republican Guards Forces Command (RGFC) invaded Kuwait.

Tensions had increased between Kuwait and Iraq over questions of oil and borders, but without warning Saddam Hussein ordered his forces to settle the disputes by military invasion. Within three days the occupation of Kuwait was complete, and Saddam Hussein announced that Kuwait was now the nineteenth province of Iraq. On August 2, after spirited discussion, the United Nations passed Resolution 660, which called upon Iraq to unconditionally end its occupation and pull its forces out of the conquered territories. Saddam Hussein forcefully rejected the resolution, and on August 3, Iraqi forces began to concentrate on the Saudi-Kuwaiti frontier. After lengthy discussions with King Fahd of Saudi Arabia, President George Bush dispatched the first American forces from Fort Bragg, North Carolina, to Saudi Arabia.

With American troops arriving in Saudi Arabia, the United Nations passed Resolution 661, which imposed an oil embargo on Iraq and demanded that the national sovereignty of Kuwait be restored. Every statement issued by the United Nations was rejected by the Baghdad government. On August 22, President Bush called up a large number of Reserve and National Guard troops for potential deployment to the Persian Gulf area. Britain, France, and Italy agreed to provide troops as part of the U.N. coalition. Troops from Egypt, Senegal, Morocco, Bangladesh, and other African and Middle Eastern nations joined the coalition in Saudi Arabia. Surprisingly, Syria indicated that they would send a contingent to Saudi Arabia as part of the coalition.

From August to early December, 1990, the Iraqi government continually refused to negotiate an end to the Gulf crisis. It had become obvious that Saddam Hussein

European nations offered economic and military support to the U.N. coalition that drove Iraqi forces out of Kuwait in early 1991. (Reuters/Win McNamee/Archive Photos)

was determined to bring the Persian Gulf region to the brink of war or worse. On December 15, the United Nations passed Resolution 678 telling Saddam Hussein to withdraw his troops from Kuwait by January 15, 1991, or the United Nations would employ force to expel them.

The process of coalition building was difficult for the United States. European nations, such as France and Britain, had great experience in war planning and modern battlefield technology. Some nations, such as Saudi Arabia, had modern equipment but had never planned for massive military operations. Other nations were at lower levels of training with very little experience. Most American senior commanders had been involved in the Vietnam War and were committed to treating the coalition as a partnership. One of the great military lessons of the Vietnam War was simply that the war in southeast Asia had been an American war with the South Vietnamese being relegated to the role of onlooker. Military commanders such as Generals H. Norman Schwartzkopf and Colin Powell were determined not to repeat that same error.

European nations made differing commitments to the coalition effort. Under the leadership of Prime Minister John Major, Great Britain ultimately sent forty-five thousand service personnel to the Gulf, making it the second largest force behind the United States. France also pledged troops for the liberation of Kuwait, and President François Mitterrand was hopeful that his country's participation would enhance its diplomatic stature in world affairs. Germany's constitution prevented it from sending troops outside its territory except as part of a NATO military exercise, but it gave generous financial support to the coalition and later provided aircraft to guard the border between its NATO ally, Turkey, and Iraq. Unwilling to violate its traditional neutrality, Austria nevertheless allowed coalition planes to fly over its airspace to reach the Gulf. The Netherlands sent supply ships to the Gulf and later deployed Patriot missiles in Turkey to protect against possible Iraqi SCUD missile attacks.

As January 15 approached, tensions in the Gulf area heightened. Saddam Hussein stated that if war started he would attack Israel. It was unclear what Iran would do once hostilities began. Some members of the coalition, such as Syria, had made no commitment to attack into either Kuwait or Iraq.

The date for the U.N.-mandated withdrawal passed with no military action, but at 2:30 A.M. on January 17, 1991, air attacks were launched against key Iraqi command and control centers. Aircraft from the "Free Kuwait" air force led the first attacks to liberate their homeland. During the late evening of January 17, Iraq launched SCUD missile attacks against Saudi Arabia and Israel.

Once it was ascertained by Israeli authorities that the SCUD missiles contained no chemical munitions, the Israeli government announced that it would not retaliate against the Baghdad government. Hussein's greatest potential weapon, the longstanding enmity between Arabs and Israelis, was no longer a valid threat to the unity of the coalition.

While the air war went on, the Iraqis launched an attack against the Saudi resort city of Khafji, but were repulsed by the U.S. Marines and Arab forces. Between February 1 and February 13, allied forces flew more than sixty thousand sorties against Iraq. Bombing then shifted to Iraqi forces in and near Kuwait in preparation for the ground offensive. On February 22, Iraq set fire to a large number of oil wells in Kuwait, and word reached General Schwartzkopf's headquarters about mounting Iraqi atrocities in Kuwait City. The next day allied troops began removing obstacles along the border, and on February 24, the allies began their attack along a several-hundred-mile front.

On February 25, it was clear that the allied advance was moving more rapidly than anyone could have predicted. With surprisingly light allied casualties, Kuwait City was liberated on February 26. In the west, the XVIII Airborne Corps, with the French, moved rapidly into the Iraqi desert crushing all opposition. Iraqi soldiers, numbed by bombing and demoralized by the lightning advance of the allies, surrendered by the tens of thousands. Iraqi forces fleeing Kuwait were caught in the open by allied planes, and the road became known as the "highway of death." The Iraqi army was in shambles when a cease fire was announced on February 28. A number of Iraqi RGFC divisions, however, made their escape back to the environs of Baghdad.

On March 2, the United Nations adopted Resolution 686, which ended combat operations, and on March 5, a still defiant Saddam Hussein rescinded all Iraqi political actions taken against Kuwait. Kuwait was independent again, but the Gulf War left behind a number of unanswered questions. First, what would be the ultimate fate of Saddam Hussein and his government? Second, how far would the U.N. coalition go to topple Saddam? When revolts broke out against Saddam, the United Nations did little but give encouragement to the rebels.

What is clear, however, is that the United States and a revitalized United Nations were able to work together to counter Iraqi aggression. European members of the U.N. coalition lent their vigorous support despite mixed public opinion about participating in the conflict. Of critical importance was the fact that, when faced with Iraq's actions against Israel, Arab states in the U.N. coalition remained focused on the military goals of the coalition.

While President Bush's "New World Order" did not emerge from the Gulf War, it was manifest that, given leadership with clear objectives, member countries of the United Nations could take decisive action against a real threat to world order and stability.   *—James J. Cooke*

ADDITIONAL READING:

Blackwell, James. *Thunder in the Desert: The Strategy and Tactics of the Gulf War.* New York: Bantam Books, 1991. This book deals strictly with the military aspects of the war.

Cooke, James J. *100 Miles from Baghdad: With the French in Desert Storm.* Westport, Conn.: Praeger Publishing, 1993. This work recounts the activities of the French unit in the Gulf War.

Pagonis, William G., and Jeffrey L. Cruikshank. *Moving Mountains: Lessons in Leadership and Logistics from the Gulf War.* Boston: Harvard Business School Press, 1992. Dealing with the question of supplies, this book by General Pagonis gives great insight into the question of war management.

Schwartzkopf, H. Norman. *The Autobiography: It Doesn't Take a Hero.* New York: Bantam Books, 1992. This autobiography sheds light on the commander's view of the war.

SEE ALSO: 1945, The United Nations Is Founded; 1966-1995, France Withdraws from NATO's Military Structure; 1991-1992, Civil War Rages in Yugoslavia.

1991-1992
CIVIL WAR RAGES IN YUGOSLAVIA

Civil war rages in Yugoslavia, unleashing ethnic violence and resulting in the atomization of Yugoslavia into separate republics.

DATE: June 25, 1991-June 1, 1992

LOCALE: Former Yugoslavia—Croatia, Slovenia, Serbia, and Bosnia-Herzegovina

CATEGORIES: Government and politics; Race and ethnicity; Wars, uprisings, and civil unrest

KEY FIGURES:

Alija Izetbegovic (born 1925), Muslim prime minister of Bosnia

Radovan Karadzic (born 1945), Bosnian Serb leader

Stjepan Klujuic, Bosnian Croat leader

Slobodan Milošević (born 1941), president of Serbia

Ratko Mladic, commander of Bosnian Serb army

Franjo Tudjman (born 1922), president of Croatia beginning in 1990

SUMMARY OF EVENT. Ever since the seventh century, when three Slavic tribes—Serbs, Croats, and Slovenes—

Residents of Sarajevo had to forage for water supplies during the Yugoslav civil war that destroyed the city's infrastructure. (Reuters/Oleg Popov/Archive Photos)

migrated from Russia to the Balkans, they had maintained their separate existence, until the formation of the Kingdom of Serbs, Croats, and Slovenes by King Aleksander on December 1, 1918. This separate existence has been the outcome of fundamental historical and cultural differences among them. Though Croats, Slovenes, Serbs, and Bosnians speak basically the same language, Serbs and Bosnians write with an eastern or Cyrillic alphabet, while Croats and Slovenes use the western or Roman alphabet. In addition, Croatians are Catholics, Serbs are Orthodox Christians, and a substantial section of the population of Bosnia-Herzegovina are Kosovo Muslims. Hostilities between Serbs and Croats date back to the Schism of 1054, while those between Serbs and Muslims may be traced to the invasion of the region by the Ottoman Turks in 1463. The feeling of "otherness" between Serbs and Croats has been further fueled by the fact that the latter had belonged to the Austro-Hungarian Empire while the former belonged to the Ottoman. The Rivers Sava and Danube, serving as borders between Croatia and Serbia, once demarcated the two imperial regions. Serbo-Croatian antagonism has also colored their relationship with the Bosnian Muslims. Croats appear to be less hostile to the

Muslims who, though viewed as heretics, could be redeemed through baptism. Serbs treat them as heretics as well as traitors. A great number of Bosnian Muslim converts had been adherents of a heretical Christian sect called *Bogomils* ("pleasing to God"), who had in fact invited the Turks with a view to protecting themselves against invasion by the Hungarian army blessed by the pope.

In 1929, Aleksander founded the state of Yugoslavia ("land of the south Slavs") by reorganizing the kingdom into six republics (Slovenia, Croatia, Bosnia-Herzegovina, Serbia, Montenegro, and Macedonia) and the two autonomous provinces of Vojvodina and Kosovo. The concept of Yugoslavism was problematic because it implied, essentially, the unification of culturally and ethnically diverse southern Slavs under Serbian hegemony. Yet, following World War II, all ethnic and religious groups of Yugoslavia remained united under the leadership of Tito's slogan of "Brotherhood and Unity" that made the Socialist Federal People's Republic of Yugoslavia a Communist state but free from Soviet control. Tito's one-party state, however, while depriving the national communities of their democratic rights, deliberately devised a constitution in 1974 to keep Serbia relatively weak while according a position of primacy to the Serbs in the bureaucracy, the secret police, and the army, and making Belgrade the national capital. Naturally, Serbs controlled the economic system.

The different levels of development among the various nationalities in Yugoslavia also paralleled their ethnocultural differences. Economically, Slovenia and Croatia are more developed than the other republics, though the lesser developed ones are more populous and Serbia and Montenegro, in particular, politically stronger. In general, however, the Yugoslav economic system was regimented by the state apparatus manned mostly by Serbs. Though the constitution of 1974 divided economic enterprises into Basic Organizations of Associated Labor and fostered a semblance of market system and private ownership, economic policies were not based on rational market criteria but were rather administrative and arbitrary. The performance of the Yugoslav economy during 1953-1989 revealed the negative outcome of a nonmarket and centralized economic system. Prime Minister Ante Markovic's attempted reforms of 1990-1991 provided for a "heavy" convertible currency, balanced budget, restrictive monetary policy, wage freezes, selective relaxation of price controls, and, above all, private enterprises. These reforms were subverted by the basic flaw of the top heavy economic system that did not allow any scope for republics to take independent action at a time when the unity of the Yugoslav market collapsed because of ethno-nationalist movements that seized the Balkan world following the breakup of the Soviet Union and the demise of Communism in Eastern Europe in 1989-1990.

Yugoslavia's political disintegration was initiated by the abortive "Croatian Spring," a separatist movement of 1970-1971 calling for the establishment of a sovereign Croatian state. This crisis prompted Serbia, led by the Socialist Party of President Slobodan Milošević, to be especially watchful of Albanian nationalist upheaval in Kosovo, considered Serbia's "mythical heart." Yet the Kosovars agitated against Serb control in 1989-1990. Kosovo's example was followed by Croatian and Slovenian secession on June 25, 1991, under the leadership of Franjo Tudjman and Milan Kucan respectively. The secession of these two republics led to the Serb realization that a Greater Serbia would be the best possible guarantee for the Serbs in diaspora (17 percent in Croatia, 34 percent in Bosnia-Herzegovina, 55 percent in Vojvodina, 10 percent in Kosovo). Hours after the Croatian-Slovenian declaration of independence, the Serb-dominated Yugoslav army moved into Slovenia. By the time the European Community endorsed the United Nations sanctions, Serbia had already controlled 30 percent of Croatian territory and revoked the autonomy of Kosovo (thus alarming the Albanian majority there) and Vojvodina (thereby making the adjacent Hungarians nervous).

The Serbo-Croatian developments impacted Bosnia-Herzegovina most heavily. Since 1971 this republic has been granted the status of "three constituent nations"—Muslims (Serbs and Croats who had converted under Ottoman rule and constituting 43 percent of the population), Serbs and Croats (17 percent)—who had to agree on any act of secession. Yet the German recognition of Croatia in January, 1992, forced Bosnia's hands. Bosnia's Muslim President Alija Izetbegovic was forced into choosing between joining the truncated Serbian Yugoslavia—something none of his people would have accepted—or declaring independence. The plebiscite of February 28 and March 1, 1992, showing a joint Croat-Muslim majority in Bosnia met with the European Community criteria of referendum validating independence but violated the 1971 principle of three constituent nations. Thus Bosnian proclamation of independence on March 1 was opposed by the Bosnian Serbs. On March 18, Izetbegovic, Radovan Karadzic (Bosnian Serb leader) and Stjepan Klujuic (Bosnian Croat leader) agreed on an ethnically based canton system for Bosnia-Herzegovina at Lisbon. Upon his return home, however, Izetbegovic was persuaded by his own hardliners to renege on the Lisbon agreement. On April 6, the weekend of formal recognition of independent Bosnia-Herzegovina by the European Community, the battle of

Sarajevo began, initially between Serbs and Croats, with Croats being aided by Bosnian Muslims. By the late spring of 1992, Serbian forces joined by the Yugoslav National Army seized Sarajevo, inhabited mostly by Muslims.

The European Community and the United Nations sponsored trade embargo against Serbia could not prevent the *de facto* proclamation of Republika Srpska by Karadzic's Serb nationalists commanded by General Ratko Mladic. Bosnia-Herzegovina witnessed massive "ethnic cleansing." The U.N. sanctions against Serbia and Montenegro (rump Yugoslavia) on June 1, 1992, failed to stop the massacre. The plight of Yugoslavia demonstrated the complexities of the New World Order that American President George Bush had announced in 1989.

—Narasingha P. Sil

ADDITIONAL READING:

Danopoulos, Constantine, and Kostas Messas, eds. *Crisis in the Balkans: Views from the Participants.* Boulder, Colo.: Westview Press, 1996. Written from the perspectives of regional and international participants in the Balkan crisis, and divided into discreet chapters on each region of Yugoslavia as well as in the Balkans, the articles provide the historical background and current concerns of each region.

Glenny, Misha. *The Fall of Yugoslavia: The Third Balkan War.* New York: Penguin Books, 1994. A single most handy volume for a quick and reliable guide to the complicated issues and developments of the civil war by a scholar journalist with linguistic competence and an intimate knowledge of Eastern Europe and the Balkans.

Held, Joseph, ed. *The Columbia History of Eastern Europe in the Twentieth Century.* New York: Columbia University Press, 1992. The article by Dimitrije Djordjevic, "The Yugoslav Phenomenon," is excellent for an analysis of the historical background of the civil war.

Pinson, Mark, ed. *The Muslims of Bosnia-Herzegovina.* Cambridge, Mass.: Harvard University Press, 1993. The five excellent articles of this anthology are a must for anyone trying to understand the history of the Muslims of Yugoslavia from the Middle Ages down to the civil war. Especially, Ivo Banac's "Bosnian Muslims: From Religious Community to Socialist Nationhood and Post-Communist Statehood, 1918-1992" is highly recommended.

Ramet, Sabrina Petra, and Ljubisa Adamovich, eds. *Beyond Yugoslavia: Politics, Economics, and Culture in a Shattered Community.* Boulder, Colo.: Westview Press, 1995. This collaborative enterprise of American, Croatian, and Serbian scholars provides an excellent analysis of the multiple issues plaguing a polyglot state.

Rieff, David. *Slaughterhouse: Bosnia and the Failure of the West.* New York: Simon & Schuster, 1996. This provocative and passionate study of the carnage in Bosnia-Herzegovina provides the most up-to-date account of the escalation of the civil war.

Thompson, Mark. *A Paper House: The Ending of Yugoslavia.* New York: Pantheon Books, 1992. This is an insightful and scholarly and yet eminently readable and dependable travelogue and firsthand account of the civil war by the London correspondent of the *Mladina* (Slovenia).

SEE ALSO: 1912-1913, Balkan Wars; 1980, Death of Tito; 1985, Gorbachev Is Elected General Secretary of the Communist Party.

1991
SOVIET UNION DISSOLVES INTO LOOSELY ALLIED REPUBLICS

The Soviet Union dissolves into loosely allied republics, altering the Eurasian map and illustrating the strength of national independence movements in the post-Cold War world.

DATE: August-December, 1991

LOCALE: The Soviet Union

CATEGORIES: Government and politics; Social reform

KEY FIGURES:

Mikhail Sergeyevich Gorbachev (born 1931), president of the Soviet Union, 1985-1991

Vytautas Landsbergis (born 1932), head of Sajudis, the Lithuanian popular front

Boris Yeltsin (born 1931), president of the Russian Federation beginning in 1991

SUMMARY OF EVENT. The Union of Soviet Socialist Republics (USSR) was established in 1922. It drew together, under a powerful, Communist Party-led government, lands which had for centuries composed the Russian empire. During World War I, that empire had fallen to the external assault from Germany and the internal assault from the Bolshevik revolutionaries. At the end of the subsequent Russian Civil War in 1920, the Bolsheviks not only succeeded in consolidating power in Russia, but also established "Soviet Socialist Republics" (SSRs) in Armenia, Azerbaijan, Belorussia, Georgia, and Ukraine. Although nominally independent, the SSRs were in fact controlled by Moscow. Moscow's power was further institutionalized on December 30, 1922, with the creation of the Soviet Union.

The Union of Soviet Socialist Republics initially con-

tained four republics: Russia, Belorussia, Ukraine, and "Transcaucasia" (which drew together Armenia, Azerbaijan, and Georgia). During the rest of the decade, the Transcaucasian SSR would again be disaggregated into its constituent parts, and additional republics—Turkmenistan, Uzbekistan, and Tajikistan—were added. The Soviet Union grew yet again in 1939, when a pact with Adolf Hitler permitted Soviet leader Joseph Stalin to seize the Baltic states of Estonia, Latvia, and Lithuania, and territories in eastern Poland and Romania. Moscow formally annexed these territories in 1940 and 1945. By the mid-1940's, after various annexations and redrawing of national boundaries, the Soviet Union comprised fifteen republics, each based on a different titular nationality.

The Soviet leadership consistently declared the Soviet Union to be a voluntary union of its constituent republics; indeed, the constitution guaranteed a right to secession. Yet it was widely understood both within the country and abroad that Moscow would never tolerate a defection from the union. The Communist Party carefully controlled nationalist symbols and writings. Independence movements were infiltrated and their leaders arrested. At the same time, official party doctrine claimed that a new Soviet "nation" was being forged as Communism took root. Soviet "nationalism" would therefore drive out the presumably anachronistic ethno-national attachments.

The party's efforts to control nationalist independence movements were largely successful until the late 1980's. At that time Soviet leader Mikhail Gorbachev was introducing democratic reforms as part of his broader effort to stabilize the country's declining economic and social conditions. Elections at the republic and federal levels did boost reformist voices in the government, as Gorbachev had wished. Yet they also provided a political base for the resurgent nationalist forces in many of the republics. The East European revolutions in 1989 provided powerful inspiration for the nationalist forces within the Soviet Union. By allowing the countries of Eastern Europe to break away from the Soviet sphere of influence, Gorbachev lent credibility to the growing belief that Moscow was unwilling to use military force against secessionists.

In reality, the Soviet leadership was deeply divided over the question of using force to protect central power, let alone the very assumption that central power should be preserved. In the months following the fall of 1989 one republic after another issued declarations of autonomy, sovereignty, or their intent to achieve independence. Lithuania was among the first to act, declaring its independence in March, 1990. Gorbachev and his allies were coming under increasing pressure from "conservatives" within the party to act. Yet Gorbachev seemed to believe that the union could be preserved only by allowing greater freedom for the republics. Then the Russian republic itself declared sovereignty on June 12, 1991. A short time before, Russia had held democratic parliamentary elections and selected Boris Yeltsin, a former member of the Soviet Politburo, as its leader. Now Gorbachev and Yeltsin competed for control over this republic which comprised three-quarters of the territory of the Soviet Union.

There ensued a "war of laws," whereby Russia and the other republics that had declared sovereignty would deliberately pass laws that conflicted with federal laws. Gorbachev responded in August with a decree that Russia's declaration of sovereignty was "null and void." At the same time, he sought to develop a new union treaty that would placate the nationalists. Most republics were skeptical. Tensions between the increasingly assertive republics and the besieged Gorbachev regime moved rapidly toward a breaking point.

In the first days of 1991, the Soviet government finally used military force against the Baltic republics, which had been among the first to declare independence. On January 2, elite "Black Beret" troops seized Latvia's press headquarters in Riga. During the next two weeks more Soviet troops entered Lithuania, seizing the national guard headquarters and the radio and television stations in Vilnius. Fourteen people were killed, and over one hundred fifty were injured. Four more people were killed on January 20, when Black Berets seized the Latvian Interior Ministry. The fighting over the Soviet Union's fate had begun.

Nationalist leaders in the different republics showed solidarity against Moscow. Yeltsin in particular seized the initiative. He signed a mutual security pact with the three Baltic states, accused Gorbachev of plotting to turn back Soviet decentralization and reform, and called upon all Russian soldiers to disobey any orders to fire on civilians. Increasingly, Yeltsin came to be seen as the leader of the forces opposed to Soviet conservatism.

With events proceeding apace, Gorbachev redoubled his efforts to contain the centripetal forces of nationalism through a new union treaty. He first arranged a country-wide referendum on preserving the country as a "renewed federation of equal sovereign republics." Only nine of the Soviet Union's fifteen republics participated in the referendum, but three-quarters of the people who did vote approved it on March 17, 1991. Gorbachev seized this as a mandate. For the next several months Gorbachev and his appointees hammered out a new union treaty, and by the end of July eight republics had ratified it. A formal signing ceremony was set for August 20, 1991.

On August 19, a group of conservative military and political leaders placed Gorbachev under house arrest and seized control of the government. In an evident effort to prevent the imminent weakening of the country through the new union treaty, the self-defined "State Committee for the State of Emergency in the USSR" issued decrees banning free speech and free movement, and directed tanks into Moscow. Yeltsin rallied thousands of citizens and soldiers against the State Committee, and the coup attempt collapsed within three days. Gorbachev was released, but popular power had clearly shifted entirely to Yeltsin.

Rather than prevent the disintegration of the Soviet Union, the coup attempt hastened it. Republican leaders who had been prepared to sign the new union treaty now balked at the idea. They wanted no part of legitimizing a political relationship with a federal government whose military and political leaders sought to reimpose the old Soviet system. By the end of August, all the republics except Russia, Kazakhstan, and Turkmenistan had declared their immediate and full independence from the Soviet Union; by fiat, at least, they had seceded. Before

In the wake of the dissolution of the Soviet Union and the resignation of Mikhail Gorbachev as president, Boris Yeltsin emerged as the leader of the newly formed Commonwealth of Independent States. (AP/Wide World Photos)

the year ended, the final three republics followed suit.

With the coup foiled, Gorbachev marginalized, and the republics seceded, all that remained was to formalize the end of the Soviet Union—a country which theoretically possessed no territory. On December 8, the three Slavic republics (Russia, Belorussia, and Ukraine) formed a Commonwealth of Independent States (CIS) to loosely coordinate their policies as a confederation. On December 21, the CIS was expanded to include eleven post-Soviet republics (only Georgia and the Baltic states remained outside the CIS). On December 25, Gorbachev delivered a speech announcing his immediate resignation as president of the Soviet Union, and the Soviet flag was lowered from atop the Kremlin for the last time.

—*Steve D. Boilard*

ADDITIONAL READING:

Adelman, Jonathan R. *Torrents of Spring: Soviet and Post-Soviet Politics*. New York: McGraw-Hill, 1995. Includes both a history of the Soviet Union through its disintegration in 1991, and several chapters focusing on the various successor states of the former Soviet Union. Also includes an extensive bibliography.

Barber-Barry, Carol, and Cynthia A. Hody. *The Politics of Change: The Transformation of the Former Soviet Union*. New York: St. Martin's Press, 1995. Although not an especially well-written book, several chapters provide a somewhat analytical examination of the Soviet Union's demise.

Daniels, Robert V., ed. *Soviet Communism from Reform to Collapse*. Lexington, Mass.: D. C. Heath, 1995. A volume of essays examining various stages of the Gorbachev period, including the disintegration of the country.

Remnick, David. *Lenin's Tomb: The Last Days of the Soviet Empire*. New York: Random House, 1993. An engaging and entertaining narrative account of the fall of the Soviet Union.

Walker, Rachel. *Six Years that Shook the World: Perestroika—the Impossible Project*. Manchester and New York: Manchester University Press, 1993. Describes the entire Gorbachev period, from the initiation of *glasnost* in 1985 to the demise of the Soviet Union at the end of 1991. Also includes brief reflections on the Commonwealth of Independent States.

SEE ALSO: 1979, Soviet Union Invades Afghanistan; 1985, Gorbachev Is Elected General Secretary of the Communist Party; 1986, Riots in Kazakhstan; 1988, Ethnic Riots Erupt in Armenia; 1989, The Berlin Wall Falls; 1989, Velvet Revolution in Czechoslovakia; 1991, Soviet Attack on Baltic Separatists; 1994, Russian Troops Invade Chechnya.

1992
PROTESTS AND VIOLENCE AGAINST IMMIGRANTS IN GERMANY

Protests and violence against immigrants in Germany in the wake of German reunification are followed by the brutal murders of ethnic minorities in November that shock the world, forcing the German government to address the problem of neo-fascism in Germany.

DATE: August-November, 1992

LOCALE: Germany

CATEGORIES: Government and politics; Race and ethnicity; Wars, uprisings, and civil unrest

KEY FIGURES:

Helmut Michael Kohl (born 1930), chancellor of the Federal Republic of Germany, 1982-1990, and later chancellor of unified Germany beginning in 1990

Volker Rühe, general secretary of the Christian Democratic Union

Rudolf Seiters (born 1937), German interior minister until his resignation in July, 1993

Wolfgang Schäuble, German interior minister beginning in 1993

Alexander von Stahl (born 1938), chief prosecutor of Germany, dismissed in July of 1993

Hans-Ludwig Zächert, head of the *Bundesdriminalamt* (BKA)

SUMMARY OF EVENT. After the reunification of Germany in October of 1990, there was an unanticipated dramatic increase in acts of violence directed against foreigners by the indigenous German population. The victims included recruited foreign laborers and their families, and refugees who had been granted political asylum in Germany. Although there are discrepancies in the data provided by various government agencies, the situation was appalling by all accounts. These estimates ranged from 1,255 to 2,426 xenophobic and racist attacks in 1991, and from 2,285 to 4,587 in 1992. Estimates of deaths from such attacks in 1992 ranged from seventeen to twenty-six.

There is no way to know how many individual acts of racially motivated violence were not included in these statistics. The apparent pattern of escalation, however, and the large-scale incidents indicated that a violent sociopolitical movement was gaining momentum, and was becoming increasingly well organized. The first highly publicized mass attack in 1991 occurred in Hoyerswerda, a town of seventy thousand people, where a mob of neo-Nazis and hundreds of local residents assaulted foreigners with baseball bats and bicycle chains and destroyed their homes. Police did nothing to stop the violence, which went on for six days, resulting in all 230 foreign-born residents being forced to leave town. Representatives of the federal government, in effect, blamed the victims, saying that they were opportunists who falsely claimed that they were fleeing political persecution in order to live off German social welfare. This incident sparked a dramatic upsurge in xenophobic violence. The head of the

the perpetrators by the government. Some politicians even expressed their sympathy for the rioters. Because of the successes in eliminating the foreign populations of Hoyerswerda and Rostock, mob violence erupted in Wismar and Quedlinburg in September of 1992, with identical results. Political refugees were attacked, their quarters

Demonstrators carrying banners and waving the Turkish flag show their support for victims of racist violence in Germany in 1992. (AP/Wide World Photos)

Bundesdriminalamt (BKA), or German national police, claimed that in October of 1992 alone, there were 904 such attacks, including more than 150 involving fire bombs.

Levels of bigotry-related violence continued to escalate in 1992, with the victims still predominantly foreigners, but also including Jews, the homeless, homosexuals, and even the physically challenged. Then, in August, 1992, in the Baltic city of Rostock, a mob burned a refugee hostel and the adjoining guest worker housing. More than one hundred Vietnamese men, women, and children barely escaped being incinerated. The fascist rioters and their supporters numbered in the thousands. As in Hoyerswerda, the police did not intervene, the foreigners were relocated, and there was only qualified condemnation of

destroyed, and they were relocated by the government.

Most observers acknowledge that a majority of German citizens disapproved of the vicious assaults and murders of foreigners. However, it may be that the ethnic nationalism and antiforeigner sentiment that formed the backdrop for those acts was much more widespread. Some authors have asserted that the answers to the questions relating to why the purveyors of xenophobic violence were repeatedly able to apply a strategy for creating "foreigner-free cities," with little federal or local government opposition, and only qualified condemnation, can be found in Germany's traditions and laws regarding citizenship and immigration, and in partisan political dynamics of the time.

The constitution and laws of contemporary Germany

are based on the historical concept that Germany is an ethnically defined country; a nation-state based on one culture. Full rights of citizenship are only constitutionally guaranteed to ethnic Germans. This basic legal fact is the basis for laws dealing with people entering from foreign countries. These policies on foreign residents distinguish rights and access to citizenship based on ethnicity. Upon entering Germany, one is either classed as an ethnic German, a recruited foreign worker, or a refugee. The concept of the ethnically defined nation means that there is an institutionalized legal structure of differential treatment of these groups. Ethnic Germans residing in the countries that were annexed by the Third Reich as of December 31, 1937, and their descendants, are considered to be eligible for German citizenship upon entering the country, as are the descendants of ethnic Germans who were scattered throughout Europe during World War II. This is not considered to be an immigration policy, but rather the repatriation of true Germans. Since the government's policy is that Germany is "not an immigration country," refugees and recruited workers are not eligible for citizenship, have significantly limited rights, and are viewed as being temporary residents, in spite of the fact that some "guest worker" families have been in the country for three generations. In 1990, legislation was passed that made it possible for second- and third-generation foreign-born residents to apply for citizenship under certain conditions, but these are still exceptions to the rule of the ethnic state. Some authors have asserted that citizenship and differential rights based on ethnicity have segmented German society, with foreigners being designated a less desirable group, and created an atmosphere in which a significant proportion of the German population felt that strong anti-foreigner sentiment was socially acceptable and justified.

The reasons for the lack of a decisive government response to the violence throughout 1991 and most of 1992 involve the political struggles of Chancellor Helmut Kohl's Christian Democratic Union (CDU) with several right-wing parties, the most prominent being the *Die Republikaner* (REP). Before East and West German reunification seemed probable, the REP had been gaining some political support with its calls for a restoration of Germany's 1937 borders and drastic reductions in the foreign population. The CDU had long advocated the reunification of East and West Germany, and, when the Berlin Wall opened with little warning in November of 1989, they were able to preempt the REP's position by actually making reunification a reality in less than one year.

Kohl, however, had promised that taxes would not be raised in the West because of reunification, and it soon became apparent that the enormous cost of shoring up the economy of the former East Germany would require just that. In the face of growing public opposition to increased taxes and reductions in public spending in the West, the CDU opened, during the summer of 1991, what was called the "Asylum Debate," through which it hoped to eliminate Article 16 of the German constitution that guaranteed asylum to foreigners fleeing political persecution. The main thrust of this event was to assert that Germany's economic problems could be alleviated by eliminating the cost of providing for refugees, and there were repeated references to "fake asylum seekers," indicating that many refugees were really "economic migrants."

Some observers have asserted that the CDU's determination to eliminate or amend Article 16 was the reason for the conditional criticism and lack of strong action following the above-mentioned mob violence in 1991 and 1992, which may have encouraged neo-Nazis to escalate levels of violence against foreigners. After the Hoyerswerda incident, for example, national-level politicians— including the federal interior minister and the general secretary of the CDU—issued statements to the effect that the violence was understandable given the strain caused by the large number of refugees that resulted from the large-scale abuse of asylum laws.

After the September incidents, the racist violence continued until, in Mölln, in November of 1992, a Turkish family was murdered in a fire bomb attack by perpetrators who shouted *"Heil Hitler."* The incident drew horrified responses from governments around the world, international human rights organizations, and a majority of the German public. This resulted in a number of government actions, including the federal state prosecutor directing law enforcement agencies to arrest members of four neo-Nazi organizations responsible for much of the violence, followed by a government ban on those organizations. The CDU had stolen the extreme right's political thunder and Article 16 had been amended to limit the admissions of those seeking asylum.

—*Jack Carter*

ADDITIONAL READING:

Betz, Hans-Georg. *Radical Right-Wing Populism in Western Europe*. New York: St. Martin's Press, 1994. This book provides an examination of the political movements in Western Europe that provide the backdrop for extremist violence.

Björgo, Tore, and Rob Witte, eds. *Racist Violence in Europe*. New York: St. Martin's Press, 1993. This volume contains chapters on racist violence throughout Europe during the 1980's and 1990's, including two on Germany.

Fekete, Liz, and Frances Webber. *Inside Racist Europe*. London: Institute of Race Relations, 1994. This work is a very concise presentation of racist and xenophobic acts and the role played by various European governments, including Germany, in discouraging, encouraging, or even participating in them.

Kemper, Franz-Josef. "New Trends in Mass Migration in Germany." In *Mass Migration in Europe: The Legacy and the Future*, edited by Russell King. London: Belhaven Press, 1993. This chapter discusses the results of recent increases in the foreign population in a society with a long tradition as an "ethnic state."

Solomos, John, and John Wrench, eds. *Racism and Migration in Western Europe*. Providence, R.I.: Berg Publishers, 1993. This collection looks at the racist and xenophobic responses to large-scale population redistribution all over Europe. Contemporary Germany is the focus of one chapter, and it is prominently mentioned in several others.

SEE ALSO: 1949, Creation of Two German Republics; 1973, West Germany Restricts Immigration of Foreign Workers; 1987, European Community Adopts the Single Europe Act; 1989, The Berlin Wall Falls; 1993, Maastricht Treaty Is Ratified.

1993
CZECHOSLOVAKIA SPLITS INTO TWO REPUBLICS

Czechoslovakia splits into two republics in a peaceful process known as the "Velvet Divorce," offering a sharp contrast to the violent breakup of Yugoslavia at roughly the same time.

DATE: January 1, 1993
LOCALE: Czechoslovakia
CATEGORY: Government and politics
KEY FIGURES:

Václav Havel (born 1936), president of Czechoslovakia, December, 1992-July, 1992; president of the Czech Republic beginning in February, 1993

Václav Klaus (born 1941), prime minister of the Czech Republic beginning in July, 1993

Vladimír Meciar (born 1942), leader of the Movement for a Democratic Slovakia; prime minister of Slovakia, intermittently beginning in June, 1990

SUMMARY OF EVENT. The victors of World War I created Czechoslovakia, along with a number of other countries, out of the territories that had belonged to the defeated Austro-Hungarian empire. The new Czechoslovakian state drew together the "Czech lands" of Bohemia and Moravia with the northern Hungarian territory of Slovakia. Czechoslovakia's population thus largely com-

prised two western Slavic peoples, the Czechs and the Slovaks. Soon after the creation of the country, leaders of both national groups argued over the structure of the government and the relative autonomy of the two peoples. The Czechs tended to prefer a more unified state, which the Slovaks feared would be a vehicle for Czech political, economic, and cultural domination.

Czechoslovakia was taken over and dismembered by Nazi Germany in 1938, and resurrected when the war ended in 1945. A Soviet-sponsored *coup d'état* in 1948 imposed a highly centralized Communist regime. After a short-lived popular rebellion in 1968 termed the "Prague Spring," the Soviets reimposed strict Communist control. This time, however, Czechoslovakia was structured as a federation, consisting of separate Czech and Slovak republics. For the next two decades dissident movements maintained pressure against the Soviet-backed regime, demanding democratic and political reforms and an end to human rights violations. The 1975 Helsinki Accords provided these groups with a link to the international community. One of the most popular and powerful of the post-Helsinki groups was Charter 77, founded in February, 1977, by several hundred Czech citizens. One of Charter 77's leaders was Václav Havel, a playwright by profession, who was repeatedly jailed for his activities and writings.

In 1989, Czechoslovakia decisively overthrew its Soviet-sponsored government in what has come to be known as the "Velvet Revolution." The Velvet Revolution occurred near the end of the series of East European revolutions in the fall of 1989, and was notable for its breathtaking speed and lack of bloodshed. Havel and other Charter 77 leaders had formed a new movement, Civic Forum, which placed unrelenting pressure on the regime. Abandoned by his Soviet patrons, the Czechoslovak president, Gustav Husák, resigned on December 9. Havel was unanimously elected president by the Federal Assembly (parliament), which itself would soon be replaced through free elections.

No sooner had Czechoslovakia become free of Soviet domination, however, than the issues of state unity and Slovakian autonomy reemerged. Slovakians had always felt dominated within the federation by the more populous and wealthy Czechs. From the time of Czechoslovakia's creation, Slovakia was less industrialized, less connected with the West, and less tied to Western capital investment. After the fall of the socialist regime, Slovakians feared that the economic reform policies pursued by the new central government would be too jarring for their more agrarian and isolated economy. The calls for Slovakian autonomy were meant to address the perceived inequality between the constituent peoples of Czechoslovakia. They also gave voice to a growing nationalist movement among Slovakians.

In an initial, symbolic move to placate Slovakian separatism, the Federal Assembly changed the country's name to the Czech and Slovak Federal Republic in early 1990. Yet Slovakians' appetites were only whetted for further redress of the perceived injustices against them. In countrywide elections in June, 1990—the first truly free elections since the country was drawn into the Soviet bloc—parties advocating Slovakian autonomy gained considerable support. This affected the cohesiveness of the country's government, and not only in the legislative branch. As president of Czechoslovakia, Havel had initially enjoyed popular support for his political reputation as a leader of the Velvet Revolution. Yet he was a Czech, and before long he was perceived by Slovakians as another manifestation of the Czech's domination of the country. The Slovakian republican government, based in Bratislava, demanded greater decentralization of economic policymaking. Sometimes Prague relented, and sometimes it insisted upon maintaining federal unity. All the while, Bratislava increasingly postured as an independent government. In the fall of 1990, for example, it established its own "Ministry for International Relations," implying that it developed its own foreign policies.

There was some disagreement among the Slovakian parties as to their ultimate goals. Some promoted a looser federation, some confederation, and still others outright secession. Over time, however, the more nationalistic, separatist groups solidified power. A turning point occurred on June 5-6, 1992, when new legislative strength shifted from the parties associated with Civic Forum and the Velvet Revolution to more nationalistic parties from both republics. As a result, Vladimír Meciar, a man firmly committed to Slovakian independence (though perhaps not secession), was returned as prime minister of Slovakia. At the same time, Slovakian opposition in the Federal Assembly foiled Havel's reelection bid. A breakup of the country seemed almost certain. On July 17, 1992, the Slovak National Council declared Slovakia as an "independent country." It was unclear what this declaration meant as a practical matter.

On the other side of the federation, Czech nationalism also was growing, largely as a reaction to perceived Slovakian insolence. In the fall of 1991, the Czech National Council passed a resolution declaring any Slovakian assertion of sovereignty unconstitutional. After Slovakia's declaration of independence in July, 1992, however, Czech leaders formally agreed to negotiate a dissolution of the federation. Most Slovakians were taken

by surprise, and not a few were somewhat worried that their brinkmanship had gone too far.

On July 23, 1992, Meciar and Czech prime minister Václav Klaus established procedures to hammer out a "divorce" between the two republics. Subsequent discussions expanded in scope to cover the most minute details, such as the division of file cabinets owned by the federal government. By the late fall of 1992 both sides found that they had arrived at an agreement. The Federal Assembly approved the separation plans in November, and several dozen agreements were signed to formalize the country's division and to establish relations between the successor states. Czechoslovakia officially dissolved into its constituent republics on January 1, 1993. The two new states, the Czech Republic and the Slovak Republic, were immediately recognized by the other countries of Europe and around the world, and received membership in the United Nations.

—Steve D. Boilard

ADDITIONAL READING:

Bugajski, Janusz. "Central European Disputes." In *Nations in Turmoil: Conflict and Cooperation in Eastern Europe*. Boulder, Colo.: Westview Press, 1995. An overview of political conflicts among different national groups in central Europe in the twentieth century, with particular emphasis on the immediate post-Cold War years. Includes notes and illustrations.

Leff, Carol Skalnik. *National Conflict in Czechoslovakia: The Making and Remaking of a State, 1918-1987*. Princeton, N.J.: Princeton University Press, 1988. Written scarcely a year before the revolutionary process liberated and divided Czechoslovakia, this sweeping historical account suffers from bad timing. Yet its detailed exploration of the nationalism that pulled at the Czechoslovakian state throughout its seventy-five years makes this volume indispensable for fully understanding the Velvet Divorce.

Rosenberg, Tina. "Czechoslovakia." In *The Haunted Land: Facing Europe's Ghosts After Communism*. New York: Random House, 1995. An engaging narrative exploring the demise of Communism in Czechoslovakia and problems that have arisen since then. The Velvet Revolution is covered thematically, not sequentially.

Stokes, Gale. *The Walls Came Tumbling Down: The Collapse of Communism in Eastern Europe*. New York: Oxford University Press, 1993. Although written before the formal division of Czechoslovakia, this book provides critical background leading up to the Velvet Divorce. Chapter 5 examines the revolutions of 1989, including Czechoslovakia's Velvet Revolution. Chapter 6 explores the revolutions' aftermath, including the growing split between Czechs and Slovakians.

Svec, Milan. "Czechoslovakia's Velvet Divorce." *Current History* 91 (November, 1992): 376-380. Briefly summarizes the events leading up to the Velvet Revolution, with particular emphasis on economic matters. Written several months before the formal division of the country, this article concludes that Czechoslovakia's breakup "seems all but certain."

Whipple, Tim D., ed. *After the Velvet Revolution: Václav Havel and the New Leaders of Czechoslovakia Speak Out*. New York: Freedom House, 1991. Although compiled before the Velvet Divorce, these speeches and writings by the architects of the Velvet Revolution convey a sense of the political problems that confronted post-Cold War Czechoslovakia.

SEE ALSO: 1968-1989, Brezhnev Doctrine; 1968, Soviet Union Invades Czechoslovakia; 1985, Gorbachev Is Elected General Secretary of the Communist Party; 1989, The Berlin Wall Falls; 1989, Velvet Revolution in Czechoslovakia; 1991, Soviet Union Dissolves into Loosely Allied Republics.

1993
MAASTRICHT TREATY IS RATIFIED

The Maastricht Treaty is ratified, establishing the criteria for a monetary union that is generally regarded as the ultimate step in a European Union.

DATE: November 1, 1993
LOCALE: Maastricht, the Netherlands
CATEGORIES: Economics; Government and politics
KEY FIGURES:

Jacques Delors (born 1925), French statesman appointed president of the new European Commission in 1985 and author of Delors Report of 1989

Jean Monnet (1888-1979), French statesman regarded as the conceptual father of a European Union

Robert Schuman (1886-1963), French foreign minister who founded the European Coal and Steel Community (ECSC)

Paul-Henri Spaak (1899-1972), Belgian statesman instrumental in Benelux accord and in Treaty of Rome negotiations

SUMMARY OF EVENT. The Maastricht Treaty on European Union, signed by member states in Maastricht, the Netherlands, on February 7, 1992, and effective November 1, 1993, brought Europe closer to economic and political union. The Maastricht accord was only the latest in a series of agreements on European community dating to 1944. The European Union traces its first roots back to the Benelux customs union. In 1947, the Organization of European Economic Cooperation was formed to help apportion Marshall Plan aid from the United States. From the beginning, a primary rationale for greater European integration was to create a united front against potential aggression from the Soviet bloc.

A French statesman, Jean Monnet, believed alliance between France and Germany might sustain the postwar peace. Monnet was also a functionalist and a pragmatist, who believed that tighter integration of European economies was dictated by the realities of market capitalism. In 1950, Robert Schuman, French minister of foreign affairs, authored the "Schuman Plan" which called for economic cooperation between Germany and France and shared ownership in iron, coal, and steel production. The Schuman Declaration would provide the basis for the six-nation European Coal and Steel Community (ECSC), in 1951. The ECSC provided the organizational skeleton for the European Economic Community created in 1957 by the Treaty of Rome. Presided over by a Belgian, Paul-Henri Spaak, the Treaty reduced trade barriers among six European nations (West Germany, France, Belgium, Netherlands, Luxembourg, and Italy) and moved toward a common European market.

In 1979, the European Monetary System (EMS) came into being. It required that participatories maintain the price of their currencies (in terms of other monies) within a narrow band—also known as the EMS "snake," and established the "ecu" as a European currency. The European Monetary System was the policy father of Maastricht and its concept of a single European currency. As head of the European Commission, Jacques Delors helped guide the Single Europe Act to passage in 1986. The Single Europe Act moved to eliminate most barriers to trade, capital, and labor mobility between European Community members, establishing a single European market (SEM) in 1992.

The stage was set for Maastricht by the Delors Report on Economic and Monetary Union in 1989, which laid out a three stage process for implementation. Subsequently, approval of the Maastricht accord was slow in forthcoming. First, twelve months of deliberations were required to establish the provisions of the treaty. On February 7, 1992, member states signed the agreement. Second, ratification of the treaty by the signatory nations was time intensive and took different forms, from referendum voting to parliamentary approval. The British parliament engaged in a particularly intense and lengthy debate of the issue. Danish voters initially defeated the Maastricht proposal in 1992, only to pass it a year later. The treaty was labeled as "unconstitutional" in a hearing before a German high court, but the motion was rejected. Finally, the European parliament (formed in 1979) had to approve the treaty.

Twenty-one months would pass between the signing of the Treaty at Maastricht and November 1, 1993, the day the Treaty became effective. With Maastricht, the European Community came to be known as the European Union (EU). The union, however, remains in name only. Maastricht established a set of rigorous criteria for membership in a monetary union which subsequently may be amended. Alternately, there may be few partners (of the fifteen EU nations) to monetary union because of the stringency of qualification criteria. In any case, Maastricht was a giant step in European economic integration.

The Delors Report stressed the point that a single European market is best served by a single currency. Maastricht established both the criteria and the process for the move to monetary union. Specifically, the treaty establishes four conditions that nations must meet to join the monetary union. First, a nation's inflation rate cannot exceed the average inflation rate of the three members with the lowest inflation rates—by more than 1.5 percentage points. Second, the prospective member must maintain a currency whose exchange rate is relatively stable and without devaluation over a two-year period. Third, a nation's long-term interest rate must be no more than 2.0 percentage points higher than the rate of the three lowest inflation members. Finally, membership in the monetary union is contingent upon fiscal restraint. A nation's national debt can be no greater than 60 percent of its gross domestic product, or GDP (subject to some exceptions) and its annual deficit no more than 3 percent of GDP. Regardless of the number of EU qualifiers who meet the conditions, the European Monetary Union (EMU) will commence on January 1, 1999.

Organization of new European monetary institutions was detailed in the Delors Report. A European bank system much like the U.S. Federal Reserve was to be established. European monetary policy would be implemented by an Executive Board of six individuals; each appointed for an eight-year, nonrenewable term. A European Central Bank would have a core system of fifteen national banks designated as the European System of Central Banks (ESCB). Overall monetary policy would be conducted by the Governing Council, consisting of the Executive Board plus fifteen central bank governors. Another institution, the European Monetary Institute, would have the responsibility for adjusting the manner in which the ESCB system will function.

The benefits of monetary union include a reduction in cross-border money exchange costs. The bid-asked spread in money exchange may account for between 0.1 and 0.5 percent of average GDP. Hence, monetary union and a single currency would effectively reallocate resources from an unproductive to a more productive use.

Another assumed benefit of monetary unification is improved price stability. Reduced European inflation during the 1980's was attributed to the EMS "snake" and the virtual tying of currencies to the stable German deutsche mark. Inflation also declined, however, in most non-EMS countries during the 1980's. It may be more accurate to state that earlier efforts toward monetary union created a greater awareness of the effects of inflation and, as a result, fostered anti-inflation policy.

Finally, it is proposed that monetary union will reduce exchange rate fluctuations and uncertainty while fostering investment and growth. Uncertainty in general, be it over the prices of currencies or inputs in production, tends to lower rather than raise investment. Certainly, the mobility of capital between EU partners is enhanced when risk is lowered by exchange rate stability. More important, a single currency lends credibility to a monetary union and the concept of European union. For the Single Europe Act (one market—uncontrolled input flows) to work well, monetary unification is necessary.

The costs of monetary union include a nation's loss of exchange rate manipulation as a means of stabilization policy. Given a demand shock that makes imports favored over domestic goods, domestic costs (labor, inputs, and so forth) may be slow to adjust, resulting in recession. Changing the exchange rate is a relatively efficient way to return demand to levels consistent with full employment. Yet the use of monetary policy to effect interest and exchange rates is surrendered under a one currency regime. Some national autonomy in fiscal policy is also surrendered under Maastricht. The preconditions for membership in EMU require that annual deficits be quite modest relative to GDP, thereby precluding deficit spending exits from recession.

As it stands, the European alliance is less than a union and more than an association. It continues to progress, but in a disjointed manner. The single currency (ecu) has been renamed the "euro." Negotiations have been scheduled to amend the Maastricht accord and to facilitate additions to its current membership of fifteen nations.

—*John A. Sondey*

ADDITIONAL READING:

Bean, Charles R. "Economic and Monetary Union in Europe." *Journal of Economic Perspectives* 6 (Fall, 1992): 31-52. Well-balanced article which examines EMU from an economic perspective, sans mathematics.

Cavazza, Fabio Luca, and Carlo Pelanda. "Maastricht: Before, After, During." *Daedalus* 123 (Spring, 1994):

53-80. Examines the EU within the framework of political science and organization theory.

Eichengreen, Barry. *Should the Maastricht Treaty Be Saved?* Princeton Studies in International Finance 74. Princeton, N.J.: International Finance Section, Department of Economics, Princeton University, 1992. Thorough theoretical examination of all aspects of monetary union in Europe.

Holland, Martin. *European Integration.* London: Pinter Publishers, 1994. A detailed account of the evolution to European Union, from 1944 to 1993, including the role of historical personages.

Jones, Barry, and Michael Keating. *The European Union and the Regions.* Oxford: Clarendon Press, 1995. The concept of European Union from the perspective of its members.

Schnitzer, Martin C. *Comparative Economic Systems.* 6th ed. Cincinnati: Southwestern Publishing, 1994. Provides a concise, readable synopsis of the evolution of EU.

SEE ALSO: 1957, Common Market Is Formed; 1961, Organization for Economic Cooperation and Development Forms; 1987, European Community Adopts the Single Europe Act; 1990, German Reunification; 1991, Sweden Applies for Membership in the European Community.

1993

ULSTER PEACE ACCORD

The Ulster Peace Accord allows the peoples of Northern Ireland (Ulster), the Republic of Ireland (Eire), and Great Britain to be involved in determining Northern Ireland's political future.

DATE: December 15, 1993
LOCALE: Ulster, Northern Ireland
CATEGORY: Diplomacy and international relations
KEY FIGURES:
Gerry Adams (born 1948), president of Sinn Féin, the Irish Republican Army's political wing, beginning in 1983
John Hume (born 1937), leader of the Social Democratic Labor Party
John Major (born 1943), British prime minister, 1990-1997
Albert Reynolds (born 1933), *taoiseach* (prime minister) of the Republic of Ireland, 1992-1994
SUMMARY OF EVENT. The Joint Declaration of Peace, also known as the Downing Street Declaration, has deep roots in Anglo-Irish history. It grew from the 1985 Anglo-Irish Agreement, which recognized three interconnections related to Northern Ireland (Ulster): the factions within Ulster itself; the Republic of Ireland and Northern Ireland;

and the Irish and British peoples. The next major step was the 1987 Enniskillen, Northern Ireland, bombing, which took place on Remembrance Day (November 8), killing eleven. As a result of that tragedy, John Hume sent a letter to Gerry Adams, stating his belief that the terrorist bombings of the Irish Republican Army (IRA) were doing more harm than good. Further, Hume contended, the focus needed to be on uniting the people rather than The Republic of Ireland and Ulster. The next major step took place in 1992, when Sinn Féin, the political wing of the IRA, issued its discussion paper, *Toward a Lasting Peace in Ireland*, in which Gerry Adams acknowledged that Northern Ireland Protestants as well as the Irish Republic had legitimate needs and concerns. Adams also cited the importance of the European Union.

The reason for the existence of Northern Ireland, separate and distinct from the Republic, dates to the twelfth and thirteenth centuries when the English slowly gained control over Ireland, using Dublin as their center of control. During the Reformation, King Henry VIII converted to Protestantism, making England a Protestant country. Ireland refused to convert, however, and to strengthen its control over Ireland, the English monarchy encouraged large numbers of English and Scottish Protestants to settle in Ulster in the seventeenth century.

Irish resistance to English rule never ended; it rose to a new level of intensity in the late nineteenth century with the Republicans—those seeking independence—centered in Dublin and the Unionists—those favoring England—in Ulster. The Unionists were unable to maintain political control and the Republicans gained power, forming Sinn Féin in 1905 to promote an independent, united Ireland. Neither side was willing to compromise, and on Easter Monday, 1916, Republicans seized control of the General Post Office in Dublin, holding it for five days until forced out by a superior force of British troops.

The urban, working-class revolutionaries, led by an intellectual elite, did not represent the majority of Irish until the British dealt harshly with the rebel leaders. Fifteen were hanged with hundreds more deported, resulting in a huge increase in Sinn Féin support. In December of 1918, Sinn Féin refused to participate with the English parliament, seized control of the Irish government and renamed it the Dáil Éireann of the Irish Republic. When the British government tried to suppress the rebellion, civil war broke out between the IRA and the Irish Constabulary, supported by the British army. A brutal and bloody conflict raged for three years, until Prime Minister David Lloyd George of Great Britain persuaded Sinn Féin to negotiate, and on December 6, 1921, the Westminster Treaty was signed. Under this agreement, ratified by members of both the British and Irish assemblies, the Republic of Ireland was recognized as a member of the British Commonwealth, with the same rights and privileges as the other member states. Known as Saorstat Eireann (the Irish Free State), it failed to include the six northern counties, known collectively as Ulster. These counties, which included a Protestant majority while the rest of Ireland was predominantly Catholic, were organized under the 1920 Government of Ireland Act, which allowed them to remain a part of the United Kingdom. The Irish Dáil narrowly approved the treaty, despite opposition from Sinn Féin and a third of the population. Eamon de Valera, president of the Irish Republic, resigned rather than swear allegiance to the English king. Over the next fifteen years, there was limited violence in the Republic and the ties with the British government were loosened as the Republicans increased control. In 1937, the Republicans severed their remaining ties with the British Commonwealth through a referendum.

Sinn Féin never gave up its goal of a united Ireland. In October of 1968, rioting broke out in Londonderry during a Catholic demonstration, following a clash with police. The next year the British government ordered troops into Ulster. In 1972, a confrontation between demonstrators and the army during a civil rights march resulted in thirteen dead, known as Bloody Sunday. Two months later, Prime Minister Edward Hume of Great Britain established direct rule of Northern Ireland from England. From that point until 1993, when the British and Irish governments issued The Joint Declaration of Peace, the violence continued, with the main combatants being the Catholic IRA

Sinn Féin president Gerry Adams assumed a higher profile in international affairs in the wake of the 1993 Ulster Peace Accord. (AP/Wide World Photos)

and the Protestant Ulster Defense Force (UDF).

A positive step toward peace was taken in 1985, when Prime Minister Margaret Thatcher of Great Britain and Taoiseach Garret FitzGerald of the Republic of Ireland signed the Anglo-Irish Agreement, which granted Ireland some say in the future of Ulster in exchange for the Republic's assistance in helping with the terrorist problem in Northern Ireland. Further steps toward peace came in 1993, when Taoiseach Albert Reynolds recognized the need for the people of Northern Ireland to determine their own fate. Without such self-determination there would be neither stability nor well being. He further noted that if there would be unification of Ireland, all parties must respect one another's civil liberties and religious liberty. Specifically cited in the Joint Declaration, the taoiseach referred to free political thought, religious expression, the right to pursue, via democratic means, political aspirations, the right to seek constitutional change through peaceful means, the right to live where one chooses without intimidation, and the right to equal opportunity without regard to class or creed.

Contained within the Joint Declaration are assurances provided by both John Major and Albert Reynolds. For his part, Major affirmed that the British would accede to the will of the majority. He noted that the British were willing to work with the Irish Free State since the issue of Ulster's place needs to be resolved by the Irish themselves, "by agreement between the two parts respectively, to exercise their right of self-determination on the basis of consent, freely and concurrently given, North and South." Reynolds pledged that Eire would use neither threat nor coercion to achieve its goal of a united Ireland. He acknowledged that the Free State's constitution, which fails to acknowledge the legitimacy of Ulster's existence, would need to be amended to recognize the rights of the people of Northern Ireland.

The taoiseach recognized the "special links that exist between the peoples of Britain and Ireland" in addition to the new economic links that exist with the rest of Europe. This trend toward unity and acceptance seemed to spring from the growing rapprochement in post nationalist Europe. Both parts of Ireland and the United Kingdom are members of the European Union (EU), and all parties understand the need to establish ways the two principal parties, along with the rest of the EU, can work and trade and live in peace with one another. The Joint Declaration devoted one of its eleven sections to the issue of these links.

To achieve a lasting peace both parties need to recognize the legitimacy of each other's history and tradition. To work toward such a solution, the taoiseach recommended the creation of a Forum for Peace and Reconciliation. The Forum's specific responsibility would be to find ways for the people of the Republic and Ulster to accept that both groups have a right to their beliefs and traditions within an environment of unity and peace. Both the prime minister and the taoiseach accept the need to create such an environment, and "they believe the framework they have set out offers the people of Ireland, North and South, whatever their tradition, the basis to agree that from now on their differences can be negotiated and resolved exclusively by peaceful political means."

—*Duncan R. Jamieson*

ADDITIONAL READING:

Arthur, Paul. "Anglo-Irish Joint Declaration: Towards a Lasting Peace?" *Government and Opposition* 29 (Spring, 1994): 218-230. Arthur focuses on the possibility for the success of the declaration.

Bardon, Jonathan. *A History of Ulster*. Belfast, Northern Ireland: Blackstaff Press, 1992. A thorough history of Northern Ireland.

Campbell, Flann. *The Dissenting Voice*. Belfast, Northern Ireland: Blackstaff Press, 1991. A history of Northern Ireland, from the Protestant perspective, from the seventeenth century to the 1990's.

Guelke, Adrian, ed. *New Perspectives on the Northern Ireland Conflict*. Brookfield, Vt.: Avebury, 1994. A solid collection of articles dealing with the variety of issues—political, social, economic, and religious—which underlie the violence in Ulster.

McKittrick, David. *Despatches from Belfast*. Belfast, Northern Ireland: Blackstaff Press, 1989. A collection of essays treating the social conditions of Ulster.

Reynolds, Albert. *The Joint Declaration of Peace*. December 15, 1993. Available online at http://www.bess.tcd.ie/dclrtn.htm. The full text of the declaration, clearly stating the positions of both the Irish taoiseach and the British prime minister.

SEE ALSO: 1972, "Bloody Sunday" in Northern Ireland; 1974, IRA Terrorists Bomb Parliament Building; 1976, IRA Hunger Striker Dies in an English Prison; 1985, Anglo-Irish Agreement Is Signed.

1994

CHANNEL TUNNEL IS OFFICIALLY OPENED

The Channel Tunnel is officially opened, linking England with the Continent and opening a new age in European rail travel and freight movement.

DATE: May 6, 1994
LOCALE: England and France
CATEGORIES: Economics; Government and politics; Science and technology; Transportation
KEY FIGURES:
André Bénard, co-chair of Eurotunnel
Elizabeth II (born 1926), queen of England beginning in 1952
Albert Mathieu-Favier, engineer who suggested a tunnel beneath the English Channel to Napoleon in 1802
François Mitterrand (1916-1996), French president, 1981-1995, and signer of Treaty of Canterbury
Sir Alastair Morton, co-chair of Eurotunnel
Margaret Thatcher (born 1925), British prime minister, 1979-1990, and signer of Treaty of Canterbury

SUMMARY OF EVENT. The Channel Tunnel between England and France had been considered a technological possibility since the eighteenth century, when scientists and engineers first proposed horse-drawn vehicles through an underwater tunnel. Economic difficulties and political tensions between England and France, however, kept postponing the project. Finally, in 1986, an Anglo-French consortium received a concession to construct the tunnel. The thirty-one-mile-long Channel Tunnel, which cost more than $15 billion to construct, was officially opened on May 6, 1994, in a ceremony attended by British and French leaders. Regular train service through the tunnel, however, was deferred to later in the year because of the need to test equipment. The Channel Tunnel became the most expensive infrastructure project ever financed privately as well as a phenomenal engineering feat.

Serious proposals for a Channel Tunnel date back about two centuries. In 1802, Albert Mathieu-Favier, a French mining engineer, suggested to Napoleon that a tunnel "accessible to men, horses, and carriages" be dug in the chalk layer underneath the English Channel. Stagecoaches would travel through with transit time estimated at five hours. Renewed war between France and England killed the project.

In the 1880's, private companies actually began work on a tunnel using primitive boring machines. More than a mile of tunnel was dug on each side of the Channel before work stopped. A press furor over the alleged threat to Britain's security caused the government to cancel the project in 1883.

In 1966, the French and British governments announced they would plan and build a tunnel. Work began in 1974 and stopped the following year. With about 1.5 miles of preliminary digging completed on each side of the Channel, the British government had to cancel the publicly financed project because of the cost. In 1978,

British Railways and the French National Railways (SNCF) again began planning for a single-track rail tunnel. This later changed to a twin-tunnel plan.

Improvements in tunneling technology gave impetus to new Channel Tunnel plans. Now the issues were financial, rather than technological or political. A new dimension entered the picture when banking studies showed that private financing was feasible.

The plan for a permanent cross-channel link was relaunched at the summit between Thatcher and Mitterrand in September, 1981. This led to a study commission which selected four plans for further consideration in 1985. These were a high suspension bridge, a bridge-tunnel road plus a railway tunnel, railway-road tunnels, and railway tunnels.

In January of 1986, a proposal by Eurotunnel (a combination of France Marche and the Channel Tunnel Group), based in London, was announced as the choice of both governments. The option chosen was a railroad system with through railroad trains and special rail shuttle trains (Le Shuttle) carrying road vehicles. Its development was agreed upon when Thatcher and Mitterrand signed the Franco-British Canterbury Treaty in February, 1986. In March of 1986, a fifty-five-year concession was signed between the two governments and what would become the Eurotunnel Group, jointly led by Bénard and Morton. Yet the treaty and concession agreement were not effective until legislation passed in both countries in July, 1987.

The tunnel was to be privately financed (with stock sales and bank loans from several international banks) by a consortium of French and British firms. The use of high-speed trains to cut surface travel time between Paris and London in half was considered to be a good investment.

Preliminary work began near Calais in late 1986 with construction work beginning on the tunnels in late 1987. Huge tunnel boring machines then drilled a tunnel through the rock at the rate of eight hundred to one thousand meters per month. The tunnel walls are precast concrete segments reinforced with steel bars, joined to each other and the rock wall using a cement grout.

The Channel Tunnel comprises three tunnels from entrances near the French and English coasts. Construction shafts were at Shakespeare Cliff near Folkestone and at Sangatte near Calais. The tunnels were dug beneath the sea in two separate sections, one from each side of the Channel to link up the terminals. There are two 7.6-meter diameter tunnels, a railway track in each, periodically connected to a 4.8-meter diameter central service tunnel. They are about 50 kilometers long, 38 kilometers of which is under the Channel.

Construction would be done by TransMarche Link ("marche" is the French term for "channel"), a consortium of five French and five British firms. Boring started on the British side in December of 1987 and in France two months later. In December of 1990, the British and French teams achieved breakthrough with the completion of the service tunnel. A worker chosen by lot became the first to walk through a newly opened linkage between bores, and thus England had rejoined the Continent. Breakthrough in the northern railway tunnel was in May, 1991, and in the southern railway tunnel in June, 1991. Installation of fixed equipment such as tracks, catenary, signals, electrical supply, lighting, and ventilation occurred in 1992-1993.

Meanwhile, equipment had to be built for the four forms of electrified rail service that would use the tunnel. The "Le Shuttle" service would carry autos, buses, and motorcycles on passenger shuttle trains with double-deck cars used for autos and single-deck cars for buses and campers. While the shuttle journey time would be about thirty-five minutes, it would be about an hour highway-to-highway. Freight shuttles with semiopen cars would carry heavy goods vehicles. The "Eurostar" service would provide for direct, high-speed passenger trains via French (SNCF), Belgian (SNCB), and British Rail lines. Freight service would be provided, too.

On May 6, 1994, Queen Elizabeth II and French president Mitterrand inaugurated the Channel Tunnel by taking their first rides. The two heads of state also opened terminals for passenger train service in their countries' capital cities. This service, utilizing high-speed Eurostar passenger trains, would connect London with Paris, France and Brussels, Belgium, but would not actually begin regular service until late that year because of the need to thoroughly test all new high-tech trains.

Limited service began at that point with some freight service starting in May. Much of the passenger service that year was of the "souvenir excursion" variety. Skeletal Eurostar service began in October. Le Shuttle opened for cars with limited service in December, and twenty-four-hour service in January of 1995. Initially, service was offered only for autos, with service for other passenger vehicles delayed into 1995.

With a maximum speed of 186 miles per hour, the tunnel portion of a Eurostar trip takes about twenty minutes. The three-hour London-Paris run was scheduled to be shortened in the twenty-first century when a high-speed rail link costing approximately $5.6 billion would be established between London and the French coast.

Eurotunnel has had a roller-coaster life since 1986, with times when the tunnel looked set to sink beyond rescue. Completion was a huge triumph for Eurotunnel and its contractors, with whom a financial deal for cost overruns was struck in April, 1994. The cost was far above estimates, and it would take a major effort to turn this asset into a profitable business. Some believed that the same overoptimism that plagued its construction phase would continue and that its forecasts for long-distance passenger traffic and freight traffic were unrealistic. Others were convinced that the tunnel was off to an encouraging but delayed start, but that it might have problems generating enough cash while it was waiting the expected three years to become profitable. Meanwhile, by the time Eurostar service was officially inaugurated on November 14, 1994, the total Eurotunnel tab would be $15.5 billion, almost exactly twice the original estimates.

Fare-paying travelers will ultimately determine whether the privately financed tunnel is an economic success. The Channel Tunnel has had and will have economic, environmental, and political implications for the United Kingdom and Europe. Much of the tunnel's trade will be diverted from other carriers, increasing competition. By its first anniversary in November of 1995, Eurostar had carried 2.5 million passengers between London and Paris, accounting for 40 percent of the total for air and rail. The successful completion of the Channel Tunnel led to interest in a rail tunnel across the Strait of Gibraltar.

—*Stephen B. Dobrow*

ADDITIONAL READING:

Hughes, Murray, ed. "The Channel Is Conquered." Supplement to *Railway Gazette International*, May, 1994. A review of the operations, marketing, and safety of the tunnel on the eve of its official opening.

Newman, Cathy. "The Light at the End of the Chunnel." *National Geographic* 185 (May, 1994): 36-47. Analysis of the effect of the Channel Tunnel.

Petroski, Henry. "The Channel Tunnel." *American Scientist* 82 (September-October, 1994): 408-411. Contains a brief history of the tunnel.

Reina, Peter. "After 99 Months' Work Channel Tunnel Prepares for Trains." *Engineering News Record* 232 (May 2, 1994): 22-25. Describes the activity just prior to the tunnel's opening.

Travis, Anthony. "Engineering and Politics: The Channel Tunnel in the 1880's." *Technology and Culture* 32 (July, 1991): 461-467. History and politics of an earlier attempt to build the tunnel.

Waller, Peter. *From the Footplate: Eurostar*. Addlestone, United Kingdom: Ian Allen, 1996. A detailed look at Eurostar operations through the tunnel.

SEE ALSO: 1854-1869, The Suez Canal Is Built; 1973, European Space Agency Is Formed; 1976, Concorde Flies Passengers at Supersonic Speeds; 1987, European Community Adopts the Single Europe Act; 1993, Maastricht Treaty Is Ratified.

1994
RUSSIAN TROOPS INVADE CHECHNYA

Russian troops invade Chechnya in an attempt to prevent its secession, but the invasion fails to end the independence movement and further erodes the popularity of Boris Yeltsin.

DATE: December 11, 1994

LOCALE: Chechnya, a province in the Caucasus region of southern Russia

CATEGORIES: Government and politics; Wars, uprisings, and civil unrest

KEY FIGURES:

Viktor Chernomyrdin (born 1938), Russian prime minister

Dzhokhar M. Dudayev (1944-1996), Chechen president, 1991-1996

Pavel S. Grachev (born 1948) Russian minister of defense

Boris Yeltsin (born 1931), president of the Russian Republic beginning in 1991

SUMMARY OF EVENT. On December 11, 1994, Russian president Boris Yeltsin ordered Russian forces to invade Chechnya in order to end the separatist movement led by Dzhokhar M. Dudayev. Dudayev, a major general in the Soviet air force, had taken advantage of the turmoil that followed the failed coup attempt against Mikhail Gorbachev in August of 1991 to seize power in Chechnya and assert its independence.

The invasion of 1994 was a dramatic episode in a long and troubled relationship between the Chechens and the Russians. During this prolonged struggle the Chechens and the related Ingush, between the seventeenth and early nineteenth centuries, converted to Islam. Islam, in its Sunni form with militant Sufi brotherhoods, subsequently became a central component of their identity. In 1783, a Chechen named Mansur led the first unified Caucasian resistance against the Russians. After Mansur, the Chechens were rallied by Shamil, an Avar from Daghestan. Although Chechnya was formally subdued in 1859, the region experienced periodic uprisings and resistance to Russian rule. During World War II, the Chechens and other Caucasian peoples charged with collaboration with the Nazis were subjected to a genocidal deportation to Kazakhstan and Kirgizia. Some estimates for the number of Chechens who died during the brutal process of forced movement run as high as three hundred thousand. Grozny, the principal Chechen city, already largely Russian, was settled with Russians and Russians and Daghestani were settled elsewhere in Chechnya. The Chechens were only rehabilitated during Khrushchev's campaign of de-Stalinization in 1956 and allowed to return to a reestablished Chechen-Ingush Autonomous Republic in 1957.

The republic was one of the least developed in Russia. Industry and the service sector provided employment for only 40 percent of the population. Despite one of the highest rates of infant mortality in the Soviet Union and one of the lowest life expectancies, the Chechen population grew. Subjected to derision by Russians, who considered them to be culturally backward and socially inferior, the Chechens controlled access to oil reserves that were of strategic interest to the Soviet Union.

Even after Stalin's death, Chechens were not often chosen to serve as administrators in the republic. The legacy of the deportations and the desire of the Chechens to control their future and, hopefully, to profit from new opportunities converged in the chaos of the disintegration of the Soviet Union. On September 15, 1991, the self-styled Executive Committee of the All National Congress of the Chechen People, headed by Dudayev, forced the disbanding of the Supreme Soviet of the Chechen-Ingush Autonomous Republic claiming that it had supported the attempted August coup in the Soviet Union.

On October 27, Dudayev was elected president by 84 percent of the electorate. Although the Ingush refused to join the Chechens, Dudayev declared Chechnya sovereign on November 1. Yeltsin on November 8 declared a state of emergency and sent troops to Grozny. The Russians completely underestimated their opponents and bungled the execution of their effort to crush Chechen separatism.

Dudayev, who dissolved the Chechen parliament on July 4, 1993, and assumed dictatorial powers, had numerous opponents in Chechnya. As Yeltsin's popularity plummeted in the wake of his October, 1993, attack on the Russian parliament, he sought to use Dudayev's opponents as his proxies. If Yeltsin could reassert Russian authority, Russia would control the crucial pipeline connecting the oil of Azerbaijan and Kazakhstan to the Black Sea. Success against the Chechens would bolster Yeltsin

Russian forces launched their invasion of Chechnya in December of 1994, with the unrealistic expectation that they could pacify the province within forty-eight hours. (AP/Wide World Photos)

against his nationalist opponents in the parliament, which was elected in December of 1993. Despite Dudayev's willingness to accept a degree of local control short of secession, Yeltsin decided to move because of his own interests. The Russian Interior Ministry forces and their Chechen collaborators, however, were humiliatingly defeated in a raid held on November 28, 1994, the fifth failed Russian attempt to oust Dudayev.

Pavel Grachev, the Russian defense minister, now decided that the honor of Russia's military was at stake. As Yeltsin retreated to the cover of a hospital, Russian forces launched their invasion on December 11. Three columns were to converge on Grozny. The plan was to allow Dudayev and his followers to withdraw to the mountains in the south, where they would be cut off and eventually forced to submit. The attack went awry from the start. The invasion united the Chechens and won them the sympathy of other Caucasian Muslims. Faced with additional humiliation, Grachev assumed personal control of the campaign and ordered one of the most difficult military tasks, the taking of a city street by street. He had earlier predicted that Chechnya would be pacified in forty-eight hours. He now asserted that Grozny would be taken in two hours. The result was disaster. Isolated Russian units were decimated. The Chechens, who were able to resupply their units at night, resisted for a month. The presidential palace, from which Dudayev directed resistance, held until January 19. The Russians were eventually forced to use their artillery and air power to level much of the city. By the end of the month, some twenty-five thousand civilians had been killed. Russia had lost at least eighteen hundred soldiers and perhaps as many as five thousand, according to some sources, and the Chechens had lost eight thousand fighters. The Chechens finally pulled out, but continued their stubborn resistance from the countryside. Prime Minister Viktor Chernomyrdin's desire for peace talks and Dudayev's willingness to negotiate was thwarted by the war party surrounding Yeltsin.

Russian attacks on Chechen villages continued through the spring. Then on the eve of the June 14 summit of the G-7 nations in Halifax, Nova Scotia, Shamil Basayev led an attack on Budyonnovsk, located two hundred miles inside Russia. Basayev, whose eleven female cousins had been raped and murdered by Russians, assumed the role of the Chechen "Abreg," or bandit of honor, who pursued the Chechen clan tradition of vendetta to the seventh generation. The Chechens, who had bribed their way past Russian security forces, killed twenty Russian policemen and held two thousand hostage in a hospital. After an inept Russian assault that led to more Russian deaths, Chernomyrdin negotiated on live television for release of the hostages. The Chechens were allowed free passage back to Chechnya and a cease-fire was negotiated. Yeltsin, who had left the country during the crisis, saw his popularity further eroded, and suffered a heart attack.

The cease-fire quickly broke down. Despite the fact that Russia committed fifty-eight thousand troops—forty thousand from the regular army and eighteen thousand from the Interior Ministry—it was not able to pacify or secure Chechnya. In September, Oleg Lobov, Yeltsin's personal representative, barely escaped assassination. General Anatoly Romanov, the Russian commander, was critically wounded in an attack on October 6. On November 20, Doku Zavgayev, the Russian appointed Chechen administrator, was injured in an assassination attempt.

In January of 1996, Salman Raduyev led a Chechen assault on Kizlar, in Daghestan, and took two thousand hostages. After negotiations, his force had won safe passage back to Chechnya, but they were stopped and surrounded at Pervomayskoye. The incompetence of the Russian forces and the lack of credibility of the Yeltsin administration were obvious in the fiasco that followed. Raduyev, a number of his band, and hostages eluded the "impenetrable" Russian circle and made it back to Chechnya. Yeltsin's desperation was palpable. Following the Communist victory in the parliamentary elections held in December of 1995, Yeltsin said that if he was to win the June presidential election, the struggle in Chechnya had to be brought to an end. Yeltsin simultaneously called for the execution of Dudayev (who was eventually killed during a missile attack in April, 1996). The Russians, however, seemed incapable of quickly achieving military victory.

—*Bernard A. Cook*

ADDITIONAL READING:

Avtorkhanov, Abdurahman. "The Chechens and the Ingush During the Soviet Period." In *The North Caucasus Barrier*, edited by Marie Broxup. New York: St. Martin's Press, 1992. An account of the Chechens under Soviet rule, including the deportations of 1943.

Galaev, Magomet. "The Chechen Crisis: Background and Future Implications." Conflict Studies Research Centre, Royal Military Academy Sandhurst, csrc1.1. http:www.nato.int/ or gopher://gopher.nato.int:70/1. Insightful analysis of the Chechen crisis easily accessible through e-mail from the NATO site's "security network."

Goldenberg, Suzanne. *Pride of Small Nations: The Caucasus and Post-Soviet Disorder*. London: Zed Books, 1994. Background material and a history of the Chechen declaration of independence and the Russian reaction.

Mesbahi, Mohiaddin, ed. *Central Asia and the Caucasus After the Soviet Union*. Gainesville: University

Press of Florida, 1994. The article by Marie Bennigsen Broxup provides useful information on the history and culture of Chechnya, and the independence movement, but the treatment ends in November of 1991.

Nichols, Johanna. "Who Are the Chechens?" *IREX News in Brief*, January-February, 1995, 3-4. Ethnographic and historical information by a Berkeley professor of linguistics. A longer version of this article with an accompanying bibliography is available at gopher://gopher.info.irex.org.

Smith, M. A. "A Chronology of the Chechen Conflict," Conflict Studies Research Centre, Royal Military Academy Sandhurst. http:www.nato.int/. A day-by-day chronology from July 4, 1994, until June 6, 1995.

SEE ALSO: 1979, Soviet Union Invades Afghanistan; 1986, Riots in Kazakhstan; 1988, Ethnic Riots Erupt in Armenia; 1991, Soviet Attack on Baltic Separatists; 1991, Soviet Union Dissolves into Loosely Allied Republics.

1995
CHIRAC TAKES OFFICE AS PRESIDENT OF FRANCE

Chirac takes office as president of France, seeking aggressively to apply his unique "Gaullist" imprint on the domestic and foreign affairs of the post-Cold War French republic.

DATE: May, 1995
LOCALE: France
CATEGORY: Government and politics
KEY FIGURES:

Jacques René Chirac (born 1936), president of France beginning in 1995

Charles de Gaulle (1890-1969), president of France, 1959-1969

Alain Juppé, prime minister under Jacques Chirac

François Mitterrand (1916-1995), president of France, 1981-1995

Georges Pompidou (1911-1974), president of France, 1969-1974

SUMMARY OF EVENT. In May, 1995, Jacques Chirac, former mayor of Paris and head of the right of center Reassemblement pour la Republique (RPR), was sworn in as the fifth president of the Fifth French Republic. Having promised his post-Cold War French constituency a brighter future, he quickly sought to establish his administration's imprint on French domestic and foreign policy.

Being born after 1968, the majority of the French electorate sought to address during the 1995 election the perceived decline in the quality of life within French

society. Dramatic economic and social changes that had gripped French society since the 1973 Organization of Petroleum Exporting Countries (OPEC) oil price increases, were a major cause of that decline. Jacques Chirac and the RPR promised the electorate that, with tough budgetary decisions over time, they would revive France's economic health.

With Chirac's relative silence during the nationwide labor strikes in December of 1995, French citizens were caught by surprise. Although referred to by former President Georges Pompidou as "le bulldozer," Chirac had adopted a noncommittal tactic that surprised the French citizenry. Later events would overshadow that troubled period of French history.

Another important domestic issue that had to be addressed by the new Chirac government involved immigrants. By 1995, many French citizens were of the opinion that France was being flooded with foreigners. A hotly contested issue during the elections, the debate was over the fate of newly naturalized citizens and recent immigrants from the Muslim homelands.

This dilemma addressed fundamental questions concerning the legitimacy of French political institutions and the nature of society. As Muslim immigrants and other disfranchised groups became part of a growing segment of the French population, issues that had been dormant since the nineteenth century began to play a larger role. The age-old debate of secularism in a predominantly Roman Catholic population resurrected the political debate of the powers inherent in the church and state. This political debate did not include the equally volatile issue of what was to define the national identity. Chirac and the RPR adopted the short-term method of limiting further immigration into France from North Africa and other Francophone nations, but also quietly adopted the long-term solution of addressing the economic and budgetary issues which, as informed policymakers, they recognized lay at the core of the immigration problem.

By reducing and rechanneling the budget, Chirac's administration placed a greater emphasis on the reform of the defense industry. By ending conscription and restructuring the armed forces, Chirac significantly reduced expenses on the military. Ending a three-year moratorium on nuclear weapons testing despite the condemnation of the policy by 75 percent of the French public, not to mention the virulent global reaction, the Chirac administration undertook a series of "final" nuclear tests in the South Pacific, which began in September, 1995. Criticizing former president François Mitterrand, Chirac sought to justify his government's decision by claiming that the earlier established moratorium of April, 1992, had been instituted "too early." Chirac further stated that if France was to sign the Comprehensive Test Ban Treaty, the series of eight tests, which would cost $20 million a piece, would allow French nuclear experts and the military to determine the aging effect on old warheads and to test the viability of the new TN-75 submarine-based warhead. Prime Minister Alain Juppe in a dramatic shift of French nuclear policy stated that "No new world order has yet replaced that of the cold war. . . . New powers are appearing on the scene, and they are not always well disposed toward us. We have the duty to tell our fellow Europeans that new threats will replace, or have already replaced, old ones." Juppe then extended the offer of a French nuclear umbrella, despite the suspicious glances of France's European neighbors. Juppe stated that once the tests were completed, the Chirac administration was hopeful that a debate would be opened, whereby "the future European defense would not be built without the French deterrent—and the British—playing some kind of role." These comments all seemed to augment former president Charles de Gaulle's model of nuclear deterrence and European security. With the demise of the Cold War, it appeared that Europe might eventually be in need of an autonomous French nuclear force. This future need, according to de Gaulle, would vindicate the French nuclear program and its military forces' high level of preparedness.

With the initial set of Pacific explosions at the Mururoa test site in September of 1995, the global reaction was immediate. Japan, Germany, Austria, Great Britain, Scandinavia, Australia, and New Zealand had instituted widespread consumer boycotts of French products. Chirac's approval rating in France dropped to 36 percent, its lowest level since his assumption of the presidency. On January 29, 1996, two days prior to his official state visit to the United States, Chirac announced an end to the controversial series of nuclear tests. Six of the eight nuclear tests were completed. With that issue behind him, Chirac and the French government would be able to concentrate on more pressing domestic and foreign issues.

During his state visit, Chirac requested that the U.S. government adopt a nonisolationist policy toward poor and developing nations, imploring the Americans that their duty and obligation to these nations be based not merely on moral grounds, but rather be perceived as being in the best interests of the West. As for Europe, Chirac adopted a new policy of returning political issues to the European Community's agenda, which had been primarily dominated by economic issues. By perceiving Europe as a political community rather than merely an economic one, the French government was hoping to create the embryonic component of an independent European union, which

Upon taking office as president of France, Jacques Chirac (right) sought to restore his country's prominence in diplomatic affairs by meeting with various world leaders, including Russian prime minister Viktor Chernomyrdin in 1996. (AP/Wide World Photos)

would function constructively without American components in its European operations. An overall renovation of the alliance seemed to be in order, important issues which Chirac discussed with President Bill Clinton during his state visit, which began February 1, 1996.

Another important decision undertaken by the Chirac government, was to reinvolve France in the military structure of the North Atlantic Treaty Organization (NATO). Although France had been an important player on the political level since the founding of NATO, President de Gaulle had withdrawn French participation in NATO's integrated military command in 1966. With the downsizing of American military presence in Europe, Chirac was hopeful that by seizing the early initiative and reviving the old Western European Union (WEU) as a new military arm for Europe, France and Germany would create the rudiments for a viable Eurocorps.

Another important political and potentially economic development for France was its attempt to normalize relations with the Islamic Republic of Iran. Following the signing of an oil deal in the summer of 1995, Chirac's government sought gradually to improve its relations with the Islamic state. Attempting to stem the wave of explosions in Paris and other urban centers within France staged by fundamentalist Islamic forces operating in Algeria, the Chirac government hoped that normalizing relations with Iran would minimize any financial support the Islamic state might be providing the fundamentalists in Algeria. This relation would also prove valuable for the West and Israel's interests in the peace process in the Middle East. Because of its funding of the terrorist activities of the HAMAS Islamic fundamentalist group in Israel, Iran was in a position to exert greater influence over the outcome of the Arab-Israeli peace process. The Chirac government hoped that improved relations with Iran would allow France to expand its role in world diplomacy.

Further on the economic front, Chirac sought to boost French trade with Southeast Asian states. On his first trip to the Asian continent since his election to office in May of 1995, Chirac attended a twenty-five-nation European-Asian summit in Bangkok, Thailand, on March 2, 1996. This meeting brought together the heads of state from the seven Association of South East Asian Nations (ASEAN), fifteen European Community members, China, Japan, and South Korea. In his stated goal over the following decade to triple France's 2 percent share of the Asian market, Chirac was determined to establish new foundations for France's relationship with its Asian partners. Aside from some quick fence-mending with Japan and some Asian states over the earlier nuclear tests, Chirac and his ministers seemed to bounce back during the government's early tenure, despite a slow start as a result of the French general strike of December, 1995. The Chirac government established the broad foundations upon which later French domestic and foreign policies would rest.

—*Talaat E. Shehata*

ADDITIONAL READING:

Aron, Robert. *An Explanation of de Gaulle*. New York: Harper & Row, 1966. A fine assessment of President de Gaulle's overall policy toward the European alliance, and France's national goals.

Fitoussi, Jean-Paul, et al. *Competitive Disinflation, the Mark and Budgetary Politics in Europe*. First Report of the International Policy Group of OFCE. New York: Oxford University Press, 1993. For the economic and financially inclined, this is a revealing study on the role of European currency in the budgetary battles and policies often pursued by most European nations.

Friend, Julius W. *Seven Years in France: François Mitterrand and the Unintended Revolution, 1981-1988*. Boulder, Colo.: Westview Press, 1989. A penetrating study that covers the impact of the domestic Socialist revolution on French institutions and affairs.

Hargreaves, Alec, ed. *Immigration in Post-War France*. London: Methuen, 1987. A good introduction to the critical issue, role, and impact of immigrants in French society.

Keohane, Robert O., Joseph S. Nye, and Stanley Hoffman, eds. *After the Cold War*. Cambridge, Mass.: Harvard University Press, 1993. Comprehensive coverage of the collapse of the Soviet Union and end to the bipolar world in 1989, brings to the forefront the evolving role of French foreign and strategic policy.

Posen, Barry. "The Security Dilemma and Ethnic Conflict." *Survival* 35 (Spring, 1993): 27-47. A well-written article on the impact of ethnic violence on stability in France.

SEE ALSO: 1966-1995, France Withdraws from NATO's Military Structure; 1969, De Gaulle Steps Down; 1981, Mitterrand Is Elected to the French Presidency; 1985, Sinking of the *Rainbow Warrior*; 1993, Maastricht Treaty Is Ratified.

1996
SCOTTISH RESEARCHERS SUCCEED IN CLONING ADULT SHEEP

A team of scientists working in Scotland achieve their goal of creating an exact copy of an adult mammal.

DATE: July 5, 1996
LOCALE: The Roslin Institute, near Edinburgh, Scotland
CATEGORY: Science and technology
KEY FIGURES:
Keith H. S. Campbell, an experiment supervisor with the Roslin Institute
J. McWhir, a researcher with the Roslin Institute
W. A. Ritchie, a researcher with the Roslin Institute
Ian Wilmut (born 1945), an embryologist with the Roslin Institute

SUMMARY OF EVENT. On February 22, 1997, officials of the Roslin Institute, a biological research institution near Edinburgh, Scotland, held a press conference to announce startling news: In July of 1996, they had succeeded in creating a clone—a biologically identical copy—from cells taken from an adult sheep. Although cloning had been performed previously with simpler organisms, the Roslin Institute experiment marked the first time that a large, complex mammal had been successfully cloned.

Cloning, or the production of genetically identical individuals, has long been a staple of science fiction and other popular literature. Clones do exist naturally, as in the example of identical twins. Scientists have long understood the process by which identical twins are created, and agricultural researchers have often dreamed of a method by which cheap identical copies of superior livestock could be created.

The discovery of the double helix structure of deoxyribonucleic acid (DNA), or the genetic code, by James Watson and Francis Crick in the 1950's led to extensive research into cloning and genetic engineering. Using the discoveries of Watson and Crick, scientists were soon able to develop techniques to clone laboratory mice; however, the cloning of complex, valuable animals such as livestock proved to be hard going.

Work had been done since the 1950's in removing embryos from animals and then replacing them, transferring them to new host mothers, or freezing them for storage and later transfer. In the 1970's, this research led to the development of methods of separating the individual cells (blastomeres) from the early two-cell, four-cell, or eight-cell embryos to make it possible to produce multiple individuals from the same original embryo. Such production of identical twins, triplets, and higher multiples is a means of artificial cloning. Work in this area was important to reproductive physiologists who were interested in how embryos develop, to researchers in other fields who needed twins for experiments in various areas, and to farmers who wanted to increase the number of specifically bred animals.

Early versions of livestock cloning were technical attempts at duplicating the natural process of fertilized egg splitting that leads to the birth of identical twins. Artificially inseminated eggs were removed, split, and then reinserted into surrogate mothers. This method proved to be overly costly for commercial purposes, a situation aggravated by a low success rate.

Researchers at the Roslin Institute found these earlier attempts to be fundamentally flawed. Even if the success rate could be improved, the number of clones created (of sheep, in this case) would still be limited. The Scots, led by embryologist Ian Wilmut and experiment supervisor Keith Campbell, decided to take an entirely different approach. The result was the first live birth of a mammal produced through a process known as "nuclear transfer."

Nuclear transfer involves the replacement of the nucleus of an immature egg with a nucleus taken from another cell. Previous attempts at nuclear transfer had cells from a single embryo divided up and implanted into an egg. Because a sheep embryo has only about forty usable cells, this method also proved limiting.

The Roslin team therefore decided to grow their own cells in a laboratory culture. They took more mature embryonic cells than those previously used, and they experimented with the use of a nutrient mixture. One of their breakthroughs occurred when they discovered that these "cell lines" grew much more quickly when certain nutrients were absent.

Using this technique, the Scots were able to produce a theoretically unlimited number of genetically identical cell lines. The next step was to transfer the cell lines of the sheep into the nucleus of unfertilized sheep eggs.

First, 277 nuclei with a full set of chromosomes were transferred to the unfertilized eggs. An electric shock was then used to cause the eggs to begin development, the shock performing the duty of fertilization. Of these eggs, twenty-nine developed enough to be inserted into surrogate mothers.

All the embryos died before birth except one: a ewe the scientists named "Dolly." Her birth on July 5, 1996, was witnessed by only a veterinarian and a few researchers. Not until the clone had survived the critical earliest stages of life was the success of the experiment disclosed; Dolly was more than seven months old by the time her birth was announced to a startled world.

The news that the cloning of sophisticated organisms had left the realm of science fiction and become a matter of accomplished scientific fact set off an immediate uproar. Ethicists and media commentators quickly began to debate the moral consequences of the use—and potential misuse—of the technology. Politicians in numerous countries responded to the news by calling for legal restrictions on cloning research. Scientists, meanwhile, speculated about the possible benefits and practical limitations of the process.

The issue that stirred the imagination of the broader public and sparked the most spirited debate was the possibility that similar experiments might soon be performed using human embryos. Although most commentators seemed to agree that such efforts would be profoundly immoral, many experts observed that they would be virtually impossible to prevent. "Could someone do this tomorrow morning on a human embryo?" Arthur L. Caplan, the director of the University of Pennsylvania's bioethics center, asked reporters. "Yes. It would not even take too much science. The embryos are out there."

Such observations conjured visions of a future that seemed marvelous to some, nightmarish to others. Optimists suggested that the best and brightest of humanity could be forever perpetuated, creating an endless supply of Einsteins and Mozarts. Pessimists warned of a world overrun by clones of self-serving narcissists and petty despots, or of the creation of a secondary class of humans to serve as organ donors for their progenitors.

The Roslin Institute's researchers steadfastly proclaimed their own opposition to human experimentation. Moreover, most scientists were quick to point out that such scenarios were far from realization, noting the extremely high failure rate involved in the creation of even a single sheep. In addition, most experts emphasized more practical possible uses of the technology: improving agricultural stock by cloning productive and disease-resistant animals, for example, or regenerating endangered or even extinct species. Even such apparently benign schemes had their detractors, however, as other observers remarked on the potential dangers of thus narrowing a species' genetic pool.

Even prior to the Roslin Institute's announcement, most European nations had adopted a bioethics code that flatly prohibited genetic experiments on human subjects. Ten days after the announcement, U.S. president Bill Clinton issued an executive order that banned the use of federal money for human cloning research, and he called on researchers in the private sector to refrain from such experiments voluntarily. Nevertheless, few observers doubted that Dolly's birth marked only the beginning of an intriguing—and possibly frightening—new chapter in the history of science.   —*Jeff Cupp*

ADDITIONAL READING:

Drlica, Karl. *Understanding DNA and Gene Cloning: A Guide for the Curious*. 3d ed. New York: John Wiley & Sons, 1997. In this third edition of his popular guide, Drlica offers a clear and accessible explanation of the techniques of cloning. Features an extensive glossary and a bibliography on cloning articles.

Thro, Ellen. *Genetic Engineering*. Science Sourcebook Series. New York: Facts On File, 1993. Written for high school students, this book provides a useful introduction for readers interested in learning more about genetic engineering and cloning.

Wheale, Peter R., and Ruth M. McNally. *Genetic Engineering: Catastrophe or Utopia?* New York: St. Martin's Press, 1988. This book, written for the general public, has a short section on nuclear transplantation (chapter 10) that discusses the concerns of science as they relate to the public. Includes a full bibliography and a glossary.

Willadsen, S. M. "Nuclear Transplantation in Sheep Embryos." *Nature* 320 (March 6, 1986): 63-65. In this well-illustrated article written at the college level, Willadsen describes a modified nuclear transplantation technique to produce viable embryos in sheep. He shows how this technique can be adapted for practical uses in animal husbandry.

Zimmerman, Burke K. *Biofuture: Confronting the Genetic Era*. New York: Plenum, 1984. Contains an excellent discussion of modern scientific methods as they relate to problems of public concern. Discusses the cloning of

animals via nuclear transplantation in chapter 1 and in the appendix, which summarizes techniques of molecular biology. Includes an annotated bibliography.

SEE ALSO: 1859, Darwin Publishes *On the Origin of Species*; 1928, Fleming Discovers Penicillin; 1951, Model of DNA Molecular Structure Is Developed.

1997

LABOUR PARTY WINS MAJORITY IN BRITISH NATIONAL ELECTIONS

The election of 418 members of the Labour Party to the British Parliament ends the Conservatives' eighteen-year hold on power.

DATE: May 1, 1997
LOCALE: Great Britain
CATEGORY: Government and politics
KEY FIGURES:

Anthony "Tony" Blair (born 1953), leader of the Labour Party since 1994 and British prime minister beginning in May, 1997

Neil Kinnock (born 1942), leader of the Labour Party, 1983-1992

John Major (born 1943), leader of the Conservative Party and British prime minister, 1990-1997

John Smith (1938-1994), leader of the Labour Party, 1992-1994

Margaret Thatcher (born 1925), British prime minister, 1979-1990

SUMMARY OF EVENT. On May 1, 1997, elections were held for the 659 seats in the House of Commons, which is the lower and more powerful house of Britain's bicameral Parliament. Like the United States, the United Kingdom elects its legislators through single-member districts. The voters of each district elect one member of Parliament to represent them in the Commons. Victory in each district is conferred to the candidate who is "first past the post," meaning the candidate who receives the most votes. This voting system tends to produce two major parties. In Britain, those parties are the Labour Party and the Conservative Party (also called the Tories). Also participating in British elections are several smaller parties, including the Liberal Democrats and nationalist parties for Wales and Scotland.

Possessing a majority in the Commons is important not only for controlling the legislature but also for controlling the executive branch. A majority vote of the members of Parliament, rather than a direct vote by the people, selects the British prime minister. Thus, the party that commands a majority in the Commons is able to place its own party

Tony Blair greets enthusiastic supporters in the wake of his victory in the British national elections held on May 1, 1997. (Express News/Archive Photos)

leader as prime minister. The prime minister then selects an executive cabinet, generally composed of other members of Parliament belonging to his or her party.

The Labour Party's previous leadership of the government ended in 1979. In that year, the Conservatives secured a parliamentary majority and placed their leader, Margaret Thatcher, as prime minister. For the next eleven years, the Conservatives embarked on a program of deregulation, privatization, and fiscal conservatism which came to be known as Thatcherism. Many similarities were observed between Thatcher's policies and those of her contemporary, U.S. president Ronald Reagan. In 1990, the Tories removed Thatcher as party leader and replaced her with John Major, thereby making Major the prime minister. The Tories believed that Thatcher's hostility to Britain's economic integration with Europe had become an electoral liability. Major took a less strident stance on European integration, but continued most of the domestic facets of Thatcherism for another six and a half years.

The Conservatives seemed to have established themselves as a permanent majority in Britain. The country's economic health improved substantially, it secured a decisive military victory in the Falkland Islands War, and it joined other Western powers in asserting global leadership in trade, finance, diplomacy, and security. The Labour Party, traditionally associated with socialist and social-democratic policies, seemed out of step with the decline of socialism witnessed in the late 1980's in Eastern Europe, the Soviet Union, and elsewhere. Indeed, in the 1980's and early 1990's, most of the large Western European countries, including Germany, France, and Italy, replaced their left-leaning governments with conservative parties or coalitions. Under the leadership of Neil Kinnock and John Smith, the British Labour Party could not garner enough electoral support to dislodge the Tories. With each of four consecutive electoral defeats, the party seemed less likely to rise again. Indeed, a well-known British political scientist wrote after the Conservative's 1992 electoral success that "the long historical era in which the two major parties in Britain alternate reasonably frequently in office [may have] finally come to an end."

In 1994, John Smith died, and the Labour Party selected Tony Blair as its new leader. Blair, who was then forty-one years old, was an Oxford-educated lawyer who had once belonged to a rock band and had been a member of Parliament since 1983. He now sought to recast the Labour Party as a more pragmatic party. "New Labour," as he called it, would not unthinkingly reverse the privatization and deregulation accomplished under the Tories. New Labour would be committed to a healthy economy as well as its more traditional social welfare concerns. In the summer of 1996, the Labour Party presented a ten-point manifesto which was notable for its uncharacteristically moderate positions on welfare reform, crime control, and limited governmental regulation of industry. The lack of a radical economic plank was perhaps not surprising, as the British economy was performing well by most accounts under Major's leadership.

The Labour Party victory in 1997 was the result of several factors. First, the Tories became divided over the issue of European integration. Even after Major assumed the party leadership, party factions continued to form and fight over this issue. Second, the Tories experienced a number of scandals in the mid-1990's. A series of incidents involving marital infidelity, political corruption, and various other peccadilloes among Tory members of Parliament were especially embarrassing given the leadership's stated commitment to emphasizing moral values. Third, Blair's recasting of the Labour Party recaptured a large bloc of middle-class voters who had defected from the party in the 1980's. Finally, Blair's party appeared to have run a more effective campaign, mobilizing resources and coordinating its campaign themes more effectively. Certainly Tony Blair was a more telegenic presence than John Major. Inevitable comparisons were made to the American presidential election between incumbent Republican George Bush and his younger Democratic challenger, Bill Clinton, in 1992.

The 1997 general election gave the Labour Party 418 seats (about 63 percent of Parliament's 659 seats). The Tories won only 165 seats (about 25 percent of the total). Several of Britain's smaller parties secured the remaining seats. The Liberal Democrats captured forty-six seats, and the remainder were divided between the Ulster Unionists, the Scottish National Party, and several tiny parties.

For the Conservative Party, the 1997 election was the worst since 1832. The Labour Party had captured a comfortable majority in the Commons, leaving the Conservatives virtually no chance of influencing policy. (The majority achieved by Thatcher's Conservatives in 1979 was only forty-four seats.) In 1997, the Tories still possessed a majority in the House of Lords, the upper house of Parliament. The political influence of that body, however, had diminished to near-symbolic importance, and the Labour Party pledged to reduce the political power of its unelected members even further. The crushing Tory defeat caused Major to lose the party leadership. The resulting intraparty conflict over selecting Major's replacement was so bitter that some speculated that the Conservative Party might even lose members to a secessionist faction (as the Labour Party had lost members to the new Social Democratic Party in the 1980's).

Although the British Labour Party traditionally championed the causes of workers, the poor, and national minorities within the United Kingdom, Blair's victory may not have been especially revolutionary for a country emerging from eighteen years of Conservative rule. In the initial weeks after the election, it was unclear precisely what effect the new Labour government would have on Britain. Tacitly conceding the success of Tory economic policies, the new leadership promised no major changes in taxing and spending. The Labour government announced that it would continue the Tory-imposed spending limits for two years, and that it would not raise income taxes for five years. Certainly the strength of trade unions and groups on the ideological left had diminished within Blair's New Labour. Even on the divisive issue of European integration, the Labour government's official position was not significantly different from that of the outgoing Major government.

Nevertheless, the Labour Party faced a number of pressing policy challenges during its first few months in power. Britain's participation in the imminent Economic and Monetary Union (EMU) of the European Union remained a thorny issue, with the country's trade position, employment levels, and inflation rate all affected. The Labour government pledged to pursue "constructive engagement" with Europe and promised to submit the issue to a national referendum. The possible devolution of certain powers from the central government to Scotland and Wales was another controversial issue, made all the more salient because of Labour's traditional support for devolution. (Under Blair, however, the party distanced itself from that position.) Electoral reform also had been a campaign issue, with the possibility of adopting proportional representation enjoying strong support with some segments of the population. (Blair had also promised a national referendum on this reform.) The future status of Northern Ireland remained a perennial problem.

During his first weeks as prime minister, Blair found himself attending summits of several international organizations to which Britain belonged, including the North Atlantic Treaty Organization, the European Union, and the Group of Seven. By most accounts, Blair handled himself admirably. Early opinion polls showed significant majorities of Britons approving of Blair's overall performance as prime minister. The long-term impact of the Labour Party victory, however, would not become evident until after Blair's policies had been implemented and given a chance to work. All that could be said in the short run was that Britain had experienced at least a temporary electoral realignment, and that the effects upon Labour, the Conservatives, and even the smaller third parties might well be substantial.   —*Steve D. Boilard*

ADDITIONAL READING:

"After the Landslide." *The Economist* 342 (May 3, 1997): 47-48. A poll sponsored by *The Economist* reveals some of the expectations British voters had of their new Labour Party government.

Hoge, Warren. "Britons Back Labor Party; Tories Routed After Eighteen Years in Majority." *The New York Times*, May 2, 1997, A1. A quick summary of the political environment that led to the Labour Party's victory and the expectations for change that accompanied the transition from Major's Conservative government to Blair's Labour government.

Mandelson, Peter, and Roger Liddle. *The Blair Revolution: Can New Labour Deliver?* Boston: Faber & Faber, 1996. Useful background information on Tony Blair and his leadership of the Labour Party. Mandelson was appointed by Blair to serve as a minister without portfolio in the Labour government, acting as a close adviser without an official cabinet post.

"A Question to Tony Blair: Will Your Government Be an Elective Dictatorship?" *The Economist* (May 24, 1997): 53-54. Offers an analytical perspective on many key decisions made by Blair and the Labour government during its first three weeks in office.

SEE ALSO: 1945, Labour Party Forms Majority Government; 1979, Margaret Thatcher Becomes Britain's First Woman Prime Minister; 1993, Maastricht Treaty Is Ratified; 1993, Ulster Peace Accord.

1997

NORTH ATLANTIC TREATY ORGANIZATION AND RUSSIA SIGN COOPERATION PACT

The signing of a cooperation pact between NATO and Russia clears one of the major obstacles to the eastward expansion of NATO.

DATE: May 27, 1997
LOCALE: Paris, France

CATEGORIES: Diplomacy and international relations; Organizations and institutions

KEY FIGURES:

Anthony "Tony" Blair (born 1953), British prime minister beginning in May, 1997

Jacques René Chirac (born 1936), president of France beginning in 1995

William Jefferson Clinton (born 1946), president of the United States beginning in 1992

Helmut Michael Kohl (born 1930), chancellor of the Federal Republic of Germany, 1982-1990, and later chancellor of unified Germany beginning in 1990

Boris Yeltsin (born 1931), president of the Russian Republic beginning in 1991

SUMMARY OF EVENT. On May 27, 1997, leaders of the sixteen member countries of the North Atlantic Treaty Organization (NATO) and Russian president Boris Yeltsin signed an agreement which institutionalized a consultative role for Russia in NATO deliberations. The agreement was widely understood to be the source of political cover that Yeltsin required to allow him to accede to NATO's expansion into Eastern European countries that once were Soviet satellites.

The North Atlantic Treaty Organization was established in 1949 as a military alliance linking the United States, Canada, and Western Europe. The organization's founding was prompted by the rapidly escalating Cold War, and by increasing tensions between the United States and the Soviet Union over Germany. In the same year, Germany was divided into a democratic West Germany that was allied with (and to a large extent controlled by) the United States, Britain, and France, and a communist East Germany that was dominated by the Soviet Union. West Germany was admitted to NATO in 1955, with East Germany being included in the newly formed Warsaw Treaty Organization (usually called the Warsaw Pact) several weeks later.

The North Atlantic Treaty placed upon NATO members obligations of mutual defense, in which an attack on any one country would be considered an attack on all. This binding of American security interests to Europe was the military centerpiece of U.S. containment policy. For four decades, NATO would be credited with preventing the spread of Soviet influence beyond its eastern sphere of influence and with permitting the rearmament of West Germany to be accomplished with sufficient international safeguards. In the words of Lord Ismay, NATO's purpose in Europe was to keep the Americans in, the Russians out, and the Germans down.

Eventually NATO expanded to sixteen member countries, including most of Western Europe. The Warsaw Pact included the Soviet Union and six East European countries: Bulgaria, Czechoslovakia, East Germany, Hungary, Poland, and Romania. The European political order thus was bipolar, centered on Washington and Moscow. The two blocs were separated by an imaginary "Iron Curtain" which ran between East and West Germany. In many respects, the existence of the two alliances ensured a "balance of power" which had eluded Europe for centuries. As a result, the great powers of Europe (and North America) did not directly fight one another for the next half-century and beyond.

In the late 1980's, however, the Soviet bloc began to fall apart. In 1989, all of the Warsaw Pact countries overthrew their Soviet-imposed Communist governments and adopted varying degrees of democratic reforms. Perhaps even more dramatically, German unification seemed increasingly likely once East Germany's communist government was eliminated. Because East Germany was arguably the most strategic country of the Warsaw Pact, German unification could well destroy what little was left of the European balance of power. Based on that logic, the Soviets insisted that any plan for the unification of Germany could not cede the territory of eastern Germany to NATO. The question of German unification thus came to hinge on the matter of NATO expansion.

By the fall of 1990, Germany did unify wholly within NATO. A few months later, the Warsaw Pact was officially dissolved. These heretofore unimaginable events were facilitated largely by Western assurances to the Soviets that NATO would not use its geographically expanded and now unchecked strength against legitimate Soviet interests. Those assurances could not protect the Soviet Union from nationalist movements within the country, however, and the Soviet Union dissolved into its fifteen constituent republics before the end of 1991.

Under President Boris Yeltsin, post-Soviet Russia sought to reestablish itself as an influential European power. The continued existence of NATO, however, served as a constant reminder that the West "won" the Cold War. Constantly chafing at this geopolitical reminder of Russia's marginalization in post-Cold War Europe, Moscow alternately called for the elimination of NATO, its conversion from a military alliance to a political one, and for Russian membership in the organization. Meanwhile, the former Warsaw Pact countries publicly expressed a desire to join NATO, as did many of the former Soviet republics. Those countries presumably wanted to institutionalize their long-sought escape from Soviet military pressure and political domination. There was significant sympathy in Western Europe and the United States for expanding NATO to those countries. In the eyes of

Moscow, however, NATO's further expansion into Eastern Europe (beyond eastern Germany) without a suitably influential Russian voice in NATO would be a violation of the spirit of NATO's promise not to take undue advantage of Moscow's weakened condition.

By the mid-1990's, an unofficial short list had emerged of countries likely to be considered for membership in an expanded NATO. That list included Poland, the Czech Republic, and Hungary. Russia vociferously opposed such proposals, arguing that expanding NATO in such a way would simply redivide Europe, which had so recently managed to draw back the Iron Curtain. Although Russian public opinion did not consider NATO expansion a particularly salient issue, Russian politicians—particularly those in the communist and nationalist parties—made it a rallying cry. Yeltsin came under increasing pressure by various opposition groups in the parliament to halt the expansion, but it was unclear exactly what Moscow could do about it.

The issue reached a climax as a July, 1997, meeting of NATO leaders neared. NATO was expected to announce at the Madrid meeting the specific countries to which an invitation to join the alliance would be extended. The NATO leaders clearly hoped to secure Yeltsin's acquiescence, however grudging, in order to prevent a major diplomatic row with Moscow. Toward that purpose, a NATO-Russia agreement was negotiated in the months leading up to the Madrid summit.

The NATO-Russia "Founding Act" was signed in Paris only weeks before the Madrid summit. It generally committed Russia and the NATO countries to cooperate in building "a stable, peaceful and undivided Europe, whole and free, to the benefit of all its peoples." More specifically, the agreement provided for the establishment of a Russia-NATO Permanent Joint Council, based in Brussels, to facilitate Russia's participation in NATO's policy discussions. (It did not, however, provide Moscow with either a vote or a veto in NATO's decision making. Yeltsin had repeatedly sought this.) The Permanent Joint Council would meet monthly to discuss matters of concern to any of the countries. The agreement also committed the countries to negotiate new national limits on the 1991 Conventional Forces in Europe Treaty. Although not specified in formal treaty commitments, NATO did reassure Russia that the alliance had neither the intention of nor the interest in deploying nuclear weapons on the territory of new member countries. For his part, Yeltsin promised that Russian nuclear weapons previously targeted at NATO countries would be dismantled.

After its signing, the Founding Act was to be considered for ratification by the legislatures of the signatory countries. The agreement was expected to encounter especially strong opposition in the Russian parliament, where Russian nationalist and communist parties held sway. At the time of the Founding Act's signing, the Russian parliament still had not ratified the 1993 START II agreement, which would cut American and Russian strategic nuclear arsenals. Indeed, the possibility of NATO expansion was one of the main issues that held up Russian ratification of START II.

In any event, the Founding Act was less important as a legal instrument than as a symbolic expression of NATO's assurances to Russia and Russia's acquiescence to NATO expansion. To be sure, Yeltsin continued to insist that NATO expansion was "a grave mistake," but he seemed to accept that it was inevitable. In that sense, the signing ceremony was a post-Cold War catharsis.

—*Steve D. Boilard*

ADDITIONAL READING:

Brenner, Michael, ed. *NATO and Collective Security.* New York: St. Martin's Press, 1997. Offers useful background information on NATO and its role in ensuring international security. Includes a bibliography.

Clemens, Clay, ed. *NATO and the Quest for Post-Cold War Security.* New York: St. Martin's Press, 1997. Published the same year as Brenner's work cited above, Cle-

mens' collection focuses primarily on NATO's complex role in furthering collective security in Western Europe without offending the national interests of individual members.

Gann, L. H., and Peter Duignan. *Contemporary Europe and the Atlantic Alliance: A Political History.* Malden, Mass.: Blackwell, 1997. An excellent overview of how NATO shaped and was shaped by postwar European political developments.

Whitney, Craig R. "Russia and NATO Sign Cooperation Pact." *The New York Times*, May 28, 1997, A1. Describes the terms of the Founding Act and the signing ceremony itself.

Wijk, Rob de. *NATO on the Brink of a New Millennium: The Battle for Consensus.* Washington, D.C.: Brassey's, 1997. Part of Brassey's Atlantic Commentaries series, this work concentrates on organizational changes within NATO that occurred after the late 1980's and how these changes shifted the balance of power among its member nations.

SEE ALSO: 1949, North Atlantic Treaty; 1966, France Withdraws from NATO's Military Structure; 1975, Helsinki Agreement; 1989, The Berlin Wall Falls; 1989, Velvet Revolution in Czechoslovakia; 1991, Civil War Rages in Yugoslavia; 1991, Soviet Union Dissolves into Loosely Allied Republics; 1993, Maastricht Treaty Is Ratified.

KEY WORD INDEX

CATEGORY LIST

NOTE: The entries in this publication are listed below under all categories that apply. The chronological order under each category corresponds to the chronological order of the entries in these volumes.

BUSINESS AND LABOR

COMMUNICATIONS

CULTURAL AND INTELLECTUAL HISTORY

HEALTH AND MEDICINE

1966	Soviet Intellectuals Express Disagreement with Party Policy
1968	French Workers Engage in a National Strike
1972	United Nations Environmental Conference
1983	Green Party Wins Seats in West German Parliament
1985	Sinking of the *Rainbow Warrior*
1989	Velvet Revolution in Czechoslovakia
1991	Soviet Union Dissolves into Loosely Allied Republics

TERRORISM AND POLITICAL ASSASSINATION

1170	Murder of Thomas à Becket
1605	The Gunpowder Plot
1911	Assassination of Peter Stolypin
1919	Rosa Luxemburg Is Assassinated
1972	Munich Olympic Massacre
1974	IRA Terrorists Bomb Parliament Building
1978	Aldo Moro Is Kidnapped and Murdered by Italian Terrorists
1986	Olof Palme Is Assassinated

TRANSPORTATION

550 B.C.	Construction of Trireme Changes Naval Warfare
312 B.C.	Building of the Appian Way
312 B.C.	First Roman Aqueduct Is Built
1150	Venetian Merchants Dominate Trade with the East
1854	Suez Canal Is Built
1906	Launching of the *Dreadnought*
1976	Concorde Flies Passengers at Supersonic Speeds
1981	Construction of Siberian Gas Pipeline Begins
1994	Channel Tunnel Is Officially Opened

WARS, UPRISINGS, AND CIVIL UNREST

736 B.C.	Spartan Conquest of Messenia
700 B.C.	Phalanx Is Developed as a Military Unit
550 B.C.	Construction of Trireme Changes Naval Warfare
480 B.C.	Persian Invasion of Greece
431 B.C.	Peloponnesian War
415 B.C.	Athenian Invasion of Sicily
401 B.C.	March of the "Ten Thousand"
338 B.C.	Battle of Chaeronea
331 B.C.	Battle of Gaugamela
264 B.C.	First Punic War
218 B.C.	Second Punic War
202 B.C.	Battle of Zama
146 B.C.	Sack of Corinth
107 B.C.	Marius Creates a Private Army
58 B.C.	Caesar's Conquest of Gaul
31 B.C.	Battle of Actium
A.D. 9	Defeat in the Teutoburger Forest
43	Roman Conquest of Britain
60	Boadicea Leads Revolt Against Roman Rule
378	Battle of Adrianople
410	Gothic Armies Sack Rome
439	Vandals Seize Carthage
445	Invasions of Attila the Hun

451	Battle of the Catalaunian Plains
476	"Fall" of Rome
533	Justinian's Wars Against the Vandals, Ostrogoths, and Visigoths
568	Lombard Conquest of Italy
711	Tarik's Crossing into Spain
732	Battle of Tours
793	Northmen Raid Lindisfarne
878	King Alfred Defeats the Danes at Edington
896	Magyar Invasions of Italy, Saxony, and Bavaria
955	Otto I Defeats the Magyars
1009	The Church of the Holy Sepulchre Is Destroyed
1014	Basil II Conquers the Bulgars
1014	Battle of Clontarf
1016	Danish Invaders Led by Canute Conquer England
1031	Fall of the Caliphate of Córdoba
1066	Battle of Hastings
1071	Battle of Manzikert
1092	El Cid Conquers Valencia and Becomes Its Ruler
1095	Pope Urban II Calls the First Crusade
1147	The Second Crusade
1169	Norman Troops Invade Ireland
1189	The Third Crusade
1204	Knights of the Fourth Crusade Capture Constantinople
1214	Battle of Bouvines
1217	The Fifth Crusade
1227	Frederick II Leads the Sixth Crusade
1240	Alexander Nevsky Defends Novgorod from Swedish Invaders
1240	Mongols Take Kiev
1248	Failure of the Seventh Crusade
1291	Fall of Acre
1314	Battle of Bannockburn
1315	Swiss Victory at Morgarten
1323	Peasants' Revolt in Flanders
1330	Basarab Defeats Hungarians
1346	Battle of Crécy
1347	Cola di Rienzo Leads Popular Uprising in Rome
1353	Ottoman Empire Establishes Foothold in Rumelia
1380	Battle of Kulikovo
1381	Wat Tyler Leads Peasants' Revolt
1389	Turkish Conquest of Serbia
1391	Timur Devastates Southern Russia
1410	Battle of Tannenburg
1429	Joan of Arc's Relief of Orléans
1442	János Hunyadi Defends Hungary Against Ottoman Invaders
1444	Albanian Chieftains Are United Under Skanderbeg
1453	English Are Driven from France
1453	Fall of Constantinople
1480	Destruction of the Golden Horde
1492	Fall of Granada
1494	Charles VIII of France Invades Italy
1514	Hungarian Peasants Revolt
1519	Cortés Conquers Aztecs in Mexico

TIME LINE

Date	Event
15,000 B.C.	Cave Paintings Provide Evidence of Magdalenian Culture
3100-1550 B.C.	Building of Stonehenge
1620-1120 B.C.	Rise of Mycenaean Civilization
1600-1500 B.C.	Flowering of Minoan Civilization
1100-500 B.C.	Hallstatt Civilization Ushers in Iron Age in Europe
1000 B.C.	Greek Alphabet Is Developed
c. 1000-900 B.C.	Ionian Confederacy
c. 800 B.C.	Homer's Composition of the *Iliad*
776 B.C.	Olympic Games
775 B.C.	Oracle at Delphi
c. 736-716 B.C.	Spartan Conquest of Messenia
c. 733 B.C.	Founding of Syracuse
700-330 B.C.	Phalanx Is Developed as a Military Unit
650 B.C.	Greek City-States Use Coins as Means of Exchange
625-509 B.C.	Rise of Etruscan Civilization in Rome
621 *or* 620 B.C.	Draco's Code
600-500 B.C.	Greek Philosophers Formulate Theories of the Cosmos
c. 594-580 B.C.	Legislation of Solon
550 B.C.	Construction of Trireme Changes Naval Warfare
c. 530 B.C.	Founding of the Pythagorean Brotherhood
c. 525 B.C.	The Sibylline Books
508-507 B.C.	Reforms of Cleisthenes
500-400 B.C.	Greek Physicians Develop Scientific Practice of Medicine
494 *or* 493 B.C.	Institution of the Plebeian Tribunate
483 B.C.	Naval Law of Themistocles
480-479 B.C.	Persian Invasion of Greece
478-448 B.C.	Athenian Empire Is Created
451-449 B.C.	The "Twelve Tables" of Roman Law
450-425 B.C.	History Develops as Scholarly Discipline
447-438 B.C.	The Parthenon Is Built
445 B.C.	The Canuleian Law
c. 440 B.C.	Teachings of the Sophists
May, 431-Sept., 404 B.C.	Peloponnesian War
June, 415-Sept., 413 B.C.	Athenian Invasion of Sicily
401-400 B.C.	March of the "Ten Thousand"
399 B.C.	Death of Socrates
c. 380 B.C.	Plato Develops His Theory of Ideas
340-338 B.C.	Origin of *Municipia*
Aug. 2, 338 B.C.	Battle of Chaeronea

Date	Event
c. 335-323 B.C.	Aristotle Writes the *Politics*
Jan. 20, 332 B.C.	Founding of Alexandria
Oct. 1, 331 B.C.	Battle of Gaugamela
325-323 B.C.	Aristotle Isolates Science as a Discipline
312-264 B.C.	Building of the Appian Way
312 B.C.	First Roman Aqueduct Is Built
c. 300 B.C.	Stoic Conception of Natural Law
287 B.C.	The *Lex Hortensia*
c. 275 B.C.	Advances in Hellenistic Astronomy
264-225 B.C.	First Punic War
c. 250 B.C.	Discoveries of Archimedes
c. 240 B.C.	Exploitation of the Arch
218 B.C.	Second Punic War
202 B.C.	Battle of Zama
180 B.C.	Establishment of the *Cursus Honorum*
146 B.C.	Sack of Corinth
133 B.C.	Pergamum Is Transferred to Rome
133 B.C.	Tribunate of Tiberius Sempronius Gracchus
109-102 B.C.	Celtic Hill Forts Appear
107-101 B.C.	Marius Creates a Private Army
90 B.C.	Julian Law
58-51 B.C.	Caesar's Conquest of Gaul
51 B.C.	Cicero Writes His *De Republica*
43-42 B.C.	Proscriptions of the Second Triumvirate
Sept. 2, 31 B.C.	Battle of Actium
27-23 B.C.	Completion of the Augustan Settlement
15 B.C.-A.D. 15	Rhine-Danube Frontier Is Established
9	Defeat in the Teutoburger Forest
43-130	Roman Conquest of Britain
c. 50	Creation of the Imperial Bureaucracy
60-61	Boadicea Leads Revolt Against Roman Rule
64-67	Nero Persecutes the Christians
Aug. 24, 79	Destruction of Pompeii
c. 110	Trajan's Religious Policy
c. 157-201	Galen Synthesizes Ancient Medical Knowledge
c. 165	Gaius' Edition of the *Institutes* of Roman Law
200	Christian Apologists Develop Concept of Theology
c. 220	Ulpian's Dictum

Date	Event
284	Inauguration of the Dominate
Oct. 28, 312	Conversion of Constantine
313-395	Inception of the Church-State Problem
325	The Nicene Creed
Nov. 24, 326-May 11, 330	Constantinople Is Founded
361-363	Failure of Julian's Pagan Revival
Aug. 9, 378	Battle of Adrianople
380-392	Theodosius' Edicts Promote Christian Orthodoxy
Aug. 24, 410	Gothic Armies Sack Rome
413-426	Augustine Writes the *City of God*
428-431	The Nestorian Controversy
439	Vandals Seize Carthage
445-453	Invasions of Attila the Hun
449	Saxon Settlement of Britain Begins
c. 450	Conversion of Ireland
451	Battle of the Catalaunian Plains
Sept. 4, 476	"Fall" of Rome
496	Baptism of Clovis
Feb. 2, 506	*Breviarium* of Alaric Is Drafted
524	Imprisonment and Death of Boethius
529-534	Justinian's *Code*
532-537	Building of Hagia Sophia
533-553	Justinian's Wars Against the Vandals, Ostrogoths, and Visigoths
568-571	Lombard Conquest of Italy
590-604	Reforms of Pope Gregory the Great
596-597	See of Canterbury Is Established
635-800	Founding of Lindisfarne and Creation of the *Book of Kells*
c. 700-1000	Use of Heavy Plow Increases Agricultural Yields
Apr., 711, *or* May, 711	Tarik's Crossing into Spain
726-843	Iconoclastic Controversy
731	Bede Concludes His *Ecclesiastical History of the English People*
Oct. 11, 732	Battle of Tours
735	Christianity Is Introduced into Germany
754	Coronation of Pepin
781	Alcuin Becomes Adviser to Charlemagne
June 7, 793	Northmen Raid Lindisfarne
843	Treaty of Verdun
c. 850	Building of the Slavic Alphabet
c. 850-900	Vikings Settle in Kiev
864	Boris Converts to Christianity

Date	Event
878	King Alfred Defeats the Danes at Edington
893	Beginning of Bulgaria's Golden Age
896	Magyar Invasions of Italy, Saxony, and Bavaria
930	Vikings Establish the Althing in Iceland
c. 950	Flourishing of the Court of Córdoba
Aug. 10, 955	Otto I Defeats the Magyars
963	Foundation of Mount Athos Monasteries
976-1025	Reign of Basil II
987	Hugh Capet Is Elected to the Throne of France
988	Vladimir, Prince of Kiev, Is Baptized
1009	The Church of the Holy Sepulchre Is Destroyed
c. 1010-1015	Avicenna Writes His *Canon of Medicine*
1014	Basil II Conquers the Bulgars
Apr. 23, 1014	Battle of Clontarf
1016	Danish Invaders Led by Canute Conquer England
c. 1025	Scholars at Chartres Revive Interest in Classical Learning
1031	Fall of the Caliphate of Córdoba
1054	Beginning of the Rome-Constantinople Schism
Oct. 14, 1066	Battle of Hastings
Aug. 26, 1071	Battle of Manzikert
1086	The Domesday Survey
Nov. 1, 1092-June 15, 1094	El Cid Conquers Valencia and Becomes Its Ruler
Nov. 27, 1095	Pope Urban II Calls the First Crusade
Mar. 21, 1098	Cistercian Monastic Order Is Founded
1100-1300	Emergence of European Universities
c. 1120	Order of the Knights Templar Is Founded
1125	Charter of Lorris
1127-1130	Kingdom of Sicily Is Created
1147-1149	The Second Crusade
c. 1150	Moors Transmit Classical Philosophy and Medicine to Europe
c. 1150	Venetian Merchants Dominate Trade with the East
c. 1150-1200	Development of Gothic Architecture
c. 1150-1200	Rise of the Hansa

Date	Event	Date	Event
1152	Frederick Barbarossa Is Elected King of Germany	Nov., 1330	Basarab Defeats Hungarians
1154-1204	Establishment of Angevin Empire	Aug. 26, 1346	Battle of Crécy
Sept. 17, 1156	Emergence of Austria	1347-1352	Invasion of the Black Death
1168	Nemanyid Dynasty Is Founded in Serbia	May 20, 1347-Oct. 8, 1354	Cola di Rienzo Leads Popular Uprising in Rome
1169-1172	Norman Troops Invade Ireland	c. 1350-1400	Petrarch and Boccaccio Recover Classical Texts
Dec. 29, 1170	Murder of Thomas à Becket	1353	Ottoman Empire Establishes Foothold in Rumelia
c. 1175	Appearance of the Waldensians		
c. 1175	Common Law Tradition Emerges in England	Jan. 10, 1356 *and* Dec. 25, 1356	The "Golden Bull"
1189-1192	The Third Crusade	1373-1400	Jean Froissart Compiles His *Chronicles*
c. 1200	Fairs of Champagne		
1204	Knights of the Fourth Crusade Capture Constantinople	1377-1378	John Wycliffe Is Condemned for Attacking Church Authority
1209-1229	Albigensian Crusade	Sept. 8, 1380	Battle of Kulikovo
1209	Founding of the Franciscans	May, 1381-June, 1381	Wat Tyler Leads Peasants' Revolt
1212	The Children's Crusade	c. 1387	Chaucer Develops Vernacular Narrative in *The Canterbury Tales*
July 27, 1214	Battle of Bouvines		
June 15, 1215	Signing of the Magna Carta		
Nov. 11, 1215-Nov. 30, 1215	Fourth Lateran Council	June 28, 1389	Turkish Conquest of Serbia
		1391-1395	Timur Devastates Southern Russia
1217-1221	The Fifth Crusade	June 17, 1397	The Kalmar Union Is Formed
1227-1230	Frederick II Leads the Sixth Crusade	1410-1440	Florentine School of Art Emerges
		July 15, 1410	Battle of Tannenburg
1228-1231	Teutonic Knights Bring Baltic Region Under Catholic Control	1414-1418	Council of Constance
		1415-1460	Prince Henry the Navigator Promotes Portuguese Exploration
1230	Kingdoms of Castile and Léon Are Unified		
c. 1233	The Papal Inquisition	July 6, 1415	Martyrdom of Jan Hus
July 15, 1240	Alexander Nevsky Defends Novgorod from Swedish Invaders	May 4, 1429-May 8, 1429	Joan of Arc's Relief of Orléans
		1440	Donation of Constantine Is Exposed as Fraudulent
Dec. 6, 1240	Mongols Take Kiev		
1248-1254	Failure of the Seventh Crusade	1442-1456	János Hunyadi Defends Hungary Against Ottoman Invaders
1258	The "Provisions of Oxford"		
c. 1265-1273	Thomas Aquinas Compiles the *Summa Theologiae*	1444-1446	Albanian Chieftains Are United Under Skanderbeg
		c. 1450	Gutenberg Pioneers the Printing Press
1271-1291	Travels of Marco Polo		
1285	Statute of Winchester	1450-1466	Second Peace of Thorn
1290-1306	Jews Are Expelled from England, France, and Southern Italy	1453	English Are Driven from France
		May 29, 1453	Fall of Constantinople
Apr., 1291	Fall of Acre	Apr. 9, 1454	Peace of Lodi
1295	The Model Parliament	1457-1504	Reign of Stephen the Great
Nov. 18, 1302	Boniface VII Issues the Bull *Unam Sanctam*	1458-1490	Hungarian Renaissance Under Mátyás Hunyadi
c. 1310-1350	William of Ockham Attacks Thomist Ideas	Oct. 19, 1469	Marriage of Ferdinand and Isabella
		Nov. 1, 1478	Establishment of the Spanish Inquisition
June 24, 1314	Battle of Bannockburn		
Nov. 15, 1315	Swiss Victory at Morgarten	1480-1502	Destruction of the Golden Horde
Aug. 1, 1323-Aug. 23, 1328	Peasants' Revolt in Flanders		

Date	Event	Date	Event
After 1480	Ivan III's Organization of the "Third Rome"	Sept. 25, 1555	Peace of Augsburg
1485-1547	Tudor Rule Is Established in England	Oct. 25, 1555-Sept. 12, 1556	Abdication of Charles V
Aug., 1487-Dec., 1488	Dias Rounds the Cape of Good Hope	May, 1559-Aug., 1561	The Scottish Reformation
1492	Expulsion of Jews from Spain	Jan., 1563	The Thirty-nine Articles of the Church of England
1492	Fall of Granada	1565	Spain Seizes the Philippines
Oct. 12, 1492	Columbus Lands in America	Feb. 25, 1570	Elizabeth I Is Excommunicated by Pius V
June 7, 1494	Treaty of Tordesillas	Oct. 7, 1571	Battle of Lepanto
Sept., 1494-Oct., 1495	Charles VIII of France Invades Italy	Aug. 24, 1572-Aug. 25, 1572	St. Bartholomew's Day Massacre
c. 1500	Botticelli Leads the Renaissance Revival of Classical Themes in Painting	1580-1595	Montaigne Publishes His *Essays*
1500-1530's	Portugal Begins to Colonize Brazil	July 26, 1581	United Provinces of the Netherlands Declare Independence from Spain
1505-1515	Portuguese Viceroys Establish Overseas Trade Empire	1583-1610	Matteo Ricci Travels to Peking as Jesuit Missionary
July, 1513-Dec., 1513	Machiavelli Writes *The Prince*	1584-1590	Raleigh Funds Expedition to North America
1514	Hungarian Peasants Revolt	1584-1613	"Time of Troubles" in Russia
1516	Sir Thomas More Publishes *Utopia*	July 7, 1585-Dec. 23, 1588	War of the Three Henrys
Mar. 14, 1516	Charles I Ascends the Throne of Spain	July 31, 1588	Defeat of the Spanish Armada
Oct. 31, 1517	Luther Posts His Ninety-five Theses	1589	Russian Patriarchate Is Established
1519-1522	Magellan Expedition Circumnavigates the Globe	c. 1589-1613	Shakespeare Writes His Dramas
Apr., 1519-Aug., 1521	Cortés Conquers Aztecs in Mexico	Aug. 2, 1589	Henry IV Ascends the Throne of France
June 28, 1519	Charles V Is Elected Holy Roman Emperor	Apr. 13, 1598	Edict of Nantes
1520-1522	Comunero Revolt	May 2, 1598	Treaty of Vervins
Apr. 17, 1521	Martin Luther Appears Before the Diet of Worms	Mar. 20, 1602	Dutch East India Company Is Founded
Aug., 1523	Franciscans Arrive in Mexico	1603-1606	Appearance of the "False Dmitry"
June, 1524-July, 1526	German Peasants' War	Mar. 24, 1603	James I Becomes King of England and Scotland
1526	Battle of Mohács	Nov. 5, 1605	The Gunpowder Plot
Feb. 27, 1531	Formation of Schmalkaldic League	May 13, 1607	English Settle Jamestown
1532-1537	Pizarro Conquers Incas in Peru	1610	Galileo Confirms Heliocentric Model of the Solar System
1534-1536	Jacques Cartier Claims St. Lawrence River Valley for France	1611	The King James Bible Is Published
Aug. 15, 1534	Founding of the Jesuits	Feb. 7, 1613	Election of Michael Romanov as Czar
Dec. 18, 1534	Act of Supremacy	May 23, 1618	Defenestration of Prague
July, 1535-Mar., 1540	Henry VIII Encourages Suppression of English Monasteries	1620	Francis Bacon Publishes *Novum Organum*
1536	Turkish Capitulations Begin	Dec. 26, 1620	Pilgrims Arrive in North America
1537	Pope Paul III Declares Rights of New World Natives	1625	Grotius Publishes *On the Law of War and Peace*
1543	Copernicus Publishes *Revolutions of the Heavenly Bodies*	May 6, 1628-June 7, 1628	Petition of Right
1545-1563	Council of Trent	Mar. 6, 1629	Edict of Restitution
Jan. 16, 1547	Coronation of Ivan IV	Nov. 10, 1630	The "Day of Dupes"
1552	Bartolomé de Las Casas Publishes *Brief Relation of the Destruction of the Indies*		

Date	Event
1632	Galileo Publishes *Dialogue on the Two Chief Systems of the World*
May 30, 1635	Peace of Prague
1637	Descartes Publishes His *Discourse on Method*
1640	Revolt of the Catalans
Oct. 23, 1641-winter, 1642	Protestant Settlers Are Killed in Ulster Insurrection
1643-1648	Peace of Westphalia
July 2, 1644	Battle of Marston Moor
1646-1649	Levellers Launch an Egalitarian Movement
1648	Beginning of the *Fronde*
Dec., 1648-Feb., 1649	Establishment of the Commonwealth in England
1651	Thomas Hobbes Publishes *Leviathan*
Oct., 1651-May, 1652	The Navigation Act and the Outbreak of the Dutch Wars
1652-1689	George Fox Organizes the Quakers
Apr. 5, 1652	Dutch Begin to Colonize Southern Africa
May, 1659-May, 1660	Restoration of Charles II
Sept. 2, 1666-Sept. 5, 1666	Great Fire of London
1667	John Milton Publishes *Paradise Lost*
Apr., 1667-June, 1671	Stenka Razin Leads Peasant Uprising in Russia
1673	The Test Act
1682	The French Court Moves to Versailles
July 14, 1683-Sept. 12, 1683	Ottoman Turks Are Defeated at Vienna
1685	Louis XIV Revokes the Edict of Nantes
Summer, 1687	Newton Formulates His Theory of Universal Gravitation
Nov., 1688-Feb., 1689	The "Glorious Revolution"
1689-Oct. 30, 1697	War of the League of Augsburg
1689-1725	Reforms of Peter the Great
1690	Locke Publishes *Two Treatises of Government*
July 27, 1694	Bank of England Is Chartered
Jan. 26, 1699	Treaty of Karlowitz
c. 1700-1750	Bach Pioneers Modern Music
Nov. 30, 1700	Battle of Narva
1701	Act of Settlement
1703-1711	Hungarian Revolt Against Habsburg Rule
Aug. 13, 1704	Battle of Blenheim

Date	Event
Feb., 1706-Apr., 1707	Act of Union Unites England and Scotland
Apr. 11, 1713-Sept. 7, 1714	Treaty of Utrecht
Sept. 18, 1739	Treaty of Belgrade
May 31, 1740	Accession of Frederick the Great
Oct. 20, 1740	Maria Theresa Succeeds to the Austrian Throne
1748	Montesquieu Publishes *The Spirit of the Laws*
1751-1772	Diderot's *Encyclopedia* Is Published
1759	Charles III Gains the Spanish Throne
1762	Rousseau Publishes His *Social Contract*
Feb. 10, 1763	Peace of Paris
1765-1769	James Watt Develops His Steam Engine
July 30, 1767	Catherine the Great's *Instruction*
Aug. 26, 1769-July 13, 1771	Cook Makes a Scientific Expedition to New Zealand
Aug. 5, 1772, Jan. 23, 1793, *and* Oct. 24, 1795	Partitioning of Poland
July 21, 1774	Treaty of Kuchuk Kainarji
1775-1790	Joseph II's Reforms
Mar. 9, 1776	Adam Smith Publishes *The Wealth of Nations*
Sept. 3, 1783	Treaty of Paris
Jan. 26, 1788	Britain Establishes Penal Colony in Australia
1789	Louis XVI Calls the Estates-General
June 20, 1789	Oath of the Tennis Court
July 14, 1789	Fall of the Bastille
1792	Mary Wollstonecraft Publishes *A Vindication of the Rights of Woman*
Mar. 16, 1792	Denmark Abolishes the Slave Trade
Jan. 21, 1793	Execution of Louis XVI
July 27, 1794-July 28, 1794	Fall of Robespierre
1798	Malthus Publishes *An Essay on the Principle of Population*
Aug. 1, 1798	Battle of Aboukir Bay
Nov. 9, 1799-Nov. 10, 1799	Napoleon Rises to Power in France
Apr. 12, 1800	Act of Union Is Passed by Parliament
Dec. 2, 1804	Coronation of Napoleon as Emperor
Dec. 2, 1805	Battle of Austerlitz
Mar. 25, 1807	British Slave Trade Is Ended by Parliament

Date	Event
May, 1808-Nov., 1813	Peninsular War
May 2, 1808	*Dos de Mayo* Insurrection in Spain
May, 1809-Nov., 1817	David Ricardo Identifies Seven Key Economic Principles
June 23, 1812-Dec. 14, 1812	Napoleon's Invasion of Russia
Oct. 16, 1813-Oct. 18, 1813	Battle of the Nations
Apr. 11, 1814-June, 1830	Restoration of the French Bourbon Kings
Aug. 13, 1814	Britain Acquires the Cape Colony
Nov. 2, 1814-June 11, 1815	Congress of Vienna
June 8, 1815	Organization of German Confederation
June 18, 1815	Battle of Waterloo
Nov., 1815	Second Peace of Paris
July, 1820-Mar., 1821	Neapolitan Revolution
Mar., 1821-Sept., 1829	Greeks Fight for Independence
Oct. 20, 1822-Oct. 30, 1822	Great Britain Withdraws from the Concert of Europe
Dec. 26, 1825	Decembrist Revolt
Feb. 26, 1828-Apr. 13, 1829	Emancipation Acts of 1828 and 1829
Sept. 24, 1829	Treaty of Adrianople
1830	France Conquers Algeria
July, 1830	Lyell Publishes His *Principles of Geology*
July 29, 1830	July Revolution Deposes Charles X
Aug. 25, 1830-May 21, 1833	Belgian Revolution
Nov., 1830-Oct., 1831	First Polish Rebellion
1831	Mazzini Founds Young Italy
Oct. 17, 1831	Faraday Converts Magnetic Force into Electricity
June 4, 1832	Reform Act of 1832
Aug. 28, 1833	Slavery Is Abolished in the British Colonies
1834	The New Poor Law
Jan. 1, 1834	German States Cooperate in Customs Union
Sept. 9, 1835	Municipal Corporations Act
May 8, 1838-Apr. 10, 1848	Chartist Movement
1845-1854	Irish Famine and the Great Emigration
June 15, 1846	Repeal of the Corn Laws
Jan., 1848-July, 1849	Revolutions of 1848 in Italy
Feb., 1848	Marx and Engels Publish the *Communist Manifesto*
Feb. 24, 1848-Dec., 1848	Paris Revolution of 1848
Mar., 1848-Nov., 1848	Prussian Revolution of 1848

Date	Event
Sept. 12, 1848	Swiss Confederation Is Formed
1851-1854	Auguste Comte Advances Theory of Positivism
Dec. 2, 1851	Louis-Napoleon Bonaparte Becomes Emperor of France
Oct., 1853-Mar. 30, 1856	The Crimean War
1854-1869	Suez Canal Is Built
1859	Darwin Publishes *On the Origin of Species*
1859	John Stuart Mill Publishes *On Liberty*
July 11, 1859	Napoleon III and Emperor Francis Joseph Meet at Villafranca
May, 1860-July, 1860	Garibaldi's Thousand "Redshirts" Land in Italy
Mar. 3, 1861	Emancipation of the Serfs
Mar. 17, 1861	Italy Is Proclaimed a Kingdom
Sept. 24, 1862	Bismarck Becomes Minister-President of Prussia
1863-1913	Greece Is Unified Under the Glucksburg Dynasty
Sept. 28, 1864	The First International Is Founded
1865	Lister Promotes Antiseptic Surgery
1866-1867	North German Confederation Is Formed
Feb., 1867	Reform Act of 1867
May 29, 1867	The Austrian *Ausgleich*
Sept. 30, 1868	Spanish Revolution of 1868
July 19, 1870-Mar., 1871	Franco-Prussian War
1871-1875	Third French Republic Is Established
Jan. 18, 1871	German States Are Unified into German Empire
Mar. 18, 1871-May 28, 1871	The Paris Commune
May 6, 1873, June 6, 1873, *and* Oct. 22, 1873	The Three Emperors' League
1876	Spanish Constitution of 1876
May 2, 1876	Bulgarian Massacres
June 13, 1878-July 13, 1878	Congress of Berlin
1882	First Birth Control Clinic Is Established in Amsterdam
1882-1884	Koch Isolates Microorganisms That Cause Tuberculosis and Cholera
May 20, 1882	The Triple Alliance
Jan., 1884	Fabian Society Is Founded
Dec. 6, 1884	Franchise Act of 1884
1886-1889	Boulanger Crisis
1889	Great Britain Strengthens the Royal Navy

Date	Event
Dec. 27, 1893-Jan. 4, 1894	Franco-Russian Alliance
1894-1906	The Dreyfus Affair
1896	Marconi Patents the Telegraph
Mar., 1898	Social-Democratic Workers' Party Is Formed
July, 1898-Mar., 1899	The Fashoda Incident
May, 1899-July, 1899	First Hague Peace Conference
Oct. 12, 1899-May 31, 1902	Boer War
1900	Freud Publishes *The Interpretation of Dreams*
Feb., 1900	British Labour Party Is Formed
1903-1906	Pogroms in Imperial Russia
Feb. 9, 1904-Sept. 5, 1905	Russo-Japanese War
Apr. 8, 1904	The Entente Cordiale
1905	Einstein Publishes His Special Theory of Relativity
Jan. 22, 1905	Bloody Sunday
Oct. 26, 1905	Norway Becomes Independent
Oct. 30, 1905	The October Manifesto
May 10, 1906-July 21, 1906	First Meeting of the Duma
Oct. 6, 1906	Launching of the *Dreadnought*
June, 1907-Oct., 1907	Second Hague Peace Conference
Aug. 31, 1907	The Triple Entente
Oct. 7, 1908	Austria Annexes Bosnia and Herzegovina
Apr., 1909-Aug., 1911	Parliament Bill
Oct. 5, 1910	Republic of Portugal Is Proclaimed
1911-1912	Italy Annexes Libya
Sept. 14, 1911	Assassination of Peter Stolypin
Apr. 11, 1912-Sept. 15, 1914	Irish Home Rule Bill
Oct. 18, 1912-Aug. 10, 1913	Balkan Wars
June 28, 1914-Aug. 4, 1914	Outbreak of World War I
Sept. 5, 1914-Sept. 9, 1914	First Battle of the Marne
Sept. 22, 1914	Germany Begins Extensive Submarine Warfare
Oct. 30, 1914	Spain Declares Neutrality in World War I
1915-1918	Armenian Genocide
Apr. 28, 1915-May 1, 1915	International Congress of Women
Feb. 21, 1916-summer, 1916	Battle of Verdun
Apr. 24, 1916-Apr. 29, 1916	Easter Rebellion

Date	Event
May 31, 1916	Battle of Jutland
1917-1920	Ukrainian Nationalists Struggle for Independence
Nov. 6, 1917-Nov. 7, 1917	October Revolution
Dec. 6, 1917-1920	Finland Gains Independence
1918-1920	Baltic States Fight for Independence
1918-1921	Russian Civil War
Feb. 6, 1918	British Women Gain the Vote
Mar., 1918-1919	Influenza Epidemic Strikes
Mar. 3, 1918	Treaty of Brest-Litovsk
1919-1933	Racist Theories Aid Nazi Rise to Political Power
Jan. 15, 1919	Rosa Luxemburg Is Assassinated
June 28, 1919	The League of Nations Is Established
June 28, 1919	Treaty of Versailles
July 31, 1919	Weimar Constitution
1921-1928	Lenin's New Economic Policy
Oct. 24, 1922-Oct. 30, 1922	Mussolini's "March on Rome"
May 3, 1926-May 12, 1926	British Workers Launch General Strike
1928	Fleming Discovers Penicillin
1928-1933	Soviet Union Launches First Five-Year Plan
1929-1940	The Maginot Line Is Built
Jan. 19, 1929	Trotsky Is Sent into Exile
Feb. 11, 1929	The Vatican Treaty
Apr. 14, 1931	Second Spanish Republic Is Proclaimed
Mar. 9, 1932	Eamon de Valera Is Elected President of the Irish Dáil
Jan. 30, 1933	Hitler Comes to Power in Germany
Feb. 27, 1933	The Reichstag Fire
Mar. 23, 1933	Enabling Act of 1933
1934-1939	Stalin Begins the Purge Trials
Feb. 6, 1934	Stavisky Riots
June 30, 1934-July 2, 1934	The Great Blood Purge
Oct. 2, 1935-May 9, 1936	Italy Conquers Ethiopia
July 17, 1936	Spanish Civil War Begins
Dec. 10, 1936	Edward VIII Abdicates the British Throne
Apr. 26, 1937	Raids on Guernica
Feb. 12, 1938-Apr. 10, 1938	The *Anschluss*
Sept. 29, 1938-Sept. 30, 1938	Munich Conference
1939-1945	Gypsies Are Exterminated in Nazi Death Camps

Date	Event
1939-1945	Nazi Extermination of the Jews
Aug. 23, 1939-Aug. 24, 1939	Nazi-Soviet Pact
Sept. 1, 1939	Germany Invades Poland
Nov. 30, 1939-Feb. 13, 1940	Russo-Finnish War
Apr. 9, 1940	German Invasion of Norway
May 10, 1940-June 22, 1940	Collapse of France
May 26, 1940-June 4, 1940	Evacuation of Dunkirk
June, 1940-Aug., 1944	The French Resistance
Late summer, 1940-1941	Battle of Britain
Aug. 12, 1941	Atlantic Charter Is Signed
Aug. 24, 1942-Jan. 31, 1943	Stand at Stalingrad
Oct. 23, 1942-Nov. 3, 1942	Battle of El Alamein
Jan. 14, 1943-Jan. 24, 1943	The Casablanca Conference
Sept. 3, 1943	Allied Invasion of Italy
June 6, 1944-Aug. 10, 1944	Allied Invasion of France
Dec. 16, 1944-Jan. 28, 1945	Battle of the Bulge
Feb. 4, 1945-Feb. 11, 1945	The Yalta Conference
Apr. 26, 1945-June 26, 1945	The United Nations Is Formed
July 17, 1945-Aug. 2, 1945	The Potsdam Conference
July 26, 1945	Labour Party Forms Majority Government
Nov. 20, 1945-Aug. 31, 1946	Nuremberg Trials
Mar. 5, 1946	Churchill's "Iron Curtain" Speech
Mar. 12, 1947	Marshall Plan Is Announced
Mar., 1948-May, 1949	Berlin Airlift
Apr. 4, 1949	North Atlantic Treaty
May 8, 1949 *and* Oct. 7, 1949	Creation of Two German Republics
1950-1963	Italy's Postwar Economic Boom
Nov. 4, 1950	European Convention on Human Rights Is Signed
Oct., 1951-1953	Model of DNA Molecular Structure Is Developed
Dec. 5, 1952-Dec. 8, 1952	London Smog Kills Thousands
Mar. 5, 1953	Death of Stalin
May 14, 1955	Warsaw Pact Is Signed
Oct., 1956-Nov., 1956	Hungarian Revolution
Mar. 25, 1957	Common Market Is Formed

Date	Event
Oct. 4, 1957	Soviet Union Launches Sputnik
Sept. 9, 1958	Race Riots Erupt in London
Apr. 12, 1961	Soviet Union Puts a Human in Space
May 28, 1961	Amnesty International Is Founded
Aug. 13, 1961	Building of the Berlin Wall
Sept. 30, 1961	Organization for Economic Cooperation and Development Forms
1963-1970	Soviet Jews Demand Cultural and Religious Rights
Aug. 5, 1963	Limited Nuclear Test Ban Treaty Is Signed
Dec. 21, 1963	Greek and Turkish Cypriots Clash over Political Rights
Oct. 13, 1964	Khrushchev Falls from Power
1966-1991	Soviet Intellectuals Express Disagreement with Party Policy
Feb., 1966-Dec. 5, 1995	France Withdraws from NATO's Military Structure
Apr. 21, 1967	Greek Coup Leads to a Military Dictatorship
Nov. 7, 1967	United Nations Issues a Declaration on Equality for Women
1968-1989	Brezhnev Doctrine
May, 1968-June, 1968	French Workers Engage in a National Strike
Aug. 20, 1968-Aug. 21, 1968	Soviet Union Invades Czechoslovakia
Sept. 27, 1968	Caetano Becomes Premier of Portugal
Apr. 28, 1969	De Gaulle Steps Down
June 18, 1969	Pesticide Poisons the Rhine River
May 29, 1970	Parliament Passes the Equal Pay Act of 1970
Jan. 30, 1972	"Bloody Sunday" in Northern Ireland
June 5, 1972-June 16, 1972	United Nations Environmental Conference
Sept. 5, 1972	Munich Olympic Massacre
June 21, 1973	East and West Germany Establish Diplomatic Relations
July 31, 1973	European Space Agency Is Formed
Nov. 23, 1973	West Germany Restricts Immigration of Foreign Workers
1974	Portugal Grants Independence to Its African Colonies
Feb. 13, 1974	Solzhenitsyn Is Expelled from the Soviet Union
June 17, 1974	IRA Terrorists Bomb Parliament Building
Aug. 1, 1975	Helsinki Agreement
Nov. 11, 1975	Death of Franco

Date	Event	Date	Event
Jan. 21, 1976	Concorde Flies Passengers at Supersonic Speeds	Dec. 8, 1987	Intermediate-Range Nuclear Forces Treaty
Feb. 12, 1976	IRA Hunger Striker Dies in an English Prison	Feb., 1988	Ethnic Riots Erupt in Armenia
Mar. 16, 1978-May 9, 1978	Aldo Moro Is Kidnapped and Murdered by Italian Terrorists	Jan., 1989-Oct., 1989	Hungary Adopts a Multiparty System
May 4, 1979	Margaret Thatcher Becomes Britain's First Woman Prime Minister	Nov. 9, 1989	The Berlin Wall Falls
		Nov. 17, 1989-Dec. 29, 1989	Velvet Revolution in Czechoslovakia
June 18, 1979	SALT II Is Signed	Dec. 25, 1989	Ceausescu Is Overthrown in Romania
Dec. 24, 1979	Soviet Union Invades Afghanistan		
May 4, 1980	Death of Tito	1990	Albania Opens Doors to Foreign Nationals
Sept., 1980	Solidarity Is Founded in Poland	Oct. 3, 1990	German Reunification
May 10, 1981	Mitterrand Is Elected to the French Presidency	1991	Sweden Applies for Membership in the European Community
Oct. 18, 1981	Greek Socialists Win Parliamentary Majority	Jan. 13, 1991	Soviet Attack on Baltic Separatists
Nov. 20, 1981	Construction of Siberian Gas Pipeline Begins	Jan. 17, 1991-Feb. 28, 1991	Coalition Defeats Iraq in Gulf War
June 14, 1982	Great Britain Recovers the Falkland Islands	June 25, 1991-June 1, 1992	Civil War Rages in Yugoslavia
Feb. 24, 1983	Klaus Barbie Faces Nazi War Crimes Charges	Aug., 1991-Dec., 1991	Soviet Union Dissolves into Loosely Allied Republics
Mar. 6, 1983	Green Party Wins Seats in West German Parliament	Sept., 1992	Protests and Violence Against Immigrants in Germany
July 21, 1983	Martial Law in Poland Ends	Jan. 1, 1993	Czechoslovakia Splits into Two Republics
Dec. 19, 1984	Britain Signs Agreement to Leave Hong Kong in 1997	Nov. 1, 1993	Maastricht Treaty Is Ratified
Mar. 11, 1985	Gorbachev Is Elected General Secretary of the Communist Party	Dec. 15, 1993	Ulster Peace Accord
		May 6, 1994	Channel Tunnel Is Officially Opened
July 10, 1985	Sinking of the Rainbow Warrior	Dec. 11, 1994	Russian Troops Invade Chechnya
Nov. 15, 1985	Anglo-Irish Agreement Is Signed	May, 1995	Chirac Takes Office as President of France
Feb. 28, 1986	Olof Palme Is Assassinated		
Apr. 26, 1986	Chernobyl Nuclear Disaster	July 5, 1996	Scottish Researchers Succeed in Cloning Adult Sheep
June 8, 1986	Election of Kurt Waldheim as President of Austria Stirs Controversy	May 1, 1997	Labour Party Wins Majority in British National Elections
Dec. 17, 1986	Riots in Kazakhstan	May 27, 1997	North Atlantic Treaty Organization and Russia Sign Cooperation Pact
July, 1987	European Community Adopts the Single Europe Act		

GEOGRAPHICAL LIST

ALBANIA
1444	Albanian Chieftains Are United Under Skanderbeg
1990	Albania Opens Doors to Foreign Nationals

AUSTRIA. *See also* AUSTRO-HUNGARIAN EMPIRE, HOLY ROMAN EMPIRE
1156	Emergence of Austria
1526	Battle of Mohács
1683	Ottoman Turks Are Defeated at Vienna
1699	Treaty of Karlowitz
1739	Treaty of Belgrade
1740	Maria Theresa Succeeds to the Austrian Throne
1772	Partitioning of Poland
1775	Joseph II's Reforms
1859	Napoleon III and Emperor Francis Joseph Meet at Villafranca
1900	Freud Publishes *The Interpretation of Dreams*
1938	The *Anschluss*
1986	Election of Kurt Waldheim as President of Austria Stirs Controversy

AUSTRO-HUNGARIAN EMPIRE
1867	The Austrian *Ausgleich*
1908	Austria Annexes Bosnia and Herzegovina
1912	Balkan Wars

BALKANS. *See also* ALBANIA, YUGOSLAVIA
1168	Nemanyid Dynasty Is Founded in Serbia
1389	Turkish Conquest of Serbia
1526	Battle of Mohács
1739	Treaty of Belgrade
1829	Treaty of Adrianople
1912	Balkan Wars

BALTIC REGION
1918	Baltic States Fight for Independence
1991	Soviet Attack on Baltic Separatists

BELGIUM
1214	Battle of Bouvines
1323	Peasants' Revolt in Flanders
1830	Belgian Revolution

BULGARIA
864	Boris Converts to Christianity
893	Beginning of Bulgaria's Golden Age
1014	Basil II Conquers the Bulgars
1876	Bulgarian Massacres

BYZANTINE EMPIRE
326	Constantinople Is Founded
361	Failure of Julian's Pagan Revival
380	Theodosius' Edicts Promote Christian Orthodoxy
428	The Nestorian Controversy
529	Justinian's *Code*
532	Building of Hagia Sophia
533	Justinian's Wars Against the Vandals, Ostrogoths, and Visigoths
726	Iconoclastic Controversy
976	Reign of Basil II
1054	Beginning of the Rome-Constantinople Schism

CRETE
1600 B.C.	Flowering of Minoan Civilization

CYPRUS
1963	Greek and Turkish Cypriots Clash over Political Rights

CZECHOSLOVAKIA. *See also* HOLY ROMAN EMPIRE
1415	Martyrdom of Jan Hus
1457	Reign of Stephen the Great
1618	Defenestration of Prague
1968	Soviet Union Invades Czechoslovakia
1989	Velvet Revolution in Czechoslovakia
1993	Czechoslovakia Splits into Two Republics

DENMARK
1397	The Kalmar Union Is Formed
1792	Denmark Abolishes the Slave Trade

ENGLAND. *See also* IRELAND AND NORTHERN IRELAND, SCOTLAND
3100 B.C.	Building of Stonehenge
43	Roman Conquest of Britain
60	Boadicea Leads Revolt Against Roman Rule
449	Saxon Settlement of Britain Begins
596	See of Canterbury Is Established
731	Bede Concludes His *Ecclesiastical History of the English People*
793	Northmen Raid Lindisfarne
878	King Alfred Defeats the Danes at Edington
1016	Danish Invaders Led by Canute Conquer England
1066	Battle of Hastings
1086	The Domesday Survey
1154	Establishment of Angevin Empire
1170	Murder of Thomas à Becket
1175	Common Law Tradition Emerges in England
1215	Signing of the Magna Carta
1258	The "Provisions of Oxford"
1285	Statute of Winchester
1290	Jews Are Expelled from England, France, and Southern Italy
1295	The Model Parliament
1310	William of Ockham Attacks Thomist Ideas
1377	John Wycliffe Is Condemned for Attacking Church Authority
1381	Wat Tyler Leads Peasants' Revolt
1387	Chaucer Develops Vernacular Narrative in *The Canterbury Tales*

1453	English Are Driven from France
1485	Tudor Rule Is Established in England
1534	Act of Supremacy
1535	Henry VIII Encourages Suppression of English Monasteries
1563	The Thirty-nine Articles of the Church of England
1570	Elizabeth I Is Excommunicated by Pius V
1584	Raleigh Funds Expedition to North America
1588	Defeat of the Spanish Armada
1589	Shakespeare Writes His Dramas
1603	James I Becomes King of England and Scotland
1605	The Gunpowder Plot
1607	English Settle Jamestown
1611	The King James Bible Is Published
1620	Francis Bacon Publishes *Novum Organum*
1620	Pilgrims Arrive in North America
1628	Petition of Right
1644	Battle of Marston Moor
1646	Levellers Launch an Egalitarian Movement
1648	Establishment of the Commonwealth in England
1651	Thomas Hobbes Publishes *Leviathan*
1651	The Navigation Act and the Outbreak of the Dutch Wars
1652	George Fox Organizes the Quakers
1659	Restoration of Charles II
1666	Great Fire of London
1667	John Milton Publishes *Paradise Lost*
1673	The Test Act
1687	Newton Formulates His Theory of Universal Gravitation
1688	The "Glorious Revolution"
1690	Locke Publishes *Two Treatises of Government*
1694	Bank of England Is Chartered
1701	Act of Settlement
1706	Act of Union Unites England and Scotland
1768	Cook Makes a Scientific Expedition to New Zealand
1776	Adam Smith Publishes *The Wealth of Nations*
1783	Treaty of Paris
1788	Britain Establishes Penal Colony in Australia
1792	Mary Wollstonecraft Publishes *A Vindication of the Rights of Woman*
1798	Malthus Publishes *An Essay on the Principle of Population*
1800	Act of Union Is Passed by Parliament
1807	British Slave Trade Is Ended by Parliament
1809	David Ricardo Identifies Seven Key Economic Principles
1814	Britain Acquires the Cape Colony
1822	Great Britain Withdraws from the Concert of Europe
1828	Emancipation Acts of 1828 and 1829
1830	Lyell Publishes His *Principles of Geology*
1831	Faraday Converts Magnetic Force into Electricity
1832	Reform Act of 1832
1833	Slavery Is Abolished in the British Colonies
1834	The New Poor Law

1835	Municipal Corporations Act
1838	Chartist Movement
1846	Repeal of the Corn Laws
1859	Darwin Publishes *On the Origin of Species*
1859	John Stuart Mill Publishes *On Liberty*
1864	The First International Is Founded
1865	Lister Promotes Antiseptic Surgery
1867	Reform Act of 1867
1884	Fabian Society Is Founded
1884	Franchise Act of 1884
1889	Great Britain Strengthens the Royal Navy
1898	The Fashoda Incident
1899	Boer War
1900	British Labour Party Is Formed
1906	Launching of the *Dreadnought*
1909	Parliament Bill
1918	British Women Gain the Vote
1926	British Workers Launch General Strike
1928	Fleming Discovers Penicillin
1936	Edward VIII Abdicates the British Throne
1941	Atlantic Charter Is Signed
1945	Labour Party Forms Majority Government
1946	Churchill's "Iron Curtain" Speech
1951	Model of DNA Molecular Structure Is Developed
1952	London Smog Kills Thousands
1958	Race Riots Erupt in London
1961	Amnesty International Is Founded
1970	Parliament Passes the Equal Pay Act of 1970
1974	IRA Terrorists Bomb Parliament Building
1976	Concorde Flies Passengers at Supersonic Speeds
1976	IRA Hunger Striker Dies in an English Prison
1979	Margaret Thatcher Becomes Britain's First Woman Prime Minister
1982	Great Britain Recovers the Falkland Islands
1984	Britain Signs Agreement to Leave Hong Kong in 1997
1985	Anglo-Irish Agreement Is Signed
1993	Ulster Peace Accord
1994	Channel Tunnel Is Officially Opened
1997	Labour Party Wins Majority in British National Elections

ESTONIA. *See* **BALTIC REGION, POLAND, and PRUSSIA**

EUROPE and INTERNATIONAL

1100 B.C.	Hallstatt Civilization Ushers in Iron Age in Europe
240 B.C.	Exploitation of the Arch
109 B.C.	Celtic Hill Forts Appear
451	Battle of the Catalaunian Plains
700	Use of Heavy Plow Increases Agricultural Yields
1009	The Church of the Holy Sepulchre Is Destroyed
1010	Avicenna Writes His *Canon of Medicine*
1100	Emergence of European Universities
1147	The Second Crusade

1189	The Third Crusade
1204	Knights of the Fourth Crusade Capture Constantinople
1212	The Children's Crusade
1217	The Fifth Crusade
1227	Frederick II Leads the Sixth Crusade
1233	The Papal Inquisition
1248	Failure of the Seventh Crusade
1265	Thomas Aquinas Compiles the *Summa Theologiae*
1291	Fall of Acre
1347	Invasion of the Black Death
1373	Jean Froissart Compiles His *Chronicles*
1516	Sir Thomas More Publishes *Utopia*
1635	Peace of Prague
1637	Descartes Publishes His *Discourse on Method*
1689	War of the League of Augsburg
1763	Peace of Paris
1783	Treaty of Paris
1798	Battle of Aboukir Bay
1805	Battle of Austerlitz
1808	Peninsular War
1813	Battle of the Nations
1814	Congress of Vienna
1815	Battle of Waterloo
1815	Second Peace of Paris
1848	Marx and Engels Publish the *Communist Manifesto*
1853	The Crimean War
1854	Suez Canal Is Built
1873	The Three Emperors' League
1878	Congress of Berlin
1882	The Triple Alliance
1899	First Hague Peace Conference
1904	The Entente Cordiale
1907	Second Hague Peace Conference
1907	The Triple Entente
1912	Balkan Wars
1914	Outbreak of World War I
1914	First Battle of the Marne
1915	International Congress of Women
1916	Battle of Verdun
1916	Battle of Jutland
1918	Influenza Epidemic Strikes
1919	The League of Nations Is Established
1919	Treaty of Versailles
1940	Evacuation of Dunkirk
1940	Battle of Britain
1942	Battle of El Alamein
1943	The Casablanca Conference
1943	Allied Invasion of Italy
1944	Allied Invasion of France
1944	Battle of the Bulge
1945	The Yalta Conference
1945	The United Nations Is Formed
1945	The Potsdam Conference
1945	Nuremberg Trials

1947	Marshall Plan Is Announced
1949	North Atlantic Treaty
1950	European Convention on Human Rights Is Signed
1955	Warsaw Pact Is Signed
1957	Common Market Is Formed
1961	Organization for Economic Cooperation and Development Forms
1963	Limited Nuclear Test Ban Treaty Is Signed
1967	United Nations Issues a Declaration on Equality for Women
1969	Pesticide Poisons the Rhine River
1972	United Nations Environmental Conference
1973	European Space Agency Is Formed
1975	Helsinki Agreement
1987	European Community Adopts the Single Europe Act
1991	Sweden Applies for Membership in the European Community
1991	Coalition Defeats Iraq in Gulf War
1993	Maastricht Treaty Is Ratified
1997	North Atlantic Treaty Organization and Russia Sign Cooperation Pact

FINLAND

1917	Finland Gains Independence
1939	Russo-Finnish War

FRANCE

15,000 B.C.	Cave Paintings Provide Evidence of Magdalenian Culture
496	Baptism of Clovis
506	*Breviarium* of Alaric Is Drafted
732	Battle of Tours
754	Coronation of Pepin
843	Treaty of Verdun
987	Hugh Capet Is Elected to the Throne of France
1025	Scholars at Chartres Revive Interest in Classical Learning
1095	Pope Urban II Calls the First Crusade
1098	Cistercian Monastic Order Is Founded
1120	Order of the Knights Templar Is Founded
1125	Charter of Lorris
1150	Development of Gothic Architecture
1175	Appearance of the Waldensians
1200	Fairs of Champagne
1209	Albigensian Crusade
1214	Battle of Bouvines
1290	Jews Are Expelled from England, France, and Southern Italy
1346	Battle of Crécy
1429	Joan of Arc's Relief of Orléans
1453	English Are Driven from France
1494	Charles VIII of France Invades Italy
1534	Jacques Cartier Claims St. Lawrence River Valley for France
1534	Founding of the Jesuits
1572	St. Bartholomew's Day Massacre
1580	Montaigne Publishes His *Essays*

1585	War of the Three Henrys
1589	Henry IV Ascends the Throne of France
1598	Edict of Nantes
1598	Treaty of Vervins
1625	Grotius Publishes *On the Law of War and Peace*
1630	The "Day of Dupes"
1648	Beginning of the *Fronde*
1682	The French Court Moves to Versailles
1685	Louis XIV Revokes the Edict of Nantes
1748	Montesquieu Publishes *The Spirit of the Laws*
1751	Diderot's *Encyclopedia* Is Published
1762	Rousseau Publishes His *Social Contract*
1763	Peace of Paris
1783	Treaty of Paris
1789	Louis XVI Calls the Estates-General
1789	Oath of the Tennis Court
1789	Fall of the Bastille
1793	Execution of Louis XVI
1794	Fall of Robespierre
1798	Battle of Aboukir Bay
1799	Napoleon Rises to Power in France
1804	Coronation of Napoleon as Emperor
1812	Napoleon's Invasion of Russia
1814	Restoration of the French Bourbon Kings
1830	France Conquers Algeria
1830	July Revolution Deposes Charles X
1848	Paris Revolution of 1848
1851	Auguste Comte Advances Theory of Positivism
1851	Louis-Napoleon Bonaparte Becomes Emperor of France
1859	Napoleon III and Emperor Francis Joseph Meet at Villafranca
1870	Franco-Prussian War
1871	Third French Republic Is Established
1871	The Paris Commune
1886	Boulanger Crisis
1893	Franco-Russian Alliance
1894	The Dreyfus Affair
1898	The Fashoda Incident
1929	The Maginot Line Is Built
1934	Stavisky Riots
1940	Collapse of France
1940	The French Resistance
1944	Allied Invasion of France
1966	France Withdraws from NATO's Military Structure
1968	French Workers Engage in a National Strike
1969	De Gaulle Steps Down
1976	Concorde Flies Passengers at Supersonic Speeds
1981	Mitterrand Is Elected to the French Presidency
1983	Klaus Barbie Faces Nazi War Crimes Charges
1985	Sinking of the *Rainbow Warrior*
1994	Channel Tunnel Is Officially Opened
1995	Chirac Takes Office as President of France
1997	North Atlantic Treaty Organization and Russia Sign Cooperation Pact

GERMANY. *See also* **HOLY ROMAN EMPIRE, PRUSSIA**

1882	Koch Isolates Microorganisms That Cause Tuberculosis and Cholera
1905	Einstein Publishes His Special Theory of Relativity
1914	Germany Begins Extensive Submarine Warfare
1918	Treaty of Brest-Litovsk
1919	Racist Theories Aid Nazi Rise to Political Power
1919	Rosa Luxemburg Is Assassinated
1919	Weimar Constitution
1933	Hitler Comes to Power in Germany
1933	The Reichstag Fire
1933	Enabling Act of 1933
1934	The Great Blood Purge
1938	The *Anschluss*
1938	Munich Conference
1939	Gypsies Are Exterminated in Nazi Death Camps
1939	Nazi Extermination of the Jews
1939	Nazi-Soviet Pact
1939	Germany Invades Poland
1940	German Invasion of Norway
1948	Berlin Airlift
1949	Creation of Two German Republics
1961	Building of the Berlin Wall
1972	Munich Olympic Massacre
1973	East and West Germany Establish Diplomatic Relations
1973	West Germany Restricts Immigration of Foreign Workers
1983	Green Party Wins Seats in West German Parliament
1989	The Berlin Wall Falls
1990	German Reunification
1992	Protests and Violence Against Immigrants in Germany

GREECE

1620 B.C.	Rise of Mycenaean Civilization
1000 B.C.	Greek Alphabet Is Developed
1000 B.C.	Ionian Confederacy
800 B.C.	Homer's Composition of the *Iliad*
776 B.C.	Olympic Games
775 B.C.	Oracle at Delphi
736 B.C.	Spartan Conquest of Messenia
733 B.C.	Founding of Syracuse
700 B.C.	Phalanx Is Developed as a Military Unit
650 B.C.	Greek City-States Use Coins as Means of Exchange
621 B.C.	Draco's Code
600 B.C.	Greek Philosophers Formulate Theories of the Cosmos
594 B.C.	Legislation of Solon
550 B.C.	Construction of Trireme Changes Naval Warfare
530 B.C.	Founding of the Pythagorean Brotherhood
508 B.C.	Reforms of Cleisthenes
500 B.C.	Greek Physicians Develop Scientific Practice of Medicine
483 B.C.	Naval Law of Themistocles

480 B.C.	Persian Invasion of Greece
478 B.C.	Athenian Empire Is Created
450 B.C.	History Develops as Scholarly Discipline
447 B.C.	The Parthenon Is Built
440 B.C.	Teachings of the Sophists
431 B.C.	Peloponnesian War
415 B.C.	Athenian Invasion of Sicily
401 B.C.	March of the "Ten Thousand"
399 B.C.	Death of Socrates
380 B.C.	Plato Develops His Theory of Ideas
338 B.C.	Battle of Chaeronea
335 B.C.	Aristotle Writes the *Politics*
332 B.C.	Founding of Alexandria
331 B.C.	Battle of Gaugamela
325 B.C.	Aristotle Isolates Science as a Discipline
300 B.C.	Stoic Conception of Natural Law
275 B.C.	Advances in Hellenistic Astronomy
250 B.C.	Discoveries of Archimedes
31 B.C.	Battle of Actium
963	Foundation of Mount Athos Monasteries
1821	Greeks Fight for Independence
1863	Greece Is Unified Under the Glucksburg Dynasty
1967	Greek Coup Leads to a Military Dictatorship
1981	Greek Socialists Win Parliamentary Majority

HOLY ROMAN EMPIRE. *See also* **AUSTRIA, CZECHOSLOVAKIA, HUNGARY, GERMANY, and PRUSSIA**

735	Christianity Is Introduced into Germany
896	Magyar Invasions of Italy, Saxony, and Bavaria
955	Otto I Defeats the Magyars
1150	Rise of the Hansa
1152	Frederick Barbarossa Is Elected King of Germany
1228	Teutonic Knights Bring Baltic Region Under Catholic Control
1356	The "Golden Bull"
1410	Battle of Tannenburg
1415	Martyrdom of Jan Hus
1450	Gutenberg Pioneers the Printing Press
1517	Luther Posts His Ninety-five Theses
1519	Charles V Is Elected Holy Roman Emperor
1521	Martin Luther Appears Before the Diet of Worms
1524	German Peasants' War
1531	Formation of Schmalkaldic League
1543	Copernicus Publishes *Revolutions of the Heavenly Bodies*
1555	Peace of Augsburg
1555	Abdication of Charles V
1629	Edict of Restitution
1635	Peace of Prague
1643	Peace of Westphalia
1700	Bach Pioneers Modern Music
1704	Battle of Blenheim
1740	Accession of Frederick the Great

HUNGARY. *See also* **AUSTRO-HUNGARIAN EMPIRE, HOLY ROMAN EMPIRE**

896	Magyar Invasions of Italy, Saxony, and Bavaria
1330	Basarab Defeats Hungarians
1442	János Hunyadi Defends Hungary Against Ottoman Invaders
1458	Hungarian Renaissance Under Mátyás Hunyadi
1514	Hungarian Peasants Revolt
1703	Hungarian Revolt Against Habsburg Rule
1956	Hungarian Revolution
1989	Hungary Adopts a Multiparty System

ICELAND

930	Vikings Establish the Althing in Iceland

IRELAND AND NORTHERN IRELAND

450	Conversion of Ireland
635	Founding of Lindisfarne and Creation of the *Book of Kells*
1014	Battle of Clontarf
1169	Norman Troops Invade Ireland
1641	Protestant Settlers Are Killed in Ulster Insurrection
1800	Act of Union Is Passed by Parliament
1845	Irish Famine and the Great Emigration
1912	Irish Home Rule Bill
1916	Easter Rebellion
1932	Eamon de Valera Is Elected President of the Irish Dáil
1972	"Bloody Sunday" in Northern Ireland
1974	IRA Terrorists Bomb Parliament Building
1976	IRA Hunger Striker Dies in an English Prison
1985	Anglo-Irish Agreement Is Signed
1993	Ulster Peace Accord

ITALY. *See also* **ROMAN EMPIRE**

524	Imprisonment and Death of Boethius
568	Lombard Conquest of Italy
590	Reforms of Pope Gregory the Great
781	Alcuin Becomes Adviser to Charlemagne
896	Magyar Invasions of Italy, Saxony, and Bavaria
1127	Kingdom of Sicily Is Created
1150	Venetian Merchants Dominate Trade with the East
1209	Founding of the Franciscans
1215	Fourth Lateran Council
1271	Travels of Marco Polo
1290	Jews Are Expelled from England, France, and Southern Italy
1302	Boniface VII Issues the Bull *Unam Sanctam*
1347	Cola di Rienzo Leads Popular Uprising in Rome
1350	Petrarch and Boccaccio Recover Classical Texts
1410	Florentine School of Art Emerges
1440	Donation of Constantine Is Exposed as Fraudulent
1454	Peace of Lodi
1494	Charles VIII of France Invades Italy
1500	Botticelli Leads the Renaissance Revival of Classical Themes in Painting

1513	Machiavelli Writes *The Prince*
1537	Pope Paul III Declares Rights of New World Natives
1545	Council of Trent
1583	Matteo Ricci Travels to Peking as Jesuit Missionary
1610	Galileo Confirms Heliocentric Model of the Solar System
1632	Galileo Publishes *Dialogue on the Two Chief Systems of the World*
1820	Neapolitan Revolution
1831	Mazzini Founds Young Italy
1848	Revolutions of 1848 in Italy
1860	Garibaldi's Thousand "Redshirts" Land in Italy
1861	Italy Is Proclaimed a Kingdom
1896	Marconi Patents the Telegraph
1911	Italy Annexes Libya
1922	Mussolini's "March on Rome"
1929	The Vatican Treaty
1935	Italy Conquers Ethiopia
1943	Allied Invasion of Italy
1950	Italy's Postwar Economic Boom
1978	Aldo Moro Is Kidnapped and Murdered by Italian Terrorists

LATVIA. *See* **BALTIC REGION, HOLY ROMAN EMPIRE, and PRUSSIA**

LITHUANIA. *See* **BALTIC REGION, POLAND, and PRUSSIA**

NETHERLANDS

1323	Peasants' Revolt in Flanders
1581	United Provinces of the Netherlands Declare Independence from Spain
1602	Dutch East India Company Is Founded
1651	The Navigation Act and the Outbreak of the Dutch Wars
1652	Dutch Begin to Colonize Southern Africa
1713	Treaty of Utrecht
1882	First Birth Control Clinic Is Established in Amsterdam

NORWAY

1397	The Kalmar Union Is Formed
1905	Norway Becomes Independent
1940	German Invasion of Norway

OTTOMAN EMPIRE

1071	Battle of Manzikert
1353	Ottoman Empire Establishes Foothold in Rumelia
1389	Turkish Conquest of Serbia
1442	János Hunyadi Defends Hungary Against Ottoman Invaders
1453	Fall of Constantinople
1526	Battle of Mohács
1536	Turkish Capitulations Begin
1571	Battle of Lepanto

1683	Ottoman Turks Are Defeated at Vienna
1699	Treaty of Karlowitz
1774	Treaty of Kuchuk Kainarji
1829	Treaty of Adrianople
1853	The Crimean War
1876	Bulgarian Massacres
1915	Armenian Genocide

POLAND

1450	Second Peace of Thorn
1772	Partitioning of Poland
1830	First Polish Rebellion
1939	Germany Invades Poland
1980	Solidarity Is Founded in Poland
1983	Martial Law in Poland Ends

PORTUGAL

1415	Prince Henry the Navigator Promotes Portuguese Exploration
1487	Dias Rounds the Cape of Good Hope
1500	Portugal Begins to Colonize Brazil
1505	Portuguese Viceroys Establish Overseas Trade Empire
1910	Republic of Portugal Is Proclaimed
1968	Caetano Becomes Premier of Portugal
1974	Portugal Grants Independence to Its African Colonies

PRUSSIA. *See also* **GERMANY, HOLY ROMAN EMPIRE**

1450	Second Peace of Thorn
1815	Organization of German Confederation
1834	German States Cooperate in Customs Union
1848	Prussian Revolution of 1848
1862	Bismarck Becomes Minister-President of Prussia
1866	North German Confederation Is Formed
1870	Franco-Prussian War
1871	German States Are Unified into German Empire

ROMAN EMPIRE. *See also* **ITALY**

625 B.C.	Rise of Etruscan Civilization in Rome
525 B.C.	The Sibylline Books
494 B.C.	Institution of the Plebeian Tribunate
451 B.C.	The "Twelve Tables" of Roman Law
445 B.C.	The Canuleian Law
340 B.C.	Origin of *Municipia*
312 B.C.	Building of the Appian Way
312 B.C.	First Roman Aqueduct Is Built
287 B.C.	The *Lex Hortensia*
264 B.C.	First Punic War
218 B.C.	Second Punic War
202 B.C.	Battle of Zama
180 B.C.	Establishment of the *Cursus Honorum*
146 B.C.	Sack of Corinth
133 B.C.	Pergamum Is Transferred to Rome
133 B.C.	Tribunate of Tiberius Sempronius Gracchus
107 B.C.	Marius Creates a Private Army

SPAIN

711	Tarik's Crossing into Spain
950	Flourishing of the Court of Córdoba
1031	Fall of the Caliphate of Córdoba
1092	El Cid Conquers Valencia and Becomes Its Ruler
1150	Moors Transmit Classical Philosophy and Medicine to Europe
1230	Kingdoms of Castile and Léon Are Unified
1469	Marriage of Ferdinand and Isabella
1478	Establishment of the Spanish Inquisition
1492	Expulsion of Jews from Spain
1492	Fall of Granada
1492	Columbus Lands in America
1494	Treaty of Tordesillas
1516	Charles I Ascends the Throne of Spain
1519	Magellan Expedition Circumnavigates the Globe
1519	Cortés Conquers Aztecs in Mexico
1520	Comunero Revolt
1523	Franciscans Arrive in Mexico
1532	Pizarro Conquers Incas in Peru
1537	Pope Paul III Declares Rights of New World Natives
1552	Bartolomé de Las Casas Publishes *Brief Relation of the Destruction of the Indies*
1565	Spain Seizes the Philippines
1588	Defeat of the Spanish Armada
1640	Revolt of the Catalans
1759	Charles III Gains the Spanish Throne
1808	Peninsular War
1808	*Dos de Mayo* Insurrection in Spain
1868	Spanish Revolution of 1868
1876	Spanish Constitution of 1876
1914	Spain Declares Neutrality in World War I
1931	Second Spanish Republic Is Proclaimed
1936	Spanish Civil War Begins
1937	Raids on Guernica
1975	Death of Franco

SWEDEN

1240	Alexander Nevsky Defends Novgorod from Swedish Invaders
1397	The Kalmar Union Is Formed
1700	Battle of Narva
1905	Norway Becomes Independent
1986	Olof Palme Is Assassinated

SWITZERLAND

1315	Swiss Victory at Morgarten
1414	Council of Constance
1848	Swiss Confederation Is Formed

TURKEY. *See* BYZANTINE EMPIRE, OTTOMAN EMPIRE

YUGOSLAVIA. *See also* BALKANS

1980	Death of Tito
1991	Civil War Rages in Yugoslavia

PERSONAGES INDEX

Goremykin, Ivan Logginovich, 962

Gorgias of Leontini, 66

Goring, George, 639

Göring, Hermann, 1059, 1062, 1064, 1071, 1080, 1103, 1107, 1112, 1137

Gort, Lord (John Standish Surtees Prendergast Vereker), 1103

Got, Bertrand de. See Clement V (pope)

Gournay, Marie le Jars de, 564

Government of Ireland Act, 1238

Goya, Francisco, 776

Gracchus, Tiberius Sempronius, 115, 117-118

Grachev, Pavel S., 1339

Graff, Michael, 1292

Gramont, duke of (Antoine Alfred Agénor), 898

Granvelle, Cardinal Antoine Perrenot de, 566

Gratian (Western Roman emperor), 164, 174, 176

Grattan, Henry, 765

Gravier, Charles. See Vergennes, comte de

Graziani, Rodolfo, 1115

Green, Charles, 728

Greene, Robert, 581

Gregorio, Leopoldo di. See Squillace, marquis of

Gregory I (pope), 214; church reforms of, 211-213

Gregory II (pope), 223, 228

Gregory IV (pope), 236

Gregory VIII (pope), 331

Gregory IX (pope), 352, 354, 358

Gregory X (pope), 372

Gregory XII (pope), 428

Gregory XIII (pope), 558

Gregory of Sinai, 257

Gregory of Tours, Saint, 197

Gregory the Great. See Gregory I (pope)

Grenville, Sir John, 657

Grey, Earl Charles, 828, 831

Grey, Sir Edward, 967-968, 984, 986

Grimaldi, marquis of, 717

Grishin, Victor, 1280

Grivas, George, 1187

Gromyko, Andrei Andreyevich, 1185, 1254, 1281, 1298

Groot, Huigh de. See Grotius, Hugo

Groot, Marie van Reigersbergh de, 618

Grósz, Károly, 1303

Grotius, Hugo, 618-620

Grouchy, Emmanuel de, 794

Grumbkow, General Friedrich Wilhelm, 707

Guacanagarí, 476

Guarnerius. See Irnerius

Guchkov, Alexander Ivanovich, 960, 962

Guelph, Count. See Welf VI

Guest, Ivor Churchill. See Wimborne, Baron

Guiscard, Robert. See Robert Guiscard

Guise, duke of (Francis de Lorraine), 584

Guise, duke of (Henry de Lorraine), 562, 576, 584

Guizot, François, 852

Gustav I Vasa (king of Sweden), 422

Gustavus II Adolphus (king of Sweden), 623

Gutenberg, Johann, 443-445

Guthrum (king of East Anglia), 244

Guyuk (Mongol khan), 363

Guzmán, Domingo de. See Dominic, Saint

Guzmán y Pimental, Gaspar de. See Olivares, count-duke of

Gylippus, 70

Haakon VII (king of Norway), 958, 1099

Hácha, Emil, 1082

Haig, Alexander, 1269

Haile Selassie I (emperor of Ethiopia), 1073

Hakam I, al- (emir of Córdoba), 253

Hakam II, al- (caliph of Córdoba), 253, 278

Hakim bi-Amrih Allāh, al-, 264

Hales, Robert, 413

Halfdan, 244

Halifax, earl of. See Montagu, Charles

Halifax, earl of (Edward Frederick Lindley Wood), 1094

Halley, Edmund, 674

Hambro, Carl Joachim, 1099

Hamilcar Barca, 101, 107

Hamilton, Alice, 997

Hamilton, Lord George Francis, 926

Hannibal, 107, 109

Hansemann, David, 855

Hardenberg, Prince Karl August von, 789, 797

Hardie, Keir, 945

Harding, Stephen, 292

Hardinge, Sir Charles, 968

Harley, Robert (earl of Oxford), 703

Harney, George Julian, 840

Haro, Luís de, 633

Harold Godwinson (king of England), 282

Harold Hardrada (king of Norway), 282

Harriot, Thomas, 571

Hartington, marquis of (Spencer Compton Cavendish), 923

Hasdrubal, 107

Hasdrubal Barca, 107, 109

Haughey, Charles, 1285

Hauteville, Robert de. See Robert Guiscard

Havel, Václav, 1307, 1331

Hawkins, John, 577

Heath, Edward, 1219

Hecataeus of Miletus, 60

Helen (grand duchess of Russia), 878

Heller, Wat. See Tyler, Wat

Heminges, John, 581

Hemingway, Ernest, 1079

Henderson, Arthur, 945

Hengist, 187

Henry (prince of Condé), 562

Henry I (king of England), 329

Henry II (king of Cyprus and king of Jerusalem). See Lusignan, Henry de

Henry II (king of England), 313, 317, 323, 325, 329

Henry II (king of France), 550, 562

Henry II (prince of Condé), 624

Henry II Jasomirgott (duke of Bavaria and duke of Austria), 315, 319

Henry III (king of England), 345, 367

Henry III (king of France), 562, 575, 584, 586; assassination of, 585

Henry IV (king of Castile), 460, 463

Henry IV (king of France), 562, 576, 579, 584, 586, 588, 672; assassination of, 586, 588; coronation of, 584-586

Henry VII (king of England), 468

Henry VIII (king of England), 468, 494, 506, 529, 531-534

Henry, Major Hubert-Joseph, 930

Henry de Bracton, 330

Henry of Navarre. See Henry IV (king of France)

Henry the Lion (duke of Saxony and duke of Bavaria), 313, 315, 319

Henry the Navigator (prince of Portugal), 430-432, 471, 476

Henry the Proud (duke of Bavaria and duke of Saxony), 319

Heraclides of Pontus, 99

Heraclitus of Ephesus, 36

Herder, Johann Gottfried, 735

Hermocrates, 70

Hernu, Charles, 1282

Herodotus, 60

SUBJECT INDEX

Abolitionist movement, 752-754, 772-774, 831-834

Aboukir Bay, Battle of, 761-763

Abraham Lincoln Brigade, 1079

Accursius, 159

Achaean League, 113

Achaean War, 113

Acre, fall of, 356, 378-380

Act of Settlement, 677, 694-696

Act of Supremacy, 495, 529-531

Act of Toleration, 654, 677

Act of Union (1706), 388, 701-703

Act of Union (1808), 765-767, 808, 981, 1238

Action Française, 1069

Action Program, 1207-1208

Actium, Battle of, 131-132

Adrianople: battle of, 173-175, 390; treaty of, 803, 810-812

Advancement of Learning, The (Bacon), 613-614

Aegina (Greek city-state), 52

Afghanistan, Soviet invasion of, 1255-1258, 1263

Africa, Vandal conquest of, 196

Afrikaners, 940

Agincourt, Battle of, 396, 429, 435, 448

Agriculture. *See* Farming and agriculture

Airplanes, 1107, 1146, 1244-1247

Aix-la-Chapelle, Treaty of, 711

Akka. *See* Acre

Akko. *See* Acre

Albania, 441; opens borders, 1312-1314

Albigensians, 349, 359; crusade against, 338-339

Alcaçovas, treaty of, 479

Alexandria (Egypt), 99; founding of, 86-87

Algeria, 1273; French conquest of, 812-813

Aliens Act, 1232

Allied invasion of France, 1121-1122

Allied invasion of Italy, 1119-1121

Allied occupation of Germany, 1133, 1145

Altamira cave paintings, 1

Althing (Icelandic legislature), 251-253

Altitudo Divini Consilii, 537

American Revolution, 739

Amnesty International, formation of, 1177-1179

Amsterdam, birth control clinic established in, 914-916

Anabaptists, 516

Andalus, al-, 253, 278, 288

Angevin dynasty, 317-319

Anglo-Irish Agreement, 1253, 1285-1287, 1335-1336

Anglo-Saxon Chronicle, 188, 235, 245, 285

Angola, 1233-1234

Anschluss, the, 1080-1081

Anti-Corn Law Circular, The , 847

Anti-Corn Law League, 841, 847-848

Antinuclear movement, 1274, 1282-1285, 1290, 1342-1343

Anti-Semitism, 349, 376-378, 398, 930, 947-948, 1025-1027, 1071, 1086-1089, 1183-1184, 1273, 1293

Antiseptic surgery, 889-890

Anti-Slavery Monthly Reporter, 832

Anti-Slavery Society, 832-833

Apollo 11, 1176

Apollo-Soyuz Test Project, 1176

Apology (Plato), 76

Appian Way, 92-93

Aqueducts, 93-96

Arbela, Battle of. *See* Gaugamela, Battle of

Archaeology, 1, 3, 6, 8, 10, 118, 149

Archias, 26

Archidamian War, 70

Archimedes, 103-105

Archimedian screw, 104

Architecture, 62, 105-107, 204. *See also* Gothic architecture, Ships and naval architecture

Archons, 39

Argentina, 1269

Arianism, 166, 176, 184, 197, 207

Armenia, 1301-1303; earthquake of 1988, 1302; genocide, 995-997

Arras, Treaty of, 448

Art of the Fugue, The (Bach), 691

Ascension of Christ and the Giving of the Keys to St. Peter (Donatello), 425

Assassination, 117, 133, 142, 161

Astronomy, 5-6, 99-101, 538, 603-605, 627-628

Athens, 35, 38, 46, 51, 56-58, 70, 76, 78; invasion of Sicily, 70-72

Atlantic Charter, 1131; signing of, 1111-1112

Atomic weapons, 1185-1187

Augsburg, Peace of, 520, 548-550

Augsburg Interim, 520

Augustan settlement, 133-135

Auschwitz, 1087-1088

Ausgleich, Austrian, 894-896

Austerlitz, Battle of, 770-772

Australia, 741

Austria, 709, 730, 791, 873, 894, 906, 919, 942, 1080, 1291; annexation of Bosnia and Herzegovina, 971-973; emergence of, 319-321. *See also* Holy Roman Empire

Austrian Nazi Party, 1080

Austrian Succession, War of, 709, 735

Auto-da-fé, 464, 473

Avignon papacy, 384, 399, 405, 428

Aztec civilization, 503-506

Bacteriology, 917

"Balance of power" theory, 804

Balkan League, 984-985

Balkan Wars, 1, 886, 911, 977-978, 984-985

Balkans, 259, 419, 810, 929

Baltic region, 313, 353, 693, 1319-1321, 1327; independence of, 1013-1015. *See also* Estonia; Latvia; Lithuania

Bank of England, 680, 1136; chartering of, 685-688

Bannockburn, Battle of, 387-389

Baroque music, 690-693

Basarab, Battle of, 393-395

Basic Treaty, 1227-1228

Basque region, 1079

Bastille, fall of the, 747-750

Battles. *See individual place names*

Bavaria, Magyar invasion of, 249-251

Bayeux Tapestry, 219

Beaver Committee on Smoke Pollution, 1160

Beer Hall Putsch, 1060

Belgian Revolution, 819-821

Belgium, 794, 819, 1126, 1149

Belgrade, Treaty of, 535, 705-707

Belzek, 1087

Benedictine order, 212

Berlin, Congress of, 971-972

Berlin Airlift, 1145-1147, 1181, 1305

Berlin Wall, 1231; building of the, 1179-1181; fall of the, 1305-1307, 1330

Bill of Rights, 622, 677, 694

Biopsychology, 944

Bireme, 40

Birmingham Political Union, 841, 924

Birth control, 759, 914-916